Wolverhampton Wanderers

The Complete Record

Wolverhampton Wanderers

The Complete Record

Every game, every scorer, every player and every attendance.
FA Cup Finals, complete history, pen pictures, manager profiles, appearance records

Tony Matthews

First published in Great Britain in 2008 by
The Breedon Books Publishing Company Limited
Breedon House, 3 The Parker Centre,
Derby, DE21 4SZ.

ISBN 978-1-85983-632-3

Printed and bound by MPG Books, Bodmin, Cornwall.

Contents

Acknowledgements

Quite a few people (some perhaps unknowingly) have assisted me in compiling this *Complete Record of Wolverhampton Wanderers*, which is an update of my previous one, published by Breedon Books in 1994.

Those who have helped most of all, and to whom I am sincerely grateful, are long-time friend and ardent Wolves supporter John Hendley, best mate Graham Hughes (Molineux museum curator), photographer Peter Harrington, journalist and author David Instone, my darling wife Margaret, David Instone, Ulf Brennmo and Urban Wigert for the overseas statistics, and three Wolves statisticians, Scott Pritchard, Mike Slater and Les Smith.

I must also say a sincere thank you to Steve Caron and Michelle Grainger of Breedon Books Publishing (Derby), who have given me terrific support and, indeed, it was Steve who asked me to 'get on and do it'! And, of course, there are the many club statisticians up and down the country from whom I have obtained some important and new statistical information on certain players.

Tony Matthews

Introduction

This book is an update of the last *Complete Record of Wolverhampton Wanderers* which I compiled 14years ago, way back in 1994.

Packed with thousands of statistics, including the date, result, scorers, attendance and line up of every single game played by Wolves at competitive level since 1883 (when the club first entered the FA Cup), biographies of all the great stars who have donned the famous gold-and-black shirt down the years, international records of players, details of all the managers who have been in charge of the team, as well as individual playing records (appearances made and goals scored) of every first-team player who has served the club since its formation way back in 1877, this book is perhaps my best on the Wanderers to date.

Putting together a publication of this magnitude has taken quite some time plus a lot of patience, and although I have written and co-compiled many other books on Wolves in the past, there is always something new to add, which I have found (or someone else has found) while scanning through old newspapers, various scrapbooks, club programmes and magazines. Those among you who enjoy dabbling in figures and statistics will surely agree with me when I say that they can be a nightmare at times as well as being a pleasure.

During my research I came across new dates concerning players' births and deaths, and also extra clubs, which have now been added to that player's career details. Certain attendances, both at home and away, have been amended as well, and alterations will continue to be made somewhere on my personal database appertaining to Wolves after publication.

At this point, I would therefore appreciate hearing of anything you might find wrong within the contents of this book or which has not been included. It is common knowledge that in the period between 1877 and 1905 quite a few errors and anomalies have been spotted in various reference books, newspaper reports and indeed programmes. Most of these have been corrected, but I am sure there are a few more which will be amended in the not-too-distant future.

I have found that most of the alterations made in updated histories or complete records of a football club appear in the period between their formation and the 1907–08 season. I believe that as shirts were numberless and players occasionally played out of position, the match reporters from that time had some difficulty identifying certain players, especially if the reporter was a neutral thrown in at the last minute to cover a match. And there are also problems the attendances. Years ago the 'gate' was rounded up by most clubs and printed likewise in newspapers, but during World War One, in 1915, certain clubs started to publish the exact attendance figure in the programme, while newspapers continued to give the crowd as round figures.

Having said that, I now believe that I have answered most of the queries that have been posed since my last *Complete Record of Wolves* and in my mind this current one is perhaps the best so far…

The History of Wolves

The formation of the club

Like many other clubs who became established in the world of football and reached a high status in the game, Wolverhampton Wanderers owe their inception to the enthusiasm, commitment and dedication of a band of young men. In their case it was scholars and choristers at St Luke's School, Blakenhall, some of whom became household names in the Black Country town.

Two of them, pupils Jack Baynton and John (Jack) Brodie, who had earlier been presented with a ball by the long-serving headmaster of St Luke's school and keen sportsman Harry Barcroft, without doubt had a huge hand in laying the foundation stones of a club that subsequently became one of the founder members of the Football League in 1888. These two youngsters were backed all the way by their manager (Mr Bancroft) and also by Jack Addenbrooke, another very competent footballer who, at the time, was in the preliminary stages of his scholastic profession and Sir Alfred Hickman, later president of the club, whose house overlooked a piece of land on Goldthorn Hill where the team would play its first home match.

An indication that St Luke's football club was to be officially formed came about on Friday 10 November 1876, at a meeting arranged by the teenagers Baynton and Brodie, a future England international.

The turnout was excellent and as a result things moved fast. At least 15 men signed up to play and, after a series of practice sessions before and after Christmas and New Year, the newly formed St Luke's team played its first game against Stafford Road reserves on a rather uneven strip of grass near to the town's orphanage on 13 January 1877.

Unfortunately, with two star players absent (Addenbrooke and Brodie) the game resulted in an 8–0 defeat for St Luke's, who fielded this 12-man team: goalkeeper Bancroft; defenders Frank Hampton, David Hedges, James Adams, Oscar Rowbotham, Tom Worrall and Walter Kendrick and forwards Baynton, Ernie Newman, Dick Myatt, Billy Jacks and Jack Foster.

Two years later, after a lot of commitment and encouragement from local folk, and with George Worrall installed as the secretary-manager, that up-and-coming team merged with the local cricket and football side, The Wanderers, to form the present-day club, Wolverhampton Wanderers, the official paperwork being registered in August 1879.

As time progressed and better players were recruited, the side got a lot stronger and more resilient. Results and performances improved considerably and the club were given the facilities of two decent stretches of land on which to play their home games – Windmill Field and John Harper's Field, both situated off Lower Villiers Street in Blakenhall. They utilised the former until May 1879 and the latter from August 1879 to April 1881.

One the better players in the team at this juncture was full-back Charlie Mason, son of the landlord of the King's Arms pub, Jeremiah Mason, a rich man who owned the land on which St Luke's school was built. Mason junior became Wolves' first England international, capped against Ireland in February 1887.

In the summer of 1881, Wolves moved to a much more substantial site in Dudley Road, directly opposite the Fighting Cocks Inn. Originally there was little or no cover for the supporters when the rain decided to come down, but this was quickly rectified and the ground remained home for Wolves for eight years, having a capacity of around 10,000.

The team as a unit improved rapidly and season 1881–82 turned out to be quite encouraging, Wolves winning 10 and drawing four of 18 games played while scoring 51 goals and conceding only 18. Their two biggest wins were both at home, 11–0 against Walsall Albion on Christmas Eve and 7–0 versus Stourbridge Standard.

More players were recruited, among them Harry Aston, cricketer-footballer Tom Blackham, Ike Griffiths and Arthur Lowder, who later became chairman of the Brewood Parish Council. The career of Blackham, a former St Luke's pupil, was cut short through injury at the age of 24, after breaking his right leg when scoring his seventh goal for Wolves in a 15–0 Birmingham Cup win over Aston Cross on Christmas Eve 1883. He subsequently became a linesman and also an influential member of the Wolves committee, acting as travel organiser. Blackham later became steward of both the Bilston and Blakenhall Conservative Clubs and licensee of the British Crown pub in Dudley Road, and also ran a general store in Coalway Road, Wolverhampton, for many years. He was 86 when he died in 1945.

Unfortunately, Wolves were desperately short of money around this time. Attendances were low, with the average home crowd hovering around the 1,500 mark, and on a miserable day only about 400 hardy supporters would bother to turn up.

Thankfully, alderman Levi Johnson, born in Macclesfield, had arrived on the scene as financial advisor in the summer of 1881 and turned things round. It was announced that the club had made a profit of £5 on the 1881–82 season, and with gate receipts topping £80, that profit was doubled the following season.

First trophy

In season 1883–84 Wolves took part in the FA Cup for the first time and also won their first trophy, the Wrekin Cup.

At this stage in the club's short history, the players wore faded red-and-white-striped jerseys and dark blue or black shorts, and the team comprised: Billy Caddick or Ike Griffiths in goal; Tommy Cliff and Charlie Mason at full-back; Alf Davidson, Jack Baynton and Tom Blackham at half-back; and James Hill, Arthur Lowder, Jack Brodie, Ted Hadley and John Griffiths in attack. In reserve were Alex Pearson, Arnold Smith and Joey Waldron.

The pressure on these players was immense. They were, of course, all amateurs (professionalism was introduced in 1885) yet week after week their supporters expected results.

In the autumn of 1883 Wolves drew 2–2 with one of the better sides from the Midland area, Stoke, in a terrific contest at Dudley Road watched by a crowd of 3,000. Goalkeeper Caddick was badly injured but battled on in pain and produced a wonderful display of courage and bravery.

In late October Wolves played their first ever game in the FA Cup, taking on Long Eaton Rangers at Dudley Road. Around 2,000 fans enjoyed a 4–1 win, with Brodie and John Griffiths both scoring twice. Wolves slipped behind in the 25th minute but recovered to register a fine victory against a very useful side.

In the second round Wolves, after a dismal performance, lost 4–2 to Wednesbury Old Athletic. However, they quickly put that horror show behind them and whipped Birmingham side St Paul's 7–0 in the first round of the Wrekin Cup, following up with a 10–0 win over Shrewsbury-based Castle Blues in the Birmingham Cup – half of the goals were scored in five minutes of the second half. Wolves also

Wrekin Cup winners, 1883–84. Back row, left to right: A. Blackham, H. Dallard (umpire), T. Cliff, J. Baynton, C. Mason, J. Brodie (captain), E. Hadley, J. Griffiths. Front row: I. Griffiths, A. Lowder, A. Davidson, A. Pearson.

knocked Stafford Rangers out of both the Walsall and Wrekin Cup competitions, but sadly lost Blackham with a broken leg in a Birmingham Cup tie against Villa Cross.

Wolves maintained their form over the festive season and into the New Year as they drove on towards the Wrekin Cup Final, beating one of the strongest sides in Wolverhampton, Stafford Road, for the first time by 5–1 at Dudley Road. In a rather one-sided Final they slaughtered Shropshire side Hadley 11–0, with Brodie scoring six times and Lowder three.

By this time Wolves had appointed their first official trainer, William Shipton, landlord of the Vine pub in Upper Vauxhall. He supervised training sessions three times a week and would often take the players on casual but enjoyable country walks.

By the summer of 1884 around 20 players were registered with the club and several more were interested in joining. Matches were becoming more competitive as other teams in the area grew in stature.

Wolves were ousted from the 1884–85 FA Cup by Derby St Luke's, losing 4–2 after extra-time in a replay, having been 2–0 up at one stage. This was one of 35 fixtures completed during the season. Twelve ended in victories and 116 goals were scored but there was disappointment as Wolves lost to Walsall Town in the Final of the very competitive Staffordshire Cup.

In June 1885, after three FA meetings, professionalism was introduced to the game, Wolves falling in line with several other leading clubs by agreeing to pay players a weekly wage. At this point Jack Addenbrooke was appointed secretary-manager of the club and immediately set about bringing in some fresh faces as many of the early players were either ready to retire, had retired or had moved to pastures new.

Baynton, Brodie, Lowder and Mason of the first generation were still prominent, while Hill turned down a move to Stoke and stayed loyal to the club. He later helped form Arsenal football club and became a director in 1891. He had a great life, living until he was 93 years of age.

Wolves fulfilled over 40 fixtures in 1885–86. They had an excellent run in the FA Cup, gaining revenge over Derby St Luke's by winning a first-round game 7–0 and following up with wins over Stafford Road 4–2 and Walsall Town Swifts 2–1 before meeting Black Country neighbours West Bromwich Albion for the very first time in the quarter-finals. Albion, though, proved too strong and won 3–1 at Stoney Lane on their way to the Final, which they lost in a replay to Blackburn Rovers.

Wolves also met Preston North End twice, losing 4–0 away and 4–1 at home, the latter attracting a crowd of 6,000 to Dudley Road. North End, referred to at the time as the 'Invincibles', were a brilliant team and that season won 49 and drew three of the 52 games played, scoring 267 goals in the process.

On 20 March 1886, Wolves played at the Molineux Grounds for the first time. A crowd of 4,000 saw them lose 1–0 to Walsall in a local Cup semi-final, but this result was far less important than the success of staging the game in the acknowledged pleasure grounds of the town, as people wondered at the time whether or not Molineux was going to become Wolves' new home. It would be another three years before that would become a reality.

Wolves' line up now comprised: I. Griffiths; Mason, Hawkins; Pearson or Davidson, J. Aston or Baynton, Evans; H. Aston, Horton or Lowder, Brodie, H. Wood and G. Wood or Cattell.

Harry Wood was born in Walsall and became one of the greatest footballers ever to play for Wolves. He amassed almost 300 appearances in two spells with the club and scored more than 125 goals. He played for England and also spent time with Southampton.

Season 1886–87 heralded the end of the first decade in the history of Wolves and it was now clear that if the pinnacles were to be reached, the affairs of the club had to be diligently directed and the public made to understand their own responsibility. At the time the population of Wolverhampton was 75,000 but the team was attracting home crowds of only 2,000–3,000, meaning that gate receipts were relatively low, certainly not adequate to sustain the aspirations of the zealots.

In 1888 Wolves became one of the 12 founders of the Football League, drawing 1–1 at home with Midland rivals Aston Villa in the very first game in the competition on 8 September. They finished in third place in that inaugural season, with 28 points out of a possible 44, well behind unbeaten champions Preston North End and runners-up Villa, as well as reaching the FA Cup Final for the first time, losing 3–0 to mighty Preston who, as a result, became the first team to complete the double.

Wolves' line up for their opening League game was: Baynton; Dickie Baugh, Mason; Albert Fletcher, who was signed for a golden sovereign from Willenhall Pickwick, Harry Allen, ex-Walsall Town Swifts, who would go on to play for England, Lowder; Tom Hunter, who also played for the Swifts, Jerry Cooper from Heathtown, local lad Nick Anderson, Halesowen-born Walter White and the versatile Alec Cannon. Wolves' first League goal was, in fact, an own-goal scored by the Villa full-back Gershom Cox!

The 1889 Cup Final was delayed due to the Boat Race and kicked off just after 4pm. Wolves played well but Preston were marginally stronger and more direct and ran out convincing winners in the end.

The Wolves team of 1888 for their first-ever League game against Aston Villa. Back row, left to right: H. Fletcher, R. Baugh, C. Mason, J. Baynton, H. Allen, A. Lowder. Front row: T. Hunter, J. Cooper, N. Anderson, W. White, A. Cannon.

The Local Government Act of 1888 raised the town of Wolverhampton to the rank of a County Borough, the status being officially adopted on 1 April 1889. And as a result it was discussed at length that it was not compatible with such dignity that the premier football team in the town, Wolves, should continue to be indifferently accommodated in as sub-standard a ground as Dudley Road. So it was agreed that a new 'stadium' was required and the obvious area on which to build was the spacious grounds that lay in the shadow of the elegant 18th-century Molineux House.

At the time, the grounds were well known all over the country. Surrounding the football pitch (on which Wolves had played a few years earlier; and, during the summer, cricket had also been played) was a quality cycling and athletics track on which several meetings had already taken place, while the grounds themselves regularly hosted festivals and garden fêtes.

After the long, laborious job of chopping down trees, uprooting flower beds, dispersing of a large lake, removing children's swings and roundabouts, lots of fencing, pathways, an iron bridge and a large bandstand, Wolves' new home, Molineux, was officially declared ready for use by the end of August 1889, and the big kick-off was set for Monday 2 September when Aston Villa took on Wolves in a friendly. A crowd of 4,000 saw Wolves win 1–0 with David Wykes, formerly of Walsall, scoring the goal.

For Wolves, season 1889–90 was a fairly good one. They finished fourth in the League and reached the semi-final of the Cup before losing 1–0 to Blackburn Rovers at Derby, having beaten the 1881 FA Cup-winners Old Carthusians 2–0 in front of 13,000 fans at Molineux in the first round and Stoke 8–0 in the third, thanks to a Jack Brodie five-timer – this after the Potters had complained about the state of the Molineux pitch and demanded a replay (Wolves won the initial game 4–0).

During the course of the season Wolves provided five players for England: Allen, Baugh, Fletcher, Mason and Wood, the latter scoring against Scotland.

In each of the next two seasons Wolves went out of the FA Cup in the third round, succumbing to bogey side Blackburn in 1891 and Aston Villa 12 months later, this being their first home Cup defeat in 20 games since 1883. At the same time they finished fourth in the League in the former campaign, despite a 9–0 drubbing by lowly Derby County, and sixth in the latter when Joe Heath had the pleasure of scoring the first ever penalty in the competition in a 5–0 home win over Accrington in September 1891. Soon afterwards Harry Allen became the first Wolves player to miss from the spot versus West Bromwich Albion.

Two key players in the side at this time were George Kinsey (signed from Mitchell St George's) and George Swift (ex-Crewe Alexandra), and both were to figure prominently in 1892–93 when Wolves lifted the FA Cup for the first time.

Cup Final joy and disappointment

En route to the Cup Final of 1893, Wolves defeated Bolton Wanderers (after a replay), Middlesbrough, Darwen and their old adversaries Blackburn Rovers 2–1 in the semis at Nottingham.

Opposing them in the Final were Everton, who would go on and finish third in the First Division and had won a League game between the clubs by 4–2 only seven days previously. In fact, after that result the Merseysiders became firm favourites to lift the trophy. But Wolves, dogged and determined, caused something of an upset by beating Everton 1–0 at Fallowfield, Manchester, in front of a then record crowd of 45,067, Allen scoring the all-important goal on 60 minutes with a long-range drive that flew high into the net.

In recognition of that magnificent win over Everton, a plaque depicting the FA Cup was strategically erected across the top of two houses on Dudley Road, numbers 329 and 330, to serve as a constant reminder to all passers-by of that wonderful achievement.

Later, a road nearby was named 'Wanderers Avenue' with houses bearing the names of several early Wolves stalwarts like Brodie and Mason, along with the 1893 Cup winners Allen, Baugh, Joe Butcher (who at 18, was the youngest player in the Final), goalkeeper Billy Rose, Alf Griffin, Kinsey, Billy Malpass, Dick Topham, Swift, Wood and David Wykes, who in October 1895, just 24 hours after a home game with Stoke, died in a Wolverhampton hospital of typhoid fever and pneumonia at the age of 28. He scored 69 goals in 179 games for the Wanderers, whom he had served since 1888.

By concentrating firmly on the Cup, Wolves' League form slumped, and they lost five games in a row either side of the Final and in the end escaped relegation by just five points. Earlier in the season they were hammered 10–1 by bottom-of-the-League Newton Heath, which still stands as the club's heaviest defeat in League football.

Three years later, having performed moderately in the League with finishes of ninth in 1894 and 11th in 1895 and failing to make much of an impact in the Cup, Wolves battled hard and long to reach their third Final in 1896, knocking out Notts County 4–3 (after a replay), Liverpool 2–0, Stoke 3–0 and Derby County 2–1 in the semis at Villa Park. The Rams included the great Steve Bloomer (from Cradley Heath) and ex-Wolves star George Kinsey in their line up.

This time their opponents at Crystal Palace were Sheffield Wednesday, whom they had beaten 4–1 at home but had lost to 3–1 away earlier in the season. Wolves had just avoided relegation by winning their last two games, against Bury 1–0 and Bolton Wanderers 5–0, and were quietly confident of success, but unfortunately on the day they failed to match the skill and commitment of the Yorkshire side and were beaten 2–1 in front of almost 49,000 spectators.

Wolves fielded this team for the Final: Billy Tennant, Baugh, Tom Dunn, Hillary Griffiths, Malpass, Billy Owen, Jack Tonks, Charlie Henderson, Billy Beats, Harry Wood and David Black – the goalscorer.

In the summer of 1896 Wolves ploughed back some of the profits made from increased gate receipts and that excellent Cup run (they received £4,600 from their share of the takings at the Cup Final) into building fully equipped dressing rooms at Molineux. The club also allocated a private room for the matchday officials, who before had to walk to the ground from a nearby hotel!

Around this time, an adult season ticket at Molineux cost one guinea (£1.05) for the main Waterloo Road Stand and 10s 6d (53p) for the Molineux Street Stand opposite. Admission to the terraces at either end of the ground was 6d (3p).

Hard times

Season 1896–97 was another generally disappointing one for Wolves, especially in the League and FA Cup, although they did reach the Final of two local Cup competitions, beating Stoke to win the Staffordshire Cup but losing to Walsall in the Birmingham Cup. Billy Smith was sent off in the latter Final – the first Wolves player to take an early bath.

Some of the players who helped Wolves reach the 1896 FA Cup Final. Back row, left to right: A. Griffin, W. Malpass, R. Baugh, W.C. Rose, T. Dunn, C. Henderson, J. Lewis (trainer). Front row: H. Griffiths, W. Beats, H. Wood, W. Owen, D. Black.

A record crowd of 27,489 saw Wolves lose 2–1 to Aston Villa at Molineux on Boxing Day 1896, but soon afterwards rivals West Bromwich Albion were thrashed 6–1 and on the last day of the campaign Bolton Wanderers were blitzed 4–0.

Goalkeeper Tom Baddeley, who had been signed from Burslem Port Vale for £40 in October 1896, took over from Tennant. He would become an England international and play for Wolves until 1907. Other new players were introduced and Wolves ended season 1897–98 in third place in the First Division – their best finish since the inaugural campaign of 1888–89. Unfortunately, things were not going too well behind the scenes.

A handful of players did not re-sign for the new season, among them the experienced Harry Wood, who reluctantly left Molineux for Southampton. George Eccles and Owen both moved to Everton and Tennant joined Walsall. Into the team came Ted 'Cock' Pheasant, a tough-tackling centre-half from Wednesbury, Welsh full-back Jack Matthias and inside-forward Tom Worton.

Wolves finished eighth in the League in 1898–99, came fourth the following season and 13th in 1900–01. By now Hillary Griffiths had left the club, having joined the Players' Union committee in 1899. Malpass had retired, George Fleming switched to Liverpool and several reserves had also found new homes. The team had changed considerably in double quick time but, sadly, strength and solidarity within the club had diminished considerably over a period of five years.

At the turn of the century there were 25 professionals at Molineux, the majority having been born within a 25-mile radius of the ground. There were several utility players in the first-team squad, one of them being Billy Wooldridge. Baddeley was the established goalkeeper; Jack Jones had bedded himself in at right-back alongside George Walker, father of Billy Walker, who was to star for Aston Villa and England in the 1920s and 1930s; Jack Whitehouse, Pheasant and Walter Annis were competent half-backs; while the forward line comprised Arthur Fellows, Adam Haywood, Beats, Wooldridge and the solid-looking Jack Miller.

Wolves settled for 14th place in the League in 1901–02 and 11th the following season while going out of the FA Cup at the first stage in both campaigns, having failed to venture beyond the third round since their Final appearance in 1896.

Dick Betteley was introduced at left-back, Albert Baynham at outside-right and the diminutive figure of Jack Smith at inside-left, and their presence certainly boosted Wolves' confidence as they edged up to eighth place in 1903–04. But it was tough going and another poor season followed before disaster struck in 1905–06: Wolves were relegated for the first time, slipping into the Second Division after finishing bottom of the table with a dismal record of only eight wins and seven draws from 38 games. They conceded 99 goals, secured a mere 23 points and used 29 players, 18 of them forwards.

Wolves were poor overall and their 23 defeats included 8–0 at Newcastle, 6–0 at Villa Park, 4–0 at Liverpool and 5–1 at Sheffield Wednesday but they at least ended their season on a note of defiance, once relegation was certain, winning their final two games 6–1 against Notts County and 7–0 against Derby County, both at Molineux.

Right-half Alf Bishop and goalscorer George Hedley (ex-Southampton) were added to the team for season 1906–07. These two players were to give Wolves excellent service over the next few years, accumulating almost 600 senior appearances between them, Hedley netting 74 goals.

Wolves' first-ever game in the Second Division was against Hull City at Molineux on 1 September 1906 and, with the temperature touching 90 degrees, they were held to a 1–1 draw in front of 6,000 spectators. The team that afternoon was: Baddeley; Ted Juggins and Jones; Bishop, Sid Corfield (ex-West Brom) and Arthur Lloyd; Jack Hopkins (once of Liverpool), Hedley, Wooldridge, policeman Jimmy Gorman and Jack Pedley, who took over from Miller after he was sold to Stoke.

The Wolves team, 1904–05.

Wolves finished a moderate sixth in the table in 1906–07 and lost in the first round of the FA Cup, 3–2 at Sheffield Wednesday, having gone out in the second round the previous season, 5–0 at the hands of Bradford City. However, that Cup form was to change dramatically in 1907–08 when the trophy was won for the second time.

FA Cup Glory

Tommy Lunn replaced Baddeley in goal and England amateur international right-half the Reverend Kenneth Hunt, an undergraduate at Queen's College, Oxford, joined the playing staff, although he could technically play for any club, being an amateur! Both players starred for Wolves in 1907–08, as did Jack Jones and his new full-back partner Ted Collins, who was recruited from Brownhills Albion; half-backs Bishop and Wooldridge, who had been switched from his forward role; right and left-wingers Billy Harrison (from Crewe Alexandra) and Jack Pedley; and the three main central strikers, Jack Shelton, Hedley and Wally Radford.

Although not performing brilliantly in the League (they eventually took ninth position) Wolves certainly produced the goods in the Cup, storming through to the Final by beating Bradford City (after a replay), Bury, Swindon Town, Stoke and Southampton before taking on the favourites Newcastle United at Crystal Palace.

Almost 75,000 spectators attended the Final, which Wolves won 3–1 with goals from Harrison, Hedley and Hunt while the only other 'H'– Howie – netted for United. It was a special day all round for Harrison, who became the father of triplets on the morning of the game.

WOLVERHAMPTON WANDERERS
LUNN
JONES
COLLINS
WOOLDRIDGE
KENNETH HUNT
BISHOP
HEDLEY
HARRISON
PEDLEY
The English Cup Team, 1908
SHELTON
RADFORD
Copyright.

Most of the players who gained Cup-winners' medals continued as members of the team over the next two seasons as Wolves battled to take seventh and eighth positions in the Second Division but did nothing in the Cup. In 1910–11, another new goalkeeper, Cradley Heath-born Frank Boxley, was installed after Lunn departed to Tottenham. George Garratly took over at left-back, Alf Groves replaced Hunt at right-half and the Needham brothers, Archie and Jack, were introduced in the two inside-forward positions.

In the five years leading up to World War One, Wolves, captained for the last three by Bishop, finished ninth, fifth, 10th, ninth and fourth in Division Two and never threatened at all in the FA Cup, although in a first-round replay in January 1912 they did whip Watford 10–0 at Molineux. In 1912–13 the club had two reverends on their books, the aforementioned Hunt and centre-forward Willie Jordan, who had played in the Cup semi-final for West Brom six years earlier and later became a director of Darlington FC (late 1930s).

Wolves played very little football during the hostilities, returning to competitive action in the Midland Victory League in March and April 1919 before embarking once again on League combat in August 1919. By this time there were several new players at the club, among them full-back Dickie Baugh junior, defenders Joe Hodnett and Maurice Woodward and forward Harry Wright, who had appeared for West Brom in the 1912 FA Cup Final.

Eight players who had performed before the War were still registered with the club, and they lined up for the first League game for four years versus Leicester Fosse in August 1919, a game Wolves won 2–1.

As the opening weeks passed by, that victory over Leicester proved a false omen and aspirations towards regaining First Division status gradually dwindled as results fluctuated. At times things got rough both on and off the pitch and during the home game with Bury in mid-October, the referee awarded the visitors a penalty. Not content merely with voicing their disapproval at the decision, a band of irate Wolves supporters raced on to the pitch and surrounded the official,

Wolverhampton Wanderers, 1907-08. Back row, left to right: A.G. Jeffs, A.J. Evans, K.R.G. Hunt, J. Jones, W. Woodridge, T. Lunn, E. Collins, A. Bishop, W. Shepherd, Dr J.A. Wolverson, A. Fletcher. Front row: J.H. Addenbrooke, E. Barker, W.E. Harrison, J. Shelton, G. Hedley, J. Radford, J. Pedley, Col G. Walton Walker, W. Fleming.

Wolves first and second teams before a pre-season public practice match, 1912–13.

Wolves in 1914–15.

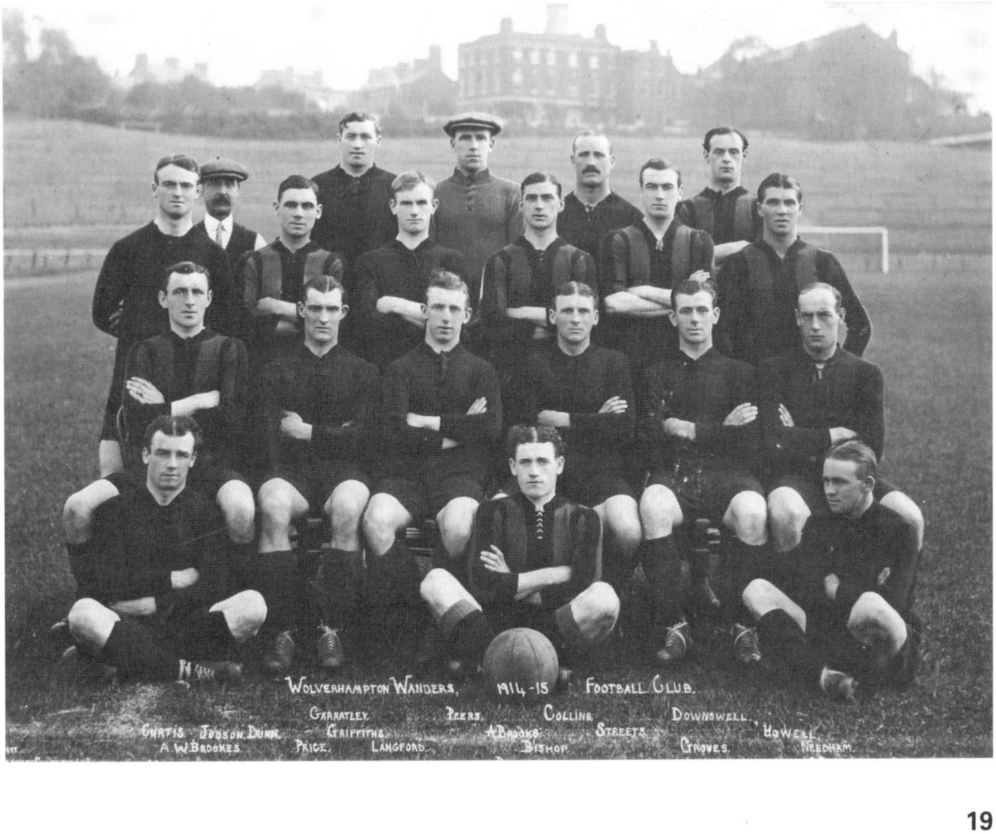

knocking him to the ground. The police were summoned, calm was eventually restored and the game continued, Wolves going on to win 1–0. This incident, however, resulted in Molineux being closed for two matches and it meant that Wolves' home League games against Barnsley and Stockport were staged at The Hawthorns, where only one point was obtained (from a draw versus Stockport).

Cup Final defeat, relegation and promotion

In 1920–21 Wolves reached their fifth FA Cup Final, but in the League they struggled, avoiding relegation by just three points, having got off to a disastrous start, winning only three of their first 15 League games.

Manager Addenbrooke made several new signings, among them wing-half Val Gregory from Arsenal for £3,500, centre-forward George Edmonds from Watford, Bill Caddick from Wellington and Fred Burrill from Southend United.

The first three all played well and Edmonds finished as top scorer with 13 goals, but he could not find the net in the Cup Final, which Wolves lost 1–0 to Tottenham Hotspur on a soggy Stamford Bridge pitch.

Wolves had knocked out Stoke, Derby County, Fulham and Chelsea in rounds three, four, five and six, before having a tough semi-final clash with Cardiff City, whom they defeated in a replay. For the Final Noel George was preferred to Teddy Peers in goal and he pulled off three fine saves in the first half. After changing their drenched shirts during the interval, Wolves came out strongly after the break but it was Spurs who scored the only goal, Jimmy Dimmock driving the ball home on 53 minutes after Maurice Woodward had miscued his clearance.

A year after this Cup defeat, Molineux was again a rather gloomy place to be as Wolves struggled in the League, escaping the drop by four points. On 25 June 1922, Dr Wolverson declared Jack Addenbrooke unfit for work and allowed the Wolves boss six months' sick leave. His health deteriorated and on 7 September he died, Albert Hoskins taking over as club secretary while George Jobey stepped in as manager-coach, bringing with him the former Sunderland player George Holley as his assistant and trainer.

In April 1922 Wolves had become a limited liability company and, despite the announcement that the club had shown a loss of £3,885 for the previous season, permission was also given to buy the freehold of Molineux for £6,000.

Despite adding some fresh blood with the acquisition of Stan Fazackerley and George Brewster from Everton, George Getgood from Southampton, Albert Legge from Lewisham and Harry Lees from Merthyr Town, things went from bad to worse out on the pitch. When the curtain came down on the 1922–23 season Wolves went down, dropping into the Third Division North after finishing bottom of the table with a dismal record of 27 points out of a possible 84. They won only nine games and lost 24, three of them rather heavily, 7–0 at Leicester, 7–1 at Coventry and 6–1 at Crystal Palace.

The average crowd at Molineux dipped to around 12,000 and only 3,822 hardy supporters turned out for the game against Hull in April, the lowest attendance since February 1915.

Being relegated was not without its benefits, for it enabled Wolves to rebuild and start afresh. More new players were brought in, among them Tommy Bowen and Ben Timmins from Walsall, Jack

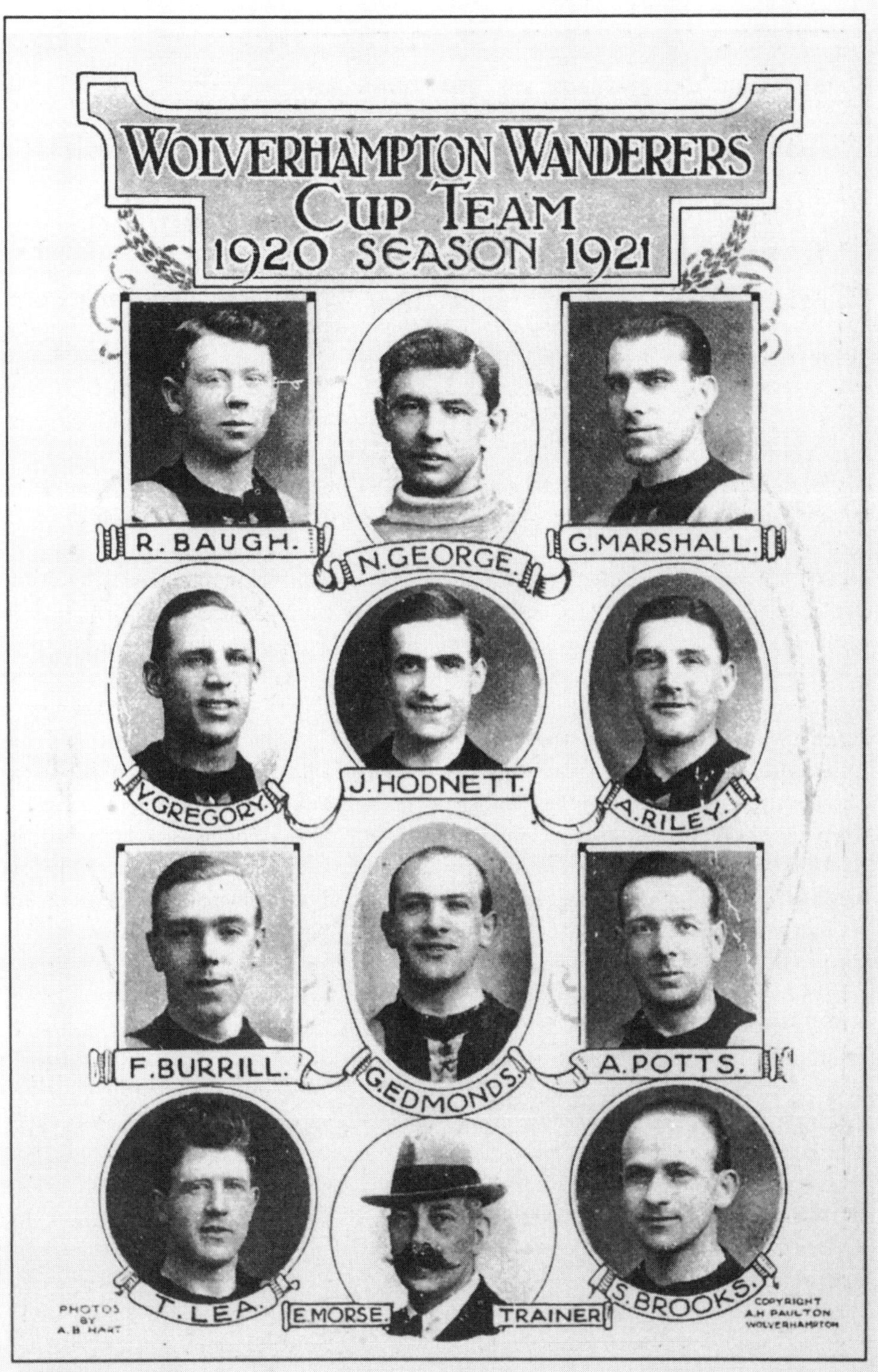
WOLVERHAMPTON WANDERERS
CUP TEAM
1920 SEASON 1921
R. BAUGH.
N. GEORGE.
G. MARSHALL.
V. GREGORY.
J. HODNETT.
A. RILEY.
F. BURRILL.
G. EDMONDS.
A. POTTS.
T. LEA.
E. MORSE.
TRAINER
S. BROOKS.
PHOTOS BY A. B. HART
COPYRIGHT A. H. PAULTON WOLVERHAMPTON

The players and staff line up before the start of the 1920–21 season.

Harrington (from Hednesford), prolific marksman Tom Phillipson from Swindon Town, full-back Harold Shaw also from Hednesford, Ted Watson from Pontypridd and Evan 'Blog' Edwards from Merthyr, and they all contributed as Wolves won the Third Division North title at the first attempt, pipping Rochdale by a single point (63 to 62) after drawing four and winning three of their last seven matches.

Three players – Lees (21), Fazackerley (14) and Phillipson (12) – scored 47 League goals between them and, in fact, only goalkeeper George remained from the 1921 Cup Final side. The average home attendance rose by 2,500 and a record crowd of 40,083 witnessed the fourth-round FA Cup replay against neighbours West Brom, which Wolves lost 2–1.

In May 1924, after successfully guiding Wolves back into the Second Division, Jobey quit as manager and secretary Hoskins stepped into the hot seat. Many supporters, however, thought the appointment was a huge gamble but nevertheless he held firm and remained in the job for almost two years, during which time Wolves finished sixth and fourth respectively in the table.

Hoskins relied on practically the same set of players who had won promotion, introducing only a handful of newcomers, one of them being half-back Jack Mitton from Sunderland.

Quite a lot of money was spent on the ground in 1924, with the Waterloo Road Stand being completed along with some smart dressing rooms and a 200ft section of the stand roof being transferred across from the Molineux Street side. However, when the north-easterly gales battered the Midlands early in 1925, the top half of the Molineux Street stand was completely blown off, while the *Express and Star* telephone box was tossed completely outside the ground and into the adjoining street, blocking the flow of traffic for four hours.

In March 1926 Lancastrian Fred Scotchbrook, aged 40 and formerly in charge of Stockport County, took over the manager's chair from Hoskins, who left to become boss of Gillingham. Unfortunately, he received little or no backing from the board of directors and on many occasions heated arguments took place between himself and certain members of the board, mainly about the lack of funds.

The 1923–24 team. Back row, left to right: J.S. Baker, A.H. Hoskins, E. Barker, T.W. Simpson, F.T. Hollins, H. Mills. Middle row: G. Jobey, G. Holley, Legge, Timmins, Caddick, George, Kay, Watson, J. Davis, A.H. Oakley, Major A. Holloway. Front row: Davison, Harrington, McMillan, Bowen, Fazackerley, Getgood, Phillipson, Lees, Edwards, Shaw.

Scotchbrook managed to secure the services of two decent players – Wilf Chadwick from Leeds United and Reg Weaver from Newport County – but he wanted more to boost his squad.

Towards the end of the 1926–27 season, with Wolves struggling to stay clear of the drop-zone, it was common knowledge that a centre-half was urgently required to bolster up a rather wobbly defence, and at the club's AGM on 27 June 1927, Scotchbrook made this clear in no uncertain terms! Unfortunately, the directors did not enjoy his remarks and he parted company with the club under a certain amount of duress.

The Buckley years

Wolves therefore required a new manager – their fifth in the 1920s – and the man handed the job was 43-year-old Manchester-born Major Frank Buckley, a former player with Aston Villa, Brighton, Manchester United, Manchester City, Birmingham, Derby County and Bradford City who had served with the 17th Middlesex Regiment during World War One.

Known as the 'Iron Major', he introduced himself to the players and staff without too much fuss or bother. He immediately instructed the players as to routine, issued each of them with a printed rule book and clearly stated that these were to be strictly obeyed at all times, with punctuality first and foremost. Buckley had no illusions whatsoever about taking the reins at Molineux and there was only one test when he moved in – the acid test. Football was like war to him; his team had to win matches to succeed. It was as simple as that.

Buckley designed a brand new strip – old gold shirts with black shorts – and his first match in charge saw Wolves held to a 2–2 home draw by his former club, Manchester City. In his first four seasons as manager, Buckley and Wolves had mixed fortunes in Division Two, finishing 16th, 17th, ninth and fourth before finally winning promotion in 1932.

In 1927–28 the first-team squad comprised 30 professionals and Buckley, a shrewd tactician, soon started to sort out his team. As the season wore on he made some significant changes in a determined effort to turn round the club's fortunes. He brought in defender Tom Pritchard from Newport County, Welsh international wing-half Dai Richards from Merthyr Town, Len Williams from Stockport County, and Lewis Botto as cover for goalkeeper Noel George, who had been suffering from rheumatoid arthritis for quite a while. Unfortunately, his health deteriorated and two years after his last game versus Bristol City in November 1927 George died in Lichfield at the age of 31.

Buckley, though, could not hold on to his ace marksman Tom Phillipson, who joined Sheffield United for £4,000, having scored 111 goals in 159 senior games for Wolves, including a club record of 37 in 1925–26. Wolves, who were £14,500 in debt at the time, simply could not refuse the bid placed by the Blades.

Wolves conceded 100 goals in Buckley's first season as manager. They crashed to an embarrassing 7–0 defeat at relegated Fulham, succumbed to a 6–0 thrashing at Swansea and, despite scoring four at Deepdale, lost a nine-goal thriller to Preston.

In 1928–29 Wolves gave away another 82 goals and were hammered 8–3 at Middlesbrough. They were also humiliated in the FA Cup, losing 1–0 to non-League side Mansfield Town in a third-round tie at Molineux. This defeat prompted Buckley to 'sort out' his defence and he did just that, not by recruiting players, but by working with those he had and introducing new ideas and tactics and getting them to be more professional.

Over a period of 17 months between 5 November 1927 and 1 April 1929, Wolves utilised six goalkeepers – George, Botto, Alf Canavon, Fred Bryce, Jack Turner and Norman Lewis, in that order – before Buckley signed Alf Tootill from Accrington. Nicknamed the 'Birdcatcher', he made his debut in a 3–1 home League win over Notts County and never looked back after that, going on to serve Wolves for over three years and make more than 140 senior appearances.

Also in season 1928–29, three sturdy defenders had their first outings for Wolves – Bill Brown and Jack Gardiner were recruited from Coventry City and Reg Hollingworth from Sutton Junction, with only Hollingworth making an impression. Wingers Jack Hetherington and Bill Barraclough also came into the team, as did Billy Hartill, who would develop into one of the greatest goalscorers in Wolves' history, and the versatile Dicky Rhodes, who would remain at Molineux until October 1935.

For the opening League game of season 1929–30 at home to rivals West Brom, which resulted in a 4–2 defeat, manager Buckley fielded five new players: right-back and penalty expert Wilf Lowton, who was signed from Exeter City; Yorkshire-born centre-half George Lax; George Bellis, a former sergeant major in the Royal Engineers based in India who arrived from Wrexham; Welsh right-winger Roy Davies from Ebbw Vale; and inside-right Dick Forshaw, who had already scored 117 goals in 266 appearances for Everton as well as assisting Liverpool. Only Lowton, Law and Bellis, however, established themselves as regulars in the first team as Buckley attempted to blend Wolves into serious promotion contenders.

After that Black Country derby defeat, results improved and by mid-October, having lost only one more game, Wolves were perched on top of the Second Division table, looking strong and positive. The front line now comprised Mark Crook (ex-Blackpool and Swindon Town), Harry Marshall (formerly of Southport), Hartill, Jimmy Deacon (who was bought from Darlington) and Barraclough, and they were playing splendidly as a unit.

Sadly, Wolves' form dipped during the winter months. Defeats of 3–1 at Southampton and 6–0 at Oldham saw them slowly slip down the ladder and their form got worse after a 7–3 drubbing by West

Brom, when goalkeeper George Walker fractured his ankle. An early exit from the FA Cup, beaten by Oldham, did not help matters and in the end Wolves had to settle for a disappointing ninth place in the table.

In May 1930 the 1926 Scottish Cup winners St Mirren beat Wolves 2–0 in a charity match at Molineux to take home a specially manufactured trophy and most of the players who played in that game started the 1930–31 season in the first team, among them Dai Richards, 'Charlie' Phillips and Walter Bottrill, ex-Middlesbrough, Rotherham United and York City. This time round Wolves did much better in the League, finishing fourth behind the champions Everton, runners-up West Brom, who beat them in the sixth round of the FA Cup, and third-placed Tottenham.

Surprisingly, Wolves were only seven points behind the unique double-winners Albion and this was due, certainly, to a poor sequence of results in February and early March, when they lost five games on the trot, and also towards the end of the campaign, when five of their last six fixtures ended in draws.

After a strenuous pre-season training programme, Wolves started the 1931–32 season in a determined and confident frame of mind, firmly believing that they could regain their First Division status after a break of some 25 years. Indeed, they began like a house on fire, whipping Spurs 4–0, Chesterfield 6–0, Bradford City 3–1 and Preston North End 3–2 in their first four home games, while also winning at Burnley and Southampton, each by 3–1.

Attendances were improving rapidly as Wolves kept on stacking up the points, and as winter drew nearer so their performances improved, with emphatic home victories over Millwall 5–0, Bristol City 4–2 and Bury 6–0 while Port Vale were thumped 7–1 in the Potteries. At this time Hartill was in brilliant form. He scored eight goals in three matches in just over a fortnight, including two hat-tricks, and as the New Year approached he was still finding the net, claiming a brace in a superb 7–0 home win over Manchester United when the crowd topped 37,000, the biggest attendance at Molineux for a League game since October 1927.

Despite losing to Preston in the fourth round of the FA Cup, Wolves surged on in the League and, as the games slowly started to run out, the title became a three-horse race with Leeds United and Stoke City also challenging for glory. It turned into a terrific battle and in the end the Championship went to Wolves, who pipped Leeds by two points (56 to 54) with Stoke in third place on 52. Buckley's braves clinched the title in April with three fine wins: 4–0 at Bristol City, 7–1 at home to Oldham Athletic and 2–0 at home to Port Vale. In fact, the League was won with that victory over the latter club when almost 29,000 fans attended Molineux. Hartill finished as top scorer for the third season running as Wolves bagged a record total of 115 goals in the League alone. Ten players made 30 appearances or more and for the first time the average League crowd at Molineux was over 20,000 (21,767).

After paying off their overdraft following a profit of more than £4,000, Wolves also had a new stand built on the Molineux Street side of the ground. This cost almost £20,500 and could accommodate 8,000 spectators, 3,400 of them seated. And with the team back in the top flight for the first time since 1906, the cash-flow situation within the club was now looking a lot healthier.

Prior to season 1932–33, manager Buckley emphasised to his players that it would be far tougher competing in the First Division than it was in the Second but knew, deep down, that there were some quality footballers at the club who could play at any level, and so it proved as the years rolled by.

Wolves did find it tough in the top Division, and in fact they just scraped clear of relegation in their first season back with the big boys, mustering only 35 points, two more than the relegated pair of

Bolton Wanderers and Blackpool. A crowd of almost 35,500 saw Wolves beat the FA Cup winners Everton 4–2 at home on the last day to stay clear of Bolton. It was a close call.

Amazingly, Wolves scored enough goals to have won the title (80) but conceded 96, suffering some big defeats in the process, among them a 7–1 reverse at the hands of the champions Arsenal (after which 'keeper Alf Tootill was sold to Fulham for £1,000), two 5–1 beatings on Merseyside to Everton and Liverpool, and a 5–3 loss at home to Sheffield Wednesday. They also suffered a 6–3 home defeat at the hands of Derby in a fourth-round FA Cup-tie.

A 10-goal thriller at Molineux in February ended Wolves 6 Huddersfield 4, Billy Hartill's hat-trick easing the pressure at a time when Buckley's team lay next to bottom.

Wolves improved in 1933–34 and finished 15th in the table. And due to a decent points tally of 40, they were actually closer to fourth-placed Derby than they were to Newcastle United in 21st position. Wolves played very well at times, whipping Manchester City 8–0, Sheffield Wednesday 6–2 and Huddersfield 5–2 at home, but on their travels they were rather poor, crashing 7–1 at Blackburn, 6–1 at Sunderland, 6–2 at Villa Park, 5–1 at Newcastle and 4–0 in the return game with Manchester City.

In the Wolves team now were several new faces, among them goalkeeper Frank Wildman, who had replaced Jack Ellis, tough-tackling coalminer Cecil Shaw at full-back, half-backs Tom Smalley and Jack Nelson, Scottish inside-right Jack Beattie, centre-forward George Goddard and Welshman Ivor Jones, who was to make his name for different reasons later on.

There were also some fine players in the second team, including Tom Galley and Bill Morris, who were both to go on to play for England, and Joe Gardiner. These three players alone made 540 senior appearances for Wolves.

To Buckley's obvious disappointment and annoyance, Wolves still struggled defensively in 1934–35, conceding another 94 League goals as they finished a poor 17th in the table, five points clear of relegation. They scored enough times themselves, 93 in all matches, and only the champions Arsenal netted more. Hartill bagged another 29, including a five-timer against Aston Villa at Molineux in September.

Among the new arrivals this season were a trio of Irishmen: Jackie Brown, David 'Boy' Martin and goalkeeper Jimmy Utterson, who sadly was to die at the age of 21 after receiving a serious head injury in the game at Middlesbrough in September 1935. Seven months earlier, Stan Cullis from Ellesmere Port made his League debut for Wolves against Huddersfield Town. Over the next 30 years he became a household name at Molineux, both as a player and manager.

Unable to get their game together in the League, Wolves came 15th in 1935–36 with 40 points, only eight fewer than runners-up Derby County. Their goal average was 77–76 and their best win was an 8–1 thrashing of relegated Blackburn Rovers. They also handed out 4–0 defeats to Everton and Middlesbrough.

Wolves again found it tough going in the FA Cup and were ousted in the third round by Leeds United, having lost to another Yorkshire club, Sheffield Wednesday, the previous season.

Manager Buckley off-loaded several players during the mid-1930s: Mark Crook and Jack Nelson both joined Luton Town; Billy Hartill, after scoring 170 goals, went to Everton (much to the annoyance of the fans); Dai Richards switched to Brentford; Dicky Rhodes, having made 159 starts for the club, signed for Sheffield United; Charlie Phillips moved to Aston Villa; Jack Dowen was snapped up by West Ham United; and Len Astill went north to Blackburn Rovers.

Always looking to rebuild his team, Buckley then transferred almost a complete team for less than £20,000 in season 1936–37. Chris Greene and George Henson both went to Swansea Town;

'Boy' Martin moved to Nottingham Forest; goalkeeper Jack Weare joined West Ham; Hartill's replacement Tom 'Pongo' Waring, the former Aston Villa centre-forward who failed to settle at Molineux, took his shooting boots to Tranmere; full-back George Laking opted to join Middlesbrough; Jackie Brown was secured by Coventry City; penalty expert Cecil Shaw, after 183 appearances for Wolves, 121 consecutively in the Football League, ventured off to West Bromwich Albion; tough-tackling Bob Iverson was recruited by Aston Villa; and outside-left Billy Wrigglesworth signed for Manchester United.

Between May 1935 and June 1939 it is believed that Major Buckley transferred as many as 30 professionals from Molineux, the majority of whom had appeared in Wolves' first team. And the club received just £110,658 in transfer fees for them all.

To replace those who left, Buckley either acquired or upgraded the following: giant goalkeeper Alex Scott, full-back brothers Frank and Jack Taylor – both of whom went on to become League club managers – defender Joe Gardiner, winger Teddy Maguire, the lanky figure of Tom Galley, David Jordan, Gordon Clayton, George Ashall and dynamic centre-forward Dennis Westcott, who would become a huge favourite with the supporters.

With so much transfer activity taking place, the supporters were somewhat concerned as to the strength of the side, but Buckley had no qualms whatsoever about the quality of the players in his squad. As a result, Wolves had their best campaign for quite some time in 1936–37, finishing fifth in the First Division – their highest placing since 1900.

Everton (7–2), Charlton (6–1), Preston (5–0), Grimsby (5–2), West Brom (5–2) and Brentford (4–0) were all blitzed at Molineux, where Wolves won 16 of their 21 League games. Unfortunately, the team suffered some heavy defeats on the road, losing 5–1 at Derby, 4–0 at Huddersfield, 4–1 at Manchester City and 6–2 at Sunderland. It was the last named club that also knocked Wolves out of the FA Cup, winning a quarter-final tie at the third attempt.

Maintaining their form, Wolves did even better in 1937–38, claiming second spot in the table, just a point behind Arsenal. After playing exceptionally well throughout the campaign and registering some superb victories, including a 10–1 home drubbing of Leicester City and a 5–0 thrashing of Portsmouth, they had to win their final game of the season to become champions. Unfortunately, they lost 1–0 at Sunderland, so handing the title to the Gunners who, earlier in the season, whipped them 5–0 at Highbury and knocked Wolves out of the FA Cup in the fourth round in front of a then record crowd of 61,267 at Molineux.

The average League attendance at Molineux in 1937–38 was 30,316 – Wolves' best ever at that time. Westcott top-scored with 22 goals in his first season with the club.

In August 1938 Bryn Jones was transferred to Arsenal for a British record fee of £14,000. The fans were shocked at his departure as the Welshman had been influential in helping the side reach second spot in the League. Sympathetic to his career choice, however, the 43,364 crowd gave Jones a standing ovation when he returned to Molineux with Arsenal at the start of the 1938–39 season – and he even helped set up the winning goal for Horace Cumner.

Wolves were again unlucky in the League in 1938–39, finishing second once more, this time to a powerful Everton side whom they slaughtered 7–0 at Molineux in late February. Wolves, in fact, were well on course to complete the double this term and reached the FA Cup Final after ousting Bradford 3–1, Leicester City 5–1, Liverpool 4–1, Everton 2–0 and Grimsby Town 5–0. A record Molineux crowd of 61,315 attended the Liverpool tie and another record turnout, 76,962, saw Westcott score four of the goals against Grimsby in the semi-final at Old Trafford. Unfortunately he forgot to take his shooting boots to Wembley where Wolves, the pre-match favourites, were well beaten 4–1 by Portsmouth. And all credit to the Wolves boss, who said after the game 'We were beaten for pace, by cleverness and even in the ability to make quick decisions. Pompey thoroughly deserved their victory. Well done.'

In February 1939 manager Buckley gave 16-year-old winger Jimmy Mullen his League debut against Leeds United and a month later he played in the semi-final, the youngest player ever to do so.

Wolves' Cup Final line up was Scott; Bill Morris (who was capped by England versus Romania that same year) and F. Taylor; Galley, Cullis and Gardiner; Burton, McIntosh, Westcott, Dorsett and Maguire. 'Dizzy' Burton, who cost £4,000 from Doncaster and made over 80 appearances for the club, was transferred to West Ham shortly afterwards for £6,000. McIntosh, a Scotsman, was recruited from Dunfermline Athletic and later played for Birmingham City and Coventry City. Dorsett, from Brownhills, scored 35 goals in only 52 games for Wolves before moving to Aston Villa, where he developed into a solid, uncompromising defender.

Wartime football and beyond

During the second half of the 1938–39 season, manager Buckley told his players that they could join the Territorial Army if they wished, as soon as the campaign was over. But with war clouds hovering perilously over Britain, they hung on until September 1939 when, after just three League matches, competitive football in England was suspended.

Skipper Stan Cullis was the first to join up. He was quickly followed by Tom Galley, Dennis Westcott and Alex Scott. Members of the Molineux groundstaff entered the Civil Defence, the police reserve and the various armed forces, while a few chose to work in local munitions factories.

After barely a fortnight without football, the Home Office allowed clubs to play again, initially forming Regional Leagues to minimise the distance teams had to travel. Wolves found it difficult at times to put out a decent team, but with the recruitment of guest players, untried youngsters and the occasional over-age professional, they battled on gamely.

During the seven-year restricted wartime period (September 1939 to April 1946) Wolves competed in over 230 matches, including four in the two-legged FA Cup competition in the transitional season of 1945–46. They did not play at all in 1940–41 when Molineux became the headquarters for the nation's Air Raid Precautions Unit.

Two trophies were won during the hostilities – the Midland Regional League Championship in 1939–40 and the Wartime League North Cup in 1941–42, when Wolves beat Sunderland in a pulsating two-legged Final that attracted an aggregate attendance figure of almost 78,000.

After knocking out Chester, both Manchester clubs (United first, City second) and neighbours West Bromwich Albion in the semi-final, Wolves drew the first leg of the Final at Roker Park 2–2 in front of 34,776 fans, Westcott scoring both goals. Over 43,000 attended the return leg, which Wolves won 4–1, with guests Jack Rowley (from Manchester United, who scored twice) and Frank Broome (Aston Villa) both figuring on the scoresheet, along with Westcott (as usual). The latter notched 91 wartime goals for Wolves, Dorsett struck 42, a young, up-and-coming Billy Wright, who made his debut at the age of 15, claimed 34 and Mullen weighed in with 28.

Full-back Derek Ashton made the most wartime appearances for Wolves with 149; Gus McLean played in 126 games and Wright in 117. In the first wartime season (1939–40) Wolves made a profit

WOLVERHAMPTON WANDERERS
MORRIS
SCOTT
TAYLOR
GALLEY
CULLIS
GARDINER
McINTOSH
WESTCOTT
DORSETT
The English Cup Team, 1939
BURTON
MAGUIRE

Wolves' first and second teams prior to the 1938–39 season. A young Billy Wright is the player second from right on the back row.

of £18,000 but lost £4,500 in 1940–41 when they never kicked a ball. The team's biggest win during the seven years was 11–1 versus Everton in a League Cup qualifying game in March 1942, when guest player Rowley netted five goals.

Major Buckley chose to resign as manager of Wolves in March 1944, handing over his duties to the former Welsh international and Bolton Wanderers FA Cup winner Ted Vizard. Vastly experienced, Vizard played over 500 games for the Trotters and remains the oldest player ever to appear for Bolton in a competitive game, aged 41 years and 287 days when he played against Sunderland in 1931.

During his short term in office Vizard signed one of the best goalscorers in the game, bringing in Jesse Pye from Notts County for £12,000 in May 1946. Pye got off to a flying start in the gold-and-black strip, scoring a hat-trick on his debut when Arsenal got walloped 6–1 in the first League game since 1939.

Wolves would have won the title in 1947 had they beaten Liverpool in their final League game. Before kick-off Wolves were a point ahead of the Merseysiders, but in front of more than 50,000 fans at Molineux they went down 2–1 and missed out on the star prize by a single point (57–56). Westcott set a new club scoring record with 38 League goals before transferring to Blackburn Rovers.

The following season Wolves were unbeaten in 28 of their 42 matches and lost in an FA Cup fourth-round replay to Everton. Hancocks and Pye were joint top scorers with 16 goals apiece and nine players made 30 or more appearances. In June 1948 Vizard was replaced as manager by 32-year-old Stan Cullis, who had been his assistant for 12 months.

The Cullis era

There is no doubt that Stan Cullis inherited a fine set of players – and he made them into a great team. An outstanding centre-half himself, he imbued his players with something of his own style –

The 1946–47 team, ready to restart League football after the break for World War Two. Back row, left to right: Ted Vizard (manager), Tom Galley, Angus McLean, Bert Williams, Billy Crook, Billy Wright, Jack Smith (coach), Jack Howley (secretary). Front row: Johnny Hancocks, Jesse Pye, Dennis Westcott, Stan Cullis, Willie Forbes, Jimmy Mullen.

shrewdness, perception, loyalty, ambition and a will to win. He devoted hours on end to the welfare of the team, and within six years of him taking charge Wolves won the two major trophies available in the game at that time – the League Championship and the FA Cup.

In his first season as manager, Cullis instilled a fighting quality in his players and also introduced a brand new style, the long ball game, using two wingers, three goal-seeking inside-forwards and an attack-minded wing-half.

The plan worked a treat with Johnny Hancocks, ex-Walsall, raiding down the right and Jimmy Mullen likewise down the left. Dunn, Pye and Irishman Sammy Smyth, formerly with Dundella, and either Bill Crook or Wright were asked to join the forward line whenever possible, leaving the rugged Bill Shorthouse and the two full-backs to defend, with Bert Williams in goal after taking over from Scott in 1946.

Prior to the start of season 1948–49, Wolves toured France and Holland, becoming the first English club to play in the latter country. On returning home, manager Cullis set out his guidelines for the new campaign, for which he had high hopes of achieving success. Jack Howley, who had joined the office staff as a youngster in 1923, was made club secretary to assist Cullis. He was to remain at the club for 20 years.

Showing strength, courage, tenacity and skill, Wolves had a wonderful season. They took sixth place in the First Division and won the FA Cup for the third time, beating Second Division strugglers Leicester City 3–1 in the Final at Wembley.

It had not been an easy passage through to the Final for Wolves. They had to beat Chesterfield, Sheffield United, Liverpool and neighbours West Brom, who at the time were going for promotion in Division Two. And this was the first time they had beaten the Baggies in five attempts in the competition, with Jimmy Mullen's floated effort doing the trick.

They reached the Final after beating the holders, Manchester United, in a tough semi-final replay at Goodison Park, having forced a draw at Hillsborough with only eight fit players on the pitch. Both full-backs, Pritchard and Kelly, were injured. The former stayed on but the latter was carried off and Pye was still trying to shake off a bout of influenza. For the replay Cullis brought back Terry Springthorpe and introduced Alf Crook (Billy's brother) at full-back, and they performed splendidly in a 1–0 win, Smyth grabbing the all-important goal.

Wolves were on a high when they met Leicester in the Final, and in a fluid, open game, with attack being the operative word, Cullis's men played tremendously well, beating the Foxes with two first-half goals from Pye (a classic header and a sweet shot on the turn) and a wonderful 68th-minute strike from Smyth.

The following year Wolves went out of the competition in the fifth round and came very close to winning the League title for the very first time.

Wolves started the 1949–50 season with a phenomenal burst of success, going 12 matches without defeat. But then they struggled, failing to register a single win between early October and Boxing Day, partly due to the fact that several key players were out injured. The goals had dried up, too, until a certain Roy Swinbourne, who had been nurtured along by former player Mark Crook in nursery side Wath Wanderers, arrived on the scene. Linking up well with Pye, Smyth and Johnny Walker, he scored seven goals during the second half of the campaign as Wolves fought it out hammer and tongs for the title with Portsmouth. Only two defeats were suffered in a run of 14 games at the end of the League programme, including a terrific final flourish which saw Wolves beat Arsenal 3–0, Bolton 4–2 and Birmingham City 6–1. But it was all in vain as Pompey took the star prize on goal-average.

Pye (18 goals) was top scorer that season, and in May 1950 Mullen became the first substitute used by England in a full international match, when he replaced the injured Jackie Milburn against Belgium in Brussels.

Billy Wright was now the Wolves and England captain, a position he would hold until his retirement in 1959. He led his country in the World Cup Finals in Brazil in June and July 1950, accompanied by goalkeeper Bert Williams and winger Jimmy Mullen, but unfortunately England failed to qualify from the group stage after being humiliated by the US in Belo Horizonte and by Spain in Rio.

At the end of the season, full-backs Springthorpe and Kelly both left Molineux, joining Coventry City and Huddersfield Town respectively.

After four very good post-war campaigns, it came as a shock for Wolves when they finished the 1950–51 season down in 14th position and lost to Newcastle United in the semi-final of the FA Cup. Their final League position was put down to a dismal run of 13 defeats and two draws in 17 games, and also to their exploits in the Cup – they played seven tough matches before losing in a replay to the eventual winners.

There were, however, portents for the future. In February 1951 inside-forward Peter Broadbent was signed from Brentford, and before the season's end he showed the quality of his footwork in nine first-team fixtures. He also helped the reserves win the Central League title for the second year running.

A year later Wolves' second string won their division again, helped this time by Norman Deeley and the versatile South African Eddie Stuart. But the first XI, minus Smyth (sold to Stoke City for £25,000) and the injured Dunn and Williams for long periods, and including a misfiring Swinbourne, slipped down to 16th in the First Division and went out of the FA Cup in the fourth round to Liverpool in front of Anfield's biggest-ever crowd, 61,905. But there was some consolation for the club when Billy Wright was voted 'Footballer of the Year'.

Once again the Central League Championship trophy found its way into the club's boardroom, and the junior team reached the Final of the FA Youth Cup, in which they were beaten 8–4 on aggregate by Manchester United's impressive Busby Babes. The seniors finished third in the League, just three points behind champions Arsenal and Preston North End. Besides the emergence of two promising youngsters, Eddie Clamp and Colin Booth, manager Cullis recruited Jack Taylor from Luton Town in a part-exchange deal involving Pye, and signed amateur international Bill Slater, who had played in the 1951 FA Cup Final for Blackpool and played for Great Britain in the 1952 Olympic Games in Helsinki. He also gave League debuts to Ron Flowers and Ronnie Stockin, while Nigel Sims proved a very capable deputy for Williams in goal and, as a massive bonus, Dennis Wilshaw was now producing the goods up front, scoring 18 goals in 29 games.

League champions

Cullis had now assembled a pretty formidable squad, and the principal players at the start of the 1953–54 season were goalkeeper Bert Williams; full-backs Jack Short and Roy Pritchard; half-backs Bill Slater, Bill Shorthouse and Billy Wright; wingers Johnny Hancocks and Jimmy Mullen; and forwards Roy Swinbourne, Peter Broadbent and Dennis Wilshaw. Full-back Eddie Stuart and half-back Ron Flowers forced their way into the team later in the season.

The season itself turned out to be a fabulous one for Wolves and their supporters as the Football League Championship trophy came to Molineux at long last. During this never-to-be-forgotten campaign, Wolves achieved some pleasing victories. They enjoyed their first win at Newcastle for 50 years, completed the first double over arch-rivals West Bromwich Albion since 1909–10, gained their first victory at The Hawthorns since November 1928 and beat the reigning champions Arsenal 3–2 at Highbury, where they had not won in 21 years. Wolves, in fact, began their League programme with a 4–1 defeat at Burnley, but from then until mid-December lost only twice in 22 games and hammered Chelsea 8–1 at Molineux in the process.

Playing some great attacking football, Wolves battled it out for glory at the top of the Division throughout the season with their Black Country neighbours Albion, and despite losing to Second Division Birmingham City in the third round of the FA Cup they powered on in the League, recording some terrific wins at home and away. Although they suffered a few hiccups here and there and at one stage looked like finishing runners-up, Wolves eventually took the star prize with four points to spare (57–53). They virtually clinched the title after the Baggies' League chances faded in the penultimate game when they went for broke in the FA Cup, a competition they won to make it a double for the Black Country.

Perhaps the turning point came in early April when Wolves won 1–0 at The Hawthorns. Both teams had key players missing due to the England-Scotland international. Albion perhaps were worse off, with their twin strikers Ronnie Allen and Wolverhampton-born Johnny Nicholls absent, and to make things harder Ray Barlow was injured early on and limped through 75 minutes of the game. Roy Swinbourne scored the all-important goal and after that Wolves never looked back. Wolves scored 96 League goals this term. Wingers Hancocks and Mullen netted 31 goals between them and Wilshaw was top marksman with 26.

The team who completed the run-in to the 1953–54 season and clinched the First Division title for the first time in Wolves' history. Back row, left to right: Gardiner (trainer), Slater, Shorthouse, Williams, Flowers, Stuart. Front row: Hancocks, Broadbent, Swinbourne, Wright, Wilshaw, Mullen.

Wolves in 1953–54 with the First Division Championship Trophy. Back row, left to right: R. Flowers, W. Shorthouse, E. Stuart, Mr S. Cullis, B. Williams, J. Gardiner, J. Mullen. W.J. Slater, R. Swinbourne. Front row: P. Broadbent, W. Wright (captain), J. Hancocks, D. Wilshaw.

International floodlit friendlies

The summer of 1953 saw the first set of floodlights installed at Molineux. They comprised 60 lamps on four giant pylons and were designed after the pattern used in New York's famous Yankee Stadium. They were officially 'switched on' for the friendly game against a South African XI on 30 September of that year, a game Wolves won 3–1.

Described at the time as being one of the greatest football teams in the world, Wolves proved this beyond all doubt when they took on and beat some of the best club sides in Europe over a period of six years, with crowds flocking to Molineux to see Stan Cullis's men produce some majestic performances.

Here are details of some of those international friendlies played by Wolves at Molineux:

30 September 1953	v South Africa XI	won 3–1
10 March 1954	v Racing Club of Buenos Aires	won 3–1
28 October 1954	v Maccabi Tel Aviv	won 10–0
16 November 1954	v Moscow Spartak	won 4–0
13 December 1954	v Honved (Hungary)	won 3–2
9 November 1955	v Moscow Dynamo	won 2–1
28 January 1956	v San Lorenzo (Argentina)	won 5–1
29 October 1956	v Bucharest CCA (Romania)	won 5–0
27 March 1957	v Borussia Dortmund	won 4–3
10 April 1957	v Valencia	won 3–0
17 October 1957	v Real Madrid	won 3–2
29 September 1958	v South Africa XI	won 1–0

Wolves were 2–0 down after just 14 minutes against Honved before storming back to beat the Hungarian champions in front of 54,998. The Honved side included the great Ferenc Puskas, inside-forward Sandor Kocsis, skipper Jozef Bozsik and wingers Laszlo Budai and Zoltan Czibor, all of whom helped Hungary beat England 6–3 at Wembley in 1953 and 7–1 in Budapest a year later.

The biggest crowd ever to attend a friendly match at Molineux – 55,480 – saw Wolves beat Moscow Spartak 4–0 in 1954, Johnny Hancocks scoring twice. Three years later, 55,169 packed into the ground to see Wolves defeat the reigning European Cup holders Real Madrid 3–2. Roy Swinbourne netted a hat-trick in the 10–0 victory over Maccabi Tel Aviv in 1954.

Wolves handed over their League crown to Chelsea in 1954–55, the Londoners having four points to spare at the death (52–48). The crucial game took place at Stamford Bridge in early April, when over 75,000 fans saw Chelsea win 1–0 courtesy of a 75th minute Peter Sillett penalty. This certainly damaged Wolves as they lost three of their last five matches and had to settle for second spot. They also went out of the FA Cup in the quarter-finals, losing to Sunderland, and were held to a 4–4 draw in a classic FA Charity Shield encounter at Molineux by Albion, for whom Ronnie Allen scored a hat-trick.

During the season Billy Wright was switched to centre-half, where he would remain until his retirement in 1959. He, Ron Flowers, Bert Williams and Dennis Wilshaw all played for England versus France in Paris, while the last named also cracked in four goals in a 7–2 win over Scotland at Wembley in April. Flowers had also played for England at Under-23 level and went on to gain 49 full caps for England. Wright would play in 105 internationals, the first player in the world to reach the century mark.

In 1955–56 Wolves finished third in the League, 11 points behind the runaway champions Manchester United, and lost to Albion in the third round of the FA Cup. They also sold three players to Aston Villa – winger Les Smith, goalkeeper Nigel Sims and full-back Roy Pritchard. Jimmy Murray made his mark as a centre-forward, scoring 11 goals, Norman Deeley was pressing hard for a place on the wing, and in September 1955 Wolves hammered Cardiff City 9–1 at Ninian Park to equal the record for the biggest away win in a First Division game. Back in 1908, Sunderland had crushed Newcastle United by the same score at St James' Park.

Both Johnny Hancocks and Roy Swinbourne scored hat-tricks against Cardiff but the latter suffered a serious injury before the turn of the year and his absence, one suspects, was why Wolves did not win the League Championship. Unfortunately, he was forced to retire shortly before his 28th birthday in 1957.

Over a period of five years – from August 1956 to April 1961 – Wolves scored a staggering 516 League goals, passing the century mark four seasons running from 1957. They were irresistible going forward and defences all over the country took a battering.

In 1956–57, despite managing a moderate sixth place in the Division – their lowest League finish for five years – they netted 94 goals. The following season, when they won the title for the second time, they bagged 103, and weighed in with 110 when they retained the title in 1958–59. A total of 106 goals were secured in 1959–60, when they were runners-up to Burnley, failing by a single point to become only the third team ever to win three successive titles, and Wolves scored 103 in 1960–61 when they came third behind double-winners Tottenham Hotspur and Sheffield Wednesday. Jimmy Murray notched 119 of those 500-plus goals and Peter Broadbent netted 80.

Wolves, 1957–58 League champions. Back row, left to right: E. Clamp, J. Murray, G. Harris, M Finlayson, W. Slater, R. Flowers, E. Stuart. Front row: R. Mason, N.Deeley, W. Wright (captain), Mr S. Cullis, P. Broadbent, C. Booth, J. Mullen.

The Wolves senior squad and their trophies in 1958–59.

In 1957–58 Wolves failed by two points to equal Arsenal's record of 66 League points when they clinched the title for the second time in four years with a superb record of 28 wins and eight draws. They finished five points clear of runners-up Preston North End and their biggest victories included 6–1 versus Bolton (who knocked Wolves out of the FA Cup in the sixth round), 5–0 versus Sunderland, 5–1 both at home and away against Birmingham, 5–1 versus Leicester City and 4–0 versus Manchester United at Old Trafford. One player who left the club was forward Dennis Wilshaw, who moved to Stoke City. He was signed as a teenager in 1943 and scored 117 goals in 232 appearances.

With the League Championship safely under their belts, Wolves entered the European Cup for the first time in 1958–59 but failed to make progress, losing 4–3 on aggregate to the German side Schalke 04 in the opening round. Peter Broadbent had the pleasure of scoring the club's first two European goals in the home leg, which ended 2–2.

Wolves lost in the annual FA Charity Shield game and also in the fourth round of the FA Cup to Bolton Wanderers. However, in the League they powered on once they had overcome a faltering start which included a 6–2 defeat at the hands of Chelsea at Stamford Bridge when a teenaged Jimmy Greaves scored five goals. Once again Wolves chalked up 28 victories as they eventually retained the title in style, finishing six points clear of second-place Manchester United. Their best win of the season was at Christmas, 7–0 at home to Portsmouth, whom they had beaten 5–3 at Fratton Park the day before, while other big wins at Molineux saw Arsenal, then topping the table, beaten 6–1, Leeds United 6–2, Blackburn Rovers and Luton Town 5–0, neighbours West Bromwich Albion 5–2 and Nottingham Forest 5–1.

Jimmy Mullen scored 114 goals in 486 appearances and retired at the end of the 1958–59 season.

The 1958–59 season proved to be the last for two major players – Billy Wright and Jimmy Mullen. The former scored 16 goals in 541 appearances for the club while Mullen netted 112 in 486. Both played in the 1949 FA Cup Final triumph and also for England. Wright had every intention of carrying on but, in a shock announcement on the eve of the 1959–60 campaign, declared he was hanging up his boots. He said farewell to the fans by playing in the pre-season public practice game at Molineux. Wright handed over the number-five shirt to George Showell and the captaincy to Eddie Stuart. When the latter lost his place in the team Bill Slater took over as skipper, guiding Wolves to FA Cup glory and runners'-up spot in the League, Burnley denying Cullis's men a third successive Championship win by just one point.

Wolves (54 pts) were sitting at the top of the table ahead of Tottenham Hotspur, having completed their 42-match programme, but third-placed Burnley had one game remaining, away at Manchester City. They had to win to pip Wolves for the title and in front of almost 66,000 fans they

The 1960 FA Cup winners. Back row, left to right: E. Clamp, R. Flowers, J. Gardiner (trainer), M. Finlayson, G. Harris, G. Showell. Front row: N. Deeley, B. Stobart, J. Murray, S. Cullis (manager), W. Slater, P. Broadbent, D. Horne.

did just that, beating City 2–1 to rob Wolves of the double. For just five days after 'losing' the League, Wolves travelled to Wembley and in front of almost 98,776 spectators defeated Blackburn Rovers 3–0 in a rather poor FA Cup Final. Norman Deeley scored two of the goals against Rovers, who were down to 10 men following Dave Whelan's injury in the first-half. Captain Slater duly collected the trophy having earlier been named Footballer of the Year.

Earlier in the season, Wolves had thrashed Fulham 9–0 at Molineux, their biggest home League win in terms of goals scored since April 1938, and they also crushed the eventual champions Burnley 6–1 as well as winning a 10-goal thriller 6–4 away at Manchester City. But their second challenge in the European Cup ended in the second round proper when they lost 9–2 on aggregate to a majestic Barcelona side.

Wolves finished third in the First Division in 1960–61, shared the Charity Shield with Burnley (2–2), lost to Huddersfield Town in the fourth round of the FA Cup and were dumped out of the European Cup-Winners' Cup by Rangers in the two-legged semi-final. Two wingers left the club – 1960 Cup-winner Des Horne joined Blackpool and Gerry Mannion moved to Norwich City – and up-and-coming centre-forward Ted Farmer scored twice on his League debut in a 3–1 win at Old Trafford. Farmer, in fact, was leading marksman with 28 goals (in 27 games), his 21st strike coming on his 21st birthday on 21 January versus Everton.

Surprisingly, Wolves finished 18th in the League table 12 months on, their lowest placing since 1933. They managed only 36 points (out of a possible 84) and were just four clear of disaster. They lost 19 matches, including a 7–2 drubbing at Blackpool, their biggest defeat for 28 years, and there's no doubt that the three points gained against relegated Chelsea over the Easter period saved their skin. They also went out of the FA Cup to rivals West Brom in the fourth round when a young full-back, Bobby Thomson, made an impressive debut.

Around this time, three loyal club men all left Molineux – Eddie Clamp signed for Arsenal for £10,000 (November 1961), Norman Deeley joined Leyton Orient (February 1962) and Eddie Stuart teamed up with his former colleague Wilshaw at Stoke City (July 1962).

An improvement was made in 1962–63 when Wolves topped the table early in the season and eventually took fifth place, 11 points behind champions Everton. Unfortunately, they failed to win 10 of their 21 home games and this perhaps ruined their chances of finishing higher. Their biggest win (of the 20 achieved) was an 8–1 opening day clattering of Manchester City, when they netted five times in the space of 15 minutes either side of half-time. New-found winger Alan Hinton top-scored with 19 goals and Bill Slater returned to his former club Brentford after making 339 senior appearances. Wolves slipped out of the FA Cup in the third round, beaten 4-3 at the City Ground by the 1959 winners Nottingham Forest.

Manager Cullis departs

Several of Wolves' performances during the 1963–64 season left a lot to be desired. With Ron Flowers leading the side, they won only two of their opening eight League games, registered just one victory in 10 starts either side of Christmas, and went out of the FA Cup in the third round to Arsenal. Thankfully they ended on a high with two 4–0 wins, which took them up to 16th place. But it was not a good season at all and there were a lot of comings and goings – out went Chris Crowe and Hinton, both to Nottingham Forest, Jimmy Murray and Barry Stobart both moved to

Manchester City, while goalkeeper Malcolm Finlayson and Ted Farmer were forced to retire. Into the camp came Ray Crawford from Ipswich Town, Bobby Woodruff from Swindon Town and Jimmy Melia from Liverpool.

In July 1964 John Ireland took over as chairman of the club, but out on the field the decline continued and with the team bottom of the table and struggling desperately, manager Stan Cullis, who had been part of the club since February 1934, was sacked in September 1964, much to the surprise of many ardent supporters.

Into his place after a six-week gap came Scotsman Andy Beattie, employed as caretaker manager. Dubbed the 'Flying Doctor', he had distinguished himself previously in spells at Nottingham Forest and Plymouth, but he failed to prevent Wolves from being demoted to the Second Division. They were relegated in 21st position with Midland neighbours Birmingham City, ironically Cullis's future club.

Striker Hugh McIlmoyle was signed from Carlisle after Cullis's departure and would make an impact when Beattie took over. The caretaker boss brought Dave Wagtaffe to Molineux, signing him from Manchester City on Boxing Day 1964. 'Waggy' would go on to enjoy a long career with Wolves and became a firm fans' favourite while Peter Knowles, given his debut by Cullis a year earlier, would start to blossom at inside-left. Out of Molineux went Peter Broadbent (to Shrewsbury Town) and George Showell (to Bristol City), while former England centre-forward Ray Crawford moved to West Brom and Johnny Kirkham to Peterborough.

Despite their horrid League form, Wolves reached the quarter-finals of the FA Cup in 1965 but found soon-to-be-champions Manchester United far too strong for them and went down 5–3 in a classic encounter in front of 53,581 fans at Molineux.

Beattie was only in office for 12 months, replaced in September 1965 by his coach Ronnie Allen. Formerly with Port Vale, West Bromwich Albion and Crystal Palace and an England international, Allen took over after a disastrous 9–3 thrashing at Southampton.

Allen quickly recruited defender John Holsgrove from his former club Palace and slowly and efficiently refloated a sinking ship. The resolution and leadership of Mike Bailey, who joined from Charlton in March 1966, the brilliant flowering of Wagstaffe's artistry, the skill and endurance of Ernie Hunt (ex-Swindon Town) and the integrity of Ron Flowers's last senior performances for the club gave a good deal of hope for the future as Wolves battled on to finish a creditable sixth at the end of their first season in Division Two for 33 years.

Again, Manchester United knocked Wolves out of the FA Cup, and in the home League game with Manchester City in August 1965 Dave Woodfield, whose senior debut had come three years earlier, became the first Wolves player to be sent off for 29 years.

The club's first spell outside the top division for 30 years would last just two seasons, as an eight-game winning run in the spring of 1967 paved the way to promotion, Wolves claiming second place, a point behind champions Coventry City.

Allen made what proved to be an outstanding signing in March 1967, capturing the services of experienced Northern Ireland international centre-forward Derek Dougan from Leicester City for £50,000. The 'Doog' became a huge favourite with the fans and scored nine important goals in 11 League games at the end of the season, including a hat-trick on his home debut against Hull City (won 4–0), braces in 4–1 wins over Bury and Norwich City and a point-saver at Millwall (1–1). He linked up superbly well with Ernie Hunt and enjoyed the wing service provided by Terry Wharton and Dave Wagstaffe. He lined up in a vital top-of-the-table clash with Coventry in late April and though the Sky

The Wolves squad at the start of the 1967–68 season under manager Ronnie Allen.

Blues won 3–1 in front of a never-to-be-bettered Highfield Road crowd of 51,455, Wolves could still have gone up as champions if they had won their final match at Crystal Palace. However, they were beaten 4–1 and City took the title.

Wolves entered the League Cup for the first time in 1966–67, losing 5–0 at Fulham in round three after dismissing Mansfield Town 2–1 at home in their first-ever tie. The holders Everton halted Wolves' progress in the FA Cup, winning a fourth-round replay 3–1 at Goodison Park.

Wolves' first-team squad (during Allen's first season in charge) comprised in the main: goalkeepers Fred Davies and the up-and-coming Phil Parkes (born in West Bromwich); full-backs Gerry Taylor, Joe Wilson (ex-Nottingham Forest) and Bobby Thomson; wing-halves Mike Bailey and Ron Flowers; defenders Graham Hawkins, John Holsgrove and Dave Woodfield; wingers Terry Wharton and Dave Wagstaffe; inside-forwards Peter Knowles, Ernie Hunt and Davey Burnside (a former teammate of Allen's at The Hawthorns); up front Hughie McIlmoyle and the irrepressible Derek Dougan.

During the summer of 1967, Wolves travelled to North America to take part in a tournament organised by the United Soccer Association. Twelve clubs were invited from Europe and South America and each one bore the name of a local team. Wolves, masquerading as 'Los Angeles Wolves', won the Western Division and went on to defeat the Eastern Division champions Washington Whips (Aberdeen of Scotland) in the match to decide the overall competition winners. The Final ended 6–5 after 30 minutes extra-time and then sudden death extra-time. This FIFA-sanctioned League merged the following season with the non-sanctioned National Professional Soccer League, which had also begun in 1967, to form the NASL (the North American Soccer League). Playing in midfield for Aberdeen was big Frank Munro who scored three goals, two of them penalties. He impressed Allen and within a matter of months had joined the ranks at Molineux, where he would stay until December 1977, making over 370 first-class appearances.

Back in the top flight of English football, season 1967–68 was not a brilliant one for Wolves, who finished 17th in the table and went out of both domestic Cup competitions in the opening round. A new full-back was signed – Derek Parkin – who would go on to make a club record 609 senior appearances. Forward Alun Evans was introduced by Allen, as were John McAlle and Les Wilson, while Hunt (sold to Everton for £80,000), Wharton (transferred to Bolton), Burnside (to Plymouth Argyle) and Fred Davies (to Cardiff City) were among those who departed.

Cup glory and dismay...then relegation

In truth, Wolves struggled in the League over the next two seasons, finishing 16th in 1968–69 and 13th the following term, during which Allen was replaced in the manager's chair by Bill McGarry (November 1968). They also failed to make headway in knockout football, losing early on in both the FA Cup and League Cup competitions and also missing out in the new Anglo-Italian tournament.

Among the major signings were those of midfielder Kenny Hibbitt (from Bradford Park Avenue), striker Hugh Curran (from Norwich City), 1966 FA Cup Finalist Jim McCalliog (from Sheffield Wednesday), winger Mike O'Grady (from Leeds United) and full-back Bernard Shaw (from Sheffield United), the latter recruited in effect to replace Bobby Thomson, who switched his allegiance to Birmingham City. And the big surprise was the retirement of the fans' favourite son, Peter Knowles, who quit football as he felt he could not continue playing and be true to his beliefs as a Jehovah's Witness.

Season 1970–71 saw Wolves claim fourth place in the League table, their highest finish since 1961, and as a result they qualified for the newly created UEFA Cup. In the FA Cup and League Cup competitions they missed out again but did have the honour of lifting the Texaco Cup, beating Heart of Midlothian 3–2 on aggregate in the two-legged Final.

Two new signings at this point were centre-forward Bobby Gould (from Arsenal) and midfielder Danny Hegan (from West Bromwich Albion) while John Holsgrove left for Sheffield Wednesday. Both the new men started the season at Newcastle and Gould went on to top-score with 24 goals while his strike partner Curran netted 20.

However, Gould, O'Grady and Woodfield all left Molineux in 1971–72 as Wolves, inspired by an exciting new goalscorer in John Richards, who had made his debut in 1969, went all the way to the UEFA Cup Final, knocking out some very useful sides. They started off by ousting Académica Coimbra (Portugal) 7–1 on aggregate, then saw off ADO Den Haag (again 7–1 over two legs), beat FC Carl Zeiss Jena (East Germany) 4–0 on aggregate, disposed of mighty Juventus 3–2 in the two-legged quarter-final and then clipped Ferencvaros of Hungary 4–3 (over two games) in the semi-final, goalkeeper Phil Parkes playing quite brilliantly in both matches, saving a penalty in each.

Unfortunately Wolves were disappointing in the first leg of the Final, losing 2–1 at home to the League Cup holders Tottenham Hotspur. They battled hard and long in the return leg at White Hart Lane, and a goal from Dave Wagstaffe earned them a 1–1 draw which was not enough, Spurs winning the contest 3–2 on aggregate.

Wolves came ninth in Division One in 1971–72, the title going to Derby County, who edged out Leeds United. In fact it was Wolves who prevented Leeds doing the double. Don Revie's team beat Arsenal 1–0 to win the FA Cup and two days later needed to win at Molineux to clinch the First Division title. However, Wolves beat them 2–1 and as the other contenders Liverpool were held 0–0 at Arsenal the same night, the crown went to Derby. In the two other competitions that season, Wolves failed miserably, going out at the first hurdle to Leicester City in the FA Cup and Manchester City in the League Cup, although they would gain revenge over the latter club at Wembley two years later.

Before then, though, in 1972–73 Wolves took fifth place in the League and reached the semi-finals of both the FA Cup and League Cup competitions, but failed to make inroads in either the Texaco or Watney Cup tournaments. They were narrowly beaten 1–0 by Leeds United in the FA Cup semi-final at Maine Road, Manchester, and went down 4–3 on aggregate to bogey side Tottenham Hotspur in the League Cup semis, having lost the first leg 2–1 at home.

John Richards became the first player since 1959–60 to score over 30 goals in a season, netting 36 in all games including 27 in the League. Dougan followed him home with 17. These same two players then netted a total of 37 goals between them in 1973–74, their combined efforts helping Wolves reach the League Cup Final for the first time after beating Halifax Town, Tranmere Rovers (in a replay), Exeter City, Liverpool and Norwich City (over two legs). Wolves fielded a handful of new players including goalkeeper Gary Pierce, forward Alan Sunderland, full-back Geoff Palmer and substitute Barry Powell, but took on and defeated Manchester City 2–1 in the Final, Kenny Hibbitt and Richards the scorers in front of 97,886 fans. This was Wolves' first major trophy win in 14 years.

Wolves hovered in mid-table throughout this term, eventually settling in 12th position while they exited the FA Cup in the third round and the UEFA Cup in the second.

Several players were not getting any younger, including Dougan, who would announce his retirement in May 1975 after making his 323rd and farewell appearance against Leeds United, but manager McGarry still considered them good enough to perform in the top flight. Wolves finished 12th again in 1974–75 but in the FA Cup, League Cup and UEFA Cup tournaments, they failed to scale the first hurdle.

After some decent campaigns, in which Wolves played close on 70 Cup matches over a period of six years, it came as a body-blow to a lot of people when they were again relegated at the end of the 1975–76 season.

Lacking personality both collectively and individually, Wolves played poorly. They won only two of their opening 15 League games, lost five in a row leading up to Christmas and then, when it mattered most, they recorded only two victories in their last nine starts. Amazingly, after playing so badly, they could have escaped the drop if they had beaten Liverpool at Molineux in their last game. A crowd of 48,900 turned up (with the Anfield 'Kop' transferring itself to the South Bank) to see the Merseysiders win 3–1 to clinch the title while sending Wolves crashing through the trapdoor with Burnley and Sheffield United.

Almost 59,500 saw Wolves draw their sixth-round FA Cup-tie with Manchester United at Old Trafford but the Reds went on to win the replay 3–2 on their way to the Final. Unfashionable and lowly Mansfield ousted Wolves from the League Cup, edging a fourth-round tie 1–0 at Field Mill.

It had certainly been a hit and miss season for Wolves. Full-back Bob McNab was surprisingly signed from Arsenal and, more surprisingly, Gould returned to Molineux from West Ham. Norman Bell, Maurice Daly, Gerry O'Hara and Martin Patching all made their senior debuts; Harry Marshall took over as club chairman from John Ireland; and the youngsters lost 5–0 on aggregate in the FA Youth Cup Final to West Bromwich Albion.

The club's image sank a peg lower when McGarry was replaced as manager by Sammy Chung and at that point few thought that the team was capable of regaining top-flight status at the first attempt. But regain it they did with some enterprising displays from midfielders Kenny Hibbitt, Willie Carr and Steve Daley; full-backs Geoff Palmer and Derek Parkin; central defenders Frank Munro and John McAlle; forwards John Richards, Alan Sunderland and (early on) Bobby Gould; and some brilliant goalkeeping by Gary Pierce, who was one of four ever presents.

Promotion was clinched with a 1–1 draw in their penultimate game at home to runners-up Chelsea, and the title was won when Bolton were defeated 1–0 at Burnden Park on the very last

Saturday, with 35,600 watching skipper Hibbitt strike the winning goal. Two Yorkshire clubs, Leeds United and Sheffield Wednesday, knocked Wolves out of the two domestic Cup competitions this season, but these results mattered little to the fans. It was promotion everyone wanted!

For the opening League game of season 1977–78, manager Sammy Chung fielded these 11 players against Bristol City at Ashton Gate: Parkes; Palmer, Daly; Daley, Parkin, McAlle; Patching, Carr, Richards, Kindon and Sunderland. Backed by 5,000 travelling supporters, Wolves battled to a 3–2 win and with an unchanged team won their next game 1–0 against QPR at Molineux.

After that bright start, results fluctuated and only one victory was secured in their next eight games, while Luton Town also knocked Wolves out of the League Cup. Attendances started to fall, dipping below the 20,000 mark, as Wolves struggled on the pitch. Alan Sunderland was transferred to Arsenal, Norman Bell and Mel Eves joined the attack and strongman Bob Hazell came into the centre of defence, with Paul Bradshaw (signed from Blackburn Rovers) taking over in goal.

Continuing to find it hard going, Wolves stumbled along and, in fact, managed only seven wins before the turn of the year. Thankfully, several teams were playing far worse than Wolves – West Ham, Newcastle United and Leicester City among them – and although beaten in the fourth round of the FA Cup by Arsenal, a five-match unbeaten run right at the end of the campaign enabled Wolves to retain their First Division status, staying up in 15th position, just four points above West Ham, relegated in 20th position.

Hopes of another Wembley appearance loomed large for Wolves in 1978–79 but the team also had to fight another relegation battle, eventually claiming 18th position, nine points above the drop-zone, with another new manager in the hot seat in the form of John Barnwell. Having been dumped out of the League Cup by Reading, Wolves' Wembley bid was made in the FA Cup and after beating Brighton and Hove Albion, Newcastle United (in a replay), Crystal Palace (when Bell fractured his right leg) and Shrewsbury Town (also in a replay) they met Arsenal in the semi-final at Villa Park. Barnwell, in charge since November 1978, was confident of beating his former club, but several players froze on the day and in the end the Gunners cruised to a comfortable 2–0 victory, the second goal being scored by former 'Wolf' Sunderland!

The Wolves squad in the late 1970s, with Sammy Chung as manager.

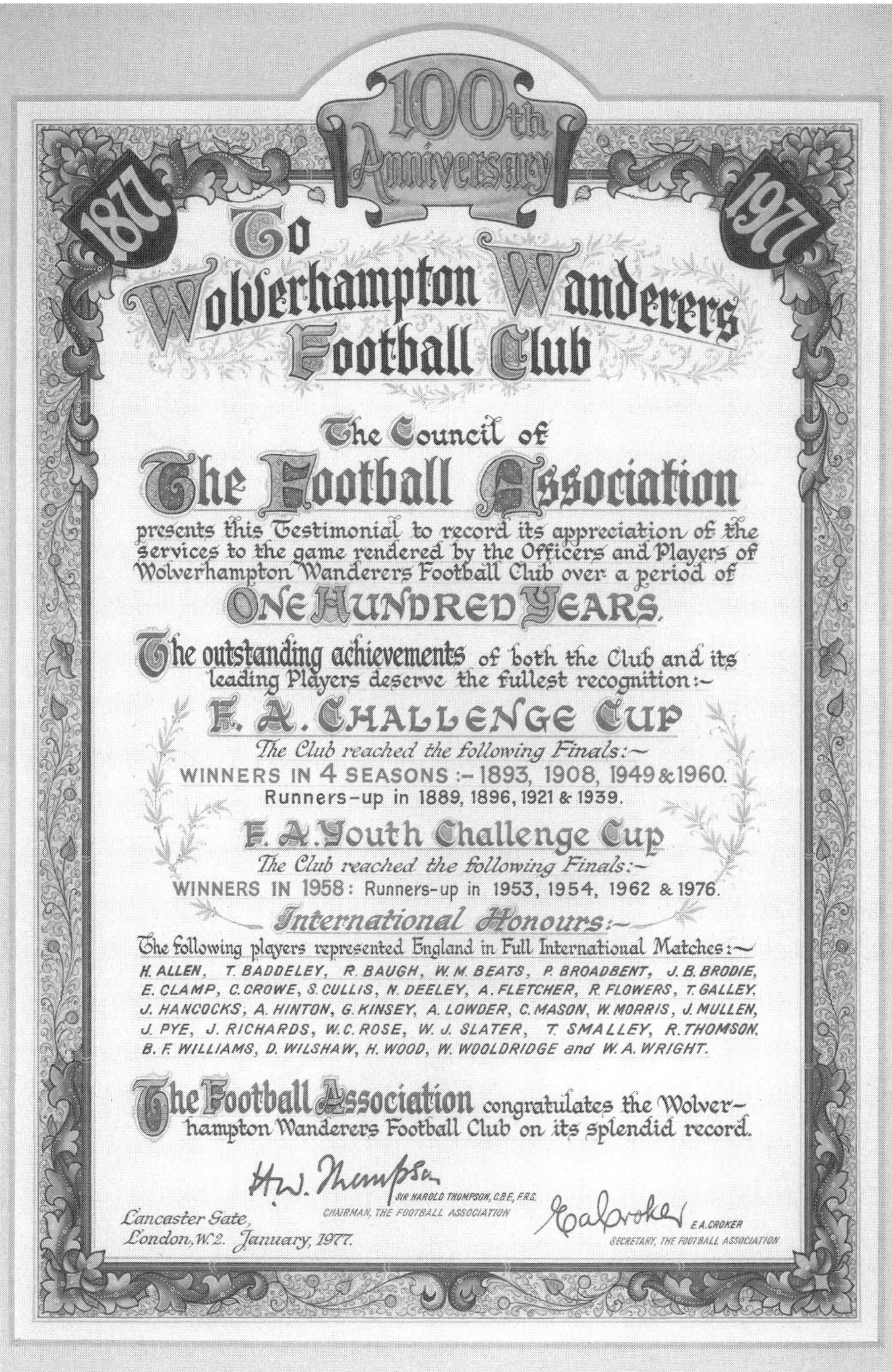

100th Anniversary

1877 1977

To
Wolverhampton Wanderers
Football Club

The Council of
The Football Association

presents this Testimonial to record its appreciation of the services to the game rendered by the Officers and Players of Wolverhampton Wanderers Football Club over a period of

ONE HUNDRED YEARS.

The outstanding achievements of both the Club and its leading Players deserve the fullest recognition:–

F. A. CHALLENGE CUP

The Club reached the following Finals:–
WINNERS IN 4 SEASONS :– 1893, 1908, 1949 & 1960.
Runners-up in 1889, 1896, 1921 & 1939.

F. A. Youth Challenge Cup

The Club reached the following Finals:–
WINNERS IN 1958: Runners-up in 1953, 1954, 1962 & 1976.

International Honours:–

The following players represented England in Full International Matches:–
H. ALLEN, T. BADDELEY, R. BAUGH, W. M. BEATS, P. BROADBENT, J. B. BRODIE, E. CLAMP, C. CROWE, S. CULLIS, N. DEELEY, A. FLETCHER, R. FLOWERS, T. GALLEY, J. HANCOCKS, A. HINTON, G. KINSEY, A. LOWDER, C. MASON, W. MORRIS, J. MULLEN, J. PYE, J. RICHARDS, W. C. ROSE, W. J. SLATER, T. SMALLEY, R. THOMSON, B. F. WILLIAMS, D. WILSHAW, H. WOOD, W. WOOLDRIDGE and W. A. WRIGHT.

The Football Association congratulates the Wolverhampton Wanderers Football Club on its splendid record.

H. W. Thompson
SIR HAROLD THOMPSON, C.B.E., F.R.S.
CHAIRMAN, THE FOOTBALL ASSOCIATION

Lancaster Gate,
London, W.2. January, 1977.

E. A. Croker
E.A. CROKER
SECRETARY, THE FOOTBALL ASSOCIATION

After the disappointment of losing to Arsenal, Barnwell, his assistant Richie Barker and the players launched a twin attack on the Empire Stadium in 1979–80, the season when football transfers went mad and Wolves were involved in two massive deals in the space of a few days in September.

On the fifth of the month Barnwell sold midfielder Steve Daley to Manchester City for £1,437,500 (including VAT and levy charges) and then, 72 hours later, he signed the Aston Villa striker Andy Gray for £1,150,000, the Scottish international putting pen to paper on the pitch before Wolves' home game with Crystal Palace.

A month earlier, Emlyn Hughes – nicknamed 'Crazy Horse' – had arrived from Liverpool for £90,000, and in October 1979 winger David Thomas was recruited from Everton for £325,000, the former QPR player choosing Molineux ahead of Old Trafford.

Hughes was handed the captaincy and proved to be a huge asset to the defence, playing alongside George Berry, while Peter Daniel (ex-Hull City), Kenny Hibbitt and Willie Carr were solid workers in midfield behind strikers Gray and John Richards and occasionally Mel Eves and Wayne Clarke. Paul Bradshaw was still in goal and the full-backs were the ever-reliable duo of Geoff Palmer and Derek Parkin.

Wolves battled on to finish sixth in the First Division and reach the fifth round of the FA Cup before losing at home to Watford. But in the League Cup, Barnwell's men went all the way and after accounting for Burnley (over two legs), Crystal Palace, QPR (in a replay), Grimsby Town (at the third attempt) and Swindon Town in the semis, they took on and beat Nottingham Forest 1–0 in the Final, Andy Gray tapping in the goal after a mix-up involving Peter Shilton and Dave Needham. This triumph, achieved against the odds as Forest were favourites and going for their third win, ensured Wolves would be back in Europe for the 1980–81 season.

Three players reached double figures in the goal stakes this term – Richards (18), Gray (15) and Hibbitt (13) – while Hughes captained England, following in the footsteps of three other Wolves players Stan Cullis, Billy Wright and Ron Flowers.

Anticipation must have been high as the 1980–81 season approached but sadly things went horribly wrong in the League, League Cup and UEFA Cup tournaments. Wolves, who lost the services of Hughes (transferred to Rotherham United) and McAlle (sold to Sheffield United), plodded along and finished 18th in the First Division, avoiding relegation by just two points thanks mainly to a win and a draw in their last three matches. They were knocked out of the League Cup by lowly Cambridge United and were beaten in the opening round of the UEFA Cup by Dutch side PSV Eindhoven.

But in the FA Cup Barnwell's men came mighty close to reaching Wembley, losing in a semi-final replay to Tottenham Hotspur. Playing with confidence and commitment in the earlier rounds despite their League troubles, Wolves beat Stoke City, Watford and Middlesbrough, all in replays, and Wrexham, but after a 2–2 draw at Hillsborough, when Kenny Hibbitt equalised late on from the penalty spot following Glenn Hoddle's foul, they succumbed to a 3–0 replay defeat at Highbury.

Sharp decline and great revival

Unfortunately, the following season Wolves carried their League troubles of 1980–81 with them and this time they failed to avoid disaster, slipping through the trapdoor and into the Second Division with 40 points, needing 45 to be safe. During the course of the season, after the club had failed to sign the French international Michel Platini, they played under three managers: Barnwell until

The Wolves squad in 1982, when Graham Hawkins was in charge.

November 1981, former Aston Villa and Liverpool defender Ian Ross as caretaker boss and finally Ian Greaves, who took charge in February 1982. He arrived via Oxford United after Alex Ferguson, then with Aberdeen, had turned down the chance of managing Wolves.

Joe Gallagher was signed from Birmingham City to bolster the defence but found it hard going, as did the rest of the players, and the team went out of both domestic Cup competitions in the opening round.

Soon after making his 500th League appearance for the club versus Middlesbrough in March 1982, Derek Parkin moved to Stoke City, joined at the Victoria Ground shortly after by George Berry. Norman Bell was transferred to Blackburn Rovers and Willie Carr signed for Millwall.

With soaring interest rates and the cost of building a new stand at Molineux, it was announced in the summer of 1982 that Wolves were around £2.5 million in debt and could go out of business! In mid-June chairman Harry Marshall resigned, allowing the former (and indeed later) Aston Villa chief Doug Ellis to take office in a boardroom shake-up. The club was in dire straits and, in fact, it was saved from extinction just 24 hours before it went into the hands of the official receiver. Ex-goalkeeper Malcolm Finlayson agreed to become vice-chairman but it was touch and go as to whether Wolves would survive. Thankfully they did, but only just: a consortium, headed by another former player, Derek Dougan, steered them to safety with barely three minutes remaining of the deadline set by the receivers. Later it was revealed that the men behind the life-saving deal were the Bhatti brothers.

The new regime brought in the commercial know-how of Eric Woodward, former chairman John Ireland returned to the club as president (the new stand at Molineux was named after him) and Greaves was replaced as manager by yet another old player, Graham Hawkins. And he got off to a flying start as Wolves won their opening League game of season 1982–83, 2–1 over Blackburn Rovers.

It turned out to be an excellent campaign all round for the savaged Wanderers, who gained promotion at the first attempt, finishing runners-up to a strong Queen's Park Rangers side who were 10 points better off at the end of the campaign (85–75). Nothing was achieved in knockout football, however, with Wolves slipping out of both the FA Cup and League Cup competitions at an early stage.

Experienced goalkeeper John Burridge and the Stoke City defender Alan Dodd were brought in by Hawkins to strengthen the defence, and right at the start of the season Wolves went eight League games without conceding a goal. With other senior professionals such as Andy Gray, Kenny Hibbitt and Mel Eves all contributing, Wolves played some excellent football, losing only one of their last 14 matches to comfortably climb back into the top flight. The average home attendance rose to 15,683 – an encouraging factor after the traumas of the previous summer.

Before the 1983–84 season got underway, 'King John' Richards left Molineux for Maritimo of Madeira in the Portuguese League. 'JR' had been at the club for 16 years, during which time he scored a record 194 goals in 486 games and had played for England. He was later to return to Wolves as a director.

After a fine performance against Liverpool on the opening day of the 1983–84 season, when full-back Geoff Palmer scored a second-minute penalty in the 1–1 draw, Wolves did not win a single game until 26 November, when they beat neighbours West Bromwich Albion 3–1. By that time they were in trouble at the foot of the table, heading quickly back to the Second Division. This was their worst-ever start to a League campaign. And the fans were not impressed, as only 8,679 turned out for the home game with Stoke City in mid-December – the lowest attendance for a League fixture at Molineux since March 1937. A rare win at Liverpool, Wolves' first at Anfield since 1950 (1–0 in January), was a moment to savour but after that it was depressing for everyone associated with the club.

Gray left for Everton and without him Wolves found goals hard to come by. They managed to scrape together just 27 in the League and four in Cup action (departing early from both the FA and League Cup competitions). They went down in last place with only 29 points, 12 fewer than Notts County (21st) and 19 fewer than Birmingham City (20th). It was a disastrous season all round as the average home gate dropped alarmingly to 12,478, with only 6,611 bothering to show their faces for the game with Ipswich Town in April 1984. Soon after this defeat Hawkins was sacked, replaced as caretaker boss by ex-goalkeeper Jim Barron.

Docherty as manager, more disaster and Fourth Division football

In June 1984 Wolves appointed Tommy Docherty as manager, but he could not turn the tide and things simply went from bad to worse. After making a decent enough start to the season, gaining six wins and three draws from their opening 16 matches, Wolves went crashing down the Second Division table at a fair rate of knots, claiming only two more victories from 26 starts (losing seven games on the trot from 1 December to 1 January) and finishing bottom of the pile for the second season running, this time with 33 points, seven short of the safety line. They also went out of both Cup competitions in the third round. The team scored only 37 League goals – the fewest in the Division – and for the third year running the average attendance at Molineux dropped again, this time to a dismal 8,376 – 4,102 fewer than in 1983–84 and the lowest since 1914–15 (7,921). The turnout of 4,422 versus Huddersfield Town on 6 May 1985 was the smallest the ground had seen for 60 years.

Dougan had resigned his position in January 1985 and Docherty's reign ended six months later. These were desperate times for Wolves, with dismal performances, dismal results, dismal attendances and players wondering whether they would be paid or not. And things would get progressively worse before they got better!

May 1985 saw the terrible fire disaster at Bradford City's Valley Parade ground and as a result safety at every football stadium in the country came under strict scrutiny. As a result, the Waterloo Road Stand and North Bank terracing at Molineux had to be closed down until they met the required standards – and that would take quite some time.

With the Bhatti brothers' company, Allied Properties, facing severe financial difficulties, Wolves were again tottering on the brink of closure, but once again enough money was found at the 11th hour to keep the team active. They set about playing Third Division football for the first time since 1924 with Irishman Sammy Chapman installed as caretaker manager. He was replaced by former boss Bill McGarry for 61 days from September before returning to the hot seat to see out the rest of the campaign, which was, sadly, another catastrophic one for Wolves. They were relegated to the Fourth Division for the first time in the club's history, and went crashing down watched by the lowest-ever average home attendance, a miserable 3,710.

Players from all over the country were drafted in as Chapman attempted (without success) to find a winning solution. Thirty-three new faces included Andy Mutch (from Southport), Micky Holmes (Burnley), Jon Purdie (Arsenal) and Floyd Streete (Derby), a returning Wayne Clarke, Stacey North and Clive Whitehead (on loan from WBA and Portsmouth respectively), Robert Rosario and Kim Wassell but they could not stop the rot as Wolves finished 23rd in the table, going down with Welsh clubs Cardiff City and Swansea along with Lincoln City. To make things worse, Wolves made an early exit from each of the three Cup competitions they entered, being blitzed 6–0 at Rotherham in the FA Cup (the heaviest defeat any Wolves team has suffered in this prestigious tournament). Only 1,618 hardy supporters bothered to attend the Freight Rover Trophy game with Torquay – the lowest turnout at Molineux since 1891 – and a mere 2,205 saw the home game versus Bury, the lowest League attendance on record.

There was talk around this time that Wolverhampton Wanderers Football Club, one of the founder members of the Football League, could well lose their status in the competition due to financial problems. This was unthinkable but true. Thankfully, on 5 August 1986, a last-minute deal involving the town council, the Asda supermarket chain and Gallagher Estates Limited, kept the club in business – but only just! The Wolverhampton town council agreed to purchase Molineux, the club's training grounds and the social club, while the other two companies jointly agreed to pay off the club's outstanding debts.

The club itself would be run by a consortium comprising Richard Homden and director Jack Harris, while the new president was to be the multi-millionaire and lifelong supporter Sir Jack Hayward OBE. Sir Jack would purchase the club in 1990 and in the period up to 2006, he put over £40 million out of his own pocket into Wolves to keep them going!

An agreed package was duly completed and accepted by the Football League on 14 August 1986. However, a day later Chapman lost his job as manager, leaving with much respect from those who admired his willingness to take on an arduous task that few would have considered in the circumstances. Into his place stepped the former Aston Villa forward Brian Little, who was given the unenviable job of steering Wolves to promotion from the Fourth Division.

Wolves get ready for a memorable 1987–88 season. Back row, left to right: Andy Mutch, David Barnes, Phil Robinson, Steve Bull, Neil Edwards, Jon Purdie, Robbie Dennison, Stephen Stoutt. Middle row: Paul Darby (physiotherapist), Nicky Clarke, Floyd Streete, Mark Kendall, Vince Bartram, Gary Bellamy, Chirs Brindley, Graham Turner (manager). Front row: Andy Thompson, Mark Jones, Matt Forman, Ally Robertson, Keith Downing, Micky Holmes, Mark Smith.

Little, the eighth full-time manager at Molineux in ten years, remained at the helm for only a short time, being replaced by Graham Turner on 7 October. If things were seen to be bad when Turner arrived, he quickly got an indication that they were far worse! That came in the shape of a humiliating first-round FA Cup defeat at the hands of non-League side Chorley, who won 3–0 at Burnden Park, Bolton, in a second replay. Two days earlier, Wolves had been thumped by the same score in a home League game against Wrexham. Not much to talk about, one might say, but in that encounter Turner fielded two new signings from West Bromwich Albion, Andy Thompson and striker Steve Bull. The latter was to become a huge favourite with the Molineux fans, and over the next 13 years broke all sorts of records with his goalscoring achievements.

As the season wore on, Turner brought in two more players from The Hawthorns in forward Robbie Dennison and defender Ally Robertson, and he also secured the services of goalkeeper Mark Kendall, thus sowing the seeds for survival but not yet promotion. Wolves finished fourth in the table and qualified for the Play-offs at the end of Turner's first season in charge but disappointingly missed out on promotion by losing in the Final to Aldershot. They also failed to make progress in the League Cup (beaten by Lincoln City) and the Freight Rover Trophy (ousted by Hereford United). Bully, as he was about to do for the next seven years, top-scored with 19 goals (in 33 games) while his strike partner Andy Mutch netted 13.

The next two seasons, 1987–88 and 1988–89, were memorable both for Wolves as a club and for one player – Steve Bull. In the former campaign, Wolves completed a 'double' by winning the Fourth Division championship (with 90 points) and lifting the Sherpa Van Trophy at Wembley, but were

Wolves at Wembly. The team celebrate winning the Sherpa Van Trophy in 1988.

knocked out of the FA Cup and League Cup without breaking sweat. Bull was magnificent. The Tipton-born striker scored 52 goals (34 in the League) to become the first player to top the half-century mark in a season since Terry Bly for Peterborough United in 1960–61. And in 1987–88 Wolves completed a record 61 first-team matches, with goalkeeper Kendall and forward Mutch appearing in them all.

On a high, Wolves carried on the good work in 1988–89 by winning the Third Division title with virtually the same squad of players – and once again Bull was in brilliant form, rattling in another 50 goals to become the first player since George Camsell of Middlesbrough in 1926–28 to complete a century of goals in the space of two seasons.

Bull also made his full international debut, becoming the first Third Division player since Peter Taylor of Crystal Palace in 1976 to appear for England when, as a substitute, he scored in a 2–0 win over Scotland at Hampden Park, joining four other Wolves players who had netted when making their England international debuts – Jack Brodie, Tom Galley, Johnny Hancocks and Dennis Wilshaw. Bull was only the fifth Third Division player to win a full England cap, the others being Tommy Lawton (Notts County), Reg Matthews (Coventry) and Johnny Byrne (Crystal Palace).

Unfortunately, despite Bull's 11 goals in the Sherpa Van Trophy Wolves failed to retain the prize, losing to Torquay United in the Southern Area Final. And there was no joy in the FA or League Cup competitions either.

Having become the first club side to win the Fourth and Third Division titles in successive years, Wolves found it much harder in the Second Division in 1989–90 as they battled to finish in 10th place, while going out of the FA Cup in round three, the League Cup in round two and the Zenith Data Systems Cup in round one. 'Bully', though, was still firing on all cylinders and he cracked in 27 more goals to earn a place in England's World Cup squad.

In the summer of 1990 Wolves bade farewell to two quality players – goalkeeper Mark Kendall and Ally Robertson, who joined Swansea City and Worcester City respectively. Also out of

Molineux went Phil Chard (to Northampton), Mick Gooding (to Reading) and Nigel Vaughan (to Hereford United). Prior to the 1990–91 season Turner recruited former loanee goalkeeper Mike Stowell (from Everton), Rob Hindmarch (from Derby County) and Brian 'Harry' Roberts (from Birmingham City). But with this trio in the side from the outset, Wolves made a poor start, gaining only 10 points out of the first 24.

Following the arrival of Kevin Ashley, also from St Andrew's, performances improved but after going out of the League Cup to Hull City on the away goals rule, injuries started to disrupt Turner's plans. As time passed by they became more and more pronounced, developing into the worst crisis in the treatment room in living memory. Five senior players were sidelined for at least five months, these being defenders Shane Westley, Mark Venus, Gary Bellamy and Ashley along with striker Mutch, and a handful of others were ruled out on a short-term basis.

Young Colin Taylor came in to assist Bull, and Turner signed Paul Stancliffe on loan from York City to fill a defensive void. Over a period of 14 weeks, going deep into February, Wolves stuck to their task positively and picked up useful League points to keep in touch with the top six, although they went out of the FA Cup (to Cambridge United) and the Zenith Data Systems Cup (to Leeds United).

During March, though, Wolves started to lose momentum, slipping down the League quickly after winning only one of 14 matches. They eventually finished in 12th place, 11 points away from the Play-offs. Bull again weighed in with 27 goals but the average League attendance at Molineux surprisingly dropped by 1,202 to 15,842.

In the summer of 1991 Sir Jack Hayward invested a large amount of money in the club, stating that work must begin in earnest on redeveloping the long-neglected parts of Molineux, especially the Waterloo Road Stand and North Bank terracing, where a brand new stand, named after former player and manager Stan Cullis, would be erected. He also put into motion plans to build a stand at the South Bank end of the ground, as well as promising manager Turner some cash to spend on rebuilding his squad.

Prospects looked good at the start of 1991–92 season but hopes of Wolves challenging for promotion gradually slipped away as injuries once again ruined Turner's team selection.

Wolves rose to fifth in the Division early on but, after a horrid display at Grimsby in the Zenith Data Systems Cup, they lost 10 of their next 12 games and slipped dangerously close to the relegation zone. Turner had to withstand a lot of criticism from the fans and the club's directors, and at one point his job was on the line. Sir Jack Hayward returned from his Bahamas home to stand among the worried supporters on the terraces for the home League game with Grimsby. Wolves won it 2–1 and Turner's position was safe – for the time being.

Results were somewhat better after this and, although Wolves were unlucky to go out of the FA Cup to Nottingham Forest, the team battled on, and after Andy Mutch's hat-trick had helped see off Newcastle United 6–2 at Molineux, Wolves settled for 11th place in the table, well short of a Play-off spot. Bull contributed 23 goals this season and, when he netted at Derby in March, he became the club's all-time record marksman, passing John Richards' tally of 194 goals.

On the eve of the final League game versus Middlesbrough at home, arsonists started fires around Molineux and live cartridges were found buried under the surface of the pitch. But after consulting the police, the game went ahead; Boro won 2–1 and with it gained promotion.

Sadly, Wolves' average home League crowd dropped again this season to 13,743 – and this was quite alarming, considering that the figure was 2,000 lower than in 1983, when the team won promotion from Division Two.

In 1992 Jonathan Hayward (Sir Jack's son) became Wolves chairman, Jack Harris joined the board along with club secretary Keith Pearson, Gary Lever was appointed commercial manager and David Clayton (formerly of Goodyear) became director of marketing and public affairs. Things were beginning to change inside the club but could manager Turner and his players change things out on the pitch? That was the question the fans were asking as another new season got under way.

Unfortunately, 1992–93 was not a happy campaign for the players as Wolves finished a moderate 11th in the table, 15 points away from the Play-offs. They also failed to make an impression in the three Cup competitions and perhaps the only bright spot being Bull's 19 goals, which took him past the 200 mark and also saw him beat Billy Hartill's record of 162 for Wolves in the League. Another highlight was Darren Roberts' hat-trick in his first League start in the televised League game at Birmingham in September (won 4–0).

Andy Mutch left the club for newly promoted Swindon Town for £250,000 in August 1993, having scored 105 goals in 338 games, and into his place alongside Bull came the Republic of Ireland international David Kelly, signed for £750,000 from Newcastle United, and veteran striker Cyrille Regis, once of West Bromwich Albion and Coventry City, who was recruited from Aston Villa. Midfielder Kevin Keen also arrived in the camp from West Ham for £600,000 and defender Peter Shirtliff was signed from Sheffield Wednesday for £250,000. And it was officially announced that Molineux was ready to become one of the best all-seater stadiums outside the Premiership, with a capacity of over 28,500, when the Billy Wright Stand opened over the Christmas period.

Expectations in and around Molineux were, once again, high when the 1993–94 season kicked-off, and Wolves made a flying start with a 3–1 win over Bristol City. With a strong-looking midfield and seemingly lethal attack, all looked rosy, but injuries started to creep in (Geoff Thomas among them) and all of a sudden the momentum slipped away. Between late September and the end of December Wolves won only four League games out of 15, dropping down to 12th in the table. They were also out of two Cup competitions.

The fans were despondent and, although he strengthened his midfield, manager Turner came under severe pressure from all quarters. He stuck in there, though, and Wolves perked up, edging slowly towards the Play-off region with some dogged performances, and although they were beaten narrowly by Chelsea in the FA Cup, three straight wins over Charlton, Bolton and Tranmere saw Wolves climb to eighth.

However, after taking some unwarranted abuse from irate supporters in a 3–0 defeat by Portsmouth at Fratton Park, 46-year-old Turner departed after seven and a half years at the helm. The local papers called it 'The Rise and Fall of Mr Nice Guy' and that summed up Turner, for he was a man of honour who had turned everything around at Molineux, bringing the club out of the doldrums and into a position from which, realistically, they could gain promotion to the Premiership.

Several names were in the melting pot as the board searched for a replacement – Shirtliff having taken over as caretaker manager – and after a fairly lengthy debate, the former England boss Graham Taylor was handed the reins. Like Turner, he had been in charge of Aston Villa.

It must be said that Taylor was not the ideal choice as far as the fans were concerned, but he moved in amid a lot of publicity and got off to a winning start as Tranmere were defeated 2–0 on 2 April. Could he steer Wolves to promotion? That was the question everyone was asking but it did not materialise and in the end the team finished a disappointing eighth, three points short of the Play-offs.

By now Molineux was a fully equipped, top-of-the-range football stadium and the average home attendance in 1993–94 was 22,008 – a rise of 8,410 on the previous season and, in fact, Wolves' best since

1980. For the first time ever, gate receipts topped £200,000 for the game against rivals West Bromwich Albion. Despite a niggling injury, Bull top-scored for the eighth consecutive season with 15 goals while Kelly netted 14. Goalkeeper Mike Stowell was the only ever present.

By the end of May 1994 manager Taylor had cleared the decks at Molineux. He made 17 players available for transfer, among them Regis, Mountfield, Kevin Ashley and Mark Burke. He signed winger Tony Daley from Aston Villa for £1.25 million and soon afterwards recruited another wide man from his former club, Steve Froggatt, for £1 million. Neil Emblen arrived from Millwall for £600,000 and two new coaches were brought in, Steve Harrison and Bobby Downes.

Wolves' first-team squad looked strong and the scene was set for a return to the big time, but 1994–95 ended in bitter disappointment yet again when, after beating Bolton 2–1 in the first leg of the Play-off semi-finals, Wolves suffered a 2–0 defeat in the second leg and lost their chance of a place in the Premiership.

Daley was injured in training early on and eventually made his debut in October. That lasted 11 minutes and his season ended there. Bull was also sidelined and during the campaign another ten players had to receive treatment. Don Goodman (ex-West Brom and Sunderland) and Dutchman John De Wolf were signed to strengthen the attack and defence but there were early exits from the League and Anglo-Italian Cup competitions. Progress, though, was made in the FA Cup, with Sheffield Wednesday knocked out in a thrilling penalty shoot-out and a record Molineux crowd of 28,544 witnessing a fifth-round win over Leicester before Crystal Palace ended Wolves' hopes of a trip to Wembley with a quarter-final replay victory.

Summer season ticket sales indicated that the fans had changed their mind about Taylor's appointment and now believed he could steer them into the top flight. Defenders Dean Richards and Eric Young were signed, the former for a club record £1.85 million from Bradford City (to replace De Wolf) and the latter from Crystal Palace. But unfortunately performances were poor and the first 10 weeks of the 1995–96 season left a lot to be desired. After a dismal 0–0 draw with Charlton in November, which saw Wolves tumble down to 19th in the table, Taylor left, to be succeeded by Scotsman and former Aberdeen, Celtic and Newcastle United striker Mark McGhee, who quit Leicester City to move to Molineux.

But 48 hours after taking charge, McGhee announced publicly that he had inherited a squad short on physical and mental strength and that certain players looked under-coached and had practically no desire to try to appreciate tactics. McGhee did his best and despite dropping out of the League Cup, progress was made in the League and also in the FA Cup. Come late March, Wolves were just outside the Play-off zone but their dismal form returned and by the end of the season the team had slipped down the ladder to 20th – just two places above the relegation trapdoor. This was the club's lowest League finish since their Fourth Division days a decade earlier.

Wolves were much more confident in 1996–97, but were pipped to the second automatic promotion place by Barnsley and lost to Crystal Palace in the Play-off semi-finals. They also went out of both Cup competitions at the first hurdle.

Defender Keith Curle from Manchester City and Steve Corica and Iwan Roberts from McGhee's former club Leicester City were brought in, while those who left included Paul Birch, De Wolf, Mark Rankine and goalkeeper Paul Jones. Bull top-scored for the 11th successive season, netting 23 goals, his best haul since 1992, while Roberts contributed 12 goals. Mike Stowell was once again an ever present between the posts.

In 1997–98 Wolves reached the FA Cup semi-finals but lost narrowly to Arsenal and went out of the League Cup in the fourth round, beaten by manager McGhee's former club Reading. In the League they huffed and puffed and finished a disappointing ninth, three wins off the Play-offs after gaining only one victory in the last eight matches. Dougie Freedman, signed from Crystal Palace for £800,000, top-scored with 12 goals while a young Robbie Keane, who netted twice on his League debut at Norwich, weighed in with 11.

Wolves won their opening four League games at the start of the 1998–99 season but then started to fall off the pace, going out of the League Cup at the same time to lowly Bournemouth. In the November, some four months into the campaign, manager McGhee left the club, to be replaced by his assistant Colin Lee. He did his best, as did the players, but the team once more missed out on the Play-offs, finishing seventh, three points off the team above them, Bolton Wanderers.

Two long-serving players – Bull and Thompson – both left in the summer of 1999: the former effectively retired and the latter joined Tranmere Rovers. Freedman also moved on, signing for Nottingham Forest for £950,000 (Wolves making a pretty good profit overall). Unfortunately, Wolves were soon to lose another star player, Robbie Keane, who would be sold to Coventry City for £6 million in August 1999.

There was more disappointment for Wolves in 1999–2000, when once again they finished in seventh place in the First Division table, this time missing the Play-offs by just two points after losing two of their last five League games. And to make things worse, they slipped out of the League Cup to unfashionable Wycombe Wanderers and lost to Sheffield Wednesday on penalties in the FA Cup. Ade Akinbiyi, signed from Bristol City to lead the attack, did well and top-scored with 16 goals but generally it was a lack of goals that was to blame for Wolves' poor season – they managed only 64 in the League when perhaps three or four more would have secured at least a top-six finish.

Those wearing the gold and black now included Akinbiyi, the versatile Keith Andrews, Darren Bazeley (from Watford), Michael Branch (from Everton), Steve Corica, Curle, Emblem, Haavard Flo (ex-Werder Bremen), the Australian defender Kevin Muscat, Lee Naylor, George Ndah (who was to be plagued by a series of injuries including a broken leg), Allan Nielsen, goalkeeper Michael Oakes (signed from Aston Villa), midfielder Simon Osborn (ex-Crystal Palace), Frenchman Ludovic Pollet, Carl Robinson, the former Spurs duo of Steve Sedgley and Andy Sinton, Paul Simpson, the evergreen Mike Stowell and Scott Taylor (ex-Leicester City).

Wolves won only five League games during the first half of the 2000–01 season and also slipped out of the League Cup. As a result, manager Lee was dismissed before Christmas with the team only a few places above the drop zone. Former Southampton boss Dave Jones was named as Lee's successor and Wolves improved during the second half of the campaign, but their dismal early season form counted against them and they were unable to achieve anything more than a mid-table finish. At the same time Jones chopped and changed his team at will, bringing in several new players, among them Cedric Roussel and Sean Connelly, while also in the side now were striker Adam Proudlock and defenders Paul Butler and Joleon Lescott.

Wolves returned to winning ways in 2001–02 and spent much of the season in the top two before being pipped to an automatic promotion spot by their deadly rivals West Bromwich Albion. In fact, the Baggies were on Wolves' heels throughout the campaign and edged beyond them inside the last month. It was so disappointing for the club and its supporters and there was more doom and gloom when defeat was suffered at the hands of Norwich City in the Play-off semi-finals. It was also a bad year in both knockout competitions, Wolves succumbing early on to Swindon Town in the League Cup and Gillingham in the FA Cup.

Several new signings were made during the season and two of them, strikers Dean Sturridge and Nathan Blake, bagged 31 League goals between them. Other new faces included four midfielders – Shaun Newton, Alex Rae, Mark Kennedy and Colin Cameron – plus striker Kenny Miller.

The team celebrate winning the Division One Play-off.

Sadly, Wolves were never in contention for an automatic promotion place during the 2002–03 season but fifth was certainly enough to clinch a Play-off spot, and after overcoming Reading in the semi-finals they faced Sheffield United in the Final at Cardiff's Millennium Stadium for a place in the Premiership. Wolves, attacking throughout and backed by over 30,000 fans, won 3–0 to reach the top flight of English football for the first time in almost 20 years – and to make it all the sweeter, they replaced their arch-rivals West Bromwich Albion. A joyful and happy Sir Jack Hayward admitted afterwards that he had spent well over £20 million in the past two seasons to achieve success.

The players who took Wolves into the Premiership, by appearing in 20 or more League games, were: Blake, Butler, Cameron, Kevin Cooper, Marc Edworthy, veteran full-back Denis Irwin and inspirational midfielder Paul Ince (both ex-Manchester United), Kennedy, Lescott, goalkeeper Matt Murray, Miller, Naylor, Ndah, Newton, Rae and Sturridge. Miller (19 goals) and Blake (12) were the leading scorers and the average League attendance at Molineux was 25,745 – the biggest since 1980.

Life in the Premiership was very hard for Wolves, who did not win until their eighth match. They did manage some decent results, in particular a 1–0 win over Manchester United in January (the first time in 25 years that United had been beaten in a competitive game by a West Midlands team other than Aston Villa or Coventry City), but their failure to win a single away game meant that their relegation battle was ultimately lost. Wolves finished bottom of the table on goal difference, bracketed together on 33 points with the two other relegated teams, Leicester City and Leeds United. It had been a tough baptism for manager Jones and his players but those who played against the likes of Arsenal, Chelsea, Liverpool, Manchester United and Newcastle United certainly learned a lot from the experience.

Having played against some of the best club sides in England the previous season, Wolves made a dismal start to the 2004–05 Championship campaign, and as a result manager Jones was sacked at the beginning of November with a second successive relegation looking a real possibility. Jones was said to be furious that the £20 million transfer kitty promised to him had never materialised as Sir Jack Hayward decided to put the club up for sale.

Coach Stuart Gray was in temporary charge of the first team for a month after Jones's dismissal, until the former Spurs and England midfielder Glenn Hoddle was appointed on a rolling one-year contract. Wolves lost only one of their final 25 League games but amazingly saw out 15 draws and in the end finished ninth in the table, not enough to qualify for the Play-offs, although they were highest-placed of the three teams relegated from the Premiership, above Leeds United (14th) and Leicester City (15th). In the League Cup and FA Cup tournaments Wolves were ousted by Arsenal and Burnley respectively, having gone out to the Gunners and West Ham the previous season.

Wolves were one of the hardest Championship teams to beat during the 2005–06 season, but failed to qualify for the Play-offs due without doubt to drawing too many games again. They finished eight points off the pace in seventh position, although at one time (mid-March) they were on course for a top-six placing. Miller top-scored this term with 12 goals while another new face, Carl Cort, weighed in with 11. Other members of the side at this juncture (and not mentioned previously) included the former England and Spurs forward Darren Anderton, Leon Clarke, defender Jody Craddock, full-back Rob Edwards, Romanian international Viorel Ganea, the Hungarian Gabor Gyepes, Scotsman Jackie McNamara (ex-Celtic), the Nigerian Seyi Olofinjana, Dutch goalkeeper Stefan Postma (from Aston Villa), England youth international Rohan Ricketts, Maurice Ross and the South Korean forward Ki-Hyeon Seol, who had completed his second full season.

Though the board expressed no displeasure with Hoddle, the season has been frowned on by both local media and, most importantly, the fan base. There was significant support for the 'Hoddle Out' campaign and he resigned as manager on 1 July 2006. Soon afterwards the club was in the news again for a totally different reason, when young striker Chris Cornes received a six-month ban after testing positive for cocaine.

In the summer of 2006 Wolves cut their wage bill considerably when no fewer than 11 senior players left Molineux, with Miller, Cameron, Lescott, Postma, Silas, Ganea, Ross, Kennedy, Seol, Ndah and Anderton all moving to pastures new. However, Wolves received a transfer fee for only two of those players – fans' favourite Lescott moving to Everton for £5 million and striker Seol joining Reading for £1.5 million.

On 21 July 2006 the former Republic of Ireland and Sunderland manager Mick McCarthy was confirmed as Hoddle's replacement, thus becoming Wolves' 15th full-time and official manager in 30 years. And then, in a boardroom shake-up at the end of the month, Rick Hayward and Paul Manduca stepped down as directors and local businessmen Kevin Threlfall and John Gough were appointed to replace them. It was all beginning to happen at Molineux and everyone was anticipating a good season.

Wolves commenced the 2006–07 season away at Plymouth with only the bare bones of a first-team squad. Manager McCarthy knew he was in for a challenge and stated to the local press 'The initials M.M. on my top stand for Mick McCarthy, not Merlin the Magician.'

After a draw at Home Park and a win at home to Ipswich Town, fans were already singing 'Merlin's' praises. And McCarthy's ambition was signalled by the acquisition of striker Jay Bothroyd and left-sided midfielder Jamie Clapham, plus the loan signings of striker Craig Davies from Verona and Guilherme Finkler, the first Brazilian ever to sign for the club.

McCarthy had already got his former captain at Sunderland, Gary Breen, at the heart of the defence and five matches into the season Wolves found themselves in third place. However, some indifferent results followed, including a 3–0 hammering at West Bromwich Albion in the first meeting between the sides for five years, and in no time at all the team had slipped down the ladder and gone out of the League Cup to lowly Chesterfield.

Despite some early setbacks, Wolves went on to win three straight matches, signalling the new manager's intention to outdo *Sky Sports'* prediction of a 14th place finish. Consistency of results was lacking, as victories and defeats came in equal measure at the end of 2006.

Several more signings were made in the January transfer window, including Michael Kightly, Andy Keogh and Stephen Ward. After exiting the FA Cup to arch-rivals Albion in the fourth round, an impressive run of form followed, including a vital 1–0 revenge victory against the Baggies at Molineux in early March. At this juncture Wolves were bedded into a Play-off position, which they eventually sealed thanks to a final day 4–1 victory at Leicester City.

They were paired with Albion again in the semi-finals, but disaster struck on the eve of the first leg when goalkeeper Matt Murray, who had been voted the club's player of the season by the supporters, broke his shoulder in the final training session, which led to Wayne Hennessey making his Wolves debut. Unfortunately, Wolves lost both legs, 3–2 at home and 1–0 away, and their season ended on a disappointing note yet again.

McCarthy echoed most commentators' sentiments – that Wolves had over-achieved – after the Play-off defeat to the Baggies when he said 'I have got nothing but pride for what our young lads have achieved this season. They have come from virtually nowhere and been brilliant. They all sat hanging their heads, but they will all look back on this as being a good season with pride and satisfaction.'

It was announced on 21 May 2007 that Sir Jack Hayward had reached an agreement to sell the club to businessman Steve Morgan for £10 in return for a £30 million investment into the club. Everyone was hoping that with a new man in the boardroom Wolves could make yet another concentrated effort to reach the Premiership for a second time.

Mick McCarthy bought in a batch of new players, but out on the pitch results did not go according to plan. The team struggled to get going and suffered a humiliating 3–1 Carling Cup home defeat at the hands of lowly Morecambe, who were playing in the competition, and indeed the Football League, for the first time.

After 12 Championship matches Wolves had only mustered 18 points out of a possible 36. They were already 11 points behind the leaders Watford and also had their arch-rivals West Brom above them in the table.

Over the next three months, in the lead-up to Christmas, only 17 points were collected, and, as 2007 gave way to 2008, Wolves found themselves languishing in eighth place, yet amazingly only two points outside the Play-off places. If only they could have managed a few more points at Molineux!

The signing of striker Sylvan Ebanks-Blake for £1.2 million from Plymouth Argyle in January, plus the arrival of midfielder David Edwards from Luton Town for £675,000, boosted the squad considerably and for a time Wolves looked a very useful outfit. But it did not last. They were knocked out of the FA Cup by former manager Dave Jones's Cardiff City in the fifth round and dropped vital League points both at home and away.

However, deep down McCarthy knew that a good run could easily see automatic promotion achieved. He swapped his team around accordingly, and after a narrow victory over Scunthorpe

United, a win at Charlton and draws against QPR and Bristol City, it was all to play for as the promotion race hotted up.

With five matches remaining (four of them at home), Wolves were still in touch with the leading pack, lying just outside the top six with a Play-off place there for the taking. Everything lay in their own hands. When they faced their fierce rivals Albion in front of a best-of-season Molineux crowd, McCarthy admitted that it was a must-win situation if automatic promotion was to be achieved. Sadly, Wolves lost 1–0 to the Baggies and it meant that, realistically, a place in the Play-offs was all they could hope for.

They battled on but in the end finished, disappointingly, in seventh position, pipped to that final Play-off place on goal-difference by Watford, who scrambled a 1–1 draw at Blackpool on the last day of the campaign. While Wolves defeated Plymouth Argyle at home 1–0, a 3–0 scoreline was needed to secure sixth spot. How close can you get?

On reflection, 2007–08 was without doubt an up-and-down season for Mick McCarthy's men, but McCarthy is quietly confident, as usual, that promotion is well within the capabilities of his team in 2008–09, while indicating that four new players would bring his senior squad up to strength and make them strong candidates to reach the Premiership for only the second time in the club's history.

Wolves' Grounds

Wolverhampton Wanderers have played their home games at Molineux since 1889. Their previous home ground was Dudley Road, which they occupied for eight years, and prior to that the team performed on Windmill Field (1877–79), John Harper's Field (1879–81) and occasionally on the Blakenhall cricket club ground.

Although there are no apparent signs of any of their former grounds, Windmill Field was situated in Goldthorn Hill and could house around 2,000 spectators at any one time. John Harper's Field lay directly opposite the Stroud Niphon Works in Lower Villiers Street and this too could accommodate 2,000 spectators, while the club's Dudley Road ground was directly opposite the Fighting Cocks pub. In fact, nearby Wanderers Avenue is named after the team that won the FA Cup in 1893. The Blakenhall cricket ground was also situated near to the Fighting Cocks pub, but Wolves only used this facility when their preferred pitch was declared unplayable.

Dudley Road was developed over the years and from having an initial capacity of 2,500, when the team moved to Molineux in 1889 it could accommodate 10,000 fans quite easily. Wolves played their first FA Cup tie at Dudley Road versus Long Eaton Rangers on 27 October 1883, winning 4–1, and five years later entertained Aston Villa there in the club's first-ever League game, which ended level at 1–1.

Molineux

Molineux was named after the famous Molineux family which first came to England with Isabella of France, wife of Edward II, some 700 years ago in 1307. At the time Flemish wool-workers were already frequenting this country, teaching the British their trade.

The Molineuxs chose to reside in a large mansion on the perimeter of Wolverhampton town centre, which was appropriately named Molineux House. The house became one of the town's most elegant and principal buildings and on local Ordnance Survey maps it was often referred to as Mr Molineux's Close, being situated between Wadham's Hill and Dunstall Lane. In 1792 the house became the residence for a family of French refugees and the adjoining grounds were eventually developed into a pleasure park by Mr A.J. Brewster, with several galas and fêtes being held there during the summer months. In 1869 a South Staffordshire Industrial Firm and Fine Arts Exhibition was staged in the grounds of Molineux House, with the old English game of croquet taking place on the lush green lawns. Some two years later, after further developments had been carried out, Molineux became an imposing and quality sporting venue incorporating some grand gardens, a spacious boating lake, an elegant bandstand and an excellent cycling and athletics track surrounding a wonderful field, the playing surface of which resembled a bowling green.

Wolves played on this field for the very first time on 20 March 1886 when they entertained Walsall Town in a local Cup semi-final – three years before they would actually move there on a permanent basis. As the team were completing their first season of League football at Dudley Road, the Northampton Brewery purchased the Molineux sports arena and a lot of surrounding land, but not the house itself – this was later converted into a small and friendly hotel.

The brewery and Wolves were united and within a matter of months developers and gardeners had made the playing area suitable (especially in size) to stage competitive League and Cup games. Two large dressing rooms were built, an office was erected, a respectable grandstand installed (capable of seating 300 spectators) and a shelter was assembled on one side of the pitch under which some 4,000 spectators could escape any inclement weather – all for an annual rent of just £50. Near the centre of Birmingham, Aston Villa were paying £200 a year to rent their Perry Barr ground.

Wolves' first official 'home' game at Molineux was a friendly against Aston Villa on Monday 2 September 1889. A crowd of 4,000 saw David Wykes score the only goal of the game to earn Wolves victory. Wolves' team for this historic encounter was: Billy Rose; Dickie Baugh, Charlie Mason; Albert Fletcher, Harry Allen, Tom Knight; Arthur Worrall, Walter Perry (guest), Wykes, Harry Wood and Charlie Booth. The first League game followed five days later when Wolves beat Notts County 2–0 (Wykes and Worrall the scorers).

During the 1890s Molineux was the chosen venue for several Football League committee meetings and in March 1891 England played Ireland in the first of four full internationals staged at the ground. A healthy crowd of 15,231 saw the Irish whipped 6–1. Two Wolves players – Billy Rose and Jack Brodie – played for England. The three other internationals were played in February 1903 when England beat Ireland 4–0, in February 1936 when Wales won 2–1, and in December 1956 when Denmark were defeated 5–2 in a World Cup qualifier. A wartime international at Molineux in October 1942 attracted a crowd of 25,000 to see Wales again beat England 2–1.

There have also been Schoolboy, Youth, Under-21 and Under-23 internationals played at Molineux as well as wartime representative matches and Inter-League games, one of these taking place in 1952 when Bolton's Nat Lofthouse scored six goals for the Football League against the Irish League. And in February 1892 the first of 10 FA Cup semi-finals was staged at Molineux when West Bromwich Albion drew 1–1 with Nottingham Forest

Molineux has also hosted Rugby Union matches and a boxing tournament – around 8,000 fans saw Henry Cooper beat Jack Bodell for the British Heavyweight title in June 1967.

Between 1889 and 1910, developments and improvements were carried out at Molineux when funds allowed and, in fact, during the early part of the 20th century the ground was rated one of the best-equipped in the Football League. Unfortunately it was allowed to deteriorate and immediately

A packed Molineux in the 1920s.

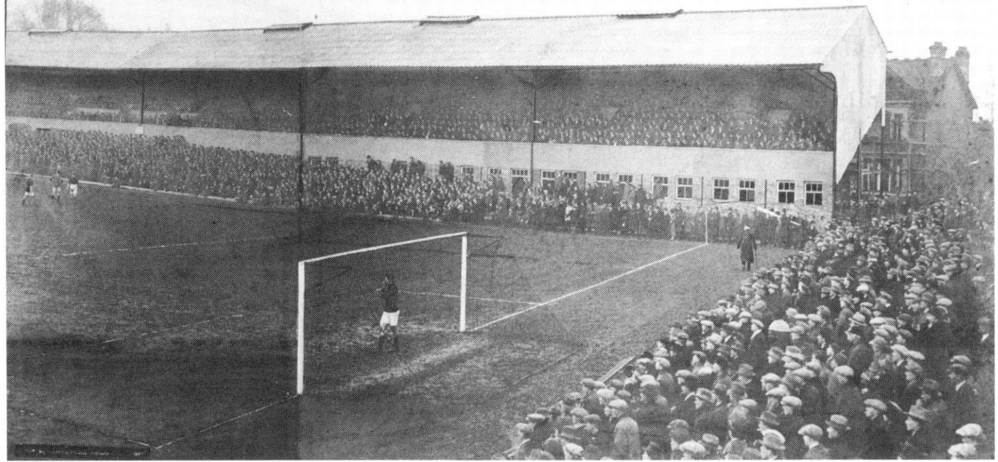

Molineux's empty terraces, 1950s.

Taken from the floodlight tower, this photograph shows a packed-out Molineux in 1957.

Molineux, seen here in 1972, remained virtually unchanged until 1991.

after World War One when Wolves were in the Second Division, it was said to be well below standard. When a large crowd was in attendance, many spectators could not see the pitch.

In the early 1920s the club decided it was time to upgrade Molineux, and they gave the task to famous football ground architect Archibald Leitch. He designed the Waterloo Road Stand which was officially opened in September 1925 by Football League president John McKenna. The new stand included dressing rooms and offices. Next step was to demolish the old North Bank stand, affectionately known as the 'Cow Shed', and erect a proper terrace with covered roof. When Wolves regained First Division status in 1932 a stand was built on the Molineux Street side of the ground. With its unusual multi-span roof, it stood there for nearly 50 years. Finally, a roof was put on the top half of the South Bank, a massive terrace which could provide standing room for 30,000 spectators. The ground then remained virtually unchanged until the Molineux Stand, later to be called the John Ireland Stand, was built in 1979. However, plans to further reshape the ground were scrapped when the club hit their financial crisis.

Between 1991 and 1993 Molineux was comprehensively redeveloped. The Waterloo Road Stand was replaced by the all-

Major redevelopment work was carried out in the early 1990s.

Molineux today is a modern all-seater stadium holding 28,500, and could be expanded to hold 40,000.

Billy Wright's statue stands outside a redeveloped Molineux.

seater Billy Wright Stand, the North Bank terracing was replaced by the Stan Cullis Stand, and the South Bank terracing was replaced by the Jack Harris Stand. Come the 1993–94 season, Molineux was one of the largest all-seater stadiums in the country with a capacity of 28,525. But by the time promotion was secured to the Premiership in 2003, the stadium itself was deemed not big enough. In fact, it was the third-smallest in the top Division, ahead of Craven Cottage (Fulham) and Fratton Park (Portsmouth).

During the previous decade, many of the smaller stadiums had either been expanded or replaced to hold a capacity of between 30,000 and 67,000 seated spectators. For the 2003–04 to 2005–06 seasons, the corner between the Billy Wright and Jack Harris Stands was filled in with temporary seating to create a further 900 seats (called the Graham Hughes area by most of the fans and now officially by the club), bringing the ground's overall capacity to 29,400. Hughes is the club's long-serving club historian. However, for the 2006–07 season the temporary seating was removed, but should Wolves gain promotion to the Premiership again, the other three corners will be filled in accordingly to push the capacity up to 32,500. Later, perhaps, the new Steve Bull and the old Billy Wright Stands would be expanded to create a ground capable of housing 40,000 fans.

Record attendance: 61,315 v Liverpool, FA Cup fifth round, 11 February 1939.

Record attendance (since redevelopment): 29,396 v Manchester United, Premiership, 16 January 2004. Capacity now reduced to 28,500.

Lowest attendance: 900 v Notts County, League, 17 October 1891, and v Blackburn Rovers, League, 28 November 1891.

Pitch measurements: 116 yards x 74 yards.

Pitch has underground heating.

Ground is approximately 480 feet above sea level.

Record gate receipts: £525,000* v West Bromwich Albion, Play-off semi-final 1st leg, 13 May 2007 (*approximate).

Matches to Remember

8 September 1888
Wolves 1 Aston Villa 1
League

A modest Dudley Road crowd witnessed Wolves' first-ever game in the Football League. It was not a classic by any means but it was interesting and those present saw a close encounter which could have gone either way, and in the end the points were shared.

Early on, Wolves' goalkeeper Jack Baynton saved well from Batt Garvey and Dennis Hodgetts, and Wolves took the lead somewhat fortuitously on the half-hour mark, after Nick Anderson had struck Villa's left upright, and visiting goalkeeper Jimmy Warner had saved well from Alec Cannon and Jerry Cooper. Walter White headed towards goal and, after the ball had bounced back to him from a scrimmage, his low shot flew between the posts at a right angle off Villa's full-back Gershom Cox. Villa hit back strongly and after a series of attacks down the centre of the pitch equalised through Tommy Green, who deflected Hodgetts's low, diagonal pass over the line via an upright.

Cooper, Albert Fletcher and Anderson all went close for Wolves during a tight second half and likewise Hodgetts and Arthur Brown for Villa, but chances were few and far between and in the end a draw was a fair result.

Wolves: Baynton, Mason, Baugh, Fletcher, Allen, Lowder, Hunter, Cooper, Anderson, White, Cannon.
Villa: Warner, Cox, Coulton, Dawson, Devey, Yates, Green, Brown, Allen, Garvey, Hodgetts.
Attendance: 2,500

15 October 1892
Newton Heath 10 Wolves 1
League

This result remains Manchester United's (formerly Newton Heath) best-ever League win and it is still Wolves' heaviest defeat.

The Heathens had been elected to the First Division only a few months earlier and, in fact, this was only their seventh League game overall – they had lost four and drawn two of their previous six. They were mightily impressive against Wolves though and tore the Midland club apart with some aggressive, all-action attacking.

Centre-forward Bob Donaldson was the star of the show. He scored a hat-trick and had a helping hand in four of his side's 10 goals, while also striking an upright and having one other effort disallowed. Willie Stewart also weighed in with a treble and he too proved quite a handful when he drove forward from centre-field. Two of his goals flew in from 25 yards. Wolves' defence simply could not cope with Donaldson's robust approach and nor could they contain flying wingers Alf Farman and debutant Jimmy Hendry, who found the net with his first touch in competitive football, giving his side the lead in the first 30 seconds.

Wolves never recovered from that early goal and were 5–0 down at half-time. To their credit, however, they never shouldered arms and despite conceding five further goals in the second half, four in the space of just 12 minutes, they did manage a consolation strike through outside-left George Kinsey, who scored with a low drive after some good work by Harry Wood. Amazingly, Newton Heath finished bottom of the table this season while Wolves won the FA Cup.

Newton Heath: Warner, Mitchell, Clements, Perrins, Stewart, Erentz, Farman, Hood, Donaldson, Carson, Hendry.

Wolves: Hassall, Baugh, Swift, Davies, Allen, Malpass, Lawrence, Devey, Griffin, Wood, Kinsey.

Attendance: 4,000

25 March 1893
Wolves 1 Everton 0
FA Cup Final

A brilliant long-range goal by Wolves skipper Harry Allen decided this tightly-fought Final at Fallowfield, Manchester.

The Merseysiders were favourites to win but Wolves, fielding a side of all Englishmen, most of them reared in the Midlands area, battled superbly well from the first to the last whistle. After

Wolves' 1893 FA Cup-winning side. Back row, left to right: R. Baugh, A. Hollingworth (chairman), J. Lewis (director), A. Blackham (linesman), H. Allen. Middle row: R. Topham, W. Malpass, W.C. Rose, G. Swift, G. Kinsey. Front row: D. Wykes, J. Butcher, H. Wood, A. Griffin, J. Addenbrooke (secretary-manager).

showing plenty of determination and commitment, they deservedly lifted the trophy for the first time in the club's history.

The hustling tactics shown by Wolves completely disrupted Everton's style of play and Dick Topham was magnificent on the right wing, causing problems all afternoon. He came close to scoring on two occasions and also created a chance for David Wykes before Allen struck on the hour mark with a rasping right-footed drive from fully 35 yards, the ball dipping under the bar at the last second. Joe Butcher, the youngest player on the pitch at 18, and Harry Wood should have increased Wolves' lead late on but some desperate yet brave defending by full-backs George Swift and Dickie Baugh prevented the Merseysiders from scoring.

Wolves: Rose, Baugh, Swift, Malpass, Allen, Kinsey, Topham, Wykes, Butcher, Wood, Griffin.
Everton: Williams, Kelso, Howarth, Boyle, Holt, Stewart, Latta, Gordon, Maxwell, Chadwick, Milward.
Attendance: 45,067

25 April 1908
Wolves 3 Newcastle United 1
FA Cup Final

Coincidentally, all four goals in this Final were scored by the only four players on the field whose surname began with the letter 'H': Hunt, Hedley and Harrison for Wolves, and Howie for Newcastle.

Heavy morning rain had given way to light drizzle as George Hedley kicked-off for Wolves. Owing to the softness of the pitch, several players lost their footing early on and their passes went astray, one almost leading to a goal for Newcastle, but Ted Collins was alert enough to clear the danger. Wolves were pegged back for long periods during the opening 30 minutes and goalkeeper Tommy Lunn made three fine saves, two from Jock Rutherford, to keep his side level.

Wolves, 1908 FA Cup winners. Back row, left to right: A. Fletcher (trainer), Revd K.R.G. Hunt, J. Jones, W. Wooldridge, T. Lunn, E. Collins, A. Bishop. Front row: W. Harrison, J. Shelton, G. Hedley, W. Radford, J. Pedley.

As time ticked away, Wolves, inspired by wing-halves the Reverend Kenneth Hunt and Alf Bishop, came more and more into the game and on 35 minutes George Hedley's shot took a wicked deflection and missed the crossbar by inches. Five minutes later Wolves went in front when Hunt, collecting Billy Harrison's low cross, drove in a shot from 25 yards and the ball went straight through 'keeper Jimmy Lawrence's hands and into the net. Two minutes before the break, having dictated proceedings since taking the lead, Wolves went 2–0 up when Hedley squeezed his shot past Lawrence from eight yards.

Wolves were now in total control, while Newcastle appeared shell-shocked as Lawrence made two brilliant saves from Hedley and Bishop just before and immediately after the break. The 'keeper then denied Walter Radford, Jack Shelton and Hedley again before Newcastle got back into the match on 73 minutes with a goal from Jim Howie, who capitalised on a weak header by Billy Wooldridge. Wolves were still positive in their approach, though, and they sealed victory three minutes from time with a brilliant individual goal by Harrison, who beat four men in a mazy dribble before finding the net from just inside the penalty area.

This was the first time a team from the Second Division had won the FA Cup since 1894.

Wolves: Lunn, Jones, Collins, Hunt, Wooldridge, Bishop, Harrison, Shelton, Hedley, Radford, Pedley.
Newcastle: Lawrence, McCracken, Pudan, Gardner, Veitch, McWilliam, Rutherford, Howie, Appleyard, Speedie, Wilson.
Attendance: 74,967

4 November 1911
Wolves 8 Hull City 0
League

A sparse crowd saw Wolves record their biggest League win in terms of goal difference for more than 21 years – since their 9–1 drubbing of Burnley in December 1889.

After a relatively quiet start, Wolves burst into life 10 minutes in when Willie Halligan scored with a low shot after some intelligent wing play by Billy Harrison and a neat touch forward by George Hedley. Before the interval Jack Needham made it 2–0 but at this juncture there was no real hint of what was to transpire during the second half.

Emerging with even more determination than in the first half, Wolves attacked the Tigers full on and increased their advantage to 4–0 in the space of five minutes. The unmarked Needham added his second goal from close range and shortly afterwards Tommy Yule, darting into space, bagged number four. Hull then lost right-winger Joe Smith to injury following a solid tackle by George Garratly. His departure heralded a stampede by Wolves, who took complete control of the game, doing as they pleased. Needham completed his hat-trick with a right-foot drive and Halligan dipped in a 20-yarder on the hour mark, making it 6–0.

Halligan then joined Needham on three goals with a crisp finish from the edge of the box and, after a series of near misses, Yule registered goal number eight two minutes from time. This win stretched Wolves' unbeaten run to six games and edged them up the Second Division table, chasing leaders Chelsea and Derby County.

Wolves: Boxley, Collins, Garratly, Groves, Hunt, Bishop, Harrison, Hedley, Halligan, Needham, Yule.
Hull City: Roughley, Nevins, McQuillan, W. Wright, A. Browell, Gordon, Smith, Chapman, T. Browell, Temple, G. Wright.
Attendance: 10,124

15 April 1938
Wolves 10 Leicester City 1
League

This win over Leicester remains Wolves' biggest in League football. After two early misses, Dennis Westcott opened the scoring for Wolves at 13 minutes after some fine wing play by Teddy Maguire. Westcott then sent a 25-yard drive narrowly wide before he set up Dicky Dorsett for number two in the 21st minute. The same combination then provided Wolves with a third goal soon afterwards and, five minutes before the interval, Bryn Jones teased two defenders and slid in the perfect pass for Dorsett to complete his hat-trick and give Wolves a commanding 4–0 lead.

Two more goals followed in quick succession as Leicester's defence crumbled at the start of the second half. Jones, cutting inside, made it 5–0 and Westcott scored number six after some fine link-up play involving Horace Wright and Dorsett. Maguire made it 7–0 in the 61st minute but Leicester, surprisingly, got a goal back seven minutes later when Stan Cullis and Cyril Sidlow got into a tangle which resulted in the former putting the ball into his own net. However, this was only a blip and Wolves powered on to score three more goals in the last seven minutes of a rather one-sided contest. Dorsett, drifting inside his full-back, smashed home his fourth goal to make it 8–1 and then Westcott bagged his third and fourth goals with a close-range tap and a 15-yard snapshot to leave the Foxes bedraggled and demoralised.

Wolves: Sidlow, Morris, Dowen, Galley, Cullis, Gardiner, Maguire, H. Wright, Westcott, Jones, Dorsett.
Leicester: McLaren, Reeday, Jones, Smith, Heywood, Coutts, Grosvenor, Dewis, Bowers, Liddle, Stubbs.
Attendance: 25,540

23 February 1939
Wolves 7 Everton 0
League

Everton won the League Championship this particular season – but they certainly did not look like title contenders when they visited Molineux to take on Wolves, who were going for the double themselves. *Daily Express* reporter John Macadam wrote 'Wolves didn't simply beat Everton, they demolished them. They are magnificent. They are unequalled. Wolves for the Cup and League double. If they cannot do it, then there isn't a football team stripped that can.'

The early exchanges were fairly even, with both sets of players sizing each other up. In fact, Everton were first to threaten through Tommy Lawton, but Wolves gradually took control and Dennis Westcott fired them in front after some clever work by 16-year-old right-winger Jimmy Mullen. Then Dicky Dorsett got to work lashing in his side's second goal at 25 minutes after a neat touch inside by Alex McIntosh, and the same player made it 3–0 10 minutes later. Collecting Tom Galley's forward pass, he turned his marker completely round before cracking a low drive past Everton's former Aston Villa 'keeper Harry Morton from fully 20 yards. Hot-shot Dorsett was at it again three minutes into the second half, driving the ball home after some smart work by Dennis Westcott and Mullen to complete his hat-trick. Six minutes later McIntosh, left free inside the box, made it 5–0 with a clinical finish. Everton were stunned and it got even worse when Teddy Maguire fed Dorsett with a peach of a pass, the ball flying into the net like a bullet for goal number six just before the hour. To round things off, Dorsett set up Westcott for the seventh goal soon afterwards.

This was the second time Wolves had put seven past Everton in three years and this defeat at Molineux was, in fact, the Goodison Park club's heaviest in the League since December 1934.
Wolves: Scott, Morris, Taylor, Galley, Cullis, Gardiner, Mullen, McIntosh, Westcott, Dorsett, Maguire.
Everton: Morton, Cook, Greenhalgh, Mercer, Jones, Thomson, Gillick, Lawton, Bell, Stevenson, Boyes.
Attendance: 39,734

25 March 1939
Wolves 5 Grimsby Town 0
FA Cup semi-final

The outcome of this encounter may well have been completely different had the Mariners' goalkeeper George Moulson remained on the pitch. Unfortunately, he was injured in a clash with Dicky Dorsett halfway through the first half and both players were carried off on stretchers. Dorsett later returned with his left leg heavily strapped while full-back Jack Hodgson took over in goal for Grimsby. Hodgson, not a tall man, was immediately peppered with a series of high balls. He was finally beaten in the 31st minute when Dennis Westcott majestically converted a left-wing cross from Jimmy Mullen. Soon afterwards the same player made it 2–0, netting with a bullet shot after beating Teddy Buck on the edge of the area.

Shortly after the break Tom Galley cracked home a penalty after Westcott had been fouled and although the 10 men of Grimsby battled on gamely, soaking up heavy pressure, they conceded two late goals, both scored by the impressive Westcott, to lose the game 5–0. It was the first time a player had

Wolves' 1939 FA Cup Final squad. Back row, left to right: Morris, Galley, Scott, Taylor, Gardiner. Front row: Mullen, Burton, McIntosh, Cullis, Westcott, Dorsett, Maguire.

netted four goals in an FA Cup semi-final since Sandy Brown of Spurs against West Bromwich Albion in 1901, and Westcott did so in front of a record Old Trafford crowd. Wolves and Grimsby attracted 76,962 spectators which remains a record attendance for Old Trafford.

Wolves: Scott, Morris, Taylor, Galley, Cullis, Gardiner, Maguire, McIntosh, Westcott, Dorsett, Mullen.
Grimsby: Moulson, Vincent, Hodgson, Hall, Betmead, Buck, Boyd, Beattie, Howe, Jones, Clark.
Attendance: 76,962

31 May 1947
Wolves 1 Liverpool 2
League

This was Wolves' final game of the first post-war League season and if they could have beaten Liverpool, they would have gone to the top of the table with only Stoke City able to overtake them.

At the time of kick-off, both Wolves and Manchester United had 56 points – one more than Liverpool and Stoke. United had finished their fixtures while Stoke were due to meet Sheffield United at home on 14 June.

A crowd of almost 51,000 eased its way into Molineux and those present saw an intriguing and tight game. Stan Cullis, playing his last game for the club, was given a tremendous ovation and he was one of the first defenders called into action, sliding in to tackle Albert Stubbins on the edge of the penalty area. It was an even contest during the first 20 minutes but then, after Wolves had gone close through Jesse Pye, Billy Liddell found space on the Wolves' right and whipped over a cross that found Jack Balmer. He exchanged passes with Bob Priday before lashing a low shot past the diving Bert Williams. Eight minutes before half-time, after Wolves had threatened again, the Merseysiders went 2–0 up through Stubbins. The robust centre-forward collected a high clearance from his teammate Eddie Spicer and ran 50 yards downfield to score a brilliant individual goal.

Wolves were not about to give up. They had most of the play up to the interval and for the first 25 minutes of the second half, during which time Jimmy Dunn scored past former Molineux goalkeeper Cyril Sidlow from 20 yards to reduce the deficit.

Wolves drove forward in search of an equaliser and all 10 outfield players twice went up for corner-kicks, but Liverpool's defence held firm and a fortnight later Liverpool celebrated as the title went to Anfield following Stoke's defeat by Sheffield United.

Wolves: Williams, McLean, W. Crook, Alderton, Cullis, W. Wright, Hancocks, Dunn, Pye, Forbes, Mullen.
Liverpool: Sidlow, Harley, Lambert, Jones, Hughes, Spicer, Watkinson, Balmer, Stubbins, Liddell, Priday.
Attendance: 50,765

30 April 1949
Wolves 3 Leicester City 1
FA Cup Final

Wolves, sitting in the top six of the First Division, had to work hard and long to overcome a relegation-threatened and injury-hit Leicester City in an excellent Final at Wembley. In the end Wolves came out on top, just, after soaking up heavy second-half pressure from the Foxes.

Skipper Billy Wright introduces the Wolves players to the Duke of Gloucester before the 1949 FA Cup Final against Leicester City.

After dominating the first 45 minutes and having eight shots on target to Leicester's two, Wolves went in at the break 2–0 in front, thanks to a brace from centre-forward Jesse Pye. His first came after 12 minutes when he got on the end of a measured right-wing cross from Johnny Hancocks to head powerfully past 'keeper Gordon Bradley. His second arrived three minutes before half-time when he pivoted around the penalty spot to crack a low drive past Bradley as the Leicester defence hesitated. In between times, Sammy Smyth (twice), Hancocks, Billy Crook and Pye had all gone close while Ken Chisholm, at the other end, mistimed his shot when in the clear following a Leicester breakaway.

During the interval Leicester manager Johnny Duncan made positional changes to his forward line and they were back in the game within two minutes of the restart, when Mal Griffiths reacted quickest, after Bert Williams had parried Chisholm's drive, to steer the ball into the net as Terry Springthorpe tried desperately to keep it out.

In the 64th minute Chisholm thought he had equalised (from Jim Harrison's looping centre) but the 'goal' was ruled out by Huddersfield referee Mortimer after consultation with his linesman – much to Leicester's annoyance. Amazingly, 30 seconds later Wolves found themselves 3–1 up. Irishman Smyth raced clear from the halfway line and darted past three defenders to score with a low drive past the diving Bradley. It was one of the best goals seen in a Final for many a year and it effectively won the Cup for Wolves, whose delighted skipper Billy Wright went up to receive the coveted trophy from HRH Princess Elizabeth.

Wolves: Williams, Pritchard, Springthorpe, Crook, Shorthouse, Wright, Hancocks, Dunn, Pye, Smyth, Mullen.

Leicester: Bradley, Jelly, Scott, W. Harrison, Plummer, King, Griffiths, Lee, J. Harrison, Chisholm, Adam.

Attendance: 98,920

The first of six goals against Manchester United at Molineux in October 1952, scored by number 10 Dennis Wilshaw. United managed two in reply.

4 October 1952
Wolves 6 Manchester United 2
League

This First Division match had everything: great goals, plenty of skill, superb defending, excitement and commitment. And although they conceded six goals to a superb Wolves side, the reigning League Champions played very well and deserved better. The game itself not only lived up to previous standards, but outdid anything seen at Molineux for many years.

United started off at a blistering pace and scored twice through former Wolves junior Jack Rowley in the 20th and 21st minutes, his first from a free-kick, his second from a splendid pass by John Scott. Then Wolves seemingly woke up and attacked United's goal with great determination, Dennis Wilshaw netting with a fine shot at 26 minutes before Roy Swinbourne swept home the equaliser 15 minutes later.

Within 30 seconds of the restart Wolves were in front. The ball reached Jimmy Mullen via the other four forwards and the winger beat 'keeper Reg Allen from the narrowest of angles. This was great stuff and, as the crowd roared for more, Wilshaw netted a fourth goal at 53 minutes after some inventive play by right-winger Les Smith and Peter Broadbent. Two minutes later Swinbourne made it 5–2 with a scorching drive from 20 yards.

The action did not finish there. Rowley hit a post and Stan Pearson fired inches wide as United hit back, but Wolves had the last laugh and added a sixth goal when Swinbourne completed a fine hat-trick from Wilshaw's deft pass with two minutes remaining. Star of the show was amateur international Bill Slater, making his Wolves debut.

Wolves: Williams, Short, Pritchard, Flowers, Shorthouse, Slater, Smith, Broadbent, Swinbourne, Wilshaw, Mullen.

United: Allen, McNulty, Aston, Carey, Chilton, Gibson, Berry, Downie, Rowley, Pearson, Scott.

Attendance: 39,667

28 September 1953
Wolves 8 Chelsea 1
League

Wolves dominated this game from start to finish and in truth they could well have won by a much wider margin, perhaps 10 or 12–1. This 8–1 victory over a poor Chelsea side was their biggest in the League since 1938 and all five forwards figured on the score sheet – only the sixth time this had happened in the club's history.

Wolves got off to the best possible start as Chelsea full-back Stan Willemse conceded a penalty in the third minute by handling Jimmy Mullen's cross, allowing Johnny Hancocks to almost rip a hole in the net with his spot-kick. Although in complete control, it took Wolves until the half-hour mark to increase their lead when Hancocks smashed home an unstoppable drive from fully 35 yards. Stan Cullis's side had two more chances before the interval, but Mullen and Roy Swinbourne both failed to hit the target.

Starting the second half as they finished the first – driving forward – Wolves went 3–0 up on 48 minutes when Dennis Wilshaw delicately steered Mullen's cross past Bill Robertson and, six minutes later, Hancocks completed his hat-trick when he nipped in on the blind side to slot home Mullen's long cross from the left. Just past the hour, Swinbourne volleyed home Bill Slater's pullback to make it 5–0 and Peter Broadbent grabbed number six, 10 minutes later, with the deftest of head flicks from another precise Mullen cross.

Wolves gave away a penalty in the 76th minute when John Short fouled Frank Blunstone, and although Williams saved Roy Bentley's 12-yard shot, the forward followed up to net the rebound. However, this was only a brief respite and three minutes later Swinbourne headed home low past Robertson from yet another exquisite cross from Mullen, and to wrap things up Mullen himself got on the score sheet four minutes from time, nodding home a Broadbent centre.

Right at the death, with Wolves on the rampage, Robertson twice saved goal-bound efforts from Hancocks while Wilshaw fired over from 10 yards. This was a magnificent win and the defeat remains Chelsea's heaviest in League football to this day.

Wolves: Williams, Short, Pritchard, Slater, Shorthouse, Wright, Hancocks, Broadbent, Swinbourne, Wilshaw, Mullen.

Chelsea: Robertson, P. Sillett, Willemse, Armstrong, Greenwood, Saunders, Bentley, J. Smith, Lewis, McNichol, Blunstone.

Attendance: 36,134

19 April 1954
Wolves 4 Huddersfield Town 0
League

This emphatic victory over third-placed Huddersfield took Wolves to within striking distance of their first-ever League Championship success. They were now on 55 points, two more than arch-rivals West Bromwich Albion and with a better goal average, and both teams had two games left.

The visitors, skippered by former Molineux full-back Laurie Kelly, found themselves a goal down after just two minutes. Johnny Hancocks raced down the right wing and fizzed over a low cross that was deflected into the path of Jimmy Mullen, whose shot beat Jack Wheeler inside his near post. Twice Jim Glazzard came close to equalising and Billy Wright made a splendid goalline clearance before Wolves were awarded a penalty in the 27th minute, when Dennis Wilshaw was brought down by Don McEvoy. Unfortunately Hancocks, who had missed from the spot in the previous home game against Charlton, blasted his kick wide. However, seven minutes later, the little winger made amends by slamming home a 30-yard free-kick (conceded by future Molineux boss Bill McGarry) to put Wolves 2–0 in front.

Wolves were generally in control and came close to adding to their goal tally either side of half-time, while Huddersfield were denied a breakthrough by a fine save from Bert Williams

Manager Stan Cullis shows off the Football League Championship trophy in 1954 watched by players, left to right: R. Flowers, W. Wright, P. Broadbent, W. Shorthouse, E. Stuart, B. Williams, J. Gardiner (trainer), J. Hancocks, J. Mullen, D. Wilshaw, W. Slater, R. Swinbourne.

and a last-ditch tackle inside the area by Wright. With 15 minutes remaining Huddersfield lost 'keeper Wheeler to an injury. He was replaced by Glazzard, and although the centre-forward was not severely tested, he did concede two late goals, Peter Broadbent bouncing in a header from Mullen's corner in the 86th minute and Wilshaw driving home from 20 yards soon afterwards.

Wolves: Williams, Stuart, Wright, Slater, Shorthouse, Flowers, Hancocks, Broadbent, Swinbourne, Wilshaw, Mullen.

Huddersfield: Wheeler, Staniforth, Kelly, McGarry, McEvoy, Battye, Burrell, Cavanagh, Glazzard, Watson, Frear.

Attendance: 42,862

29 September 1954
Wolves 4 West Bromwich Albion 4
FA Charity Shield

This was a terrific game of football, with end-to-end attacking, chances galore, great skill and some brilliant goals. Both teams were minus key players but that was only a minor detail. The 24 who did appear gave the 45,000-plus crowd plenty to cheer about – and more!

Wolves took the lead after 12 minutes through Roy Swinbourne, who collected Eddie Russell's long ball and lobbed home from 15 yards. Wilf Carter and Reg Ryan should have equalised for Albion, the latter missing from two yards, while Norman Deeley fired into the side netting when well placed for Wolves.

Inside the first minute of the second half, Wolves increased their lead through Deeley, who headed home, unchallenged, after Peter Broadbent had flicked on a Johnny Hancocks free-kick. On 56 minutes Ronnie Allen blasted home from 20 yards as the Wolves defence retreated and, 90 seconds later, the England centre-forward again beat Bert Williams with a superb long-range drive to bring the scores level. This was tremendous football and it got better.

Albion were denied what seemed to be two clear penalties before Wolves reclaimed the lead on 62 minutes as Swinbourne's low shot eluded the diving Jim Sanders. In the 73rd minute Wolves went 4–2 up when Hancocks, cutting inside Len Millard, fired home a rasping shot from 20 yards. But back came Albion in the 77th minute as Ryan cracked in a 30-yard drive which Williams seemed to have covered but unfortunately let slip through his fingers, and two minutes later Allen, left on his own, tapped in the equaliser to complete his hat-trick, after Stan Rickaby's fierce shot had rebounded off the crossbar.

With time running out, Allen smashed a free-kick high into Wolves' net and Albion thought they had won the shield but referee George Gibson from Manchester ruled his effort out, stating that the ball had not rolled its full circumference when touched forward by Ryan. By such margins, trophies are won and lost – on this occasion, it was shared.

Wolves: Williams, Guttridge, Shorthouse, Flowers, Russell, Clamp, Hancocks, Broadbent, Swinbourne, Deeley, Wilshaw.

Albion: Sanders, Rickaby, Millard, Dudley (Dugdale), Kennedy, Brookes, Griffin, Ryan, Allen, Carter, Lee (Hodgkisson).

Attendance: 45,035

13 December 1954
Wolves 3 Honved 2
Friendly

Earlier in the year Wolves had beaten Racing Club of Buenos Aires, Maccabi Tel Aviv and Moscow Spartak under the Molineux floodlights and they were confident of defeating probably the greatest club side in Europe (at that time) to keep their run going. However, they got a shock, conceding two goals in the first 14 minutes against their slick Hungarian opponents, who included a handful of the players who had helped destroy England 6–3 at Wembley and 7–1 in Budapest the previous season.

Displaying superb ball skills, Honved took the lead inside five minutes when Sandor Kocsis, regarded as the best header of the ball in the world, rose majestically to steer home a free-kick flighted in from the left by Ferenc Puskas. After a couple of Wolves attacks had petered out, Kocsis sent Machos racing through to make it 2–0. The visitors continued to press forward and Wolves goalkeeper Bert Williams pulled off two excellent saves from Budai and Puskas. In fact, Wolves hardly got a look-in during the first half but after the break, with TV viewers tuned in, they were a different team, especially after Welsh referee Mervyn Griffiths awarded them a dubious penalty in the 49th minute. Johnny Hancocks smashed the ball past Farago and the Wanderers were back in the game.

Pressure on the Honved goal increased and with their fans roaring them on, Wolves drove forward. Roy Swinbourne went close with two forceful headers, Peter Broadbent fired inches wide, Les Smith's cross flew agonisingly across the face of the goal and Hancocks bent the crossbar with a 25-yard pile-driver.

Lining up before the famous win over Honved in their satin shirts are (left to right): Wright, Shorthouse, Broadbent, Smith, Wilshaw, Hancocks, Flowers, Stuart, Slater, Williams and Swinbourne.

With time fast running out, Dennis Wilshaw, who had been kept quiet by the brilliance of Jozsef Bozsik, found enough space to clip in a short cross which Swinbourne headed firmly home on 76 minutes. Bill Shorthouse won a 50–50 challenge in centre-field a minute later. He exchanged passes with Smith and found Wilshaw, who in turn spotted Swinbourne, and the centre-forward did the rest with a brilliant hook shot which flew past Farago to give Wolves a famous victory.

Wolves: Williams, Stuart, Shorthouse, Slater, Wright, Flowers, Hancocks, Broadbent, Swinbourne, Wilshaw, Smith.

Honved: Farago, Rakoczi, Kovacs, Bozsik, Lorant, Banyai, Budai, Kocsis, Machos (Tichy), Puskas, Czibor.

Attendance: 54,998

3 September 1955
Cardiff City 1 Wolves 9
League

Not since 1908 had a team won an away First Division game by a margin of eight goals, and this victory by Wolves would have been much bigger if Cardiff 'keeper Ron Howells had not produced four brilliant second-half saves.

Wolves got off to a flier with Johnny Hancocks tapping home a goal after only 55 seconds after Jimmy Mullen had struck the bar. Hancocks was on target again in the 10th minute, striking home Mullen's pass from 12 yards. With Cardiff struggling defensively, Mullen grabbed a third goal in the 13th minute after a Broadbent–Hancocks move, and another superb Mullen

Roy Swinbourne scoring the sixth in the 9–1 drubbing of Cardiff City in 1955.

cross was flicked home by Roy Swinbourne seven minutes later. Driving forward, Wolves grabbed a fifth goal in the 34th minute when Hancocks completed his hat-trick from another excellent cross by Mullen.

Either side of half-time, Hancocks, Swinbourne and Eddie Clamp all went close to adding to Wolves' tally before Swinbourne made it 6–0 in the 54th minute, netting with a smart back-heel following a corner by Hancocks and a return from Mullen. Broadbent got in on the act in the 66th minute, side-footing home Mullen's left-wing corner, and Broadbent notched his second in the 75th minute by sweeping in yet another exquisite pass from Mullen.

To round things off, Mullen's impressive drive was deflected wide of Howells by the alert Swinbourne for his hat-trick and Wolves's ninth goal in the 81st minute. Not surprisingly, Mullen was Man of the Match.

Cardiff – outplayed, outfought and outclassed – snatched a goal via ex-Wolves player Ronnie Stockin in the 83rd minute, but it was only a consolation for this was a majestic display by a wonderful Wolves side.

Cardiff: Howells, Sherwood, Stitfall, Harrington, Gale, Sullivan, Dixon, Kirtley, Hitchens, Stockin, McSeveney.

Wolves: Williams, Stuart, Shorthouse, Slater, Wright, Clamp, Hancocks, Broadbent, Swinbourne, Booth, Mullen.

Attendance: 40,060

17 October 1957
Wolves 3 Real Madrid 2
Friendly

Real Madrid had defeated Reims 4–3 and Fiorentina 2–0 in the 1956 and 1957 European Cup Finals and would go on to win their third Final 3–2 against AC Milan in 1958. Meanwhile Wolves, one of the three best club sides in Great Britain, had won the League title in 1954, finished runners-up in 1955, were third in 1956, sixth in 1957 and would subsequently win their second Championship in 1958.

Real were expected to win this friendly but their huge reputation took a hefty knock after losing this five-goal thriller to a resilient and confident Wolves side. Fielding internationals Jose Santamaria, Jose Zarraga, French goal-ace Raymond Kopa, the great Alfredo Di Stefano, Jose Hector Rial and wing-wizard Francisco Gento, Real set the early pace and took the lead after 14 minutes, Ramon Marsal meeting Jose Joseito's corner to steer a header past Malcolm Finlayson.

Real came close to scoring twice before the interval and soon after the restart when Finlayson saved from Kopa. It was not until seven minutes after half-time that Wolves finally equalised. Jimmy Murray nodded on Finlayson's long downfield clearance for Peter Broadbent to collect and lob smartly over goalkeeper Ernesto Dominguez from 15 yards. Dennis Wilshaw then clipped an upright and on 60 minutes Wolves were ahead when Murray headed home a Norman Deeley corner.

Within nine minutes Marsal scrambled his second goal and all was set for a grandstand finish. Wolves grabbed the glory when Wilshaw hooked the ball home from Jimmy Mullen's terrific cross from the left. There was still time for Murray and Wilshaw to fire wide before the final whistle signalled another famous floodlit victory. It was achieved without skipper Billy Wright, who was with the England squad preparing for an international. Eddie Stuart led the side magnificently in his absence while George Showell, Wright's deputy, did a superb job marking Di Stefano.

Wolves: Finlayson, Stuart, Harris, Clamp, Showell, Flowers, Deeley, Broadbent, Murray, Wilshaw, Mullen.

Real Madrid: Dominguez, Atienza (Marquitos), Lesmes, Santisteban, Santamaria, Zarraga (Ruiz), Joseito (Kopa), Kopa (Marsal), Di Stefano, Marsal (Rial), Gento (Joseito).

Attendance: 55,169

7 May 1960
Wolves 3 Blackburn Rovers 0
FA Cup Final

This was not a great Final for many: one newspaper reporter described it as a 'Dustbin Final' but as far as Wolves and their supporters were concerned, it was well worth the trip to Wembley!

In the opening five minutes, Wolves' defenders put in a series of crunching tackles on their Rovers counterparts and this set the pattern for the rest of the game. Although Wolves were on top for long periods, they created very little in front of goal. Until the 41st minute, that is, when Mick McGrath diverted the ball past his own goalkeeper after young Barry Stobart had sold full-back Jack Bray the perfect dummy. Shortly afterwards, Dave Whelan tried to beat Norman Deeley by turning on the ball, but his whole body and right limb twisted under him with his studs gripped in the turf...he fell and something had to give – a leg bone snapped. With Blackburn a goal and a man down, the match was now a formality of uneven odds.

Blackburn's Mick McGrath puts through his own goal in the 1960 FA Cup Final.

Wolves pushed forward after the interval and were camped in the Blackburn half for the first 20 minutes without really troubling Leyland. Then on 68 minutes Deeley, nipping into the penalty area unnoticed, ran the ball over the line after some smart wing play by the South African Des Horne. Blackburn, who included future Molineux star Derek Dougan, were struggling but Wolves, although in complete control, had to wait until the 88th minute before netting their third goal, Deeley firing high into the net with a powerful right-foot shot. Ron Flowers and Jimmy Murray both had goals disallowed in a poor Final which left a lot to be desired.

When Wolves skipper Bill Slater went up to receive the Cup he was greeted by a crescendo of boos and jeers which drowned the cheering of his own supporters. And then, as Stan Cullis took his players down the tunnel with the trophy, disgruntled Rovers supporters showered them all with orange peel, apple cores, stale sandwiches, plastic cups and general rubbish. It was all disgusting – sour grapes really – after their team had lost hands down,

Wolves: Finlayson, Showell, Harris, Clamp, Slater, Flowers, Deeley, Stobart, Murray, Broadbent, Horne.

Blackburn: Leyland, Bray, Whelan, Clayton, Woods, McGrath, Bimpson, Dobing, Dougan, Douglas, McLeod.

Attendance: 98,776

16 March 1963
Wolves 7 West Bromwich Albion 0
League

Wolves completely dominated this rearranged Black Country derby after the initial encounter had been abandoned because of snow on Boxing Day when Albion were 2–0 adrift.

Winger Terry Wharton was the star man as Wolves blitzed the Baggies with some powerful and thrustful attacking, aimed mainly down Albion's left flank. Barry Stobart, avoiding a casual lunge by Stan Jones, swept Wolves in front at nine minutes and added a second in the 26th minute with another crisp finish after a weak clearance by Ron Bradley, who was later to become a coach at Molineux. Although leading by only two goals at half-time, Wolves had dominated the opening 45 minutes with Albion managing just two efforts at Fred Davies' goal.

It was much the same after the break yet it took Wolves 21 minutes to claim their third goal, when Alan Hinton smashed home an unstoppable shot after a clever pass from Chris Crowe. Three minutes later Wharton netted the first of his three goals with a strong right-foot shot, and he struck home his second goal in the 81st minute as Albion's defence caved in. Pushing men forward at will, Wolves scored twice more through Hinton (87 minutes) and Wharton (89), and Wharton missed a sitter from three yards right at the death.

This had been a nightmare evening for Albion's future Welsh international goalkeeper Tony Millington, who earlier in the season had conceded eight goals in a Central League game on the same ground! Nevertheless, this 7–0 romp still remains Wolves' best win over their arch-rivals at senior level.

Wolves: Davies, Showell, Thomson, Kirkham, Woodfield, Flowers, Wharton, Crowe, Stobart, Broadbent, Hinton.

Albion: Millington, Howe, G. Williams, Cram, Jones, Bradley, Foggo, Fenton, Smith, Hope, Clark.

Attendance: 22,618

A Wolves goal for Bobby Gould in the centenary match at The Hawthorns in March 1971.

20 March 1971
West Bromwich Albion 2 Wolves 4
League

This was the 100th League game between Albion and Wolves and it was the visitors who came out on top, winning a six-goal thriller with Hugh Curran scoring two superb goals.

The game was evenly balanced for the opening half-hour, Jeff Astle going close for Albion, and Curran and Dave Wagstaffe for Wolves. The first goal arrived in the 31st minute as George McVitie, cutting in from the wing, fired Albion ahead with a low drive past Phil Parkes's right hand. It was cut and thrust up to the break and at the start of the second half before Wolves went into overdrive, scoring three times in 11 minutes to leave the Baggies demoralised. First, Scotsman Curran equalised in the 52nd minute after racing through a spreadeagled Albion defence, and five minutes later he was there again to drill a shot past the stranded Jim Cumbes. Albion, who had John Kaye playing as a makeshift right-back, could not cope at all with the wing play of Wagstaffe, especially as he helped set up Mike Bailey's fine goal in the 63rd minute. Tony Brown's penalty shortly afterwards gave Albion hope but Bobby Gould, soon to move to The Hawthorns and later to manage the Baggies, wrapped up the points with a fourth goal at 79 minutes.

This was Wolves' best win on Albion soil (in terms of goal difference) for 13 years and it was the first time they had ever scored four at The Hawthorns.

Albion: Cumbes, Kaye, Wilson, Lovett, Wile, Merrick, McVitie, T. Brown, Astle, Hope, Hartford.
Wolves: Parkes, Shaw, Parkin, Bailey, Munro, McAlle, McCalliog, Hibbitt (O'Grady), Gould, Curran, Wagstaffe.
Attendance: 35,716

17 May 1972
Tottenham Hotspur 1 Wolves 1
UEFA Cup Final second leg

The Molineux leg of this initial UEFA Cup Final, played a fortnight earlier, had ended in a 2–1 win for Spurs, with Martin Chivers netting twice, and Wolves knew it would take a monumental effort for them to win at White Hart Lane. Backed by over 6,000 travelling supporters, they played exceptionally well and, on reflection, only an inspired display of goalkeeping by Northern Ireland international Pat Jennings denied Wolves a victory. He was quite brilliant, pulling off superb saves in each half from Derek Dougan (twice), Dave Wagstaffe, Jim McCalliog's piledriver and late on from John Richards.

Spurs, confident in their approach, almost went in front after six minutes when Alan Gilzean's header was tipped over by Phil Parkes. The Londoners took the lead after 30 minutes through midfielder Alan Mullery, whose diving header from Martin Peters' free-kick, followed by an astute Martin Chivers dummy, flew hard and low past Parkes as Wolves' defence stood watching.

Pressing forward with great determination, Wolves equalised 10 minutes later through Wagstaffe, whose low shot from the edge of the area eluded Jennings and flew into the net. Both teams went in search of a winning goal after the break. Parkes saved well from Chivers and Gilzean while, at the other end of the field, Jennings was absolutely brilliant, his last-ditch save from Richards quite outstanding.

At the final whistle it was Spurs who lifted the Cup, winning the tie 3–2 on aggregate to become the first British club to lift two different European trophies.

Tottenham: Jennings, Kinnear, Knowles, Mullery, England, Beal, Gilzean, Perryman, Chivers, Peters, Coates.

Wolves: Parkes, Shaw, Taylor, Hegan, Munro, McAlle, McCalliog, Hibbitt (Bailey), Richards, Dougan (Curran), Wagstaffe.

Attendance: 52,891

2 March 1974
Wolves 2 Manchester City 1
League Cup Final

This was Wolves' first appearance in a League Cup Final and only their fourth visit to Wembley Stadium. Around 30,000 fans went along with them to see them beat the 1970 winners Manchester City, thanks to a fine volleyed goal from Kenny Hibbitt and a spanking effort from leading scorer John Richards.

Wolves' manager Bill McGarry chose Gary Pierce, to deputise for injured Phil Parkes, in goal while City had no worries, fielding their strongest side – and they were clear favourites to lift the trophy. However, Wolves matched them kick for kick throughout the first half and both 'keepers were kept busy, dealing mainly with high crosses, Pierce being the busier on his 23rd birthday. It was Wolves who went in at the interval a goal to the good, scored by Hibbitt from the edge of the penalty area in the 43rd minute.

Immediately after the break, City's Denis Law, Rodney Marsh and Francis Lee were all denied by the agility and awareness of Pierce before Colin Bell equalised in the 53rd minute, beating the Wolves 'keeper with a snap shot after some slack marking in defence. But Wolves battled on and took the game to City, whose 'keeper Keith MacRae saved well from Derek Dougan and Alan Sunderland.

Wolves skipper Mike Bailey holds aloft the Football League Cup at Wembley in 1974.

The substitution of Barry Powell for the limping Dave Wagstaffe (a former City player, incidentally) proved crucial as it gave Wolves more drive in midfield and, after a creative build-up between Powell and influential skipper Mike Bailey, Sunderland slipped the ball across via the heel of Rodney Marsh's boot for Richards to smash home the winner with nine minutes remaining. Shell-shocked City threw players forward in a desperate attempt to save the game, but Wolves' rearguard held firm to claim a famous victory.

Wolves: Pierce, Palmer, Parkin, Bailey, Munro, McAlle, Hibbitt, Sunderland, Richards, Dougan, Wagstaffe (Powell).

City: MacCrae, Pardoe, Donachie, Doyle, Booth, Towers, Summerbee, Bell, Lee, Law, Marsh. Substitute not used: Carrodus.

Attendance: 97,886

15 March 1980
Wolves 1 Nottingham Forest 0
League Cup Final

A bizarre tap-in goal from three yards by striker Andy Gray won this tight and rather disappointing Final for Wolves, and robbed Nottingham Forest of a third consecutive League Cup victory.

The game itself was scrappy. Neither side really got going, although Wolves, backed by some 35,000 supporters, were perhaps the more forceful and threatening team overall, certainly having the better of the midfield exchanges.

There were only six worthwhile efforts on goal during the first 45 minutes, three to each side, with Gray going the closest for Wolves and Trevor Francis likewise for Forest. Francis, in fact, was well shackled by Emlyn 'Crazy Horse' Hughes, who had a storming game at the heart of the Wolves defence.

In the second period, play was much more open but a lack of composure in dangerous areas let both teams down badly. Then out of the blue, Peter Daniel, Wolves' right-half, pumped a long ball deep into the Forest half. Centre-half Dave Needham let it bounce, thinking his goalkeeper Peter Shilton would come out and collect it. However, he didn't and both Forest players hesitated, allowing a delighted Andy Gray to run in and score the easiest goal of his career. It was enough to decide the game and Wolves celebrated victory over one of the most successful club sides from that era. A delighted Hughes received the trophy and simultaneously completed a full set of winners' medals for triumphs in the League Championship, FA Cup, European Cup and League Cup.

The gate receipts of £625,400 created a new record for this 20-year-old competition.

Wolves: Bradshaw, Palmer, Parkin, Daniel, Hughes, Berry, Hibbitt, Carr, A. Gray, Richards, Eves.

Forest: Shilton, Anderson, F. Gray, McGovern, Needham, Burns, O'Neill, Bowyer, Birtles, Francis, Robertson.

Attendance: 96,527

29 May 1988
Wolves 2 Burnley 0
Sherpa Van Trophy Final

Wolves, playing at Wembley for the third time in 14 years, made the early running and peppered the Burnley goal without really causing 'keeper Chris Pearce too much trouble, Gary Bellamy's rising shot

Andy Mutch glances a header home to give Wolves the lead in the 1988 Sherpa Van Trophy Final at Wembley. The ball had been hooked across goal by the grounded Steve Bull (centre).

being the only effort of note. However, in the 23rd minute, after a couple of close shaves, Wolves broke the deadlockfrom a right wing corner when Steve Bull hooked the ball back across the six-yard line for his strike-partner Andy Mutch to glide forward and glance a header into the Burnley net. Burnley hit back and Mark Kendall had to be alert to thwart Tony Oghani and Steve Taylor.

Wolves started the second half again on the offensive and, roared on by some 50,000 supporters, they struck again in the 51st minute when Northern Ireland international Robbie Dennison majestically curled a free-kick past former Molineux trainee Pearce. Burnley then took over and controlled the remainder of the game but never really troubled the Wolves defence minus Ally Robertson, who had to go off injured. Floyd Streete was immense at the back and so too was Bellamy, while Kendall was as safe as houses on his line. Right at the death Bull and Mutch both went close to adding to Wolves' tally, the latter striking the woodwork.

Wolves: Kendall, Bellamy, Thompson, Streete, Robertson (Gallagher), Robinson, Dennison, Downing, Bull, Mutch, Holmes (Vaughan).

Burnley: Pearce, Daniel, Deakin, Britton, Davis, Gardner, Farrell, Oghani, Taylor, Comstive, McGrory (James).

Attendance: 80,841

26 November 1988
Wolves 6 Preston North End 0
League

Wolves were brilliant in this game while Preston were poor, very poor. And for one man – Steve Bull – it was a time to celebrate as he struck home the first four-timer of his senior career in a romping 6–0 victory.

Wolves opened their account in the 13th minute when Sam Allardyce, the Preston defender, failed to clear Andy Mutch's looping cross, leaving Bull free to drive the ball into the bottom corner of the net. Then just after the half-hour mark, Bull collected a weak back pass by Richard Mooney and raced 40 yards downfield, unchallenged, to make it 2–0. Mutch weighed in with a third goal on 35 minutes before Bull struck again just before the hour, completing his sixth hat-trick for the club with a thumping drive from 10 yards, after Mutch had created the chance by robbing Bob Atkins. Wolves were now in total control and Nigel Vaughan made it 5–0 with a sweetly struck shot in the 71st minute before Bull completed the rout with his fourth goal, 14 minutes from time, after some fine work involving Mark Venus and Keith Downing down the left. The ball found its way to Bull near the penalty spot and the Preston 'keeper could only blink as it whizzed past him.

Earlier in his career 'Bully' had scored seven goals in one game for his junior team, Princes End Colts, and struck a five-timer in a Central League game for Wolves.

Wolves: Kendall, Bellamy, Venus, Street, Robertson, Vaughan (Bennett), Thompson, Downing (Gallagher), Bull, Mutch, Dennison.

Preston: Brown, Williams, Rathbone, Atkins, Wrightson (Hughes), Allardyce, Mooney, Joyce, Ellis, Brazil, Patterson.

Attendance: 13,180

Photograph © Action Images / Michael Regan

Kenny Miller celebrates after scoring the third goal against Sheffield United.

26 May 2003
Wolves 3 Sheffield United 0
Division One Play-off Final

Almost 70,000 spectators were inside the Millennium Stadium for this Play-off Final, the prize for the winners being a place in the Premiership. It was Wolves who got off to a superb start, taking the lead in the sixth minute through Mark Kennedy. Kenny Miller neatly controlled the ball before setting up his wing partner to beat Paddy Kenny with a cracking drive. As the Blades readjusted, so Wolves drove forward and they twice came close to increasing their lead before United had their first attempt on goal in the 19th minute. Keeping up the pressure, Wolves scored again two minutes later when Nathan Blake found the net after finding space behind the back four, and it was game over just before the interval as Miller neatly and precisely glanced a deft header wide of Kenny.

Wolves were on the brink of returning to the top flight of English football for the first time since 1984, but they were made to work much harder in the second half as United pressed forward. Paul Butler was unlucky to concede a penalty but 'keeper Matt Murray saved from the spot. Then Kennedy was fortunate not to give away a second spot-kick while Joleon Lescott cleared from almost under his own crossbar.

With millionaire owner Sir Jack Hayward waving to the fans from the royal box, Wolves saw out time with ease, and when the final whistle sounded there were scenes of joy all around the stadium. Wolves were back – but for how long?

Wolves: Murray, Irwin, Naylor, Ince, Butler, Lescott, Newton, Cameron, Blake (Proudlock), Miller (Sturridge), Kennedy.

Sheffield United: Kenny, Curtis, Kozluk, Brown, Jagielka, Page, Ndlovu (Peschisolido), Rankine (McCall), Asaba (Allison), Kabba, Tonge.

Attendance: 69,473

17 January 2004
Wolves 1 Manchester United 0
Premiership

In front of the live Sky Sports cameras, Wolves caused a major upset by beating the reigning champions and League leaders, Manchester United, 1–0 at Molineux to record only their fourth victory in the Premiership.

Wolves certainly played well, matching their more illustrious opponents kick for kick during the first half when both goalkeepers were continually in action. However, it was difficult to assess how well Wolves were really performing because United were certainly below par, with Ryan Giggs and Gary Neville both sidelined. But give credit where it's due, halfway through the second half Scotsman Kenny Miller proved his worth when he scored a dramatic winning goal, driving the ball home after a smart build-up involving four players.

United counter-attacked – as they always do – but found Wolves' back line immovable, as Paul Butler and Jody Craddock stopped everything before them, while 'keeper Michael Oakes saved superbly from Ruud van Nistelrooy and Paul Scholes. Miller almost scored again late on, and just before the final whistle substitute Diego Forlan fired wide for the Reds. This was a great day for two former United players, Denis Irwin and Paul Ince.

Wolves: Oakes, Irwin, Naylor, Ince, Butler, Craddock, Newton, Rae, Iversen (Ganea), Miller, Kennedy.
United: Howard, O'Shea, Fortune, Ferdinand (Brown), Keane, Silvestre, Fletcher (Bellion), P. Neville (Forlan), van Nistelrooy, Scholes, Ronaldo.
Attendance: 29,396 (ground record since redevelopment)

Kenny Miller celebrates his goal against Manchester United.

4 May 2008
Wolves 1 Plymouth Argyle 0
Championship

Going into this final Championship game of the season against a useful Plymouth Argyle side, Wolves knew they had to win – and win well – to stand any chance of claiming the sixth and final Play-off place.

Watford, with a slightly better goal-difference, were just two points above Wolves in the table – and they had a tricky away fixture at Blackpool, while Ipswich Town and even Sheffield United could also squeeze into the frame if results went their way. In the end, despite beating the Pilgrims 1–0, thanks to a late Seyi Olofinjana strike, a one-goal victory was not enough to see Wolves leap-frog the Hornets, who managed to scramble a 1–1 draw at Bloomfield Road despite playing 75 minutes with 10 men.

Although this was not the greatest match of season 2007–08, this encounter was certainly a crucial one for Wolves as a club, and certainly for the players and supporters, especially as their arch-rivals West Bromwich Albion had already clinched a place in the Premiership.

Wolves knew they had to score at least a couple of goals – a win margin of 2–0, 3–0 or even better was needed to stand any chance of grabbing that final Play-off spot. In the very first minute Andy Keogh's teasing cross was hacked clear before Krisztian Timar had to head a Matt Jarvis centre over his own crossbar. Ex-Argyle striker Sylvan Ebanks-Blake fired wide from 20 yards as Wolves continued

Seyi Olofinjana celebrates scoring the first goal with teammates.

Photograph © Action Images / Paul Dowker

their siege on the visitors' goal, and in fact, during the opening 15 minutes, Wolves' 'keeper Wayne Hennessey's only action was to deal with Jody Craddock's back pass.

After former Molineux youth-team player Jermaine Easter was yellow-carded following a foul on Wolves defender Gary Breen, both sides had opportunities to take the lead. Michael Kightly shot wide for Wolves while Rory Fallon hit his effort into the side netting for the Devon side.

With the news known by everyone inside Molineux that Blackpool were 1–0 up on Watford, and a goal would move Wolves up into sixth place in the table, they continued to drive forward but could not find a way past Argyle 'keeper Luke McCormack.

The breakthrough almost arrived early in the second-half. Kightly fed Ebanks-Blake but his low cross struck a defender and then Keogh before bouncing a yard wide. Plymouth responded and a glancing header from Jamie Mackie was grabbed at the second attempt by Hennessey. After Henry had been booked for a late challenge on Mackie, Anderson's last-ditch tackle stopped Ebanks-Blake from having a clear run at goal.

Just past the hour mark, Molineux fell silent as news filtered through that Watford had equalised at Blackpool. At this juncture, Wolves were pushing forward but simply could not find a way through a well-organised defence. The fans were becoming more irritable by the minute, and finger nails were getting shorter as the tension mounted.

Mick McCarthy replaced Keogh with Freddy Eastwood in an attempt to add more bite up front after Henry had miscued from 20 yards and Jarvis had seen his fiercely struck shot blocked by a defender. Plymouth's captain, Timur, was then carried off on a stretcher with his neck in a brace.

With just three minutes of normal time remaining, Wolves finally grabbed the lead. Kevin Foley found Eastwood, whose lofted pass dropped into the path of Olofinjana. He controlled his lob perfectly, guiding the ball over McCormick and into the net.

Then, shortly after the goal celebrations had died down, the crowd erupted again when it was reported on the radio that Blackpool had been awarded a penalty. However, within seconds the euphoria died down when it became apparent that Blackpool had not, in fact, been awarded the spot-kick.

The fourth official then held the board up stating that there would be eight minutes of added time. Up went the roars again, only to fall quiet just as quickly when Luke Summerfield's long-range shot took a deflection and flew narrowly wide of Hennessey's goal. Wolves failed to create a single chance in added time, and although they won the game it was a sad occasion when the final result came in from Bloomfield Road.

Wolves: Hennessey, Foley (Elliott), Elokobi, Henry, Craddock, Breen, Kightly (Gray), Keogh (Eastwood), Ebanks-Blake, Olofinjana, Jarvis.

Plymouth: McCormick, Doumbe, Timar (Folly), Anderson, Abdou, Mackie, Fallon, Sawyer, Summerfield, Clark (Teale), Easter (MacLean).

Attendance: 26,293.

100 Wolves Stars

Harry Allen

Centre-half: 153 apps, 13 goals.

Born: 19 January 1866, Walsall. Died: 23 February 1895, Walsall.
Career: Walsall Town Swifts, WOLVES (August 1886–October 1894).

■ Although imprudent at times, Harry Allen was a splendid centre-half and captain of Wolves. Quite unflagging, especially good in the air, strong in the tackle and a fine passer, he always tried to find a teammate when clearing his lines rather than just hoofing the ball downfield. After doing well with Walsall Town Swifts, Harry joined Wolves in 1886 and scored on his debut in a 6–0 FA Cup win over Matlock Town. He hit another goal in his second Cup appearance when Crosswell's Brewery were thrashed 14–0 – Wolves' record victory at senior level. Virtually an ever present in his first two seasons, he won three of his five England caps in that time and he also lined up for Wolves in their first-ever Football League match, against Aston Villa in September 1888. He played in every game that season, including the defeat to double winners Preston in the FA Cup Final. Four years later, Wolves again reached the Cup Final and this time they triumphed, beating Everton 1–0 in Manchester, Harry scoring the vital goal on the hour. Illness, coupled with a tedious back injury, forced him to retire in 1894, at which point he became a publican in Wolverhampton.

Tom Baddeley

Goalkeeper: 315 apps.

Born: 2 November 1874, Bycars, Burslem, Stoke-on-Trent. Died: 24 September 1946, Hartshill, Stoke-on-Trent.
Career: Burslem Swifts, Burslem Port Vale, WOLVES (October 1896–July 1907), Bradford Park Avenue, Stoke, Whitfield Colliery, England (5 caps).

■ An excellent goalkeeper, brave and consistent, with outstanding agility and capable of dealing

with any type of shot, Tom Baddeley spent 18 years in the game, 11 with Wolves, and was the first player to appear in 300 matches for the club. Although on the small side at 5ft 9in, he was never afraid to defend where it hurt, often diving at the feet of opponents and contesting high balls with rugged, powerful centre-forwards. He could throw a ball up to 50 yards and often turned defence into attack with one almighty swing of his right arm. He made his debut for Port Vale as a 19-year-old and joined Wolves for £50 in 1896. His first months were spent in the second XI before taking over from Billy Tennant. Tom was at his peak in 1902–03 and 1903–04 when he gained England recognition, securing the first of five full caps against Ireland at Molineux in February 1903. He was lucky not to suffer too many injuries during his career and, in fact, was out of action only half-a-dozen times mainly due to a niggling back problem. Making his last appearance for Wolves at Burton in March 1907, Tom left Molineux to become a founder member of Bradford Park Avenue. He played in the Yorkshire club's first-ever League game against Hull in September 1908 but failed to hold down a regular place in the side, switching to Stoke in March 1910. After a handful of games for the Potters, he rounded off his career with Whitfield Colliery, retiring in May 1911.

Mike Bailey

Midfield: 432+4 apps, 24 goals.

Born: 27 February 1942, Wisbech, Cambridgeshire.

Career: Charlton Athletic, WOLVES (February 1966–January 1977), Minnesota Kicks (NASL), Hereford United (player-manager), Bexleyheath (player-manager), England (five Under-23 and two full caps), Charlton (manager), Brighton & Hove Albion (manager), Fisher Athletic (manager), Leatherhead (manager).

■ Mike Bailey suffered two massive injury scares as a Charlton player but regained his fitness, his confidence and self-belief and, indeed, his form to become one of the finest half-backs in the

country, as well as being an inspirational captain at both Charlton and Wolves. He won all his England honours during his time at The Valley – his two full caps coming in 1964 against the US and Wales. He also represented the Football League on three occasions. Mike made almost 170 appearances for the Addicks before moving to Molineux in 1966, signed by Ronnie Allen for £35,000. He was outstanding as Wolves regained their top-flight status in 1967 and was duly voted Midland Footballer of the Year. The team's driving force, he produced some outstanding performances as Wolves won the Texaco Cup in 1971, reached the UEFA Cup Final the following year and lifted the League Cup in 1974. Unfortunately, Wolves were relegated two years later and at this juncture Mike was starting to feel the pinch. Nevertheless, after his testimonial match against West Bromwich Albion, he battled on gamely and helped Wolves win the Second Division title at the first attempt. This was his last season at Molineux and with Steve Daley, Kenny Hibbitt and Willie Carr in midfield, he joined the NASL club Minnesota Kicks for £15,000. In 1978 he returned to the UK as player-manager of Hereford and later scouted for his former club Charlton, whom he also managed, steering the Addicks to promotion in 1981. After a spell in charge of Brighton, he worked a minor miracle by keeping Fisher Athletic in the Conference in 1990.

Dicky Baugh (senior)

Full-back: 229 apps, 1 goal.

Born: 14 February 1864, Wolverhampton. Died: 14 August 1929, Wolverhampton.
Career: Rose Villa, Wolverhampton Rangers, Stafford Road, WOLVES (May 1886–September 1896), Walsall, England (2 caps).

■ Dicky Baugh was a redoubtable full-back with a tremendous appetite for hard work. Well built, he was quick in recovery and headed the ball powerfully, yet despite his aggressiveness was never sent off and rarely cautioned. A pupil at St Luke's School, Blakenhall, he was 22 when he joined Wolves as a professional in May 1886 from Stafford Road, having gained his first England cap against Ireland two months earlier. He immediately established himself in the first team, partnering Charlie Mason, and both players were ever present in the first season of League football in 1888–89, playing in the 3–0 FA Cup Final defeat by Preston. The following year (March 1890) both Dickie and Mason were England's full-backs when Ireland were whipped 9–1 in Belfast. Two more Cup Final appearances came Dickie's way – in 1893 when Wolves beat Everton, and in 1896 when Sheffield Wednesday won the trophy. After 10 years' service, Dickie was transferred to Walsall in 1896. He remained with the Saddlers for one season before retiring with a knee injury which had been troubling him for a long time. Only six players have appeared in more FA Cup games for Wolves than Dickie who, without doubt, was a genuinely fine footballer, a dedicated club man whose son, Richard Baugh junior, also played for Wolves for six years after World War One.

Jack Baynton

Centre-half/goalkeeper: 28 apps.

Born: 20 March 1859, Rushtock Wood, Worcestershire. Died: 17 May 1939, Alfreton, Derbyshire.
Career: Blakenhall St Luke's, WOLVES (August 1877–May 1899), Kidderminster Olympic.

■ Although he made only 28 appearances for Wolves, Jack Baynton was one of the most inspirational and respected persons in the club's early years. A pupil and teacher at St Luke's School, Blakenhall, for whom he played as a centre-half, he helped form Wolves in 1877 with his best friend, John Brodie, and was skipper when the club won its first trophy – the Wrekin Cup in 1884. A versatile footballer who occupied eight different positions, Jack's last outing for Wolves was in goal in the 1889 FA Cup Final defeat by double-chasing Preston. Able to perform at right-back, in all three half-back positions and as a forward, it is on record that in one local Cup tie he scored a goal

from almost 100 yards by fly-kicking the ball downfield, watching it bounce once and land between the posts. He always preferred to keep goal and was in that position for Wolves' first League game, against Aston Villa in September 1888, when he produced some fine saves in a 1–1 draw. Five years earlier he figured in Wolves' first FA Cup tie against Long Eaton Rangers – as a centre-half. After leaving Wolves (owing to school commitments), Jack assisted Kidderminster Olympic and looked on, sitting on a chair in his goalmouth, smoking a pipe, as Hereford Thistle were thumped 25–0 in a Birmingham Cup tie. Jack became an English and maths teacher at All Saints School, Hockley, Birmingham, and spent his weekends refereeing.

Billy Beats

Forward: 218 apps, 73 goals.

Born: 13 November 1871, Wolstanton, Stoke-on-Trent. Died: 6 April 1939, Reading.

Career: Porthill Victoria, Port Vale Rovers, Burslem Port Vale, WOLVES (June 1895–May 1903), Bristol Rovers, Port Vale, Reading, England (2 caps).

■ Keen and aggressive with a powerful right-foot shot, Billy Beats joined Wolves in 1895 for £80 plus a guarantee of a further £50 from a benefit match: an agreement made after he had scored a hat-trick for Port Vale in their Staffordshire Cup Final win over Wolves a year earlier. Billy loved to run at defenders and was a clever footballer in his own right, often deceiving his opponent with smart footwork or by dropping his shoulder and turning completely around, with or without the ball. A lot of his goals were scored with deliberate or well-directed shots, several from inside the penalty area, although at times he would choose to unleash a stinging drive from fully 20–25 yards. He spent eight seasons at Molineux, during which time he represented England against Wales in 1901 and Scotland in 1902. He also played in the ill-fated international match against Scotland at Ibrox Park in April 1902 when 25 spectators were killed and over 500 injured after wooden terracing collapsed behind one of the goals. A regular in the Wolves side until shortly after the start of the 1902–03 campaign, he was leading scorer twice and his best season was his first, when he netted 14 times, collecting an FA Cup runners-up medal.

Towards the end of his Molineux career Billy began to lose his form, although an ankle injury did not help his cause. He left the club reluctantly for Bristol Rovers in 1903 and two years later returned to Port Vale, later assisting Reading as a player and trainer and also acting as spongeman at Reading. In 1917 he took over the Truro Inn in Castle Street, Reading.

Gary Bellamy

Full-back: 161+3 apps, 9 goals.

Born: 4 July 1962, Worksop, Nottinghamshire.

Career: Chesterfield, WOLVES (September 1987–September 1992), Cardiff City, Leyton Orient, Chelmsford City, Dover Athletic (manager).

■ Signed in 1987 by Graham Turner for £17,000 from Chesterfield, for whom he had appeared in more than 200 games, Gary Bellamy made his debut for Wolves 48 hours after joining the club but had to work hard to gain a regular place in the side, owing to the form of Steve Stoutt. Partnering Andy Thompson, he actually shared the right-back duties with Stoutt during that season, helping Wolves win the Fourth Division Championship (just as he had done with his former club Chesterfield in 1985) and also lift the Sherpa Van Trophy. Also capable of playing in the centre-half position (and as the anchor man in midfield if required), Gary certainly bolstered a previously leaky Wolves defence and, over the next four years, he produced some terrific performances as the Molineux side charged through the Third Division and into the Second in rapid time. His positive, tireless displays down the right flank enabled Wolves to attack much more than in the past and in some cases he was classed as an extra forward – a winger in fact, whose crosses were usually delivered into the danger zone perfectly for prolific striker Steve Bull and his partner Andy Mutch. Losing his place to Kevin Ashley, Gary remained at the club as an important and certainly valuable reserve. He had a loan spell with Cardiff, during which time he won a Welsh Cup-winners' medal, before moving to Leyton Orient for £30,000 in 1992. He made 150 appearances with the London club prior to his appointment as player-coach/commercial manager of Chelmsford City in 1996, and later bossed Dover Athletic.

Gary Bellamy

George Berry

Defender: 160 apps, 6 goals.

Born: 19 November 1957, Rostrop, West Germany.

Career: WOLVES (April 1974–August 1982), Stoke City, Doncaster Rovers, Peterborough United, Preston North End, Aldershot, Stafford Rangers, Wales (5 caps).

■ George Berry, loose-limbed with a deceptively casual style, was a strong-tackling, wholehearted central-defender who became a firm favourite with the Molineux fans. Born to a Welsh mother (from Mountain Ash, Glamorgan) and a Jamaican father, he moved to England as a child and attended school in Blackpool and Handsworth, Birmingham. He had an unsuccessful trial with Ipswich before joining Wolves as an apprentice in 1974, turning professional on his 18th birthday and making his debut against Chelsea in the penultimate

George Berry, left, with manager John Barnwell.

game of the 1976–77 season, when both clubs were chasing the Second Division title, which Wolves won. George gained a regular place in the side in 1978–79 and during the season George won the first of his five full caps for Wales, ironically against the country of his birth, West Germany. His other international appearances came against the Republic of Ireland, West Germany (again) and Turkey in 1979–80 and England in 1982–83. George helped Wolves win the 1980 League Cup but injuries and suspension affected his performances and, after an uneasy 1981–82 season ended in relegation, George was re-united with his former Molineux colleagues Derek Parkin and manager Sammy Chung at Stoke City. He made 260 appearances for the Potters in eight years, scoring 30 goals, a third of them penalties. In later years he promoted soccer in various schools and youth clubs while running his own BBC radio programme.

Alf Bishop

Half-back: 382 apps, 6 goals.

Born: 8 April 1886, Stourbridge. Died: 8 August 1938, Wolverhampton.

Career: Halesowen Town, WOLVES (June 1906–July 1920), Merthyr Town, Wrexham.

■ Originally a self-disciplined full-back with Halesowen, Alf Bishop joined Wolves as a professional in June 1906 and after spending a season in the reserves, where he was converted into a right-half, he made his League debut on the opening day of the 1906–07 Second Division campaign, against Hull City at Molineux. He retained his place in the side and eventually took over at centre-half from Billy Wooldridge, who switched to centre-forward, as Wolves battled in vain to regain their First Division status. Alf moved over to left-half halfway through 1907–08, forming a superb middle-line trio along with the Reverend Kenneth Hunt and Wooldridge, who returned to the pivotal berth. Alf was outstanding as progress was made in the FA Cup and some excellent performances saw Wolves reach the Final, where they beat red-hot favourites

Newcastle to lift the trophy for the second time. However, the main priority at this juncture was to regain First Division status, and despite the drive and commitment, skill and endeavour of Alf, unfortunately promotion eluded Wolves. Alf never shirked a tackle or, indeed, a challenge and always gave encouragement to his colleagues as he continued to do the business on the field, skippering the team on occasions. Unfortunately he was not getting any younger; his legs were beginning to feel the pressure and, after guesting for Merthyr Town in 1917 and playing in the Victory League for Wolves in 1919, he left Molineux in May 1920 for Wrexham. Injuries started to catch up with him and, after working in a local department store, he returned to Wolverhampton. Sadly, Alf never gained international recognition.

Paul Bradshaw

Goalkeeper: 243 apps.

Born: 28 April 1956, Altrincham, Cheshire.

Career: Blackburn Rovers, WOLVES (September 1977–August 1984), Vancouver Whitecaps (NASL), West Bromwich Albion (2 spells), Bristol Rovers, Newport County, Walsall, Peterborough United, England (4 Under-21 caps).

■ Paul Bradshaw represented Altrincham &

Cheshire Boys and had a trial with Manchester United before joining Blackburn Rovers as an apprentice in January 1972, turning professional 18 months later. After making more than 80 appearances for the Ewood Park club and gaining the first two of his four England Under-21 caps against Wales and Scotland, he was transferred to Wolves for £150,000 in September 1977, manager Sammy Chung recruiting him to take over from Gary Pierce. Tall, agile and strong with a safe pair of hands, Paul was also courageous, a fine shot-stopper who would often fling himself at the feet of opposing forwards. He proved to be an excellent signing and went on to appear in 243 competitive games for the club, gaining a League Cup-winners' medal in 1980 against Nottingham Forest. He also won two more Under-21 caps, lining up against Finland and Yugoslavia in 1978–79. In his first season at Molineux (1977–78) Paul made 37 appearances. He missed only 13 games over the next three years before being an ever present player in 1981–82 when, sadly, Wolves were relegated to the Second Division. He was twice voted Wolves' Player of the Year (1981 and 1982). Once Graham Hawkins had taken over as manager, Paul was replaced by the experienced John Burridge. Promotion was subsequently gained at the first attempt but Paul, disappointed at not being part of the triumphant team, was still playing second fiddle and had to fight his way back into the side, mustering only 12 outings in 1983–84 before transferring to Vancouver Whitecaps. He returned to Football League action with West Bromwich Albion in February 1985, served as coach at Walsall for a short time, played briefly for Bristol Rovers and Newport County, and had a second spell at The Hawthorns (1988–90) before rounding off his career with Peterborough United, retiring in May 1991. Paul later returned to Wolverhampton to work as a security officer and is a member of the Wolves Former Players' Association.

Peter Broadbent

Inside-forward: 497 apps, 145 goals.
Born: 15 May 1933, Elvington near Dover, Kent.
Career: Dover, Brentford, WOLVES (February 1951–January 1965), Shrewsbury Town, Aston Villa, Stockport County, Bromsgrove Rovers, England (1 B, 1 Under-23 and 7 full caps).

■ Peter Broadbent, the son of a miner, was signed by Wolves as a 17-year-old from Brentford for a record £10,000 in 1951. He quickly settled in at Molineux and reached great heights, eventually playing almost 500 games for the club. He gained three League Championship medals in the 1950s, won the FA Cup in 1960, played for England at three levels, participated in the World Cup Finals in 1958 and twice represented the Football League. He certainly deserved more honours but was unfortunate to have several other quality players to compete with for a place in the national team, including Johnny Haynes, Bobby Robson and even Bobby Charlton. A hard-working, scheming, ball-playing midfielder who loved to drive forward and have a crack at goal, Peter made the Wolves side tick in the 1950s. An elegantly, beautifully balanced player who preferred the inside-right position, he was a complete master on the ball and his passes, long or short, were often inch-

perfect. After gaining a regular place in the team in 1952, Peter remained a permanent fixture in manager Stan Cullis's side for 12 years, his name being one of the first on the team sheet. He netted 12 goals when the League title was won in 1954, struck 17 more when the Championship was won again in 1958 and added another 20 to his tally when Wolves secured the star prize for a third time in 1959. Peter also had the pleasure of scoring Wolves' first goal in a major European tournament, doubling up against Schalke '04 in the European Cup in 1958 – the same year he made his senior international debut, collecting his first cap against the USSR in the World Cup Finals. He later played in the win over Scotland, when his teammate Billy Wright won his 100th senior cap. Peter played his last game for Wolves on Boxing Day 1964. A month later he joined Shrewsbury, switched to Aston Villa in 1966, spent a season with Stockport and ended his career with Bromsgrove Rovers. He later ran a babywear shop in Halesowen and lived in Codsall but, sadly, is now in a nursing home, suffering from Alzheimer's disease. Peter was also a champion golfer, winning both the professional footballers' and the Staffordshire amateur titles.

John Brodie

Forward: 65 apps, 44 goals.

Born: 30 August 1862, Wightwick, Wolverhampton. Died: 16 February 1925, Wolverhampton.

Career: WOLVES (August 1877–May 1891), West Bromwich Albion (guest), England (3 full caps).

■ Educated at St Luke's School, Blakenhall, Jack Brodie was one of the founder members of the club in 1877 and while things were being developed behind the scenes – fixtures being arranged, players signed, ground sorted out – he attended Saltley College, Birmingham, for two years (1880–82) before continuing his football career. Able to occupy a variety of positions but preferring the centre-forward berth, he scored twice on his senior debut for Wolves in a 4–1 win over Long Eaton Rangers in a first-round FA Cup tie in October 1883 – this being Wolves' first-ever game in this competition. By the time League football arrived in September 1888, Jack had already hit 15 goals for Wolves, including his first hat-trick in a 14–0 home win over Crosswell's Brewery in November 1886. In the inaugural League season he scored once in each of nine successive games between 20 October and 22 December,

helped Wolves reach the Cup Final for the first time, where they lost to double winners Preston North End, and twice represented England, scoring on his debut in a 6–1 win over Ireland. He later added a third cap to his collection against Ireland in 1891, at Molineux. Jack continued playing until May 1891 when he retired through injury. In later life he had a pronounced limp, a legacy of his footballing days. Jack took up refereeing on a part-time basis as well as being headmaster at St Peter's School, Wolverhampton. In August 1913 he joined the board of directors at Molineux and regularly livened up many a dull meeting with his witty and devilish remarks. He remained a director until the early-1920s, when he resigned to spend more time on his teaching.

Sammy Brooks

Winger: 246 apps, 53 goals.

Born: 28 March 1890, Brierley Hill, Staffordshire. Died: 13 January 1960, Brierley Hill, Staffordshire.
Career: Brierley Hill Corinthians, Brierley Hill Alliance, Bilston United, WOLVES (July 1909–July 1922), Tottenham Hotspur, Southend United, Cradley Heath (2 spells), Kidderminster Harriers, Stourbridge, England (1 Victory cap).

■ A tricky 5ft 2in tall left-winger known as 'Little Giant', Sammy Brooks spent 13 years at Molineux during which time he averaged a goal every five games, appeared in the 1921 FA Cup Final, was capped by England in a Victory international and represented the Football League against the Irish League. One of the smallest and lightest players ever to play for Wolves, he was always involved in the action and he certainly enjoyed a challenge, often giving as good as he got when opposed by a rock solid full-back. He had his best season in terms of appearances in 1914–15, when he was absent from the side just once. He also netted 18 goals that term – his best seasonal tally. In the first season after World War One he had five different partners on the left wing, while producing some fine displays. The following

year, he again performed admirably as Wolves swept all before them to reach the Cup Final. Unfortunately, on a tacky, wet Chelsea pitch they lost 1–0 to Spurs, the team Sammy would join 15 months later. Switched to the right wing by secretary-manager Jack Addenbrooke, who wanted to accommodate fresh players, Sammy struggled during 1921–22 and when George Jobey took charge of the team he was transferred to Spurs, where he linked up with 'Fanny' Walden who was an inch taller. Sammy disappointed at White Hart Lane and in May 1924, after just 16 appearances, he moved to Southend United, later assisting three Midland clubs before retiring in May 1927.

Steve Bull, MBE

Striker: 545+16 apps, 306 goals.

Born: 28 March 1965, Tipton, West Midlands.
Career: Newey Goodman, Red Lion, Tipton Town (2 spells), West Bromwich Albion (2 spells), WOLVES (November 1986–July 1999), Hereford United, Stafford Rangers (manager), England (5 Under-21, 5 B and 13 full caps).

■ The greatest goalscorer in the long and eventful history of Wolverhampton Wanderers football club, Steve Bull played for his school teams, Ocker Hill Infants and Willingsworth High, as well as two local junior teams before joining Tipton Town. His goalscoring expertise

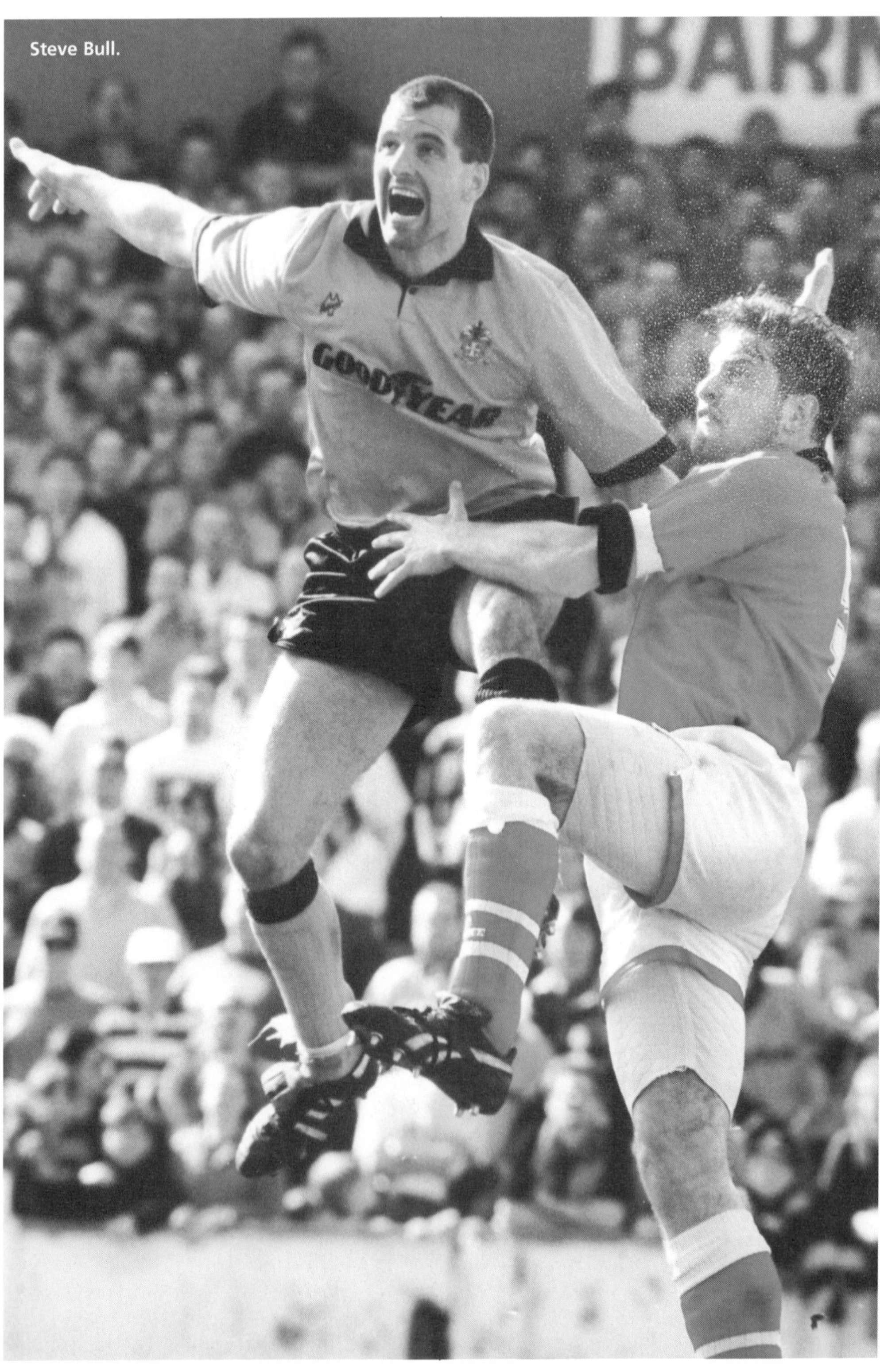

Steve Bull.

was noted by West Bromwich Albion and he signed professional forms at The Hawthorns in August 1985. Steve scored three goals in nine games for the Baggies before transferring to Wolves in November 1986, along with Andy Thompson in a combined deal worth £70,000, of which Steve was valued at £50,000. 'Bully', as he became known to every Wolves supporter, made his debut against Wrexham 48 hours later in front of 5,252 fans. The team were struggling in the Fourth Division at the time and Molineux was a very depressing place to be. Worse was to come when, on the following Monday evening, cup-tied Steve sat in the stand and watched as Wolves suffered the worst humiliation in their history, crashing out of the FA Cup to non-League Chorley. Steve was straight back into the team after that disaster and scored the first of his 306 goals for Wolves in a Freight Rover Trophy game at Cardiff, following up with his first goal in the League to earn a 1–0 victory at Hartlepool. He claimed five more goals up to February 1987, when Wolves met Stockport at Molineux, a game many people saw as the turning point for the club. Trailing 1–0 with 14 minutes to go, Wolves suddenly clicked into gear and scored three times to win the game, Steve netting once. Only three of the remaining 22 games that season ended in defeats and, amazingly, Wolves just missed out on promotion, losing to Aldershot in the Play-off Final. In 1986–87 Steve scored 19 goals, including his first hat-trick for the club in a 4–1 win over Hartlepool. He already had many admirers, but in 1987–88 Steve became a hero as Wolves won the Fourth Division Championship and beat Burnley 2–0 to lift the Sherpa Van Trophy at Wembley. That season Steve scored 52 times, 34 in the League, making him the first player to claim half a century of goals in a season of English football since Peterborough's Terry Bly almost 30 years earlier. The following season, he netted four hat-tricks and two four-timers in another 50-goal haul as Wolves won the Third Division title and came within a whisker of returning to Wembley. Bull's half century of goals in successive seasons remains a unique feat. Legendary Middlesbrough centre-forward George Camsell also scored 100 goals in the space of two seasons but his haul consisted of 63 in 1926–27 and 37 in 1927–28. Steve's marksmanship brought him international recognition, and he was capped by England for the first time against Scotland at Hampden Park in May 1989, scoring in a 2–0 win. The following April he netted twice against Czechoslovakia to clinch a place in the squad for the World Cup Finals in Italy. Steve won 13 full caps in total, eight of them as a substitute, and scored four goals. He also played in five B and five Under-21 internationals. In March 1992 Steve broke the Wolves scoring record set by John Richards when he netted his 195th goal (against Derby County). After remaining loyal to the club by resisting the temptation to join a team in the Premiership, he scored his 300th goal for Wolves in February 1998, following up six months later with his record-breaking 18th hat-trick. Steve went on to appear in 561 games for Wolves (474 in the Football League) and scored 306 goals (250 in the League) before a knee injury forced him to quit top-line soccer in the summer of 1999. He joined Conference side Hereford United the following season but didn't play much, retiring to concentrate on his work at Molineux in a PR capacity. Awarded the MBE in the Millennium New Year's honours list for services to football, he took over as manager of Stafford Rangers in 2007–08.

Billy Caddick

Defender: 154 apps, 2 goals.

Born: 14 March 1898, Wellington, Shropshire.
Died: 13 June 1981, Maldon, Essex.
Career: All Saints, Wellington Town (2 spells), WOLVES (December 1920–May 1927), Stafford Rangers.

■ Billy Caddick spent seven years at Molineux and was a first-team regular in five of those campaigns. He scored two goals in a total of 154 senior appearances. A pupil at St Luke's School, Blakenhall, until he was 15, he then played for local team All Saints prior to joining the 3rd

Battalion Grenadier Guards (also the Household battalion), serving behind enemy lines between 1916 and 1919. After the war he signed for the Birmingham & District League side Wellington Town and did extremely well at the heart of their defence. Watched by scouts from several major clubs, including Aston Villa and Wolves, he was eventually recruited as a professional by the latter in December 1920. Acting as cover for Maurice Woodward and Joe Hodnett, Bill had to wait three months before making his first-team debut in the Staffordshire derby at Stoke, in front of 13,500 spectators. There was a possibility that he might just creep into that season's FA Cup Final team but in the end he had to settle for a seat in the stand as Wolves lost 1–0 to Spurs at Stamford Bridge. Bill always worked hard at his game and within seven months he had established himself in the first XI. Playing alongside skipper Val Gregory and left-half Alf Riley, he produced some excellent performances as Wolves just scraped clear of relegation. Bill actually scored his first goal for the club this term, in a 3–2 home win over South Shields on Christmas Eve. A year on, Bill struggled with a tedious ankle injury as Wolves desperately fought a losing battle, slipping into the Third Division North for the first time in the club's history. Disillusioned of course, Bill nevertheless continued to fight on and, having been joined in the middle line by George Getgood and Albert Kay, he missed only six games in 1923–24 when the Third Division North title was won at the first time of asking, Wolves pipping Rochdale by one point to claim top spot in the table. An injury suffered in September 1925 saw Bill replaced by Sam Charnley. He attained full fitness but had to wait a while before regaining his first-team place – celebrating with a goal in a 4–0 win over Nottingham Forest. In 1926–27 Bill entered the reserves and at that point his Wolves career ended. He joined Wellington Town and a year later switched to Stafford Rangers, helping them twice win the Keys Cup (1928 and 1929). Retiring in May 1931, he became licensee of the Hop Pole, Oxley Moor Road, Wolverhampton. Bill's grandfather, also named Bill, was a goalkeeper with Wolves in the early 1880s.

Willie Carr

Midfield: 282+7 apps, 26 goals.

Born: 6 January 1950, Glasgow.

Career: Coventry City, WOLVES (March 1975–August 1982), Millwall, Worcester City, Willenhall Town, Stourbridge, Scotland (4 Under-23, 6 full caps).

■ Willie Carr, educated in Cambridge and a star of Coventry City's 1968 Youth team, scored 37 goals in 298 games for the Sky Blues before joining Wolves for £80,000 in March 1975. Twelve months earlier, Molineux boss Bill McGarry had offered £240,000 for Willie's services but pulled out of the deal when the player failed a medical. At only 23 years old, Willie severely injured his knee at Liverpool in April 1973 and it took some time for him to recover – at one time he was under intense daily treatment. He played in only 13 League games the following season. Thankfully, all was well in the end and he performed superbly well for Wolves for seven years, up to August 1982 when

he was transferred to Millwall. A tireless worker in the engine room, Willie had flair, ability, vision, skill, aggression (when required) and could pass a ball with great precision. He was able to manufacture openings out of nothing for his strikers and he certainly contributed greatly when Wolves won the Second Division Championship in 1977 and the League Cup in 1980. Replacing Steve Daley in midfield, Willie made a terrific start to his Wolves career, scoring on his debut in an emphatic 7–1 home League win over Chelsea. He appeared in 35 League games in 1975–76 when Wolves were relegated, and performed with great commitment when promotion was achieved at the first attempt, netting crucial goals against Sheffield United (2–2) and Nottingham Forest (won 2–1). Between 1977 and 1980 he continued to do the business and missed only 14 games out of a possible 126 in the League as Wolves re-established themselves in the top flight and proceeded to Wembley, where they lifted the League Cup for the second time in six years, beating Nottingham Forest 1–0. Manager John Barnwell and his replacement Ian Greaves kept faith with the red-haired Scot for another two seasons, during which Wolves were beaten by Arsenal in the FA Cup semi-final of 1981. But then, after Graham Hawkins had taken charge, Willie moved to Millwall and later joined Worcester City to start a succession of moves around the West Midlands, which included a spell as player-manager of Willenhall Town, before he finally hung up his boots in 1988. Willie, who was part of that infamous 'donkey-kick' routine (involving the former Wolves player Ernie Hunt when playing for Coventry against Everton in October 1970), won the first of his six full caps for Scotland against Northern Ireland in 1969 and the last in 1972 against Peru. He would have gained more honours had he been with a bigger club than Coventry, with whom he won all his caps. Nevertheless, he did a fine job for his club and country. Willie now lives in Shropshire.

Eddie Clamp

Wing-half: 237 apps, 25 goals.

Born: 14 September 1934, Coalville, Leicestershire. Died: 10 November 1995, Wolverhampton.

Career: WOLVES (September 1949–November 1961), Arsenal, Stoke City, Peterborough United, Worcester City, Lower Gornal, England (4 full caps).

■ A pupil at Bridge Road Secondary School, Coalville, Eddie Clamp represented both Leicestershire and England Schoolboys before joining Wolves as an amateur early in the 1949–50 season. After impressing the Molineux coaching staff and, indeed, his manager Stan Cullis, he was taken on to the professional staff in April 1952 and made his League debut against Manchester United in front of 39,000 spectators at Old Trafford almost two years later. At the time of his debut, Wolves were battling it out with neighbours West Bromwich Albion for the First Division title and at the end of the season, a delighted Eddie, despite figuring in only two games, duly celebrated the Championship triumph with his teammates. Eddie had to fight for his place in the team, simply because Wolves were blessed with quality half-backs in the 1950s such as Bill Slater, Ron

Flowers and Billy Wright. He made only 11 senior appearances in 1954–55 but upped his tally to 28 the following season, when he became an established member of the first-team squad. However, he spent most of 1956–57 in the reserves before bedding down at right-half in place of Bill Slater for the 1957–58 campaign, when Wolves performed splendidly to claim their second League title in four years. Nicknamed 'Chopper', Eddie was strong and resolute with a crunching tackle, and his form earned him a call-up to England's World Cup squad of 1958 and an international debut against the USSR, before the Finals in Sweden. He was then selected in three games in the tournament proper, against the USSR, Brazil and Austria, when his two half-back colleagues were Molineux buddies Billy Wright and Bill Slater. Another Wolves star, Peter Broadbent, was also in the squad. Adding a second League Championship medal to his collection in 1959, Eddie continued to impress at club level and a year later helped Wolves beat Blackburn 3–0 in the FA Cup Final – only his second visit to Wembley having also played there in a Schoolboy international. He followed that success with another fine season as Wolves finished third in the League but then, four months into the 1961–62 campaign, he was replaced by Johnny Kirkham. In November 1961 he was sold to Arsenal for £34,000 and in September 1962, after making 24 appearances for the Gunners, he was sold by his former teammate Billy Wright to Stoke City for £12,000. The recipient of a Second Division Championship medal with the Potters in his first season at the Victoria Ground, Eddie went on to assist Peterborough before entering non-League football with Worcester City in 1965, retiring two years later. Thereafter, he ran his own business and was a regular visitor to Molineux right up until his death. Eddie's mother was employed as the laundry lady at Molineux for many years.

Wayne Clarke

Striker: 147+24 apps, 33 goals.

Born: 28 February 1961, Willenhall.

Career: WOLVES (June 1976–August 1984), Birmingham City, Everton, Leicester City, Manchester City, Shrewsbury Town (2 spells), Stoke City, WOLVES (loan, September 1991), Walsall, Telford United (player and manager).

■ One of five footballing brothers (the others being England striker Allan, Frank, Derek and Kelvin), striker Wayne Clarke played for England at Schoolboy and Youth team levels and also represented West Midlands Schools as a teenager. He joined Wolves as a 15-year-old in June 1976 and, after developing through the intermediate and reserve teams, he signed as a full-time professional at Molineux in March 1978. Although Mel Eves, John Richards and Billy Rafferty were ahead of him in the pecking order for a place in the first-team forward line, Wayne was given his League debut (in place of Rafferty) by manager Sammy Chung against Ipswich Town at Molineux in September 1978. Although Wolves lost 3–1 to the FA Cup holders, Wayne kept his place and quickly scored his first League goal in a 3–3 draw at Queen's Park Rangers. When Wolves added Andy Gray to their strike-force at the start of the 1979–80 season, it looked as though Wayne's chances of first-team football would be restricted even more, but he stuck in there and played in 16 games that term. Then Norman Bell came along to boost Wolves' attacking options even further but Wayne remained loyal to the club and had 22 outings during 1980–81 and 26 the following season, when Wolves were demoted to the Second Division. Under new boss Graham Hawkins, Wayne was first choice in 1982–83 and hit 12 goals as promotion was achieved at the first attempt. Sadly, 1983–84 proved to be another disappointing season for Wayne and Wolves when relegation was suffered once more. At that point, Wayne was transferred to Birmingham City for £80,000. After scoring 43 times in 105 outings for Blues, he switched to Everton for £500,000 in March 1987, teaming up at Goodison Park with his former Molineux colleague Andy Gray. He helped the Merseysiders win the League title in his first season and scored the winning goal in the Charity Shield game at Wembley against Coventry City before moving to Leicester in July 1989. Six months later he switched his allegiance to Manchester City, also for £500,000, and after loan spells with Shrewsbury, Stoke and Wolves – when he partnered Steve Bull in the game at Southend – he left Maine Road to join Kenny Hibbitt's Walsall (August 1992). He later spent another two seasons with Shrewsbury,

gaining a Third Division-winners' medal in 1994 before taking over as player-manager of Telford United, resigning in November 1996. Wayne's career realised 151 goals in 511 appearances. He later became a postman.

Billy Crook

Half-back: 221 apps, 3 goals.

Born: 7 June 1926, Wolverhampton.

Career: Boulton & Paul, WOLVES (August 1940–October 1954), guest for Aldershot and Chelsea during World War Two, Walsall, Wellington Town.

■ Billy Crook was a part-time player at Molineux, earning his keep in two ways – as a footballer with Wolves and as a structural draughtsman with the local engineering company, Rubery Owen & Co (Darlaston), for whom he worked full-time after retiring from the game at the age of 34. Spotted playing in the local junior League, he joined Wolves as a 14-year-old in August 1940 and signed amateur forms in July 1941 after leaving grammar school. He developed his game during the war and eventually became a part-time professional in August 1943. A guest player for Aldershot and Chelsea during the hostilities, he made 121 wartime appearances for Wolves before League football recommenced in August 1946. At that juncture, he was already an established member of the side and missed only three games in the initial post-World War Two campaign as Wolves finished third in Division One. Two seasons later he helped Wolves win the FA Cup. Wolves manager Stan Cullis certainly admired Billy as a player, describing him as 'highly skilled, constructive, technical and a model of precision, whose many attributes included those of consistency and sportsmanship. There was nothing untidy about his play whatsoever'. Billy continued to perform with grim determination and conviction, making 41 appearances in 1949–50 followed by 27 and 20 in the next two campaigns. Early in 1952–53 he lost his place to Ron Flowers but maintained a high level of performance in the second XI before leaving Molineux in October 1954, joining

Walsall. Billy remained a Saddler for two years and retired in 1960 after a spell in non-League football. He was awarded a benefit in September 1950 after 10 years' service with Wolves. Billy was also keen on Dixieland jazz and travelled miles to watch and listen to a quality group playing his kind of music. Billy now lives in Cheshire. His brother, Alf Crook, also played for Wolves, from 1942–49.

Stan Cullis

Defender: 171 apps.

Born: 25 October 1916, Ellesmere Port, Cheshire.
Died: 27 February 2001, Malvern.
Career: Bolton Wanderers (amateur), Ellesmere Port Wednesday, WOLVES (February 1934–May 1947; assistant manager season 1947–48; manager May 1948–September 1964), guest for Aldershot, Fulham and Liverpool during World War Two, England (12 full and 20 wartime caps), Birmingham City (manager).

■ Stan Cullis served Wolves as a player and manager for 30 years, and there is no doubt that he had a huge hand in the team's success on the field during the 1950s, when he was regarded by many as the best manager in the country. As a player he quickly established himself as a centre-half after a few games as a half-back. A powerful tackler and strong in the air, he would try to hold the ball until he could use it and then, if possible, deliver a defence-splitting pass or perhaps take it through with his ungainly, crouching, dribbling style. Very rarely did he lose possession but, if he did, he was quick to regain his defensive position. As well as performing superbly well for Wolves, he did likewise for England, gaining 32 caps in total, captaining the team at the age of 22 against Romania in 1939. In fact, during World War Two Stan formed part of a magnificent England half-back line with Cliff Britton and Joe Mercer. He also played for the Football League on three occasions and starred in several representative matches when serving in the Army. After his Wolves debut in 1935, Stan had to wait until the second half of 1936–37 before finally establishing himself in the first team, taking over from Bill Morris at centre-half. He skippered Wolves for several years and led them in the 1939 FA Cup Final, which sadly they lost 4–1 to Portsmouth. This was a huge disappointment for Stan but he later made up for it with some great achievements as a manager. He missed only eight League games in the last two campaigns before World War Two and then, during the hostilities, made 34 appearances in regional competitions before continuing at senior level in 1946–47, when Wolves finished third in Division One. Before the final game of that season Stan, who was now prone to concussive injuries, announced his retirement as a player to become assistant to manager Ted Vizard, and when Vizard was sacked a year later Stan took charge of the team. As a manager he instilled a fighting quality into his players and built a side which thrived on the quick, long pass – some even called it the big boot. It worked wonders as Wolves, playing a unique brand of direct, robust football and stretching their opponents with wing-to-wing crosses, packed Molineux for most home games. Ten years after losing a Cup Final, Stan was a winner in 1949 when Wolves beat Leicester 3–1. Five years later, he guided the club to their first-ever League Championship and followed up with two more Division One triumphs in 1958 and 1959, and a second Cup success in 1960. In between times, he saw Wolves beat the cream of Europe, including Moscow Spartak, Honved, Moscow Dynamo and Real Madrid, in high-profile floodlit games at Molineux and, above all, he signed and developed some terrific footballers. Alas, things started to go wrong in 1961 and, although he tried his best to get things back on track, he was sacked in September 1964. His dismissal led to bitter recriminations from fans and media alike: how could a man who had served his club so well for so long be so shabbily treated? That question was never answered. For the next 15 months Stan worked as a sales representative for the Coventry City chairman Derrick Robbins before becoming manager of Birmingham City in December 1965. He remained at St Andrew's until March 1970, having taken Blues to the semi-finals of both the League Cup in 1967 and FA Cup in 1968, and signed some footballing greats including Trevor Francis! After ending his football career, Stan took a job with a travel agency and scribed a witty column in the local *Sporting Star*.

Hugh Curran

Striker: 91+7 apps, 47 goals.

Born: 25 September 1943, Carstairs, Glasgow.
Career: Manchester United (apprentice), Shamrock Rovers, Third Lanark, Millwall, Corby Town, Norwich City, WOLVES (January 1969–September 1972), Oxford United (2 spells), Bolton Wanderers, Scotland (5 full caps).

■ A determination to score goals continually made striker Hugh Curran happy to go in 'where it hurt'. He was quite fearless, had an abundance of attacking flair and possessed a strong left-foot shot. Despite having five cartilage operations in 10 years, his brave efforts in a 15-year Football League career (1964–79) brought him 164 goals in 403 appearances. And if his Cup record was added, then his overall record was more impressive: 184 goals in 462 matches. Released by Manchester United, he assisted Shamrock Rovers before spending two years with Third Lanark. Spotted by Millwall manager Billy Gray, he signed for the Lions in March 1964 and stayed at The Den for almost two years. He then served Norwich City until January 1969, when Wolves boss Bill McGarry secured his services for £60,000. He helped Wolves win the Texaco Cup and in November 1969 collected the first of his five full caps for Scotland, his others following in 1970–71. With John Richards ready to make his mark in attack, Hugh found himself out of favour and, after coming on as a sub in the second leg of the 1972 UEFA Cup Final, he was transferred to Oxford for £50,000 a few months later. Curran did superbly well at the Manor Ground and then did likewise at Bolton before returning to Oxford in 1977. He retired just before his 35th birthday and returned to Carstairs to run his own hairdressing business, later taking over a string of grocery shops before becoming a licensee in Chorlton-cum-Hardy, and then manager of a hotel in Lanarkshire.

Steve Daley

Midfielder: 218+26 apps, 43 goals.

Born: 15 April 1953, Barnsley.
Career: WOLVES (May 1969–September 1979), Manchester City, Seattle Sounders (NASL), San Diego Sockers (NASL), Walsall, Lye Town, Kettering Town, Old Wulfrunians, England (6 B caps), Telford United (manager), Bromsgrove Rovers (manager), Bilston Town (manager).

■ On 5 September 1979, Steve Daley became the most expensive footballer in the UK when he joined Manchester City from Wolves for £1,437,500. The previous record was set when Trevor Francis switched from Birmingham to Nottingham Forest, seven months earlier, for a shade over £1 million. Highly rated as a youngster, Steve signed for Wolves at the age of 16 and turned professional in 1971. Four months later, he made his League debut against Nottingham Forest. He developed fast and helped Wolves win the Second Division title at the first attempt, contributing 13 goals. He then scored in his final outing for Wolves in a 3–2 defeat against Manchester United in May 1979. Steve spent less than two years at Maine Road, and after a spell in the NASL he joined Burnley in 1983. Following a second summer in America, he signed for Walsall in 1985 and wound down his

career in non-League circles before having a brief career with a Midlands-based brewery. Steve's father, Alan, was a professional with Mansfield, Hull, Doncaster, Scunthorpe, Stockport, Crewe and Coventry between 1946 and 1961.

Peter Daniel

Full-back/midfield: 194 apps, 16 goals.

Born: 12 December 1955, Hull.

Career: Hull City, WOLVES (May 1978–May 1984), Minnesota Kicks (NASL), Sunderland, Lincoln City, Burnley, England (7 Under-21 caps).

■ Initially a right-back, Peter Daniel was the driving force in midfield for Wolves for six seasons. He played in 134 games for the Tigers and gained seven England Under-21 caps before joining Wolves for £82,000 in May 1978. He made an immediate impact with his determination, commitment, intelligence and mobility. Shortly after a Midlands debut at Villa Park on the opening day of 1978–79, Peter moved into midfield, where he linked up with Kenny Hibbitt and Willie Carr. John Barnwell took over from Sammy Chung in November 1979 and subsequently became a great admirer of Peter, declaring 'He will run through a brick wall if he has to; he's totally committed, a grand player to have around.' Peter, who grew a beard presumably to look more fearsome than he really was, struck some cracking goals for Wolves, most of them from a distance. His efforts against Queen's Park Rangers, Leeds and Birmingham in 1978–79 and Everton and Manchester City the following season all contributed to gaining vital points. In 1980 Peter played his part in helping Wolves win the League Cup. He scored in the first leg of the semi-final at Swindon, and when Nottingham Forest were defeated 1–0 it was his long punt downfield that led to Andy Gray's tap-in goal. In February 1981 Peter broke his leg in a League game against Aston Villa and missed the FA Cup semi-final defeat by Arsenal. He regained full fitness and was back in the side at the start of the new campaign which, sadly, was to end in relegation. But all was not lost, and under new boss Graham Hawkins promotion was gained at the first attempt. At this juncture Peter's position in the team came under threat, and after another relegation campaign he moved to Minnesota Kicks in May 1984, later playing for Sunderland, Lincoln City and Burnley. He retired in May 1988 with almost 400 League appearances under his belt. He is now living in his native Hull.

Jimmy Deacon

Forward: 158 apps, 56 goals.

Born: 23 January 1906, Glasgow. Died: c.1984, Scotland.

Career: Darlington, WOLVES (June 1929–October 1934), Southend United, Hartlepools United.

■ Jimmy Deacon was a key player in the Wolves team between 1929 and 1934. Born to Irish parents, he worked as a fitter before starting his League career with Darlington, for whom he made two appearances in the Third Division North before moving to Molineux for £250 in 1929. At 5ft 7in tall and 11st, he was certainly not the biggest or, indeed, the strongest of forwards, but he always gave a good, honest account of himself when playing against sturdy and rugged defenders, and he formed a fine partnership with Billy Hartill. Quick over the ground, he possessed good skills and a splendid body-swerve, but above all he was a sharp-shooter who often fired the ball at goal from fully 30 yards. He was also clever at sneaking in on the blind side of a defender and at least half of his goals came from inside the penalty area. He scored on his Wolves debut at Bradford and in 1931–32 gained a Second Division Championship medal. Jimmy started off well in the First Division, scoring seven goals in the opening 11 games, but after that he struggled and, after losing his place to Bryn Jones, he was transferred to Southend United. He later assisted Hartlepools United (1938–40) and after World War Two he returned to Glasgow to work in industry as well as running a pub. Jimmy's brother, Richard Deacon, also played for Wolves (1930–31) and West Ham United.

Norman Deeley

Winger: 237 apps, 75 goals.

Born: 30 November 1933, Wednesbury, Staffordshire. Died: 3 September 2007, Wednesbury, Staffordshire.

Career: WOLVES (April 1949–February 1962), Leyton Orient, Worcester City, Bromsgrove Rovers, Darlaston, England (2 full caps).

■ An England Schoolboy international in 1948, Norman Deeley made his League debut as a 17-year-old for Wolves, against Arsenal at Molineux in August 1951. After the game, he was highly praised by Gunners manager Tom Whittaker, who said 'Well played young 'un – a fine debut;

now grow a bit taller!' Norman did just that, rising from 4ft 11in to a maximum of 5ft 4in. An inside-forward or half-back in his early career, it took Norman time to establish himself and he made only 37 League appearances in six years. Even when he switched to the wing his chances were still limited as Wolves signed Harry Hooper to replace veteran Johnny Hancocks. However, when Hooper fell out of favour with manager Cullis, Norman was given the opportunity to make the right-wing position his own. He scored 23 goals in the 1957–58 season, which ended in glory as Wolves won the League title for the second time. He gained a second League Championship medal a year later and was rewarded for his efforts with two England caps against Brazil and Peru. Norman continued to impress, and in 1959–60 he helped Wolves win the FA Cup and finish runners-up in the League. In the Cup Final he scored twice in a 3–0 win over Blackburn and was voted Man of the Match after teasing and tormenting the Rovers defence all afternoon. Earlier that season, Norman had netted four times in a 9–0 League win over Fulham and afterwards England skipper Johnny Haynes, who had missed the action through injury, said 'You were brilliant, Norm, absolutely brilliant.' Maintaining his form throughout 1960–61, Norman then lost his way somewhat and when manager Stan Cullis introduced wingers Terry Wharton and Alan Hinton, and signed Peter McParland, Norman reluctantly moved on, joining Leyton Orient in February 1962. In the summer of 1964 he signed for Worcester, and after spells with Bromsgrove and Darlaston, announced his retirement in 1974. Residing in his native Wednesbury, Norman became manager of the Caldmore Community Centre in Walsall and for many years was the steward for the guest lounge at Walsall FC.

Robbie Dennison

Winger: 316+37 apps, 49 goals.

Born: 30 April 1963, Banbridge, Northern Ireland.

Career: Glenavon, West Bromwich Albion,

WOLVES (March 1987–July 1997), Swansea City (loan), Hednesford Town, Hereford United, Warley Borough, Warley Rangers, Northern Ireland (18 full and 3 B caps).

■ Wolves signed Robbie Dennison for a bargain fee of just £20,000 – half what Albion had paid Irish League club Glenavon for him two years earlier. There is no doubt that he added purpose, skill and, more significantly, width to Graham Turner's side. A positive footballer who loved to hug the touchline, Robbie could occupy both flanks, preferring the left wing to the right. He enjoyed running at defenders, had a trick or two in both feet, centred the ball well and, when given the chance, could shoot with power and direction. He was also spot on with corner-kicks and quite often was given the chance to try his luck when a free-kick was awarded within shooting range. Robbie followed Steve Bull and Andy Thompson to Molineux from The Hawthorns, and he quickly became a huge favourite with the fans and manager; his and Bull's names invariably being first and second on the team sheet. Robbie played his part in helping Wolves win the Fourth Division title and the Sherpa Van Trophy in his first full season at the club (1987–88). The following year he played a major part as Wolves clinched promotion for the second year running as champions of Division Three. At the same time, he established himself in the Northern Ireland squad, winning the first of 18 caps against France in April 1987. An ever-present player for the first time in 1989–90, Robbie continued to supply crosses for 'Bully' and Andy Mutch, but in 1991–92 he badly injured his leg which set him back. Regaining full fitness, he was never the same again, and after a spell with Swansea he moved to Hednesford in 1997. Rewarded with a testimonial by Wolves, Robbie later rejoined his former manager Graham Turner at Hereford before quitting football in 2002 to run a sports trophy business.

Dicky Dorsett

Forward: 52 apps, 35 goals.

Born: 3 December 1919, Brownhills, Staffordshire.
Died: 1998, Brownhills, Staffordshire.
Career: WOLVES (May 1935–September 1946), Aston Villa (player, then coach), guest for Brentford, Grimsby Town, Liverpool, Queen's Park Rangers and Southampton during World War Two, Liverpool (assistant trainer), Brownhills Boys' Club (manager/coach).

■ Known as the 'Iron Man' and also the 'Brownhills Bomber', play-anywhere Dicky Dorsett was as tough as they come: a rock-solid footballer, as strong as an ox and a player who never shirked a tackle. He shoulder-charged his opponents with aggressiveness and total commitment, was rugged to the last and, above all, his general outfield play was exceptional. Signed by Wolves as a 15-year-old amateur having been spotted playing (and scoring goals) for Walsall Boys and the Birmingham County FA, he turned professional in December 1936 and went on to spend the next 10 years at Molineux, although seven were lost to the war. Completely out of the blue, he grabbed four goals in a record 10–1 home League win over Leicester in April 1938 – in only his fourth senior game. He then netted Wolves' goal in their FA Cup Final defeat by Portsmouth in 1939. After the war, and having helped Wolves

win the League North Cup in 1942, Dorsett was sent off during a tour of Denmark in May/June 1946. This incident upset the club and as a result Dorsett never played for Wolves again. He was transferred to Aston Villa for £3,000 in September 1946 and over the next seven years added a further 271 appearances to his career record. In January 1950 Dorsett's playing days almost came to an abrupt end when he was involved in a serious car crash. Retiring in 1953, he became youth team coach at Villa Park and was later assistant trainer at Anfield. He was the nephew of the former West Bromwich Albion brothers George and Joe Dorsett.

Derek Dougan

Centre-forward: 307+16 apps, 123 goals.

Born: 20 January 1938, Belfast, Northern Ireland.
Died: 24 June 2007, Wolverhampton.
Career: Distillery, Portsmouth, Blackburn Rovers, Aston Villa, Peterborough United, Leicester City, WOLVES (March 1967–May 1975), Northern Ireland (6 amateur, 4 Schoolboy, 6 Youth, 43 full and 2 B caps). Also Kettering Town (manager), WOLVES (chief executive, August 1982–May 1985).

Dougan in action agaist Tottenham Hotspur in 1972.

■ One of the most colourful and controversial figures in soccer, Derek Dougan became the idol of the terraces when he joined Wolves for £50,000 from Leicester City in 1967. His cause was greatly assisted when he netted a hat-trick on his home debut against Hull City. However, when he returned to the club as chief executive under the notorious reign of the Bhatti brothers in 1982, the fortunes of Wolves spiralled out of control and Dougan appeared to lose favour with the team's supporters and, indeed, the local community. He played for Distillery before joining Portsmouth for £25,000 in August 1957, having already gained international caps at three levels as a wing-half and defender. After switching to centre-forward at Fratton Park, he went on to score a career total of 262 goals in 692 games, 222 of them in 546 League games – the most by an Irishman in English football. He also notched eight goals in his 43 full internationals. Nicknamed 'the Doog', he was transferred to Blackburn in March 1959 and a little over a year later played in the FA Cup Final against Wolves. He left Ewood Park for Aston Villa in a £15,000 deal in 1961 and two years later switched to Peterborough. He went to Leicester in 1965, before Wolves manager Ronnie Allen put the icing on the club's promotion challenge by bringing 'the Doog' to Molineux. By scoring nine goals in 11 games at the end of that 1966–67 campaign, he helped Wolves clinch a place in the First Division. Dougan was top scorer with 17 goals in 1967–68 and 14 in 1968–69 but his most prolific campaign came in 1971–72. Joined in the attack by John Richards, he claimed 24 goals, 12 of them in the UEFA Cup, the Final of which Wolves lost to Spurs. Two years later, though, he celebrated when the League Cup was won for the first time. Dougan, who retired in 1975, went to manage Kettering and was PFA chairman before his ill-fated return to Molineux. He was deeply involved in a fund-raising scheme for the Duncan Edwards Medical Centre (Dudley) as well as being the author of several books.

Jimmy Dunn

Inside-forward: 131 apps, 33 goals.

Born: 25 November 1923, Edinburgh.
Career: WOLVES (May 1941–November 1952), Derby County, Worcester City, Runcorn, West Bromwich Albion (trainer).

■ Son of Jimmy Dunn, the famous Scottish international from the 1920s, young Jimmy was not as good as his father but still a fine footballer whose career was severely disrupted by World War Two. He joined Wolves in 1941, turned professional a year later and made 100 appearances during the hostilities, scoring 15 goals, which put him in good stead for the re-commencement of League football in 1946. Jimmy, however, had to bide his time in the reserves before gaining regular outings in 1947–48. Switched to inside-left halfway through the following season, he helped Wolves win the FA Cup but a serious back injury affected his game in 1949–50. With Peter Broadbent now in the side and manager Cullis planning for the future, Jimmy became superfluous and was transferred to Derby County in 1952. He later assisted Worcester City and Runcorn before returning to Wolverhampton to run the Roebuck pub in Penn. In the mid-1960s Jimmy became coach at The Hawthorns and twice went to Wembley with Albion, losing in the 1967 League Cup Final but winning the FA Cup a year later. A qualified physiotherapist, he worked at an Edgbaston Clinic (Birmingham) after leaving the Baggies and later ran his own gymnasium in Birmingham's jewellery quarter.

Sylvan Augustus Ebanks-Blake

Striker: 20 apps. 11 goals.

Born: 29 March 1986, Cambridge.
Career: Cherry Hinton Lions, Fulbourn Falcons, Manchester United, Royal Antwerp (loan), Plymouth Argyle, WOLVES (January 2008).

■ Perhaps Sylvan Ebanks-Blake was signed just a fraction too late. There is no doubt his goals almost earned Wolves a Play-off spot, but just think what might have happened if Mick

Photograph © Action Images / John Marsh

McCarthy had recruited the former Manchester United striker a month, even two months, earlier. He scored 12 goals in his 20 League games for Wolves, following his £1.5 million transfer from Plymouth Argyle when the transfer window opened in January 2008, and his presence out on the pitch certainly added some much-needed venom and, indeed, some enthusiasm to the Wanderers' attack as the team battled away to try and claim a place in the top six of the Championship.

Strong and powerful with a good turn of foot and a cracking right-foot shot, Sylvan played for two Cambridge-based junior clubs, before joining Manchester United in the summer of 2003, turning professional in February 2005. He scored once in his two League Cup outings for the Reds and also netted four times in nine outings when on loan to Royal Antwerp (January–April 2006) before leaving Old Trafford for Home Park in a £200,000 deal in July 2006 as manager Ian Holloway's first signing for the Pilgrims. He became a hero with the Devon club, for whom he scored some terrific goals in his haul of 21 in 66 League matches, before his transfer to Molineux. Now he wants to continue scoring for Wolves.

George Edmonds

Centre-forward: 126 apps, 42 goals.

Born: 4 April 1893, Holborn, London. Died: 10 December 1989, Ryde, Isle of Wight.

Career: St Stephen's FC, Andrew's FC, St Albans City, Watford, WOLVES (August 1920–October 1926), Fulham, Northfleet.

■ George Edmonds spent two seasons with St Albans City before joining Watford in 1912. An out-and-out striker, he helped the Hornets win the Southern League title in 1915 before joining Wolves for £150 in 1920. Making an immediate impact, his goals saved the team from relegation and helped them reach the FA Cup Final, although they were beaten 1–0 by Spurs. In the home game against Bristol City in September 1920, a shot from Edmonds went straight through the net. The referee disallowed the 'goal'

and the game ended in a 0–0 draw. Well built with a powerful right-foot shot, George was aggressive, dangerous in the air and knew no fear. He formed an excellent partnership with Stan Fazackerley, the pair sharing 27 goals in 1922–23. Their efforts, however, were all in vain as Wolves were relegated to the Third Division North for the first time in their history. Disappointed, George asked for a transfer and was sold to Fulham for £250. He netted 26 goals in 73 games for the Cottagers before returning to Watford in 1926, later assisting Northfleet and retiring in 1929. George lived until he was 96.

Mel Eves

Forward: 202+12 apps, 53 goals.

Born: 10 September 1956, Wednesbury.

Career: WOLVES (July 1973–November 1984), Huddersfield Town, Sheffield United, Gillingham, Mansfield Town, West Bromwich Albion (reserves), Telford United, Cheltenham Town, Old Wulfrunians, England (3 B caps), Willenhall Town (manager).

Eves (left) with former player Derek Dougan.

■ Mel Eves spent 11 years at Molineux, helping Wolves win the League Cup in 1980 – the highlight of his career. He joined the club in 1973 and turned professional two years later. However, with John Richards, Bobby Gould and Steve Kindon, and then Norman Bell and Alan Sunderland all ahead of him in the pecking order, he spent two seasons in the reserves, finally making the breakthrough in 1977 when manager Sammy Chung gave him his debut against Ipswich. After John Barnwell had taken over as manager, Mel had Andy Gray as his strike partner and won a League Cup-winners' medal in 1980 as Wolves beat Nottingham Forest 1–0. Despite topping the scoring charts, Mel's goals failed to prevent Wolves from being relegated to the Second Division. Thankfully, promotion was gained at the first attempt but, after another relegation campaign and a loan spell at Huddersfield, Tommy Docherty – the sixth manager at Molineux in 10 years – sold Mel to Sheffield United in 1984. Two years later he switched to Gillingham and, following spells with several other clubs, quit competitive football in 1989 with a satisfactory career record under his belt of 69 goals in 273 games. He won three England B caps against Singapore (twice) and New Zealand in 1978. He became a football agent and entered management for the first time with Willenhall Town in 2006.

Ted Farmer

Centre-forward: 62 apps, 44 goals.

Born: 21 January 1940, Rowley Regis, Staffordshire.

Career: Wednesbury Commercial, Wednesbury Youth Club, WOLVES (June 1956–April 1964), England (2 Under-23 caps).

■ Unfortunately Ted Farmer played only four seasons of League football before injury forced him to retire at the age of 24. A prolific marksman for Wednesbury High School, Rowley Regis Boys, Dudley & District Schools, Wednesbury Commercial and Wednesbury Youth Clubs, he once netted 11 goals in one game and nine in another and often starred in two games on the same day. In November 1955 he struck 21 goals in three hours of football – 13 in the morning and eight in the afternoon. Signed after a trial in 1956, Ted struck 86 goals

for Wolves' junior side in his first season and never looked back. He made his First Division debut against Manchester United at Old Trafford in September 1960 and scored twice in a 3–1 win, finishing that season as top marksman with 28 goals. Shortly after gaining two England Under-23 caps, Ted broke his right leg at Fulham in 1961 and was out for four months. He came back but injuries continued to plague him and although he had many memorable scoring moments, he sadly announced his retirement in 1964. Ted went through hell, and only his close friends, trainers and manager knew the extent of his injuries, of which he had many, including a damaged bladder, broken leg, numerous dislocations, a couple of bad twists, a handful of cracked ribs, a few chipped bones, concussion (twice) plus the familiar sprains and strains; even boxers do not suffer this sort of torture. In the late 1960s, Ted took over The Lamp Tavern in Dudley and in 1986 wrote a book about his short career.

Malcolm Finlayson

Goalkeeper: 203 apps.

Born: 14 June 1930, Alexandria, Dunbartonshire, Scotland.
Career: Renfrew Juniors, Millwall, WOLVES (August 1956–May 1964).

■ Malcolm Finlayson was signed as cover for Bert Williams having made 251 appearances for Millwall. Ideally built for a goalkeeper, he was agile, had a safe pair of hands, was courageous and commanded his area well. He gained two League Championship medals (1958 and 1959) and played his part in Wolves' FA Cup Final victory over Blackburn Rovers in 1960. Malcolm went on to appear in over 200 games for Wolves before announcing his retirement in May 1964. Many people were surprised that he never received international recognition, considering the goalkeeping dilemma that faced Scotland during the 1950s and early 1960s. Later in life he became a director of R & F Stockholders of Kingswinford near Dudley, and in 1982 took over as vice-chairman of Wolves, but his appointment

only lasted a short while, ending when the new regime (the Bhatti brothers) took over.

Albert Fletcher

Defender: 76 apps, 2 goals.

Born: 4 June 1867, Wolverhampton. Died: 8 August 1938, Wolverhampton.
Career: Willenhall Pickwick, WOLVES (August 1886–July 1891; later club trainer), England (2 caps).

■ Albert Fletcher received a golden sovereign from secretary-manager Jack Addenbrooke when he joined Wolves in 1886. He had to wait a year before making his debut, starring in a first-round FA Cup win over Walsall Town. From that day on he remained a permanent fixture in the side, producing some brilliant performances. He played in Wolves' first-ever League match against Aston Villa in September 1888 and gained an FA Cup runners-up medal that season. Maintaining his form, he was capped twice by England against Wales, but unfortunately broke his right leg in a Birmingham Cup tie against Villa in March 1891. He failed to regain full fitness and was

forced to retire prematurely at the age of 24. Albert immediately became the club's assistant trainer and five years later (May 1896) was upgraded to head trainer at Molineux, going on to serve the club in that capacity for the next 24 years. Albert continued to visit Molineux as often as he could until his death in 1938.

Ron Flowers

Wing-half: 515 apps, 37 goals.

Born: 28 July 1934, Edlington, near Doncaster, South Yorkshire.

Career: Wath Wanderers, WOLVES (May 1952–September 1967), Northampton Town, Wellington Town, England (49 full, 2 Under-23 caps), Telford United (player-manager).

■ Ron Flowers developed through the junior ranks at Molineux before making a major contribution to Wolves' success during the 1950s. A terrific athlete and fine passer of the ball, he gained three League Championship medals (1954, 1958 and 1959) and an FA Cup-winners' medal in 1960, when he linked up superbly with Peter Broadbent. Ron went on to serve Wolves for 15 years, becoming the fifth-highest appearance-maker in the club's history. Between 1955 and 1966 Ron scored 10 goals (six from the penalty spot) in 49 internationals for England. He appeared in the 1962 World Cup Finals and was a member of Alf Ramsey's squad in 1966 and almost played in the Final when there was a last-minute doubt about centre-half Jack Chasrlton. He also represented his country at Under-23 level and starred for the Football League on several occasions. He stayed at Molineux just long enough to see Wolves regain their First Division status after relegation in 1965 before joining Northampton Town. He later took over as player-coach of the Cobblers before becoming player-manager of Telford United. Ron's father and brother both played for Doncaster Rovers.

Tom Galley

Forward/half-back: 204 apps, 49 goals.

Born: 4 August 1915, Hednesford, Staffordshire.

Died: 12 July 2000, Cannock.

Career: Cannock Town, Notts County (amateur), WOLVES (August 1933–November 1947), guest for Aldershot, Clapton Orient, Leeds United and

Watford during World War Two, Grimsby Town, Kidderminster Harriers, Clacton Town, England (2 caps).

■ Tom Galley was a utility player who preferred the right-half position. Tall and rangy, he had an attacking flair and proved to be a loyal and dedicated club man who served Wolves for 14 years, during which time he appeared in over 200 first-class games and 74 during World War Two, scoring almost 60 goals in total. An amateur with Notts County, he joined Wolves as a part-timer in 1933, turning professional in 1934. Initially a centre-forward, he made his League debut at Sunderland halfway through the 1934–35 season, replacing the injured David 'Boy' Martin as leader of the attack. After that, he bided his time in the reserves before gaining a regular place in the first team in the 1935–36 campaign, when he switched to wing-half. In May 1937 he won his first England cap, scoring in a 6–0 win over Norway in Oslo. His second cap followed 72 hours later in a 4–0 win over Sweden, and in 1938 he represented the Football League against the Scottish League. Tom had Dennis Westcott as his strike partner in 1937–38 and between them they scored 33 goals. However, Tom switched to right-half the following season and helped Wolves finish runners-up in the League and FA Cup. During the war, Tom served in France and Germany with the Royal Artillery and helped Wolves win the League North Cup in 1942. After the hostilities, he scored his first hat-trick for Wolves in an 8–1 Cup win over Lovells in January 1946 before transferring to Grimsby, whom he captained for a season before injuries caught up with him. He later assisted Kidderminster (1949–50) and was player-coach of Clacton Town before managing a local team in Cannock. Tom's nephew, John Galley, played for Wolves in the 1960s and also Rotherham, Bristol City, Nottingham Forest, Peterborough and Hereford United.

Joe Gardiner

Defender: 139 apps, 2 goals.

Born: 23 August 1916, Bearpark, County Durham. Died: 1997, Sedgley, Wolverhampton. Career: WOLVES (December 1932–May 1944), later trainer at Molineux and Birmingham City.

■ One of Major Frank Buckley's 'Molineux Babes', Joe Gardiner was 18 when he made his

League debut against West Bromwich Albion in February 1935 and, when Dai Richards joined Brentford nine months later, he stepped forward again and made 21 first-team appearances that season, forming a fine middle line trio with Tom Smalley and Stan Cullis. Originally a bustling centre-forward, Joe developed into a tough-tackling defender who held no prisoners, and was regarded as one of the most reliable and committed in the First Division. Over a period of four years, leading up to World War Two, he was one of Wolves' unsung heroes as he twice helped Wolves finish runners-up in Division One and was a member of the FA Cup Final side in 1939. Joe played throughout the war, making almost 50 appearances in regional competitions before May 1944. He remained on the club's training staff and went on to become trainer. Joe made 188 first-team appearances for Wolves (including wartime). He represented the Football League against the Scottish League in 1938 and as a trainer, collecting awards when Wolves won the FA Cup in 1949 and 1960, and the League title in 1954, 1958 and 1959. When Cullis took over as manager of Birmingham City in December 1965, Joe joined him at St Andrew's as first-team trainer. Four years later, he returned to Molineux as a scout and, all told, served the club for 51 years. Joe represented Durham County Boys as a teenager before joining Wolves as an amateur in December 1932, turning professional nine months later.

Noel George

Goalkeeper: 42 apps.

Born: 26 December 1897, Lichfield. Died: 16 October 1929, Lichfield.

Career: Hednesford Town, WOLVES (July 1919–October 1929).

■ Not the tallest of goalkeepers, Noel George was cool, confident, reliable, agile, a safe handler of the ball, and as bold and brave as anyone. During World War One, when serving in the Royal Artillery Second Command in

Greece, Noel went in goal for his unit in an emergency. He did well, kept his position and in April 1919 represented a Salonika Select XI against an Italian XI at Aldershot. He played exceptionally and never looked back. On his demob in July 1919 he joined Wolves, and within 18 months had established himself in the League side, playing in the 1921 FA Cup Final defeat by Tottenham Hotspur. Following relegation he was in top form and kept 23 clean sheets in 1923–24, helping Wolves win the Third Division North title at the first attempt. At this point, he was in line for an England call-up but missed out to Sewell of Blackburn and Huddersfield's Taylor. Noel continued to produce quality performances over the next two seasons, being an ever present for a third time in 1924–25. However, he started to struggle with injuries and complained of feeling unwell with head and neck pains. Sadly, after a 4–0 League defeat at Bristol City in November 1927, Noel was admitted to a Wolverhampton hospital with a terminal illness. He bravely held his own for almost two years before passing away in his sleep in a Lichfield infirmary.

Andy Gray celebrates his winning goal in the 1980 League Cup Final.

Andy Gray

Striker: 159+3 apps, 45 goals.

Born: 30 November 1955, Gorbals, Glasgow.
Career: Clydebank Strollers, Clydesdale Juniors, Dundee United, Aston Villa, WOLVES (September 1979–November 1983), Everton, Aston Villa, Notts County, West Bromwich Albion, Glasgow Rangers, Cheltenham Town, Scotland (20 full, 4 Youth, 4 Under-23 caps).

■ Striker Andy Gray became the most expensive footballer in Britain when Wolves paid Aston Villa over £1 million for his services in 1979. He completed the move by signing on the Molineux pitch before Wolves' League game with Crystal Palace. A colourful figure wherever he played, Andy was brave, determined, totally committed and a tremendous header of the ball, netting plenty of goals with both head and feet. He gained a 1974 Scottish Cup runners-up medal with Dundee United, played in the two drawn games of the 1977 League Cup Final for Villa versus Everton and was voted Player of the Year and Young Player of the Year by the PFA. He scored the winner for Wolves against Nottingham Forest in the 1980 League Cup Final and continued to score regularly for Everton (23 goals in 71 games). During his time at Goodison Park, he collected winners' medals in three competitions – the FA Cup, League Championship and European Cup-winners' Cup. He returned to Villa Park, had a loan spell with Notts County and assisted West Bromwich Albion before helping Rangers win the League Cup and Premier League, then retired to pursue a career in television. Capped 20 times by Scotland, Andy scored over 200 goals in more than 600 senior club matches.

Val Gregory

Half-back: 106 apps, 2 goals.

Born: 14 February 1888, Hendon, Middlesex.
Died: 10 March 1940, Heathtown, Wolverhampton.
Career: Reading, Watford, Arsenal, WOLVES (May 1920–May 1925).

■ Val Gregory was an exceptionally smart tackler, aggressive and perceptive, and a purveyor of passes that could split the tightest

defence; at times he was coolness personified. He joined Wolves for £3,000 in 1920, at a time when manager Jack Addenbrooke wanted some authority in the middle of the park. Despite not having played in the Football League, Val impressed Jack and quickly slotted into the team at right-half. Wolves' form improved greatly as Val, who was made captain, urged his players on with some gritty performances, especially in the FA Cup. Wolves reached the Final but lost 1–0 to Spurs. After two moderate campaigns in 1922–23, Wolves, for the first time in the club's history, slipped into the Third Division North. No blame was placed on Val as he continued to play his heart out. It was a lack of goals – only 42 scored in 42 games – that was Wolves' downfall. Val remained at Molineux until the summer of 1925, when he retired. At that juncture, he took over as coach and later assisted the club as a trainer. Ill health caused him to quit football in 1938. The son of a schoolteacher, Val previously spent two seasons with Reading, three with Watford and six with Arsenal, for whom he failed to make a single first-team appearance due to World War One.

Albert Groves

Half-back: 217 apps, 20 goals.

Born: 13 January 1886, Newport, Monmouthshire. Died: 15 May 1960, Willenhall.

Career: Aberdare Athletic, WOLVES (June 1909–May 1920), Walsall (player-manager), Willenhall Town.

■ One of the smallest right-halves, and certainly centre-halves, ever to play for Wolves, Albert Groves was only 5ft 7in tall and weighed less than 12st. Yet he was always a giant on the field, giving many outstanding performances at the heart of the defence. He spent 11 years at Molineux, losing four to World War One, and in that time made well over 200 appearances, scoring 20 goals. Strong in the tackle and of thoughtful bent, Albert was a superb passer of the ball and was a huge favourite with the fans. He played a few games of rugby at school but preferred the round ball game and, after developing as an inside-forward with Aberdare, for whom he scored 22 goals in 1908–09, he joined Wolves. Albert spent his first season at Molineux in the reserves, eventually making his debut on the very last day of the 1909–10 campaign, at home to Manchester City. The following season he took over the right-half

position and was an ever present, missing only one game in each of the following two campaigns, during which time he was switched to centre-half. The next season he netted 10 times as an emergency inside-right and centre-forward. After serving in the army during the war, Albert's last season with Wolves was in 1919–20. He then became player-manager of Birmingham League side Walsall. He suffered a serious knee injury in February 1924 and retired three months later. At 38, he was the oldest player at that time to have appeared in a League game for the Saddlers. After assisting Willenhall, Albert became mine host of the Hope and Anchor pub in Willenhall.

Johnny Hancocks

Winger: 378 apps, 167 goals.

Born: 30 April 1919, Oakengates, Shropshire. Died: 19 February, 1994, Oakengates.

Career: Oakengates Town, Walsall, guest for Chester, Crewe Alexandra and Wrexham during World War Two, WOLVES (May 1946–June 1957), Wellington Town (player-manager), Cambridge United, Oswestry Town, GKN Sankey, England (3 full caps).

■ One of the smallest players in first-class football at 5ft 4in, during the late 1940s and early 1950s versatile winger Johnny Hancocks possessed a cracking right-foot shot, and often tested goalkeepers from long distance, letting fly when least expected. He was also a lethal penalty taker and missed only a handful of more than 40 spot-kicks awarded to Wolves during his time at the club. He put his shooting power down to incessant practice on waste ground near his Shropshire home, saying 'I loved to kick the ball as hard as I could!' He made his mark with Walsall either side of World War Two, playing in the Football League South where he became known as the 'Southern Stan Matthews'. Wolves manager Ted Vizard monitored his performances carefully before bringing him to Molineux in 1946. He became an instant hit with the Wolves fans, and his brilliant form earned him his first England cap against Switzerland at Highbury in December

1948, when he scored twice in a 6–0 win from the outside-left berth. It was a pity that there were so many excellent wingers in the top-class game at that time, because Johnny certainly deserved more honours. He gained an FA Cup-winners' medal in 1949 and scored 24 goals when the League Championship came to Molineux for the first time in 1954. In fact, no other winger has scored more goals for Wolves than the Oakengates sharpshooter's 167. He lost his place in the Wolves side to Harry Hooper in 1956 but, for the 1956–57 season he drew crowds of 5,000-plus to Molineux when he turned out for the reserves.

Gerry Harris

Full-back: 270 apps, 2 goals.

Born: 8 October 1935, Claverley, near Bridgnorth.
Career: Bobbington, West Bromwich Albion (trial), WOLVES (September 1953–April 1966), Walsall, England (4 Under-23 caps).

■ Gerry Harris played as a left-winger for Bobbington, an amateur club, and had trials for West Bromwich Albion before signing amateur forms for Wolves in 1953. He made excellent

progress and took professional status in January 1954. Converted into a left-back, he had to wait two and a half years before making his League debut against Luton in a nine-goal thriller at Molineux. Five weeks later, when Bill Shorthouse was injured, Gerry took over the number-three shirt on a regular basis. He never looked back, went from strength to strength, and helped Wolves win the League title in 1957–58 and 1958–59, as well as gaining an FA Cup-winners' medal in 1960. In 1962 Gerry slipped into the reserves and stayed there until the start of the 1964–65 season, when he was reinstated at left-back following the departure of George Showell. Unfortunately, Wolves suffered relegation for the first time since 1923, and a year later Gerry left Molineux to sign for Walsall, retiring through injury after 12 months. A keen bowls player, Gerry captained the Bridgnorth club, Bylet. Today he lives in his native Claverley.

Billy Harrison

Outside-right: 345 apps, 49 goals.

Born: 27 December 1886, Wybunbury, Staffordshire. Died: 12 August 1948, Wolverhampton.

Career: Hough United, Crewe South End, Willaston White Star, Crewe Alexandra, WOLVES (May 1907–October 1920), guest for Stoke during World War One, Manchester United, Port Vale, Wrexham.

■ Billy Harrison helped Wolves win the 1908 FA Cup when he scored three minutes from full-time to sew up a 3–1 victory over Newcastle. Meanwhile, his wife had already given birth to triplets! He went on to have a long and consistent association with Wolves, playing in almost 350 games in a little over nine seasons before succeeding wing-wizard Billy Meredith at Manchester United. He did well at Old Trafford for two years, but when United were relegated from the top flight in 1922 he switched to Port Vale. After recovering from a broken ankle, he joined Wrexham in 1923 before retiring in May 1924 with 411 League appearances under his belt. Billy, who was only 5ft 4½in tall and weighed just over 11st, was blessed with a remarkable turn of speed and was the idol of the Molineux faithful, who loved his all-action style, his pace and his trickery. He was two-footed but preferred his right to his left, and he always enjoyed a challenge, never flinching or shying

away when matched against a bigger and seemingly burlier opponent. After retiring, Billy became a champion crown green bowler and managed the Rose and Crown public house in Tettenhall for many years.

Billy Hartill

Centre-forward: 234 apps, 169 goals.

Born: 18 July 1905, Wolverhampton. Died: 12 August 1980, Walsall.

Career: WOLVES (August 1928–July 1935), Everton, Liverpool, Bristol Rovers.

■ Centre-forward Billy 'Artillery' Hartill was born near to his future playing colleague Dickie Rhodes, with whom he represented the Wolverhampton Town side as a schoolboy. After scoring goals galore at junior level, Billy became a bombardier with the Royal Horse Artillery and, while in the services, netted more than 70 times in two seasons before he was demobbed. Wolves signed him in August 1928 and after making a big impression in the second team, Major Frank Buckley blooded him in the first XI at Bradford three months later. However, it was not until mid-March 1929 that he got back into

the first team, and from then on he was a star act. In 1929–30 he struck 33 goals, including the first of 16 hat-tricks for the club. The following year, Billy scored 30 times and at this point was regarded as one of the finest strikers outside the top flight. In 1931–32 another 30–goal haul helped Wolves win the Second Division title and put him in line for an England cap. After firing in his 100th goal for the club, Billy ended the 1932–33 campaign with another 33 in his locker. He started to struggle with injuries yet still managed his fair share of strikes. In 1935 Major Buckley began to rebuild his team and surprisingly Billy was transferred to Everton, after scoring 170 goals (a new club record which stood for 46 years, until John Richards beat it in April 1980). After spells with Liverpool and Bristol Rovers, Billy retired in 1940. His only representative honour was to play for the Football League against a Midland XI in 1935.

George Hedley

Centre-forward: 214 apps, 74 goals.

Born: 20 July 1876, Southbank, Northumberland. Died: 16 August 1942, Wolverhampton.

Career: South Bank, Sheffield United, Southampton, WOLVES (May 1906–April 1913), Bristol City (manager), England (1 cap).

■ Robust, opportunist centre-forward George Hedley was very much an advocate of the open game, and was regarded as a veteran when he joined relegated Wolves in 1906. Nevertheless, he formed a splendid partnership in attack with Billy Wooldridge and became a firm favourite with the fans. With Sheffield United, he gained FA Cup-winners' medals in 1899 and 1902, and he also played for England against Ireland in 1901, as well as representing the Football League. He proceeded successfully with Southampton, scoring 34 goals in three years and helping them win the Southern League title before his surprise switch to Molineux. He served Wolves exceptionally well for seven years, gaining a third FA Cup-winners' medal in 1908 when he scored in a 3–1 Final win over Newcastle. After netting a goal every three

Photograph © Action Images / Michael Regan

games, George announced his retirement in 1913. He had a brief, two-season managerial flirtation with Bristol City before becoming a licensee in Bristol, a job he held for 23 years (1918–41). He and his wife were running a boarding house in Wolverhampton when he died at the age of 66 after a short illness. It is rumoured that George wore the same pair of boots for 10 years, finally discarding them in 1908 with 17 patches on them!

Wayne Robert Hennessey

Goalkeeper: 51 apps.

Born: 24 January 1987, Anglesey, North Wales.
Career: WOLVES (apprentice June 2003, professional April 2005), Stockport County (loan), Wales (Youth, 4 Under-21 and 10 full caps).

■ Goalkeeper Wayne Hennessey was the only ever-present in Wolves' first team in 2007–08, having previously played in just two Play-off games for the club and in 15 League matches while on loan to Stockport County during the second half of the 2006–07 season. In fact, his first nine outings for the Hatters all ended in victories without conceding a single goal, which set a new Football League record at that time. He has also established himself in the full Welsh team and is set for an exceptionally fine career in the game. Able to kick with both feet, he is agile, has good positional sense and is never afraid to dive at opponents' feet when danger threatens. He had the pleasure of saving a late Zoltan Gera penalty against arch-rivals West Bromwich Albion in the Championship game at The Hawthorns in November 2007, which ultimately earned his side a point from a 0–0 draw.

Kenny Hibbitt

Midfield: 552+22 apps, 114 goals.

Born: 3 January 1951, Bradford, Yorkshire.
Career: Bradford Park Avenue, WOLVES (November 1968–August 1984), Coventry City, Bristol Rovers (player-assistant manager), Walsall (manager), Cardiff City (manager, 3 spells, coach/director of football), Hednesford Town (manager).

■ Kenny Hibbitt starred in the Wolves midfield for 16 years, amassing more than 550 appearances and scoring over 100 goals. Signed

by Ronnie Allen for £5,000 from Bradford in 1968, he made a scoring debut in a 2–2 draw against Chelsea, when Wolves were under the leadership of Bill McGarry. Kenny helped Wolves win the Texaco Cup in 1971 and the following season gained a runners-up medal when Tottenham Hotspur beat them to win the UEFA Cup. In 1972–73 he produced some superb displays, particularly when Wolves came within a whisker of reaching both the FA Cup and League Cup Finals. After those disappointments, Kenny finally won a major prize when Wolves beat Manchester City in the 1974 League Cup Final, and six years later added a second League Cup-winners' prize to his collection when Nottingham Forest were defeated 1–0. The driving force in centre-field, Kenny netted all of Wolves' goals in a 4–2 League win over Newcastle in 1974, but his efforts were all in vain as relegation was suffered the following season. Battling on, he played his part in helping win promotion before two more Cup semi-final defeats in 1979 and 1981. After a second relegation and immediate promotion, plus a well-deserved testimonial, Kenny left Molineux for Coventry, switching to Bristol Rovers in 1986. His illustrious playing career ended in February 1988 when he broke a leg playing for Rovers against Sunderland. As assistant to Gerry Francis, he helped the Bristol club win the Third Division title and reach the Leyland DAF Final. As manager of Walsall, he steered the Saddlers into the Third Division Play-offs. His brother Terry, a midfielder for Newcastle, Leeds and Birmingham City, died of cancer in 1994, aged 46.

Reg Hollingworth

Defender: 180 apps, 8 goals.

Born: 17 October 1909, Rainworth, near Mansfield. Died: 8 July 1969, Sparkbrook, Birmingham.

Career: Nuffield Colliery, Sutton Junction, WOLVES (November 1928–May 1936).

■ Centre-half Reg Hollingworth was one of the unluckiest footballers ever to play for Wolves. Plagued by a series of leg, hip and back injuries, he was out of action for long periods through illness, suffered concussion on three occasions, twice dislocated his shoulder and had over a dozen stitches in various head wounds. In March 1932, having been selected to play for England against The Rest in an international

trial, he damaged his ankle in a League game at Barnsley ahead of the senior game against Scotland at Wembley and never got another chance. Four years later, he suffered a serious leg injury which ended his career. Tall and strong, solid in the tackle and a good, clean header and kicker of the ball, Reg joined Wolves in 1928 and made his debut against West Bromwich Albion 48 hours later. He finally gained a regular place in the half-back line at the start of the 1930–31 campaign and scored his first goal for the club in a 3–1 League win over Reading that same season. A year later he helped Wolves win the Second Division title but then, unfortunately, injuries started to affect his game. He was switched to right-back after an injury to Wilf Lowton but did not particularly like playing there and, as the injuries persisted, he announced his retirement in 1936 and subsequently joined the Staffordshire police force. Later employed at the Goodyear tyre factory, Wolverhampton, he was manager of Batchelor Robinson in Balsall Heath at the time of his tragic death, from a heart attack, while driving his car in Sparkbrook in 1969.

John Holsgrove

Defender: 200+2 apps, 7 goals.

Born: 27 September 1945, Southwark, Middlesex.
Career: Arsenal, Tottenham Hotspur, Crystal Palace, WOLVES (May 1965–June 1971), Sheffield Wednesday, Stockport County.

■ A tall, well built defender, John Holsgrove proved to be a wonderful signing by Wolves manager Andy Beattie, who paid Crystal Palace £18,000 for his services in 1965. Registered as an amateur at Highbury and White Hart Lane, John represented England at Youth team level and made 22 appearances for Palace before moving to Molineux. He played in 25 games in his first season before helping Wolves gain promotion in the following year as runners-up behind Coventry City. An ever-present player in his debut season in Division One, John produced some fine performances at the heart of the defence, resulting in an unbeaten run of

almost 100 matches in the first team. Composed and comfortable on the ball, John was strong in the air and possessed a telling tackle, hardly ever being reckless with his challenges. As time went by, he was switched around in defence and consequently moved to pastures new, when Sheffield Wednesday eventually recruited him in a £50,000 deal in 1971 after more than 200 appearances. John spent four seasons at Hillsborough, during which time he made a further 115 appearances before rounding off his career with Stockport and retiring in 1976. He now works as a financial advisor in the West Midlands. His son, Paul, played for Aldershot and Luton and had loan spells with Wimbledon, West Bromwich Albion and Stoke, among others.

Emlyn Hughes, OBE

Defender: 75+2 apps, 2 goals.

Born: 28 August 1947, Barrow-in-Furness. Died: 9 November 2004, Sheffield.
Career: Roose FC, Blackpool, Liverpool, WOLVES (August 1979–July 1981), Rotherham United (player-manager), Hull City, Mansfield Town, Swansea City, England (62 full and 8 Under-23 caps).

■ Emlyn Hughes had a wonderful career that spanned almost 20 years. He represented North Lancashire Schools and Roose FC (Blackpool) before becoming a professional with Blackpool in 1964. Two and a half years later, he moved to Liverpool for £65,000 and made 665 appearances for the Merseysiders up to August 1979, when he joined Wolves for £90,000. Emlyn spent two seasons at Molineux before leaving to join Rotherham as player-manager, later playing for Hull City, Mansfield and Swansea before retiring in 1983 through injury. Nicknamed 'Crazy Horse', he loved the game. Tough and resilient, he always gave 100 per cent and as one scribe wrote 'He was strong, durable and courageous, the soul of consistency, never ruffled, with a big heart, a tenacious player of the bulldog breed.' Emlyn helped Liverpool win two European Cups, two UEFA Cups, the European Super Cup, four League Championships (in 10 years), the FA Cup and two FA Charity Shields, and he was also voted Footballer of the Year in 1977. He replaced John McAlle at the heart of the Wolves defence, and in his first season skippered the team to victory in the League Cup Final. He formed an excellent defensive barrier with George Berry, and his encouragement and drive proved to be endearing to the fans. In fact, some thought he played better in his second season with Wolves than he did in his first. Emlyn moved on at the end of the 1981–82 campaign, having contributed a lot to Wolves' cause in a relatively short period of time. Capped 62 times by England between 1970 and 1980, Emlyn also represented his country at Under-21 level and played for the Football League. He amassed over 900 appearances at club and international level and, after retiring, became a TV personality, captaining one of the teams in a *Question of Sport*. Emlyn sadly died of cancer at the age of 57. Emlyn's father was a Rugby League international who played for Barrow. His brother and uncle also played rugby, while his aunt represented England at hockey.

Kenneth Hunt (Reverend)

Wing-half: 61 apps, 2 goals.

Born: 24 February 1884, Oxford. Died: 28 April 1949, Oxford.

Career: Trent College, Queen's College (Oxford), Leyton, Oxford City, Crystal Palace, Oxford University, Corinthians, WOLVES (various times between March 1907 and April 1920), England (2 full and 20 amateur caps).

■ The Revd Kenneth Hunt played for Wolverhampton Grammar School for four years, and after serving with several amateur and university teams he was registered with Wolves in March 1907. Unfortunately, he could not be lured away on a permanent basis from his studies at Oxford University, much to the disappointment of the Wolves board. However, he certainly produced the goods when available, scoring a fine long-range goal in the 1908 FA Cup Final win over Newcastle. He was an inspirational and muscular player, strong in defence as well as in attack, although he did not score too many goals (at any level). An Oxford Blue, Kenneth gained a gold medal when Great Britain won the Olympic Games soccer tournament in London in 1908. He also played

in the Amateur Cup Final for Oxford City. An amateur throughout his career, Kenneth won 20 caps for England at this level (1907–20) and played twice for the senior side against Wales and Scotland in 1911. Ordained in 1909, he became housemaster at Highgate School, London, where he was heavily involved in public schools soccer until 1945. He served on the FA Council from 1946 to 1949, when he retired through ill health.

Paul Ince

Midfield: 122+8 apps, 12 goals.

Born: 21 October 1967, Ilford, Essex.

Career: West Ham United, Manchester United, Inter Milan, Liverpool, Middlesbrough, WOLVES (August 2002–August 2006), England (53 full, 1 B, 2 Under-21 caps), Macclesfield Town (manager), Milton Keynes Dons (manager), Blackburn Rovers (manager).

■ Strong-running, hard-working, full of heart and energy, blessed with a powerful right-foot shot and a persistent approach, Paul Ince did a tremendous job in midfield. He made almost 100 appearances for West Ham, 281 in six seasons with Manchester United, had over 50 outings for Inter Milan after signing for £8 million in July 1995, played in 81 games for Liverpool (after a £4.2 million move) and starred in 106 first-class matches for Middlesbrough before joining Wolves on a free transfer in August 2002. He arrived at Molineux with 17 years' experience and nine winners' medals to his credit (all with Manchester United). His magic moments included two Premiership titles, two FA Cup Final victories, European Cup-winners' Cup glory, European Super Cup success and triumphs in both the League Cup and FA Charity Shield. He was also an experienced international, having represented England at Youth, Under-21, B and senior levels, featuring in the 1996 European Championships and the World Cup Finals two years later. He was voted runner-up to Paul McGrath in the PFA Player of the Year poll in 1993. Paul's sheer presence lifted Wolves, his encouragement beaming through as captain. Competitive and ambitious, he played in 45 out of 55 games in his first season at Molineux, helping Wolves gain a place in the Premiership via the Play-offs. He managed another 35 games in the top flight while at the same time edging past the milestone of 700 games in his club career. He then became a successful manager, having guided MK Dons to promotion in 2008 before being given the Blackburn Rovers hot seat in June. Paul's cousin is the former boxing champion Nigel Benn.

Bryn Jones

Inside-forward: 177 apps, 57 goals.

Born: 2 February 1912, Penyard, Merthyr Tydfil. Died: 18 October 1985, Wood Green, London. Career: Merthyr Amateurs, Plymouth United, Southend United (trial), Glenavon, Aberaman, WOLVES (November 1933–August 1938), Arsenal, Norwich City, Wales (17 caps).

■ Bryn Jones' soccer career began at Queen's Road School, Merthyr. At the age of 14 he took virtually the only option open to him for work, which was to go down the pit. Playing in the South Wales District League, he had a trial with Southend and played in Ireland and then for Aberaman before joining Wolves for £1,500 in November 1933. He scored 10 goals in his first season at Molineux but managed only seven in 1934–35, yet still became the idol of the Wolves supporters with his excellent ball control and unselfish play. Bryn's skills were quickly being recognised, and he was chosen to play for Wales against Northern Ireland in 1935 – the first of 17 full caps. Bryn grabbed his first-ever League hat-trick against Preston in April 1936, adding more caps to his collection for the Principality. Continuing to star for club and country, Bryn caused outrage in August 1938 when he chose to leave Wolves for Arsenal for a then record British fee of £14,000. Such was the popularity of the 5ft 6in Welshman that there was a four-hour demonstration outside Molineux when he left. He scored 57 goals in 177 games for the Wanderers. Serving in the 34th Light AA Regiment in North Africa and Italy during World War Two, he remained at Highbury until 1949, when he was appointed player-coach of Norwich City. After two seasons with the Canaries, his doctor advised him to quit the game because of a chest condition. Returning to London, he ran a newsagent-tobacconist shop in Stoke Newington, near Highbury, from September 1951 to April 1979. Bryn had four footballing brothers: Ivor (West Bromwich Albion, Swansea and Wales), Bill (Merthyr Town), Emlyn (Merthyr, Everton and Southend) and Bert (Southend and Wolves). He was also an uncle to Cliff Jones (ex-Spurs and Wales).

Jack Jones

Full-back: 336 apps, 16 goals.

Born: 16 March 1877, Wellington, Salop. Died: 20 August 1945, Wolverhampton. Career: Wrockwardine Wood, Lanesfield FC, WOLVES (June 1900–May 1913, later trainer).

■ Jack Jones was 23 when he joined Wolves in 1900. He eventually took over from Harry Davies, having made the first of 336 senior appearances at the start of the 1901–02 season against Nottingham Forest. A very consistent defender, he was chosen to represent the Football League against the Scottish League in 1905 and, three years later, helped Wolves win the FA Cup. A terrific performer whose skill complemented a fine physique, Jack was a solid kicker of a ball, clearing his lines efficiently from any angle. He was able to contain the most difficult opponent, never really getting the run-around from a winger, and he was always in control of things in tight situations – although he did concede two own-goals during his time at Molineux. In January 1910 Jack became the first Wolves player to appear in 300 League

games, and he also holds the record for most ever-present campaigns, with five. At this juncture he was on top of his game, but during the build-up to the 1910–11 season he badly twisted his ankle and lost his place to George Garratly. Jack never really got back into the team and in 1913, at the age of 36, he announced his retirement. Remaining loyal to Wolves, he continued to work for the club as assistant trainer (to Albert Fletcher), retaining his position until after World War One, when Elijah Morse arrived on the scene. When Jack died in 1945, part of the club's history went with him. He was known as a great and wonderful club man. His brother Joe, also a full-back, played for Wolves from 1898 to 1903.

Albert Kay

Defender: 295 apps, 2 goals.

Born: 22 November 1895, Sheffield. Died: c 1975, Wolverhampton.
Career: Tinsley FC, Birmingham (trialist), Willenhall, WOLVES (July 1921–1932).

■ Albert Kay was a versatile defender who was 25 when he joined Wolves in 1921 as a reserve to Val Gregory, Joe Hodnett, Bill Caddick and Alf Riley. After doing well in the second XI, he gained his place in the first team in the relegation season of 1922–23 but Wolves won promotion at the first attempt. Predominantly a defensive wing-half, Albert could also play in a variety of positions and took over in goal twice in reserve games, saving a penalty in the process. A gentlemanly player, exceptional in that very few forwards got the better of him, he was surprisingly replaced in the team by Jack Bradford but came back strongly in 1925–26 and with some resolute performances kept his place. In 1931–32, his last season at Molineux, Albert helped Wolves win the Second Division title before retiring with almost 300 appearances under his belt – a worthy effort by any standards. He remained local, residing in the Tettenhall and then Codsall area until his death in 1975.

Mark Kendall

Goalkeeper: 177 apps.

Born: 20 September 1958, Blackwood, Monmouthshire. Died: 1 May 2008, Blackwood, Monmouthshire.
Career: Tottenham Hotspur, Chesterfield, Newport County, WOLVES (December 1986–July 1990), Swansea City, Burnley, Newport AFC, Wales (1 Under-21 cap).

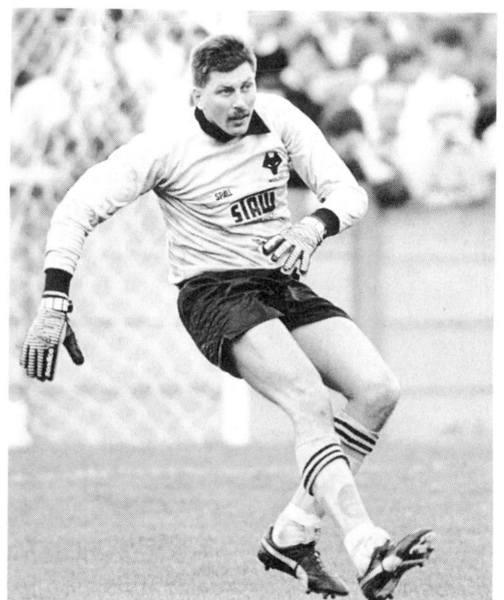

■ Signed by manager Graham Turner halfway through the 1986–87 season, after Wolves had used four different goalkeepers in nine months, Mark Kendall made rapid progress at Molineux, helping the team reach the Play-off Final which they disappointingly lost to Aldershot. Standing 6ft tall and weighing 13st 9lbs, Mark was strong in the air, had a safe pair of hands, commanded his area well and was brave and decisive in his actions. An ever present when Wolves won the Fourth Division title and Sherpa Van Trophy in 1988, he was quite outstanding the following season when he added a Third Division Championship medal to his collection. Battling with Tony Lange for a first-team place after that, he was eventually replaced between the posts by Mike Stowell, at which point Mark was sold to Swansea City for £25,000. He had served Wolves extremely well and reached two milestones – 500 career appearances and 450 League outings. He spent 18 months at the Vetch Field and, after a loan spell with Burnley, Mark assisted Newport AFC before joining the South Wales police force. As a youngster, Mark represented Tredegar and Gwent schools, made 36 appearances for Spurs and gained a Welsh Under-21 cap against Scotland in 1978. He played in 317 first-class matches for Newport County. In his one game for Cwmbran against Barry Town in 2000-2001, Mark's son Lee, now at WPL side Rhyl, was in the other goal as Cwmbran ran out 3-0 winners. After hanging up his gloves Mark joined Gwent Police and was named police trainer of the year in 2007. He sadly died from a heart attack in his home village of Blackwood in 2008.

Andrew Declan Keogh

Forward: 57 (+10) apps. 16 goals.

Born: 16 May 1986, Dublin.

Career: Leeds United, Scunthorpe United (loan), Bury (loan), Scunthorpe United, Wolves (January 2007), Republic of Ireland (Youth, 7 Under-21, 1 B and 5 full caps).

■ Andy formed a very successful partnership with hot-shot Billy Sharp at Scunthorpe, and during his two spells with the Iron he scored a total of 25 goals in 109 appearances. Signed by Wolves for £600,000, rising to £850,000, he is a tall, quick, skilful forward, possesses some neat touches and is perhaps now regarded as a maker of rather than a taker of chances, although he has already netted 16 times for Wolves, finishing second in the scoring charts behind Ebanks-Blake in 2007–08. Recognised at four different

Photograph © Action Images / Keith Williams

levels by the Republic of Ireland, Andy gained his first full cap in May 2007 in a friendly against Ecuador in the Giants Stadium, New York. He has a great appetite for the game, and hopefully he can go on and give Wolves solid and sound service for many years to come.

George Kinsey

Half-back: 83 apps, 3 goals.

Born: 20 June 1866, Burton upon Trent. Died: 3 January 1911, Aston, Birmingham.

Career: Burton Crusaders, Burton Swifts, Mitchell St George's, WOLVES (July 1891–June 1894), Aston Villa, Derby County, Notts County, Eastville (Bristol) Rovers, Burton Early Closing FC, England (4 caps).

■ Tough-tackling defender George Kinsey's footballing career spanned 23 years, from 1883–1906. He made his League debut in 1891 for Wolves against Sunderland. A resolute footballer, short and stocky, hard-working with a very strong left foot, his excellent performances earned him four England caps, and some say he deserved more. Enthusiastic and regarded as a 'fetch and carry' player, he often delivered passes of up to 40–50 yards. The Wolves fans loved him, especially in 1893 when he helped the team win the FA Cup at Everton's expense. George left Molineux in the summer of 1894 for Villa Park, signed to replace Bob Chatt. He joined Derby County in the summer of 1895 and helped the Rams take the runners-up spot in Division One and reach the FA Cup semi-final. George later helped Bristol Rovers establish themselves in the Southern League before playing his last game at the age of 40. On retiring, George returned to the Midlands and worked in industry for a short time before settling down in Birmingham. He was 44 when he died in 1911.

Peter Knowles

Forward: 188+3 apps, 64 goals.

Born: 30 September 1945, Fitzwilliam, near Frickley, Yorkshire.

Career: Wath Wanderers, WOLVES (June 1961–September 1969), England (4 Under-23 caps).

■ The skilful Peter Knowles had every trick in the book. Predominantly a goalscoring inside-forward, he also created opportunities for his colleagues with deft touches, clever flicks, reverse passes and neat headers while regularly drawing defenders out of position with his excellent positional play and off-the-ball

running. He top-scored in 1965–66 with 21 goals, including hat-tricks against Carlisle (won 3–0) and Derby (won 4–0). He subsequently drew up a terrific understanding with Derek Dougan, who started at the tail-end of the 1966–67 season, as Wolves switched into top gear on their way to gaining promotion from the Second Division. In 1967–68 Peter netted 12 times as Wolves tried, successfully, to re-adjust to life back in the top flight. Manager Ronnie Allen believed there and then that Peter was destined for full international honours after playing in four Under-23 matches for England and having earlier helped his country win the International Youth tournament in Holland, scoring in the Final against Spain. Peter then began to star under new manager Bill McGarry but, amazingly, he rocked Molineux by announcing his retirement at the age of 24. He decided he could not continue to play football and be true to his beliefs as a Jehovah's Witness. Peter's registration was retained by Wolves, who repeatedly asked him in vain to reconsider his decision. A song by Billy Bragg – *God's Footballer* – was dedicated to Peter. Peter's brother was the late Cyril Knowles, who played for Tottenham Hotspur and managed Hartlepool United.

Joleon Lescott

Defender: 228+7 apps, 13 goals.

Born: 16 August 1982, Birmingham.

Career: WOLVES (August 1998–June 2006), Everton, England (4 Youth, 1 B, 2 Under-21 and 5 full caps).

■ Joleon Lescott was originally with Wolves' Centre of Excellence. He gained England international honours at Under-18 level and, after a season in which his mature displays belied his tender years, was named the club's Young Player of the Year for 2000–01, taking the same award the following season. His strong control of Wolves' central defence led to him being called-up to England's Under-20 squad, and he quickly graduated to the Under-21s. A member of Wolves' Play-off Final-winning side

that reached the Premiership in 2003, his form in later years earned him widespread acclaim. However, he had set his sights on bigger things and when Everton came in with an offer Wolves could not refuse, he moved to Goodison Park for £5 million in June 2006, and a year later gained his first full England cap in the European Championship qualifying round.

Wilf Lowton

Full-back: 209 apps, 27 goals.

Born: 3 October 1899, Exeter, Devon. Died: 12 January 1963, Exeter.

Career: Heavitree United, Exeter City, WOLVES (August 1929–May 1935), Exeter City.

■ Right-back Wilf Lowton was one of the most powerful kickers of a dead ball in the game during the 1930s. He took all Wolves' penalties and free-kicks within reasonable distance, and some of his enormous clearances, from a standing position with hardly any run-up, often went sailing downfield, first bounce, into the goalkeeper's arms 100 yards away! Captaining the side for several years, he rendered yeoman service to Wolves, who signed him for just £1,400 from Exeter City prior to the start of the 1929–30 season – having missed only two of 224 games for

the Grecians in five years. Wilf was in fine form when Wolves won the Second Division Championship, contributing nine goals from the penalty spot – two in a 7–1 win at Port Vale. Back in the top flight, Wilf maintained his form in a struggling team. In the mid-1930s, manager Frank Buckley was ready to make changes to his team and, at this point, Wilf knew his days were numbered at Molineux. At the end of the 1934–35 season he returned to Exeter City having accumulated a fine record with Wolves. Retiring in May 1936, Wilf remained at St James Park as trainer for three months before illness forced him to give up. He lived in Devon until his death in January 1963, aged 63.

Tommy Lunn

Goalkeeper: 142 apps.

Born: 9 July 1883, Bishop Auckland, County Durham. Died: 29 March 1960, Edmonton, London.

Career: Brownhills Albion, WOLVES (August 1904–April 1910), Tottenham Hotspur, Stockport County.

■ Five months after gaining an FA Cup-winners' medal with Wolves, Tommy Lunn played in goal against Tottenham Hotspur in the first-ever League game staged at White Hart Lane, on 1 September 1908. Eighteen months later he was transferred from Molineux to Spurs for £500. Strong and agile with a good positional sense, Tommy was not a big man but challenging for high balls with big, burly centre-forwards never seemed to worry him. Confident on his line, he became Wolves' permanent 'keeper in March 1907 having understudied England's Tom Baddeley over the previous two and a half years. Tommy, who always wore a flat cap and often punched the ball rather than collect it in his hands, kept his place for over two years before his transfer to Spurs. He represented the Football League against the Southern League at White Hart Lane in November 1910, his only representative honour. Early in 1913, he obtained a publican's licence, which was frowned upon by the Spurs hierarchy and considered a breach of contract. Suspended as a consequence, Tommy did not play again for the Londoners and, in June of that year, signed for Stockport County. Forced to retire with a serious leg injury in 1914, he was approaching his 77th birthday when he died.

John McAlle

Defender: 495+13 apps, 3 goals.

Born: 31 January 1950, Liverpool.
Career: WOLVES (July 1965–August 1981), Sheffield United, Derby County, Harrisons FC.

■ John McAlle had a magnificent career with Wolves. He made his debut as a teenager and went on to star in more than 500 games, making him the sixth-highest appearance-maker in the club's history. He joined the first team at Molineux in 1970 when he replaced John Holsgrove to become Frank Munro's central-defensive partner. Strong and mobile, he tackled well but more importantly had exceptional positional sense, and very rarely did he venture over the halfway line. A very positive footballer, he helped Wolves win the Texaco Cup in 1971 and was an ever-present player in the side that reached the 1972 UEFA Cup Final (beaten by Spurs). Club commitments denied him an England Under-23 cap, but he won a League Cup-winners' medal in 1974 and was a key member of the side that lifted the Second Division title three years later. Soon afterwards, he was awarded a richly deserved testimonial. In February 1980 John came off the subs' bench during an FA Cup tie against Watford, but before he had touched the ball he fractured his leg. He was never the same player again, and in 1981 was transferred to Sheffield United, moving to Derby County two years later. He left the Rams in 1984 after relegation to the Third Division and, after assisting non-League side Harrisons FC, he became head groundsman at the Merryhill shopping centre, Brierley Hill, before starting his own landscape gardening business near Wolverhampton.

Jim McCalliog

Midfield: 204+6 apps, 48 goals.

Born: Glasgow, 23 September 1946.
Career: Leeds United, Chelsea, Sheffield Wednesday, WOLVES (August 1969–March 1974), Manchester United, Southampton, Chicago Sting (NASL), Lyn Oslo, Lincoln City, Runcorn, Halifax Town (manager), Scotland (2 Youth, 2 Under-23 and 5 full caps).

■ Jim McCalliog was an amateur with Leeds United and had limited success with Chelsea before moving to Sheffield Wednesday in 1965 for £37,500 – Britain's costliest teenager at the time. He played in the Owls' 1966 FA Cup Final

defeat by Everton before becoming the first Wednesday player to represent Scotland for 47 years when he scored against England at Wembley in April 1967 – the first defeat inflicted upon the world champions since they lifted the Jules Rimet Trophy. Jim became unsettled at Hillsborough and as a result moved to Wolves for £60,000 in August 1969. The money was well spent as he remained at Molineux for almost five years, making over 200 appearances and scoring almost 50 goals. He linked up well in midfield with Kenny Hibbitt and often brought left-winger Dave Wagstaffe into the game. He captained Wolves several times during 1971–72, when they reached the Final of the UEFA Cup, but dropped out of favour when Steve Daley appeared on the scene. Jim was subsequently sold to Manchester United and, after helping the Reds regain their First Division status, he switched to Southampton, gaining an FA Cup-winners' medal in 1976 when Saints beat his former club Manchester United in the Final. Jim left The Dell for the NASL in 1977 and, after a brief coaching appointment in Nigeria, he made his 423rd and final League appearance as player-coach with Lincoln City in October 1978. After playing in Norway, Jim became player-manager of Runcorn in 1979 and after more than 10 years out of the game running a pub, he surprisingly returned as manager of Fourth Division Halifax Town in 1990. It was a thankless task and he left after a year.

Bobby Mason

Forward: 173 apps, 54 goals.

Born: 22 March 1936, Tipton, Staffordshire.
Career: WOLVES (July 1951–June 1962), Chelmsford City, Leyton Orient, Poole Town.

■ Bobby Mason spent 11 years at Molineux and was a regular member of the first team between November 1957 and November 1961. He joined the club as an amateur and turned professional at the age of 18, but with so many other quality forwards at the club he was nurtured along in the reserves, scoring plenty of goals and helping

them win the Central League title in 1953 and 1958, the year he established himself in the first XI. Blessed with a sturdy little frame, Bobby was one of the nearest things to perpetual motion one could find in top-flight football. Fired by tremendous determination, he gave nothing less than 100 per cent on the field and often received high praise from his manager Stan Cullis. He helped Wolves win successive League titles in 1958 and 1959 but missed the 1960 FA Cup Final win over Blackburn. He left Molineux for Chelmsford City and later played with Leyton Orient and Poole Town. He retired in 1965 and went on to reside in Christchurch (Dorset) and later Swadlincote.

Bill Morris

Defender: 197 apps, 3 goals.
Born: 26 March 1913, Handsworth, Birmingham.
Died: 11 November 1995, Dudley.
Career: Handsworth Old Boys, West Bromwich Albion, Halesowen Town, WOLVES (May 1933–May 1947), guest for Wrexham during World War Two, Dudley Town, England (3 caps).

■ A natural footballer, Bill Morris was able to occupy almost any outfield position but

preferred to defend rather than attack. After starring in all three half-back berths and as an inside-forward for Albion's third team and Halesowen, he settled down at centre-half for Wolves, a position he held until the mid-1930s. Bill was then switched by manager Frank Buckley to right-back, where he became a grandly mobile performer and gained three England caps in 1938–39, against Ireland, Scotland and Romania, as well as appearing in that season's FA Cup Final defeat by Portsmouth. Signed for just £100, Bill was a strong kicker and tackler, mobile with great positional sense, whose League debut came as an emergency centre-forward against his former club WBA in 1934. In later years Bill was rated one of the best full-backs in the country, and although World War Two disrupted his career, he eventually appeared in 264 first-team games for Wolves (including regional fixtures). When new Wolves boss Ted Vizard switched Gus McLean to right-back, Bill moved to Dudley Town, spending two seasons in the Birmingham League as a centre-forward before retiring in 1949. He was 82 when he died in an old people's home in 1995.

Jimmy Mullen

Outside-left: 486 apps, 112 goals.
Born: 6 January 1923, Newcastle-on-Tyne. Died: October 1987, Wolverhampton.
Career: WOLVES (July 1937–May 1960), guest for Leicester City, Newcastle United and Darlington during World War Two, England (12 full, 2 wartime, 2 Victory and 3 B caps).

■ With Johnny Hancocks on the right wing and Jimmy Mullen on the left, the Wolves attack was regarded as one of the most potent in the Football League from 1946 to 1956. Whereas Hancocks could score cracking goals with powerful shots, Jimmy was the more cultured footballer, possessing great skill, exceptional speed over 30–40 yards, vision and alertness, while his crossing, especially on the run, was second to none. At times, he was so accurate from the touchline and corner flag that the player he was aiming for hardly had to move. Jimmy's left foot was pure magic, but it was used more to provide than as a weapon for shooting – although he did net his fair share of goals, averaging one every four games for Wolves. Jimmy was only 16 when he was handed his League debut by Wolves manager Major Frank Buckley in 1939. In fact, he is one of the youngest footballers ever to appear in an FA Cup semi-final, doing so against Grimsby just five weeks

after his League baptism. In his fourth international appearance, against Belgium in Brussels in 1950, Jimmy became England's first-ever substitute when he replaced the injured Jackie Milburn in a 4–1 victory. Jimmy gave Wolves 23 years' excellent service, accumulating well over 570 first-team appearances (including wartime) before retiring in the summer of 1959 after gaining his third League Championship medal, following earlier ones in 1954 and 1958. He also helped Wolves win the FA Cup in 1949.

Frank Munro

Defender: 365+6 apps, 19 goals.

Born: Dundee, Scotland, 25 October 1947.

Career: Chelsea, Dundee United, Aberdeen, WOLVES (January 1968–December 1977), Celtic, Hellas (Australia), Scotland (9 full, 2 amateur, 4 Youth and 4 Under-23 caps), Albion Rovers (coach), Australian football (coach).

■ In the summer of 1967, shortly after regaining their First Division status, Wolves, masquerading as 'Los Angeles Wolves', took part in (and won) a North American international soccer tournament. In the Final, they defeated Aberdeen, for whom wing-half Frank Munro scored a hat-trick including two penalties. Impressed with what he saw, manager Ronnie Allen opened negotiations with the Pittodrie Park club and signed the Scot for £55,000 six months later. Frank, who was once on Chelsea's ground staff, started his League career with Dundee United and won four youth caps and played in two amateur internationals for his country before 1963. He then gained a Scottish Cup runners'-up medal in 1967, and was in line to become Scotland's next international centre-half. Big and burly, Frank was terrific in the air and went on to form a fine partnership with John Holsgrove at the heart of the Wolves defence. He helped Wolves win the Texaco Cup in 1971 and soon afterwards gained the first two of his nine full caps for Scotland, as a substitute against Northern Ireland and England. Frank also won four Under-23 caps between 1969–71. The following year, bitterly disappointed when Wolves lost to Tottenham Hotspur in the 1972 UEFA Cup Final, he cursed his luck again when two major semi-finals were lost, but, in 1974 Frank starred in Wolves' League Cup Final win over Manchester City. Frank went on to amass over 370 appearances for Wolves before leaving the club in 1977, signing for Celtic for £20,000. After playing in the 1978 Scottish Cup Final defeat by Rangers, he had a spell in Australian football before holding coaching positions with Albion Rovers and later Hamlyn Rangers and Keilor FC in Australia. After returning to England, Frank suffered the first of two strokes in 1993.

Jimmy Murray

Forward: 299 apps, 166 goals.

Born: 11 October 1935, Dover.
Career: WOLVES (November 1951–November 1963), Manchester City, Walsall, Telford United.

■ Wolves manager Stan Cullis always believed that Jimmy Murray would become a top-class goalscorer and so it proved. Having joined the Molineux club as a youngster – spotted by scout George Poyser – Jimmy was doing his National Service at Lichfield when, 24 hours before a home friendly with Moscow Dynamo in November 1955, he picked up a newspaper and saw the headline 'Unknown to lead Wolves.' He was staggered but the news was true and soon afterwards, following a telephone call from his boss, he went out and helped Wolves beat the Russians 2–1 before a crowd of more than 55,000. Jimmy never looked back, developing into a superb marksman; razor-sharp with the knack of being in the right place at the right time. He scored some wonderful goals and was leading marksman in Wolves' First Division Championship-winning campaigns of 1957–58 and 1958–59, and again in 1959–60 when the FA Cup was won. His exquisite scoring exploits were not confined to the first XI, as in 1961 he hit six goals in a reserve game against Chesterfield. On leaving Molineux in 1963, Jimmy linked up with former West Bromwich Albion striker Derek Kevan at Manchester City, whom he helped win the Second Division title in 1966. After that, he played for Walsall and Telford United, starring for the latter in two FA Trophy Finals before retiring in 1971. Jimmy went on to run a greengrocery business in Tamworth and a contract car hire company in Lichfield.

Andy Mutch

Striker: 275+13 apps, 106 goals.

Born: 28 December 1963, Liverpool.
Career: Everton, Liverpool, Southport, WOLVES (February 1986–August 1993), Swindon Town, Wigan Athletic, Stockport County, Barrow, Southport, Telford United, England B (3 caps).

■ Plucked out of non-League obscurity by Wolves boss Sammy Chapman in 1986, Andy

Mutch formed a prolific seven and a half year partnership with Steve Bull that yielded 301 goals, 84 of which were Andy's. An apprentice with both Merseyside clubs, Andy spent two seasons with Southport before arriving at Molineux when Wolves were heading into the Fourth Division. Bull arrived the following season and their partnership took off straightaway. The Fourth Division Championship and Sherpa Van Trophy were both won in 1988 as ever-present Andy struck 23 goals, including one at Wembley in the SVT win over Burnley. The following season, his 21 goals helped Wolves clinch the Third Division title and earned him three England B caps. He continued to score for Wolves, and when he left Molineux for Swindon for £250,000, his goal-tally had passed the century mark. A loan spell with Wigan preceded a stint with Stockport, whom he helped gain promotion to the First Division in 1997. After that he assisted Barrow, his former club Southport and Telford United, the last of these as assistant manager.

Seyi George Olofinjana

Midfielder: 134 (+13) apps. 18 goals.

Born: 30 June 1980, Lagos, Nigeria.
Career: FC Crown Ogbomoso, Kwara United, SK Brann Bergen, Norway, WOLVES (August 2004), Nigeria (20 full caps).

■ Nigerian international Seyi Olofinjana cost Wolves £1.7 million when he signed from the Norwegian side SK Brann Bergen in readiness for the 2004–05 season. Standing 6ft 4ins tall and weighing almost 12st, he is an imposing presence out on the field and gives defenders plenty to think about during the course of a game. He scored five League goals in his first season in English football but failed to make an impact in 2005–06, mainly due to a cracked bone in his back, which kept him out of the African Cup of Nations. He then returned full of enthusiasm and commitment and top scored with 10 goals in 2006–07 before weighing in with just three in 2007–08, including a late winner against Plymouth Argyle on the very last day of the League programme. His efforts are much appreciated by the supporters, who will be hoping he can find the net on a more regular basis in the years to come. Capped 20 times by Nigeria, Seyi made his international debut on 6 June 2000 in a 3–2 friendly win over Malawi. He also played in the 2004 African Cup of Nations in Tunisia, helping Nigeria finish third, and participated in the same tournament in 2008 when Nigeria lost in the quarter-finals. He signed a contract extension with Wolves in October 2007 which will keep him at Molineux until 2011, but in the summer of 2008 he moved to Stoke City to play in the Preimership.

Photograph © AAction Images / Andrew Boyers

Seyi is a Chemical Engineering graduate from the Ladoke Akintola University Of Technology, Ogbomoso, and also sat exams as part of his Masters degree in Chemical Engineering in July 2007.

Geoff Palmer

Full-back: 489+6 apps, 16 goals.

Born: 11 July 1954, Cannock, Staffordshire.
Career: WOLVES (July 1970–November 1984), Burnley, WOLVES (December 1985–May 1986), Cannock Police team, Bromsgrove Rovers (coach), England Under-23 (2 caps).

■ Uncompromising full-back Geoff Palmer had two spells with Wolves and, in all, spent 16 years at Molineux, amassing almost 500 senior appearances. A sterling performer, full of energy and commitment, he was a strong kicker and was able to contain the trickiest of wingers. Twice a League Cup winner with Wolves – in 1974 against Manchester City and 1980 against Nottingham Forest – he helped the team gain promotion from the old Second Division in 1977 (as champions) and 1983 (as runners-up), and played in all four Divisions of the Football League before the Premiership was introduced in 1992. He also gained two England Under-23 caps against Wales and Portugal in the mid-1970s. He made his League debut against Birmingham City, 11 games into the 1973–74 season, and never looked back after that. Firmly establishing himself as Derek Parkin's full-back partner, Geoff performed consistently until manager Tommy Docherty took charge. Geoff's position immediately came under threat and he quickly moved to Burnley, returning to Wolves 13 months later, re-signed by his former boss Bill McGarry. Unfortunately, Wolves were now in the Third Division and it got no better as Geoff went down to Division Four with his teammates at the end of the 1985–86 campaign. He played just once at this level before retiring to join the police, initially based in Cannock. He played for the police team in the Midland Combination and later assisted ex-Wolves star Steve Daley as coach of Bromsgrove Rovers (1998–99).

Phil Parkes

Goalkeeper: 382 apps.

Born: West Bromwich, 14 July 1947.
Career: WOLVES (August 1962–May 1978), Vancouver Whitecaps, Chicago Sting, Toronto Blizzard, San Jose Earthquakes (all NASL), Marstons FC, Bromsgrove Rovers (coach).

■ Phil 'Lofty' Parkes supported West Bromwich Albion as a lad, attended the local grammar school and represented the town's football team before joining Wolves. Confined to the inermediate, youth and reserve teams for four years, he made his League debut against Preston in November 1966 and saved a penalty in a 3–2 win. He made 14 appearances that season, helping Wolves regain promotion. Four years later, after being in and out of the team, he was in the side which won the Texaco Cup and a year

later appeared in the UEFA Cup Final defeat by Spurs. Wolves losing two major Cup semi-finals in quick succession and Phil's injury and replacement by Gary Pierce for the 1974 League Cup Final meant that, unfortunately, Phil never played at Wembley. Pierce, in fact, brought an end to his record-breaking run of 127 consecutive League appearances (from 1 September 1970) and 171 in all competitions. Retiring from League football after his testimonial match in 1978, Phil went to America and assisted four clubs in the NASL, winning the Soccer Bowl with the Whitecaps in 1979. Only Mike Stowell and Bert Williams have made more appearances in goal for Wolves than 'Lofty'.

Derek Parkin

Full-back: 507+2 apps, 10 goals.

Born: Newcastle-upon-Tyne, 2 January 1946.
Career: Huddersfield Town, WOLVES (February 1968–March 1982), Stoke City, England (5 Under-23 caps).

■ Derek 'Squeak' Parkin was one of the best left-backs in the First Division between 1969 and 1979. He represented England in five Under-23 internationals and also played for the Football League but missed out on a full cap. A stylish defender who relied on skill, interception and anticipation, he became the first player to appear in 600 games for the club and also the first to top 500 in the Football League, reaching the latter milestone in March 1982 at Villa Park. A very consistent performer, Derek appeared in 50 or more competitive games per season for Wolves no fewer than five times (another record). He was an ever present in League action on four occasions and had one run of 134 consecutive first-team outings from his debut (in his home town) until 14 November 1970. Signed by Ronnie Allen for £80,000 in 1968, he helped Wolves win the Texaco Cup in 1971, reach the UEFA Cup Final a year later, lift the League Cup in 1974 and 1980, and gain promotion as Second Division champions. After 14 years' service, Derek moved to Stoke City on a free transfer in 1982, teaming up with future Wolves player Alan Dodd and soon to be joined by his old Molineux teammate George Berry. Derek made 45 appearances for the Potters before retiring in May 1983 to concentrate on a new career in landscape gardening. He now resides in the same locality near Bridgnorth as ex-Wolves players Willie Carr and Bert Williams.

Teddy Peers

Goalkeeper: 198 apps.

Born: 31 December 1886, Connah's Quay, Flintshire. Died: 20 September 1935, Wolverhampton.
Career: Oswestry St Clare's, Chirk, Shrewsbury Town (trial), Connah's Quay Juniors, Connah's Quay Victoria, Connah's Quay, WOLVES (April 1911–January 1922), guest for Stoke and Walsall during World War One, Hednesford Town (2 spells), Port Vale, Wales (12 full caps, 1 Victory cap).

■ Teddy Peers won several honours as a teenager, including a Welsh Amateur Cup-winners' medal and a Chester League Championship medal. He joined Wolves at the age of 24 and proved to be a loyal servant to the club, accumulating almost 200 senior appearances. He was virtually an ever present for three years, having a splendid run of 71 consecutive first-team outings in the Second Division before World War One. During the hostilities he helped Port Vale win the Lancashire Section Championship in 1917–18. Teddy, who always wore a rather tatty-looking flat cap, was agile and consistent, and got tremendous distance with his clearances. A jovial character, he was replaced in the Wolves goal by Noel George in 1921 and, as a result, missed that year's FA Cup Final defeat by Spurs. He was capped on 12 occasions – eight of them while with Wolves – and picked up his first against Ireland in 1913. He moved to Port Vale in 1922 (after six months with Hednesford) and was a member of the Valiants' Staffordshire Infirmary Cup-winning team before returning to Hednesford in 1923. Retiring three years later, he went on to run several pubs in Wolverhampton, the first being the New Inn on Bilston Road.

Ted Pheasant

Defender: 168 apps, 19 goals.

Born: 15 February 1877, Darlaston. Died: 17 July 1910, Wolverhampton.

Career: Wednesbury Excelsior, Wednesbury Old Athletic, WOLVES (August 1895–November 1904), West Bromwich Albion, Leicester Fosse.

■ Ted 'Cock' Pheasant was a bustling forward when he joined Wolves in 1895. Standing 6ft 2in and weighing 15st, he always looked super-fit and, as time progressed, he was used in a variety of positions, eventually settling down as a centre-half. As hard as nails, he always rolled up the sleeves of his jersey, making him look as fearsome as possible to the opposing team. After taking over from Billy Malpass as Wolves' centre-half, he never looked back and went on to make almost 170 appearances for the club. Twice an ever-present player, he always performed with aggression, determination and confidence, and in 1902 scored a hat-trick from his defensive position in a 3–0 home win over Newcastle. Ted received a specially designed gold medal for that treble, presented to him by club chairman Mr T.H. Slaney. It would be another 93 years before another Wolves defender achieved the same feat. Such was his commitment to the club, Ted turned down the chance to represent the Football League against the Irish League so that he could play in a League game for Wolves. A spate of injuries eventually led to his departure from Wolves, transferring to neighbours West Bromwich Albion for £500 in November 1904. He went on to appear in 152 games for the Baggies, scoring 22 goals before joining Leicester Fosse for £300 in 1910. Ted never played a game for the Foxes. Two weeks after leaving The Hawthorns, he was admitted to a Birmingham hospital with peritonitis, presumably contracted after diving into a canal to rescue someone from under a barge. Sadly he failed to recover from that illness and died at the age of 33. Hundreds turned out for his funeral in Darlaston.

Tom Phillipson

Centre-forward: 159 apps, 111 goals.

Born: 31 October 1898, Ryton-on-Tyne, County Durham. Died: 19 November 1965, Wolverhampton.

Career: Scotswood, Newcastle United, Swindon Town, WOLVES (December 1923–March 1928), Sheffield United, Bilston United (player-manager), Walsall.

■ Tom Phillipson is regarded as being one of the greatest goalscorers in Wolves' history. In a brilliant junior career he netted at will, once scoring 14 of his side's 15 goals and following up with 10 out of 12 in his next match. Capped twice by England as a schoolboy in 1913, he served in the West Yorkshire Regiment in Russia during World War One and signed for Newcastle in 1919. Yet surprisingly, he never got going at St James' Park and joined Swindon for £500 in 1921, switching to Molineux for £1,000 in December 1923. He helped Wolves win the Third Division North title in his first season, scoring 14 goals including a hat-trick against Ashington. He was top scorer with 16 goals in 1924–25 and in 1925–26 rattled in a total of 37, a club record at that time. He struck hat-tricks

against Middlesbrough and Stockport and a four-timer past Barnsley, but his efforts were all in vain as Wolves missed promotion, finishing fourth. Despite Tom bagging another 31 goals the following season (including a five-timer against Bradford), Wolves slumped to 15th in the table. In May 1927 Wolves appointed Major Frank Buckley as manager and the change of leadership seemed to affect Tom, who netted only 11 times in 24 games that season, a fair strike-rate but below what the Major expected from him. He played his last game for Wolves in a 2–2 draw away to Stoke in March 1928 and soon afterwards was sold to Sheffield United for £2,600. Tom spent two seasons with the Blades and after assisting Bilston United as player-manager and then Walsall, he retired to start his own business in Wolverhampton, later entering local government and becoming mayor of the town in 1938. Tom's record of scoring in 13 consecutive League matches in 1926–27 has never been equalled in English football.

Jesse Pye

Centre-forward: 209 apps, 95 goals.

Born: 22 December 1919, Treeton, Rotherham. Died: 19 February 1984, Blackpool.

Career: Catliffe FC, Treeton FC, Sheffield United (trial), Notts County, WOLVES (May 1946–July 1952), Luton Town, Derby County, Wisbech Town (player-manager), England (1 full, 1 Victory and 3 B caps).

■ Jesse Pye played village football in Yorkshire and had a trial with Sheffield United before World War Two broke out. He served with the Royal Engineers and played with some star footballers during the hostilities, once scoring seven goals (three penalties) in a game. Jesse joined Notts County in 1945 but spent less than a year at Meadow Lane despite representing England in a Victory international. A rugged, all-action goalscorer, he switched to Wolves for a record £12,000 in 1946 and immediately became a hero with the Molineux fans after netting a hat-trick on his debut, in a 6–1 win over Arsenal. He struck 20 League goals in his first season with Wolves, netted 16 the following campaign and was leading marksman with 21 in 1948–49, two of which came in the FA Cup Final win over Leicester. Jesse continued to find the net regularly until leaving for Luton in 1952. He represented the Football League, gained three England B caps and won one full cap against the Republic of Ireland in 1949. From Kenilworth Road, Jesse joined Derby County in 1954 but, after the Rams had slipped into the Third Division North, he left to become player-manager of Wisbech Town in 1960.

Dicky Rhodes

Wing-half: 156 apps, 10 goals.

Born: 18 February 1908, Wolverhampton. Died: 21 January 1993, Wolverhampton.
Career: Redditch United, WOLVES (July 1926–October 1935), Sheffield Wednesday, Swansea Town, Rochdale.

■ Capped by England at schoolboy level, Dicky Rhodes began as a centre-forward, scoring plenty of goals. He continued to impress with Redditch United and netted 75 times in three seasons of non-League football. Wolves had monitored his progress closely and signed him as a professional in 1926. Dicky became a star, serving Wolves for over nine years and gaining a Second Division Championship medal in 1932. Converted into a right-half by Major Frank Buckley in 1930, Dicky held that position until Tom Smalley arrived in 1933, at which point he slipped into the reserves, but was always ready to step up when required. Rated

one of the best half-backs in the Second Division during the late 1920s and early 1930s, one felt that if Wolves had been in the top flight Dicky would certainly have earned a full England cap. A gifted footballer and full of energy, he was thoughtful with his passing, often playing the ball short and precise rather than thumping it aimlessly downfield. He captained Wolves occasionally and in 1931–32, when the Second Division title was won, he missed only two games. A niggling knee injury kept him out of action for long periods and in October 1935 he moved to Sheffield Wednesday, later assisting Swansea Town and Rochdale. World War Two effectively ended his career and he returned to Wolverhampton after the hostilities to become mine host of the Posada Inn. In his spare time Dicky was a champion canary breeder, winning the national title in 1973.

John Richards

Striker: 461+25 apps, 194 goals.

Born: 9 November 1950, Warrington.

Career: WOLVES (July 1966–August 1983), Derby County, Maritimo Funchal (Madeira), WOLVES (director), England (1 full, 2 Under-21 and 6 Under-23 caps).

■ Known as 'King John', 'J.R' or 'Richie', John Richards was a superb striker: skilful, quick, alert and decisive with a tally of 194 goals that remained a club record until 1992 and earned him a place in the memories of those who saw him play forever. John played both rugby and soccer at school but chose the round ball game and represented Lancashire Grammar Schools, scoring six goals against an English public school team in 1966. After tentative approaches from Derby and Sheffield Wednesday, he signed for Wolves after a trial. He turned professional in July 1969 and made his debut against West Brom that season. In September 1970 John netted the first of his 144 League goals and helped Wolves reach the Final of the UEFA Cup the following season. In superb form in 1972–73 with a goal tally of 37, his efforts earned him his only full England cap against Northern Ireland, although he had earlier played at Youth, Under-21 and Under-23 levels. John, whose goal beat Manchester City in the 1974 League Cup Final, was Wolves' leading marksman in six out of seven seasons in which he also suffered relegation, enjoyed immediate promotion and won a second League Cup-winners' medal after Nottingham Forest were defeated in the 1980 Final. Come 1982, John's Molineux career was nearing an end. He had a loan spell with Derby County, and after a spell in Madeira with Maritimo Funchal he retired to take employment with the Wolverhampton Leisure Services Department. He returned to Molineux as a director following the death of Billy Wright in 1994 and was later appointed managing director, holding the position until 2000. He now works in sports ground development in the West Midlands.

William Crispin Rose

Goalkeeper: 165 apps.

Born: 3 April 1861, St Pancras, London. Died: 4

February 1937, Wolverhampton.
Career: Small Heath, London Swifts, Preston North End, Stoke, WOLVES (January 1889–February 1894), Loughborough Town, WOLVES (August 1895–May 1896), England (5 full caps).

■ Billy Crispin Rose was rightly regarded as one of the best goalkeepers of his time. Larger than life and twice as eccentric, he was agile, solid and strong. Quite brilliant at times, he was always in command of his area, punched the ball regularly and often raced out from his goal area to fly-kick the ball upfield or into touch. He failed to make an impact with Small Heath, but after joining London Swifts he won his first England cap against Ireland (later adding four more to his tally). He then signed for Preston North End, and after assisting Stoke moved to Wolves in 1889. Maintaining a high level of consistency throughout his career, he was superb during Wolves' FA Cup winning run of 1893. Instrumental in forming the Players' Union (now the PFA), Billy had a dispute with Wolves in 1895 and joined Loughborough but returned to Molineux 18 months later and held his place until the end of the season, when he retired. He went on to become a publican in Birmingham and Wolverhampton, and also ran a corner shop near St Andrew's.

Alex (Bob) Scott

Goalkeeper: 120 apps.

Born: 29 October 1913, Liverpool. Died: 1962, Wolverhampton.
Career: Forest Dynamos, Liverpool, Burnley, WOLVES (February 1936–August 1947), wartime guest of Aston Villa and Southport, Crewe Alexandra.

■ Bob Scott failed to make the grade at Anfield owing to the presence of Elisha Scott and Arthur Riley and, seeking first-team football, he moved to Turf Moor in 1933, helping Burnley reach the FA Cup semi-final two years later. He cost Wolves £1,250 when signed in 1936. Tall, well built, eminently safe and with a huge kick, he brought a secure style of goalkeeping to Molineux which was to be of inestimable value over the next 10 years, during which time he made 129 appearances for Wolves. Of those, 85 came during World War Two, when he represented an All British XI having earlier played for a Football League XI. The recipient of two First Division runners-up medals in 1938 and 1939, he also collected an FA Cup runners-up medal at the end of that latter campaign. In December 1936 Bob was sent off against Leeds and Huddersfield. These two indiscretions cost him £10 (in wages and a fine)

and 13 days' suspension. When Bert Williams took over as Wolves' first-choice 'keeper after World War Two, Bob moved to Crewe Alexandra in 1947, retiring two years later. He then ran a general store in Whitmore Reans before becoming a policeman and subsequently a detective in the local constabulary. Originally a centre-half, Bob played for England Boys in that position and, as a youngster, was good at baseball, starring for Oakmere in Liverpool's Zingari League.

Harold Shaw

Full-back: 249 apps.

Born: 22 May 1905, Hednesford, Staffordshire.
Died: 7 June 1984, Cannock, Staffordshire.
Career: Hednesford Town, WOLVES (May 1923–February 1930), Sunderland (later coach).

■ Harold Shaw was a great defender who occupied both full-back positions. He was a fine leader, fair and reliable and described as 'a stylist of the first water'. He served Wolves for seven years, making almost 250 appearances. A former engineer's fitter, he moved to Molineux on his 18th birthday and went straight into the first team, replacing George Marshall in Wolves' first-ever game in the Third Division North. The baby of the side, Harold was outstanding, and he helped bring the Third Division North Championship to the club at the first attempt. Certainly a classy defender, Harold was surprisingly transferred by Major Frank Buckley to Sunderland for £7,000 in February 1930 and played in an FA Cup tie against Derby in March 1933 which attracted the biggest-ever crowd to Roker Park – 75,118. He was forced to retire in 1936 after adding 217 appearances to his career record with Sunderland. Often considered unlucky not to gain representative honours, the nearest Harold came to a full cap was to play for England against The Rest in an international trial. In later years he returned to the Midlands and joined the South Staffs and Penn golf club while also working at Cannock colliery.

Bill Shorthouse

Defender: 376 apps, 1 goal.
Born: 27 May 1922, Bilston.
Career: St Martin's Old Boys, WOLVES (November 1941–May 1957, later coach), Aston Villa (coach) and Birmingham City (coach).

■ Bill Shorthouse had the unenviable task of replacing Stan Cullis in the Wolves side, but he took to it like a duck to water and went on to give the club grand service. He served with the Royal Engineers during World War Two and participated in the D-Day landings. He returned to England after being badly wounded and on his recovery played for Wolves' reserves, making his senior debut in 1947 at full-back, a position he later filled with great efficiency. He moved into the centre of the defence within two months. A wholehearted and thoroughly determined footballer, Bill – nicknamed the Baron – had tremendous grit, was a strong tackler and very consistent, missing only 32 League games out of 378 between October 1947 and September 1956, gaining an FA Cup-winners' medal in 1949 and a League Championship medal in 1954. He was only ever out of the side through injury and received very few cautions. When he switched to full-back, his

place at centre-half went to Billy Wright. Bill's only goal for Wolves was a terrific drive in a 2–0 victory over Charlton at Molineux in November 1955. After retiring in 1957 he became coach at Molineux, later taking similar positions with Aston Villa and Birmingham City as well as taking charge of the England Youth team in 1970–71.

Bill Slater, OBE, CBE

Half-back: 334 apps, 30 goals.

Born: 29 April 1927, Clitheroe, Lancashire.
Career: Yorkshire Amateurs, Leeds University, Blackpool, Brentford, WOLVES (August 1952–May 1963), Brentford, Northern Nomads, England (12 full and 8 amateur caps).

■ Bill Slater played for Blackpool in the 1951 FA Cup Final defeat by Newcastle United, but nine years later he did manage to gain a winners' medal when he skippered Wolves to victory over Blackburn from the centre-half position. Bill played for Yorkshire Amateurs and Leeds University before joining Blackpool in 1944. He then had a spell with Brentford before switching to Wolves in 1952. When Wolves won the League title in 1954, Bill missed only three matches while occupying the right-half position with England's Billy Wright alongside him. Over the next six years he played superbly well and gained two more League Championship medals (1958 and 1959), as well as appearing in 12 internationals for England having previously represented his country as an amateur. In the 1958 World Cup Finals in Sweden he was part of an all-Wolves half-back line against USSR, Brazil and Austria, the other two players being Wright and Eddie Clamp. In 1960, Bill obtained a BSc degree and was voted Footballer of the Year. In the summer of 1963 he returned to Brentford and later assisted Northern Nomads, retiring in 1964. Bill then became deputy director of the Crystal Palace Sports Centre while also working as a director of PE at both Liverpool and Birmingham Universities. In 1982 he was awarded the OBE for services to sport and in 1998 received the CBE too. From 1984 to 1989, he was director of National Services and in July 1989 was elected president of the British Gymnastics Association. Later a member of the National Olympic Committee, he served on the panel of the National Lottery. His daughter Barbara, a former national champion gymnast, represented Britain in the 1976 Olympic Games and later worked for Central TV.

Mike Stowell

Goalkeeper: 447+1 apps.

Born: 19 April 1965, Portsmouth.
Career: Leyland Motors, Preston North End, Everton, Chester City, York City, Manchester City, Port Vale, WOLVES (loan, March–April 1989), Preston North End, WOLVES (June 1990–June 2001), Bristol City.

■ Mike Stowell holds the record for making the most appearances as a goalkeeper for Wolves, accumulating 448 – 28 more than Bert Williams. He turned professional in 1985 and remained in League football for 20 years, assisting eight clubs. He was farmed out on loan by Everton to gain experience, and made seven appearances in the Third Division for Wolves before returning to Molineux on a permanent basis for £250,000 in 1990. Mike, 6ft 2in tall and over 14st in weight, was a fine shot-stopper with splendid reflexes and good positional sense. In November 1990 he hired a tractor to beat the severe snow storms in the Midlands and link up with the England B team for a friendly with Algeria, which never materialised due to the atrocious weather. He loved his football and this proved it. Mike was outstanding in the early 1990s. Unfortunately, he never won a prize with Wolves, losing three semi-final showdowns. He eventually left Molineux for Bristol City on a free transfer in 2001, and was 40 years of age when he announced his retirement in 2005 having amassed a career total of 525 club appearances.

Eddie Stuart

Defender: 322 apps, 1 goal.

Born: 12 May 1931, Johannesburg, South Africa.
Career: Johannesburg Rangers, WOLVES (January 1951–July 1962), Stoke City, Tranmere Rovers, Stockport County, Worcester City (player-manager).

■ Eddie Stuart made rapid progress in his home country, winning the South African Cup with Johannesburg Rangers. At the age of 19, he joined Wolves and his first game was at centre-half in a reserve game at West Bromwich Albion. He continued playing at the heart of the second XI defence until April 1952, when he made his senior debut, ironically also against the Baggies, deputising for Roy Swinbourne at centre-forward and scoring in a 4–1 defeat. At the end of that season, Eddie went home to celebrate his 21st birthday, but unfortunately on his return he had contracted a tropical virus which doctors could not diagnose. Admitted to hospital, he slowly recovered, regained full fitness and after a year out of the game returned to reserve team football. He went on to serve Wolves for another nine years, amassing over 320 appearances. He was outstanding in the last 12 games of Wolves' Championship-winning season of 1953–54 and missed only 26 games over the next three years. In 1958 and 1959 he played in two more Championship-winning teams and when Billy Wright retired he was made captain of the side. After helping Wolves win the Charity Shield at the start of the 1959–60 campaign, he was eventually replaced at full-back by George Showell and as skipper by Bil Slater and missed that season's FA Cup Final win over Blackburn. 'As 12th man I received a winners' medal but it wasn't the same,' said Eddie. Over the next two seasons, he played in

74 out of 93 games before joining Stoke City for £8,000. He helped the Potters win the Second Division title before moving to Tranmere Rovers for £4,000, ending his career at Stockport County, with whom he gained a Fourth Division Championship medal in 1967. After a spell as player-manager of Worcester City, Eddie retired in 1970 with 565 club appearances to his credit. He became a local businessman.

Roy Swinbourne

Centre-forward: 230 apps, 114 goals.

Born: 25 August 1929, Denaby Main, Yorkshire.
Career: Wath Wanderers, WOLVES (August 1944–May 1957), England (1 B cap).

■ Roy Swinbourne was a fine goalscoring centre-forward; sharp, decisive and clever, his career came to an abrupt end in 1957 after a serious knee injury. The son of a former Aston Villa defender, he played for Wolves' nursery side, Wath Wanderers, as a 15-year-old, turned professional after the war and scored his first senior goal for Wolves against Aston Villa in only his third outing in the League. He established himself in the first XI in 1950–51, taking over from Jesse Pye. He netted 22 goals in 48 outings and although injuries disrupted his progress the following season, he bounced back in style in 1952–53 with a further 21 goals. Then, playing in a forward line with Johnny Hancocks, Peter Broadbent, Dennis Wilshaw and Jimmy Mullen, his 24 goals helped bring the League Championship to Molineux in 1953–54. However, after netting 17 times in the opening 12 League games of the 1955–56 campaign, he badly injured his knee as he tried to avoid a group of cameramen near the byline in an away game at Luton. He returned to play in one more match, at Preston, but badly injured the knee again and was destined never to play for Wolves again. There is no doubt he was a quality goalscorer who would surely have played for England had he not been injured. He now lives in Kinver.

Andy Thompson

Utility: 431+20 apps, 45 goals.

Born: 9 November 1967, Featherstone, Staffordshire.
Career: West Bromwich Albion, WOLVES (November 1986–July 1997), Tranmere Rovers, Crewe Alexandra, Cardiff City, Shrewsbury Town, Hednesford Town.

■ For a small man, Andy Thompson was a very capable footballer who occupied a variety of positions, choosing left-back as his best. Tough and resilient, quick and decisive, he was a fine crosser of the ball, packed a powerful shot and was an expert penalty taker. He was never able to establish himself at The Hawthorns and in 1986 was transferred to Wolves with Steve Bull in a combined deal worth £70,000, Andy being valued at £20,000. He took time to bed into his new surroundings but, once he had, his form was outstanding, playing out of his skin when Wolves won the Fourth Division title and the Sherpa Van Trophy in 1988. An ever present the following season when Wolves clinched the Third Division title, his consistency was worth its weight in gold. Andy avoided serious injury, missing only the odd game here and there. Unfortunately, he had his worst season as a professional in 1991–92, with leg injuries seriously affecting his performances. In 1994–95 Wolves qualified for the Play-offs but lost to Bolton in the semi-final with the Premiership beckoning. Amazingly, a year later, Andy's experience helped Wolves escape relegation. Granted a testimonial match against Chelsea in 1996, Andy left Molineux for Tranmere the following year, later assisting Crewe (loan), Cardiff City, whom he helped gain promotion to the Second Division, Shrewsbury Town (loan) and Hednesford Town. He retired in 2005.

Bobby Thomson

Full-back: 299+1 apps, 3 goals.

Born: 5 December 1943, Smethwick, Staffordshire.

Career: WOLVES (June 1959–March 1969), Birmingham City, Walsall, Luton Town, Connecticut Bicentennials (NASL), Port Vale, Worcester City, Stafford Rangers, Worcester City, Stafford Rangers, Memphis Rogues (NASL), Brewood, Solihull Borough, Tipton Town, England (8 full and 15 Under-23 caps).

■ Plucked from schoolboy football by Wolves manager Stan Cullis, Bobby Thomson made his senior debut in an FA Cup tie against West Bromwich Albion in 1962 and, over the next seven years, gave the supporters something to cheer about with some enterprising displays. Blessed with an astonishing burst of speed, he could attack with great determination down the

flank, often putting defenders under pressure. His efforts were rewarded with eight England caps between November 1963 and December 1964, his first coming against Northern Ireland (won 8–3). He then played in a 10–0 victory over the US and followed up with games against Portugal, Argentina, Northern Ireland (again), Belgium, Wales and Holland. A regular in the Wolves team right up to his move to Birmingham City in March 1969 (signed by his former boss Stan Cullis), Bobby did reasonably well at St Andrew's before having a loan spell with Walsall. Transferred to Luton Town, Bobby spent four years with the Hatters and then served in the NASL with Connecticut Bicentennials before ending his League career with Port Vale. Afterwards, he assisted several non-League clubs, returned for a second spell in the States and also appeared in several charity matches, mostly for the WBA All Stars. He ran a sportswear shop in Sedgley, near Wolverhampton, for many years.

Mark Venus

Full-back: 320+18 apps, 10 goals.

Born: 6 April 1967, Hartlepool.
Career: Hartlepool United, Leicester City, WOLVES (March 1988–June 1997), Ipswich Town, Cambridge United, Hornchurch (player-manager), Hibernian (assistant manager), West Bromwich Albion (assistant manager).

■ Mark Venus made almost 340 appearances for Wolves in nine years, having his best seasons in 1991–92, when he was an ever-present player, 1993–94 and 1994–95. Signing as a professional for Hartlepool at the age of 18, he moved to Leicester in 1985 on a free transfer and was recruited by Wolves boss Graham Turner for £40,000 in 1988. He had four outings at the end of Wolves' Fourth Division Championship-winning season and came into his own in 1988–89, appearing in 45 games (35 in the League) as Wolves won the Third Division title. The following season, he scored his first goal in a 5–0 win over Portsmouth. Mark developed into an outstanding defender, capable of occupying several positions and he even played in midfield.

Blessed with a fine physique, he had good pace, a powerful kick and could deliver a cross from the left flank to perfection. Injured early in 1990–91, Mark took a while to regain his fitness and, indeed, his place in the side. By the mid-1990s, he was back to his best and netted in the Play-off semi-final against Bolton Wanderers, although it counted for nothing as Wolves lost 3–2 on aggregate. A later Play-off semi-final defeat against Crystal Palace was equally disappointing. In 1997 – having donned nine different shirts during his time at Molineux – Mark was transferred to Ipswich Town for £150,000. He spent almost six years at Portman Road, adding 184 appearances to his tally before joining Cambridge United in 2003. A spell as player-manager of Hornchurch followed and he later acted as assistant manager to Tony Mowbray at Hibernian and then The Hawthorns.

Dave Wagstaffe

Outside-left: 404 apps, 32 goals.

Born: 5 April 1943, Manchester.
Career: Manchester City, WOLVES (December 1964–January 1976), Blackburn Rovers, Blackpool, Blackburn Rovers.

■ Dave Wagstaffe was one of the finest wingers in the country in the late 1960s, early 1970s. A great crosser of the ball, especially on the run, he was fast and clever, and possessed a superb body-swerve and strong shot. Although on the slim side, he was courageous, never letting the sturdier defenders worry him unduly. Manager Andy Beattie signed him in 1964 for £30,000 and he quickly became a huge favourite with the Molineux fans, but his presence and skill could not save Wolves from slipping into the Second Division for the first time since 1932. When Ronnie Allen took over as boss, Wolves' form improved considerably, and once Derek Dougan had been introduced to the attack, Waggy's form got better and better, as did his crosses. Promotion was duly achieved with Waggy being an ever-present player. He laid on many chances for his colleagues and netted some crucial goals himself. He was superb in the 7–1 win over Cardiff, setting up three goals, and doing the same in the 4–0 and 5–2 wins over Hull and Bolton respectively. After helping Wolves win the Texaco Cup, reach the Final of the UEFA Cup and win the League Cup against his former club Manchester City, he began to suffer with a knee injury but remained a key member of the squad. However, with various formations being used around that time, Waggy found himself in and out of the team and, with relegation looming, he left Molineux for Blackburn early in 1976. Nine months later, he had the misfortune to become the first player in English football to receive a red card, dismissed against Bolton on 2 October 1976. He went on to play for Blackpool and Blackburn again before ending his career in 1979 with 671 club appearances under his belt and 48 goals. He also represented the Football League against the Scottish League in 1971–72 and won England Schoolboy and Youth caps as a teenager. In later life, Waggy was steward of the Old Wulfrunians club, Castlecroft and the Wolves social club and after that ran Waggy's Bar at Molinuex. In 2008 penned his autobiography, *Waggy's Tales*.

Dennis Westcott

Centre-forward: 144 apps, 134 goals.

Born: 2 July 1917, Wallasey, Lancashire. Died: 13 July 1960, Stafford.

Career: West Ham United (trial), New Brighton, WOLVES (July 1936–April 1948), Blackburn Rovers, Manchester City, Chesterfield, Stafford Rangers, England (4 Victory caps).

■ Dennis Westcott was a supreme goalscorer with dynamite in his boots. He played for England schoolboys and, after a trial with West Ham, joined New Brighton in 1932. He moved to Molineux in 1936 and, after taking over from Billy Hartill, developed into one of the greatest marksmen in the country. Over a period of 10 years (1938–48), he averaged almost a goal a game for Wolves – 215 in 220 appearances in League, FA Cup and wartime football. And if you add in his 'other' matches, his overall record was even better. He was the club's top scorer in 1937–38, 1938–39, 1939–40, 1941–42, 1942–43 and 1946–47, and his tally of 43 goals in 1938–39, which included a four-timer against Grimsby in the FA Cup semi-final, remained a club record until it was beaten by Steve Bull in

1987–88. An FA Cup Final defeat to Portsmouth in 1939 saw Dennis have his worst game of that season but he bounced back and helped Wolves win the 1942 Wartime League Cup Final. Desperately unlucky not to gain a full England cap, Dennis represented his country in four wartime internationals (1940–43) and played for the Football League XI against the Scottish League in 1947. After leaving Molineux, he continued to find the net for Blackburn – scoring a goal every other game – and did likewise for Manchester City and Chesterfield before retiring from first-class soccer in 1953 with a League record of 321 appearances and 210 goals. Dennis finally hung up his boots in May 1949 after a spell with Stafford Rangers. His 38 goals in the 1946–47 campaign remains the biggest total by any Wolves player in a League season.

Bert Williams

Goalkeeper: 420 apps.

Born: 31 January 1922, Bradley, Bilston.
Career: Thompson's FC, Walsall, WOLVES (September 1945–May 1957), England (24 full, 2 wartime, 2 Victory and 1 B caps).

■ Bert Williams was a great goalkeeper – one of the best in England between 1949 and 1955, when he won all of his England caps. Virtually first choice at Molineux for the 12

seasons up to 1957, he made over 400 appearances for the club, a record for a goalkeeper that stood for more than 40 years, until bettered by Mike Stowell in 1999. Quite brilliant at times, Bert was agile, alert, fearless and utterly reliable. Known as 'The Cat', he played in the 1950 World Cup Finals and was unlucky to have been standing between the posts when the US inflicted that embarrassing 1–0 defeat on England in Belo Horizonte. But he quickly put that nightmare behind him and starred on many occasions as the last line of defence for both club and country. Signed by Walsall from Thompson's FC, his game got better and better under the tutorship of Harry Wait at Fellows Park and after serving in the RAF during the war – reaching the rank of sergeant – he joined Wolves. He missed very few games through injury and, in fact, most of his absences were due to international call-ups. An FA Cup winner in 1949 and the recipient of a Division One Championship medal in 1954, Bert retired in the summer of 1957, handing over the goalkeeping duties to Malcolm Finlayson. For many years afterwards he ran a successful sports-outfitters shop in Bilston and a goalkeeping school in the Black Country area. He now lives near Bridgnorth and is one of Wolves' oldest former players, and has recently released a book.

Dennis Wilshaw

Forward: 219 apps, 112 goals.

Born: 11 March 1926, Stoke on Trent. Died: 10 May 2004, Stoke on Trent.
Career: Packmoor Boys Club, WOLVES (August 1943–December 1957), England (2 B and 12 full caps).

■ Dennis Wilshaw was a natural goalscorer, strong, determined and sharp with both feet and his head. A junior with Packmoor Boys Club, for whom he once scored 10 goals in a 16–0 victory over Michelin Tyres, he was a wartime signing by Wolves and was loaned out to Walsall before returning to Molineux in September 1948. Full of confidence and determination, he went on to score a hat-trick on his First Division debut against Newcastle. During his association with Wolves, Dennis played in four front line positions, outside-right being the odd one out. He established himself in the first team in 1952 and two years later starred in the Championship-winning team, netting 26 League goals. He was the first player to net four times in a major game at Wembley – doing so in England's 7–2 win over Scotland in April 1955. It was a shock to some people when he left Molineux for Stoke City in 1957 – signed by former Wolves player Frank Taylor. He became a vital cog in the Potters' forward line, finishing up as top scorer in his first season. Unfortunately, Dennis's career ended in tragic circumstances when he broke his leg against Newcastle in an FA Cup tie in 1961. It was coincidental that he should play the first and last senior games of his career against the 'Geordies'. On leaving football, he continued his profession as a schoolmaster, acting as a scout for Stoke for a short while. Dennis recovered from a heart attack in 1993.

Harry Wood

Forward: 289 apps, 126 goals.

Born: 2 August 1868, Walsall. Died: 5 July 1951, Portsmouth.
Career: Walsall Town Swifts, Kidderminster Harriers, WOLVES (August 1885–July 1891), Walsall, WOLVES (November 1891–May 1898), Southampton, England (3 caps), Portsmouth (trainer).

■ Harry Wood, one of the outstanding forwards of the 1890s, was a gentleman on and off the field. A model professional, he played the game with great skill and enthusiasm; his clever, cunning passing, direct shooting and all-out

commitment earning him a huge reputation in Wolverhampton and, indeed, with the rest of his teammates. He played for Walsall Town Swifts and Kidderminster Harriers before joining Wolves as a 17-year-old. After starring in several friendly matches, he scored on his senior debut against Derby St Luke's in a first-round FA Cup tie in October 1885. Harry continued to play magnificently and appeared in 87 out of a possible 93 competitive matches, scoring 46 goals, 14 in the first League season of 1888–89 when he was Wolves' top marksman. He also struck his first hat-trick in a 6–0 home win over Derby but, like the rest of his colleagues, was bitterly disappointed when Preston beat Wolves 3–0 in the FA Cup Final. The following year, he again topped the club's scoring charts but then surprisingly left Molineux, only to return after spending four months with Walsall. Quickly back into his stride, he helped Wolves win the FA Cup in 1893 and was leading scorer yet again in 1894–95 and 1895–96, the latter campaign seeing him (and Wolves) suffer more disappointment with a second FA Cup Final defeat. Nicknamed 'Woolf', he was capped only three times by England. He did, however, represent the Football League on four occasions and star in two international trials, although he deserved far more. He refused to sign a new contract with Wolves in 1898 and as a result moved to Southampton, completing the formalities in a waiting room on Snow Hill railway station, Birmingham. He became a star at The Dell, scoring 65 goals in 180 games in seven years. He played in two more FA Cup Finals (1900 and 1902), losing both, and won four Southern League Championship medals between 1899 and 1904. On his retirement in May 1905 Harry was appointed trainer of Portsmouth, a position he held until 1912. He later ran the Milton Arms pub near Fratton Park.

David Woodfield

Defender/forward: 273+3 apps, 15 goals.

Born: 11 October 1943, Leamington Spa, Warwickshire.

Career: WOLVES (January 1959–September 1971), Watford.

■ Dave Woodfield, one of Wolves' unsung heroes during his 12½ years at Molineux, could occupy a variety of positions, although centre-half was undoubtedly his best. Dark-haired with a solid physique, he was an old-fashioned defender: strong in the tackle and, most significantly, totally reliable. He joined Wolves as an amateur in 1959, turned professional in 1960 and, after being nurtured through the youth, intermediate and second XIs, made his League debut against Chelsea in April 1962. The following season he became a first-team regular, retaining his place (injuries apart) for four years. Disappointed with relegation in 1965, he buckled down to life in the Second Division and produced some superb displays in both defence and attack, and in 1966–67 he and his colleagues produced some excellent football to steer Wolves back into the top flight. Dave got to grips with First Division football but was now beginning to feel the pace and, with John McAlle added to the defence, he had to work overtime to retain his position. Battling on, he took his appearance record past the 275 mark before joining Watford for £30,000 in 1971. Unfortunately, a niggling knee injury eventually forced Dave into retirement in the summer of 1974 – shortly after a well-deserved testimonial match at Molineux.

Billy Wright, CBE

Half-back/inside-forward: 541 apps, 16 goals.

Born: 6 February 1924, Ironbridge, Shropshire. Died: 3 December 1994, Barnet.

Career: Cradley Heath, WOLVES (August 1938–May 1959), Leicester City guest during World War Two, England (105 full caps, 4 Victory caps, 4 England XI apps), Arsenal (manager), England Youth and Under-23 team (manager), WOLVES (director).

■ Billy Wright was only 14 years old when he made his debut as a forward for Wolves' B team against Walsall Wood in the Walsall Minor League, after being accepted on an eight-month trial by Major Frank Buckley. He made his first-team debut at the age of 15 in a 2–1 win at Notts County in 1939 and signed professional forms on his 17th birthday. However, World War Two forced the League/FA to suspend competitive football and, during the hostilities, Billy managed to appear in 112 regional games as well as guesting for Leicester with Jimmy Mullen. After the war, he settled into his football at Molineux and became one of the greatest defenders ever to play for the club and, indeed, for England, being the first footballer in history to win a century of caps for his country. He also played in four Victory internationals, represented an England XI on four occasions, played in 21 Inter-League games and played for the Rest of the United Kingdom. Ted Vizard converted him into a cool, calm and confident half-back, and later under Stan Cullis he skippered Wolves to victory in the 1949 FA Cup Final. Five years on and by now a regular in the England side, he lifted the League Championship trophy, following up with two more League titles in 1958 and 1959 before announcing his retirement on the eve of the 1959–60 season. He accumulated almost 500 League appearances for Wolves and played in over 650 first-team matches overall. As fair a player as you could ever wish to see, he was never dropped, cautioned or sent off and only absent through injury, illness or international calls; a true gentleman both on and off the field. In the summer of 1959 Bill received the CBE for services to football and then, in a blaze of publicity in October 1960, he was appointed manager of the England Youth team, later taking charge of the Under-23 side. In May 1962, with the press and media again taking full advantage of the story, Billy became manager of Arsenal, a position he held for four years. After that he controlled sports coverage on ATV until his retirement in 1989. He was then made an honorary member of the FA and also became a member of the Pilkington Commission on Television Broadcasting before joining the board of directors at Molineux in May 1990 – a position he held until his death in 1996. Billy married one of the Beverley sisters, Joy, and had a stand at Molineux named after him. Today there is a statue standing proudly outside the main entrance to the Wolves stadium – in recognition of the service he gave to the club over many years, first as a player and then as a director.

Wolves Managers

George Worrall*	1877–1885
John Addenbrooke*	1885–1922
George Jobey	1922–24
Albert Hoskins*	1924–26
Fred Scotchbrook	1926–27
Major Frank Buckley	1927–44
Ted Vizard	1944–48
Stan Cullis	1948–64
Andy Beattie	1964–65
Ronnie Allen	1966–68
Bill McGarry	1968–76
Sammy Chung	1976–78
John Barnwell	1978–81
Ian Greaves	1982
Graham Hawkins	1982–84
Tommy Docherty	1984–85
Bill McGarry	1985
Sammy Chapman	1985–86
Brian Little	1986
Graham Turner	1986–94
Graham Taylor	1994–95
Mark McGhee	1995–98
Colin Lee	1998–2000
Dave Jones	2001–04
Glenn Hoddle	2004–06
Mick McCarthy	2006 to date

* Served as secretary-manager

GEORGE WORRALL was one of Wolves' early players who acted as team manager, club secretary and committee member for a period of eight years from the summer of 1877 until April 1885. His position at the club was secretary rather than manager but he had a huge say regarding team selection. Born in Wolverhampton in 1855, he was a football man through and through, and after leaving office he remained a true and avid supporter of the team until his death in 1930.

JOHN ADDENBROOKE was Wolves' manager from August 1885 until June 1922. Always referred to as Jack, he was born in Wolverhampton on 6 June 1865 and for two years (1875–77) played for the St Luke's school team. He was actually appointed secretary of the side at the age of 10. He attended Saltley College, Birmingham, from the age of 14 and qualified as a teacher, taking a position at Bushbury School in Wolverhampton. During his time there he played for Wolves' reserve team, and then, shortly before the start of the 1885–86 season, he became the first paid secretary-manager of the club, a position he was to retain for 37 years. Unfortunately he was taken ill in June 1922 and within three days was declared unfit for work by Dr Wolverson. Allowed six months' leave, Addenbrooke never recovered and on 7 September 1922 died in his sleep, leaving George Jobey to take over his duties. During his time as manager, Wolves entered the Football League, moved to Molineux and twice won the FA Cup, as well as carrying off several local prizes including the Birmingham Senior, Lord Mayor of Birmingham Charity and the Staffordshire Senior Cups. In 1909, when the Football League celebrated its 21st anniversary, Addenbrooke and his counterpart at Aston Villa, George

Ramsay, were both presented with long service medals by the League. Besides being an exceptionally fine and dedicated office worker (he knew everything there was to know about being the secretary of a company), Addenbrooke also ran a tobacconists in Wolverhampton. And he could certainly spot a good footballer when he saw one. Among those he signed for Wolves (with the assistance of others, including scouts and ex-professionals) were: goalkeepers Tom Baddeley, Noel George, Tommy Lunn, Teddy Peers, Billy Rose and Billy Tennant; defenders Harry Allen, Dickie Baugh, Alf Bishop, Arthur Fletcher, George Garratly, Val Gregory, Jack Jones, George Kinsey, Billy Malpass, Charlie Mason, George Swift, the Reverend Kenneth Hunt, George Fleming and the versatile Billy Wooldridge; wingers Sammy Brooks, Billy Harrison, Jack Miller and Jack Pedley; and forwards Billy Beats, George Edmonds, Willie Halligan, George Hedley, Ted Pheasant, Harry Wood and David Wykes. Several of these players became internationals as well as giving Wolves wonderful service. Addenbrooke held the Molineux fortress manfully during World War One and was certainly responsible for arranging and overseeing major developments at the ground. When League football resumed in 1919, he was at the heart of everything – sorting out players' contracts, making a few extra signings and overseeing the general running of the club. A vice-president of the Staffordshire County FA, he served on the committee for 28 years and was without doubt a wonderful football man.

GEORGE JOBEY was manager at Molineux for two seasons, leaving in May 1924. He had as his assistant the former Sunderland and England forward George Holley, who had toured South Africa with the FA party in 1910. Given the official title of manager-coach, Jobey found the going exceedingly tough in his first season, as Wolves slipped into the Third Division North for the first time in the club's history. But surprisingly, and quite dramatically, he turned things around immediately and promotion was achieved at the first attempt, Wolves climbing back as champions. Born in Heddon near Newcastle upon Tyne in July 1885, as a player Jobey was of the zealous type, revealing no appreciable degree of outstanding ability. He served with Morpeth Harriers, Newcastle United (for whom he appeared in the 1911 FA Cup Final) and Arsenal, scoring the first-ever Arsenal goal at Highbury, versus Leicester Fosse in 1913. He then assisted Bradford (1914–15) and linked up with Hamilton Academical during World War One before winding down his career with Leicester City and finally Northampton Town, the last of these as player-coach. He quit football in April 1922 to enter the hotel business but was enticed back into the game following Addenbrooke's death. Jobey spent a year out of the game after leaving Molineux, returning as Derby County manager in July 1925. He remained at the Baseball Ground until 1938 but some years later a joint FA and Football League Commission, sitting at the Midland Hotel, Derby, found that during those 13 years Derby County and Jobey himself had paid out illegal bonuses and inducements to

certain players, balancing the club's books with some inventive entries. Jobey was found guilty and banned from football permanently. County's directors all received *sine die* suspensions and the club itself was fined £500. Although Jobey's ban was lifted in 1945, it was not until 1952 that he re-entered football, this time as manager of Mansfield Town, a position he held for only a short period of time. He died in Derby on 9 March 1962, aged 76.

ALBERT HOSKINS played as a forward for Freemantle FC (Hampshire), Southampton and Shrewsbury Town before joining Wolves in May 1908. He scored twice in 14 senior outings for the club, who released him in April 1909 when he signed for Dudley Town. He later assisted St Peter's FC, Darlaston and Wellington Town and returned to Wolves as assistant to secretary-manager Jack Addenbrooke in August 1919. He was perhaps disappointed not to be offered the manager's job when Addenbrooke died in the summer of 1922, but Hoskins nevertheless remained loyal to the club and continued as secretary for two years before being appointed secretary-manager in June 1924. In his first season in charge, Wolves, based in the Second Division, finished a creditable sixth and then fourth the following season. However, Hoskins surprisingly left Molineux in March 1926 to join Gillingham as secretary-manager. After a spell at Torquay United he worked as a trainer, coach and scout for a number of non-League clubs, but on the outbreak of war in 1939 he left football for good. He was born in Southampton in March 1885 and died in the same town on 6 February 1968.

FRED SCOTCHBROOK was a Lancastrian, born in Horwich near Bolton in April 1886, who followed his father (an ex-player) by joining Bolton Wanderers just before the start of World War One. However, he decided he wasn't good enough for League football and retired to become a coach at Burnden Park, later taking over as assistant-secretary before joining Stockport County as manager in November 1924. Unfortunately, Stockport finished a disappointing 19th in Division Two that season, only three points clear of relegation, and the team started their second season even worse, losing six of their first seven matches. Scotchbrook was subsequently sacked in February 1926 as County were staring relegation in the face, but his poor record did not deter Wolves from appointing him as their new manager the very next month. Though never given full control at Molineux, he did his best but became disheartened when the club's directors began to make decisions on a whim, which he could do nothing about. In fact, Scotchbrook blamed the directors for the club's lack of success and he left Molineux shortly after criticising club policy at the annual meeting in the summer of 1927. Quitting football for good, he returned to Lancashire where he died in 1959.

MAJOR FRANK BUCKLEY was born on 9 November 1883 in Urmston, Manchester, and was manager of Wolves for almost 17 years, from July 1927 until March 1944. Unfortunately, none of his sides ever won a major honour, although Wolves did come agonisingly close to completing the League and FA Cup double in 1939 when they finished runners-up in both competitions. They did lift the 1942 Wartime League Cup, but this was scant reward for one of the most famous managers in the history of the game. The Major – as he was called after his army service – won fame as a shrewd dealer in the transfer market. People said he was ahead of his time but his patriarchal, disciplined approach seemed to suit the era in which he managed. In 1898 he joined the army, and after serving in the Boer War became a professional with Aston Villa in 1903 but never made the first team. A rugged centre-half, he went on to appear in 165 League games for five other clubs: Manchester United, Manchester City, Birmingham, Derby County and Bradford City. He also assisted Brighton and Hove Albion and gained one England cap versus Ireland in 1914 before becoming a commanding officer in the Footballers' Battalion (the Middlesex Regiment). After his demob in 1919 he was appointed player-manager of Southern League side Norwich City but, following a crisis at the club which resulted in six directors resigning, he too quit the Canaries. Out of the game for three years, during which time he worked as a commercial traveller, he returned to football management with Blackpool, taking the hot seat at Molineux in the summer of 1927 as successor to Fred Scotchbrook. The Major immediately began to turn young unknowns into stars, and in 1932 Wolves regained their First Division status after trying for 26 years. Keeping the directors happy, he signed and developed some brilliant players including Stan Cullis, Dennis Westcott, Jimmy Mullen, Bryn Jones and a certain Billy Wright, although at first he didn't think Wright was tall or strong enough to become a footballer and sent him away to build up his strength. Over a period of four years, from 1935 to 1939, Wolves received a massive amount in transfer fees and it was all due to the Major's inspired dealings in the transfer market. However, with things going extremely well on the pitch, it came as a body blow, especially to him, when the team surprisingly lost 4–1 to underdogs Portsmouth in the 1939 FA Cup Final and also missed out on winning their first-ever League Championship in the same month. In 1944, after admitting that he was now 'feeling vulnerable', Buckley resigned as Wolves manager and later took charge of Blackpool, Notts County, Hull City,

Leeds United and Walsall before pulling out of the game in September 1955. Some of the Major's methods were certainly controversial, like his 'monkey gland injections' which, in effect, were simply inoculations against colds. He also sent players to see a psychologist in his search for that elusive self-confidence boost and he would often arrange for the pitch to be watered prior to a Wolves home game – simply because he loved playing on soft ground. The Major had five brothers, one of whom, Chris, also played for Aston Villa as well as Arsenal, and was chairman at Villa Park from 1955 to 1966. Regarded as one of the finest managers of all time, Major Frank Buckley died on 22 December 1964 in Walsall.

TED VIZARD served Bolton Wanderers for 21 years, up to 1931, and was among the first 11 players to be placed in the Lancashire club's Hall of Fame in 2002. Born in Cogan, South Wales, on 7 June 1889, he played rugby for Penarth and football for Barry Town before signing for Bolton in September 1910. He made his League debut before the turn of the year and never looked back, making the outside-left position his own for the next 18 seasons. In that time he made over 500 senior appearances for the Trotters, scoring 70 goals. He starred in two FA Cup Final victories, – 1923 (the first at Wembley) and 1926 – and also won 22 full caps for Wales. At the time of his retirement at the age of 41, Vizard was the oldest player ever to play for Bolton, a record broken in 1995 by Peter Shilton. He first took charge of Bolton's A team and the youth side before taking over from Sam Allen as manager of Swindon Town (1933), initially on a salary of £6 per week. Vizard's first action was to release almost the entire first-team squad, leaving only Arthur Briggs, Alec Lambie, Cyril Quinn and Harry Cousins – even the legendary Harry Morris was allowed to leave. He was given just £200 to spend on new players and after a promising first season, which saw Swindon finish eighth in the Third Division, performances began to deteriorate. Two seasons later in 1935–36, after a disastrous FA Cup defeat to non-League Southall and a final League placing of 19th, Vizard offered his resignation to the board but was persuaded to stay, and he guided the team to respectable mid-table positions over the following three seasons. Vizard also broke the four-figure transfer barrier for the first time, signing Ben Morton from Torquay United. In the summer of 1939, Vizard left the County Ground to take over the reins at Queen's Park Rangers, no doubt attracted by the reported £1,000 a year salary. He succeeded Billy Birrell at Loftus Road, but because of World War Two he never had the chance to manage them in a competitive game. In 1944 he replaced Major Buckley as manager of Wolves, being chosen ahead of more than 100 other applicaants. But despite taking the Wanderers to third place in the First Division in the first peacetime season in 1946–47, he was replaced by ex-player Stan Cullis in June 1948. Vizard later managed non-League side Cradley Heath before taking over a pub in Wolverhampton. He died on Christmas Day 1973, aged 84.

STAN CULLIS – see Star Players

ANDY BEATTIE was involved with more than 20 clubs during an exciting career in professional football. Born in the village of Kintore, Aberdeenshire, on 11 August 1913, he began his playing days with Kilmarnock before joining Preston North End as a full-time professional in 1935. He appeared in the 1937 and 1938 FA Cup Finals for the Deepdale club and won seven Scottish caps between April 1937 and December 1938, plus another five in wartime internationals. He also guested for Aldershot, Bradford City, Clapton Orient, Derby County, Leicester City, Manchester City, Northampton Town and Notts County during World War Two. On his retirement in May 1947, he was appointed secretary-manager of Barrow, but after producing a new-found team spirit he had a disagreement with the club chairman and resigned, only to be reinstated when the other directors forced the chairman to leave instead! After moving to Stockport County in a similar capacity in March 1949, he was enticed to Huddersfield Town in April 1952 and, although he was too late to stave off relegation, he guided the Terriers to promotion the following season. He twice served as team manager of Scotland, firstly from February to June 1954, when he took them to the World Cup Finals, and for a brief period in 1959–60. Resigning from his position with Huddersfield in 1956, Beattie then had a decent spell in charge of Carlisle United (from May 1958 to March 1960) before replacing Billy Walker in the hot seat at Nottingham Forest. He spent three seasons at the City Ground prior to joining Plymouth Argyle as caretaker manager in October 1963, saving the Pilgrims from relegation by the smallest of margins. In November 1964 Beattie was appointed caretaker manager of Wolves, and during his first season at Molineux he used 28 players as the campaign ended in relegation to the Second Division. Following a 9–3 defeat

Andy Beattie, pictured here on the left.

at Southampton and with his wife quite ill, Beattie decided that he had had enough and resigned. In December 1965 he joined Notts County as general manager and later held coaching and scouting positions with Sheffield United, Brentford, Wolves again, Walsall and Liverpool. Enjoying a long and successful career in the game, he left his mark on many clubs in the Football League. Beattie died in Rushcliffe on 20 September 1983, aged 70.

RONNIE ALLEN was born in Fenton, Stoke-on-Trent on 15 January 1929. He was soon finding the net in local junior football and in 1944 signed for Port Vale. He top scored in 1947–48 with 13 goals, including hat-tricks in the wins over Aldershot and Watford and went on to net 38 times in 135 games before transferring to West Bromwich Albion for £20,100 in March 1950. He scored on his Baggies debut in a 1–1 draw at home to Wolves and over the next 11 seasons he bagged a then club record 234 goals in 458 first-team appearances. He also won five full England caps and scored twice when Albion beat Preston 3–2 to lift the FA Cup in 1954. In May 1961 Allen

moved to Crystal Palace and scored 37 goals in 109 games before retiring. He then became coach at Molineux before taking over as manager when Andy Beattie departed. When Allen took charge, Wolves were struggling near the foot of the Second Division but he bought wisely, signing both Mike Bailey and Derek Dougan, who in 1966–67 helped the team to promotion. However, when things started to go wrong at Molineux, Allen was sacked and subsequently spent four years abroad managing Athletic Bilbao (1969–71) and Sporting Lisbon (1972–73) before returning to England to take charge at Walsall. He later went back to The Hawthorns, first as scouting adviser (January 1977) and then as manager (from December 1977). After coaching the Saudi Arabia national side (1978–80) and also Panathinaikos of Athens (1980–81), he returned to manage Albion for a second time, leading the Baggies to the semi-finals of both the League Cup and FA Cup competitions in season 1981–82. He actually played his last game of football at the age of 66 – for Albion in a friendly against Cheltenham Town in 1995, when he was employed by the club as a part-time coach. Allen died at Great Wyrley, Walsall, on 9 June 2001.

BILL McGARRY, a well-balanced wing-half, was also discovered by Port Vale in 1945. He played in over 150 games for the Valiants before switching to Huddersfield Town for £12,000 in March 1951. He soon established himself at a higher level and in 1954 won the first of four England caps when he played in the World Cup Finals in Switzerland. He was also capped for England B, played for the Football League and went on the FA's 1956 South African tour. Bill scored 26 goals in 381 games for the Yorkshire club before becoming Bournemouth's first player-manager, appointed in March 1961. After that he managed Watford before taking charge of Ipswich Town in October 1964. In 1967–68 he guided the Portman Road club to the Second Division Championship, but in November 1968 he quit to take over at Wolves. Renowned for his competitiveness as a player, McGarry certainly carried that approach into his managerial career at Molineux and he successfully led Wolves into Europe, where they reached the Final of the UEFA Cup, beaten over two legs by Spurs in 1972. He also celebrated a League Cup Final win in 1974 before being sacked in the summer of 1976 after the club had been relegated. McGarry later coached in Saudi Arabia and managed Newcastle United as well as having spells as a coach for Brighton, a coach for Power Dynamo FC (Zambia) and also serving as manager of the Zambian national team. He then returned to Molineux for a second spell as manager but spent only 61 days in charge. Disillusioned, he quit the game before returning to South Africa to coach Bophuthatswana. McGarry died in March 2005 after a long illness.

SAMMY CHUNG, whose father was Chinese and his mother English, was a utility player who began his career as a part-time centre-forward with Headington United (now Oxford United). He later joined Reading but didn't sign professional forms until he had completed his national service. After a spell with Norwich City

he joined Watford and played in 240 games for them, gaining his FA coaching badge while with that club. On leaving Watford and his role as player-coach, he joined Ipswich Town as coach under Bill McGarry, who had also been his boss at Watford. When McGarry became Wolves manager, Chung followed him to Molineux as trainer-coach before succeeding him in June 1976. His time wasn't a happy one, and with the fans calling for his head he was sacked. Chung later coached in the UAE, managed Stoke City and Tamworth, scouted for Blackburn Rovers, managed Doncaster Rovers and also served as director of football in Barbados.

JOHN BARNWELL was born on 24 December 1938 in High Heaton, Newcastle upon Tyne, and was manager of Wolves from November 1978 until November 1981. As a player he served with Bishop Auckland, Arsenal, Nottingham Forest and Sheffield United and after retiring in June 1971 took over as coach at Hereford United. He held a similar position with Peterborough United, whom he also managed, before taking over the reins at Molineux from Sammy Chung, having missed out on becoming boss of Sunderland when that job went to ex-Wolves player Ken Knighton. A powerful, workmanlike and very effective inside-forward, he moved to Highbury in 1955 and scored 24 goals in 155 appearances for Arsenal, staying until 1964 when he transferred to Nottingham Forest for £30,000. He added a further 25 goals to his tally (in 201 games) during his six years at the City Ground before netting twice in 13 outings for Sheffield United. An England Youth international, Barnwell later gained one Under-23 cap as well as representing the RASC during his national service. He quickly turned things round at Molineux and towards the end of his first season came mightily close to taking Wolves to the FA Cup Final, losing in the semi-final to his former club Arsenal at Villa Park. However, shortly afterwards Barnwell almost lost his life in a road traffic accident which saw him hospitalised with a fractured skull. Richie Barker took over as caretaker boss with player-coach Brian Garvey assisting too. Thankfully Barnwell recovered in time for the start of the new season and almost immediately bolstered his defence by signing the Liverpool and England star Emlyn Hughes for £90,000. Soon afterwards he had the world talking when he smashed the British transfer record by selling midfielder Steve Daley to Manchester City for £1,437,500 (5 September) and then, 72 hours later, paid out £1,150,000 for

the Aston Villa striker Andy Gray. Winger David Thomas also arrived from QPR and all of a sudden there was a buzz of excitement within the club. The team's League performances, however, were rather inconsistent, and Barnwell wasn't all that happy. Yet in the League Cup it was a completely different story, as slowly but surely Wolves edged their way to the Final. On 15 March 1980, Barnwell proudly led his players out at Wembley to take on his former club Nottingham Forest, managed by Brian Clough. A tight game ended in triumph for Wolves, Gray's tap-in goal deciding the contest to book Wolves a place in the UEFA Cup. Barnwell was very optimistic about 1980–81 and, in an effort to improve his squad, he made enquiries about the availability of the French international Michel Platini and Poland's Zbigniew Boniek but had to settle for the Uruguayan Rafael Villazan instead. Wolves finished 18th in the First Division, went out of the League Cup and UEFA Cup competitions early on and lost in the FA Cup semi-final to Tottenham Hotspur after a replay. Despite a cluster of new signings, the first half of the 1981–82 campaign was very disappointing and after a series of defeats Wolves found themselves at the wrong end of the table. As a result Barnwell lost his job, his contract being terminated. After a coaching appointment in Saudi Arabia, he took over as coach of AEK Athens, only to be banned from working in Greece in January 1984. Three years later he became manager of Notts County and was in charge of Walsall in 1989–90 before becoming a consultant at Northampton Town (1992–93). Appointed Chief Executive of the Football League Managers' Association in July 1997, Barnwell has also been involved with Grantham Town.

IAN GREAVES joined Manchester United as a full-back in the early 1950s but found his first-team opportunities rare. He did win a League Championship medal in 1955–56 by appearing in the last 14 games of the season, but it was the Munich air crash which provided the unhappy opening for his breakthrough. He played in the 1958 FA Cup Final, but after 75 appearances for United he moved to Lincoln City before ending his playing career with Oldham Athletic. Greaves' first managerial post was with Huddersfield Town and in 1970 he took them to the Second Division title. After two seasons in the top flight, the Yorkshire club suffered successive relegations to the Third Division, and after a boardroom struggle he walked out to take charge at Bolton Wanderers. He took Bolton to the semi-finals of the League Cup in 1977 and the following season to the Second Division Championship. In January 1980, with Bolton firmly rooted to the foot of the First Division, he was dismissed. After a spell in charge at Oxford United, he became manager at Wolves. Although he was highly regarded by the club's supporters, Greaves failed to halt Wolves' decline. After only five wins in six months at Molineux, he was sacked by the new regime led by Derek Dougan. In 1983 he became manager of Mansfield Town, leading them to promotion and victory at Wembley in the Freight Rover Trophy Final. As a club manager Greaves was in charge for 855 games.

GRAHAM HAWKINS began his playing career as a central-defender in the First Division with Wolves and made his League debut against West Bromwich Albion in October 1964. He was never a regular at Molineux, and after only 35 appearances in four seasons he moved to Preston North End. Seen as a successor to Tony Singleton, he did not make too many appearances in his early days owing to the misfortune of being injured on his debut. He was one of the club's youngest-ever captains at 22, and went on to make 245 League appearances for the Deepdale club before joining neighbours Blackburn Rovers in June 1974. There he played 109 League games before moving to Port Vale, where he ended his playing career. After a spell as assistant manager at

Shrewsbury Town, he was employed by Derek Dougan when the Irish international became chief executive at Molineux and helped the club regain their top-flight status as runners-up to Queen's Park Rangers in 1982–83. He made some shrewd signings but after Wolves failed to win any of their first 16 games in the First Division and were relegated straight back, it came as no surprise that he was sacked.

Glasgow-born **TOMMY DOCHERTY** had worked his way up through Celtic's junior ranks and served with the Highland Light Infantry for two years in Palestine before joining Preston North End in November 1949 for £4,000. A fearless wing-half, he was capable of dispossessing the best of opponents and instantly turning defence into attack with the drive of an aggressive ball player. A terror in the tackle, 'The Doc' had the cure for most inside-forwards. He won the first of 25 Scottish caps against Wales in 1952, and after playing in 324 out of a possible 356 games, missing 21 through injury and seven through international calls and playing in an FA Cup Final, he moved to Arsenal for £28,000 in August 1958. Tragically ironic for Docherty was the misfortune of breaking a leg when playing for the Gunners against Preston. He packed away his boots to become senior coach to Chelsea before being appointed caretaker manager in September 1961. Four months later his appointment was confirmed on a permanent basis and in 1967 he took the young Chelsea side to the FA Cup Final, which they lost 2–1 to Spurs. One of the game's most controversial characters, he was an outspoken and much-travelled manager. He left Chelsea in 1967 and after a year in charge of Rotherham United he took on the challenge of Queen's Park Rangers, but he left within a month. He then joined Aston Villa but, following one of the worst seasons in the club's history, he was sacked in January 1970. After a spell with Porto he was appointed Scotland's manager, giving them an immediate boost, before succeeding Frank O'Farrell at Manchester United. In four and a half seasons at Old Trafford he assembled an exciting side and led them to success in the FA Cup Final of 1977. He later managed Derby County, QPR (for a second time) and, after a spell in Australia, Preston North End (again). In June 1984 he was appointed manager of Wolves but the club finished bottom of the Second Division in 1984–85, and though Docherty tried his best to save them, a run of 21 games without a win meant the situation couldn't be salvaged and in July 1985 he was sacked. Docherty is now a well-established after-dinner speaker.

SAMMY CHAPMAN was an attacking wing-half and a great favourite at Mansfield Town, where he scored 41 goals in 168 games. After a spell with Portsmouth he became coach at Crewe Alexandra before joining Wolves as chief scout. Following the departure of Tommy Docherty, Chapman was appointed caretaker manager until the arrival of Bill McGarry in September 1985. He was then certainly the surprise choice to take over on a full-time basis when McGarry left after just 61 days. Wolves had just been relegated to the Third Division for the first time since 1923, but sadly he was not cut out to be boss again and when relegation was suffered again at the end of 1985–86 he was relieved of his duties. He later worked as a scout and youth development officer at Leicester and then became coach of Broadbridge Heath FC (West Sussex).

BRIAN LITTLE began his career with Aston Villa, where he played an important part in the club's FA Youth Cup success. He went on to win League Cup-winners' medals in 1975 and 1977, scoring two of Villa's goals in the 3–2 win over Everton in the third match of that Final at Old Trafford. He was the Second Division's leading scorer in 1974–75 with 20 goals, including a hat-trick in a 5–0 win over Oldham Athletic. At the end of that season, he won his only England cap when he came on as a substitute for the final 10 minutes of the match against Wales at Wembley. Forced to give up playing football on medical grounds, he had a spell working in the club's promotion department before moving to Molineux as first-team coach. Little then replaced Sammy Chapman as manager, but was replaced by Graham Turner a few weeks later. After leaving the club, Little was employed as a coach by Middlesbrough before going on to manage Darlington, whom he guided back into the Football League as Nationwide Conference Champions in 1990, Leicester City (1991–94), his former club Aston Villa (1994–98), Stoke City (1998–99), West Bromwich Albion (1999–2000), Hull City, Tranmere Rovers and Wrexham, the latter slipping out of the Football League when he was in charge (2008). Little was born in Peterlee, County Durham, on 25 November 1953. His brother, Alan, also played for Aston Villa (1971–74) as well as a number of other League clubs before he too took up management, first with York City and then with Southend United.

GRAHAM TURNER was born in Ellesmere Port, Cheshire, on 5 October 1947. An England Youth international, he signed professional forms for Wrexham in July 1965 and made 77 League appearances before joining Chester in January 1968. A hard-working player, tenacious in the tackle, and equally effective in defence or midfield, he netted five goals in 218 League outings for Chester before switching his allegiance to Shrewsbury Town in January 1973, signed for a then record fee of £30,000. The Shrews were relegated to the Fourth Division in 1974 but gained promotion as runners-up straightaway, and four years later Turner was appointed player-manager at Gay Meadow, going on to appear in almost 400 games for the club, 355 of them in the Football League, before retiring in 1984. In 1978–79 Shrewsbury won the Third Division Championship with 61 points, their success being based on a strong defence, which was to become Turner's priority to a certain extent when he became Wolves' manager in 1986. However, before he set foot inside Molineux, Turner spent two moderate years in charge of First Division side Aston Villa, leading them into the League Cup semi-finals before he was sacked in September 1986. A month later he replaced ex-Villa star Brian Little in the hot seat at Wolves, and after a steady start he transformed the Wanderers from an ordinary run-of-the-mill Fourth Division team into one capable, perhaps, of holding its own in the top flight (if they had got there). He took over when Wolves were at their lowest ebb, having just been relegated from the Third Division. He was given a tough time by the passionate fans early on, especially after non-League side Chorley knocked Wolves out of the FA Cup, but he gradually won them over – especially after he recruited Steve Bull and Andy Thompson and then Ally Robertson and Robbie Dennison, all from neighbours West Bromwich Albion, for a relatively small amount of money. And everyone knows what 'Bully' did for Wolves, proving to be the bargain of the century as far as all of Wolves'

supporters are concerned. Turner also signed some significant other players, among them Paul Birch, Gary Bellamy, Paul Cook, Mark Venus, Shane Westley and Derek Mountfield. At the end of the 1986–87 season Turner got Wolves into the Fourth Division Play-offs but they surprisingly they lost to Aldershot. The following season, however, the team walked away with the Fourth Division Championship and doubled up by winning the Sherpa Van Trophy at Wembley. Then, in 1988–89, they won the Third Division title in style, finishing eight points clear of second-placed Sheffield United. At this juncture Molineux was being completely redesigned, which certainly hampered Graham's ambitions in the transfer market. As a result, and a lot of people will agree with this assumption, it meant that Wolves missed out on a chance of reaching the top flight under his control. After a disappointing run of results at the start of 1991–92 it was thought that Turner would be dismissed, but he got the team rolling again on the pitch and the rumours quickly died down. Unfortunately Wolves then had a very moderate 1992–93 campaign, one of the main reasons being that top scorer Bull was completely out of form. Turner, nevertheless, kept his job until March 1994 when, after seven and a half years of dedicated service, he was shown the door, replaced by caretaker manager Peter Shirtliff. Of his 412 games in charge, Wolves won 179, drew 109 and lost 124, scoring 634 goals and conceding 476. He was out of football for a quite some time before returning as manager of Hereford United in June 1996. Unfortunately, under his control the Bulls lost their Football League status in May 1997 after failing to win their last home game of the season against Brighton and Hove Albion. In 1999 Graham was appointed chairman and director for football at Edgar Street and later took over again as team manager, guiding the club back into the Football League in 2006 and promotion in 2008.

After a lengthy playing career with Scunthorpe United (amateur), Grimsby Town and Lincoln City, **GRAHAM TAYLOR** took his first managerial appointment with Lincoln in December 1972 and four years later guided the Imps to the Fourth Division title. In June 1977 he received an offer he couldn't refuse from Sir Elton John to take over at Watford. He stayed at Vicarage Road for over 10 years, steering the Hornets from the Fourth Division to runners'-up spot in the First Division in 1982–83 and the following season leading them out in their first-ever FA Cup Final, which they lost to Everton. Deciding he needed a fresh challenge, he became manager of Aston Villa in July 1987. At that time the club were in the Second Division and by the end of his first season in charge they were back in the First, after finishing runners-up to Millwall. After Villa just escaped relegation in 1988–89, they amazed everyone by finishing second behind Liverpool the very next season. His efforts saw him leave Villa Park in May 1990 to take over from Bobby Robson as England manager. However, his career hit rock-bottom at the European Championships of 1992, and within days of England failing to qualify for the

1994 World Cup Finals he had resigned. In April 1994 he was appointed manager of Wolves and in his first season took them to fourth place in Division One and into the Play-offs. But despite beating Bolton Wanderers 2–1 at home in the first leg of the semi-final, they lost the return fixture 2–0. Expectations were high for the 1995–96 season, especially as money had been spent, but performances out on the pitch left a lot to be desired and certainly didn't match up to the financial outlay. As a result, in December 1995 Taylor departed, to be replaced by Mark McGhee. Taylor later returned to Vicarage Road as general manager and helped the Hornets win promotion to the Premier League and also managed Villa once more in 2002–03.. He is now a match summariser, covering games for Sky Sports, ITV and Radio Five Live. Taylor was born in Worksop on 15 September 1944.

MARK McGHEE was born on 20 May 1957 in Glasgow. He played for Cumbernauld Burgh, Bristol City (1973), Greenock Morton (1975), Newcastle United (signed for £150,000, December 1977), Aberdeen (£80,000, March 1979), SV Hamburg (£285,000, May 1984), Celtic (£200,000, November 1985), Newcastle United again (£200,000, July 1989), IK Braga, Sweden (April 1991) and Reading (player-manager, May 1991). He was voted the Scottish PFA Players' Player of the Year in 1982 as well as gaining four caps and scoring two goals for the Scotland national team. After his spell in charge of Reading, he managed Leicester City before taking over the reins at Wolves in December 1995. On his departure from Molineux he became manager of Millwall and later took charge of Brighton and Hove Albion, appointed in October 2003 after Steve Coppell had moved to one of McGhee's former clubs, Reading. In his first season at Brighton, the team gained promotion to the Football League Championship, having been relegated the previous season. McGhee's popularity surged, with the humorous terrace chant of 'Drinking Pints of Whisky, Mark McGhee' (sung to the tune of The Beatles' *Let It Be*) being enjoyed by both fans and staff alike, as well as pundits working on Sky's *Soccer Saturday*. On 17 April 2006, a 2–0 home defeat by Sheffield Wednesday condemned Brighton to relegation to League One, and several poor performances that season saw many fans turn against McGhee. In early September 2006, McGhee was sacked by Brighton after nearly three years with the club. His biggest successes as a manager include winning the Division Two title with Reading in 1994 and Millwall in 2001, as well as reaching the FA Cup semi-final with Wolves in 1998. He also won the Division Two Play-off Final with Brighton in 2004 and during the 2006–07 season was linked with the vacant managerial post at Irish club Bohemians. He then became manager of Motherwell, 2007–08.

COLIN LEE was born on 12 June 1956 in Torquay, Devon. He began his football career as an apprentice with Bristol City, turning professional in July 1974, but failed to break into the first team. He joined Hereford United on loan in November 1974, playing nine times before returning to the reserves at Ashton Gate. He moved to Torquay United in January 1977, quickly establishing himself in Frank O'Farrell's side and attracting attention from clubs at a higher level. In October 1977, after 14 goals in 35 games, he left Plainmoor to join Tottenham Hotspur for £60,000, making an immediate impact by scoring four goals on his debut in a 9–0 win over Bristol Rovers. In January 1980 he moved to Chelsea for a fee of £200,000, having scored 18 times in 62 games for Spurs. He stayed at Stamford Bridge for over seven years, scoring 36 goals in 185 League games and playing as a central-defender towards the end of his time there. In July 1987 a fee of £17,500 took him to Brentford, where he combined playing with being youth development officer. He retired from playing in the summer of 1989 after one goal in 24 games. He was later appointed youth coach at Watford, taking over as manager in March 1990. He was sacked in November of the following season after a dismal start saw Watford win only two games when they had been hoping for a promotion challenge in the Second Division. In 1991 Lee returned to the game as youth coach at Reading, later becoming assistant manager to Mark McGhee. He helped them win the Division Two Championship in 1994 and followed McGhee to Leicester a few months later. When McGhee ended his year-long reign at Filbert Street to take charge of Wolves, he again followed McGhee. During Lee's time as coach, Wolves were semi-finalists in the Division One Play-offs and the FA Cup, and Lee was promoted to the manager's seat in November 1998 when McGhee was sacked, his initial caretaker spell beginning with a 6–1 win against Bristol City at Ashton Gate. The next two seasons saw Wolves just miss out on the Division One Play-offs, and he was sacked in December 2000 with the Midlanders struggling in the bottom half of the division. After leaving Molineux he joined Leeds United as a scout, a job he held until March 2001, when he was called in by Torquay United chairman Mike Bateson as a consultant to the under-pressure manager Wes Saunders in a desperate battle to keep Torquay out of the Conference. When Saunders was sacked soon after (on 28 March 2001), Lee took over as caretaker manager until the end of the season and guided the side to the heights of 21st place and safety, thanks to a nerve-wracking win at Barnet on the final day of the season which saw their opponents relegated. After much negotiating at the end of the season, Lee verbally agreed to become the new manager of Torquay. However, on 2 July, the day on which he was expected to formally sign his contract, he turned down the offer, leaving Torquay managerless less than a week before the start of pre-season training. The reason he gave was that he was still looking for a job at a higher level, although in November 2001 he was still scouting for Leeds United, as well as working for both television and radio. The following month he was appointed assistant manager at Second Division Wigan Athletic and in January 2002, Lee was named as manager of Division One strugglers Walsall, and against all odds kept them clear of relegation for the next two seasons. However, he was sacked in March 2004 after allegedly talking to Plymouth Argyle about the possibility of replacing Paul Sturrock as manager, and his successor Paul Merson was unable to stave off relegation. While Walsall actually gave permission for Lee to speak to Plymouth, and Lee publicly turned the job down, Walsall owner Jeff Bonser claimed that if Lee was truly committed then he wouldn't have even spoken to Plymouth. He said that, as his actions were tantamount to misconduct, he would not receive any compensation (though Bonser eventually paid up Lee's contract after intervention from the League Managers' Association). Lee began his fourth full-time manager's job in July 2005 with Millwall, succeeding Steve Claridge, who had been sacked after just 36 days at the helm by the club's new owners. But Millwall were bottom for much of the first half of the 2005–06 Championship campaign, and just before Christmas Lee became director of football. Defender David Tuttle took over the managerial duties, with Lee leaving Millwall in January 2006. A year later he returned to the coaching staff at struggling Torquay United.

DAVE JONES was born in Liverpool on 17 August 1956 and, like most professional managers in the game today, enjoyed a career as a player. He started out as a defender with Everton, whom he served for seven years, during which time he represented England at Youth and Under-21 levels. He moved from Goodison Park to Coventry City in 1981 for £275,000 but picked up a knee injury which threatened to end his football career. After regaining his fitness,

Jones spent two seasons with FC Seiko in Hong Kong and one with Preston before retiring to become assistant manager at Mossley AFC. In July 1990 he was appointed Stockport County's youth-team manager before taking charge of the first team when Danny Bergara left in March 1995. He successfully guided County into the First Division (now the Championship) via an automatic promotion place in 1997 and this success brought him to the attention of Southampton, who offered him a managerial contract in 1999. However, his reign was rocked in 2000 by his arrest on charges of child abuse during his employment as a care worker in the late 1980s. The case put tremendous strain on Jones, who was forced to defend his case back on Merseyside while managing a team based several hundred miles away on the south coast. In January 2000 Southampton decided to suspend him on full pay until the case was resolved, with Glenn Hoddle taking over his managerial duties. When the case eventually came to court, it was thrown out in its first week – the judge recording a 'not guilty' verdict and commenting that the case should never have reached the trial stage. Southampton paid off the remainder of Jones' contract and he was free to leave the club. Jones contended that this amounted to unfair dismissal and took the case to industrial tribunal but their decision was upheld. He took over at Wolves in January 2001 and guided the team to 12th position in the table that season. In 2001–02 he took them to a clear 11-point lead over their arch-rivals West Bromwich Albion but a poor run of results from March onwards saw an automatic promotion place slip by. Thankfully, the very next season Jones was over the moon as Wolves reached the Play-off Final and qualified for the Premiership after beating Sheffield United 3–0 at the Millennium Stadium. Back in the top flight for the first time in 19 years, Wolves failed to cope with a higher grade of football and were relegated to the Championship after one season. Following a poor run of form at the start of the 2004–05 campaign, Jones was sacked in the November and the following year took over as manager of Cardiff City. During his first season in charge the Bluebirds achieved a respectable mid-table placing and in 2006–07 they were doing pretty well in the top group before eventually fading away and finishing in mid-table. However, the 2007–08 season brought a trip to Wembley Stadium for the FA Cup Final, which Portsmouth won 1–0.

GLENN HODDLE was born on 27 October 1957 in Hayes, Middlesex. He was signed as an apprentice by Tottenham Hotspur in April 1974 and turned professional 12 months later. He scored on his full debut for Spurs and also for England when winning the first of his 53 full caps against Bulgaria in a European Championship qualifier at Wembley in November 1979. An FA Cup winner in 1981 and 1982, his penalty in the latter Final replay beat QPR 1–0. His 590th and last outing for Spurs came in the 1987 FA Cup Final, which Coventry City won 3–2. Soon afterwards Hoddle moved to the French club AS Monaco for £750,000 and played under Arsene Wenger, gaining a French First Division Championship-winners' medal before returning to England with Chelsea in January 1991. Unfortunately, he was plagued by injury at Stamford Bridge and left to become player-manager of Swindon Town eight weeks later. He scored for the Robins in the Division One Play-off Final as they reached the Premier League in 1993. Following that triumph he returned to Chelsea as player-manager (signed for £75,000), helping the Blues reach the FA Cup Final in 1994 (where they were beaten 4–0 by Manchester United). Hoddle succeeded Terry Venables as England coach after Euro '96, going on to take the team to the 1998 World Cup in France following a 0–0 draw with Italy in Rome. Unfortunately, England lost in the second round of the World Cup to Argentina on penalties and afterwards Hoddle insisted that his only mistake had been to leave faith healer Eileen Drewery in England! And when Hoddle's book *World Cup Diaries* was published, the contents caused controversy and consternation. Leading figures accused him of betraying his players after he revealed certain incidents, including Gascoigne's reaction at being dropped from the squad. Further controversy plagued Hoddle after an alleged row with striker Alan Shearer over the team's tactics in a 3–0 win over Luxembourg, and he faced widespread criticism following alleged remarks he made about disabled people. In an interview with *The Times* newspaper, he suggested disabled people were paying for sins in a previous life. He was sacked as England coach by the FA in August 1998 and was out of the game until being recruited as manager by Southampton in January 2000, a position he held until April 2001 when he returned 'home' to White Hart Lane as Spurs manager. He remained in charge until July 2003, and after a spell as a TV matchday summariser he was handed the manager's job at Wolves in December 2004, but failed to produce the goods and was replaced by Mick McCarthy for the 2006–07 season, having seen the team finish ninth and seventh respectively in the Championship during his term in office.

MICK McCARTHY was handed the manager's job at Molineux in July 2006 – only a few weeks after being sacked as boss of relegated Sunderland. Born in Barnsley on 7 February 1959, McCarthy made his League debut for his home-town club in 1977. A strong central-defender, he amassed 315 appearances for the Tykes before joining Manchester City in December 1983. He switched to Celtic in May 1987 after adding a further 163 appearances to his tally and, following a spell with the French club Olympique Lyon (from June 1989 to March 1990), he ended his playing days at Millwall, retiring as a player in May 1991 to become assistant manager and coach at The Den. He made well over 500 club appearances. McCarthy's father, Charles, was Irish, meaning that his son was eligible for the Republic of Ireland's national team, and after making his international debut in 1984 he went on to win 57 caps, being a well-respected captain for his side. Perhaps the biggest feat for 'Captain Fantastic' was the second-round penalty shoot-out win over Romania in Italia '90 which took Eire into a crunch tie with the hosts in the quarter-final. Although Ireland were beaten 1–0 they were resilient opponents and were considered unfortunate not to progress to the semi-finals. McCarthy succeeded Bruce Rioch as Millwall manager in March 1992 and remained with the Lions for four years, during which time he was a relative success. No doubt this went in his favour when he was appointed successor to Jack Charlton as Republic of Ireland manager in February 1996. Millwall went on to be relegated that season under Jimmy Nicholl. Despite failure to qualify for the 1998 World Cup or for Euro 2000, McCarthy retained his job. The Republic of Ireland qualified for the 2002 World Cup in Korea and Japan, but their tournament was overshadowed by a very public and bitter spat between McCarthy and one of the team's star players, Roy Keane, who was sent home by the manager without having kicked a ball. McCarthy was criticised by some for his handling of the player. Nevertheless, he had a successful campaign, reaching the second round only to be eliminated by Spain in a penalty shoot-out. The general feeling in Ireland was to get McCarthy out as quickly as possible, and 'Keano' back in. The media's vilification became increasingly intense and personal, and after a poor start to their qualifying campaign for Euro 2004, McCarthy resigned from the post on 5 November 2002. During his time in charge, Eire won 29, drew 19 and lost 20 of the 68 games played. In mid-March 2003 McCarthy was appointed manager of struggling Sunderland as an immediate replacement for Howard Wilkinson, who was sacked after six successive Premiership defeats left the club facing near-certain relegation. McCarthy could not stop Sunderland's slide, and the Black Cats were relegated at the end of the season. However, he largely escaped blame, and was retained as manager. The following season, McCarthy got Sunderland into the First Division promotion Play-offs, but the team lost in a penalty shoot-out to Crystal Palace after the London club scored a disputed stoppage-time equaliser. This was a remarkable achievement considering the players sold and huge debt that the club were in. McCarthy then went on to complete a miraculous recovery in 2004–05 when Sunderland secured automatic promotion to the Premiership as champions. After a disappointing 2005–06 season that left the club 16 points from safety with only ten games remaining, McCarthy was dismissed as manager in March 2006. Several members of the media and certainly the supporters did not believe the problem lay with McCarthy, blaming the board instead, with chairman Bob Murray reluctant to release funds needed to survive in the top flight. Kevin Ball was appointed caretaker manager for the remainder of the season. On 21 July 2006 McCarthy bounced back into football when he was appointed manager of Wolves, taking over from Hoddle, who had departed a fortnight earlier. He was officially unveiled as the new boss three days later at a press conference at Molineux, and then, in his first season in charge, McCarthy guided Wolves into the Championship Play-offs where, disappointingly, they lost to arch-rivals West Bromwich Albion in the semi-final.

CARETAKER MANAGERS

For the seven games from 19 September to 31 October 1964, following the sacking of Stan Cullis, the team was chosen by the training staff in consultation with the directors, until Andy Beattie officially moved into office.

Ex-player Jack Dowen (then the club's trainer) was briefly in charge before Ronnie Allen took over in 1965, Dowen and coach Gerry Summers were placed in charge of the team against Newcastle United on 23 November 1968 prior to the arrival of manager Bill McGarry.

Senior coach Brian Garvey acted as caretaker manager for two League games on 11 and 18 November 1978 before John Barnwell took charge.

Ian Ross held office as caretaker manager for four games between 16 January and 16 February prior to the arrival at Molineux of Ian Greaves.

Jim Barron had a two-week spell as caretaker manager covering five League games from 28 April to 12 May 1984 – then Tommy Docherty took over the reins.

Brian Little was in charge of the team from August to October 1986.

Peter Shirtliff was handed control of the team during March 1984, between the reigns of the two Grahams, Turner and Taylor.

Bobby Downes was caretaker boss for some four weeks, from mid-November to mid-December 1995.

Colin Lee took over on a short-term basis from Mark McGhee in November 1998.

John Ward was briefly in charge during December 2000–January 2001 – after Lee's departure.

Stuart Gray was caretaker manager at Molineux twice: in December 2004, before Hoddle's appointment, and prior to McCarthy's arrival for the 2006–07 season.

RESERVE-TEAM MANAGER

In July 1892 Wolves appointed Harry Dillard as the club's first ever second-team manager. He held the position until 1918.

PLAYER TO MANAGER

Several men who did well as players with Wolves later became League club managers. Among them were Mike Bailey, Jock Basford, Phil Chard, Steve Claridge, Keith Curle, Peter Daniel, Fred Davies, Keith Downing, Darren Ferguson, Ron Flowers, Bobby Gould (won the FA Cup with Wimbledon in 1988), Jack Hamilton, Ray Hankin, John Harris, Joe Harvey, George Hedley, Kenny Hibbitt, Don Howe (amateur with Wolves), Emlyn Hughes OBE, Paul Ince, Eric Jones, Robert Kelly, Andy King, Ken Knighton, Jim McCalliog, Angus McLean, Jimmy Melia (took Brighton & Hove Albion to the 1983 FA Cup Final), Rob Newman, Graham Rodger, Ian Ross, brothers Arthur and Jack Rowley, John Rudge (spent 15 years in charge of Port Vale), Peter Shirtliff, Paul Simpson, Jack Smith (guided West Bromwich Albion to promotion from Division Two in 1949), Cyril Spiers, George Swift, Frank Taylor, Jack Taylor, Harry Thompson, Les Wilson (manager of the Canadian national team), Peter Withe and Billy Wright.

SIR JACK HAYWARD

Although he was never in the frame to become manager at Molineux, Sir Jack Hayward has, for many years, been affectionately known as 'Mr Wolverhampton Wanderers'. Born on 14 June 1923 at Dunstall, Wolverhampton, the multi-millionaire businessman, who has been an avid supporter since he was a boy, bought the club in May 1990 for £2.1 million from Gallagher Estates, and immediately placed his son Jonathan and former player Billy Wright on the board of directors. He quickly set about redeveloping Molineux and over the next seven years ploughed almost £20 million into making the ground a 28,500 all-seater stadium with facilities on a par with those of most Premiership clubs.

A pupil at Stowe Public School, he used to crawl under the turnstiles to watch Wolves' home games in the 1930s. In 1941 he joined the RAF, obtaining his wings after training in Canada and the US, and as a glider pilot he took on the Japanese on the India/Burma border before his demob in 1946, having attained the rank of flight lieutenant. After that Sir Jack worked in South Africa before taking control of his father's business in America.

The business flourished and was subsequently moved to the Bahamas, then part of the British Empire. Over the next 42 or so years, this one-time desolate island was converted into a thriving economy, with an efficient airport and seaport, a major tanker terminal and top electrical and water companies, all owned by Sir Jack, who also purchased Lundy Island, off the coast of Devon, for the National Trust in 1969 and obtained the first ever iron ship, Brunel's SS *Great Britain.* He paid £1 million for a hospital in Port Stanley and also made a huge donation to help build MCC's indoor cricket school. For all his efforts Jack was knighted by the Queen in 1986 at a time when his beloved Wolves were struggling desperately in the Fourth Division. His money – a lot of it – and the assistance of manager

Graham Turner especially, helped turn the club around but Wolves simply couldn't regain their top-flight status. In May 1997 Sir Jack vowed he would not continue to bail the club out of trouble, claiming it was being run 'sloppily'. Four months later he took over as chairman, relegating his son, Jonathan, who had held the position previously, to vice-chairman. He also appointed former player John Richards as marketing director. Richards had been a director since 1994.

Four weeks after taking the chair, Sir Jack paid off the club's £8 million bank overdraft, and later in the year it was revealed that he had forked out around £30 million from his own account to keep Wolves going. In March 1998 Sir Jack underwent a triple heart bypass in Los Angeles. He recovered in time to see Wolves lose to Arsenal in that year's FA Cup semi-final, and four months into the next season he sacked manager Mark McGhee. Confident that Premiership football would soon be seen at Molineux, Sir Jack revealed in January 1999 that he had filed papers at the High Court, suing his son Jonathan, solicitor James Nicholas Stones and his firm, Wiggin & Company over alleged financial irregularities totalling £237,400.

The action surrounded the movement of monies within the club without authority from Sir Jack, when Jonathan was chairman. Sir Jack was successful. With nothing forthcoming on the playing side, another manager (Colin Lee) left halfway through the 2000–01 season and into his place stepped Dave Jones, backed all the way by Sir Jack, who had earlier brought in Jez Moxley from Stoke City to be chief executive which soon prompted the departure of managing director John Richards. Sir Jack was on a high when Wolves reached the First Division Play-offs in 2002, but his joy quickly turned to despair as Norwich City won the two-legged semi-final. Bitterly disappointed, he kept faith with Jones and a year later was overcome with joy as Wolves finally made it into the top-flight, beating Sheffield United 3–0 in the Play-off Final. Unfortunately only one season was spent competing with the likes of Arsenal, Chelsea, Liverpool and Manchester United. Following relegation, Glenn Hoddle and Mick McCarthy have both served as manager and Sir Jack's second son, Rick Hayward, has been appointed as chairman. In May 2007 Sir Jack announced that he had sold the club to businessman Steve Morgan for £10 in return for a £30 million investment into the club. Sir Jack – now believed to be the world's 120th richest man – would love to see Wolves back in the Premiership before he leaves this world.

Sir Jack Hayward lives, eats and breathes Wolves!

League Record against other clubs

Club			*Home*					*Away*		
	P	*W*	*D*	*L*	*F*	*A*	*W*	*D*	*L*	*F*	*A*
Accrington	10	5	0	0	19	4	1	1	3	11	18
Accrington Stanley	2	1	0	0	5	1	0	0	1	0	1
Aldershot	4	2	0	0	4	0	2	0	0	4	2
Arsenal	92	18	11	17	82	70	8	13	25	65	111
Ashington	2	1	0	0	1	0	1	0	0	7	1
Aston Villa	98	21	12	16	86	72	12	10	27	66	112
Barnet	2	1	0	0	5	0	0	0	1	1	2
Barnsley	74	22	8	7 *	80	34	8	9	20	43	74
Birmingham City	114	37	7	13	109	60	18	19	20	79	80
Blackburn Rovers	82	24	9	8	106	61	8	9	24	46	90
Blackpool	92	27	9	10	88	56	16	8	22	60	80
Bolton Wanderers	112	34	10	12	131	59	14	11	31	71	109
Bournemouth	4	1	0	1	3	4	0	1	1	3	4
Bradford City	30	8	4	3	34	15	4	5	6	22	29
Bradford Park Avenue	24	5	6	1	24	10	3	3	6	11	20
Brentford	16	5	0	3	19	13	2	1	5	10	18
Brighton & Hove Albion	20	2	2	6	10	16	1	4	5	9	22
Bristol City	52	14	10	2	48	21	11	4	11	37	32
Bristol Rovers	12	2	1	3	12	10	1	5	0	9	5
Burton United	2	1	0	0	3	0	0	0	1	1	4
Burnley	114	37	9	11	130	52	21	14	22	90	93
Bury	50	15	8	2	54	16	4	1	20	20	50
Cambridge United	10	2	1	2	8	6	0	3	2	4	6
Cardiff City	44	13	3	6	50	26	8	9	5	40	31
Carlisle United	14	5	1	1	15	5	4	0	3	9	6
Charlton Athletic	66	21	7	5	72	32	13	6	14	50	54
Chelsea	94	21	12	14	97	66	15	14	18	73	92
Chester City	2	1	0	0	3	1	0	1	0	1	1
Chesterfield	14	6	1	0	15	2	2	2	3	8	10
Colchester United	8	4	0	0	6	0	1	1	2	3	5
Coventry City	56	11	7	10	29	26	8	5	15	27	48
Crewe Alexandra	20	4	4	2	13	8	5	3	2	17	6
Crystal Palace	48	12	6	6	30	23	7	9	8	33	37
Darlington	10	5	0	0	12	5	1	2	2	9	11
Darwen	4	1	1	0	4	3	1	0	1	5	4
Derby County	130	28	17	20	123	82	19	11	35	103	148
Doncaster Rovers	4	1	0	1	2	2	2	0	0	3	0
Durham City	2	1	0	0	2	1	1	0	0	3	2
Everton	116	30	9	19	114	78	11	11	36	51	120

Club				Home					Away		
	P	W	D	L	F	A	W	D	L	F	A
Exeter City	4	1	1	0	5	2	2	0	0	7	3
Fulham	66	18	10	5	65	34	11	8	14	37	50
Gainsborough Trinity	12	4	2	0	8	1	3	0	3	6	4
Gillingham	12	3	2	1	18	7	3	0	3	10	7
Glossop North End	20	8	2	0	27	3	5	1	4	16	17
Grimsby Town	68	22	5	7	91	30	11	6	17	33	47
Halifax Town	6	1	0	2	5	3	1	1	1	7	7
Hartlepool United	6	3	0	0	8	2	2	1	0	2	0
Hereford United	6	3	0	0	5	1	2	0	1	8	4
Huddersfield Town	68	19	8	7	89	47	10	4	20	34	56
Hull City	52	13	5	8	53	31	7	3	16	24	61
Ipswich Town	64	15	12	5	42	28	7	4	21	32	59
Leeds City	20	7	1	2	30	14	1	3	6	10	23
Leeds United	78	20	10	9	64	37	7	9	23	31	66
Leicester City	100	24	16	10	93	48	12	15	23	48	78
Leyton Orient	46	15	2	6	49	25	6	6	11	26	32
Lincoln City	22	10	1	0	29	5	3	2	6	16	19
Liverpool	88	21	9	14	66	37	8	7	29	40	79
Luton Town	28	7	2	5	29	21	5	3	6	23	28
Manchester City	102	29	12	10	127	71	12	11	28	75	123
Manchester United	82	22	9	10	82	55	9	5	27	44	81
Mansfield Town	1	1	0	0	6	2	0	0	1	1	3
Middlesbrough	80	18	7	15	75	54	4	12	24	37	76
Millwall	32	9	4	3	32	13	4	5	7	16	19
New Brighton	2	1	0	0	5	1	1	0	0	1	0
Newcastle United	78	25	9	5	79	37	8	9	22	49	90
Newport County	4	1	1	0	3	3	1	0	1	4	4
Northampton Town	6	2	1	0	5	3	1	0	2	6	5
Norwich City	42	16	4	1	45	14	8	7	6	26	19
Nottingham Forest	112	40	9	7	130	59	11	15	30	62	107
Notts County	66	20	8	5	67	32	7	11	15	40	71
Oldham Athletic	38	9	6	4	34	19	4	2	13	19	42
Oxford United	18	5	2	2	16	10	1	4	4	7	15
Peterborough United	8	1	1	2	5	8	3	1	0	6	3
Plymouth Argyle	26	8	4	1	22	12	3	5	5	14	18
Portsmouth	82	22	14	5	96	41	12	10	19	46	61
Port Vale	42	13	4	4	45	21	11	6	4	39	24
Preston North End	106	29	11	13	106	62	13	12	28	78	116
Queen's Park Rangers	30	8	4	3	29	22	3	8	4	18	20
Reading	28	8	2	4	23	15	4	3	7	15	25
Rochdale	6	1	2	0	2	0	2	1	0	4	0
Rotherham United	24	9	2	1	24	6	3	4	5	16	17

Club		Home					Away				
	P	W	D	L	F	A	W	D	L	F	A
Scarborough	2	1	0	1	0	0	0	1	0	2	2
Scunthorpe United	6	3	0	0	7	2	3	0	0	5	0
Sheffield United	94	21	16	10	89	56	7	16	24	65	97
Sheffield Wednesday	92	28	12	6	100	54	10	14	22	54	85
Shrewsbury Town	4	0	1	1	2	3	1	0	1	3	2
Southampton	54	11	10	6	41	35	5	5	17	31	57
Southend United	18	6	2	1	22	7	3	3	3	9	9
Southport	2	1	0	0	2	1	0	1	0	0	0
South Shields	16	7	1	0	15	4	3	4	1	13	11
Stockport County	38	13	5 *	1	39	17	6	7	6	25	25
Stoke City	132	36	17	13	129	72	21	13	32	82	109
Sunderland	96	23	11	14	79	66	10	11	27	58	107
Swansea City	24	5	4	3	22	15	4	4	4	18	22
Swindon Town	14	3	3	1	10	8	2	0	5	7	11
Torquay United	4	1	0	1	2	2	1	1	0	2	1
Tottenham Hotspur	76	20	7	11	76	54	4	7	27	51	99
Tranmere Rovers	22	8	1	2	23	10	3	4	4	12	15
Walsall	10	2	2	1	7	3	2	2	1	7	4
Watford	28	4	8	2	17	14	1	5	8	13	25
West Bromwich Albion	142	34	17	20	130	95	17	22	32	92	123
West Ham United	54	14	6	7	44	31	3	7	17	25	61
Wigan Athletic	6	1	2	0	7	6	0	1	2	4	8
Wigan Borough	2	0	1	0	3	3	0	1	0	1	1
Wimbledon	8	1	2	1	5	5	1	2	1	5	5
Wrexham	6	1	0	2	3	5	0	2	1	4	6
York City	2	1	0	0	3	2	0	0	1	1	2

* One game played at The Hawthorns

League Play-offs

Club	P	W	D	L	F	A	W	D	L	F	A
Aldershot	2	0	0	1	0	1	0	0	1	0	2
Bolton Wanderers	2	1	0	0	2	1	0	0	1	0	2
Colchester United	2	0	1	0	0	0	1	0	0	2	0
Crystal Palace	2	1	0	0	2	1	0	0	1	1	3
Norwich City	2	1	0	0	1	0	0	0	1	1	3
Reading	2	1	0	0	2	1	1	0	0	1	0
Sheffield United	1	0	0	0	0	0	1 *	0	0	3	0
West Bromwich Albion	2	0	0	1	2	3	0	0	1	0	1

* Played at The Millennium Stadium, Cardiff

Wolves' League Records 1888–2008

			Final	No of			Home					Away		
No	Season	Div.	Pos	Games	W	D	L	F	A	W	D	L	F	A
1	1888–89	1	3	22	8	2	1	31	14	4	2	5	20	23
2	1889–90	1	4	22	6	3	2	28	14	4	2	5	23	24
3	1890–91	1	4	22	8	1	2	23	8	4	1	6	16	42
4	1891–92	1	6	26	8	2	3	34	15	3	2	8	25	31
5	1892–93	1	11	30	11	2	2	32	17	1	2	12	15	51
6	1893–94	1	9	30	11	1	3	34	24	3	2	10	18	39
7	1894–95	1	11	30	7	4	4	24	25	2	3	10	19	38
8	1895–96	1	14	30	10	0	5	43	18	0	1	14	18	47
9	1896–97	1	10	30	6	4	5	26	14	5	2	8	19	27
10	1897–98	1	3	30	10	4	1	36	14	4	3	8	21	27
11	1898–99	1	8	34	9	5	3	30	13	5	2	10	24	35
12	1899–1900	1	4	34	8	4	5	28	16	7	5	5	20	21
13	1900–01	1	13	34	6	10	1	21	15	3	3	11	18	40
14	1901–02	1	14	34	12	3	2	32	13	1	3	13	14	44
15	1902–03	1	11	34	12	2	3	34	17	2	3	12	14	40
16	1903–04	1	8	34	10	6	1	29	23	4	2	11	15	43
17	1904–05	1	14	34	10	2	5	30	23	1	2	14	17	50
18	1905–06	1	20	38	7	5	7	38	28	1	2	16	20	71
19	1906–07	2	6	38	13	4	2	49	16	4	3	12	17	37
20	1907–08	2	9	38	11	4	4	34	11	4	3	12	16	34
21	1908–09	2	7	38	10	6	3	32	12	4	5	10	24	36
22	1909–10	2	8	38	14	3	2	51	22	3	3	13	13	41
23	1910–11	2	9	38	10	5	4	26	16	5	3	11	25	36
24	1911–12	2	5	38	12	3	4	41	10	4	7	8	16	23
25	1912–13	2	10	38	10	6	3	34	16	4	4	11	22	38
26	1913–14	2	9	38	14	1	4	33	16	4	4	11	18	36
27	1914–15	2	4	38	12	4	3	47	13	7	3	9	30	39
Competition suspended due to World War One														
28	1919–20	2	19	42	8	4	9	41	32	2	6	13	14	48
29	1920–21	2	15	42	11	4	6	34	24	5	2	14	15	42
30	1921–22	2	17	42	8	7	6	28	19	5	4	12	16	30
31	1922–23	2	22	42	9	4	8	32	26	0	5	16	10	51
32	1923–24	3N	1	42	18	3	0	51	10	6	12	3	25	17
33	1924–25	2	6	42	14	1	6	29	19	6	5	10	26	32
34	1925–26	2	4	42	15	4	2	55	15	6	3	12	29	45
35	1926–27	2	15	42	10	4	7	54	30	4	3	14	19	45
36	1927–28	2	16	42	11	5	5	43	31	2	5	14	20	60
37	1928–29	2	17	42	9	6	6	41	31	6	1	14	36	50
38	1929–30	2	9	42	14	3	4	53	24	2	6	13	24	55

			Final	*No of*			*Home*					*Away*		
No	*Season*	*Div.*	*Pos*	*Games*	*W*	*D*	*L*	*F*	*A*	*W*	*D*	*L*	*F*	*A*
39	1930–31	2	4	42	15	2	4	56	25	6	3	12	28	42
40	1931–32	2	1	42	17	3	1	71	11	7	5	9	44	38
41	1932–33	1	20	42	10	4	7	56	48	3	5	13	24	48
42	1933–34	1	15	42	13	4	4	50	28	1	8	12	25	58
43	1934–35	1	17	42	13	3	5	65	38	2	5	14	23	56
44	1935–36	1	15	42	13	7	1	59	28	2	3	16	18	48
45	1936–37	1	5	42	16	2	3	63	24	5	3	13	21	43
46	1937–38	1	2	42	11	8	2	47	21	9	3	9	25	28
47	1938–39	1	2	42	14	6	1	55	12	8	5	8	33	27
48	1939–40*	1	16	3	0	1	0	2	2	0	1	1	2	2
* Fixtures subsequently declared null and void, competition suspended due to World War Two														
49	1946–47	1	3	42	15	1	5	66	31	10	5	6	32	25
50	1947–48	1	5	42	12	4	5	45	29	7	5	9	38	41
51	1948–49	1	6	42	13	5	3	48	19	4	7	10	31	47
52	1949–50	1	2	42	11	8	2	47	21	9	5	7	29	28
53	1950–51	1	14	42	9	3	9	44	30	6	5	10	30	31
54	1951–52	1	16	42	8	6	7	40	33	4	8	9	33	40
55	1952–53	1	3	42	13	5	3	54	27	6	8	7	32	36
56	1953–54	1	1	42	16	1	4	61	25	9	6	6	35	31
57	1954–55	1	2	42	13	5	3	58	30	6	5	10	31	40
58	1955–56	1	3	42	15	2	4	51	27	5	7	9	38	38
59	1956–57	1	6	42	17	2	2	70	29	3	6	12	24	41
60	1957–58	1	1	42	17	3	1	60	21	11	5	5	43	26
61	1958–59	1	1	42	15	3	3	68	19	13	2	6	42	30
62	1959–60	1	2	42	15	3	3	63	28	9	3	9	43	39
63	1960–61	1	3	42	17	2	2	61	32	8	5	8	42	43
64	1961–62	1	18	42	8	7	6	38	34	5	3	13	35	52
65	1962–63	1	5	42	11	6	4	51	25	9	4	8	42	40
66	1963–64	1	16	42	6	9	6	36	34	6	6	9	34	46
67	1964–65	1	21	42	8	2	11	33	36	5	2	14	26	53
68	1965–66	2	6	42	15	4	2	52	18	5	6	10	35	43
69	1966–67	2	2	42	15	4	2	53	20	10	4	7	35	28
70	1967–68	1	17	42	10	4	7	45	36	4	4	13	21	39
71	1968–69	1	16	42	7	10	4	26	22	3	5	13	15	36
72	1969–70	1	13	42	8	8	5	30	23	4	8	9	25	34
73	1970–71	1	4	42	13	3	5	33	22	9	5	7	31	32
74	1971–72	1	9	42	10	7	4	35	23	8	4	9	30	34
75	1972–73	1	5	42	13	3	5	43	23	5	8	8	23	31
76	1973–74	1	12	42	11	6	4	30	18	2	9	10	19	31
77	1974–75	1	12	42	12	5	4	43	21	2	6	13	14	33
78	1975–76	1	20	42	7	6	8	27	25	3	4	14	24	43
79	1976–77	2	1	42	15	3	3	48	21	7	10	4	36	24

			Final	No of	Home					Away				
No	Season	Div.	Pos	Games	W	D	L	F	A	W	D	L	F	A
80	1977–78	1	15	42	7	8	6	30	27	5	4	12	21	37
81	1978–79	1	18	42	10	4	7	26	26	3	4	14	18	42
82	1979–80	1	6	42	9	6	6	29	20	10	3	8	29	27
83	1980–81	1	18	42	11	2	8	26	20	2	7	12	17	35
84	1981–82	1	21	42	8	5	8	19	20	2	5	14	13	43
85	1982–83	2	2	42	14	5	2	42	16	6	10	5	26	28
86	1983–84	1	22	42	4	8	9	15	28	2	3	16	12	52
87	1984–85	2	22	42	5	4	12	18	32	3	5	13	19	47
88	1985–86	3	23	46	6	6	11	29	47	5	4	14	28	51
89	1986–87	4	4	46	12	3	8	36	24	12	4	7	33	26
90	1987–88	4	1	46	15	3	5	47	19	12	6	5	35	24
91	1988–89	3	1	46	18	4	1	61	19	8	10	5	35	30
92	1989–90	2	10	46	12	5	6	37	20	6	8	9	30	40
93	1990–91	2	12	46	11	6	6	45	35	2	13	8	18	28
94	1991–92	2	11	46	11	6	6	36	24	7	4	12	25	30
95	1992–93	1	11	46	11	6	6	37	26	5	7	11	20	30
96	1993–94	1	8	46	10	10	3	34	19	7	7	9	26	28
97	1994–95	1	4	46	15	5	3	39	18	6	8	9	38	43
98	1995–96	1	20	46	8	9	6	34	28	5	7	11	22	34
99	1996–97	1	3	46	10	5	8	31	24	12	5	6	37	27
100	1997–98	1	9	46	13	6	4	42	25	5	5	13	15	28
101	1998–99	1	7	46	11	10	2	37	19	8	6	9	27	24
102	1999–2000	1	7	46	15	5	3	45	20	6	6	11	19	28
103	2000–01	1	12	46	7	9	7	25	20	7	4	12	20	28
104	2001–02	1	3	46	13	4	6	33	18	12	7	4	43	25
105	2002–03	1	5	46	9	10	4	40	19	11	6	6	41	25
106	2003–04	PL	20	38	7	5	7	23	35	0	7	12	15	42
107	2004–05	1	9	46	9	11	3	40	26	6	10	7	32	33
108	2005–06	LC	7	46	9	10	4	24	18	7	9	7	26	24
109	2006–07	LC	5	46	12	5	6	33	28	10	5	8	26	28
110	2007–08	LC	7	46	11	6	6	31	25	7	10	6	22	23

Summary of League Seasons

No	Season	Points	Players Used	Top goalscorer	Total Goals	Home League Attendances Aggregate	Average
1	1888–89	28	19	Harry Wood	13	43,978	3,998
2	1889–90	25	19	David Wykes	15	59,797	5,436
3	1890–91	26	19	Sam Thomson, Harry Wood	9	54,791	4,981
4	1891–92	26	22	Will Devey	12	59,593	4,584
5	1892–93	28	22	Harry Wood	16	79,802	5,320
6	1893–94	31	19	Joe Butcher	13	96,003	6,400
7	1894–95	25	22	Harry Wood	10	79,515	5,301
8	1895–96	21	21	Harry Wood	14	85,320	5,688
9	1896–97	28	20	Billy Beats	8	96,045	6,403
10	1897–98	35	22	Beats, Bill Smith, Wood	11	105,602	7,040
11	1898–99	35	22	Jack Miller	12	114,632	6,743
12	1899–1900	39	20	George Harper	10	120,581	7,093
13	1900–01	31	21	George Bowen, George Harper, Billy Wooldridge	6	113,492	6,676
14	1901–02	32	21	Billy Wooldridge	13	110,449	6,497
15	1902–03	33	19	Adam Haywood	11	100,573	5,916
16	1903–04	36	18	Billy Wooldridge	17	122,434	7,202
17	1904–05	26	22	Billy Wooldridge	13	125,987	7,411
18	1905–06	23	29	Billy Wooldridge	12	118,998	6,263
19	1906–07	41	21	Jack Roberts	14	109,497	5,763
20	1907–08	37	27	George Hedley	12	179,989	9,473
21	1908–09	39	25	Wally Radford	21	160,494	8,447
22	1909–10	40	25	Billy Blunt	23	139,004	7,316
23	1910–11	38	19	Jack Needham	13	150,498	7,921
24	1911–12	42	21	Billy Halligan	19	204,991	10,789
25	1912–13	38	22	Billy Halligan	15	149,492	7,868
26	1913–14	41	25	Sammy Brooks	11	203,091	10,689
27	1914–15	45	20	Frank Curtis	25	150,497	7,921
Competition suspended due to World War One							
28	1919–20	30	31	Dick Richards	10	245,931	11,711
29	1920–21	38	25	George Edmonds	11	395,304	18,824
30	1921–22	37	25	George Edmonds	13	270,565	12,884
31	1922–23	27	28	George Edmonds	14	252,231	12,011
32	1923–24	63	24	Harry Lees	21	308,196	14,676
33	1924–25	46	25	Tom Phillipson	16	343,686	16,366
34	1925–26	49	28	Tom Phillipson	36	323,904	15,424
35	1926–27	35	28	Tom Phillipson	31	266,553	12,694
36	1927–28	36	32	Wilf Chadwick	19	336,378	16,018
37	1928–29	37	30	Reg Weaver	18	284,685	13,555
38	1929–30	41	28	Billy Hartill	33	288,940	13,759

No	Season	Points	Players Used	Top goalscorer	Total Goals	Home League Attendances Aggregate	Average
39	1930–31	47	26	Billy Hartill	24	351,372	16,732
40	1931–32	56	22	Billy Hartill	30	457,107	21,767
41	1932–33	35	28	Billy Hartill	33	570,423	27,163
42	1933–34	40	27	Billy Hartill, Charlie Phillips	13	528,045	25,145
43	1934–35	38	32	Billy Hartill	27	503,160	23,960
44	1935–36	40	29	Billy Wrigglesworth	12	521,368	24,827
45	1936–37	47	29	Gordon Clayton	24	515,529	24,549
46	1937–38	51	24	Dennis Westcott	19	636,637	30,316
47	1938–39	55	28	Dennis Westcott	32	616,035	29,335
48	1939–40*	2	12	Richard Dorsett, Gerald McAloon, Dennis Westcott	1	41,222	41,222
* Fixtures subsequently declared null and void, competition suspended due to World War Two							
49	1946–47	56	23	Dennis Westcott	38	909,447	43,307
50	1947–48	47	23	Johnny Hancocks, Jesse Pye	16	827,337	39,397
51	1948–49	46	24	Jesse Pye	17	917,491	43,690
52	1949–50	53	24	Jesse Pye	18	952,266	45,346
53	1950–51	38	21	Roy Swinbourne	20	843,549	40,169
54	1951–52	38	27	Jesse Pye	15	739,704	35,224
55	1952–53	51	23	Roy Swinbourne	21	769,063	36,622
56	1953–54	57	22	Dennis Wilshaw	26	726,558	34,598
57	1954–55	48	22	Johnny Hancocks	26	765,996	36,476
58	1955–56	49	24	Johnny Hancocks	18	737,353	35,112
59	1956–57	48	23	Harry Hooper	19	744,345	35,445
60	1957–58	64	21	Jimmy Murray	29	783,447	37,307
61	1958–59	61	22	Jimmy Murray	21	807,261	38,441
62	1959–60	54	21	Jimmy Murray	29	715,261	34,060
63	1960–61	57	21	Ted Farmer	28	638,001	30,381
64	1961–62	36	27	Jimmy Murray	16	520,359	24,779
65	1962–63	50	20	Alan Hinton	19	520,863	24,803
66	1963–64	39	22	Ray Crawford	26	483,441	23,021
67	1964–65	30	28	Ray Crawford	13	451,478	21,499
68	1965–66	50	21	Peter Knowles	19	455,637	21,697
69	1966–67	58	24	Ernie Hunt	20	520,023	24,763
70	1967–68	36	25	Derek Dougan	17	698,544	33,264
71	1968–69	35	28	Derek Dougan	11	644,868	30,708
72	1969–70	40	23	Hugh Curran	20	644,847	30,707
73	1970–71	52	21	Bobby Gould	17	576,387	27,447
74	1971–72	47	22	Derek Dougan	15	586,908	27,948
75	1972–73	47	21	John Richards	27	492,493	23,452
76	1973–74	41	22	Derek Dougan	10	537,789	25,609
77	1974–75	39	22	Kenny Hibbitt	17	491,421	23,401
78	1975–76	30	25	John Richards	17	485,310	23,110
79	1976–77	57	19	Kenny Hibbitt	17	444,802	21,181

No	Season	Points	Players Used	Top goalscorer	Total Goals	Home League Attendances Aggregate	Average
80	1977–78	36	24	John Richards	11	468,636	22,316
81	1978–79	34	21	John Richards	9	437,451	20,831
82	1979–80	47	22	John Richards	13	540,835	25,754
83	1980–81	35	23	John Richards	13	434,259	20,679
84	1981–82	40	25	Mel Eves	7	320,166	15,246
85	1982–83	75	21	Mel Eves	18	329,365	15,684
86	1983–84	29	32	Wayne Clarke	6	262,038	12,478
87	1984–85	33	30	Alan Ainscow, Mark Buckland, Anthony Evans	5	171,885	8,185
88	1985–86	43	33	Andy King	10	85,330	3,710
89	1986–87	79	31	Steve Bull	15	132,434	5,758
90	1987–88	90	22	Steve Bull	34	225,515	9,805
91	1988–89	92	21	Steve Bull	37	329,591	14,330
92	1989–90	67	22	Steve Bull	24	392.082	17,047
93	1990–91	58	27	Steve Bull	26	364,182	15,834
94	1991–92	64	23	Steve Bull	20	315,790	13,730
95	1992–93	61	26	Steve Bull	16	300,196	13,052
96	1993–94	68	26	Steve Bull	14	505,908	21,996
97	1994–95	76	29	Steve Bull	16	570,216	24,792
98	1995–96	55	33	Don Goodman	16	521,134	22,658
99	1996–97	76	30	Steve Bull	23	569,549	24,763
100	1997–98	65	35	Robbie Keane	11	535,371	23,277
101	1998–99	73	25	Robbie Keane	11	520,260	22,620
102	1999–2000	74	26	Ade Akinbiyi	16	493,810	21,470
103	2000–01	55	30	Adam Proudlock	8	442,934	19,258
104	2001–02	86	26	Dean Sturridge	20	547,309	23,796
105	2002–03	76	24	Kenny Miller	19	592,135	25,745
106	2003–04	33	27	Henri Camara	7	548,416	28,864
107	2004–05	66	25	Kenny Miller	19	612,260	26,620
108	2005–06	67	30	Carl Cort	10	543,352	23,624
109	2006–07	76	33	Jay Bothroyd	9	482,265	20,968
110	2007–08	70	26	Sylvan Ebanks-Blake	12	540,421	23,496

Wolves' Playing Record at First-Team Level: 1883–2008

Competition	P	W	D	L	F	A
Premiership	38	7	12	19	38	77
Football League	4,334	1,760	1,026	1,548	7,032	6,382
Play-offs	13	7	1	5	15	14
FA Cup	356	167	80	109	643	455
League Cup	120	52	22	46	186	162
European Cup	8	2	2	4	12	16
Cup-Winners' Cup	4	1	1	2	6	5
UEFA Cup	20	13	3	4	41	23
FA Charity Shield	5	1	3	1	11	12
Texaco Cup	12	6	2	4	20	9
Watney Cup	1	0	0	1	0	2
Anglo-Italian Cup	12	5	3	4	17	15
FAT/SVT	20	13	5	2	43	16
ZDS Cup	4	1	0	3	2	4
War Football	235	98	50	87	451	421
Totals	**5,182**	**2,133**	**1,210**	**1,839**	**8,517**	**7,613**

Results do not include games decided by a penalty shoot-out

Wolves' League Sequences

- Record unbeaten run in League football is 21 matches, between January and August 2005.
- Best unbeaten home League run is 27 matches, from March 1923 until September 1924.
- Went 19 League games without a win between December 1984 and April 1985.
- Best run of successive League wins is eight, achieved four times in 1915, 1967, 1987 and 1988.
- Suffered a club record of eight successive League defeats in season 1981–82.
- Played 12 home games without a League win between November 1984 and April 1985.
- Remained unbeaten in 11 successive away League games in 1953–54 (September to January).
- Won 14 successive home League games between March and November 1953.
- Failed to win any of their 32 away League games between March 1922 and October 1923.
- Drew a club record six League games in a row between April and August 1995.
- Went eight League games without conceding a goal in 1982–83.
- Scored at least one goal in 41 successive League games between December 1958 and December 1959.
- Went seven League games without scoring between February and March 1985.

1888-89

Football League

Manager: Jack Addenbrooke

	P	W	D	L	F	A	Pts
Preston North End	22	18	4	0	74	15	40
Aston Villa	22	12	5	5	61	43	29
Wolverhampton Wanderers	22	12	4	6	51	37	28
Blackburn Rovers	22	10	6	6	66	45	26
Bolton Wanderers	22	10	2	10	63	59	22
West Bromwich Albion	22	10	2	10	40	46	22
Accrington	22	6	8	8	48	48	20
Everton	22	9	2	11	35	47	20
Burnley	22	7	3	12	42	62	17
Derby County	22	7	2	13	41	61	16
Notts County	22	5	2	15	40	73	12
Stoke	22	4	4	14	26	51	12

Match No.	Date		Venue	Opponents	Result		Scorers
1	Sep	8	H	Aston Villa	D	1-1	Cox (og)
2		15	H	Preston North End	L	0-4	
3		22	H	Burnley	W	4-1	Hunter, Knight, White 2
4		29	H	Blackburn Rovers	D	2-2	Cooper, Wykes
5	Oct	6	A	Accrington	D	4-4	Knight, Wood, Fletcher, Stevenson (og
6		13	A	Burnley	W	4-0	Wood 2, Knight, Hunter
7		20	A	Blackburn Rovers	D	2-2	Wood, Brodie
8		27	A	Preston North End	L	2-5	Brodie, Wykes
9	Nov	3	H	Derby County	W	4-1	Wood 3, Brodie
10		10	H	Bolton Wanderers	W	3-2	Brodie, Cooper, Knight
11		17	A	Stoke	W	1-0	Brodie
12		24	A	Aston Villa	L	1-2	Brodie
13	Dec	8	H	Accrington	W	4-0	Brodie, Cooper 2, Wykes
14		15	H	West Bromwich Albion	W	2-1	Hunter, Brodie
15		22	H	Stoke	W	4-1	Brodie, Wood 2, Wykes
16		29	A	Bolton Wanderers	L	1-2	Cooper
17	Jan	5	A	West Bromwich Albion	W	3-1	Brodie, Hunter, Cooper
18		12	A	Derby County	L	0-3	
19		19	A	Notts County	L	0-3	
20		26	H	Everton	W	5-0	Lowder, Brodie, Wood 2, Knight
21	Feb	9	A	Everton	W	2-1	Wood, Knight
22		23	H	Notts County	W	2-1	Wood, Knight

Appea

Two own-goals

FA Cup

R1	Feb	2	H	Old Carthusians	W	4-3	Wykes, Knight 2, Mason
R2		16	H	Walsall Town Swifts	W	6-1	Knight 3, Brodie, Hunter, Lowder
R3	Mar	2	H	The Wednesday	W	3-0	Wykes 2, Fletcher
SF		16	N	Blackburn Rovers	D	1-1	Wykes
rep		23	N	Blackburn Rovers	W	3-1	Hunter, Allen, Wood
F		30	N	Preston North End	L	0-3	

SF and replay at the Alexandra Recreation Ground, Crewe. Final at The Oval.

Appea

Did you know that?

- Two players shared the captaincy this season – Dicky Baugh and Jack Brodie.
- Wolves' first League goal was scored by an Aston Villa player, full-back Gershom Cox.
- The first Wolves player to score a League goal was Walter White versus Burnley in September.
- Harry Wood scored Wolves' first League hat-trick versus Derby County (h) in November.
- Jack Brodie scored on his international debut for England against Ireland in March.
- The average price of a season ticket (in 1888–89) was 5s (25p).

	Baugh R	Mason C	Fletcher A	Allen H	Lowder A	Hunter T	Cooper J	Anderson N	White W	Cannon A	Benton J	Wykes D	Knight T	Wood H	Brodie JB	Rose WC	Tomkys T	Dudley R
1	2	3	4	5	6	7	8	9	10	11								
2	2	3	4	5		7	8	9	10		6	11						
3	2	3	4	5		7	8		10	6		9	11					
4	2	3	4	5	6	7	8		10			9	11					
5	2	3	4	5	6	7	8					9	11	10				
6	2	3	4	5	6	7	8					9	11	10				
7	2	3	4	5	6	7	8					11		10	9			
8	2	3	4	5	6	7	8					11		10	9			
9	2	3	4	5	6	7	8					11		10	9			
10	2		4	5	3	7	8			6			11	10	9			
11	2		4	5	3	7	8			6			11	10	9			
12	2	3	4	5	6	7	8						11	10	9			
13	2	3		5	6	7	8					11	4	10	9			
14	2	3		5	6	7	8					11	4	10	9			
15	2	3		5	6		8			4		7	11	10	9			
16	2	3		5	6	7	8					11	4	10	9			
17	2	3		5	6	7	8					11	4	10	9			
18	2	3	4	5	6		8					11	7	10	9			
19	2	3	4	5		7	8			6		11	10			1	9	
20	2	3	4	5	6	7						8	11	10	9	1		
21	2	3	4	5	6	7	9					8	11	10		1		
22	2	3		5		7	8			4		9	11	10		1		6
	2	20	16	22	18	20	21	2	4	7	1	18	17	17	13	4	1	1
			1		1	4	6		2			4	7	13	11			
R1		3	4	5	6	7						8	11	10	9			
R2		3	4	5	6	7						8	11	10	9			
R3		3	4	5	6	7				9		8	11	10				
SF		3	4	5	6	7				9		8	11	10				
rep		3	4	5	6	7						8	11	10	9			
F		3	4	5	6	7						8	11	10	9			
		6	6	6	6	6				2		6	6	6	4			
		1	1	1	1	2						4	5	1	1			

1889-90

Football League

Manager: Jack Addenbrooke

	P	W	D	L	F	A	Pts
Preston North End	22	15	3	4	71	30	33
Everton	22	14	3	5	65	40	31
Blackburn Rovers	22	12	3	7	78	41	27
Wolverhampton Wanderers	22	10	5	7	51	38	25
West Bromwich Albion	22	11	3	8	47	50	25
Accrington	22	9	6	7	53	56	24
Derby County	22	9	3	10	43	55	21
Aston Villa	22	7	5	10	43	51	19
Bolton Wanderers	22	9	1	12	54	65	19
Notts County	22	6	5	11	43	51	17
Burnley	22	4	5	13	36	65	13
Stoke	22	3	4	15	27	69	10

Match No.	Date		Venue	Opponents	Result		Scorers
1	Sep	7	H	Notts County	W	2-0	Worrall, Wykes
2		14	A	Blackburn Rovers	L	3-4	Wykes 2, Perry
3		16	H	Everton	W	2-1	Knight, Worrall
4		28	A	Stoke	L	1-2	Wood
5		30	A	Everton	D	1-1	Wykes
6	Oct	5	H	Accrington	W	2-1	Brodie, Wood
7		12	H	Stoke	D	2-2	Wood, Worrall
8		19	A	West Bromwich Albion	W	4-1	Booth, Brodie, Wood, Worrall
9		26	A	Preston North End	W	2-0	Worrall, Wykes
10	Nov	2	A	Aston Villa	L	1-2	Brodie
11		9	A	Burnley	W	2-1	Wood 2
12		23	A	Derby County	D	3-3	Perry, Wykes, Wood
13	Dec	7	H	Burnley	W	9-1	Allen 2, Brodie 2, Wood 2, Wykes 2, Worra
14		14	A	Notts County	W	2-0	Wykes 2
15		21	H	Aston Villa	D	1-1	Wood
16		26	H	Blackburn Rovers	L	2-4	Booth, Wykes
17		28	H	West Bromwich Albion	D	1-1	Wood
18	Jan	1	A	Accrington	L	3-6	Wood 2, Wykes
19		4	H	Preston North End	L	0-1	
20		25	H	Derby County	W	2-1	Brodie, Mason
21	Feb	24	A	Bolton Wanderers	L	1-4	Perry
22	Mar	15	H	Bolton Wanderers	W	5-1	Wykes 3, Brodie, Worrall

Appea

FA Cup

R1	Jan	18	H	Old Carthusians	W	2-0	Wood 2
R2	Feb	1	H	Small Heath	W	2-1	Fletcher, Speller (og)
R3	Feb	15	H	Stoke	W	4-0	Worrall 2, Brodie, Wood
R3R		22	H	Stoke	W	8-0	Brodie 5, Wood 2, Allen
SF	Mar	8	N	Blackburn Rovers	L	0-1	

SF at County Ground, Derby.

Appea

A first R3 meeting with Stoke was replayed after protest over the pitch.

One own-goal

Did you know that?

- Wolves moved from their Dudley Road ground to Molineux and the first League game to be played there was against Notts County on 7 September.
- David Wykes scored the first League goal at Molineux (against Notts County).
- Jack Brodie became the first Wolves player to score five goals in a competitive game – doing so against Stoke in an FA Cup tie in February.
- Wolves' full-back pairing of Dickie Baugh and Charlie Mason played alongside each other for England against Ireland in Belfast.
- February 1890 saw the lowest-ever crowd for an FA Cup tie at Molineux – just 3,000.

	Baugh R	Mason C	Fletcher AA	Allen H	Knight T	Worrall AJ	Perry W	Wykes D	Wood H	Booth C	Lowder A	Mason J	Cooper J	Brodie JB	Oldershaw W	Griffiths H	Johnson T	Pickerell J
1	2	3	4	5	6	7	8	9	10	11								
2	2	3	4	5	7		8	9	10	11	6							
3	2	3	4	5	7	8		9	10	11	6							
4		5	4		2	8	7	9	10	11	6	3						
5	2	3	4	5		8		9	10	11	6		7					
6	2	3	4	5		7		8	10	11	6			9				
7	2	3	4	5		7		8	10	11	6			9				
8	2	3	4	5		9		8	10	11	6			7				
9	2	3	4	5		9		8	10	11	6			7				
10	2	3	4	5		9		8	10	11	6			7				
11	2	3	4	5		9	7	8	10	11	6							
12	2	3	4	5		9	7	8	10	11	6							
13	2		4	5		9		8	10	11	6	3		7				
14	2		4	5		9		8	10	11	6	3		7				
15	2	3	4	5		9		8	10	11		6		7				
16	2	3	4	5			8	7	10	11	6			9				
17		3	4	5		9		7	10	11	6	2		8				
18	2		4	5		9	7	8	10	11	6				3			
19	2	3	4	5		9		8	10	11	6			7				
20	2	3	4	5		9		8	10	11	6			7				
21	2	3	4	5		9	7	8	10	11	6							
22				5		8		7		11	6	3		9		4	2	10
	9	18	21	21	4	20	8	22	21	22	20	6	1	13	1	1	1	1
		1		2	1	7	3	15	13	2				7				
R1		3	4	5		7		8	10	11	6			9				
R2		3	4	5		7		8	10	11		6		9				
R3		3	4	5		7	8		10	11	6			9				
R3R		3	4	5		7		8	10	11	6			9				
SF		3	4	5		7		8	10	11	6			9				
		5	5	5		5		5	5	5	4	1		5				
			1	1		2			5					6				

1890-91

Football League

Manager: Jack Addenbrooke

	P	W	D	L	F	A	Pts
Everton	22	14	1	7	63	29	29
Preston North End	22	12	3	7	44	23	27
Notts County	22	11	4	7	52	35	26
Wolverhampton Wanderers	22	12	2	8	39	50	26
Bolton Wanderers	22	12	1	9	47	34	25
Blackburn Rovers	22	11	2	9	52	43	24
Sunderland	22	10	5	7	51	31	23
Burnley	22	9	3	10	52	63	21
Aston Villa	22	7	4	11	45	58	18
Accrington	22	6	4	12	28	50	16
Derby County	22	7	1	14	47	81	15
West Bromwich Albion	22	5	2	15	34	57	12

Match No.	Date		Venue	Opponents	Result		Scorers
1	Sep	6	H	Aston Villa	W	2-1	Thomson, Worrall
2		13	A	Everton	L	0-5	
3		15	A	Sunderland	W	4-3	Bowdler, Thomson, Wood, Wykes
4		22	H	Notts County	D	1-1	Wood
5		27	A	Blackburn Rovers	W	3-2	Booth, Brodie, Thomson
6	Oct	4	H	Accrington	W	3-0	Brodie, Thomson, Wood
7		11	H	Derby County	W	5-1	Brodie 2, Thomson, Wood, Wykes
8		18	A	Preston North End	L	1-5	Thomson
9		25	H	Burnley	W	3-1	Allen, Thomson, Wykes
10	Nov	1	A	Burnley	L	2-4	Booth, Wood
11		8	H	Bolton Wanderers	W	1-0	Wood
12		22	A	Notts County	D	1-1	Wykes
13		29	H	Preston North End	W	2-0	Bowdler, Wykes
14	Dec	6	H	Everton	L	0-1	
15		13	A	West Bromwich Albion	W	1-0	Worrall
16		26	H	Blackburn Rovers	W	2-0	Allen, Wood
17		27	H	Sunderland	L	0-3	
18		29	A	Bolton Wanderers	L	0-6	
19	Jan	1	A	Accrington	W	2-1	Thomson, Worrall
20		3	H	West Bromwich Albion	W	4-0	Wood 2, Thomson, Wykes
21		10	A	Derby County	L	0-9	
22	Mar	14	A	Aston Villa	L	2-6	Topham 2

Appea

FA Cup

R1	Jan	17	A	Long Eaton Rangers	W	2-1	Wood 2
R2		31	A	Accrington	W	3-2	Booth, Wood, Worrall
R3	Feb	14	A	Blackburn Rovers	L	0-2	

R1 and R2 aet

Appea

Did you know that?

- Wolves were fined £50 by the Football League for illegally signing the Preston North End forward Sammy Thomson.
- Harry Wood was Wolves' top scorer for the third successive season (all competitions).
- When losing 9–0 at Derby in January, Wolves never had a single shot at goal. Johnny McMillan scored five times for the Rams.
- Dick Topham scored twice on his League debut for Wolves against Aston Villa in April.
- Jack Bowdler was the first Wolves player to represent Wales (against Scotland in March).

Baugh R	Brodie JB	Fletcher AA	Allen H	Lowder A	Wykes D	Worrall AJ	Thomson S	Wood H	Bowdler JCH	Mason C	Davies J	Booth C	Rutter H	Griffiths I	Cooper J	Griffiths H	Topham R	
2	3	4	5	6	7	8	9	10	11									1
2		4	5	6	7	8	9	10	11	3								2
2		4	5		7		9	10	11	3	6	8						3
		4	5	6	7		9	10	11	3		8	2					4
2	6	4	5		7		9	10	11	3		8						5
2	6	4	5		7		9	10	11	3		8						6
2	6	4	5		7		9	10	11	3		8						7
2	6	4	5		7		9	10	11	3		8						8
	6	4	5		7		9	10	11	3		8	2	1				9
2	6	4	5		7		9	10	11	3		8						10
2	6	4	5		7		9	10	11	3		8						11
2	6	4	5		7	9		10	11	3		8						12
2	6	4	5		7		9	10	11	3		8						13
2	6	4	5		7	8	9	10		3		11						14
2	6	4	5			8	9	10		3		11			7			15
2	6	4	5		7		9	10	11	3		8						16
2	6	4	5			8	9	10		3		11			7			17
2		4	5		7	8	9	10		3	6	11						18
2		4	5	6	7	8	9	10				11				3		19
2		4	5	6	7	8	9	10		3		11						20
2	3	4	5	6	7		9	10	11			8						21
	3		5	6	7		8	10	11	2		4					9	22
9	16	21	22	7	20	9	21	22	16	19	2	20	2	1	2	1	1	
	4		2		6	3	9	9	2			2					2	

Baugh R	Brodie JB	Fletcher AA	Allen H	Lowder A	Wykes D	Worrall AJ	Thomson S	Wood H	Bowdler JCH	Mason C	Davies J	Booth C	
2		4	5	6		9	7	10	11	3		8	R1
2		4	5		7	9	8	10		3	6	11	R2
2	6	4			7	9	8	10		3	5	11	R3
3	1	3	2	1	2	3	3	3	1	3	2	3	
						1		3				1	

1891-92

Football League

Manager: Jack Addenbrooke

	P	W	D	L	F	A	Pts
Sunderland	26	21	0	5	93	36	42
Preston North End	26	18	1	7	61	31	37
Bolton Wanderers	26	17	2	7	51	37	36
Aston Villa	26	15	0	11	89	56	30
Everton	26	12	4	10	49	49	28
Wolverhampton Wanderers	26	11	4	11	59	46	26
Burnley	26	11	4	11	49	45	26
Notts County	26	11	4	11	55	51	26
Blackburn Rovers	26	10	6	10	58	65	26
Derby County	26	10	4	12	46	52	24
Accrington	26	8	4	14	40	78	20
West Bromwich Albion	26	6	6	14	51	58	18
Stoke	26	5	4	17	38	61	14
Darwen	26	4	3	19	38	112	11

Match No.	Date		Venue	Opponents	Result		Scorers
1	Sep	5	A	Sunderland	L	2-5	Allen, Wykes
2		12	A	Stoke	W	3-1	Allen, Baker, Booth
3		14	H	Accrington	W	5-0	Heath 2, Allen, Baker, Devey
4		19	A	West Bromwich Albion	L	3-4	Booth 2, Heath
5		26	H	Derby County	L	1-3	Devey
6		28	H	Darwen	D	2-2	Devey, Topham
7	Oct	3	A	Preston North End	L	0-2	
8		10	A	Blackburn Rovers	L	0-2	
9		17	H	Notts County	W	2-1	Bowdler, Topham
10		24	A	Accrington	L	2-3	Baker, Wykes
11		31	A	Derby County	L	1-2	Baker
12	Nov	7	H	Burnley	D	0-0	
13		14	A	Notts County	D	2-2	Devey, Topham
14		21	H	Everton	W	5-1	Topham 2, Devey, Booth, Wykes
15		28	H	Blackburn Rovers	W	6-1	Topham 3, Wykes 2, Devey
16	Dec	5	A	Bolton Wanderers	L	0-3	
17		12	A	Everton	L	1-2	Devey
18		19	H	Aston Villa	W	2-0	Devey, Wykes
19		26	H	Sunderland	L	1-3	Topham
20		28	H	West Bromwich Albion	W	2-1	Devey, Topham
21	Jan	2	H	Stoke	W	4-1	Wood 2, Heath, Wykes
22	Mar	1	A	Darwen	W	4-1	Baker, Booth, Devey, Wood
23		26	A	Burnley	D	1-1	Wykes
24	Apr	2	H	Preston North End	W	3-0	Devey, Johnson, Wood
25		16	H	Bolton Wanderers	L	1-2	Wood
26		18	A	Aston Villa	W	6-3	Wood 3, Johnson 2, Devey

Appear

FA Cup

R1	Jan	16	H	Crewe Alexandra	D	2-2	Wykes, Devey
rep		23	A	Crewe Alexandra	W	4-1	Baker 2, Wykes, Heath
R2		30	H	Sheffield United	W	3-1	Baker 2, Topham
R3	Feb	13	H	Aston Villa	L	1-3	Topham

R1 aet

Appear

Did you know that?

- Wolves' 3-1 defeat by Aston Villa in the third round of the FA Cup was their first at home in the competition for 20 matches.
- Joe Heath scored the first-ever penalty in a Football League game – for Wolves against Accrington on 14 September.
- Harry Allen became the first Wolves player to miss a penalty – in the away League game against West Bromwich Albion on 19 September.
- The Wolves against Sunderland League game on Boxing Day attracted the first 20,000 crowd to Molineux.

	Baugh R	Dunn T	Davies J	Allen H	Kinsey G	Baker C	Devey W	Heath JF	Wykes D	Bowdler JCH	Booth C	Burleigh J	Swift GH	Malpass AW	Bradley C	Topham R	Bailey H	Mason C	Wood H	Lowder A	Johnston J
1	2	3	4	5	6	7	8	9	10	11											
2	2	3	4	5	6	7	8	9			10	11									
3		2	4	5	6	7	8	9	10		11		3								
4	2	3		5	6	7	8	9			11	10		4							
5	2		4	5	6	7	8	9		11	10		3								
6	2			5	6		8		7	11	10		3		4	9					
7	2	3		5	6	7	8			11	10				4	9					
8	2			5	6	7	8			11	10				4		9	3			
9	2		4	5	6	8	10		7	11						9		3			
10	2		4	5		8	10	9	7		11				6			3			
11	2			5	6	8	10	9	7		11				4			3			
12	2			5	6	8	10		7	11					4	9		3			
13	2		4	5	6	8	10		7	11						9		3			
14	2		4	5	6	8	10		7		11					9		3			
15	2		4	5	6	8	10		7		11					9		3			
16	2		4	5	6	8	9		7		11							3	10		
17	2		4		6	8	9		7		11			5				3	10		
18	2		4		6		8		7		11			5		9		3	10		
19	2				6	8	10		7		11			5		9		3		4	
20		2	4		6	8	10		7		11			5		9		3			
21	2		4	5	6	8		9	7		11							3	10		
22	2			5	6	8	9		7		11			4				3	10		
23	2			5	6	8	9		7		11			4				3			10
24	2			5	6	8	9		7					4				3	10		11
25	2			5	6	8	9		7					4				3	10		11
26	2			5	6	8	9		7				3	4					10		11
	4	6	14	22	25	24	25	8	21	8	19	2	4	10	6	10	1	18	8	1	4
				3		5	12	4	8	1	5					10			8		3

	Baugh R	Dunn T	Davies J	Allen H	Kinsey G	Baker C	Devey W	Heath JF	Wykes D	Bowdler JCH	Booth C	Burleigh J	Swift GH	Malpass AW	Bradley C	Topham R	Bailey H	Mason C	Wood H	Lowder A	Johnston J
R1			4	5	6	8	10	9	7		11							3			
rep		3	4		6	8		10	7		11			5		9					
R2			4		6	8		10	7		11			5		9		3			
R3		3		5	6	8		10	7		11			4		9					
		2	3	2	4	4	1	4	4		4			3		3		2			
						4	1	1	2							2					

1892-93

Division One

Manager: Jack Addenbrooke

	P	W	D	L	F	A	Pts
Sunderland	30	22	4	4	100	36	48
Preston North End	30	17	3	10	57	39	37
Everton	30	16	4	10	74	51	36
Aston Villa	30	16	3	11	73	62	35
Bolton Wanderers	30	13	6	11	56	55	32
Burnley	30	13	4	13	51	44	30
Stoke	30	12	5	13	58	48	29
West Bromwich Albion	30	12	5	13	58	69	29
Blackburn Rovers	30	8	13	9	47	56	29
Nottingham Forest	30	10	8	12	48	52	28
Wolverhampton Wanderers	30	12	4	14	47	68	28
The Wednesday	30	12	3	15	55	65	27
Derby County	30	9	9	12	52	64	27
Notts County	30	10	4	16	53	61	24
Accrington	30	6	11	13	57	81	23
Newton Heath	30	6	6	18	50	85	18

Match No.	Date		Venue	Opponents	Result		Scorers
1	Sep	3	H	Burnley	W	1-0	Wykes
2		10	H	Blackburn Rovers	W	4-2	Wood 2, Kinsey, Wykes
3		17	A	West Bromwich Albion	L	1-2	Wykes
4		24	H	Notts County	W	3-0	Wykes 2, Butcher
5	Oct	1	A	Bolton Wanderers	L	1-3	Wykes
6		8	H	Aston Villa	W	2-1	Wood, Devey
7		15	A	Newton Heath	L	1-10	Kinsey
8		22	H	Bolton Wanderers	L	1-2	Wood
9		29	A	Stoke	L	1-2	Topham
10	Nov	5	H	Nottingham Forest	D	2-2	Devey 2
11		12	A	Blackburn Rovers	D	3-3	Devey, Baker, Wood
12		19	H	Accrington	W	5-3	Butcher 5
13		26	A	Derby County	D	2-2	Wood, Devey
14	Dec	3	H	Stoke	W	1-0	Wood
15		10	A	Everton	L	2-3	Wood 2
16		17	H	Newton Heath	W	2-0	Wykes, Butcher
17		24	A	Nottingham Forest	L	1-3	Wood
18		26	H	Sunderland	W	2-0	Wood 2
19		27	H	West Bromwich Albion	D	1-1	Swift
20		31	A	Accrington	L	0-4	
21	Jan	2	A	Sunderland	L	2-5	Allen, Butcher
22	Feb	11	H	The Wednesday	W	2-0	Butcher, Wood
23		25	H	Derby County	W	2-1	Wood, Butcher
24	Mar	11	A	The Wednesday	W	1-0	Wood
25		18	H	Everton	L	2-4	Butcher, Wood
26	Apr	1	A	Burnley	L	0-2	
27		3	A	Aston Villa	L	0-5	
28		8	A	Notts County	L	0-3	
29		10	A	Preston North End	L	0-4	
30		15	H	Preston North End	W	2-1	Johnston 2

Appear

FA Cup

R1	Jan	21	A	Bolton Wanderers	D	1-1	Johnston
rep		28	H	Bolton Wanderers	W	2-1	Wood, Wykes
R2	Feb	4	H	Middlesbrough	W	2-1	Butcher, Wykes
R3		18	H	Darwen	W	5-0	Topham 2, Butcher, Griffin, Wykes
SF	Mar	4	N	Blackburn Rovers	W	2-1	Butcher, Topham
F		25	N	Everton	W	1-0	Allen

SF at Town Ground, Nottingham. Final at Fallowfield, Manchester.

Appear

R1 and R2 aet

Did you know that?

- Wolves' 10–1 League defeat at the hands of Newton Heath in mid-October remains their heaviest in competitive football.

- A record crowd of 45,067 attended the FA Cup Final at Fallowfield, Manchester.

- Joe Butcher (signed from Wolverhampton East End) became the first Wolves player to score five goals in a League game, against Accrington in November.

- Charlie Baker and Will Devey both played their last games for Wolves this season.

Swift GH	Malpass AW	Allen H	Kinsey G	Wykes D	Baker C	Devey W	Wood H	Johnston J	Hassall J	Davies J	Butcher J	Lawrence J	Topham R	Griffin A	Woodhall G	Wilson J	Dunn T	Fletcher AA	Griffiths H	
3	4	5	6	7	8	9	10	11												1
3		5	6	7	8	9	10	11	1	4										2
3		5	6	7	8	9	10	11	1	4										3
3		5	6	7	8		10	11	1	4	9									4
3	5		6	9	7	8	10	11		4										5
3		5	6	8		11	10		1	4		7	9							6
3	6	5	11			8	10		1	4		7		9						7
3		5	6			7	10	11	1	4	8		9							8
3		5	6			7	10			4	8		9		11					9
3	6	5			11	7	10			4			9		8					10
3	6	5			7	11	10			4	9				8					11
3	6	5			10	9	11			4	8				7					12
3	6	5			8	11	10			4	9				7					13
3	6	5			8		10			4	9				7	11				14
3	6	5			8	11	10			4	9				7					15
3	6	5		8			10			4	9				7	11				16
3	4	5	6	8	7	11	10				9									17
3	4	5	6	8		11	10				9		7							18
3	4	5	6	8	7	11	10				9									19
3	4	5	6	8			10	11			9				7					20
3		5	6	8			10			4	9		11		7					21
3	4	5	6	8			10				9		7	11			2			22
3	4	5	6	8			10		1		9			11	7					23
3	4	5	6	8			10	9						11				7		24
3	4	5	6	8			10				9		7	11						25
3		5		8			10	11		6	9				7				4	26
3		5	6	8			10		1	4	9		7	11			2			27
3	4	5	6	8				11	1		9			10	7					28
3	4	5	6				10	11	1		9			8	7					29
3		5	6	8			10	11	1		9		7						4	30
30	20	29	22	20	13	16	29	12	11	18	22	2	10	8	14	2	2	1	2	
1		1	2	7	1	5	16	2			11		1							

Swift GH	Malpass AW	Allen H	Kinsey G	Wykes D	Baker C	Devey W	Wood H	Johnston J	Hassall J	Davies J	Butcher J	Lawrence J	Topham R	Griffin A	Woodhall G	Wilson J	Dunn T	Fletcher AA	Griffiths H	
3	4	5	6	8			10	11			9		7							R1
3	4	5	6	8			10	11			9		7							rep
3	4	5	6	8			10	11			9		7				2			R2
3	4	5	6	8			10				9		7	11						R3
3	4	5	6	8			10				9		7	11						SF
3	4	5	6	8			10				9		7	11						F
6	6	6	6	6			6	3			6		6	3			1			
		1		3			1	1			3		3	1						

1893-94

Division One

Manager: Jack Addenbrooke

	P	W	D	L	F	A	Pts
Aston Villa	30	19	6	5	84	42	44
Sunderland	30	17	4	9	72	44	38
Derby County	30	16	4	10	73	62	36
Blackburn Rovers	30	16	2	12	69	53	34
Burnley	30	15	4	11	61	51	34
Everton	30	15	3	12	90	57	33
Nottingham Forest	30	14	4	12	57	48	32
West Bromwich Albion	30	14	4	12	66	59	32
Wolverhampton Wanderers	30	14	3	13	52	63	31
Sheffield United	30	13	5	12	47	61	31
Stoke	30	13	3	14	65	79	29
The Wednesday	30	9	8	13	48	57	26
Bolton Wanderers	30	10	4	16	38	52	24
Preston North End	30	10	3	17	44	56	23
Darwen	30	7	5	18	37	83	19
Newton Heath	30	6	2	22	36	72	14

Match No.	Date		Venue	Opponents	Result		Scorers	At
1	Sep	2	A	Nottingham Forest	L	1-7	Butcher	
2		4	H	The Wednesday	W	3-1	Wood 2, Black	
3		9	H	Bolton Wanderers	W	2-1	Black, Butcher	
4		18	H	Darwen	W	2-1	Woodhall, Wood	
5		23	A	Blackburn Rovers	L	0-3		
6		30	H	Sheffield United	L	3-4	Butcher, Wykes, Wood	
7	Oct	7	A	West Bromwich Albion	D	0-0		1
8		14	H	Nottingham Forest	W	3-1	Butcher 2, Wood	
9		21	A	Bolton Wanderers	L	0-2		
10		28	H	Newton Heath	W	2-0	Butcher, Wykes	
11	Nov	4	A	Sunderland	L	0-6		
12		11	A	Newton Heath	L	0-1		
13		25	H	Stoke	W	4-2	Butcher 3, Wood	
14	Dec	2	A	The Wednesday	W	4-1	Griffin, Wood, Edge, Butcher	
15		4	H	Everton	W	2-0	Butcher, Wood	
16		9	H	Preston North End	D	0-0		
17		16	A	Preston North End	W	3-1	Wykes 2, Owen	
18		23	H	Aston Villa	W	3-0	Butcher, Owen, Wykes	1
19		26	H	Blackburn Rovers	W	5-1	Griffin, Edge 2, Wykes 2	1
20		27	H	West Bromwich Albion	L	0-8		
21		30	A	Stoke	W	3-0	Griffin, Wood, Edge	
22	Jan	6	H	Sunderland	W	2-1	Wykes, Wood	
23		13	A	Sheffield United	L	2-3	Edge, Owen	
24		20	H	Derby County	L	2-4	Butcher, Wood	
25	Feb	3	A	Derby County	L	1-4	Edge	
26	Mar	3	H	Burnley	W	1-0	Malpass	
27		10	A	Darwen	L	1-3	Black	
28		24	A	Everton	L	0-3		
29		26	A	Aston Villa	D	1-1	Kinsey	1
30	Apr	14	A	Burnley	L	2-4	Wood, Wykes	

Appeara

FA Cup

R1	Jan	27	A	Aston Villa	L	2-4	Butcher, Wood	2

Appeara

* Some reference books give the score of the Wolves-Stoke League game played on 25 November 1893 as 5–2 with Butcher scoring four goals.

Did you know that?

- Wolves' home League game with Everton on 18 November was abandoned with the visitors leading 2–0. Wolves won the 'replay' 2–0.
- In April 1894 Wolves played Celtic for the first time, losing 4–2 in a friendly in Glasgow.
- Wolves signed outside-left David Black from Middlesbrough.
- Defenders Harry Haynes and Dave Robson both made their League debuts for Wolves.

Baugh R	Swift GH	Malpass AW	Haynes AH	Kinsey G	Wykes D	Butcher J	Griffin A	Wood H	Black DG	Griffiths H	Dunn T	Woodhall G	Owen W	Allen H	Edge R	Hassall J	Robson D	
2	3	4	5	6	7	8	9	10	11									1
2	3			6	8	9		10	11	4	5	7						2
2				6	8	9		10	11	4	5	7	3					3
2				6	8	9		10	11	4		7	3	5				4
2				6		9	8	10	11	4		7	3	5				5
2		4		6	7	8	9	10	11				3	5				6
2	3			6	7	9	8	10	11	4				5				7
	3			6	7	9	8	10	11	4	2			5				8
	3				7	9	8	10	11	4	2		6	5				9
2	3			6	7	9	8	10	11	4	5							10
2	3			6	7	9	8	10	11	4	5							11
2	3			6	7	9	8	10	11	4			5					12
2	3			6		9	8	10	11	4				5	7			13
2	3			6	7	9	8	10		4			5		11			14
2	3			6	7	8	9	10		4			5		11			15
2	3			6	7	8	9	10		4			5		11			16
	3			6	7	8	9	10		4	2		5		11			17
	3			6	7	8	9	10		4	2		5		11			18
	3			6	7	8	9	10		4	2		5		11			19
	3			6	7	8	9	10		4	2		5		11			20
	3			6	7	8	9	10		4	2		5		11	1		21
	3	6			7	8	9	10		4	2		5		11			22
	3	6			7	8	9	10		4	2		5		11			23
2	3	6			7	8	9	10		4			5		11			24
	3	6			7	8	9	10		4	2		5		11	1		25
	3	5		6	7		9	10	8	4	2				11	1		26
2	3	5		6	7		9	10	8	4					11	1		27
2	3	5		6	7		9	10	8	4					11	1		28
2	3	5		6	7		9	10	8	4					11	1		29
2		5	9	6	7			10	8	4					11	1	3	30
19	25	11	2	25	28	25	26	30	18	28	15	4	18	7	18	7	1	
		1		1	9	13	3	12	3			1	3		6			

Baugh R	Swift GH	Malpass AW	Haynes AH	Kinsey G	Wykes D	Butcher J	Griffin A	Wood H	Black DG	Griffiths H	Dunn T	Woodhall G	Owen W	Allen H	Edge R	Hassall J	Robson D	
	3			6	7	8	9	10		4	2		5		11			R1
	1			1	1	1	1	1		1	1		1		1			
						1		1										

1894-95

Division One

Manager: Jack Addenbrooke

	P	W	D	L	F	A	Pts
Sunderland	30	21	5	4	80	37	47
Everton	30	18	6	6	82	50	42
Aston Villa	30	17	5	8	82	43	39
Preston North End	30	15	5	10	62	46	35
Blackburn Rovers	30	11	10	9	59	49	32
Sheffield United	30	14	4	12	57	55	32
Nottingham Forest	30	13	5	12	50	56	31
The Wednesday	30	12	4	14	50	55	28
Burnley	30	11	4	15	44	56	26
Bolton Wanderers	30	9	7	14	61	62	25
Wolverhampton Wanderers	30	9	7	14	43	63	25
Small Heath	30	9	7	14	50	74	25
West Bromwich Albion	30	10	4	16	51	66	24
Stoke	30	9	6	15	50	67	24
Derby County	30	7	9	14	45	68	23
Liverpool	30	7	8	15	51	70	22

Match No.	Date		Venue	Opponents	Result		Scorers	At
1	Sep	1	H	Preston North End	L	1-3	Wood	
2		3	H	Sheffield United	L	0-3		
3		8	A	West Bromwich Albion	L	1-5	Griffin	
4		15	H	Small Heath	W	2-1	Wood, Butcher	
5		22	A	Burnley	L	1-2	Reynolds	
6		29	H	Liverpool	W	3-1	Reynolds, Black, Wood	
7	Oct	6	A	Small Heath	L	3-4	Butcher, Wood, Black	
8		13	H	The Wednesday	W	2-0	Wood 2	
9		20	A	Preston North End	L	0-2		
10		27	H	Bolton Wanderers	W	4-2	Bell 2, Haynes, Wood	
11	Nov	3	A	Sunderland	L	0-2		
12		10	H	Nottingham Forest	D	1-1	Wood	
13		17	A	The Wednesday	L	1-3	Reynolds	
14		24	H	Stoke	D	0-0		
15	Dec	1	A	Liverpool	D	3-3	Reynolds 2, Baugh	
16		8	H	Derby County	D	2-2	Fleming, Wood	
17		15	A	Bolton Wanderers	L	1-6	Wykes	
18		22	H	Aston Villa	L	0-4		
19		26	H	Burnley	W	1-0	Wykes	
20		27	H	West Bromwich Albion	W	3-1	Wykes, Fleming, Griffin	
21	Jan	5	H	Everton	W	1-0	Griffin	
22		12	H	Sunderland	L	1-4	Haynes	
23		19	A	Sheffield United	L	0-1		
24		26	A	Derby County	W	3-1	Griffin, Fleming 2	
25	Feb	4	A	Stoke	D	0-0		
26		23	H	Blackburn Rovers	D	3-3	Griffin 2, Malpass	
27	Mar	23	A	Blackburn Rovers	L	1-5	Edge	
28	Apr	8	A	Everton	L	1-2	Wykes	
29		13	A	Nottingham Forest	W	2-0	Griffin, Wood	
30		15	A	Aston Villa	D	2-2	Wykes, Griffin	

Appeara

FA Cup

R1	Feb	2	A	Darwen	D	0-0		
rep		6	H	Darwen	W	2-0	Griffin, Wykes	
R2		16	H	Stoke	W	2-0	Wykes 2	
R3	Mar	2	A	West Bromwich Albion	L	0-1		2

Appeara

Did you know that?

• Wolves sacked goalkeeper Billy Rose in July 1894 after a letter was circulated indicating that he was forming a players' union – the forerunner to the current PFA.

• Dicky Baugh became the first full-back to score in a League game for Wolves (against Liverpool in December).

• In October 1894, former club captain Harry Allen retired after 152 senior appearances for Wolves.

• Two Georges left Molineux – Kinsey (to Aston Villa) and Swift (to Loughborough Town).

	Robson D	Griffiths H	Malpass AW	Hamilton AJ	Wykes D	Fleming G	Black DG	Wood H	Bell J	Haynes AH	Brocksopp A	Dunn T	Reynolds J	Griffin A	Butcher J	Crump WH	Edge R	Lester F	Roberts J	Nurse DG	Tonks J	
	3	4	5	6	7	8	9	10	11													1
	3	4		6	7	9	8	10		5	11											2
	3	4		6			7	10			11	5	8	9								3
	3	4		6			8	10		5	11		7		9							4
		4	6				8	10		5		3	7	11	9							5
		4	6				8	10		5		3	7	11	9							6
		4	6				8	10		5		3	7	11	9							7
		4	6				8	10		5		3	7	11	9							8
		4	6				8	10		5		3	7	11	9							9
		4	6				8	10	9	5		3	7	11								10
		4	6				8	10		5		3	7	11	9							11
		4	6		7		8	10		5		3		11	9							12
		4	6		7		8	10	9	5		3	11					2				13
		4	6				8	10		5		3	7		9				11			14
		4	6			11	8	10		5		3	7	9								15
		4	6			11	8	10		5		3	7	9								16
		4	6		7	11	8	10		5		3			9							17
		4	6			11		10	9	5		3	7		8							18
		4	6		7		8	10		5		3		11	9							19
		4	6		7	10	8	2		5		3		11	9							20
		4	6		7	10	8	2		5		3		11	9							21
		4	6		7	10	8	2		5		3		11	9							22
		4	6		7	10	8	2		5		3		11	9							23
		4	5		7	10	8	6				3		11	9							24
		4			7	10	8	6	9	5		3		11								25
			5		7	10	8	6				3		11	9					4		26
			5		7		8	10				3		11		6	9			4		27
			5		7	4	8		10			3		11			9			6		28
			5		7	4	8	10				3		9			11			6		29
			5		7	6	8	10				3		9			11			4		30
5	4	25	26	4	17	16	29	29	6	22	3	27	14	23	18	1	4	1	1	5		
			1		5	4	2	10	2	2			5	8	2		1					

	Robson D	Griffiths H	Malpass AW	Hamilton AJ	Wykes D	Fleming G	Black DG	Wood H	Bell J	Haynes AH	Brocksopp A	Dunn T	Reynolds J	Griffin A	Butcher J	Crump WH	Edge R	Lester F	Roberts J	Nurse DG	Tonks J	
2		4	5		7	10	8	6				3		11	9							R1
2		4	5		7	10	8	6				3		11	9							rep
2		4	5		7	10	8	6				3		11	9							R2
2		4	5		7	10	8	6				3			9						11	R3
4		4	4		4	4	4	4				4		3	4						1	
					3									1								

1895-96

Division One

Manager: Jack Addenbrooke

	P	W	D	L	F	A	Pts
Aston Villa	30	20	5	5	78	45	45
Derby County	30	17	7	6	68	35	41
Everton	30	16	7	7	66	43	39
Bolton Wanderers	30	16	5	9	49	37	37
Sunderland	30	15	7	8	52	41	37
Stoke	30	15	0	15	56	47	30
The Wednesday	30	12	5	13	44	53	29
Blackburn Rovers	30	12	5	13	40	50	29
Preston North End	30	11	6	13	44	48	28
Burnley	30	10	7	13	48	44	27
Bury	30	12	3	15	50	54	27
Sheffield United	30	10	6	14	40	50	26
Nottingham Forest	30	11	3	16	42	57	25
Wolverhampton Wanderers	30	10	1	19	61	65	21
Small Heath	30	8	4	18	39	79	20
West Bromwich Albion	30	6	7	17	30	59	19

Match No.	Date		Venue	Opponents	Result		Scorers
1	Sep	2	H	Burnley	W	5-1	Beats, Henderson, Malpass, Wood, Wykes
2		7	A	Preston North End	L	3-4	Beats, Tonks, Wood
3		14	H	The Wednesday	W	4-0	Beats, Griffin, Henderson, Wykes
4		21	A	Sunderland	D	2-2	Wood, Wykes
5		28	H	Everton	L	2-3	Beats, Wood
6	Oct	5	H	Stoke	W	1-0	Wood
7		12	A	The Wednesday	L	1-3	Black
8		19	H	Sheffield United	W	4-1	Black 2, Beats, Tonks
9		26	A	Derby County	L	2-5	Beats, Wood
10	Nov	2	A	Everton	L	0-2	
11		9	A	Blackburn Rovers	L	1-3	Black
12		16	H	Derby County	W	2-0	Beats, Henderson
13		23	A	Stoke	L	1-4	Wood
14		30	A	West Bromwich Albion	L	1-2	Henderson
15	Dec	14	H	Blackburn Rovers	L	1-2	Black
16		21	H	Preston North End	W	2-1	Black, Wood
17		26	H	Aston Villa	L	1-2	Owen
18		27	H	Sunderland	L	1-3	Topham
19	Jan	4	A	Bolton Wanderers	L	0-4	
20		18	A	Small Heath	L	2-3	Henderson, Wood
21		25	H	Small Heath	W	7-2	Beats 2, Wood 2, Black, Henderson, Malpass
22	Feb	8	A	Sheffield United	L	1-2	Beats
23		18	A	Bury	L	0-3	
24		22	A	Burnley	L	1-3	Beats
25	Mar	7	H	West Bromwich Albion	L	1-2	Malpass
26		28	H	Nottingham Forest	W	6-1	Beats 2, Wood 2, Black, Henderson
27	Apr	4	A	Nottingham Forest	L	2-3	Fleming, Alsop (og)
28		6	A	Aston Villa	L	1-4	Tonks
29		7	H	Bury	W	1-0	Tonks
30		11	H	Bolton Wanderers	W	5-0	Henderson 2, Black, Tonks, Wood

Appeara

FA Cup

R1	Feb	1	H	Notts County	D	2-2	Henderson, Malpass
rep		5	A	Notts County	W	4-3	Wood 2, Beats, Black
R2		15	H	Liverpool	W	2-0	Owen, Wood
R3		29	H	Stoke	W	3-0	Henderson, Malpass, Tonks
SF	Mar	21	N	Derby County	W	2-1	Malpass, Tonks
F	Apr	18	N	The Wednesday	L	1-2	Black

SF at Perry Barr. Final at Crystal Palace.

Appeara

Did you know that?

- Forward David Wykes died in a Wolverhampton hospital from typhoid fever just 24 hours after playing for Wolves against Stoke on 5 October. He was only 28 years old.
- Billy Beats was signed for £80 (plus the proceeds from a benefit match) from Burslem Port Vale, Jack Miller came from Hednesford, Ted 'Cock' Pheasant arrived from Wednesbury Old Athletic and goalkeeper Billy Tennant moved from Hartshill Unity. Joe Butcher was sold to neighbours West Bromwich Albion.
- The attendance at the FA Cup Final was a new competition record at that time.
- The Final itself was refereed by an army lieutenant (William Simpson).

ugh R	Dunn T	Nurse DG	Malpass AW	Owen W	Wykes D	Henderson C	Beats WE	Wood H	Griffin A	Tonks J	Black DG	Fleming G	Green A	Swallow JE	Griffiths H	Topham R	Bunch W	Miller TJ	Tennant W	
	3	4	5	6	7	8	9	10	11											1
	3	4	5	6		8	9	10	11	7										2
	3	4	5	6	7	8	9	10	11											3
	3	4	5	6	7	8	9	10			11									4
	3	4	5	6	7	8	9	10	11											5
	3	4		5	7	8	9	10			11	6								6
	3	4	5	6		8	9	10		7	11									7
	3	4	5	6		8	9		10	7	11									8
	3	4	5	6		8	9	10		7	11									9
	3	4	5	6		8	9	10		7	11									10
	3	4	5	6		8	9	10	7		11									11
	3	4	5	6		8	9	10	7		11									12
	3	4	5	6		8	9	10	7		11									13
2	3	4	5	6		8		10	7		11		9							14
	3		5	6		8		10	9	7	11			1	4					15
2	3	4	5	6		8	9	10	7		11									16
2	3	4	5	6		8	9	10			11					7				17
	3	4	5	6		8	9	2			11	10				7				18
2		4		5		8		10		7		6	9				3	11		19
2	3		5	6		8		10	9	7	11			1	4					20
2	3		5	6		8	9	10		7	11				4					21
2	3		5	6		8	9	10		7	11	4							1	22
2	3		5	6		8	9	10		7					4			11	1	23
2			5	6		8	9	10		7	11	4					3		1	24
2	3		5	6		8	9	10		7	11				4				1	25
2	3		5	6		8	9	10		7	11				4				1	26
2	3		5	6		8	9			7	11	10			4				1	27
2	3		5	6		8	9	10		7	11				4				1	28
2	3		5	6		8	9	10		7	11	4							1	29
2	3		5	6		8	9	10		7	11				4				1	30
29	28	18	28	30	5	30	26	28	12	18	24	7	2	2	9	2	2	2	9	
			3	1	3	9	13	14	1	5	9	1				1				
2	3		5	6		8	9	10		7	11				4					R1
2	3		5	6		8	9	10		7	11				4					rep
2	3		5	6		8	9	10		7	11				4				1	R2
2	3		5	6		8	9	10		7	11				4				1	R3
2	3		5	6		8	9	10		7	11				4				1	SF
2	3		5	6		8	9	10		7	11				4				1	F
6	6		6	6		6	6	6		6	6				6				4	
			3	1		2	1	3		2	2									

1896-97

Division One

Manager: Jack Addenbrooke

	P	W	D	L	F	A	Pts
Aston Villa	30	21	5	4	73	38	47
Sheffield United	30	13	10	7	42	29	36
Derby County	30	16	4	10	70	50	36
Preston North End	30	11	12	7	55	40	34
Liverpool	30	12	9	9	46	38	33
The Wednesday	30	10	11	9	42	37	31
Everton	30	14	3	13	62	57	31
Bolton Wanderers	30	12	6	12	40	43	30
Bury	30	10	10	10	39	44	30
Wolverhampton Wanderers	30	11	6	13	45	41	28
Nottingham Forest	30	9	8	13	44	49	26
West Bromwich Albion	30	10	6	14	33	56	26
Stoke	30	11	3	16	48	59	25
Blackburn Rovers	30	11	3	16	35	62	25
Sunderland	30	7	9	14	34	47	23
Burnley	30	6	7	17	43	61	19

Match No.	Date		Venue	Opponents	Result		Scorers	Att
1	Sep	1	H	Derby County	W	1-0	Black	
2		5	A	Stoke	L	1-2	Edge	
3		12	H	Everton	L	0-1		
4		19	A	Derby County	L	3-4	Beats 2, Wood	
5		26	H	Blackburn Rovers	D	1-1	Miller	
6	Oct	3	A	Sunderland	W	3-0	Wood, Pheasant, Beats	
7		10	H	Stoke	L	1-2	Owen	
8		17	A	West Bromwich Albion	L	0-1		
9		24	H	Sunderland	L	0-1		
10		31	A	Everton	D	0-0		
11	Nov	21	H	Burnley	W	2-0	Nicholls 2	
12		28	A	Bury	L	2-3	Miller 2	
13	Dec	5	H	Nottingham Forest	W	4-1	McMain, Miller, Smith, Tonks	
14		12	A	The Wednesday	D	0-0		
15		19	H	Preston North End	D	1-1	Lyden	
16		26	H	Aston Villa	L	1-2	Malpass	2
17		28	H	West Bromwich Albion	W	6-1	Smith, Lyden 2, Owen, McMain 2	1
18	Jan	2	A	Blackburn Rovers	L	0-2		
19		9	H	Liverpool	L	1-2	McMain	
20		16	A	Preston North End	L	0-4		
21		23	A	Sheffield United	W	3-1	McMain, Miller, Tonks	
22	Feb	27	H	Bury	D	1-1	McMain	
23	Mar	4	A	Liverpool	L	0-3		
24		6	H	Sheffield United	D	1-1	Miller	
25		13	H	The Wednesday	W	2-0	Beats 2	
26		20	A	Burnley	W	3-0	Beats 2, Miller	
27	Apr	5	A	Bolton Wanderers	W	2-1	Tonks, Wood	
28		10	A	Nottingham Forest	W	2-1	Smith, Eccles	
29		19	A	Aston Villa	L	0-5		3
30		20	H	Bolton Wanderers	W	4-0	Smith 2, Wood, Beats	

Appeara

G

FA Cup

R1	Jan	30	A	Millwall Athletic	W	2-1	Beats, Tonks	1
R2	Feb	13	A	Blackburn Rovers	L	1-2	Beats	8

Appeara

G

Did you know that?

- The first Wolves player to be sent off during a competitive game was Billy Smith in the Final of the Birmingham Cup, which Walsall won 2–1.
- Goalkeeper Tom Baddeley and full-back George Eccles were both recruited from Burslem Port Vale, and Joe Blackett was secured from Loughborough Town.
- Billy Malpass took over as team captain from Harry Wood.
- Wolves recorded their biggest League win over rivals West Bromwich Albion so far, beating the Baggies 6–1 in December.

Eccles GS	Dunn T	Griffiths H	Malpass AW	Owen W	Tonks J	Nicholls A	Beats WE	Wood H	Black DG	Edge R	Nurse DG	Pheasant E	Miller TJ	Bunch W	Smith W	Fleming G	McMain J	Lyden J	
2	3	4	5	6	7	8	9	10	11										1
2	3	4	5	6	7		9	10	11	8									2
2	3	4	5	6	7		9	10	11		8								3
2	3	4	5	6	7		9	10				8	11						4
	3	4	5	6	7		9	10				8	11	2					5
	3	4	5	6	7		9	10				8	11	2					6
	3	4	5	6	7		9	10				8	11	2					7
	3	4	5	6	7		9	10				8	11	2					8
	3	4	5	6	7		9	10				8	11	2					9
2	3	4	5	6	7		9	10				8	11						10
2		4	5	6	7	8	9	3					11		10				11
2		4		6	7	8	9	3				5	11		10				12
2		4		5	7		9	3					11		10	6	8		13
2		4		5	7			3					11		10	6	8	9	14
2			4	5	7			3					11		10	6	8	9	15
2		4	5	6	7			3					11		10		8	9	16
2		4		5	7		9	3							11	6	10	8	17
2		4		5	7		11	3							10	6	8	9	18
2		4		5	7		9	3							11	6	10	8	19
		4	6	5			9	3		7					11	2	10	8	20
		4	5	6	7		9	3					11		10	2	8		21
		4	5	6	7		9	3					11		10	2	8		22
		4	5	6			9	3					11		10	2	8	7	23
		4	5	6	7		9	3					11		10	2	8		24
		4	6	5	7		9	3					11		10	2	8		25
		4	6	5	7		9	3					11		10	2	8		26
2		4	6	5	7		9	10							11	3	8		27
2		4	6	5	7		9	10							11	3	8		28
2		4	6	5	7		9	10							11	3	8		29
2		4	6	5	7		9	10							11	3	8		30
8	10	29	24	30	28	3	27	30	3	2	1	8	19	5	20	17	18	8	
1			1	2	3	2	8	4	1	1		1	7		5		6	3	

Eccles GS	Dunn T	Griffiths H	Malpass AW	Owen W	Tonks J	Nicholls A	Beats WE	Wood H	Black DG	Edge R	Nurse DG	Pheasant E	Miller TJ	Bunch W	Smith W	Fleming G	McMain J	Lyden J	
		4	6	5	7		9	3					11		10	2	8		R1
		4	6	5	7		9	3					11		10	2	8		R2
		2	2	2	2		2	2					2		2	2	2		
					1		2												

1897-98

Division One

Manager: Jack Addenbrooke

	P	W	D	L	F	A	Pts
Sheffield United	30	17	8	5	56	31	42
Sunderland	30	16	5	9	43	30	37
Wolverhampton Wanderers	30	14	7	9	57	41	35
Everton	30	13	9	8	48	39	35
The Wednesday	30	15	3	12	51	42	33
Aston Villa	30	14	5	11	61	51	33
West Bromwich Albion	30	11	10	9	44	45	32
Nottingham Forest	30	11	9	10	47	49	31
Liverpool	30	11	6	13	48	45	28
Derby County	30	11	6	13	57	61	28
Bolton Wanderers	30	11	4	15	28	41	26
Preston North End	30	8	8	14	35	43	24
Notts County	30	8	8	14	36	46	24
Bury	30	8	8	14	39	51	24
Blackburn Rovers	30	7	10	13	39	54	24
Stoke	30	8	8	14	35	55	24

Did you know that?

- By scoring against Preston North End on the opening day of the season, Harry Wood became the first player to reach the milestone of 100 League goals for Wolves. He moved to Southampton at the end of the campaign.
- Winger David Black was transferred to Burnley and Billy Tennant to Walsall, the latter for £75.
- Hillary Griffiths was appointed team captain.

Match No.	Date		Venue	Opponents	Result		Scorers
1	Sep	1	H	Preston North End	W	3-0	Tonks, McMain, Wood
2		4	H	Bury	W	3-0	Wood, Tonks, Miller
3		11	A	Sunderland	L	2-3	McMain, Beats
4		18	A	Everton	L	0-3	
5		25	H	Nottingham Forest	D	0-0	
6	Oct	2	H	Sheffield United	D	1-1	McMain
7		9	H	Everton	L	2-3	Tonks, Beats
8		16	A	Stoke	W	2-0	Smith, Wood
9		23	A	West Bromwich Albion	D	2-2	Smith, Miller
10		30	H	Notts County	W	3-1	Beats, Wood, Tonks
11	Nov	6	A	Bury	L	1-2	Smith
12		13	H	Sunderland	W	4-2	Wood, Smith, Tonks 2
13		20	A	Liverpool	L	0-1	
14		27	A	Preston North End	W	2-1	Smith, Wood
15	Dec	4	H	Derby County	W	2-0	Smith, Harper
16		11	H	Liverpool	W	2-1	Harper, Beats
17		18	A	Notts County	D	2-2	Owen, Miller
18		27	H	Aston Villa	D	1-1	Beats
19		28	H	West Bromwich Albion	D	1-1	Wood
20	Jan	8	A	Derby County	L	2-3	Miller, Fryer (og)
21		22	A	Sheffield United	L	1-2	Smith
22	Feb	5	H	Stoke	W	4-2	Tonks, Beats, Wood, Griffiths
23		26	A	Blackburn Rovers	W	3-2	Beats, Smith, Wood
24	Mar	5	A	The Wednesday	L	0-2	
25		12	A	Bolton Wanderers	L	1-2	Beats
26	Apr	2	H	Blackburn Rovers	W	3-2	Beats, Wood, Smith
27		8	A	Nottingham Forest	D	1-1	Beats
28		9	H	Bolton Wanderers	W	2-0	McMain 2
29		11	A	Aston Villa	W	2-1	Wood, Evans (og)
30		16	H	The Wednesday	W	5-0	Smith 2, Beats, Blackett, Chadburn

Appear

Two own-goals

FA Cup

R1	Jan	29	A	Notts County	W	1-0	Beats
R2	Feb	12	H	Derby County	L	0-1	

Appear

	Eccles GS	Blackett J	Griffiths H	Owen W	Fleming G	Tonks J	McMain J	Beats WE	Wood H	Miller TJ	Smith W	Matthias JS	Chadburn J	Harper G	Malpass AW	Nurse DG	Harris G	Tuft WE	Davies HJ	Greatwich FE	Smith J
1	2	3	4	5	6	7	8	9	10	11											
2	2	3	4	5	6	7	8	9	10	11											
3	2	3	4	5	6	7	8	9	10	11											
4	2	3	4	5	6	7	8	9	10	11											
5	2	3	4	5	6	7	8	9	10	11											
6	2	3	4	5	6	7	8	9	10	11											
7	2	3	4	5	6	7	8	9	10		11										
8		2	4	5	6	7		9	8	11	10	3									
9		2	4	5	6	7		9	8	11	10	3									
10		2	4	5	6	7		9	8	11	10	3									
11		2	4	5	6	7	9		8	11	10	3									
12	2	3	4	5	6	7		9	8	11	10										
13	2	3	4	5	6	7		9	8	11	10										
14	2	3	4	5	6			9	8	11	10		7								
15	2	3	4	5	6			9		11	10		7	8							
16	2	3		5	6			9		11	10		7	8	4						
17	2	3		5	6	7		9	8	11	10				4						
18	2	3		5	6	7		9	8	11	10				4						
19	2	3		5	6	7		9	8	11	10				4						
20	2	3			6	7		9	8	11	10				5	4					
21	2	3	4		6	7		9	8	11	10				5						
22		3	4	5	6	7		9	8	11	10				2						
23		3	4	5	2	7		9	8	11	10				6						
24		3	4	5	2	7		9	8	11	10				6						
25	2	3	4	5	6	7		9	8	11	10										
26		3	4	5	6			9	8	11	10		7				1	2			
27		3	4	5	6			9	8	11	10		7						2		
28		3	4	5	6		9			11	10								2	7	8
29		3	4	5	6			9	8	11	10								2	7	
30		3	4	5	6			9	8	11	10		7						2		
	8	30	25	28	30	22	9	28	27	29	24	4	6	2	9	1	1	1	4	2	1
		1	1	1		7	5	11	11	4	11		1	2							

	Eccles GS	Blackett J	Griffiths H	Owen W	Fleming G	Tonks J	McMain J	Beats WE	Wood H	Miller TJ	Smith W	Matthias JS	Chadburn J	Harper G	Malpass AW	Nurse DG	Harris G	Tuft WE	Davies HJ	Greatwich FE	Smith J
R1		3	4	5	6	7		9	8	11	10										
R2		3	4	5	2	7		9	8	11	10				6						
		2	2	2	2	2		2	2	2	2				1						
								1													

1898-99

Division One

Manager: Jack Addenbrooke

	P	W	D	L	F	A	Pts
Aston Villa	34	19	7	8	76	40	45
Liverpool	34	19	5	10	49	33	43
Burnley	34	15	9	10	45	47	39
Everton	34	15	8	11	48	41	38
Notts County	34	12	13	9	47	51	37
Blackburn Rovers	34	14	8	12	60	52	36
Sunderland	34	15	6	13	41	41	36
Wolverhampton Wanderers	34	14	7	13	54	48	35
Derby County	34	12	11	11	62	57	35
Bury	34	14	7	13	48	49	35
Nottingham Forest	34	11	11	12	42	42	33
Stoke	34	13	7	14	47	52	33
Newcastle United	34	11	8	15	49	48	30
West Bromwich Albion	34	12	6	16	42	57	30
Preston North End	34	10	9	15	44	47	29
Sheffield United	34	9	11	14	45	51	29
Bolton Wanderers	34	9	7	18	37	51	25
The Wednesday	34	8	8	18	32	61	24

Did you know that?

- Walter Annis was signed from neighbours Stafford Road FC.
- Three players who left Molineux were George Eccles and Billy Owen (both to Everton) and Billy Smith (to Portsmouth).
- The First Division was expanded to 18 clubs.
- League champions Aston Villa suffered their heaviest defeat of the season at Molineux, losing 4–0 in April.
- Wolves players, between them, missed four penalties this season.

Match No.	Date		Venue	Opponents	Result		Scorers
1	Sep	3	A	Newcastle United	W	4-2	Beats 2, R Davies, Miller
2		10	H	Preston North End	D	0-0	
3		12	A	Sheffield United	L	0-1	
4		17	A	Liverpool	L	0-1	
5		24	H	Nottingham Forest	L	0-2	
6	Oct	1	A	Bolton Wanderers	L	1-2	McMain
7		8	H	Derby County	D	2-2	Miller, Nurse
8		15	A	West Bromwich Albion	W	2-1	Miller, Worton
9		22	H	Blackburn Rovers	W	2-1	Smith 2
10		29	A	The Wednesday	L	0-3	
11	Nov	5	H	Sunderland	W	2-0	Blackett, Smith
12		12	H	Bury	L	1-2	Beats
13		19	A	Everton	L	1-2	Miller
14		26	H	Notts County	W	1-0	Fleming
15	Dec	3	A	Stoke	W	4-2	McMain 2, Blackett. Miller
16		10	A	Aston Villa	D	1-1	McMain
17		17	A	Burnley	L	2-4	McMain, Miller
18		24	H	Sheffield United	W	4-1	Blackett 3, Miller
19		27	H	West Bromwich Albion	W	5-1	Blackett 2, McMain 2, Miller
20		31	H	Newcastle United	D	0-0	
21	Jan	7	A	Preston North End	L	1-2	R Davies
22		14	H	Liverpool	D	0-0	
23		21	A	Nottingham Forest	L	0-3	
24	Feb	4	A	Derby County	L	2-6	Blackett, McMain
25		18	A	Blackburn Rovers	D	2-2	Miller 2
26		25	H	The Wednesday	D	0-0	
27	Mar	4	A	Sunderland	L	0-3	
28		14	A	Bury	W	2-0	Beats 2
29		25	A	Notts County	W	2-0	Tonks, Worton
30	Apr	1	H	Stoke	W	3-2	Beats 2, Worton
31		3	H	Aston Villa	W	4-0	Worton 2, Blackett, Tonks
32		4	H	Bolton Wanderers	W	1-0	Miller
33		15	H	Burnley	W	4-0	Beats 2, Miller, Tonks
34		29	H	Everton	L	1-2	Harper

Appear

FA Cup

R1	Jan	28	H	Bolton Wanderers	D	0-0	
rep	Feb	1	A	Bolton Wanderers	W	1-0	Blackett
R2		11	A	Derby County	L	1-2	Beats

Appear

Davies HJ	Blackett J	Griffiths H	Malpass AW	Fleming G	Tonks J	Davies RH	Beats WE	Smith W	Miller TJ	McMain J	Chadburn J	Pheasant E	Harris G	Matthias JS	Harper G	Nurse DG	Worton T	Tuft WE	Annis W	Platt D	
2	3	4	5	6	7	8	9	10	11												1
2	3	4	5	6	7	8	9	10	11												2
2	3	4	5	6	7	8		10		9	11										3
2	3	4		6	7	8		10	11	9		5									4
2	3	4	5	6	7	8	9	10	11												5
	3	4	5	6				10	11	9	7		1	2	8						6
	3			6				10	11	9	7	5	1	2	8	4					7
	3	4		6	7		9	10	11			5	1	2			8				8
	3	4		6	7		9	10	11			5	1	2			8				9
	3	4		6	7		9	10	11			5		2			8				10
	3	4		6	7		9	10	11			5		2			8				11
	3	4		6	7		9	10	11			5		2			8				12
	3	4		6	7		9	10	11			5		2			8				13
3	10	4		6	7		9		11	8		5		2							14
3	10	4		6	7		9		11	8		5		2							15
3	10	4		6	7		9		11	8				2			5				16
3	10			6	7		9		11	8				2		4	5				17
3	10	4		6	7		9		11	8		5		2							18
3	10	4		6	7	9			11	8		5		2							19
3	10	4		6	7	9			11	8		5		2							20
3	10	4		6	7	9			11	8		5		2							21
3	10	4		6	7	9			11	8		5		2							22
3	10	4		6		8	9		11		7	5		2							23
	10	4		6			9		11	8	7	5		2				3			24
	3	4		6	7		9		11	8		5					10	2			25
	3	4		6	7		9	10	11	8		5						2			26
	10	4		6	7		9		11	8		5		3				2			27
3	10	4		5			9		11					2			8		6	7	28
3		4		5	7		9		11	8				2			10		6		29
3	10	4		5	7		9		11					2			8		6		30
2	3	4		6	7		9		11			5			8		10				31
2	3	4		6	7	8	9		11			5					10				32
2	3	4		6	7		9		11	8		5					10				33
2	3	4		6	7		9		11			5			8		10				34
2	33	32	5	34	29	11	26	14	33	19	5	24	4	23	4	2	16	4	3	1	
	9			1	3	2	9	3	12	8					1	1	5				

Davies HJ	Blackett J	Griffiths H	Malpass AW	Fleming G	Tonks J	Davies RH	Beats WE	Smith W	Miller TJ	McMain J	Chadburn J	Pheasant E	Harris G	Matthias JS	Harper G	Nurse DG	Worton T	Tuft WE	Annis W	Platt D	
3	10	4	8	6	7		9		11	2		5									R1
3	10	4	8	6			9		11	2	7	5									rep
2	3	4	8	6	7		9		11			5					10				R2
3	3	3	3	3	2		3		3	2	1	3					1				
	1						1														

1899-1900

Division One

Manager: Jack Addenbrooke

	P	W	D	L	F	A	Pts
Aston Villa	34	22	6	6	77	35	50
Sheffield United	34	18	12	4	63	33	48
Sunderland	34	19	3	12	50	35	41
Wolverhampton Wanderers	34	15	9	10	48	37	39
Newcastle United	34	13	10	11	53	43	36
Derby County	34	14	8	12	45	43	36
Manchester City	34	13	8	13	50	44	34
Nottingham Forest	34	13	8	13	56	55	34
Stoke	34	13	8	13	37	45	34
Liverpool	34	14	5	15	49	45	33
Everton	34	13	7	14	47	49	33
Bury	34	13	6	15	40	44	32
West Bromwich Albion	34	11	8	15	43	51	30
Blackburn Rovers	34	13	4	17	49	61	30
Notts County	34	9	11	14	46	60	29
Preston North End	34	12	4	18	38	48	28
Burnley	34	11	5	18	34	54	27
Glossop	34	4	10	20	31	74	18

Match No.	Date		Venue	Opponents	Result		Scorers	At
1	Sep	2	A	Bury	L	0-3		
2		9	H	Nottingham Forest	D	2-2	Owen 2	
3		16	A	Notts County	D	0-0		
4		18	A	Stoke	W	3-1	Beats, Bryan, Miller	
5		23	H	Glossop	W	4-0	Beats 2, Miller, Worton	
6		30	A	Manchester City	D	1-1	Bryan	
7	Oct	7	H	Stoke	L	0-2		
8		14	A	Sheffield United	L	2-5	Blackett, Worton	
9		28	A	Newcastle United	W	1-0	Owen	
10	Nov	4	H	West Bromwich Albion	W	2-0	Beats, Worton	
11		11	A	Aston Villa	D	0-0		
12		25	A	Liverpool	D	1-1	Worton	
13	Dec	2	H	Blackburn Rovers	W	4-0	Bowen 2, Harper 2	
14		9	A	Burnley	W	1-0	Tonks	
15		16	A	Derby County	W	2-0	Harper, Worton	
16		23	H	Preston North End	L	1-3	Harper	
17		26	H	Sunderland	W	1-0	Bowen	
18		30	H	Bury	W	1-0	Pheasant	
19	Jan	1	A	Sunderland	W	2-1	Harper, Tonks	
20		6	A	Nottingham Forest	D	0-0		
21		13	H	Notts County	D	2-2	Bowen Pheasant	
22		20	A	Glossop	W	3-2	Beats, Harper, Pheasant	
23	Feb	3	H	Manchester City	D	1-1	Bowen	
24	Mar	3	H	Newcastle United	D	1-1	Beats	
25		10	A	West Bromwich Albion	L	2-3	Harper, Miller	
26		17	H	Everton	W	2-1	Bowen, Harper	
27		24	A	Everton	W	1-0	Bowen	
28		31	H	Liverpool	L	0-1		
29	Apr	7	A	Blackburn Rovers	L	1-2	Pheasant	
30		14	H	Burnley	W	3-0	Beats, Harper, Worton	
31		16	H	Aston Villa	L	0-1		
32		17	H	Sheffield United	L	1-2	Colley	
33		21	H	Derby County	W	3-0	Beats 2, Harper	
34		28	A	Preston North End	L	0-2		

Appeara

FA Cup

R1	Jan	27	A	Queen's Park Rangers	D	1-1	Miller
rep		31	H	Queen's Park Rangers	L	0-1	

Replay aet

Appeara

Did you know that?

- Billy Wooldridge was signed from Cradley St Luke's. He would go on to serve Wolves for 13 years, making over 350 appearances.
- Other new signings included George Bowen (from Bridgetown Amateurs) and George Walker (from Willenhall Pickwick).
- Out of Molineux went Joe Blackett (to Derby County), Joe McMain (to Notts County) and Billy Malpass who retired after making 155 senior appearances for the club.
- Sheffield United defender Peter Boyle scored a goal from 50 yards in Wolves' 5–2 defeat at Bramall Lane in October.
- Wolves' FA Cup conquerors, QPR, were members of the Southern League.

	Matthias JS	Blackett J	Griffiths H	Pheasant E	Fleming G	Tonks J	Owen T	Beats WE	Worton T	Miller TJ	Bryan JT	Tuft WE	Nurse DG	Platt D	Harper G	Davies HJ	Bowen G	Colley R	Harris G
1	2	3	4	5	6	7	8	9	10	11									
2	2	3	4	5	6		8	9	10	11	7								
3	2	3	4	5	6		8	9	10	11	7								
4	2	3	4	5	6		8	9	10	11	7								
5		3		5	6		8	9	10	11	7	2	4						
6		3		5	6			9	10		11	2	4	7	8				
7		3		5	6			9	10	11	7	2	4		8				
8		3	4	5	6		8	9	10	11				7		2			
9		3	4	5	6		8	9	10	11				7		2			
10		3	4	5	6		8	9	10	11				7		2			
11		3	4	5	6		9		10	11				7	8	2			
12		3	4	5	6	7			10	11					8	2	9		
13		3	4	5	6	7			10	11					8	2	9		
14		3	4	5	6	7			10	11					8	2	9		
15		3	4	5	6	7			10	11					8	2	9		
16		3	4	5	6	7			10	11					8	2	9		
17		3	4	5	6	7			10	11					8	2	9		
18		3	4	5	6	7			10	11					8	2	9		
19		3	4	5	6	7			10	11					8	2	9		
20		3	4	5	6				10	11					8	2	9	7	1
21		3	4	5	6		8		10	11					7		9		
22		3		5	6			9	10	11			4		8		7		1
23		3	4	5	6		10				11				8	2	9	7	
24		3	4	5	6			9	10	11					8	2	7		
25		3		5	6			9	10	11			4		8	2	7		
26		3	4	5	6			9	10	11					8	2	7		
27		3	4	5	6			9	10	11					8	2	7		
28		3		5	6			9	10		11		4		8	2	7		
29		3	4	5	6			9	10	11					8	2	7		
30		3	4	5	6			9	10	11					8	2		7	
31		3	4	5	6			9	10	11					8			7	
32		3	4	5	6			9	10		11				8			7	
33		3	4	5	6			9	10	11					8	2		7	
34			4	5	6			9	10	11					8	2		7	
		33	28	34	34	9	11	22	33	30	9	3	6	5	26	23	18	7	2
		1		4		2	3	9	6	3	2				10		7	1	
R1		3	4	5	6			9	10	11					8	2	7		
rep		3	4	5	6		10			11	7				8	2	9		
		2	2	2	2		1	1	1	2	1				2	2	2		
										1									

1900-01

Division One

Manager: Jack Addenbrooke

	P	W	D	L	F	A	Pts
Liverpool	34	19	7	8	59	35	45
Sunderland	34	15	13	6	57	26	43
Notts County	34	18	4	12	54	46	40
Nottingham Forest	34	16	7	11	53	36	39
Bury	34	16	7	11	53	37	39
Newcastle United	34	14	10	10	42	37	38
Everton	34	16	5	13	55	42	37
The Wednesday	34	13	10	11	52	42	36
Blackburn Rovers	34	12	9	13	39	47	33
Bolton Wanderers	34	13	7	14	39	55	33
Manchester City	34	13	6	15	48	58	32
Derby County	34	12	7	15	55	42	31
Wolverhampton Wanderers	34	9	13	12	39	55	31
Sheffield United	34	12	7	15	35	52	31
Aston Villa	34	10	10	14	45	51	30
Stoke	34	11	5	18	46	57	27
Preston North End	34	9	7	18	49	75	25
West Bromwich Albion	34	7	8	19	35	62	22

Did you know that?

- Of the 25-strong professional squad at Molineux, 21 were Staffordshire-born; the other four came from Cheshire.
- Two Jacks joined Wolves – Jack Whitehouse from Wednesbury Town and Jack Jones from Lanesfield. Both would go on to give the club excellent service.
- Three players who left Molineux were Jack Tonks (to Walsall), George Harper (to Grimsby Town) and Dan Nurse, who joined West Bromwich Albion at the end of the season.
- Wolves visited The Hawthorns for the first time, beating Albion 2–1, a result that helped send the Baggies into the Second Division.

Match No.	Date		Venue	Opponents	Result		Scorers
1	Sep	1	H	West Bromwich Albion	D	0-0	
2		3	H	Notts County	W	3-2	Colley, Miller, Worton
3		8	A	Everton	L	1-5	Poppitt
4		15	H	Sunderland	D	2-2	Bowen, Pheasant
5		22	A	Derby County	W	5-4	Beats 2, Harper 2, Miller
6		29	H	Bolton Wanderers	D	1-1	Harper
7	Oct	6	A	Notts County	L	1-4	Harper
8		13	H	Preston North End	D	2-2	Miller, Poppitt
9		27	A	Aston Villa	D	0-0	
10	Nov	3	H	Liverpool	W	2-1	Bowen 2
11		10	A	Newcastle United	L	1-3	Harper
12		17	H	Sheffield United	W	3-0	Bowen 2, Pheasant
13		24	A	Manchester City	L	2-3	Harper, Poppitt
14	Dec	1	H	Bury	D	1-1	Beats
15		8	A	Nottingham Forest	L	1-2	Beats
16		15	H	Blackburn Rovers	D	2-2	Miller, Pheasant
17		22	A	Stoke	L	0-3	
18		26	H	The Wednesday	D	1-1	Miller
19		29	A	West Bromwich Albion	W	2-1	Wooldridge 2
20	Jan	1	A	The Wednesday	L	0-2	
21		5	H	Everton	D	1-1	Wooldridge
22		12	A	Sunderland	L	2-7	Wooldridge 2
23		19	H	Derby County	D	0-0	
24	Feb	16	A	Preston North End	D	1-1	Bowen
25	Mar	9	A	Liverpool	L	0-1	
26		16	H	Newcastle United	W	1-0	Wooldridge
27		25	A	Sheffield United	D	1-1	Annis
28		30	H	Manchester City	W	1-0	Pheasant
29	Apr	6	A	Bury	W	1-0	Fleming
30		8	H	Aston Villa	D	0-0	
31		9	H	Stoke	L	0-2	
32		13	H	Nottingham Forest	W	1-0	Beats
33		20	A	Blackburn Rovers	L	0-2	
34		29	A	Bolton Wanderers	L	0-1	

Appeara

FA Cup

R1	Feb	9	H	New Brighton Tower	W	5-1	Bowen 2, Wooldridge 3
R2		23	A	Notts County	W	3-2	Harper 2, Beats
R3	Mar	23	H	Sheffield United	L	0-4	

Appeara

Davies HJ	Matthias JS	Griffiths H	Pheasant E	Fleming G	Poppitt J	Harper G	Beats WE	Worton T	Miller TJ	Nurse DG	Colley R	Bowen G	Walker WG	Annis W	Howell WT	Wooldridge WT	Barker G	Pope FH	Jones JW	
2	3	4	5	6	7	8	9	10	11											1
2	3		5	6	7		9	10	11	4	8									2
2	3		5	6	7	8	9	10	11	4										3
2			5	3	7	8	9	6	11	4		10								4
2			5	3	7	8	9	6	11	4		10								5
2			5		7	8	9	6	11	4		10	3							6
			5	2	7	8	9		11	4		10	3	6						7
3			5	4	8	10	9		11			7	2	6						8
3			5	6	8	10	9		11			7	2	4						9
3			5	6	8	10	9		11			7	2	4						10
3			5	6	8	10	9		11			7	2	4						11
3			5	6	8	10	9		11			7	2	4						12
3			5	6	8	10	9		11			7	2	4						13
3			5	6	8	10	9		11			7	2	4						14
3			5	6	8	10	9		11			7	2	4						15
			5	6	8	10	9		11			7	2	4	3					16
	3		5	6	8	10	9		11			7	2	4						17
	3		5	6	8		9		11			7	2	4		10				18
	3		5	6		8	9		11			7	2	4		10				19
	3		5	6		8	9		11			7	2	4		10				20
	3		5	6		8	9		11			7	2	4		10				21
3			5	6		8	9		11			7		4		10	2			22
			5	6		10			11			7	3	4		9	2	8		23
			5	6		8	9		11			7	3	4		10	2			24
			5	6		8	9		11			7	3	4		10	2			25
3			5	6	8		9		11			7		4		10	2			26
3			5	6		8	9		11			7		4		10	2			27
			5	6		8	9		11			7	3	4		10	2			28
			5	6		8	9					7	3	4		10	2		11	29
			5	6			9	8				7	3	4		10	2		11	30
			5	6			9	8				7	3	4		10	2		11	31
			5	6		8	9					7	3	4		10	2		11	32
			5	6	7	8	9						3	4		10	2		11	33
			5	6		8	9					7	3	4		10	2		11	34
7	8	1	34	33	20	29	33	8	28	6	1	30	26	28	1	17	13	1	6	
			4	1	3	6	5	1	5		1	6		1		6				

Davies HJ	Matthias JS	Griffiths H	Pheasant E	Fleming G	Poppitt J	Harper G	Beats WE	Worton T	Miller TJ	Nurse DG	Colley R	Bowen G	Walker WG	Annis W	Howell WT	Wooldridge WT	Barker G	Pope FH	Jones JW	
			5	6		8	9		11			7	3	4		10	2			R1
			5	6		8	9		11			7	3	4		10	2			R2
3			5	6		8	9		11			7		4		10	2			R3
1			3	3		3	3		3			3	2	3		3	3			
						2	1					2				3				

1901-02

Division One

Manager: Jack Addenbrooke

	P	W	D	L	F	A	Pts
Sunderland	34	19	6	9	50	35	44
Everton	34	17	7	10	53	35	41
Newcastle United	34	14	9	11	48	34	37
Blackburn Rovers	34	15	6	13	52	48	36
Nottingham Forest	34	13	9	12	43	43	35
Derby County	34	13	9	12	39	41	35
Bury	34	13	8	13	44	38	34
Aston Villa	34	13	8	13	42	40	34
The Wednesday	34	13	8	13	48	52	34
Sheffield United	34	13	7	14	53	48	33
Liverpool	34	10	12	12	42	38	32
Bolton Wanderers	34	12	8	14	51	56	32
Notts County	34	14	4	16	51	57	32
Wolverhampton Wanderers	34	13	6	15	46	57	32
Grimsby Town	34	13	6	15	44	60	32
Stoke	34	11	9	14	45	55	31
Small Heath	34	11	8	15	47	45	30
Manchester City	34	11	6	17	42	58	28

Did you know that?

- Centre-half Ted Pheasant became the first Wolves defender to score a hat-trick when Newcastle United were defeated 3–0 on 10 March.
- Goalkeeper Jimmy Stringer conceded five goals when making his League debut for Wolves against Notts County in March.
- Wolves' Billy Wooldridge scored four goals in England's 10–0 'unofficial' international win over Germany in Manchester. In the same year Wooldridge also scored a hat-trick for the Football League in a 9–0 win over the Irish League.
- Dick Betteley was signed from Bilston United, while Hillary Griffiths moved to Burton Swifts.

Match No.	Date		Venue	Opponents	Result		Scorers	Atten
1	Sep	2	H	Nottingham Forest	W	2-0	Haywood, JW Jones	4
2		7	A	Everton	L	1-6	Wooldridge	25
3		14	H	Sunderland	W	4-2	Beats, Haywood, Miller, Wooldridge	6
4		21	A	Small Heath	W	2-1	Beats, Haywood	17
5		28	H	Derby County	D	0-0		8
6	Oct	5	A	The Wednesday	D	1-1	Wooldridge	6
7		12	H	Notts County	W	3-1	Miller, Pope, Wooldridge	5
8		19	A	Bolton Wanderers	D	2-2	Haywood, Pheasant	9
9		26	H	Manchester City	D	0-0		8
10	Nov	2	H	Grimsby Town	W	2-0	Swift, Wooldridge	6
11		9	A	Liverpool	L	1-4	Guelliam	16
12		11	A	Stoke	L	0-3		8
13		23	A	Aston Villa	L	1-2	Wooldridge	20
14		30	H	Sheffield United	D	1-1	Wooldridge	6
15	Dec	7	A	Nottingham Forest	L	0-2		5
16		14	H	Bury	W	1-0	Wooldridge	4
17		21	A	Blackburn Rovers	L	0-2		4
18		25	A	Derby County	L	1-3	Wooldridge	13
19		26	H	Everton	W	2-1	Beats, Haywood	10
20		28	H	Stoke	W	4-1	Beats 2, Fellows, Miller	7
21	Jan	11	A	Sunderland	L	0-2		15
22		18	H	Small Heath	W	2-1	Beats, Rowbotham	9
23	Feb	1	H	The Wednesday	W	1-0	Beats	5
24		15	H	Bolton Wanderers	L	1-2	Wooldridge	4
25		22	A	Manchester City	L	0-3		16
26	Mar	1	A	Grimsby Town	L	0-3		4
27		8	H	Liverpool	W	3-1	Miller, Preston, Wooldridge	6
28		10	H	Newcastle United	W	3-0	Pheasant 3	2
29		15	A	Newcastle United	L	1-3	Beats	7
30		22	H	Aston Villa	L	0-2		18
31		28	A	Notts County	L	3-5	Wooldridge 2, Fellows	4
32		29	A	Sheffield United	D	0-0		12
33		31	H	Blackburn Rovers	W	3-1	Pheasant 2, Fellows	1
34	Apr	12	A	Bury	L	1-2	Pheasant	2

Appearar

G

FA Cup

R1	Jan	25	H	Bolton Wanderers	L	0-2	16

Appearar

…nes J	Walker WG	Whitehouse J	Pheasant E	Annis W	Jones JW	Haywood A	Beats WE	Wooldridge WT	Miller TJ	Pope FH	Fellows A	Swift G	Preston H	Guelliam RC	Robotham H	Poppitt J	Dean J	Stringer J	Betteley RH	
	3	4	5	6	7	8	9	10	11											1
	3	4	5	6	7	8	9	10	11											2
	3	4	5	6	7	8	9	10	11											3
	3	4	5	6	7	8	9	10	11											4
	3	4	5	6	7	8	9	10	11											5
	3	4	5	6	7	8		10	11	9										6
	3	4	5	6	7	8		10	11	9										7
	3	4	5	6		8		10	11	9	7									8
	3	4	5	6	7	8		10	11	9										9
	3	4	5	6				10	11		7	8	9							10
	3	4	5	6		8			11		7		9	10						11
	3	4	5	6		8		9	11		7			10						12
	3	4		6		8		10	11		7		9		5					13
	3	4	5	6		8		10	11		7		9							14
	3	4	5	6	7	8		10			11					9				15
	3	4	5	6		8	9	10			7						11			16
	3	4	5	6		8	9	10			7						11			17
	3	4	5	6		8	9	10			7						11			18
	3	4	5			8	9	10	11		7				6					19
	3	4	5			8	9	10	11		7				6					20
	3		5	6		8	9	10	11		7				4					21
	3	4	5	6			9	10	11		7				8					22
	3		5	6		8	9	10	11		7				4					23
	3	4	5	6		8	9	10	11		7									24
	3	4	5	6		8	9	10	11		7									25
	3	4	5	6		8	9	10	11		7									26
	3	4	5	6		8		10	11		7		9							27
	3	4	5	6		8		10	11		7		9							28
	3	4	5	6		8	9	10	11		7									29
	3	4	5	6		8		10	11		7		9							30
		4	5	6			9	10	11		7		8					1	3	31
		4	5	6		8		10	11		7		9					1	3	32
		4	5	6		8		10	11		7		9					1	3	33
		4	5	6		8	9	10	11		7							1	3	34
	30	32	33	32	9	31	19	33	30	4	26	1	10	2	6	1	3	4	4	
			7		1	5	8	13	4	1	3	1	1	1	1					
	3	4	5	6		8	9	10	11		7									R1
	1	1	1	1		1	1	1	1		1									

1902-03

Division One

Manager: Jack Addenbrooke

	P	W	D	L	F	A	Pts
The Wednesday	34	19	4	11	54	36	42
Aston Villa	34	19	3	12	61	40	41
Sunderland	34	16	9	9	51	36	41
Sheffield United	34	17	5	12	58	44	39
Liverpool	34	17	4	13	68	49	38
Stoke	34	15	7	12	46	38	37
West Bromwich Albion	34	16	4	14	54	53	36
Bury	34	16	3	15	54	43	35
Derby County	34	16	3	15	50	47	35
Nottingham Forest	34	14	7	13	49	47	35
Wolverhampton Wanderers	34	14	5	15	48	57	33
Everton	34	13	6	15	45	47	32
Middlesbrough	34	14	4	16	41	50	32
Newcastle United	34	14	4	16	41	51	32
Notts County	34	12	7	15	41	49	31
Blackburn Rovers	34	12	5	17	44	63	29
Grimsby Town	34	8	9	17	43	62	25
Bolton Wanderers	34	8	3	23	37	73	19

Match No.	Date		Venue	Opponents	Result		Scorers
1	Sep	1	H	Derby County	W	3-0	Smith 2, Miller
2		6	H	Sunderland	D	3-3	Beats,Smith, Wooldridge
3		13	A	Stoke	L	0-3	
4		20	H	Everton	D	1-1	Wooldridge
5		27	A	The Wednesday	D	1-1	Smith
6	Oct	4	H	West Bromwich Albion	L	1-2	Smith
7		11	A	Notts County	D	0-0	
8		18	H	Bolton Wanderers	W	3-1	Fellows, Haywood, Wooldridge
9		25	A	Middlesbrough	L	0-2	
10	Nov	1	H	Newcastle United	W	3-0	Haywood 2, Miller
11		8	A	Derby County	L	1-3	Beats
12		15	A	Liverpool	L	1-4	Miller
13		22	H	Sheffield United	L	1-3	Wooldridge
14		29	A	Grimsby Town	W	2-1	Fellows, Haywood
15	Dec	6	H	Aston Villa	W	2-1	Haywood, Smith
16		13	A	Nottingham Forest	L	0-2	
17		20	H	Bury	W	3-2	Haywood 2, Fellows
18		26	H	Middlesbrough	W	2-0	Haywood 2
19		27	H	Blackburn Rovers	W	2-0	Fellows, Smith
20	Jan	1	A	Blackburn Rovers	L	0-1	
21		3	A	Sunderland	L	0-3	
22		10	H	Stoke	W	1-0	Wooldridge
23		17	A	Everton	L	1-2	Beats
24		24	H	The Wednesday	W	2-1	Smith, Walker
25		31	A	West Bromwich Albion	D	2-2	Bowen, Wooldridge
26	Feb	14	A	Bolton Wanderers	L	1-4	Wooldridge
27		28	A	Newcastle United	W	4-2	Beats, Jones, Miller, Smith
28	Mar	21	A	Sheffield United	L	0-3	
29		28	H	Grimsby Town	W	3-0	Haywood, Miller, Wooldridge
30	Apr	4	A	Aston Villa	L	1-3	Walker
31		11	H	Nottingham Forest	W	2-1	Fellows, Haywood
32		13	H	Notts County	W	2-0	Pheasant, Wooldridge
33		22	A	Bury	L	0-4	
34		27	H	Liverpool	L	0-2	

Appea

FA Cup

R1	Feb	7	A	Bury	L	0-1	

Appea

Did you know that?

- In February, Wolves' goalkeeper Tom Baddeley won the first of his five England caps at Molineux against Ireland in a 4–0 win.

- After scoring 73 goals in 199 senior games for Wolves, Billy Beats left Molineux in May 1903 to join Bristol Rovers.

- Bury, who ousted Wolves in the first round of the FA Cup, went on to win the Final, beating Derby County by a record score of 6–0.

Match	Betteley RH	Whitehouse J	Pheasant E	Annis W	Fellows A	Smith J	Beats WE	Wooldridge WT	Miller TJ	Dean J	Robotham H	Haywood A	Stringer J	Walker WG	Preston H	Holyhead J	Bowen G
1	3	4	5	6	7	8	9	10	11								
2	3	4	5	6	7	8	9	10	11								
3	3	4	5	6	7	8	9	10	11								
4	3	4	5	6	7	8	9	10	11								
5	3	4	5	6		8	9	10	11	7							
6	3	4		6		8	9	10	11		5	7					
7	3	4		6		8	9	10	11				1	5	7		
8	3	5		6	7		9	10	11			8	1			4	
9	3	5		6	7		9	10	11			8	1			4	
10	3	5		6	7		9	10	11			8				4	
11	3	5		6	7		9	10	11			8				4	
12	3	4	5	6	7		9	10	11			8					
13	3	5		6	7		9	10	11			8				4	
14	3	4		6	7	9		10	11			8		5			
15	3	4		6	7	9		10	11			8		5			
16	3	4		6	7	9		10	11			8		5			
17	3	4		6	7	9		10	11			8		5			
18	3	4		6	7	9		10	11			8		5			
19	3	4		6	7	9		10	11			8		5			
20	3	4		6	7	9		10	11			8	1	5			
21	3	4		6	7	9		10	11			8	1	5			
22	3	4		6	7	9		10	11			8	1	5			
23	3	4		6	7	9	8	10	11					5			
24	3	4		6		9	8	10	11					5			7
25	3	4		6		9		10	11			8		5			7
26	3	4				9	8	10	11				1	5		6	7
27	3	4		6	7	10	9	8	11					5			
28	3	4		6	7	9		8	11			10		5			
29	3	4		6	7		9	8	11			10		5			
30	3	4	5	6	7			8	11			10	1	9			
31	3		5	6	7	9		8	11			10		4			
32	3		5	6	7	9		8	11			10		4			
33	3		5	6	7	9		8	11			10		4			
34	3	4	5	6	7			8	11			10		9			
	34	31	11	33	28	25	18	34	34	1	1	24	8	22	1	6	3
			1		5	9	4	9	5			11		2			1

Match	Betteley RH	Whitehouse J	Pheasant E	Annis W	Fellows A	Smith J	Beats WE	Wooldridge WT	Miller TJ	Dean J	Robotham H	Haywood A	Stringer J	Walker WG	Preston H	Holyhead J	Bowen G
R1	3	4		6		9	7	10	11			8		5			
	1	1		1		1	1	1	1			1		1			

1903-04

Division One

Manager: Jack Addenbrooke

	P	W	D	L	F	A	Pts
The Wednesday	34	20	7	7	48	28	47
Manchester City	34	19	6	9	71	45	44
Everton	34	19	5	10	59	32	43
Newcastle United	34	18	6	10	58	45	42
Aston Villa	34	17	7	10	70	48	41
Sunderland	34	17	5	12	63	49	39
Sheffield United	34	15	8	11	62	57	38
Wolverhampton Wanderers	34	14	8	12	44	66	36
Nottingham Forest	34	11	9	14	57	57	31
Middlesbrough	34	9	12	13	46	47	30
Small Heath	34	11	8	15	39	52	30
Bury	34	7	15	12	40	53	29
Notts County	34	12	5	17	37	61	29
Derby County	34	9	10	15	58	60	28
Blackburn Rovers	34	11	6	17	48	60	28
Stoke	34	10	7	17	54	57	27
Liverpool	34	9	8	17	49	62	26
West Bromwich Albion	34	7	10	17	36	60	24

Match No.	Date		Venue	Opponents	Result		Scorers
1	Sep	5	A	Derby County	L	1-2	Smith
2		12	H	Blackburn Rovers	W	1-0	Haywood
3		19	A	Manchester City	L	1-4	Pheasant
4		26	H	Nottingham Forest	W	3-2	Wooldridge 2, Pheaasant
5	Oct	3	A	Notts County	W	2-0	Miller 2
6		10	H	The Wednesday	W	2-1	Miller, Wooldridge
7		17	A	Sheffield United	L	2-7	Wooldridge 2
8		24	H	Sunderland	W	2-1	Haywood, Miller
9		31	A	Newcastle United	L	0-3	
10	Nov	7	H	West Bromwich Albion	W	1-0	Haywood
11		14	A	Aston Villa	L	0-2	
12		21	H	Small Heath	W	1-0	Haywood
13		28	A	Middlesbrough	W	2-1	Miller, Wooldridge
14	Dec	5	H	Everton	D	2-2	Miller, Wooldridge
15		12	A	Liverpool	W	2-1	Jones, Wooldridge
16		19	A	Stoke	L	1-5	Haywood
17		26	H	Bury	D	0-0	
18		28	H	Liverpool	W	4-2	Haywood 2, Wooldridge 2
19	Jan	1	A	The Wednesday	L	0-4	
20		2	H	Derby County	D	2-2	Smith, Wooldridge
21		9	A	Blackburn Rovers	D	1-1	Wooldridge
22		23	A	Nottingham Forest	L	0-5	
23		30	H	Notts County	D	1-1	Smith
24	Feb	13	H	Sheffield United	W	1-0	Wooldridge
25		27	H	Newcastle United	W	3-2	Haywood, Smith, Wooldridge
26	Mar	5	A	West Bromwich Albion	W	2-1	Bevin, Smith
27		12	H	Aston Villa	W	3-2	Smith 2, Bevin
28		19	A	Small Heath	L	0-3	
29		21	H	Manchester City	L	1-6	Pilsbury
30		26	H	Middlesbrough	D	2-2	Wooldridge 2
31	Apr	1	A	Sunderland	L	1-2	Wooldridge
32		2	A	Everton	L	0-2	
33		4	H	Stoke	D	0-0	
34		23	A	Bury	D	0-0	

Appear

FA Cup

R1	Feb	6	A	Stockton	W	4-1	Smith 2, Wooldridge, Logan (og)
R2		20	A	Derby County	D	2-2	Whitehouse, Wooldridge
rep		24	H	Derby County	D	2-2	Baynham, Miller
rep2		29	N	Derby County	L	0-1	

Second replay at Villa Park, Birmingham.

Appear

R2 replay aet

One own-goal

Did you know that?

- Despite finishing eighth, Wolves conceded 66 goals – the worst defensive record in the First Division.
- Wolves signed Albert Baynham from Halesowen while transferring Arthur Fellows to Darlaston and Ted Pheasant to neighbours West Bromwich Albion. Baynham scored his first goal for the club in the FA Cup second-round replay against Derby County.
- Wolves' 7–2 defeat at Bramall Lane is the heaviest they have ever suffered against Sheffield United.

Jones J	Betteley RH	Whitehouse J	Pheasant E	Annis W	Baynham A	Haywood A	Wooldridge WT	Smith J	Miller TJ	Preston H	Walker J	Walker WG	Stringer J	Bevin FW	Pisbury C	Smith E	
2	3	4	5	6	7	8	9	10	11								1
2	3	4	5	6	7	8	9	10	11								2
2	3	4	5	6	7	8	9	10	11								3
2	3	4	5	6	7	8	9		11	10							4
2	3	4	5	6	7	8	9		11	10							5
2	3	4		6	7	8	9		11	10	5						6
2	3	4		6	7	8	9		11	10	5						7
2	3	4	5	6	7	8	9		11	10							8
2	3	4	5	6	7	8	9		11	10							9
2	3	4		6	7	8	9		11	10	5						10
2	3	4			7	8	9		11	10	5	6					11
2	3	4		6	7	8	9	10	11		5						12
2	3	4		6	7	8	9	10	11		5						13
2	3	4		6	7	8	9	10	11		5						14
2	3	4		6	7	8	9	10	11		5						15
2	3	4		6	7	8	9	10	11		5						16
2	3	4		6	7	8	9	10	11		5						17
2	3	4		6	7	8	9	10	11		5						18
2	3	4		6	7	8	9	10	11		5						19
2	3	4		6	7	8	9	10	11		5						20
2	3	4	5	6	7	8	9	10	11				1				21
2	3	4	5	6	7	8	9	10	11								22
2	3	4		6	7	8	9	10	11		5						23
2	3	4		6	7	8	9	10	11		5						24
2	3	4		6	7	8	9	10	11		5						25
2	3	4		6	7	8		10		9	5			11			26
2	3	4		6	7	8		10		9	5		1	11			27
2	3	4		6	7	8		10		9	5			11			28
		4	5	6	7	8		10						11	9	3	29
2	3	4	5	6	7	8	9		11					10			30
2	3	4	5	6	7	8	9		11					10			31
2	3	4	5	6	7	8	9		11					10			32
2	3	4	5		7	8	9		11			6	1	10			33
2	3	4	5	6	7	8	9		11					10			34
4	33	34	15	32	34	34	30	21	30	11	19	2	3	9	1	1	
			2			8	17	7	6					2	1		

Jones J	Betteley RH	Whitehouse J	Pheasant E	Annis W	Baynham A	Haywood A	Wooldridge WT	Smith J	Miller TJ	Preston H	Walker J	Walker WG	Stringer J	Bevin FW	Pisbury C	Smith E	
2	3	4		6	7	8	9	10	11		5						R1
2	3	4		6	7	8	9	10	11		5						R2
2	3	4		6	7	8	9	10	11		5						rep
2	3	4		6	7	8	9	10	11		5		1				rep2
	4	4		4	4	4	4	4	4		4		1				
		1			1		2	2	1								

1904-05

Division One

Manager: Jack Addenbrooke

	P	W	D	L	F	A	Pts
Newcastle United	34	23	2	9	72	33	48
Everton	34	21	5	8	63	36	47
Manchester City	34	20	6	8	66	37	46
Aston Villa	34	19	4	11	63	43	42
Sunderland	34	16	8	10	60	44	40
Sheffield United	34	19	2	13	64	56	40
Small Heath	34	17	5	12	54	38	39
Preston North End	34	13	10	11	42	37	36
The Wednesday	34	14	5	15	61	57	33
Woolwich Arsenal	34	12	9	13	36	40	33
Derby County	34	12	8	14	37	48	32
Stoke	34	13	4	17	40	58	30
Blackburn Rovers	34	11	5	18	40	51	27
Wolverhampton Wanderers	34	11	4	19	47	73	26
Middlesbrough	34	9	8	17	36	56	26
Nottingham Forest	34	9	7	18	40	61	25
Bury	34	10	4	20	47	67	24
Notts County	34	5	8	21	36	69	18

Match No.	Date		Venue	Opponents	Result		Scorers	Att
1	Sep	3	H	Nottingham Forest	W	3-2	Haywood, Jones, Wooldridge	
2		5	H	Sheffield United	W	4-2	Haywood, Miller, Smith, Wooldridge	
3		10	A	The Wednesday	L	0-4		
4		17	H	Sunderland	W	1-0	Wooldridge	
5		24	A	Woolwich Arsenal	L	0-2		
6	Oct	1	H	Derby County	W	2-0	Baynham, Smith	
7		8	A	Everton	L	1-2	Wooldridge	
8		15	H	Small Heath	L	0-1		
9		29	H	Notts County	W	3-1	Smith 2, Wooldridge	
10	Nov	5	A	Sheffield United	L	2-4	Haywood, Smith	
11		12	H	Newcastle United	L	1-3	Haywood	
12		14	A	Manchester City	L	1-5	Hopkins	
13		19	A	Preston North End	D	2-2	Smith 2	
14		26	H	Middlesbrough	W	5-3	Bevin 3, Hopkins, Veysey	
15	Dec	3	A	Stoke	L	1-2	Veysey	
16		10	A	Bury	L	1-3	Wooldridge	
17		17	H	Aston Villa	D	1-1	Wooldridge	
18		24	A	Blackburn Rovers	L	0-3		
19		26	H	Everton	L	0-3		
20		31	A	Nottingham Forest	D	2-2	Wooldridge 2	
21	Jan	7	H	The Wednesday	W	1-0	Wooldridge	
22		14	A	Sunderland	L	0-3		
23		21	H	Woolwich Arsenal	W	4-1	Bevin, Smith, Wooldridge, Hopkins	
24		28	A	Derby County	L	1-2	Hopkins	
25	Feb	11	A	Small Heath	L	1-4	Hopkins	
26		25	A	Notts County	W	4-3	Bevin 2, Smith, Wooldridge	
27	Mar	11	A	Newcastle United	L	0-3		
28		18	H	Preston North End	D	0-0		
29		25	A	Middlesbrough	L	1-3	Layton	
30	Apr	1	H	Stoke	L	1-3	Betteley	
31		8	H	Bury	W	2-0	Smith 2	
32		22	H	Blackburn Rovers	W	2-0	Smith, Wooldridge	
33		24	H	Manchester City	L	0-3		
34		27	A	Aston Villa	L	0-3		

Appear

FA Cup

R1	Feb	4	A	Sunderland	D	1-1	Wooldridge	
rep		8	H	Sunderland	W	1-0	Smith	
R2		18	H	Southampton	L	2-3	Bevin, Smith	

Appear

Did you know that?

- Reserve left-winger Arthur Veysey scored in each of his two senior games for Wolves this season.
- Wolves' goalkeeper Tom Baddeley was sent off in the away League game at Nottingham Forest in December.
- Goalkeeper Tommy Lunn, signed from Brownhills Albion, conceded a total of 10 goals in his first four League games for Wolves.
- In May 1905 forward Adam Haywood moved to West Bromwich Albion having scored 28 goals in 113 appearances for Wolves.

etteley RH	Whitehouse J	Walker WG	Annis W	Baynham A	Haywood A	Wooldridge WT	Smith J	Miller TJ	Juggins E	Layton W	Williams W	Bevin FW	Smith E	Preston H	Hopkins J	Lunn TH	Veysey AJ	Grosvenor SG	Walker D	
3	4	5	6	7	8	9	10	11												1
3	4	5	6	7	8	9	10	11												2
3	4	5	6	7	8	9	10	11												3
3	4	5	6	7	8	9	10	11												4
3	4	5	6	7	8	9	10	11												5
3	4	5	6	7	8	9	10	11												6
3	4	5	6	7	8	9	10	11												7
3	4	5	6		8	9	10	11	2	7										8
3	4	5		7	8	9	10	11			6									9
3	4		6	7	8	9	10	11			5									10
3	4	5		7	8		9	11			6	10								11
	4	5		7			8		2		6	10	3	9	11					12
3		5				9	8			7	4	10	6		11	1				13
3						9	8		5		4	10	6		11	1	7			14
3		5				9	8		4		6	10			11	1	7			15
3		5		7		9	8		4		6	10			11	1				16
3	4				8	9	10	11	5		6	7								17
3	4				8	9	10		5		6	7			11					18
3	4				8	9	10		5		6	7			11					19
3	4					9	8		5	7	6	10			11					20
3	4					9	8			7	5		6	10	11					21
3	4					9	8			7	5	10	6		11					22
3		5				9	8			7	4	10	6		11	1				23
3		5				9	8			7	4	10	6		11	1		2		24
		5				9	8			7	4		6	10	11	1		3		25
3	4					9	8			7	5	10	6		11	1				26
3	4	5				9	8			7		10	6		11	1				27
3	4	5					8			7	6	10			11	1			9	28
3	4	5				9	8			7		10	6		11	1				29
3	4					9				7	5		6	10	11				8	30
3	4	5		7	8	9	10	11			6									31
3	4	5		7	8	9	10	11			6									32
3	4	5			8	9	10	11			6	7								33
3	4	5			8	9		11		7	6	10				1				34
32	27	24	9	14	18	31	32	16	9	14	24	19	12	4	18	12	2	2	2	
1				1	4	13	12	1		1		6			5		2			

etteley RH	Whitehouse J	Walker WG	Annis W	Baynham A	Haywood A	Wooldridge WT	Smith J	Miller TJ	Juggins E	Layton W	Williams W	Bevin FW	Smith E	Preston H	Hopkins J	Lunn TH	Veysey AJ	Grosvenor SG	Walker D	
3		5				9	8			7	4	10	6		11					R1
3		5				9	8			7	4	10	6		11					rep
3		5				9	8			7	4	10	6		11					R2
3		3				3	3			3	3	3	3		3					
						1	2					1								

1905-06

Division One

Manager: Jack Addenbrooke

	P	W	D	L	F	A	Pts
Liverpool	38	23	5	10	79	46	51
Preston North End	38	17	13	8	54	39	47
The Wednesday	38	18	8	12	63	52	44
Newcastle United	38	18	7	13	74	48	43
Manchester City	38	19	5	14	73	54	43
Bolton Wanderers	38	17	7	14	81	67	41
Birmingham	38	17	7	14	65	59	41
Aston Villa	38	17	6	15	72	56	40
Blackburn Rovers	38	16	8	14	54	52	40
Stoke	38	16	7	15	54	55	39
Everton	38	15	7	16	70	66	37
Woolwich Arsenal	38	15	7	16	62	64	37
Sheffield United	38	15	6	17	57	62	36
Sunderland	38	15	5	18	61	70	35
Derby County	38	14	7	17	39	58	35
Notts County	38	11	12	15	55	71	34
Bury	38	11	10	17	57	74	32
Middlesbrough	38	10	11	17	56	71	31
Nottingham Forest	38	13	5	20	58	79	31
Wolverhampton Wanderers	38	8	7	23	58	99	23

Did you know that?

• Wolves were relegated to the Second Division for the first time.

• Archie Goodall played his last game for Wolves on 2 December against Everton aged 41 years, five months and two days – the oldest player ever to appear in a competitive game for the club.

• Wolves conceded a club record 99 League goals.

• Arthur Lloyd (from Halesowen), Jack Pedley (from Wednesbury Old Athletic) and George Hedley (from Southampton) were among the new faces at Molineux.

• Dick Betteley and Jack Miller both left the club, joining West Bromwich Albion and Stoke respectively.

Match No.	Date		Venue	Opponents	Result		Scorers
1	Sep	2	A	Nottingham Forest	L	1-3	Smith
2		4	H	The Wednesday	D	0-0	
3		9	H	Stoke	L	1-2	Pope
4		11	H	Bury	D	2-2	Boon, Smith
5		16	A	Manchester City	L	0-4	
6		23	H	Bolton Wanderers	W	2-0	Smith, Wooldridge
7		30	A	Bury	W	1-0	Wooldridge
8	Oct	5	A	Notts County	L	2-5	Williams, Wooldridge
9		7	H	Woolwich Arsenal	L	0-2	
10		14	A	Middlesbrough	L	1-3	Jones
11		21	H	Blackburn Rovers	W	2-1	Layton, Wooldridge
12		28	A	Preston North End	L	2-3	Wooldridge 2
13	Nov	4	H	Sunderland	W	5-2	Wooldridge 2, Breakwell, Corfield, Jones
14		11	A	Newcastle United	L	0-8	
15		18	H	Birmingham	D	0-0	
16		25	A	Aston Villa	L	0-6	
17	Dec	2	H	Everton	L	2-5	Smith 2
18		9	A	Liverpool	L	0-4	
19		16	A	Derby County	L	0-2	
20		23	H	Sheffield United	D	1-1	Smith
21		26	A	The Wednesday	L	1-5	Smith
22		30	H	Nottingham Forest	W	2-1	Layton, Pedley
23	Jan	6	A	Stoke	L	0-4	
24		20	H	Manchester City	L	2-3	Jones, Layton
25		27	A	Bolton Wanderers	L	2-3	Baynham, Corfield
26	Feb	10	A	Woolwich Arsenal	L	1-2	Jones
27		17	H	Middlesbrough	D	0-0	
28		24	A	Blackburn Rovers	L	1-3	Pedley
29	Mar	3	H	Preston North End	L	2-3	Corfield, Pedley
30		10	A	Sunderland	L	2-7	Hopkins, Pedley
31		17	H	Newcastle United	L	0-2	
32		19	A	Sheffield United	L	1-4	Pedley
33		24	A	Birmingham	D	3-3	Pedley, Smith, Wooldridge
34		31	H	Aston Villa	W	4-1	Hopkins 2, Pedley, Smith
35	Apr	7	A	Everton	D	2-2	Hopkins 2
36		14	H	Liverpool	L	0-2	
37		16	H	Notts County	W	6-1	Pedley 3, Pope 2, Smith
38		21	H	Derby County	W	7-0	Wooldridge 3, Gorman 2, Breakwell, Lloy

Appea

FA Cup

R1	Jan	13	A	Bishop Auckland	W	3-0	Baynham, Pedley, Smith
R2	Feb	3	A	Bradford City	L	0-5	

Appea

Betteley RH	Whitehouse J	Raybould T	Williams G	Baynham A	Henshall AV	Wooldridge WT	Smith J	Hopkins J	Bevin RW	Stanley J	Pope FH	Boon R	Hughes H	James EJ	Breakwell AJ	Williams W	Goodall JA	Layton W	Corfield S	Pedley J	Wilkes GH	Lloyd AA	Juggins E	Lunn TH	Radford WR	Gorman J	
3	4	5	6	7	8	9	10	11																			1
3	4	5	6	7	8		10	11	9																		2
	4	5	6	7			10	11		3	8	9															3
	4	5		7			10	11		3	8	9	6														4
	4			7		9	8	11		3			5	6	10												5
3	5			7		9	8						4	6	10	11											6
3	5		4	7		9	8							6	10	11											7
3	5		4	7		9	8							6	10	11											8
	5			7		9	8			3		10	4	6		11											9
3	4	5		7		9	8		11					6	10												10
3	4			7		9								6	11		5	8	10								11
	4			7		9				3				6	11		5	8	10								12
	4			7		9				3				6	11		5	8	10								13
	4			7		9				3				6	11		5	8	10								14
	4			7		9				3				6	11		5	8	10								15
3	4			7		9	8							6	11		5		10								16
3	4			7			9						5	6	11		8		10								17
3			4	7		9	10						6					8	5	11							18
	8		4	7		9				3			6						5	11	10						19
	8		4	7		9	10			3									5	11		6					20
	8		4	7		9	10												5	11		6	3				21
			4			9	10			3	8							7	5	11		6					22
			4			9	10			3					8			7	5	11		6					23
			4	7		9				3					10			8	5	11		6		1			24
			4	7		9	10			3								8	5	11		6		1			25
	8		4			9				3								7	5	11		6			10		26
	4		7			9			10	3									5	11		6			8		27
		4				9			10	3			5	6				7	8	11							28
						9		7	10	3			4	6					8	11		5					29
3						9	8	7	10					6					4	11		5					30
3			4			9	10							6	8			7		11		5					31
			4			9	10			3	8							7	5	11		6					32
			4			9	10				8				7				5	11		6	2				33
			4			9	10	7			8								5	11		6	2				34
			4			9	10	7							8				5	11		6	2				35
			4			9	10	7			8								5	11		6	2				36
			4				10				9				7			8	5	11		6	2	1			37
	4					9			7	3					8				5	11		6				10	38
12	23	6	22	23	2	33	26	10	7	20	8	3	9	17	19	4	7	15	27	21	1	18	6	3	2	1	
				1		12	10	5			3	1			2	1		3	3	10		1				2	

Betteley RH	Whitehouse J	Raybould T	Williams G	Baynham A	Henshall AV	Wooldridge WT	Smith J	Hopkins J	Bevin RW	Stanley J	Pope FH	Boon R	Hughes H	James EJ	Breakwell AJ	Williams W	Goodall JA	Layton W	Corfield S	Pedley J	Wilkes GH	Lloyd AA	Juggins E	Lunn TH	Radford WR	Gorman J	
	4		6	7		9	10			3								8	5	11				1			R1
	4		6	7		9	10			3								8	5	11				1			R2
	2		2	2		2	2			2								2	2	2				2			
				1			1													1							

1906-07

Division Two

Manager: Jack Addenbrooke

	P	W	D	L	F	A	Pts
Nottingham Forest	38	28	4	6	74	36	60
Chelsea	38	26	5	7	80	34	57
Leicester Fosse	38	20	8	10	62	39	48
West Bromwich Albion	38	21	5	12	83	45	47
Bradford City	38	21	5	12	70	53	47
Wolverhampton Wanderers	38	17	7	14	66	53	41
Burnley	38	17	6	15	62	47	40
Barnsley	38	15	8	15	73	55	38
Hull City	38	15	7	16	65	57	37
Leeds City	38	13	10	15	55	63	36
Grimsby Town	38	16	3	19	57	62	35
Stockport County	38	12	11	15	42	52	35
Blackpool	38	11	11	16	33	51	33
Gainsborough Trinity	38	14	5	19	45	72	33
Glossop	38	13	6	19	53	79	32
Burslem Port Vale	38	12	7	19	60	83	31
Clapton Orient	38	11	8	19	45	67	30
Chesterfield Town	38	11	7	20	50	66	29
Lincoln City	38	12	4	22	46	73	28
Burton United	38	8	7	23	34	68	23

Did you know that?

• Full-back Jackery Jones set a club record by being ever present for the fifth time in succession.

• Jones also had the pleasure of scoring Wolves' first goal in the Second Division, against Hull City in September, when the temperature inside Molineux was almost 90 degrees Fahrenheit.

• Jack Shelton and Alf Bishop joined Wolves from Compton Rovers and Halesowen respectively, while three players left – Jack Smith (to Birmingham), Jack Whitehouse (to Stoke) and Albert Baynham (retired).

Match No.	Date		Venue	Opponents	Result		Scorers
1	Sep	1	H	Hull City	D	1-1	Jones
2		3	H	Gainsborough Trinity	W	1-0	Jones
3		8	A	Glossop	L	1-2	Hedley
4		15	H	Blackpool	D	1-1	Gorman
5		22	A	Bradford City	W	3-2	Roberts 2
6		29	H	West Bromwich Albion	L	0-3	
7	Oct	6	A	Leicester Fosse	L	0-2	
8		13	H	Nottingham Forest	W	2-0	Hawkins, Roberts
9		20	A	Lincoln City	W	4-0	Hawkins, Hedley, Roberts, Williams
10		24	A	Gainsborough Trinity	L	0-1	
11		27	H	Burton United	W	3-0	Hawkins 2, Roberts
12	Nov	3	A	Grimsby Town	L	1-2	Hawkins
13		10	H	Burslem Port Vale	W	6-2	Hedley 3, Hawkins, Pedley, Roberts
14		17	A	Burnley	L	0-3	
15		24	H	Leeds City	W	3-2	Hedley, Jones, Pedley
16	Dec	1	A	Barnsley	W	1-0	Hedley
17		8	H	Chelsea	L	1-2	Hawkins
18		15	H	Chesterfield Town	W	2-1	Pedley, Roberts
19		22	A	Clapton Orient	L	0-4	
20		26	H	Stockport County	D	1-1	Roberts
21		27	H	Clapton Orient	W	6-1	Hawkins 2, Roberts 2, Pedley, Williams
22		29	A	Hull City	L	1-5	Pedley
23	Jan	5	H	Glossop	W	4-0	Hedley 2, Roberts 2
24		19	A	Blackpool	W	2-1	Hopkins 2
25		26	H	Bradford City	D	1-1	Jones
26	Feb	9	H	Leicester Fosse	W	1-0	Roberts
27		16	A	Nottingham Forest	L	0-1	
28		23	H	Lincoln City	W	3-0	Hedley, Hopkins, Raybould
29	Mar	2	A	Burton United	L	1-4	Ward
30		9	H	Grimsby Town	W	5-0	Wooldridge 2, Bishop, Breakwell, Hopkins
31		16	A	Burslem Port Vale	D	0-0	
32		23	H	Burnley	W	3-0	Gorman, Wooldridge, Dixon (og)
33		29	A	Stockport County	D	0-0	
34		30	A	Leeds City	L	0-2	
35	Apr	1	A	West Bromwich Albion	D	1-1	Corbett
36		6	H	Barnsley	W	5-1	Bishop 2, Wooldridge 2, Williams
37		13	A	Chelsea	L	0-4	
38		20	A	Chesterfield Town	L	2-3	Hedley, Pedley

Appear

One own-goal

FA Cup

R1	Jan	12	A	The Wednesday	L	2-3	Pedley, Wooldridge

Appear

Jones J	Bishop AJ	Corfield S	Lloyd AA	Hopkins J	Hedley GA	Wooldridge WT	Gorman J	Pedley J	Ward S	Breakwell AJ	Raybould T	Williams W	Hawkins A	Roberts J	Lunn TH	Hunt KRG	Corbett PB	Price ABR	
3	4	5	6	7	8	9	10	11											1
3	4	5		7	8	9	10	11	6										2
3	4	5			8	9	10	11	6	7									3
3	4	5			8	9	10	11			6	7							4
3	4		6		8	5		11				7	9	10					5
3	4		6		8	5		11				7	9	10					6
3	4		6		8	5		11				7	9	10					7
2	4	5	6		8			11	3			7	9	10	1				8
2	4		6		8	5		11	3			7	9	10					9
2	4		6		8	5		11	3			7	9	10					10
2	4		6		8	5		11	3			7	9	10					11
2	4		6		8	5		11	3			7	9	10					12
2	4		6		8	5		11	3			7	9	10					13
2	4		6		8	5		11	3			7	9	10					14
2	4		6		8	5		11	3			7	9	10					15
2	3	4	6		8	5		11				7	9	10					16
2	3	4	6		8	5		11				7	9	10					17
2	3	4	6		8	5		11				7	9	10					18
2	3	4	6	7	8	5		11					9	10					19
2	5	4	6	7	8			11	3				9	10					20
2	5	4	6		8			11	3			7	9	10					21
2	5	4	6		8			11	3			7	9	10					22
2	5	4	6	7	8	9		11	3					10					23
2	5	4	6	7	8			11	3				9	10					24
2	5	4	6	7	8			11	3				9	10	1				25
2	5	4	6	7	8	9		11	3					10					26
2	5	4	6	7	8	9		11	3					10					27
2	5		6	7	8	9		11	3		4			10					28
2	5		6		8	9		11	3	10	4	7							29
2	5		6	7	8	9		11	3	10	4				1				30
2	5		6	7	8	9		11	3	10	4				1				31
2	5		6	7	8	9	10	11	3						1	4			32
2	5		6	7	8	9	10	11	3		4				1				33
2	5		6		8	9	10	11	3		4	7			1				34
2	5		6	7	8	9		11	3		4				1		10		35
2	5		6			9		11	3	8		7			1	4	10		36
2	5		6		8	9	10	11	3		4	7			1				37
2	5		6		10	9		11	3			7			1	4		8	38
38	38	17	35	15	37	32	8	38	29	5	9	22	20	24	11	3	2	1	
4	3			4	11	5	2	6	1	1	1	3	9	14			1		

Jones J	Bishop AJ	Corfield S	Lloyd AA	Hopkins J	Hedley GA	Wooldridge WT	Gorman J	Pedley J	Ward S	Breakwell AJ	Raybould T	Williams W	Hawkins A	Roberts J	Lunn TH	Hunt KRG	Corbett PB	Price ABR	
2	5	4	6	7	8	9		11	3					10					R1
1	1	1	1	1	1	1		1	1					1					
						1		1											

1907-08

Division Two

Manager: Jack Addenbrooke

	P	W	D	L	F	A	Pts
Bradford City	38	24	6	8	90	42	54
Leicester Fosse	38	21	10	7	72	47	52
Oldham Athletic	38	22	6	10	76	42	50
Fulham	38	22	5	11	82	49	49
West Bromwich Albion	38	19	9	10	61	39	47
Derby County	38	21	4	13	77	45	46
Burnley	38	20	6	12	67	50	46
Hull City	38	21	4	13	73	62	46
Wolverhampton Wanderers	38	15	7	16	50	45	37
Stoke	38	16	5	17	57	52	37
Gainsborough Trinity	38	14	7	17	47	71	35
Leeds City	38	12	8	18	53	65	32
Stockport County	38	12	8	18	48	67	32
Clapton Orient	38	11	10	17	40	65	32
Blackpool	38	11	9	18	51	58	31
Barnsley	38	12	6	20	54	68	30
Glossop	38	11	8	19	54	74	30
Grimsby Town	38	11	8	19	43	71	30
Chesterfield Town	38	6	11	21	46	92	23
Lincoln City	38	9	3	26	46	83	21

Did you know that?

• After finishing ninth in the Second Division, Wolves went on to win the FA Cup and are still the lowest-placed League side to lift the coveted trophy.

• The surnames of all four goalscorers in the FA Cup Final began with the letter 'H'– and they were the only players on the field whose names started with that letter.

• Ted Collins (from Brownhills Albion), Billy Harrison (from Crewe Alexandra) and Wally Radford (from Southampton) were among the new recruits.

• Out of Molineux went experienced goalkeeper Tom Baddeley, who joined Bradford Park Avenue having made 315 senior appearances for Wolves since joining in 1896.

Match No.	Date		Venue	Opponents	Result		Scorers
1	Sep	2	H	West Bromwich Albion	L	1-2	Wooldridge
2		7	A	Glossop	D	1-1	Radford
3		9	A	Leicester Fosse	L	0-1	
4		14	H	Leicester Fosse	D	0-0	
5		21	A	Blackpool	W	2-0	Jones, Pedley
6		28	H	Stoke	W	2-0	Bould, Hedley
7	Oct	5	A	West Bromwich Albion	L	0-1	
8		12	H	Bradford City	D	0-0	
9		19	A	Hull City	L	0-2	
10		23	A	Gainsborough Trinity	W	1-0	Wooldridge
11		26	H	Derby County	D	2-2	Hedley, Wooldridge
12	Nov	2	A	Lincoln City	L	1-3	Hedley
13		9	H	Fulham	W	2-0	Pedley, Wooldridge
14		16	A	Barnsley	L	0-5	
15		23	H	Chesterfield Town	D	0-0	
16		30	A	Burnley	L	0-1	
17	Dec	14	A	Clapton Orient	D	1-1	Shelton
18		21	H	Leeds City	W	2-0	Hedley, Radford
19		25	H	Gainsborough Trinity	W	1-0	Harrison
20		26	H	Stockport County	L	0-1	
21		28	H	Grimsby Town	W	5-1	Shelton 3, Hedley 2
22	Jan	1	A	Stockport County	W	3-1	Harrison, Pedley, Radford
23		4	H	Glossop	W	5-0	Corbett 2, Shelton 2, Hedley
24		18	H	Blackpool	W	1-0	Lloyd
25		25	A	Stoke	D	0-0	
26	Feb	8	A	Bradford City	L	2-6	Harrison, Radford
27		15	H	Hull City	L	1-2	Radford
28		29	H	Lincoln City	W	3-0	Hedley, Lloyd, Shelton
29	Mar	14	H	Barnsley	L	0-1	
30		16	H	Burnley	W	5-1	Hedley 2, Radford 2, Shelton
31		21	A	Chesterfield Town	L	0-2	
32	Apr	1	A	Fulham	L	1-2	Wake
33		4	A	Oldham Athletic	L	0-2	
34		8	A	Derby County	L	2-3	Hedley, Pedley
35		11	H	Clapton Orient	W	2-0	Hedley, Radford
36		17	A	Grimsby Town	W	1-0	Harrison
37		18	A	Leeds City	L	1-3	Mason
38		20	H	Oldham Athletic	W	2-1	Radford, Shelton

Appeara

FA Cup

R1	Jan	11	A	Bradford City	D	1-1	Shelton
rep		15	H	Bradford City	W	1-0	Hedley
R2	Feb	1	H	Bury	W	2-0	Radford 2
R3		22	H	Swindon Town	W	2-0	Harrison, Hedley
R4	Mar	7	A	Stoke	W	1-0	Radford
SF		28	N	Southampton	W	2-0	Hedley, Radford
F	Apr	25	N	Newcastle United	W	3-1	Harrison, Hedley, Hunt

SF at Stamford Bridge. Final at Crystal Palace.

Appeara

Jones J	Collins E	Hunt KRG	Bishop AJ	Lloyd AA	Harrison WE	Holt S	Wooldridge WT	Radford WR	Pedley J	Hedley GA	Corbett PB	Bould G	Ward S	Williams W	Shelton J	Cartwright A	Callanan WD	Ferris WF	Jeavons W	Fownes WJ	Metcalf TC	Mason J	Wake B	Tatem FE	Payne CE	
	3	4	5	6	7	8	9	10	11																	1
	3	4	5	6	7	8	9	10	11																	2
	3	4	5	6	7	8	9	10	11																	3
	3	4	5	6	7	9			11	8	10															4
	3	4	5	6	7		9		11	10		8														5
	3	4	5	6	7		9		11	10		8														6
	3	4	5	6	7		9		11	10		8														7
	3	4	5	6	7		9		11	10		8														8
	3		5	4	7	9				10		8	6	11												9
	3		5	4		8	9	11		10			6	7												10
	3		5	6		8	9		11	10				7	4											11
	3		5	6			9		11	10				7	4	8										12
	3		6		7		9	10	11	8					4		5									13
	3		6		7		9	10	11	8					4		5	1								14
	3		4		7			9	11	10					8		5		6							15
	3		9	6	8		5	7	11	10					4											16
			4	6	7		5	9	11	10			2		8					3						17
	3	4	6		7		5	9	11	10			2		8											18
	3		6	4	7		5	9	11	10					8											19
	3	4	6		7		5	9	11	10						8										20
	3	4	6		7		5		11	9	10				8											21
	3	4	6		7		5	10	11	9					8											22
		4	6		7		5		11	9	10		3		8											23
	3	4	6	5	7			9	11		10		2		8											24
			6	4	7		5	10	11	9			3		8											25
	3		6	5	7	9		10	11				4		8											26
	3		6	4	7			10	11				2					1			5	8	9			27
	3		6	4	7		5	10	11	9					8											28
	3	4	6		7		5	10	11	9					8											29
	3	4	6		7			10	11	9					8						5					30
	3		6	4	7		5	10	11	9					8									1		31
	3	4	6		7		5	10	11						8								9			32
	3	4		6				10	11				2	7	8						5		9			33
		4		6					11	9			3	7							5	10	8			34
	3	4		6			5	10		9				11	8										7	35
	3			6	7		5		11	9			2		8						4	10				36
				6			5	10				8	3	11							4	9		1	7	37
	3	4	6		7			10	11	9			2		8						5					38
	33	21	33	26	31	8	28	26	34	29	4	6	14	8	24	2	3	2	1	1	7	4	4	2	2	
				2	4		4	9	4	12	2	1			9							1	1			

Jones J	Collins E	Hunt KRG	Bishop AJ	Lloyd AA	Harrison WE	Holt S	Wooldridge WT	Radford WR	Pedley J	Hedley GA	Corbett PB	Bould G	Ward S	Williams W	Shelton J	Cartwright A	Callanan WD	Ferris WF	Jeavons W	Fownes WJ	Metcalf TC	Mason J	Wake B	Tatem FE	Payne CE	
	3	4	6		7		5		11	9	10				8											R1
	3	4	6		7		5		11	9	10				8											rep
	3	4	6		7		5	10	11	9					8											R2
	3	4	6		7		5	10	11	9					8											R3
	3	4	6		7		5	10	11	9					8											R4
	3	4	6		7		5	10	11	9					8											SF
	3	4	6		7		5	10	11	9					8											F
	7	7	7		7		7	5	7	7	2				7											
		1			2			4		4					1											

1908-09

Division Two

Manager: Jack Addenbrooke

	P	W	D	L	F	A	Pts
Bolton Wanderers	38	24	4	10	59	28	52
Tottenham Hotspur	38	20	11	7	67	32	51
West Bromwich Albion	38	19	13	6	56	27	51
Hull City	38	19	6	13	63	39	44
Derby County	38	16	11	11	55	41	43
Oldham Athletic	38	17	6	15	55	43	40
Wolverhampton Wanderers	38	14	11	13	56	48	39
Glossop	38	15	8	15	57	53	38
Gainsborough Trinity	38	15	8	15	49	70	38
Fulham	38	13	11	14	58	48	37
Birmingham	38	14	9	15	58	61	37
Leeds City	38	14	7	17	43	53	35
Grimsby Town	38	14	7	17	41	54	35
Burnley	38	13	7	18	51	58	33
Clapton Orient	38	12	9	17	37	49	33
Bradford Park Avenue	38	13	6	19	51	59	32
Barnsley	38	11	10	17	48	57	32
Stockport County	38	14	3	21	39	71	31
Chesterfield Town	38	11	8	19	37	67	30
Blackpool	38	9	11	18	46	68	29

Match No.	Date		Venue	Opponents	Result		Scorers	A
1	Sep	1	A	Tottenham Hotspur	L	0-3		
2		5	H	Blackpool	D	2-2	Hedley, Shelton	
3		7	A	West Bromwich Albion	W	2-0	Hedley, Radford	
4		12	A	Chesterfield Town	D	1-1	Hoskins	
5		16	A	Derby County	L	1-2	Harrison	
6		19	H	Glossop	D	0-0		
7		26	A	Stockport County	L	0-1		
8	Oct	3	H	West Bromwich Albion	L	0-1		
9		10	A	Birmingham	D	1-1	Shelton	
10		17	H	Gainsborough Trinity	W	4-0	Radford 2, Hedley, Pedley	
11		24	A	Grimsby Town	L	0-3		
12		31	H	Fulham	L	0-1		
13	Nov	7	A	Burnley	W	5-3	Radford 3, Harrison 2	
14		14	H	Bradford Park Avenue	D	1-1	Harris	
15		21	A	Bolton Wanderers	D	1-1	Radford	
16		28	A	Oldham Athletic	L	1-2	Radford	
17	Dec	5	H	Clapton Orient	W	5-1	Blunt 2, Hedley, Pedley, Radford	
18		12	A	Leeds City	L	2-5	Blunt, Hedley	
19		19	H	Barnsley	W	2-0	Blunt, Hedley	
20		25	H	Derby County	D	1-1	Radford	
21		26	H	Hull City	W	3-0	Radford 2, Hedley	
22		28	H	Tottenham Hotspur	W	1-0	Blunt	
23	Jan	2	A	Blackpool	L	1-3	Jones	
24		9	H	Chesterfield Town	W	3-0	Hedley 2, Radford	
25		23	A	Glossop	L	2-3	Radford, Shelton	
26		30	H	Stockport County	W	2-0	Jones, Radford	
27	Feb	13	H	Birmingham	W	2-0	Hedley 2	
28		20	A	Gainsborough Trinity	L	0-1		
29		27	H	Grimsby Town	D	0-0		
30	Mar	6	A	Fulham	D	1-1	Pedley	
31		13	H	Burnley	W	2-1	Radford 2	
32		20	A	Bradford Park Avenue	L	1-4	Radford	
33		27	H	Bolton Wanderers	L	1-2	Radford	
34	Apr	3	H	Oldham Athletic	D	1-1	Blunt	
35		10	A	Clapton Orient	W	3-1	Blunt, Radford, Shelton	
36		12	A	Hull City	W	1-0	Radford	
37		17	H	Leeds City	W	2-1	Blunt, Hunt	
38		24	A	Barnsley	D	1-1	Hoskins	

Appear

FA Cup

R1	Jan	16	H	Crystal Palace	D	2-2	Radford 2
rep		21	A	Crystal Palace	L	2-4	Hedley, Radford

Appear

Did you know that?

- FA Cup holders Wolves were knocked out of the FA Cup by Southern League side Crystal Palace.
- Centre-forward Billy Blunt joined Wolves from Stafford Rangers and had an excellent first season scoring eight goals.
- Arthur Lloyd was transferred to Hednesford Town in August.
- Jack Gregory made his only League appearance for Wolves this season against Leeds City at Molineux – and he had a hand in both goals in a 2–1 win.

Collins E	Hunt KRG	Wooldridge WT	Bishop AJ	Harrison WE	Shelton J	Hedley GA	Radford WR	Pedley J	Metcalf TC	Jeavons W	Hoskins AH	Harris WT	Arrowsmith A	Conway AJ	Payne CE	May GJ	Blunt W	Pemble A	Ward S	Hardware J	Mason J	Gregory JT	
3	4	5	6	7	8	9	10	11															1
3		5	6	7	8	9	10	11	4														2
3		5		7	4	9	10	11		6	8												3
3		5	6	7		9	10	11		4	8												4
3	4	5	6	7		9	10	11			8												5
3	4	5	6	7		9	10	11			8												6
3		5	6	7	8	9	10	11		4													7
3		5	6	7	4	9	10	11			8												8
3		5	4	7	8			11		6		9	10										9
3			4	7	8	9	10	11		6				5									10
3			4	7	8		10	11		6		9		5									11
3		5	4	8	9		10	11		6					7								12
3		5	4	7	8		10	11				9				6							13
3		5	4	7	8		10	11				9				6							14
3			4	7		9	10	11	5			8				6							15
3		5	6	7	4	9	10	11									8						16
3		5	6	7	4	9	10	11									8						17
3		5	6		4	9	10	11							7		8						18
3			5	7	4	9	10	11								6	8						19
3			5	7	4	9	10	11								6	8						20
3	4		5	7	8	9	10	11								6							21
3	4		5	7	8		10	11								6	9						22
3	4		5	7	8	9	10	11								6		1					23
3	4	5	6	7	8	9	10	11															24
		5	4	7	8		10	11								6	9	1	3				25
3		5	4		8		10	11							7	6	9						26
3		5	4	7	8	9	10	11								6							27
3		5	4	7	8		10				11					6	9						28
3		5	6	7	8		10	11									9			4			29
3	5		6	7	8		10	11												4	9		30
3		5	6	7	8		10	11												4	9		31
3		5	6	7	8		10	11												4	9		32
3			5	7	8		10	11								6			2	4	9		33
3			5	7			10	11			8					6	9			4			34
3	4	5	6	7	8		10				11						9						35
3		5	6		8		10	11							7		9			4			36
3	4	5	6	11	8		10										9					7	37
3		5		7	8		10				11					6	9			4			38
37	10	27	36	35	33	19	37	34	2	7	9	5	1	2	4	15	15	2	2	8	4	1	
	1			3	4	11	21	3			2	1					8						

Collins E	Hunt KRG	Wooldridge WT	Bishop AJ	Harrison WE	Shelton J	Hedley GA	Radford WR	Pedley J	Metcalf TC	Jeavons W	Hoskins AH	Harris WT	Arrowsmith A	Conway AJ	Payne CE	May GJ	Blunt W	Pemble A	Ward S	Hardware J	Mason J	Gregory JT	
3	4	5	6	7	8	9	10	11															R1
3	5		6	7	4	9	10	11									8						rep
2	2	1	2	2	2	2	2	2									1						
						1	3																

1909-10

Division Two

Manager: Jack Addenbrooke

	P	W	D	L	F	A	Pts
Manchester City	38	23	8	7	81	40	54
Oldham Athletic	38	23	7	8	79	39	53
Hull City	38	23	7	8	80	46	53
Derby County	38	22	9	7	72	47	53
Leicester Fosse	38	20	4	14	79	58	44
Glossop	38	18	7	13	64	57	43
Fulham	38	14	13	11	51	43	41
Wolverhampton Wanderers	38	17	6	15	64	63	40
Barnsley	38	16	7	15	62	59	39
Bradford Park Avenue	38	17	4	17	64	59	38
West Bromwich Albion	38	16	5	17	58	56	37
Blackpool	38	14	8	16	50	52	36
Stockport County	38	13	8	17	50	47	34
Burnley	38	14	6	18	62	61	34
Lincoln City	38	10	11	17	42	69	31
Clapton Orient	38	12	6	20	37	60	30
Leeds City	38	10	7	21	46	80	27
Gainsborough Trinity	38	10	6	22	33	75	26
Grimsby Town	38	9	6	23	50	77	24
Birmingham	38	8	7	23	42	78	23

Did you know that?

• Wolves' first-round FA Cup tie was scheduled to take place at Elm Park but the club paid Southern League side Reading £450 and the game was duly switched to Molineux.

• Frank Boxley (from Cradley St Luke's), George Garratly (from Walsall) and Albert Groves (from Aberdare Athletic) were among the new players to arrive at Molineux.

• Billy Blunt became the first Wolves player to score two League hat-tricks in the same season. He also netted four in the FA Cup tie against Reading.

• Wolves' 8–1 home win over Grimsby was their biggest so far in League football.

Match No.	Date		Venue	Opponents	Result		Scorers
1	Sep	1	A	Leicester Fosse	L	1-2	Hedley
2		4	A	Blackpool	L	0-2	
3		11	H	Hull City	D	2-2	Jones, Radford
4		13	H	Clapton Orient	W	3-1	Blunt 2, Radford
5		18	A	Derby County	L	0-5	
6		25	H	Stockport County	W	2-1	Hedley, Shinton
7	Oct	2	A	Glossop	L	0-2	
8		9	H	Birmingham	W	4-2	Blunt 2, Harrison, Shelton
9		16	H	West Bromwich Albion	W	3-1	Blunt, Harrrison, Wooldridge
10		23	H	Oldham Athletic	W	1-0	Blunt
11		25	A	Clapton Orient	L	0-1	
12		30	A	Barnsley	L	1-7	Shelton
13	Nov	6	H	Fulham	D	1-1	Hedley
14		13	A	Burnley	L	2-4	Blunt, Radford
15		20	H	Leeds City	W	5-0	Hedley 2, Pedley, Radford, Shelton
16		27	H	Bradford Park Avenue	L	0-2	
17	Dec	4	A	Gainsborough Trinity	W	2-0	Harrison, Radford
18		11	H	Grimsby Town	W	8-1	Blunt 2, Hedley 2, Pedley 2, Radford 2
19		18	A	Manchester City	L	0-6	
20		25	A	West Bromwich Albion	W	1-0	Harrison
21		27	H	Lincoln City	W	4-2	Harrison 2, Blunt, Radford
22		28	H	Leicester Fosse	W	4-1	Blunt 4
23	Jan	8	H	Blackpool	W	2-1	Blunt, Harrison
24		22	A	Hull City	D	2-2	Blunt, Radford
25		29	H	Derby County	L	2-3	Radford 2
26	Feb	12	H	Glossop	W	3-1	Blunt 2, Hedley
27		19	A	Birmingham	L	0-1	
28	Mar	5	A	Oldham Athletic	L	0-3	
29		12	H	Barnsley	W	1-0	Hedley
30		19	A	Fulham	D	0-0	
31		25	A	Lincoln City	L	0-1	
32		26	H	Burnley	W	3-1	Blunt 3
33		28	A	Stockport County	D	1-1	Blunt
34	Apr	2	A	Leeds City	L	0-1	
35		9	A	Bradford Park Avenue	W	3-2	Hedley, Jones, Payne
36		16	H	Gainsborough Trinity	D	0-0	
37		23	A	Grimsby Town	L	0-1	
38		30	H	Manchester City	W	3-2	Bishop, Blunt, Needham

Appear

FA Cup

R1	Jan	15	H	Reading	W	5-0	Blunt 4, Harrison
R2	Feb	5	H	West Ham United	L	1-5	Wooldridge

Appeara

Jones J	Collins E	Shelton J	Wooldridge WT	Bishop AJ	Harrison WE	Blunt W	Hedley GA	Radford WR	Pedley J	Hunt KRG	Payne CE	Hardware J	Perrett W	Shinton B	Conway AJ	Boxley F	Garratly G	Hoskins AH	May GJ	Hill JT	Groves A	Needham J	Walker AJ	
2	3	4	5	6	7	8	9	10	11															1
2	3		5	6	7	8	9	10	11	4														2
2	3		5	6	7	8	9	10	11	4														3
2	3		5	6	7	8	9	10	11	4														4
2	3	4	5	6		8	9	10	11		7													5
2	3			6		9	10		11		7	4	5	8										6
2	3	8	5	6		9	10		11		7				4									7
2	3	8	5	6	7	9	10		11						4									8
2	3	8	5	6	7	9	10		11						4									9
2	3	8	5	6	7	9	10		11						4									10
2	3	8	5	6	7	9	10		11						4									11
2	3	8	5	6	7	9	10		11						4									12
2	3	8	5	6	7	9	10		11						4	1								13
2	3	8	5	6	7	9	10	11							4	1								14
2	3	8	5	6	7		9	10	11						4									15
	3	8	5	6	7		9	10	11						4		2							16
	3		5	6	7	8	9	10	11						4		2							17
2	3		5	6	7	8	9	10	11						4									18
2	3		5	6	7	8	9	10	11						4									19
2	3	8	5	6	7		9	10	11						4									20
2	3	8		6	7	9		10	11	5					4									21
2		8	5	6	7	9	10	11		4							3							22
2	3	8	5	6	7	9	10	11		4														23
2		8	5	6	7	9		11							4		3	10						24
2		8	5	6	7	9		11							4		3	10						25
2	3	8	5	6	7	9	10								4			11						26
2	3	8	5	6	7	9	10								4	1		11						27
2	3	8	5	6	7	9		10	11						4									28
2		8	5	6	7	9	10								4		3	11						29
2		8	5	6	7	9	10		11	4							3							30
2		8	5	6	7	9	10		11						4		3							31
2		8	5	6	7	9	10		11						4		3							32
	2	8	5	6	7	9	10		11						4		3							33
2			5	6	7	9	10		11		8				4		3							34
2			5	6	7		9	10	11		8				4		3							35
2	3			5	8	9	10		11		7				4				6					36
2	3		5	6	7	8	9	10	11						4					1				37
	3		5	6	7	9	8									1	2				4	10	11	38
4	29	26	35	38	35	34	34	20	29	7	6	1	1	1	28	4	13	5	1	1	1	1	1	
2		3	1	1	7	23	10	11	3		1			1								1		

Jones J	Collins E	Shelton J	Wooldridge WT	Bishop AJ	Harrison WE	Blunt W	Hedley GA	Radford WR	Pedley J	Hunt KRG	Payne CE	Hardware J	Perrett W	Shinton B	Conway AJ	Boxley F	Garratly G	Hoskins AH	May GJ	Hill JT	Groves A	Needham J	Walker AJ	
		8	5	6	7	9	10	11		4							3							R1
2	3	8	5	6	7	9	10	11		4														R2
	1	2	2	2	2	2	2	2		2							1							
			1		1	4																		

1910-11

Division Two

Manager: Jack Addenbrooke

	P	W	D	L	F	A	Pts
West Bromwich Albion	38	22	9	7	67	41	53
Bolton Wanderers	38	21	9	8	69	40	51
Chelsea	38	20	9	9	71	35	49
Clapton Orient	38	19	7	12	44	35	45
Hull City	38	14	16	8	55	39	44
Derby County	38	17	8	13	73	52	42
Blackpool	38	16	10	12	49	38	42
Burnley	38	13	15	10	45	45	41
Wolverhampton Wanderers	38	15	8	15	51	52	38
Fulham	38	15	7	16	52	48	37
Leeds City	38	15	7	16	58	56	37
Bradford Park Avenue	38	14	9	15	53	55	37
Huddersfield Town	38	13	8	17	57	58	34
Glossop	38	13	8	17	48	62	34
Leicester Fosse	38	14	5	19	52	62	33
Birmingham	38	12	8	18	42	64	32
Stockport County	38	11	8	19	47	79	30
Gainsborough Trinity	38	9	11	18	37	55	29
Barnsley	38	7	14	17	52	62	28
Lincoln City	38	7	10	21	28	72	24

Did you know that?

- Three 1908 FA Cup winners all left the club – Tommy Lunn (to Tottenham Hotspur), Billy Wooldridge (to Croydon Common) and Jack Shelton (to Port Vale). Wally Radford also left Molineux, signing for Southport Central.
- Wooldridge scored 90 goals in 356 senior appearances for the club.
- Sammy Brooks (from Cradley Heath) and Jack Needham (from Birmingham) were among the new signings.
- Wolves had a settled team, with 10 players making 31 or more appearances at League level.
- The first 30,000-plus crowd at Molineux (33,028) saw Wolves lose to Chelsea in the third round of the FA Cup.

Match No.	Date		Venue	Opponents	Result		Scorers
1	Sep	3	A	Barnsley	D	2-2	Blunt 2
2		5	H	Derby County	L	1-2	Blunt
3		10	H	Leicester Fosse	W	1-0	J Needham
4		17	H	Bolton Wanderers	W	3-0	Blunt 3
5		24	A	Chelsea	L	0-2	
6	Oct	1	H	Clapton Orient	W	1-0	J Needham
7		8	A	Blackpool	L	0-2	
8		15	H	Glossop	W	2-0	Blunt, Harrison
9		22	A	Lincoln City	W	5-1	Hedley 2, J Needham 2, A Needham
10		29	H	Huddersfield Town	L	0-3	
11	Nov	5	A	Birmingham	W	3-1	J Needham 2, Walker
12		12	H	West Bromwich Albion	L	2-3	Harrison, Hedley
13		19	A	Hull City	D	2-2	Hedley, J Needham
14		26	H	Fulham	W	5-1	Harrison, Hedley, A Needham, J Needham, Wooldridge
15	Dec	3	A	Bradford Park Avenue	L	0-1	
16		10	H	Burnley	W	1-0	J Needham
17		17	A	Gainsborough Trinity	W	3-1	Harrison 2, Bishop
18		24	H	Leeds City	W	3-1	Harrison, Hedley, J Needham
19		26	H	Stockport County	D	0-0	
20		27	A	Derby County	L	0-2	
21		31	H	Barnsley	W	1-0	A Needham
22	Jan	7	A	Leicester Fosse	W	3-2	Harrison, Hedley, J Needham
23		21	A	Bolton Wanderers	L	1-4	J Needham
24		28	H	Chelsea	D	0-0	
25	Feb	11	H	Blackpool	L	0-3	
26		18	A	Glossop	L	1-5	J Needham
27	Mar	4	A	Huddersfield Town	L	1-3	Hedley
28		11	H	Birmingham	W	3-1	Deakin, Hedley, A Needham
29		18	A	West Bromwich Albion	L	1-2	Walker
30		20	A	Clapton Orient	L	1-3	Harrison
31		25	H	Hull City	D	0-0	
32	Apr	1	A	Fulham	W	1-0	Harrison
33		8	H	Bradford Park Avenue	D	0-0	
34		14	A	Stockport County	L	0-1	
35		15	A	Burnley	D	1-1	A Needham
36		22	H	Gainsborough Trinity	D	1-1	A Needham
37		24	H	Lincoln City	W	2-1	Hedley 2
38		29	A	Leeds City	L	0-1	

Appeara

FA Cup

R1	Jan	14	H	Accrington	W	2-0	Hedley 2
R2	Feb	4	H	Manchester City	W	1-0	A Needham
R3		25	H	Chelsea	L	0-2	

Appeara

rratty G	Collins E	Groves A	Wooldridge WT	Bishop AJ	Harrison WE	Needham A	Blunt W	Needham J	Walker AJ	Micklewright W	Hedley GA	Hunt KRG	Deakin E	Jones H	Hill WA	Fownes WJ	Brooks SE	
2	3	4	5	6	7	8	9	10	11									1
2	3	4	5	6	7	8	9	10	11									2
[illegible]	3	4	5	6		8	9	10	11	7								3
2	3	4	5	6		8	9	10	11	7								4
[illegible]	3	4	5	6		8	9	10	11	7								5
2	3	4	5	6			9	10	11	7	8							6
2	3	4	5	6			9	10	11	7	8							7
2	3	4	5	6	7		9	10	11		8							8
2	3	4	5	6	7	8		10	11		9							9
2	3	4	5	6	7	8		10	11		9							10
2	3	4	5	6	7	8		10	11		9							11
2	3	4	5	6	7	8		10	11		9							12
2	3	4	5	6	7	8		10	11		9							13
2	3	4	5	6	7	8		10	11		9							14
2	3	4	5	6	7	8		10	11		9							15
2	3	4	5	6	7	8		10	11		9							16
2	3	4	5	6	7	8		10	11		9							17
3	2	4		6	7	8		10	11		9	5						18
3	2	4	5	6	7	8		10	11		9							19
3	2	8	5	6	7	9						4	10	11				20
3	2	4	5	6	7	8		10	11		9							21
3	2	4	5	6	7	8		10	11		9							22
3	2	4	5	6	7	8		10	11		9							23
3	2	4	5	6	7	8		10			9			11	1			24
3	2	4	5	6	7	8		10	11		9							25
3	2	4	5	6	7	8		10					9	11	1			26
3	2	4	5	6	7	8		10	11		9							27
3	2	4	5	6	7	8			11		9		10					28
3	2	4	5	6	7	8		10	11		9							29
3	2	5		6	7	9		10	11		4		8					30
3	2	5		6	7	9		10	11		4		8					31
3	5	4		6	8			10	7		9			11		2		32
3		4		6	8			10	7		9	5				2	11	33
3		4		6	8			10	7		9	5				2	11	34
3	5	4		6	7	8		10			9					2	11	35
3	5	4		6	7	8		10			9					2	11	36
3	5	4		6	7	8		10			9					2	11	37
3	5	4		6	7	8		10			9					2	11	38
38	36	38	28	38	33	32	8	36	31	5	31	4	5	4	2	7	6	
			1	1	9	6	7	13	2		11		1					

rratty G	Collins E	Groves A	Wooldridge WT	Bishop AJ	Harrison WE	Needham A	Blunt W	Needham J	Walker AJ	Micklewright W	Hedley GA	Hunt KRG	Deakin E	Jones H	Hill WA	Fownes WJ	Brooks SE	
3	2	4	5	6	7	8		10	11		9							R1
3	2	4	5	6	7	8		10	11		9							R2
3	2	4	5	6	7	8		10	11		9							R3
3	3	3	3	3	3	3		3	3		3							
						1					2							

1911-12

Division Two

Manager: Jack Addenbrooke

	P	W	D	L	F	A	Pts
Derby County	38	23	8	7	74	28	54
Chelsea	38	24	6	8	64	34	54
Burnley	38	22	8	8	77	41	52
Clapton Orient	38	21	3	14	61	44	45
Wolverhampton Wanderers	38	16	10	12	57	33	42
Barnsley	38	15	12	11	45	42	42
Hull City	38	17	8	13	54	51	42
Fulham	38	16	7	15	66	58	39
Grimsby Town	38	15	9	14	48	55	39
Leicester Fosse	38	15	7	16	49	66	37
Bradford Park Avenue	38	13	9	16	44	45	35
Birmingham	38	14	6	18	55	59	34
Bristol City	38	14	6	18	41	60	34
Blackpool	38	13	8	17	32	52	34
Nottingham Forest	38	13	7	18	46	48	33
Stockport County	38	11	11	16	47	54	33
Huddersfield Town	38	13	6	19	50	64	32
Glossop	38	8	12	18	42	56	28
Leeds City	38	10	8	20	50	78	28
Gainsborough Trinity	38	5	13	20	30	64	23

Match No.		Date	Venue	Opponents	Result		Scorers	Attend
1	Sep	2	A	Grimsby Town	D	0-0		6,
2		4	H	Bristol City	W	3-1	Needham, Parsonage, Yule	8,
3		9	H	Nottingham Forest	W	1-0	Parsonage	12,
4		16	A	Chelsea	L	0-4		32,
5		23	H	Clapton Orient	L	0-1		10,
6		30	A	Bristol City	W	3-0	Halligan, Needham, Yule	7,
7	Oct	7	H	Birmingham	W	1-0	Harrison	12,
8		14	A	Huddersfield Town	D	1-1	Garratty	4,
9		21	H	Blackpool	W	3-0	Halligan 2, Needham	10,
10		28	A	Glossop	W	1-0	Halligan	5,
11	Nov	4	H	Hull City	W	8-0	Halligan 3, Needham 3, Yule 2	10,
12		11	A	Barnsley	L	1-2	Harrison	7,
13		18	H	Bradford Park Avenue	D	1-1	Harrison	15,
14		25	A	Fulham	D	1-1	Yule	10,
15	Dec	2	H	Derby County	L	0-1		20,
16		9	A	Stockport County	W	2-1	Halligan 2	8,
17		16	H	Leeds City	W	5-0	Halligan 2, Harrison, Young, Yule	8,
18		23	A	Burnley	L	1-2	Harrison	7,
19		25	A	Leicester Fosse	D	1-1	Harrison	10,
20		26	H	Leicester Fosse	W	1-0	Hedley	18,
21		30	H	Grimsby Town	L	1-2	Young	10,
22	Jan	6	A	Nottingham Forest	D	0-0		8,
23		20	H	Chelsea	W	3-1	Brooks, Halligan, Hedley	9,
24		27	A	Clapton Orient	L	0-1		7,
25	Feb	10	A	Birmingham	L	1-3	Needham	25,
26		17	H	Huddersfield Town	L	1-2	Hedley	10,
27	Mar	2	H	Glossop	D	1-1	Halligan	7,
28		9	A	Hull City	L	0-3		6,
29		16	H	Barnsley	W	5-0	Halligan 3, Hedley, Needham	7,
30		23	A	Bradford Park Avenue	W	2-0	Young 2	8
31		30	H	Fulham	D	0-0		8,
32	Apr	5	A	Gainsborough Trinity	L	0-1		4
33		6	A	Derby County	D	1-1	Halligan	10
34		8	H	Gainsborough Trinity	W	1-0	Young	8
35		13	H	Stockport County	W	4-0	Hedley 2, Parsonage 2	3
36		17	A	Blackpool	L	0-1		6,
37		20	A	Leeds City	D	1-1	Hedley	5
38		27	H	Burnley	W	2-0	Halligan 2	18,

Appearan

G

FA Cup

R1	Jan	13	A	Watford	D	0-0		7
rep		24	H	Watford	W	10-0	Halligan 3, Brooks 2, Needham 2, Harrison, Hedley, Young	8
R2	Feb	3	H	Lincoln City	W	2-1	Groves, Hedley	19
R3		24	A	Blackburn Rovers	L	2-3	Halligan 2	45

Appearan

G

Did you know that?

- Wolves beat Watford 10–0 to register their biggest-ever FA Cup win at Molineux.
- Billy Halligan (signed from Derby County) was the first Wolves player to be capped by Ireland against England in Dublin in February.
- Teddy Peers (from Connah's Quay) and Bob Young (from Everton) were two other new recruits.
- Out of Molineux went goalkeeper Frank Boxley, who joined Shrewsbury Town.

	Boxley F	Fownes WJ	Garratly G	Groves A	Collins E	Bishop AJ	Harrison WE	Halligan W	Parsonage H	Needham J	Yule T	Perrett W	Sheargold AL	Hedley GA	Jones J	Hunt KRG	Young RT	Brooks SE	Blunt W	Peers EJ	Brookes AW
1	1	2	3	4	5	6	7	8	9	10	11										
2	1	2	3	4	5	6	7	8	9	10	11										
3	1	2	3	4	5	6	7	8	9	10	11										
4	1	2	3	4	5	6	7	8	9	10	11										
5	1		3	6	2		7	8	9	10	11	5	4								
6	1		3	4	2	6	7	9		10	11	5		8							
7	1		3	4	2	6	7	9		10	11	5		8							
8	1		3	4	2	6	7	9		10	11			8	5						
9	1		3	4	2	6	7	9		10	11		5	8							
10	1		3	4	2	6	7	9		10	11		5	8							
11	1		3	4	2	6	7	9		10	11			8		5					
12	1		3	4	2	6	7	9		10	11		5	8							
13	1		3	4	2	6	7	9		10	11			8			5				
14	1		3	4	2	6	7	9		10	11			8			5				
15	1		3	4	2	6	7	9		10	11			8			5				
16	1		3	4	2	6	7	9		10	11			8			5				
17	1		3	4	2	6	7	9	10		11			8			5				
18	1		3	4	2	6	7	9	10		11			8			5				
19	1		3	4	2	6	7	9		10	11			8			5				
20	1		3		2	6	7	9		10	11			8		4	5				
21	1		3	4	2	6	7	9		10	11			8			5				
22	1		3	4		6	7	9		10	11			8	2		5				
23			3	4	2	6	7	9		10				8			5	11			
24			3	4	2	6	7	9		10				8			5	11			
25			3	4	2	6	7			10	8						5	11	9		
26			3	4	2	6	7	9		10				8			5	11			
27			3	4	2		7	9		10				8			5	11		1	6
28			3	4	2		7	9		10				8			5	11		1	6
29			3	4	2	6	7	9		10				8			5	11		1	
30			3	4	2	6	7	9		10				8			5	11		1	
31			3	4	2	6	7	9		10				8			5	11		1	
32			3	4	2	6	7	9		10				8			5	11		1	
33			3	4	2	6	7	9		10				8				11		1	5
34			3	4	2	6	7	9		10				8			5	11		1	
35			3	4	2	6	7		9	10				8			5	11		1	
36			3	4	2	6	7		9	10				8			5	11		1	
37			3	4	2	6	7	9		10	11			8			5				
38			3	4	2	6	7	9		10	11			8			5			1	
	7	4	38	37	37	35	38	35	9	36	25	3	4	32	2	2	25	14	1	11	3
			1				6	19	4	8	6			7			5	1			

	Boxley F	Fownes WJ	Garratly G	Groves A	Collins E	Bishop AJ	Harrison WE	Halligan W	Parsonage H	Needham J	Yule T	Perrett W	Sheargold AL	Hedley GA	Jones J	Hunt KRG	Young RT	Brooks SE	Blunt W	Peers EJ	Brookes AW
R1			3	4	2	6	7	9		10				8			5	11			
rep			3	4	2	6	7	9		10				8			5	11			
R2			3	4	2	6	7	9		10				8			5	11			
R3			3	4	2	6	7	9		10				8			5	11			
			4	4	4	4	4	4		4				4			4	4			
				1			1	5		2				2			1	2			

1912-13

Division Two

Manager: Jack Addenbrooke

	P	W	D	L	F	A	Pts
Preston North End	38	19	15	4	56	33	53
Burnley	38	21	8	9	88	53	50
Birmingham	38	18	10	10	59	44	46
Barnsley	38	19	7	12	57	47	45
Huddersfield Town	38	17	9	12	66	40	43
Leeds City	38	15	10	13	70	64	40
Grimsby Town	38	15	10	13	51	50	40
Lincoln City	38	15	10	13	50	52	40
Fulham	38	17	5	16	65	55	39
Wolverhampton Wanderers	38	14	10	14	56	54	38
Bury	38	15	8	15	53	57	38
Hull City	38	15	6	17	60	55	36
Bradford Park Avenue	38	14	8	16	60	60	36
Clapton Orient	38	10	14	14	34	47	34
Leicester Fosse	38	13	7	18	49	65	33
Bristol City	38	9	15	14	46	72	33
Nottingham Forest	38	12	8	18	58	59	32
Glossop	38	12	8	18	49	68	32
Stockport County	38	8	10	20	56	78	26
Blackpool	38	9	8	21	39	69	26

Did you know that?

- Wolves had two reverends on their books this season: Kenneth Hunt, who made two appearances; and Billy Jordan, who played in three games and netted two goals.
- George Hedley, having scored 74 goals in 214 appearances, left Molineux to become manager of Bristol City, while centre-forward Billy Blunt joined Bristol Rovers.
- Alf Bishop was appointed team captain in place of the departed Wooldridge.
- Bert Smart, brother of Tommy (of Aston Villa fame), made his League debut for Wolves.

Match No.	Date		Venue	Opponents	Result		Scorers	Attenda
1	Sep	2	H	Lincoln City	W	2-0	Needham, Young	5,0
2		7	H	Bristol City	D	1-1	Jordan	14,0
3		14	A	Birmingham	D	0-0		30,0
4		16	H	Nottingham Forest	L	2-3	Needham, Parsonage	10,0
5		21	H	Huddersfield Town	W	2-0	Halligan, Jordan	12,0
6		28	A	Leeds City	D	2-2	Halligan, Young	20,0
7	Oct	5	H	Grimsby Town	W	3-0	Brooks, Needham, Yule	9,5
8		12	A	Bury	L	0-1		4,0
9		19	H	Fulham	W	2-1	Halligan, Harrison	12,5
10		26	A	Barnsley	L	2-3	Brooks, Needham	6,0
11	Nov	2	H	Bradford Park Avenue	D	0-0		14,0
12		9	A	Blackpool	W	2-1	Halligan, Mulholland	5,0
13		16	A	Leicester Fosse	W	1-0	Brooks	7,5
14		23	H	Stockport County	W	1-0	Hedley	6,0
15		30	A	Preston North End	D	1-1	Young	10,0
16	Dec	7	H	Burnley	L	0-2		6,0
17		14	A	Hull City	W	1-0	Hedley	7,0
18		21	H	Glossop	W	3-1	Brooks, Garratty, Halligan	5,0
19		25	A	Nottingham Forest	L	0-2		10,0
20		26	H	Clapton Orient	D	1-1	Groves	8,0
21		28	A	Bristol City	L	1-3	Groves	8,0
22	Jan	4	H	Birmingham	D	2-2	Halligan 2	7,0
23		25	H	Leeds City	D	2-2	Hedley, Foley (og)	8,0
24	Feb	8	A	Grimsby Town	L	1-2	Brooks	5,0
25		15	H	Bury	W	3-1	Groves 2, Parsonage	4,0
26		22	A	Fulham	L	2-4	Groves 2	15,0
27	Mar	1	H	Barnsley	W	3-0	Halligan 2, Needham	3,0
28		12	A	Huddersfield Town	L	1-2	Groves	6,0
29		15	H	Blackpool	W	4-0	Halligan 2, Groves, Needham	2,5
30		21	A	Clapton Orient	D	0-0		4,0
31		22	H	Leicester Fosse	D	1-1	Harrison	4,0
32		24	A	Lincoln City	L	1-2	Halligan	3,0
33		29	A	Stockport County	L	1-5	Halligan	3,5
34	Apr	5	H	Preston North End	W	2-0	Halligan, Needham	13,0
35		12	A	Burnley	L	2-4	Halligan, Harrison	5,
36		16	A	Bradford Park Avenue	L	1-5	Needham	8,0
37		19	H	Hull City	L	0-1		6,0
38		26	A	Glossop	W	3-1	Groves 2, Brooks	1,5
								Appearanc
							One own-goal	Go

FA Cup

R1	Jan	18	H	London Caledonians	W	3-1	Halligan 2, Needham	18,
R2	Feb	1	A	Bradford Park Avenue	L	0-3		24,
								Appearanc
								Go

Garratly G	Groves A	Young RT	Bishop AJ	Harrison WE	Hedley GA	Halligan W	Needham J	Brooks SE	Jordan WC	Yule T	Parsonage H	Brookes AW	Mulholland T	Hunt KRG	Jones J	Smart B	Price F	Crabtree J	Dunn R	
3	4	5	6	7	8	9	10	11												1
3	4	5	6	7		9	10	11	8											2
3	4	5	6	7		9	10		8	11										3
3	4	5	6	7		9	10			11	8									4
3	4	5	6	7		9	10		8	11										5
3	4	5	6			9	10	7		11	8									6
3	4	5	6		8	9	10	7		11										7
3	4	5	6		8	9	10	7		11										8
3		5	6	7	8	9	10	11				4								9
3	4	5	6	7	8	9	10	11												10
3	4	5	6	7		9	10	11					8							11
3	4	5	6	7		9	10	11					8							12
3	4	5	6	7	10			11			9		8							13
3	4	5	6	7	10	9		11					8							14
3	4	5	6	7		9	10	11					8							15
3	4	5	6	7		9	10	11					8							16
3	4	5	6	7	8	9	10	11												17
3	4		6	7	8	9	10	11				5								18
3	4	5	6	7		9	10	11			8									19
3	8	5	6	7			10	11			9			4						20
	8		6				10	7		11	9	5		4	2					21
	4	5	3	7	8	9	10	11				6								22
	4	5	3	7	8	9	10	11				6								23
	8	5	6	7		9		11			10					3	4			24
	8	5	6	7			10	11			9					3	4			25
	8	5		7			10	11			9					3	4	6		26
3	8	5	6	7		9	10	11									4			27
3	8	5	6	7		9	10	11									4			28
3	8	5	6	7		9	10	11									4			29
3	8	5	6	7		9	10	11									4			30
3	8	5	6	7		9	10	11									4			31
3	8	5	6	7		9	10			11							4			32
3	8		6	7		9	10	11				5					4			33
3	8	5	6	7		9	10	11									4			34
3	8	5	6	7		9	10	11									4			35
3	6			7		9	10	11			8						4		5	36
3	8	5	6	7		9	10	11									4			37
3	9	5	6	7			10	11			8						4			38
32	37	34	36	34	11	32	35	34	3	8	11	6	6	2	1	3	15	1	1	
1	10	3		3	3	15	8	6	2	1	2		1							

Garratly G	Groves A	Young RT	Bishop AJ	Harrison WE	Hedley GA	Halligan W	Needham J	Brooks SE	Jordan WC	Yule T	Parsonage H	Brookes AW	Mulholland T	Hunt KRG	Jones J	Smart B	Price F	Crabtree J	Dunn R	
	4	5	3	7	8	9	10	11				6								R1
3	4	5	6	7	8	9	10	11												R2
1	2	2	2	2	2	2	2	2				1								
						2	1													

1913-14

Division Two

Manager: Jack Addenbrooke

	P	W	D	L	F	A	Pts
Notts County	38	23	7	8	77	36	53
Bradford Park Avenue	38	23	3	12	71	47	49
Woolwich Arsenal	38	20	9	9	54	38	49
Leeds City	38	20	7	11	76	46	47
Barnsley	38	19	7	12	51	45	45
Clapton Orient	38	16	11	11	47	35	43
Hull City	38	16	9	13	53	37	41
Bristol City	38	16	9	13	52	50	41
Wolverhampton Wanderers	38	18	5	15	51	52	41
Bury	38	15	10	13	39	40	40
Fulham	38	16	6	16	46	43	38
Stockport County	38	13	10	15	55	57	36
Huddersfield Town	38	13	8	17	47	53	34
Birmingham	38	12	10	16	48	60	34
Grimsby Town	38	13	8	17	42	58	34
Blackpool	38	9	14	15	33	44	32
Glossop	38	11	6	21	51	67	28
Leicester Fosse	38	11	4	23	45	61	26
Lincoln City	38	10	6	22	36	66	26
Nottingham Forest	38	7	9	22	37	76	23

Did you know that?

- After netting 41 goals in 73 games for Wolves, Billy Halligan joined Hull City for a record fee of £600. On 6 December he produced a brilliant display, scoring four goals as the Tigers whipped his former club 7–1 in a League game.

- Tansey Lea and Dick Richards both joined Wolves from Oswestry United while Alf Riley arrived from Stafford Rangers. Lea and Riley would later play in the 1921 FA Cup Final.

Match No.	Date		Venue	Opponents	Result		Scorers
1	Sep	1	H	Lincoln City	W	1-0	Needham
2		6	A	Nottingham Forest	W	3-1	Brooks, Harrison, Lloyd
3		9	A	Huddersfield Town	D	0-0	
4		13	H	Woolwich Arsenal	L	1-2	Young
5		20	A	Grimsby Town	L	0-1	
6		27	H	Birmingham	W	1-0	Young
7	Oct	4	A	Bristol City	D	0-0	
8		11	H	Leeds City	L	1-3	Groves
9		18	A	Clapton Orient	D	2-2	Francis, Richards
10		25	H	Glossop	W	1-0	Francis
11	Nov	1	A	Stockport County	D	0-0	
12		8	H	Bradford Park Avenue	W	1-0	Brooks
13		15	A	Notts County	L	0-2	
14		22	H	Leicester Fosse	W	2-1	Francis, Lockett
15		29	H	Fulham	W	1-0	Brooks
16	Dec	6	A	Hull City	L	1-7	Harrison
17		13	H	Barnsley	L	0-1	
18		20	A	Bury	W	4-1	Brooks 2, Groves, Hughes
19		26	H	Blackpool	W	1-0	Brooks
20		27	H	Nottingham Forest	W	4-1	Brooks 2, Harrison, Hughes
21	Jan	1	A	Blackpool	L	0-2	
22		3	A	Woolwich Arsenal	L	1-3	Needham
23		17	H	Grimsby Town	W	4-1	Brooks, Harrison, Hughes, Needham
24		24	A	Birmingham	L	1-4	Hughes
25	Feb	7	H	Bristol City	L	0-2	
26		14	A	Leeds City	L	0-5	
27		21	H	Clapton Orient	W	2-1	Harrison, Hughes
28		28	A	Glossop	W	2-1	Brooks, Hughes
29	Mar	7	H	Stockport County	W	3-1	Hughes, Lockett, Needham
30		14	A	Bradford Park Avenue	L	0-1	
31		21	H	Notts County	W	4-1	Richards 2, Groves, Hughes
32		28	A	Leicester Fosse	W	3-2	Hughes 2, Harrison
33	Apr	4	A	Fulham	L	0-1	
34		10	A	Lincoln City	L	0-1	
35		11	H	Hull City	W	1-0	Griffiths
36		13	H	Huddersfield Town	D	2-2	Needham 2
37		18	A	Barnsley	L	1-2	Griffiths
38		25	H	Bury	W	3-0	Brooks, Garratty, Needham

Appea

FA Cup

R1	Jan	10	H	Southampton	W	3-0	Groves, Howell, Needham
R2		31	H	Sheffield Wednesday	D	1-1	Howell
rep	Feb	4	A	Sheffield Wednesday	L	0-1	

Appea

	Collins E	Garratly G	Price F	Young RT	Bishop AJ	Harrison WE	Lloyd H	Groves A	Needham J	Brooks SE	Lockett WC	Hughes WH	Brookes AW	Francis E	Richards RW	Marr A	Crabtree J	Brooks A	Lea T	Howell H	Hayes JW	Griffiths CR	Riley A	Streets JW
1	2	3	4	5	6	7	8	9	10	11														
2	2	3	4	5	6	7	8	9	10	11														
3	2	3	4	5	6	7	8	9	10	11														
4	2	3	4	5	6	7	8	9	10	11														
5	2	3	4	5	6	7			10	11	8	9												
6	2	3	4	5	6	7			10	11	8	9												
7	2	3	4	5	6	7			10	11	8	9												
8	2	3	4		6	7		8	10	11		9	5											
9	2	3	4		6	7		8		11			5	9	10									
10	2	3	4	5	6			8		11				9	10	7								
11	2	3	4		5			8		11				9	10	7	6							
12	3		4		5			8		11				9	10	7	6	2						
13	3		4		5	7		8		11				9	10		6	2						
14	3		4		5	7			10	11	8			9			6	2						
15	3		4		5	7			10	11		8		9			6	2						
16	3	2	4			7			6			8		9	10		5		11					
17	3	2	4			7	8	5	10	11				9			6							
18	3		4			7	8	5	10	11		9	6					2						
19	3		4		6	7	8	5	10	11		9						2						
20	3		4		6	7	8	5	10	11		9						2						
21	3		4		6	7		5	10			9						2	11	8				
22	3		4		6	7		5	10			9			11			2		8				
23	3		4		6	7		5	10	11		9						2		8				
24	3		4		6	7		5	10	11		9						2		8				
25		2	4		3	7		5	10	11				9			6			8				
26	2	3	4		6	7		5	10	11	9									8				
27	2	3	4		6	7		5	10	11		9								8				
28	2	3	4		6	7		5	10	11		9								8	1			
29	2	3	4		6	7		5	10	11	8	9												
30	2	3	4		6	7		5	10			9			11					8				
31	2	3	4		6	7		5	10			9			11					8				
32	2	3	4		6	7		5	10	11		9								8				
33	2	3	4		6	7		5	10	11		9								8				
34	2	3	4		6	7		5	10			9			11					8				
35	2	3	4		6	7		5	10	11										8		9		
36	2	3	4		6	7			10	11										8		9	5	
37	2	3	4			7		5	10	11							6				1	9		8
38	2	3	4		6	7		5	10	11												9		8
	7	27	38	8	34	35	8	31	33	32	6	21	3	10	10	3	9	11	2	15	2	4	1	2
		1		2		6	1	3	7	11	2	10		3	3							2		

	Collins E	Garratly G	Price F	Young RT	Bishop AJ	Harrison WE	Lloyd H	Groves A	Needham J	Brooks SE	Lockett WC	Hughes WH	Brookes AW	Francis E	Richards RW	Marr A	Crabtree J	Brooks A	Lea T	Howell H	Hayes JW	Griffiths CR	Riley A	Streets JW
R1	3		4		6	7		5	10	11		9						2		8				
R2	3		4		6	7		5	10	11		9						2		8				
rep		3	4			7		5	10	11		9					6	2		8				
	2	1	3		2	3		3	3	3		3					1	3		3				
								1	1											2				

1914-15

Division Two

Manager: Jack Addenbrooke

	P	W	D	L	F	A	Pts
Derby County	38	23	7	8	71	33	53
Preston North End	38	20	10	8	61	42	50
Barnsley	38	22	3	13	51	51	47
Wolverhampton Wanderers	38	19	7	12	77	52	45
Arsenal	38	19	5	14	69	41	43
Birmingham	38	17	9	12	62	39	43
Hull City	38	19	5	14	65	54	43
Huddersfield Town	38	17	8	13	61	42	42
Clapton Orient	38	16	9	13	50	48	41
Blackpool	38	17	5	16	58	57	39
Bury	38	15	8	15	61	56	38
Fulham	38	15	7	16	53	47	37
Bristol City	38	15	7	16	62	56	37
Stockport County	38	15	7	16	54	60	37
Leeds City	38	14	4	20	65	64	32
Lincoln City	38	11	9	18	46	65	31
Grimsby Town	38	11	9	18	48	76	31
Nottingham Forest	38	10	9	19	43	77	29
Leicester Fosse	38	10	4	24	47	88	24
Glossop	38	6	6	26	31	87	18

Did you know that?

- Wolves were the Second Division's top scorers with 77 goals.
- Frank Curtis was top scorer with 25 League goals, including four against Leicester Fosse in November. Curtis had joined the club from Llanelli.
- Bob Young announced his retirement through injury.
- This was the last League season for four years, as the competition was postponed due to World War One.

Match No.	Date		Venue	Opponents	Result		Scorers
1	Sep	1	A	Clapton Orient	D	1-1	Langford
2		5	H	Arsenal	W	1-0	Curtis
3		7	H	Clapton Orient	D	0-0	
4		12	A	Derby County	L	1-3	Langford
5		19	H	Lincoln City	W	3-1	Curtis 2, Langford
6		26	A	Birmingham	W	2-1	Brooks, Garratty
7	Oct	3	H	Grimsby Town	L	0-1	
8		10	A	Huddersfield Town	L	0-2	
9		17	H	Bristol City	D	2-2	Brooks, Curtis
10		24	A	Bury	L	1-4	Brooks
11		31	H	Preston North End	W	2-0	Brooks, Needham
12	Nov	7	A	Nottingham Forest	L	1-3	Dunn
13		14	H	Leicester Fosse	W	7-0	Curtis 4, Needham 3
14		21	A	Barnsley	L	1-2	Brooks
15		28	H	Glossop	W	4-0	Brooks, Curtis, Dunn, Needham
16	Dec	5	A	Blackpool	L	0-1	
17		12	A	Fulham	W	1-0	Curtis
18		19	H	Stockport County	W	4-1	Richards 3, Brooks
19		25	A	Hull City	L	1-5	Curtis
20		26	H	Hull City	L	1-2	Garratty
21	Jan	2	A	Arsenal	L	1-5	Howell
22		16	H	Derby County	L	0-1	
23		23	A	Lincoln City	D	2-2	Curtis, Needham
24	Feb	6	A	Grimsby Town	W	4-1	Curtis 2, Brooks, Garratty
25		13	H	Huddersfield Town	W	4-1	Brooks, Curtis, Dunn, Needham
26		20	A	Bristol City	W	1-0	Needham
27		27	H	Bury	D	1-1	Needham
28	Mar	6	A	Preston North End	L	3-5	Curtis 2, Brooks
29		13	H	Nottingham Forest	W	5-1	Curtis 2, Needham 2, Howell
30		20	A	Leicester Fosse	W	3-0	Brooks 2, Harrison
31		27	H	Barnsley	W	4-1	Bishop, Brooks, Howell, Needham
32	Apr	3	A	Glossop	W	2-0	Brooks, Needham
33		5	H	Leeds City	W	5-1	Curtis 2, Needham 2, Brooks
34		6	A	Leeds City	W	3-2	Brooks 2, Curtis
35		10	H	Blackpool	W	2-0	Brooks, Curtis
36		17	H	Fulham	W	2-0	Curtis, Groves
37		19	H	Birmingham	D	0-0	
38		24	A	Stockport County	D	2-2	Curtis, Howell

Appear

FA Cup

R1	Jan	9	A	Reading	W	1-0	Harrison
R2		30	A	Sheffield Wednesday	L	0-2	

Appear

Garratly G	Collins E	Price F	Groves A	Bishop AJ	Harrison WE	Curtis F	Langford TS	Needham J	Brooks SE	Griffiths CR	Parfitt G	Richards RW	Dunn E	Brookes AW	Riley A	Howell H	Brooks A	Lea T	
2	3	4	5	6	7	8	9	10	11										1
2	3	4	5	6	7	8		10	11	9									2
2	3	4	5	6	7	8		10	11	9									3
2	3	4	5	6	7	8	9	10	11										4
2	3	4	5	6	7	8	9	10	11										5
2	3	4	5	6	7	8	10		11	9									6
2		4	5	6	7	8	10		11	9	3								7
2	3	4	5	6	7	8	10			9		11							8
2	3	4	5	6	7	9	10		11				8						9
2	3	4	5	6	7	9		10	11				8						10
2	3	4	5	6	7	9		10	11				8						11
2	3	4		5	7	9		10	11				8	6					12
2	3	4		6	7	9		10	11				8		5				13
2	3	4		6	7	9		10	11				8		5				14
2	3	4		6	7	9		10	11				8		5				15
2	3	4		6	7	9		10	11				8		5				16
2	3	4		6	7	8		10	11	9					5				17
2	3		4	6	7	8			11	9		10			5				18
2	3		4	6	7	8			11	9		10			5				19
2	3		4	6	7	8		10	11	9					5				20
2	3	4	9	6	7			10	11						5	8			21
	3	4	5	6	7	9		10	11				8				2		22
	3	4		6	7	9		10	11				8		5		2		23
2	3	4	5	6	7	9		10	11				8						24
2	3	4	5	6	7	9		10	11				8						25
2	3	4	5	6	7	9		10	11				8						26
2	3	4	5	6	7	9		10	11				8						27
2	3	4	5	6	7	9		10	11							8			28
2	3	4	5	6	7	9		10	11							8			29
2	3	4	5	6	7	9		10	11							8			30
2	3	4	5	6	7	9		10	11							8			31
2	3	4	5	6	7	9		10	11							8			32
2	3	4	5	6	7	9		10	11							8			33
2	3	4	5	6		9		10	11							8		7	34
2	3	4	5	6		9		10	11							8		7	35
2	3	4	5	6	7	9		10	11							8			36
	3	4	5	6	7	9		10	11							8	2		37
	3	4	5	6		9		10	11							8	2	7	38
34	37	35	31	38	35	37	7	32	37	9	1	3	14	1	10	12	4	3	
3			1	1	1	25	3	15	18			3	3			4			

Garratly G	Collins E	Price F	Groves A	Bishop AJ	Harrison WE	Curtis F	Langford TS	Needham J	Brooks SE	Griffiths CR	Parfitt G	Richards RW	Dunn E	Brookes AW	Riley A	Howell H	Brooks A	Lea T	
2	3	4	5	6	7	9		10	11				8						R1
2	3	4	5	6	7	9		10	11				8						R2
2	2	2	2	2	2	2		2	2				2						
					1														

1919-20

Division Two

Manager: Jack Addenbrooke

	P	W	D	L	F	A	Pts
Tottenham Hotspur	42	32	6	4	102	32	70
Huddersfield Town	42	28	8	6	97	38	64
Birmingham	42	24	8	10	85	34	56
Blackpool	42	21	10	11	65	47	52
Bury	42	20	8	14	60	44	48
Fulham	42	19	9	14	61	50	47
West Ham United	42	19	9	14	47	40	47
Bristol City	42	13	17	12	46	43	43
South Shields	42	15	12	15	58	48	42
Stoke	42	18	6	18	60	54	42
Hull City	42	18	6	18	78	72	42
Barnsley	42	15	10	17	61	55	40
Port Vale	42	16	8	18	59	62	40
Leicester City	42	15	10	17	41	61	40
Clapton Orient	42	16	6	20	51	59	38
Stockport County	42	14	9	19	52	61	37
Rotherham County	42	13	8	21	51	83	34
Nottingham Forest	42	11	9	22	43	73	31
Wolverhampton Wanderers	42	10	10	22	55	80	30
Coventry City	42	9	11	22	35	73	29
Lincoln City	42	9	9	24	44	101	27
Grimsby Town	42	10	5	27	34	75	25

Did you know that?

- Following crowd trouble at Molineux, Wolves were made to play two home League games at The Hawthorns (against Barnsley and Stockport County).
- Wolves' 10–3 League defeat at Hull is the second-heaviest in the club's history.
- Harry Dillard left Wolves after serving as second-team trainer for 27 years.
- A total of 17 players made their Football League debuts for Wolves this season.
- Jack Needham moved to Hull City and Fred Price to Port Vale, while both George Garratly and Jackery Jones announced their retirement, the latter after making 336 senior appearances for the club.

Match No.	Date		Venue	Opponents	Result		Scorers
1	Aug	30	A	Leicester City	W	2-1	Bate, Harrison
2	Sep	1	H	Grimsby Town	W	6-1	Brooks 2, Bate, Harrison, Howell, Needham
3		6	H	Leicester City	D	1-1	Bate
4		8	A	Grimsby Town	W	1-0	Bate
5		13	A	Clapton Orient	D	0-0	
6		20	H	Clapton Orient	L	1-2	Needham
7		27	A	Leeds City	D	1-1	Howell
8	Oct	4	H	Leeds City	L	2-4	Bate, Brooks
9		11	A	Bury	L	0-2	
10		18	H	Bury	L	0-1	
11		25	A	Nottingham Forest	L	0-1	
12	Nov	1	H	Nottingham Forest	W	4-0	Groves 3, Harrison
13		8	A	Birmingham	L	0-2	
14		15	H	Birmingham	L	0-2	
15		22	A	Barnsley	L	1-4	Green
16		29	H	Barnsley	L	2-4	Brooks, Williams (og)
17	Dec	6	H	Stockport County	D	2-2	Smart, Wright
18		13	A	Stockport County	L	1-4	Wright
19		20	H	Hull City	W	4-2	Brooks 2, Needham, Sambrook
20		26	H	South Shields	D	0-0	
21		27	A	Hull City	L	3-10	Needham, Richards, Wright
22	Jan	1	A	South Shields	D	0-0	
23		3	H	Lincoln City	W	4-0	Groves, Hodnett, Needham, Sambrook
24		17	A	Lincoln City	L	0-4	
25		24	A	Fulham	D	1-1	Richards
26	Feb	7	A	Coventry City	L	0-1	
27		14	H	Coventry City	W	2-0	Cutler, Richards
28		23	H	Fulham	W	2-1	Richards, Sambrook
29		28	H	Huddersfield Town	L	2-3	Richards 2
30	Mar	6	H	Blackpool	L	0-3	
31		13	A	Blackpool	D	1-1	Cutler
32		20	A	Bristol City	D	1-1	Wright
33	Apr	2	A	Tottenham Hotspur	L	2-4	Cutler, Richards
34		3	H	West Ham United	D	1-1	Richards
35		5	H	Tottenham Hotspur	L	1-3	Woodward
36		10	A	West Ham United	L	0-4	
37		14	A	Huddersfield Town	L	0-2	
38		17	H	Rotherham County	L	0-1	
39		19	H	Bristol City	W	3-1	Sambrook 2, Richards
40		24	A	Rotherham County	L	0-2	
41		26	H	Stoke	W	4-0	Lea 2, Cutler, Richards
42	May	1	A	Stoke	L	0-3	

Appeara

One own-goal

FA Cup

R1	Jan	10	A	Blackburn Rovers	D	2-2	Richards 2
rep		15	H	Blackburn Rovers	W	1-0	Lea
R2		31	H	Cardiff City	L	1-2	Harrison

Appeara

Garratty G	Price F	Groves A	Bishop AJ	Harrison WE	Howell H	Bate W	Needham J	Brooks SE	Lea T	Rostance JC	Basford G	Richards RW	Riley A	Higgs H	Green JA	Baugh RH	Parfitt G	Curtis F	Bird H	Wright HF	Smart HH	Hodnett JE	Sambrook JH	Nightingale JG	Cutler ER	Roper FL	Woodward M	Hunt KRG	
3	4	5	6	7	8	9	10	11																					1
3	4	5	6	7	8	9	10	11																					2
3	4	5	6	7		9	10	11	8																				3
3	4	5	6			9	10	7		1	8	11																	4
3	4	5		7	8	9	10	11					6																5
3	4	5		7	8	9	10	11					6																6
3	4	5	6	7	8	9	10	11																					7
3		5	6	7	8	9		11		1		10	4																8
3		5	6	7		9	10					11	4	1	8														9
	4	5	6	7	9			11		1		10			8	2	3												10
	4	5	6	7		9		11				10			8		3												11
3	4	9	6	7	10			11					5					8											12
3	4	9	6	7	10			11					5		8														13
3	4	9	6		10			7				11	5					8											14
	4	5				9		11	10				6		8		3		7										15
	4	5	6	7				11	10							2		9		8									16
	4	5	3					11	9	1			6						7	8	10								17
	4	5	3					11	9	1			6						7	8	10								18
3		4		7			10	11		1			6			2				8		5	9						19
3		4		7			10	11		1			6			2				8		5	9						20
3		4		7			10			1		11	6			2				8	9	5							21
3		4		7			10					11	6	1		2				8		5	9						22
3		4					10	11					6			2				8		5	9	7					23
	4	5										11		1		2				8	10	6	9	7					24
3	4	5		7			9	11				10	6			2				8									25
3	4			7				11				10	6		8	2						5	9						26
3			6	7				11				10	5			2						4	9		8				27
3	4		6	7				11				10				2						5	9		8				28
3	4		6	7				11				10				2						5	9		8				29
3	4		6	7					11			10				2						5			8	9			30
3			5					11				10	6			2				8		4		7	9				31
3	4		5	7				11				10	6			2				8					9				32
3	4		5	7				11				10	6			2				8					9				33
3	4		6	7				11				10				2				8					9		5		34
3	4		6					11				10				2				8			9		7		5		35
3	4		6					11				10				2				8			9		7		5		36
3	7		6					11				10	4			2				8			9				5		37
3			6	7	8				11			10	4			2							9				5		38
3			6	7					11	1		10	4			2							9		8		5		39
3			6	7					11			10	4			2				8			9				5		40
3			6	7				11	9			10				2									8		5	4	41
3			6	7				11	9			10	4			2									8		5		42
35	28	25	31	31	11	11	14	34	11	9	1	27	26	3	6	26	3	3	3	18	4	12	15	3	13	1	9	1	
		4		3	2	5	5	6	2			10			1					4	1	1	5		4		1		

Garratty G	Price F	Groves A	Bishop AJ	Harrison WE	Howell H	Bate W	Needham J	Brooks SE	Lea T	Rostance JC	Basford G	Richards RW	Riley A	Higgs H	Green JA	Baugh RH	Parfitt G	Curtis F	Bird H	Wright HF	Smart HH	Hodnett JE	Sambrook JH	Nightingale JG	Cutler ER	Roper FL	Woodward M	Hunt KRG	
3	4	5		7				11	9			10	6			2				8									R1
3	4	5		7				11	9			10	6			2				8									rep
3	4	5		7			9	11				10	6			2				8									R2
3	3	3		3			1	3	2			3	3			3				3									
				1					1			2																	

1920-21

Division Two

Manager: Jack Addenbrooke

	P	W	D	L	F	A	Pts
Birmingham	42	24	10	8	79	38	58
Cardiff City	42	24	10	8	59	32	58
Bristol City	42	19	13	10	49	29	51
Blackpool	42	20	10	12	54	42	50
West Ham United	42	19	10	13	51	30	48
Notts County	42	18	11	13	55	40	47
Clapton Orient	42	16	13	13	43	42	45
South Shields	42	17	10	15	61	46	44
Fulham	42	16	10	16	43	47	42
The Wednesday	42	15	11	16	48	48	41
Bury	42	15	10	17	45	49	40
Leicester City	42	12	16	14	39	46	40
Hull City	42	10	20	12	43	53	40
Leeds United	42	14	10	18	40	45	38
Wolverhampton Wanderers	42	16	6	20	49	66	38
Barnsley	42	10	16	16	48	50	36
Port Vale	42	11	14	17	43	49	36
Nottingham Forest	42	12	12	18	48	55	36
Rotherham County	42	12	12	18	37	53	36
Stoke	42	12	11	19	46	56	35
Coventry City	42	12	11	19	39	70	35
Stockport County	42	9	12	21	42	75	30

Did you know that?

• In the home game with Bristol City on 25 September 1920 a shot from Wolves forward George Edmonds went straight through the net but the referee refused to award a goal. The match ended 0–0.

• David Stokes was 40 years of age when he played for Wolves against The Wednesday in April 1921.

• In December 1920, former Wolves forward Henry Howell played cricket for England against Australia in Melbourne. He went on to appear in four more Tests.

• Val Gregory was appointed team captain.

Match No.	Date		Venue	Opponents	Result		Scorers
1	Aug	28	A	Fulham	L	0-2	
2		30	H	West Ham United	L	1-2	Burrill
3	Sep	4	H	Fulham	W	1-0	Jones
4		6	A	West Ham United	L	0-1	
5		11	H	Bury	W	2-1	Potts, Brooks
6		18	A	Bury	L	1-3	Burrill
7		25	H	Bristol City	D	0-0	
8	Oct	2	A	Bristol City	L	0-2	
9		9	H	Barnsley	D	1-1	Edmonds
10		16	A	Barnsley	L	2-3	Harrison, Potts
11		23	H	Rotherham County	W	3-0	Potts 2, Edmonds
12		30	A	Rotherham County	L	0-1	
13	Nov	6	H	Birmingham	L	0-3	
14		13	A	Birmingham	L	1-4	Brooks
15		20	H	Port Vale	D	2-2	Edmonds, Brooks
16		27	A	Port Vale	W	3-2	Potts, Edmonds, Gregory
17	Dec	4	A	South Shields	W	2-1	Price, Potts
18		11	H	South Shields	W	3-0	Edmonds, Burrill, Potts
19		18	A	Hull City	W	1-0	Gregory
20		25	A	Stockport County	W	2-1	Potts, Burrill
21		27	H	Stockport County	W	2-0	Edmonds 2
22	Jan	1	H	Hull City	L	1-3	Hodnett
23		15	H	Leeds United	W	3-0	Brooks, Burrill, Richards
24		22	A	Leeds United	L	0-3	
25	Feb	5	A	Nottingham Forest	D	1-1	Edmonds
26		12	H	Coventry City	W	1-0	Hodnett
27		14	H	Nottingham Forest	W	2-1	Hales, Hodnett
28		24	A	Coventry City	L	0-4	
29		26	H	Stoke	D	3-3	Burrill 3
30	Mar	10	A	Stoke	L	0-1	
31		12	H	The Wednesday	L	1-2	Sambrook
32		25	A	Clapton Orient	W	1-0	Sambrook
33		26	A	Notts County	L	1-2	Richards
34		28	H	Clapton Orient	L	0-2	
35	Apr	2	H	Notts County	W	1-0	Edmonds
36		9	A	Blackpool	L	0-3	
37		11	A	The Wednesday	L	0-6	
38		16	H	Blackpool	W	3-1	Potts, Burrill, Brooks
39		28	A	Leicester City	D	0-0	
40		30	H	Leicester City	W	3-0	Brooks, Edmonds, Riley
41	May	2	A	Cardiff City	L	0-2	
42		7	H	Cardiff City	L	1-3	Edmonds

Appeara

FA Cup

R1	Jan	8	H	Stoke	W	3-2	Edmonds 2, Burrill
R2		29	A	Derby County	D	1-1	Wightman (og)
rep	Feb	2	H	Derby County	W	1-0	Richards
R3		19	A	Fulham	W	1-0	Potts
R4	Mar	5	A	Everton	W	1-0	Edmonds
SF		19	N	Cardiff City	D	0-0	
rep		23	N	Cardiff City	W	3-1	Brooks, Edmonds, Richards
F	Apr	23	N	Tottenham Hotspur	L	0-1	

SF at Anfield, replay at Old Trafford. Final at Stamford Bridge.

Appeara

One own-goal

	…es JH	Marshall GH	Gregory VF	Woodward M	Riley A	Harrison WE	Cutler ER	Edmonds GWN	Burrill F	Richards RW	Brooks SE	Potts AA	Hodnett JE	Lea T	Stokes D	Baugh RH	Price JA	Sambrook JH	Thomas A	George FN	Hales FF	Caddick W	Newell P	Hartland F
1		3	4	5	6	7	8	9	10	11														
2		3	4	5	6	7		9	8	10	11													
3		3	4	5	6	7		9	8	10	11													
4		3	4	5	6	7		9	8		11	10												
5		3	4	5	6	7		9	8		11	10												
6		3	4	5	6	7		9	8		11	10												
7		3	4	5	6	7		9	8		11	10												
8		3	4	5	6	7		9	8		11	10												
9		3	4		6	7		9	8		11		5	10										
10		3	4	5	6	7		9	8		11	10												
11		3		5	6		7	9	8		11	10	4											
12		3	5		6		7	9	8		11	10	4											
13		3	5		6			9	8		11	10	4		7									
14		3	4	5	6			9			11	10				2	7	8						
15		3	4		6			9	8		11	10	5			2	7							
16		3	4		6			9	8		11	10	5			2	7							
17		3	4		6			9	8		11	10	5			2	7							
18		3	4		6			9	8		11	10	5			2	7							
19		3	4		6			9	8		11	10	5			2	7							
20		3			6			9	8		11	10	5				7		4					
21		3			6			9	8		11	10	5				7		4					
22		3			6			9	8	11	7	10	5			2			4					
23		3	4		6			9	8	10	11		5	7		2								
24		3	4		6			9	8	11		10	5	7		2								
25		3	4	5	6			9	8	10	11			7		2				1				
26		3	4		6			9		10	11		5	7		2	8			1				
27		3			6					11		10	5			2	7	9	4	1	8			
28		3	4		6			9		11		10	5	7		2				1	8			
29		3			6			9	8		11	10	5	7		2			4	1				
30		3			6		8	9		10	11				7	2			4	1		5		
31			4		6				8	10	11		5	7		2		9		1				
32				6			8			11		10		7		3		9	4	1		5	2	
33				6						10		8		11	7			9	4			5	2	
34			4	3	6			9		10			5	11	7				8				2	
35		3	4		6			9		8	11	10	5		7	2								
36		3	4		6			9	8		11	10	5		7	2								1
37		3	4	5	6				8	11		10			7	2		9						
38		3	4	2	6			9	8		11	10		7								5		
39	2	3		4	6			9	8	10			5	11			7							
40		3	4	2	6			9	8	10	11		5	7										
41		3	4	2	6			9	8	10	11		5	7										
42		3	4	2	6			9	8	10	11		5	7										
	8	38	32	21	40	10	5	37	33	21	33	28	26	16	7	20	11	6	9	8	2	4	3	1
			2		1	1		11	9	2	6	9	3				1	2			1			
R1		3	4		6			9	8		11	10	5	7		2								
R2		3	4		6			9	8		11	10	5	7		2								
rep		3	4		6			9	8	10	11		5	7		2				1				
R3		3	4		6			9	8		11	10	5	7		2				1				
R4		3	4		6			9	8		11	10	5	7		2				1				
SF			4	3	6			9	8		11	10	5	7		2				1				
rep			4	3	6			9		8	11	10	5	7		2				1				
F		3	4	2	6			9	8		11	10	5	7						1				
		6	8	3	8			8	7	2	8	7	8	8		7				6				
								4	1	2	1	1												

1921-22

Division Two

Manager: Jack Addenbrooke

	P	W	D	L	F	A	Pts
Nottingham Forest	42	22	12	8	51	30	56
Stoke	42	18	16	8	60	44	52
Barnsley	42	22	8	12	67	52	52
West Ham United	42	20	8	14	52	39	48
Hull City	42	19	10	13	51	41	48
South Shields	42	17	12	13	43	38	46
Fulham	42	18	9	15	57	38	45
Leeds United	42	16	13	13	48	38	45
Leicester City	42	14	17	11	39	34	45
The Wednesday	42	15	14	13	47	50	44
Bury	42	15	10	17	54	55	40
Derby County	42	15	9	18	60	64	39
Notts County	42	12	15	15	47	51	39
Crystal Palace	42	13	13	16	45	51	39
Clapton Orient	42	15	9	18	43	50	39
Rotherham County	42	14	11	17	32	43	39
Wolverhampton Wanderers	42	13	11	18	44	49	37
Port Vale	42	14	8	20	43	57	36
Blackpool	42	15	5	22	44	57	35
Coventry City	42	12	10	20	51	60	34
Bradford Park Avenue	42	12	9	21	46	62	33
Bristol City	42	12	9	21	37	58	33

Did you know that?

- Wolves signed George Bissett (from Manchester United), Harold Hargreaves (from Nelson), Albert Kay (from Willenhall) and Ted Watson (from Pontypridd).
- Goalkeeper Teddy Peers was transferred to Port Vale having made 198 appearances for the club.
- On 25 June 1922, secretary-manager Jack Addenbrooke was advised to take six months' rest after illness.
- Wolves used five players in the outside-left position.

Match No.	Date		Venue	Opponents	Result		Scorers
1	Aug	27	A	Rotherham County	L	0-1	
2		29	H	Notts County	L	1-2	Burrill
3	Sep	3	H	Rotherham County	W	3-1	Baugh, Edmonds 2
4		5	A	Notts County	L	0-4	
5		10	A	Barnsley	L	1-2	Burrill
6		17	H	Barnsley	W	2-0	Lea, Smart
7		24	A	Coventry City	L	1-3	Edmonds
8	Oct	1	H	Coventry City	W	1-0	Burrill
9		8	A	Derby County	W	3-2	Edmonds 2, Burrill
10		15	H	Derby County	L	0-3	
11		22	A	Leicester City	W	1-0	Brooks
12		29	H	Leicester City	D	1-1	Edmonds
13	Nov	5	A	West Ham United	L	0-2	
14		12	H	West Ham United	L	0-1	
15		19	H	Crystal Palace	L	0-1	
16	Dec	3	H	Port Vale	W	2-0	Richards, Bissett
17		7	A	Crystal Palace	D	1-1	Edmonds
18		10	A	Port Vale	W	2-0	Baugh, Richards
19		17	A	South Shields	W	2-0	Brooks, Bissett
20		24	H	South Shields	W	3-2	Edmonds 2, Caddick
21		26	A	Nottingham Forest	D	0-0	
22		27	H	Nottingham Forest	W	2-0	Bissett 2
23		31	A	Bristol City	L	0-2	
24	Jan	14	H	Bristol City	D	2-2	Hargreaves, Bissett
25		28	H	The Wednesday	D	0-0	
26	Feb	4	A	Fulham	L	0-1	
27		11	H	Fulham	D	0-0	
28		13	A	The Wednesday	L	1-3	Bissett
29		18	A	Blackpool	W	3-1	Bissett, Edmonds, Hargreaves
30		25	H	Blackpool	W	4-0	Richard, Hargreaves 2, Baugh
31	Mar	4	A	Bradford Park Avenue	D	0-0	
32		11	H	Bradford Park Avenue	W	5-0	Richards, Edmonds 2, Bissett 2
33		18	H	Clapton Orient	L	0-2	
34		25	A	Clapton Orient	L	0-1	
35	Apr	1	H	Stoke	D	1-1	Hargreaves
36		8	A	Stoke	L	0-3	
37		14	A	Bury	L	1-2	Marshall
38		15	H	Leeds United	D	0-0	
39		17	H	Bury	D	1-1	Edmonds
40		22	A	Leeds United	D	0-0	
41		29	H	Hull City	L	0-2	
42	May	6	A	Hull City	L	0-2	

Appeara

G

FA Cup

R1	Jan	7	A	Preston North End	L	0-3	

Appeara

Marshall GH	Gregory V	Hodnett JE	Riley A	Burrill F	Potts AA	Edmonds GWN	Mayson T	Brooks S	Lea T	Richards RW	Woodward M	Smart FL	Carter ET	Gill J	Watson EG	Caddick W	Rouse VA	Price J	Hargreaves H	Bissett G	Thomas A	Newell P	
3	4	5	6	7	8	9	10	11															1
3	4	5	6	8	10	9		11	7														2
3	4	5	6		8	9		11	7	10													3
3	4	5	6		8	9		11	7	10													4
	4	5	6	8		9			7	11	3	10											5
	4	5		8		9			7	11	3	10	6										6
	4	5		8		9			7	11	3	10	6										7
3	4	5		8	10	9			7				6	11									8
3	4	5		8	10	9			7				6	11									9
3	4	5		8	10	9			7				6	11									10
	4			10				7					6	11	3	5	8	9					11
	4					9	10	7					6	11	3	5	8						12
	4					9		7		10			6	11	3	5	8						13
	4			9				7	10				6	11	3	5	8						14
3	4		6	8		9		7	11							5			10				15
3			6			9		7		11						5	4		10	8			16
3	4		6			9		7		11						5			10	8			17
3	4		6			9		7		11						5			10	8			18
3	4		6			9		7		11						5			10	8			19
3	4		6			9		7		11						5			10	8			20
3			6			9		7		11						5			10	8	4		21
3	4		6			9		7		11						5			10	8			22
3	4		6	8		9				11						5		7	10				23
3			6	7		9				11						5			10	8	4		24
3	4		6			9		7		11						5			10	8			25
3	4			10		9		7					6			5			11	8			26
3	4		6	7		9		11								5			10	8			27
3	4	5	6			9		7		11									10	8			28
3	4		6			9		7		11						5			10	8			29
3	4		6			9		7		11						5			10	8			30
3	4		6			9		7		11						5			10	8			31
3	4		6			9		7		11						5			10	8			32
3	4		6	9				7		11						5			10	8			33
	4		6			9		7		11					3	5			10	8			34
3	4		6			9		7		11						5			10	8			35
3	4	5	6			9		7		11									10	8			36
3	4	5	6			9		7		11									10	8			37
3	4		6			9		7		11						5			10	8		2	38
3	4	5	6			9		7	11										10	8			39
3	4		6			9		7	11							5			10	8			40
3	4		6			9		7	11						2	5			10	8			41
3	4		6			9		7	11							5			10	8			42
34	39	14	32	16	7	39	2	34	15	27	3	3	10	7	6	28	5	2	28	26	2	1	
1				4		13		2	1	4		1				1			5	9			

Marshall GH	Gregory V	Hodnett JE	Riley A	Burrill F	Potts AA	Edmonds GWN	Mayson T	Brooks S	Lea T	Richards RW	Woodward M	Smart FL	Carter ET	Gill J	Watson EG	Caddick W	Rouse VA	Price J	Hargreaves H	Bissett G	Thomas A	Newell P	
3			6			9			7	11	4					5			10	8			R1
1			1			1			1	1	1					1			1	1			

1922-23

Division Two

Manager: George Jobey

	P	W	D	L	F	A	Pts
Notts County	42	23	7	12	46	34	53
West Ham United	42	20	11	11	63	38	51
Leicester City	42	21	9	12	65	44	51
Manchester United	42	17	14	11	51	36	48
Blackpool	42	18	11	13	60	43	47
Bury	42	18	11	13	55	46	47
Leeds United	42	18	11	13	43	36	47
The Wednesday	42	17	12	13	54	47	46
Barnsley	42	17	11	14	62	51	45
Fulham	42	16	12	14	43	32	44
Southampton	42	14	14	14	40	40	42
Hull City	42	14	14	14	43	45	42
South Shields	42	15	10	17	35	44	40
Derby County	42	14	11	17	46	50	39
Bradford City	42	12	13	17	41	45	37
Crystal Palace	42	13	11	18	54	62	37
Port Vale	42	14	9	19	39	51	37
Coventry City	42	15	7	20	46	63	37
Clapton Orient	42	12	12	18	40	50	36
Stockport County	42	14	8	20	43	58	36
Rotherham County	42	13	9	20	44	63	35
Wolverhampton Wanderers	42	9	9	24	42	77	27

Did you know that?

• George Jobey became Wolves' new manager, and former boss Jack Addenbrooke died in September 1922. Jobey brought with him as trainer the former Sunderland inside-forward George Holley.

• Several players were signed, among them Stan Fazackerley and George Brewster (from Everton),George Getgood (from Southampton), Harry Lees (from Ebbw Vale), Albert Legge (from Lewisham Athletic) and Harold Shaw (from Hednesford Town).

• Tansey Lea, Dick Richards and Alf Riley all left Molineux.

• In December Wolves forward Harry Hargreaves was sent off during the home League game against Leeds United.

• The club became Wolverhampton Wanderers (1923) Ltd.

Match No.	Date		Venue	Opponents	Result		Scorers
1	Aug	26	H	Derby County	L	0-1	
2		28	A	Fulham	L	0-2	
3	Sep	2	A	Derby County	D	1-1	Baugh
4		4	H	Fulham	D	0-0	
5		9	H	Manchester United	L	0-1	
6		16	A	Manchester United	L	0-1	
7		23	H	Bury	D	1-1	Hodnett
8		30	A	Bury	L	0-3	
9	Oct	7	H	Rotherham County	W	3-2	McCall, Edmonds, Bissett
10		14	A	Rotherham County	L	2-3	Edmonds, Hargreaves
11		21	H	Southampton	D	0-0	
12		28	A	Southampton	L	0-3	
13	Nov	4	A	Stockport County	D	1-1	Edmonds
14		11	H	Stockport County	W	3-1	Edmonds 2, Hargreaves
15		18	A	Notts County	L	1-4	Edmonds
16		25	H	Notts County	W	1-0	Fazackerley
17	Dec	2	A	Leeds United	L	0-1	
18		9	H	Leeds United	L	0-1	
19		16	H	West Ham United	L	1-4	Edmonds
20		23	A	West Ham United	L	0-1	
21		25	A	Coventry City	L	1-7	Fazackerley
22		26	H	Coventry City	L	1-2	E White
23		30	H	South Shields	W	1-0	E White
24	Jan	6	A	South Shields	D	1-1	Fazackerley
25		20	H	Clapton Orient	L	1-3	Edmonds
26		27	A	Clapton Orient	L	1-4	Fazackerley
27	Feb	10	A	Bradford City	D	1-1	Fazackerley
28		17	H	Blackpool	L	3-4	Fazackerley 2, Caddick
29		19	H	Bradford City	W	4-1	Burrill 3, E White
30		24	A	Blackpool	L	1-3	Fazackerley
31	Mar	3	H	Leicester City	L	1-2	Fazackerley
32		10	A	Leicester City	L	0-7	
33		17	A	Barnsley	L	0-1	
34		24	H	Barnsley	D	3-3	McMillan, Edmonds 2
35		30	A	Port Vale	L	0-1	
36		31	A	The Wednesday	L	0-1	
37	Apr	2	H	Port Vale	W	3-0	Edmonds 3
38		7	H	The Wednesday	W	2-0	Fazackerley, Rhodes
39		14	A	Hull City	D	0-0	
40		23	H	Hull City	W	3-0	Edmonds, Fazackerley 2
41		28	A	Crystal Palace	L	0-5	
42	May	5	H	Crystal Palace	W	1-0	Hargreaves

Appear

FA Cup

R1	Sep	13	A	Merthyr Town	W	1-0	Fazackerley
R2	Feb	3	H	Liverpool	L	0-2	

Appear

	Marshall GH	Gregory VF	Hodnett JE	Riley A	Bissett G	Burrill F	Edmonds GWN	Hargreaves H	McCall W	Hampton JW	Caddick W	Kay AE	McMillan ST	Whatmore EL	Best R	Watson EG	Rhodes L	Brewster G	Fazackerley SN	Carter ET	White E	Newell P	Picken AH	White J	Getgood G	Lees HH
1	3	4	5	6	7	8	9	10	11																	
2	3	4	5	6	7	8	9	10	11	1																
3	3		4		8	10			11	1	5	6	7	9												
4	3		4		8		9	10	11	1	5	6	7													
5	3		4		8			10	11	1	5	6	7	9												
6	3		4		8		9		11	1	5	6	10		7											
7	3		4		8		9		11	1	5	6	10		7											
8	3	4			8	10		9	11		5	6			7											
9	3	4			8		9	10	11		5	6			7											
10	3	4			8		9	10	11		5	6			7											
11	3	4			8		9	10	11	1	5	6			7											
12	3	4	5		10		9		11	1		6	8		7											
13			4				9	10		1	5	6	8		7	3	11									
14			4				9	10		1		6			7	3	11	5	8							
15			4	6			9	10		1					7	3	11	5	8							
16			4				9	10		1		6			7	3	11	5	8							
17					4		9	10		1		6			7	3	11	5	8							
18	3	4					9	10		1					7		11	5	8	6						
19	3		4		8		9		11	1					7			5	10	6						
20	3		4				9			1					7		11	5	8	6	10					
21	3		4				9			1					7		11	5	8	6	10					
22	3		4				9	11		1	5				7				8	6	10	2				
23	3		4				9				5				7				8	6	10	2	11			
24		3	4						11		6				7			5	9		10	2		8		
25	3	6	4		8		10		11						7			5	9			2				
26	3	2	4				9				5				7		11		8		10				6	
27		2					6				5		7			3			8		10		11		4	9
28		2					6				5		7			3			8		10		11		4	9
29		2				9	6						7			3		5	8		10		11		4	
30		2	5			9	6						7			3			8		10		11		4	
31		2	5			9	6						7			3			8		10		11		4	
32		2	5				10					6	7			3			8				11		4	9
33	3	2				8	9	10			5	6	7				11								4	
34	3	2				8	9	10			5	6	7				11								4	
35	3	2				8	9	10			5	6	7				11								4	
36	3	2				8	9	10			5	6	7				11								4	
37	3	2			8		9	10			5	6	7				11								4	
38	3						9	10			5	6	7				11		8			2			4	
39	3						9	10			5	6	7				11		8			2			4	
40	3	2					9	10			5	6			7		11		8						4	
41	3	2					9	10			5	6	7				11		8						4	
42	3	2					9	10			5	6	7				11		8						4	
	30	25	23	3	16	11	38	25	15	18	26	25	22	2	22	11	19	11	24	6	11	6	7	1	17	3
			1		1	3	14	3	1		1		1				1		12		3					

	Marshall GH	Gregory VF	Hodnett JE	Riley A	Bissett G	Burrill F	Edmonds GWN	Hargreaves H	McCall W	Hampton JW	Caddick W	Kay AE	McMillan ST	Whatmore EL	Best R	Watson EG	Rhodes L	Brewster G	Fazackerley SN	Carter ET	White E	Newell P	Picken AH	White J	Getgood G	Lees HH
R1	3	6	4		8		10		11						7			5	9							
R2	3	2	4		8	10	6	11					7					5	9							
	2	2	2		2	1	2	1	1				1		1			2	2							
																			1							

1923-24

Division Three North

Manager: George Jobey

	P	W	D	L	F	A	Pts
Wolverhampton Wanderers	42	24	15	3	76	27	63
Rochdale	42	25	12	5	60	26	62
Chesterfield	42	22	10	10	70	39	54
Rotherham County	42	23	6	13	70	43	52
Bradford Park Avenue	42	21	10	11	69	43	52
Darlington	42	20	8	14	70	53	48
Southport	42	16	14	12	44	42	46
Ashington	42	18	8	16	59	61	44
Doncaster Rovers	42	15	12	15	59	53	42
Wigan Borough	42	14	14	14	55	53	42
Grimsby Town	42	14	13	15	49	47	41
Tranmere Rovers	42	13	15	14	51	60	41
Accrington Stanley	42	16	8	18	48	61	40
Halifax Town	42	15	10	17	42	59	40
Durham City	42	15	9	18	59	60	39
Wrexham	42	10	18	14	37	44	38
Walsall	42	14	8	20	44	59	36
New Brighton	42	11	13	18	40	53	35
Lincoln City	42	10	12	20	48	59	32
Crewe Alexandra	42	7	13	22	32	58	27
Hartlepools United	42	7	11	24	33	70	25
Barrow	42	8	9	25	35	80	25

Did you know that?

• Wolves' 20-match unbeaten run in 1923–24 remains their best in the Football League.

• Harry Lees scored Wolves' first-ever goal in Third Division football against Rotherham on 27 August.

• Stan Fazackerley became the first Wolves player to be sent off in an FA Cup tie, against Charlton.

• In December 1923 Wolves paid £1,000 to Swindon Town for centre-forward Tom Phillipson.

• Wolves met 15 clubs in competitive games for the first time: Accrington Stanley, Ashington, Barrow, Crewe Alexandra, Darlington, Doncaster Rovers, Durham City, Halifax Town, Hartlepools United, New Brighton, Rochdale, Southport, Tranmere Rovers, Walsall and Wigan Borough.

Match No.	Date		Venue	Opponents	Result		Scorers
1	Aug	25	A	Chesterfield	D	0-0	
2		27	H	Rotherham County	W	3-0	Lees 2, Fazackerley
3	Sep	1	H	Chesterfield	W	2-1	Lees, Harrington
4		3	A	Rotherham County	D	1-1	Legge
5		8	A	Crewe Alexandra	D	0-0	
6		15	H	Crewe Alexandra	W	1-0	Kay
7		22	A	Accrington Stanley	L	0-1	
8		29	H	Accrington Stanley	W	5-1	McMillan, Fazackerley 3, Lees
9	Oct	6	A	Halifax Town	D	2-2	McMillan, Fazackerley
10		13	H	Halifax Town	W	4-0	Legge, McMillan 2, Edwards
11		20	A	Bradford Park Avenue	W	1-0	Lees
12		27	H	Bradford Park Avenue	W	2-0	Edwards, Getgood
13	Nov	3	H	Grimsby Town	W	4-1	Martin 2, Fazackerley 2
14		10	A	Grimsby Town	L	0-2	
15		24	H	New Brighton	W	5-1	Lees 3, Martin 2
16	Dec	1	A	New Brighton	W	1-0	Fazackerley
17		8	A	Hartlepools United	W	1-0	Legge
18		22	H	Walsall	D	0-0	
19		26	H	Durham City	W	2-1	Lees 2
20		29	H	Ashington	W	1-0	Lees
21	Jan	1	A	Durham City	W	3-2	Fazackerley, Lees 2
22		5	A	Ashington	W	7-1	Phillipson 3, Fazackerley 2, Lees 2
23		19	A	Wrexham	D	2-2	Phillipson, Lees
24		26	H	Wrexham	W	3-0	Lees 3
25	Feb	9	H	Doncaster Rovers	W	1-0	Fazackerley
26		11	H	Hartlepools United	W	2-1	Fazackerley, Phillipson
27		16	A	Rochdale	D	0-0	
28	Mar	1	A	Southport	D	0-0	
29		8	H	Southport	W	2-1	Edwards 2
30		15	H	Darlington	W	2-0	Martin, Phillipson
31		22	A	Darlington	D	1-1	Martin
32		26	H	Rochdale	D	0-0	
33		29	H	Barrow	W	3-0	Fazackerley, Harrington 2
34	Apr	5	A	Barrow	D	2-2	Marson 2
35		7	A	Walsall	L	1-2	Edwards
36		12	A	Lincoln City	D	0-0	
37		19	H	Lincoln City	W	3-0	Phillipson 2, Lees
38		21	H	Wigan Borough	D	3-3	Davison, Edwards, Phillipson
39		22	A	Wigan Borough	D	1-1	Edwards
40		26	H	Tranmere Rovers	W	3-0	Lees, Phillipson, Bowen
41	May	1	A	Doncaster Rovers	W	2-0	Phillipson 2
42		3	A	Tranmere Rovers	D	0-0	

Appea

FA Cup

R1	Jan	12	H	Darlington	W	3-1	Phillipson 2, Lees
R2	Feb	2	A	Charlton Athletic	D	0-0	
rep		6	H	Charlton Athletic	W	1-0	Fazackerley
R3		23	A	West Bromwich Albion	D	1-1	Fazackerley
rep		27	H	West Bromwich Albion	L	0-2	

Appea

	Watson EG	Shaw HV	Getgood G	Caddick W	Kay AE	Harrington JW	Fazackerley SN	Legge AE	Lees HH	Edwards EJ	McMillan ST	Marson F	Edmonds GWN	Martin JC	Picken AH	Phillipson WT	Crewe W	Davison TR	Carter ET	Timmins B	Bradford J	Baugh RH	Bowen TG
1	2	3	4	5	6	7	8	9	10	11													
2	2	3	4	5	6	7	8	9	10	11													
3	2	3	4	5	6	7	8	9	10	11													
4	2	3	4	5	6	7	8	9	10	11													
5	2	3	4	5	6	7	8	9	10	11													
6	2	3	4	5	6		8		9	11	7	10											
7	2	3	4	5	6		8		10	11	7		9										
8	2	3	4	5	6		8	9	10	11	7												
9	2	3	4	5	6		8	9	10	11	7												
10	2	3	4	5	6		8	9	10	11	7												
11	2	3	4	5	6		8		10	11	7			9									
12	2	3	4	5	6		8		10	11	7			9									
13	2	3	4	5	6		8		10	11	7			9									
14	2	3	4	5	6		8		10	11	7			9									
15	2	3	4	5	6	7	8		10	11				9									
16	2	3	4	5	6	7	8		10					9	11								
17	2	3	4	5	6	7	8	9	10	11													
18	2	3	4	5	6	7	8	9	10	11													
19	2	3	4	5	6	7	8		10	11						9							
20	2	3			6	7	8		10	11						9	4	5					
21	2	3			6	7	8		10						11	9	4	5					
22	2	3			6	7	8		10	11						9	4	5					
23	2	3			6	7	8		10	11						9	4	5					
24	2	3	4	5	6		8		10	11	7					9							
25	2	3	4	5	6		8		10	11	7					9							
26	2	3	4	5			8		10	11	7					9			6				
27	2	3	4	5	6		8		10		7				11	9							
28	2	3	4	5	6	7	8		10	11						9							
29	2		6	5		7	8		10	11						9	4			3			
30	2	3		5	6	7			10	11				9		8	4						
31	2	3	4	5	6	7			10	11				9		8							
32	2	3	4	5	6	7			10	11				9		8							
33	2	3	4	5		7	8		10					9	11						6		
34	2	3	4	5	6	7	8			11		10				9							
35		3		5			8			11	7	10				9	4				6	2	
36	2	3	4	5	6			7	10	11				9		8							
37	2	3	4		6	7	8		10	11						9		5					
38	2	3	4		6	7	8		10	11						9		5					
39	2		4	5	6	7			10	11						9				3			8
40	2		4	5	6	7			10	11						9				3			8
41	2		4	5	6	7			10	11						9				3			8
42	2		4	5	6	7			10	11						9				3			8
	1	37	36	36	38	27	34	11	40	38	14	3	1	11	4	23	7	6	1	5	2	1	4
			1		1	3	14	3	21	7	4	2		6		12		1					1

	Watson EG	Shaw HV	Getgood G	Caddick W	Kay AE	Harrington JW	Fazackerley SN	Legge AE	Lees HH	Edwards EJ	McMillan ST	Marson F	Edmonds GWN	Martin JC	Picken AH	Phillipson WT	Crewe W	Davison TR
R1	2	3			6	7	8		10	11						9	4	5
R2	2	3	4	5	6		8		10	11	7					9		
rep	2	3	4	5	6		8		10	11	7					9		
R3	2	3	4	5	6	7	8		10	11						9		
rep	2	3	4	5	6	7	8		10	11						9		
	5	5	4	4	5	3	5		5	5	2					5	1	1
							2		1							2		

1924-25

Division Two

Manager: Alfred Hoskins

	P	W	D	L	F	A	Pts
Leicester City	42	24	11	7	90	32	59
Manchester United	42	23	11	8	57	23	57
Derby County	42	22	11	9	71	36	55
Portsmouth	42	15	18	9	58	50	48
Chelsea	42	16	15	11	51	37	47
Wolverhampton Wanderers	42	20	6	16	55	51	46
Southampton	42	13	18	11	40	36	44
Port Vale	42	17	8	17	48	56	42
South Shields	42	12	17	13	42	38	41
Hull City	42	15	11	16	50	49	41
Clapton Orient	42	14	12	16	42	42	40
Fulham	42	15	10	17	41	56	40
Middlesbrough	42	10	19	13	36	44	39
The Wednesday	42	15	8	19	50	56	38
Barnsley	42	13	12	17	46	59	38
Bradford City	42	13	12	17	37	50	38
Blackpool	42	14	9	19	65	61	37
Oldham Athletic	42	13	11	18	35	51	37
Stockport County	42	13	11	18	37	57	37
Stoke	42	12	11	19	34	46	35
Crystal Palace	42	12	10	20	38	54	34
Coventry City	42	11	9	22	45	84	31

Did you know that?

- The Waterloo Road Stand was completed at Molineux and new dressing rooms installed. The old Waterloo Road cover was moved to the Molineux Street side of the ground but was blown away in a severe gale.
- Goalkeeper Noel George completed his third successive season as an ever present.
- Jack Mitton (from Sunderland), Vic Fox (from Middlesbrough) and Jack Bradford (from Grimsby Town) were among the new faces at Molineux.
- Four players who left the club were Dicky Baugh (to West Bromwich Albion), Stan Fazackerley (to Derby County), George Getgood (to Kidderminster Harriers) and George Bissett (to Pontypridd).
- Tom Phillipson was appointed team captain in place of Getgood.

Match No.	Date		Venue	Opponents	Result		Scorers	At
1	Aug	30	A	Port Vale	W	3-1	Bowen, Edwards, Lees	
2	Sep	1	A	Barnsley	D	0-0		
3		6	H	Bradford City	W	2-0	Edwards, Phillipson	
4		10	A	Middlesbrough	L	0-2		
5		13	A	South Shields	D	3-3	Mitton 2, Lees	
6		20	H	Derby County	L	0-4		
7		27	A	Blackpool	W	4-2	O'Conner 2, Lees 2	
8	Oct	4	H	Hull City	W	2-1	Phillipson 2	
9		11	A	Portsmouth	D	2-2	Bowen , Lees	
10		18	H	Fulham	W	2-1	Lees, Phillipson	
11		25	H	Manchester United	D	0-0		
12	Nov	1	A	Leicester City	L	0-2		
13		8	H	Stoke	W	1-0	Phillipson	
14		15	A	Coventry City	W	4-2	Bowen, Lees, Phillipson, Harrington	
15		22	H	Oldham Athletic	W	2-0	Phillipson, Gummery	
16		29	A	The Wednesday	L	0-2		
17	Dec	6	H	Clapton Orient	L	1-2	Phillipson	
18		13	A	Crystal Palace	L	1-2	Fazackerley	
19		20	H	Southampton	W	3-0	Edwards 2, Fazackerley	
20		25	A	Chelsea	L	0-1		
21		26	H	Chelsea	L	0-1		
22		27	H	Port Vale	W	1-0	Lees	
23	Jan	1	A	Stockport County	D	1-1	Marson	
24		3	A	Bradford City	L	1-3	Marson	
25		17	H	South Shields	W	2-1	Fazackerley, Bowen	
26		24	A	Derby County	W	1-0	Harris	
27	Feb	7	A	Hull City	W	1-0	Harris	
28		14	H	Portsmouth	L	0-5		
29		21	A	Fulham	L	0-1		
30		28	A	Manchester United	L	0-3		
31	Mar	14	A	Stoke	W	3-0	Phillipson 2, Bowen	
32		21	H	Coventry City	W	3-1	Lees, Bowen, Phillipson	
33		23	H	Blackpool	W	2-0	Phillipson, Lees	
34		28	A	Oldham Athletic	L	0-2		
35		30	H	Leicester City	L	0-1		
36	Apr	4	H	The Wednesday	W	1-0	Bowen	
37		11	A	Clapton Orient	L	1-2	Edwards	
38		13	H	Stockport County	W	3-0	Phillipson 2, Lees	
39		18	H	Crystal Palace	W	3-1	Phillipson 2, Bowen	
40		25	A	Southampton	D	1-1	Lees	
41		27	H	Barnsley	L	0-1		
42	May	2	H	Middlesbrough	W	1-0	Harrington	

Appeara

FA Cup

R1	Jan	10	A	Hull City	D	1-1	Edwards	
rep		15	H	Hull City	L	0-1		

R1 replay aet

Appeara

Watson EG	Timmins B	Mitton J	Caddick W	Bradford J	Harrington JW	Bowen TG	Phillipson WT	Lees HH	Edwards EJ	Shaw HV	O'Connor JP	Legge AE	Tyler S	Kay AE	Gummery WH	Fazackerley SN	Getgood G	Marson F	Harris J	Picken AH	Davison TR	Bradley PJ	Fox WV	
2	3	4	5	6	7	8	9	10	11															1
2	3	4	5	6	7	8	9	10	11															2
2		4	5	6		8	9	10	11	3	7													3
2		4	5	6			9	10	11	3	8	7												4
2		4	5	6			9	10	11	3	8	7												5
2	3	4	5	6			9	10	11		8	7												6
		4	5	6		8	9	10		3	7		2	11										7
		4	5	6		8	9	10		3	7		2	11										8
2		4	5	6		8	9	10	11	3	7													9
2		4	5	6	7		9	10	11	3	8													10
2		4	5	6	7		9	10	11	3	8													11
2		4	5	6	7	8	9	10	11	3														12
2		4	5	6	7	8	9	10		3					11									13
2		4	5	6	7	8	9	10		3					11									14
2		4	5	6	7	8	9	10		3					11									15
2		4	5	6	7	8	9	10		3					11									16
2		4	5	6			9	10		3		7			11	8								17
2		4	5	6			9	10		3		7			11	8								18
2		4	5	6			9	10	11	3		7				8								19
2		4	5	6			9	10	11	3		7				8								20
2		4	5	6			9	10	11	3		7				8								21
2			5	6				9		3		7			11	8	4	10						22
2			5	6				9		3		7			11	8	4	10						23
2		4	5	6				9		3		7			11	8		10						24
			5	4	7	10				3				6		8			9	11				25
				4		10	7	11		3			2	6		8			9		5			26
	4					10	7	11		3			2	6		8			9		5			27
	2			4		10	7	11		3				6		8			9		5			28
		4	5	6		8				3		7			11			10	9					29
		4	5	6					11	3	8	7						10	9					30
		4	5	6	7	8	9	10	11	3														31
		4	5	6	7	8	9	10	11	3														32
		4	5	6	7	8	9	10	11	3														33
		4	5	6	7	8	9	10	11	3														34
		4	5		7		9	10	11		8			6									3	35
		4	5		7	8	9	10	11					6									3	36
		4	5		7	8	9	10	11					6									3	37
		4	5	6	7	8	9	10	11														3	38
		4	5	6	7	8	9	10	11														3	39
		4	5	6	7	8	9	10	11														3	40
		4	5	6	7	8	9	10	11														3	41
		4	5	6	7	8	9	10														11	3	42
	5	36	39	38	22	27	36	39	25	31	11	13	4	9	10	12	2	5	6	1	3	1	8	
		2			2	8	16	12	5		2				1	3		2	2					

Watson EG	Timmins B	Mitton J	Caddick W	Bradford J	Harrington JW	Bowen TG	Phillipson WT	Lees HH	Edwards EJ	Shaw HV	O'Connor JP	Legge AE	Tyler S	Kay AE	Gummery WH	Fazackerley SN	Getgood G	Marson F	Harris J	Picken AH	Davison TR	Bradley PJ	Fox WV	
		4	5	6		10	8	9	11	3		7												R1
		4	5	6		10	8	9	11	3		7												rep
		2	2	2		2	2	2	2	2		2												
									1															

1925-26

Division Two

Manager: Alfred Hoskins (to March)
Fred Scotchbrook

	P	W	D	L	F	A	Pts
The Wednesday	42	27	6	9	88	48	60
Derby County	42	25	7	10	77	42	57
Chelsea	42	19	14	9	76	49	52
Wolverhampton Wanderers	42	21	7	14	84	60	49
Swansea Town	42	19	11	12	77	57	49
Blackpool	42	17	11	14	76	69	45
Oldham Athletic	42	18	8	16	74	62	44
Port Vale	42	19	6	17	79	69	44
South Shields	42	18	8	16	74	65	44
Middlesbrough	42	21	2	19	77	68	44
Portsmouth	42	17	10	15	79	74	44
Preston North End	42	18	7	17	71	84	43
Hull City	42	16	9	17	63	61	41
Southampton	42	15	8	19	63	63	38
Darlington	42	14	10	18	72	77	38
Bradford City	42	13	10	19	47	66	36
Nottingham Forest	42	14	8	20	51	73	36
Barnsley	42	12	12	18	58	84	36
Fulham	42	11	12	19	46	77	34
Clapton Orient	42	12	9	21	50	65	33
Stoke City	42	12	8	22	54	77	32
Stockport County	42	8	9	25	51	97	25

Did you know that?

- The new Molineux stand was officially opened on the first day of the season for the game against Preston North End.
- Striker Tom Phillipson became the first Wolves player to score three League hat-tricks in a season. He also netted in 10 successive League games, starting on 6 February and finishing on 27 March – a club record.
- Evan Edwards was transferred to Mid-Rhondda and Val Gregory retired, having made 106 senior appearances for the club.

Match No.	Date		Venue	Opponents	Result		Scorers
1	Aug	29	H	Preston North End	W	3-0	Phillipson 2, Keetley
2	Sep	5	A	Middlesbrough	L	1-4	Keetley
3		7	A	South Shields	L	1-3	Bowen
4		12	H	Portsmouth	W	4-1	Bowen, Kerr, Keetley, Price
5		14	H	South Shields	W	2-0	Bowen 2
6		19	A	Nottingham Forest	W	4-1	Bowen, Kerr 2, Keetley
7		26	A	Swansea Town	W	4-2	Kerr 2, Keetley, Price
8	Oct	3	H	The Wednesday	L	1-2	Mitton
9		5	A	Fulham	W	2-1	Harrington 2
10		10	A	Stoke City	D	0-0	
11		17	H	Southampton	W	4-1	Mitton, Bowen, Phiilipson 2
12		24	A	Blackpool	L	0-4	
13		31	H	Bradford City	D	1-1	Bowen
14	Nov	7	A	Derby County	L	0-2	
15		14	H	Chelsea	D	0-0	
16		21	A	Clapton Orient	L	1-2	Price
17	Dec	5	A	Port Vale	L	0-3	
18		12	H	Blackpool	D	0-0	
19		19	A	Hull City	L	1-3	Price
20		25	A	Oldham Athletic	W	2-1	Phillipson 2
21		26	H	Oldham Athletic	W	2-1	Phillipson, Meek
22	Jan	2	A	Preston North End	L	0-1	
23		16	H	Middlesbrough	W	3-1	Phillipson 3
24		23	A	Portsmouth	L	0-3	
25	Feb	6	H	Swansea Town	L	2-3	Phillipson 2
26		8	H	Nottingham Forest	W	4-0	Caddick, Phillipson 2, Homer
27		13	A	The Wednesday	L	1-2	Phillipson
28		20	H	Stoke City	W	5-1	Phillipson 2, Lees, Price 2
29		27	A	Southampton	L	2-4	Phillipson , Price
30	Mar	1	H	Darlington	W	1-0	Phillipson
31		6	A	Barnsley	D	1-1	Phillipson
32		13	A	Bradford City	W	2-1	Phillipson, Price
33		20	H	Derby County	W	2-0	Phillipson 2
34		27	A	Chelsea	D	3-3	Scott 2, Phillipson
35	Apr	2	A	Stockport County	L	0-1	
36		3	H	Clapton Orient	W	3-0	Caddick, Scott, Phillipson
37		5	H	Stockport County	W	5-1	Scott, Phillipson 3, Hann
38		12	H	Fulham	D	0-0	
39		17	H	Port Vale	W	3-1	Mitton, Phillipson 2
40		24	A	Darlington	W	4-3	Scott, Phillipson, Lees 2
41		26	H	Barnsley	W	7-1	Homer, Phillipson 4, Lees, Barnett (og)
42	May	1	H	Hull City	W	3-1	Phillipson, Lees, Hann

Appear

One own-goal

FA Cup

R3	Jan	9	H	Arsenal	D	1-1	Phillipson
rep		13	A	Arsenal	L	0-1	

Appear

Watson EG	Timmins B	Mitton J	Caddick W	Kay AE	Harrington JW	Bowen TG	Phillipson WT	Keetley JF	Price FT	Shaw HV	Charnley S	Kerr RC	Scott H	Lees HH	Bradford J	Legge AE	Fox WV	MacDougall AL	Burns W	Meek HL	Hampton JW	Bradley PJ	Homer S	Tyler S	Canavon A	Hann CW	
2	3	4	5	6	7	8	9	10	11																		1
2		4	5	6	7	8	9	10	11	3																	2
2		4	5	6	7	8	9	10	11	3																	3
2		4		6	7	8		10	11	3	5	9															4
2		4		6	7	8		10	11	3	5	9															5
2		4		6	7	8		10	11	3	5	9															6
2		4		6	7	8		10	11	3	5	9															7
2		4		6	7	8		10	11	3	5	9															8
2		4		6	7		9		11	3	5		8	10													9
2		4		6	7		9		11	3	5		8	10													10
2		4		6	7	8	9		11	3	5			10													11
2		4		6	7	8	9		11	3	5			10													12
2		4		6	7	8		10	11	3					5	9											13
2		4				8		10	11	3	5	9			6	7											14
		4				10			11	3	5	9	8		6	7	2										15
		4				10			11	3	5	9	8		6	7	2										16
		4		6	7	8			11	3	5	9		10			2										17
					7	8			11	3		9		10	6		2	4	5								18
		4			7		10		11	3	5	9	8		6		2										19
2		4			7		9		11		5		8		6		3			10							20
2		4					9		11		5		8		6	7	3			10							21
2		4			7		9		11		5		8		6		3			10							22
		4		6			9			3	5		8			7	2			10	1	11					23
		4		6	7		9		11	3	5		8				2			10	1						24
		4		6			9		11	3	5		8				2			10	1		7				25
		4	5	6			9		11	3			8	10			2				1		7				26
		4	5	6			9		11	3			8	10							1		7	2			27
		4	5	6			9		11	3			8	10							1		7	2			28
2		4	5	6			9		11	3			8	10									7				29
2		4	5	6			9			3			8	10								11	7		1		30
2		4		6			9			3	5		8	10									7		1	11	31
		4		6			9		11	3	5		8	10							1		7	2			32
		4		6			9		11	3	5		8	10							1		7	2			33
		4		6			9		11	3	5		8	10							1		7	2			34
		4		6			9		11	3	5		8	10							1		7	2			35
2		4	5	6			9			3			8	10							1		7			11	36
2		4	5	6			9			3		10	8								1		7			11	37
2		4	5				9			3		10	8		6						1		7			11	38
2		4					9		11	3	5		8	10	6						1		7				39
2		4					9		11	3	5		8	10	6						1		7				40
2							9		11	3	5		8	10	6			4			1		7				41
2							9			3	5		8	10	6			4			1		7			11	42
7	1	39	11	29	19	16	31	10	35	38	29	13	28	21	14	6	12	3	1	6	17	2	18	6	2	5	
		3	2		2	7	36	5	8			5	5	5						1			2			2	

Watson EG	Timmins B	Mitton J	Caddick W	Kay AE	Harrington JW	Bowen TG	Phillipson WT	Keetley JF	Price FT	Shaw HV	Charnley S	Kerr RC	Scott H	Lees HH	Bradford J	Legge AE	Fox WV	MacDougall AL	Burns W	Meek HL	Hampton JW	Bradley PJ	Homer S	Tyler S	Canavon A	Hann CW	
2		4			7		9		11		5		8		6		3			10							R3
		4		6			9		11	3	5		8			7	2			10							rep
1		2		1	1		2		2	1	2		2		1	1	2			2							
									1																		

1926-27

Division Two

Manager: Fred Scotchbrook

	P	W	D	L	F	A	Pts
Middlesbrough	42	27	8	7	122	60	62
Portsmouth	42	23	8	11	87	49	54
Manchester City	42	22	10	10	108	61	54
Chelsea	42	20	12	10	62	52	52
Nottingham Forest	42	18	14	10	80	55	50
Preston North End	42	20	9	13	74	72	49
Hull City	42	20	7	15	63	52	47
Port Vale	42	16	13	13	88	78	45
Blackpool	42	18	8	16	95	80	44
Oldham Athletic	42	19	6	17	74	84	44
Barnsley	42	17	9	16	88	87	43
Swansea Town	42	16	11	15	68	72	43
Southampton	42	15	12	15	60	62	42
Reading	42	16	8	18	64	72	40
Wolverhampton Wanderers	42	14	7	21	73	75	35
Notts County	42	15	5	22	70	96	35
Grimsby Town	42	11	12	19	74	91	34
Fulham	42	13	8	21	58	92	34
South Shields	42	11	11	20	71	96	33
Clapton Orient	42	12	7	23	60	96	31
Darlington	42	12	6	24	79	98	30
Bradford City	42	7	9	26	50	88	23

Did you know that?

- Tom Phillipson broke his own club record by scoring in 13 consecutive League matches from 6 November to 9 February inclusive, a record in English League football that has never been beaten.
- Wilf Chadwick (from Leeds United), Reg Weaver (from Newport County) and Dicky Rhodes (from Redditch United) were three new recruits.
- In his first full season as Wolves manager, Fred Scotchbrook utilised 28 players.
- The Staffordshire FA celebrated its Jubilee with a game at Molineux. A crowd of 5,848 saw an FA XI beat a Staffordshire FA XI 6–4. Dixie Dean scored twice for the winners.

Match No.	Date		Venue	Opponents	Result		Scorers	Atten
1	Aug	28	A	Hull City	L	0-1		8,
2		30	H	Chelsea	L	0-3		16,
3	Sep	4	H	Swansea Town	D	2-2	Lees, Milton	15,
4		11	H	Notts County	L	0-1		14,
5		13	H	Preston North End	L	1-2	Scott	8
6		18	A	Clapton Orient	L	0-2		15,
7		25	H	Middlesbrough	L	1-2	Chadwick	14
8		27	A	Preston North End	L	0-2		13
9	Oct	2	A	Port Vale	D	1-1	Boswell	14
10		9	H	Southampton	D	2-2	Boswell, Chadwick	11
11		16	A	Blackpool	W	3-2	Phillipson 2, Chadwick	9
12		23	H	Reading	D	1-1	Boswell	19
13		30	A	Nottingham Forest	D	1-1	Weaver	10
14	Nov	6	H	Barnsley	W	9-1	* see below	9
15		13	A	Manchester City	L	1-2	Phillipson	24
16		20	H	Darlington	W	2-1	Harrington, Phillipson	7
17		27	A	Portsmouth	L	1-2	Phillipson	15
18	Dec	4	H	Oldham Athletic	D	1-1	Phillipson	14
19		11	A	Fulham	L	1-4	Phillipson	17
20		18	H	Grimsby Town	L	3-4	Legge, Phillipson, Weaver	9
21		25	H	Bradford City	W	7-2	Phillipson 5, Bowen, Weaver	10
22		27	A	Bradford City	W	2-1	Lees, Phillipson	26
23	Jan	15	H	Hull City	W	5-2	Chadwick 2, Phillipson 2, Weaver	16
24		22	A	Swansea Town	L	1-4	Phillipson	14
25	Feb	5	H	Clapton Orient	W	5-0	Phillipson 3, Bowen 2	11
26		9	A	Notts County	D	2-2	Phillipson, Watson	5
27		12	A	Middlesbrough	L	0-2		26
28		26	A	Southampton	L	0-1		7
29	Mar	12	A	Reading	W	2-1	Phillipson 2	14
30		19	H	Nottingham Forest	W	2-0	Phillipson 2	15
31		21	H	Blackpool	W	4-1	Phillipson 2, Higham, McDougall	6
32		26	A	Barnsley	L	1-4	Chadwick	8
33	Apr	2	H	Manchester City	W	4-1	Chadwick 2, Harrington, Weaver	11
34		9	A	Darlington	L	1-3	Phillipson	7
35		16	H	Portsmouth	L	0-1		18
36		18	A	Chelsea	L	0-1		28
37		19	H	Port Vale	L	1-2	Weaver	11
38		23	A	Oldham Athletic	L	0-2		7
39		25	H	South Shields	W	2-0	Kerr 2	4
40		30	H	Fulham	W	2-1	Chadwick, Weaver	8
41	May	2	A	South Shields	W	2-1	Boswell 2	
42		7	A	Grimsby Town	L	0-6		

Scorers in game 14: Chadwick 3, Phillipson 3, Legge, Watson, Weaver.

Appeara

G

FA Cup

R3	Jan	8	A	Carlisle United	W	2-0	Lees, Weaver	1
R4		29	H	Nottingham Forest	W	2-0	Phillipson, Weaver	4
R5	Feb	19	H	Hull City	W	1-0	Lees	4
R6	Mar	5	A	Arsenal	L	1-2	Phillipson	5

Appeara

G

Match	Tyler S	Shaw HV	Mitton J	Charnley S	Kay AE	Homer S	Scott H	Phillipson WT	Lees HH	Hann CW	George FN	Caddick W	Bradford J	Legge AE	Bowen TG	Price FT	Watson EG	MacDougall AL	Kerr RC	Chadwick W	Bradley PJ	Boswell W	Weaver W	Harrington JW	Higham F	Fox WV	Baker JE
1	2	3	4	5	6	7	8	9	10	11																	
2	2	3	4	5	6	7	8	9	10	11																	
3	2	3	4					9	10		1	5	6	7	8	11											
4		3						9	10		1	5	6	7	8	11	2	4									
5		3	4	5	6	7	8	9	10	11	1						2										
6		3	4	5	6	7	8		10	11	1				9		2										
7		3	4	5	6	7	8				1						2		9	10	11						
8	2	3			6	7					1	5	4	8					9	10	11						
9	2	3	5		6	7	8			11	1		4							10		9					
10	2	3	5		6	7	8			11	1		4							10		9					
11	2	3	5		6	7		9			1		4							10		8	11				
12	2	3	5		6	7		9			1		4							10		8	11				
13		3	5		6			9			1		4	8			2			10			11	7			
14		3	5		6			9			1		4	8			2			10			11	7			
15		3	5		6			9			1		4	8			2			10			11	7			
16		3	5		6			9			1		4	8			2			10			11	7			
17		3	5		6			9			1			8			2			10			11	7	4		
18		3	5		6			9			1		4	8			2			10			11	7			
19		3	5		6			9	10		1		4	8			2						11	7			
20		3	5		6			9					4	8			2			10			11	7			
21		3	5		6			9	10					7	8		2	4					11				
22		3	5		6			9	10					7	8		2						11		4		
23		3	5		6			9							8		2			10			11	7	4		
24		3		5	6			9							8		2			10			11	7	4		
25		3	5		6			9		11					8		2			10				7	4		
26		3	5		6			9	10						8	11	2							7	4		
27				5	6				10		1				8	11	2					9		7	4	3	
28				5	6			9			1				8		2			10			11	7	4	3	
29		3			5			9							8		2	6		10			11	7	4		
30		3			5			9			1				8		2	6		10			11	7	4		
31		3			5			9			1				8		2	6		10			11	7	4		
32		3			5			9			1			8			2			10		6	11	7	4		
33		3		5	6			9			1				8		2			10			11	7	4		
34		3		5	6			9		11	1				8		2			10				7	4		
35		3	4	5				9			1		6		8		2			10			11	7			
36		3		5				9					6	8	10		2						11	7	4		
37		3	4	5		7		9					6	8			2			10			11				
38		3		5									6	7	8		2			10		9	11		4		
39		3		5						11			6	7	8		2		9	10					4		
40		3		5							1		6	7	8		2		9	10			11				4
41		3		5							1		6	7	8		2		9	10		11					4
42		3		5				9	11		1		6		8		2			10				7			4
Totals	8	40	25	18	32	11	7	32	12	9	28	3	22	20	23	4	34	5	5	30	2	8	25	23	17	2	3
Totals (second row)			1				1	31	2					2	3		2	1	2	12		5	8	2	1		
R3		3		5	6			9	10						8		2						11	7	4		
R4		3	5		6			9							8		2			10			11	7	4		
R5		3	5		6			9	10		1				8								11	7	4	2	
R6		3	5		6			9			1				8		2			10			11	7	4		
Cup totals		4	3	1	4			4	2		2				4		3			2			4	4	4	1	
Cup totals (second row)								2	2														2				

1927-28

Division Two

Manager: Major Frank Buckley

	P	W	D	L	F	A	Pts
Manchester City	42	25	9	8	100	59	59
Leeds United	42	25	7	10	98	49	57
Chelsea	42	23	8	11	75	45	54
Preston North End	42	22	9	11	100	66	53
Stoke City	42	22	8	12	78	59	52
Swansea Town	42	18	12	12	75	63	48
Oldham Athletic	42	19	8	15	75	51	46
West Bromwich Albion	42	17	12	13	90	70	46
Port Vale	42	18	8	16	68	57	44
Nottingham Forest	42	15	10	17	83	84	40
Grimsby Town	42	14	12	16	69	83	40
Bristol City	42	15	9	18	76	79	39
Barnsley	42	14	11	17	65	85	39
Hull City	42	12	15	15	41	54	39
Notts County	42	13	12	17	68	74	38
Wolverhampton Wanderers	42	13	10	19	63	91	36
Southampton	42	14	7	21	68	77	35
Reading	42	11	13	18	53	75	35
Blackpool	42	13	8	21	83	101	34
Clapton Orient	42	11	12	19	55	85	34
Fulham	42	13	7	22	68	89	33
South Shields	42	7	9	26	56	111	23

Did you know that?

- Major Frank Buckley was appointed team manager in June 1927.
- Goalkeeper Noel George played his last game for the club against Bristol City on 5 November, and he died two years later.
- A total of 32 players appeared in Wolves' first team this season – a new club record and the most since 1919–20, when 31 were used.
- Harry Marshall (from Southport), Tom Pritchard (from Newport County) and Dai Richards (from Merthyr Town) were recruited. Those who left the club included Tom Phillipson (to Sheffield United), Jack Bradford (to Bournemouth), Billy Caddick (to Wellington Town), Jack Harrington (to Northampton Town), Albert Legge (to Gillingham), Harry Lees (to Darlington) and Jack Mitton (to Southampton).

Match No.	Date		Venue	Opponents	Result		Scorers	A
1	Aug	27	H	Manchester City	D	2-2	Phillipson, W Weaver	
2	Sep	3	A	Hull City	L	0-2		
3		5	H	South Shields	W	2-1	Chadwick, Phillipson	
4		10	H	Preston North End	L	2-3	Chadwick 2	
5		12	A	South Shields	D	2-2	Chadwick 2	
6		17	A	Swansea Town	L	0-6		
7		24	H	Fulham	W	3-1	Chadwick 2, Watson	
8	Oct	1	A	Barnsley	D	2-2	Chadwick. Higham	
9		8	H	West Bromwich Albion	W	4-1	Chadwick 2, Bowen, Phillipson	
10		15	H	Port Vale	W	2-1	Cock, W Weaver	
11		22	A	Southampton	L	1-4	Bowen	
12		29	H	Stoke City	L	1-2	W Weaver	
13	Nov	5	A	Bristol City	L	1-4	Rotton	
14		12	H	Notts County	D	2-2	Chadwick, Green	
15		19	A	Oldham Athletic	L	0-3		
16		26	H	Blackpool	L	2-4	Phillipson, W Richards	
17	Dec	3	A	Reading	L	1-2	Chadwick	
18		10	H	Grimsby Town	L	0-1		
19		17	A	Chelsea	L	0-2		
20		24	H	Clapton Orient	W	5-3	Baxter 2, Bowen, Chadwick, Phillipson	
21		26	A	Nottingham Forest	L	2-3	Bowen, Phillipson	
22		27	H	Nottingham Forest	W	1-0	Baxter	
23		31	A	Manchester City	L	0-3		
24	Jan	7	H	Hull City	D	1-1	Bowen	
25		21	A	Preston North End	L	4-5	Phillipson 2, Chadwick, Charnley	
26	Feb	4	A	Fulham	L	0-7		
27		11	H	Barnsley	W	2-1	Phillipson, Watson	
28		18	A	West Bromwich Albion	L	0-4		
29		25	A	Port Vale	D	2-2	Chadwick, R Weaver	
30	Mar	3	H	Southampton	W	2-1	Chadwick, R Weaver	
31		10	A	Stoke City	D	2-2	Chadwick, R Weaver	
32		17	H	Bristol City	W	5-2	R Weaver 3, Chadwick, Marshall	
33		24	A	Notts County	W	2-1	R Weaver 2	
34		31	H	Oldham Athletic	W	3-1	R Weaver 2, Chadwick	
35	Apr	7	A	Blackpool	L	0-3		
36		9	H	Leeds United	D	0-0		
37		10	A	Leeds United	L	0-3		
38		14	H	Reading	W	2-1	Harrington, Marshall	
39		21	A	Grimsby Town	W	1-0	Baxter	
40		28	H	Chelsea	L	1-2	R Weaver	
41		30	H	Swansea Town	D	1-1	Marshall	
42	May	5	A	Clapton Orient	D	0-0		

Appear

FA Cup

R3	Jan	14	H	Chelsea	W	2-1	Baxter, Phillipson
R4		28	A	Sheffield United	L	1-3	Phillipson

Appear

	Watson EG	Shaw HV	Higham F	Williams WJ	Kay AE	Harrington JW	Cock DJ	Phillipson WT	Chadwick W	Weaver W	Fox WV	Richards WE	Lees HH	Bradford J	Bowen TG	Charnley S	MacDougall AL	Pritchard TF	Boswell W	Legge AE	Rotton WH	Botto LA	Weaver RW	Green F	Canavon A	Baker JE	Baxter TW	Bryce F	Williams LH	Richards DT	Marshall WH
1	2	3	4	5	6	7	8	9	10	11																					
2	2		4	5	6			9	8	11	3	7	10																		
3	2			5	6			9	8	11	3	7	10	4																	
4	2				6			9	8	11	3	7	10		4	5															
5	2	3			6			9	10	11		7	8			5	4														
6					6			9	10	11	3	7	8			5	4														
7			4		6			9	10	11	3	7			8			5													
8	2		4		6			9	10	11	3	7			8			5													
9			4		6			9	10	11	3	7			8			5													
10			4		6		9		10	11	3	7			8			5													
11			4		6				10	11	3	7			8			5	9												
12			4		6	7			10	11	3				8			5		9											
13			4		6				10	11	3	7						5		8	9										
14		3	4		6				10	11		7						5				1	8	9							
15		3	4		6				10	11		7						5				1	8	9							
16		3	4		6			9	10	11		7						5				1	8								
17						7			10	11	3						6	5		8			9		1	4					
18						7	9		10	11	3						6	5					8		1	4					
19		3				7		9			6				10		4	5					8		1		11				
20					6	7		9	10		3				8		4	5							1		11				
21					6	7		9			3				8		4	5			10				1		11				
22						7		9			3				8		6	5			10				1	4	11				
23					6	7		9			3				8		4	5			10				1		11				
24					6	7		9			3				8		4	5						10	1		11				
25								9	10		3	7			8	4	6	5									11	1			
26								9	10		3				8		6	5					7			4	11	1			
27		3			6			9				7						5					8	10	1	4	11				
28		3			6			9	10			7			8	5									1	4	11				
29		3	4		6				10			7						5					9		1		11		2	8	
30		3	4		6			8	10			7						5				1	9				11		2		
31		3	4		6			8	10			7						5				1	9				11		2		
32		3	4		6				10			7						5				1	9				11		2		8
33		3	4		6				10			7						5				1	9				11		2		8
34		3	4		6				10			7						5				1	9				11		2		8
35		3	4		6	7			10									5				1	9				11		2		8
36		3	4		6	7												5				1	9	10			11		2		8
37		3			6	7												5				1	9	10		4	11		2		8
38		3			6	7												5				1	9	10		4	11		2		8
39		3			6	7			10									5				1	9			4	11		2		8
40		3			6	7			10									5				1	9			4	11		2		8
41		3			6				10			7						5				1	9				11		2	4	8
42					6				10		3	7						5				1	9				11		2	4	8
Apps		21	20	3	36	16	3	22	33	18	22	25	5	1	16	5	12	35	1	3	4	16	22	7	11	10	24	2	14	3	11
Goals			1			1	1	9	19	3		1			5	1					1		11	1			4				3
R3			4			7		9	10		3				8		6	5							1		11				
R4						7		9	10		3				8		6	5							1	4	11				
Cup apps			1			2		2	2		2				2		2	2							2	1	2				
Cup goals								2																			1				

1928-29

Division Two

Manager: Major Frank Buckley

	P	W	D	L	F	A	Pts
Middlesbrough	42	22	11	9	92	57	55
Grimsby Town	42	24	5	13	82	61	53
Bradford Park Avenue	42	22	4	16	88	70	48
Southampton	42	17	14	11	74	60	48
Notts County	42	19	9	14	78	65	47
Stoke City	42	17	12	13	74	51	46
West Bromwich Albion	42	19	8	15	80	79	46
Blackpool	42	19	7	16	92	76	45
Chelsea	42	17	10	15	64	65	44
Tottenham Hotspur	42	17	9	16	75	81	43
Nottingham Forest	42	15	12	15	71	70	42
Hull City	42	13	14	15	58	63	40
Preston North End	42	15	9	18	78	79	39
Millwall	42	16	7	19	71	86	39
Reading	42	15	9	18	63	86	39
Barnsley	42	16	6	20	69	66	38
Wolverhampton Wanderers	42	15	7	20	77	81	37
Oldham Athletic	42	16	5	21	54	75	37
Swansea Town	42	13	10	19	62	75	36
Bristol City	42	13	10	19	58	72	36
Port Vale	42	15	4	23	71	86	34
Clapton Orient	42	12	8	22	45	72	32

Did you know that?

- Wolves signed defender Reg Hollingworth from Sutton Junction appointing him team captain.
- Bill Barraclough also joined Wolves (from Hull City) while moving to pastures new were: Ted Watson and George Bowen (both to Coventry City), Tom Baxter (to Mansfield Town) and Sam Charnley (to York City).
- Tom Pritchard became the first Wolves centre-half to score a League goal since April 1926 when he netted against Bristol City in October.
- Wolves' 8–3 League defeat at Middlesbrough remains their heaviest against the Teeside club to this day. Three penalties were awarded in the game, Boro scoring both of theirs.

Match No.	Date		Venue	Opponents	Result		Scorers
1	Aug	25	A	Port Vale	W	4-1	Marshall 2, Chadwick, Weaver
2		27	H	Millwall	L	0-1	
3	Sep	1	H	Hull City	L	2-4	Baxter, Chadwick
4		3	A	Millwall	W	5-0	Weaver 3, Baxter 2
5		8	A	Tottenham Hotspur	L	2-3	Baxter, Weaver
6		15	H	Reading	W	2-0	Baxter, Green
7		22	A	Preston North End	L	1-5	Weaver
8		29	H	Middlesbrough	D	3-3	Green 2, Weaver
9	Oct	6	A	Oldham Athletic	W	4-0	Chadwick 2, Baxter, Weaver
10		13	H	Southampton	D	1-1	Green
11		20	H	Bristol City	W	2-1	Chadwick, Pritchard
12		27	A	Barnsley	D	2-2	Baxter, Chadwick
13	Nov	3	H	Chelsea	D	1-1	Chadwick
14		10	A	West Bromwich Albion	W	2-0	Coundon, Weaver
15		17	H	Swansea Town	D	0-0	
16		24	A	Bradford Park Avenue	L	1-4	Baxter
17	Dec	1	H	Grimsby Town	D	2-2	Green, Kay
18		8	A	Stoke City	L	3-4	Chadwick, Green, Weaver
19		15	H	Clapton Orient	W	3-2	Chadwick, W Richards, Weaver
20		22	A	Blackpool	L	0-3	
21		25	H	Nottingham Forest	L	2-3	Green, Johnson
22		26	A	Nottingham Forest	L	1-2	Green
23		29	H	Port Vale	W	4-0	Weaver 2, Chadwick, Green
24	Jan	5	A	Hull City	W	3-1	Baxter, Marshall, Weaver
25		19	H	Tottenham Hotspur	W	4-2	Weaver 2, Baxter, Chadwick
26	Feb	2	H	Preston North End	L	1-2	Chadwick
27		9	A	Middlesbrough	L	3-8	Chadwick, Ferguson, Pritchard
28		16	H	Oldham Athletic	D	0-0	
29		23	A	Southampton	L	1-2	Pritchard
30	Mar	2	A	Bristol City	L	2-3	Featherby, Ferguson
31		9	H	Barnsley	W	3-1	Weaver 2, Ferguson
32		13	A	Reading	L	0-3	
33		16	A	Chelsea	W	2-0	Hartill 2
34		23	H	West Bromwich Albion	L	0-1	
35		30	A	Swansea Town	L	0-2	
36	Apr	1	A	Notts County	L	0-3	
37		2	H	Notts County	W	3-1	Green 3
38		6	H	Bradford Park Avenue	W	3-1	Green 2, Featherby
39		13	A	Grimsby Town	L	0-2	
40		20	H	Stoke City	W	4-0	Green 2, Featherby, Ferguson
41		27	A	Clapton Orient	L	0-2	
42	May	4	H	Blackpool	L	1-5	Johnson

Appear

FA Cup

R3	Jan	12	H	Mansfield Town	L	0-1	

Appear

iams LH	Cross CA	Brown W	Burns W	Gardiner JG	Coundon C	Marshall WH	Weaver RW	Chadwick W	Baxter TW	Shaw HV	Pritchard TF	Richards DT	Green F	Kay AE	Lewis AN	Watson EG	Baker JE	Hollingworth R	Hartill WJ	Richards WE	Barraclough W	Johnson M	Thorpe AE	Ferguson JJ	Featherby WL	Hetherington JA	Rhodes RA	Tootill A	
	3	4	5	6	7	8	9	10	11																				1
	3	4	5	6	7	8	9	10	11																				2
	3	4	5	6	7	8	9	10	11																				3
		4			7		9	10	11	3	5	6	8																4
		4			7		9	10	11	3	5	6	8																5
		4				7	9	10	11	3	5		8	6															6
		4				7	9	10	11	3	5		8	6															7
		4				7	9	10	11	3	5		8	6	1														8
		4				7	9	10	11	3	5		8	6	1														9
		4			7		9	10	11	3	5		8	6	1	2													10
		4			7	8	9	10	11	3	5			6	1	2													11
					7		9	10	11	3	5		8	6	1	2	4												12
		5			7		9	10	11	3			8	6	1		4												13
		4			7		9	10	11	3			8	6	1			5											14
					7		9	10	11	3		4	8	6	1			5											15
					7		9		11	3		4	10	6	1			5	8										16
					7			10	11	3		4	8	6	1			5	9										17
							9	10	11	3		4	8	6	1			5		7									18
		4					9	10		3			8	6	1			5		7	11								19
		4					9	10		3			8	6	1			5		7	11								20
		4						10	11	3			8	6	1			5		7		9							21
								10	11	3	5		8	6	1					7		9	4						22
2							9	10	11	3		4	8	6	1			5						7					23
		4				10	9		11	3			8	6	1			5						7					24
		4					9	10	11	3	5		8	6	1									7					25
2		4				8	9	10	11	3	5			6	1									7					26
							9	10	11	3	5	4	8	6	1									7					27
		4					9	10	11	3	5	6			1	2								7	8				28
		4					9			3	5	6			1	2						10		7	8	11			29
		4					9			3	5	6			1	2						10		7	8	11			30
		4					9	10		3	5	6			1	2								7	8	11			31
		4								3	5	6			1	2			9			10		7	8	11			32
		4						10		3	5			6	1	2			9					7		11	8		33
2		4						10		3	5		8	6	1				9					7		11			34
2		4						10		3	5			6	1				9		11			7			8		35
2						4		10		3				6	1		5		9					7	8	11			36
2		4				6				3			9	5								10		7	8	11		1	37
2		4				6				3			9	5								10		7	8	11		1	38
2		4				6		10		3			9	5										7	8	11		1	39
2		4				6		10		3			9	5										7	8	11		1	40
2		4				6		10		3			9	5										7	8	11		1	41
2		4				6				3			9	5								10		7	8	11		1	42
3	3	33	3	3	13	17	28	34	26	39	21	13	29	32	29	9	3	10	7	5	3	8	1	20	12	13	2	6	
					1	3	18	13	10		3		16	1					2	1		2		4	3				
2		4				10	9		11	3			8	6	1			5		7									R3
1		1				1	1		1	1			1	1	1			1		1									

1929-30

Division Two

Manager: Major Frank Buckley

	P	W	D	L	F	A	Pts
Blackpool	42	27	4	11	98	67	58
Chelsea	42	22	11	9	74	46	55
Oldham Athletic	42	21	11	10	90	51	53
Bradford Park Avenue	42	19	12	11	91	70	50
Bury	42	22	5	15	78	67	49
West Bromwich Albion	42	21	5	16	105	73	47
Southampton	42	17	11	14	77	76	45
Cardiff City	42	18	8	16	61	59	44
Wolverhampton Wanderers	42	16	9	17	77	79	41
Nottingham Forest	42	13	15	14	55	69	41
Stoke City	42	16	8	18	74	72	40
Tottenham Hotspur	42	15	9	18	59	61	39
Charlton Athletic	42	14	11	17	59	63	39
Millwall	42	12	15	15	57	73	39
Swansea Town	42	14	9	19	57	61	37
Preston North End	42	13	11	18	65	80	37
Barnsley	42	14	8	20	56	71	36
Bradford City	42	12	12	18	60	77	36
Reading	42	12	11	19	54	67	35
Bristol City	42	13	9	20	61	83	35
Hull City	42	14	7	21	51	78	35
Notts County	42	9	15	18	54	70	33

Did you know that?

- Wolves defender Vic Fox scored 1,457 runs (an average of 31 per game) for Worcestershire CCC during the summer of 1929.
- Roy Davies was sent off against Hull City at Molineux in September.
- Goalkeeper Billy Walker fractured his right leg before half-time in the League game against West Bromwich Albion in December. He was sorely missed as Wolves lost 7–3 – their heaviest defeat at The Hawthorns.
- Cecil Shaw, Mark Crook, the Deacon brothers (James and Richard), Wilf Lowton, Charlie Phillips and George Lax were all signed.
- Those who left Molineux included Harold Shaw (to Sunderland), Tom Baxter (to Port Vale), Wilf Chadwick (to Stoke City) and Tom Pritchard (to Charlton).

Match No.	Date		Venue	Opponents	Result		Scorers	Atte
1	Aug	31	H	West Bromwich Albion	L	2-4	Featherby, Forshaw	2
2	Sep	4	A	Reading	L	1-3	Forshaw	1
3		7	A	Bradford City	D	2-2	Deacon, Hartill	1
4		9	H	Reading	W	2-1	Hartill 2	
5		14	H	Swansea Town	W	4-1	Forshaw 2, Deacon, Hartill	1
6		21	A	Cardiff City	D	0-0		1
7		23	H	Hull City	W	4-2	Marshall 2, Barraclough, Featherby	
8		28	H	Preston North End	W	4-0	Hartill 3, Marshall	1
9		30	A	Stoke City	L	0-3		
10	Oct	5	A	Bristol City	W	2-1	Hartill 2	
11		12	H	Notts County	W	5-1	Hartill 5	1
12		19	H	Tottenham Hotspur	W	3-0	Deacon, Hartill, Cable (og)	2
13		26	A	Southampton	L	1-3	Marshall	1
14	Nov	2	H	Millwall	D	1-1	Hartill	1
15		9	A	Oldham Athletic	L	0-6		1
16		16	H	Nottingham Forest	W	2-1	Lawton, Marshall	
17		23	A	Chelsea	D	1-1	Rhodes	1
18		30	H	Bury	W	2-0	Lowton, Rhodes	1
19	Dec	7	A	Blackpool	L	2-3	Hartill, Hetherington	
20		14	H	Barnsley	W	3-0	Hartill 2, Deacon	1
21		21	A	Bradford Park Avenue	D	0-0		1
22		26	H	Charlton Athletic	L	0-4		2
23		28	A	West Bromwich Albion	L	3-7	White 2, Featherby	2
24	Jan	1	A	Charlton Athletic	L	0-2		
25		4	H	Bradford City	W	6-0	* see below	1
26		18	A	Swansea Town	D	2-2	Hartill 2	
27	Feb	1	A	Preston North End	D	1-1	Hartill	1
28		8	H	Bristol City	W	1-0	Hetherington	1
29		15	A	Notts County	W	3-0	Hartill, Marshall, Bisby (og)	11
30		22	A	Tottenham Hotspur	L	2-4	Deacon, Hetherington	2
31	Mar	1	H	Southampton	W	2-0	Hartill 2	1
32		8	A	Millwall	L	0-4		2
33		15	H	Oldham Athletic	D	1-1	Hartill	
34		22	A	Nottingham Forest	L	2-5	Hartill, Hetherington	
35		29	H	Chelsea	L	0-1		1
36	Apr	5	A	Bury	L	1-3	Hetherington	
37		12	H	Blackpool	L	1-2	Deacon	1
38		14	H	Cardiff City	W	4-0	Rhodes 2, Crook, Deacon	
39		19	A	Barnsley	L	1-3	Rhodes	3
40		21	H	Stoke City	W	2-1	Hartill, Richards	15
41		26	H	Bradford Park Avenue	D	4-4	Hartill 3, Hetherington	
42	May	3	A	Hull City	L	0-2		8

Scorers in game 25: Deacon 2, Hartill 2, Hetherington, Marson. Appearar

Two own-goals G

FA Cup

R3	Jan	11	A	Oldham Athletic	L	0-1		32

Appearar

	Lowton WG	Shaw HV	Lax G	Bellis GA	Marshall WH	Davies R	Forshaw R	Rhodes RA	Featherby WL	Hetherington JA	Green F	Hollingworth R	Hartill WJ	Deacon J	Barraclough W	Kay AE	Richards DT	Crook MS	White RN	Walker WS	Williams LH	Phillips C	Bartley JP	Richardson JT	Hill AE	Griffiths J	Shaw CE
1	2	3	4	5	6	7	8	9	10	11																	
2	2	3	4	5	6	7	8		10	11	9																
3	2	3	4		6	7	8					5	9	10	11												
4	2	3	4			7	8					5	9	10	11	6											
5	2	3	4			7	8					5	9	10	11		6										
6	2	3	4			7	8		10			5	9		11		6										
7	2	3	4		8	7			10			5	9		11		6										
8	2	3	4	5	8	7			10				9		11		6										
9	2	3	4	5	8	7			10				9		11		6										
10	2	3	4	5	8								9	10	11		6	7									
11	2	3	4	5	8								9	10	11		6	7									
12	2	3	4	5	8								9	10	11		6	7									
13	2	3	4	5	8								9	10	11		6	7									
14	2	3	4	5	8								9	10	11		6	7									
15	2	3	4	5	8				6					10	11			7	9								
16	2	3	4	5	8								9	10	11		6	7									
17	2	3	4					8					9	10	11	5	6	7									
18	2	3	4					8					9	10	11	5	6	7									
19	2	3	4					8		11			9	10		5	6	7									
20	2	3	4					8		11			9	10		5	6	7									
21	2	3	4		8					11			9	10		5	6	7									
22	2	3	4		6			8					9	10	11	5		7									
23		3	4		6				8					10	11	5		7	9	1	2						
24		3	4	5					8					10	11	6		7	9		2						
25	2	3	4	5	8					11			9	10		6		7									
26	2	3	4	5	8					11			9	10		6		7									
27	2	3	4	5	8					11			9	10		6		7									
28	2	3	4		8					11		5	9	10		6		7									
29	2	3	4	5	8					11			9	10		6		7									
30	2		4	5	8					11			9	10		3	6	7									
31	2		4	5	8					11			9	10		3	6	7									
32	2		4	5	8					11			9	10		3	6	7									
33	2		4	5						11			9	10		3	6	7				8					
34	2		4	5						11			9	10		3	6	7				8					
35	2		4	5						11			9	10		3	6	7				8					
36	2		4	5						11			9	10		3	6	7					8				
37	2		4									5	9	10	11	3	6	7					8				
38	2		4					8		11		5		10		6		7						3	9		
39	2		4					8		11		5		10			6	7						3	9		
40	2		4					8		11		5	9			6	10					7		3			
41	2							8		11		5	9	10		6	4					7				3	
42	2			4				8		11		5	9	10			6	7									3
	40	29	40	24	24	9	6	11	9	22	1	12	35	35	20	25	28	31	3	1	2	5	2	3	2	1	1
	2				7		4	5	3	7			33	9	1		1	1	2								
R3	2	3	4	5	8					11			9	10		6		7									
	1	1	1	1	1					1			1	1		1		1									

1930-31

Division Two

Manager: Major Frank Buckley

	P	W	D	L	F	A	Pts
Everton	42	28	5	9	121	66	61
West Bromwich Albion	42	22	10	10	83	49	54
Tottenham Hotspur	42	22	7	13	88	55	51
Wolverhampton Wanderers	42	21	5	16	84	67	47
Port Vale	42	21	5	16	67	61	47
Bradford Park Avenue	42	18	10	14	97	66	46
Preston North End	42	17	11	14	83	64	45
Burnley	42	17	11	14	81	77	45
Southampton	42	19	6	17	74	62	44
Bradford City	42	17	10	15	61	63	44
Stoke City	42	17	10	15	64	71	44
Oldham Athletic	42	16	10	16	61	72	42
Bury	42	19	3	20	75	82	41
Millwall	42	16	7	19	71	80	39
Charlton Athletic	42	15	9	18	59	86	39
Bristol City	42	15	8	19	54	82	38
Nottingham Forest	42	14	9	19	80	85	37
Plymouth Argyle	42	14	8	20	76	84	36
Barnsley	42	13	9	20	59	79	35
Swansea Town	42	12	10	20	51	74	34
Reading	42	12	6	24	72	96	30
Cardiff City	42	8	9	25	47	87	25

Did you know that?

- Brothers Richard and James Deacon both played for Wolves – the former replacing the latter in three League games.
- Walter Bottrill was signed from York City while Harry Marshall and Vic Fox moved on, joining Port Vale and Newport County respectively.
- A record mid-week crowd of 46,860 attended Molineux for the FA Cup sixth-round replay with West Bromwich Albion.
- Billy Hartill became the first player to score more than 20 League goals in successive seasons for Wolves since Tom Phillipson in 1925–27.

Match No.	Date		Venue	Opponents	Result		Scorers	Atten
1	Aug	30	A	Nottingham Forest	W	4-3	Lowton, Hartill 2, Thompson (og)	10
2	Sep	1	H	Millwall	W	2-0	Phillips, Lowton	15
3		6	H	Tottenham Hotspur	W	3-1	J Deacon 2, Lowton	24
4		8	H	Stoke City	W	5-1	Hartill 3, Hetherington, Bottrill	16
5		13	A	Preston North End	L	4-5	Bottrill, Hartill, Phillips, Hetherington	15
6		15	A	Stoke City	W	2-1	Bottrill, Lax	13
7		20	H	Burnley	L	2-4	Hetherington, J Deacon	18
8		27	A	Southampton	L	0-2		13
9	Oct	4	H	Reading	W	3-1	J Deacon, Hollingworth, Hartill	14
10		11	A	West Bromwich Albion	L	1-2	Lowton	40
11		18	H	Bradford City	L	0-1		15
12		25	A	Port Vale	W	1-0	Lowton	9
13	Nov	1	H	Bury	W	7-0	Hartill 3, Lowton, Phillips, J Deacon, Bottrill	10
14		8	A	Everton	L	0-4		32
15		15	H	Barnsley	W	2-0	J Deacon, Hartill	9
16		22	A	Bristol City	W	3-0	Hartill 3	8
17		29	H	Cardiff City	W	4-1	J Deacon, Hartill, Bottrill, Lowton	6
18	Dec	6	A	Charlton Athletic	W	2-1	Bottrill, Hartill	7
19		13	H	Swansea Town	W	3-1	Bottrill, Hartill, J Deacon	14
20		20	A	Plymouth Argyle	L	2-3	Bottrill, Phillips	22
21		25	A	Oldham Athletic	L	0-2		18
22		26	H	Oldham Athletic	W	3-0	Hartill, Bottrill 2	23
23		27	H	Nottingham Forest	W	4-2	Hartill 2, Phillips, J Deacon	20
24	Jan	3	A	Tottenham Hotspur	L	0-1		26
25		17	H	Preston North End	W	2-0	Bottrill 2	18
26		31	H	Southampton	W	3-2	Hollingworth, J Deacon, Hartill	9
27	Feb	3	A	Burnley	L	2-4	Martin, Phillips	8
28		7	A	Reading	L	0-3		8
29		18	H	West Bromwich Albion	L	1-4	Phillips	36
30		21	A	Bradford City	L	1-4	Hartill	14
31	Mar	7	A	Bury	L	0-1		4
32		11	H	Port Vale	W	3-0	R Deacon, Hartill, Hetherington	4
33		21	A	Barnsley	L	0-3		5
34		25	H	Everton	W	3-1	Martin, J Deacon, Bottrill	9
35		28	H	Bristol City	L	0-1		9
36	Apr	4	A	Cardiff City	W	3-0	Martin, Bottrill, J Deacon	6
37		6	A	Bradford Park Avenue	D	1-1	Barraclough	7
38		7	H	Bradford Park Avenue	D	1-1	Martin	11
39		11	H	Charlton Athletic	D	1-1	Martin	9
40		18	A	Swansea Town	D	1-1	Hartill	9
41		25	H	Plymouth Argyle	W	4-3	J Deacon, Martin 2, Phillips	3
42	May	2	A	Millwall	D	1-1	Martin	13

Appeara

One own-goal G

FA Cup

R3	Jan	10	H	Wrexham	W	9-1	Hartill 4, Phillips 3, Hollingworth, J Deacon	28
R4		24	A	Bradford City	D	0-0		2
rep		28	H	Bradford City	W	4-2	Bottrill 2, J Deacon, Hartill	22
R5	Feb	14	A	Barnsley	W	3-1	Barraclough, J Deacon, Hartill	33
R6		28	A	West Bromwich Albion	D	1-1	Shaw (og)	52
rep	Mar	4	H	West Bromwich Albion	L	1-2	J Deacon	46

Appeara

One own-goal G

	...ith WG	Lumberg AA	Lax G	Hollingworth R	Richards DT	Phillips C	Bottrill WG	Hartill WJ	Deacon J	Hetherington JA	Kay AE	Rhodes RA	Hemingway CF	Barraclough W	Crook MS	Martin TJ	Whittaker P	Smith AJ	Bellis GA	Griffiths JR	Hatfield E	Reed J	Deacon R	Anderson EW	Shaw CE
1		3	4	5	6	7	8	9	10	11															
2		3	4	5	6	7	8	9	10	11															
3		3	4	5	6	7	8	9	10	11															
4		3	4	5	6	7	8	9	10	11															
5		3	4	5	6	7	8	9	10	11															
6		3	4	5	6	7	8	9	10	11															
7		3	4	5	6	7	8	9	10	11															
8				5	6	7		9	10	11	3	4	8												
9				5	6	7		9	10		3	4	8	11											
10			4	5	6		8	9		11	3		10		7										
11			4	5	6		8			11	3		10		7	9									
12				5	6	7	8	9	10	11	3	4													
13				5	6	7	8	9	10		3	4		11											
14				5	6	7	8	9	10		3	4		11											
15				5	6	7	8	9	10		3	4		11											
16				5	6	7	8	9	10		3	4		11											
17				5	6	7	8	9	10		3	4		11											
18				5	6	7	8	9	10		3	4		11											
19				5	6	7	8	9	10		3	4		11											
20				5	6	7	8	9	10		3	4		11											
21				5	6	7	8	9	10		3	4		11											
22				5	6	7	8	9	10		3	4		11											
23				5	6	7	8	9	10	11	3	4													
24				5	6	7	8	9	10		3	4		11											
25				5	6	7	8	9	10		3	4		11			1								
26				5		7	8	9	10		3	4		11			1	6							
27		3				7	8		10	11		4				9	1	6	5						
28		3	4	5		7	8		10			6		11			1			9					
29			4	5		7		9	10		3	6		11		8	1				2				
30		2	4	5		7		9	10		3			11			1	6				8			
31			4	5		7	8	9			3	6		11							2		10		
32			4	5			8	9		11	3				7						2		10	6	
33		3	4	5			8	9	10	11		6			7										
34	2		4	5		7	8		10					11		9								6	3
35			4	5		7	8		10					11		9								6	3
36	[illegible]			5		7	8		10			4		11		9		6							3
37	2		6	5		8			10			4		11	7	9									3
38	[illegible]		8	5	6	7						4		11		9							10		3
39	[illegible]			5	6	7		8	10			4		11		9									3
40	2			5	6	7		8	10			4		11		9									3
41	2			5	6	7		8	10			4		11		9									3
42	2			5	6	7	8		10			4		11		9									3
	8	11	19	41	30	38	33	33	37	15	23	29	4	27	5	12	6	4	1	1	3	1	3	3	9
	[illegible]		1	2		8	14	24	13	4				1		8							1		

	...ith WG	Lumberg AA	Lax G	Hollingworth R	Richards DT	Phillips C	Bottrill WG	Hartill WJ	Deacon J	Hetherington JA	Kay AE	Rhodes RA	Hemingway CF	Barraclough W	Crook MS	Martin TJ	Whittaker P	Smith AJ	Bellis GA	Griffiths JR	Hatfield E	Reed J	Deacon R	Anderson EW	Shaw CE
R3	2	3		5	6	7	8	9	10			4		11											
R4	2			5	6	7	8	9	10		3	4		11			1								
rep	2		4	5	6	7	8	9	10		3			11			1								
R5			4	5		7	8	9	10		3	6		11			1				2				
R6	2		4	5		7	8	9	10		3	6		11											
rep	2		4	5		7	8	9	10		3	6		11											
	5	1	4	6	3	6	6	6	6		5	5		6			3				1				
				1		3	2	6	4					1											

1931-32

Division Two

Manager: Major Frank Buckley

	P	W	D	L	F	A	Pts
Wolverhampton Wanderers	42	24	8	10	115	49	56
Leeds United	42	22	10	10	78	54	54
Stoke City	42	19	14	9	69	48	52
Plymouth Argyle	42	20	9	13	100	66	49
Bury	42	21	7	14	70	58	49
Bradford Park Avenue	42	21	7	14	72	63	49
Bradford City	42	16	13	13	80	61	45
Tottenham Hotspur	42	16	11	15	87	78	43
Millwall	42	17	9	16	61	61	43
Charlton Athletic	42	17	9	16	61	66	43
Nottingham Forest	42	16	10	16	77	72	42
Manchester United	42	17	8	17	71	72	42
Preston North End	42	16	10	16	75	77	42
Southampton	42	17	7	18	66	77	41
Swansea Town	42	16	7	19	73	75	39
Notts County	42	13	12	17	75	75	38
Chesterfield	42	13	11	18	64	86	37
Oldham Athletic	42	13	10	19	62	84	36
Burnley	42	13	9	20	59	87	35
Port Vale	42	13	7	22	58	89	33
Barnsley	42	12	9	21	55	91	33
Bristol City	42	6	11	25	39	78	23

Did you know that?

• The 7–0 home win over Manchester United in December remains Wolves' best-ever over the Old Trafford club.

• Winger Billy Barraclough was sent off during the away League game with Stoke City in February.

• Wolves' reserve team won the Central League Championship for the first time with a record number of points (61).

• Wolves signed future England international Tom Smalley and Frank Wildman from South Kirkby Colliery.

• George Law was transferred to Barnsley, while Albert Kay retired having made 295 senior appearances for Wolves.

Match No.	Date		Venue	Opponents	Result		Scorers	Att
1	Aug	29	H	Tottenham Hotspur	W	4-0	Bottrill, Barraclough, Phillips, Hollingworth	
2	Sep	5	A	Nottingham Forest	L	0-2		
3		7	A	Bradford City	D	2-2	Deacon, Barraclough	
4		12	H	Chesterfield	W	6-0	Buttery, Phillips 2, Bottrill 2, Hollingworth	
5		14	H	Bradford City	W	3-1	Hartill, Bottrill, Buttery	
6		19	A	Burnley	W	3-1	Bottrill, Buttery, Phillips	
7		26	H	Preston North End	W	3-2	Hartill, Bottrill, Lowton	
8	Oct	3	A	Southampton	W	3-1	Phillips, Bottrill, Buttery	
9		10	H	Stoke City	L	0-1		
10		17	A	Leeds United	L	1-2	Phillips	
11		24	H	Swansea Town	W	2-0	Martin, Buttery	
12		31	A	Barnsley	D	2-2	Buttery, Bottrill	
13	Nov	7	H	Millwall	W	5-0	Deacon, Hartill 3, Bottrill	
14		14	A	Plymouth Argyle	D	3-3	Hartill 2, Hollingworth	
15		21	H	Bristol City	W	4-2	Phillips, Hartill 3	
16		28	A	Oldham Athletic	W	2-0	Bottrill 2	
17	Dec	5	H	Bury	W	6-0	Hartill, Phillips 2, Deacon 2, Barraclough	
18		12	A	Port Vale	W	7-1	Bottrill, Barraclough, Deacon, Hartill, Lowton 2, Phillips	
19		19	H	Notts County	D	0-0		
20		25	A	Manchester United	L	2-3	Bottrill, Phillips	
21		26	H	Manchester United	W	7-0	Deacon, Hartill 2, Bottrill 2, Barraclough, Phillips	
22		28	H	Charlton Athletic	W	3-1	Barraclough, Hartill 2	
23	Jan	2	A	Tottenham Hotspur	D	3-3	Phillips 2, Bottrill	
24		16	H	Nottingham Forest	D	0-0		
25		27	A	Chesterfield	W	2-1	Hartill 2	
26		30	H	Burnley	W	3-1	Deacon, Richards, Bottrill	
27	Feb	6	A	Preston North End	L	2-4	Lowton, Phillips	
28		13	H	Southampton	W	5-1	Hollingworth, Deacon, Hartill 3	
29		20	A	Stoke City	L	1-2	Hartill	
30		27	H	Leeds United	D	1-1	Phillips	
31	Mar	5	A	Swansea Town	D	1-1	Phillips	
32		12	H	Barnsley	W	2-0	Lowton, Hartill	
33		19	A	Millwall	W	2-1	Bottrill, Deacon	
34		26	H	Plymouth Argyle	W	2-0	Lowton, Phillips	
35		28	H	Bradford Park Avenue	W	6-0	Deacon 2, Bottrill 2, Hartill, Lowton	
36		29	A	Bradford Park Avenue	L	1-2	Ward (og)	
37	Apr	2	A	Bristol City	W	4-0	Bottrill 2, Lowton, Crook	
38		9	H	Oldham Athletic	W	7-1	Hartill 3, Crook, Barraclough, Lowton, Deacon	
39		16	A	Bury	L	0-1		
40		23	H	Port Vale	W	2-0	Hartill 2	
41		30	A	Notts County	L	1-3	Deacon	
42	May	7	A	Charlton Athletic	L	2-3	Smalley, Redfern	

One own-goal

FA Cup

R3	Jan	9	A	Luton Town	W	2-1	Lowton, Phillips	
R4		23	A	Preston North End	L	0-2		

	…bill A	Lowton WG	Kay AE	Rhodes RA	Hollingworth R	Richards DT	Phillips C	Bottrill WG	Harrill WJ	Deacon J	Barraclough W	Buttery A	Lax G	Shaw CE	Martin TJ	Griffiths J	Smalley T	Redfern L	Smith AJ	Hetherington JA	Bellis GA	Crook MS	Whittaker P	Lumberg A
1		2	3	4	5	6	7	8	9	10	11													
2		2	3	4	5	6	7	8	9	10	11													
3		2	3	4	5	6	7	8	9	10	11													
4		2	3	4	5	6	7	8	9		11	10												
5		2	3	4	5	6	7	8	9		11	10												
6		2	3		5	6	7	8	9		11	10	4											
7		2	3		5	6	7	8	9		11	10	4											
8		2		4	5	6	7	8	9		11	10		3										
9		2		4	5	6	7	8	9		11	10		3										
10		2	3	4	5	6	7	8			11	10			9									
11		2	3	4	5	6	7	8			11	10			9									
12		2	3	4	5	6	7	8	9		11	10												
13		2	3	4	5	6	7	8	9	10	11													
14		2	3	4	5	6	7	8	9	10	11													
15		2	3	4	5	6	7	8	9	10	11													
16		2	3	4	5	6	7	8	9	10	11													
17		2	3	4	5	6	7	8	9	10	11													
18		2	3	4	5	6	7	8	9	10	11													
19		2	3	4	5	6	7	8	9	10	11													
20		2	3	4	5	6	7	8	9	10	11													
21		2	3	4	5	6	7	8	9	10	11													
22		2	3	4	5	6	7	8	9	10	11													
23		2	3	4	5	6	7	8	9	10	11													
24		2	3	4	5	6	7	8		10	11				9									
25		2		4	5	6	7	8	9	10	11					3								
26		2		4	5	6	7	8	9	10	11					3								
27		2		4	5	6	7		9	10	11					3	8							
28		2	3	4	5	6	7		9	10	11							8						
29		2	3	4	5	6	7	8	9		11							10						
30		2	3	4	5	6	7	8	9		11							10						
31		2	3	4	5	6	7		9	10	11							8						
32		2	3	4	5		7	8	9	10									6	11				
33		2	3	4			7	8	9	10									6		5	11		
34		2	3	4			7	8	9	10	11								6		5			
35		2		4			7	8	9	10	11			3					6		5			
36		2		4			7	8	9	10	11			3					6		5			
37		2		4				8	9	10	11			3					6		5	7		
38		2		4				8	9	10	11			3					6		5	7		
39		2		4				8	9	10	11			3					6		5	7		
40		2		4		6	7	8	9	10	11			3							5			
41		2		4		6		8	9	10	11			3							5	7		
42				4							11	10		3		2	9	8	6		5	7		
		41	29	40	32	33	37	38	38	30	40	10	2	10	3	4	2	5	9	1	10	6		
		9			4	1	18	21	30	13	7	6			1		1	1				2		
R3		2		4	5	6	7	8	9	10	11												1	3
R4		2		4	5	6	7	8	9	10	11					3								
		2		2	2	2	2	2	2	2	2					1								
		1					1																	

1932-33

Division One

Manager: Major Frank Buckley

	P	W	D	L	F	A	Pts
Arsenal	42	25	8	9	118	61	58
Aston Villa	42	23	8	11	92	67	54
Sheffield Wednesday	42	21	9	12	80	68	51
West Bromwich Albion	42	20	9	13	83	70	49
Newcastle United	42	22	5	15	71	63	49
Huddersfield Town	42	18	11	13	66	53	47
Derby County	42	15	14	13	76	69	44
Leeds United	42	15	14	13	59	62	44
Portsmouth	42	18	7	17	74	76	43
Sheffield United	42	17	9	16	74	80	43
Everton	42	16	9	17	81	74	41
Sunderland	42	15	10	17	63	80	40
Birmingham	42	14	11	17	57	57	39
Liverpool	42	14	11	17	79	84	39
Blackburn Rovers	42	14	10	18	76	102	38
Manchester City	42	16	5	21	68	71	37
Middlesbrough	42	14	9	19	63	73	37
Chelsea	42	14	7	21	63	73	35
Leicester City	42	11	13	18	75	89	35
Wolverhampton Wanderers	42	13	9	20	80	96	35
Bolton Wanderers	42	12	9	21	78	92	33
Blackpool	42	14	5	23	69	85	33

Did you know that?

- After conceding seven goals against Arsenal in November, Wolves 'keeper Alf Tootill was transferred to Fulham for £1,000.
- For the fourth successive season, Billy Hartill scored three League hat-tricks for Wolves.
- Billy Wrigglesworth (from Chesterfield), Gordon Clayton (from Shotton Colliery) and Jack Nelson (from Preston North End) joined the club.
- Wolves avoided relegation by beating the FA Cup winners Everton 4–2 at Molineux on the last day of the season.

Match No.	Date		Venue	Opponents	Result		Scorers	Atten
1	Aug	27	A	Liverpool	L	1-5	Phillips	33
2		29	H	Bolton Wanderers	W	4-1	Bottrill, Hartill, Deacon, Barraclough	28
3	Sep	3	H	Leicester City	D	1-1	Deacon	32
4		5	A	Bolton Wanderers	L	0-2		11
5		10	A	Portsmouth	L	0-2		20
6		17	H	Chelsea	L	1-2	Hartill	31,
7		24	A	Huddersfield Town	L	2-3	Hartill, Barraclough	13
8	Oct	1	H	Sheffield United	W	5-1	Deacon 2, Hartill 2, Bottrill	22
9		8	A	West Bromwich Albion	L	1-4	Hartill	30
10		15	A	Newcastle United	L	2-3	Deacon, Hartill	23
11		22	H	Sheffield Wednesday	L	3-5	Deacon 2, Hartill	24,
12		29	A	Leeds United	L	0-2		11
13	Nov	5	H	Arsenal	L	1-7	Bottrill	43
14		12	A	Manchester City	L	1-4	Hartill	20
15		19	H	Sunderland	L	0-2		18
16		26	A	Birmingham	D	0-0		24,
17	Dec	3	H	Blackburn Rovers	W	5-3	Hartill 3, Bottrill, Hetherington	20
18		10	A	Derby County	D	4-4	Hartill 3, Hetherington	13
19		17	H	Blackpool	L	2-3	Barraclough 2	21,
20		24	A	Everton	L	1-5	Hartill	21
21		26	A	Aston Villa	W	3-1	Deacon 2, Crook	48
22		27	H	Aston Villa	L	2-4	Deacon, Hartill	52,
23		31	H	Liverpool	W	3-1	Bottrill, Hartill, Deacon	19
24	Jan	7	A	Leicester City	D	2-2	Crook, Hetherington	14,
25		21	H	Portsmouth	W	5-2	Bottrill, Hartill, Deacon, Crook, Lowton	18,
26		28	A	Chelsea	L	1-3	Hartill	16,
27	Feb	4	H	Huddersfield Town	W	6-4	Young (og), Bottrill, Hartill 4	22,
28		11	A	Sheffield United	D	0-0		15,
29		18	H	West Bromwich Albion	D	3-3	Deacon, Hartill, Richards	34,
30	Mar	4	A	Sheffield Wednesday	L	0-2		12,
31		6	H	Newcastle United	D	1-1	Hartill	16,
32		11	H	Leeds United	D	3-3	Deacon, Crook 2	24,
33		18	A	Arsenal	W	2-1	Hartill, Nelson	44,
34		25	H	Manchester City	L	1-2	Deacon	26,
35	Apr	1	A	Sunderland	W	1-0	Hartill	8,
36		8	H	Birmingham	W	1-0	Hartill	25,
37		14	H	Middlesbrough	W	2-0	Hartill, Crook	28,
38		15	A	Blackburn Rovers	L	0-1		9,
39		17	A	Middlesbrough	L	1-2	Hartill	16,
40		22	H	Derby County	W	3-1	Hartill, Hetherington, Rhodes	21,
41		29	A	Blackpool	D	2-2	Hartill, Crook	16,
42	May	6	H	Everton	W	4-2	Hetherington 2, Phillips, Crook	34,
								Appearan
							One own-goal	Gc

FA Cup

R3	Jan	14	H	Derby County	L	3-6	Crook 2, Lowton	31,
								Appearan
								Gc

Lowton WG	Lumberg AA	Rhodes RA	Bellis GA	Richards DT	Phillips C	Bottrill WG	Hartill WJ	Deacon J	Barraclough W	Shaw CE	Smalley T	Smith AJ	Smith WC	Farrow GH	Crook MS	Ivill E	Pincott FC	Ellis J	Nelson JH	Hetherington JA	Hollingworth R	Heelbeck LW	Bryant W	Wildman FR	Wildsmith T	Redfern L	Whittaker P	
2	3	4	5	6	7	8	9	10	11																			1
2		4	5	6	7	8	9	10	11	3																		2
2		4	5	6	7	8	9	10	11	3																		3
2		4	5	6	7		9	10	11	3	8																	4
2		4	5	6	7		9	10	11	3	8																	5
2		4	5	6	7		9	10	11	3	8																	6
2		4		6	7	8	9	10	11			3	5															7
2				6	7	8	9	10	11			3	5	4														8
2				6	7	8	9	10	11			3	5	4														9
				6		8	9	10	11	3		2	5	4	7													10
				6	7	8	9	10	11	3		2	5	4														11
2	3	4	5	6		8	9	10	11						7													12
2		4		6		8	9	10	11						7	3	5											13
2		4		6		8	9	10	11						7	3	5	1										14
2				6		8	9	10						4	7	3		1	5	11								15
2	3				7	8	9		11					4				1		10	5	6						16
2	3					8	9		11					4				1		10	5	6	7					17
2	3					8	9		11					4				1	5	10		6	7					18
2						8	9		11					4		3		1	5	10		6	7					19
2	3					8	9	10	11					4					5			6	7	1				20
2		4		6		8	9	10	11			3			7				5					1				21
2		4		6		8	9	10	11			3			7				5					1				22
2		4		6		8	9	10	11			3			7				5					1				23
2		4		6			9	10	11			3			7				5	8				1				24
2		4		6		8	9	10	11			3			7				5					1				25
2		4		6		8	9	10	11			3			7				5					1				26
2				6	7	8	9	10	11			3							4		5			1				27
2				6	7	8	9	10	11			3						1			5				4			28
2				6	7	8	9	10	11			3						1	4		5							29
	2			6		8	9	10	11	3					7			1	4		5							30
	2			6		8	9	10	11	3					7			1	4		5							31
	2			6			9	10	11	3				4	7			1	5							8		32
2						8	9	10	11	3					7			1	4		5	6						33
2				6		8	9	10	11	3					7			1	4		5							34
2		4		6			9	10	11	3					7			1		8	5							35
2		4		6			9	10	11	3					7			1		8	5							36
2		4		6			9	10	11	3					7			1		8	5							37
2		4		6		8	9	10		3					7			1	5	11								38
2		4		6	11		9	10		3					7			1	5	8								39
2		4		6	11		9	10		3					7			1	5	8								40
2		4		6	11		9	10		3					7			1	5	8								41
2		4		6	11		9	10		3					7			1	5	8								42
7	9	24	7	36	18	30	42	38	36	20	3	14	5	11	24	4	2	21	22	14	12	6	4	8	1	1		
		1		1	2	7	33	15	4						8				1	6								

Lowton WG	Lumberg AA	Rhodes RA	Bellis GA	Richards DT	Phillips C	Bottrill WG	Hartill WJ	Deacon J	Barraclough W	Shaw CE	Smalley T	Smith AJ	Smith WC	Farrow GH	Crook MS	Ivill E	Pincott FC	Ellis J	Nelson JH	Hetherington JA	Hollingworth R	Heelbeck LW	Bryant W	Wildman FR	Wildsmith T	Redfern L	Whittaker P	
2		4		6			9		11		10	3		8	7				5								1	R3
		1		1			1		1		1	1		1	1				1									
															2													

1933-34

Division One

Manager: Major Frank Buckley

	P	W	D	L	F	A	Pts
Arsenal	42	25	9	8	75	47	59
Huddersfield Town	42	23	10	9	90	61	56
Tottenham Hotspur	42	21	7	14	79	56	49
Derby County	42	17	11	14	68	54	45
Manchester City	42	17	11	14	65	72	45
Sunderland	42	16	12	14	81	56	44
West Bromwich Albion	42	17	10	15	78	70	44
Blackburn Rovers	42	18	7	17	74	81	43
Leeds United	42	17	8	17	75	66	42
Portsmouth	42	15	12	15	52	55	42
Sheffield Wednesday	42	16	9	17	62	67	41
Stoke City	42	15	11	16	58	71	41
Aston Villa	42	14	12	16	78	75	40
Everton	42	12	16	14	62	63	40
Wolverhampton Wanderers	42	14	12	16	74	86	40
Middlesbrough	42	16	7	19	68	80	39
Leicester City	42	14	11	17	59	74	39
Liverpool	42	14	10	18	79	87	38
Chelsea	42	14	8	20	67	69	36
Birmingham	42	12	12	18	54	56	36
Newcastle United	42	10	14	18	68	77	34
Sheffield United	42	12	7	23	58	101	31

Did you know that?

• Wolves' pre-season friendly against Nice in France ended in disarray when civil disobedience led to Major Frank Buckley escorting his players off the pitch before the final whistle.

• In April 1934 six Wolves players – Barraclough, James Deacon, Hollingworth, Lowton, Rhodes and Hartill – were all granted benefits of £100 each by the management committee, a Football League record.

• Wolves scored four goals in seven minutes during their 5–2 win over Huddersfield Town in September.

• The lowest Hillsborough League crowd on record, just 5,182, attended the Sheffield Wednesday – Wolves game in March.

Match No.	Date		Venue	Opponents	Result		Scorers
1	Aug	26	H	Liverpool	W	3-2	Phillips, Hartill, Barraclough
2		28	A	Tottenham Hotspur	L	0-4	
3	Sep	2	A	Chelsea	L	2-5	Nelson, Hartill
4		4	H	Tottenham Hotspur	W	1-0	Hartill
5		9	H	Sunderland	L	1-6	Barraclough
6		16	A	Portsmouth	D	1-1	Hartill
7		23	H	Huddersfield Town	W	5-2	Beattie, Hetherington 3, Lowton
8		30	A	Stoke City	D	1-1	Barraclough
9	Oct	7	H	West Bromwich Albion	D	0-0	
10		14	H	Sheffield United	W	3-2	Hartill 2, Philips
11		21	A	Birmingham	D	0-0	
12		28	H	Sheffield Wednesday	W	6-2	Lowton, Beattie, Barraclough, Hartill, Phillips 2
13	Nov	4	A	Blackburn Rovers	L	1-7	Hetherington
14		11	H	Arsenal	L	0-1	
15		18	A	Everton	W	2-1	Phillips, Lowton
16		25	H	Middlesbrough	L	0-1	
17	Dec	2	A	Derby County	L	1-3	Jones
18		9	H	Newcastle United	W	2-1	Lowton, Barraclough
19		16	A	Leeds United	D	3-3	Beattie, Jones, Barraclough
20		23	H	Manchester City	W	8-0	Beattie 2, Phillips 3, Jones 2, Goddard
21		25	A	Aston Villa	L	2-6	Goddard, Phillips
22		26	H	Aston Villa	W	4-3	Hartill, Phillips, Lowton, Jones
23		30	A	Liverpool	D	1-1	Goddard
24	Jan	6	H	Chelsea	D	1-1	Goddard
25		20	A	Sunderland	D	3-3	Phillips, Goddard 2
26	Feb	3	A	Huddersfield Town	L	1-3	Hartill
27		7	H	Portsmouth	D	1-1	Lowton
28		10	H	Stoke City	L	0-2	
29		17	A	West Bromwich Albion	L	0-2	
30		24	A	Sheffield United	L	1-3	Hartill
31	Mar	3	H	Birmingham	W	2-0	Jones, Goddard
32		10	A	Sheffield Wednesday	L	1-2	Beattie
33		17	H	Blackburn Rovers	W	5-3	Jones 2, Goddard, Beattie, Phillips
34		24	A	Arsenal	L	2-3	Nelson, Goddard
35		31	H	Everton	W	2-0	Jones, Goddard
36	Apr	2	H	Leicester City	D	1-1	Phillips
37		3	A	Leicester City	D	1-1	Goddard
38		7	A	Middlesbrough	D	0-0	
39		14	H	Derby County	W	3-0	Jones, Hartill 2
40		21	A	Newcastle United	L	1-5	Davidson (og)
41		28	H	Leeds United	W	2-0	Richards, Hartill
42	May	5	A	Manchester City	L	0-4	

Appeara

One own-goal

FA Cup

R3	Jan	13	H	Newcastle United	W	1-0	Phillips
R4		27	A	Derby County	L	0-3	

Appeara

Lowton WG	Shaw CE	Rhodes RA	Nelson JH	Richard DT	Phillips C	Hetherington JA	Hartill WJ	Deacon J	Barraclough W	Harwood I	Bryant W	Smith AJ	Crook MS	Hollingworth R	Beattie JM	Wildman FR	Heelbeck LW	Smalley T	Jones B	Goddard G	Spiers CH	Morris WW	Clayton JGT	Weare AJ	Preece JC	
2	3	4	5	6	7	8	9	10	11																	1
2	3	4	5	6	7		9	10	11	8																2
2	3	4	5	6	8		9	10	11		7															3
	3	4	5	6	8		9	10	11			2	7													4
	3	4	5		7		9	10	11			2		6	8											5
2	3	4				10	9		11				7	5	8	1	6									6
2	3		4	6		10	9		11				7	5	8	1										7
2	3		5	6	4	10	9		11				7		8	1										8
2	3	4	5	6		10	9		11				7		8	1										9
2	3	4	5	6	7	10	9		11						8	1										10
2	3		5	6	7	10	9		11						8	1		4								11
2			5	6	7	10	9		11			3			8	1		4								12
2	3	6	5			10	9		11				7		8	1		4								13
2	3		5	6	7	10	9		11						8	1		4								14
2	3		5	6	7		9	10	11							1		4	8							15
2	3		5	6	7		9	10	11						8	1		4								16
2	3	4	5	6	7	8	9		11							1			10							17
2	3		5	6	7				11						8	1		4	10	9						18
2	3		5	6	7				11						8	1		4	10	9						19
2	3			6	7				11					5	8	1		4	10	9						20
2	3			6	7				11					5	8	1		4	10	9						21
2	3		5	6	7		9		11						8	1		4	10							22
2	3			6	7				11					5	8	1		4	10	9						23
2	3			6	7				11					5	8	1		4	10	9						24
2	3			6	7				11	8				5		1		4	10	9						25
2	3			6	7	11	9							5				4	10	8	1					26
2	3				7			10	11					5			6	4	8	9	1					27
2	3			6	7		9		11	8				5		1		4	10							28
2	3	4		6	7				11	8				5		1			10			9				29
2	3	4		6	7	11	8							5		1			10			9				30
2	3		5	6	7				11						8	1		4	10	9						31
2	3		5	6	7				11						8	1		4	10	9						32
2	3		5	6	7				11						8	1		4	10	9						33
2	3		5	6	7				11						8	1		4	10	9						34
2	3		5	6	7				11						8	1		4	10	9						35
2	3		5	6	7				11						8	1		4	10	9						36
2	3	6	5		8				11				7			1		4	10	9						37
2	3	6	5		7		9		11	8						1		4	10							38
2	3		5	6	7		9		11	8						1		4	10							39
2	3		5	6	7		9		11									4	10				8	1		40
	3	6	5	11	7		9								8			4	10		1				2	41
	3		5	6	7	11	9								8			4	10		1				2	42
8	41	15	31	36	38	14	26	8	38	6	1	3	7	13	26	32	2	29	27	16	4	2	1	1	2	
6			2	1	13	4	13		5						7				10	12						

Lowton WG	Shaw CE	Rhodes RA	Nelson JH	Richard DT	Phillips C	Hetherington JA	Hartill WJ	Deacon J	Barraclough W	Harwood I	Bryant W	Smith AJ	Crook MS	Hollingworth R	Beattie JM	Wildman FR	Heelbeck LW	Smalley T	Jones B	Goddard G	Spiers CH	Morris WW	Clayton JGT	Weare AJ	Preece JC	
2	3			6	7		9		11					5	8	1		4	10							R3
2	3			6	7				11					5	8	1		4	10	9						R4
2	2			2	2		1		2					2	2	2		2	2	1						
					1																					

1934-35

Division One

Manager: Major Frank Buckley

	P	W	D	L	F	A	Pts
Arsenal	42	23	12	7	115	46	58
Sunderland	42	19	16	7	90	51	54
Sheffield Wednesday	42	18	13	11	70	64	49
Manchester City	42	20	8	14	82	67	48
Grimsby Town	42	17	11	14	78	60	45
Derby County	42	18	9	15	81	66	45
Liverpool	42	19	7	16	85	88	45
Everton	42	16	12	14	89	88	44
West Bromwich Albion	42	17	10	15	83	83	44
Stoke City	42	18	6	18	71	70	42
Preston North End	42	15	12	15	62	67	42
Chelsea	42	16	9	17	73	82	41
Aston Villa	42	14	13	15	74	88	41
Portsmouth	42	15	10	17	71	72	40
Blackburn Rovers	42	14	11	17	66	78	39
Huddersfield Town	42	14	10	18	76	71	38
Wolverhampton Wanderers	42	15	8	19	88	94	38
Leeds United	42	13	12	17	75	92	38
Birmingham	42	13	10	19	63	81	36
Middlesbrough	42	10	14	18	70	90	34
Leicester City	42	12	9	21	61	86	33
Tottenham Hotspur	42	10	10	22	54	93	30

Did you know that?

- The £2 season ticket came into force for the first time at Molineux this season.
- Billy Hartill became the first Wolves player to twice score five goals in a game – when he went up against Aston Villa in September. He later moved to Everton.
- Also on the move this season were Bill Barraclough (to Chelsea), Jack Beattie (to Blackburn Rovers), Mark Crook (to Luton Town) and Jimmy Deacon (to Southend United).
- Tom Galley, one of the tallest outfield players ever to serve the club, made his League debut as centre-forward against Sunderland in January.

Match No.	Date		Venue	Opponents	Result		Scorers	Atten
1	Aug	25	A	Leicester City	D	1-1	Hartill	21,
2		27	A	Aston Villa	L	1-2	Hetherington	34,
3	Sep	1	H	Sunderland	L	1-2	Beattie	29,
4		3	H	Aston Villa	W	5-2	Hartill 5	29,
5		8	A	Tottenham Hotspur	L	1-3	Nelson	37
6		15	H	Preston North End	D	2-2	Deacon, Crook	26
7		22	A	Grimsby Town	L	1-2	Beattie	9
8		29	H	Everton	W	4-2	Beattie 2, Hartill, Crook	15,
9	Oct	6	A	Huddersfield Town	L	1-4	Hartill	11,
10		13	H	West Bromwich Albion	W	3-2	Hartill, Beattie, Hetherington	35
11		20	A	Sheffield Wednesday	L	1-3	Hartill	14,
12		27	H	Birmingham	W	3-1	Hartill 2, Beattie	22
13	Nov	3	A	Liverpool	L	1-2	Rhodes	19
14		10	H	Leeds United	L	1-2	Hetherington	13
15		17	A	Middlesbrough	D	2-2	Clayton, Hartill	10
16		24	H	Blackburn Rovers	W	2-1	Clayton 2	16
17	Dec	1	A	Arsenal	L	0-7		39
18		8	H	Portsmouth	L	2-3	Jones, Phillips	16
19		15	A	Stoke City	W	2-1	Spencer (og), Wrigglesworth	18
20		22	H	Manchester City	W	5-0	Hartill, Hollingworth, Jones, Wrigglesworth 2	27
21		25	H	Derby County	W	5-1	Martin 2, Phillips 3	36
22		26	A	Derby County	L	0-2		35
23		29	H	Leicester City	W	3-1	Phillips, Hartill, Crook	24
24	Jan	5	A	Sunderland	D	0-0		26
25		19	H	Tottenham Hotspur	W	6-2	Hartill 3, Martin, Jones, Phillips	28
26		28	A	Preston North End	L	1-2	Martin	10
27	Feb	2	H	Grimsby Town	L	0-3		21
28		9	A	Everton	L	2-5	Richards, Jones	28
29		16	H	Huddersfield Town	L	2-3	Martin 2	16
30		23	A	West Bromwich Albion	L	2-5	Iverson, Martin	31
31	Mar	4	H	Sheffield Wednesday	D	2-2	Shaw, Iverson	12
32		9	A	Birmingham	D	1-1	Phillips	1
33		16	H	Liverpool	W	5-3	Wrigglesworth 2, Iverson 2, Hartill	1
34		23	A	Leeds United	D	1-1	Wrigglesworth	
35		30	H	Middlesbrough	W	5-3	Phillips 2, Hartill, Jones, Stuart (og)	1
36	Apr	6	A	Blackburn Rovers	L	2-4	Hartill 2	
37		13	H	Arsenal	D	1-1	Jones	4
38		19	A	Chelsea	L	2-4	Phillips, Hartill	4
39		20	A	Portsmouth	W	1-0	Hartill	1
40		22	H	Chelsea	W	6-1	Phillips, Jones, Galley, Wrigglesworth, Hartill, Shaw	3
41		27	H	Stoke City	W	2-1	Hartill 2	1
42	May	4	A	Manchester City	L	0-5		1

Appeara

Two own-goals G

FA Cup

R3	Jan	12	H	Notts County	W	4-0	Brown, Hartill, Martin, Phillips	2
R4		26	H	Sheffield Wednesday	L	1-2	Hartill	5

Appeara

G

Match	Hollingworth R	Shaw CE	Smalley T	Nelson JH	Hetherington JA	Phillips C	Beattie JM	Hartill WJ	Jones B	Barraclough W	Richards DT	Goddard G	Rhodes RA	Crook MS	Deacon J	Lutterlock BR	Spiers CH	Lowton WG	Clayton JGT	Utterson J	Wigglesworth W	Martin DK	Dowen JS	Morris WW	Galley T	Brown J	Greene C	Cullis S	Weare AJ	Gardiner JB	Iverson RTJ	Astill LV
1	2	3	4	5	6	7	8	9	10	11																						
2	2	3	4	5	10	7	8	9		11	6																					
3	2	3	4	5			8	9	10	11	6	7																				
4	2	3		5	8		7	9	10	11	6		4																			
5	2	3		5	8		7	9	10	11	6		4																			
6	2	3		5	8			9		11	6		4	7	10																	
7	2	3		5		7	8	9	10	11	6		4																			
8	2	3	6	5	10		8	9		11			4	7																		
9	2	3	6	5	10		8	9			11		4	7																		
10	2	3	6	5	11	7	8	9					4			10																
11	2	3	6	5	11	7	8	9					4			10																
12	2	3	6	5	11	7	8	9	10				4																			
13	2	3	6	5	11	7	8	9	10				4																			
14	2	3	6	5	11	7	8	9	10				4																			
15	5	3	6		11	7	8	9					4				1	2	10													
16	5	3	6		11	7	8	9					4				1	2	10													
17	5	3	6			7	8	9			11		4				1	2	10													
18		3		5	11	7	8	9	10		6		4				1	2														
19	2	3	5			7	8	9	10		6		4							1	11											
20	2	3	5			7		8	10		6		4							1	11	9										
21	2	3	5			7		8	10		6		4							1	11	9										
22		3	5		11	7			10		6								8	1		9	2	4								
23	2	3	5			7		8	10		6		4	11						1		9										
24	2	3	5			7		8	10		6		4	11						1					9							
25	2	3	5			11		8	10		6		4							1		9				7						
26	2	3	5					8	10		6									1	11	9				7	4					
27	2	3	5					8	10		6									1	11				9	7	4					
28	2	3	5					8	10		6		4							1	11	9				7						
29	2	3	5			11		8	10		6									1		9				7		4				
30	2	3				11			10													9		5		7		4	1	6	8	
31		3						9	10		6										11		2	5		7		4	1		8	
32		3	4			7		9	10		6										11		2	5					1		8	
33		3	4			7		9	10		6										11		2	5					1		8	
34		3	4			7		9	10		6										11		2	5					1		8	
35		3	4			7		9	10		6										11		2	5					1		8	
36	5	3	4			7		9	10												11		2	6					1		8	
37	2	3	4	5		7		9	10		6										11								1		8	
38	2	3	4	5		7		9	10		6										11								1		8	
39	2	3	4	5		7		9	10		6										11				8				1			
40	2	3	4	5		7		9	10		6										11				8				1			
41	2	3	4	5		7		9	10		6														8				1			11
42	2	3	4	5		7		9	10		6														8				1			11
	35	42	35	21	16	32	18	40	33	8	31	1	22	5	1	2	4	4	4	11	16	9	7	8	6	7	2	3	13	1	9	2
	1	2		1	3	11	6	27	7		1		1	3	1				3		7	7			1						4	

Round	Hollingworth R	Shaw CE	Smalley T	Nelson JH	Hetherington JA	Phillips C	Beattie JM	Hartill WJ	Jones B	Barraclough W	Richards DT	Goddard G	Rhodes RA	Crook MS	Deacon J	Lutterlock BR	Spiers CH	Lowton WG	Clayton JGT	Utterson J	Wigglesworth W	Martin DK	Dowen JS	Morris WW	Galley T	Brown J	Greene C	Cullis S	Weare AJ	Gardiner JB	Iverson RTJ	Astill LV
R3	2	3	5			11		8	10		6		4									9				7			1			
R4	2	3	5					8	10		6		4	11								9				7			1			
	2	2	2			1		2	2		2		2	1								2				2			2			
						1		2														1				1						

1935-36

Division One

Manager: Major Frank Buckley

	P	W	D	L	F	A	Pts
Sunderland	42	25	6	11	109	74	56
Derby County	42	18	12	12	61	52	48
Huddersfield Town	42	18	12	12	59	56	48
Stoke City	42	20	7	15	57	57	47
Brentford	42	17	12	13	81	60	46
Arsenal	42	15	15	12	78	48	45
Preston North End	42	18	8	16	67	64	44
Chelsea	42	15	13	14	65	72	43
Manchester City	42	17	8	17	68	60	42
Portsmouth	42	17	8	17	54	67	42
Leeds United	42	15	11	16	66	64	41
Birmingham	42	15	11	16	61	63	41
Bolton Wanderers	42	14	13	15	67	76	41
Middlesbrough	42	15	10	17	84	70	40
Wolverhampton Wanderers	42	15	10	17	77	76	40
Everton	42	13	13	16	89	89	39
Grimsby Town	42	17	5	20	65	73	39
West Bromwich Albion	42	16	6	20	89	88	38
Liverpool	42	13	12	17	60	64	38
Sheffield Wednesday	42	13	12	17	63	77	38
Aston Villa	42	13	9	20	81	110	35
Blackburn Rovers	42	12	9	21	55	96	33

Did you know that?

- In December, Charlie Phillips received his second sending off as a Wolves player, this time against Bolton Wanderers at Molineux.
- Full-back Wilf Lowton returned to his former club, Exeter City, after making 209 senior appearances for Wolves. Jack Nelson joined Luton Town and Dai Richards switched to Brentford.
- Giant goalkeeper Alex Scott was recruited from Burnley and George Ashall arrived from Frickley Colliery.
- Stan Cullis took over as team captain.

Match No.	Date		Venue	Opponents	Result		Scorers	Atten
1	Aug	31	H	Birmingham	W	3-1	Shaw, Brown 2	33
2	Sep	2	H	Huddersfield Town	D	2-2	Jones, Martin	20
3		7	A	Sheffield Wednesday	D	0-0		21
4		11	A	Huddersfield Town	L	0-3		12
5		14	H	Portsmouth	W	2-0	Jones, Greene	24
6		18	A	Middlesbrough	L	2-4	Brown, Greene	15
7		21	A	Preston North End	L	0-2		17
8		28	H	Brentford	W	3-2	Martin 2, Phillips	28
9	Oct	5	A	Derby County	L	1-3	Smalley	20
10		12	H	Everton	W	4-0	Thompson, Smalley, Shaw, Phillips	30
11		19	H	Sunderland	L	3-4	Thompson, Martin, Shaw	29
12		26	A	West Bromwich Albion	L	1-2	Wrigglesworth	42
13	Nov	2	H	Leeds United	W	3-0	Smalley 2, Phillips	22
14		9	A	Grimsby Town	L	1-2	Thompson	10
15		16	H	Liverpool	W	3-1	Smalley 2, Wrigglesworth	22
16		23	A	Arsenal	L	0-4		39
17		30	H	Blackburn Rovers	W	8-1	Jones, Thompson, Wrigglesworth 2, Gardiner, Phillips 2, Crook (og)	18
18	Dec	7	A	Stoke City	L	1-4	Turner (og)	20
19		14	H	Manchester City	W	4-3	Wrigglesworth 2, Phillips, Smalley	20
20		21	A	Chelsea	D	2-2	Smalley, Morris	20
21		25	A	Bolton Wanderers	W	3-0	Iverson, Wrigglesworth, Smalley	30
22		26	H	Bolton Wanderers	D	3-3	Wrigglesworth, Phillips, Iverson	35
23		28	A	Birmingham	D	0-0		37
24	Jan	4	H	Sheffield Wednesday	W	2-1	Wrigglesworth 2	25
25		18	A	Portsmouth	L	0-1		15
26	Feb	1	A	Brentford	L	0-5		25
27		8	H	Derby County	D	0-0		23
28		15	A	Everton	L	1-4	Martin	27
29		22	A	Sunderland	L	1-3	Martin	26
30	Mar	4	H	Grimsby Town	W	1-0	Ashall	8
31		7	A	Blackburn Rovers	L	0-1		
32		14	H	West Bromwich Albion	W	2-0	Jones, Ashall	34
33		21	A	Liverpool	W	2-0	Thompson, Gardiner	23
34		28	H	Arsenal	D	2-2	Thompson. Martin	3
35	Apr	4	A	Leeds United	L	0-2		1
36		10	A	Aston Villa	L	2-4	Clayton 2	5
37		11	H	Stoke City	D	1-1	Shaw	2
38		13	H	Aston Villa	D	2-2	Henson, Jones	4
39		18	A	Manchester City	L	1-2	Ashall	2
40		20	H	Preston North End	W	4-2	Jones 3, Shaw	1
41		25	H	Chelsea	D	3-3	Shaw, Martin 2	1
42	May	2	H	Middlesbrough	W	4-0	Wrigglesworth 2, Jones, Martin	1

Appeara

Two own-goals

FA Cup

R3	Jan	11	H	Leeds United	D	1-1	Wrigglesworth	3
rep		15	A	Leeds United	L	1-3	Morris	3

Appeara

…llingworth R	Shaw CE	Smalley T	Morris WW	Rhodes RA	Phillips C	Galley T	Martin DK	Jones B	Brown J	Iverson RTJ	Henson GH	Richards DT	Greene C	Utterson J	Dowen JS	Wigglesworth W	Gardiner JB	Thompson H	Cullis S	Laking GE	Curnow JL	Clayton JGT	Taylor J	Scott RA	Marsden F	Ashall GH	Whittam EA	
2	3	4	5	6	7	8	9	10	11																			1
2	3	4	5	6	7	8	9	10	11																			2
2	3	4	5	6	7		9	10	11	8																		3
2	3	4	5	6	7			10	11	8	9																	4
2	3	4	5		11			10	7		9	6	8															5
2	3	4	5		11			10	7		9	6	8	1	2													6
2	3	4	5		7			10	11		9	6	8															7
2	3	4	5		8		9	10	7			6				11												8
2	3	9	5	4					7							11	6	8	10									9
2	3	9	5	4	7			10				6				11		8										10
2	3	4	5		7		9	10				6				11		8										11
2	3	4	5		7		9	10				6				11		8										12
2	3	9	5		7	4		10				6				11		8										13
2	3	9	5		7	4		10								11	6	8		2								14
2	3	9	5		7	4		10								11	6	8		2								15
2	3	9	5		7	4		10								11	6	8		2								16
2	3	9	5		7	4		10								11	6	8		2								17
2	3	9	5		7	4		10								11	6	8		2								18
2	3	9	5		7	4		10		6						11		8		2								19
2	3	9	5		7			10		8			4			11	6			2	1							20
2	3	9	5		7			10		8			4			11	6			2								21
2	3	9	5		7	4		10		8						11	6			2								22
2	3	9	5		7	4		10		8						11	6			2	1							23
2	3	9	5		7	4		10		8						11	6			2	1							24
2	3	9	5			4			7	8						11	6			2	1	10						25
2	3	9	5			4		7								11	6	8			1	10	2					26
2	3	6	5			4		10	7	8	9					11				2				1				27
2	3	6	5			4	9	10	7	8						11								1	2			28
2	3	4	5			6	9	7		10						11	8			2	1							29
2	3	4	5			6	9	7		10							8			2				1		11		30
2	3	4	9			6		7		8									5				2	1		11	10	31
2	3	4	9			6		7		8							10		5				2	1		11		32
2	3	4				6		7		10							9	8	5				2	1		11		33
2	3	4				6	7	10									9	8	5				2	1		11		34
2	3	4				6	9	7									10	8	5				2	1		11		35
2	3	4	9					7		6								8	5			10	2	1		11		36
2	3	4	5				9	7		6						11		8				10	2	1				37
2	3	4	5					7		10	9							8	6				2	1		11		38
2	3	4	5				9	10	7									8	6				2			11		39
2	3	4	5				9	10								7		8	6	2						11		40
2	3	4	5				9	10								7		8	6	2						11		41
2	3	4	5				9	10								7		8	6	2						11		42
	42	42	39	6	23	23	16	40	13	19	6	8	5	1	1	26	19	22	12	18	6	4	10	11	1	12	1	
	6	9	1		7		10	9	3	2	1		2			12	2	6				2				3		

…llingworth R	Shaw CE	Smalley T	Morris WW	Rhodes RA	Phillips C	Galley T	Martin DK	Jones B	Brown J	Iverson RTJ	Henson GH	Richards DT	Greene C	Utterson J	Dowen JS	Wigglesworth W	Gardiner JB	Thompson H	Cullis S	Laking GE	Curnow JL	Clayton JGT	Taylor J	Scott RA	Marsden F	Ashall GH	Whittam EA	
	3	9	5			4		10	7	8						11	6			2	1							R3
	3	9	5			4		10	7	8						11	6			2	1							rep
	2	2	2			2		2	2	2						2	2			2	2							
			1													1												

1936-37

Division One

Manager: Major Frank Buckley

	P	W	D	L	F	A	Pts
Manchester City	42	22	13	7	107	61	57
Charlton Athletic	42	21	12	9	58	49	54
Arsenal	42	18	16	8	80	49	52
Derby County	42	21	7	14	96	90	49
Wolverhampton Wanderers	42	21	5	16	84	67	47
Brentford	42	18	10	14	82	78	46
Middlesbrough	42	19	8	15	74	71	46
Sunderland	42	19	6	17	89	87	44
Portsmouth	42	17	10	15	62	66	44
Stoke City	42	15	12	15	72	57	42
Birmingham	42	13	15	14	64	60	41
Grimsby Town	42	17	7	18	86	81	41
Chelsea	42	14	13	15	52	55	41
Preston North End	42	14	13	15	56	67	41
Huddersfield Town	42	12	15	15	62	64	39
West Bromwich Albion	42	16	6	20	77	98	38
Everton	42	14	9	19	81	78	37
Liverpool	42	12	11	19	62	84	35
Leeds United	42	15	4	23	60	80	34
Bolton Wanderers	42	10	14	18	43	66	34
Manchester United	42	10	12	20	55	78	32
Sheffield Wednesday	42	9	12	21	53	69	30

Did you know that?

- Wolves goalkeeper Alex Scott was sent off twice this season against two Yorkshire clubs – Huddersfield Town and Leeds United.
- David Jordan became the first Wolves player to gain a full cap for the Republic of Ireland (against Switzerland).
- A record crowd of 31,653 attended the Grimsby Town versus Wolves FA Cup tie at Blundell Park in March.
- Dennis Westcott was signed from New Brighton and Teddy Maguire from Willington, while Billy Wrigglesworth joined Manchester United and Charlie Phillips switched to Aston Villa.

Match No.	Date		Venue	Opponents	Result		Scorers
1	Aug	29	A	Manchester United	D	1-1	Ashall
2		31	H	Middlesbrough	L	0-1	
3	Sep	5	H	Sheffield Wednesday	W	4-3	B Jones 2, Waring, Wrigglesworth
4		9	A	Middlesbrough	L	0-1	
5		12	A	Preston North End	W	3-1	Iverson, Clayton, Waring
6		19	H	Arsenal	W	2-0	B Jones, Brown
7		23	A	Derby County	L	1-5	B Jones
8		26	A	Brentford	L	2-3	Brown, B Jones
9	Oct	3	H	Bolton Wanderers	L	2-3	B Jones, Waring
10		10	A	Everton	L	0-1	
11		17	A	West Bromwich Albion	L	1-2	Brown
12		24	H	Manchester City	W	2-1	Ashall, Galley
13		31	A	Portsmouth	D	1-1	Clayton
14	Nov	7	H	Chelsea	L	1-2	Wrigglesworth
15		14	A	Stoke City	L	1-2	B Jones
16		21	H	Charlton Athletic	W	6-1	Galley, B Jones 2, Ashall 2, Clayton
17		28	A	Grimsby Town	D	1-1	Galley
18	Dec	5	H	Liverpool	W	2-0	Clayton 2
19		19	H	Birmingham	W	2-1	Clayton, Galley
20		25	H	Huddersfield Town	W	3-1	Clayton, Goodall (og), Galley
21		26	H	Manchester United	W	3-1	Ashall, Galley 2
22		28	A	Huddersfield Town	L	0-4	
23	Jan	2	A	Sheffield Wednesday	W	3-1	Galley 2, Clayton
24		9	H	Preston North End	W	5-0	Galley, Ashall, Clayton 2, B Jones
25		23	A	Arsenal	L	0-3	
26	Feb	6	A	Bolton Wanderers	W	2-1	Galley, Clayton
27		10	H	Brentford	W	4-0	Thompson, Clayton 2, Wharton
28		13	H	Everton	W	7-2	Clayton 4, Galley 2, Ashall
29		27	A	Manchester City	L	1-4	Thompson
30	Mar	13	A	Chelsea	W	1-0	Clayton
31		17	H	Portsmouth	D	1-1	Thompson
32		20	H	Stoke City	W	2-1	Westcott 2
33		26	A	Sunderland	L	2-6	B Jones, Thompson
34		27	A	Charlton Athletic	L	0-4	
35		29	H	Sunderland	D	1-1	Westcott
36	Apr	3	H	Grimsby Town	W	5-2	Thompson, Clayton 3, Ashall
37		10	A	Liverpool	L	0-1	
38		14	H	West Bromwich Albion	W	5-2	C Shaw (og), Ashall, Thompson, Clayton, Wharton
39		17	H	Leeds United	W	3-0	Clayton 2, Thompson
40		21	A	Leeds United	W	1-0	Morris
41		24	A	Birmingham	L	0-1	
42	May	1	H	Derby County	W	3-1	Ashall, Westcott 2

Appeara

Two own-goals

FA Cup

R3	Jan	16	H	Middlesbrough	W	6-1	Ashall 2, Clayton, Galley, B Jones, Smalley
R4		30	H	Sheffield United	D	2-2	Clayton, Johnson (og)
rep	Feb	4	A	Sheffield United	W	2-1	Ashall, Clayton
R5		20	A	Grimsby Town	D	1-1	Galley
rep		24	H	Grimsby Town	W	6-2	Ashall 2, Clayton 2, B Jones, Westcott
R6	Mar	6	H	Sunderland	D	1-1	B Jones
rep		10	A	Sunderland	D	2-2	Galley, Thompson
rep2		15	N	Sunderland	L	0-4	

R6 replay aet

R6 replay 2 at Hillsborough, Sheffield.

Appear

One own-goal

	Shaw CE	Smalley T	Morris WW	Galley T	Wrigglesworth W	Thompson H	Waring T	Jones B	Ashall GH	Iverson RJT	Scott RA	Clayton JGT	Brown J	Taylor J	Cullis S	Wharton G	Jordan D	Gardiner JB	Maguire JE	Gold W	Ordish CS	Westcott D	Dowen JS	Taylor F	Coley WE	Jones EN	Keetley A
1	3	4	5	6	7	8	9	10	11																		
2	3	4	5	6	7	8	9		11	10																	
3	3	4	5	6	7	8	9	10	11																		
4	3	4	5	6	7	8	9	10	11																		
5	3	4	5	6			9		7	8	1	10	11														
6	3	4	5	6			9	8	7		1	10	11														
7		4	5	6			9	8	7		1	10	11	3													
8	3	4	5	6			9	8	7		1	10	11														
9	3	4	5	6			9	8	7		1	10	11														
10	3	4	2	6			9	7		8	1	10	11		5												
11	3		2	6					7	8	1	10	11		5	4	9										
12	3	6	2	9	11			10	7	8	1				5	4											
13	3	6	2		11			10	7	8	1	9			5	4											
14		6	2		11			10	7	8	1	9		3	5	4											
15		4	2	8				10	11		1	9		3	5			6	7								
16		4	2	8				10	11		1	9		3	5			6	7								
17		4	2	8				10	11		1	9		3	5			6	7								
18		4	2	8				10	11		1	9		3	5			6	7								
19		4	2	8				10	11		1	9		3		5		6	7								
20		4	2	8				10	11		1	9		3		5		6	7								
21		4	2	8				10	11		1	9		3		5		6	7								
22		4	2	8	7			10	11		1	9		3		5		6									
23			2	8				10	11		1	9		3	5	4		6	7								
24			2	8				10	11			9		3	5	4		6	7	1							
25		7	2	8				10	11		1	9		3	5	4		6									
26		7	2	8		10			11			9		3	5	4		6		1							
27		7	2	8		10			11			9		3	5	4		6		1							
28		7	2	8		10			11			9		3	5	4		6		1							
29		5		8		10						9		3		4		6		1	2	7	11				
30		5				10		8	11			9		3		4				1		7		2	6		
31		5		8		10			7					3		4				1		9		2	6	11	
32		5		8				10	11					3		4		6		1		9		2		7	
33		5				10		8	11					3		4		6		1		9		2		7	
34		4	2	8				10	11			9		3	5			6		1		7					
35		4	2	6		10		8	11		1	9		3	5							7					
36		4	2	8		10			11		1	9		3	5			6									7
37		4	2			10			11		1			3	5	8	9	6									7
38		4	2			10			11		1	9		3	5	8		6	7								
39		4	2	8		10			11		1	9		3	5			6	7								
40		4	2	8		10			11		1	9		3	5			6	7								
41		4		8		10			11		1			3	5		9	6	7					2			
42		4	2	8		10			11		1			3	5			6	7			9					
	12	39	36	36	8	19	10	27	40	7	28	31	7	30	24	21	3	25	14	10	1	8	1	5	2	3	2
			1	13	2	7	3	11	10	1		24	3			2						5					
R3		7	2	8				10	11		1	9		3	5	4		6									
R4		7	2	8		10			11		1	9		3	5	4		6									
rep		7	2	8				10	11			9		3	5	4		6		1							
R5		7	2	8		10			11			9		3	5	4		6		1							
rep		5	2	8				10	11			9		3		4		6		1		7					
R6		7	2	8				10	11			9		3	5	4		6		1							
rep		4	2	8		10		7	11			9		3	5			6		1							
rep2		4	2			10		8	11			9		3	5			6		1		7					
		8	8	7		4		6	8		2	8		8	7	6		8		6		2					
		1		3		1		3	5			5										1					

1937-38

Division One

Manager: Major Frank Buckley

	P	W	D	L	F	A	Pts
Arsenal	42	21	10	11	77	44	52
Wolverhampton Wanderers	42	20	11	11	72	49	51
Preston North End	42	16	17	9	64	44	49
Charlton Athletic	42	16	14	12	65	51	46
Middlesbrough	42	19	8	15	72	65	46
Brentford	42	18	9	15	69	59	45
Bolton Wanderers	42	15	15	12	64	60	45
Sunderland	42	14	16	12	55	57	44
Leeds United	42	14	15	13	64	69	43
Chelsea	42	14	13	15	65	65	41
Liverpool	42	15	11	16	65	71	41
Blackpool	42	16	8	18	61	66	40
Derby County	42	15	10	17	66	87	40
Everton	42	16	7	19	79	75	39
Huddersfield Town	42	17	5	20	55	68	39
Leicester City	42	14	11	17	54	75	39
Stoke City	42	13	12	17	58	59	38
Birmingham	42	10	18	14	58	62	38
Portsmouth	42	13	12	17	62	68	38
Grimsby Town	42	13	12	17	51	68	38
Manchester City	42	14	8	20	80	77	36
West Bromwich Albion	42	14	8	20	74	91	36

Did you know that?

- The 10–1 victory over Leicester City at Molineux in April still remains Wolves' biggest in the competition (home or away). Two players scored four goals each – the first time this had happened in a Wolves League game.
- A record crowd at Molineux – 61,267 – attended the FA Cup fourth-round tie against Arsenal in January.
- Stan Cullis became the first Wolves player to appear at Wembley, lining up for England against Scotland on 9 April.
- Wolves beat Arsenal 1–0 to win the Colchester Charity Cup Final at Layer Road.
- Not one single member of Wolves' 40-strong playing squad this season was married.

Match No.	Date		Venue	Opponents	Result		Scorers	Attend
1	Aug	28	H	Manchester City	W	3-1	Clayton 3	39,
2	Sep	1	A	Derby County	W	2-1	Clayton, Thompson	23,
3		4	A	Arsenal	L	0-5		67,
4		6	H	Derby County	D	2-2	Clayton, Howe (og)	28,
5		11	H	Blackpool	W	1-0	Thompson	30,
6		15	H	Sunderland	W	4-0	Westcott 2, Galley, Jones	25,
7		18	A	Brentford	L	1-2	Jones	28,
8		25	H	Bolton Wanderers	D	1-1	Maguire	36,
9	Oct	2	A	Huddersfield Town	L	0-1		19,
10		9	H	Everton	W	2-0	Galley, Maguire	30,
11		16	H	Liverpool	W	2-0	Westcott 2	27,
12		23	A	Leeds United	W	2-1	Jones 2	13,
13		30	H	Grimsby Town	D	1-1	Galley	28,
14	Nov	6	A	Stoke City	D	1-1	Galley	38,
15		13	H	Charlton Athletic	D	1-1	Jones	31,
16		20	A	Birmingham	L	0-2		35,
17		27	H	Portsmouth	W	5-0	Jones 2, Wescott 2, Smalley	21,
18	Dec	4	A	Preston North End	L	0-2		15,
19		18	A	Chelsea	W	2-0	Westcott 2	31,
20		27	A	West Bromwich Albion	D	2-2	Westcott 2	55,
21	Jan	1	A	Manchester City	W	4-2	Galley 2, Jones, Westcott	49,
22		15	H	Arsenal	W	3-1	Kirkham 2, Jones	39,
23		26	A	Blackpool	W	2-0	Galley, Jones	13
24		29	H	Brentford	W	2-1	Jones, Langley	35,
25	Feb	5	A	Bolton Wanderers	W	2-1	Galley, Jones	38,
26		16	H	Huddersfield Town	L	1-4	Langley	16,
27		19	A	Everton	W	1-0	Langley	39,
28		26	A	Liverpool	W	1-0	Ashall	32,
29	Mar	5	H	Leeds United	D	1-1	Jones	38,
30		12	A	Grimsby Town	L	0-1		17,
31		19	H	Stoke City	D	2-2	Galley, Thompson	32
32		23	H	Middlesbrough	L	0-1		22
33		26	A	Charlton Athletic	L	1-4	Galley	38
34	Apr	2	H	Birmingham	W	3-2	Westcott 2, Maguire	27
35		9	A	Portsmouth	L	0-1		28
36		15	H	Leicester City	W	10-1	Dorsett 4, Westcott 4, Jones, Maguire	24
37		16	H	Preston North End	D	0-0		42
38		18	A	Leicester City	D	1-1	Jones	30
39		23	A	Middlesbrough	W	3-0	Dorsett, Maguire, Westcott	26
40		30	H	Chelsea	D	1-1	Galley	27
41	May	2	H	West Bromwich Albion	W	2-1	Dorsett, Westcott	43
42		7	A	Sunderland	L	0-1		21

Appearan

One own-goal G

FA Cup

R3	Jan	8	A	Swansea Town	W	4-0	Westcott 3, Jones	19
R4		22	H	Arsenal	L	1-2	Jones	61

Appearan

G

orris WW	Taylor J	Wharton G	Cullis S	Gardiner JB	Jones B	Galley T	Clayton JGT	Thompson H	Ashall GH	Maguire JE	Smalley T	Westcott D	McIntosh A	Ordish CS	Kirkham RJ	Smith RGC	Taylor F	Langley WE	Dorsett R	Sidlow C	Dowen JS	Wright HR	
	3	4	5	6	7	8	9	10	11														1
	3	4	5	6		8	9	10	11	7													2
	3	4		6	8		9	10	11	7	5												3
	3	4	5	6		8	9	10	11	7													4
	3	4	5	6		8	9	10	11	7													5
	3		5	6	10	8			11	7	4	9											6
	3		5	6	10	8			11	7	4	9											7
	3		5	6	10	8			11	7	4	9											8
	3	8	5	6			9		11	7	4	10											9
	3		5	6	10	8	9		11	7	4												10
	3		5	6	10	8			11	7	4	9											11
	3	6			10	5			11	7	4	9	8										12
	3	6	5			10			11	7	4	9	8										13
	3		5	6	10	9			11	7	4		8										14
	3		5	6	10	9			11		4		8	7									15
	3		5	6	10	9			7		4		8		11								16
	3		5	6	10	8			11	7	4	9											17
	3		5	6	10	8			11	7	4	9											18
	3		5	6	8					7	4	9			11	10							19
	3		5	6	8				7		4	9			11	10							20
	3		5	6	8	10			7		4	9			11		2						21
	3		5	6	10	8			7		4	9			11								22
	3			6	8	5		10	11	7	4	9											23
	3			6	10	5		8	11	7	4							9					24
	3		5	6	10	8			11	7	4							9					25
	3		5	6	10	8			11	7	4						2	9					26
	3		5	6	10			8	11	7	4							9					27
	3		5	6	10			8	11	7	4							9					28
	3		5	6	10			8	11	7	4							9					29
	3		5	6		10		8		7	4	9			11								30
	3		5	6	7	8		10			4	9			11								31
	3		5	6	10	8			7		4	9			11								32
	3			6	10	5			11	7			8					9	4				33
	3		5		10	6		8	11	7		9							4	1			34
	3			6	10	5		8	11	7		9							4	1			35
			5	6	10	4				7		9							11	1	3	8	36
			5	6	10	4				7		9							11		3	8	37
			5	6	10	4		8				9							11		3	7	38
	3		5	6	10	4				7		9	8						11				39
	3		5	6	10	4				7		9	8						11				40
	3		5		10	4		8		7	6	9							11				41
	3		5	6	10	4		8		7		9							11				42
	39	8	36	38	36	35	7	17	32	33	29	26	8	1	8	2	2	7	10	3	3	3	
					15	11	5	3	1	5	1	19			2			3	6				
	3		5	6	10	8			7		4	9			11								R3
	3		5	6	10	8			7		4	9			11								R4
	2		2	2	2	2			2		2	2			2								
					2							3											

1938-39

Division One

Manager: Major Frank Buckley

	P	W	D	L	F	A	Pts
Everton	42	27	5	10	88	52	59
Wolverhampton Wanderers	42	22	11	9	88	39	55
Charlton Athletic	42	22	6	14	75	59	50
Middlesbrough	42	20	9	13	93	74	49
Arsenal	42	19	9	14	55	41	47
Derby County	42	19	8	15	66	55	46
Stoke City	42	17	12	13	71	68	46
Bolton Wanderers	42	15	15	12	67	58	45
Preston North End	42	16	12	14	63	59	44
Grimsby Town	42	16	11	15	61	69	43
Liverpool	42	14	14	14	62	63	42
Aston Villa	42	16	9	17	71	60	41
Leeds United	42	16	9	17	59	67	41
Manchester United	42	11	16	15	57	65	38
Blackpool	42	12	14	16	56	68	38
Sunderland	42	13	12	17	54	67	38
Portsmouth	42	12	13	17	47	70	37
Brentford	42	14	8	20	53	74	36
Huddersfield Town	42	12	11	19	58	64	35
Chelsea	42	12	9	21	64	80	33
Birmingham	42	12	8	22	62	84	32
Leicester City	42	9	11	22	48	82	29

Did you know that?

• Jimmy Mullen made his League debut this season at the age of 16 years and 43 days against Leeds United in February, and Stan Cullis became England's captain at the age of 22.

• When taking on Portsmouth at Wembley, Wolves became the first club to play in an FA Cup Final on five different grounds.

• The biggest-ever crowd at Molineux – 61,305 – saw Wolves beat Liverpool 4–1 in a fifth-round FA Cup tie in February. A then record crowd of 76,962 witnessed Wolves versus Grimsby Town FA Cup semi-final game at Old Trafford.

• Billy Wright, aged 14, had a trial in Wolves' third team this season.

Match No.	Date		Venue	Opponents	Result		Scorers
1	Aug	27	A	Derby County	D	2-2	Kirkham, Barlow
2		29	H	Leicester City	D	0-0	
3	Sep	3	H	Blackpool	D	1-1	Galley
4		7	A	Sunderland	D	1-1	Kirkham
5		10	A	Brentford	W	1-0	Kirkham
6		17	H	Arsenal	L	0-1	
7		24	A	Portsmouth	L	0-1	
8	Oct	1	H	Huddersfield Town	W	3-0	Galley, McIntosh, Burton
9		8	A	Everton	L	0-1	
10		15	A	Leeds United	L	0-1	
11		22	H	Liverpool	D	2-2	McIntosh, Westcott
12		29	A	Middlesbrough	L	0-1	
13	Nov	5	H	Birmingham	W	2-1	McIntosh, Westcott
14		12	A	Manchester United	W	3-1	Burton, Dorsett, Westcott
15		19	H	Stoke City	W	3-0	Burton, Dorsett, Westcott
16		26	A	Chelsea	W	3-1	Westcott 3
17	Dec	3	H	Preston North End	W	3-0	Galley 2, Dorsett
18		10	A	Charlton Athletic	W	4-0	Westcott 2, Dorsett 2
19		17	H	Bolton Wanderers	D	1-1	Galley
20		24	H	Derby County	D	0-0	
21		26	A	Grimsby Town	W	4-2	McIntosh 2, Galley, Dorsett
22		27	H	Grimsby Town	W	5-0	Dorsett, Westcott 3, Maguire
23		31	A	Blackpool	L	0-1	
24	Jan	14	H	Brentford	W	5-2	Dorsett 2, Westcott 3
25		28	H	Portsmouth	W	3-0	Dorsett 2, Westcott
26	Feb	1	A	Arsenal	D	0-0	
27		4	A	Huddersfield Town	W	2-1	McIntosh, Westcott
28		18	H	Leeds United	W	4-1	Westcott 2, Galley, Dorsett
29		22	H	Everton	W	7-0	Dorsett 4, Westcott 2, McIntosh
30		25	A	Liverpool	W	2-0	Westcott, Dorsett
31	Mar	8	H	Middlesbrough	W	6-1	Westcott 2, Dorsett 2, Galley, Maguire
32		11	A	Birmingham	L	2-3	Dorsett, Galley
33		18	H	Manchester United	W	3-0	Dorsett, Galley, Steen
34		29	A	Stoke City	L	3-5	Westcott 2, McAloon
35	Apr	1	H	Chelsea	W	2-0	Westcott, Dorsett
36		8	A	Preston North End	L	2-4	Dorsett 2
37		10	H	Aston Villa	W	2-1	Galley, Westcott
38		11	A	Aston Villa	D	2-2	Westcott, Wright
39		15	H	Charlton Athletic	W	3-1	Dorsett 2, Westcott
40		22	A	Bolton Wanderers	D	0-0	
41	May	4	A	Leicester City	W	2-0	Westcott 2
42		6	H	Sunderland	D	0-0	

Appea

FA Cup

R3	Jan	7	H	Bradford Park Avenue	W	3-1	Westcott 2, McIntosh
R4		21	H	Leicester City	W	5-1	Maguire 2, Westcott 2, Dorsett
R5	Feb	11	H	Liverpool	W	4-1	Burton, Dorsett, McIntosh, Westcott
R6	Mar	4	H	Everton	W	2-0	Westcott 2
SF		25	N	Grimsby Town	W	5-0	Westcott 4, Galley
F	Apr	29	N	Portsmouth	L	1-4	Dorsett

SF at Old Trafford, Manchester. Final at Wembley Stadium.

Appea

…rns WW	Taylor F	Galley T	Cullis S	Gardiner JB	Maguire JE	Barlow H	Kirkham RJ	Thompson H	Dorsett R	Westcott D	Myers JH	Burton S	Wright HR	McIntosh A	Parker WD	McMahon D	Mullen J	Goddard R	Steen AW	McAloon GP	Sidlow C	McDonald JC	Tagg E	Rooney J	Brown HS	Marshall J	
	3	4	5	6	7	8	9	10	11																		1
	3	4	5	6	7	8	9	10	11																		2
	3	8	5	6		7		10	4	9	11																3
	3	8	5	6	7		11	10	4	9																	4
	3	8	5	6	11		9		4			7	10														5
	3	8	5	6	11		9		4			7	10														6
	3	4	5	6				10	11	9		7		8													7
	3	4	5	6	11			10		9		7		8													8
	3	4	5	6	11			10		9		7		8													9
	3	4	5	6	11			10		9		7		8													10
	3	4	5	6	11			10		9		7		8													11
	3	4	5	6	11			10		9		7		8													12
	3	4	5	6				10	11	9		7		8													13
		4	5	6	11				10	9		7		8	3												14
	3	4	5	6	11				10	9		7		8													15
	3	4	5	6	11				10	9		7		8													16
	3	4	5	6	11				10	9		7		8													17
	3	4	5	6	11				10	9		7		8													18
	3	4	5	6	11				10	9		7		8													19
	3	4	5	6	11				10	9		7		8													20
	3	4	5	6	11				10	9		7		8													21
	3	4	5	6	11				10	9		7		8													22
	3	4	5	6	11				10	9		7				8											23
	3	4	5	6	11				10	9		7		8													24
	3	4	5	6	11				10	9		7		8													25
	3	4	5	6	11				10	9		7		8													26
	3	4	5	6					10	9	11	7		8													27
	3	4	5	6	11				10	9				8			7										28
	3	4	5	6	11				10	9				8			7										29
	3	4	5	6	11				10	9				8			7										30
	3	4	5	6	11				10	9		7		8													31
	3	4	5	6	11				10			7	9	8													32
	3	4	5						10	9							11	6	7	8							33
	3	4	5							9	11	7		8				6		10							34
	3	4	5	6					10	9				8			7				1	11					35
	3	4	5	6					10	9				8			7					11					36
	3	4	5	6	11				10	9				8									7				37
	3	4		6	11					9		7	10	8	2									5			38
	3	4			11				10	9		7		8	2			6						5			39
	3	4	5		11				10	9				8				6							7		40
	3	4	5	6					10	9				8			11								7		41
	3	4	5	6					10	9			8				11									7	42
	41	42	40	38	32	3	5	11	35	37	3	28	5	33	3	1	8	4	1	2	1	2	1	2	2	1	
		11			2	1	3		26	32		3	1	7					1	1							

…rns WW	Taylor F	Galley T	Cullis S	Gardiner JB	Maguire JE	Barlow H	Kirkham RJ	Thompson H	Dorsett R	Westcott D	Myers JH	Burton S	Wright HR	McIntosh A	Parker WD	McMahon D	Mullen J	Goddard R	Steen AW	McAloon GP	Sidlow C	McDonald JC	Tagg E	Rooney J	Brown HS	Marshall J	
	3	4	5	6	11				10	9		7		8													R3
	3	4	5	6	11				10	9		7		8													R4
	3	4	5	6	11				10	9		7		8													R5
	3	4	5	6	11				10	9				8			7										R6
	3	4	5	6	7				10	9				8			11										SF
	3	4	5	6	11				10	9		7		8													F
	6	6	6	6	6				6	6		4		6			2										
		1			2				3	11		1		2													

1946-47

Division One

Manager: Ted Vizard

	P	W	D	L	F	A	Pts
Liverpool	42	25	7	10	84	52	57
Manchester United	42	22	12	8	95	54	56
Wolverhampton Wanderers	42	25	6	11	98	56	56
Stoke City	42	24	7	11	90	53	55
Blackpool	42	22	6	14	71	70	50
Sheffield United	42	21	7	14	89	75	49
Preston North End	42	18	11	13	76	74	47
Aston Villa	42	18	9	15	67	53	45
Sunderland	42	18	8	16	65	66	44
Everton	42	17	9	16	62	67	43
Middlesbrough	42	17	8	17	73	68	42
Portsmouth	42	16	9	17	66	60	41
Arsenal	42	16	9	17	72	70	41
Derby County	42	18	5	19	73	79	41
Chelsea	42	16	7	19	69	84	39
Grimsby Town	42	13	12	17	61	82	38
Blackburn Rovers	42	14	8	20	45	53	36
Bolton Wanderers	42	13	8	21	57	69	34
Charlton Athletic	42	11	12	19	57	71	34
Huddersfield Town	42	13	7	22	53	79	33
Brentford	42	9	7	26	45	88	25
Leeds United	42	6	6	30	45	90	18

Did you know that?

- Dennis Westcott was the Football League's top scorer this season with 38 goals. His haul still remains a Wolves record for most scored in any division.
- Jesse Pye scored a hat-trick on his League debut for Wolves against Arsenal.
- Billy Wright won the first of his record-breaking 105 caps for England against Northern Ireland in Belfast in September.
- A total of 16 players made their Football League debuts for Wolves this season.
- This remains the longest League season on record, at 274 days.
- Stan Cullis retired as a player after making 171 senior appearances for Wolves.

Match No.	Date		Venue	Opponents	Result		Scorers	At
1	Aug	31	H	Arsenal	W	6-1	Pye 3, Westcott 2, Mullen	
2	Sep	3	A	Grimsby Town	D	0-0		
3		7	A	Blackpool	L	0-2		
4		11	H	Aston Villa	L	1-2	Pye	
5		14	H	Brentford	L	1-2	Westcott	
6		16	A	Aston Villa	L	0-3		
7		21	A	Blackburn Rovers	W	2-1	Westcott 2	
8		23	H	Grimsby Town	W	2-0	Pye 2	
9		28	H	Portsmouth	W	3-1	Galley (pen), King, Westcott	
10	Oct	5	A	Everton	W	2-0	Westcott, Wright	
11		12	H	Huddersfield Town	W	6-1	Pye 2, Crook, Galley (pen), Hancocks, Westcott	
12		19	H	Leeds United	W	1-0	Hancocks	
13		26	A	Stoke City	W	3-0	Pye 2, Mullen	
14	Nov	2	H	Middlesbrough	L	2-4	Mullen, Pye	
15		9	A	Charlton Athletic	W	4-1	Mullen 2, Westcott 2	
16		16	H	Sheffield United	W	3-1	Westcott 2, Pye	
17		23	A	Preston North End	D	2-2	Forbes 2	
18		30	H	Manchester United	W	3-2	Westcott 2, Hancocks	
19	Dec	7	A	Liverpool	W	5-1	Westcott 4, Mullen	
20		14	H	Bolton Wanderers	W	5-0	Westcott 4, Pye	
21		21	A	Chelsea	W	2-1	Forbes, Mullen	
22		25	A	Sunderland	W	1-0	Hancocks	
23		26	H	Sunderland	W	2-1	Galley, King	
24		28	A	Arsenal	D	1-1	King	
25	Jan	4	H	Blackpool	W	3-1	Forbes, Pye, Westcott	
26		18	A	Brentford	L	1-4	Westcott	
27	Feb	22	A	Leeds United	W	1-0	Westcott	
28	Mar	1	H	Stoke City	W	3-0	Mullen, Forbes, Westcott	
29		8	A	Middlesbrough	D	1-1	Westcott	
30		15	H	Charlton Athletic	W	2-0	Mullen, Westcott	
31		22	A	Sheffield United	L	0-2		
32		29	H	Preston North End	W	4-1	Hancocks, Pye, Ramscar, Westcott	
33	Apr	5	A	Manchester United	L	1-3	Westcott	
34		7	A	Derby County	L	1-2	Westcott	
35		8	H	Derby County	W	7-2	Pye 3, Westcott 2, Forbes, Hancocks	
36		19	A	Bolton Wanderers	W	3-0	Hancocks, Mullen, Pye	
37		26	H	Chelsea	W	6-4	Forbes 2, Hancocks 2, Westcott 2	
38	May	3	A	Portsmouth	D	1-1	Westcott	
39		10	H	Everton	L	2-3	Mullen, Westcott	
40		17	H	Blackburn Rovers	D	3-3	Galley, Pye, Westcott	
41		26	A	Huddersfield Town	W	1-0	Hancocks	
42		31	H	Liverpool	L	1-2	Dunn	

Appear

FA Cup

R3	Jan	11	H	Rotherham United	W	3-0	Hancocks, Pye, Westcott
R4		25	H	Sheffield United	D	0-0	
rep		29	A	Sheffield United	L	0-2	

Appear

Morris WW	McLean A	Galley T	Cullis S	Wright WA	Hancocks J	Pye J	Westcott D	Ramscar FT	Mullen J	Dorsett R	Crook WC	Chatham RH	McIntosh A	Alderton JH	Ratcliffe PC	King FAR	Elliott E	Pritchard RT	Forbes W	Dunn J	Miller D	
2	3	4	5	6	7	8	9	10	11													1
2	3	4	5	6	7	8	9		11	10												2
2	3	5		6	7	8	9	10	11		4											3
2	3	4	5	6	7	8		10	11			9										4
2	3	5		6	7		9	10	11		4		8									5
2	5	6					9	10	11		8			4	3	7						6
2	3	4	5		7	8	9	10	11		6											7
2		4	5	10	7	8	9		11		6				3		1					8
2	3	4	5			8	9	10	11		6					7	1					9
2	3	4	5	10	11	8	9				6					7	1					10
	2	4	5	6	7	8	9		11		10							3				11
	2	4	5	6	7	8	9	10	11		3											12
	2	4	5	6	7	9			11		3			8					10			13
	2		5	6	7	9		10	11		3			8						4		14
	2		5	4	7	8	9		11		3								10		6	15
	2	4	5	6	7	8	9		11		3								10			16
	2	4	5	6	7	8	9		11		3								10			17
	2	4	5	6	7	8	9		11		3								10			18
	2	4	5	6	7	8	9		11		3								10			19
	2	4	5	6	7	8	9		11		3								10			20
	2	4	5	6	7	9			11		3		8						10			21
	2	4	5	6	7	8	9		11		3								10			22
	2	4	5	6	11		9				3		8			7			10			23
	2	4	5	6	11			8			3	9				7			10			24
	2		5	6	11	8	9				4					7		3	10			25
	2		5		7	8	9		11		4							3	10		6	26
	2	4	5	6	7	8	9		11		3								10			27
	2	4	5	6	7		9	8	11		3								10			28
	2	4	5		7		9	8	11		3			6					10			29
	2	5		6	7		9	8	11		3			4					10			30
	2	5		6	7		9	8	11		3			4					10			31
	2	4	5	6	7	10	9	8	11		3											32
	2	4	5	6	7	8	9	10	11		3											33
	2	4	5	6	7	8	9		11		3								10			34
	2		5	6	7	8	9		11		3			4					10			35
	2	4	5	6	7	8	9		11		3								10			36
	2	4	5	6	7	8	9		11		3								10			37
	2	4	5		7	8	9		11		3			6					10			38
	2	4	5	6	7	8	9		11		3								10			39
	2	4	5		7	8	9		11		3			6					10			40
	2		5		7	9			11		4			6				3	10	8		41
	2		5	6	7	9			11		3			4					10	8		42
0	41	35	37	34	40	34	35	16	38	1	39	2	3	11	2	6	3	4	27	3	2	
		4		1	10	20	38	1	11		1					3			8	1		
	2	4	5	6	11	8	9				3					7			10			R3
	3		5	6	11	8	9				4					7			10			R4
	2	4	5	6	11	8	9	10			3					7						rep
	3	2	3	3	3	3	3	1			3					3			2			
					1	1	1															

1947-48

Division One

Manager: Ted Vizard

	P	W	D	L	F	A	Pts
Arsenal	42	23	13	6	81	32	59
Manchester United	42	19	14	9	81	48	52
Burnley	42	20	12	10	56	43	52
Derby County	42	19	12	11	77	57	50
Wolverhampton Wanderers	42	19	9	14	83	70	47
Aston Villa	42	19	9	14	65	57	47
Preston North End	42	20	7	15	67	68	47
Portsmouth	42	19	7	16	68	50	45
Blackpool	42	17	10	15	57	41	44
Manchester City	42	15	12	15	52	47	42
Liverpool	42	16	10	16	65	61	42
Sheffield United	42	16	10	16	65	70	42
Charlton Athletic	42	17	6	19	57	66	40
Everton	42	17	6	19	52	66	40
Stoke City	42	14	10	18	41	55	38
Middlesbrough	42	14	9	19	71	73	37
Bolton Wanderers	42	16	5	21	46	58	37
Chelsea	42	14	9	19	53	71	37
Huddersfield Town	42	12	12	18	51	60	36
Sunderland	42	13	10	19	56	67	36
Blackburn Rovers	42	11	10	21	54	72	32
Grimsby Town	42	8	6	28	45	111	22

Did you know that?

- For safety reasons, some 5,000 fans were locked out of the Aston Villa versus Wolves League game on Boxing Day.
- Billy Crook took over the captaincy from Stan Cullis.
- Sammy Smyth was signed from the Irish club Dundella and Gordon Brice arrived from Luton Town.
- Out of Molineux went Dennis Westcott, sold to Blackburn Rovers after scoring 124 goals in 144 League and Cup games, Alex Scott to Crewe Alexandra, Teddy Maguire to Swindon Town and Tom Galley to Grimsby Town.
- Stan Cullis became the first former Wolves player to manage the club since Jack Addenbrooke in 1922.

Match No.	Date		Venue	Opponents	Result		Scorers	Atte
1	Aug	23	A	Manchester City	L	3-4	Galley (pen), Hancocks, Westcott	6
2		27	H	Grimsby Town	W	8-1	Pye 3, Smyth 2, Westcott 2, Hancocks	4
3		30	H	Blackburn Rovers	W	5-1	Hancocks, Mullen, Pye, Smith, Westcott	4
4	Sep	3	A	Grimsby Town	W	4-0	Forbes 2, Hancocks, Pye	2
5		6	A	Blackpool	D	2-2	Forbes, Hancocks	3
6		10	H	Middlesbrough	L	1-3	Mullen	4
7		13	H	Derby County	W	1-0	Pye	5
8		20	A	Huddersfield Town	W	1-0	Pye	2
9		27	H	Chelsea	W	1-0	Forbes	5
10	Oct	4	A	Everton	D	1-1	Hancocks	4
11		11	A	Charlton Athletic	L	1-5	Mullen	4
12		18	H	Arsenal	D	1-1	Pye	5
13		25	A	Sheffield United	D	2-2	Smyth, Wright	4
14	Nov	1	H	Manchester United	L	2-6	Dunn, Hancocks (pen)	4
15		8	A	Burnley	D	1-1	Mullen	3
16		15	H	Portsmouth	W	3-1	Forbes 2, Mullen	3
17		22	A	Preston North End	W	3-1	Forbes, McLean, Pye	2
18		29	H	Stoke City	L	1-2	Pye	3
19	Dec	6	A	Bolton Wanderers	L	2-3	Mullen, Smyth	2
20		13	H	Liverpool	L	1-2	Forbes	3
21		20	H	Manchester City	W	1-0	Westcott	3
22		26	A	Aston Villa	W	2-1	Hancocks, Westcott	6
23		27	H	Aston Villa	W	4-1	Hancocks 2, Mullen, Westcott	5
24	Jan	1	A	Middlesbrough	W	4-2	Westcott 3, Hancocks	3
25		3	A	Blackburn Rovers	L	0-1		2
26		17	H	Blackpool	D	1-1	Hancocks	4
27	Feb	7	H	Huddersfield Town	W	2-1	Dunn, Wright	3
28		14	A	Chelsea	D	1-1	Hancocks (pen)	5
29		21	H	Everton	L	2-4	Dunn, Westcott	2
30		28	H	Charlton Athletic	W	2-0	Hancocks, Pye	2
31	Mar	6	A	Arsenal	L	2-5	Hancocks, Smyth	5
32		13	H	Sheffield United	D	1-1	Wright	3
33		20	A	Manchester United	L	2-3	Dunn, Smyth	5
34		26	A	Sunderland	L	1-2	Wright	5
35		27	H	Burnley	D	1-1	Dunn	3
36		29	H	Sunderland	W	2-1	Smyth, Wright	3
37	Apr	3	A	Portsmouth	L	0-2		2
38		10	H	Preston North End	W	4-2	Pye 2, Dunn, Hancocks (pen)	2
39		14	A	Derby County	W	2-1	Dunn, Pye	1
40		17	A	Stoke City	W	3-2	Dunn, Mullen, Pye	2
41		24	H	Bolton Wanderers	W	1-0	Dunn	2
42	May	1	A	Liverpool	L	1-2	Pye	3

Appeara

FA Cup

R3	Jan	10	A	Bournemouth	W	2-1	Mullen 2	2
R4		24	H	Everton	D	1-1	Westcott	4
rep		31	A	Everton	L	2-3	Westcott 2	

R4 and R4 replay aet

Appeara

McLean A	Shorthouse WH	Galley T	Brice GHJ	Wright WA	Hancocks J	Pye J	Westcott D	Smyth S	Mullen J	Pritchard RT	Forbes W	Crook WC	Dunn J	Elliott E	Kelly L	Stevenson E	Mynard LD	Springthorpe TA	Chatham RH	Simpson A	Smith LJ	
2	3	4	5	6	7	8	9	10	11													1
2		4	5	6	7	8	9	10	11	3												2
2		4	5	6	7	8	9	10	11	3												3
2		4	5	6	7	8		10	11	3	9											4
2			5	6	7	8		10	11	3	9	4										5
2		4	5	6	7	8		10	11	3	9											6
2			5	6	7	8	9		11	3	10	4										7
2			5		7	8	9	10	11	3	6	4										8
2			5	6	7	8		10	11	3	9	4										9
2		4	5	6	7	8			11	3	9		10									10
2			5	6	7	8		10	11	3	9	4										11
2	5				7	8	9	10	11	3	6	4		1								12
	5			6	7	8	9	10	11	3	4											13
	5			6	7		9	10	11	3	4		8									14
	5			6	7			10	11	3	9	4	8									15
	5			6	7			10	11	3	9	4	8									16
	5			6	7	8		10	11	3	9	4										17
	5			6	7	8		10	11	3	9	4										18
	5			6	7	8		10	11	3	9	4										19
			5	6		8		10	11		9	4	7		2							20
	5			6	7	8	9		11			4	10		2							21
	5			6	7	8	9		11			4	10		2							22
	5			6	7	8	9		11			4	10		2							23
	5			6	7		9		11			4	8		2	10						24
	5			6	7				11		9	4	8		2	10						25
	5			6	7		9		11			4	8		2	10						26
	5			6	7		9				10	4	8	1	2		11					27
	5			6	7		9					4	8	1	2	10	11					28
	5			6	7		9					4	8	1	2	10	11					29
	5			6	11	8	9	10		3		4	7									30
	5			6	11	8	9	10		3		4	7									31
	5			6	11	8	9	10				4	7		2			3				32
	5			6	11	8	9	10				4	7		2			3				33
	5			6	7	8	9	10	11			4			2			3				34
	5			6	7	9		10	11			4	8		2			3				35
	5			8			9	10	11			4	7		2			3	6			36
	5			6		9		10	11		8		7		2			3	4			37
	5				7	9		10	11			6	8		2			3	4			38
	5			4	11	9						7	8		2	10		3	6			39
				6		9		10	11			4	8		2			3		5	7	40
	5			6	7	9		10	11				8		2			3	4			41
	5			6		9		10	11				8		2			3	4		7	42
	30	6	12	39	37	32	22	30	34	20	20	31	26	4	21	6	3	11	6	1	2	
		1		5	16	16	11	8	8		8		9									

McLean A	Shorthouse WH	Galley T	Brice GHJ	Wright WA	Hancocks J	Pye J	Westcott D	Smyth S	Mullen J	Pritchard RT	Forbes W	Crook WC	Dunn J	Elliott E	Kelly L	Stevenson E	Mynard LD	Springthorpe TA	Chatham RH	Simpson A	Smith LJ	
	5			6	7		9		11			4	8		2	10						R3
	5			6	7	8	9		11		10	4			2							R4
	5			6	7		9		11		10	4	8		2							rep
	3			3	3	1	3		3		2	3	2		3	1						
							3		2													

1948-49

Division One

Manager: Stan Cullis

	P	W	D	L	F	A	Pts
Portsmouth	42	25	8	9	84	42	58
Manchester United	42	21	11	10	77	44	53
Derby County	42	22	9	11	74	55	53
Newcastle United	42	20	12	10	70	56	52
Arsenal	42	18	13	11	74	44	49
Wolverhampton Wanderers	42	17	12	13	79	66	46
Manchester City	42	15	15	12	47	51	45
Sunderland	42	13	17	12	49	58	43
Charlton Athletic	42	15	12	15	63	67	42
Aston Villa	42	16	10	16	60	76	42
Stoke City	42	16	9	17	66	68	41
Liverpool	42	13	14	15	53	43	40
Chelsea	42	12	14	16	69	68	38
Bolton Wanderers	42	14	10	18	59	68	38
Burnley	42	12	14	16	43	50	38
Blackpool	42	11	16	15	54	67	38
Birmingham City	42	11	15	16	36	38	37
Everton	42	13	11	18	41	63	37
Middlesbrough	42	11	12	19	46	57	34
Huddersfield Town	42	12	10	20	40	69	34
Preston North End	42	11	11	20	62	75	33
Sheffield United	42	11	11	20	57	78	33

Did you know that?

- Dennis Wilshaw scored a hat-trick on his League debut for Wolves versus Newcastle United in mid-March.
- Alf Crook made his debut for Wolves in the FA Cup semi-final replay against Manchester United and his League debut followed four days later. These were his only two first-class appearances for the club he served for seven years (1942–49).
- Ernie Stevenson moved to Cardiff City and goalkeeper Nigel Sims was signed from Stapenhill (as cover for Bert Williams).
- The biggest crowd ever to watch a Wolves team in action – almost 99,000 – attended the FA Cup Final.

Match No.	Date		Venue	Opponents	Result		Scorers
1	Aug	21	H	Birmingham City	D	2-2	Pye, Smith
2		25	H	Sunderland	L	0-1	
3		28	A	Bolton Wanderers	W	5-0	Hancocks 2, Mullen 2, Pye
4	Sep	1	A	Sunderland	D	3-3	Hancocks 2 (1 pen), Pye
5		4	H	Liverpool	D	0-0	
6		8	H	Manchester United	W	3-2	Hancocks 2, Smyth
7		11	A	Blackpool	W	3-1	Smyth 2, Dunn
8		15	A	Manchester United	L	0-2	
9		18	H	Derby County	D	2-2	Hancocks, Mullen
10		25	A	Arsenal	L	1-3	Smyth
11	Oct	2	H	Huddersfield Town	W	7-1	Pye 3, Forbes 2, Hancocks 2 (1 pen)
12		9	H	Middlesbrough	L	0-3	
13		16	A	Newcastle United	L	1-3	Smith
14		23	H	Portsmouth	W	3-0	Hancocks, Ferrier, Wright
15		30	A	Manchester City	D	3-3	Pye, Smith, McDowall (og)
16	Nov	6	H	Charlton Athletic	W	2-0	Smyth, Wright
17		13	A	Stoke City	L	1-2	Smyth
18		20	H	Burnley	W	3-0	Mullen, Pye, Smyth
19		27	A	Preston North End	D	1-1	Pye
20	Dec	4	H	Everton	W	1-0	Pye
21		11	A	Chelsea	L	1-4	Hancocks
22		18	A	Birmingham City	W	1-0	Pye
23		25	H	Aston Villa	W	4-0	Pye 2, Smyth 2
24		27	A	Aston Villa	L	1-5	Dunn
25	Jan	1	H	Bolton Wanderers	W	2-0	Mullen 2
26		22	H	Blackpool	W	2-1	Dunn, Pye
27	Feb	5	A	Derby County	L	2-3	Smyth 2
28		19	H	Arsenal	L	1-3	Pye (pen)
29	Mar	5	A	Middlesbrough	D	4-4	Pye 2, Mullen, Smyth
30		12	H	Newcastle United	W	3-0	Wilshaw 3
31		19	A	Burnley	D	0-0	
32	Apr	6	A	Liverpool	D	0-0	
33		9	H	Stoke City	W	3-1	Wilshaw 2, Dunn
34		13	A	Charlton Athletic	W	3-2	Wilshaw 2, Smyth
35		16	A	Portsmouth	L	0-5	
36		18	A	Sheffield United	D	1-1	Mullen
37		19	H	Sheffield United	W	6-0	Dunn 2, Mullen 2, Wilshaw 2
38		23	H	Manchester City	D	1-1	Wilshaw
39	May	2	H	Preston North End	W	2-1	Hancocks, Mullen
40		4	A	Everton	L	0-1	
41		5	A	Huddersfield Town	L	0-4	
42		7	H	Chelsea	D	1-1	Mullen

Appear

Two own-goals

FA Cup

R3	Jan	8	H	Chesterfield	W	6-0	Pye 2, Smyth 2, Hancocks, Mullen
R4		29	A	Sheffield United	W	3-0	Hancocks 2, Dunn
R5	Feb	12	H	Liverpool	W	3-1	Dunn, Mullen, Smyth
R6		26	H	West Bromwich Albion	W	1-0	Mullen
SF	Mar	26	N	Manchester United	D	1-1	Smyth
rep	Apr	2	N	Manchester United	W	1-0	Smyth
F		30	N	Leicester City	W	3-1	Pye 2, Smyth

SF at Hillsborough, aet SF replay at Goodison Park. Appear

Final at Wembley Stadium.

McLean A	Springthorpe TA	Chatham RH	Shorthouse WH	Wright WA	Hancocks J	Dunn J	Pye J	Smyth S	Mullen J	Forbes W	Crook WC	Stevenson E	Simpson A	Pritchard RT	Kelly L	Baxter W	Parsons DR	Russell ET	Smith LJ	Wishaw DJ	Crook AR	Sims ND	
2	3	4	5	6	7	8	9	10	11														1
2	3		5	6	7	8	9	10	11	4													2
2	3		5	6	7		9	8	11	10	4												3
2	3		5	6	7		9	8	11	10	4												4
2	3		5		7		9	8	11	6	4	10											5
2	3		5	6	7	8	9	10	11		4												6
2	3		5	6	7	8	9	10	11		4												7
2	3		5	6	7	8	9	10	11		4												8
2	3			4	7	8	9	10	11	6			5										9
2			5		7	8	9	10	11	6	4			3									10
2			5	6	7	8	9		11	10	4			3									11
			5		7	8	9		11	6	4	10		3	2								12
2			5	6	7		9	8	11	10	4			3									13
			5	6	7		9	10	11	8	4			3	2								14
			5	6	7	8	9	10	11		4			3	2								15
			5	6	7		9	10	11	8	4			3	2								16
			5	6	7		9	10	11	8	4			3	2								17
			5	6	7		9	10	11	8	4			3	2								18
			5	6	7	8	9	10	11	4				3	2								19
			5	6	7		9	10	11	8				3	2	4							20
			5	6	7	8	9	10	11					3	2	4							21
			5	6	7	8	9	10	11		4			3	2								22
			5	6	7	8	9	10	11		4			3	2								23
			5	6	7	8	9	10	11		4			3	2		1						24
			5	6	7	10	9	8	11		4			3	2								25
			5	6	7	10	9	8	11		4			3	2								26
			5	6	7	10	9	8	11		4			3	2								27
3			5	6			9	10	11		8				2			4	7				28
			5	6		10	9	8	11		4			3	2				7				29
			5	6		10	9	8			4			3	2				7	11			30
			5	6		10	9	8	11		4			3	2				7				31
	3		5		7	10	9	8	11		6					4					2		32
	3		5		7	10		8	11		6			2		4				9			33
	3		5	6	7	10		8	11		4			2						9			34
	3	5			11	8				10	6			2		4			7	9			35
	3		5	6	7	10		8	11		4			2						9		1	36
	3	5		6	7	10		8	11		4			2						9		1	37
	3		5	6	7	10		8	11		4			2						9		1	38
	3		5	6	7		9	8	11		4			2						10			39
			5	6	11			10			8			3	2			4	7	9			40
	3	6	5		11			10			8				2			4	7	9			41
	3		5	6	7			10	11		8			2				4		9		1	42
3	19	4	39	35	38	28	33	39	38	16	36	2	1	30	21	5	1	4	7	11	1	4	
				2	12	6	17	16	12	2										10			

McLean A	Springthorpe TA	Chatham RH	Shorthouse WH	Wright WA	Hancocks J	Dunn J	Pye J	Smyth S	Mullen J	Forbes W	Crook WC	Stevenson E	Simpson A	Pritchard RT	Kelly L	Baxter W	Parsons DR	Russell ET	Smith LJ	Wishaw DJ	Crook AR	Sims ND	
			5	6	7	10	9	8	11		4			3	2								R3
			5	6	7	10	9	8	11		4			3	2								R4
			5	6	7	10	9	8	11		4			3	2								R5
			5	6	7	10	9	8	11		4			3	2								R6
			5	6	7	10	9	8	11		4			3	2								SF
	3		5	6	7	10	9	8	11		4										2		rep
	3		5	6	7	10	9	8	11		4			2									F
	2		7	7	7	7	7	7	7		7			6	5						1		
					3	2	4	6	3														

1949-50

Division One

Manager: Stan Cullis

	P	W	D	L	F	A	Pts
Portsmouth	42	22	9	11	74	38	53
Wolverhampton Wanderers	42	20	13	9	76	49	53
Sunderland	42	21	10	11	83	62	52
Manchester United	42	18	14	10	69	44	50
Newcastle United	42	19	12	11	77	55	50
Arsenal	42	19	11	12	79	55	49
Blackpool	42	17	15	10	46	35	49
Liverpool	42	17	14	11	64	54	48
Middlesbrough	42	20	7	15	59	48	47
Burnley	42	16	13	13	40	40	45
Derby County	42	17	10	15	69	61	44
Aston Villa	42	15	12	15	61	61	42
Chelsea	42	12	16	14	58	65	40
West Bromwich Albion	42	14	12	16	47	53	40
Huddersfield Town	42	14	9	19	52	73	37
Bolton Wanderers	42	10	14	18	45	59	34
Fulham	42	10	14	18	41	54	34
Everton	42	10	14	18	42	66	34
Stoke City	42	11	12	19	45	75	34
Charlton Athletic	42	13	6	23	53	65	32
Manchester City	42	8	13	21	36	68	29
Birmingham City	42	7	14	21	31	67	28

Did you know that?

• Wolves winger Jimmy Mullen became England's first-ever substitute when he replaced the injured Jackie Milburn against Belgium in Brussels in May 1950.

• Wolves achieved their best seasonal average League attendance this season – 46,295.

• A record Hawthorns League crowd of 60,945 witnessed the derby between Albion and Wolves in March – the day future Wolves manager Ronnie Allen made his debut for the Baggies.

• Three Wolves players – Jimmy Mullen, Bert Williams and Billy Wright – went to the World Cup Finals with England.

• Willie Forbes (to Preston North End), Laurie Kelly (to Huddersfield Town) and Terry Springthorpe (to Coventry City) were among the players who left Molineux this season.

Match No.	Date		Venue	Opponents	Result		Scorers
1	Aug	20	A	Fulham	W	2-1	Hancocks, Mullen
2		24	A	Charlton Athletic	W	3-2	Forbes, Pye, Wright
3		27	H	Newcastle United	W	2-1	Forbes, Pye
4		29	H	Charlton Athletic	W	2-1	Smyth, Wright
5	Sep	3	A	Blackpool	W	2-1	Mullen, Smyth
6		10	H	Middlesbrough	W	3-1	Dunn, Hancocks (pen), Smyth
7		14	A	Birmingham City	D	1-1	Dorman (og)
8		17	A	Everton	W	2-1	Mullen, Pye
9		24	H	Huddersfield Town	W	7-1	Pye 3, Forbes 2, Mullen, Smyth
10	Oct	1	A	Portsmouth	D	1-1	Pye
11		8	A	Derby County	W	2-1	Hancocks, Mullen
12		15	H	West Bromwich Albion	D	1-1	Pye
13		22	A	Manchester United	L	0-3	
14		29	H	Chelsea	D	2-2	Smyth 2
15	Nov	5	A	Stoke City	L	1-2	Hancocks
16		12	H	Burnley	D	0-0	
17		19	A	Sunderland	L	1-3	Forbes
18		26	H	Liverpool	D	1-1	Wilshaw
19	Dec	3	A	Arsenal	D	1-1	Mullen
20		10	H	Bolton Wanderers	D	1-1	Wilshaw
21		17	H	Fulham	D	1-1	Pye
22		24	A	Newcastle United	L	0-2	
23		26	H	Aston Villa	L	2-3	Smyth, Swinbourne
24		27	A	Aston Villa	W	4-1	Swinbourne 2, Pye, Smyth
25		31	H	Blackpool	W	3-0	Hancocks, Mullen, Pye
26	Jan	14	A	Middlesbrough	L	0-2	
27		21	H	Everton	D	1-1	Wilshaw
28	Feb	4	A	Huddersfield Town	L	0-1	
29		18	H	Portsmouth	W	1-0	McLean
30		25	H	Derby County	W	4-1	Pye 2, Walker 2
31	Mar	4	A	West Bromwich Albion	D	1-1	Hancocks
32		11	H	Sunderland	L	1-3	Smyth
33		18	A	Liverpool	W	2-0	Hancocks, Swinbourne
34		25	H	Stoke City	W	2-1	Hancocks (pen), Swinbourne
35	Apr	1	A	Burnley	W	1-0	Walker
36		8	H	Manchester United	D	1-1	Walker
37		10	A	Manchester City	L	1-2	Walker
38		11	H	Manchester City	W	3-0	Hancocks (pen), Pye, Swinbourne
39		15	A	Chelsea	D	0-0	
40		22	H	Arsenal	W	3-0	Walker 2, Pye
41		29	A	Bolton Wanderers	W	4-2	Hancocks, Mullen, Pye, Wright
42	May	6	H	Birmingham City	W	6-1	Mullen 2, Pye 2, Swinbourne, Walker

Appea

One own-goal

FA Cup

R3	Jan	7	A	Plymouth Argyle	D	1-1	Smyth
rep		11	H	Plymouth Argyle	W	3-0	Hancocks (pen), Smyth, Swinbourne
R4		28	H	Sheffield United	D	0-0	
rep	Feb	1	A	Sheffield United	W	4-3	Hancocks 2 (1 pen), Mullen, Smyth
R5		11	H	Blackpool	D	0-0	
rep		15	A	Blackpool	L	0-1	

Appea

	Kelly L	Pritchard RT	Crook WC	Shorthouse WH	Wright WA	Hancocks J	Smyth S	Pye J	Dunn J	Mullen J	Forbes W	McLean A	Wilshaw DJ	Springthorpe TA	Parsons DR	Russell ET	Smith LJ	Chatham RH	Swinbourne RH	Baxter W	Rowley KF	Walker JH	Sims ND
1	2	3	4	5	6	7	8	9	10	11													
2	2	3	4	5	6	7	8	9		11	10												
3	2	3	4	5	6	7	8	9		11	10												
4	2	3	4	5	6	7	10	9		11	8												
5		3	4	5	6	7	8	9		11		2	10										
6		3	4	5	6	7	8	9	10	11		2											
7		3	4	5	6	7	8	9	10	11		2											
8		3	4	5	6	7	10	9		11	8	2											
9		3	4	5	6	7	10	9		11	8	2											
10	2		4	5	6	7		9		11	8		10	3									
11	2		4	5	6	7	8	9	10	11				3									
12	2		4	5			8	9	10	11				3	1	6	7						
13	2		6			7	8	9	10	11				3	1	4		5					
14	2		6	5		7	8	9	10	11		3			1	4							
15	2		8	5	6	7	10	9		11		3			1	4							
16	2	3		5	6	7	10	9		11	8					4							
17		3		5	6	7	10	9		11	8	2				4							
18		3		5	4	7	10	8		11		2	9			6							
19		3		5	4	7	10	8		11		2	9			6							
20		3		5	6	7	10	8		11		2	9			4							
21		3	4	5			10	9		11		2				6	7		8				
22		3	4	5	6			9		11		2				10	7		8				
23		3	4	5	6	7	10	9		11		2							8				
24		3	4		6	7	10	9		11		2						5	8				
25	2	3	4			7	10	9		11		6						5	8				
26	2	3	4	5	6	7	10						11					9	8				
27		3	4	5		7	10	9				2	11			6			8				
28	3			5	6	7	8	9		11		2			1					4	10		
29	2	3		5	6					11		9					7		10	4		8	
30		3	4	5	6	7		9		11		2							10			8	
31		3	4	5	6	7		9		11		2							10			8	
32				5	6	7	10	9		11		2		3						4		8	
33		3	4	5	6	7		10		11		2							9			8	
34		3	4	5	6	7		10		11		2							9			8	
35	[illegible]		4	5	6	7		10		11		2							9			8	
36	[illegible]		4	5	6	7		10		11		2							9			8	
37	[illegible]		4	5	6	7				11		2	10						9			8	
38			4	3	6	7	8	10		11		2						5	9				
39			4	3		7	8	10		11		2				6		5	9				1
40			4	3	6	7		10		11		2						5	9			8	
41			4	3	6	7		10		11		2						5	9			8	
42			4	3	6	7		10		11		2						5	9			8	
	3	26	34	39	35	38	29	39	7	40	8	32	8	5	5	13	4	9	20	3	1	12	1
					3	10	9	18	1	10	5	1	3						7			8	

	Kelly L	Pritchard RT	Crook WC	Shorthouse WH	Wright WA	Hancocks J	Smyth S	Pye J	Dunn J	Mullen J	Forbes W	McLean A	Wilshaw DJ	Springthorpe TA	Parsons DR	Russell ET	Smith LJ	Chatham RH	Swinbourne RH	Baxter W	Rowley KF	Walker JH	Sims ND
R3		3	4		6	7	10	9		11		2						5	8				
rep		3	4		6	7	10	9		11		2						5	8				
R4		3	4	5	6	7	10	9		11		2									8		
rep		3	4	5	6	7	8	9		11		2									10		
R5		3	4	5	6	7	8	9		11		2							10				
rep		3	4	5	6		8	9		11		2					7		10				
		6	6	4	6	5	6	6		6		6					1	2	4		2		
						3	3			1									1				

1950-51

Division One

Manager: Stan Cullis

	P	W	D	L	F	A	Pts
Tottenham Hotspur	42	25	10	7	82	44	60
Manchester United	42	24	8	10	74	40	56
Blackpool	42	20	10	12	79	53	50
Newcastle United	42	18	13	11	62	53	49
Arsenal	42	19	9	14	73	56	47
Middlesbrough	42	18	11	13	76	65	47
Portsmouth	42	16	15	11	71	68	47
Bolton Wanderers	42	19	7	16	64	61	45
Liverpool	42	16	11	15	53	59	43
Burnley	42	14	14	14	48	43	42
Derby County	42	16	8	18	81	75	40
Sunderland	42	12	16	14	63	73	40
Stoke City	42	13	14	15	50	59	40
Wolverhampton Wanderers	42	15	8	19	74	61	38
Aston Villa	42	12	13	17	66	68	37
West Bromwich Albion	42	13	11	18	53	61	37
Charlton Athletic	42	14	9	19	63	80	37
Fulham	42	13	11	18	52	68	37
Huddersfield Town	42	15	6	21	64	92	36
Chelsea	42	12	8	22	53	65	32
Sheffield Wednesday	42	12	8	22	64	83	32
Everton	42	12	8	22	48	86	32

Did you know that?

- Bert Williams became England's first-choice goalkeeper.
- Inside-forward Peter Broadbent was signed from Brentford and Gus McLean left the club to sign for Aberystwyth.
- During May and June 1951, Wolves toured South Africa and scored 60 goals in 12 victories, including a 13–0 win over Eastern Transvaal.
- Johnny Hancocks became the first Wolves player to score a League hat-trick against arch-rivals West Bromwich Albion (December 1950).
- Wolves slipped from Championship contenders to relegation candidates in the space of two months (March and April).

Match No.	Date		Venue	Opponents	Result		Scorers	A
1	Aug	19	H	Liverpool	W	2-0	Crook, Swinbourne	
2		23	A	Derby County	W	2-1	Walker 2	
3		26	A	Fulham	L	1-2	Swinbourne	
4		28	H	Derby County	L	2-3	Dunn, Pye	
5	Sep	2	H	Bolton Wanderers	W	7-1	Swinbourne 3, Hancocks 2, Dunn, Mullen	
6		6	H	Sunderland	W	2-1	Hancocks (pen), Pye	
7		9	A	Blackpool	D	1-1	Swinbourne	
8		16	H	Tottenham Hotspur	W	2-1	Hancocks, Swinbourne	
9		23	A	Charlton Athletic	L	2-3	Mullen, Swinbourne	
10		30	H	Manchester United	D	0-0		
11	Oct	7	H	Middlesbrough	L	3-4	Dunn, Hancocks, Swinbourne	
12		14	A	Sheffield Wednesday	D	2-2	Hancocks, Mullen	
13		21	H	Chelsea	W	2-1	Hancocks, Swinbourne	
14		28	A	Portsmouth	W	4-1	Hancocks 2 (1 pen), Walker 2	
15	Nov	4	H	Arsenal	L	0-1		
16		11	A	Burnley	L	0-2		
17		18	H	Everton	W	4-0	Dunn, Hancocks (pen), Mullen, Swinbourne	
18		25	A	Stoke City	W	1-0	Dunn	
19	Dec	2	H	West Bromwich Albion	W	3-1	Hancocks 3	
20		9	A	Newcastle United	D	1-1	Hancocks	
21		16	A	Liverpool	W	4-1	Walker 2, Swinbourne, Wilshaw	
22		23	H	Fulham	D	1-1	Wilshaw	
23		25	A	Huddersfield Town	W	2-1	Swinbourne, Walker	
24		26	H	Huddersfield Town	W	3-1	Dunn, Hancocks (pen), Swinbourne	
25	Jan	13	H	Blackpool	D	1-1	Walker	
26		20	A	Tottenham Hotspur	L	1-2	Walker	
27	Feb	3	H	Charlton Athletic	L	2-3	Mullen, Walker	
28		17	A	Manchester United	L	1-2	Wilshaw	
29	Mar	3	H	Sheffield Wednesday	W	4-0	Hancocks 2, Swinbourne 2	
30		17	H	Portsmouth	L	2-3	Swinbourne, Walker	
31		24	A	Arsenal	L	1-2	Wilshaw	
32		26	H	Aston Villa	L	2-3	Hancocks (pen), Wilshaw	
33		27	A	Aston Villa	L	0-1		
34		31	H	Burnley	L	0-1		
35	Apr	7	A	Everton	D	1-1	Pye	
36		11	A	Middlesbrough	W	2-1	Swinbourne 2	
37		14	H	Stoke City	L	2-3	Dunn, Smith	
38		21	A	West Bromwich Albion	L	2-3	Broadbent, Hancocks (pen)	
39		25	A	Chelsea	L	1-2	Swinbourne	
40		28	A	Bolton Wanderers	L	1-2	Pye	
41	May	2	H	Newcastle United	L	0-1		
42		5	A	Sunderland	D	0-0		

Appear

FA Cup

R3	Jan	6	A	Plymouth Argyle	W	2-1	Dunn, Walker	
R4		27	H	Aston Villa	W	3-1	Mullen, Swinbourne, Walker	
R5	Feb	10	H	Huddersfield Town	W	2-0	Dunn 2	
R6		24	A	Sunderland	D	1-1	Walker	
rep		28	H	Sunderland	W	3-1	Dunn, Swinbourne, Walker	
SF	Mar	10	N	Newcastle United	D	0-0		
rep		14	N	Newcastle United	L	1-2	Walker	

SF at Hillsborough, Sheffield. SF replay at Leeds Road, Huddersfield.

Appeara

	McLean A	Shorthouse WH	Crook WC	Chatham RH	Wright WA	Dunn J	Walker JH	Swinbourne RH	Pye J	Mullen J	Pritchard RT	Hancocks J	Wilshaw DJ	Parsons DR	Russell ET	Smyth S	Short J	Broadbent PF	Smith LJ	Baxter W
1		3	4	5	6	7	8	9	10	11										
2		3	4	5	6	7	8	9	10	11										
3			4	5	6	7	8	9	10	11	3									
4		3	4	5	6	7	8	9	10	11										
5		3	4	5	6	8		9	10	11		7								
6		3	4	5	6	8		9	10	11		7								
7		3	4	5	6	8		9	10			7	11							
8		3	4	5	6	8		9	10	11		7								
9		3	4	5	6	8		9	10	11		7								
10		3	4	5	6	8		9	10	11		7		1						
11		3	4	5		8		9	10	11		7			6					
12		3	4	5	6	10		9	8	11		7								
13		2	4	5	6	10		9		11	3	7				8				
14		5		4	6		8	9	10	11	3	7								
15		5		4	6		8	9	10	11	3	7								
16		5		4	6	8		9	10	11	3	7								
17		5	4		6	8		9	10	11	3	7								
18		5	4		6	8		9	10	11	3	7								
19		5	4		6	8		9		11	3	7				10	2			
20		5	4		6	8		9		11	3	7				10	2			
21		5		4	6	8	10	9			3	7	11				2			
22		5		4	6	8	10	9			3	7	11	1			2			
23		5		4	6	8	10	9			3	7	11	1			2			
24		5	6	4	10	8		9			3	7	11				2			
25		5		4	6	8	10	9			3	7	11				2			
26		5	4		6	10	8	9		11	3	7					2			
27		5	4		6	10	8	9		11	3	7		1			2			
28		5			6		10		8	11	3	7	9				2			
29					6	10	8	9		11	3	7			4		2			
30		5			4		10	9		11	3	7			6		2	8		
31		5			6		8	9		11	3		10		4			7		
32		5			6			9	8	11	3	7	10		4		2			
33		5			6		8	9		11	3	7			4		2	10		
34		5			6		8	9		11	3	7			4			10		
35		5			6	10		9	8		3		11		4				7	
36		5	6			10		9	8		3		11	1	4				7	
37		5	6			10		9	8		3		11	1	4				7	
38		5	4		6		10	9			3	7	11					8		
39		5	4		6		10	9		11	3						2	8	7	
40			6			10		9	8	11	3				5		2	7		4
41			4		6	10		9		11		7			5		3	8		
42					6	10		9					11		5		3	8	7	4
		37	26	21	38	32	20	41	23	31	29	31	14	6	13	3	18	9	5	2
			1			7	11	20	4	5		19	5					1	1	

	McLean A	Shorthouse WH	Crook WC	Chatham RH	Wright WA	Dunn J	Walker JH	Swinbourne RH	Pye J	Mullen J	Pritchard RT	Hancocks J	Wilshaw DJ	Parsons DR	Russell ET	Smyth S	Short J	Broadbent PF	Smith LJ	Baxter W
R3		5		4	6	8	10	9			3	7	11				2			
R4		5	4		6	10	8	9		11	3	7					2			
R5		5		4	6	10	8	9		11	3	7					2			
R6		5			6	10	8	9		11	3	7			4		2			
rep		5			6	10	8	9		11	3	7			4		2			
SF		5			6	10	8	9		11	3	7			4		2			
rep		5			6	10	8	9		11	3	7			4		2			
		7	1	2	7	7	7	7		6	7	7	1		4		7			
						4	5	2		1										

1951-52

Division One

Manager: Stan Cullis

	P	W	D	L	F	A	Pts
Manchester United	42	23	11	8	95	52	57
Tottenham Hotspur	42	22	9	11	76	51	53
Arsenal	42	21	11	10	80	61	53
Portsmouth	42	20	8	14	68	58	48
Bolton Wanderers	42	19	10	13	65	61	48
Aston Villa	42	19	9	14	79	70	47
Preston North End	42	17	12	13	74	54	46
Newcastle United	42	18	9	15	98	73	45
Blackpool	42	18	9	15	64	64	45
Charlton Athletic	42	17	10	15	68	63	44
Liverpool	42	12	19	11	57	61	43
Sunderland	42	15	12	15	70	61	42
West Bromwich Albion	42	14	13	15	74	77	41
Burnley	42	15	10	17	56	63	40
Manchester City	42	13	13	16	58	61	39
Wolverhampton Wanderers	42	12	14	16	73	73	38
Derby County	42	15	7	20	63	80	37
Middlesbrough	42	15	6	21	64	88	36
Chelsea	42	14	8	20	52	72	36
Stoke City	42	12	7	23	49	88	31
Huddersfield Town	42	10	8	24	49	82	28
Fulham	42	8	11	23	58	77	27

Did you know that?

• Four goals were scored in the last five minutes of the Wolves versus Chelsea League game in September. The scoreline jumped from 4–0 to 5–3.

• Full-back Jack Short, playing as an emergency centre-forward, scored his only goals for Wolves in a 4–1 FA Cup win over Manchester City in January.

• Wolves captain Billy Wright was voted Footballer of the Year this season.

• Anfield's biggest-ever crowd – 61,905 – attended the FA Cup tie between Liverpool and Wolves in February.

• Eddie Stuart joined Wolves from Rangers FC (South Africa), while forwards Sammy Smyth and Jesse Pye moved to Stoke City and to Luton Town respectively.

Match No.	Date		Venue	Opponents	Result		Scorers	Att
1	Aug	18	A	Manchester City	D	0-0		4
2		22	H	Derby County	L	1-2	Hancocks	3
3		25	H	Arsenal	W	2-1	Hancocks (pen), Swinbourne	4
4		29	A	Derby County	W	3-1	Wilshaw 2, Dunn	2
5	Sep	1	A	Blackpool	L	2-3	Mullen, Smyth	3
6		8	H	Liverpool	W	2-1	Pye, Wilshaw	3
7		15	A	Portsmouth	W	3-2	Dunn, Hancocks, Mullen	3
8		22	H	Chelsea	W	5-3	Pye 2, Dunn, Hancocks (pen), Wilshaw	3
9		29	A	Huddersfield Town	W	7-1	Dunn 3, Mullen 2, Hancocks, Pye	3
10	Oct	6	A	Newcastle United	L	1-3	Walker	5
11		13	H	Bolton Wanderers	W	5-1	Pye 3, Dunn, Hancocks	3
12		20	A	Stoke City	L	0-1		4
13		27	H	Manchester United	L	0-2		4
14	Nov	3	A	Tottenham Hotspur	L	2-4	Mullen, Pye	6
15		10	H	Preston North End	L	1-4	Mullen	3
16		17	A	Burnley	D	2-2	Pye 2	2
17		24	H	Charlton Athletic	D	2-2	Dunn, Swinbourne	2
18	Dec	1	A	Fulham	D	2-2	Pye, Smith	3
19		8	H	Middlesbrough	W	4-0	Pye 2, Mullen, Swinbourne	2
20		15	H	Manchester City	D	2-2	Smith 2	2
21		22	A	Arsenal	D	2-2	Smith, Walker	4
22		25	A	Aston Villa	D	3-3	Baxter, Smith, Wilshaw	4
23		26	H	Aston Villa	L	1-2	Smith (pen)	5
24		29	H	Blackpool	W	3-0	Whitfield 3	3
25	Jan	1	A	Sunderland	D	1-1	Mullen	3
26		5	A	Liverpool	D	1-1	Smith	4
27		19	H	Portsmouth	D	1-1	Broadbent	
28		26	A	Chelsea	W	1-0	Hancocks	
29	Feb	9	H	Huddersfield Town	D	0-0		
30		16	H	Newcastle United	W	3-0	Hancocks 2 (1 pen), Dunn	
31		23	H	Sunderland	L	0-3		
32	Mar	1	A	Bolton Wanderers	D	2-2	Mullen, Pye	
33		8	H	Stoke City	W	3-0	Hancocks 2, Mullen	
34		15	A	Manchester United	L	0-2		
35		22	H	Tottenham Hotspur	D	1-1	Pye	
36		29	A	Preston North End	L	0-3		
37	Apr	5	H	Burnley	L	1-2	Hancocks	
38		12	A	Charlton Athletic	L	0-1		
39		14	A	West Bromwich Albion	L	1-2	Birch	
40		15	H	West Bromwich Albion	L	1-4	Stuart	
41		19	H	Fulham	D	2-2	Mullen, Swinbourne	
42		26	A	Middlesbrough	L	0-4		

Appear

FA Cup

R3	Jan	12	A	Manchester City	D	2-2	Broadbent, Whitfield	
rep		16	H	Manchester City	W	4-1	Mullen 2, Short 2	
R4	Feb	2	A	Liverpool	L	1-2	Mullen	

Appear

…J	Pritchard RT	Baxter W	Shorthouse WH	Wright WA	Hancocks J	Dunn J	Swinbourne RH	Pye J	Mullen J	Deeley NV	Crook WC	Wilshaw DJ	Chatham RH	Smyth S	Gibbons L	Walker JH	Sims ND	Smith LJ	Whitfield K	Parsons DR	Guttridge WH	Broadbent PF	Clews MD	Birch B	Stuart EA	
	3	4	5	6	7	8	9	10	11																	1
	3	4	5	6	7	8	9	10	11																	2
	3		5	6	7	8	9	10	11	4																3
	3		5	6	7	8		10	11		4	9														4
			3	6	7	10			11		4	9	5	8												5
	3		5	6	7	8		10	11		4	9														6
			5	6	7	8		10	11		4	9			3											7
	3		5	6	7	8		10	11		4	9														8
	3		5	4	7	8	9	10	11		6															9
	3		5	4	7	8	9		11		6					10										10
			5	6	7	8		10	11	4		9			3											11
	3		5		7	8		10	11	6	4	9					1									12
	3			6	7	8		10	11		4	9	5													13
	3		5	6		8		10	11		4	9						7								14
	2		5	6		8		10	11		4	9			3		1	7								15
	3	6	5			8	4	10	11									7	9							16
	3	4	5	6		8	9	10	11									7								17
	3	4	5	6		8	9	10	11								1	7								18
	3	4	5	6		8	9	10	11									7		1						19
	3	4	5	6		8	9	10	11									7		1						20
		4		6			9		11			10	5		3	8		7		1						21
		4		6				10	11			9	5			8		7		1	3					22
		4		6				9	11			10	5			8		7		1	3					23
		4	2	6	7	10			11				5		3				9	1		8				24
		4	2	6		10			11				5		3			7	9	1		8				25
		4	2	6		10							5		3			7	9	1		8	11			26
		6	2	4	7				11				5		3			8		1		10				27
		6	2	4	7			10	11				5		3					1		8				28
		6	2	4	7	10			11				5		3					1		8				29
		4	2	6	7	10			11				5		3				9			8				30
		4	2	6	7				11				5		3	10			9			8				31
			2	6	7		9	10	11		4		5		3							8				32
			2	4	7	10	9	8	11		6		5		3											33
			2	4	11		9				6	10	5		3			7				8				34
			2	4	7		9	8	11		6		5		3							10				35
	2			4	7		9	8	11		6		5		3							10				36
			2		7		8	9	11	6	4		5		3							10				37
			2	4	7				11		6		5		3			8	9					10		38
			2	6	7				11		4		5		3				9			8		10		39
			2	6	7				11		4		5		3							8		10	9	40
		4	2	6	7		9		11	8			5		3							10				41
	3	4	2	6	7		9	10	11	8							1								5	42
5	19	20	37	39	30	26	19	27	40	6	20	14	23	1	22	5	4	15	8	11	2	16	1	3	2	
		1			12	9	4	15	11			5		1		2		7	3			1		1	1	

…J	Pritchard RT	Baxter W	Shorthouse WH	Wright WA	Hancocks J	Dunn J	Swinbourne RH	Pye J	Mullen J	Deeley NV	Crook WC	Wilshaw DJ	Chatham RH	Smyth S	Gibbons L	Walker JH	Sims ND	Smith LJ	Whitfield K	Parsons DR	Guttridge WH	Broadbent PF	Clews MD	Birch B	Stuart EA	
		4	2	6	7			10	11				5		3				9	1		8				R3
9		4	2	6	7			10	11				5		3					1		8				rep
		6	2	4	7		9	10	11				5		3					1		8				R4
1		3	3	3	3		1	3	3				3		3				1	3		3				
2									3										1			1				

1952-53

Division One

Manager: Stan Cullis

	P	W	D	L	F	A	Pts
Arsenal	42	21	12	9	97	64	54
Preston North End	42	21	12	9	85	60	54
Wolverhampton Wanderers	42	19	13	10	86	63	51
West Bromwich Albion	42	21	8	13	66	60	50
Charlton Athletic	42	19	11	12	77	63	49
Burnley	42	18	12	12	67	52	48
Blackpool	42	19	9	14	71	70	47
Manchester United	42	18	10	14	69	72	46
Sunderland	42	15	13	14	68	82	43
Tottenham Hotspur	42	15	11	16	78	69	41
Aston Villa	42	14	13	15	63	61	41
Cardiff City	42	14	12	16	54	46	40
Middlesbrough	42	14	11	17	70	77	39
Bolton Wanderers	42	15	9	18	61	69	39
Portsmouth	42	14	10	18	74	83	38
Newcastle United	42	14	9	19	59	70	37
Liverpool	42	14	8	20	61	82	36
Sheffield Wednesday	42	12	11	19	62	72	35
Chelsea	42	12	11	19	56	66	35
Manchester City	42	14	7	21	72	87	35
Stoke City	42	12	10	20	53	66	34
Derby County	42	11	10	21	59	74	32

Did you know that?

- Centre-forward Roy Swinbourne scored a 20-minute hat-trick as Wolves beat Manchester City 7–3 in their 1,000th home League game in November.
- Wolves' second XI won the Central League title for the third season running.
- Wolves' youngsters were beaten by Manchester United over two legs in the FA Youth Cup Final.
- Wolves beat West Bromwich Albion 3–1 to win the Coronation Cup at The Hawthorns.
- Bill Slater was signed from Brentford, while Billy Crook moved to Walsall and Jimmy Dunn to Derby County.

Match No.	Date		Venue	Opponents	Result		Scorers	Atte
1	Aug	23	H	Cardiff City	W	1-0	Mullen	5
2		25	H	Bolton Wanderers	W	3-1	Swinbourne 2, Broadbent	3
3		30	A	Charlton Athletic	D	2-2	Hancocks, Swinbourne	2
4	Sep	1	A	Bolton Wanderers	L	1-2	Swinbourne	2
5		6	H	Arsenal	D	1-1	Swinbourne	4
6		8	H	Aston Villa	W	2-1	Broadbent, Taylor	3
7		13	A	Derby County	W	3-2	Hancocks, Mullen, Swinbourne	2
8		15	A	Aston Villa	W	1-0	Mullen	2
9		20	H	Blackpool	L	2-5	Flowers, Swinbourne	4
10		27	A	Chelsea	W	2-1	Smith, Wilshaw	6
11	Oct	4	H	Manchester United	W	6-2	Swinbourne 3, Wilshaw 2, Mullen	3
12		11	H	Newcastle United	W	2-0	Broadbent, Batty (og)	4
13		18	A	West Bromwich Albion	D	1-1	Smith	54
14		25	H	Middlesbrough	D	3-3	Smith, Swinbourne, Wilshaw	3
15	Nov	1	A	Liverpool	L	1-2	Broadbent	4
16		8	H	Manchester City	W	7-3	Swinbourne 3, Smith 2, Mullen, Wilshaw	3
17		15	A	Stoke City	W	2-1	Mullen, Swinbourne	28
18		22	H	Preston North End	L	0-2		32
19		29	A	Burnley	D	0-0		3
20	Dec	6	H	Tottenham Hotspur	D	0-0		37
21		13	A	Sheffield Wednesday	W	3-2	Slater, Smith, Swinbourne	4
22		20	A	Cardiff City	D	0-0		25
23		26	H	Sunderland	D	1-1	Swinbourne	51
24		27	A	Sunderland	L	2-5	Broadbent, Smith (pen)	41
25	Jan	3	H	Charlton Athletic	L	1-2	Swinbourne	33
26		17	A	Arsenal	L	3-5	Hancocks 2, Mullen	57
27		24	H	Derby County	W	3-1	Hancocks, Mullen, Wilshaw	29
28		31	H	Sheffield Wednesday	W	3-1	Hancocks (pen), Wilshaw, Curtis (og)	28
29	Feb	7	A	Blackpool	L	0-2		21
30		18	H	Chelsea	D	2-2	Stockin, Wilshaw	13
31		21	A	Manchester United	W	3-0	Mullen 2, Wilshaw	40
32		28	A	Newcastle United	D	1-1	Wilshaw	46
33	Mar	7	H	West Bromwich Albion	W	2-0	Wilshaw 2	48
34		14	A	Middlesbrough	D	1-1	Wilshaw	24
35		21	H	Liverpool	W	3-0	Hancocks, Swinbourne, Wright	29
36		28	A	Manchester City	L	1-3	Swinbourne	27
37	Apr	3	A	Portsmouth	D	2-2	Slater, Swinbourne	39
38		4	H	Stoke City	W	3-0	Stockin 2, Wilshaw	30
39		6	H	Portsmouth	W	4-1	Wilshaw 2, Hancocks, Stockin	29
40		11	A	Preston North End	D	1-1	Slater	35
41		18	H	Burnley	W	5-1	Stockin 2, Hancocks, Mullen, Wilshaw	33
42		25	A	Tottenham Hotspur	L	2-3	Hancocks, Stockin	48

Appearan

Two own-goals G

FA Cup

R3	Jan	10	A	Preston North End	L	2-5	Smith, Wilshaw	32

Appearan

G

Pritchard RT	Crook WC	Chatham RH	Wright WA	Hancocks J	Taylor JE	Swinbourne RH	Dunn J	Mullen J	Broadbent PF	Flowers R	Short J	Smith LJ	Wilshaw DJ	Slater WJ	Sims ND	Whitfield K	Baxter W	Gibbons L	Guttridge WH	Stockin R	
3	4	5	6	7	8	9	10	11													1
3	4	5	6	7	8	9		11	10												2
3	4	5	6	7	8	9		11	10												3
3	4	5	6	7	8	9		11	10												4
3	4	5	6	7	8	9		11	10												5
3	4	5	6	7	8	9		11	10												6
3	4	5	6	7	8	9		11	10												7
3	4	5	6	7	8	9		11	10												8
3	4		6	7	8	9		11	10	5											9
3	4		6			9		11	8		2	7	10								10
3						9		11	8	4	2	7	10	6							11
3			6			9		11	8	4	2	7	10								12
3			6			9		11	8	4	2	7	10		1						13
3			6			9		11	8	4	2	7	10								14
3			6			9		11	8	4	2	7	10								15
3			6			9		11	8	4	2	7	10		1						16
3			6			9		11	8	4	2	7	10		1						17
3			6					11	8	4	2	7	10		1	9					18
3			6		8	9		11	10		2	7					4				19
3			6			9		11	8		2	7		10			4				20
3			6			9		11	8		2	7		10			4				21
3			6			9		11	8		2	7		10			4				22
3			4			9		11	8		2	7	10	6							23
3		5	6			9		11	8		2	7	10				4				24
2		5	6	7		9		11	8				10				4	3			25
			6	7		9		11	8		2		10				4		3		26
			6	7		9		11		4	2		10	8					3		27
3			6	7		9		11		4	2		10							8	28
3			6	7		9				4	2		11	8						10	29
3			6	7		9		11			2		10				4			8	30
3				7		9		11		4	2		10	6	1					8	31
3				7		9		11		4	2		10	6	1					8	32
3			4	7		9		11			2		10	6	1					8	33
3			4	7		9		11			2		10	6	1					8	34
3			6	7		9		11		4	2		10		1					8	35
3			6	7		9		11		4	2		10		1					8	36
3			4	7		9		11			2		10	6	1					8	37
3			5	7		9		11		4	2		10	6	1					8	38
3			4	7		9		11			2		10	6	1					8	39
3			2	7		9		11		4			10	6						8	40
3				7		9		11		4			10	6				2		8	41
3			2	7		9		11		4			10	6						8	42
40	10	10	38	27	10	41	1	41	25	20	29	15	29	17	13	1	8	2	2	15	
			1	10	1	21		11	5	1		7	17	3						7	
2		5	6			9		11	8			7	10				4	3			R3
1		1	1			1		1	1			1	1				1	1			
												1	1								

1953-54

Division One

Manager: Stan Cullis

	P	W	D	L	F	A	Pts
Wolverhampton Wanderers	42	25	7	10	96	56	57
West Bromwich Albion	42	22	9	11	86	63	53
Huddersfield Town	42	20	11	11	78	61	51
Manchester United	42	18	12	12	73	58	48
Bolton Wanderers	42	18	12	12	75	60	48
Blackpool	42	19	10	13	80	69	48
Burnley	42	21	4	17	78	67	46
Chelsea	42	16	12	14	74	68	44
Charlton Athletic	42	19	6	17	75	77	44
Cardiff City	42	18	8	16	51	71	44
Preston North End	42	19	5	18	87	58	43
Arsenal	42	15	13	14	75	73	43
Aston Villa	42	16	9	17	70	68	41
Portsmouth	42	14	11	17	81	89	39
Newcastle United	42	14	10	18	72	77	38
Tottenham Hotspur	42	16	5	21	65	76	37
Manchester City	42	14	9	19	62	77	37
Sunderland	42	14	8	20	81	89	36
Sheffield Wednesday	42	15	6	21	70	91	36
Sheffield United	42	11	11	20	69	90	33
Middlesbrough	42	10	10	22	60	91	30
Liverpool	42	9	10	23	68	97	28

Did you know that?

- Wolves' best-ever unbeaten away run (11 matches) came to an end at Portsmouth in late January.
- Wolves did the double over their arch-rivals West Bromwich Albion and the four points gained was enough to see them win the League title for the first time in the club's history.
- In November 1953, wing-half Bill Baxter was transferred to Aston Villa after making a record 213 Central League appearances for Wolves.
- Ray Chatham and Jack Short also left Wolves – for Notts County and Stoke City respectively.
- Floodlights were installed at Molineux for the first time.

Match No.	Date		Venue	Opponents	Result		Scorers	Atten
1	Aug	19	A	Burnley	L	1-4	Swinbourne	32,
2		22	A	Manchester City	W	4-0	Swinbourne 2, Slater, Wilshaw	22,
3		26	A	Sunderland	L	2-3	Hancocks (pen), Wilshaw	57,
4		29	H	Cardiff City	W	3-1	Hancocks (pen), Mullen, Wilshaw	33,
5		31	H	Sunderland	W	3-1	Mullen, Swinbourne, Wilshaw	41,
6	Sep	5	A	Arsenal	W	3-2	Broadbent, Hancocks, Wilshaw	60
7		7	H	Liverpool	W	2-1	Broadbent, Swinbourne	35
8		12	H	Portsmouth	W	4-3	Wilshaw 3, Swinbourne	36
9		16	A	Liverpool	D	1-1	Wilshaw	29
10		19	A	Blackpool	D	0-0		35
11		26	H	Chelsea	W	8-1	Hancocks 3(1 pen),Swinbourne 2,Broadbent,Mullen,Wilshaw	36
12	Oct	3	A	Sheffield United	D	3-3	Hancocks, Swinbourne, Wilshaw	35
13		10	A	Newcastle United	W	2-1	Smith, Swinbourne	39
14		17	H	Manchester United	W	3-1	Broadbent, Hancocks (pen), Swinbourne	40
15		24	A	Bolton Wanderers	D	1-1	Hancocks	40
16		31	H	Preston North End	W	1-0	Wilshaw	34
17	Nov	7	A	Middlesbrough	D	3-3	Hancocks, Swinbourne, Wilshaw	24
18		14	H	West Bromwich Albion	W	1-0	Mullen	56
19		21	A	Charlton Athletic	W	2-0	Broadbent, Hancocks	35
20		28	H	Sheffield Wednesday	W	4-1	Hancocks (pen), Swinbourne 2, Wilshaw	35
21	Dec	5	A	Tottenham Hotspur	W	3-2	Broadbent, Hancocks, Wilshaw	48
22		12	H	Burnley	L	1-2	Hancocks	35
23		19	H	Manchester City	W	3-1	Hancocks 2 (1 pen), Wilshaw	27
24		24	H	Aston Villa	L	1-2	Wilshaw	40
25		26	A	Aston Villa	W	2-1	Hancocks, Wilshaw	49
26	Jan	2	A	Cardiff City	W	3-1	Hancocks, Swinbourne, Wilshaw	42
27		16	H	Arsenal	L	0-2		45
28		23	A	Portsmouth	L	0-2		35
29	Feb	6	H	Blackpool	W	4-1	Swinbourne 3, Hancocks	27
30		13	A	Chelsea	L	2-4	Swinbourne, Wilshaw	60
31		20	H	Sheffield United	W	6-1	Hancocks 2, Swinbourne 2, Broadbent, Wilshaw	27
32		27	H	Newcastle United	W	3-2	Broadbent, Slater, Wilshaw	38
33	Mar	6	A	Manchester United	L	0-1		40
34		20	A	Preston North End	W	1-0	Wilshaw	24
35		24	H	Bolton Wanderers	D	1-1	Broadbent	19
36		27	H	Middlesbrough	L	2-4	Broadbent 2	29
37	Apr	3	A	West Bromwich Albion	W	1-0	Swinbourne	49
38		10	H	Charlton Athletic	W	5-0	Hancocks 2, Mullen 2, Wilshaw	35
39		17	A	Sheffield Wednesday	D	0-0		40
40		19	H	Huddersfield Town	W	4-0	Broadbent, Hancocks, Mullen, Wilshaw	42
41		20	A	Huddersfield Town	L	1-2	Wilshaw	35
42		24	H	Tottenham Hotspur	W	2-0	Swinbourne 2	44

Appearar

G

FA Cup

R3	Jan	9	H	Birmingham City	L	1-2	Wilshaw	36

Appeara

G

Short J	Pritchard RT	Slater WJ	Shorthouse WH	Wright WA	Hancocks J	Stockin R	Swinbourne RH	Wilshaw DJ	Mullen J	Broadbent PF	Williams BF	Gibbons L	Deeley NV	Baxter W	Chatham RH	Flowers R	Smith JL	Guttridge WH	Stuart EA	Clamp HE	
2	3	4	5	6	7	8	9	10	11												1
2	3	4	5	6	7	8	9	10	11												2
2	3	4	5	6	7	8	9	10	11												3
2	3	4	5	6	7		9	10	11	8											4
2	3	4	5	6	7		9	10	11	8											5
2	3	4	5	6	7		9	10	11	8	1										6
2	3	4	5	6	7		9	10	11	8	1										7
	3		5	6	7		9	10	11	8	1	2	4								8
	3	6	5	2	7		9	10	11	8	1		4								9
	3		5	2	7		9	10	11	8	1			6	4						10
2	3	4	5	6	7		9	10	11	8	1										11
2	3	4	5	6	7		9	10	11	8	1										12
2	3	4	5		7	10	9			8	1					6	11				13
2		4	5	6	7		9	10	11	8	1							3			14
2		6	5		7		9	10	11	8	1			4				3			15
2		6	5	3	7	10		9	11	8	1			4							16
2		6	5	3	7		9	10	11	8	1			4							17
2	3		5	6	7	8	9	10	11		1			4							18
2	3	4	5	6	7		9	10	11	8	1										19
2	3	4	5	6	7		9	10	11	8	1										20
2	3	4	5	6	7		9	10	11	8	1										21
2	3	4	5	6	7		9	10	11	8	1										22
2	3	4	5	6	7		9	10	11	8	1										23
2	3	4	5	6	7		9	10	11	8											24
2	3	4	5	6	7		9	10	11	8											25
	3	4	5	2	7		9	10	11	8						6					26
2	3	4		5	7		9	10	11	8	1					6					27
2		4	5	3	7		9		11	10	1		8			6					28
2	3	4	5	6	7		9	10	11		1					8					29
2	3	4	5	6	7		9	10	11		1					8					30
	3	4		5	7		9	10	11	8	1					6			2		31
		4	3	5	7		9	10	11	8	1					6			2		32
		4	3	5	7			10	11	8	1					9			2	6	33
		4	3	5	7		9	10		8	1		6				11		2		34
		4	3	5	7		9			8	1		6				11		2	10	35
		4	3	5	7		9	10	11	8	1		6						2		36
	3	4	5		11		9	10		8	1					6	7		2		37
		4	5	3	7		9	10	11	8	1					6			2		38
		4	5	3	7		9	10	11	8	1					6			2		39
		4	5	3	7		9	10	11	8	1					6			2		40
		4	5	3	7		9	10	11	8	1					6			2		41
		4	5	3	7		9	10	11	8	1					6			2		42
26	27	39	40	39	42	6	40	39	38	36	34	1	6	5	1	15	4	2	12	2	
		2			24		24	26	7	12							1				

Short J	Pritchard RT	Slater WJ	Shorthouse WH	Wright WA	Hancocks J	Stockin R	Swinbourne RH	Wilshaw DJ	Mullen J	Broadbent PF	
2	3	4	5	6	7		9	10	11	8	R3
1	1	1	1	1	1		1	1	1	1	
								1			

1954-55

Division One

Manager: Stan Cullis

	P	W	D	L	F	A	Pts
Chelsea	42	20	12	10	81	57	52
Wolverhampton Wanderers	42	19	10	13	89	70	48
Portsmouth	42	18	12	12	74	62	48
Sunderland	42	15	18	9	64	54	48
Manchester United	42	20	7	15	84	74	47
Aston Villa	42	20	7	15	72	73	47
Manchester City	42	18	10	14	76	69	46
Newcastle United	42	17	9	16	89	77	43
Arsenal	42	17	9	16	69	63	43
Burnley	42	17	9	16	51	48	43
Everton	42	16	10	16	62	68	42
Huddersfield Town	42	14	13	15	63	68	41
Sheffield United	42	17	7	18	70	86	41
Preston North End	42	16	8	18	83	64	40
Charlton Athletic	42	15	10	17	76	75	40
Tottenham Hotspur	42	16	8	18	72	73	40
West Bromwich Albion	42	16	8	18	76	96	40
Bolton Wanderers	42	13	13	16	62	69	39
Blackpool	42	14	10	18	60	64	38
Cardiff City	42	13	11	18	62	76	37
Leicester City	42	12	11	19	74	86	35
Sheffield Wednesday	42	8	10	24	63	100	26

Did you know that?

- The match against Everton at Goodison Park attracted a crowd of 75,322 – the biggest-ever to watch a League game involving Wolves.
- Wolves striker Dennis Wilshaw became the first player to score four goals in a game at Wembley when he helped England whip Scotland 7–2 in April.
- Four Wolves players – Wilshaw, Billy Wright, Bert Williams and Ron Flowers – played for England against France in Paris in May.
- Wolves beat Spartak Moscow 4–0 and Honved 3–2 in two prestigious friendly games at Molineux in November and December.

Match No.	Date		Venue	Opponents	Result		Scorers	Att
1	Aug	21	H	Sheffield Wednesday	W	4-2	Swinbourne 2, Mullen, Wilshaw	4
2		25	A	Tottenham Hotspur	L	2-3	Wright, Wetton (og)	4
3		28	A	Portsmouth	D	0-0		4
4		30	H	Tottenham Hotspur	W	4-2	Mullen, Swinbourne, Wilshaw, Wetton (og)	3
5	Sep	4	H	Blackpool	W	1-0	Slater	5
6		8	H	Sunderland	W	2-0	Wilshaw 2	3
7		11	A	Charlton Athletic	W	3-1	Slater, Smith, Swinbourne	3
8		15	A	Sunderland	D	0-0		4
9		18	H	Bolton Wanderers	L	1-2	Smith	4
10		25	A	Huddersfield Town	L	0-2		3
11	Oct	2	H	Manchester United	W	4-2	Hancocks 2, Broadbent, Swinbourne	3
12		9	H	Manchester City	D	2-2	Deeley, Mullen	4
13		16	H	Cardiff City	D	1-1	Slater	3
14		23	H	West Bromwich Albion	W	4-0	Hancocks 2, Swinbourne 2	5
15		30	A	Newcastle United	W	3-2	Smith, Swinbourne, Wilshaw	4
16	Nov	6	H	Burnley	W	5-0	Flowers 2, Swinbourne 2, Hancocks (pen)	2
17		13	A	Preston North End	D	3-3	Broadbent, Hancocks, Wilshaw	2
18		20	H	Sheffield United	W	4-1	Broadbent, Hancocks, Wilshaw, Smith	2
19		27	A	Arsenal	D	1-1	Hancocks	5
20	Dec	4	H	Chelsea	L	3-4	Broadbent, Hancocks (pen), Swinbourne	3
21		11	A	Leicester City	W	2-1	Hancocks 2	3
22		18	A	Sheffield Wednesday	D	2-2	Mullen, Wilshaw	3
23		25	H	Everton	L	1-3	Wilshaw	2
24		27	A	Everton	L	2-3	Broadbent, Wilshaw	7
25	Jan	1	H	Portsmouth	D	2-2	Mullen, Wilshaw	3
26		15	A	Blackpool	W	2-0	Swinbourne, Wilshaw	14
27		22	H	Charlton Athletic	W	2-1	Hancocks 2	32
28	Feb	5	A	Bolton Wanderers	L	1-6	Wilshaw	37
29		12	H	Huddersfield Town	W	6-4	Hancocks 3 (1 pen), Wilshaw 2, Slater	30
30		23	A	Manchester United	W	4-2	Flowers, Hancocks, Smith, Wilshaw	17
31	Mar	5	H	Leicester City	W	5-0	Hancocks 2, Smith, Swinbourne, Wilshaw	41
32		16	A	West Bromwich Albion	L	0-1		28
33		19	H	Newcastle United	D	2-2	Hancocks, Swinbourne	36
34		26	A	Burnley	L	0-1		23
35	Apr	2	H	Preston North End	D	1-1	Hancocks	28
36		9	A	Chelsea	L	0-1		75
37		11	H	Aston Villa	W	1-0	Flowers	33
38		12	A	Aston Villa	L	2-4	Hancocks, Wilshaw	44
39		16	H	Arsenal	W	3-1	Hancocks 3	34
40		20	A	Manchester City	L	0-3		50
41		23	A	Sheffield United	W	2-1	Hancocks, Wilshaw	24
42		30	A	Cardiff City	L	2-3	Flowers, Wilshaw	30

Appearar

Two own-goals G

FA Cup

R3	Jan	8	A	Grimsby Town	W	5-2	Wilshaw 2, McDonald, Smith, Swinbourne	25
R4		29	H	Arsenal	W	1-0	Swinbourne	52
R5	Feb	19	H	Charlton Athletic	W	4-1	Wilshaw 3, Hancocks	49
R6	Mar	12	A	Sunderland	L	0-2		54

Appearan

G

	Williams BF	Stuart EA	Pritchard RT	Slater WJ	Shorthouse WH	Wright WA	Hancocks J	Broadbent PF	Swinbourne RH	Wilshaw DJ	Mullen J	Flowers R	Smith JL	Russell WP	Clamp HE	Deeley NV	McDonald T	Baillie J	Sims DN	Showell GW	Booth C	Taylor D
1		2	3	4	5	6	7	8	9	10	11											
2		2	3	4	5	6	7	8	9	10	11											
3		2	3	4	5	6	7	8	9	10	11											
4		2	3	4		5		8	9	10	11	6	7									
5		2	3	4		5		8	9	10	11	6	7									
6		2	3	4		5		8	9	10	11	6	7									
7		2		4	3	5		8	9	10	11	6	7									
8		2		4	3	5	7	8	9	10		6	11									
9		2		4	3	5		8	9	10	11	6	7									
10		2	3	4		5		8	9	10	11	6	7									
11		2			3		7	8	9	11		4		5	6	10						
12		2		4	3	5	7	8	9		11	6				10						
13		2		8	3	5	7		9		11	4			6	10						
14		2		4	3	5	7	8	9	10		6	11									
15		2		4	3	5	7	8	9	10		6	11									
16		2		4	3	5	7	8	9	10		6	11									
17		2		4	3	5	7	8	9	10			11		6							
18		2		4	3	5	7	8	9	10		6	11									
19		2			3	5	7	8	9	10		4	11		6							
20		2		4	3	5	7	8	9	10		6	11									
21		2		4	3	5	7	8	9	10		6	11									
22		2		4	3	5		8	9	10	11	6	7									
23		2		4	3	5	7	8	9	10		6	11									
24		2		4	3			8	9	10	11	6	7	5								
25		2		4	3	5		8	9	10	11	6	7									
26		2		4	3	5			9	10		6	11			8	7					
27		2		4	3	5	7	8	9	10		6	11									
28		2		4	3	5	7	8	9	10		6	11									
29				4	3	5	7	8	9	10		6	11					2				
30		2			3	5	7	8	9	10		4	11		6				1			
31		2		4	3	5	7	8	9	10		6	11									
32		2				3	7	10	9		11	5	8		6	4						
33		2		4		3	7	8	9	10		5	11		6							
34		2		4	3	5	7	8	9	10			11		6							
35				4	3		7	8	9			5	11		6	10			1	2		
36				4	3	5	7	8	9	10		6	11							2		
37				4	3	5	7			10		9	11		6					2	8	
38				4	3	5	7			10		6	11			8			1	2		9
39				4	3	5	7	8		10	11	6								2		9
40				4	3	5	7	8		10	11	6								2		9
41				4	3	5	7	8		9		6	11							2	10	
42				4	3	5	7	8		9		6	11							2	10	
		33	7	38	36	39	32	38	36	38	17	37	34	2	10	7	1	1	3	8	3	3
				4		1	26	5	14	20	5	5	6			1						

	Williams BF	Stuart EA	Pritchard RT	Slater WJ	Shorthouse WH	Wright WA	Hancocks J	Broadbent PF	Swinbourne RH	Wilshaw DJ	Mullen J	Flowers R	Smith JL	Russell WP	Clamp HE	Deeley NV	McDonald T	Baillie J	Sims DN	Showell GW	Booth C	Taylor D
R3		2		4	3	5		8	9	10		6	11				7					
R4		2		4	3	5	7	8	9	10		6	11									
R5		2		4	3	5	7	8	9	10		6	11									
R6		2		4	3	5	7	8	9	10		6	11									
		4		4	4	4	3	4	4	4		4	4				1					
							1		2	5			1				1					

1955-56

Division One

Manager: Stan Cullis

	P	W	D	L	F	A	Pts
Manchester United	42	25	10	7	83	51	60
Blackpool	42	20	9	13	86	62	49
Wolverhampton Wanderers	42	20	9	13	89	65	49
Manchester City	42	18	10	14	82	69	46
Arsenal	42	18	10	14	60	61	46
Birmingham City	42	18	9	15	75	57	45
Burnley	42	18	8	16	64	54	44
Bolton Wanderers	42	18	7	17	71	58	43
Sunderland	42	17	9	16	80	95	43
Luton Town	42	17	8	17	66	64	42
Newcastle United	42	17	7	18	85	70	41
Portsmouth	42	16	9	17	78	85	41
West Bromwich Albion	42	18	5	19	58	70	41
Charlton Athletic	42	17	6	19	75	81	40
Everton	42	15	10	17	55	69	40
Chelsea	42	14	11	17	64	77	39
Cardiff City	42	15	9	18	55	69	39
Tottenham Hotspur	42	15	7	20	61	71	37
Preston North End	42	14	8	20	73	72	36
Aston Villa	42	11	13	18	52	69	35
Huddersfield Town	42	14	7	21	54	83	35
Sheffield United	42	12	9	21	63	77	33

Did you know that?

- Wolves equalled the best-ever away League win in First Division history when they hammered Cardiff City 9–1 at Ninian Park in September.
- A crowd of 55,480 saw Wolves beat Dynamo Moscow 2–1 in a floodlit friendly at Molineux in November.
- Kenilworth Road's biggest-ever crowd – 27,911 – witnessed the Luton Town versus Wolves League encounter in November 1955, and Blackpool registered their biggest home crowd when 38,098 attended the League game versus Wolves in September.
- Three players – Les Smith, Roy Pritchard and Nigel Sims – all left Wolves for Aston Villa.

Match No.	Date		Venue	Opponents	Result		Scorers	Atter
1	Aug	20	A	West Bromwich Albion	D	1-1	Swinbourne	45
2		24	A	Portsmouth	L	1-2	Hancocks	30
3		27	H	Manchester City	W	7-2	Swinbourne 4, Hancocks 2, Booth	38
4		31	H	Portsmouth	W	3-1	Broadbent, Mullen, Swinbourne	41
5	Sep	3	A	Cardiff City	W	9-1	Hancocks 3, Swinbourne 3, Broadbent 2, Mullen	42
6		10	H	Huddersfield Town	W	4-0	Swinbourne 3, Slater	43
7		17	A	Blackpool	L	1-2	Hancocks	38
8		24	H	Chelsea	W	2-1	Swinbourne 2	43
9	Oct	1	A	Bolton Wanderers	L	1-2	Slater	34
10		8	A	Manchester United	L	3-4	Swinbourne 2, Slater	48
11		15	H	Sheffield United	W	3-2	Hancocks (pen), Swinbourne, Wilshaw	33
12		22	A	Newcastle United	L	1-3	McDonald	34
13		29	H	Birmingham City	W	1-0	Wilshaw	47
14	Nov	5	A	Luton Town	L	1-5	Hancocks	27
15		12	H	Charlton Athletic	W	2-0	Mullen, Shorthouse	36,
16		19	A	Tottenham Hotspur	L	1-2	Broadbent,	51
17		26	H	Everton	W	1-0	Murray	31
18	Dec	3	A	Preston North End	L	0-2		26,
19		10	H	Burnley	W	3-1	Hancocks 2, Clamp	24
20		17	H	West Bromwich Albion	W	3-2	Hancocks 2 (1 pen), Murray	31
21		24	A	Manchester City	D	2-2	Hancocks, Murray	32
22		26	H	Arsenal	D	3-3	Booth 2, Hancocks	43
23		27	A	Arsenal	D	2-2	Mullen, Murray	61,
24		31	H	Cardiff City	L	0-2		36,
25	Jan	2	A	Sunderland	D	1-1	Flowers	48,
26		14	A	Huddersfield Town	W	3-1	Murray 2, Broadbent	14,
27		21	H	Blackpool	L	2-3	Hancocks (pen), Murray	46,
28	Feb	4	A	Chelsea	W	3-2	Broadbent 2, Murray	37,
29		11	H	Bolton Wanderers	W	4-2	Broadbent 2, Hancocks, Dean (og)	24,
30		18	H	Manchester United	L	0-2		40,
31	Mar	10	A	Birmingham City	D	0-0		45,
32		17	H	Luton Town	L	1-2	Hancocks	32,
33		24	A	Charlton Athletic	W	2-0	Wilshaw, Murray	27,
34		31	H	Newcastle United	W	2-1	Mullen, Murray	31,
35	Apr	2	H	Aston Villa	D	0-0		33,
36		3	A	Aston Villa	D	0-0		39,
37		7	A	Everton	L	1-2	Mullen	37,
38		14	H	Preston North End	W	2-1	Slater (pen), Wilshaw	18,
39		18	H	Tottenham Hotspur	W	5-1	Slater 2 (2 pen), Broadbent, Murray, Wilshaw	29,
40		21	A	Burnley	W	2-1	Booth, Deeley	22,
41		28	H	Sunderland	W	3-1	Mullen, Slater (pen), Wilshaw	29,
42	May	2	A	Sheffield United	D	3-3	Booth 3	12,
								Appearan
							One own-goal	Go

FA Cup

R3	Jan	7	H	West Bromwich Albion	L	1-2	Slater	55,
								Appearan
								Go

Stuart EA	Shorthouse WH	Slater WJ	Wright WA	Flowers R	Hancocks J	Broadbent PF	Swinbourne RH	Wilshaw DJ	Smith LJ	Showell GW	Mullen J	Clamp HE	Booth C	Sims ND	Russell PW	McDonald T	Mason RH	Murray JR	Deeley NV	Jones G	Howells R	Middleton H	
2	3	4	5	6	7	8	9	10	11														1
2		4	5	6	7	8	9	10		3	11												2
2	3	4	5		7	8	9				11	6	10										3
2	3	4	5		7	8	9				11	6	10										4
2	3	4	5		7	8	9				11	6	10										5
2	3	4	5		7	8	9				11	6	10										6
2	3		5	4	7	8	9				11	6	10										7
2	3	4		5	7		9	10			11	6	8										8
2	3	4		5	7		9	10			11	6	8										9
	3	4	5		7	8	9	10		2	11	6											10
	3	4	5		7	8	9	10		2	11	6											11
	3	4				8	9			2	11	6	10	1	5	7							12
	3	4	5	6	7	8		9		2	11		10										13
	3	4	5		7	6	9	10		2	11						8						14
2	3	4	5		7	8		10			11	6						9					15
2	3	4	5			8		10	7		11	6						9					16
2	3	4	5			8					11	6	10					9	7				17
2	3	4	5			8	9	10			11	6							7				18
2	3	4	5		7	8					11	6	10					9					19
2				4	7	8				5	11	6	10					9		3			20
2	3		5	4	7	8		10			11	6						9					21
2	3		5	4	7	8					11	6	10					9					22
2	3	4	5		7	8					11	6	10	1				9					23
2	3		5	4	7	8					11	6	10	1				9					24
2	3	4	5	9	7	8					11	6	10	1									25
2		4	5	3	7	8						6	10					9	11				26
2		4	3		7	8				5	11	6						9	10				27
2	3	4	5		7	8		10				6						9	11				28
2	3		5	4	7	8						6	10					9	11				29
2	3		5	4	7	8		11				6	10	1				9					30
2	3	4	5	6		8		11					10					9	7				31
2	3	4	5	6	7	8		9			11		10										32
2	3	4	5	6		8		10			11					7		9					33
2	3	4	5	6		8		10			11					7		9					34
2	3	4	5			8		10			11	6				7		9					35
2	3	6	5		7	8		10			11							9			4		36
2	3	4	5			8		10			11							9			6	7	37
2	3	4				7		10		5	11		8					9			6		38
2	3	4	5			7		10			11		8					9			6		39
2	3	4	5					10			11		8					9	7		6		40
2	3	4	5			7		10			11		8					9			6		41
2	3		4			7		10		5	11		8					9			6		42
7	38	34	37	18	28	39	14	26	2	10	36	27	26	5	1	4	1	25	8	1	7	1	
	1	7		1	18	10	17	6			7	1	7			1		11	1				

Stuart EA	Shorthouse WH	Slater WJ	Wright WA	Flowers R	Hancocks J	Broadbent PF	Swinbourne RH	Wilshaw DJ	Smith LJ	Showell GW	Mullen J	Clamp HE	Booth C	Sims ND	Russell PW	McDonald T	Mason RH	Murray JR	Deeley NV	Jones G	Howells R	Middleton H	
	3	4	5	9	7	8					11	6	10										R3
	1	1	1	1	1	1					1	1	1										
		1																					

1956-57

Division One

Manager: Stan Cullis

	P	W	D	L	F	A	Pts
Manchester United	42	28	8	6	103	54	64
Tottenham Hotspur	42	22	12	8	104	56	56
Preston North End	42	23	10	9	84	56	56
Blackpool	42	22	9	11	93	65	53
Arsenal	42	21	8	13	85	69	50
Wolverhampton Wanderers	42	20	8	14	94	70	48
Burnley	42	18	10	14	56	50	46
Leeds United	42	15	14	13	72	63	44
Bolton Wanderers	42	16	12	14	65	65	44
Aston Villa	42	14	15	13	65	55	43
West Bromwich Albion	42	14	14	14	59	61	42
Chelsea	42	13	13	16	73	73	39
Birmingham City	42	15	9	18	69	69	39
Sheffield Wednesday	42	16	6	20	82	88	38
Everton	42	14	10	18	61	79	38
Luton Town	42	14	9	19	58	76	37
Newcastle United	42	14	8	20	67	87	36
Manchester City	42	13	9	20	78	88	35
Portsmouth	42	10	13	19	62	92	33
Sunderland	42	12	8	22	67	88	32
Cardiff City	42	10	9	23	53	88	29
Charlton Athletic	42	9	4	29	62	120	22

Did you know that?

• Winger Harry Hooper, in his first season with the club, finished up as top scorer with 19 League goals.

• Ex-West Bromwich Albion winger Reg Cutler scored Bournemouth's goal in the Cherries' FA Cup win at Molineux – and also broke an upright at the South Bank End of the ground.

• Wolves again toured South Africa at the end of the season, winning all eight games and scoring 49 goals. Their two biggest wins were 10–1 and 11–1 over Southern Rhodesia and Northern Rhodesia respectively.

• Wolves played their last-ever League game on a Christmas Day this season.

Match No.	Date		Venue	Opponents	Result		Scorers	A
1	Aug	18	H	Manchester City	W	5-1	Murray 4, Hooper	
2		22	A	Luton Town	L	0-1		
3		25	A	Blackpool	L	2-3	Murray, Slater	
4		29	H	Luton Town	W	5-4	Murray 2, Broadbent, Mullen, Slater	
5	Sep	1	H	Everton	W	2-1	Booth, Slater	
6		8	A	Tottenham Hotspur	L	1-4	Hooper	
7		12	H	Sunderland	D	2-2	Broadbent, Murray	
8		15	H	Leeds United	L	1-2	Broadbent	
9		22	A	Bolton Wanderers	W	3-0	Booth, Mullen, Wilshaw	
10		29	H	Birmingham City	W	3-0	Hooper (pen), Murray, Wilshaw	
11	Oct	6	A	West Bromwich Albion	D	1-1	Hooper	
12		13	H	Portsmouth	W	6-0	Wilshaw 2, Flowers, Hooper, Murray, Gunter (og)	
13		20	A	Chelsea	D	3-3	Flowers, Hooper, Murray	
14		27	H	Cardiff City	W	3-1	Booth, Hooper (pen), Mullen	
15	Nov	3	A	Manchester United	L	0-3		
16		10	H	Arsenal	W	5-2	Booth 4, Murray	
17		17	A	Burnley	L	0-3		
18		24	H	Preston North End	W	4-3	Hooper 3 (1 pen), Mason	
19	Dec	1	A	Newcastle United	L	1-2	Hooper	
20		8	H	Sheffield Wednesday	W	2-1	Broadbent, Hooper	
21		15	A	Manchester City	W	3-2	Broadbent, Murray, Neil	
22		22	H	Blackpool	W	4-1	Wilshaw 3, Hooper	
23		25	A	Charlton Athletic	L	1-2	Booth	
24		29	A	Everton	L	1-3	Broadbent	
25	Jan	1	A	Sunderland	W	3-2	Broadbent 2, Flowers	
26		12	H	Tottenham Hotspur	W	3-0	Broadbent 2, Mason	
27		19	A	Leeds United	D	0-0		
28	Feb	2	H	Bolton Wanderers	W	3-2	Hooper 2, Murray	
29		9	A	Birmingham City	D	2-2	Hooper, Murray	
30		16	H	Charlton Athletic	W	7-3	Murray 2, Clamp, Broadbent 2, Bonson, Hooper	
31		23	A	Cardiff City	D	2-2	Bonson 2	
32	Mar	2	H	Chelsea	W	3-1	Bonson, Broadbent, Mason	
33		9	A	Sheffield Wednesday	L	1-2	Hooper (pen)	
34		16	H	Manchester United	D	1-1	Broadbent	
35		23	A	Arsenal	D	0-0		
36		30	H	Burnley	L	1-2	Slater	
37	Apr	6	A	Preston North End	L	0-1		
38		13	H	Newcastle United	W	2-0	Thomson, Wilshaw	
39		15	H	West Bromwich Albion	W	5-2	Booth, Broadbent, Deeley, Hooper, Wilshaw	
40		20	A	Portsmouth	L	0-1		
41		22	A	Aston Villa	L	0-4		
42		23	H	Aston Villa	W	3-0	Broadbent 2, Wilshaw	
								Appear
							One own-goal	

FA Cup

R3	Jan	5	H	Swansea Town	W	5-3	Bonson 2, Broadbent, Flowers, Mullen	
R4		26	H	Bournemouth	L	0-1		
								Appear

Stuart EA	Shorthouse WH	Slater WJ	Wright WA	Flowers R	Hooper H	Broadbent PF	Murray JR	Booth C	Mullen J	Harris GW	Finlayson MJ	Wilshaw DJ	Showell GW	Clamp HE	Mason RH	Neil PT	Bonson J	Deeley NV	Tether C	Thomson RGMcK	Jones G	
2	3	4	5	6	7	8	9	10	11													1
2	3	4	5	6	7	8	9	10	11													2
2	3	4	5	6	7	8	9	10	11													3
2		4	5	6	7	8	9	10	11	3												4
2	3	4	5	6	7	8	9	10	11													5
2	3	4	5	6	7	8	9	10	11													6
2	3	4	5	6	7	8	9	10	11													7
2	3	4	5	6	7	8	9		11		1	10										8
2	3	4	5	6	7	10		8	11		1	9										9
2	3	4	5	6	7	10	8		11		1	9										10
2		4		6	7	10	9	8	11	3	1		5									11
2		4	5	6	7		10	8	11	3	1	9										12
2		4	5	6	7		10	8	11	3	1	9										13
2		4	5	6	7		10	8	11	3	1	9										14
2		4	5	6	7		10	8	11	3	1	9										15
		4	5	6	7		10	8	11	3	1	9	2									16
		4	5	6	7	10	9	8	11	3	1		2									17
		4	5		7		10		11	3	1	9	2	6	8							18
		4	5	6	7	8	10		11	3	1	9	2									19
		4	5	6	7	10			11	3		9	2		8							20
		4	5	6	7	10	9			3			2		8	11						21
2		4	5	6	7	10	8			3		9				11						22
2		4	5	6	7	10	9	8		3						11						23
2		4	5	6	7	10	9			3					8	11						24
2		4	5	6	7	10			11	3					8		9					25
2		4	5	6	7	10			11	3					8		9					26
2		4	5	6	7	10			11	3					8		9					27
2			5	6	7	10	8		11	3				4			9					28
2			5	6	7	10	8		11	3				4			9					29
2			5	6	7	10	8		11	3				4			9					30
2			5	6	7	10	8			3				4			9	11				31
2			5	6		10		7		3				4	8		9	11				32
			5	6	7	10	8			3				4			9	11	2			33
2			5	6	7	10	8			3		9		4				11				34
2			5	6		10	8		11	3		9		4				7				35
2		4	5		7	10	8		11	3		9		6								36
2				6	7	10		8		3			5	4			9	11				37
			5	6	7	10				3		9	2	4				11		8		38
		4	5	6	7	10		8		3		9	2					11				39
		4	5	6	7		10	8		3		9	2					11				40
		4	5	6		10	8		11			9	2					7			3	41
		4	5		7	10	8		11		1	9	2	6							3	42
0	9	32	40	39	39	35	33	20	30	31	13	20	13	13	8	4	10	10	1	1	2	
		4		3	19	17	17	9	3			10		1	3	1	4	1		1		

Stuart EA	Shorthouse WH	Slater WJ	Wright WA	Flowers R	Hooper H	Broadbent PF	Murray JR	Booth C	Mullen J	Harris GW	Finlayson MJ	Wilshaw DJ	Showell GW	Clamp HE	Mason RH	Neil PT	Bonson J	Deeley NV	Tether C	Thomson RGMcK	Jones G	
2		4	5	6	7	10			11	3					8		9					R3
2		4	5	6	7	10		8	11	3							9					R4
2		2	2	2	2	2		1	2	2					1		2					
				1		1			1								2					

1957-58

Division One

Manager: Stan Cullis

	P	W	D	L	F	A	Pts
Wolverhampton Wanderers	42	28	8	6	103	47	64
Preston North End	42	26	7	9	100	51	59
Tottenham Hotspur	42	21	9	12	93	77	51
West Bromwich Albion	42	18	14	10	92	70	50
Manchester City	42	22	5	15	104	100	49
Burnley	42	21	5	16	80	74	47
Blackpool	42	19	6	17	80	67	44
Luton Town	42	19	6	17	69	63	44
Manchester United	42	16	11	15	85	75	43
Nottingham Forest	42	16	10	16	69	63	42
Chelsea	42	15	12	15	83	79	42
Arsenal	42	16	7	19	73	85	39
Birmingham City	42	14	11	17	76	89	39
Aston Villa	42	16	7	19	73	86	39
Bolton Wanderers	42	14	10	18	65	87	38
Everton	42	13	11	18	65	75	37
Leeds United	42	14	9	19	51	63	37
Leicester City	42	14	5	23	91	112	33
Newcastle United	42	12	8	22	73	81	32
Portsmouth	42	12	8	22	73	88	32
Sunderland	42	10	12	20	54	97	32
Sheffield Wednesday	42	12	7	23	69	92	31

Did you know that?

- The Wolves trio of Eddie Clamp, Billy Wright and Bill Slater formed England's half-back line in four internationals during May and June 1958 (against USSR twice, Brazil and Austria).
- Wolves' teenagers won the FA Youth Cup, beating Chelsea 7–6 on aggregate after coming back from a 5–1 first leg deficit.
- Wolves' first, second, third and fourth teams all won their respective League titles.
- A crowd of 55,169 saw Wolves beat mighty Real Madrid 3–2 in a floodlit friendly at Molineux in October.
- Jackie Henderson was signed from Portsmouth, while Dennis Wilshaw moved to Stoke City.

Match No.	Date		Venue	Opponents	Result		Scorers	Atten
1	Aug	24	A	Everton	L	0-1		58,
2		28	H	Bolton Wanderers	W	6-1	Deeley 2, Murray 2, Booth, Broadbent	30,
3		31	H	Sunderland	W	5-0	Murray 2, Booth, Deeley, Mullen	38,
4	Sep	4	A	Bolton Wanderers	D	1-1	Deeley	25
5		7	A	Luton Town	L	1-3	Wilshaw	22,
6		14	H	Blackpool	W	3-1	Broadbent, Mullen, Murray	38
7		16	H	Aston Villa	W	2-1	Deeley, Murray	26
8		21	A	Leicester City	W	3-2	Murray 2, Clamp (pen)	35
9		23	A	Aston Villa	W	3-2	Broadbent, Deeley, Murray	20
10		28	H	Manchester United	W	3-1	Deeley 2, Wilshaw	48
11	Oct	2	H	Tottenham Hotspur	W	4-0	Broadbent 2, Flowers, Murray	36
12		5	A	Leeds United	D	1-1	Deeley	28
13		12	A	Birmingham City	W	5-1	Clamp 2 (2 pen), Deeley, Murray, Wilshaw	43
14		19	H	Chelsea	W	2-1	Deeley, Wilshaw	37
15		26	A	Newcastle United	D	1-1	Deeley	44
16	Nov	2	H	Nottingham Forest	W	2-0	Broadbent, Deeley	47
17		9	A	Portsmouth	D	1-1	Clamp	38
18		16	H	West Bromwich Albion	D	1-1	Clamp (pen)	55
19		23	A	Manchester City	W	4-3	Murray 2, Broadbent, Mason	45
20		30	H	Burnley	W	2-1	Broadbent, Murray	32
21	Dec	7	A	Preston North End	W	2-1	Lill, Murray	22
22		14	H	Sheffield Wednesday	W	4-3	Broadbent, Clamp (pen), Mason, Murray	28
23		21	H	Everton	W	2-0	Clamp, Mullen	29
24		26	A	Tottenham Hotspur	L	0-1		58
25		28	A	Sunderland	W	2-0	Broadbent, Murray	46
26	Jan	11	H	Luton Town	D	1-1	Mason	30
27		18	A	Blackpool	L	2-3	Deeley, Murray	17
28	Feb	1	H	Leicester City	W	5-1	Murray 2, Broadbent, Deeley, Mason	36
29		19	H	Leeds United	W	3-2	Broadbent, Deeley, Mason	35
30		22	H	Birmingham City	W	5-1	Murray 3, Deeley 2	36
31	Mar	8	H	Newcastle United	W	3-1	Broadbent, Deeley, Mason	34
32		11	A	Chelsea	W	2-1	Deeley, Showell	46
33		15	A	Nottingham Forest	W	4-1	Murray 3, Broadbent	40
34		22	H	Manchester City	D	3-3	Deeley, Mullen, Ewing (og)	34
35		29	A	West Bromwich Albion	W	3-0	Murray 2, Mason	5
36	Apr	5	H	Portsmouth	W	1-0	Clamp (pen)	3
37		7	A	Arsenal	W	2-0	Broadbent, Murray	5
38		8	H	Arsenal	L	1-2	Broadbent	4
39		12	A	Burnley	D	1-1	Clamp (pen)	2
40		19	H	Preston North End	W	2-0	Deeley, Milne (og)	4
41		21	A	Manchester United	W	4-0	Broadbent, Clamp, Deeley, Flowers	3
42		26	A	Sheffield Wednesday	L	1-2	Flowers	2

Appeara

Two own-goals

FA Cup

R3	Jan	4	A	Lincoln City	W	1-0	Mullen	2
R4		25	H	Portsmouth	W	5-1	Broadbent 2, Mason, Mullen, Rutter (og)	4
R5	Feb	15	H	Darlington	W	6-1	Murray, 3, Broadbent 2, Mason	5
R6	Mar	1	A	Bolton Wanderers	L	1-2	Mason	5

Appeara

One own-goal

…EA	Harris GW	Clamp HE	Wright WA	Flowers R	Deeley NV	Booth C	Murray JR	Broadbent PF	Mullen J	Wilshaw DJ	Mason RH	Dwyer NM	Showell GW	Jones G	Lill MJ	Slater WJ	Howells R	Jackson A	Henderson JG	
	3	4	5	6	7	8	9	10	11											1
	3	4	5	6	7	8	9	10	11											2
	3	4	5	6	7	10	9	8	11											3
	3	4	5	6	7	10	9	8	11											4
	3	4	5	6	7	10	9	8		11										5
	3	4	5	6	7		9	10	11		8									6
	3	4	5	6	7		9	10	11		8									7
	3	4	5	6		7	9	8	11	10										8
		4	5	6	7		9	8	11	10		1	3							9
	3	4	5	6	7		9	8	11	10			2							10
	3	4	5	6	7		9	8	11	10										11
	3	4	5	6	7	10		8	11	9										12
	3	4	5	6	7		9	8	11	10										13
	3	4		6	7		9	8	11	10			5	2						14
	3	4	5	6	7		9	8	11	10										15
	3	4	5	6	7		9	8	11	10										16
	3	4	5	6	7		9	8	11	10		1								17
	3	4	5	6	7		9	8	11	10		1								18
	3	4	5	6	7		9	8	11		10	1								19
	3	4	5	6	7		9	8	11		10									20
	3	4	5	6	7	10	9	8							11					21
	3	4	5	6	7		9	8	11		10									22
	3	4	5	6	7		9		11		10					8				23
	3	4	5		7		9	8	11		10					6				24
	3	4			7		9	8	11		10		5			6				25
	3	4	5		7		9	8	11		10					6				26
	3	4	5		7		9	8	11		10					6				27
	3	4	5		7		9	8	11		10					6				28
	3	4	5		7		9	8	11		10					6				29
	3	4	5		7	10	9	8	11							6				30
	3	4	5		7		9	8	11		10						6			31
		4	5		7		9	8	11		10		3				6			32
	3	4	5		7		9	8	11		10					6				33
	3	4	5		7		9	8	11		10					6				34
	3	4	5		7		9	8	11		10					6				35
	3	4	5		7		9	8	11		10					6				36
	3	4	5	6	7		9	8			10							11		37
	3	4	5		7		9	8			10					6		11		38
	3	4		6	7	10	9	8	11				5							39
	3	4		6	7	10	9	8	11				5							40
		4	5	6	7	10	9	8	11			1		3						41
	3		5	6	7	10	9		11							4			8	42
0	39	41	38	28	41	13	41	40	38	12	20	5	7	2	1	14	2	2	1	
		10		3	23	2	29	17	4	4	7		1		1					
	3	4	5		7		9	8	11		10					6				R3
	3	4	5		7		9	8	11		10					6				R4
	3	4	5		7		9	8	11		10					6				R5
	3	4	5	6	7		9	8	11		10									R6
	4	4	4	1	4		4	4	4		4					3				
		4					3		2		3									

1958-59

Division One

Manager: Stan Cullis

	P	W	D	L	F	A	Pts
Wolverhampton Wanderers	42	28	5	9	110	49	61
Manchester United	42	24	7	11	103	66	55
Arsenal	42	21	8	13	88	68	50
Bolton Wanderers	42	20	10	12	79	66	50
West Bromwich Albion	42	18	13	11	88	68	49
West Ham United	42	21	6	15	85	70	48
Burnley	42	19	10	13	81	70	48
Blackpool	42	18	11	13	66	49	47
Birmingham City	42	20	6	16	84	68	46
Blackburn Rovers	42	17	10	15	76	70	44
Newcastle United	42	17	7	18	80	80	41
Preston North End	42	17	7	18	70	77	41
Nottingham Forest	42	17	6	19	71	74	40
Chelsea	42	18	4	20	77	98	40
Leeds United	42	15	9	18	57	74	39
Everton	42	17	4	21	71	87	38
Luton Town	42	12	13	17	68	71	37
Tottenham Hotspur	42	13	10	19	85	95	36
Leicester City	42	11	10	21	67	98	32
Manchester City	42	11	9	22	64	95	31
Aston Villa	42	11	8	23	58	87	30
Portsmouth	42	6	9	27	64	112	21

Match No.	Date		Venue	Opponents	Result		Scorers	Atten
1	Aug	23	H	Nottingham Forest	W	5-1	Mason 3, Broadbent, Deeley	52
2		25	A	West Ham United	L	0-2		37
3		30	A	Chelsea	L	2-6	Mason, Slater (pen)	62
4	Sep	3	H	West Ham United	D	1-1	Broadbent	52
5		6	H	Blackpool	W	2-0	Broadbent, Henderson	46
6		8	A	Aston Villa	W	3-1	Booth, Broadbent, Murray	43
7		13	A	Blackburn Rovers	W	2-1	Home, Woods (og)	43
8		17	H	Aston Villa	W	4-0	Henderson 2, Murray 2	41
9		20	H	Newcastle United	L	1-3	Broadbent	39
10		27	A	Tottenham Hotspur	L	1-2	Clamp (pen)	48
11	Oct	4	H	Manchester United	W	4-0	Murray 2, Mason, Mullen	36
12		11	H	Manchester City	W	2-0	Broadbent, Deeley	33
13		18	A	Arsenal	D	1-1	Showell	49
14		25	H	Birmingham City	W	3-1	Mullen 2, Showell	36
15	Nov	1	A	West Bromwich Albion	L	1-2	Deeley	48
16		8	H	Preston North End	W	2-0	Mason 2	35
17		15	A	Burnley	W	2-0	Deeley, Jackson	23
18		22	H	Bolton Wanderers	L	1-2	Deeley	33
19		29	A	Luton Town	W	1-0	Mullen	20
20	Dec	6	H	Everton	W	1-0	Broadbent	27
21		13	A	Leicester City	L	0-1		25
22		20	A	Nottingham Forest	W	3-1	Broadbent, Horne, Mason	28
23		26	A	Portsmouth	W	5-3	Broadbent 3, Booth, Deeley	28
24		27	H	Portsmouth	W	7-0	Booth 3, Deeley 3, Horne	41
25	Jan	3	H	Chelsea	L	1-2	Deeley	36
26		31	H	Blackburn Rovers	W	5-0	Mason 2, Deeley, Lill, Murray	30
27	Feb	7	A	Newcastle United	W	4-3	Lill 2, Mason, Murray	42
28		14	H	Leeds United	W	6-2	Broadbent 2, Deeley 2, Murray 2	26
29		21	A	Manchester United	L	1-2	Mason	62
30		28	A	Manchester City	W	4-1	Murray 2, Lill, Brannagan (og)	42
31	Mar	2	H	Tottenham Hotspur	D	1-1	Lill	30
32		7	H	Arsenal	W	6-1	Broadbent 2, Deeley 2, Lill, Murray	40
33		14	A	Birmingham City	W	3-0	Murray 2, Broadbent	37
34		21	H	West Bromwich Albion	W	5-2	Lill 3, Deeley, Mason	44
35		28	A	Preston North End	W	2-1	Lill 2	22
36		31	A	Leeds United	W	3-1	Broadbent, Clamp, Murray	35
37	Apr	4	H	Burnley	D	3-3	Broadbent, Harris, Murray	39
38		11	A	Bolton Wanderers	D	2-2	Booth, Murray	26
39		13	A	Blackpool	W	1-0	Murray	2
40		18	H	Luton Town	W	5-0	Broadbent 2, Booth, Clamp, Murray	40
41		22	H	Leicester City	W	3-0	Deeley, Lill, Murray	4
42		25	A	Everton	W	1-0	Murray	2

Appeara

Two own-goals G

FA Cup

R3	Jan	10	A	Barrow	W	4-2	Deeley 2, Booth, Lill	1
R4		24	H	Bolton Wanderers	L	1-2	Hennin (og)	5

Appeara

One own-goal G

Did you know that?

- In October 1958 Wolves featured in the first-ever League game played on a Saturday night, beating Manchester United 4–0 at Molineux.

- Peter Broadbent scored Wolves' first-ever European goal against German side Schalke 04.

- Billy Wright made his 100th international appearance for England, celebrating the occasion with a 1–0 win over Scotland at Wembley. He also retired as a Wolves player with 541 appearances under his belt.

- Wolves' second team won the Central League title for the second season in succession and for the fifth time in nine years. They netted a record 131 goals in the process.

uart EA	Harris GW	Slater WJ	Wright WA	Flowers R	Deeley NV	Broadbent PF	Henderson JG	Mason RH	Horne DT	Mullen J	Booth C	Clamp HE	Murray JR	Lill MJ	Showell GW	Durandt CM	Sidebottom G	Jackson A	Jones G	Kelly JPV	
2	3	4	5	6	7	8	9	10	11												1
2	3	4	5	6	7	8	9	10	11												2
2	3	4	5	6	7	8	9	10		11											3
2	3	4	5	6	7	8	9			11	10										4
2	3	4	5		7	8	11	10				6	9								5
2	3	4	5		7	8				11	10	6	9								6
2	3		5	4	7	8			11		10	6	9								7
2	3	6	5		7	8	11				10	4	9								8
2	3	6	5			8	11				10	4	9	7							9
2	3	4	5			8	7	10		11		6	9								10
2	3	4			7			10		11		6	9		5	8					11
2	3	4	5		7	8		10		11		6	9								12
2	3	4	5		7	8		10		11		6			9						13
2	3	4	5	6	7	8		10		11					9						14
2	3	4	5	6	7	8		10		11					9		1				15
2	3	4	5	6	7	8		10		11					9		1				16
2	3		5	6	7	8		10	11			4					1	9			17
2	3	4	5		7	8		10		11		6						9			18
2	3	4	5	6	7	8		10		11			9								19
2	3	4	5	6	7	8		10		11			9								20
2	3	4	5	6	7	8		10		11			9								21
2	3	4	5	6	7	9		8	11		10										22
2	3	4	5	6	7	9		8	11		10										23
2	3	4	5	6	7	9		8	11		10										24
	3	4	5	6	7	9		8	11		10										25
		4	5	6	11	10		8					9	7					3		26
		4	5		11	10		8				6	9	7					3		27
	3		5	6	11	10		8				4	9	7							28
	3		5	6	11	10		8				4	9	7							29
	3		5	6		10		8		11		4	9	7							30
	3		5	6		10		8		11		4	9	7							31
	3		5	6	11	10		8				4	9	7							32
	3		5	6	11	10		8				4	9	7							33
	3		5	6	11	10		8				4	9	7							34
	3		5	6	11	10		8				4	9	7					2		35
	3		5	6	11	10		8				4	9	7	2						36
	3		5	6	11	10		8				4	9	7					2		37
	3	6			11			8			10	4	9	7	5					2	38
	3		5	6	11	10		8				4	9	7							39
	3		5	6	11	10					8	4	9	7							40
	3		5	6	11	10					8	4	9	7							41
	3	4		6	11	10					8		9	7	5						42
	40	27	39	31	38	40	8	34	8	16	13	26	28	18	8	1	3	2	4	1	
	1	1			17	20	3	13	3	4	7	3	21	12	2			1			

uart EA	Harris GW	Slater WJ	Wright WA	Flowers R	Deeley NV	Broadbent PF	Henderson JG	Mason RH	Horne DT	Mullen J	Booth C	Clamp HE	Murray JR	Lill MJ	Showell GW	Durandt CM	Sidebottom G	Jackson A	Jones G	Kelly JPV	
	3	4	5	6	11	9		8			10			7							R3
	3	4	5	6	7	9		8	11		10										R4
	2	2	2	2	2	2		2	1		2			1							
					2						1			1							

1959-60

Division One

Manager: Stan Cullis

	P	W	D	L	F	A	Pts
Burnley	42	24	7	11	85	61	55
Wolverhampton Wanderers	42	24	6	12	106	67	54
Tottenham Hotspur	42	21	11	10	86	50	53
West Bromwich Albion	42	19	11	12	83	57	49
Sheffield Wednesday	42	19	11	12	80	59	49
Bolton Wanderers	42	20	8	14	59	51	48
Manchester United	42	19	7	16	102	80	45
Newcastle United	42	18	8	16	82	78	44
Preston North End	42	16	12	14	79	76	44
Fulham	42	17	10	15	73	80	44
Blackpool	42	15	10	17	59	71	40
Leicester City	42	13	13	16	66	75	39
Arsenal	42	15	9	18	68	80	39
West Ham United	42	16	6	20	75	91	38
Everton	42	13	11	18	73	78	37
Manchester City	42	17	3	22	78	84	37
Blackburn Rovers	42	16	5	21	60	70	37
Chelsea	42	14	9	19	76	91	37
Birmingham City	42	13	10	19	63	80	36
Nottingham Forest	42	13	9	20	50	74	35
Leeds United	42	12	10	20	65	92	34
Luton Town	42	9	12	21	50	73	30

Did you know that?

- Wolves missed completing the League and Cup double this season by a single point.
- Bill Slater, took over as captain from Eddie Stuart and was named Footballer of the Year in 1960 after lifting the FA Cup at Wembley.
- Wolves became the first club to score a century of League goals in three successive seasons, with 103, 110 and 106. The following season they made it four in a row with another haul of 103.
- Four Scottish-born goalkeepers were registered with Wolves this season – Finlayson, Brodie, McLaren and Evans.
- Colin Booth moved to Nottingham Forest.

Match No.	Date		Venue	Opponents	Result		Scorers	Atte
1	Aug	22	A	Birmingham City	W	1-0	Mason	41
2		26	H	Sheffield Wednesday	W	3-1	Murray 2, Clamp	37
3		29	H	Arsenal	D	3-3	Deeley 2, Lill	45
4	Sep	2	A	Sheffield Wednesday	D	2-2	Murray 2	44
5		5	A	Manchester City	W	6-4	Murray 2, Slater 2, Deeley, Lill	43
6		9	A	Fulham	L	1-3	Deeley	32
7		12	H	Blackburn Rovers	W	3-1	Mason 2, Deeley	3
8		16	H	Fulham	W	9-0	Deeley 4 (1 pen), Broadbent, Clamp, Flowers, Mason, Murray	4
9		19	A	Blackpool	L	1-3	Deeley	3
10		26	H	Everton	W	2-0	Broadbent, Clamp	3
11	Oct	3	A	Luton Town	W	5-1	Deeley 2, Booth, Broadbent, Murray	2
12		10	A	Tottenham Hotspur	L	1-5	Mason	5
13		17	H	Manchester United	W	3-2	Murray 2, Broadbent	4
14		24	A	Preston North End	L	3-4	Horne 2, Murray	2
15		31	H	Newcastle United	W	2-0	Broadbent, Murray	3
16	Nov	7	A	Burnley	L	1-4	Mason	2
17		14	H	Leeds United	W	4-2	Mason 2, Horne, Murray	2
18		21	A	West Ham United	L	2-3	Broadbent, Mason	3
19		28	H	Chelsea	W	3-1	Flowers 2, Clamp	3
20	Dec	5	A	West Bromwich Albion	W	1-0	Murray	4
21		12	H	Leicester City	L	0-3		2
22		19	H	Birmingham City	W	2-0	Mason 2	2
23		26	A	Bolton Wanderers	L	1-2	Murray	3
24		28	H	Bolton Wanderers	L	0-1		2
25	Jan	2	A	Arsenal	D	4-4	Clamp, Horne, Mason, Murray	4
26		16	H	Manchester City	W	4-2	Broadbent 2, Clamp (pen), Murray	2
27		23	A	Blackburn Rovers	W	1-0	Woods (og)	3
28	Feb	6	H	Blackpool	D	1-1	Murray	3
29		13	A	Everton	W	2-0	Murray 2	5
30		23	H	Luton Town	W	3-2	Broadbent, Horne, Murray	3
31		27	H	West Bromwich Albion	W	3-1	Clamp, Deeley, Murray	4
32	Mar	5	A	Manchester United	W	2-0	Deeley, Stobart	6
33		16	H	Preston North End	D	3-3	Broadbent 2, Stobart	2
34		19	A	Leicester City	L	1-2	Murray	2
35		30	H	Burnley	W	6-1	Mannion 2, Broadbent, Horne, Mason, Murray	3
36	Apr	2	A	Leeds United	W	3-0	Mannion 3	2
37		11	H	West Ham United	W	5-0	Murray 2, Clamp, Horne, Mannion	4
38		16	A	Newcastle United	L	0-1		4
39		18	H	Nottingham Forest	W	3-1	Murray 2, McDonald (og)	3
40		19	A	Nottingham Forest	D	0-0		4
41		23	H	Tottenham Hotspur	L	1-3	Broadbent	5
42		30	A	Chelsea	W	5-1	Horne 2, Broadbent, Flowers (pen), Murray	6

Appeara

Two own-goals

FA Cup

R3	Jan	9	A	Newcastle United	D	2-2	Clamp (pen), Flowers	6
rep		13	H	Newcastle United	W	4-2	Deeley, Flowers, Horne, Murray	3
R4		30	H	Charlton Athletic	W	2-1	Broadbent, Horne	3
R5	Feb	20	A	Luton Town	W	4-1	Mason 2, Clamp, Murray	2
R6	Mar	12	A	Leicester City	W	2-1	Broadbent, Chalmers (og)	4
SF		26	N	Aston Villa	W	1-0	Deeley	5
F	May	7	N	Blackburn Rovers	W	3-0	Deeley 2, McGrath (og)	[illegible]

SF at The Hawthorns. Final at Wembley Stadium.

Appear

Two own-goals

son MJ	Stuart EA	Jones G	Clamp HE	Showell GW	Flowers R	Lill MJ	Mason RH	Murray JR	Broadbent PF	Deeley NV	Booth C	Harris GW	Durandt CM	Slater WJ	Horne DT	Kelly JPV	Kirkham JK	Sidebottom G	Mannion GP	Stobart BH	
	2	3	4	5	6	7	8	9	10	11											1
	2	3	4	5	6	7	8	9		11	10										2
	2		4	5	6	7	8	9		11		3	10								3
	2	3	4	5	6	7	8	9		11			10								4
	2		4	5	6	7	8	9		11		3		10							5
	2		4	5	6	7	8	9		11		3		10							6
	2		6	5		7	8	9	10	11		3		4							7
	2		6	5	4	7	8	9	10	11		3									8
	2		6	5	4	7	8	9	10	11		3									9
	2		6	5		7	8	9	10	11		3		4							10
		2		5	6			9	10	7	8	3		4	11						11
	2		6		5	7	8	9		11	10	3		4							12
	5							9	10	7		3	8	4	11	2	6				13
	5				6			9	10	7		3	8	4	11	2					14
	5				6		8	9	10	7		3		4	11	2					15
	5		4		6		8	9	10	7		3			11	2					16
	2		4	5	6		8	9	10	7		3			11						17
	2		4	5	6		8	9	10	7		3			11						18
	2		4		6		8	9	10	7		3		5	11						19
	2		4	5	6		8	9	10	7		3			11						20
	2		4	5	6		8	9	10	7		3			11						21
	2		4	5			8	9		7		3	10	6	11						22
	2		4	5	6		8	9	10	7		3			11						23
	2		4		6		8	9	10	7		3		5	11						24
			4	2	6		8	9	10	7		3		5	11						25
			4	2	6		8	9	10	7		3		5	11						26
	2		6				8	9	10	7		3		5	11		4				27
		3	4	2	6		8	9	10	7				5	11						28
	2		4		6		8	9	10	7		3		5	11			1			29
	3		4	2	6		10	9	8	7				5	11			1			30
			4	2	6		10	9	8	7		3		5	11			1			31
			4	2	6		10		8	11		3		5				1	7	9	32
			4	2			8		10	11		3		5			6	1	7	9	33
	2		4		6			8	10	11		3		5				1	7	9	34
			4	2	6		8	9	10			3		5	11			1	7		35
			4	2	6		8	9	10			3		5	11				7		36
			4	2	6		8	9	10			3		5	11				7		37
			4	2	6		8	9				3	10	5	11				7		38
			4	2	6		8	9	10	11		3		5					7		39
	5		4	2			10	9				3	8	6	11				7		40
			4	2	6		8	9	10	11		3		5					7		41
			4	2	6			9	10	7		3		5	11					8	42
	28	5	38	32	35	11	37	40	33	37	3	37	7	30	26	4	3	7	10	4	
			8		4	2	13	29	14	14	1			2	9				6	2	
	2		4		6		8	9	10	7		3		5	11						R3
	2		4		6		8	9	10	7		3		5	11						rep
	2		4		6		8	9	10	7		3		5	11						R4
	2		4		6		8	9	10	7		3		5	11			1			R5
			4	2	6		8		10	7		3		5	11			1		9	R6
			4	2	6		8	9	10	11		3		5					7		SF
			4	2	6			9	10	7		3		5	11					8	F
	4		7	3	7		6	6	7	7		7		7	6			2	1	2	
			2		2		2	2	2	4					2						

1960-61

Division One

Manager: Stan Cullis

	P	W	D	L	F	A	Pts
Tottenham Hotspur	42	31	4	7	115	55	66
Sheffield Wednesday	42	23	12	7	78	47	58
Wolverhampton Wanderers	42	25	7	10	103	75	57
Burnley	42	22	7	13	102	77	51
Everton	42	22	6	14	87	69	50
Leicester City	42	18	9	15	87	70	45
Manchester United	42	18	9	15	88	76	45
Blackburn Rovers	42	15	13	14	77	76	43
Aston Villa	42	17	9	16	78	77	43
West Bromwich Albion	42	18	5	19	67	71	41
Arsenal	42	15	11	16	77	85	41
Chelsea	42	15	7	20	98	100	37
Manchester City	42	13	11	18	79	90	37
Nottingham Forest	42	14	9	19	62	78	37
Cardiff City	42	13	11	18	60	85	37
West Ham United	42	13	10	19	77	88	36
Fulham	42	14	8	20	72	95	36
Bolton Wanderers	42	12	11	19	58	73	35
Birmingham City	42	14	6	22	62	84	34
Blackpool	42	12	9	21	68	73	33
Newcastle United	42	11	10	21	86	109	32
Preston North End	42	10	10	22	43	71	30

Did you know that?

- Wolves became the first English club to compete in the European Cup-winners' Cup competition.
- Ted Farmer netted twice on his League debut for Wolves in their 3–1 win at Old Trafford in September and finished up as leading scorer in his first season.
- Wingers Des Horne and Gerry Mannion both left Molineux, joining Blackpool and Norwich City respectively.

Match No.	Date		Venue	Opponents	Result		Scorers	Atte
1	Aug	20	H	West Ham United	W	4-2	Flowers 2, Broadbent, Murray	37
2		24	A	Bolton Wanderers	W	2-0	Horne, Murray	20
3		27	A	Chelsea	D	3-3	Murray 2, Horne	41
4		31	H	Bolton Wanderers	W	3-1	Broadbent, Deeley, Horne	37
5	Sep	3	H	Blackpool	W	1-0	Mason	34
6		7	H	Leicester City	W	3-2	Murray 2, Broadbent	33
7		10	A	Everton	L	1-3	Flowers	53
8		14	A	Leicester City	L	0-2		20
9		17	H	Blackburn Rovers	D	0-0		28
10		24	A	Manchester United	W	3-1	Farmer 2, Horne	44
11	Oct	1	H	Tottenham Hotspur	L	0-4		52
12		8	H	Cardiff City	D	2-2	Farmer 2	23
13		15	A	Newcastle United	D	4-4	Broadbent 2, Farmer, Murray	23
14		22	H	Sheffield Wednesday	W	4-1	Murray 2, Broadbent, Deeley	30
15		29	A	Birmingham City	W	2-1	Mason, Murray	32
16	Nov	5	H	Nottingham Forest	W	5-3	Farmer 2, Broadbent, Deeley, Palmer (og)	24
17		12	A	Burnley	L	3-5	Farmer 2, Broadbent	26
18		19	H	Preston North End	W	3-0	Broadbent, Farmer, Mason	23
19		26	A	Fulham	W	3-1	Farmer 2, Mason	23
20	Dec	3	H	Arsenal	W	5-3	Farmer 3, Deeley, Groves (og)	25
21		10	A	Manchester City	W	4-2	Durandt, Farmer, Flowers, Mason	30
22		17	A	West Ham United	L	0-5		22
23		24	A	Aston Villa	W	2-0	Durandt, Farmer	49
24		26	H	Aston Villa	W	3-2	Farmer 2, Murray (pen)	43
25		31	H	Chelsea	W	6-1	Murray 3, Durandt, Farmer, Kirkham	28
26	Jan	21	H	Everton	W	4-1	Murray 2, Deeley, Farmer	31
27		28	H	West Bromwich Albion	W	4-2	Murray 2 (1pen), Deeley, Durandt	31
28	Feb	4	A	Blackburn Rovers	L	1-2	Durandt	15
29		11	H	Manchester United	W	2-1	Flowers, Brennan (og)	38
30		22	A	Tottenham Hotspur	D	1-1	Farmer	62
31		25	A	Cardiff City	L	2-3	Farmer 2	24
32	Mar	4	A	Blackpool	L	2-5	Durandt 2	15
33		8	H	Newcastle United	W	2-1	Broadbent, Murray (pen)	24
34		11	A	Sheffield Wednesday	D	0-0		33
35		18	H	Birmingham City	W	5-1	Farmer 4, Murray	23
36		25	A	Nottingham Forest	D	1-1	Murray (pen)	24
37	Apr	1	H	Manchester City	W	1-0	Murray	25
38		3	A	West Bromwich Albion	L	1-2	Stobart	34
39		8	A	Preston North End	W	2-1	Mannion, Stobart	18
40		15	H	Burnley	W	2-1	Durandt, Kirkham	25
41		22	A	Arsenal	W	5-1	Stobart 2, Broadbent, Mason, Murray	34
42		29	H	Fulham	L	2-4	Deeley, Stobart	24
								Appearan
							Three own-goals	Go

FA Cup

R3	Jan	7	H	Huddersfield Town	D	1-1	Kirkham	31
rep		11	A	Huddersfield Town	L	1-2	Murray (pen)	46
								Appearan
								Go

	Showell GW	Harris GW	Clamp HE	Stuart EA	Flowers R	Deeley NV	Mason RH	Murray JR	Broadbent PF	Horne DT	Slater WJ	Mannion GP	Stobart BH	Durandt CM	Kelly JPV	Farmer JE	Finlayson MJ	Kirkham JK	Cocker LJR	Brodie CTG	Hinton AT
1	2	3	4	5	6	7	8	9	10	11											
2	2	3	4		6	7	8	9	10	11	5										
3	2	3	4		6	7	8	9	10	11	5										
4	2	3	4		6	7	8	9	10	11	5										
5	2	3	4		6	11	8	9	10		5	7									
6	2	3	4		6	11	8	9	10		5	7									
7	2	3	4		6	11	8	9			5		7	10							
8	2	3	4		6	11	7	9	10		5		8								
9	3		4	5	6	7	10	9	8				11		2						
10	2	3	4	5	6	7	10		8	11						9					
11	2	3	4	5	6	7	10		8	11						9					
12	2	3	4	5		11			10		6	7	8			9					
13	3			5	6	11	7	8	10		4				2	9					
14	3		4	2	6	11	7	8	10		5					9	1				
15	3		4	2	6	11	7	8	10		5					9	1				
16	3		4	2	6	11	7	8	10		5					9	1				
17	2	3	4		6		7	8	10		5			11		9	1				
18		3	4	2	6	7	8		10		5			11		9					
19		3	4	2	6	7	8		10		5			11		9					
20		3	4	2	6	7	8		10		5			11		9					
21		3	4	2	6	7	8		10		5			11		9					
22		3	4	2		7			10		5		8	11		9		6			
23		3	6	2	4	7		8	10		5			11		9	1				
24	2	3	6			7		8	10		5			11		9	1	4			
25		3	6	2		7		8	10		5			11		9	1	4			
26	3		6	2		7		8	10		5			11		9	1	4			
27	3			2	6	7		8	10		5			11		9	1	4			
28	3		4	2	6	7			10		5			11		9	1		8		
29	3		4	2	8	7			10		5			11		9		6		1	
30	3		4	2	6	7		8	10		5			11		9	1				
31	5	3	4	2	6	7		8	10					11		9	1				
32	5	3	4	2	6	7		8	10					11		9	1				
33	5	3	4	2	6	11	8	9	10			7					1				
34	5	3	4	2	6	11	10	8				7				9	1				
35	3		4	2	6	7	10	8			5			11		9	1				
36	3		4	2	6	7	10	8			5			11		9	1				
37	3		4	2	6	7	10	8			5			11		9	1				
38	3		4	2	6	11		8	10		5	7	9				1				
39	3		10	2	6			8			5	7	9	11			1	4			
40	3		4	2		7	8		10		5		9	11			1	6			
41		3	4		6	11	7	8	10		5		9		2		1				
42		3	4		6	11	7	8	10		5		9		2		1				
	3	26	40	31	36	40	28	31	36	6	34	7	10	22	4	27	23	8	1	1	
					5	7	6	23	11	4		1	5	8		28		2			

	Showell GW	Harris GW	Clamp HE	Stuart EA	Flowers R	Deeley NV	Mason RH	Murray JR	Broadbent PF	Horne DT	Slater WJ	Mannion GP	Stobart BH	Durandt CM	Kelly JPV	Farmer JE	Finlayson MJ	Kirkham JK	Cocker LJR	Brodie CTG	Hinton AT
R3	5	3	6	2		7		8	10							9	1	4			11
rep	3		4	2		7		8	10		5			11		9	1	6			
	2	1	2	2		2		2	2		1			1		2	2	2			1
								1										1			

1961-62

Division One

Manager: Stan Cullis

	P	W	D	L	F	A	Pts
Ipswich Town	42	24	8	10	93	67	56
Burnley	42	21	11	10	101	67	53
Tottenham Hotspur	42	21	10	11	88	69	52
Everton	42	20	11	11	88	54	51
Sheffield United	42	19	9	14	61	69	47
Sheffield Wednesday	42	20	6	16	72	58	46
Aston Villa	42	18	8	16	65	56	44
West Ham United	42	17	10	15	76	82	44
West Bromwich Albion	42	15	13	14	83	67	43
Arsenal	42	16	11	15	71	72	43
Bolton Wanderers	42	16	10	16	62	66	42
Manchester City	42	17	7	18	78	81	41
Blackpool	42	15	11	16	70	75	41
Leicester City	42	17	6	19	72	71	40
Manchester United	42	15	9	18	72	75	39
Blackburn Rovers	42	14	11	17	50	58	39
Birmingham City	42	14	10	18	65	81	38
Wolverhampton Wanderers	42	13	10	19	73	86	36
Nottingham Forest	42	13	10	19	63	79	36
Fulham	42	13	7	22	66	74	33
Cardiff City	42	9	14	19	50	81	32
Chelsea	42	9	10	23	63	94	28

Did you know that?

- Future England full-back Bobby Thomson made his senior debut for Wolves in the fourth-round FA Cup tie against West Bromwich Albion, as did goalkeeper Fred Davies and half-back Freddie Goodwin.
- Wolves' youngsters were defeated by Newcastle United in the FA Youth Cup Final.
- Ted Farmer scored four goals in his two outings for England's Under-23 side this season, including a hat-trick against Holland.
- Billy Wright and Jimmy Mullen shared a benefit match at Molineux in April, when Wolves drew 4–4 with an International XI.
- New recruits included Chris Crowe (from Leeds) and Peter McParland (from Aston Villa), while Eddie Clamp (to Arsenal), Eddie Stuart (to Stoke) and Norman Deeley (to Leyton Orient) were all sold.

Match No.	Date		Venue	Opponents	Result		Scorers	A
1	Aug	19	A	Sheffield United	L	1-2	Flowers	
2		26	H	West Ham United	W	3-2	Murray 2, Deeley	
3		28	H	Aston Villa	D	2-2	Farmer 2	
4	Sep	2	A	Blackburn Rovers	L	1-2	Farmer	
5		9	H	Blackpool	D	2-2	Murray 2	
6		16	A	Tottenham Hotspur	L	0-1		
7		19	A	Nottingham Forest	L	1-3	Murray	
8		23	H	Cardiff City	D	1-1	Farmer	
9		27	H	Nottingham Forest	W	2-1	Kirkham 2	
10		30	A	Manchester United	W	2-0	Broadbent, Kirkham	
11	Oct	2	A	Aston Villa	L	0-1		
12		7	A	Birmingham City	W	6-3	Mason 2, Deeley, Lazarus, Murray, Slater	
13		14	H	Everton	L	0-3		
14		21	A	Bolton Wanderers	L	0-1		
15		28	H	Manchester City	W	4-1	Durandt, Hinton, Lazarus, Murray (pen)	
16	Nov	4	A	Leicester City	L	0-3		
17		11	H	Ipswich Town	W	2-0	Hinton, Wharton	
18		18	A	Burnley	D	3-3	Flowers, Hinton, Murray	
19		25	H	Arsenal	L	2-3	Wharton 2	
20	Dec	2	A	Fulham	W	1-0	Murray	
21		9	H	Sheffield Wednesday	W	3-0	Hinton, Lazarus, Wharton	
22		16	H	Sheffield United	L	0-1		
23		18	A	West Ham United	L	2-4	Murray 2	
24		26	A	West Bromwich Albion	D	1-1	Murray	
25	Jan	13	H	Blackburn Rovers	L	0-2		
26		20	A	Blackpool	L	2-7	Murray (pen), Wharton	
27	Feb	3	H	Tottenham Hotspur	W	3-1	Crowe, McParland, Wharton	
28		9	A	Cardiff City	W	3-2	Wharton 2, McParland	
29		24	H	Birmingham City	W	2-1	McParland, Wharton	
30		28	H	Manchester United	D	2-2	Crowe, Murray	
31	Mar	3	A	Everton	L	0-4		
32		10	H	Bolton Wanderers	W	5-1	McParland 2, Broadbent, Crowe, Murray	
33		17	A	Manchester City	D	2-2	Crowe, Wharton	
34		24	H	Leicester City	D	1-1	Hinton	
35		28	H	West Bromwich Albion	L	1-5	Broadbent	
36		31	A	Ipswich Town	L	2-3	Flowers, McParland	
37	Apr	7	H	Burnley	D	1-1	Crowe	
38		14	A	Arsenal	L	1-3	Murray	
39		20	A	Chelsea	W	5-4	Crowe 2, Kirkham, McParland, Whartor	
40		21	H	Fulham	L	1-3	Broadbent	
41		23	H	Chelsea	D	1-1	Broadbent	
42		28	A	Sheffield Wednesday	L	2-3	Farmer, Flowers	

Appeara

FA Cup

R3	Jan	8	H	Carlisle United	W	3-1	Wharton, 2, Broadbent	
R4		27	H	West Bromwich Albion	L	1-2	Murray	

Appeara

	Stuart EA	Showell GW	Clamp E	Slater WJ	Flowers R	Deeley NV	Mason RH	Murray JR	Broadbent PF	Durandt CM	Harris DJ	Hinton AT	Farmer JE	Jones G	Stobart BH	Kirkham J	Kelly JPV	Lazarus M	Harris GW	Wharton TJ	Davies F	Thomson RA	Crowe C	McParland P	Goodwin FJ	Woodfield D
1	2	3	4	5	6	7	8	9	10	11																
2	2		4	5	6	7	8	9	10		3	11														
3	2		4	5	6	7	8	10			3	11	9													
4	2		4	5	6	8		10				11	9	3	7											
5	2		4	5	6	7		10		11			9	3	8											
6	2		4	5	6	11		8		10			9	3	7											
7	2		4	5		11	7	9	10	8				3		6										
8			4	5	6		11	8	10				9	3			2	7								
9	2		4	5		11	7	10	8				9			6			3							
10	2		4	5		11	7	10	8				9			6			3							
11	2		4	5		11		10	8				9			6		7	3							
12	2		4	5	6	11	7	10	8									9	3							
13	2		4	5		11		10	8	7						6		9	3							
14	2		4	5	6	11	7	10	8									9	3							
15	2		4	5	6		8	9		10		11						7	3							
16	2		4	5	6		8	9		10		11						7	3							
17	2		4	5	6		8	9	10			11							3	7						
18	2			5	6		8	9	10			11				4			3	7						
19	2			5	6		8	9	10			11				4			3	7						
20		2		5	6			8	10			11	9			4			3	7						
21	2			5	6					10		11			9	4	3	8		7						
22	2			5	6					10		11			9	4	3	8		7						
23	2			5	6			9	10	8		11				4	3			7						
24	2			5	6		8	9	10			11				4	3			7						
25	2			5	6		8	9	10			11				4	3			7						
26	2	5		4	6		8	9	10			11					3			7						
27	2			5	6			9	10							4				7	1	3	8	11		
28				5	6			9	10					3		4				7	1	2	8	11		
29	2	5			6			9	10							4				7	1	3	8	11		
30	2	5			6			9	10							4				7	1	3	8	11		
31	2			5				9		10				6		4				7	1	3	8	11		
32	2			5	6			9	10							4				7	1	3	8	11		
33	2			5	6			9	10							4				7	1	3	8	11		
34	2			5	6			9	10			11				4				7		3	8			
35	2			5	6			9	10							4				7		3	8	11		
36	2	3		5	6			8	10							4				11			7	9		
37	2			5	6			8	10							4				11		3	7	9		
38	2			5				8	10							6				7	1	3	11	9	4	
39	2	3		5	4			9	10							6				7	1		8	11		
40		2		5	4			9	10							6				7	1	3	8	11		
41		2			4				10	8			9			6				7	1	3		11		5
42		2			4		8		10	7			9			6					1	3		11		5
	6	10	17	38	35	13	18	38	33	13	2	16	11	7	5	29	7	9	12	25	12	14	14	15	1	2
				1	4	2	2	16	5	1		5	5			4		3		11			7	7		
R3	2			5	6	11	8	9	10							4	3			7						
R4	2			5	6			8	10	11					9					7	1	3			4	
	2			2	2	1	1	2	2	1					1	1	1			2	1	1			1	
								1	1											2						

1962-63

Division One

Manager: Stan Cullis

	P	W	D	L	F	A	Pts
Everton	42	25	11	6	84	42	61
Tottenham Hotspur	42	23	9	10	111	62	55
Burnley	42	22	10	10	78	57	54
Leicester City	42	20	12	10	79	53	52
Wolverhampton Wanderers	42	20	10	12	93	65	50
Sheffield Wednesday	42	19	10	13	77	63	48
Arsenal	42	18	10	14	86	77	46
Liverpool	42	17	10	15	71	59	44
Nottingham Forest	42	17	10	15	67	69	44
Sheffield United	42	16	12	14	58	60	44
Blackburn Rovers	42	15	12	15	79	71	42
West Ham United	42	14	12	16	73	69	40
Blackpool	42	13	14	15	58	64	40
West Bromwich Albion	42	16	7	19	71	79	39
Aston Villa	42	15	8	19	62	68	38
Fulham	42	14	10	18	50	71	38
Ipswich Town	42	12	11	19	59	78	35
Bolton Wanderers	42	15	5	22	55	75	35
Manchester United	42	12	10	20	67	81	34
Birmingham City	42	10	13	19	63	90	33
Manchester City	42	10	11	21	58	102	31
Leyton Orient	42	6	9	27	37	81	21

Did you know that?

- Wolves scored five goals in 15 minutes either side of half-time in their 8–1 win over Manchester City on the opening day of the season.
- On 6 April 1963, Ron Flowers played for England against Scotland in the 148th successive England international to include a Wolves player (since 26 October 1938).
- Wolves toured the USA and Canada in May and June, winning nine and drawing one of their 10 games.
- Following Bill Slater's departure to Brentford, Ron Flowers took over as captain.
- The Queen visited Molineux for the first time in the summer of 1962.

Match No.	Date		Venue	Opponents	Result		Scorers
1	Aug	18	H	Manchester City	W	8-1	Farmer 4, Murray 2, Hinton, Wharton
2		20	A	West Ham United	W	4-1	Farmer 2, Crowe, Wharton
3		25	A	Blackpool	W	2-0	Crowe 2
4		29	H	West Ham United	D	0-0	
5	Sep	1	H	Blackburn Rovers	W	4-2	Hinton 2, Crowe, Farmer
6		8	A	Sheffield United	W	2-1	Farmer, Wharton
7		12	A	Tottenham Hotspur	W	2-1	Crowe, Wharton
8		15	H	Nottingham Forest	D	1-1	Wharton
9		19	H	Tottenham Hotspur	D	2-2	Murray 2
10		22	A	Ipswich Town	W	3-2	McParland 2, Hinton
11		29	H	Liverpool	W	3-2	Crowe, Murray (pen), Wharton
12	Oct	6	H	Everton	L	0-2	
13		13	A	Bolton Wanderers	L	0-3	
14		24	H	Birmingham City	L	0-2	
15		27	A	Arsenal	L	4-5	Broadbent, Crowe, Flowers (pen), McParland
16	Nov	3	H	Sheffield Wednesday	D	2-2	Kirkham 2
17		10	A	Burnley	L	0-2	
18		17	H	Manchester United	L	2-3	Stobart 2
19		24	A	Leyton Orient	W	4-0	Stobart 2, Crowe, Hinton
20	Dec	1	H	Leicester City	L	1-3	Hinton
21		8	A	Fulham	W	5-0	Hinton 3, Galley, Stobart
22		15	A	Manchester City	D	3-3	Crowe, Galley, Stobart
23	Jan	19	H	Sheffield United	D	0-0	
24	Feb	16	A	Liverpool	L	1-4	Murray
25		23	A	Everton	D	0-0	
26	Mar	9	A	Birmingham City	W	4-3	Broadbent, Kirkham, Stobart, Wharton
27		16	H	West Bromwich Albion	W	7-0	Wharton 3, Hinton 2, Stobart 2
28		20	H	Bolton Wanderers	W	4-0	Crowe, Kirkham, Stobart, Wharton
29		23	A	Sheffield Wednesday	L	1-3	Hinton
30		30	H	Leyton Orient	W	2-1	Stobart, Wharton
31	Apr	3	A	West Bromwich Albion	D	2-2	Hinton, Stobart
32		8	H	Arsenal	W	1-0	Wharton
33		13	H	Burnley	W	7-2	Broadbent 2, Hinton 2, Murray, Wharton, Angus (og)
34		15	H	Aston Villa	W	3-1	Hinton, Murray, Wharton
35		16	A	Aston Villa	W	2-0	Hinton, Wharton
36		20	A	Leicester City	D	1-1	Hinton
37		22	A	Manchester United	L	1-2	Dunne (og)
38		27	H	Fulham	W	2-1	Flowers, Hinton
39		30	A	Nottingham Forest	L	0-2	
40	May	4	H	Ipswich Town	D	0-0	
41		9	H	Blackpool	W	2-0	Broadbent, Farmer
42		13	A	Blackburn Rovers	L	1-5	Crowe

Two own-goals

FA Cup

R3	Jan	29	A	Nottingham Forest	L	3-4	Stobart 2, Broadbent

Thomson RA	Goodwin FJ	Woodfield D	Flowers R	Wharton TJ	Crowe C	Farmer E	Murray JR	Hinton AT	Harris GW	McParland PJ	Kirkham J	Broadbent PF	Stobart BH	Slater WJ	Galley JE	Harris DJ	Finlayson MJ	
3	4	5	6	7	8	9	10	11										1
3	4	5	6	7	8	9	10	11										2
3	4	5	6	7	8	9	10	11										3
3	4	5	6	7	8	9	10	11										4
3	4	5	6	7	8	9	10	11										5
2	4	5	6	7	8	9	10	11	3									6
3	4	5	6	7	8	9	10	11										7
3	4	5	6	7	8	9	10	11										8
3	4	5	6	7	8	9	10	11										9
3	4	5	6	7	8		10	11		9								10
3	4	5	6	7	8	9	10	11										11
3	4	5		7	8		10	11		9	6							12
3	4	5	6	7	8		10	11		9								13
3	4	5	6	7	8		10	11		9								14
3		5	6	7	8		9			11	4	10						15
3		5	6		7		8	11			4	10	9					16
3		5	6		8		7			11	4	10	9					17
3		5	6	7	8			11			4	10	9					18
3			6	7	8			11			4	10	9	5				19
3			6	7	8			11			4	10	9	5				20
3			6		8			11			4	7	10	5	9			21
3			6		8			11			4	7	10	5	9	2		22
2		5	6		8			11	3		4	7	10		9			23
3		5	6	11	8		9				4	7	10				1	24
3		5	6	7	8			11			4	10	9					25
3		5	6	7	8			11			4	10	9					26
3		5	6	7	8			11			4	10	9					27
3			6	7	8			11			4	10	9	5				28
3		5	6	7	8			11			4	10	9					29
3		5	6	7	8			11			4	10	9					30
3		5	6	7			8	11			4	10	9					31
3		5	6	7			8	11			4	10	9					32
3		5	6	7			8	11			4	10	9					33
3		5	6	7			8	11			4	10	9					34
3		5	6	7	8		9	11			4	10						35
3			6	7			8	11	2		4	10	9					36
3	6	5		11	7		8				4	10	9					37
3		5	6	7	8		9	11			4	10						38
2		5	6		7		8	11	3		4	10	9					39
2		5	6		7	9	8	11	3		4	10						40
2			6		7	9	8	11	3		4	10		5				41
2			6	7	8	9		11	3		4		10	5				42
42	15	34	40	34	37	13	29	38	7	6	29	27	23	7	3	1	1	
			2	16	11	9	8	19		3	4	5	12		2			

Thomson RA	Goodwin FJ	Woodfield D	Flowers R	Wharton TJ	Crowe C	Farmer E	Murray JR	Hinton AT	Harris GW	McParland PJ	Kirkham J	Broadbent PF	Stobart BH	Slater WJ	Galley JE	Harris DJ	Finlayson MJ	
3		5	6		8			11			4	7	10		9			R3
1		1	1		1			1			1	1	1		1			
												1	2					

1963-64

Division One

Manager: Stan Cullis

	P	W	D	L	F	A	Pts
Liverpool	42	26	5	11	92	45	57
Manchester United	42	23	7	12	90	62	53
Everton	42	21	10	11	84	64	52
Tottenham Hotspur	42	22	7	13	97	81	51
Chelsea	42	20	10	12	72	56	50
Sheffield Wednesday	42	19	11	12	84	67	49
Blackburn Rovers	42	18	10	14	89	65	46
Arsenal	42	17	11	14	90	82	45
Burnley	42	17	10	15	71	64	44
West Bromwich Albion	42	16	11	15	70	61	43
Leicester City	42	16	11	15	61	58	43
Sheffield United	42	16	11	15	61	64	43
Nottingham Forest	42	16	9	17	64	68	41
West Ham United	42	14	12	16	69	74	40
Fulham	42	13	13	16	58	65	39
Wolverhampton Wanderers	42	12	15	15	70	80	39
Stoke City	42	14	10	18	77	78	38
Blackpool	42	13	9	20	52	73	35
Aston Villa	42	11	12	19	62	71	34
Birmingham City	42	11	7	24	54	92	29
Bolton Wanderers	42	10	8	24	48	80	28
Ipswich Town	42	9	7	26	56	121	25

Did you know that?

- After scoring twice, Ray Crawford took over in goal from Fred Davies during Wolves' 4–3 defeat by Sheffield United at Bramall Lane in March.
- Wolves toured the Caribbean in May and June and played eight games, five against Chelsea!
- Wolves kicked off at the start of each half in their home League game with Stoke City in August.
- Out of Molineux went Alan Hinton to Nottingham Forest and both Jimmy Murray and Barry Stobart to Manchester City, while into the camp came Ray Crawford (from Ipswich), Bobby Woodruff (from Swindon) and Jimmy Melia (from Liverpool).

Match No.	Date		Venue	Opponents	Result		Scorers
1	Aug	24	A	Arsenal	W	3-1	Crowe, Hinton, Murray
2		28	H	Tottenham Hotspur	L	1-4	Hinton
3		31	H	Stoke City	W	2-1	Crowe, Farmer
4	Sep	4	A	Tottenham Hotspur	L	3-4	Hinton, Crowe, Kirkham
5		7	A	Nottingham Forest	L	0-3	
6		9	H	Liverpool	L	1-3	Flowers
7		14	H	Blackburn Rovers	L	1-5	Farmer
8		16	A	Liverpool	L	0-6	
9		21	A	Blackpool	W	2-1	Crawford 2
10		28	H	Chelsea	W	4-1	Wharton 2, Crawford, Broadbent
11	Oct	2	H	West Bromwich Albion	D	0-0	
12		5	A	West Ham United	D	1-1	Hinton
13		14	A	Leicester City	W	1-0	Crawford
14		19	H	Bolton Wanderers	D	2-2	Knowles, Broadbent
15		26	A	Birmingham City	D	2-2	Hinton, Wharton
16	Nov	2	H	Manchester United	W	2-0	Wharton, Crawford
17		9	A	Burnley	L	0-1	
18		16	H	Ipswich Town	W	2-1	Crawford, Knowles
19		23	A	Sheffield Wednesday	L	0-5	
20		30	H	Everton	D	0-0	
21	Dec	7	A	Fulham	L	1-4	Crawford
22		14	H	Arsenal	D	2-2	Crowe, Flowers
23		21	A	Stoke City	W	2-0	Crawford 2
24		26	H	Aston Villa	D	3-3	Wharton, Crawford 2
25		28	A	Aston Villa	D	2-2	Crawford, Crowe
26	Jan	11	H	Nottingham Forest	L	2-3	Broadbent, Crowe
27		18	A	Blackburn Rovers	D	1-1	Stobart
28	Feb	1	H	Blackpool	D	1-1	Crawford
29		8	A	Chelsea	W	3-2	Crawford 2, Le Flem
30		17	H	West Ham United	L	0-2	
31		22	H	Leicester City	L	1-2	Broadbent (pen)
32		29	A	West Bromwich Albion	L	1-3	Le Flem
33	Mar	7	H	Birmingham City	W	5-1	Wharton 2, Crawford, Flowers, Le Flem
34		21	H	Burnley	D	1-1	Wharton
35		28	A	Manchester United	D	2-2	Crawford 2
36		30	H	Sheffield United	D	1-1	Crawford
37		31	A	Sheffield United	L	3-4	Melia, Crawford 2
38	Apr	4	H	Sheffield Wednesday	D	1-1	Melia
39		11	A	Everton	D	3-3	Crawford 2, Wharton
40		14	A	Ipswich Town	L	0-1	
41		18	H	Fulham	W	4-0	Melia 2, Le Flem, Knowles
42		24	A	Bolton Wanderers	W	4-0	Crawford 3, Knowles

Appear

FA Cup

R3	Jan	4	A	Arsenal	L	1-2	Wharton

Appear

Thomson RA	Kirkham J	Woodfield D	Flowers R	Wharton TJ	Crowe C	Farmer JE	Murray JR	Hinton AT	Broadbent PF	Stobart BH	Goodwin FJ	Finlayson MJ	Harris GW	Crawford R	Knowles PR	Barron J	Le Flem RP	Woodruff RW	Melia J	
3	4	5	6	7	8	9	10	11												1
3	4	5	6	7	8	9	10	11												2
3	4	5	6	7	8	9	10	11												3
3	4	5	6	7	8		9	11	10											4
3	4	5	6	7	10		9	11	8											5
3		5	6	7	10		9	11	4	8										6
3	6	5		7	8	9		11	10		4									7
2	4		6	11	7		8		10			1	3	9						8
2		5	6	11	7				10	8	4		3	9						9
2		5	6	11	7				10	8	4		3	9						10
2			5	7	10			11	6	8	4		3	9						11
2		5	6	7	8			11	10		4		3	9						12
3		5	6		7		10	11			4			9	8					13
3	6		5		7			11	10		4			9	8					14
3		5	6	7				11	10		4			9	8					15
3		5	6	7				11	10		4			9	8					16
3		5	6	7				11	10		4			9	8					17
3		5	6	7				11	10		4			9	8					18
2		5	6	11		8				7	4		3	9	10					19
3		5	6	11	7				10		4			9	8	1				20
3		5	6	7	10			11			4			9	8					21
3		5	6	7	10			11			4			9	8					22
3	6		5	7	8			11	10		4			9		1				23
3	6		5	7	8			11	10		4			9		1				24
3	6	5		7	8			11	10		4			9		1				25
3	6	5	4	7	8			11	10					9		1				26
3	6		5	7	8				10	11	4			9		1				27
3	6		5	7	8				10		4			9			11			28
3		5	6	7	10				4					9	8		11			29
3		5	6	7	10				4					9	8		11			30
3		5	6	7					10	8	4			9			11			31
2	4	5	6	7	8	9			10				3				11			32
3		5	4	7	8				10					9			11	6		33
3		5	4	7					10					9			11	6	8	34
3		5	4	7					10					9			11	6	8	35
3		5	4	7					10					9			11	6	8	36
3		5	4	7	10									9			11	6	8	37
3		5	4	7					10					9		1	11	6	8	38
3		5	4	11	7				10					9				6	8	39
3		5	4	11	7				10					9				6	8	40
3		5	4		7									9	8		11	6	10	41
3		5	4		7									9	8		11	6	10	42
42	15	35	40	38	32	6	8	21	32	7	21	1	7	34	14	7	13	10	9	
	1		3	9	6	2	1	5	4	1				26	4		4		4	
3	6		5	7	8			11	10		4			9						R3
1	1		1	1	1			1	1		1			1						
				1																

1964-65

Division One

Manager: Stan Cullis (to September) then Andy Beattie (November)

	P	W	D	L	F	A	Pts
Manchester United	42	26	9	7	89	39	61
Leeds United	42	26	9	7	83	52	61
Chelsea	42	24	8	10	89	54	56
Everton	42	17	15	10	69	60	49
Nottingham Forest	42	17	13	12	71	67	47
Tottenham Hotspur	42	19	7	16	87	71	45
Liverpool	42	17	10	15	67	73	44
Sheffield Wednesday	42	16	11	15	57	55	43
West Ham United	42	19	4	19	82	71	42
Blackburn Rovers	42	16	10	16	83	79	42
Stoke City	42	16	10	16	67	66	42
Burnley	42	16	10	16	70	70	42
Arsenal	42	17	7	18	69	75	41
West Bromwich Albion	42	13	13	16	70	65	39
Sunderland	42	14	9	19	64	74	37
Aston Villa	42	16	5	21	57	82	37
Blackpool	42	12	11	19	67	78	35
Leicester City	42	11	13	18	69	85	35
Sheffield United	42	12	11	19	50	64	35
Fulham	42	11	12	19	60	78	34
Wolverhampton Wanderers	42	13	4	25	59	89	30
Birmingham City	42	8	11	23	64	96	27

Did you know that?

- All three of Bobby Woodruff's goals against Sunderland in April came from powerful headers.
- Wolves were relegated to the Second Division for the first time since 1932.
- An International XI beat Wolves 8–5 in Peter Broadbent's testimonial match in March.
- Wolves signed Hugh McIlmoyle (from Carlisle) and Dave Wagstaffe (from Manchester City), and transferred Peter Broadbent (to Shrewsbury), Ray Crawford (to WBA), John Kirkham (to Peterborough) and George Showell (to Bristol City).

Match No.	Date		Venue	Opponents	Result		Scorers
1	Aug	22	H	Chelsea	L	0-3	
2		26	A	Leicester City	L	2-3	Knowles, Wharton
3		29	A	Leeds United	L	2-3	Crawford, Knowles
4	Sep	2	H	Leicester City	D	1-1	Crawford
5		5	H	Arsenal	L	0-1	
6		7	A	West Ham United	L	0-5	
7		12	A	Blackburn Rovers	L	1-4	Thompson
8		14	H	West Ham United	W	4-3	Crawford 2, Harris, Knowles
9		19	H	Blackpool	L	1-2	Crawford
10		26	A	Sheffield Wednesday	L	0-2	
11		30	H	Birmingham City	L	0-2	
12	Oct	10	A	West Bromwich Albion	L	1-5	Knowles
13		17	H	Manchester United	L	2-4	Crawford 2
14		24	A	Fulham	L	0-2	
15		31	H	Nottingham Forest	L	1-2	Crawford
16	Nov	7	A	Stoke City	W	2-0	Wharton, Woodfield
17		14	H	Tottenham Hotspur	W	3-1	Wharton, Le Flem, Crawford
18		21	A	Burnley	D	1-1	Crawford
19		28	H	Sheffield United	W	1-0	Woodfield
20	Dec	5	A	Everton	L	0-5	
21		12	A	Chelsea	L	1-2	Crawford
22		19	H	Leeds United	L	0-1	
23		26	H	Aston Villa	L	0-1	
24	Jan	2	A	Arsenal	L	1-4	Crawford
25		16	H	Blackburn Rovers	W	4-2	Woodruff 2, Crawford, McIlmoyle
26		23	A	Blackpool	D	1-1	Wagstaffe
27	Feb	6	H	Sheffield Wednesday	W	3-1	Wharton, Miller 2
28		13	A	Liverpool	L	1-2	Woodruff
29		27	A	Manchester United	L	0-3	
30	Mar	13	A	Birmingham City	W	1-0	Wharton
31		15	H	West Bromwich Albion	W	3-2	McIlmoyle 2, Woodruff
32		20	H	Stoke City	W	3-1	Buckley, Woodruff, Wharton
33		22	A	Aston Villa	L	2-3	Woodruff, McIlmoyle
34		27	A	Tottenham Hotspur	L	4-7	Buckley, McIlmoyle, Kirkham, Wharton
35		30	H	Fulham	D	0-0	
36	Apr	3	H	Burnley	L	1-2	Flowers
37		10	A	Sheffield United	W	2-0	Knowles, Woodruff
38		16	A	Sunderland	W	2-1	McIlmoyle, Knowles
39		17	H	Everton	L	2-4	Woodruff, Wharton
40		20	H	Sunderland	W	3-0	Woodruff 3
41		24	A	Nottingham Forest	W	2-0	McIlmoyle, Buckley
42		26	H	Liverpool	L	1-3	Miller

Appea

FA Cup

R3	Jan	9	A	Portsmouth	D	0-0	
rep		12	H	Portsmouth	W	3-2	McIlmoyle 2, Crawford
R4		30	H	Rotherham United	D	2-2	Crawford, Flowers
rep	Feb	2	A	Rotherham United	W	3-0	Wagstaffe, Wharton, Woodruff
R5		20	A	Aston Villa	D	1-1	Woodruff
rep		24	H	Aston Villa	D	0-0	
rep2	Mar	1	N	Aston Villa	W	3-1	McIlmoyle, 3
R6		10	H	Manchester United	L	3-5	McIlmoyle 2, Knowles

R5 replay aet

Appea

R5 replay 2 at The Hawthorns.

Thomson RA	Harris GW	Flowers R	Woodfield D	Woodruff RW	Wharton TJ	Melia J	Crawford R	Broadbent PF	Ford C	Goodwin FJ	Knowles PR	Thompson D	Kirkham J	Barron J	Showell GW	Galley J	Buckley P	Hawkins G	McIlmoyle H	Le Flem RP	Miller G	Kemp FG	Wagstaffe D	MacLaren D	Knighton K	Wilson J	
2	3	4	5	6	7	8	9	10	11																		1
2	3	5		6	11	10	9	7		4	8																2
2	3	5		6	11	10	9	7		4	8																3
2	3	5		6	11	10	9	7		4	8																4
2	3	5		6	11	10	9	8		4		7															5
2	3	5		6	11	10	9	7		4			8														6
2	3	4		6	11	10					8	7		1	5	9											7
2	3			6	11		9	10		4	8	7			5												8
2	3	4		6	11		9	10			8	7			5												9
2	3	4		6	11			8	9		10	7			5												10
3		5		6	7			8		4	10				2	9	11										11
3		4		6		8	9				10	7			2		11	5									12
2	3	4	9	6	7		10	8							5		11										13
2	3	4	9	6	7		8								5				10	11							14
2	3	4	5		7	8	9										11		10		6						15
2	3	4	5		7	8	9										11		10		6						16
2	3	4	5		7	8	9												10	11	6						17
2	3	4	5		7	8	9												10	11	6						18
2	3	4	5		7	8	9												10	11	6						19
2	3	4	5		7	8	9												10	11	6						20
2	3	4	5		7	8	9												10	11	6						21
2	3	4	5		7		9	8									11				6	10					22
2	3	4	5		7		9	8													6	10	11				23
2	3	4	5	8	7		9														6	10	11	1			24
2	3	4	5	8			10					7							9		6		11				25
2	3	4	5	8			10					7							9		6		11				26
2	3	4	5	8	7								6						9		10		11				27
2	3	5		8	7								4						9		10		11		6		28
2	3	4	5	8	7						10		6								9		11				29
2	3	4	5	8	7						10								9		6		11				30
2	3	5		8	7						10		4				11		9		6						31
2	3	5		8	7						10		4				11		9		6						32
2	3	5		8	7						10		4				11		9		6						33
2	3	5		8	7						10		4				11		9		6						34
	3	5		8	7						10		4				11		9		6			1		2	35
	3	5		8	7						10		4						9		6		11	1		2	36
3		5		8	7						10		4						9		6		11	1		2	37
3		5		8	7						10		4						9		6		11	1		2	38
3		5		8	7						10		4				11		9		6			1		2	39
3		5		8	7						10		4				11		9		6			1	2		40
3		5		8	7						10		4				11		9		6			1	2		41
3		5		8	7						10		4				11		9		6			1	2		42
0	34	41	18	33	39	15	23	13	2	7	23	8	16	1	8	2	15	1	25	6	28	3	11	9	4	5	
	1	1	2	11	8		13				6	1	1				3		7	1	3		1				

Thomson RA	Harris GW	Flowers R	Woodfield D	Woodruff RW	Wharton TJ	Melia J	Crawford R	Broadbent PF	Ford C	Goodwin FJ	Knowles PR	Thompson D	Kirkham J	Barron J	Showell GW	Galley J	Buckley P	Hawkins G	McIlmoyle H	Le Flem RP	Miller G	Kemp FG	Wagstaffe D	MacLaren D	Knighton K	Wilson J	
2	3		5	8	7		9						4								6	10	11				R3
2	3	4	5	8			10					7							9		6		11				rep
2	3	4	5	8			10					7							9		6		11				R4
2	3	4	5	8	7								6						9		10		11				rep
2	3	4	5	8	7								6						9		10		11				R5
2	3	4	5	8	7								6						9		10		11				rep
2	3	4	5	8	7						10								9		6		11				rep2
2	3	4	5	8	7						10								9		6		11				R6
8	8	7	8	8	6		3				2	2	4						7		8	1	8				
		1		2	1		2				1								7				1				

1965-66

Division Two

Manager: Andy Beattie (to September) then Ronnie Allen

	P	W	D	L	F	A	Pts
Manchester City	42	22	15	5	76	44	59
Southampton	42	22	10	10	85	56	54
Coventry City	42	20	13	9	73	53	53
Huddersfield Town	42	19	13	10	62	36	51
Bristol City	42	17	17	8	63	48	51
Wolverhampton Wanderers	42	20	10	12	87	61	50
Rotherham United	42	16	14	12	75	74	46
Derby County	42	16	11	15	71	68	43
Bolton Wanderers	42	16	9	17	62	59	41
Birmingham City	42	16	9	17	70	75	41
Crystal Palace	42	14	13	15	47	52	41
Portsmouth	42	16	8	18	74	78	40
Norwich City	42	12	15	15	52	52	39
Carlisle United	42	17	5	20	60	63	39
Ipswich Town	42	15	9	18	58	66	39
Charlton Athletic	42	12	14	16	61	70	38
Preston North End	42	11	15	16	62	70	37
Plymouth Argyle	42	12	13	17	54	63	37
Bury	42	14	7	21	62	76	35
Cardiff City	42	12	10	20	71	91	34
Middlesbrough	42	10	13	19	58	86	33
Leyton Orient	42	5	13	24	38	80	23

Did you know that?

• When he was dismissed against Manchester City at Molineux in August, David Woodfield became the first Wolves player to be sent off in a League game for 29 years.

• Substitutes were introduced in League games this season and Wolves' first number-12 to be used was Fred Goodwin against Middlesbrough in October.

• Wolves had four goalkeepers over 6ft tall on their books: Phil Parkes (6ft 3in), Dave McLaren (6ft 1½in), Bob Knight (6ft) and Fred Davies (6ft).

• Mike Bailey was signed from Charlton Athletic in March 1966.

Match No.	Date		Venue	Opponents	Result		Scorers	Atten
1	Aug	21	A	Coventry City	L	1-2	McIlmoyle	36
2		25	A	Manchester City	L	1-2	Knowles	25
3		28	H	Carlisle United	W	3-0	Knowles 3	18
4		30	H	Manchester City	L	2-4	Wagstaffe, Woodruff	22
5	Sep	4	A	Cardiff City	W	4-1	McIlmoyle 2, Williams (og), Wagstaffe	19
6		7	A	Rotherham United	L	3-4	Wagstaffe, Knowles, Wharton (pen)	11
7		11	H	Derby County	W	4-0	Knowles 3, Woodruff	17
8		13	H	Rotherham United	W	4-1	McIlmoyle, Wagstaffe, Knowles, Woodfield	20
9		18	A	Southampton	L	3-9	Knapp (og), Woodruff, Knowles	23
10		25	H	Bury	W	3-0	Wagstaffe, Knowles, Wharton	15
11	Oct	2	A	Norwich City	W	3-0	Wagstaffe, Wharton, Knowles	20
12		9	A	Leyton Orient	W	3-0	Wagstaffe, Ferry 2 (2 og)	11
13		16	H	Middlesbrough	W	3-0	Knowles, Hunt, Woodfield	20
14		23	A	Huddersfield Town	D	1-1	Wharton	19
15		30	H	Crystal Palace	W	1-0	Knowles	21
16	Nov	6	A	Preston North End	D	2-2	Knowles, Wharton	15
17		13	H	Charlton Athletic	D	2-2	McIlmoyle, Hunt	20
18		20	A	Plymouth Argyle	D	2-2	McIlmoyle 2	17
19		27	H	Portsmouth	W	8-2	Woodruff 2, Wagstaffe, McIlmoyle 2, Flowers, Holsgrove 2	17
20	Dec	4	A	Bolton Wanderers	L	1-2	McIlmoyle	12
21		11	H	Ipswich Town	W	4-1	Hunt, Woodruff, McIlmoyle, Wharton	1
22		18	A	Middlesbrough	L	1-3	Knowles	1
23		27	H	Bristol City	D	1-1	Buckley	3
24		28	A	Bristol City	W	1-0	Knowles	3
25	Jan	1	H	Leyton Orient	W	2-1	Wharton, Hunt	2
26		8	A	Charlton Athletic	D	1-1	Burridge (og)	14
27		15	H	Huddersfield Town	W	2-1	Hunt, Woodruff	2
28		29	H	Coventry City	L	0-1		44
29	Feb	5	A	Carlisle United	L	1-2	Wagstaffe	1
30		19	H	Cardiff City	W	2-1	Wharton 2	2
31		26	A	Derby County	D	2-2	Hunt, McIlmoyle	2
32	Mar	12	H	Southampton	D	1-1	Hunt	2
33		19	A	Bury	L	0-1		
34		26	H	Norwich City	W	2-1	Woodfield 2	1
35	Apr	2	H	Preston North End	W	3-0	Hunt, McIlmoyle, Woodfield	1
36		9	A	Crystal Palace	W	1-0	Woodfield	1
37		11	A	Birmingham City	D	2-2	Woodfield, Hunt	2
38		12	H	Birmingham City	W	2-0	McIlmoyle, Hunt	3
39		16	H	Plymouth Argyle	D	0-0		2
40		23	A	Portsmouth	L	0-2		2
41		30	H	Bolton Wanderers	W	3-1	Knowles, McIlmoyle, Wharton	1
42	May	7	A	Ipswich Town	L	2-5	Buckley, Knowles	1
								Appeara
								Sub appeara
							Five own-goals	G

FA Cup

R3	Jan	22	H	Altrincham	W	5-0	Hunt 2, McIlmoyle, Woodruff, Dewar (og)	3
R4	Feb	12	H	Sheffield United	W	3-0	Knowles 2, McIlmoyle	3
R5	Mar	5	H	Manchester United	L	2-4	Wharton 2 (2 pen)	5
								Appeara
							One own-goal	G

Knighton K	Thomson RA	Flowers R	Woodfield D	Miller G	Wharton TJ	Woodruff RW	McIlmoyle H	Knowles PR	Wagstaffe D	Harris GW	Wilson J	Holsgrove JW	Hunt RP	Goodwin F	Buckley P	Davies F	Hawkins GN	Wilson LJ	Bailey MA	
2	3	4	5	6	7	8	9	10	11											1
2	3	4	5	6	7	8	9	10	11											2
2	3	4	5	6	7	8	9	10	11											3
	2	4	5	6	7	8	9	10	11	3										4
	3	4	5	6	7	8	9	10	11		2									5
	3	4	5	6	7	8	9	10	11		2									6
	3	4	5	6	7	8	9	10	11		2									7
	3	4	5	6	7	8	9	10	11		2									8
	3	4	5	6	7	8	9	10	11		2									9
	3	4	5		7		9	10	11		2	6	8							10
	3	4	5		7		9	10	11		2	6	8							11
	3	4	5		7		9	10	11		2	6	8							12
	3	4	5		7		9	10	11		2	6	**8**	12						13
	3	4	5		7		9	10	11		2	6			8					14
	3	4	5		7		9	10	11		2	6	8							15
	3	4	5		7		9	10	11		2	6	8							16
	3	4	5		7		9	10	11		2	6	8			1				17
	3	4	5		7		9	10	11		2	6	8			1				18
	3	4	5		7	10	9		11		2	6	8			1				19
2	3	4	5		7	10	9		11		2	**6**	8			1				20
2	3	**4**			7	6	9	10	11		2		8			1	5			21
	3		5		7	4	9	10	11		2		8			1		6		22
	3		5		7	4	9	10			2	6	8		11	1				23
	3		5		7	4	9	10			2	6	8		11	1				24
	3		5		7	4	9	10			2	6	8		11					25
	3	4	5		7	10	9		11		2	6	8							26
	3	4	5		7	10	9		11		2	6	8							27
	3	4	5		7	10	9		11		2	6	8							28
	3	4	5		7	10	9		11		2	6	8							29
	3	4	5		7		9	10	11		2	6	8							30
	3	4	5		7		9	10	11		2	6	8							31
	3	5	12		7		9	10	11		2	6	8						4	32
		5	9		7			10	11	3	2	6	8						4	33
	3	4	9		7		10		11		2						5		8	34
	3	6	9		7		10		11		2		8				5		4	35
	3	6	9		7		10		11		2		8				5		4	36
	3	6	9		7		10		11		2		8				5		4	37
	3	6	9				10	7	11		2		8				5		4	38
	3	6	9				10	7	11		2		8				5		4	39
	3	6	9				10		11		2		8		7		5		4	40
	3	6	12		7		9	10	11		**2**		8				5		4	41
2	**3**	6	2		7		9	10					8		11		5		4	42
	41	38	39	9	39	20	41	31	38	2	37	22	31		6	8	10	1	11	
			2											1						
		1	7		10	7	15	19	9			2	10		2					

Knighton K	Thomson RA	Flowers R	Woodfield D	Miller G	Wharton TJ	Woodruff RW	McIlmoyle H	Knowles PR	Wagstaffe D	Harris GW	Wilson J	Holsgrove JW	Hunt RP	Goodwin F	Buckley P	Davies F	Hawkins GN	Wilson LJ	Bailey MA	
	3	4	5		7	10	9		11		2	6	8							R3
	3	4	5		7		9	10	11		2	6	8							R4
	3	4	5		7		9	10	11		2	6	8							R5
	3	3	3		3	1	3	2	3		3	3	3							
					2	1	2	2					2							

1966-67

Division Two

Manager: Ronnie Allen

	P	W	D	L	F	A	Pts
Coventry City	42	23	13	6	74	43	59
Wolverhampton Wanderers	42	25	8	9	88	48	58
Carlisle United	42	23	6	13	71	54	52
Blackburn Rovers	42	19	13	10	56	46	51
Ipswich Town	42	17	16	9	70	54	50
Huddersfield Town	42	20	9	13	58	46	49
Crystal Palace	42	19	10	13	61	55	48
Millwall	42	18	9	15	49	58	45
Bolton Wanderers	42	14	14	14	64	58	42
Birmingham City	42	16	8	18	70	66	40
Norwich City	42	13	14	15	49	55	40
Hull City	42	16	7	19	77	72	39
Preston North End	42	16	7	19	65	67	39
Portsmouth	42	13	13	16	59	70	39
Bristol City	42	12	14	16	56	62	38
Plymouth Argyle	42	14	9	19	59	58	37
Derby County	42	12	12	18	68	72	36
Rotherham United	42	13	10	19	61	70	36
Charlton Athletic	42	13	9	20	49	53	35
Cardiff City	42	12	9	21	61	87	33
Northampton Town	42	12	6	24	47	84	30
Bury	42	11	6	25	49	83	28

Did you know that?

- Bob Hatton scored after just 29 seconds of his League debut for Wolves against Portsmouth in October. A month earlier, Hatton had the pleasure of scoring the winning goal in the League Cup clash with Mansfield Town on his first-team debut.
- Wolves had two players sent off during the League game at Blackburn in January – Dave Woodfield and Dave Wagstaffe.
- Derek Dougan was signed from Leicester City.
- Pat Buckley scored a record 33 Central League goals for Wolves.
- Masquerading as Los Angeles Wolves, in the summer of 1967 Wolves won the USA International tournament, beating Aberdeen 6–5 after extra-time in the Final.
- In April 1967 a record Highfield Road crowd of 51,455 attended the Coventry versus Wolves League game.

Match No.	Date		Venue	Opponents	Result		Scorers
1	Aug	20	H	Birmingham City	L	1-2	McIlmoyle
2		27	A	Ipswich Town	L	1-3	McIlmoyle
3		31	A	Cardiff City	W	3-0	McIlmoyle 2, Buckley
4	Sep	3	H	Bristol City	D	1-1	Knowles
5		7	H	Crystal Palace	D	1-1	Burnside
6		10	A	Carlisle United	W	3-1	Hunt 2, Holsgrove
7		17	H	Blackburn Rovers	W	4-0	Hunt 2, Burnside, Wharton (pen)
8		21	H	Cardiff City	W	7-1	Wharton 3 (2 pens), Hunt, Thomson, McIlmoyle, Wagstaffe
9		24	A	Bolton Wanderers	D	0-0	
10	Oct	1	H	Charlton Athletic	W	1-0	McIlmoyle
11		8	H	Portsmouth	W	3-1	Hatton, Hunt, Wharton
12		15	A	Hull City	L	1-3	Bailey
13		22	H	Plymouth Argyle	W	2-1	Woodfield, Hunt
14		29	A	Northampton Town	W	4-0	Hunt 3, McIlmoyle
15	Nov	5	H	Millwall	W	2-0	McIlmoyle 2
16		12	A	Rotherham United	D	2-2	Wagstaffe, McIlmoyle
17		19	H	Preston North End	W	3-2	McIlmoyle, Wharton 2 (1 pen)
18		26	A	Bury	L	1-2	Hunt
19	Dec	3	H	Coventry City	L	1-3	Burnside
20		10	A	Norwich City	W	2-1	Knowles, Wagstaffe
21		17	A	Birmingham City	L	2-3	Wagstaffe, Bailey
22		24	H	Derby County	W	5-3	McIlmoyle, Wharton 2 (1 pen), Hatton 2
23		26	A	Derby County	W	3-0	Hatton, McIlmoyle, Wharton
24		31	H	Ipswich Town	D	0-0	
25	Jan	7	A	Bristol City	L	0-1	
26		14	H	Carlisle United	D	1-1	Hunt
27		21	A	Blackburn Rovers	D	0-0	
28	Feb	4	H	Bolton Wanderers	W	5-2	Hunt 2, Hatton 2, Wagstaffe
29		11	A	Charlton Athletic	W	3-1	Hatton, Woodfield, Knowles
30		25	A	Portsmouth	W	3-2	Bailey, Knowles, Hunt
31	Mar	4	H	Northampton Town	W	1-0	Wagstaffe
32		18	A	Plymouth Argyle	W	1-0	Knowles
33		25	H	Hull City	W	4-0	Dougan 3, Knowles
34		27	A	Huddersfield Town	W	1-0	Wharton
35		28	H	Huddersfield Town	W	1-0	Knowles
36	Apr	1	A	Millwall	D	1-1	Dougan
37		8	H	Rotherham United	W	2-0	Hunt, Dougan
38		15	A	Preston North End	W	2-1	Hunt 2
39		22	H	Bury	W	4-1	Wharton (pen), Dougan 2, Burnside
40		29	A	Coventry City	L	1-3	Knowles
41	May	6	H	Norwich City	W	4-1	Dougan 2, Wharton, Hunt
42		13	A	Crystal Palace	L	1-4	Hunt

Appeara

Sub appeara

FA Cup

R3	Jan	28	A	Oldham Athletic	D	2-2	Bailey, Thomson
rep	Feb	1	H	Oldham Athletic	W	4-1	Hunt, McIlmoyle, Wharton, Woodfield
R4		18	H	Everton	D	1-1	Wharton
rep		21	A	Everton	L	1-3	Wharton

Appeara

Sub appeara

League Cup

R2	Sep	13	H	Mansfield Town	W	2-1	Hatton, Wharton
R3	Oct	5	A	Fulham	L	0-5	

Appeara

Thomson RA	Bailey MA	Flowers R	Holsgrove JW	Farrington JR	Knowles PR	McIlmoyle H	Hunt RP	Wagstaffe D	Davies F	Woodfield D	Wilson L	Buckley PM	Wilson J	Wharton TJ	Burnside D	Hawkins GN	Wallace I	Hatton RJ	Parkes P	Taylor GW	Dougan AD	
3	4	5	6	7	8	9	10	11														1
3	4		6	7	8	9	10	11	1	5	12											2
3	4		6		8	9	10	11	1	5		7	2									3
3	4		6		10	9	8	11	1	5	2	7										4
3	4		6			9	8	11	1	5			2	7	10							5
3	4		6			9	8	11	1	5			2	7	10							6
	4					9	**8**	11	1	5			2	7	10	6	12					7
3	4					9	8	11	1	5			2	7	10	6						8
3	4		12		8	9		11	1	5			2	7	**10**	6						9
3	4				8	9		11	1	5			2	7	10	6						10
	4		6			9	8	11	1	**5**			2	7		12		10				11
	4		6			9	8	11	1				2	7		5		10				12
3	4	6				9	8	11	1	5			2	7	10							13
3	4	6				9	8	11	1	5			2	7	10							14
3	4	6				9	8	11	1	5			2	7	10							15
3	4	6				9	8	11	1	5			2	7	10							16
3	4	6				9	8	11		5			2	7	10				1			17
3	4	6				9	8	11	1	5			2	7	10							18
3	4	6				9	8	11	1	5			2	7	10							19
3	4	6			9		8	11	1	5				7	10	2						20
3	4	2			9		8	11	1	5				7	10	6						21
3	4	2				9	8	11	1	5				7		6		10				22
3	4	2	12			9	8	11	1	5				7		**6**		10				23
3	4	6				9	8	11	1	5				7				10		2		24
3	4	6				9	8	11	1	5				7				10		2		25
3	4		6		10	9	8	11	1	5				7						2		26
3	4		6		10		8	11	1	5				7				9		2		27
3	4		6		10		8	11	1	5				7				9		2		28
3	4		6		10		8	11	1	5				7				9		2		29
3	4		6		10		8	11		5				7	9				1	2		30
3	4		6		9		8	11		5				**7**	12			10	1	2		31
3	**4**		6		10		8	11		5				7		12			1	2	9	32
3	4		6		10		**8**	11		5				7	12				1	2	9	33
3	4		6		10			11		5				**7**	8	12			1	2	9	34
3	4		6	7	10			11		5					8				1	2	9	35
3	4		6	7	**8**			11		5	12				10				1	2	9	36
3	4		6				8	11		5				7	10				1	2	9	37
3	4		6		7		8	11		**5**				12	10				1	2	9	38
3	4		6		12		8	11						7	10	5			1	**2**	9	39
3	4		6		4		8	11						7	10	5			1		9	40
3	**4**		6				8	11		5			2	7	10	12			1		9	41
3			6		12		8	11		5				**7**	10	4			1	2	9	42
39	41	14	25	4	21	24	37	42	27	38	1	2	17	35	25	12		10	14	17	11	
			2		2						2			1	2	4	1					
1	3		1		8	13	20	6		2		1		13	4			7			9	
3	4		6		10	9	8	11	1	5				7						2		R3
3	4		6		10	9	**8**	11	1	5	12			7						2		rep
3	4		6		**10**	12	8	11	1	5				7				9		2		R4
3	4		6		10		8	11	1	5				7				9		2		rep
4	4		4		4	2	4	4	4	4				4				2		4		
						1					1											
	1					1	1			1				3								
3	4		6			9	8	11	1	5			2	7				10				R2
3	4				8	9		11	1	5			2	7	10	6						R3
2	2		1		1	2	1	2	2	2			2	2	1	1		1				
														1				1				

1967-68

Division One

Manager: Ronnie Allen

	P	W	D	L	F	A	Pts
Manchester City	42	26	6	10	86	43	58
Manchester United	42	24	8	10	89	55	56
Liverpool	42	22	11	9	71	40	55
Leeds United	42	22	9	11	71	41	53
Everton	42	23	6	13	67	40	52
Chelsea	42	18	12	12	62	68	48
Tottenham Hotspur	42	19	9	14	70	59	47
West Bromwich Albion	42	17	12	13	75	62	46
Arsenal	42	17	10	15	60	56	44
Newcastle United	42	13	15	14	54	67	41
Nottingham Forest	42	14	11	17	52	64	39
West Ham United	42	14	10	18	73	69	38
Leicester City	42	13	12	17	64	69	38
Burnley	42	14	10	18	64	71	38
Sunderland	42	13	11	18	51	61	37
Southampton	42	13	11	18	66	83	37
Wolverhampton Wanderers	42	14	8	20	66	75	36
Stoke City	42	14	7	21	50	73	35
Sheffield Wednesday	42	11	12	19	51	63	34
Coventry City	42	9	15	18	51	71	33
Sheffield United	42	11	10	21	49	70	32
Fulham	42	10	7	25	56	98	27

Did you know that?

- Goalkeeper Phil Parkes was sent off late on during Wolves' home League game against West Bromwich Albion in August.
- Les Wilson, on for Dave Wagstaffe, became the first substitute to score for Wolves, netting against Everton in September.
- In June 1968 Jack Howley ended his 20-year reign as Wolves' secretary.
- Wolves' first-ever club shop was officially opened behind the North Bank at Molineux.
- Frank Munro (from Aberdeen), Derek Parkin (from Huddersfield) and Frank Wignall (from Nottingham Forest) were recruited, while those who departed included Ernie Hunt (to Everton), Terry Wharton (to Bolton) and Davey Burnside (to Plymouth Argyle).

Match No.	Date		Venue	Opponents	Result		Scorers
1	Aug	19	A	Fulham	W	2-1	Bailey, Dougan
2		23	H	West Bromwich Albion	D	3-3	Bailey, Burnside, Hunt
3		26	H	Leeds United	W	2-0	Dougan 2
4		30	A	West Bromwich Albion	L	1-4	Bailey
5	Sep	2	A	Everton	L	2-4	Wharton (pen), Wilson
6		6	A	Tottenham Hotspur	L	1-2	Hunt
7		9	H	Leicester City	L	1-3	Knowles
8		16	A	West Ham United	W	2-1	Dougan 2
9		23	H	Burnley	W	3-2	Knowles 2, Evans
10		30	A	Sheffield Wednesday	D	2-2	Evans, Knowles
11	Oct	7	H	Newcastle United	D	2-2	Holsgrove, Wharton
12		14	A	Manchester City	L	0-2	
13		23	H	Arsenal	W	3-2	Dougan 2, Evans
14		28	A	Sheffield United	D	1-1	Dougan
15	Nov	4	H	Coventry City	W	2-0	Knowles 2
16		11	A	Nottingham Forest	L	1-3	Thomson
17		18	H	Stoke City	L	3-4	Buckley, Holsgrove, Knowles (pen)
18		25	A	Liverpool	L	1-2	Evans
19	Dec	2	H	Southampton	W	2-0	Dougan, Knowles
20		16	H	Fulham	W	3-2	Knowles 2, Woodfield
21		23	A	Leeds United	L	1-2	Dougan
22		26	A	Manchester United	L	0-4	
23		30	H	Manchester United	L	2-3	Bailey, Buckley
24	Jan	6	H	Everton	L	1-3	Knowles
25		13	A	Leicester City	L	1-3	Kenning
26		20	H	West Ham United	L	1-2	Dougan
27	Feb	3	A	Burnley	D	1-1	Dougan
28		24	A	Newcastle United	L	0-2	
29	Mar	2	H	Liverpool	D	1-1	Dougan
30		9	H	Sunderland	W	2-1	Dougan, Kenning (pen)
31		16	A	Arsenal	W	2-0	Holsgrove, Wignall
32		19	H	Sheffield Wednesday	L	2-3	Holsgrove, Wignall
33		23	H	Sheffield United	L	1-3	Farrington
34		30	A	Coventry City	L	0-1	
35	Apr	6	H	Nottingham Forest	W	6-1	Dougan 3, Wignall 2, Kenning
36		13	A	Stoke City	W	2-0	Knowles, Wignall
37		15	A	Sunderland	L	0-2	
38		20	H	Manchester City	D	0-0	
39		27	A	Southampton	D	1-1	Wagstaffe
40		29	A	Chelsea	L	0-1	
41	May	4	H	Chelsea	W	3-0	Wignall 3
42		11	H	Tottenham Hotspur	W	2-1	Parkin, Wignall

Appear

Sub appear

FA Cup

R3	Jan	27	A	Rotherham United	L	0-1	

Appeara

League Cup

R2	Sep	12	A	Huddersfield Town	L	0-1	

Appeara

Taylor GW	Thomson RA	Bailey MA	Woodfield D	Holsgrove JW	Wharton TJ	Hunt RP	Dougan AD	Burnside DG	Wagstaffe D	Wilson LJ	Knowles PR	Davies F	Buckley PM	Evans AW	Hawkins GN	Farrington JR	Williams SE	Ross S	Munro FM	Kenning MJ	Parkin D	Wignall F	McAlle JE	
2	3	4	5	6	7	8	9	10	11															1
2	3	4	5	6	7	8	9	10	11															2
2		4	5	6	7	8	9	10	11	3														3
2		4	5	6	7	**8**	9	10	11	3	12													4
2	3	4	5	6	7	8	9	10	**11**	12														5
2	3	4	5	6	**7**	8	9	10		12	11	1												6
2	3	4	5	6			9	10	7		8	1	11											7
2	3	4	5	6	7		9		11		8			10										8
2	3	4	5	6	7		**9**		11	12	8			10										9
2	3	4	5	6	7		9		11		10			8										10
2	3	4	5	6	7		**9**		11		10			8	12									11
2	3	4	5	6	7		9		11		10			8										12
2	3	4	5	6	7		9		11		10			8			1							13
2	3	4	5	6	7		9		11		10			8			1							14
2	3	4	5	6			9		**11**		10			8	12	7	1							15
2	3	4	5	6			9				10		12	8	**11**	7	1							16
2	3	4	5	6			9				10		11	8		7	1							17
	3	4		6			9	10		2			11	8	5	7	1							18
	3	4	5	6			9	10		2	11			8		7	1							19
	3	4	5	6			9	10	11	2	8					7	1							20
	3	4		6			**9**	10		2	8		11	7	5	12	1							21
2	3	4		6				10	11	7	9			8	5		1							22
12	3	4		6					11	2	8		9	7	**5**		1	10						23
	3	**4**	5	6			9		11	2	10			8			1	12	7					24
2			5	6			9	10		3	11			8					4	7				25
2		4	5	6			9			3	8					11	1		10	7				26
2		10	5	6			9		11	3	8								4	7				27
	3	10	5	6			9			11	8								4	7	2			28
	3	4	5	6			9		11		10			**8**		12				7	2			29
	3	4	5	6			9		11										10	7	2	8		30
	3	4	5	6			9		11		10									7	2	8		31
	3	4	5	6			9		11		10									7	2	8		32
		4	5	6					11	3	10			9		7				12	2	**8**		33
	3	10	5	6					11		8								4	7	2	9		34
	3	4	5	6			9		11		10								12	7	2	**8**		35
	3	4	5	6			9		11		10									7	2	8		36
	3	4	5	6			9		11		10									7	2	8		37
	3	4	5	6			9		11		10									7	2	8		38
	3	4	5	6			9		11		10									7	2	8		39
	3	4	5	6			9		11		10			12						7	2		**8**	40
	3	4	5	6			9		11		10									**7**	2	8	12	41
	3	4	5	6			9		11		10									7	2	8		42
21	36	41	38	42	13	6	38	13	33	14	35	2	5	19	5	8	13	1	7	17	15	12	1	
1										3	1		1	1	2	2		1	1	1			1	
	1	4	1	4	2	2	17	1	1	1	12		2	4		1				3	1	9		
2		4	5	6			9	10	11	3	8									7				R3
1		1	1	1			1	1	1	1	1									1				
2		4	5	6			9	10	11	3	8					7								R2
1		1	1	1			1	1	1	1	1					1								

1968-69

Division One

Manager: Ronnie Allen (to November) then Bill McGarry

	P	W	D	L	F	A	Pts
Leeds United	42	27	13	2	66	26	67
Liverpool	42	25	11	6	63	24	61
Everton	42	21	15	6	77	36	57
Arsenal	42	22	12	8	56	27	56
Chelsea	42	20	10	12	73	53	50
Tottenham Hotspur	42	14	17	11	61	51	45
Southampton	42	16	13	13	57	48	45
West Ham United	42	13	18	11	66	50	44
Newcastle United	42	15	14	13	61	55	44
West Bromwich Albion	42	16	11	15	64	67	43
Manchester United	42	15	12	15	57	53	42
Ipswich Town	42	15	11	16	59	60	41
Manchester City	42	15	10	17	64	55	40
Burnley	42	15	9	18	55	82	39
Sheffield Wednesday	42	10	16	16	41	54	36
Wolverhampton Wanderers	42	10	15	17	41	58	35
Sunderland	42	11	12	19	43	67	34
Nottingham Forest	42	10	13	19	45	57	33
Stoke City	42	9	15	18	40	63	33
Coventry City	42	10	11	21	46	64	31
Leicester City	42	9	12	21	39	68	30
Queen's Park Rangers	42	4	10	28	39	95	18

Did you know that?

- Alun Evans became Britain's costliest teenager when he was transferred from Wolves to Liverpool for £100,000 in September 1968.
- Also on the move were full-back Bobby Thomson to Birmingham City and Frank Wignall to Derby County. Kenny Hibbitt was signed from Bradford Park Avenue and Hugh Curran from Norwich City.
- Wolves played eight games (two each against Aston Villa, West Ham, Dundee United and Kilmarnock) in a summer tournament in the USA.

Match No.	Date		Venue	Opponents	Result		Scorers	Attenda
1	Aug	10	A	Ipswich Town	L	0-1		25,8
2		14	A	Manchester City	L	2-3	Wignall 2	35,8
3		17	H	Queen's Park Rangers	W	3-1	Bailey, Dougan, Wignall	30,8
4		21	H	Arsenal	D	0-0		36,6
5		24	A	Southampton	L	1-2	Wagstaffe	19,7
6		28	H	Leicester City	W	1-0	Dougan	33,4
7		31	H	Stoke City	D	1-1	Bailey	31,0
8	Sep	7	A	Leeds United	L	1-2	Munro	31,2
9		14	H	Sunderland	D	1-1	Wignall	27,2
10		21	A	West Bromwich Albion	D	0-0		35,1
11		28	H	Liverpool	L	0-6		39,8
12	Oct	5	A	Coventry City	W	1-0	Dougan	39,2
13		9	A	Leicester City	L	0-2		27,0
14		12	H	Chelsea	D	1-1	Knowles	27,8
15		19	A	Sheffield Wednesday	W	2-0	Dougan, Knowles (pen)	23,9
16		26	H	Everton	L	1-2	Knowles	34,7
17	Nov	2	A	Nottingham Forest	D	0-0		19,4
18		9	H	West Ham United	W	2-0	Bailey, Farrington	29,
19		16	A	Burnley	D	1-1	Dougan	20,8
20		23	H	Newcastle United	W	5-0	Dougan 2, Knowles 2, Wignall	25,4
21		30	A	Manchester United	L	0-2		50,1
22	Dec	7	H	Tottenham Hotspur	W	2-0	Dougan, Wignall	30,8
23		14	A	Chelsea	D	1-1	Kenning (pen)	26,1
24		21	H	Sheffield Wednesday	L	0-3		24,7
25	Jan	11	H	Nottingham Forest	W	1-0	Knowles	24,
26		28	A	Everton	L	0-4		48,0
27	Feb	1	H	Burnley	D	1-1	Knowles	27,
28		15	H	Manchester United	D	2-2	Curran, Dougan	44,
29		22	A	Tottenham Hotspur	D	1-1	Curran	35,
30	Mar	1	H	Ipswich Town	D	1-1	Kenning	25,
31		8	A	Queen's Park Rangers	W	1-0	Dougan	17,
32		15	H	Southampton	D	0-0		24,
33		22	A	Stoke City	L	1-4	Curran	19,
34		24	A	West Ham United	L	1-3	Wilson	25,
35		29	H	Leeds United	D	0-0		27,
36	Apr	5	A	Liverpool	L	0-1		45,
37		7	A	Arsenal	L	1-3	Wilson	31,
38		8	H	Manchester City	W	3-1	Dougan, Knowles, Munro	28,
39		12	H	West Bromwich Albion	L	0-1		37,
40		15	H	Coventry City	D	1-1	Knowles	32,
41		19	A	Sunderland	L	0-2		21,
42		21	A	Newcastle United	L	1-4	Curran	24,

Appearan
Sub appearan
G

FA Cup

R3	Jan	4	A	Hull City	W	3-1	Dougan 2, Wignall	27,
R4		25	A	Tottenham Hotspur	L	1-2	Wagstaffe	48,

Appearan
Sub appearan
G

League Cup

R2	Sep	4	H	Southend United	W	1-0	Farrington	18,
R3		25	H	Millwall	W	5-1	Farrington 2, Dougan, Kenning (pen), Munro	17,
R4	Oct	16	A	Blackpool	L	1-2	Wagstaffe	16,

Appearan
G

Match	rkin D	Thomson RA	Bailey MA	Woodfield D	Holsgrove JW	Kenning MJ	Wignall F	Dougan AD	Knowles PR	Wagstaffe D	McAlle JE	Wilson LJ	Farrington J	Evans AW	Clarke D	Munro FM	Boswell AH	Ross S	Taylor GW	Curran HP	Galvin D	Seal J	Lutton RJ	Hibbitt K	McVeigh J	Walker PG	Williams E
1		3	4	**5**	6	7	8	9	10	11	12																
2		3	4	5	**6**	7	8	9	10	11	12																
3		3	4	5	6	7	8	9	10	11																	
4		3	4	5	6	7	8	9	10	11																	
5			4	5	6	7	8	9	10	11		3															
6			4	5	6	11	8	**9**	10			3	7	12													
7			4	5	6	**11**	9		10			3	7	8	12												
8			4	5	6	11	8	9				3	7			10											
9			4	5	6		9		8	11		3	7			10	1										
10	2		4	5	6	7	9		8	**11**		3				10	1	12									
11	2	12	4	5	6	11		9	8			3	**7**			10	1										
12	2	3	4	5	6	11	10	9	8			7					1										
13	2	3	4	5	6	11	10	9	8			7					1										
14	2		4	5	6		10	9	8	11		3	7				1										
15	2	3	4	5	6			9	**8**	11	12	10	7				1										
16	2	3	4	5	6	12		9	**8**	11		10	7				1										
17	2	3	4	5	6			9	8	11	12	10	7														
18	2	3	4	5	6			9	8	11		10	7														
19	2	3		5	6	**7**	4	9	8	11		10				12											
20	2	3	4	5	6	12	**7**	9	8	11		10															
21	2	3	4	**5**	6	12	7	9	8	11		10															
22	2	3	4		5	7	10	9	8	11		6															
23	2	3	4		5	7	10	9	8			11					1		6								
24	2	3	4		5	7	10	9	8	11		6					1										
25	2	3	4		5	7	10	9	**8**	11		6				12											
26	2	3	4		5	12		9	8	**11**		6	7			10											
27	2	3	4		**5**			9	8	11		6	7			12				10							
28	2	3	4	5				9	8	11		7							6	10							
29	2	3	4	5	6			9	8	11		7								10							
30	2	3	4	5	6	12		9	8	11		**7**								10							
31	2	3	4	5	6	11		9	8			7								10							
32	3		4	**5**	6			9	8	11		7	12						2	10							
33	3		4		6			9	8		12	7			11				2	**10**	5						
34	3		4		5			9	8		6	7	11						2			10					
35	3		4		5			9	8		6	10	7			11			2								
36	3				5			9	8		6	10	**7**		12	11			2		4						
37	3				5			9	8		6	10	7		12	11			2		**4**						
38	3				5			9	8		6	4	7			10			2				11				
39	3				5			9	8		6	4	**7**			10			2				11	12			
40	3				5			9	8	11	6	4				12			**2**	10			7				
41	2				5			9		11	6	7				**8**				10	4				3	12	
42	2				5			9		11	6					8				10	4				3	7	
	42	23	34	26	41	18	20	39	39	27	9	37	18	1	1	12	10		11	10	5	1	3		2	1	
		1				5					5		1	1	3	4		1						1		1	
			3			2	6	11	9	1		2	1			2				4							

Round	rkin D	Thomson RA	Bailey MA	Woodfield D	Holsgrove JW	Kenning MJ	Wignall F	Dougan AD	Knowles PR	Wagstaffe D	McAlle JE	Wilson LJ
R3	2	3	4		5	7	10	9	8	11		6
R4	2	3	4	5		**7**	12	9	8	11	6	10
	2	2	2	1	1	2	1	2	2	2	1	2
							1					
							1	2		1		

Round	rkin D	Thomson RA	Bailey MA	Woodfield D	Holsgrove JW	Kenning MJ	Wignall F	Dougan AD	Knowles PR	Wagstaffe D	McAlle JE	Wilson LJ	Farrington J	Evans AW	Clarke D	Munro FM	Boswell AH	Ross S	Taylor GW	Curran HP	Galvin D	Seal J	Lutton RJ	Hibbitt K	McVeigh J	Walker PG	Williams E
R2	2		4	5	6	11	8	9	10			3	7														
R3	2		4	5	6	11		9	8			3	7			10											1
R4	2		4	5	6		10	9	8	11		3	7														1
	3		3	3	3	2	2	3	3	1		3	3			1											2
						1		1		1			3			1											

1969-70

Division One

Manager: Bill McGarry

	P	W	D	L	F	A	Pts
Everton	42	29	8	5	72	34	66
Leeds United	42	21	15	6	84	49	57
Chelsea	42	21	13	8	70	50	55
Derby County	42	22	9	11	64	37	53
Liverpool	42	20	11	11	65	42	51
Coventry City	42	19	11	12	58	48	49
Newcastle United	42	17	13	12	57	35	47
Manchester United	42	14	17	11	66	61	45
Stoke City	42	15	15	12	56	52	45
Manchester City	42	16	11	15	55	48	43
Tottenham Hotspur	42	17	9	16	54	55	43
Arsenal	42	12	18	12	51	49	42
Wolverhampton Wanderers	42	12	16	14	55	57	40
Burnley	42	12	15	15	56	61	39
Nottingham Forest	42	10	18	14	50	71	38
West Bromwich Albion	42	14	9	19	58	66	37
West Ham United	42	12	12	18	51	60	36
Ipswich Town	42	10	11	21	40	63	31
Southampton	42	6	17	19	46	67	29
Crystal Palace	42	6	15	21	34	68	27
Sunderland	42	6	14	22	30	68	26
Sheffield Wednesday	42	8	9	25	40	71	25

Did you know that?

- Derek Dougan was sent off twice in three months – against Sheffield Wednesday in August and Everton in October.
- In September 1969 24-year-old Peter Knowles announced that he was quitting football to become a Jehovah's Witness.
- When Derek Parkin and Les Wilson netted against Southampton in August, it was the first time both full-backs had scored for Wolves in the same League game.
- Hugh Curran became the first Wolves player to win a full cap for Scotland (against Austria in Vienna in November).
- Jim McCalliog (from Sheffield Wednesday), Mike O'Grady (from Leeds) and Bernard Shaw (from Sheffield United) were all signed.

Match No.	Date		Venue	Opponents	Result		Scorers	Att
1	Aug	9	H	Stoke City	W	3-1	Dougan 2, Knowles	3
2		13	H	Southampton	W	2-1	Knowles, Munro	3
3		16	A	Sheffield Wednesday	W	3-2	Curran, Knowles, McCalliog	2
4		20	A	Southampton	W	3-2	Bailey, Parkin, Wilson	2
5		23	H	Manchester United	D	0-0		5
6		27	H	Derby County	D	1-1	Dougan	4
7		30	A	Coventry City	L	0-1		3
8	Sep	6	H	Nottingham Forest	D	3-3	Curran 2, Dougan	3
9		13	A	Chelsea	D	2-2	Curran 2	3
10		16	A	Ipswich Town	D	1-1	Dougan	2
11		20	H	Burnley	D	1-1	McCalliog	2
12		27	A	Newcastle United	D	1-1	McCalliog	3
13	Oct	4	H	Everton	L	2-3	Curran 2 (1 pen)	4
14		8	H	Sheffield Wednesday	D	2-2	Dougan, O'Grady	2
15		11	A	Tottenham Hotspur	W	1-0	Curran	3
16		18	H	West Ham United	W	1-0	McCalliog	2
17		25	A	Manchester City	L	0-1		3
18	Nov	1	H	West Bromwich Albion	W	1-0	O'Grady	3
19		8	A	Liverpool	D	0-0		3
20		15	H	Arsenal	W	2-0	Curran, Lutton	2
21		22	A	Crystal Palace	L	1-2	Wagstaffe	2
22		29	H	Sunderland	W	1-0	Curran	2
23	Dec	6	A	Leeds United	L	1-3	Wilson	3
24		13	H	Chelsea	W	3-0	Curran 2, Wagstaffe	2
25		20	A	Nottingham Forest	L	2-4	McCalliog, Wilson	1
26		26	A	Manchester United	D	0-0		5
27	Jan	10	A	Burnley	W	3-1	Bailey, McCalliog, O'Grady	1
28		17	H	Newcastle United	D	1-1	Curran	2
29		24	H	Ipswich Town	W	2-0	Curran, Dougan	2
30		31	A	Everton	L	0-1		4
31	Feb	7	H	Tottenham Hotspur	D	2-2	Bailey, Woodfield	2
32		14	A	Stoke City	D	1-1	Curran	2
33		21	H	Manchester City	L	1-3	Wilson	3
34		28	A	West Bromwich Albion	D	3-3	Curran 2 (1 pen), O'Grady	3
35	Mar	14	A	Sunderland	L	1-2	McCalliog	1
36		18	H	Crystal Palace	D	1-1	Curran	2
37		21	H	Leeds United	L	1-2	Curran	3
38		28	A	Arsenal	D	2-2	Curran, Dougan	3
39		30	H	Liverpool	L	0-1		2
40		31	A	West Ham United	L	0-3		2
41	Apr	4	A	Derby County	L	0-2		3
42		10	H	Coventry City	L	0-1		2

Appeara
Sub appeara
G

FA Cup

R3	Jan	3	A	Burnley	L	0-3		1

Appeara

League Cup

R2	Sep	3	H	Tottenham Hotspur	W	1-0	McCalliog	34
R3		24	A	Brighton & Hove Albion	W	3-2	Curran 2, Woodfield	3
R4	Oct	14	A	Queen's Park Rangers	L	1-3	Wilson	2

Appeara
Sub appeara
G

ylor G	Parkin D	Bailey M	Holsgrove J	Munro F	McCalliog J	Knowles P	Dougan D	Curran H	Wagstaffe D	Wilson L	Lutton B	Walker P	McAlle J	Farrington J	O'Grady M	Woodfield D	Shaw B	Oldfield J	Clarke D	Richards J	Kent M	
	3	4	5	6	7	8	9	10	**11**	12												1
	3	4	5	6	7	8	9	10		12	11											2
	3	4	**5**	6	7	8	9	10		2		11	12									3
	3	4	5	6	7	8	9	10		2		11										4
	3	4	5	6	7	8	9	10		2		11										5
	3	4	5	6	7	8	9	10		2		**11**	12									6
	3	4	5	6	7	8	9	10		2			12	**11**								7
	3	4	5	6	7	8	9	10	11	2												8
	3	4	5	6	7		9	10		2	12	11	**8**									9
	3	4	5	6	7		9	10	11	2		8										10
	3		5	6	7		9	10	11	2		8	4									11
	3	4	5	6	7				11	**2**	12	10			8	9						12
	3	4	5	**6**	7		9	10	11	2		12			8							13
	3	4	5	6	7		9	10	11						8		2					14
	3	4	5	6	**7**		9	10	11	12					8		2					15
	3		5	6	7		9	10	11	4					8							16
	3	4	5	**6**	7		9		11	10			12		8							17
	3	4	5		7		9	10	11						8	6						18
	3	4	5		7			10	11			9			**8**	6	12					19
	3	4	5		7			10	11		8	**9**	12			6						20
	3	4	5		7			10	11		**9**		12		8	6						21
	3	4	5	**9**	7			10	11		12				8	6						22
	3	4	5	12	7			10	**11**	9	8					6						23
	3		5	9	7			10	11	4	8					6	2					24
	3		5	**9**	7			10	11	4	8	12				6						25
	3	10	5	9	7				11	4	**8**	12				6						26
	3	4	5	10	7		9		11	12					**8**	6		1				27
	3	4	5		7		9	10	11						8	6		1				28
	3	4	5		7		9	10	11		8					6		1				29
	3	**4**	5		7		9	10	11	6	8					12		1				30
	3	4	5		7			10	11	12	**8**					6	2	1	9			31
	3	4	5	8	9			10	11			12	**6**		7		2	1				32
	3	4	5	8	9			10	11	**6**		12			7		2	1				33
	3	4		6	8			10	11			12			**7**	5	2	1		9		34
	3	4		6	7			10	**11**						8	5	2	1		9	12	35
	3	4		6	7			10	11						8	5	2	1		9		36
	3	4	5	6	7			10	11	2					8		12	1		**9**		37
	3	4	5	6	7		9	10		2			8		11			1				38
	3	4	5	6	7		9	10	**11**	2	12		8					1				39
2	3	8	5		7		9	10		4	11						6					40
2	3	8	5	6	7		9	10		4		12			**11**							41
2	3	4	5	6	7		9	10		8	11							1				42
9	42	38	39	32	42	8	26	38	31	25	12	10	5	1	20	17	10	14	1	4		
				1						5	4	7	6			1	2				1	
	1	3		1	7	3	8	20	2	4	1				4	1						

ylor G	Parkin D	Bailey M	Holsgrove J	Munro F	McCalliog J	Knowles P	Dougan D	Curran H	Wagstaffe D	Wilson L	Lutton B	Walker P	McAlle J	Farrington J	O'Grady M	Woodfield D	Shaw B	Oldfield J	Clarke D	Richards J	Kent M	
2	3	4	5		7		9		11	10					8	6						R3
1	1	1	1		1		1		1	1					1	1						

ylor G	Parkin D	Bailey M	Holsgrove J	Munro F	McCalliog J	Knowles P	Dougan D	Curran H	Wagstaffe D	Wilson L	Lutton B	Walker P	McAlle J	Farrington J	O'Grady M	Woodfield D	Shaw B	Oldfield J	Clarke D	Richards J	Kent M	
	3	4	5	6	7	8	9	10	11	2												R2
	3		5	6	7			10	11	4	8					9	2					R3
	3		5	6			9	10	**11**	4	7	12			8		2					R4
	3	1	3	3	2	1	2	3	3	3	2				1	1	2					
												1										
					1			2		1						1						

1970-71

Division One

Manager: Bill McGarry

	P	W	D	L	F	A	Pts
Arsenal	42	29	7	6	71	29	65
Leeds United	42	27	10	5	72	30	64
Tottenham Hotspur	42	19	14	9	54	33	52
Wolverhampton Wanderers	42	22	8	12	64	54	52
Liverpool	42	17	17	8	42	24	51
Chelsea	42	18	15	9	52	42	51
Southampton	42	17	12	13	56	44	46
Manchester United	42	16	11	15	65	66	43
Derby County	42	16	10	16	56	54	42
Coventry City	42	16	10	16	37	38	42
Manchester City	42	12	17	13	47	42	41
Newcastle United	42	14	13	15	44	46	41
Stoke City	42	12	13	17	44	48	37
Everton	42	12	13	17	54	60	37
Huddersfield Town	42	11	14	17	40	49	36
Nottingham Forest	42	14	8	20	42	61	36
West Bromwich Albion	42	10	15	17	58	75	35
Crystal Palace	42	12	11	19	39	57	35
Ipswich Town	42	12	10	20	42	48	34
West Ham United	42	10	14	18	47	60	34
Burnley	42	7	13	22	29	63	27
Blackpool	42	4	15	23	34	66	23

Did you know that?

- Bobby Gould joined Wolves from Arsenal and finished the season as top scorer with 24 goals.
- Danny Hegan was also signed, from Gould's future club, West Bromwich Albion.
- Out of Molineux went Les Wilson (to Bristol City) and John Holsgrove (to Sheffield Wednesday).
- Derek Dougan came off the bench to score with his first touch in Wolves' 3–2 win at Burnley in September.
- Wolves beat an England XI 8–4 in the Ron Flowers testimonial match in October.

Match No.	Date		Venue	Opponents	Result		Scorers	Atte
1	Aug	15	A	Newcastle United	L	2-3	Dougan, Curran	3
2		19	H	Derby County	L	2-4	Dougan, Curran	2
3		22	H	Tottenham Hotspur	L	0-3		2
4		25	A	Coventry City	W	1-0	Curran	3
5		29	A	Nottingham Forest	L	1-4	Curran	2
6	Sep	1	A	Ipswich Town	W	3-2	Gould, Curran 2	1
7		5	H	Stoke City	D	1-1	Curran	2
8		12	A	Chelsea	D	2-2	McCalliog, Hibbitt	3
9		19	H	Huddersfield Town	W	3-1	Gould, Curran, Richards	1
10		26	A	Burnley	W	3-2	McCalliog, Dougan, Gould	1
11	Oct	3	H	Manchester United	W	3-2	Gould 3	3
12		10	A	Southampton	W	2-1	Dougan, Wagstaffe	2
13		17	H	Newcastle United	W	3-2	Bailey, Gould, Wagstaffe	2
14		24	H	Manchester City	W	3-0	Gould 2, McCalliog (pen)	3
15		31	A	Liverpool	L	0-2		45
16	Nov	7	H	West Bromwich Albion	W	2-1	Dougan, Wagstaffe	39
17		14	A	West Ham United	D	3-3	McCalliog 2, Gould	2
18		21	H	Leeds United	L	2-3	Gould, Curran	40
19		28	A	Crystal Palace	D	1-1	Curran	26
20	Dec	5	H	Blackpool	W	1-0	Allcock (og)	22
21		12	A	Arsenal	L	1-2	Dougan	38
22		19	A	Tottenham Hotspur	D	0-0		3
23		26	H	Everton	W	2-0	Dougan 2	30
24	Jan	9	A	Derby County	W	2-1	Shaw, Gould	34
25		16	H	Coventry City	D	0-0		27
26		30	H	Crystal Palace	W	2-1	Dougan 2	20
27	Feb	6	A	Blackpool	W	2-0	McCalliog, Dougan	19
28		13	H	Chelsea	W	1-0	Hibbitt	34
29		20	A	Leeds United	L	0-3		37
30		27	H	Liverpool	W	1-0	O'Grady	34
31	Mar	2	H	Arsenal	L	0-3		33
32		6	A	Manchester City	D	0-0		24
33		13	H	West Ham United	W	2-0	Gould 2	25
34		20	A	West Bromwich Albion	W	4-2	Curran 2, Bailey, Gould	36
35	Apr	3	H	Nottingham Forest	W	4-0	Curran 3, Gould	20
36		7	A	Stoke City	L	0-1		22
37		10	A	Everton	W	2-1	Bailey, Gould	35
38		12	A	Manchester United	L	0-1		39
39		17	H	Southampton	L	0-1		23
40		24	A	Huddersfield Town	W	2-1	Curran, McCalliog	13
41		28	H	Ipswich Town	D	0-0		18
42	May	1	H	Burnley	W	1-0	Dougan	19

Appearar

Sub appearar

One own-goal G

FA Cup

R3	Jan	2	H	Norwich City	W	5-1	Gould 2, McCalliog 2 (1 pen), Hibbitt	29
R4		23	A	Derby County	L	1-2	Richards	40

Appearar

Sub appearar

G

League Cup

R2	Sep	9	A	Oxford United	L	0-1		15

Appearar

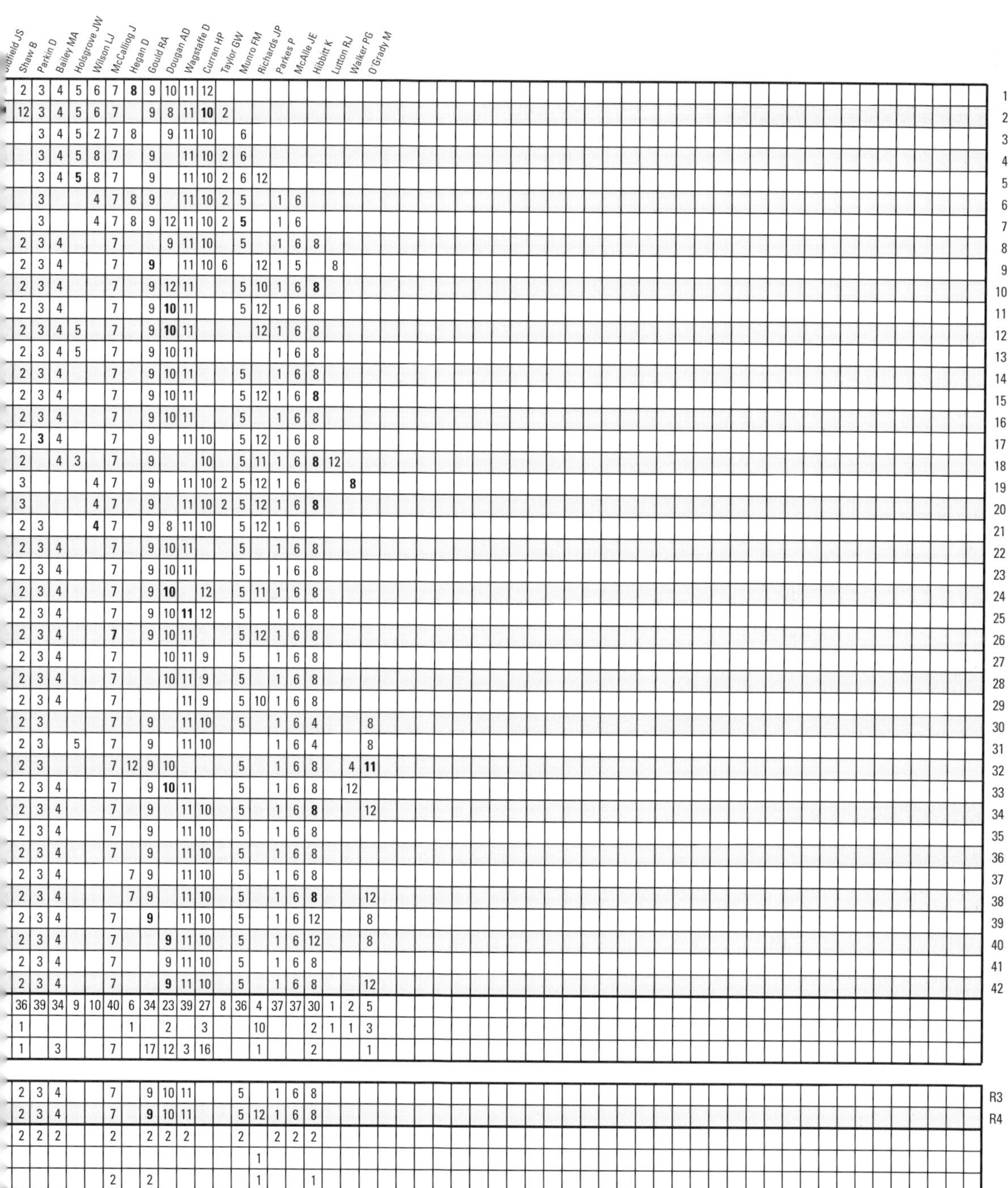

Oldfield JS	Shaw B	Parkin D	Bailey MA	Holsgrove JW	Wilson LJ	McCalliog J	Hegan D	Gould RA	Dougan AD	Wagstaffe D	Curran HP	Taylor GW	Munro FM	Richards JP	Parkes P	McAlle JE	Hibbitt K	Lutton RJ	Walker PG	O'Grady M	
	2	3	4	5	6	7	**8**	9	10	11	12										1
	12	3	4	5	6	7		9	8	11	**10**	2									2
		3	4	5	2	7	8		9	11	10		6								3
		3	4	5	8	7		9		11	10	2	6								4
		3	4	**5**	8	7		9		11	10	2	6	12							5
		3			4	7	8	9		11	10	2	5		1	6					6
		3			4	7	8	9	12	11	10	2	**5**		1	6					7
	2	3	4			7			9	11	10		5		1	6	8				8
	2	3	4			7		**9**		11	10	6		12	1	5		8			9
	2	3	4			7		9	12	11			5	10	1	6	**8**				10
	2	3	4			7		9	**10**	11			5	12	1	6	8				11
	2	3	4	5		7		9	**10**	11				12	1	6	8				12
	2	3	4	5		7		9	10	11					1	6	8				13
	2	3	4			7		9	10	11			5		1	6	8				14
	2	3	4			7		9	10	11			5	12	1	6	**8**				15
	2	3	4			7		9	10	11			5		1	6	8				16
	2	**3**	4			7		9		11	10		5	12	1	6	8				17
	2		4	3		7		9			10		5	11	1	6	**8**	12			18
	3				4	7		9		11	10	2	5	12	1	6			**8**		19
	3				4	7		9		11	10	2	5	12	1	6	**8**				20
	2	3			**4**	7		9	8	11	10		5	12	1	6					21
	2	3	4			7		9	10	11			5		1	6	8				22
	2	3	4			7		9	10	11			5		1	6	8				23
	2	3	4			7		9	**10**		12		5	11	1	6	8				24
	2	3	4			7		9	10	**11**	12		5		1	6	8				25
	2	3	4			**7**		9	10	11			5	12	1	6	8				26
	2	3	4			7			10	11	9		5		1	6	8				27
	2	3	4			7			10	11	9		5		1	6	8				28
	2	3	4			7				11	9		5	10	1	6	8				29
	2	3				7		9		11	10		5		1	6	4			8	30
	2	3		5		7		9		11	10				1	6	4			8	31
	2	3				7	12	9	10				5		1	6	8		4	**11**	32
	2	3	4			7		9	**10**	11			5		1	6	8		12		33
	2	3	4			7		9		11	10		5		1	6	**8**			12	34
	2	3	4			7		9		11	10		5		1	6	8				35
	2	3	4			7		9		11	10		5		1	6	8				36
	2	3	4				7	9		11	10		5		1	6	8				37
	2	3	4				7	9		11	10		5		1	6	**8**			12	38
	2	3	4			7		**9**		11	10		5		1	6	12			8	39
	2	3	4			7			**9**	11	10		5		1	6	12			8	40
	2	3	4			7			9	11	10		5		1	6	8				41
	2	3	4			7			**9**	11	10		5		1	6	8			12	42
	36	39	34	9	10	40	6	34	23	39	27	8	36	4	37	37	30	1	2	5	
	1						1		2		3			10			2	1	1	3	
	1		3			7		17	12	3	16			1			2			1	

Oldfield JS	Shaw B	Parkin D	Bailey MA	Holsgrove JW	Wilson LJ	McCalliog J	Hegan D	Gould RA	Dougan AD	Wagstaffe D	Curran HP	Taylor GW	Munro FM	Richards JP	Parkes P	McAlle JE	Hibbitt K	Lutton RJ	Walker PG	O'Grady M	
	2	3	4			7		9	10	11			5		1	6	8				R3
	2	3	4			7		**9**	10	11			5	12	1	6	8				R4
	2	2	2			2		2	2	2			2		2	2	2				
														1							
						2		2						1			1				

Oldfield JS	Shaw B	Parkin D	Bailey MA	Holsgrove JW	Wilson LJ	McCalliog J	Hegan D	Gould RA	Dougan AD	Wagstaffe D	Curran HP	Taylor GW	Munro FM	Richards JP	Parkes P	McAlle JE	Hibbitt K	Lutton RJ	Walker PG	O'Grady M	
	2	3	4		8	7		9	5	11	10				1	6					R2
	1	1	1		1	1		1	1	1	1				1	1					

1971-72

Division One

Manager: Bill McGarry

	P	W	D	L	F	A	Pts
Derby County	42	24	10	8	69	33	58
Leeds United	42	24	9	9	73	31	57
Liverpool	42	24	9	9	64	30	57
Manchester City	42	23	11	8	77	45	57
Arsenal	42	22	8	12	58	40	52
Tottenham Hotspur	42	19	13	10	63	42	51
Chelsea	42	18	12	12	58	49	48
Manchester United	42	19	10	13	69	61	48
Wolverhampton Wanderers	42	18	11	13	65	57	47
Sheffield United	42	17	12	13	61	60	46
Newcastle United	42	15	11	16	49	52	41
Leicester City	42	13	13	16	41	46	39
Ipswich Town	42	11	16	15	39	53	38
West Ham United	42	12	12	18	47	51	36
Everton	42	9	18	15	37	48	36
West Bromwich Albion	42	12	11	19	42	54	35
Stoke City	42	10	15	17	39	56	35
Coventry City	42	9	15	18	44	67	33
Southampton	42	12	7	23	52	80	31
Crystal Palace	42	8	13	21	39	65	29
Nottingham Forest	42	8	9	25	47	81	25
Huddersfield Town	42	6	13	23	27	59	25

Did you know that?

- Wolves became the first Midland team for 11 years to appear in a major European Final, losing to Spurs over two legs in the UEFA Cup.
- Derek Dougan scored Wolves' first European hat-trick in this competition against Academica Coimbra (a) in September. In this same game, Danny Hegan became the first Wolves player to be sent off in a European competition.
- Wolves beat a Jersey Select XI 9–0 in a friendly on the island in February.
- Wolves played Aberdeen in four exhibition games in the USA and Canada in May 1972. They won two and lost two.

Match No.	Date		Venue	Opponents	Result		Scorers	Atten
1	Aug	14	H	Tottenham Hotspur	D	2-2	Gould, McCalliog (pen)	30,
2		17	A	Liverpool	L	2-3	Dougan, Hibbitt	51,
3		21	A	Leeds United	D	0-0		20,
4		24	H	Manchester City	W	2-1	Hibbitt, McCalliog	26,
5		28	H	Manchester United	D	1-1	Shaw	46
6		31	H	Crystal Palace	W	1-0	Bailey	24,
7	Sep	4	A	Stoke City	W	1-0	Hegan	29,
8		11	H	Everton	D	1-1	Hegan	26,
9		18	A	Newcastle United	L	0-2		29,
10		25	H	Nottingham Forest	W	4-2	Dougan 3, McCalliog	20,
11	Oct	2	A	Chelsea	L	1-3	McCalliog	42,
12		9	H	Southampton	W	4-2	Dougan 2, Daley, Parkin (pen)	21,
13		16	A	Tottenham Hotspur	L	1-4	Bailey	36,
14		23	A	West Ham United	L	0-1		33,
15		30	H	Coventry City	D	1-1	Munro	25,
16	Nov	6	A	Ipswich Town	L	1-2	Dougan	21,
17		13	H	Derby County	W	2-1	Richards 2	32,
18		20	H	Arsenal	W	5-1	Dougan 2, Hibbitt, McCalliog (pen), Wagstaffe	28
19		27	A	West Bromwich Albion	W	3-2	McCalliog, Richards, Wagstaffe	37,
20	Dec	4	H	Huddersfield Town	D	2-2	Dougan, Richards	21,
21		11	A	Sheffield United	D	2-2	Richards, Colquhoun (og)	29,
22		18	H	Stoke City	W	2-0	Dougan, Bloor (og)	25,
23		27	A	Leicester City	W	2-1	Dougan, Munro	37,
24	Jan	1	H	Newcastle United	W	2-0	Parkin, Richards	26,
25		8	A	Manchester United	W	3-1	Dougan, McCalliog (pen), Richards	47,
26		22	H	Liverpool	D	0-0		33,
27		29	A	Manchester City	L	2-5	Richards 2	37,
28	Feb	12	H	West Ham United	W	1-0	Richards	26,
29		19	A	Coventry City	D	0-0		22,
30		26	H	Ipswich Town	D	2-2	Hibbitt, McCalliog (pen)	19,
31	Mar	4	A	Derby County	L	1-2	McCalliog (pen)	33,
32		11	A	Southampton	W	2-1	McCalliog, Taylor	16,
33		18	A	Crystal Palace	W	2-0	Dougan, McCalliog	24,
34		25	A	Everton	D	2-2	Hibbitt 2	29,
35	Apr	1	H	Leicester City	L	0-1		23,
36		8	A	Arsenal	L	1-2	Richards	38,
37		12	H	Chelsea	L	0-2		24,
38		15	H	West Bromwich Albion	L	0-1		30,
39		22	A	Huddersfield Town	W	1-0	Daley	11,
40		25	A	Nottingham Forest	W	3-1	Hegan, Hibbitt, Richards	16,
41		28	H	Sheffield United	L	1-2	Richards	17,
42	May	8	H	Leeds United	W	2-1	Dougan, Munro	53,
								Appearanc
								Sub appearanc
							Two own-goals	Goa

FA Cup

R3	Jan	15	H	Leicester City	D	1-1	McCalliog	38,
rep		19	A	Leicester City	L	0-2		37,
								Appearanc
								Sub appearanc
								Goa

League Cup

R2	Sep	8	A	Manchester City	L	3-4	Hegan, McAlle, Parkin (pen)	29,1
								Appearanc
								Goa

	Parkin D	Walker PG	Munro FM	McAlle JE	Hibbitt K	McCalliog J	Gould RA	Dougan AD	Wagstaffe D	Richards JP	Wilson LJ	Sunderland A	Taylor GW	Hegan D	Bailey MA	O'Grady M	Daley SJ	Curran HP	Eastoe PR	Kent MJ
1	3	4	5	6	7	8	9	10	11											
2	3	**4**	5	6	7	8	9	10	11	12										
3	3	4	5	6		7	12	**10**	11	9	8									
4	3		5	6	7	8	9		11	10		4								
5	3			6	7	**8**	9	10	11			4	5	12						
6	3			6	8		9	10	11			7	5		4					
7	3		5	6	8			**10**	11	9			12	7	4					
8	3		5	6	8			10	11	9				7	4					
9	3		5	6				10	11	**9**		12		7	4	8				
10	3		5	6		9		10	11					7	4	**8**	12			
11	3		5	6		9		10	11					7	4	**8**	12			
12	3			6		**9**		10	11				5	7	4		8	12		
13	3	11		6		9				10			5	7	4		8			
14	3			6	11	8		10		9	12		5	**7**	4					
15	3		5	6		7		10	11	9					4		8			
16	3		5	6	8	7		9	11	12			2		4			**10**		
17	3		5	6	8	7		10	11	9					4					
18	3		5	6	8	7		10	11	9					4					
19	3		5	6	**8**	7		10	11	9					4	12				
20	3		5	6	8	**7**		10	11	9				12	4					
21	3		5	6	8	7		10	11	9					4					
22	3		5	6	8	7		10	11	9					4					
23	3		5	6	8	7		10	11	9					4					
24	3		5	6	8	7		10	11	9					4					
25	3		5	6	8	7		**10**	11	9					4			12		
26	3		5	6		7		**10**	11			4		8				9	12	
27	3		5	6	8	7		10	11	9		4								
28	3		5	6	8	7		10	11	9			4							
29	3		5	6	8	7		10	11	9			4							
30	**3**		5	6	8	7		10	11	9		12	4							
31			5	6	8	7		10	11	9			3	4						
32			5	6	8	7		10	11	9			3	4						12
33			5	6	8	7		10	11	9			**3**	4			12			
34			5	6	8	7		10	11	9			3	4						
35			5	6	**8**	7		10	11	9			3	4			12			
36	3		5	6	8	7			**11**	9			12	4					10	
37	**3**		5	6	8	7			11	9				4			12		10	
38			5	6	8	7		10	11	9		12	3	4						
39			5	6	12	7		**10**	11	9			3	4			8			
40			5	6	8	7		10		9			3	4			11			
41			5	6	8	7		10	11	9			3	4						
42			5	6	8	7		10	11	9			3	4						
	32	4	37	42	33	38	5	38	39	33	1	5	19	21	20	3	5	2	2	
					1		1			2	1	3	2	2		1	5	2	1	1
	2		3		7	11	1	15	2	13			1	3	2		2			

	Parkin D	Walker PG	Munro FM	McAlle JE	Hibbitt K	McCalliog J	Gould RA	Dougan AD	Wagstaffe D	Richards JP	Wilson LJ	Sunderland A	Taylor GW	Hegan D	Bailey MA	O'Grady M	Daley SJ	Curran HP	Eastoe PR	Kent MJ
R3	3		5	6	8	7			11	9			12		**4**			10		
rep	3		5	6	8	7			11	9		4						10		
	2		2	2	2	2			2	2		1			1			2		
													1							
						1														

	Parkin D	Walker PG	Munro FM	McAlle JE	Hibbitt K	McCalliog J	Gould RA	Dougan AD	Wagstaffe D	Richards JP	Wilson LJ	Sunderland A	Taylor GW	Hegan D	Bailey MA	O'Grady M	Daley SJ	Curran HP	Eastoe PR	Kent MJ
R2	3		5	6	8			10	11	9				7	4					
	1		1	1	1			1	1	1				1	1					
	1			1										1						

1972-73

Division One

Manager: Bill McGarry

	P	W	D	L	F	A	Pts
Liverpool	42	25	10	7	72	42	60
Arsenal	42	23	11	8	57	43	57
Leeds United	42	21	11	10	71	45	53
Ipswich Town	42	17	14	11	55	45	48
Wolverhampton Wanderers	42	18	11	13	66	54	47
West Ham United	42	17	12	13	67	53	46
Derby County	42	19	8	15	56	54	46
Tottenham Hotspur	42	16	13	13	58	48	45
Newcastle United	42	16	13	13	60	51	45
Birmingham City	42	15	12	15	53	54	42
Manchester City	42	15	11	16	57	60	41
Chelsea	42	13	14	15	49	51	40
Southampton	42	11	18	13	47	52	40
Sheffield United	42	15	10	17	51	59	40
Stoke City	42	14	10	18	61	56	38
Leicester City	42	10	17	15	40	46	37
Everton	42	13	11	18	41	49	37
Manchester United	42	12	13	17	44	60	37
Coventry City	42	13	9	20	40	55	35
Norwich City	42	11	10	21	36	63	32
Crystal Palace	42	9	12	21	41	58	30
West Bromwich Albion	42	9	10	23	38	62	28

Did you know that?

- Wolves striker John Richards was voted Young Footballer of the Year in 1973.
- Derek Dougan scored the 200th League goal of his career for Wolves against West Ham United at Molineux in August 1972.
- Tottenham Hotspur inflicted upon Wolves their first home defeat in the League Cup, winning 2–1 in the first leg of the semi-final at Molineux in December.
- Steve Kindon was used as a substitute by Wolves on 15 occasions.
- Wolves entered four Cup competitions this season and reached the semi-final in two of them.

Match No.	Date		Venue	Opponents	Result		Scorers	A
1	Aug	12	A	Newcastle United	L	1-2	Kindon	
2		15	A	Arsenal	L	2-5	Richards, Simpson (og)	
3		19	H	Tottenham Hotspur	W	3-2	Richards 2, Hibbitt	
4		22	H	West Ham United	W	3-0	McCalliog, Dougan, Richards	
5		26	A	Southampton	D	1-1	McCalliog	
6		29	A	Coventry City	W	1-0	Richards	
7	Sep	2	H	Birmingham City	W	3-2	Munro, McCalliog 2 (1 pen)	
8		9	A	Liverpool	L	2-4	Kindon, Richards	
9		16	H	Manchester United	W	2-0	Dougan, Richards	
10		23	A	Leicester City	D	1-1	Hegan	
11		30	H	Stoke City	W	5-3	Richards 3, Dougan, Hegan	
12	Oct	7	A	Manchester City	D	1-1	Dougan	
13		14	H	Crystal Palace	D	1-1	Dougan	
14		21	A	West Bromwich Albion	L	0-1		
15		28	H	Leeds United	L	0-2		
16	Nov	4	A	West Ham United	D	2-2	Kindon 2	
17		11	H	Arsenal	L	1-3	Richards	
18		18	H	Ipswich Town	L	0-1		
19		25	A	Sheffield United	W	2-1	Richards, Hibbitt	
20	Dec	2	H	Derby County	L	1-2	Richards	
21		9	A	Everton	W	1-0	Hibbitt	
22		16	H	Chelsea	W	1-0	Sunderland	
23		23	A	Norwich City	D	1-1	Dougan	
24		26	H	Leicester City	W	2-0	Richards, Dougan	
25	Jan	6	H	Southampton	L	0-1		
26		27	H	Liverpool	W	2-1	Hughes (og), Richards	
27	Feb	10	A	Manchester United	L	1-2	Hegan	
28		17	H	Newcastle United	D	1-1	Hibbitt	
29		27	A	Birmingham City	W	1-0	Dougan	
30	Mar	3	H	Manchester City	W	5-1	Dougan 3, Richards 2	
31		6	A	Chelsea	W	2-0	Dougan, Richards	
32		10	A	Crystal Palace	D	1-1	Munro	
33		20	H	West Bromwich Albion	W	2-0	Hibbitt, Richards	
34		24	A	Leeds United	D	0-0		
35		31	H	Sheffield United	D	1-1	Richards	
36	Apr	14	H	Everton	W	4-2	Richards 3, Hibbitt	
37		21	A	Ipswich Town	L	1-2	Richards	
38		23	H	Norwich City	W	3-0	Sunderland 2, Richards	
39		24	A	Stoke City	L	0-2		
40		28	H	Coventry City	W	3-0	Sunderland, Richards, Powell	
41		30	A	Tottenham Hotspur	D	2-2	Sunderland, Richards	
42	May	4	A	Derby County	L	0-3		

Appear

Sub appear

Two own-goals

FA Cup

R3	Jan	13	H	Manchester United	W	1-0	Bailey
R4	Feb	3	H	Bristol City	W	1-0	Richards
R5		24	H	Millwall	W	1-0	Richards
R6	Mar	17	H	Coventry City	W	2-0	Hibbitt (pen), Richards
SF	Apr	7	N	Leeds United	L	0-1	

SF at Maine Road, Manchester.

Appear

Sub appear

League Cup

R2	Sep	5	H	Orient	W	2-1	Dougan, Richards
R3	Oct	4	H	Sheffield Wednesday	W	3-1	Dougan, Hibbitt (pen), Munro
R4		31	H	Bristol Rovers	W	4-0	McCalliog 2, Kindon, Richards
R5	Nov	21	H	Blackpool	D	1-1	McCalliog
rep		28	A	Blackpool	W	1-0	Dougan
SF1	Dec	20	H	Tottenham Hotspur	L	1-2	Hibbitt (pen)
SF2		30	A	Tottenham Hotspur	D	2-2	Richards, Naylor (og)

SF2 aet

Appear

Sub appear

One own-goal

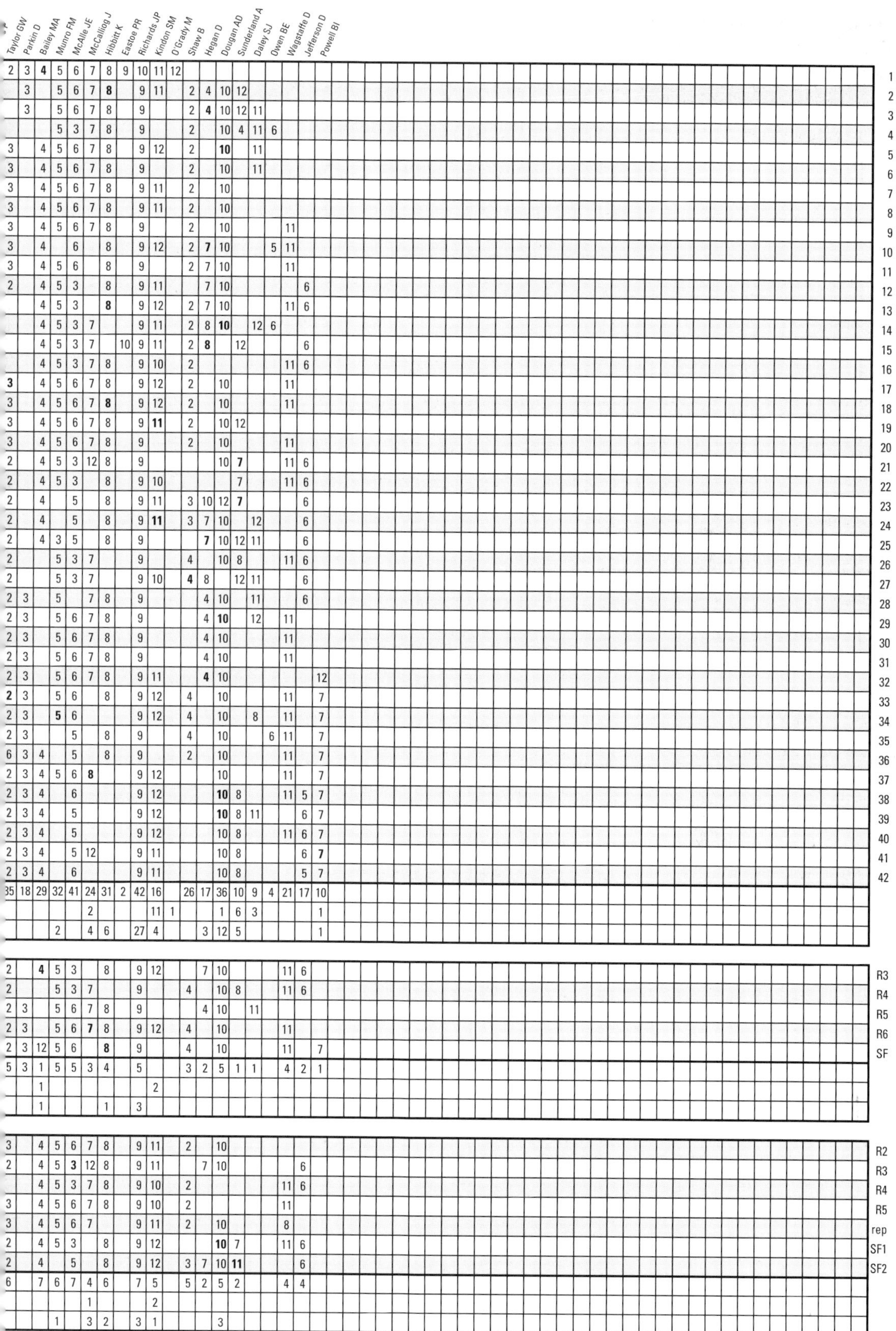

	Taylor GW	Parkin D	Bailey MA	Munro FM	McAlle JE	McCalliog J	Hibbitt K	Eastoe PR	Richards JP	Kindon SM	O'Grady M	Shaw B	Hegan D	Dougan AD	Sunderland A	Daley SJ	Owen BE	Wagstaffe D	Jefferson D	Powell BI
1	2	3	**4**	5	6	7	8	9	10	11	12									
2		3		5	6	**7**	**8**		9	11		2	4	10	12					
3		3		5	6	7	8		9			2	**4**	10	12	11				
4				5	3	7	8		9			2		10	4	11	6			
5	3		4	5	6	7	8		9	12		2		**10**		11				
6	3		4	5	6	7	8		9			2		10		11				
7	3		4	5	6	7	8		9	11		2		10						
8	3		4	5	6	7	8		9	11		2		10						
9	3		4	5	6	7	8		9			2		10				11		
10	3		4		6		8		9	12		2	**7**	10			5	11		
11	3		4	5	6		8		9			2	7	10				11		
12	2		4	5	3		8		9	11			7	10					6	
13			4	5	3		**8**		9	12		2	7	10				11	6	
14			4	5	3	7			9	11		2	8	**10**		12	6			
15			4	5	3	7		10	9	11		2	**8**		12				6	
16			4	5	3	7	8		9	10		2						11	6	
17	**3**		4	5	6	7	8		9	12		2		10				11		
18	3		4	5	6	7	**8**		9	12		2		10				11		
19	3		4	5	6	7	8		9	**11**		2		10	12					
20	3		4	5	6	7	8		9			2		10				11		
21	2		4	5	3	12	8		9					10	**7**			11	6	
22	2		4	5	3		8		9	10					7			11	6	
23	2		4		5		8		9	11		3	10	12	**7**				6	
24	2		4		5		8		9	**11**		3	7	10		12			6	
25	2		4	3	5		8		9				**7**	10	12	11			6	
26	2			5	3	7			9			4		10	8			11	6	
27	2			5	3	7			9	10		**4**	8		12	11			6	
28	2	3		5		7	8		9				4	10		11			6	
29	2	3		5	6	7	8		9				4	**10**		12		11		
30	2	3		5	6	7	8		9				4	10				11		
31	2	3		5	6	7	8		9				4	10				11		
32	2	3		5	6	7	8		9	11			**4**	10						12
33	**2**	3		5	6		8		9	12		4		10				11		7
34	2	3		**5**	6				9	12		4		10		8		11		7
35	2	3			5		8		9			4		10			6	11		7
36	6	3	4		5		8		9			2		10				11		7
37	2	3	4	5	6	**8**			9	12				10				11		7
38	2	3	4		6				9	12				**10**	8			11	5	7
39	2	3	4		5				9	12				**10**	8	11			6	7
40	2	3	4		5				9	12				10	8			11	6	7
41	2	3	4		5	12			9	11				10	8				6	**7**
42	2	3	4		6				9	11				10	8				5	7
	35	18	29	32	41	24	31	2	42	16		26	17	36	10	9	4	21	17	10
						2				11	1			1	6	3				1
				2		4	6		27	4			3	12	5					1

	Taylor GW	Parkin D	Bailey MA	Munro FM	McAlle JE	McCalliog J	Hibbitt K	Eastoe PR	Richards JP	Kindon SM	O'Grady M	Shaw B	Hegan D	Dougan AD	Sunderland A	Daley SJ	Owen BE	Wagstaffe D	Jefferson D	Powell BI
R3	2		**4**	5	3		8		9	12			7	10				11	6	
R4	2			5	3	7			9			4		10	8			11	6	
R5	2	3		5	6	7	8		9				4	10		11				
R6	2	3		5	6	**7**	8		9	12		4		10				11		
SF	2	3	12	5	6		**8**		9			4		10				11		7
	5	3	1	5	5	3	4		5			3	2	5	1	1		4	2	1
			1							2										
			1				1		3											

	Taylor GW	Parkin D	Bailey MA	Munro FM	McAlle JE	McCalliog J	Hibbitt K	Eastoe PR	Richards JP	Kindon SM	O'Grady M	Shaw B	Hegan D	Dougan AD	Sunderland A	Daley SJ	Owen BE	Wagstaffe D	Jefferson D	Powell BI
R2	3		4	5	6	7	8		9	11		2		10						
R3	2		4	5	**3**	12	8		9	11			7	10					6	
R4			4	5	3	7	8		9	10		2						11	6	
R5	3		4	5	6	7	8		9	10		2						11		
rep	3		4	5	6	7			9	11		2		10				8		
SF1	2		4	5	3		8		9	12				**10**	7			11	6	
SF2	2		4		5		8		9	12		3	7	10	**11**				6	
	6		7	6	7	4	6		7	5		5	2	5	2			4	4	
						1				2										
				1		3	2		3	1				3						

1973-74

Division One

Manager: Bill McGarry

	P	W	D	L	F	A	Pts
Leeds United	42	24	14	4	66	31	62
Liverpool	42	22	13	7	52	31	57
Derby County	42	17	14	11	52	42	48
Ipswich Town	42	18	11	13	67	58	47
Stoke City	42	15	16	11	54	42	46
Burnley	42	16	14	12	56	53	46
Everton	42	16	12	14	50	48	44
Queen's Park Rangers	42	13	17	12	56	52	43
Leicester City	42	13	16	13	51	41	42
Arsenal	42	14	14	14	49	51	42
Tottenham Hotspur	42	14	14	14	45	50	42
Wolverhampton Wanderers	42	13	15	14	49	49	41
Sheffield United	42	14	12	16	44	49	40
Manchester City	42	14	12	16	39	46	40
Newcastle United	42	13	12	17	49	48	38
Coventry City	42	14	10	18	43	54	38
Chelsea	42	12	13	17	56	60	37
West Ham United	42	11	15	16	55	60	37
Birmingham City	42	12	13	17	52	64	37
Southampton	42	11	14	17	47	68	36
Manchester United	42	10	12	20	38	48	32
Norwich City	42	7	15	20	37	62	29

Did you know that?

- In September 1973 goalkeeper Phil Parkes made his 127th consecutive League appearance for Wolves, beating Noel George's club record.
- John Richards was sent off in the UEFA Cup game in Belenenses in September.
- Peter Withe scored on his League debut for Wolves at Ipswich in March.
- Owing to the three-day working week and electricity cuts, Wolves played afternoon games in the League Cup against Tranmere Rovers, Exeter City and Liverpool – hence the relatively small crowds.
- Derek Dougan became the first Wolves player to score in the first four matches of a League season since Johnny Hancocks in 1947–48.

Match No.	Date		Venue	Opponents	Result		Scorers
1	Aug	25	H	Norwich City	W	3-1	Dougan 2, McCalliog
2		28	H	Sheffield United	W	2-0	Dougan, McCalliog
3	Sep	1	A	Southampton	L	1-2	Dougan
4		5	A	Leeds United	L	1-4	Dougan
5		8	H	Burnley	L	0-2	
6		11	H	Leeds United	L	0-2	
7		15	A	Newcastle United	L	0-2	
8		22	H	Everton	D	1-1	Dougan
9		29	A	Chelsea	D	2-2	McCalliog 2
10	Oct	6	H	Manchester United	W	2-1	Dougan, McCalliog
11		13	A	Birmingham City	L	1-2	Richards
12		20	H	Queen's Park Rangers	L	2-4	Daley, Richards
13		27	A	Ipswich Town	L	0-2	
14	Nov	3	H	Manchester City	D	0-0	
15		10	A	Liverpool	L	0-1	
16		17	H	West Ham United	D	0-0	
17		24	A	Tottenham Hotspur	W	3-1	Hibbitt, Palmer, Powell
18	Dec	4	A	Arsenal	D	2-2	Dougan, Richards
19		8	A	Coventry City	L	0-1	
20		15	A	Stoke City	W	3-2	Hibbitt, Munro, Richards
21		22	H	Chelsea	W	2-0	Richards 2
22		26	A	Leicester City	D	2-2	Richards, Sunderland
23		29	A	Burnley	D	1-1	Powell
24	Jan	1	H	Southampton	W	2-1	Richards, Wagstaffe
25		12	H	Newcastle United	W	1-0	Richards
26		19	A	Norwich City	D	1-1	Dougan
27	Feb	2	H	Stoke City	D	1-1	Pejic (og)
28		5	A	Sheffield United	L	0-1	
29		9	A	Everton	L	1-2	Sunderland
30		16	H	Birmingham City	W	1-0	Munro
31		23	A	Manchester United	D	0-0	
32	Mar	9	H	Ipswich Town	W	3-1	Dougan, Sunderland, Withe
33		16	A	Queen's Park Rangers	D	0-0	
34		23	H	Liverpool	L	0-1	
35		30	A	Manchester City	D	1-1	Kindon
36	Apr	6	H	Tottenham Hotspur	D	1-1	Powell
37		9	H	Derby County	W	4-0	Kindon 2, Powell, Sunderland
38		13	A	West Ham United	D	0-0	
39		15	H	Arsenal	W	3-1	Sunderland 2, Kindon
40		20	H	Coventry City	D	1-1	Cross (og)
41		23	H	Leicester City	W	1-0	Sunderland
42		27	A	Derby County	L	0-2	

Appeara

Sub appeara

Two own-goals

FA Cup

R3	Jan	5	H	Leeds United	D	1-1	Richards
rep		9	A	Leeds United	L	0-1	

Appeara

League Cup

R2	Oct	8	A	Halifax Town	W	3-0	Dougan, Richards, Sunderland
R3		31	A	Tranmere Rovers	D	1-1	Sunderland
rep	Nov	13	H	Tranmere Rovers	W	2-1	Dougan, Powell
R4		20	H	Exeter City	W	5-1	Hibbitt 2, Richards 2, Dougan
R5	Dec	19	H	Liverpool	W	1-0	Richards
SF1	Jan	23	A	Norwich City	D	1-1	Richards
SF2		26	H	Norwich City	W	1-0	Richards
F	Mar	2	N	Manchester City	W	2-1	Hibbitt, Richards

Final at Wembley Stadium.

Appeara

Sub appeara

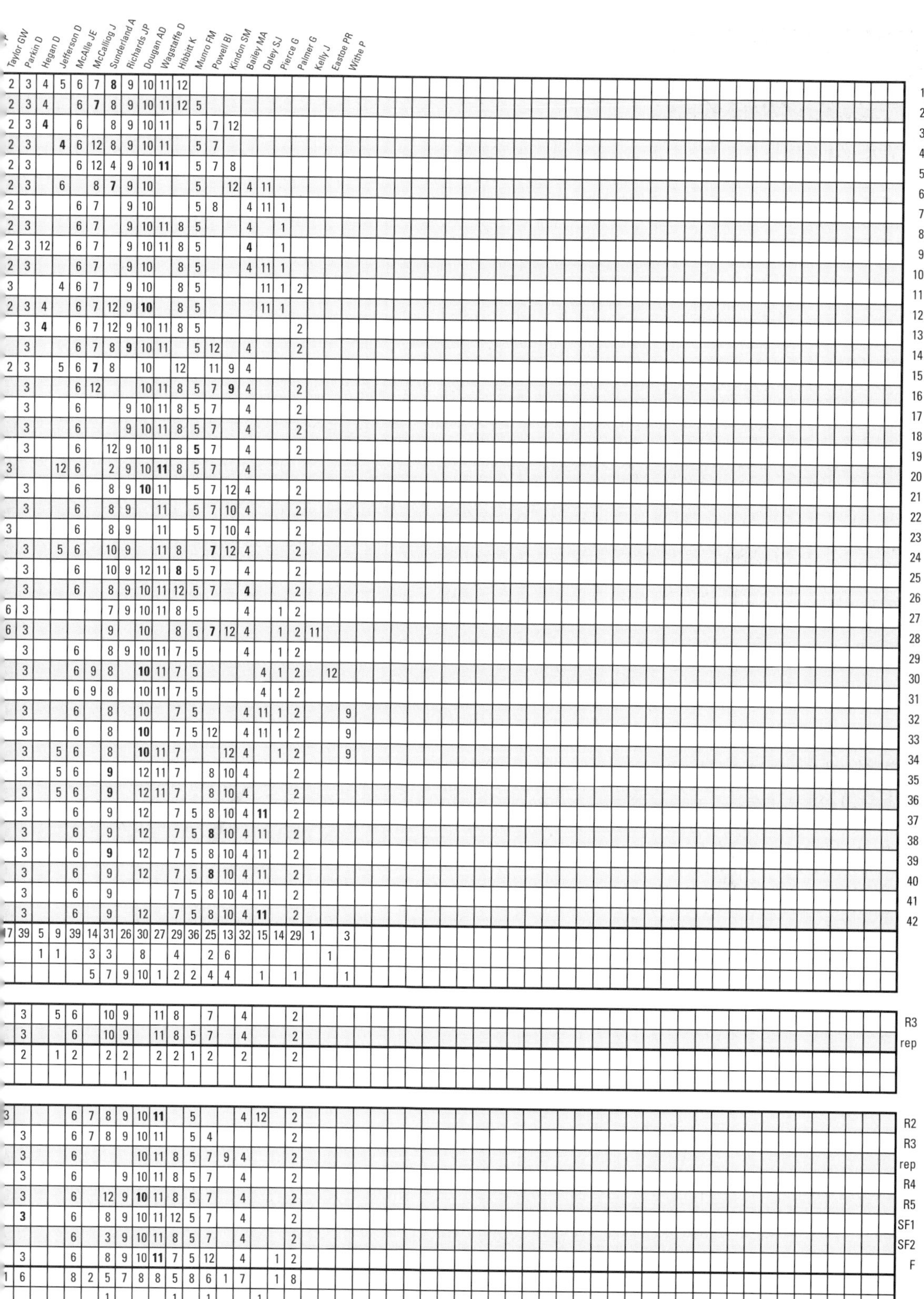

Taylor GW	Parkin D	Hegan D	Jefferson D	McAlle JE	McCalliog J	Sunderland A	Richards JP	Dougan AD	Wagstaffe D	Hibbitt K	Munro FM	Powell BI	Kindon SM	Bailey MA	Daley SJ	Pierce G	Palmer G	Kelly J	Eastoe PR	Withe P	
2	3	4	5	6	7	**8**	9	10	11	12											1
2	3	4		6	**7**	8	9	10	11	12	5										2
2	3	**4**		6		8	9	10	11		5	7	12								3
2	3		**4**	6	12	8	9	10	11		5	7									4
2	3			6	12	4	9	10	**11**		5	7	8								5
2	3		6		8	**7**	9	10			5		12	4	11						6
2	3			6	7		9	10			5	8		4	11	1					7
2	3			6	7		9	10	11	8	5			4		1					8
2	3	12		6	7		9	10	11	8	5			**4**		1					9
2	3			6	7		9	10		8	5			4	11	1					10
3			4	6	7		9	10		8	5				11	1	2				11
2	3	4		6	7	12	9	**10**		8	5				11	1					12
	3	**4**		6	7	12	9	10	11	8	5						2				13
	3			6	7	8	**9**	10	11		5	12		4			2				14
2	3		5	6	**7**	8		10		12		11	9	4							15
	3			6	12			10	11	8	5	7	**9**	4			2				16
	3			6			9	10	11	8	5	7		4			2				17
	3			6			9	10	11	8	5	7		4			2				18
	3			6		12	9	10	11	8	**5**	7		4			2				19
3			12	6		2	9	10	**11**	8	5	7		4							20
	3			6		8	9	**10**	11		5	7	12	4			2				21
	3			6		8	9		11		5	7	10	4			2				22
3				6		8	9		11		5	7	10	4			2				23
	3		5	6		10	9		11	8		**7**	12	4			2				24
	3			6		10	9	12	11	**8**	5	7		4			2				25
	3			6		8	9	10	11	12	5	7		**4**			2				26
6	3					7	9	10	11	8	5			4		1	2				27
6	3					9		10		8	5	**7**	12	4		1	2	11			28
	3			6		8	9	10	11	7	5			4		1	2				29
	3			6	9	8		**10**	11	7	5				4	1	2		12		30
	3			6	9	8		10	11	7	5				4	1	2				31
	3			6		8		10		7	5			4	11	1	2			9	32
	3			6		8		**10**		7	5	12		4	11	1	2			9	33
	3		5	6		8		**10**	11	7			12	4		1	2			9	34
	3		5	6		**9**		12	11	7		8	10	4			2				35
	3		5	6		**9**		12	11	7		8	10	4			2				36
	3			6		9		12		7	5	8	10	4	**11**		2				37
	3			6		9		12		7	5	**8**	10	4	11		2				38
	3			6		**9**		12		7	5	8	10	4	11		2				39
	3			6		9		12		7	5	**8**	10	4	11		2				40
	3			6		9				7	5	8	10	4	11		2				41
	3			6		9		12		7	5	8	10	4	**11**		2				42
17	39	5	9	39	14	31	26	30	27	29	36	25	13	32	15	14	29	1		3	
		1	1		3	3		8		4		2	6						1		
					5	7	9	10	1	2	2	4	4		1		1			1	

Taylor GW	Parkin D	Hegan D	Jefferson D	McAlle JE	McCalliog J	Sunderland A	Richards JP	Dougan AD	Wagstaffe D	Hibbitt K	Munro FM	Powell BI	Kindon SM	Bailey MA	Daley SJ	Pierce G	Palmer G	Kelly J	Eastoe PR	Withe P	
	3		5	6		10	9		11	8		7		4			2				R3
	3			6		10	9		11	8	5	7		4			2				rep
	2		1	2		2	2		2	2	1	2		2			2				
							1														

Taylor GW	Parkin D	Hegan D	Jefferson D	McAlle JE	McCalliog J	Sunderland A	Richards JP	Dougan AD	Wagstaffe D	Hibbitt K	Munro FM	Powell BI	Kindon SM	Bailey MA	Daley SJ	Pierce G	Palmer G	Kelly J	Eastoe PR	Withe P	
3				6	7	8	9	10	**11**		5			4	12		2				R2
	3			6	7	8	9	10	11		5	4					2				R3
	3			6				10	11	8	5	7	9	4			2				rep
	3			6			9	10	11	8	5	7		4			2				R4
	3			6		12	9	**10**	11	8	5	7		4			2				R5
	3			6		8	9	10	11	12	5	7		4			2				SF1
				6		3	9	10	11	8	5	7		4			2				SF2
	3			6		8	9	10	**11**	7	5	12		4		1	2				F
1	6			8	2	5	7	8	8	5	8	6	1	7		1	8				
						1				1		1			1						
						2	7	3		3		1									

1974-75

Division One

Manager: Bill McGarry

	P	W	D	L	F	A	Pts
Derby County	42	21	11	10	67	49	53
Liverpool	42	20	11	11	60	39	51
Ipswich Town	42	23	5	14	66	44	51
Everton	42	16	18	8	56	42	50
Stoke City	42	17	15	10	64	48	49
Sheffield United	42	18	13	11	58	51	49
Middlesbrough	42	18	12	12	54	40	48
Manchester City	42	18	10	14	54	54	46
Leeds United	42	16	13	13	57	49	45
Burnley	42	17	11	14	68	67	45
Queen's Park Rangers	42	16	10	16	54	54	42
Wolverhampton Wanderers	42	14	11	17	57	54	39
West Ham United	42	13	13	16	58	59	39
Coventry City	42	12	15	15	51	62	39
Newcastle United	42	15	9	18	59	72	39
Arsenal	42	13	11	18	47	49	37
Birmingham City	42	14	9	19	53	61	37
Leicester City	42	12	12	18	46	60	36
Tottenham Hotspur	42	13	8	21	52	63	34
Luton Town	42	11	11	20	47	65	33
Chelsea	42	9	15	18	42	72	33
Carlisle United	42	12	5	25	43	59	29

Did you know that?

- Derek Dougan announced his retirement after a farewell game against Leeds United.
- Kenny Hibbitt, who scored a then record nine penalties for Wolves this season, was the first recognised midfield player to score four goals in a League game for the club, doing so at home to Newcastle United in August. He was also the first midfielder to score two League hat-tricks in a season.
- The price of a matchday seat at Molineux rose to £1 for the first time this season.
- Willie Carr was signed from Coventry City, taking over in midfield from the departed Barry Powell, who switched to Highfield Road.

Match No.	Date		Venue	Opponents	Result		Scorers
1	Aug	17	A	Burnley	W	2-1	Palmer, Richards
2		20	H	Liverpool	D	0-0	
3		24	H	Newcastle United	W	4-2	Hibbitt 4 (1 pen)
4		27	A	Liverpool	L	0-2	
5		31	A	Birmingham City	D	1-1	Richards
6	Sep	7	H	Leicester City	D	1-1	Richards
7		14	A	Everton	D	0-0	
8		21	H	Tottenham Hotspur	L	2-3	Parkin, Evans (og)
9		24	H	Sheffield United	D	1-1	Daley
10		28	A	Chelsea	W	1-0	Richards
11	Oct	5	A	Middlesbrough	L	1-2	Dougan
12		12	H	Carlisle United	W	2-0	Parkin, Withe
13		16	A	Newcastle United	D	0-0	
14		19	A	Leeds United	L	0-2	
15		26	H	Queen's Park Rangers	L	1-2	Hibbitt (pen)
16	Nov	2	A	Arsenal	D	0-0	
17		9	H	Ipswich Town	W	2-1	Hibbitt, Munro
18		16	A	West Ham United	L	2-5	Kindon, Richards
19		23	H	Stoke City	D	2-2	Hibbitt (pen), Powell
20	Dec	7	H	Coventry City	W	2-0	Kindon 2
21		14	H	Burnley	W	4-2	Kindon 2, Richards 2
22		21	A	Manchester City	D	0-0	
23		26	H	Everton	W	2-0	Hibbitt (pen), Kindon
24		28	A	Luton Town	L	2-3	Munro, Powell
25	Jan	11	A	Coventry City	L	1-2	Kindon
26		18	H	Derby County	L	0-1	
27	Feb	1	A	Ipswich Town	L	0-2	
28		8	H	Arsenal	W	1-0	Hibbitt (pen)
29		15	A	Stoke City	D	2-2	Hibbitt (pen), Munro
30		22	H	West Ham United	W	3-1	Richards 2, Kindon
31	Mar	1	H	Birmingham City	L	0-1	
32		8	A	Sheffield United	L	0-1	
33		15	H	Chelsea	W	7-1	Richards 2, Bailey, Carr, Hibbitt, Kindon, Wagstaffe
34		22	A	Leicester City	L	2-3	Kindon, Richards
35		28	A	Tottenham Hotspur	L	0-3	
36		29	H	Manchester City	W	1-0	Hibbitt (pen)
37		31	H	Luton Town	W	5-2	Hibbitt 3 (1 pen), Carr, Withe
38	Apr	5	A	Queen's Park Rangers	L	0-2	
39		9	A	Derby County	L	0-1	
40		12	H	Middlesbrough	W	2-0	Hibbitt 2 (1 pen)
41		19	A	Carlisle United	L	0-1	
42		26	H	Leeds United	D	1-1	Richards

Appeara
Sub appeara
One own-goal G

FA Cup

R3	Jan	4	H	Ipswich Town	L	1-2	Richards

Appeara
G

League Cup

R2	Sep	11	H	Fulham	L	1-3	Richards

Appeara
Sub appeara
G

	Parkin D	Bailey MA	Munro FM	McAlle JE	Hibbitt K	Powell BI	Richards JP	Sunderland A	Farley JD	Kindon SM	Daley SJ	Dougan AD	Taylor GW	Williams NJ	Withe P	Jefferson D	Pierce G	Wagstaffe D	Carr WMcI	Gardner CD
1	3	4	5	6	7	8	9	10	11											
2	3	4	5	6	7	8	9	10		11										
3	3	4	5	6	7	8	9	10		11										
4	3	4	5	6	7	**8**	9	10		11	12									
5	3	4	5	6	7	8	9	10		**11**	12									
6	3	4	5	6	7	8	9	10	11											
7	3	4	5	6	7	8	**9**	12	11			10								
8	3	4	5	6	7	8		9	11	10			2							
9	3	4	5	6	7			**9**	11	10	8			2	12					
10	3	4	5	6	7		9	8	11		10			2						
11	3	4		6	7		9	11		**10**	8	12				5				
12	3	4		6	**7**		9	11			8	10			12	5	1			
13	3	4	5	6	7	8	9	**11**			12				10		1			
14	3	4	5	6	7	**8**	9	11			12				10		1			
15	3	4	5	6	7	8	9	12							**10**		1	11		
16	3	4	5	6	7	8	9	10	11								1			
17	3	4	5	6	7	8	9	10	11											
18	3	4		6	7	8	9		11	10						5				
19	3	4	5	6	7	8	9			10								11		
20	3	4	5	6	7	8	9			10								11		
21	3	4	5	6	7	8	9		11	10										
22	3	4	5	6	7	8	9		11	10										
23	3	4	5	6	7	8	9		11	10				2						
24	3	4	5	6	**7**	8	9		11	10	12			2						
25	3	4	5	6	7	**8**	9			10	12							11		
26	3	4	5	6	7	12	9			10	8							11		
27	3	4		6	**7**	8	9			10	11			2	12	5				
28		4	5		7	8	9		11	10			3	2		6	1			
29	3	4	5		7		9		11	10	8			2		6	1			
30	3	4	5		7		9			10	8					6	1	11		
31	3	4	5		7		9			10	8		6				1	11		
32	3	4	5	6	7		9			10	8			2	12		1	**11**		
33	3	4	5	6	7		9			10							1	11	8	
34	3	4	5	6		12	**9**			10	7						1	11	8	
35	3		5	6	7					10	4	12			**9**		1	11	8	
36	3		5	6	7					10		**9**			12	4	1	11	8	
37	3		5	6	7					**10**	11			2	9	4	1		8	12
38	3		5	6	7	12					11			**2**	9	4	1		8	10
39	3	4		6	7				10		**11**				9	5	1		8	12
40	3	4		6	7		**9**		11		12				10	5	1		8	
41	3	4		6	7				11	10	12				**9**	5	1		8	
42	3	4	5	6	7		9			**10**		12					1	11	8	
	41	38	35	38	41	23	34	15	18	29	15	3	3	10	9	13	20	13	10	1
						3		2			8	3			5					2
	2	1	3		17	2	13			10	1	1			2			1	2	
R3	3	4	5	6	7	8	9		11	10										
	1	1	1	1	1	1	1		1	1										
							1													
R2	**3**	4	5	6	7	12	9	8	11			10								
	1	1	1	1	1		1	1	1			1								
						1														
							1													

1975-76

Division One

Manager: Bill McGarry

	P	W	D	L	F	A	Pts
Liverpool	42	23	14	5	66	31	60
Queen's Park Rangers	42	24	11	7	67	33	59
Manchester United	42	23	10	9	68	42	56
Derby County	42	21	11	10	75	58	53
Leeds United	42	21	9	12	65	46	51
Ipswich Town	42	16	14	12	54	48	46
Leicester City	42	13	19	10	48	51	45
Manchester City	42	16	11	15	64	46	43
Tottenham Hotspur	42	14	15	13	63	63	43
Norwich City	42	16	10	16	58	58	42
Everton	42	15	12	15	60	66	42
Stoke City	42	15	11	16	48	50	41
Middlesbrough	42	15	10	17	46	45	40
Coventry City	42	13	14	15	47	57	40
Newcastle United	42	15	9	18	71	62	39
Aston Villa	42	11	17	14	51	59	39
Arsenal	42	13	10	19	47	53	36
West Ham United	42	13	10	19	48	71	36
Birmingham City	42	13	7	22	57	75	33
Wolverhampton Wanderers	42	10	10	22	51	68	30
Burnley	42	9	10	23	43	66	28
Sheffield United	42	6	10	26	33	82	22

Did you know that?

- Wolves were defeated 5–0 on aggregate in the FA Youth Cup Final by arch-rivals West Bromwich Albion.
- John Richards scored the fastest goal in the club's history, netting after just 12 seconds against Burnley in November 1975.
- Bobby Gould was re-signed from West Ham and Bob McNab arrived from Arsenal.
- Dave Wagstaffe joined Blackburn Rovers, Peter Withe signed for Birmingham City and Gerry Taylor retired to become a policeman.
- Wolves won all four games on their Swedish tour in May 1976.
- Wolves won the National five-a-side tournament, beating Tottenham Hotspur in the Final.

Match No.	Date		Venue	Opponents	Result		Scorers
1	Aug	16	H	Manchester United	L	0-2	
2		20	A	Stoke City	D	2-2	Carr, Richards
3		23	A	Middlesbrough	L	0-1	
4		26	H	Queen's Park Rangers	D	2-2	Hibbitt (pen), Richards
5		30	H	Arsenal	D	0-0	
6	Sep	6	A	Leeds United	L	0-3	
7		13	H	Birmingham City	W	2-0	Carr 2
8		20	A	Newcastle United	L	1-5	Daley
9		23	H	Aston Villa	D	0-0	
10		27	H	West Ham United	L	0-1	
11	Oct	4	A	Liverpool	L	0-2	
12		11	H	Sheffield United	W	5-1	Hibbitt 2, Richards 2, Carr
13		18	A	Derby County	L	2-3	Kindon, Richards
14		25	H	Everton	L	1-2	Hibbitt
15	Nov	1	A	Tottenham Hotspur	L	1-2	Daley
16		8	H	Ipswich Town	W	1-0	Daley
17		15	A	Burnley	W	5-1	Daley 2, Richards 2, Hibbitt
18		22	H	Derby County	D	0-0	
19		29	H	Manchester City	L	0-4	
20	Dec	6	A	Leicester City	L	0-2	
21		13	H	Middlesbrough	L	1-2	Hibbitt (pen)
22		20	A	Manchester United	L	0-1	
23		26	H	Coventry City	L	0-1	
24		27	A	Norwich City	D	1-1	Bell
25	Jan	10	A	Birmingham City	W	1-0	Carr (pen)
26		17	H	Leeds United	D	1-1	Gould
27		31	H	Stoke City	W	2-1	Bell, Carr (pen)
28	Feb	7	A	Queen's Park Rangers	L	2-4	Gould 2
29		17	A	Ipswich Town	L	0-3	
30		21	H	Burnley	W	3-2	Richards 2, Bell
31		24	A	Aston Villa	D	1-1	Richards
32		28	A	Everton	L	0-3	
33	Mar	13	A	Sheffield United	W	4-1	Kindon 2, Palmer, Richards
34		16	H	Tottenham Hotspur	L	0-1	
35		20	A	Manchester City	L	2-3	Daley, Kindon
36		27	H	Leicester City	D	2-2	Hibbitt, Richards
37	Apr	3	A	West Ham United	D	0-0	
38		10	H	Newcastle United	W	5-0	Richards 3, Carr, Hibbitt
39		13	A	Arsenal	L	1-2	Richards
40		17	A	Coventry City	L	1-3	Bell
41		19	H	Norwich City	W	1-0	Richards
42	May	4	H	Liverpool	L	1-3	Kindon

Appeara

Sub appeara

FA Cup

R3	Jan	3	H	Arsenal	W	3-0	Bell, Hibbitt, Richards
R4		24	A	Ipswich Town	D	0-0	
rep		27	H	Ipswich Town	W	1-0	Gould
R5	Feb	14	H	Charlton Athletic	W	3-0	Richards 3
R6	Mar	6	A	Manchester United	D	1-1	Richards
rep		9	H	Manchester United	L	2-3	Kindon, Richards

R6 replay aet

Appeara

Sub appeara

League Cup

R2	Sep	9	A	Swindon Town	D	2-2	Richards, Sunderland
rep		16	H	Swindon Town	W	3-2	Hibbitt, Richards, Sunderland
R3	Oct	7	A	Birmingham City	W	2-0	Hibbitt 2
R4	Nov	12	A	Mansfield Town	L	0-1	

Appeara

Sub appeara

arkin D	McNab R	Bailey MA	Munro FM	McAlle JE	Sunderland A	Carr WMcI	Richards JP	Kindon SM	Wagstaffe D	Hibbitt K	Farley JD	Taylor GW	Daley SJ	Pierce G	Palmer G	Jefferson D	Bell N	Patching M	Daly MC	Gould RA	O'Hara GJ	Williams NJ	Kelly J	
[illegible]	3	4	5	6	7	8	9	10	11	12														1
	3	4	5	6	12	8	9	10		7	11													2
[illegible]	3	4		6		8	9	10		7	11	5	12											3
2	3	4	5	6	12	8	9	10		7	11													4
	3	4	5	6	12	8	9	10		7			11	1	2									5
	3	4	5	6	10	8	9			7			11	1										6
2	3	4	5	6	10	8	9		11	7				1										7
3		4		6	10	8	9			7	12		11	1	2	5								8
	3	4	5	6		8		10	11	7				1	2		9							9
	3	4	5	6	12	8	9	10		7			11	1	2									10
	3	4	5	6		8	9	10		7			11	1	2		12							11
	3	4	5	6		8	9	10		7			11	1	2			12						12
	3	4	5	6	12	8	9	10		7			11	1	2									13
3		4	5	6		8	9	10		7	12		11	1	2									14
3	2	4	5	6	10	8	9			7	11		12	1										15
3			5	6	10	8	9			7	11		4	1	2				12					16
3		4	5	6		12	9	10		7	11		8	1	2									17
3		4	5	6		12	9	10		7	11		8	1	2									18
		4	5	6		12	9	10		7	11		8	1	2				3					19
		4	5	6			9	12		7	11		8	1	2				3	10				20
3		4	5	6			9	12		7	11		8	1	2					10				21
3		4	5	6	11		12	9		7			8		2					10				22
3		4	5	6	11		10	9		7			8		2									23
3		4		6	2	8		12		7	11						9		5	10				24
3		4		5	2	8	11	12		7			6				9			10				25
3		4	5	6		8	11	12		7					2		9			10				26
3			5	6	7	8	11										9			10	4	2		27
3			5	6	2	8	11			4							9			10	7			28
3				6		8	11			4			9		2	5	12			10	7			29
3			5	6	2	8	11			4							9			10	7			30
3			5	6	2	8	11			4			12				9			10	7			31
3			5	6	2	8	9	12		4	11		7							10				32
		4		5	2	8	10	9		7			6		3								11	33
		4		5	2	8	10	9		7			6		3								11	34
		4		5	2	8	10	9		7			6		3								11	35
		4		5	2	8	10	9		7			6		3						12		11	36
5		4		6	2	8		9		12			7		3					10			11	37
3		4	5	6	2	8	10			7							9			12			11	38
3			5	6	2	8	10			7			4					9		12			11	39
3			5	6		8	10			7	11		4		2		9			12				40
3				6	2	8	10			7			12	1	5		9	4					11	41
6		5			2	8	10	9		7			4	1	3					12			11	42
30	13	32	30	41	24	35	38	22	3	39	13	1	27	19	26	2	11	2	3	13	5	1	9	
					5	3	1	6		2	2		4				2	1	1	4	1			
						7	17	5		8			6		1		4			3				

arkin D	McNab R	Bailey MA	Munro FM	McAlle JE	Sunderland A	Carr WMcI	Richards JP	Kindon SM	Wagstaffe D	Hibbitt K	Farley JD	Taylor GW	Daley SJ	Pierce G	Palmer G	Jefferson D	Bell N	Patching M	Daly MC	Gould RA	O'Hara GJ	Williams NJ	Kelly J	
3		4		5	2	8	11			7			6				9			10				R3
3		4	5	6	2	8	11			7							9			10				R4
3		4	5	6	2	8	11	12									9			10	7			rep
3			5	6	2	8	12		11	4							9			10	7			R5
3			5	6	2	8	11	9		7			4		12					10				R6
3		12	5	6	2	8	11	9		7			4							10				rep
6		3	5	6	6	6	5	2	1	5			3				4			6	2			
		1					1	1							1									
							6	1		1							1			1				

arkin D	McNab R	Bailey MA	Munro FM	McAlle JE	Sunderland A	Carr WMcI	Richards JP	Kindon SM	Wagstaffe D	Hibbitt K	Farley JD	Taylor GW	Daley SJ	Pierce G	Palmer G	Jefferson D	Bell N	Patching M	Daly MC	Gould RA	O'Hara GJ	Williams NJ	Kelly J	
2	3	4	5	6	10	8	9		11	7				1										R2
2	3	4		6	10	8	9		11	7				1		5								rep
	3	4	5	6		8	9	10		7	12		11	1	2									R3
3		4	5	6	10	8	9	12		7			11	1	2									R4
3	3	4	3	4	3	4	4	1	2	4			2	4	2	1								
								1			1													
					2		2			3														

1976-77

Division Two

Manager: Sammy Chung

	P	W	D	L	F	A	Pts
Wolverhampton Wanderers	42	22	13	7	84	45	57
Chelsea	42	21	13	8	73	53	55
Nottingham Forest	42	21	10	11	77	43	52
Bolton Wanderers	42	20	11	11	75	54	51
Blackpool	42	17	17	8	58	42	51
Luton Town	42	21	6	15	67	48	48
Charlton Athletic	42	16	16	10	71	58	48
Notts County	42	19	10	13	65	60	48
Southampton	42	17	10	15	72	67	44
Millwall	42	15	13	14	57	53	43
Sheffield United	42	14	12	16	54	63	40
Blackburn Rovers	42	15	9	18	42	54	39
Oldham Athletic	42	14	10	18	52	64	38
Hull City	42	10	17	15	45	53	37
Bristol Rovers	42	12	13	17	53	68	37
Burnley	42	11	14	17	46	64	36
Fulham	42	11	13	18	54	61	35
Cardiff City	42	12	10	20	56	67	34
Orient	42	9	16	17	37	55	34
Carlisle United	42	11	12	19	49	75	34
Plymouth Argyle	42	8	16	18	46	65	32
Hereford United	42	8	15	19	57	78	31

Did you know that?

- Wolves retained their National five-a-side title after beating Stoke City in the Final.
- Mike Bailey left Molineux for Minnesota Kicks after making 436 senior appearances in 11 years.
- Kenny Hibbitt took over as team captain.
- Bobby Gould moved to Bristol Rovers and Frank Munro signed for Celtic.
- Wolves clinched the Second Division title after a last-match victory at Bolton.
- George Berry made his League debut in the penultimate League game of the season against fellow title contenders Chelsea.

Match No.	Date		Venue	Opponents	Result		Scorers	Atte
1	Aug	21	H	Burnley	D	0-0		1
2		24	A	Sheffield United	D	2-2	Carr, Sunderland	1
3		28	A	Nottingham Forest	W	3-1	Gould 2, Daley	1
4	Sep	4	H	Charlton Athletic	W	3-0	Gould 2, Sunderland	1
5		11	A	Fulham	D	0-0		2
6		18	H	Oldham Athletic	W	5-0	Kindon 2, Daley, Hibbitt, Sunderland	1
7		25	H	Luton Town	L	1-2	Hibbitt	1
8	Oct	2	A	Hereford United	W	6-1	Gould 2, Carr, Daley, Kindon, Sunderland	1
9		5	H	Southampton	L	2-6	Daley, Hibbitt (pen)	2
10		16	A	Hull City	L	0-2		1
11		23	H	Carlisle United	W	4-0	Sunderland 3, Carr	1
12		30	A	Blackpool	D	2-2	Hibbitt, Munro	21
13	Nov	6	H	Millwall	W	3-1	Sunderland 2, Daley	1
14		13	A	Notts County	D	1-1	Gould	14
15		20	H	Blackburn Rovers	L	1-2	Sunderland	1
16		27	A	Orient	W	4-2	Richards 3 (1 pen), Gould	[illegible]
17	Dec	4	H	Plymouth Argyle	W	4-0	Richards 2, Hibbitt, Sunderland	16
18		11	A	Chelsea	D	3-3	Richards 2, Gould	3
19		18	H	Bolton Wanderers	W	1-0	Gould	1
20		27	A	Bristol Rovers	W	5-1	Sunderland 2, Daley, Hibbitt, Kindon	2
21	Jan	1	A	Millwall	D	1-1	Hibbitt	16
22		22	A	Burnley	D	0-0		13
23	Feb	5	H	Nottingham Forest	W	2-1	Carr, Richards	3
24		9	H	Sheffield United	W	2-1	Richards, Sunderland	2
25		12	A	Charlton Athletic	D	1-1	Patching	17
26		19	H	Fulham	W	5-1	Daley 2, Hibbitt 2 (1 pen), Richards	2
27	Mar	1	H	Blackpool	W	2-1	Daley, Hibbitt	23
28		5	A	Luton Town	L	0-2		19
29		12	H	Hereford United	W	2-1	Hibbitt, Todd	22
30		15	A	Oldham Athletic	W	2-0	Daley, Sunderland	12
31		26	H	Hull City	W	2-1	Hibbitt, Richards	1
32	Apr	5	H	Bristol Rovers	W	1-0	Daley	1
33		9	A	Cardiff City	D	2-2	Daley, Hibbitt	1
34		11	H	Notts County	D	2-2	Daley, Richards	2
35		16	A	Blackburn Rovers	W	2-0	Hibbitt (pen), Richards	11
36		19	A	Carlisle United	L	1-2	Hibbitt	[illegible]
37		23	H	Orient	W	1-0	Richards	19
38		26	H	Cardiff City	W	4-1	Hibbitt, Palmer, Patching, Sunderland	21
39		30	A	Plymouth Argyle	D	0-0		16
40	May	3	A	Southampton	L	0-1		20
41		7	H	Chelsea	D	1-1	Richards	34
42		14	A	Bolton Wanderers	W	1-0	Hibbitt	36

Appearan

Sub appearar

G

FA Cup

R3	Jan	8	H	Rotherham United	W	3-2	Richards 2, Daley	23
R4		29	A	Ipswich Town	D	2-2	Richards 2	32
rep	Feb	2	H	Ipswich Town	W	1-0	Richards	33
R5		26	H	Chester	W	1-0	Hibbitt	37
R6	Mar	19	H	Leeds United	L	0-1		49,

Appearan

Sub appearan

G

League Cup

R2	Aug	31	H	Sheffield Wednesday	L	1-2	Parkin	15,

Appearan

G

Parkin D	Daley SJ	Bailey MA	McAlle JE	Hibbitt K	Carr WMcI	Sunderland A	Kindon SM	O'Hara GJ	Kelly J	Gould RA	Patching M	Munro FM	Todd K	Richards JP	Brazier CJ	Berry GF	
3	4	5	6	7	8	9	10	11									1
3	4	5	6	**7**	8	9	10	12	11								2
3	4	5	6	7	8	11	10			9							3
3	4	5	6	7	8	11	10			9							4
3	4	5	6	7	8	11	10			9							5
3	4	5	6	7	8	11	10			9							6
3	4	5	6	7	8	11	**10**			9	12						7
3	4	5	6	7	8	11	10			9							8
3	4	5	6	7	8	11	10			**9**	12						9
3	4		6	7	8	9	**10**	11			12	5					10
3	4	12	6	**7**	8	9	10		11			5					11
3	11	**4**	6	7	8	9	10				12	5					12
3	4		6	7		9	10				11	5	8				13
3	4		6	7		9	10			12	11	5	**8**				14
3	4		6	7		8	**10**			12	11	5		9			15
3	4		6	**7**		8	12			10	11	5		9			16
3	4		6	7		8				10	11	5		9			17
3	4		6	7		8				10	11	5		9			18
3	4		6	7		8	10			9	11	5					19
3	4		6	7		8	10				11	5		9			20
3	4		6	7		8	10				11	5		9			21
3	4		6	7	11	8	10					5		9			22
3	4		6	7	11	**8**	12				10	5		9			23
3	4		6	7	11	**8**			12		10	5		9			24
3	4		6	7	11		9				10	5		8			25
3	4		6	7	11	8					10	5		9			26
3	4		6	7	11	**8**	12				10	5		9			27
3	4		6	7	11	8				12	**10**	5		9			28
3	4		6	7		8	10					5	11	9			29
3	4		6	7	11	8	10					5		9			30
3	4		6	7	11	**8**	10				12	5		9			31
3	4		6		11	8	10				7	5		9			32
3	4		6	12	11	8	**10**				7	5		9			33
3	4		6	7	11	8					10	5		9			34
3	4		6	7	11	8				12	10	5		9			35
3	4		6	7	11	8					10	5		9			36
3	4		6	7	11	8					10	5		9			37
3	4		6	7	11	8					10	5		9			38
3	4		**6**	7	11	8					10	5	12	9			39
3	4			7	11	8					10	5		9	6		40
3	4			7	11	**8**				12	10	5		9		6	41
3	4			7	11	8				12	10	**5**		9	6		42
42	42	10	39	40	32	41	25	2	2	11	26	33	3	27	2	1	
		1		1			3	1	1	6	5		1				
	13			17	4	16	4			10	2	1	1	15			

Parkin D	Daley SJ	Bailey MA	McAlle JE	Hibbitt K	Carr WMcI	Sunderland A	Kindon SM	O'Hara GJ	Kelly J	Gould RA	Patching M	Munro FM	Todd K	Richards JP	Brazier CJ	Berry GF	
3	4		6	7	12	8	10				**11**	5		9			R3
3	4		6	7	11	8	12				10	**5**		9			R4
3	4		6	7	11	8					10			9	5		rep
3	4		6	7	11	8	12				**10**	5		9			R5
3	4		6	7	11	**8**	10			12		5		9			R6
5	5		5	5	4	5	2				4	4		5	1		
					1		2			1							
	1			1										5			

Parkin D	Daley SJ	Bailey MA	McAlle JE	Hibbitt K	Carr WMcI	Sunderland A	Kindon SM	O'Hara GJ	Kelly J	Gould RA	Patching M	Munro FM	Todd K	Richards JP	Brazier CJ	Berry GF	
3	4	5	6	7	8	11	10			9							R2
1	1	1	1	1	1	1	1			1							
1																	

1977-78

Division One

Manager: Sammy Chung (to November) then John Barnwell

	P	W	D	L	F	A	Pts
Nottingham Forest	42	25	14	3	69	24	64
Liverpool	42	24	9	9	65	34	57
Everton	42	22	11	9	76	45	55
Manchester City	42	20	12	10	74	51	52
Arsenal	42	21	10	11	60	37	52
West Bromwich Albion	42	18	14	10	62	53	50
Coventry City	42	18	12	12	75	62	48
Aston Villa	42	18	10	14	57	42	46
Leeds United	42	18	10	14	63	53	46
Manchester United	42	16	10	16	67	63	42
Birmingham City	42	16	9	17	55	60	41
Derby County	42	14	13	15	54	59	41
Norwich City	42	11	18	13	52	66	40
Middlesbrough	42	12	15	15	42	54	39
Wolverhampton Wanderers	42	12	12	18	51	64	36
Chelsea	42	11	14	17	46	69	36
Bristol City	42	11	13	18	49	53	35
Ipswich Town	42	11	13	18	47	61	35
Queen's Park Rangers	42	9	15	18	47	64	33
West Ham United	42	12	8	22	52	69	32
Newcastle United	42	6	10	26	42	78	22
Leicester City	42	5	12	25	26	70	22

Did you know that?

- Alan Sunderland was sold to Arsenal for a record fee of £240,000 and Steve Kindon went to Burnley.
- Billy Rafferty was signed from Carlisle and goalkeeper Paul Bradshaw from Blackburn Rovers.
- Wolves won five and drew one of their six games on tour in Sweden in May.
- Wolves won the Football League's Fair Play League this season. Only one player was sent off – defender Bob Hazell against Arsenal in the FA Cup.
- Four penalties were awarded in the Bristol City versus Wolves League game in August 1977.

Match No.	Date		Venue	Opponents	Result		Scorers
1	Aug	20	A	Bristol City	W	3-2	Carr (pen), Patching, Sunderland
2		23	H	Queen's Park Rangers	W	1-0	Richards
3		27	H	Arsenal	D	1-1	Kindon
4	Sep	3	A	Everton	D	0-0	
5		10	H	Nottingham Forest	L	2-3	Bell, Daley (pen)
6		17	A	West Bromwich Albion	D	2-2	Bell, Daley
7		23	A	Aston Villa	L	0-2	
8	Oct	1	H	Leicester City	W	3-0	Richards 3
9		4	H	Derby County	L	1-2	Hibbitt
10		8	A	Norwich City	L	1-2	Sunderland
11		15	H	West Ham United	D	2-2	Hibbitt, Richards
12		22	A	Manchester City	W	2-0	Richards 2
13		29	H	Coventry City	L	1-3	Hibbitt
14	Nov	5	A	Birmingham City	L	1-2	Patching
15		12	H	Newcastle United	W	1-0	Patching
16		19	A	Middlesbrough	D	0-0	
17		26	H	Ipswich Town	D	0-0	
18	Dec	3	A	Manchester United	L	1-3	Richards
19		10	H	Chelsea	L	1-3	Carr
20		17	A	Newcastle United	L	0-4	
21		26	H	Leeds United	W	3-1	Richards 2, Patching
22		27	A	Liverpool	L	0-1	
23		31	A	Queen's Park Rangers	W	3-1	Bell 2, Daley
24	Jan	2	H	Bristol City	D	0-0	
25		14	A	Arsenal	L	1-3	Young (og)
26		21	H	Everton	W	3-1	Hibbitt 2, Daley
27	Feb	4	A	Nottingham Forest	L	0-2	
28		25	A	Leicester City	L	0-1	
29	Mar	4	H	Norwich City	D	3-3	Daley 2, Hibbitt
30		11	A	West Ham United	W	2-1	Carr, Rafferty
31		14	H	West Bromwich Albion	D	1-1	Daley
32		18	H	Manchester City	D	1-1	Hazell
33		25	H	Liverpool	L	1-3	Patching
34		27	A	Leeds United	L	1-2	Daley
35		28	A	Coventry City	L	0-4	
36	Apr	1	H	Birmingham City	L	0-1	
37		8	A	Derby County	L	1-3	Patching
38		15	H	Middlesbrough	D	0-0	
39		22	A	Chelsea	D	1-1	Eves
40		29	H	Manchester United	W	2-1	Eves, Patching
41	May	2	H	Aston Villa	W	3-1	Eves, Rafferty, Richards
42		9	A	Ipswich Town	W	2-1	Rafferty 2

Appeara

Sub appear

One own-goal

FA Cup

R3	Jan	7	A	Exeter City	D	2-2	Carr, Daley
rep		10	H	Exeter City	W	3-1	Daley, Hibbitt, Richards
R4		28	A	Arsenal	L	1-2	Hibbitt

Appeara

Sub appeara

League Cup

R2	Aug	30	H	Luton Town	L	1-3	Richards

Appeara

Daly MC	Daley SJ	Parkin D	McAlle JE	Patching M	Carr WMcI	Richards JP	Kindon SM	Sunderland A	Todd K	Bell N	Brazier CJ	Hibbitt K	Bradshaw PW	Farley JD	Kelly J	Eves MJ	Hazell RJ	Black J	Berry GF	Rafferty WH	Clarke W	
3	4	5	6	7	8	9	10	11														1
3	4	5	6	7	8	9	10	11														2
3	4	5	6	7	8	9	10	11														3
3	4	5	6	7	8	9	10	11														4
3	4	5	6	7	8	9		11	**10**	12												5
3	4		6	10	8			11		9	5	7										6
3	4		6	**10**	8	9		11		12	5	7										7
3	4		6		8	9	10	11			5	7	1									8
3	4	5	6	12	8	9	**10**	11				7	1									9
3	4	6		10	8	9	12	11			5	7	1									10
3		6		4	8	9		11		10	5	7	1									11
		3	6	4	8	9		11		10	5	7	1									12
		3	6	4	8	9		11		10	5	**7**	1	12								13
	5	3	6	4	8	9				10		7	1		11							14
2	5	3	6	4	8	9				**10**		7	1	12	11							15
2	5	3	6	4	8	9						7	1	10	11							16
	5	3	6	4	8	9						7	1		11	10						17
11	5	3	6	4	8	9						7	1			10						18
11	5	3	6	4	8	9							1	7	12	10						19
	4	3	6		8	9						7	1	11		10	5					20
	4	3	6	11	8	9				10		7	1				5					21
11	4	3	6		8	9				10		7	1	12			5					22
2	4	3	6		8	9				10		7	1				5	11				23
	4	3	6		8	9				10		7	1				5	11				24
11	4	3	6		8	9				12		7	1			**10**	5					25
11	4	3	6	9	8					10		7	1				5					26
11	4	3	6		8	9				10		7	1						5			27
11	4	3	6	10	8	9						7	1						5			28
12	4	3	6	11	8							**7**	1	9			5			10		29
12	4	3	6	**11**	8	9					7						5			10		30
3	4		6	11	8	9					7		1				5	12		10		31
	4	3	6	11	8	9							1				5	7		10		32
	4	3	6	7	8	9							1		11		5			10		33
11	4	3	6	7	8					9	12		1				5			**10**		34
11	4	3	6	7	8						10		1			9	5					35
	4	3	6	7	**8**	9					5		1		11	12				10		36
12	4	3	6	7		9					8		1		**11**		5			10		37
3	4	2	6	**7**		9							1		11	12	5		8	10		38
	4	3	6	7		9							1			11	5		8	10		39
	4	3	6	7		9							1			11	5		8	10		40
	4	3	6	7		9							1			11	5		8	10		41
	4	3	6	7		9							1			**11**	5		8	10	12	42
25	39	38	40	34	36	37	6	13	1	13	12	23	34	4	8	10	20	3	7	13		
3				1			1			3	1			3	1	2		1			1	
	8			7	3	11	1	2		4		6				3	1			4		

Daly MC	Daley SJ	Parkin D	McAlle JE	Patching M	Carr WMcI	Richards JP	Kindon SM	Sunderland A	Todd K	Bell N	Brazier CJ	Hibbitt K	Bradshaw PW	Farley JD	Kelly J	Eves MJ	Hazell RJ	Black J	Berry GF	Rafferty WH	Clarke W	
12	4	3	6		8	9				10		7	1		**11**		5					R3
11	4	3	6		8	9				10		7	1				5					rep
11	4	3	6	12	8	9				10		7	1				5					R4
2	3	3	3		3	3				3		3	3		1		3					
1				1																		
	2				1	1						2										

Daly MC	Daley SJ	Parkin D	McAlle JE	Patching M	Carr WMcI	Richards JP	Kindon SM	Sunderland A	Todd K	Bell N	Brazier CJ	Hibbitt K	Bradshaw PW	Farley JD	Kelly J	Eves MJ	Hazell RJ	Black J	Berry GF	Rafferty WH	Clarke W	
3	4	5	6	7	8	9	10	11														R2
1	1	1	1	1	1	1	1	1														
						1																

1978-79

Division One

Manager: John Barnwell

	P	W	D	L	F	A	Pts
Liverpool	42	30	8	4	85	16	68
Nottingham Forest	42	21	18	3	61	26	60
West Bromwich Albion	42	24	11	7	72	35	59
Everton	42	17	17	8	52	40	51
Leeds United	42	18	14	10	70	52	50
Ipswich Town	42	20	9	13	63	49	49
Arsenal	42	17	14	11	61	48	48
Aston Villa	42	15	16	11	59	49	46
Manchester United	42	15	15	12	60	63	45
Coventry City	42	14	16	12	58	68	44
Tottenham Hotspur	42	13	15	14	48	61	41
Middlesbrough	42	15	10	17	57	50	40
Bristol City	42	15	10	17	47	51	40
Southampton	42	12	16	14	47	53	40
Manchester City	42	13	13	16	58	56	39
Norwich City	42	7	23	12	51	57	37
Bolton Wanderers	42	12	11	19	54	75	35
Wolverhampton Wanderers	42	13	8	21	44	68	34
Derby County	42	10	11	21	44	71	31
Queen's Park Rangers	42	6	13	23	45	73	25
Birmingham City	42	6	10	26	37	64	22
Chelsea	42	5	10	27	44	92	20

Did you know that?

- Former World Cup Final referee Jack Taylor was appointed Wolves' first commercial manager.
- Peter Daniel was signed from Hull City.
- Bob Hazell moved to QPR and 1974 League Cup Final hero Gary Pierce went to Barnsley.
- Norman Bell broke his leg during the fifth-round FA Cup tie against Crystal Palace.
- One of Arsenal's goals in the FA Cup semi-final was scored by former Wolves star Alan Sunderland.

Match No.	Date		Venue	Opponents	Result		Scorers
1	Aug	19	A	Aston Villa	L	0-1	
2		22	H	Chelsea	L	0-1	
3		26	A	Leeds United	L	0-3	
4	Sep	2	H	Bristol City	W	2-0	Hibbitt, Rodgers (og)
5		9	A	Southampton	L	2-3	Bell, Daniel (pen)
6		16	H	Ipswich Town	L	1-3	Beattie (og)
7		23	A	Everton	L	0-2	
8		30	H	Queen's Park Rangers	W	1-0	Daniel (pen)
9	Oct	7	A	Nottingham Forest	L	1-3	Eves
10		14	H	Arsenal	W	1-0	Eves
11		21	A	Middlesbrough	L	0-2	
12		28	H	Manchester United	L	2-4	Daley, Hibbitt
13	Nov	4	A	Derby County	L	1-4	Carr
14		11	H	Aston Villa	L	0-4	
15		18	H	Leeds United	D	1-1	Daniel
16		21	A	Bristol City	W	1-0	Daley
17		25	A	Tottenham Hotspur	L	0-1	
18	Dec	9	A	Bolton Wanderers	L	1-3	Berry
19		16	H	West Bromwich Albion	L	0-3	
20		26	H	Birmingham City	W	2-1	Daniel (pen), Hibbitt
21		30	H	Coventry City	D	1-1	Daley
22	Jan	17	H	Southampton	W	2-0	Bell, Carr
23		20	A	Ipswich Town	L	1-3	Berry
24	Feb	3	H	Everton	W	1-0	Daley
25		10	A	Queen's Park Rangers	D	3-3	Bell, Clarke, Patching
26		24	A	Arsenal	W	1-0	Richards
27	Mar	3	H	Middlesbrough	L	1-3	Richards
28		7	A	Norwich City	D	0-0	
29		20	A	Liverpool	L	0-2	
30		24	A	Chelsea	W	2-1	Rafferty, Richards
31		27	H	Manchester City	D	1-1	Carr
32	Apr	3	H	Tottenham Hotspur	W	3-2	Daley, Hibbitt, Richards
33		7	A	Manchester City	L	1-3	Hibbitt
34		10	H	Liverpool	L	0-1	
35		14	A	Birmingham City	D	1-1	Richards
36		16	H	Norwich City	W	1-0	Hibbitt
37		21	A	West Bromwich Albion	D	1-1	Richards
38		24	H	Derby County	W	4-0	Berry, Daley, Daniel, Rafferty
39		28	H	Bolton Wanderers	D	1-1	Richards
40		30	H	Nottingham Forest	W	1-0	Richards
41	May	5	A	Coventry City	L	0-3	
42		7	A	Manchester United	L	2-3	Daley, Richards

Appear

Sub appear

Two own-goals

FA Cup

R3	Jan	9	A	Brighton & Hove Albion	W	3-2	Bell, Williams (og), Daley
R4		27	A	Newcastle United	D	1-1	Hibbitt
rep	Feb	22	H	Newcastle United	W	1-0	Bell
R5		26	A	Crystal Palace	W	1-0	Patching
R6	Mar	10	H	Shrewsbury Town	D	1-1	Rafferty
rep		13	A	Shrewsbury Town	W	3-1	Carr, Daniel (pen), Rafferty
SF		31	N	Arsenal	L	0-2	

SF at Villa Park.

Appear

Sub appear

One own-goal

League Cup

R2	Aug	30	A	Reading	L	0-1	

Appear

Sub appear

…aw PW

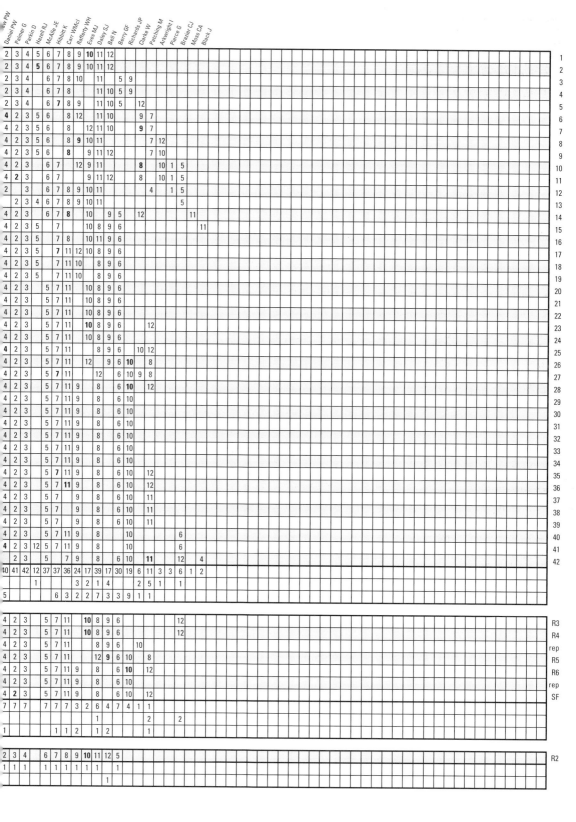

Daniel PW	Palmer G	Parkin D	Hazell RJ	McAlle JE	Hibbitt K	Carr WMcI	Rafferty WH	Eves MJ	Daley SJ	Bell N	Berry GF	Richards JP	Clarke W	Patching M	Arkwright I	Pierce G	Brazier CJ	Moss CA	Black J	
2	3	4	5	6	7	8	9	**10**	11	12										1
2	3	4	**5**	6	7	8	9	10	11	12										2
2	3	4		6	7	8	10		11		5	9								3
2	3	4		6	7	8			11	10	5	9								4
2	3	4		6	**7**	8	9		11	10	5		12							5
4	2	3	5	6		8	12		11	10			9	7						6
4	2	3	5	6		8		12	11	10			**9**	7						7
4	2	3	5	6		8	**9**	10	11					7	12					8
4	2	3	5	6		**8**		9	11	12				7	10					9
4	2	3		6	7		12	9	11				**8**		10	1	5			10
4	**2**	3		6	7			9	11	12			8		10	1	5			11
2		3		6	7	8	9	10	11					4		1	5			12
	2	3	4	6	7	8	9	10	11								5			13
4	2	3		6	7	**8**		10		9	5		12					11		14
4	2	3	5		7			10	8	9	6								11	15
4	2	3	5		7	8		10	11	9	6									16
4	2	3	5		**7**	11	12	10	8	9	6									17
4	2	3	5		7	11	10		8	9	6									18
4	2	3	5		7	11	10		8	9	6									19
4	2	3		5	7	11		10	8	9	6									20
4	2	3		5	7	11		10	8	9	6									21
4	2	3		5	7	11		10	8	9	6									22
4	2	3		5	7	11		**10**	8	9	6			12						23
4	2	3		5	7	11		10	8	9	6									24
4	2	3		5	7	11			8	9	6		10	12						25
4	2	3		5	7	11		12		9	6	**10**		8						26
4	2	3		5	**7**	11			12		6	10	9	8						27
4	2	3		5	7	11	9		8		6	**10**		12						28
4	2	3		5	7	11	9		8		6	10								29
4	2	3		5	7	11	9		8		6	10								30
4	2	3		5	7	11	9		8		6	10								31
4	2	3		5	7	11	9		8		6	10								32
4	2	3		5	7	11	9		8		6	10								33
4	2	3		5	7	11	9		8		6	10								34
4	2	3		5	**7**	11	9		8		6	10		12						35
4	2	3		5	7	**11**	9		8		6	10		12						36
4	2	3		5	7		9		8		6	10		11						37
4	2	3		5	7		9		8		6	10		11						38
4	2	3		5	7		9		8		6	10		11						39
4	2	3		5	7	11	9		8			10					6			40
4	2	3	12	5	7	11	9		8			10					6			41
	2	3		5		7	9		8		6	10		**11**			12		4	42
40	41	42	12	37	37	36	24	17	39	17	30	19	6	11	3	3	6	1	2	
			1				3	2	1	4			2	5	1		1			
5					6	3	2	2	7	3	3	9	1	1						
4	2	3		5	7	11		**10**	8	9	6						12			R3
4	2	3		5	7	11		**10**	8	9	6						12			R4
4	2	3		5	7	11			8	9	6		10							rep
4	2	3		5	7	11			12	**9**	6	10		8						R5
4	2	3		5	7	11	9		8		6	**10**		12						R6
4	2	3		5	7	11	9		8		6	10								rep
4	**2**	3		5	7	11	9		8		6	10		12						SF
7	7	7		7	7	7	3	2	6	4	7	4	1	1						
									1					2			2			
1					1	1	2		1	2				1						
2	3	4		6	7	8	9	**10**	11	12	5									R2
1	1	1		1	1	1	1	1	1		1									
										1										

1979-80

Division One

Manager: John Barnwell

	P	W	D	L	F	A	Pts
Liverpool	42	25	10	7	81	30	60
Manchester United	42	24	10	8	65	35	58
Ipswich Town	42	22	9	11	68	39	53
Arsenal	42	18	16	8	52	36	52
Nottingham Forest	42	20	8	14	63	43	48
Wolverhampton Wanderers	42	19	9	14	58	47	47
Aston Villa	42	16	14	12	51	50	46
Southampton	42	18	9	15	65	53	45
Middlesbrough	42	16	12	14	50	44	44
West Bromwich Albion	42	11	19	12	54	50	41
Leeds United	42	13	14	15	46	50	40
Norwich City	42	13	14	15	58	66	40
Crystal Palace	42	12	16	14	41	50	40
Tottenham Hotspur	42	15	10	17	52	62	40
Coventry City	42	16	7	19	56	66	39
Brighton & Hove Albion	42	11	15	16	47	57	37
Manchester City	42	12	13	17	43	66	37
Stoke City	42	13	10	19	44	58	36
Everton	42	9	17	16	43	51	35
Bristol City	42	9	13	20	37	66	31
Derby County	42	11	8	23	47	67	30
Bolton Wanderers	42	5	15	22	38	73	25

Did you know that?

- Wolves transferred midfielder Steve Daley to Manchester City for £1·44 million and signed striker Andy Gray for £1·15 million (£1·44 million with VAT and levy charges added) in the space of three days in September.
- Dave Thomas (from Everton) was also signed, while Martin Patching (to Watford) and Billy Rafferty (to Newcastle United) both departed.
- New signing Emlyn Hughes (from Liverpool) replaced Kenny Hibbitt as team captain.
- John Richards became the first Wolves player to be sent off in a local derby. He was dismissed in the Molineux fixture in October against Aston Villa.
- At Wembley for the second time in six years, Wolves won the League Cup courtesy of Andy Gray's tap-in from four yards.

Match No.	Date		Venue	Opponents	Result		Scorers	Att
1	Aug	22	A	Derby County	W	1-0	Clarke	2
2		25	H	Ipswich Town	W	3-0	Carr, Daniel, Eves	2
3	Sep	1	A	Bristol City	L	0-2		1
4		8	H	Crystal Palace	D	1-1	Clarke	2
5		15	A	Everton	W	3-2	Daniel (pen), Gray, Richards	3
6		22	H	Manchester United	W	3-1	Gray, Hibbitt, Richards	3
7		29	A	Arsenal	W	3-2	Gray 2, Hibbitt	4
8	Oct	6	A	Nottingham Forest	L	2-3	Daniel (pen), Richards	2
9		9	H	Derby County	D	0-0		3
10		13	H	Norwich City	W	1-0	Carr	2
11		20	A	Middlesbrough	L	0-1		1
12		27	H	Aston Villa	D	1-1	Gray	3
13	Nov	3	A	Liverpool	L	0-3		4
14		10	A	Stoke City	W	1-0	Hibbitt	2
15		17	H	Coventry City	L	0-3		2
16		24	H	West Bromwich Albion	D	0-0		3
17	Dec	1	A	Manchester City	W	3-2	Daniel, Gray, Hibbitt	3
18		8	H	Bolton Wanderers	W	3-1	Gray 2, Walsh (og)	2
19		15	A	Leeds United	L	0-3		2
20		21	H	Brighton & Hove Albion	L	1-3	Eves	1
21		26	H	Southampton	D	0-0		2
22		29	A	Ipswich Town	L	0-1		2
23	Jan	12	H	Bristol City	W	3-0	Daniel, Gray, Richards	1
24		19	A	Crystal Palace	L	0-1		2
25	Feb	2	H	Everton	D	0-0		2
26		9	A	Manchester United	W	1-0	Eves	5
27		23	A	Norwich City	W	4-0	Hibbitt 2 (2 pens), Eves, Richards	1
28		26	H	Liverpool	W	1-0	Richards	3
29	Mar	1	H	Middlesbrough	L	0-2		2
30		10	A	Aston Villa	W	3-1	Bell, Brazier, Daniel	3
31		22	H	Stoke City	W	3-0	Eves, Gray, Richards	2
32		29	A	Coventry City	W	3-1	Richards 2, Atkinson	1
33	Apr	5	H	Tottenham Hotspur	L	1-2	Richards	3
34		7	A	Southampton	W	3-0	Gray 2, Bell	2
35		8	A	Brighton & Hove Albion	L	0-3		2
36		12	H	Manchester City	L	1-2	Futcher (og)	2
37		19	A	West Bromwich Albion	D	0-0		3
38		23	A	Tottenham Hotspur	D	2-2	Bell, Hibbitt	1
39		26	H	Leeds United	W	3-1	Eves, Hibbitt, Richards	2
40	May	3	A	Bolton Wanderers	D	0-0		1
41		12	H	Nottingham Forest	W	3-1	Hibbitt (pen), Palmer, Richards	2
42		16	H	Arsenal	L	1-2	Richards	2

Appeara

Sub appeara

Two own-goals G

Parkin D	Daniel PW	Hughes EW	Berry GF	Hibbitt K	Carr WMcI	Rafferty WH	Clarke W	Patching M	Eves MJ	Gray AM	Richards JP	Brazier CJ	Thomas D	McAlle JE	Atkinson HA	Bell N	Moss CA	Humphrey J	Kearns M	
3	4	5	6	7	8	9	10	11	12											1
3	4	5	6	7	8	9	10	11	12											2
3	4	5	6	7	8	9	10	11												3
3	4	5	6	7	8	9	10	11	12											4
3	4	5	6	7	8				11	9	10	12								5
3	4	5	6	7	8				11	9	10									6
3	4	5	6	7	8				11	9	10									7
3	4	5	6	7	8				11	9	10									8
3	4	5	6	7	8					9	10		11							9
3	4	5	6	7	8					9	10		11							10
3	4	5	6	7	8					9	10		11							11
3	4	5	6	7	8				12	9	10		11							12
3		5	6	7	8			4		9	10		11							13
3	4		6	7	8		10			9	11			5						14
3	4	12	6	7	8				11	9	10			5						15
3	4	5	6	7	8					9	10		11							16
3	4	5	6	7	8					9	10		11							17
3	4	5	6	7	8				11	9	10	12								18
3	4		6	7	8		10		11	9		5								19
3		5	6	7	8		9		10			12	11	4						20
	4		6	7	8				11	9	10	3		5						21
	4		6	7	8		12		11	9	10	3		5						22
3	4		6		8					9	10		11	5	7					23
3	4	7	6		8					9	10		11	5						24
3	4	5	6	7	8		10		11	9										25
3	4		6	7	8				11	9	10			5						26
3	4	5	6	7	8				11	9	10									27
3	4	5	6	7	8				11	9	10									28
3	4	5	6	7	8		12		11	9	10									29
3	4	5	6		8		9					7				10	11			30
3		5	6		8				11	9	10	7			4					31
3		5	6		8				11	9	10	7			4					32
3		5	6		8		12		11	9	10	7			4					33
3	4	5	6		8		10		11	9		7				12		2		34
3	4	5	6		8		10		11	9		7						2		35
3	4	5	6		8		10		11	9		7				12				36
3	4		6		8		10		11	9		5			7	12			1	37
3	4	5	6	10	8				11			7			12	9				38
3	4	12	6	7	8				11	9	10	5							1	39
3	4	5		7	8				11	9	10	6							1	40
3	4	5	6	7					11	9	10	8							1	41
3	4	5	6	7					11	9	10	8			12				1	42
40	37	33	41	32	40	4	13	5	27	35	29	16	10	8	5	2	1	2	5	
		2					3		4			3			2	3				
	6			9	2		2		6	12	13	1			1	3				

1979-80

Cont.

Match No.	Date		Venue	Opponents	Result		Scorers
FA Cup							
R3	Jan	5	A	Notts County	W	3-1	Berry, Carr, Richards
R4		26	H	Norwich City	D	1-1	Gray
rep		30	A	Norwich City	W	3-2	Berry, Eves, Richards
R5	Feb	16	H	Watford	L	0-3	

Appea
Sub appea

Match No.	Date		Venue	Opponents	Result		Scorers
League Cup							
R2	Aug	28	A	Burnley	D	1-1	Palmer
rep	Sep	4	H	Burnley	W	2-0	Hibbitt, Palmer
R3		25	A	Crystal Palace	W	2-1	Eves, Hibbitt
R4	Oct	30	A	Queen's Park Rangers	D	1-1	Hibbitt
rep	Nov	6	H	Queen's Park Rangers	W	1-0	Carr
R5	Dec	4	A	Grimsby Town	D	0-0	
rep		11	H	Grimsby Town	D	1-1	Gray
rep2		18	N	Grimsby Town	W	2-0	Hibbitt (pen), Richards
SF1	Jan	22	A	Swindon Town	L	1-2	Daniel
SF2	Feb	12	H	Swindon Town	W	3-1	Richards 2, Eves
F	Mar	15	N	Nottingham Forest	W	1-0	Gray

R5 replay 2 at the Baseball Ground, Derby. Final at Wembley Stadium. Appea

R5 replay aet Sub appea

Palmer G	Parkin D	Daniel PW	Hughes EW	Berry GF	Hibbitt K	Carr WMcI	Rafferty WH	Clarke W	Patching M	Eves MJ	Gray AM	Richards JP	Brazier CJ	Thomas D	McAlle JE	Atkinson HA	Bell N	Moss CA	Humphrey J	Kearns M	
2		4		6	7	8		12		11	9	10	3		5						R3
2	3	4	5	6	7	8					9	10		11							R4
2	3	4	5	6	7	8				11	9	10									rep
2	3	4	5	6	7	8				11	9	10			12					1	R5
4	3	4	3	4	4	4				3	4	4	1	1	1					1	
								1							1						
				2		1				1	1	2									

Palmer G	Parkin D	Daniel PW	Hughes EW	Berry GF	Hibbitt K	Carr WMcI	Rafferty WH	Clarke W	Patching M	Eves MJ	Gray AM	Richards JP	Brazier CJ	Thomas D	McAlle JE	Atkinson HA	Bell N	Moss CA	Humphrey J	Kearns M	
2	3	4	5	6	7	8	9	10	11												R2
2	3	4	5	6	7	8	9	10	11	12											rep
2	3	4	5	6	7	8				11	9	10									R3
2	3	4	5	6	7	8		10			9		12	11							R4
2	3	4	5	6	7	8					9	10	12	11							rep
2	3	4	5	6	7	8				11	9	10									R5
2	3	4	5	6	7	8					9	10	12	11							rep
2	3		5	6	7	8				11	9	10			4						rep2
2	3	4		6	7	8					9	10		11	5						SF1
2	3	4	5	6	7	8				11	9	10									SF2
2	3	4	5	6	7	8				11	9	10									F
11	11	10	10	11	11	11	2	3	2	5	9	8		4	2						
										1			3								
2		1			4	1				2	2	3									

1980-81

Division One

Manager: John Barnwell

	P	W	D	L	F	A	Pts
Aston Villa	42	26	8	8	72	40	60
Ipswich Town	42	23	10	9	77	43	56
Arsenal	42	19	15	8	61	45	53
West Bromwich Albion	42	20	12	10	60	42	52
Liverpool	42	17	17	8	62	42	51
Southampton	42	20	10	12	76	56	50
Nottingham Forest	42	19	12	11	62	44	50
Manchester United	42	15	18	9	51	36	48
Leeds United	42	17	10	15	39	47	44
Tottenham Hotspur	42	14	15	13	70	68	43
Stoke City	42	12	18	12	51	60	42
Manchester City	42	14	11	17	56	59	39
Birmingham City	42	13	12	17	50	61	38
Middlesbrough	42	16	5	21	53	61	37
Everton	42	13	10	19	55	58	36
Coventry City	42	13	10	19	48	68	36
Sunderland	42	14	7	21	52	53	35
Wolverhampton Wanderers	42	13	9	20	43	55	35
Brighton & Hove Albion	42	14	7	21	54	67	35
Norwich City	42	13	7	22	49	73	33
Leicester City	42	13	6	23	40	67	32
Crystal Palace	42	6	7	29	47	83	19

Did you know that?

- Full-back Geoff Palmer was sent off in the League game against Sunderland in November.
- Kenny Hibbitt, reinstated as team captain, equalised for Wolves with 30 seconds remaining of the FA Cup semi-final clash with Spurs in April.
- John McAlle was transferred to Sheffield United, Emlyn Hughes to Rotherham United and goalkeeper Mick Kearns to Walsall.
- For the first time, Wolves had to replay four FA Cup games in the same season.
- Wolves' best win of the season was against reigning champions Liverpool at Molineux.

Match No.	Date		Venue	Opponents	Result		Scorers
1	Aug	16	A	Brighton & Hove Albion	L	0-2	
2		19	H	Manchester United	W	1-0	Berry
3		23	A	West Bromwich Albion	D	1-1	Gray
4		30	H	Crystal Palace	W	2-0	Gray, Richards
5	Sep	6	A	Everton	L	0-2	
6		13	H	Coventry City	L	0-1	
7		20	A	Aston Villa	L	1-2	Eves
8		27	H	Ipswich Town	L	0-2	
9	Oct	4	H	Birmingham City	W	1-0	Richards
10		7	A	Southampton	L	2-4	Gray, Richards
11		11	A	Norwich City	D	1-1	Hibbitt
12		18	H	Leeds United	W	2-1	Hughes, Richards
13		25	A	Leicester City	L	0-2	
14	Nov	1	H	Sunderland	W	2-1	Clarke 2
15		8	A	Tottenham Hotspur	D	2-2	Richards, Atkinson
16		12	A	Manchester United	D	0-0	
17		15	H	Brighton & Hove Albion	L	0-2	
18		22	A	Middlesbrough	L	0-2	
19		25	H	Liverpool	W	4-1	Hughes, Richards, Eves, Bell
20		29	H	Stoke City	W	1-0	Bell
21	Dec	6	A	Arsenal	D	1-1	Richards
22		13	H	Southampton	D	1-1	Bell
23		20	A	Liverpool	L	0-1	
24		26	H	Nottingham Forest	L	1-4	Richards (pen)
25		27	A	Manchester City	L	0-4	
26	Jan	10	H	Middlesbrough	W	3-0	Eves 2, Hibbitt
27		17	A	Crystal Palace	D	0-0	
28		31	H	West Bromwich Albion	W	2-0	Gray, Eves
29	Feb	7	A	Coventry City	D	2-2	Gray, Richards
30		21	A	Ipswich Town	L	1-3	Gray
31		28	H	Aston Villa	L	0-1	
32	Mar	14	H	Norwich City	W	3-0	Palmer, Richards, McDowell (og)
33		17	A	Birmingham City	L	0-1	
34		21	A	Leeds United	W	3-1	Gray, Richards, Clarke
35		28	H	Leicester City	L	0-1	
36	Apr	4	A	Sunderland	W	1-0	Gray
37		18	H	Manchester City	L	1-3	Richards
38		20	A	Nottingham Forest	L	0-1	
39		25	H	Arsenal	L	1-2	Richards
40		30	H	Tottenham Hotspur	W	1-0	Gray
41	May	2	A	Stoke City	L	2-3	Hibbitt, Evans (og)
42		4	H	Everton	D	0-0	

Appeara

Sub appeara

Two own-goals

FA Cup

R3	Jan	3	A	Stoke City	D	2-2	Bell, Eves
rep		6	H	Stoke City	W	2-1	Eves, Hibbitt
R4		24	A	Watford	D	1-1	Richards
rep		27	H	Watford	W	2-1	Parkin, Richards (pen)
R5	Feb	14	H	Wrexham	W	3-1	Richards, Bell 2
R6	Mar	7	A	Middlesbrough	D	1-1	Gray
rep		10	H	Middlesbrough	W	3-1	Richards, Eves, Bell
SF	Apr	11	N	Tottenham Hotspur	D	2-2	Carr (pen), Hibbitt
rep		15	N	Tottenham Hotspur	L	0-3	

SF at Hillsborough. SF replay at Highbury.

R6 replay and SF aet

Appeara

Sub appeara

League Cup

R2/1	Aug	26	A	Cambridge United	L	1-3	Daniel (pen)
R2/2	Sep	2	H	Cambridge United	L	0-1	

Appeara

Sub appeara

almer G	Parkin D	Daniel PW	Hughes EW	Berry GF	Brazier CJ	Carr WMcI	Gray AM	Richards JP	Eves MJ	Clarke W	Hibbitt K	Villazan R	Atkinson HA	Bell N	Humphrey J	Hollifield M	McAlle JE	Teasdale JS	Moss CA	Kearns M	Matthews M	
	3	4	5	6	7	8	9	10	**11**	12												1
	3	4	5	6	7	8	9	10	11	12												2
		4	5	6	3	8	**9**	10	11	12	7											3
		4	5	6	**3**	8	9	10	11	12		7										4
	3	4	5	6		8	9	10	11	12		**7**										5
	3	**4**	5	6		8	9	10	11	7		12										6
			5	6	3	8		10	11	12		7	4	**9**								7
	3	4	5		6		9	12	11	**10**		7	8									8
	3	4	5		12	8	9	10	11		**7**	6										9
	3	4	5			8	9	10	11		7	6		12	2							10
		4	5		3	8	9	10	11		7	6			2							11
		4	5			8	9	10	11		7	6			2							12
		4		5	12	**8**		10	11	9	7	6			2							13
		4			5	12		10	11	**9**	7	6	8		2							14
		4			5	12		10	11	9	7	**6**	8		2	3						15
		4	6		5			10	11	9	7		8		2	3						16
		4	6		5	12		10	11	9	7		8			3						17
		4	6		5			10	12	9	7		8		2	3						18
		4	6		5			10	11		7		8	9	2	3						19
		4	6		5			10	11		7		8	9	2	3						20
		4	6		5			10	11		7		8	9	2	3						21
		4	6		5			10	11		7		8	9		3						22
		4	6		5			10	11		7		8	9		3						23
		4	6		5		12	10	11		7		**8**	9		3						24
2			6	4	5	**8**	11	10			7		12	9		3						25
2		4		6				10	11		7		8	9		3	5					26
2	12	**4**		6				10	11		7		8	9		3	5					27
2	3	**4**		6			9	10	11		7		8	12			5					28
2	3			6			9	10	**11**	4	7		8	12			5					29
2	3	**4**		6			9	10	11		7		8	12			5					30
2	3	**4**		6		8	9	10	11		7			12			5					31
2	3			6		8	9	10	11	4	7						5					32
2	3		7	6		8	9	10	11	**4**				12			5					33
2	3			6		8	9	10	**11**	4	7			12			5					34
2	3			6		8	9	10	11	**4**	7			12			5					35
2	3			6		8	12		**11**	4			7	9			5	10				36
	3			6				10		**4**	7		8	9	2		5	12	11			37
2	3			6		8	9	10	**11**	4	7						5	12				38
2	3			6		8	9	10		4	7						5	11		1		39
2				6	4	8	**9**	10			7		12			3	5	11		1		40
2				6	**4**	8	9	10			7		12			3	5	11		1		41
2					6		9	10		4	7					3	5	11		1	8	42
4	19	28	23	25	22	23	25	40	35	18	33	11	20	12	12	16	17	5	1	4	1	
	1				2	3	2	1	1	6		1	3	8				2				
1			2	1			9	13	5	3	3		1	3								

almer G	Parkin D	Daniel PW	Hughes EW	Berry GF	Brazier CJ	Carr WMcI	Gray AM	Richards JP	Eves MJ	Clarke W	Hibbitt K	Villazan R	Atkinson HA	Bell N	Humphrey J	Hollifield M	McAlle JE	Teasdale JS	Moss CA	Kearns M	Matthews M	
2		4		6	5			10	11		7		8	9		3						R3
2		4		6				10	11		7		8	9		3	5					rep
2	12	4		6			9	10	11		7		**8**			3	5					R4
2	8	4		6			9	10	11		7					3	5					rep
2	3			6			9	10	**11**	4	7		8	12			5					R5
2	3			6		8	9	10	11	**4**	7			12			5					R6
2	3			6		8	9	10	11	**4**	7			12			5					rep
2	3		11	6		8	9	10		**4**	7			12			5					SF
2	3		**4**	6		8		10	11	12	7			9			5					rep
9	6	4	2	9	1	4	6	9	8	4	9		4	3		4	8					
	1									1				4								
	1					1	1	4	3		2			4								

almer G	Parkin D	Daniel PW	Hughes EW	Berry GF	Brazier CJ	Carr WMcI	Gray AM	Richards JP	Eves MJ	Clarke W	Hibbitt K	Villazan R	Atkinson HA	Bell N	Humphrey J	Hollifield M	McAlle JE	Teasdale JS	Moss CA	Kearns M	Matthews M	
2		4	5	6	3	8	9	10	11	12	**7**											R2/1
2	3	4	5	**6**		8	9	10	11	12		7										R2/2
2	1	2	2	2	1	2	2	2	2		1	1										
										1												
		1																				

1981-82

Division One

Manager: John Barnwell (to November) Ian Ross (caretaker manager) then Ian Greaves.

	P	W	D	L	F	A	Pts
Liverpool	42	26	9	7	80	32	87
Ipswich Town	42	26	5	11	75	53	83
Manchester United	42	22	12	8	59	29	78
Tottenham Hotspur	42	20	11	11	67	48	71
Arsenal	42	20	11	11	48	37	71
Swansea City	42	21	6	15	58	51	69
Southampton	42	19	9	14	72	67	66
Everton	42	17	13	12	56	50	64
West Ham United	42	14	16	12	66	57	58
Manchester City	42	15	13	14	49	50	58
Aston Villa	42	15	12	15	55	53	57
Nottingham Forest	42	15	12	15	42	48	57
Brighton & Hove Albion	42	13	13	16	43	52	52
Coventry City	42	13	11	18	56	62	50
Notts County	42	13	8	21	61	69	47
Birmingham City	42	10	14	18	53	61	44
West Bromwich Albion	42	11	11	20	46	57	44
Stoke City	42	12	8	22	44	63	44
Sunderland	42	11	11	20	38	58	44
Leeds United	42	10	12	20	39	61	42
Wolverhampton Wanderers	42	10	10	22	32	63	40
Middlesbrough	42	8	15	19	34	52	39

Did you know that?

• Derek Parkin became the first Wolves player to appear in 500 League games when he took the field against Middlesbrough in March. He joined Stoke City at the end of the season with teammate George Berry.

• Other players who left the club included Colin Brazier (to Jacksonville Tea Men) and Willie Carr (to Millwall), while Joe Gallagher (from Birmingham City) was the only major signing.

• In October 1981 Andy Gray became the first Wolves player to be sent off in a League Cup tie, against his former club Aston Villa. In April 1982, he was also red-carded when playing against Stoke City at the Victoria Ground.

• Wolves, after being relegated to the Second Division, were declared bankrupt.

Match No.	Date		Venue	Opponents	Result		Scorers	Att
1	Aug	29	H	Liverpool	W	1-0	Matthews	2
2	Sep	1	A	Southampton	L	1-4	Clarke	2
3		5	A	Leeds United	L	0-3		2
4		12	H	Tottenham Hotspur	L	0-1		1
5		19	A	Sunderland	D	0-0		2
6		22	H	Brighton & Hove Albion	L	0-1		1
7		26	H	Notts County	W	3-2	Daniel, Eves 2	1
8	Oct	3	A	Manchester United	L	0-5		4
9		10	A	Ipswich Town	L	0-1		2
10		17	H	Middlesbrough	D	0-0		1
11		24	H	Aston Villa	L	0-3		1
12		31	A	Swansea City	D	0-0		1
13	Nov	7	H	Coventry City	W	1-0	Eves	1
14		21	A	Birmingham City	W	3-0	Gray, Richards, Brazier	1
15		24	H	Southampton	D	0-0		1
16		28	H	Stoke City	W	2-0	Palmer (pen), Matthews	1
17	Dec	5	A	West Bromwich Albion	L	0-3		2
18		28	A	Manchester City	L	1-2	Daniel	4
19	Jan	16	A	Liverpool	L	1-2	Atkinson	2
20		23	H	Everton	L	0-3		1
21		30	H	Sunderland	L	0-1		1
22	Feb	2	A	Arsenal	L	1-2	Hibbitt	1
23		6	A	Tottenham Hotspur	L	1-6	Hibbitt	2
24		13	H	Manchester United	L	0-1		2
25		16	H	Nottingham Forest	D	0-0		1
26		20	A	Notts County	L	0-4		1
27		27	H	Ipswich Town	W	2-1	Clarke 2	1
28	Mar	6	A	Middlesbrough	D	0-0		1
29		13	A	Aston Villa	L	1-3	Clarke	2
30		16	H	Leeds United	W	1-0	Eves	1
31		20	H	Swansea City	L	0-1		1
32		27	A	Coventry City	D	0-0		1
33	Apr	3	H	Arsenal	D	1-1	Eves	1
34		6	A	West Ham United	L	1-3	Richards	2
35		10	A	Nottingham Forest	W	1-0	Gray	1
36		12	H	Manchester City	W	4-1	Hibbitt, Gray, Clarke, Eves	1
37		17	H	Birmingham City	D	1-1	Gray	1
38		24	A	Stoke City	L	1-2	Hibbitt	1
39	May	1	H	West Bromwich Albion	L	1-2	Gray	1
40		4	A	Brighton & Hove Albion	L	0-2		1
41		8	A	Everton	D	1-1	Clarke	2
42		15	H	West Ham United	W	2-1	Richards, Eves	1

Appeara
Sub appeara
G

FA Cup

R3	Jan	2	H	Leeds United	L	1-3	Gray	2

Appeara
G

League Cup

R2/1	Oct	7	A	Aston Villa	L	2-3	Gallagher, Gray	2
R2/2		27	H	Aston Villa	L	1-2	Richards	1

Appeara
Sub appeara
G

…lmer G

Parkin D	Daniel PW	Gallagher JA	Villazan R	Birch A	Hibbitt K	Gray AM	Clarke W	Matthews M	Bell N	Richards JP	Humphrey J	Berry GF	Coy RA	Carr WMcI	Eves MJ	Atkinson HA	Brazier CJ	Hollifield M	Teasdale JS	Moss CA	Pender JP	Kernan AP	
3	4	5	6	7	**8**	9	10	11	12														1
3	4	5	6	**7**	8	9	10	11		12													2
3	4	5	6	7	**8**	9	10	11		12													3
3	**4**			11	7				9	8	2	5	6	10									4
3	4	5		11	7		8	**10**	9	12	2	6											5
3	4	5		7	8	9	10	**11**	12		2	6											6
3	4	5		8	**7**	9		11		12		6			10								7
3	4	5		**8**	7	9		11		10		6				12							8
3		5	6		7	9	8	**11**	10							4	12						9
3		5	6	11	7	9	12	4		10						**8**							10
3		5	6	7			8	4						11	9		10						11
3	8			**7**			12	4		10		5			9	11	6						12
3	8			7				4		10		5			9	11	6						13
3	4	5				9		7		10		6			11		8						14
3	4	5		12		9		**7**		10		6			8		11						15
3	4	5				9		7		10		6			8		11						16
	4	5		12		9		7		10	**3**	6			8		11						17
3	4	5		**7**		9		12		10		6			8		11						18
3	4	5				9	8	7		10		6				11							19
	4	5			8			7		10		**6**				12		3	9	11			20
		5	12		7	9				10	3	6			8	4	11						21
		5	12		7	9				10	3	6			**8**	4	11						22
		5			7	9	12			10	3	6			8	4	**11**						23
	8				7	9	12			10	3	6	5	**11**		4							24
	8	5			7	9	11			10	3		6			4							25
	8	5			7	9	11			10	3		6		12	**4**							26
3		5			7	9	11	4		10			6	8									27
3		5			7	9	11	4		10			6	8									28
3		5	4		7		11	12		**10**			6	8	9								29
		5	4		7		11	10			2		6	8	9								30
					7	9	11	4			2		6	8	10						5		31
					7	9		4			2		6	8	10						5	11	32
					7		11	4		9	2		6	8	10						5		33
					7		11	4		9	2		6	8	10						5		34
			4		7	12	11			9	2		6	8	10						5		35
					7	9	11			10	2		6	8	4			3			5		36
					7	9	11			10	2		6	8	4						5		37
					7	9	11	12		**10**	2	5	6	8	4			3					38
					7	9	11	10			2	5	6	8	4			3					39
					7		11	9		10	2		6	8	4	12		**3**			5		40
		5			7		11	9		10	2		6	8	4	3							41
		5			7		11	9		10	2		6	8	4	3							42
21	20	28	9	13	33	28	25	29	3	30	23	20	20	19	26	13	11	5	1	1	8	1	
			2	2		1	4	3	2	4					1	3	1						
	2				4	5	6	2		3					7	1	1						
3	4	5		7		9				10		6			8		11						R3
1	1	1		1		1				1		1			1		1						
						1																	
3		5	6	8	7	9		11	12	10						**4**							R2/1
3	10	5		7			8	4		12				**11**	9		6						R2/2
2	1	2	1	2	1	1	1	2		1				1	1	1	1						
									1	1													
		1				1				1													

1982-83

Division Two

Manager: Graham Hawkins

	P	W	D	L	F	A	Pts
Queen's Park Rangers	42	26	7	9	77	36	85
Wolverhampton Wanderers	42	20	15	7	68	44	75
Leicester City	42	20	10	12	72	44	70
Fulham	42	20	9	13	64	47	69
Newcastle United	42	18	13	11	75	53	67
Sheffield Wednesday	42	16	15	11	60	47	63
Oldham Athletic	42	14	19	9	64	47	61
Leeds United	42	13	21	8	51	46	60
Shrewsbury Town	42	15	14	13	48	48	59
Barnsley	42	14	15	13	57	55	57
Blackburn Rovers	42	15	12	15	58	58	57
Cambridge United	42	13	12	17	42	60	51
Derby County	42	10	19	13	49	58	49
Carlisle United	42	12	12	18	68	70	48
Crystal Palace	42	12	12	18	43	52	48
Middlesbrough	42	11	15	16	46	67	48
Charlton Athletic	42	13	9	20	63	86	48
Chelsea	42	11	14	17	51	61	47
Grimsby Town	42	12	11	19	45	70	47
Rotherham United	42	10	15	17	45	68	45
Burnley	42	12	8	22	56	66	44
Bolton Wanderers	42	11	11	20	42	61	44

Did you know that?

- From late August to early October, Wolves went eight League games without conceding a single goal. Under new owners, they gained promotion at the first attempt.
- Former player Graham Hawkins replaced Greaves as team manager and signed two experienced campaigners, goalkeeper John Burridge from QPR and defender Alan Dodd from Stoke City. Out of Molineux went Joe Gallagher, sold to West Ham United.
- Geoff Palmer and Kenny Hibbitt shared the captaincy.

Match No.	Date		Venue	Opponents	Result		Scorers
1	Aug	28	H	Blackburn Rovers	W	2-1	Eves 2
2		31	A	Chelsea	D	0-0	
3	Sep	4	A	Leeds United	D	0-0	
4		7	H	Charlton Athletic	W	5-0	Palmer, Clarke, Eves, Matthews, Gray
5		11	H	Barnsley	W	2-0	Humphrey, Eves
6		18	A	Bolton Wanderers	W	1-0	Livingstone
7		25	H	Rotherham United	W	2-0	Humphrey, Clarke
8	Oct	2	A	Carlisle United	W	2-0	Livingstone, Smith
9		9	A	Sheffield Wednesday	D	0-0	
10		16	H	Leicester City	L	0-3	
11		30	H	Derby County	W	2-1	Palmer (pen), Gray
12	Nov	2	A	Cambridge United	L	1-2	Eves
13		6	H	Grimsby Town	W	3-0	Clarke, Eves, Gray
14		13	A	Oldham Athletic	L	1-4	Hibbitt
15		20	H	Fulham	L	2-4	Clarke, Gray
16		27	A	Crystal Palace	W	4-3	Clarke, Matthews 2, Gray
17	Dec	4	H	Middlesbrough	W	4-0	Eves 2, Cartwright, Dodd
18		11	A	Newcastle United	D	1-1	Eves
19		18	H	Queen's Park Rangers	W	4-0	Humphrey, Palmer (pen), Clarke, Dod
20		27	A	Shrewsbury Town	W	2-0	Clarke 2
21		28	H	Burnley	W	2-0	Eves, Gray
22	Jan	1	A	Fulham	W	3-1	Pender, Clarke, Eves
23		3	H	Leeds United	W	3-0	Clarke, Eves, Gray
24		15	A	Blackburn Rovers	D	2-2	Matthews, Dodd
25		22	H	Chelsea	W	2-1	Clarke, Eves
26	Feb	5	A	Barnsley	L	1-2	Smith
27		12	H	Carlisle United	W	2-1	Livingstone, Eves
28		26	A	Leicester City	L	0-5	
29	Mar	1	H	Sheffield Wednesday	W	1-0	Clarke (pen)
30		5	H	Cambridge United	D	1-1	Eves
31		12	A	Derby County	D	1-1	Kellock
32		19	A	Grimsby Town	D	1-1	Eves
33		26	H	Oldham Athletic	D	0-0	
34	Apr	2	A	Burnley	W	1-0	Palmer
35		4	H	Shrewsbury Town	D	2-2	Palmer (pen), Eves
36		9	A	Rotherham United	D	1-1	Hibbitt
37		16	H	Bolton Wanderers	D	0-0	
38		23	A	Middlesbrough	D	0-0	
39		30	H	Crystal Palace	W	1-0	Gray
40	May	2	A	Charlton Athletic	D	3-3	Eves, Kellock 2
41		7	A	Queen's Park Rangers	L	1-2	Gray
42		14	H	Newcastle United	D	2-2	Matthews, Gray

Appea

Sub appea

FA Cup

R3	Jan	8	A	Tranmere Rovers	W	1-0	Hibbitt
R4		29	A	Aston Villa	L	0-1	

Appea

League Cup

R2/1	Oct	5	H	Sunderland	D	1-1	Eves
R2/2		27	A	Sunderland	L	0-5	

Appea

Sub appea

Burridge J	Humphrey J	Wintersgill D	Palmer G	Pender JP	Coy RA	Daniel PW	Clarke W	Livingstone W	Eves MJ	Matthews M	Butler PJ	Smith GM	Gray AM	Hibbitt K	Gallagher JA	Cartwright IJ	Dodd A	Rudge DA	Kellock W	Richards JP	
	2	3	4	5	6	7	8	**9**	10	11	12										1
	2	**3**	4	5	6	7	8	9	10	11		12									2
	2		3	5	6	7	8		10	11		4	9								3
	2		3	5	6	7	8		10	11	12	4	**9**								4
	2		3	5	6	7	8	**9**	10	11	12	4									5
	2		3	5	6	7	8	9	10	11		4									6
	2		3	5	6	7	8	9	10	11		4									7
	2		3	5	6	7	8	9	10	11		4									8
	2		3	5	6	7	8	**9**	10	11		4		12							9
	2		3	5	6	7	8	9	10	11		**4**		12							10
	2		3	5	6		8		10	4	11		9	7							11
	2		3	5	6		8	**11**	10	4	12		9	7							12
	2		**3**		6	7	8		10	11	12		9	4	5						13
	2		3		6	7	**8**		10	11			9	4	5	12					14
	2		3		6	7	8		**10**	11			9	4	5	12					15
	2		3	5			8		10	11			9	4		7	6				16
	2		3	5			8		10	11			9	4		7	6				17
	2		3	5			8		10	11			9	4		7	6				18
	2		3	5			8		10	11			9	7			6	4			19
	2		3	5	12		8		10	**11**			9	4			6	7			20
	2		3	5	12		8		10			11	9	7			6	**4**			21
	2		3	5			8		10	11		4	9	7			6				22
	2		3	**5**	12		8		10	11		4	9	7			6				23
	2		3	5			8		10	11		4	9	7			6				24
	2		3	5			8		10	11		4	9	7			6				25
	2		3	5			8		10	11		4	9				6	7			26
	2		3	5			8	12	10	**11**			9	7			6	4			27
	2		**3**	5			8		10	11		12	9	7			6	4			28
	2			5			8		10	11		3	9	7			6	4			29
	2		12	5			8		10	11		3	9	7			6	**4**			30
	2		3	5					10	11		4	9	7			6		8		31
	2		3	5			8		10	**11**		4	9				6		7	12	32
	2		3	5			8		10	11		4	9	12			6		**7**		33
	2		3	5			8		10	11		4		12			6		**7**	9	34
	2		3	5			8		10	11		4	9				6		7		35
	2		3	5					10	11		4	9	7			6		**8**	12	36
	2		3	5			**8**			11	12	4	9	7			6			10	37
	2		3	5			8	10		11		12	**9**	7		4	6				38
	2		3	5			8		**10**	11	12		9	7		4	6				39
	2		3	5			8		10				9	7		4	6		11		40
	2		3	5					10	11			9	7		4	6		8		41
	2		3	5			12		10	**11**		4	9	7			6		8		42
	42	2	40	39	15	13	38	10	40	40	1	24	33	27	3	7	27	8	9	2	
			1		3		1	1			7	3		4		2				2	
	3		5	1			12	3	18	5		2	10	2		1	3		3		
	2		3	5			8		10	11		4	9	7			6				R3
	2		3	5					10	11		4	9	7			6	8			R4
	2		2	2			1		2	2		2	2	2			2	1			
														1							
	2		3	5	6	7	8	**9**	10	11	12	4									R2/1
	2		3	5	6	7	8		10	**11**	12		9	4							R2/2
	2		2	2	2	2	2	1	2	2		1	1	1							
										2											
									1												

1983-84

Division One

Manager: Graham Hawkins (to April) then Jim Barron (caretaker manager) to May

	P	W	D	L	F	A	Pts
Liverpool	42	22	14	6	73	32	80
Southampton	42	22	11	9	66	38	77
Nottingham Forest	42	22	8	12	76	45	74
Manchester United	42	20	14	8	71	41	74
Queen's Park Rangers	42	22	7	13	67	37	73
Arsenal	42	18	9	15	74	60	63
Everton	42	16	14	12	44	42	62
Tottenham Hotspur	42	17	10	15	64	65	61
West Ham United	42	17	9	16	60	55	60
Aston Villa	42	17	9	16	59	61	60
Watford	42	16	9	17	68	77	57
Ipswich Town	42	15	8	19	55	57	53
Sunderland	42	13	13	16	42	53	52
Norwich City	42	12	15	15	48	49	51
Leicester City	42	13	12	17	65	68	51
Luton Town	42	14	9	19	53	66	51
West Bromwich Albion	42	14	9	19	48	62	51
Stoke City	42	13	11	18	44	63	50
Coventry City	42	13	11	18	57	77	50
Birmingham City	42	12	12	18	39	50	48
Notts County	42	10	11	21	50	72	41
Wolverhampton Wanderers	42	6	11	25	27	80	29

Did you know that?

- Wolves won four and lost one of their five pre-season tour games in Sweden in July/August 1983.
- Wolves suffered their worst-ever start to a season when they failed to win any of their first 16 League and Cup games.
- The attendance of 8,679 for the Wolves versus Stoke City game was the lowest for a League game at Molineux since March 1937.
- Kenny Hibbitt moved to Coventry City after scoring 114 goals in 574 appearances for Wolves; John Richards joined the Portuguese side Maritimo Funchal, after scoring a then record 194 goals in 486 first-class matches for the club; Andy Gray switched to Everton; Paul Bradshaw moved to Vancouver Whitecaps and Wayne Clarke left for Birmingham City.

Match No.		Date	Venue	Opponents	Result		Scorers	Attendan
1	Aug	27	H	Liverpool	D	1-1	Palmer (pen)	26,24
2		29	H	Arsenal	L	1-2	Clarke	18,57
3	Sep	3	A	Norwich City	L	0-3		12,99
4		7	A	Sunderland	L	2-3	Eves, Towner	12,96
5		10	H	Birmingham City	D	1-1	Eves	15,93
6		17	A	Luton Town	L	0-4		10,97
7		24	H	Queen's Park Rangers	L	0-4		11,51
8	Oct	1	A	Southampton	L	0-1		16,58
9		15	H	Tottenham Hotspur	L	2-3	Gray 2	12,52
10		23	H	Aston Villa	D	1-1	Clarke	13,20
11		29	A	Manchester United	L	0-3		41,88
12	Nov	5	A	Nottingham Forest	L	0-5		13,85
13		12	H	West Ham United	L	0-3		12,06
14		19	H	Coventry City	D	0-0		11,41
15		26	A	West Bromwich Albion	W	3-1	Clarke, Crainie 2	17,94
16	Dec	3	H	Watford	L	0-5		11,90
17		10	A	Leicester City	L	1-5	Clarke	10,97
18		17	H	Stoke City	D	0-0		8,67
19		26	A	Ipswich Town	L	1-3	Clarke (pen)	14,02
20		27	H	Everton	W	3-0	Eves, Clarke, Crainie	12,76
21		31	H	Norwich City	W	2-0	Towner, Troughton	10,72
22	Jan	2	A	Queen's Park Rangers	L	1-2	Dawes (og)	12,87
23		14	A	Liverpool	W	1-0	Mardenborough	23,32
24		21	H	Luton Town	L	1-2	Pender	11,59
25	Feb	4	H	Southampton	L	0-1		9,94
26		11	A	Birmingham City	D	0-0		14,31
27		18	H	Manchester United	D	1-1	Troughton	20,67
28		25	A	Aston Villa	L	0-4		18,25
29	Mar	3	H	Nottingham Forest	W	1-0	Hart (og)	10,47
30		10	A	West Ham United	D	1-1	McGarvey	18,11
31		17	H	Sunderland	D	0-0		9,11
32		24	A	Arsenal	L	1-4	McGarvey	18,61
33		31	A	Tottenham Hotspur	L	0-1		19,29
34	Apr	7	H	Notts County	L	0-1		7,45
35		14	A	Coventry City	L	1-2	Livingstone	8,43
36		21	H	Ipswich Town	L	0-3		6,61
37		23	A	Everton	L	0-2		17,09
38		28	H	West Bromwich Albion	D	0-0		13,20
39	May	1	A	Notts County	L	0-4		5,37
40		5	A	Watford	D	0-0		13,53
41		7	H	Leicester City	W	1-0	Smith	7,4
42		12	A	Stoke City	L	0-4		18,97

Appearanc
Sub appearanc
Two own-goals Goa

FA Cup

R3	Jan	7	A	Coventry City	D	1-1	Clarke	15,8
rep		10	H	Coventry City	D	1-1	Eves	19,2
rep2		16	A	Coventry City	L	0-3		18,0

R3 replay aet

Appearanc
Sub appearanc
Goa

League Cup

R2/1	Oct	4	H	Preston North End	L	2-3	Clarke 2	7,7
R2/2		25	A	Preston North End	L	0-1		8,8

Appearanc
Sub appearanc
Goa

Humphrey J	Palmer G	Smith GM	Pender JP	Dodd A	Daniel PW	Rudge DA	Gray AM	Eves MJ	Kellock W	Towner AJ	Clarke W	Livingstone W	Cartwright IJ	Hibbitt K	Matthews M	Bradshaw PW	Bennett M	Coy RA	Blair A	Mardenborough SA	Crainie D	Wintersgill D	Butler PJ	Troughton SE	Buckland MC	McGarvey ST	Watkiss SP	Bayly MJ	Rodger G	Dougherty PD	Jackson JG	
2	3	4	5	6	7	**8**	9	10	11	12																						1
2	3	4	5	6	7		**9**	10	11	12	8																					2
2	3	4	5	6	8			9	**11**	7	12	10																				3
2	3		5	6	8	11		10		**7**	12	**9**	4																			4
2	3		5	6	**8**	4	10	9		11		12	7																			5
2	**3**		5	6		4	10	9		11		8	7	12																		6
2	3	4	5	6			10			12	8	**9**	7		11																	7
2				6	4		10			12	8		9	7	**11**	1	3	5														8
2	10			6	**4**	12	9			11	8			7		1	3	5														9
2	10	4		6		11	9				8			7		1	3	5														10
2	**10**	4		6		11					8			7	12	1	3	5	9													11
2				6		12	9				8			7		1	**3**	5	4	10	11											12
2			5	6		12					8		9	7		1	**3**		4	10	11											13
2			5	6		3					8		9	7		1			4	10	11											14
2	12		5	6		3					8		9	7		1			4	**10**	11											15
2			5	6		3					8		9	7		1			**4**	10	11	12										16
2			5	6		3					8		9	7		1			4	10	11		12									17
	3		5	6	2			12			8		**9**	7					4	10	11											18
	3		5	6	2			10		12	8		9						4		11			**7**								19
2	3		5	6				10		7	8								4		11			9								20
2	3		**5**	6				10		7	8		4								11		12	9								21
4	3			6	2			10		7	8		5								11		12	**9**								22
2	3		5	6	4					7	8									10	11			9								23
2	3		5	6	4			10		7	8										11			9								24
2	3		5	6	4					**7**	8			12						10	11			9								25
	12		5	6	4					7	8			3							**11**	10		9	2							26
	12		5	6	4			10		7	8			3							11			9	2							27
	3		5	6	4			10		7	8										11			9	2							28
	3		5	6		4				7	8										11			9	2	10						29
	3		5	6		4				7	8										11			9	2	10						30
	3		5		4					7	8										11			9	2	10	6					31
	3			6	4					7	8			12							11			**9**	2	10	5					32
	3		5	6	4					7	**8**			12							11			9	2	10						33
	3		5	6						7		12	4	8							11			9	**2**	10						34
	3		5	6		10				12	**8**	9	4	7							11				2							35
	3			6		12				10		9		7							11				2	8		4	5			36
3			5	6						11		9		7										8	2	10		4				37
2		3	5	6						7		10		8												9		4		11		38
2		3	5	6						7		**10**													12	9		4		11	8	39
2		3	5	6				**10**		7				8							12					9		4		11		40
		8	5	6		3						10									7				2	9		4		11		41
2		8	5	6		3						**10**									7				12	9		4		11		42
28	27	11	34	41	19	15	9	14	3	25	29	11	16	19	2	10	6	5	10	9	27	1		17	13	13	2	7	1	5	1	
	3					4		1		6	2	2		4	1						1	1	3		2							
	1	1	1				2	3		2	6	1								1	3			2		2						

Humphrey J	Palmer G	Smith GM	Pender JP	Dodd A	Daniel PW	Rudge DA	Gray AM	Eves MJ	Kellock W	Towner AJ	Clarke W	Livingstone W	Cartwright IJ	Hibbitt K	Matthews M	Bradshaw PW	Bennett M	Coy RA	Blair A	Mardenborough SA	Crainie D	Wintersgill D	Butler PJ	Troughton SE	Buckland MC	McGarvey ST	Watkiss SP	Bayly MJ	Rodger G	Dougherty PD	Jackson JG	
2	3		5	6	4			10		7	8										11			9								R3
2	3		5	6	4			10		7	8										11			9								rep
2	3		5	6	4			10		7	**8**									12	11			9								rep2
3	3		3	3	3			3		3	3										3			3								
																				1												
								1			1																					

Humphrey J	Palmer G	Smith GM	Pender JP	Dodd A	Daniel PW	Rudge DA	Gray AM	Eves MJ	Kellock W	Towner AJ	Clarke W	Livingstone W	Cartwright IJ	Hibbitt K	Matthews M	Bradshaw PW	Bennett M	Coy RA	Blair A	Mardenborough SA	Crainie D	Wintersgill D	Butler PJ	Troughton SE	Buckland MC	McGarvey ST	Watkiss SP	Bayly MJ	Rodger G	Dougherty PD	Jackson JG	
2				6	4			**10**		11	8			7	9	1	3	5		12												R2/1
2	10	4		6		**11**	9				8			7		1	3	5					12									R2/2
2	1	1		2	1	1	1	1		1	2			2	1	2	2	2														
																				1			1									
											2																					

1984-85

Division Two

Manager: Tommy Docherty

	P	W	D	L	F	A	Pts
Oxford United	42	25	9	8	84	36	84
Birmingham City	42	25	7	10	59	33	82
Manchester City	42	21	11	10	66	40	74
Portsmouth	42	20	14	8	69	50	74
Blackburn Rovers	42	21	10	11	66	41	73
Brighton & Hove Albion	42	20	12	10	54	34	72
Leeds United	42	19	12	11	66	43	69
Shrewsbury Town	42	18	11	13	66	53	65
Fulham	42	19	8	15	68	64	65
Grimsby Town	42	18	8	16	72	64	62
Barnsley	42	14	16	12	42	42	58
Wimbledon	42	16	10	16	71	75	58
Huddersfield Town	42	15	10	17	52	64	55
Oldham Athletic	42	15	8	19	49	67	53
Crystal Palace	42	12	12	18	46	65	48
Carlisle United	42	13	8	21	50	67	47
Charlton Athletic	42	11	12	19	51	63	45
Sheffield United	42	10	14	18	54	66	44
Middlesbrough	42	10	10	22	41	57	40
Notts County	42	10	7	25	45	73	37
Cardiff City	42	9	8	25	47	79	35
Wolverhampton Wanderers	42	8	9	25	37	79	33

Did you know that?

- Between 17 November 1984 and 13 April 1985, Wolves went 1,002 minutes without scoring a home goal.
- Wolves beat an Isle of Man XI 11–0 in a friendly on the island in February.
- Wolves played two friendly games in Malta during May 1985, winning both.
- New faces included former WBA midfielder Andy King (from SC Cambuur), Steve Stoutt (Huddersfield) and Peter Zelem (Chester), while those who left included Geoff Palmer (to Burnley), Mel Eves (Sheffield United), Alan Dodd (Stoke City), Peter Daniel (Sunderland), John Pender and John Humphrey (both to Charlton) and Tony Evans (Exeter City).

Match No.	Date		Venue	Opponents	Result		Scorers
1	Aug	25	H	Sheffield United	D	2-2	Dodd, Langley
2	Sep	1	A	Leeds United	L	2-3	Dougherty, Ainscow
3		4	H	Manchester City	W	2-0	Dougherty, McCarthy (og)
4		8	H	Charlton Athletic	W	1-0	Langley
5		15	A	Middlesbrough	D	1-1	Buckland
6		19	A	Oxford United	L	1-3	Langan (og)
7		22	H	Birmingham City	L	0-2	
8		29	A	Barnsley	L	1-5	Dodd
9	Oct	6	H	Notts County	L	2-3	Langley, Buckland
10		13	A	Oldham Athletic	L	2-3	Evans 2
11		20	H	Crystal Palace	W	2-1	Evans, Melrose
12		27	A	Portsmouth	W	1-0	Melrose
13	Nov	3	H	Cardiff City	W	3-0	Pender, Evans, Buckland
14		10	A	Grimsby Town	L	1-5	Langley
15		17	H	Wimbledon	D	3-3	Ainscow, Butler, Barnes
16		24	A	Fulham	W	2-1	Cartwright, Buckland
17	Dec	1	H	Brighton & Hove Albion	L	0-1	
18		8	A	Huddersfield Town	L	1-3	Buckland
19		15	H	Blackburn Rovers	L	0-3	
20		22	H	Leeds United	L	0-2	
21		26	A	Shrewsbury Town	L	1-2	Ainscow
22		29	A	Manchester City	L	0-4	
23	Jan	1	H	Carlisle United	L	0-2	
24		12	H	Middlesbrough	D	0-0	
25		26	A	Sheffield United	D	2-2	Butler, Chapman
26	Feb	2	H	Barnsley	L	0-1	
27		23	A	Cardiff City	D	0-0	
28	Mar	2	H	Portsmouth	D	0-0	
29		5	H	Grimsby Town	L	0-1	
30		9	A	Crystal Palace	D	0-0	
31		12	A	Charlton Athletic	L	0-1	
32		16	H	Oldham Athletic	L	0-3	
33		23	A	Notts County	L	1-4	Hankin
34		30	A	Birmingham City	L	0-1	
35	Apr	6	H	Shrewsbury Town	L	0-1	
36		8	A	Carlisle United	W	1-0	Evans
37		13	H	Oxford United	L	1-2	Chapman
38		20	A	Wimbledon	D	1-1	Ainscow
39		27	H	Fulham	L	0-4	
40	May	4	A	Brighton & Hove Albion	L	1-5	O'Reilly (og)
41		6	H	Huddersfield Town	W	2-1	Ainscow, Ryan
42		11	A	Blackburn Rovers	L	0-3	

Appeara

Sub appeara

Three own-goals G

FA Cup

R3	Jan	5	H	Huddersfield Town	D	1-1	Pender
rep		23	A	Huddersfield Town	L	1-3	Ainscow

Appeara

Sub appeara

G

League Cup

R2/1	Sep	24	A	Port Vale	W	2-1	Dodd, Evans
R2/2	Oct	9	H	Port Vale	D	0-0	
R3		30	A	Southampton	D	2-2	Melrose 2
rep	Nov	6	H	Southampton	L	0-2	

Appearar

Sub appearar

G

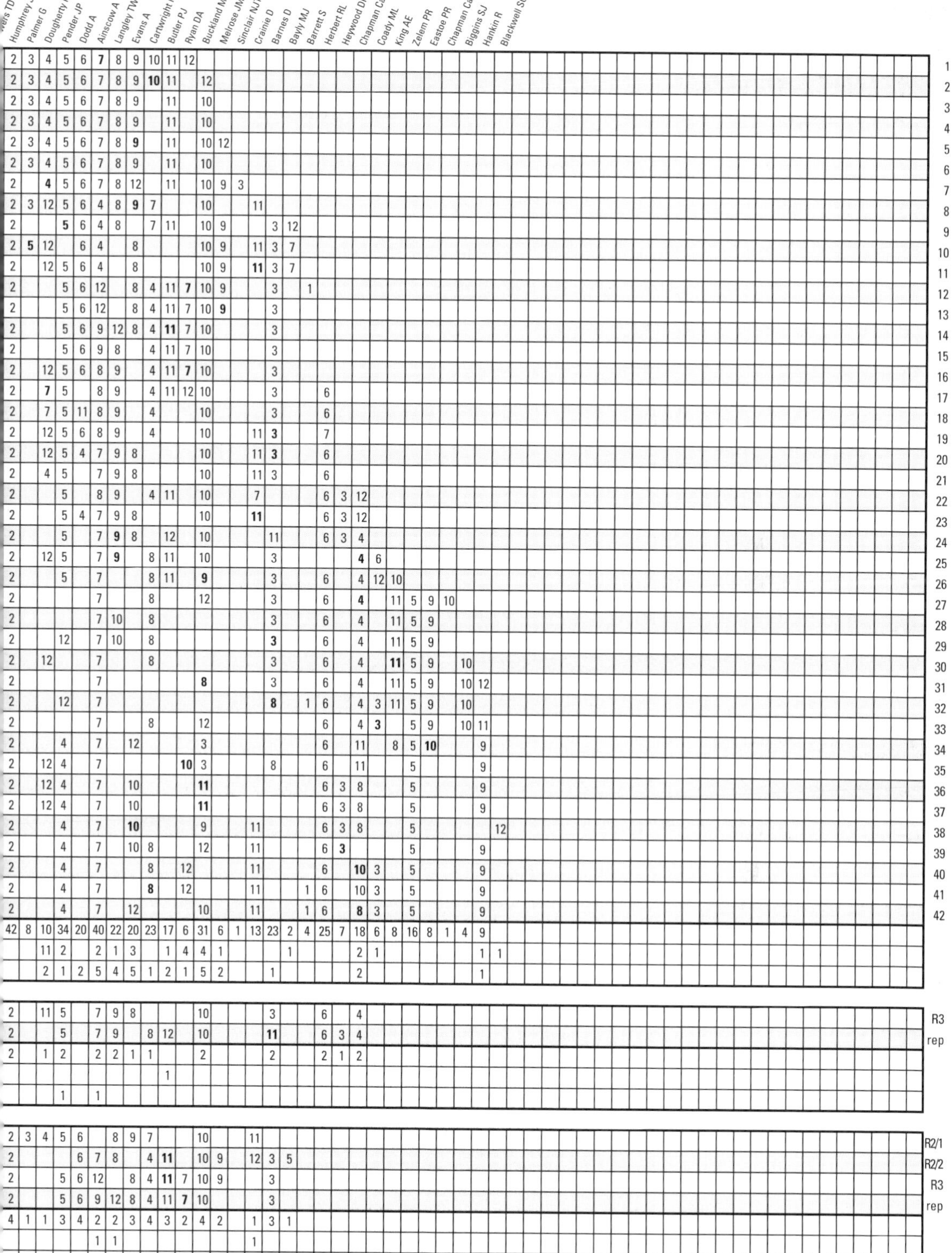

Humphrey J	Palmer G	Dougherty PD	Pender JP	Dodd A	Ainscow A	Langley TW	Evans A	Cartwright IJ	Butler PJ	Ryan DA	Buckland MC	Melrose JM	Sinclair NJT	Crainie D	Barnes D	Bayly MJ	Barrett S	Herbert RL	Heywood DI	Chapman Campbell	Coady ML	King AE	Zelem PR	Eastoe PR	Chapman Cavan	Biggins SJ	Hankin R	Blackwell SG	
2	3	4	5	6	**7**	8	9	10	11	12																			1
2	3	4	5	6	7	8	9	**10**	11		12																		2
2	3	4	5	6	7	8	9		11		10																		3
2	3	4	5	6	7	8	9		11		10																		4
2	3	4	5	6	7	8	**9**		11		10	12																	5
2	3	4	5	6	7	8	9		11		10																		6
2		**4**	5	6	7	8	12		11		10	9	3																7
2	3	12	5	6	4	8	**9**	7			10			11															8
2			**5**	6	4	8		7	11		10	9			3	12													9
2	**5**	12		6	4		8				10	9		11	3	7													10
2		12	5	6	4		8				10	9		**11**	3	7													11
2			5	6	12		8	4	11	**7**	10	9			3		1												12
2			5	6	12		8	4	11	7	10	**9**			3														13
2			5	6	9	12	8	4	**11**	7	10				3														14
2			5	6	9	8		4	11	7	10				3														15
2		12	5	6	8	9		4	11	**7**	10				3														16
2		**7**	5		8	9		4	11	12	10				3			6											17
2		7	5	11	8	9		4			10				3			6											18
2		12	5	6	8	9		4			10			11	**3**			7											19
2		12	5	4	7	9	8				10			11	**3**			6											20
2		4	5		7	9	8				10			11	3			6											21
2			5		8	9		4	11		10			7				6	3	12									22
2			5	4	7	9	8				10			**11**				6	3	12									23
2			5		7	**9**	8		12		10				11			6	3	4									24
2		12	5		7	**9**		8	11		10				3					**4**	6								25
2			5		7			8	11		**9**				3			6		4	12	10							26
2					7			8			12				3			6		**4**		11	5	9	10				27
2					7	10		8							3			6		4		11	5	9					28
2			12		7	10		8							**3**			6		4		11	5	9					29
2		12			7			8							3			6		4		**11**	5	9		10			30
2					7						**8**				3			6		4		11	5	9		10	12		31
2			12		7										**8**		1	6		4	3	11	5	9		10			32
2					7			8			12							6		4	**3**		5	9		10	11		33
2			4		7		12				3							6		11		8	5	**10**			9		34
2		12	4		7					**10**	3				8			6		11			5				9		35
2		12	4		7		10				**11**							6	3	8			5				9		36
2		12	4		7		10				**11**							6	3	8			5				9		37
2			4		7		**10**				9			11				6	3	8			5					12	38
2			4		7		10	8			12			11				6	**3**				5				9		39
2			4		7			8		12				11				6		**10**	3		5				9		40
2			4		7			**8**		12				11			1	6		10	3		5				9		41
2			4		7		12				10			11			1	6		**8**	3		5				9		42
42	8	10	34	20	40	22	20	23	17	6	31	6	1	13	23	2	4	25	7	18	6	8	16	8	1	4	9		
		11	2		2	1	3		1	4	4	1				1				2	1						1	1	
		2	1	2	5	4	5	1	2	1	5	2			1					2							1		

Humphrey J	Palmer G	Dougherty PD	Pender JP	Dodd A	Ainscow A	Langley TW	Evans A	Cartwright IJ	Butler PJ	Ryan DA	Buckland MC	Melrose JM	Sinclair NJT	Crainie D	Barnes D	Bayly MJ	Barrett S	Herbert RL	Heywood DI	Chapman Campbell	Coady ML	King AE	Zelem PR	Eastoe PR	Chapman Cavan	Biggins SJ	Hankin R	Blackwell SG	
2		11	5		7	9	8				10				3			6		4									R3
2			5		7	9		8	12		10				**11**			6	3	4									rep
2		1	2		2	2	1	1			2				2			2	1	2									
									1																				
			1		1																								

Humphrey J	Palmer G	Dougherty PD	Pender JP	Dodd A	Ainscow A	Langley TW	Evans A	Cartwright IJ	Butler PJ	Ryan DA	Buckland MC	Melrose JM	Sinclair NJT	Crainie D	Barnes D	Bayly MJ	Barrett S	Herbert RL	Heywood DI	Chapman Campbell	Coady ML	King AE	Zelem PR	Eastoe PR	Chapman Cavan	Biggins SJ	Hankin R	Blackwell SG	
2	3	4	5	6		8	9	7			10			11															R2/1
2				6	7	8		4	**11**		10	9		12	3	5													R2/2
2			5	6	12		8	4	**11**	7	10	9			3														R3
2			5	6	9	12	8	4	11	**7**	10				3														rep
4	1	1	3	4	2	2	3	4	3	2	4	2		1	3	1													
					1	1								1															
				1			1					2																	

1985-86

Division Three

Manager: Sammy Chapman (caretaker to September) then Bill McGarry (to November) then Chapman (again)

	P	W	D	L	F	A	Pts
Reading	46	29	7	10	67	51	94
Plymouth Argyle	46	26	9	11	88	53	87
Derby County	46	23	15	8	80	41	84
Wigan Athletic	46	23	14	9	82	48	83
Gillingham	46	22	13	11	81	54	79
Walsall	46	22	9	15	90	64	75
York City	46	20	11	15	77	58	71
Notts County	46	19	14	13	71	60	71
Bristol City	46	18	14	14	69	60	68
Brentford	46	18	12	16	58	61	66
Doncaster Rovers	46	16	16	14	45	52	64
Blackpool	46	17	12	17	66	55	63
Darlington	46	15	13	18	61	78	58
Rotherham United	46	15	12	19	61	59	57
Bournemouth	46	15	9	22	65	72	54
Bristol Rovers	46	14	12	20	51	75	54
Chesterfield	46	13	14	19	61	64	53
Bolton Wanderers	46	15	8	23	54	68	53
Newport County	46	11	18	17	52	65	51
Bury	46	12	13	21	63	67	49
Lincoln City	46	10	16	20	55	77	46
Cardiff City	46	12	9	25	53	83	45
Wolverhampton Wanderers	46	11	10	25	57	98	43
Swansea City	46	11	10	25	43	87	43

Did you know that?

- Rotherham United inflicted Wolves' heaviest defeat in FA Cup football with a 6–0 hammering at Millmoor in November 1985.
- Wolves' average home League attendance was an all-time low – just 3,710.
- Two players were sent off in away games – ex-Derby County defender Floyd Streete (at Bristol Rovers) and David Barnes (at Gillingham).
- Andy Mutch was signed from Southport and Micky Holmes arrived from Burnley.
- Andy King left for Luton Town, Danny Crainie moved to Dundee and Tim Flowers signed for Southampton.

Match No.	Date		Venue	Opponents	Result		Scorers	Attend
1	Aug	17	A	Brentford	L	1-2	N.Edwards	5,5
2		24	H	Newport County	L	1-2	Clarke	6,0
3		26	A	Derby County	L	2-4	N.Edwards, Purdie	13,1
4		31	H	York City	W	3-2	N.Edwards, King (pen), Coady	4,4
5	Sep	7	A	Bolton Wanderers	L	1-4	Morrissey	4,9
6		14	H	Swansea City	L	1-5	King	4,0
7		17	H	Bristol Rovers	L	3-4	N.Edwards, King 2 (1 pen)	3,2
8		21	A	Plymouth Argyle	L	1-3	N.Edwards	5,2
9		28	H	Lincoln City	D	1-1	King (pen)	3,5
10	Oct	1	A	Bury	L	1-3	King	3,2
11		5	A	Rotherham United	W	2-1	N.Edwards 2	4,0
12		12	H	Doncaster Rovers	L	1-2	King	4,3
13		19	H	Walsall	D	0-0		7,5
14		23	A	Reading	D	2-2	Ryan 2	13,4
15		26	A	Bristol City	L	0-3		7,1
16	Nov	2	H	Darlington	W	2-1	Purdie, Ryan	3,8
17		5	H	Blackpool	W	2-1	Purdie, Crainie	3,6
18		9	A	Bournemouth	L	2-3	Barnes, King	4,1
19		23	H	Gillingham	L	1-3	King	3,
20		30	A	Cardiff City	D	1-1	King	2,4
21	Dec	14	H	Wigan Athletic	D	2-2	Ryan, Holmes	3,
22		21	A	Newport County	L	1-3	Purdie	2,
23		26	A	Notts County	L	0-4		5,
24		28	H	Derby County	L	0-4		9,
25	Jan	1	H	Chesterfield	W	1-0	Purdie	3,
26		11	A	York City	L	1-2	Rosario	4,
27		18	H	Brentford	L	1-4	D.Edwards	3,
28		25	A	Swansea City	W	2-0	Cartwright, Streete	4,
29	Feb	1	H	Bolton Wanderers	L	0-2		3,
30		9	A	Walsall	D	1-1	Holmes	10,
31	Mar	8	H	Rotherham United	D	0-0		2,
32		11	H	Plymouth Argyle	L	0-3		2,
33		15	A	Doncaster Rovers	W	1-0	Chapman	2,
34		18	H	Bury	D	1-1	Chapman	2,
35		22	H	Bristol City	W	2-1	D.Edwards, Mutch	3,
36		25	A	Bristol Rovers	D	1-1	Mutch	3,
37		29	A	Chesterfield	L	0-3		2,
38		31	H	Notts County	D	2-2	D.Edwards, Mutch	3,
39	Apr	2	A	Darlington	L	1-2	Mutch	3,
40		5	A	Blackpool	W	1-0	D.Edwards	4,
41		8	H	Reading	L	2-3	D.Edwards, Lockhart	4,
42		12	H	Bournemouth	L	0-3		3,
43		19	A	Gillingham	L	0-2		3,
44		26	H	Cardiff City	W	3-1	Holmes, Mutch, Lockhart	3,
45	May	3	A	Wigan Athletic	L	3-5	Dougherty, D.Edwards, Mutch	4,
46		5	A	Lincoln City	W	3-2	Purdie, D.Edwards, Mutch	2,

Appearan
Sub appearan
Go

FA Cup

R1	Nov	16	A	Rotherham United	L	0-6		

Appearan

League Cup

R1/1	Aug	20	A	Walsall	D	1-1	Purdie	11,
R1/2	Sep	3	H	Walsall	L	0-1		11,

Appearan
Sub appearan
Go

Barrett S	Herbert RL	Barnes D	Zelem PR	Clarke NJ	Chapman Campbe	Morrissey JJ	Edwards NA	Purdie J	King AE	Crainie D	Stoutt SP	Smith RF	Ryan DA	Flowers TD	Coady ML	Dougherty PD	Ainscow A	Cartwright IJ	Hazell RJ	Wright DJ	Streete FA	Wassell KD	Lomax GW	North SS	Edwards DS	Holmes MA	Raynes W	Palmer G	Whitehead CR	Rosario RM	Eli R	Mutch AT	Lockhart KS	
1	**2**	3	4	5	6	7	8	9	10	11	12																							1
1		3	4	5	6	**7**	8	9	10	11	2	12																						2
1		3	4	5	6	**7**	8	9	10	11	2		12																					3
		3		5		12	8	9	10	11	2			1	4	6	7																	4
		3		5	**6**	12	8	9	10	11	2			1	4		7																	5
		3		5		12	8	**9**	10	11	2			1	4		7	6																6
		3		4		7	9		10	11	2		12	1			6	8	**5**															7
		3		5		12	9		10	11	4			1		**7**	8	6		2														8
	2	3		5		7	9		**10**	11	4		12	1			8	6																9
	2	3		5		12	9	**7**	10	11	4			1			8	6																10
1	2	3		5			9	7	10	11							8	6			4													11
1	2	3		5			9	7	10	**11**	12						8	6			4													12
1	2	3			12		**9**	7	10	11	5		6				8				4													13
1	2	3		**5**	12			7	10		6		8				9				4	11												14
1	2	3		5	12			7	10		6		8				9				4	**11**												15
1		3			9			7	10	11	5		6				8				4		2											16
1		3		12	9			7	10	11	5		6				8				**4**		2											17
1	12	3		**4**	9			7	10	11	5		6				8						2											18
	5	3			**9**			7	10	11			8	1			6						2	4	12									19
	5	3			11			7	10				9	1		8							2	4		6								20
	5	3			**11**			10			8		9	1	2	12								4		6	7							21
	5	3			10			8		11	2		9	1	4	12										6	**7**							22
	5	3			10			**8**		11			9	1	4	12										6	7	2						23
	5	3			**10**					11	6		9	1	4										12	8	7	2						24
	5	**3**		4				10		11			9	1				6							12	8	7	2						25
	5			4				10		11				1	2			6								**7**	12	3	8	9				26
				5				12		11				1				2			4				10		**8**	3	6	9	7			27
	3		5		12			**11**					9	1				6			4				10	8		2			7			28
	3		5					11					9	1				6			4				10	8		2			7			29
1	3		5		11			9										6			4				10	8		2			7			30
1		3	5		11			6													4				10	8		2			7	9		31
1		3	5		11			6					12								4				10	8		2			7	**9**		32
1		3	5		11			6								12					4				10	8		2			7	**9**		33
1		3	5		11			6								12					4				10	8		2			**7**	9		34
1		3	5		11			6													4				10	8		2				9	7	35
1			5		11			6													4				10	8		3			2	9	7	36
1		3	5		11			6													4				10	8		12			**2**	9	7	37
1		3	5		11			6													4				10	8		2				9	7	38
1		3			11			6			5										4				10	8		2				9	7	39
		3			11			6			5			1							4				10	8		2				9	7	40
		3			11			6			5			1											10	8		2			4	9	7	41
		3		12	**11**			6			5			1											10	8		2			4	9	7	42
		3			11			9			5		12	1							4				10	8		2			**6**		7	43
		3		5				**11**			2			1		12					4				10	8					6	9	7	44
				5	3			7			2			1		6					4				10	8						9	11	45
				5	7			11			2			1		6					4				10	8						9	3	46
21	19	38	14	21	29	5	13	41	20	23	26		15	25	8	5	16	13	1	1	25	2	5	3	20	26	6	20	2	2	14	15	12	
	1			2	4	5		1			2	1	5			6									3		1	1						
		1		1	2	1	7	6	10	1			4		1	1		1			1				7	3				1		7	2	

Barrett S	Herbert RL	Barnes D	Zelem PR	Clarke NJ	Chapman Campbe	Morrissey JJ	Edwards NA	Purdie J	King AE	Crainie D	Stoutt SP	Smith RF	Ryan DA	Flowers TD	Coady ML	Dougherty PD	Ainscow A	Cartwright IJ	Hazell RJ	Wright DJ	Streete FA	Wassell KD	Lomax GW	North SS	Edwards DS	Holmes MA	Raynes W	Palmer G	Whitehead CR	Rosario RM	Eli R	Mutch AT	Lockhart KS	
1	5	3		4	10			7		11	2		8			6	9																	R1
1	1	1		1	1			1		1	1		1			1	1																	

Barrett S	Herbert RL	Barnes D	Zelem PR	Clarke NJ	Chapman Campbe	Morrissey JJ	Edwards NA	Purdie J	King AE	Crainie D	Stoutt SP	Smith RF	Ryan DA	Flowers TD	Coady ML	Dougherty PD	Ainscow A	Cartwright IJ	Hazell RJ	Wright DJ	Streete FA	Wassell KD	Lomax GW	North SS	Edwards DS	Holmes MA	Raynes W	Palmer G	Whitehead CR	Rosario RM	Eli R	Mutch AT	Lockhart KS	
1		3	4	5	6	**7**	8	9	10	11	2		12																					R1/1
		3	4	5	6		8	9	10	11	**2**			1		12	7																	R1/2
1		2	2	2	2	1	2	2	2	2	2			1			1																	
													1			1																		
								1																										

1986-87

Division Four

Manager: Brian Little (to October) then Graham Turner

	P	W	D	L	F	A	Pts
Northampton Town	46	30	9	7	103	53	99
Preston North End	46	26	12	8	72	47	90
Southend United	46	25	5	16	68	55	80
Wolverhampton Wanderers	46	24	7	15	69	50	79
Colchester United	46	21	7	18	64	56	70
Aldershot	46	20	10	16	64	57	70
Orient	46	20	9	17	64	61	69
Scunthorpe United	46	18	12	16	73	57	66
Wrexham	46	15	20	11	70	51	65
Peterborough United	46	17	14	15	57	50	65
Cambridge United	46	17	11	18	60	62	62
Swansea City	46	17	11	18	56	61	62
Cardiff City	46	15	16	15	48	50	61
Exeter City	46	11	23	12	53	49	56
Halifax Town	46	15	10	21	59	74	55
Hereford United	46	14	11	21	60	61	53
Crewe Alexandra	46	13	14	19	70	72	53
Hartlepool United	46	11	18	17	44	65	51
Stockport County	46	13	12	21	40	69	51
Tranmere Rovers	46	11	17	18	54	72	50
Rochdale	46	11	17	18	54	73	50
Burnley	46	12	13	21	53	74	49
Torquay United	46	10	18	18	56	72	48
Lincoln City	46	12	12	22	45	65	48

Did you know that?

- When Graham Turner became manager in October one of his early signings, striker Steve Bull, scored the first of his record 306 goals for Wolves in a 1–0 Freight Rover Trophy win at Cardiff two months later.
- The club was saved from extinction at the 11th hour.
- Defender Peter Zelem scored Wolves' first-ever goal in the Fourth Division against Cambridge United (in August).
- Wolves had four players sent off in League games.
- Ally Robertson and Floyd Streete shared the captaincy.

Match No.	Date		Venue	Opponents	Result		Scorers	Attenda
1	Aug	23	H	Cambridge United	L	1-2	Zelem (pen)	6,0
2		30	A	Aldershot	W	2-1	Mutch, Lockhart	2,9
3	Sep	6	H	Cardiff City	L	0-1		5,7
4		13	A	Crewe Alexandra	D	1-1	Stoutt	2,5
5		15	A	Stockport County	W	2-0	Lockhart, D.Edwards	2,7
6		20	H	Burnley	L	0-1		5,7
7		27	A	Northampton Town	L	1-2	Mutch	5,7
8		30	H	Preston North End	W	1-0	Mutch	4,4
9	Oct	5	A	Scunthorpe United	W	2-0	Forman, D.Edwards	3,2
10		11	H	Tranmere Rovers	W	2-1	Forman, Mutch	5,4
11		18	A	Swansea City	L	0-1		5,8
12		21	H	Halifax Town	L	1-2	Handysides	4,3
13		25	H	Orient	W	3-1	Mutch, Stoutt, Handysides (pen)	4,3
14		31	A	Colchester United	L	0-3		4,7
15	Nov	4	H	Rochdale	D	0-0		3,9
16		8	A	Torquay United	W	2-1	Forman, Purdie	2,9
17		22	H	Wrexham	L	0-3		5,2
18		29	A	Lincoln City	L	0-3		2,2
19	Dec	13	A	Hartlepool United	W	1-0	Bull	1,7
20		20	H	Southend United	L	1-2	Bull	4,1
21		26	A	Hereford United	L	0-2		5,8
22		27	H	Exeter City	D	2-2	Thompson, Bull	4,6
23	Jan	1	H	Peterborough United	L	0-3		4,3
24		3	A	Wrexham	D	0-0		4,6
25		10	A	Cambridge United	D	0-0		2,7
26		24	A	Cardiff City	W	2-0	Thompson (pen), Bull	3,3
27		31	H	Crewe Alexandra	L	2-3	Holmes, Thompson (pen)	3,7
28	Feb	7	H	Stockport County	W	3-1	Holmes, Thompson (pen), Bull	3,2
29		14	A	Burnley	W	5-2	Barnes, Holmes, Mutch, Purdie, Thompson	2,9
30		17	H	Aldershot	W	3-0	Holmes, Mutch 2	3,3
31		21	H	Northampton Town	D	1-1	Holmes	9,9
32		28	A	Preston North End	D	2-2	Holmes, Stoutt	12,57
33	Mar	3	H	Colchester United	W	2-0	Holmes, Bull	5,7
34		7	A	Orient	L	1-3	Bull	4,60
35		14	H	Swansea City	W	4-0	Holmes, Mutch, Purdie, Thompson (pen)	7,6
36		17	A	Halifax Town	W	4-3	Mutch 2, Stoutt, Thompson	2,01
37		21	A	Tranmere Rovers	W	1-0	Dennison	3,6
38		28	H	Scunthorpe United	W	1-0	Bull	7,34
39	Apr	4	H	Torquay United	W	1-0	Dennison	6,10
40		11	A	Rochdale	W	3-0	Purdie, Kelly, Dennison	3,81
41		18	A	Peterborough United	W	1-0	Bull	9,54
42		20	H	Hereford United	W	1-0	Purdie	10,73
43		24	A	Southend United	L	0-1		10,70
44	May	2	H	Lincoln City	W	3-0	Barnes, Bull 2	7,28
45		4	A	Exeter City	W	3-1	Forman, Bull, Kelly	4,91
46		9	H	Hartlepool United	W	4-1	Bull 3, Thompson (pen)	8,61

Appearance

Sub appearance

Goa

Oldroyd DR	Barnes D	Streete FA	Zelem PR	Hellin MK	Forman MC	Holmes MA	Mutch AT	Edwards NA	Purdie J	Stoutt SP	Lockhart KS	Ryan DA	Eli R	Nixon EW	Clarke NJ	Edwards DS	Robertson A	Handysides IR	Palmer G	Thompson AR	Bull SG	Barrett S	Powell BI	Dougherty PD	Brindley CP	Kendall M	Caswell BL	Kelly RA	Dennison RS	
2	3	4	5	6	7	8	9	10	11																					1
2		**4**	5			8	9		11	6	7	10	12	1	3															2
2	3	4	5			8	**9**		11	6	7	10	12	1																3
2	3	4	5				9		11	6	7		8	1		10														4
2	3	4	5				9		11	6	7		**8**	1	12	10														5
2		4	5			12	9		11	8	7			1	3	10	**6**													6
2	3	4	5			12	9			8	7			1		11	6	10												7
		4	5			8	9	12			7			1	3	11	6	10	**2**											8
		4			5	8	9		7	2	3			1		11	6	10												9
	3	4			5	8	9			2	7			1		11	6	10												10
		4			5	8	9		12	2	7			1	3	11	**6**	10												11
	3	4	6		5	8	9	11	12	2	**7**			1				10												12
2		4	6		5	8	9	11	7	3				1				10												13
2		4	6		5	8	9	11	7	3				1				10												14
	12	4	6		5	**8**	9	11	7	3				1			2	10												15
		4	6		5	8	**9**	11	7	3	12			1			2	10												16
	3	4			5		9			2	11	12		1			6	10		**7**	8									17
	3		6		**5**		12		7	2					4					8	9	1	10	11						18
	3		**5**			12	10		7	2					6					8	9	1	4	11						19
[illegible]	3						10		7	5					6					8	9	1	4	11						20
	3	4				12	10		7	2										8	9	1	6	**11**	5					21
	3					11	**10**	12	7	2					6					8	9	1	4		5					22
					11		10	12	7	2					3		6			**8**	9		4		5	1				23
	3				11		10	8	7	2					5		6				9		4			1				24
	3				11		10	8	7	2					5		6			12	9		**4**			1				25
	3	4					10	7		2					5		6			11	9					1	8			26
		4			11	12	10	8		2					3		**6**			7	9				5	1				27
						11	10	8	7	2					3		6			4	9				5	1				28
	3				12	11	10	**8**	7	2					5		6			4	9					1				29
	3	12			8	11	10		**7**	2					5		6			4	9					1				30
	3	8				11	10		7	2					5		6			4	9					1				31
		4			8	11	10		7	2							6			3	9				5	1				32
		4			8	11	10		**7**	2							6			3	9				5	1		12		33
	3	4				11	10			2					5		6			8	9					1		7		34
	3					11	10		12	2					5		6			7	9					1		4	**8**	35
	3					11	10			2					5		6			7	9					1		4	8	36
		12				11	10		**7**	2					5		6			3	9					1		4	8	37
		4				11	10		7	2					**5**					3	9		12			1		6	8	38
		4			7	11	**10**		12	2							6			3	9					1		5	8	39
		4			10	11			7	2							6			3	**9**		12			1		5	8	40
		4			10	11			7	2							6			3	9					1		5	8	41
		4			**10**	11			7	2							6			3	9		12			1		5	8	42
		4				11			7	2							6			3	9		10			1		5	8	43
	12	4				11			7	2							6			3	9		**10**			1		5	8	44
	3	4			8	11	12		**7**	2							6			10	9					1		5		45
	3	4			8	11	12		7	**2**					6					10	9					1		5		46
[illegible]	24	33	15	1	24	32	38	12	34	44	12	2	2	16	23	8	31	11	1	28	30	5	10	4	7	24	1	13	10	
	2	2			1	5	3	3	4		1	1	2		1					1			3					1		
	2		1		4	8	11		5	4	2					2		2		8	15							2	3	

1986-87

Cont.

Match No.	Date		Venue	Opponents	Result		Scorers
Play-offs							
SF1	May	14	A	Colchester United	W	2-0	Bull, Kelly
SF2		17	H	Colchester United	D	0-0	
F1		22	A	Aldershot	L	0-2	
F2		25	H	Aldershot	L	0-1	

Appea
Sub appea

FA Cup

Match No.	Date		Venue	Opponents	Result		Scorers
R1	Nov	15	N	Chorley	D	1-1	Mutch
rep		18	H	Chorley	D	1-1	Forman
rep2		24	N	Chorley	L	0-3	

R1 replay aet

R1 and R1 replay 2 played at Burnden Park, Bolton.

Appea
Sub appea

League Cup

Match No.	Date		Venue	Opponents	Result		Scorers
R1/1	Aug	26	H	Lincoln City	L	1-2	Mutch
R1/2	Sep	2	A	Lincoln City	W	1-0	Lockhart

Appear
Sub appear

	Oldroyd DR	Barnes D	Streete FA	Zelem PR	Hellin MK	Forman MC	Holmes MA	Mutch AT	Edwards NA	Purdie J	Stoutt SP	Lockhart KS	Ryan DA	Eli R	Nixon EW	Clarke NJ	Edwards DS	Robertson A	Handysides IR	Palmer G	Thompson AR	Bull SG	Barrett S	Powell BI	Dougherty PD	Brindley CP	Kendall M	Caswell BL	Kelly RA	Dennison RS
SF1		3	4				11	10		7	2							6			8	9					1		5	
SF2		3	4				11	10		12	2							6			8	9					1		5	**7**
F1		3	4				11	10		7	2					6					8	9					1		5	
F2		3	4				11	10		12	2					6					8	9		5			1			**7**
		4	4				4	4		2	4					2		2			4	4		1			4		3	2
										2																				
																						1							1	
R1		3	4	6		5	8	9	11		2	10						7												
rep		3	4	6		5	8	9	**11**		2	10					12	7												
rep2		3		6		5	8	9	**10**	11	2	7				12		4												
		3	2	3		3	3	3	3	1	3	3						3												
																1	1													
						1		1																						
R1/1	2	**3**	4	5			8	9		11	6	7	10	12																
R1/2	2			5			8	9	12	11	6	7	10	4		**3**														
	2	1	1	2			2	2		2	2	2	2	1		1														
									1					1																
								1				1																		

1987-88

Division Four

Manager: Graham Turner

	P	W	D	L	F	A	Pts
Wolverhampton Wanderers	46	27	9	10	82	43	90
Cardiff City	46	24	13	9	66	41	85
Bolton Wanderers	46	22	12	12	66	42	78
Scunthorpe United	46	20	17	9	76	51	77
Torquay United	46	21	14	11	66	41	77
Swansea City	46	20	10	16	62	56	70
Peterborough United	46	20	10	16	52	53	70
Leyton Orient	46	19	12	15	85	63	69
Colchester United	46	19	10	17	47	51	67
Burnley	46	20	7	19	57	62	67
Wrexham	46	20	6	20	69	58	66
Scarborough	46	17	14	15	56	48	65
Darlington	46	18	11	17	71	69	65
Tranmere Rovers	46	19	9	18	61	53	64
Cambridge United	46	16	13	17	50	52	61
Hartlepool United	46	15	14	17	50	57	59
Crewe Alexandra	46	13	19	14	57	53	58
Halifax Town	46	14	14	18	54	59	55
Hereford United	46	14	12	20	41	59	54
Stockport County	46	12	15	19	44	58	51
Rochdale	46	11	15	20	47	76	48
Exeter City	46	11	13	22	53	68	46
Carlisle United	46	12	8	26	57	86	44
Newport County	46	6	7	33	35	105	25

Did you know that?

- Scarborough's first-ever League game was against Wolves at the McCain Stadium on 15 August, when crowd disturbances marred the 2–2 draw.
- Wolves completed a club record 61 competitive games this season – and Mark Kendall and Andy Mutch played in them all.
- Wolves returned to Wembley for the first time in eight years to beat Burnley 2–0 in the Final of the Sherpa Van Trophy.
- Steve Bull became the first player for 27 years to score 50 goals in a season, finishing with a total of 52. He was also sent off twice.
- Two substitutes were used in a game for the first time this season.

Match No.	Date		Venue	Opponents	Result		Scorers	Att
1	Aug	15	A	Scarborough	D	2-2	Stoutt, Bull	
2		22	H	Halifax Town	L	0-1		
3		29	A	Hereford United	W	2-1	Bull, Mutch	
4		31	H	Scunthorpe United	W	4-1	Bull 2, Mutch 2	
5	Sep	5	A	Cardiff City	L	2-3	Bull, Vaughan	
6		12	H	Crewe Alexandra	D	2-2	Bull, Gallagher	
7		16	A	Peterborough United	D	1-1	Bull	
8		19	A	Stockport County	W	2-0	Robinson, Mutch	
9		26	H	Torquay United	L	1-2	Bull	
10		29	H	Rochdale	W	2-0	Bull, Mutch	
11	Oct	3	A	Bolton Wanderers	L	0-1		
12		10	A	Carlisle United	W	1-0	Bull	
13		17	H	Tranmere Rovers	W	3-0	Bull, Mutch, Vaughan	
14		20	H	Cambridge United	W	3-0	Bull, Mutch, Vaughan	
15		24	A	Darlington	D	2-2	Mutch 2	
16		31	H	Newport County	W	2-1	Mutch, Vaughan	
17	Nov	3	A	Swansea City	W	2-1	Bull, Gallagher	
18		7	H	Burnley	W	3-0	Downing, Gallagher, Vaughan	1
19		21	A	Colchester United	W	1-0	Thompson (pen)	
20		28	H	Wrexham	L	0-2		
21	Dec	12	A	Hartlepool United	D	0-0		
22		19	H	Leyton Orient	W	2-0	Bull 2	1
23		28	H	Exeter City	W	3-0	Thompson (pen), Dennison, Mutch	1
24	Jan	1	H	Hereford United	W	2-0	Bull 2	1
25		2	A	Crewe Alexandra	W	2-0	Mutch 2	
26		16	H	Stockport County	D	1-1	Vaughan	
27		30	A	Scunthorpe United	W	1-0	Mutch	
28	Feb	6	H	Cardiff City	L	1-4	Bull	1
29		13	A	Exeter City	W	4-2	Bull 3, Purdie	
30		16	A	Halifax Town	L	1-2	Bellamy	
31		19	H	Scarborough	D	0-0		1
32		23	A	Torquay United	D	0-0		
33		27	H	Bolton Wanderers	W	4-0	Robinson, Dennison, Bull 2	1
34	Mar	1	A	Rochdale	W	1-0	Holmes	
35		4	A	Tranmere Rovers	L	0-3		
36		12	H	Carlisle United	W	3-1	Mutch, Bellamy, Clark (og)	
37		22	H	Peterborough United	L	0-1		
38		26	H	Darlington	W	5-3	Robinson, Bull 3, Chard	
39	Apr	2	A	Burnley	W	3-0	Bull, Mutch, Holmes	1
40		4	H	Colchester United	W	2-0	Bull 2	1
41		10	A	Cambridge United	D	1-1	Mutch	
42		23	H	Swansea City	W	2-0	Robinson, Bull	1
43		26	A	Newport County	W	3-1	Bull 2, Mutch	
44		30	A	Wrexham	L	2-4	Mutch, Chard	
45	May	2	H	Hartlepool United	W	2-0	Bull 2	1
46		7	A	Leyton Orient	W	2-0	Robinson, Dennison	

Appeara

Sub appeara

One own-goal G

FA Cup

R1	Nov	14	H	Cheltenham Town	W	5-1	Bull 3, Downing, Vaughan	1
R2	Dec	5	A	Wigan Athletic	W	3-1	Robinson, Dennison, Gallagher	
R3	Jan	9	A	Bradford City	L	1-2	Sinnott (og)	1

Appeara

Sub appeara

One own-goal G

League Cup

R1/1	Aug	18	H	Notts County	W	3-0	Mutch 2, Yates (og)	
R1/2		25	A	Notts County	W	2-1	Bull 2	
R2/1	Sep	22	A	Manchester City	W	2-1	Dennison, Bull	8
R2/2	Oct	6	H	Manchester City	L	0-2		13

Appeara

Sub appeara

One own-goal G

	Stout SP	Barnes D	Streete FA	Robertson A	Robinson PJ	Thompson AR	Dennison RS	Bull SG	Mutch AT	Holmes MA	Downing KG	Clarke NJ	Gallagher JC	Vaughan NM	Bellamy G	Purdie J	Edwards NA	Powell BI	McDonald RW	Venus M	Chard PJ
1	2	3	4	5	6	7	**8**	9	10	11	12										
2	2		4	5	6	8	7	9	**10**		11	3	12								
3	2		4	5	6	8	7	9	10		11	3									
4	2		4	5	6	8	7	9	10		11	**3**	12								
5	2		4	5	6	8	**7**	9	10		11	3	12	14							
6	2		4	5	6	3	7	9	**10**				14	8	2	11					
7	2		4		6	3	7	9	10					8	5	11					
8			4	5	6	3	7	9	10					8	2	11					
9			4	5	6	3	7	9	10				12	8	2	**11**					
10			4	5	6	3	**7**	9	10		12			8	2	11					
11			4	5	6	3	7	9	**10**				12	8	2	11					
12			4	5	6	3	**7**	9	10		11		12	8	2						
13			4	5	6	3	7	9	**10**		11		12	8	2						
14	2		4	5	**6**	3	7	9	10		11		12	8							
15	2		4	5		3	7	9	10	6	11			8							
16	2		4	5		3	7		10	**6**			9	8			11	12			
17	2		4	5		3	7	9	10		11		6	8							
18	2		4	5		3	7	9	10		11		6	8							
19	2		4		12	3	7	9	10		**11**	5	6	8							
20	2		**4**	5	6	3	7	9	10	14		12	11	8							
21	2		4	5	6	3	7		10		11		9	8							
22	2		4	5	6	3	7	9	10		11			8							
23	2		4		6	3	7	9	10		11	5		8							
24	2		4	5	6	3	7	9	10		11			8							
25	2		4	5	6	3	7	9	10		11			8							
26	**2**		4	5	6	3	7	9	10	12	11		14	8							
27			4	5	6	3	7	9	10		11			8	2						
28				5	6	3	7	9	10		11	4		8	2						
29			4	5	6	3	7	**9**	10		11			8	2	12					
30			4	5	6	3		9	10	12	11		14	8	**2**	7					
31			4	5	6	2	7	9	10		**11**		12	8					3		
32			4	5	6	2	7	9	10	11				8					3		
33			4	5	6	2	7	9	10	11	12			**8**					3		
34			4	**5**	6	2	7	9	10	11	12			8					3		
35			4		6	**2**	7	9	10	11	12			8	5				3		
36			4	5	6		7	9	10	11				8	2				3		
37	2			5	6		7	9	10	11	14		12	**8**	4					3	
38			4	5	6		7	9	10	11					2					3	8
39			4	5	6	12	**7**	9	10	11					2					3	8
40			4	5	**6**		7	9	10	11				12	2					3	8
41			4	5		3		9	10	11	6			7	2						8
42			4	5	6	3	**7**	9	10	14	11				2	12					8
43	5		4		6	3		9	10	7	11				2						8
44			4	5	**6**	3	7	9	10	11	12				2						8
45			4	5	6	3	7	9	10		11				2						8
46			4	5	**6**	3	11	9	10	7	8			14	2						12
	21	1	44	41	40	41	43	44	46	16	27	7	6	33	24	7	1		6	4	8
	1				1	1				4	7	1	13	3		2		1			1
	1				5	2	3	34	19	2	1		3	6	2	1					2

	Stout SP	Barnes D	Streete FA	Robertson A	Robinson PJ	Thompson AR	Dennison RS	Bull SG	Mutch AT	Holmes MA	Downing KG	Clarke NJ	Gallagher JC	Vaughan NM	Bellamy G	Purdie J	Edwards NA	Powell BI	McDonald RW	Venus M	Chard PJ
R1	2		4	**5**		3	7	9	10		11	13	6	8				12			
R2	2		4	5	6	3	7		10		11		9	8							
R3	2		4	5	6	3	7	9	10	12	**11**			8							
	3		3	3	2	3	3	2	3		3		2	3							
										1		1						1			
					1		1	3			1		1	1							

	Stout SP	Barnes D	Streete FA	Robertson A	Robinson PJ	Thompson AR	Dennison RS	Bull SG	Mutch AT	Holmes MA	Downing KG	Clarke NJ	Gallagher JC	Vaughan NM	Bellamy G	Purdie J	Edwards NA	Powell BI	McDonald RW	Venus M	Chard PJ
R1/1	2	3	4	5	6	7	8	9	10	**11**	12										
R1/2	2		4	5	6	8	**7**	9	10		11	3	12								
R2/1			4	5	6	3	7	9	10					8	2	11					
R2/2			4	5	6	3	7	9	10		11			8	2						
	2	1	4	4	4	4	4	4	4	1	2	1		2	2	1					
											1		1								
							1	3	2												

1988-89

Division Three

Manager: Graham Turner

	P	W	D	L	F	A	Pts
Wolverhampton Wanderers	46	26	14	6	96	49	92
Sheffield United	46	25	9	12	93	54	84
Port Vale	46	24	12	10	78	48	84
Fulham	46	22	9	15	69	67	75
Bristol Rovers	46	19	17	10	67	51	74
Preston North End	46	19	15	12	79	60	72
Brentford	46	18	14	14	66	61	68
Chester City	46	19	11	16	64	61	68
Notts County	46	18	13	15	64	54	67
Bolton Wanderers	46	16	16	14	58	54	64
Bristol City	46	18	9	19	53	55	63
Swansea City	46	15	16	15	51	53	61
Bury	46	16	13	17	55	67	61
Huddersfield Town	46	17	9	20	63	73	60
Mansfield Town	46	14	17	15	48	52	59
Cardiff City	46	14	15	17	44	56	57
Wigan Athletic	46	14	14	18	55	53	56
Reading	46	15	11	20	68	72	56
Blackpool	46	14	13	19	56	59	55
Northampton Town	46	16	6	24	66	76	54
Southend United	46	13	15	18	56	75	54
Chesterfield	46	14	7	25	51	86	49
Gillingham	46	12	4	30	47	81	40
Aldershot	46	8	13	25	48	78	37

Did you know that?

- By clinching the Third Division Championship, Wolves created history by becoming the first team to win five sections of the Football League (Divs. 1, 2, 3, 3N and 4).
- Steve Bull won the first of his 13 full England caps against Scotland in May 1989.
- 'Bully' also became the first player since George Camsell of Middlesbrough (1926–28) to score a total of more than 100 goals in two seasons (amassing 102 in all).
- Defenders Ally Robertson and Floyd Streete were both sent off this season.
- Andy Thompson captained Wolves.

Match No.	Date		Venue	Opponents	Result		Scorers	Att
1	Aug	27	A	Bury	L	1-3	Streete	
2	Sep	3	H	Reading	W	2-1	Chard (pen), Dennison	1
3		10	A	Chesterfield	W	3-0	Robinson, Chard, Dennison	
4		17	H	Notts County	D	0-0		1
5		20	H	Aldershot	W	1-0	Bull	
6		24	A	Swansea City	W	5-2	Robinson, Chard, Bull 2, Dennison	
7	Oct	1	H	Port Vale	D	3-3	Thompson (pen), Bull 2	1
8		5	A	Fulham	D	2-2	Mutch, Gooding	
9		8	A	Sheffield United	L	0-2		1
10		15	H	Wigan Athletic	W	2-1	Bull, Gallagher	1
11		22	A	Bolton Wanderers	W	2-1	Bull, Dennison	
12		25	H	Blackpool	W	2-1	Mutch 2	1
13		29	A	Gillingham	W	3-1	Robinson, Bull, Mutch	
14	Nov	5	H	Southend United	W	3-0	Streete, Bull, Downing	1
15		8	A	Bristol City	W	1-0	Mutch	1
16		12	H	Huddersfield Town	W	4-1	Streete, Bull 2, Mutch	1
17		26	H	Preston North End	W	6-0	Vaughan, Bull 4, Mutch	1
18	Dec	4	A	Northampton Town	L	1-3	Dennison	
19		17	H	Mansfield Town	W	6-2	Thompson, Bull 3, Mutch, Gooding	1
20		26	A	Bristol Rovers	D	0-0		
21		31	A	Brentford	D	2-2	Bull, Mutch	
22	Jan	2	H	Chester City	W	3-1	Bull, Mutch, Gooding	2
23		10	H	Cardiff City	W	2-0	Bull, Mutch	14
24		14	A	Reading	W	2-0	Mutch 2	
25		21	H	Chesterfield	W	1-0	Vaughan	1
26		29	A	Notts County	D	1-1	Mutch	
27	Feb	4	A	Port Vale	D	0-0		1
28		11	H	Fulham	W	5-2	Bull 3, Thompson (pen), Thomas (og)	1
29		28	A	Blackpool	W	2-0	Vaughan, Bull	
30	Mar	4	H	Bolton Wanderers	W	1-0	Bull	1
31		10	A	Southend United	L	1-3	Streete	
32		14	H	Gillingham	W	6-1	Thompson (pen), Bull, Mutch 2, Dennison, Steele	
33		18	H	Bury	W	4-0	Bull 3, Mutch	1
34		25	A	Chester City	D	1-1	Mutch	7
35		27	H	Bristol Rovers	L	0-1		2
36	Apr	1	A	Mansfield Town	L	1-3	Bull	9
37		4	A	Cardiff City	D	1-1	Thompson (pen)	7
38		8	H	Brentford	W	2-0	Streete, Bull	14
39		15	A	Aldershot	W	2-1	Bull, Dennison	5
40		22	H	Swansea City	D	1-1	Vaughan	1
41		29	A	Huddersfield Town	D	0-0		8
42	May	1	H	Bristol City	W	2-0	Bull 2	17
43		6	H	Northampton Town	W	3-2	Thompson (pen), Bull, Mutch	15
44		9	H	Sheffield United	D	2-2	Bull, Dennison	24
45		13	A	Preston North End	D	3-3	Bellamy, Mutch 2	14
46		16	A	Wigan Athletic	D	1-1	Gooding	5

Appearar
Sub appearar
One own-goal G

FA Cup

R1	Nov	19	A	Grimsby Town	L	0-1		7

Appearan
Sub appearan

League Cup

R1/1	Aug	30	H	Birmingham City	W	3-2	Bull 2, Dennison	11
R1/2	Sep	6	A	Birmingham City	L	0-1		8

Appearan
Sub appearan
G

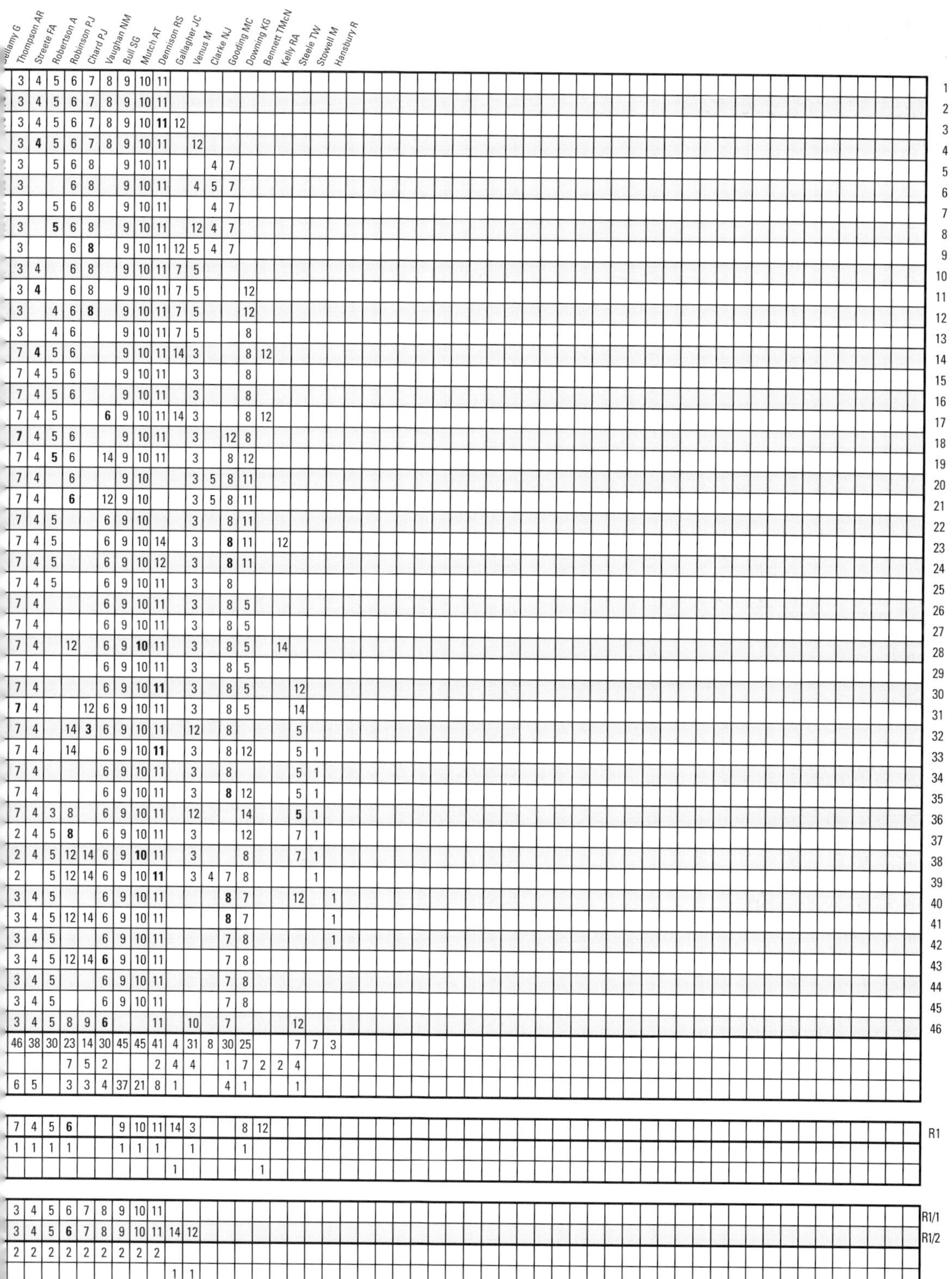

	Bellamy G	Thompson AR	Streete FA	Robertson A	Robinson PJ	Chard PJ	Vaughan NM	Bull SG	Mutch AT	Dennison RS	Gallagher JC	Venus M	Clarke NJ	Gooding MC	Downing KG	Bennett TMcN	Kelly RA	Steele TW	Stowell M	Hansbury R
1		3	4	5	6	7	8	9	10	11										
2		3	4	5	6	7	8	9	10	11										
3		3	4	5	6	7	8	9	10	**11**	12									
4		3	**4**	5	6	7	8	9	10	11		12								
5		3		5	6	8		9	10	11			4	7						
6		3			6	8		9	10	11		4	5	7						
7		3		5	6	8		9	10	11			4	7						
8		3		**5**	6	8		9	10	11		12	4	7						
9		3			6	**8**		9	10	11	12	5	4	7						
10		3	4		6	8		9	10	11	7	5								
11		3	**4**		6	8		9	10	11	7	5			12					
12		3		4	6	**8**		9	10	11	7	5			12					
13		3		4	6			9	10	11	7	5			8					
14		7	**4**	5	6			9	10	11	14	3			8	12				
15		7	4	5	6			9	10	11		3			8					
16		7	4	5	6			9	10	11		3			8					
17		7	4	5			**6**	9	10	11	14	3			8	12				
18		**7**	4	5	6			9	10	11		3		12	8					
19		7	4	**5**	6		14	9	10	11		3		8	12					
20		7	4		6			9	10			3	5	8	11					
21		7	4		**6**		12	9	10			3	5	8	11					
22		7	4	5			6	9	10			3		8	11					
23		7	4	5			6	9	10	14		3		**8**	11		12			
24		7	4	5			6	9	10	12		3		**8**	11					
25		7	4	5			6	9	10	11		3		8						
26		7	4				6	9	10	11		3		8	5					
27		7	4				6	9	10	11		3		8	5					
28		7	4		12		6	9	**10**	11		3		8	5		14			
29		7	4				6	9	10	11		3		8	5					
30		7	4				6	9	10	**11**		3		8	5			12		
31		**7**	4			12	6	9	10	11		3		8	5			14		
32		7	4		14	**3**	6	9	10	11		12		8				5		
33		7	4		14		6	9	10	**11**		3		8	12			5	1	
34		7	4				6	9	10	11		3		8				5	1	
35		7	4				6	9	10	11		3		**8**	12			5	1	
36		7	4	3	8		6	9	10	11		12			14			**5**	1	
37		2	4	5	**8**		6	9	10	11		3			12			7	1	
38		2	4	5	12	14	6	9	**10**	11		3			8			7	1	
39		2		5	12	14	6	9	10	**11**		3	4	7	8				1	
40		3	4	5			6	9	10	11				**8**	7			12		1
41		3	4	5	12	14	6	9	10	11				**8**	7					1
42		3	4	5			6	9	10	11				7	8					1
43		3	4	5	12	14	**6**	9	10	11				7	8					
44		3	4	5			6	9	10	11				7	8					
45		3	4	5			6	9	10	11				7	8					
46		3	4	5	8	9	**6**			11		10		7				12		
		46	38	30	23	14	30	45	45	41	4	31	8	30	25			7	7	3
					7	5	2			2	4	4		1	7	2	2	4		
		6	5		3	3	4	37	21	8	1			4	1			1		
R1		7	4	5	**6**			9	10	11	14	3			8	12				
		1	1	1	1			1	1	1		1			1					
											1					1				
R1/1		3	4	5	6	7	8	9	10	11										
R1/2		3	4	5	**6**	7	8	9	10	11	14	12								
		2	2	2	2	2	2	2	2	2										
											1	1								
								2		1										

1989-90

Division Two

Manager: Graham Turner

	P	W	D	L	F	A	Pts
Leeds United	46	24	13	9	79	52	85
Sheffield United	46	24	13	9	78	58	85
Newcastle United	46	22	14	10	80	55	80
Swindon Town	46	20	14	12	79	59	74
Blackburn Rovers	46	19	17	10	74	59	74
Sunderland	46	20	14	12	70	64	74
West Ham United	46	20	12	14	80	57	72
Oldham Athletic	46	19	14	13	70	57	71
Ipswich Town	46	19	12	15	67	66	69
Wolverhampton Wanderers	46	18	13	15	67	60	67
Port Vale	46	15	16	15	62	57	61
Portsmouth	46	15	16	15	62	65	61
Leicester City	46	15	14	17	67	79	59
Hull City	46	14	16	16	58	65	58
Watford	46	14	15	17	58	60	57
Plymouth Argyle	46	14	13	19	58	63	55
Oxford United	46	15	9	22	57	66	54
Brighton & Hove Albion	46	15	9	22	56	72	54
Barnsley	46	13	15	18	49	71	54
West Bromwich Albion	46	12	15	19	67	71	51
Middlesbrough	46	13	11	22	52	63	50
Bournemouth	46	12	12	22	57	76	48
Bradford City	46	9	14	23	44	68	41
Stoke City	46	6	19	21	35	63	37

Did you know that?

- In 1990 Sir Jack Hayward bought his beloved Wolverhampton Wanderers football club.
- Steve Bull, Shane Westley (signed from Southend United) and Andy Mutch were all sent off during the season.
- Paul Cook (from Norwich City) was among the new faces at Molineux.
- Out of the club went Mick Gooding, who was sold to Reading, and Ally Robertson, who moved to Worcester City.
- Gary Bellamy acted as team captain this season.

Match No.	Date		Venue	Opponents	Result		Scorers
1	Aug	19	A	Middlesbrough	L	2-4	Thompson (pen), Mutch
2		26	H	Bradford City	D	1-1	Bull
3	Sep	3	A	Swindon Town	L	1-3	Thompson (pen)
4		9	H	Stoke City	D	0-0	
5		12	H	Brighton & Hove Albion	L	2-4	Bull, Mutch
6		16	A	Ipswich Town	W	3-1	Bellamy, Mutch 2
7		23	H	Plymouth Argyle	W	1-0	Paskin
8		26	A	Barnsley	D	2-2	Bull 2
9		30	H	Portsmouth	W	5-0	Venus, Bull 2, Dennison 2
10	Oct	7	H	Sheffield United	L	1-2	Hill (og)
11		15	A	West Bromwich Albion	W	2-1	Bull, Dennison
12		17	H	Port Vale	W	2-0	Bull, Mutch
13		21	A	Leeds United	L	0-1	
14		28	H	Oldham Athletic	D	1-1	Thompson (pen)
15	Nov	1	A	Leicester City	D	0-0	
16		4	H	West Ham United	W	1-0	Bull
17		11	A	Sunderland	D	1-1	Mutch
18		18	H	Blackburn Rovers	L	1-2	Paskin
19		25	A	Watford	L	1-3	Mutch
20	Dec	2	H	Middlesbrough	W	2-0	Thompson (pen), Cook
21		9	A	Brighton & Hove Albion	D	1-1	Dennison
22		16	A	Oxford United	D	2-2	Venus, Dennison
23		26	H	Hull City	L	1-2	Bull
24		30	H	Bournemouth	W	3-1	Mutch, Dennison, Downing
25	Jan	1	A	Newcastle United	W	4-1	Bull 4
26		13	A	Bradford City	D	1-1	Bull
27		20	H	Swindon Town	W	2-1	McLoughlin 2
28	Feb	3	A	Plymouth Argyle	W	1-0	Mutch
29		10	H	Ipswich Town	W	2-1	Bull, Linighan (og)
30		17	A	Stoke City	L	0-2	
31		24	H	Watford	D	1-1	Bull
32	Mar	3	A	Blackburn Rovers	W	3-2	Downing, McLoughlin 2
33		6	A	Portsmouth	W	3-1	Bellamy, Fillery (og), Bull
34		10	H	Barnsley	D	1-1	Bull
35		17	A	Sheffield United	L	0-3	
36		20	H	West Bromwich Albion	W	2-1	Bull, Cook
37		24	A	Port Vale	L	1-3	Mutch
38		31	H	Leeds United	W	1-0	Mutch
39	Apr	3	A	Bournemouth	D	1-1	Bellamy
40		10	H	Leicester City	W	5-0	Bull 3, Dennison 2
41		14	H	Newcastle United	L	0-1	
42		16	A	Hull City	L	0-2	
43		21	H	Oxford United	W	2-0	Bull, Downing
44		28	H	Sunderland	L	0-1	
45	May	3	A	Oldham Athletic	D	1-1	Steele
46		5	A	West Ham United	L	0-4	

Appear

Sub appear

Three own-goals

FA Cup

R3	Jan	6	H	Sheffield Wednesday	L	1-2	Bull

Appear

Sub appear

League Cup

R1/1	Aug	22	H	Lincoln City	W	1-0	Westley
R1/2		30	A	Lincoln City	W	2-0	Bull, Dennison
R2/1	Sep	20	A	Aston Villa	L	1-2	Mutch
R2/2	Oct	4	H	Aston Villa	D	1-1	Bull

Appear

Sub appear

Bellamy G	Venus M	Robertson A	Westley SLM	Vaughan NM	Thompson AR	Gooding MC	Bull SG	Mutch AT	Dennison RS	Downing KG	Chard PJ	Steele TW	Paskin WJ	McLoughlin PB	Kendall M	Streete FA	Bennett TMcN	Clarke NJ	Cook PA	Jones PA	
2	3	4	5	6	7	8	9	10	11	12											1
	3	4	5	6	7	8	9	10	11	**2**	12										2
	3	4	5	**6**	7	8	9	10	11		2	12									3
	3	4	5	6	7	8	9	10	11		**2**		12								4
2	3	4	5	6	7	**8**	9	10	11				12	14							5
2	3		5	6		8		10	11				9		1	4	7				6
2	3			6		8	9	10	**11**	12			14		1	4	7	5			7
2	3			6		8	9		11				10		1	4	7	5			8
2	3		4	6		**8**	9		11	12	14		10		1		7	5			9
2	3		5	6		8	9	10	11		7				1	4					10
2	3		5	**6**	7	8	9	10	11	12					1	4					11
	3		5	6	7		9	10	11	8	4				1		2				12
4	3		5	14	**7**	8	9	10	11	6			12		1		2				13
4	3		5		7	8	9	10	11	6					1		2				14
4	3		5		7		9	10	11	6					1		2		8		15
4	3		5		7		9	10	11	6					1		2		8		16
4	3		5	8	7		9	10	11	6					1		2				17
4	3		5	12	7			10	11	**6**			9	14	1		2		8		18
4	3		5	2	7			10	11				9	14	1	6			**8**	12	19
4	3		5	2	7			**10**	11				9	12	1	6			8		20
4	3		5	2	7		9	10	11						1	6			8		21
4	3		5	2	7		9	10	11						1	6			8		22
4	3		5	**2**	7		9	10	11	12			14		1	6			8		23
4	3						9	10	11	5			7		1	6	2		8		24
4	3						9	10	11	**5**			7	14	1	6	2		8	12	25
4	3						9	10	11	5				12	1	6	2		**8**	7	26
4	3						9	**10**	11	5				12	1	6	2		8	7	27
	3		4		12		9	10	11	**5**					1	6	2		8	7	28
	3		4				9	10	11	5					1	6	2		8	7	29
	3		4				9	10	11	5				12	1	6	2		8	**7**	30
6	3		4		2		9		11	5		7		10	1				8		31
6	3		4		2		9		11	**5**		7		10	1				8	12	32
6	3		4		2		9		11	5		7		10	1				8		33
6	3		4		2		9	12	11			**7**		10	1				8	5	34
6	3		4		14		9	12	11	5				10	1		2		8	**7**	35
6	3		4		5		9	10	11			7			1		2		8		36
6	3		4		5		9	10	11			7			1		2		8		37
6	3		4				9	**10**	11	5		7		12	1		2		8		38
6	3		4				9	10	11	5		7			1		2		8		39
6			4	8	3		9	10	11	**5**		7			1		2			12	40
6	4			8	3		9	10	11			7		14	1		2		**5**	12	41
6			4	5	3		9	**10**	11			7		12	1		2		8		42
6	4			5	3		9		11	8		7	12	**10**	1		2				43
6	4			5	3		9		11	8		7	12	**10**	1		2				44
6	4		5		3		9		**11**	8		12	10		1		2		7		45
6	4		5		3		9		11	8			10	14	1		2		**7**	12	46
39	44	5	37	23	31	13	42	35	46	26	4	13	10	7	41	17	30	3	28	7	
				2	2			2		5	2	2	7	12						6	
3	2				4		24	11	8	3		1	2	4					2		

Bellamy G	Venus M	Robertson A	Westley SLM	Vaughan NM	Thompson AR	Gooding MC	Bull SG	Mutch AT	Dennison RS	Downing KG	Chard PJ	Steele TW	Paskin WJ	McLoughlin PB	Kendall M	Streete FA	Bennett TMcN	Clarke NJ	Cook PA	Jones PA	
4	3						9	10	11	5			**7**		1	6	2		8	12	R3
1	1						1	1	1	1			1		1	1	1		1		
																				1	
							1														

Bellamy G	Venus M	Robertson A	Westley SLM	Vaughan NM	Thompson AR	Gooding MC	Bull SG	Mutch AT	Dennison RS	Downing KG	Chard PJ	Steele TW	Paskin WJ	McLoughlin PB	Kendall M	Streete FA	Bennett TMcN	Clarke NJ	Cook PA	Jones PA	
	3	4	5	6	7	8	9	10	11	2											R1/1
	3	4	5	6	7	8	9	10	11		2										R1/2
2	3			**6**		8	9	10	11	12			14		1	4	7	5			R2/1
2	3		5	6		8	9		11	12	14		10		1	**4**	7				R2/2
2	4	2	3	4	2	4	4	3	4	1	1		1		2	2	2	1			
										2	1		1								
			1				2	1	1												

1990-91

Division Two

Manager: Graham Turner

	P	W	D	L	F	A	Pts
Oldham Athletic	46	25	13	8	83	53	88
West Ham United	46	24	15	7	60	34	87
Sheffield Wednesday	46	22	16	8	80	51	82
Notts County	46	23	11	12	76	55	80
Millwall	46	20	13	13	70	51	73
Brighton & Hove Albion	46	21	7	18	63	69	70
Middlesbrough	46	20	9	17	66	47	69
Barnsley	46	19	12	15	63	48	69
Bristol City	46	20	7	19	68	71	67
Oxford United	46	14	19	13	69	66	61
Newcastle United	46	14	17	15	49	56	59
Wolverhampton Wanderers	46	13	19	14	63	63	58
Bristol Rovers	46	15	13	18	56	59	58
Ipswich Town	46	13	18	15	60	68	57
Port Vale	46	15	12	19	56	64	57
Charlton Athletic	46	13	17	16	57	61	56
Portsmouth	46	14	11	21	58	70	53
Plymouth Argyle	46	12	17	17	54	68	53
Blackburn Rovers	46	14	10	22	51	66	52
Watford	46	12	15	19	45	59	51
Swindon Town	46	12	14	20	65	73	50
Leicester City	46	14	8	24	60	83	50
West Bromwich Albion	46	10	18	18	52	61	48
Hull City	46	10	15	21	57	85	45

Did you know that?

- Wolves drew 19 of their 46 Second Division games this season.
- Ex-Birmingham City full-back Kevin Ashley and Paul Cook were sent off in away League games at Barnsley and Bristol City respectively.
- Paul Birch (from Aston Villa) and Mark Burke (ex-Middlesbrough) joined the club, while those who left included Mark Kendall to Swansea City and Floyd Streete to Reading.
- Gary Bellamy, Steve Bull and Rob Hindmarch all captained Wolves.

Match No.	Date		Venue	Opponents	Result		Scorers	Atten
1	Aug	25	H	Oldham Athletic	L	2-3	Bull 2	20
2		28	A	Port Vale	W	2-1	Bellamy, Bull	12
3	Sep	1	A	Brighton & Hove Albion	D	1-1	Cook	9,
4		8	H	Bristol Rovers	D	1-1	Dennison	17,
5		15	A	West Ham United	D	1-1	Bull	23,
6		18	A	Swindon Town	L	0-1		12,
7		22	H	Plymouth Argyle	W	3-1	Bull 2, Mutch	15,
8		29	A	Oxford United	D	1-1	Dennison	7,
9	Oct	2	H	Charlton Athletic	W	3-0	Thompson, Bull 2	14,
10		6	H	Bristol City	W	4-0	Thompson, Bull 3	17,
11		13	A	Notts County	D	1-1	Westley	12,
12		20	A	Hull City	W	2-1	Bull, Dennison	7,
13		23	H	Middlesbrough	W	1-0	Bull	17,
14		27	H	Blackburn Rovers	L	2-3	Cook, Steele	17,
15	Nov	3	A	Portsmouth	D	0-0		14,
16		10	H	Newcastle United	W	2-1	Bellamy, Steele	18,
17		17	A	Leicester City	L	0-1		16,
18		24	A	Barnsley	D	1-1	Cook	9,
19	Dec	1	H	Ipswich Town	D	2-2	Bull 2	15,
20		15	A	Oldham Athletic	L	1-4	Thompson	11,
21		22	H	Millwall	W	4-1	Bellamy, Bull, Taylor 2	14,
22		26	A	Sheffield Wednesday	D	2-2	Cook, Bull	29,
23		29	A	West Bromwich Albion	D	1-1	Hindmarch	28,
24	Jan	1	H	Watford	D	0-0		18,
25		12	H	Brighton & Hove Albion	L	2-3	Bull, Mutch	12,
26		19	A	Bristol Rovers	D	1-1	Twentyman (og)	6,
27	Feb	2	H	West Ham United	W	2-1	Bull, Birch	19,
28		23	A	Newcastle United	D	0-0		18,
29		26	H	Port Vale	W	3-1	Bull 2, Mutch	15,
30	Mar	2	A	Ipswich Town	D	0-0		13,
31		5	H	Leicester City	W	2-1	Bull, Mutch	15,
32		9	H	Barnsley	L	0-5		15,
33		12	A	Charlton Athletic	L	0-1		6,
34		16	H	Oxford United	D	3-3	Bull 3	11,
35		19	H	Notts County	L	0-2		12,
36		23	A	Bristol City	D	1-1	Dennison	15,
37		30	H	Sheffield Wednesday	W	3-2	Bull, Mutch 2	18,
38	Apr	3	A	Millwall	L	1-2	Cook	13,
39		6	H	West Bromwich Albion	D	2-2	Mutch, Dennison	22,
40		9	A	Plymouth Argyle	L	0-1		7,
41		13	A	Watford	L	1-3	Cook (pen)	12,
42		16	H	Swindon Town	L	1-2	Hindmarch	9,
43		20	H	Hull City	D	0-0		9,
44		27	A	Middlesbrough	L	0-2		16,
45	May	4	A	Blackburn Rovers	D	1-1	Paskin	9,
46		11	H	Portsmouth	W	3-1	Downing, Mutch, Birch	12,
								Appearanc
								Sub appearanc
							One own-goal	Go

FA Cup

R3	Jan	5	H	Cambridge United	L	0-1		15,1
								Appearanc
								Sub appearanc

League Cup

R2/1	Sep	25	A	Hull City	D	0-0		5,
R2/2	Oct	9	H	Hull City	D	1-1	Steele	14,
R2/2 lost on away goals aet								Appearanc
								Sub appearanc
								Go

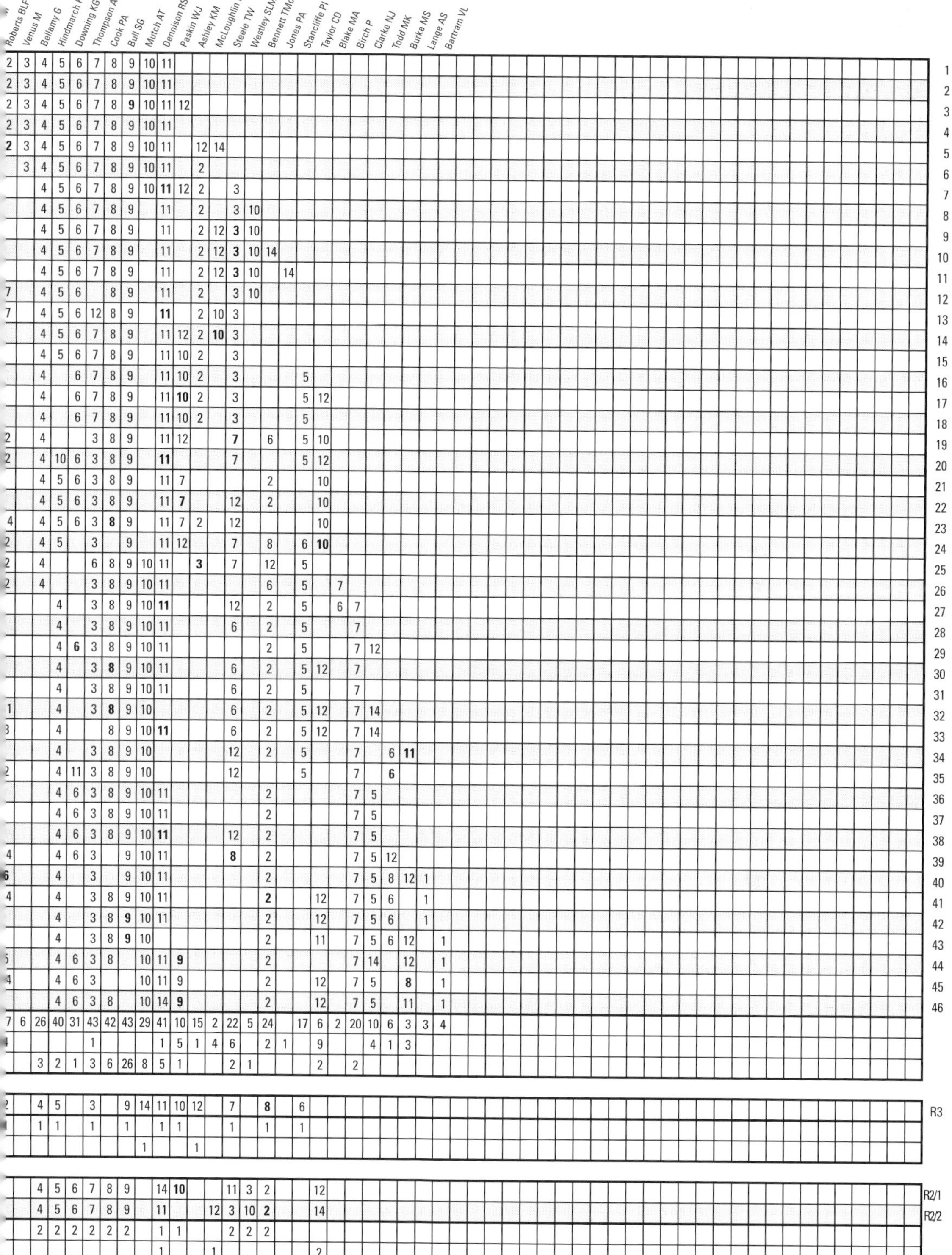

Roberts BLF	Venus M	Bellamy G	Hindmarch R	Downing KG	Thompson AR	Cook PA	Bull SG	Mutch AT	Dennison RS	Paskin WJ	Ashley KM	McLoughlin PB	Steele TW	Westley SLM	Bennett TMcN	Jones PA	Stancliffe PI	Taylor CD	Blake MA	Birch P	Clarke NJ	Todd MK	Burke MS	Lange AS	Bartram VL	
2	3	4	5	6	7	8	9	10	11																	1
2	3	4	5	6	7	8	9	10	11																	2
2	3	4	5	6	7	8	**9**	10	11	12																3
2	3	4	5	6	7	8	9	10	11																	4
2	3	4	5	6	7	8	9	10	11		12	14														5
	3	4	5	6	7	8	9	10	11		2															6
		4	5	6	7	8	9	10	**11**	12	2		3													7
		4	5	6	7	8	9		11		2		3	10												8
		4	5	6	7	8	9		11		2	12	**3**	10												9
		4	5	6	7	8	9		11		2	12	**3**	10	14											10
		4	5	6	7	8	9		11		2	12	**3**	10		14										11
7		4	5	6		8	9		11		2		3	10												12
7		4	5	6	12	8	9		**11**		2	10	3													13
		4	5	6	7	8	9		11	12	2	**10**	3													14
		4	5	6	7	8	9		11	10	2		3													15
		4		6	7	8	9		11	10	2		3				5									16
		4		6	7	8	9		11	**10**	2		3				5	12								17
		4		6	7	8	9		11	10	2		3				5									18
2		4			3	8	9		11	12			**7**		6		5	10								19
2		4	10	6	3	8	9		**11**				7				5	12								20
		4	5	6	3	8	9		11	7					2			10								21
		4	5	6	3	8	9		11	**7**			12		2			10								22
4		4	5	6	3	**8**	9		11	7	2		12					10								23
2		4	5		3		9		11	12			7		8		6	**10**								24
2		4			6	8	9	10	11		**3**		7		12		5									25
2		4			3	8	9	10	11						6		5		7							26
			4		3	8	9	10	**11**				12		2		5		6	7						27
			4		3	8	9	10	11				6		2		5			7						28
			4	**6**	3	8	9	10	11						2		5			7	12					29
			4		3	**8**	9	10	11				6		2		5	12		7						30
			4		3	8	9	10	11				6		2		5			7						31
1			4		3	**8**	9	10					6		2		5	12		7	14					32
3			4			8	9	10	**11**				6		2		5	12		7	14					33
			4		3	8	9	10					12		2		5			7		6	**11**			34
2			4	11	3	8	9	10					12				5			7		**6**				35
			4	6	3	8	9	10	11						2					7	5					36
			4	6	3	8	9	10	11						2					7	5					37
			4	6	3	8	9	10	**11**				12		2					7	5					38
4			4	6	3		9	10	11				**8**		2					7	5	12				39
6			4		3		9	10	11						2					7	5	8	12	1		40
4			4		3	8	9	10	11						**2**			12		7	5	6		1		41
			4		3	8	**9**	10	11						2			12		7	5	6		1		42
			4		3	8	**9**	10							2			11		7	5	6	12		1	43
5			4	6	3	8		10	11	**9**					2					7	14		12		1	44
4			4	6	3			10	11	9					2			12		7	5		**8**		1	45
			4	6	3	8		10	14	**9**					2			12		7	5		11		1	46
7	6	26	40	31	43	42	43	29	41	10	15	2	22	5	24		17	6	2	20	10	6	3	3	4	
4					1				1	5	1	4	6		2	1		9			4	1	3			
		3	2	1	3	6	26	8	5	1			2	1				2		2						
2		4	5		3		9	14	11	10	12		7		**8**		6									R3
1		1	1		1		1		1	1			1		1		1									
								1			1															
		4	5	6	7	8	9		14	**10**			11	3	2			12								R2/1
		4	5	6	7	8	9		11			12	3	10	**2**			14								R2/2
		2	2	2	2	2	2		1	1			2	2	2											
									1			1						2								
													1													

1991-92

Division Two

Manager: Graham Turner

	P	W	D	L	F	A	Pts
Ipswich Town	46	24	12	10	70	50	84
Middlesbrough	46	23	11	12	58	41	80
Derby County	46	23	9	14	69	51	78
Leicester City	46	23	8	15	62	55	77
Cambridge United	46	19	17	10	65	47	74
Blackburn Rovers	46	21	11	14	70	53	74
Charlton Athletic	46	20	11	15	54	48	71
Swindon Town	46	18	15	13	69	55	69
Portsmouth	46	19	12	15	65	51	69
Watford	46	18	11	17	51	48	65
Wolverhampton Wanderers	46	18	10	18	61	54	64
Southend United	46	17	11	18	63	63	62
Bristol Rovers	46	16	14	16	60	63	62
Tranmere Rovers	46	14	19	13	56	56	61
Millwall	46	17	10	19	64	71	61
Barnsley	46	16	11	19	46	57	59
Bristol City	46	13	15	18	55	71	54
Sunderland	46	14	11	21	61	65	53
Grimsby Town	46	14	11	21	47	62	53
Newcastle United	46	13	13	20	66	84	52
Oxford United	46	13	11	22	66	73	50
Plymouth Argyle	46	13	9	24	42	64	48
Brighton & Hove Albion	46	12	11	23	56	77	47
Port Vale	46	10	15	21	42	59	45

Did you know that?

- Steve Bull netted his 150th goal for Wolves in a 4–3 League defeat at Tranmere Rovers in February.
- Ex-Sheffield Wednesday defender Lawrie Madden and former Aston Villa man Derek Mountfield were sent off against Derby County and Barnsley respectively.
- Mark Rankine (from Doncaster Rovers) and Paul Jones (from Kidderminster Harriers) were signed.
- Madden and Mark Venus acted as Wolves' captains this season.
- Defender Nicky Clarke was transferred to Mansfield Town.

Match No.	Date		Venue	Opponents	Result		Scorers
1	Aug	17	A	Watford	W	2-0	Bull, Mutch
2		24	H	Charlton Athletic	D	1-1	Bull
3		31	A	Brighton & Hove Albion	D	3-3	Bull, Mutch 2
4	Sep	3	H	Port Vale	L	0-2	
5		7	H	Oxford United	W	3-1	Bull, Dennison, Steele
6		14	A	Newcastle United	W	2-1	Bull, Steele
7		17	A	Cambridge United	L	1-2	Bull
8		21	H	Swindon Town	W	2-1	Bull, Steele
9		28	A	Southend United	W	2-0	Ashley, Birch
10	Oct	5	H	Barnsley	L	1-2	Cook
11		12	A	Middlesbrough	D	0-0	
12		19	A	Leicester City	L	0-3	
13		26	H	Tranmere Rovers	D	1-1	Birch
14	Nov	2	A	Plymouth Argyle	L	0-1	
15		5	H	Bristol Rovers	L	2-3	Bull 2
16		9	H	Derby County	L	2-3	Coleman (og), Cook (pen)
17		16	A	Millwall	L	1-2	Cook (pen)
18		23	H	Ipswich Town	L	1-2	Birch
19		26	H	Grimsby Town	W	2-1	Madden, Birch
20		30	A	Portsmouth	L	0-1	
21	Dec	7	H	Sunderland	W	1-0	Cook
22		21	A	Port Vale	D	1-1	Bull
23		26	H	Blackburn Rovers	D	0-0	
24		28	H	Brighton & Hove Albion	W	2-0	Mutch, Burke
25	Jan	1	A	Grimsby Town	W	2-0	Birch, Cook
26		15	A	Charlton Athletic	W	2-0	Bennett, Bull
27		18	H	Watford	W	3-0	Cook, Bull, Holdsworth (og)
28	Feb	1	H	Leicester City	W	1-0	Bull
29		8	A	Tranmere Rovers	L	3-4	Cook, Bull, Burke
30		22	H	Portsmouth	D	0-0	
31		29	A	Sunderland	L	0-1	
32	Mar	7	H	Bristol City	D	1-1	Bull
33		11	A	Bristol Rovers	D	1-1	Bull
34		14	H	Plymouth Argyle	W	1-0	Venus
35		17	A	Bristol City	L	0-2	
36		21	A	Derby County	W	2-1	Birch (pen), Bull
37		28	H	Millwall	D	0-0	
38		31	H	Newcastle United	W	6-2	Bennett, Cook, Bull, Mutch 3
39	Apr	4	A	Oxford United	L	0-1	
40		7	A	Ipswich Town	L	1-2	Mutch
41		11	H	Cambridge United	W	2-1	Mutch, Rankine
42		14	A	Blackburn Rovers	W	2-1	Birch, Bull
43		18	A	Swindon Town	L	0-1	
44		20	H	Southend United	W	3-1	Birch, Bull, Mountfield
45		25	A	Barnsley	L	0-2	
46	May	2	H	Middlesbrough	L	1-2	Mutch

Appeara

Sub appeara

Two own-goals

FA Cup

R3	Jan	4	A	Nottingham Forest	L	0-1	

Appeara

Sub appeara

League Cup

R2/1	Sep	24	H	Shrewsbury Town	W	6-1	Steele, Birch 2, Bull 2, Burke
R2/2	Oct	8	A	Shrewsbury Town	L	1-3	Steele
R3		30	A	Everton	L	1-4	Bull

Appeara

Ashley KM	Venus M	Bennett TMcN	Madden LD	Downing KG	Birch P	Cook PA	Bull SG	Mutch AT	Dennison RS	Steele TW	Bellamy G	Burke MS	Clarke W	Bradbury S	Thompson AR	Paskin WJ	Taylor CD	McLoughlin PB	Mountfield DN	Clarke NJ	Rankine SM	Kelly J	
2	3	4	5	6	7	8	9	10	11														1
2	3	4	5	6	**7**	8	9	10	11	12													2
2	3	4	5	6	7	8	9	10	11														3
2	3	4	5	6	7	8	9	10	**11**	12													4
2	3	4	5	6		8	9	10	11	7	12												5
2	3	4	5	**6**	12	8	9	10	11	7													6
2	3	4	5	6	12	8	9	10	**11**	7													7
2	3	4	5	6	11	8	9			**7**	12	10											8
2	3	4	5	6	7	8	9		12		11		**10**										9
2	3	4	5	**6**	7	8	9		12	10		11											10
2	3	4	5		7	**8**	9		12	6					11	10							11
2	3	4	5	6	7		9	**10**	12	8					11	14							12
2	3	4	5	6	7		9	**10**	11	8							12						13
2	3	4	5	6	7	8			**11**	10					12		9						14
2	3	4	5	6	7		9		**11**	14	12	8						10					15
2	3	4	5	6	**7**	11	9	10											8				16
2	3	4	5	**6**	7	11	9	10		12									8				17
2	3	**4**		6	7	11	9	10	12										8	5			18
2	3	4	5	6	7	8	9	10											11				19
2	3	**4**	5		7	8		10	6	12					14			9	11				20
2	3	4	5		7	8		10		**11**		12			6		14	9					21
2	3	4	5		7	8	9	10							11				6				22
2	3	**4**	5		7	8	9	10				12			11				6				23
2	3		5		7	8	9	10				4			11				6				24
2	3	14	5		**7**	8	9	10	12			4			11				6				25
2	3	4	5		7	8	9	10							11				6				26
2	3	4	5		7	8	9	**10**				12			11				6				27
2	3	4	5		7	**8**	9					10			11				6		12		28
2	3	4	5		7	**8**	9		12			10			11						6		29
2	3	4			7	8	9	14	12			10			11				5		6		30
	3	4	6	2	7	8	9	10				14			**11**				5		12		31
2	3	4		**6**	7	8	9	10	11			12							5		14		32
2	3	4	6	11	7	8	9	**10**											5		12		33
2	3	4	6		7	8	9								11				5		10		34
2	3	4	6		7	8	9	12							**11**				5		10		35
2	3	4	6	12	7	8	9	10				11									5		36
	3	4	5	12	7	8	9	10	14			11							2		**6**		37
2	3	4	5	11	7	8	9	10											6			12	38
2	3	**4**	5	11	7	8	9	10											6		14	12	39
2	3		5	11	7	8	9	10											6		4		40
2	3		5	11	7	8	9	10											6		4		41
2	3		5	11	7	8	9	10											6		4		42
2	3		5	11	7	8	9	10		12									6		4		43
2	3		5	11	7	8	9	10				4							6				44
2	3		5	11	**7**	8	9	10		14		4							6			12	45
2	3		5	**11**	7	8	9	10	12			4							6				46
4	46	37	43	30	43	43	43	35	12	10	1	13	1		15	1	1	3	28	1	10		
		1		2	2			2	10	7	3	5			2	1	2				5	3	
	1	2	1		8	8	20	10	1	3		2							1		1		

Ashley KM	Venus M	Bennett TMcN	Madden LD	Downing KG	Birch P	Cook PA	Bull SG	Mutch AT	Dennison RS	Steele TW	Bellamy G	Burke MS	Clarke W	Bradbury S	Thompson AR	Paskin WJ	Taylor CD	McLoughlin PB	Mountfield DN	Clarke NJ	Rankine SM	Kelly J	
2	3	6	5		7	8	9	10	12			**4**			11								R3
	1	1	1		1	1	1	1				1			1								
									1														

Ashley KM	Venus M	Bennett TMcN	Madden LD	Downing KG	Birch P	Cook PA	Bull SG	Mutch AT	Dennison RS	Steele TW	Bellamy G	Burke MS	Clarke W	Bradbury S	Thompson AR	Paskin WJ	Taylor CD	McLoughlin PB	Mountfield DN	Clarke NJ	Rankine SM	Kelly J	
2	3	4	5	6	11	8	9			7		10											R2/1
2	3	4	5		7	8				10	6			9	11								R2/2
2	3	4	5	6	7		9	10	11	8													R3
3	3	3	3	2	3	2	2	1	1	3	1	1		1	1								
					2		3			2		1											

1992-93

Division Two

Manager: Graham Turner

	P	W	D	L	F	A	Pts
Newcastle United	46	29	9	8	92	38	96
West Ham United	46	26	10	10	81	41	88
Portsmouth	46	26	10	10	80	46	88
Tranmere Rovers	46	23	10	13	72	56	79
Swindon Town	46	21	13	12	74	59	76
Leicester City	46	22	10	14	71	64	76
Millwall	46	18	16	12	65	53	70
Derby County	46	19	9	18	68	57	66
Grimsby Town	46	19	7	20	58	57	64
Peterborough United	46	16	14	16	55	63	62
Wolverhampton Wanderers	46	16	13	17	57	56	61
Charlton Athletic	46	16	13	17	49	46	61
Barnsley	46	17	9	20	56	60	60
Oxford United	46	14	14	18	53	56	56
Bristol City	46	14	14	18	49	67	56
Watford	46	14	13	19	57	71	55
Notts County	46	12	16	18	55	70	52
Southend United	46	13	13	20	54	64	52
Birmingham City	46	13	12	21	50	72	51
Luton Town	46	10	21	15	48	62	51
Sunderland	46	13	11	22	50	64	50
Brentford	46	13	10	23	52	71	49
Cambridge United	46	11	16	19	48	69	49
Bristol Rovers	46	10	11	25	55	87	41

Did you know that?

- Striker Darren Roberts scored a hat-trick on his first League start for Wolves in the televised game against Birmingham City in September. His three previous League appearances had been as a substitute.
- Midfielder Paul Birch was sent off at Charlton.
- Steve Bull and Derek Mountfield both skippered Wolves.
- Keith Downing was transferred to Birmingham City and Andy Mutch to Swindon Town, the latter after scoring 106 goals in 338 first-class games for Wolves.

Match No.	Date		Venue	Opponents	Result		Scorers
1	Aug	15	A	Brentford	W	2-0	Bull, Dennison
2		18	H	Leicester City	W	3-0	Birch (pen), Bull, Mutch
3		22	H	Swindon Town	D	2-2	Downing, Mutch
4		29	A	Oxford United	D	0-0	
5	Sep	1	A	Barnsley	W	1-0	Birch
6		5	H	Peterborough United	W	4-3	Bull, Mutch 2, Burke
7		13	A	Leicester City	D	0-0	
8		19	H	Watford	D	2-2	Bull 2
9		27	A	Birmingham City	W	4-0	Downing, Roberts 3
10	Oct	4	H	West Ham United	D	0-0	
11		10	A	Southend United	D	1-1	Mutch
12		17	H	Portsmouth	D	1-1	Birch
13		25	A	Millwall	L	0-2	
14		31	H	Derby County	L	0-2	
15	Nov	3	A	Sunderland	L	0-2	
16		7	H	Bristol Rovers	W	5-1	Bull 2, Dennison, Burke 2
17		14	A	Notts County	D	2-2	Bull, Dennison
18		22	H	Charlton Athletic	W	2-1	Roberts, Burke
19		28	H	Grimsby Town	W	2-1	Burke, Mountfield
20	Dec	5	A	Cambridge United	D	1-1	Bull
21		12	H	Luton Town	L	1-2	Blades
22		19	A	Tranmere Rovers	L	0-3	
23		26	A	Newcastle United	L	1-2	Cook
24		28	H	Bristol City	D	0-0	
25	Jan	9	A	Watford	L	1-3	Mountfield
26		17	H	Birmingham City	W	2-1	Mutch, Burke
27		27	H	Barnsley	W	1-0	Mutch
28		30	A	Swindon Town	L	0-1	
29	Feb	6	H	Brentford	L	1-2	Mutch
30		13	A	Peterborough United	W	3-2	Roberts, Burke, Philliskirk (og)
31		20	H	Oxford United	L	0-1	
32		27	H	Southend United	D	1-1	Bull
33	Mar	6	A	West Ham United	L	1-3	Bull
34		9	H	Notts County	W	3-0	Bull 2, Johnson (og)
35		13	A	Bristol Rovers	D	1-1	Bull
36		20	H	Cambridge United	L	1-2	Bull
37		23	A	Charlton Athletic	W	1-0	Dennison
38		27	H	Sunderland	W	2-1	Dennison, Sampson (og)
39	Apr	3	A	Grimsby Town	L	0-1	
40		7	A	Luton Town	D	1-1	Bull
41		10	H	Newcastle United	W	1-0	Mutch
42		12	A	Bristol City	L	0-1	
43		17	H	Tranmere Rovers	L	0-2	
44		24	A	Portsmouth	L	0-2	
45	May	1	H	Millwall	W	3-1	Burke, Bradbury 2
46		8	A	Derby County	L	0-2	

Appeara
Sub appeara
Three own-goals

FA Cup

R3	Jan	2	A	Watford	W	4-1	Downing, Bull, Mutch, Holdsworth (og)
R4		24	H	Bolton Wanderers	L	0-2	

Appeara
Sub appeara
One own-goal

League Cup

R2/1	Sep	22	A	Notts County	L	2-3	Cook (pen), Bull
R2/2	Oct	7	H	Notts County	L	0-1	

Appeara
Sub appeara

vell M	Ashley KM	Thompson AR	Downing KG	Westley SLM	Blades PA	Birch P	Cook PA	Bull SG	Mutch AT	Dennison RS	Edwards PR	Madden LD	Roberts DA	Burke MS	Mountfield DN	Bennett TMcN	Rankine SM	Jones PS	Venus M	Taylor CD	Beasant DJ	Steele TW	Simkin DS	Bradbury SD	Turner GM	
	2	3	4	5	6	7	8	9	10	11																1
	2	3	4	5	6	7	8	9	10	11																2
	2	3	4	5	6	7	8	9	10	**11**	12															3
	2	3	4	**5**	6	7	8	9	10	11		12	14													4
	2		4	12	6	7		9	10	11	3	**5**	14	8												5
	2	14	4	12	6	7	8	9	10		3	**5**		11												6
	2		4	5		7	8	9	10		3			**11**	6	12										7
	2		**4**	5		7	8	9	10	12	3		14		6		11									8
	2	14	4			7	8	9		12	3	5	**10**		6		11									9
	2		4		6	7	8	9	12		3		**10**		5		11									10
	2		**4**		6	7	8	9	10	12	3				5		11									11
	2		**4**		6	7	8	9	10	12	3				5		11									12
	2		4		6	7	8	9	10	12	3				5		**11**									13
	2		4		6	**7**	8	9	10	11	3			12	5		14									14
	2				6	7	8	9	10	11	3			12	5		**4**	1								15
	2				6	7	8	9	**10**	11	3		12	4	5			1								16
	2				6	7	8	9		11	3		**10**	4	5		12	1								17
	2				6	7	8	9		11	3		10	4	5			1								18
	2				6	7	8	9		11	3		10	4	5			1								19
	2		12		6	7	8	9		**11**	3		10	4	5			1								20
	2		11		6	7	8	9			**3**	12	10	4	5			1								21
	2		7		6		8	9			3		**10**	4	5			1	11	12						22
	2		10		12		8	9	14		3	6		4	**5**		7	1	11							23
	2		7		6		8	9	12		3	5		4			10	1	11							24
		3	7		6	11	**8**	9	10			2		12	5		4	1								25
			7			**11**	8	9	10	12	3	6		2	5		4				1					26
			7		12		8	9	10	11	3	6	14	2	5		**4**				1					27
			7		2		8	9	10	**11**	3	6	12	4	5						1					28
			7		2		8	9	10	11	3	6		4	5		12				1					29
			7		2		8		10	11	3	6	9	4	5			1				12				30
					2		8		10	11	3	6	9	4	5		12	1				**7**				31
					2		8	9	10	11	3	6		4	5		7	1								32
		10			2		8	9	12	11		6		4	5		**7**		3							33
		10	5		2		8	9	12	11	**3**	6		4			7									34
		3	5		2		8	9	10	11		6		4	12		**7**									35
	5	14			**2**		8	9	10	11	3	6		4	12		7									36
	6	12			2	4	8		10	11	**3**		9	14	5		7									37
	6	3			2	4	8		10	11			**9**	12	5		7									38
	6		8		2	4		9	10	11					5		7		3							39
		12	4		6		8	**9**	10	11					5		7		3				2			40
		9	4		6		8		10	11		12			5		7		3				**2**			41
		9	4		**6**	14	8		10	11		12			5		7		3				2			42
		9				**7**	8		10	11	14	6	12	4	5				3				2			43
		9					8		10	11	7	**6**	14	4	5				3			12	2			44
		9			5		8		10	11	3		12	4				1	6				2	**7**		45
		9			5		8		10		3	14		4				1	6			12	2	**7**	11	46
	28	15	30	6	38	27	44	36	34	31	33	19	12	27	34		23	16	12		4	1	7	2	1	
		5	1	2	2	1			5	6	2	5	9	5	2	1	4			1		3				
			2		1	3	1	16	9	5			5	8	2									2		

vell M	Ashley KM	Thompson AR	Downing KG	Westley SLM	Blades PA	Birch P	Cook PA	Bull SG	Mutch AT	Dennison RS	Edwards PR	Madden LD	Roberts DA	Burke MS	Mountfield DN	Bennett TMcN	Rankine SM	Jones PS	Venus M	Taylor CD	Beasant DJ	Steele TW	Simkin DS	Bradbury SD	Turner GM	
			7		6	12	8	9	10		3	2			5		4	1	**11**							R3
			7				8	9	10	11	3	6		2	5		4				1					R4
			2		1		2	2	2	1	2	2		1	2		2	1	1		1					
						1																				
			1					1	1																	

vell M	Ashley KM	Thompson AR	Downing KG	Westley SLM	Blades PA	Birch P	Cook PA	Bull SG	Mutch AT	Dennison RS	Edwards PR	Madden LD	Roberts DA	Burke MS	Mountfield DN	Bennett TMcN	Rankine SM	Jones PS	Venus M	Taylor CD	Beasant DJ	Steele TW	Simkin DS	Bradbury SD	Turner GM	
	2		4			7	8	9	10	12	3	5			6		**11**									R2/1
	2		4		**6**	7	8	9	10	14	3		12		5		11									R2/2
	2		2		1	2	2	2	2		2	1			2		2									
										2			1													
							1	1																		

1993-94

Division One

Manager: Graham Turner (to March) then Peter Shirtliff (caretaker manager) then Graham Taylor

	P	W	D	L	F	A	Pts
Crystal Palace	46	27	9	10	73	46	90
Nottingham Forest	46	23	14	9	74	49	83
Millwall	46	19	17	10	58	49	74
Leicester City	46	19	16	11	72	59	73
Tranmere Rovers	46	21	9	16	69	53	72
Derby County	46	20	11	15	73	68	71
Notts County	46	20	8	18	65	69	68
Wolverhampton Wanderers	46	17	17	12	60	47	68
Middlesbrough	46	18	13	15	66	54	67
Stoke City	46	18	13	15	57	59	67
Charlton Athletic	46	19	8	19	61	58	65
Sunderland	46	19	8	19	54	57	65
Bristol City	46	16	16	14	47	50	64
Bolton Wanderers	46	15	14	17	63	64	59
Southend United	46	17	8	21	63	67	59
Grimsby Town	46	13	20	13	52	47	59
Portsmouth	46	15	13	18	52	58	58
Barnsley	46	16	7	23	55	67	55
Watford	46	15	9	22	66	80	54
Luton Town	46	14	11	21	56	60	53
West Bromwich Albion	46	13	12	21	60	69	51
Birmingham City	46	13	12	21	52	69	51
Oxford United	46	13	10	23	54	75	49
Peterborough United	46	8	13	25	48	76	37

Did you know that?

- Despite missing 20 games through injury, Steve Bull still finished up as Wolves' leading scorer with 15 goals.
- Wolves striker Cyrille Regis became the first player to appear in League games for four West Midlands clubs, having earlier assisted West Bromwich Albion, Coventry City and Aston Villa.
- The rebuilding of the 'new' Molineux was completed in December 1993.

Match No.	Date		Venue	Opponents	Result		Scorers
1	Aug	14	H	Bristol City	W	3-1	Mountfield, Bull 2
2		22	A	Birmingham City	D	2-2	Venus, Thomas
3		25	H	Millwall	W	2-0	Bull, D.Kelly
4		28	H	Middlesbrough	L	2-3	Thomas, D.Kelly
5	Sep	5	A	West Bromwich Albion	L	2-3	Thomas, Bull
6		7	A	Watford	L	0-1	
7		11	H	Portsmouth	D	1-1	D.Kelly
8		18	A	Sunderland	W	2-0	Thomas, Small
9		25	A	Grimsby Town	L	0-2	
10	Oct	2	H	Charlton Athletic	D	1-1	Keen
11		17	A	Crystal Palace	D	1-1	D.Kelly
12		23	H	Stoke City	D	1-1	D.Kelly
13		30	A	Southend United	D	1-1	Cook (pen)
14	Nov	2	H	Notts County	W	3-0	Birch, Bull, Keen
15		7	A	Derby County	W	4-0	Bull 3, Keen
16		10	H	Nottingham Forest	D	1-1	D.Kelly
17		13	H	Barnsley	D	1-1	D.Kelly
18		27	A	Leicester City	D	2-2	Bull 2
19	Dec	5	H	Derby County	D	2-2	Bull, D.Kelly
20		11	H	Watford	W	2-0	Bull, Dennison
21		18	A	Bristol City	L	1-2	D.Kelly
22		27	A	Tranmere Rovers	D	1-1	Bull
23		28	H	Oxford United	W	2-1	Cook (pen), Keen
24	Jan	1	A	Peterborough United	W	1-0	Regis
25		3	H	Bolton Wanderers	W	1-0	Dennison
26		15	H	Crystal Palace	W	2-0	Keen, Thompson (pen)
27		23	A	Nottingham Forest	D	0-0	
28	Feb	5	A	Stoke City	D	1-1	Blades
29		12	H	Southend United	L	0-1	
30		22	H	Birmingham City	W	3-0	D.Kelly, Keen, Regis
31		26	H	West Bromwich Albion	L	1-2	Keen
32	Mar	5	A	Middlesbrough	L	0-1	
33		15	A	Portsmouth	L	0-3	
34		19	H	Grimsby Town	D	0-0	
35		26	A	Charlton Athletic	W	1-0	Whittingham
36		29	A	Bolton Wanderers	W	3-1	Thompson, Whittingham 2
37	Apr	2	H	Tranmere Rovers	W	2-1	Mills, Whittingham
38		4	A	Oxford United	L	0-4	
39		9	H	Peterborough United	D	1-1	Whittingham
40		12	A	Luton Town	W	2-0	Burke, Whittingham
41		16	A	Notts County	W	2-0	Thompson (pen), Whittingham
42		20	A	Millwall	L	0-1	
43		23	H	Luton Town	W	1-0	Whittingham
44		30	A	Barnsley	L	0-2	
45	May	3	H	Sunderland	D	1-1	Bull
46		8	H	Leicester City	D	1-1	D.Kelly

Appeara

Sub appeara

G

FA Cup

R3	Jan	8	H	Crystal Palace	W	1-0	D.Kelly
R4		29	A	Port Vale	W	2-0	Blades, Keen
R5	Feb	19	H	Ipswich Town	D	1-1	D.Kelly
rep	Mar	2	A	Ipswich Town	W	2-1	Thompson, Mills
R6		13	A	Chelsea	L	0-1	

Appearar

Sub appearar

G

League Cup

R2/1	Sep	22	A	Swindon Town	L	0-2	
R2/2	Oct	5	H	Swindon Town	W	2-1	Mountfield, Burke

Appearar

G

Rankine SM	Venus M	Cook PA	Mountfield DN	Blades PA	Birch P	Thomas GR	Bull SG	Kelly DT	Keen KI	Regis C	Shirtliff PA	Burke MS	Thompson AR	Mills RL	Dennison RS	Small MA	Simkin DS	Kelly J	Edwards PR	Bennett TMcN	Masters NB	Marsden C	Ferguson D	Whittingham G	
2	3	4	5	6	7	8	9	**10**	11	12															1
2	3	4	5		7	8	9	**10**	11	12	6														2
2	3	**4**		5	7	8	9	10	11		6	12													3
2		4	5	6	7	8	9	10	11				3												4
2	6	4		5	7	8	**9**	10	11	12			3												5
2	6	4	12	5	7	8			11	9		10	3	14											6
2	6	**4**		5	14	8		10	11	9	3	7			12										7
2	3		5	7	12	**8**		10	11		6	4				9									8
2	3		5	7	8		**9**	10	11		6	4				12									9
	3	7	5					10	11		6	4		12		**9**	2	8							10
	3	7	5	**4**				10		9	6				11		2	8	12						11
	3	7	5					10	12	9	6		4		11		2	**8**							12
	3	7	5				9	10	14	12	6		4		11		2	**8**							13
	4	7	5		8		9	10	11		6		12				2		3						14
2	3	**7**	5		8		9	10	11		6		2						4						15
	3	8	5		7		9	10	11		6		2						4						16
	3	8	5		7		9	10	11		6		2						4						17
	3	8			**7**		9	10	11		6		2		12		5		4						18
	3			5	8		9	10	11	12	6		2		7		14		**4**						19
	3	7		5	8		9	10			**6**		2		11				4	12					20
2	3	7			8		9	10	14				2		11		5		**6**	4					21
	3	7		5	8		9	10	11		6		2								4				22
	3	8		**5**			9	10	11	12	6		2		7				4						23
	3	7		5	8		9	10	11	12	6								**4**						24
	4			5	**8**		9	10	11	14	6		3		7					12					25
	4			5			9	10	11		6		3									7	8		26
	4			5			9	10	11		6		3									7	8		27
	4			5				10	11	9	6		3									7	8		28
	4			5				10	11	9	6	14	3		12							7	8		29
2	3			5				10	11	**9**	6		2								4	7	8		30
	3			5				10	11	**9**	6		2	12	7						4		8		31
	3	12		5				10	11		6		2	14	8						**4**	7		9	32
	4	12	**5**	6	14			10	11				3									7	8	9	33
	4	8		5				10	11		6		3	9								**7**	12		34
	4	**8**		5	12			10	11		6		3	14									7	9	35
	4	**8**		5	12				11		6		3	10									7	9	36
	4	**8**		5	12				11	14	6		3	10									7	9	37
	4	**8**	5	6	14				11	12			3	10									7	9	38
		8	5	4					**11**	12	6		3	10	14								7	9	39
	4	8	14	5	7						6	11	3	10						2			12	9	40
		8	5		7		**9**				6	11	3	12						4				10	41
		8		5	7		9		12		6	11	3	14						4				10	42
		8		5	7		9				6	11	3							4				10	43
		8		5	7		9		12		6	11	3	14						4				10	44
		8		5	7		9	12	11		6		3							4				**10**	45
	12	**8**		5	7		9	10	11		6		3							4					46
	38	34	17	35	25	8	27	35	36	8	39	10	36	6	10	2	7	4	10	8	4	8	12	13	
	1	2	2		7			1	5	11		2	1	8	4	1	1		1	2			2		
	1	2	1	1	1	4	14	11	7	2		1	3	1	2	1								8	

Rankine SM	Venus M	Cook PA	Mountfield DN	Blades PA	Birch P	Thomas GR	Bull SG	Kelly DT	Keen KI	Regis C	Shirtliff PA	Burke MS	Thompson AR	Mills RL	Dennison RS	Small MA	Simkin DS	Kelly J	Edwards PR	Bennett TMcN	Masters NB	Marsden C	Ferguson D	Whittingham G	
	4	8		5			**9**	10	11	12	6		3		7										R3
	4			5			**9**	10	11	12	6		3									7	8		R4
	4			5				10	11	9	6		3		12							7	8		R5
	3	12		5				10	11		6		2	9	7								**8**		rep
	4	12		5				10	11		6		3									7	**8**	9	R6
	5	1		5			2	5	5	1	5		5	1	2							3	4	1	
		2								2					1										
				1				2	1				1	1											

Rankine SM	Venus M	Cook PA	Mountfield DN	Blades PA	Birch P	Thomas GR	Bull SG	Kelly DT	Keen KI	Regis C	Shirtliff PA	Burke MS	Thompson AR	Mills RL	Dennison RS	Small MA	Simkin DS	Kelly J	Edwards PR	Bennett TMcN	Masters NB	Marsden C	Ferguson D	Whittingham G	
	3		5	7	8			10	11		6	4				9									R2/1
	3	7	5					10	11		6	4		9			2	8							R2/2
	2	1	2	1	1			2	2		2	2		1		1	1	1							
			1									1													

1994-95

Division One

Manager: Graham Taylor

	P	W	D	L	F	A	Pts
Middlesbrough	46	23	13	10	67	40	82
Reading	46	23	10	13	58	44	79
Bolton Wanderers	46	21	14	11	67	45	77
Wolverhampton Wanderers	46	21	13	12	77	61	76
Tranmere Rovers	46	22	10	14	67	58	76
Barnsley	46	20	12	14	63	52	72
Watford	46	19	13	14	52	46	70
Sheffield United	46	17	17	12	74	55	68
Derby County	46	18	12	16	66	51	66
Grimsby Town	46	17	14	15	62	56	65
Stoke City	46	16	15	15	50	53	63
Millwall	46	16	14	16	60	60	62
Southend United	46	18	8	20	54	73	62
Oldham Athletic	46	16	13	17	60	60	61
Charlton Athletic	46	16	11	19	58	66	59
Luton Town	46	15	13	18	61	64	58
Port Vale	46	15	13	18	58	64	58
Portsmouth	46	15	13	18	53	63	58
West Bromwich Albion	46	16	10	20	51	57	58
Sunderland	46	12	18	16	41	45	54
Swindon Town	46	12	12	22	54	73	48
Burnley	46	11	13	22	49	74	46
Bristol City	46	11	12	23	42	63	45
Notts County	46	9	13	24	45	66	40

Did you know that?

• Dutchman John de Wolf became the first defender to score a hat-trick for Wolves since Ted Pheasant back in March 1902, when he grabbed three goals in a 4–2 win over Port Vale in February.

• In February 1995 the Wolves versus Leicester City FA Cup tie realised record gate receipts for a game at Molineux – £236,972.

• In May 1995 Wolves paid a record £1.85 million to Bradford City for defender Dean Richards, who had been on loan for two months.

• Jamie Smith was sent off in the Black Country League derby at The Hawthorns – the first Wolves player ever dismissed on Albion territory.

Match No.	Date		Venue	Opponents	Result		Scorers
1	Aug	13	H	Reading	W	1-0	Froggatt
2		21	A	Notts County	D	1-1	Thompson (pen)
3		28	H	West Bromwich Albion	W	2-0	Thompson (pen), Kelly
4		30	A	Watford	L	1-2	Emblen
5	Sep	3	A	Sunderland	D	1-1	Venus
6		10	H	Tranmere Rovers	W	2-0	Emblen, Stewart
7		13	H	Southend United	W	5-0	Emblen, Bull, Kelly, Froggatt, Walters
8		17	A	Burnley	W	1-0	Bull
9		24	A	Portsmouth	W	2-1	Kelly, Walters
10	Oct	1	H	Port Vale	W	2-1	Thompson 2 (2 pens)
11		8	A	Swindon Town	L	2-3	Kelly 2
12		15	H	Grimsby Town	W	2-1	Thompson (pen), Venus
13		22	H	Millwall	D	3-3	Bull 2, Venus
14		30	A	Stoke City	D	1-1	Bull
15	Nov	1	A	Bristol City	W	5-1	Thompson (pen), Kelly 3, Walters
16		5	H	Luton Town	L	2-3	Stewart, Johnson (og)
17		20	A	Middlesbrough	L	0-1	
18		23	H	Bolton Wanderers	W	3-1	Thompson (pen), Birch, Coleman (og)
19		27	H	Derby County	L	0-2	
20	Dec	4	A	Millwall	L	0-1	
21		10	H	Notts County	W	1-0	Bull
22		18	A	Reading	L	2-4	Bull, Quinn (og)
23		26	A	Oldham Athletic	L	1-4	Dennison
24		28	H	Charlton Athletic	W	2-0	Bull, Chapple (og)
25		31	A	Barnsley	W	3-1	Emblen, Mills, Dennison
26	Jan	2	H	Sheffield United	D	2-2	Emblen, de Wolf (pen)
27		14	H	Stoke City	W	2-0	Kelly, Dennison
28	Feb	4	A	Bolton Wanderers	L	1-5	Goodman
29		11	H	Bristol City	W	2-0	Kelly, Dennison
30		21	H	Middlesbrough	L	0-2	
31		25	A	Port Vale	W	4-2	Bull, de Wolf 3 (1 pen)
32	Mar	5	H	Portsmouth	W	1-0	Bull
33		8	H	Sunderland	W	1-0	Thompson (pen)
34		15	A	West Bromwich Albion	L	0-2	
35		18	H	Watford	D	1-1	Thomas
36		24	H	Burnley	W	2-0	Emblen, Bull
37	Apr	1	A	Southend United	W	1-0	Bull
38		4	A	Luton Town	D	3-3	Emblen, Kelly 2
39		8	H	Barnsley	D	0-0	
40		12	A	Derby County	D	3-3	Goodman, Richards 2
41		15	A	Charlton Athletic	L	2-3	Bull 2
42		17	H	Oldham Athletic	W	2-1	Kelly 2
43		22	A	Sheffield United	D	3-3	Bull, Kelly, Goodman
44		29	A	Grimsby Town	D	0-0	
45	May	3	A	Tranmere Rovers	D	1-1	Bull
46		7	H	Swindon Town	D	1-1	Thompson (pen)
							Appea
							Sub appea
							Four own-goals

owell M	Smith JJA	Thompson AR	Ferguson D	Emblen NR	Shirtliff PA	Keen KI	Thomas GR	Bull SG	Kelly DT	Froggatt SJ	Mills RL	Blades PA	Venus M	Rankine SM	Birch P	Stewart PA	Walters ME	Daley AM	Bennett TMcN	de Wolf J	Goodman DR	Jones PS	Law BJ	Cowans GS	Dennison RS	Masters NB	Wright JM	Richards DI	
	2	3	4	5	6	7	8	**9**	10	11	12																		1
	2	3	4		6		8		10	11		5	7	9															2
	2	3	4	**7**	6		8		10	11		5	12		9														3
	2	3	4	7	6		8		**10**	11		5	14	12	9														4
	2	3	11	4	6				**10**			5	8	12	7	9													5
	2	3	8	4	6			9	12	11			5			**10**	7												6
	2	3	8	4	6			9	10	11			5				7												7
	2	3	8	4	6			9	10	11			5				7												8
	2	3	8		6			9	10	11		5	4				7												9
	2	3	8		6			9		11		5	4	10			7												10
	2	3	8		6			9	10			5	4		7		11												11
	2	3	**8**		6			9	10	11		5	4	12			7												12
	2	3	8		6			9	10	11		5	4				**7**	12											13
	2	3	14	4			8	9	10	11		5	6			12	7												14
	2	3	4				8	**9**	10	11		5	6			12	7												15
	2	3	4	14			8	9	10	11		5	6			12	**7**												16
		3	**4**	7			8		10	11		5	6	2	12	9													17
		3	4	12			8		10	11		5	**6**	2	7	9													18
	12	**3**	4	14			8		10	11		5	6	2	7	9													19
	2		**4**	7			8	9	10	11	12	5	6						3										20
	2		4	6				9	12	11		14	3	**7**					10	5	8								21
	2		10	4				9		**11**	14	6	3	7	12					5	8								22
	2		**10**	4							9		3	7						5		1	6	8	11	12			23
				4				9			8	2	3						14	5	**7**	1	6	10	11	12			24
				4					12		**9**	2	3						8	5	7	1	6	10	11				25
				4					8		9	2	3							5	7	1	6	10	11				26
				4					8		9	2	3		7					5		1	6	10	11				27
		3		**4**			14		8		9	2							12	5	7	1	6	10	11				28
		3		**4**					8		14	2		7					12	5	9	1	6	10	11				29
		3			14		4		8		12		**2**	7						5	9	1	6	10	11				30
		3			6			**9**	8			2	12	4						5	7	1		10	11				31
		3			6			9	8			2		4						5	7			10	11				32
	2	3			6			9	8					4					12	**5**	7			10	11		14		33
	2	3		14	6			**9**	8					4							7		5	10	11		12		34
		3			6		8		9			2	14	**7**					4		10		5		11		12		35
				10	6			9	8			2	3	4							7		5		11				36
				4				9	8			2	10								7		5		11	3		6	37
				4				9	14			2	11		7						8		5	10	12	**3**		6	38
			14	**4**	12			9	8					2							7		5	10	11	3		6	39
	3				6			9	8				11	4							7		5	**10**			12	2	40
	3				**6**			9	8			12	11	4							7		5	10			14	2	41
					6			9	8				3	4							7		5	10	11			2	42
		12			6			9	8			**2**	3	4							7			10	11			5	43
		2			6			9	8				3	4							7			10	11			5	44
		2			6			9	8				3	4							7			10	11			5	45
		2			6			9	8				3	4							7			10	**11**		12	5	46
	24	30	22	23	26	1	13	31	38	20	6	30	35	24	8	5	11		4	13	24	9	17	21	21	3		10	
	1	1	2	4	2		1		4		5	2	4	3	2	3		1	4						1	2	6		
		9		7			1	16	15	2	1		3		1	2	3			4	3				4			2	

1994-95

Cont.

Match No.	Date		Venue	Opponents	Result		Scorers	Attenda
Play-offs								
SF1	May	14	H	Bolton Wanderers	W	2-1	Bull, Venus	26,1
SF2		17	A	Bolton Wanderers	L	0-2		20,0
SF2 aet								Appearanc
								Sub appearanc
								Goa

Match No.	Date		Venue	Opponents	Result		Scorers	Attenda
FA Cup								
R3	Jan	7	A	Mansfield Town	W	3-2	Kelly, Mills, Dennison	6,7
R4		30	A	Sheffield Wednesday	D	0-0		21,7
rep	Feb	8	H	Sheffield Wednesday	D	1-1	Kelly	28,1
R5		18	H	Leicester City	W	1-0	Kelly	28,5
R6	Mar	11	A	Crystal Palace	D	1-1	Cowans	14,6
rep		22	H	Crystal Palace	L	1-4	Kelly	27,5
R4 replay won 4–3 on penalties aet								Appearanc
								Sub appearanc
								Goa

Match No.	Date		Venue	Opponents	Result		Scorers	Attenda
League Cup								
R2/1	Sep	20	A	Chesterfield	W	3-1	Bull 2, Kelly	5,8
R2/2		27	H	Chesterfield	D	1-1	Froggatt	14,8
R3	Oct	26	H	Nottm Forest	L	2-3	Kelly, Birch	28,3
								Appearanc
								Sub appearanc
								Go

	…owell M	Smith JJA	Thompson AR	Ferguson D	Emblen NR	Shirtliff PA	Keen KI	Thomas GR	Bull SG	Kelly DT	Froggatt SJ	Mills RL	Blades PA	Venus M	Rankine SM	Birch P	Stewart PA	Walters ME	Daley AM	Bennett TMcN	de Wolf J	Goodman DR	Jones PS	Law BJ	Cowans GS	Dennison RS	Masters NB	Wright JM	Richards DI
SF1			2			6			9	8				3	4							7			10	11			5
SF2			2			6			9	8				3	4							7			10	**11**		12	5
			2			2			2	2				2	2							2			2	2			2
																												1	
									1					1															

	…owell M	Smith JJA	Thompson AR	Ferguson D	Emblen NR	Shirtliff PA	Keen KI	Thomas GR	Bull SG	Kelly DT	Froggatt SJ	Mills RL	Blades PA	Venus M	Rankine SM	Birch P	Stewart PA	Walters ME	Daley AM	Bennett TMcN	de Wolf J	Goodman DR	Jones PS	Law BJ	Cowans GS	Dennison RS	Masters NB	Wright JM	Richards DI
R3					4					8		9	2	3	12						**5**	7	1	6	10	11			
R4			3		4					8		9	2	12		**7**					5	14	1	6	10	11			
rep			3		4					8		12	**2**		7					14	5	9	1	6	10	11			
R5			3							8				2	7					4	5	9	1	6	10	11			
R6		2	3		12	6			9	8					4							7		5	10	**11**			
rep			3		12	6			9	8				10	2					**4**		7		5		11			
		1	5		3	2			2	6		2	3	3	4	1				2	4	5	4	6	5	6			
					2							1		1	1					1		1							
										4		1													1	1			

	…owell M	Smith JJA	Thompson AR	Ferguson D	Emblen NR	Shirtliff PA	Keen KI	Thomas GR	Bull SG	Kelly DT	Froggatt SJ	Mills RL	Blades PA	Venus M	Rankine SM	Birch P	Stewart PA	Walters ME	Daley AM	Bennett TMcN	de Wolf J	Goodman DR	Jones PS	Law BJ	Cowans GS	Dennison RS	Masters NB	Wright JM	Richards DI
R2/1		2	3	8	**4**	6			9	10	11		12	5		7													
R2/2		2	3	8		6	14		**9**	10	11		5	4	12	7													
R3		2	3	**6**	12			8	9	10	11		5	4		7													
		3	3	3	1	2		1	3	3	3		2	3		3													
					1		1						1		1														
									2	2	1					1													

1995-96

Division One

Manager: Graham Taylor (to November) then Bobby Downes (caretaker to December) then Mark McGhee

	P	W	D	L	F	A	Pts
Sunderland	46	22	17	7	59	33	83
Derby County	46	21	16	9	71	51	79
Crystal Palace	46	20	15	11	67	48	75
Stoke City	46	20	13	13	60	49	73
Leicester City	46	19	14	13	66	60	71
Charlton Athletic	46	17	20	9	57	45	71
Ipswich Town	46	19	12	15	79	69	69
Huddersfield Town	46	17	12	17	61	58	63
Sheffield United	46	16	14	16	57	54	62
Barnsley	46	14	18	14	60	66	60
West Bromwich Albion	46	16	12	18	60	68	60
Port Vale	46	15	15	16	59	66	60
Tranmere Rovers	46	14	17	15	64	60	59
Southend United	46	15	14	17	52	61	59
Birmingham City	46	15	13	18	61	64	58
Norwich City	46	14	15	17	59	55	57
Grimsby Town	46	14	14	18	55	69	56
Oldham Athletic	46	14	14	18	54	50	56
Reading	46	13	17	16	54	63	56
Wolverhampton Wanderers	46	13	16	17	56	62	55
Portsmouth	46	13	13	20	61	69	52
Millwall	46	13	13	20	43	63	52
Watford	46	10	18	18	62	70	48
Luton Town	46	11	12	23	40	64	45

Did you know that?

- Wolves had three players sent off early in the season – Geoff Thomas against Sunderland, Steve Bull against Norwich City and Mark Rankine against Port Vale.
- This season saw the three-substitute rule introduced.
- The Wolves versus Tottenham Hotspur FA Cup tie on 7 February produced record gate receipts for a game at Molineux – £276,168.

Match No.	Date		Venue	Opponents	Result		Scorers	Attenda
1	Aug	12	A	Tranmere Rovers	D	2-2	Bull, Goodman	11,8
2		20	H	West Bromwich Albion	D	1-1	Mardon (og)	26,3
3		26	A	Sunderland	L	0-2		16,8
4		30	H	Derby County	W	3-0	Daley, Goodman, de Wolf	26,0
5	Sep	2	A	Leicester City	L	0-1		19,2
6		9	H	Grimsby Town	W	4-1	Bull 2, Goodman 2	23,6
7		13	H	Norwich City	L	0-2		27,0
8		16	A	Southend United	L	1-2	Goodman	6,3
9		23	H	Luton Town	D	0-0		23,6
10		30	A	Port Vale	D	2-2	Daley, Goodman	11,7
11	Oct	7	A	Ipswich Town	W	2-1	Goodman, Atkins	15,2
12		14	H	Stoke City	L	1-4	Thompson (pen)	26,4
13		21	A	Watford	D	1-1	Daley	11,3
14		28	H	Sheffield United	W	1-0	Bull	23,8
15	Nov	4	A	Barnsley	L	0-1		9,6
16		12	H	Charlton Athletic	D	0-0		20,4
17		18	H	Oldham Athletic	L	1-3	Emblen	23,1
18		22	A	Crystal Palace	L	2-3	Thompson (pen), Young	13,3
19		25	A	Huddersfield Town	L	1-2	Bull	16,4
20	Dec	3	H	Ipswich Town	D	2-2	Goodman 2	20,8
21		10	A	Luton Town	W	3-2	Richards, Bull, Goodman	6,9
22		16	H	Port Vale	L	0-1		23,8
23		26	H	Millwall	D	1-1	Bull	25,5
24		30	H	Portsmouth	D	2-2	Bull, Goodman	24,7
25	Jan	13	A	West Bromwich Albion	D	0-0		21,6
26		20	H	Tranmere Rovers	W	2-1	Bull, Goodman	24,1
27	Feb	3	H	Sunderland	W	3-0	Thompson (pen), Goodman, Atkins	26,5
28		10	A	Derby County	D	0-0		17,4
29		17	A	Norwich City	W	3-2	Bull 2, Goodman	14,6
30		21	H	Leicester City	L	2-3	Bull, Law	27,3
31		24	H	Southend United	W	2-0	Thompson, Young	24,6
32	Mar	2	A	Millwall	W	1-0	Bull	9,1
33		5	A	Birmingham City	L	0-2		22,0
34		9	H	Reading	D	1-1	Atkins	25,9
35		12	A	Grimsby Town	L	0-3		5,5
36		16	A	Portsmouth	W	2-0	Emblen, Goodman	11,7
37		23	H	Birmingham City	W	3-2	Thompson (pen), Bull, Goodman	26,2
38		30	H	Watford	W	3-0	Froggatt, Osborn 2	25,8
39	Apr	3	A	Stoke City	L	0-2		16,3
40		6	A	Sheffield United	L	1-2	Thompson (pen)	16,
41		8	H	Barnsley	D	2-2	Bull, Ferguson (pen)	23,7
42		13	A	Oldham Athletic	D	0-0		7,
43		20	H	Crystal Palace	L	0-2		24,3
44		27	H	Huddersfield Town	D	0-0		25,
45		30	A	Reading	L	0-3		12,
46	May	5	A	Charlton Athletic	D	1-1	Crowe	14,
								Appearan
								Sub appearan
							One own-goal	Go

	Thompson AR	Masters NB	Emblen NR	Shirtliff PA	Richards DI	Daley AM	Kelly DT	Bull SG	Cowans GS	Goodman DR	Stowell M	Froggatt SJ	Rankine SM	de Wolf J	Thomas GR	Ferguson D	Pearce DA	Smith JJA	Young E	Atkins MN	Wright JM	Williams MF	Venus M	Birch P	Foley DJ	Law BJ	Osborn SE	Samways V	Corica SC	Crowe GM	Dennison RS
1	2	3	4	5	6	7	8	9	10	11																					
2	2	3	4	5	6	7	**8**	9	10	11	1	12																			
3	2	**3**			6	13	8	9	10	7	1	11	4	5	12																
4	[illegible]		4		6	7		9		8	1	11	**2**	5		10	12														
5	[illegible]		**4**		6	7	13	9		8	1		2	5	12	10	11														
6					6	7		9	12	8	1	11	4	5		10	**3**														
7			12		6	7	13	9	14	8	1	11	4	5		*10*	**3**														
8					6	7		9		8	1	11	4			10		2	5												
9					6	7		9	12	8	1		2			10			5	**4**	11	13									
10	[illegible]				6	7			9	8	1		2			10			5	4		**11**	12								
11					6	**7**			12	8	1		2			10			5	4	13	11	9								
12			2		6			12	13	8	*1*					**10**		14	5	4	7	11	9								
13	[illegible]				6	7		9	10	8			2						5	4				11							
14			12		**6**			9	10	8			2						5	4	7			11							
15	[illegible]		12			**7**		9	10	8			2	6					5	4	13			11							
16	[illegible]		9			7		12	10	8			**2**	6					5	4	13	11									
17			4			11		9	10	8			2	6					5	12		*13*		**7**	14						
18			4		12			9	10	8			2	6					5		**11**			7	13						
19			4		6			9		8			2	5		12				10			7		**11**						
20			**11**		6			9		8	1		2			4				10			7	12		5					
21			11		6			9		8	1		2			4				10			7			5					
22			11		6	12		9		8	1		2	**5**		4				10			7	13							
23			5		6	*7*		9	12	8	1		14			13				4			2				10	**11**			
24			5		6	**7**		9		8	1		13			12				4			2				10	11			
25					6			9		8	1		2			**10**			4	12			5		13		7	11			
26					6			9		8	1		2			10			4	11			5				7				
27			5					9		8	1		2			10			4	11			6				7				
28			5					9		8	1			6		10			4	11			3				7				
29			5					9		8	1			**6**		10			3	4						12	11		7		
30			5					9		8	1	12							4	10		13	3			6	11		**7**		
31			5					9		8	1					10			4	3						6	11		7		
32			5		**6**			9		8	1					10			4	3						12	11		7		
33			5					9		8	1	12				10			4	**3**		13				6	11		7		
34			5		6			9		8	1	12				**10**			4	3							11		7		
35			**5**		6			9		8	1	13				10		12	4	7		14	*3*				11				
36			5		6			9		8	1	10						2	4								11		7		
37			5		6			9		8	1	10						2	**4**	12							11		7		
38			5		6			9		8	1	10				12		2	4				13				11		**7**		
39					6			9		8	1	10	12			13		*2*	4	14			5				**11**		7		
40					6			9		8	1	3	12	*5*		11		13	4	**10**		14							7		
41					6			9		8	1	3	5			11		2	4	**10**			12						7		
42			5		6			9		8	1	10	12			11		2	4			13							**7**		
43			5		6			9		12	1	3	*8*	13								**10**	4		14		11		7		
44			5		6			9		**8**	1		10			12		3					4				11		7		
45			5		6			9			1		**10**			8		3		12			4				11		7	13	
46					6			9			1		*10*			12	13	3	5	14			4				11		**7**	8	
		3	30	2	36	16	3	42	10	43	38	13	27	14		26	3	10	30	26	4	5	19	5	1	5	21	3	17	1	
			3		1	2	2	2	6	1		5	5	1	2	7	2	3		6	3	7	3	2	4	2				1	
			2		1	3		15		16		1		1		1			2	3						1	2			1	

1995-96

Cont.

Match No.	Date		Venue	Opponents	Result		Scorers	Atte
FA Cup								
R3	Jan	6	A	Birmingham City	D	1-1	Bull	21
rep		17	H	Birmingham City	W	2-1	Bull, Ferguson	28
R4		27	A	Tottenham Hotspur	D	1-1	Goodman	32
rep	Feb	7	H	Tottenham Hotspur	L	0-2		27
								Appeara
								Sub appeara
								G

Match No.	Date		Venue	Opponents	Result		Scorers	Atte
League Cup								
R2/1	Sep	20	H	Fulham	W	2-0	Goodman, Wright	20
R2/2	Oct	3	A	Fulham	W	5-1	Daley, Goodman 2, Williams, Atkins	[illegible]
R3		25	H	Charlton Athletic	D	0-0		2
rep	Nov	8	A	Charlton Athletic	W	2-1	Emblen, Atkins	1
R4		29	H	Coventry City	W	2-1	Ferguson, Venus	2
R5	Jan	10	A	Aston Villa	L	0-1		3
R3 replay aet								Appeara
								Sub appeara
								G

Jones PS	Thompson AR	Masters NB	Emblen NR	Shirtliff PA	Richards DI	Daley AM	Kelly DT	Bull SG	Cowans GS	Goodman DR	Stowell M	Froggatt SJ	Rankine SM	de Wolf J	Thomas GR	Ferguson D	Pearce DA	Smith JJA	Young E	Atkins MN	Wright JM	Williams MF	Venus M	Birch P	Foley DJ	Law BJ	Osborn SE	Samways V	Corica SC	Crowe GM	Dennison RS	
	2		**5**		6			9		8	1		*12*			13	11		3	4		7			14		10					R3
	3							9		8	1		2			10			4	11			5			6	7					rep
	3		5		6			9		8	1		2			10			4	7							11					R4
	3		5			12		9		8	1		**2**			10			4	7			6				11					rep
	4		3		2			4		4	4		3			3	1		4	4		1	2			1	4					
						1							1			1									1							
								2		1						1																

Jones PS	Thompson AR	Masters NB	Emblen NR	Shirtliff PA	Richards DI	Daley AM	Kelly DT	Bull SG	Cowans GS	Goodman DR	Stowell M	Froggatt SJ	Rankine SM	de Wolf J	Thomas GR	Ferguson D	Pearce DA	Smith JJA	Young E	Atkins MN	Wright JM	Williams MF	Venus M	Birch P	Foley DJ	Law BJ	Osborn SE	Samways V	Corica SC	Crowe GM	Dennison RS	
	3		12		6	7		9		8	1		4			10		**2**	5		11	13										R2/1
	3				6	7				8	1		2			10			5	4		11	9									R2/2
1	3				6	7		9	10	8			2						5	4	12			**11**								R3
1	3		9			7		13	10	8			2	**6**					5	4		11		12								rep
	3				6			9		8	1		2			4				10			7	11		5						R4
	2				6			9		8	1		7			10	*11*		3	4			5		13	12					14	R5
2	6		1		5	4		4	2	6	4		6	1		4	1	1	5	5	1	2	3	2		1						
			1					1													1	1		1	1	1					1	
			1			1				3						1				2	1	1	1									

1996-97

Division One

Manager: Mark McGhee

Match No.	Date		Venue	Opponents	Result		Scorers	Attend
1	Aug	17	A	Grimsby Town	W	3-1	Bull 3	7,9
2		24	H	Bradford City	W	1-0	Bull	24,1
3		28	H	Queen's Park Rangers	D	1-1	Osborn	25,7
4		31	A	Norwich City	L	0-1		14,4
5	Sep	6	H	Charlton Athletic	W	1-0	Thompson (pen)	21,0
6		10	A	Oxford United	D	1-1	Roberts	7,4
7		15	A	West Bromwich Albion	W	4-2	Bull, Roberts 3	20,7
8		21	H	Sheffield United	L	1-2	Thompson (pen)	25,1
9		27	A	Swindon Town	W	2-1	Ferguson, Foley	9,2
10	Oct	2	H	Bolton Wanderers	L	1-2	Ferguson	26,5
11		5	H	Reading	L	0-1		23,1
12		13	A	Southend United	D	1-1	Bull	5,3
13		15	A	Portsmouth	W	2-0	Bull 2	7,4
14		19	H	Port Vale	L	0-1		22,7
15		27	A	Manchester City	W	1-0	Bull	27,2
16		30	H	Huddersfield Town	D	0-0		22,3
17	Nov	2	H	Barnsley	D	3-3	Bull, Roberts, Goodman	22,8
18		17	H	Birmingham City	L	1-2	Bull	22,6
19		23	A	Crystal Palace	W	3-2	Corica 2, Thomas	21,4
20	Dec	1	H	Manchester City	W	3-0	Roberts 2, Dennison	23,9
21		7	A	Ipswich Town	D	0-0		11,8
22		14	H	Oldham Athletic	L	0-1		22,5
23		21	A	Tranmere Rovers	W	2-0	Bull, Osborn (pen)	9,6
24		26	H	Oxford United	W	3-1	Osborn 2, Goodman	26,5
25		28	A	Charlton Athletic	D	0-0		12,2
26	Jan	12	H	West Bromwich Albion	W	2-0	Richards, Roberts	27,3
27		18	A	Bolton Wanderers	L	0-3		18,9
28		24	A	Sheffield United	W	3-2	Atkins, Bull, Osborn	17,4
29		29	H	Swindon Town	W	1-0	Bull	23,0
30	Feb	1	H	Stoke City	W	2-0	Bull 2	27,4
31		8	A	Huddersfield Town	W	2-0	Froggatt, Bull	15,2
32		15	H	Crystal Palace	L	0-3		25,9
33		22	A	Barnsley	W	3-1	Froggatt, Bull, Roberts	17,8
34	Mar	1	H	Ipswich Town	D	0-0		26,7
35		4	A	Birmingham City	W	2-1	Bull, Goodman	19,8
36		8	H	Tranmere Rovers	W	3-2	Bull 2, Roberts	26,1
37		15	A	Oldham Athletic	L	2-3	Bull, Roberts	9,6
38		18	A	Stoke City	L	0-1		15,6
39		22	A	Bradford City	L	1-2	Goodman	15,3
40		31	A	Queen's Park Rangers	D	2-2	Curle (pen), Goodman	17,3
41	Apr	5	H	Norwich City	W	3-2	Roberts, Curle (pen), Thomas	26,9
42		12	A	Reading	L	1-2	Atkins	14,8
43		19	H	Southend United	W	4-1	Atkins, Bull, Ferguson, Goodman	25,0
44		23	H	Grimsby Town	D	1-1	Gilkes	25,4
45		27	A	Port Vale	W	2-1	Atkins, Thomas	13,6
46	May	4	H	Portsmouth	L	0-1		26,0

Appearance

Sub appearanc

Goa

	P	W	D	L	F	A	Pts
Bolton Wanderers	46	28	14	4	100	53	98
Barnsley	46	22	14	10	76	55	80
Wolverhampton Wanderers	46	22	10	14	68	51	76
Ipswich Town	46	20	14	12	68	50	74
Sheffield United	46	20	13	13	75	52	73
Crystal Palace	46	19	14	13	78	48	71
Portsmouth	46	20	8	18	59	53	68
Port Vale	46	17	16	13	58	55	67
Queen's Park Rangers	46	18	12	16	64	60	66
Birmingham City	46	17	15	14	52	48	66
Tranmere Rovers	46	17	14	15	63	56	65
Stoke City	46	18	10	18	51	57	64
Norwich City	46	17	12	17	63	68	63
Manchester City	46	17	10	19	59	60	61
Charlton Athletic	46	16	11	19	52	66	59
West Bromwich Albion	46	14	15	17	68	72	57
Oxford United	46	16	9	21	64	68	57
Reading	46	15	12	19	58	67	57
Swindon Town	46	15	9	22	52	71	54
Huddersfield Town	46	13	15	18	48	61	54
Bradford City	46	12	12	22	47	72	48
Grimsby Town	46	11	13	22	60	81	46
Oldham Athletic	46	10	13	23	51	66	43
Southend United	46	8	15	23	42	86	39

Did you know that?

- Defender Dean Richards was appointed captain in place of John de Wolf.
- In February 1997, Steve Bull celebrated his 500th appearance for Wolves with a goal against Huddersfield Town.
- Wolves suffered their 100th defeat in the FA Cup against Portsmouth.
- Darren Ferguson and Bull were both sent off this term against Bolton Wanderers and Oldham Athletic respectively.
- Dutch defender de Wolf signed for Feyenoord, Paul Birch for Doncaster Rovers, Mark Rankine for Preston North End and Paul Jones for Stockport County.

Romano S	Froggatt SJ	Atkins MN	Venus M	Richards DI	Thompson AR	Corica SC	Bull SG	Roberts IW	Osborn SE	Ferguson D	Smith JJA	Curle K	Wright JM	Emblen NR	Foley DJ	Crowe GM	Van der Laan RP	Dowe J	Pearce DA	Dennison RS	Leadbeater RP	Young E	Goodman DR	Thomas GR	Williams A	Law BJ	Gilkes MEGMc	Robinson CP	
2	3	4	5	6	7	8	9	10	11	12																			1
	3	4	**5**	6	7	8	9	10	11	12	2																		2
	3	4	5	6	7	8	9	10	11		2																		3
	3	4	5	6	7	8	9	10	11		2																		4
	3	4	5	6	7	**8**	9	10	11	12	2																		5
	3	**4**	5	6	7	8	9	10	11		2	12	13																6
	3	4	5	6	7	8	9	10	11		2																		7
	3	4	5	6	7	**8**	9	10	11		2		12																8
	3	4	5	6	7	12	9	10		8	2			**11**	13														9
	3	4	5	6	7	12	9	10		8	2			**11**	13														10
12	3	4	5	6	7	*11*	9	10		8	**2**			13		14													11
12	3	4	5	6		8	9				**2**					11	7	10			13								12
12	**3**	4	5	6		8	9				2				13	11	7	10											13
		4	5			**8**	9				2				12	11	7	10	3	13		6							14
		4	5	6			9				2			8			7	**10**	3	11			12						15
		4	5	6			9		12		2			8			7	**10**	3	11			13						16
		4	5	6			9	12	11		2			10			**7**	13	*3*	14			8						17
		4	5	6	3		9	10	11		2						7			12			**8**	13					18
		4	5		2	7	9	10	11					6						3				8					19
		4	5		2	**7**	9	10	11					6				12		3				8					20
		4	5		**2**	7	9	10	11		12			6						3			13	8					21
		4	5	12		7	9	10	11		2			**6**				13		3			14	8					22
		4	5	12		7	9		11		2			6						3			10	**8**					23
		4	5			7	9		11		2			6						3			10	8					24
		4	5			7	9		11		2			6						3			10	8					25
	3		4	6	12		9	10	11		2	5		7										8					26
	3	12	4	6	13		9	10	11		2	5		*7*									14	**8**					27
	3	4			2	7	9		11			6		8									10		5				28
	3	4				7	9		11		2	6		8									10		5				29
	3	4			2	7	9	12	11			6		8									**10**		5				30
	3	4			2	7	9		11			6		8									10		5				31
	3	4	12		2	*7*	9	13	11			6		8									10	14	**5**				32
	3	4	5		12	**7**	9	10	11		2	6		*8*									13	14					33
	3	*4*	5		12	7	9	10	11		**2**	6		8									13	14					34
	3	4	5		2	7	9	12	11		13	6		8									**10**						35
		4	5		3	7	9	12	11	13	2	6		8									**10**						36
		4	5		3	*7*	9	12	11	13	2	6		**8**									10			14			37
		4	3		2	**7**	9	10	11	12		6		5						14			13	*8*					38
		4	5		3	7	9	12	11		2	6		8									**10**	13					39
	3	4	5			**7**		9	11	8	2	6											10	12		13			40
	3	4						9	**11**	8	2	5											10	6			7	12	41
	3	11	13		12			9		8	2	5											10	6		4	7		42
	3	11			12		9	13		8	2	5		*6*									10	14		4	7		43
		11	12		**3**	13	9	14		8	2	5											*10*	6		4	7		44
		4	12			7	9		13	8	2	6				10								11	*5*	14	**3**		45
		4	5		3		*9*			**8**	2		12		14	10				13				11		6		7	46
1	27	44	36	19	26	33	43	24	33	10	36	20		27		5	7	5	4	9		1	19	15	6	4	5	1	
3		1	4	2	6	3		9	2	6	2	1	3	1	5	1		3		5	1		8	7		3		1	
	2	4		1	2	2	23	12	5	3		2			1					1			6	3			1		

1996-97

Cont.

Match No.	Date		Venue	Opponents	Result		Scorers	At
Play-offs								
SF1	May	10	A	Crystal Palace	L	1-3	Bull	
SF2		14	H	Crystal Palace	W	2-1	Atkins, Williams	

Appear
Sub appear

Match No.	Date		Venue	Opponents	Result		Scorers	
FA Cup								
R3	Jan	4	H	Portsmouth	L	1-2	Ferguson	

Appeara
Sub appeara

Match No.	Date		Venue	Opponents	Result		Scorers	
League Cup								
R1/1	Aug	20	A	Swindon Town	L	0-2		
R1/2	Sep	4	H	Swindon Town	W	1-0	Osborn	

Appeara
Sub appeara

ill M	Romano S	Froggatt SJ	Atkins MN	Venus M	Richards DI	Thompson AR	Corica SC	Bull SG	Roberts IW	Osborn SE	Ferguson D	Smith JJA	Curle K	Wright JM	Emblen NR	Foley DJ	Crowe GM	Van der Laan RP	Dowe J	Pearce DA	Dennison RS	Leadbeater RP	Young E	Goodman DR	Thomas GR	Williams A	Law BJ	Gilkes MEGMc	Robinson CP	
			4			3		**9**	10	11	8	2	6			12									7	5				SF1
			4					9	10	**11**	8	2	6			12								7	3	5				SF2
			2			1		2	2	2	2	2	2											1	2	2				
																2														
			1					1																		1				
			4	5			**7**	9	13	11	12	2			6						3			10	8					R3
			1	1			1	1		1		1			1						1			1	1					
									1		1																			
											1																			
	2	3	4	5	6	7	8	9	10		11	12		13																R1/1
		3	4	5	6	7	**8**	9	10	11		2		12																R1/2
	1	2	2	2	2	2	2	2	2	1	1	1																		
												1		2																
										1																				

1997-98

Division One

Manager: Mark McGhee

	P	W	D	L	F	A	Pts
Nottingham Forest	46	28	10	8	82	42	94
Middlesbrough	46	27	10	9	77	41	91
Sunderland	46	26	12	8	86	50	90
Charlton Athletic	46	26	10	10	80	49	88
Ipswich Town	46	23	14	9	77	43	83
Sheffield United	46	19	17	10	69	54	74
Birmingham City	46	19	17	10	60	35	74
Stockport County	46	19	8	19	71	69	65
Wolverhampton Wanderers	46	18	11	17	57	53	65
West Bromwich Albion	46	16	13	17	50	56	61
Crewe Alexandra	46	18	5	23	58	65	59
Oxford United	46	16	10	20	60	64	58
Bradford City	46	14	15	17	46	59	57
Tranmere Rovers	46	14	14	18	54	57	56
Norwich City	46	14	13	19	52	69	55
Huddersfield Town	46	14	11	21	50	72	53
Bury	46	11	19	16	42	58	52
Swindon Town	46	14	10	22	42	73	52
Port Vale	46	13	10	23	56	66	49
Portsmouth	46	13	10	23	51	63	49
Queen's Park Rangers	46	10	19	17	51	63	49
Manchester City	46	12	12	22	56	57	48
Stoke City	46	11	13	22	44	74	46
Reading	46	11	9	26	39	78	42

Did you know that?

• Robbie Keane scored twice on his League debut for Wolves in a 2–0 win at Norwich in August. In the same month Wolves accepted a record £2 million fee from Crystal Palace for Neil Emblen.

• In February 1998 Steve Bull scored his 300th senior goal for Wolves against Bradford City.

• Chris and Matthew Clarke became the first set of twins to join Wolves when they signed apprentice forms on 2 June 1997.

• In September 1997 Rachael Heyhoe Flint MBE became the first female to be elected to the Wolves board of directors.

• Steve Sedgley was sent off twice this season – against Portsmouth (a) and Manchester City (h).

• Although still to make his first-team debut, defender Ryan Green becames Wales' youngest ever international when he faced Malta in Valletta on 3 June 1998 aged 17 years 226 days.

Match No.	Date		Venue	Opponents	Result		Scorers	Attend.
1	Aug	9	A	Norwich City	W	2-0	Keane 2	17,2
2		16	H	Sheffield United	D	0-0		23,1
3		24	A	West Bromwich Albion	L	0-1		21,5
4		30	H	Bury	W	4-2	Keane 2, Bull 2	21,1
5	Sep	3	H	Port Vale	D	1-1	Bull	21,5
6		7	A	Oxford United	L	0-3		6,9
7		13	H	Charlton Athletic	W	3-1	Bull 2, Froggatt	22,6
8		20	A	Sunderland	D	1-1	Melville (og)	31,2
9		27	H	Huddersfield Town	D	1-1	Bull	21,
10	Oct	4	A	Bradford City	L	0-2		15,2
11		12	A	Birmingham City	L	0-1		17,
12		18	H	Swindon Town	W	3-1	Curle, Simpson, Freedman	21,
13		22	H	Tranmere Rovers	W	2-1	Robinson, Freedman	20,
14		25	A	Stockport County	L	0-1		9,
15	Nov	1	H	Middlesbrough	W	1-0	Keane	26,
16		4	A	Crewe Alexandra	W	2-0	Freedman, Muscat	5,
17		8	A	Stoke City	L	0-3		18,
18		15	H	Ipswich Town	D	1-1	Keane	21,
19		29	H	Queen's Park Rangers	W	3-2	Goodman 2, Osborn	23,
20	Dec	6	A	Manchester City	W	1-0	Symons (og)	28,
21		9	A	Portsmouth	L	2-3	Froggatt, Westwood	8,
22		14	H	Nottingham Forest	W	2-1	Robinson, Freedman	24,
23		20	A	Reading	D	0-0		11,
24		26	H	Oxford United	W	1-0	Goodman	26,
25		28	A	Port Vale	W	2-0	Freedman, Muscat	10,
26	Jan	10	H	Norwich City	W	5-0	Keane, Goodman, Freedman 3	23,
27		17	A	Sheffield United	L	0-1		22,
28		27	A	Bury	W	3-1	Keane, Simpson 2	6,
29		31	H	West Bromwich Albion	L	0-1		28,
30	Feb	7	H	Sunderland	L	0-1		27,
31		18	H	Bradford City	W	2-1	Bull, Robinson	21,
32		21	A	Huddersfield Town	L	0-1		12,
33		28	H	Birmingham City	L	1-3	Freedman	25,
34	Mar	4	H	Stoke City	D	1-1	Freedman	21,
35		14	H	Crewe Alexandra	W	1-0	Keane	24,
36		18	A	Swindon Town	D	0-0		8,
37		21	A	Ipswich Town	L	0-3		21,
38		29	H	Portsmouth	W	2-0	Goodman, Osborn	20,
39	Apr	1	A	Queen's Park Rangers	D	0-0		12,
40		7	A	Charlton Athletic	L	0-1		13,
41		11	H	Manchester City	D	2-2	Margetson (og), Simpson	24,
42		13	A	Nottingham Forest	L	0-3		22,
43		18	H	Reading	W	3-1	Goodman 2, Muscat	19,
44		25	H	Stockport County	L	3-4	Atkins, Keane 2	22,
45		29	A	Middlesbrough	D	1-1	Atkins	29,
46	May	3	A	Tranmere Rovers	L	1-2	Goodman	11,
								Appearances
								Sub appearances
							Three own-goals	Goals

Stowell M	Smith JJA	Kubicki D	Atkins MN	Sedgley SP	Curle K	Keane RD	Ferguson D	Bull SG	Goodman DR	Froggatt SJ	Wright JM	Paatelainen MM	Robinson CP	Coleman S	Crowe GM	Diaz I	Williams A	Garcia J	Westwood CJ	Foley DJ	Freedman DA	Simpson PD	Naylor LM	Muscat KV	Corica SC	Gilkes MEGMc	Osborn SE	Richards DI	Daley AM	Segers JCA	Slater RD	Emblen NR	Claridge SE	Wright S	
1	2	3	4	5	6	7	8	9	10	11																									1
1	**2**	3	4	5	6	7	8	9	10	11	12	13																							2
1	2	3	4	5	6	**7**	8	9	10	11		12																							3
1	2	3	4	**5**		7	8	9	10	11	12		6																						4
1	2	3	4			7	8	9	**10**	11			6	5	12																				5
1	**2**	3	4			7	8	9		11	12	13	6	5		10																			6
1	2	**3**	4			7	8	9		11	12	10	6	5																					7
1	2	3	4			7	8	9				10	6	12			**5**	11	13																8
1	2	3			6	7	8	**9**	12			10	4				5	11		13															9
1	2	3	4		6	7	8	9	10			12					5	**11**																	10
1	2		4		6	7	8	9					12				5	**11**		13		10	3												11
1		3	2		6	**7**	8	9					4				5			12	10	11	13												12
1			3		6		8	9					4				5			7	10	11		2											13
1			3		6		8	9		**7**			4				5			12	10	11		2	13										14
1					6	7	8	9		3			4				5				10	11		2											15
1					6	7	8	9		3			4				5				10	11		2											16
1					6	7	8	9		3			**4**				5				10	11	12	2											17
1			2		6	9	8			7		12	4				5				10	**11**				3	13								18
1			8		6	9	12		7	3		13					5		4		10					2	**11**								19
1			8	4	6	9			7	3		12							5		10					**2**	11								20
1		**2**	8	4	6	9	12		7	3		13							5		10	14					*11*								21
1			2	4	6	9	12		7	3			5								**10**	8					11								22
1			2	4	6	**9**	12		7	3			5								10	8					11								23
1			2		6	9			7	3			4								**10**	8		12			11	5							24
1			4		6	**9**			7	3		13	12								10	8		2			11	5							25
1			4		6	*9*	8		7	3		13	12								10			2			**11**	5	14						26
1			4	11	6	**9**	8		7	3		12	13								*10*			2				5	14						27
1			12	4	6	**9**			7	3			8								10	11		2				5							28
1			12	4	6	9			7	**3**		13	8								10	11		2				5							29
1				4	6	9	8		7				11								10		3	2				5							30
1			2		6			12	**7**			9	4		13						10	8	3				11	5							31
1			8		6			12				9	7				4				**10**		3	2			11	5							32
1			4		6	**9**		12				7	8								10	13	3	2			11	5							33
			2		6	7		9				12	8								**10**	4	3	13			11	5		1					34
					6	9		12	7	4			8				5				**10**	13	3	2			11			1					35
					6			12	7	4		9	8				5				**10**		3	2			11			1					36
			12		6	13		9		7		*10*	8				5				14		**3**				11	4		1				2	37
				4	6	12		13	10	3							5					14					11			1	**7**	8	9	2	38
				4		12		9		3							5				13	7		2			**11**	6		1		8	10		39
				4	6				9	7							5				13	12	**3**	2			*11*			1	14	8	10		40
				5	6	**10**		9	7	3												4					11			1	8	12		2	41
				4	6			**9**	7	3							5				12	10		2			11			1	8				42
			12	5	6	13		14	9				**8**									7	3	2			11			1	*4*		10		43
			4		6	10		9	7				12									**8**	3	2			11			1	13	5			44
1			4		6	**10**			7	12		9										8	3	2			11					5			45
1			4	12	6		**8**	10	7	13		9										*11*	3	2								5	14		46
35	11	12	30	18	40	34	22	24	29	31		10	27	3		1	20	4	3	1	25	23	14	22		3	23	13		11	4	6	4	3	
			4	1		4	4	7	1	2	4	13	5	1	2				1	4	4	5	2	2	1		1		2		2	1	1		
			2		1	11		7	8	2			3						1		10	4		3			2								

1997-98

Cont.

FA Cup

Match No.	Date		Venue	Opponents	Result		Scorers	Attendance
R3	Jan	14	A	Darlington	W	4-0	Ferguson, Paatelainen 2, Freedman	5,018
R4		24	A	Charlton Athletic	D	1-1	Richards	15,540
rep	Feb	3	H	Charlton Athletic	W	3-0	Curle (pen), Paatelainen, Naylor	20,429
R5		14	A	Wimbledon	D	1-1	Paatelainen	15,322
rep		25	H	Wimbledon	W	2-1	Robinson, Freedman	25,112
R6	Mar	7	A	Leeds United	W	1-0	Goodman	39,902
SF	Apr	5	N	Arsenal	L	0-1		39,372

SF at Villa Park.

Appearances
Sub appearances
Goals

League Cup

Match No.	Date		Venue	Opponents	Result		Scorers	Attendance
R1/1	Aug	12	A	Queen's Park Rangers	W	2-0	Froggatt, Paatelainen	8,355
R1/2		27	H	Queen's Park Rangers	L	1-2	Ferguson (pen)	18,398
R2/1	Sep	16	A	Fulham	W	1-0	Garcia	5,933
R2/2		24	H	Fulham	W	1-0	Goodman	17,862
R3	Oct	14	A	Reading	L	2-4	Bull 2	11,080

Appearances
Sub appearances
Goals

Smith JJA	Kubicki D	Atkins MN	Sedgley SP	Curle K	Keane RD	Ferguson D	Bull SG	Goodman DR	Froggatt SJ	Wright JM	Paatelainen MM	Robinson CP	Coleman S	Crowe GM	Diaz I	Williams A	Garcia J	Westwood CJ	Foley DJ	Freedman DA	Simpson PD	Naylor LM	Muscat KV	Corica SC	Gilkes MEGMc	Osborn SE	Richards DI	Daley AM	Segers JCA	Slater RD	Emblen NR	Claridge SE	Wright S	
		4	11	6		8		**7**	3		12	9								10			2				5	13						R3
		4	11	6				7	3		9	8								10			2				5							R4
		12	4	6		8		7			9	11								10	13	3	2				**5**							rep
		2	**4**	6				7			9	10				13				12	8	3				11	5							R5
		2	**4**	6	9		14				7	8				13				*10*	12	3				11	5							rep
				6	**12**		9	7				8				4				10		3	2			11	5		1					R6
			8	6	12		13	7	3			*10*				5					9		**2**				4		1	14		11		SF
		4	6	7	1	2	1	6	3		4	7				2				5	2	4	5			3	7		2			1		
		1			2		2				1					2				1	2							1		1				
				1		1		1			4	1								2		1					1							

Smith JJA	Kubicki D	Atkins MN	Sedgley SP	Curle K	Keane RD	Ferguson D	Bull SG	Goodman DR	Froggatt SJ	Wright JM	Paatelainen MM	Robinson CP	Coleman S	Crowe GM	Diaz I	Williams A	Garcia J	Westwood CJ	Foley DJ	Freedman DA	Simpson PD	Naylor LM	Muscat KV	Corica SC	Gilkes MEGMc	Osborn SE	Richards DI	Daley AM	Segers JCA	Slater RD	Emblen NR	Claridge SE	Wright S	
2	3	4	5	6	**7**	8	9	10	11		12																							R1/1
2	3	4	5			8	9	10	11		7	6																						R1/2
2	3	4			7	8	**9**		11		10	6					13	5	12															R2/1
2	3	**4**			7	8	9	13			10	6				5	11	12																R2/2
2		4		6	12	**8**	9				10	7				5	11		13			3												R3
5	4	5	2	2	3	5	5	2	3		4	4				2	2	1				1												
					1			1			1						1	1	2															
						1	2	1	1		1								1															

1998-99

Division One

Manager: Mark McGhee (to November) then Colin Lee

	P	W	D	L	F	A	Pts
Sunderland	46	31	12	3	91	28	105
Bradford City	46	26	9	11	82	47	87
Ipswich Town	46	26	8	12	69	32	86
Birmingham City	46	23	12	11	66	37	81
Watford	46	21	14	11	65	56	77
Bolton Wanderers	46	20	16	10	78	59	76
Wolverhampton Wanderers	46	19	16	11	64	43	73
Sheffield United	46	18	13	15	71	66	67
Norwich City	46	15	17	14	62	61	62
Huddersfield Town	46	15	16	15	62	71	61
Grimsby Town	46	17	10	19	40	52	61
West Bromwich Albion	46	16	11	19	69	76	59
Barnsley	46	14	17	15	59	56	59
Crystal Palace	46	14	16	16	58	71	58
Tranmere Rovers	46	12	20	14	63	61	56
Stockport County	46	12	17	17	49	60	53
Swindon Town	46	13	11	22	59	81	50
Crewe Alexandra	46	12	12	22	54	78	48
Portsmouth	46	11	14	21	57	73	47
Queen's Park Rangers	46	12	11	23	52	61	47
Port Vale	46	13	8	25	45	75	47
Bury	46	10	17	19	35	60	47
Oxford United	46	10	14	22	48	71	44
Bristol City	46	9	15	22	57	80	42

Did you know that?

- In January 1999 the Wolves versus Arsenal FA Cup tie realised record gate receipts for a game at Molineux – £319,141.
- Wolves met Barnet in a competitive game for the first time this season.
- In February 1999 Wolves played their 2,000th home League game (against Huddersfield).
- In February 1999 Wolves invited 48 Irish schoolboys for trials at Molineux.

Match No.	Date		Venue	Opponents	Result		Scorers
1	Aug	8	H	Tranmere Rovers	W	2-0	Curle (pen), Keane
2		15	A	Oxford United	W	2-0	Bull, Osborn
3		22	H	Swindon Town	W	1-0	Curle (pen)
4		28	A	Watford	W	2-0	Bull, Keane
5		31	H	Stockport County	D	2-2	Richards, Gomez
6	Sep	8	A	Port Vale	L	1-2	Keane
7		12	H	Sunderland	D	1-1	Keane
8		19	A	Huddersfield Town	L	1-2	Keane
9		26	H	Bury	W	1-0	Bull
10		29	H	Queen's Park Rangers	L	1-2	Foley
11	Oct	3	A	Crewe Alexandra	D	0-0	
12		17	A	Portsmouth	L	0-1	
13		20	A	Crystal Palace	L	2-3	Sedgley 2
14		24	H	Grimsby Town	W	2-0	Curle (pen), Foley
15		31	H	Barnsley	D	1-1	Muscat (pen)
16	Nov	3	A	Ipswich Town	L	0-2	
17		7	A	Bristol City	W	6-1	Robinson, Connolly 4, Whittingham
18		10	H	Sheffield United	W	2-1	Robinson, Connolly
19		14	A	Norwich City	D	0-0	
20		22	H	Birmingham City	W	3-1	Robinson 2, Naylor
21		29	A	West Bromwich Albion	L	0-2	
22	Dec	5	H	Bolton Wanderers	D	1-1	Emblen
23		12	H	Norwich City	D	2-2	Keane 2
24		19	A	Bradford City	L	1-2	Keane
25		26	A	Swindon Town	L	0-1	
26		28	H	Ipswich Town	W	1-0	Muscat
27	Jan	8	A	Tranmere Rovers	W	2-1	Keane, Gomez
28		16	H	Watford	D	0-0	
29		30	A	Stockport County	W	2-1	Richards, Robinson
30	Feb	6	H	Oxford United	D	1-1	Keane
31		13	H	Port Vale	W	3-1	Curle (pen), Keane, Simpson
32		20	A	Sunderland	L	1-2	Melville (og)
33		27	H	Huddersfield Town	D	2-2	Robinson, Gray (og)
34	Mar	6	A	Queen's Park Rangers	W	1-0	Sedgley
35		13	H	Bristol City	W	3-0	Flo 2, Sebok (og)
36		16	A	Bury	D	0-0	
37		20	A	Barnsley	W	3-2	Richards, Emblen, Connolly
38		30	H	Crewe Alexandra	W	3-0	Muscat (pen), Robinson, Flo
39	Apr	3	H	Portsmouth	W	2-0	Muscat, Flo
40		5	A	Sheffield United	D	1-1	Osborn
41		10	H	Crystal Palace	D	0-0	
42		17	A	Birmingham City	W	1-0	Corica
43		25	H	West Bromwich Albion	D	1-1	Robinson
44		30	A	Bolton Wanderers	D	1-1	Corica
45	May	4	A	Grimsby Town	D	0-0	
46		9	H	Bradford City	L	2-3	Simpson, Flo

Appeara

Sub appeara

Three own-goals

FA Cup

R3	Jan	2	A	Bolton Wanderers	W	2-1	Keane 2
R4		24	H	Arsenal	L	1-2	Flo

Appeara

Sub appeara

League Cup

R1/1	Aug	11	A	Barnet	L	1-2	Osborn
R1/2		18	H	Barnet	W	5-0	Bull 3, Keane 2
R2/1	Sep	15	A	Bournemouth	D	1-1	Ferguson
R2/2		22	H	Bournemouth	L	1-2	Keane

Appeara

Sub appeara

Stowell M	Muscat KV	Froggatt SJ	Richards DI	Emblen NR	Curle K	Corica SC	Robinson CP	Bull SG	Keane RD	Osborn SE	Sedgley SP	Naylor LM	Gomez F	Connolly DJ	Gilkes MEGMc	Foley DJ	Atkins MN	Ferguson D	Whittingham G	Jones MA	Green R	Niestroj R	Flo H	Simpson PD	Williams A	
	2	3	4	5	6	**7**	8	9	10	11	12															1
	2	7	4		6			9	10	11	5	3	8													2
	2	7	4		6			9	**10**	11	5	3	8	12												3
	2	7	4		6			9	**10**	11	5	3	8	12												4
	2	7	4		6			9	10	11	5	**3**	8	12												5
	2	7	4		6			9	10	11	5	**3**	8	12												6
	2	7	4		6			9	**10**	11	5	3	8	12												7
	2	7	4		6			9	10	11	5	**3**	8	12												8
	2		4	8	6			9	10	**11**	5	3	12	7	13											9
	2		4	8	6			9	10		5	**3**	11	7	12	13										10
	2		4		6	8	7	9	10		5		11		3											11
				4	6	7	8				5	12	10	9	**3**		2	11								12
	2			**4**	6	7	8				5	12	10	9	3	13		11								13
	2		4		6	7	8				5		11	9	3	10										14
	2		4	6		7	8				5		11	9	3	10										15
	2			4	6	7	**8**			11	5	12		9	3	13			10							16
	2			4	6	7	13			11	5	3	**8**	*9*				12	10	14						17
				4	6	7	13			11	5	3	8	9				12	10		**2**					18
			4	5	6	7	8		12	11		3		9			2		**10**							19
	2		4		6	**7**	8		12	11	5	3		9					10							20
	2		4		6	12	8		**7**	11	5	3		9					10			13				21
	2		4	12	6	**7**	8		10	11	5	3		13					9							22
	2		4	12	6	7	8		10	**11**	*5*	3		13	14				9							23
			4	11	6	**7**	8		10		5	3		9	13		2		12							24
			4	7	6		8		10	11	5			9	3		2									25
	3		4	10	6	12	8			11	*5*		13		14		2		9			**7**				26
	3		12	5	6	9	8		10		13		**4**	14	11		2					7				27
	3		5		6	12	8		10	11			**4**		7		2						9			28
	3		5	**4**	6		8		10	11	12				7		2						9			29
	3		5		6		**8**		10	11	4			12	7		2						9	13		30
	3		5	12	6		**8**		10	11	4	13		14			2						*9*	7		31
	3		5	8	6				10	11	4						2						9	7		32
			5	8	6		7		**10**	11	4				3		2			12			9			33
			5	8	6	12	13		10	11	4				3		2						9	**7**		34
			5	8	6	12	13		10	**11**	4			14	3		2						9	*7*		35
			5	8	6	12			10	11	4			13	3		2						9	**7**		36
	2		5	8	6	**7**			10	11	4			13	3							12	9			37
	2		5	8		7	6			11	4	12		10	**3**							13	9	14		38
	2		5	8	6	12	7			11	**4**			10	3								9			39
	2		5	8	6	12	7			11	4			**10**	3								9			40
	2		5	8	6	12	7			11	4	13		**10**	3								9			41
	2		5	8	6	10	7	12			4				3								**9**	11		42
	2		5	8	6	10	7	12	13	14	4				3								**9**	*11*		43
	2		5	8	6	9	7		**10**	11	4				3								12			44
	2		5	8	6	12	7	13	**10**	11	4				3								9	14		45
	2		5	8	6	12	13	14	**10**	11	4				3								*9*	7		46
	37	8	40	30	44	20	29	11	30	36	41	17	17	18	25	2	15	2	9		1	2	18	8		
			1	3		11	5	4	3	1	3	6	2	14	5	3		2	1	2		3	1	3		
	4		3	2	4	2	8	3	11	2	3	1	2	6		2			1				5	2		

Stowell M	Muscat KV	Froggatt SJ	Richards DI	Emblen NR	Curle K	Corica SC	Robinson CP	Bull SG	Keane RD	Osborn SE	Sedgley SP	Naylor LM	Gomez F	Connolly DJ	Gilkes MEGMc	Foley DJ	Atkins MN	Ferguson D	Whittingham G	Jones MA	Green R	Niestroj R	Flo H	Simpson PD	Williams A	
	3			5	6	9	8		10				4		11		2					7				R3
	3		5	4	6		8		10	11	14			12	*7*		**2**						9	13		R4
	2		1	2	2	1	2		2	1			1		2		2					1	1			
											1			1										1		
									2														1			

Stowell M	Muscat KV	Froggatt SJ	Richards DI	Emblen NR	Curle K	Corica SC	Robinson CP	Bull SG	Keane RD	Osborn SE	Sedgley SP	Naylor LM	Gomez F	Connolly DJ	Gilkes MEGMc	Foley DJ	Atkins MN	Ferguson D	Whittingham G	Jones MA	Green R	Niestroj R	Flo H	Simpson PD	Williams A	
	2	12	4	5	6		8	9	10	7		**3**					13							11		R1/1
	2	7	4		6			9	10	11	5	**3**	8		12					13						R1/2
	2	7	4	13		8			*10*	11	5	**3**		9				12		14					6	R2/1
	2		4	7	6	13			10	11	**5**	3	8	9				12								R2/2
	4	2	4	2	3	1	1	2	4	4	3	4	2	2										1	1	
		1		1		1									1		1	2		2						
								3	3	1								1								

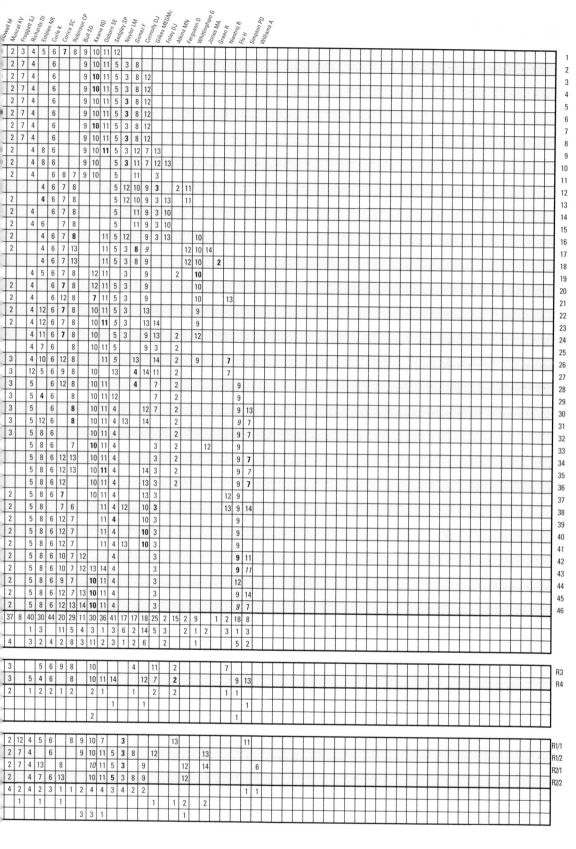

1999-2000

Division One

Manager: Colin Lee

	P	W	D	L	F	A	Pts
Charlton Athletic	46	27	10	9	79	45	91
Manchester City	46	26	11	9	78	40	89
Ipswich Town	46	25	12	9	71	42	87
Barnsley	46	24	10	12	88	67	82
Birmingham City	46	22	11	13	65	44	77
Bolton Wanderers	46	21	13	12	69	50	76
Wolverhampton Wanderers	46	21	11	14	64	48	74
Huddersfield Town	46	21	11	14	62	49	74
Fulham	46	17	16	13	49	41	67
Queen's Park Rangers	46	16	18	12	62	53	66
Blackburn Rovers	46	15	17	14	55	51	62
Norwich City	46	14	15	17	45	50	57
Tranmere Rovers	46	15	12	19	57	68	57
Nottingham Forest	46	14	14	18	53	55	56
Crystal Palace	46	13	15	18	57	67	54
Sheffield United	46	13	15	18	59	71	54
Stockport County	46	13	15	18	55	67	54
Portsmouth	46	13	12	21	55	66	51
Crewe Alexandra	46	14	9	23	46	67	51
Grimsby Town	46	13	12	21	41	67	51
West Bromwich Albion	46	10	19	17	43	60	49
Walsall	46	11	13	22	52	77	46
Port Vale	46	7	15	24	48	69	36
Swindon Town	46	8	12	26	38	77	36

Did you know that?

- Wolves missed out on a Play-off spot by just two points – the defeat at Bolton in their penultimate League game proving fatal.
- Striker Ade Akinbiyi, signed from Bristol City for a club record £3.5 million, top scored for Wolves with 16 goals in his first season with the club.
- Other new recruits this term included Darren Bazeley from Watford, Michael Branch from Everton, George Ndah from Swindon Town, Michael Oakes from Aston Villa, Ludovic Pollet from Le Havre, Andy Sinton from Tottenham Hotspur and Scott Taylor from Leicester City.
- Defender Dean Richards was transferred to Southampton in July 1999.
- Robbie Keane became the most expensive teenager in Britain when he was transferred by Wolves to Coventry City for a record fee of £6 million.

Match No.	Date		Venue	Opponents	Result		Scorers	Atten
1	Aug	8	A	Manchester City	W	1-0	Keane	31,
2		14	H	Portsmouth	D	1-1	Keane	21
3		21	A	Queen's Park Rangers	D	1-1	Corica	13,
4		28	H	Walsall	L	1-2	Robinson	24,
5	Sep	11	H	Huddersfield Town	L	0-1		20,
6		19	A	Nottingham Forest	D	1-1	Bazeley	20,
7		25	A	Sheffield United	L	0-3		14,
8		28	A	Crystal Palace	D	1-1	Akinbiyi	12,
9	Oct	3	H	West Bromwich Albion	D	1-1	Akinbiyi	25,
10		9	H	Bolton Wanderers	W	1-0	Akinbiyi	18,
11		16	A	Barnsley	W	2-1	Akinbiyi, Taylor	14,
12		19	A	Fulham	W	1-0	Emblen	13,
13		23	H	Port Vale	D	2-2	Curle (pen), Sedgley	20,
14		26	H	Sheffield United	W	1-0	Emblen	24,
15		31	A	West Bromwich Albion	D	1-1	Akinbiyi	21,
16	Nov	6	H	Grimsby Town	W	3-0	Akinbiyi 3	19,
17		20	H	Swindon Town	D	1-1	Flo	19,
18		24	A	Ipswich Town	L	0-1		15,
19		27	A	Tranmere Rovers	L	0-1		8,
20	Dec	3	H	Manchester City	W	4-1	Muscat, Akinbiyi, Branch 2	21,
21		14	A	Crewe Alexandra	L	0-1		6,
22		17	H	Birmingham City	W	2-1	Akinbiyi, Pollet	19,
23		26	A	Stockport County	L	2-3	Emblen, Pollet	10,
24		28	H	Norwich City	W	1-0	Branch	25,
25	Jan	3	A	Blackburn Rovers	D	1-1	Naylor	24,
26		11	H	Charlton Athletic	L	2-3	Flo, Pringle (og)	18,
27		15	A	Portsmouth	W	3-2	Sedgley, Akinbiyi, Branch	13,
28		22	H	Queen's Park Rangers	W	3-2	Sedgley, Akinbiyi, Branch	20,
29		29	A	Walsall	D	1-1	Emblen	9,
30	Feb	5	H	Crystal Palace	W	2-1	Sedgley, Pollet	20,
31		12	A	Charlton Athletic	L	0-2		20,
32		16	H	Tranmere Rovers	W	4-0	Naylor, Bazeley, Akinbiyi 2	18,
33		26	H	Nottingham Forest	W	3-0	Bazeley, Pollet, Branch	24,
34	Mar	4	A	Huddersfield Town	L	0-2		17,
35		7	A	Grimsby Town	L	0-1		5,
36		11	H	Ipswich Town	W	2-1	Flo 2	22,
37		18	A	Swindon Town	W	2-1	Muscat, Robinson	8,
38		21	H	Crewe Alexandra	W	2-0	Sedgley, Taylor	20,
39		25	H	Stockport County	D	2-2	Curle (pen), Emblen	25,
40	Apr	1	A	Birmingham City	L	0-1		29,
41		8	H	Blackburn Rovers	W	2-1	Muscat (pen), Nielsen	22,
42		15	A	Norwich City	L	0-1		15,
43		22	H	Barnsley	W	2-0	Akinbiyi 2	21,
44		30	H	Fulham	W	3-0	Muscat (pen), Taylor, Nielsen	19,
45	May	3	A	Bolton Wanderers	L	1-2	Pollet	18,
46		7	A	Port Vale	W	1-0	Robinson	8,
								Appearanc
								Sub appearanc
							One own-goal	Go

FA Cup

R3	Dec	11	A	Wigan Athletic	W	1-0	Robinson	10,
R4	Jan	8	A	Sheffield Wednesday	D	1-1	Sedgley	18,
rep		18	H	Sheffield Wednesday	D	0-0		25,
R4 replay lost 3–4 on penalties aet								Appearanc
								Sub appearanc
								Go

League Cup

R1/1	Aug	10	A	Wycombe Wanderers	W	1-0	Curle (pen)	4,
R1/2		24	H	Wycombe Wanderers	L	2-4	Emblen, Larkin	13,
								Appearanc
								Sub appearanc
								Go

Muscat KV	Naylor LM	Robinson CP	Curle K	Emblen NR	Bazeley DS	Osborn SE	Flo H	Keane RD	Sinton A	Sedgley SP	Corica SC	Simpson PD	Larkin C	Pollet L	Akinbiyi AP	Niestroj RW	Jones MA	Taylor SD	Ndah GE	Oakes MC	Branch PM	Andrews KJ	Williams A	Nielsen A	
2	3	4	5	6	7	**8**	9	10	11	12	13	14													1
2	3	4	5	6	7		9	10	11	8															2
2	3	4	5	6	7		9		11	8	**10**	12													3
3	12	4	5	6	2	7	9		11	13	**10**		8												4
2	**3**	4	5	6	8	7	9		11			12		13	10										5
2	3	4	5	6	8	7	12		11		**10**	13			9										6
2	3	4	5	6	8	7			**11**		*10*	12			9	13	14								7
3		12	5	8	2	11				4	10			6	9			**7**							8
3		8	5	10	2	11				4				6	9			7							9
3	12		5	8	2	11				4	10	13		6	9			**7**							10
3	12	13	**5**	8	2	11				4	*10*	14		6	9			7							11
3	12		5	8	2	11				4	**10**			6	9			7							12
3		12	5	10	2	11			13	4				6	9			**7**	8						13
3			5	10	2	11			12	4				6	9			**7**	8						14
3		12	5	10	2	11			13	4	14			**6**	9			*7*	8						15
	3	12	5	6	2	7			11	4	**10**	13			9			8							16
3			5	4	2	**7**	13		11	12	10			6	9			8							17
3		**8**	5	10	2	11	12		13	4				6	9			7							18
3		12	5	*4*	2	7	13		11	14				6	9			8		1	**10**				19
2	3		5	4	8	7			11		12			6	9			13		1	**10**				20
2	3		5	4	8	7			11					6	9					1	10				21
2	3		5	4	8	7			11					6	9			12		1	**10**				22
2	3	8	5	4	7	11	12					13		6	9					1	**10**				23
2	3	8	5	4	7		12		11					6	9					1	**10**				24
2	3	8	*5*	4	7				**11**	14		12		6	9			13		1	10				25
2	3	8	12	4	7		9		11	5	13			**6**						1	10				26
2	3	**8**	5	4	7				11	12				6	9					1	10				27
2	3	12	5	13	7	8			11	4				6	9					1	**10**				28
2	3	8		4	7				11	5				6	9					1	10				29
2	3		5	8	7				11	4				6	9					1	10				30
3		7	5	8	2		12		*11*	4		14		6	9			13		1	**10**				31
2	3	12	5	10	7		13		*11*	4		14		6	9			**8**		1					32
2	3	12	5	8	7				11	**4**	13			6	9			14		1	*10*				33
2	3		5	8	7		12		11	4				6	9			13		1	**10**				34
2	3		5	10	7					4		**11**		6	9			8		1	12				35
3		7	5	8	2		9		11	4				6						1	10				36
3	12	7	5	8	2		**9**		11	4				*6*						1	10	14	13		37
3		7	5	9	2				11	4				6				**8**		1	10	12			38
3			5	9	2				11	4				6	12			7		1	10			**8**	39
3		**7**	5	10	2				11	4				6	9				13	1	12			8	40
3		7	5	11	2		12			4				6	**9**			13		1	10			8	41
3			5	11	2	12	9			4				6				**7**		1	10			8	42
3			5	7	2	12			**11**	4				6	9			13		1	10			8	43
3	13	12	5	7	2				11	4				**6**	9			14		1	10			*8*	44
2	3	12	5	11	7					4				6	9			13		1	10			**8**	45
2	3	12	5	11	7	13				4				6	9			8		1	**10**				46
45	24	21	44	45	46	22	9	2	31	32	10	1	1	38	36			18	3	28	25			7	
	6	12	1	1		3	10		4	6	5	12		1	1	1	1	10	1		2	2	1		
4	2	3	2	5	3		4	2		5	1			5	16			3			6			2	

Muscat KV	Naylor LM	Robinson CP	Curle K	Emblen NR	Bazeley DS	Osborn SE	Flo H	Keane RD	Sinton A	Sedgley SP	Corica SC	Simpson PD	Larkin C	Pollet L	Akinbiyi AP	Niestroj RW	Jones MA	Taylor SD	Ndah GE	Oakes MC	Branch PM	Andrews KJ	Williams A	Nielsen A	
2	3	8	5	4	7		12		11		**10**	13		6	9					1					R3
2	3	8		4	7		12		11	5				6	**9**					1	10				R4
	3	**7**	5	8	2	12			*11*	4	13	14		6	9					1	10				rep
2	3	3	2	3	3				3	2	1			3	3					3	2				
						1	2				1	2													
		1								1															

Muscat KV	Naylor LM	Robinson CP	Curle K	Emblen NR	Bazeley DS	Osborn SE	Flo H	Keane RD	Sinton A	Sedgley SP	Corica SC	Simpson PD	Larkin C	Pollet L	Akinbiyi AP	Niestroj RW	Jones MA	Taylor SD	Ndah GE	Oakes MC	Branch PM	Andrews KJ	Williams A	Nielsen A	
2	3	4	5	6	7		9	12	11	8	**10**														R1/1
2	3	4	5	6	7		**9**		11	8	10	12	13												R1/2
2	2	2	2	2	2		2		2	2	2														
								1				1	1												
			1	1								1													

2000-01

Division One

Manager: Mark McGhee then Dave Jones from January

	P	W	D	L	F	A	Pts
Fulham	46	30	11	5	90	32	101
Blackburn Rovers	46	26	13	7	76	39	91
Bolton Wanderers	46	24	15	7	76	45	87
Preston North End	46	23	9	14	64	52	78
Birmingham City	46	23	9	14	59	48	78
West Bromwich Albion	46	21	11	14	60	52	74
Burnley	46	21	9	16	50	54	72
Wimbledon	46	17	18	11	71	50	69
Watford	46	20	9	17	76	67	69
Sheffield United	46	19	11	16	52	49	68
Nottingham Forest	46	20	8	18	55	53	68
Wolverhampton Wanderers	46	14	13	19	45	48	55
Gillingham	46	13	16	17	61	66	55
Crewe Alexandra	46	15	10	21	47	62	55
Norwich City	46	14	12	20	46	58	54
Barnsley	46	15	9	22	49	62	54
Sheffield Wednesday	46	15	8	23	52	71	53
Grimsby Town	46	14	10	22	43	62	52
Stockport County	46	11	18	17	58	65	51
Portsmouth	46	10	19	17	47	59	49
Crystal Palace	46	12	13	21	57	70	49
Huddersfield Town	46	11	15	20	48	57	48
Queen's Park Rangers	46	7	19	20	45	75	40
Tranmere Rovers	46	9	11	26	46	77	38

Did you know that?

- In July 2000 Wolves transferred Ade Akinbiyi to Leicester City for a record fee of £5 million.
- Dave Jones was appointed Wolves manager in January 2001 in succession to Colin Lee, and he quickly signed defender Paul Butler from Sunderland.
- Players who made an impact this season were Australian international Kevin Muscat and three youngsters – Joleon Lescott, Keith Andrews and Lee Naylor.
- Wolves rose to a high of eighth and slipped to a low of 21st in the Division this season.
- Carl Robinson and Adam Proudlock scored in all three competitions: League, FA Cup and League Cup.

Match No.	Date		Venue	Opponents	Result		Scorers	Attenda
1	Aug	13	H	Sheffield Wednesday	D	1-1	Ketsbaia	19,08
2		19	A	Stockport County	D	1-1	Bazeley	7,75
3		26	H	Burnley	W	1-0	Sedgley	20,1
4		28	A	Portsmouth	L	1-3	Ketsbaia	14,1
5	Sep	2	A	Gillingham	L	0-1		10,0
6		9	H	Tranmere Rovers	L	1-2	Robinson	17,2
7		12	H	Sheffield United	D	0-0		14,8
8		16	A	Wimbledon	D	1-1	Lescott	8,7
9		24	H	Norwich City	W	4-0	Branch, Robinson, Proudlock, Dinning	15,1
10		30	A	Nottingham Forest	D	0-0		19,1
11	Oct	14	A	Bolton Wanderers	L	1-2	Dinning (pen)	15,5
12		17	A	West Bromwich Albion	L	0-1		21,4
13		21	H	Fulham	D	0-0		21,0
14		24	A	Barnsley	W	2-1	Muscat, Ketsbaia	13,3
15		28	H	Watford	D	2-2	Muscat (pen), Dinning	20,2
16	Nov	4	A	Crewe Alexandra	L	0-2		7,1
17		11	H	Crystal Palace	L	1-3	Branch	17,6
18		18	A	Blackburn Rovers	L	0-1		20,3
19		21	H	Grimsby Town	W	2-0	Ndah, Dinning	16,0
20		25	A	Queen's Park Rangers	D	2-2	Pollet, Ndah	11,1
21	Dec	2	H	Barnsley	W	2-0	Robinson, Dinning	17,3
22		9	A	Huddersfield Town	L	0-3		11,5
23		17	H	Birmingham City	L	0-1		19,9
24		23	A	Sheffield Wednesday	W	1-0	Muscat	17,7
25		26	H	Preston North End	L	0-1		24,3
26		30	H	Stockport County	W	3-2	Branch, Proudlock, Wiss (og)	16,6
27	Jan	1	A	Burnley	W	2-1	Naylor, Proudlock	14,3
28		13	H	Portsmouth	D	1-1	Sinton	20,8
29	Feb	3	H	Gillingham	D	1-1	Branch	26,6
30		10	A	Tranmere Rovers	W	2-0	Flynn (og), Proudlock	9,6
31		20	A	Sheffield United	L	0-1		20,4
32		24	A	Norwich City	L	0-1		17,2
33	Mar	3	H	Nottingham Forest	W	2-0	Edds (og), Proudlock	20,2
34		10	A	Grimsby Town	W	2-0	Proudlock, Dinning	4,8
35		14	A	Preston North End	L	0-2		15,4
36		18	H	West Bromwich Albion	W	3-1	Pollet, Ndah 2	25,0
37	Apr	1	A	Birmingham City	W	1-0	Ndah	24,
38		4	H	Wimbledon	L	0-1		16,7
39		7	H	Huddersfield Town	L	0-1		19,3
40		14	H	Crewe Alexandra	D	0-0		20,3
41		17	A	Watford	L	2-3	Ndah (pen), Proudlock	13,7
42		21	H	Blackburn Rovers	D	0-0		20,0
43		24	A	Fulham	L	0-2		15,3
44		28	A	Crystal Palace	W	2-0	Sinton, Proudlock	18,9
45	May	1	H	Bolton Wanderers	L	0-2		16,2
46		6	H	Queen's Park Rangers	D	1-1	Lescott	17,4
								Appearanc
								Sub appearanc
							Three own-goals	Go

FA Cup

R3	Jan	7	A	Nottingham Forest	W	1-0	Proudlock	14,
R4		27	A	Wycombe Wanderers	L	1-2	Robinson	9,
								Appearanc
								Sub appearanc
								Go

League Cup

R1/1	Aug	22	H	Oxford United	L	0-1		9,
R1/2	Sep	5	A	Oxford United	W	3-1	R.Taylor, Robinson, Proudlock	4,
R2/1		26	A	Grimsby Town	L	2-3	R.Taylor 2	2,
R2/2	Oct	2	H	Grimsby Town	W	2-0	Muscat (pen), Proudlock	8,
R3	Nov	1	A	Fulham	L	2-3	Osborn, Ketsbaia	6,
								Appearan
								Sub appearan
								Go

Muscat KV	Naylor LM	Lescott JP	Pollet L	Emblen NR	Bazeley DS	Osborn SE	Ketsbaia T	Branch PM	Sinton A	Taylor SD	Taylor RA	Ndah GE	Sedgley SP	Thetis M	Camara M	Robinson CP	Larkin C	Green R	Proudlock AD	Al-Jaber SA	Dinning A	Peacock D	Butler PJ	Tudor SA	Andrews KJ	Roussel C	Connelly SP	Stowell M	
2	3	4	5	6	7	8	9	10	11																				1
2	3	5		6	7	8	10		**11**	4	9	12																	2
2	3	5		8	7		10		**11**		9	12	4	6	13														3
2	3	5		8	7	12	10			13		9	**4**	6	11	14													4
3	12	5		2	13	8	10			7		*9*	4	6	**11**		14												5
2	3	13		5	7	12		14		**8**	9		6			4		*11*	10										6
2	3	5		11	7	**8**	12		13		9		6			4			10										7
2	3	5		6	7			9	12						**8**	4		11	10	13									8
	3			5	7		8	*9*	11		12				13	4		2	**10**	14	6								9
2	3	5			7			**9**	11							4		8	10	12	6								10
	3	12	**6**	*2*	7	8	13	9	11							4			10		5	14							11
	3	12	**6**	*11*	7	8		9			13					14		2	10		4	5							12
2	3	5	6	10	7	8	9		**11**						12				13		4								13
2	3	6			7	8	9	**10**	11		12					13					4	5							14
2	3	5	6		7	8	9	10	**11**							12					4	13							15
2	3	5		6	**7**	8	9	11				13				4			12		10								16
2	3	5	**6**	11	7	8		9				12				*4*		14	13		10								17
2	3		6	**11**	7			10				9			12	4			13		8		5						18
2	3		6	11	7	8		12				**9**				4			13		10		5						19
2	3		6	11	7	8						**9**				4			12		10		5						20
2	3		6	**11**	7	8		12				9			13	4					10		5						21
2	3	12	6		**7**	*8*		11			13	9				4				14	10		5						22
2	3	5	6	11	7		12	14			*10*	9			13	4					**8**								23
2	3	5	6		7			12	11			**9**				4			10					13	8				24
2	3	5	6			12		13	*11*			9			14	4			10		8				**7**				25
2	3	5	6			12		11				9			13	4			10		**8**				7				26
2	3	5	*6*	12				11				9			13	**4**		14	10		8				7				27
2	3	5		12		8	13	9	11							4			10		6				**7**				28
2	3		6					9	**11**			12				4			10		8		5		7				29
	3	12	**6**				13	9	11							4			10		8		5		7				30
	3		6					9	11			12			13	4			10		8		5		7				31
2	3		6				12	10	11			9				**4**					8		5		7	13			32
2	3		6					7	11			9				4			10		8		5						33
	3	12	**6**					7	11						13	4			10		8		5		14	*9*			34
	3	5						7	**11**			9			12	4			10		8		6		13	14			35
	3	5	6					7	11			9				4			10						8				36
	3	5	6	12				7	**11**			9				4			10						8		2		37
	3	5	6				12	**7**	11			9				4			10						8	13	2		38
	3	5	6	12			13	7	11			9				4			10						**8**	14	2		39
	3	5	6					12	**11**			9				4			10						7	8	2		40
	12	5	**6**	3				11				9			10	4			13						7	8	2		41
	3	5		12			**8**		11			9			13	4			10		6				7				42
	3	5	6					11				9			12	4			10		**8**				7	13			43
	3	5		12			**9**	7	11							4			10		6				8				44
	3	5		12			9	7	11							**4**			10		6				8	13			45
	3	5		4			9	7	**11**								12		10		6				8		2	13	46
7	44	31	29	21	23	16	14	31	28	3	5	23	5	3	4	36		5	28		31	2	12		20	3	6		
	2	6		7	1	4	8	7	2	1	4	6			14	4	2	2	7	4		2		1	2	6		1	
	1	2	2		1		3	4	2			6	1			3			8		6								

Muscat KV	Naylor LM	Lescott JP	Pollet L	Emblen NR	Bazeley DS	Osborn SE	Ketsbaia T	Branch PM	Sinton A	Taylor SD	Taylor RA	Ndah GE	Sedgley SP	Thetis M	Camara M	Robinson CP	Larkin C	Green R	Proudlock AD	Al-Jaber SA	Dinning A	Peacock D	Butler PJ	Tudor SA	Andrews KJ	Roussel C	Connelly SP	Stowell M	
	3	5		12		**8**		9	11							4		13	10		6				7				R3
	3	5	6	2		8		9	*11*			13			14	4		12	10						**7**			1	R4
	2	2	1	1		2		2	2							2			2		1				2			1	
				1								1			1			2											
																1			1										

Muscat KV	Naylor LM	Lescott JP	Pollet L	Emblen NR	Bazeley DS	Osborn SE	Ketsbaia T	Branch PM	Sinton A	Taylor SD	Taylor RA	Ndah GE	Sedgley SP	Thetis M	Camara M	Robinson CP	Larkin C	Green R	Proudlock AD	Al-Jaber SA	Dinning A	Peacock D	Butler PJ	Tudor SA	Andrews KJ	Roussel C	Connelly SP	Stowell M	
	3	5		6	7	8	10		*11*	**4**	9	14	12			13													R1/1
	3	5			7		12			8	9		6			4		11	**10**										R1/2
	3	5		6	7		8	13	14		**9**				*11*	4			12	10								1	R2/1
	3	5		6	7			9	11							4		8	10										R2/2
	3	6		2	7	8	9	11							12	4			**10**			5							R3
	5	5		4	5	2	3	2	2	2	3		1		1	4		2	3	1		1						1	
							1	1	1			1	1		1	1			1										
						1	1				3					1			2										

2001-02

Division One

Manager: Dave Jones

	P	W	D	L	F	A	Pts
Manchester City	46	31	6	9	108	52	99
West Bromwich Albion	46	27	8	11	61	29	89
Wolverhampton Wanderers	46	25	11	10	76	43	86
Millwall	46	22	11	13	69	48	77
Birmingham City	46	21	13	12	70	49	76
Norwich City	46	22	9	15	60	51	75
Burnley	46	21	12	13	70	62	75
Preston North End	46	20	12	14	71	59	72
Wimbledon	46	18	13	15	63	57	67
Crystal Palace	46	20	6	20	70	62	66
Coventry City	46	20	6	20	59	53	66
Gillingham	46	18	10	18	64	67	64
Sheffield United	46	15	15	16	53	54	60
Watford	46	16	11	19	62	56	59
Bradford City	46	15	10	21	69	76	55
Nottingham Forest	46	12	18	16	50	51	54
Portsmouth	46	13	14	19	60	72	53
Walsall	46	13	12	21	51	71	51
Grimsby Town	46	12	14	20	50	72	50
Sheffield Wednesday	46	12	14	20	49	71	50
Rotherham United	46	10	19	17	52	66	49
Crewe Alexandra	46	12	13	21	47	76	49
Barnsley	46	11	15	20	59	86	48
Stockport County	46	6	8	32	42	102	26

Did you know that?

- Kenny Miller was bought for £3 million from Rangers in December, equalling the club's record signing.
- Record gate receipts for a game at Molineux – £369,232 – were banked from the Play-off semi-final encounter against Norwich City in May 2002.
- Wolves were never out of the top three in the League table from mid-September until the season's end.
- Midfielder Alex Rae was signed from Sunderland for £1.2 million (September).

Match No.	Date		Venue	Opponents	Result		Scorers	Atte
1	Aug	11	H	Portsmouth	D	2-2	Newton, Roussel	23
2		19	A	Coventry City	W	1-0	Robinson	22
3		25	H	Watford	W	1-0	Vega (og)	20
4		27	A	Sheffield United	D	2-2	Lescott, Roussel	16
5	Sep	8	A	Preston North End	W	2-1	Lescott, Sinton	14
6		15	H	Stockport County	D	2-2	Robinson, Blake	20
7		18	A	Gillingham	W	3-2	Newton, Miller, Blake	8
8		21	A	Walsall	W	3-0	Newton, Kennedy, Miller	8
9		25	H	Nottingham Forest	W	1-0	Newton	24
10		29	A	Rotherham United	W	3-0	Kennedy, Cameron, Rae	8
11	Oct	13	A	Bradford City	W	3-0	Proudlock 3	16
12		16	H	Crewe Alexandra	L	0-1		22
13		20	H	Crystal Palace	L	0-1		26
14		25	A	West Bromwich Albion	D	1-1	Blake	26
15		28	H	Burnley	W	3-0	Taylor (og), Rae, Cook (og)	24
16		31	H	Millwall	W	1-0	Rae	23
17	Nov	3	A	Norwich City	L	0-2		20
18		18	H	Sheffield Wednesday	D	0-0		1
19		24	A	Wimbledon	W	1-0	Sturridge	
20		27	H	Barnsley	W	4-1	Newton, Sturridge 3	1
21	Dec	2	H	West Bromwich Albion	L	0-1		27
22		7	A	Grimsby Town	D	1-1	Groves (og)	
23		11	A	Manchester City	L	0-1		3
24		16	H	Birmingham City	W	2-1	Blake, Rae	2
25		22	A	Watford	D	1-1	Newton	1
26		26	H	Preston North End	L	2-3	Blake, Sturridge	2
27		29	H	Sheffield United	W	1-0	Sturridge	2
28	Jan	13	H	Coventry City	W	3-1	Cameron, Sturridge 2	2
29		17	A	Portsmouth	W	3-2	Blake, Rae, Sturridge	1
30		29	A	Barnsley	L	0-1		1
31	Feb	2	H	Rotherham United	W	2-1	Ndah, Sturridge	2
32		7	A	Crystal Palace	W	2-0	Newton, Sturridge	1
33		16	H	Bradford City	W	3-1	Newton, Sturridge 2 (1 pen)	2
34		20	A	Crewe Alexandra	W	4-1	Kennedy, Blake 2, Rae	
35		23	A	Stockport County	W	4-1	Kennedy 2, Sturridge 2 (1 pen)	
36		26	H	Walsall	W	3-0	Blake, Sturridge 2	2
37	Mar	2	H	Gillingham	W	2-0	Blake, Rae	2
38		6	A	Nottingham Forest	D	2-2	Lescott, Sturridge	2
39		9	A	Birmingham City	D	2-2	Lescott, Butler	2
40		16	H	Grimsby Town	L	0-1		2
41		23	H	Norwich City	D	0-0		2
42		30	A	Burnley	W	3-2	Cameron, Sturridge 2	2
43	Apr	1	H	Manchester City	L	0-2		2
44		5	A	Millwall	L	0-1		1
45		14	H	Wimbledon	W	1-0	Blake	2
46		21	A	Sheffield Wednesday	D	2-2	Lescott, Cameron	2

Appeara

Sub appeara

Four own-goals (

Play-offs

SF1	Apr	28	A	Norwich City	L	1-3	Sturridge	2
SF2	May	1	H	Norwich City	W	1-0	Cooper	2

Appeara

Sub appeara

(

FA Cup

R3	Jan	5	H	Gillingham	L	0-1	1

Appeara

Sub appeara

League Cup

R1	Aug	22	H	Swindon Town	L	1-2	Dinning

Appeara

Sub appeara

(

Oakes MC	Muscat KV	Naylor LM	Robinson CP	Lescott JP	Butler PJ	Newton SO'N	Dinning T	Roussel C	Proudlock AD	Kennedy MJ	Connelly SP	Ketsbaia T	Cameron C	Sinton A	Ndah GE	Miller K	Blake NA	Rae AS	Branch PM	Sturridge DC	Camara M	Pollet L	Andrews KJ	Halle G	Cooper KL	
1	2	**3**	4	5	6	7	8	9	10	11	12															1
1	2	3	4	5	6	7	8	**9**	10	11		12														2
1	2	3	4	5	6	7	8	9	**10**	*11*		12	13	14												3
1	2	3		5	6	7	8	9	**10**				4	11	12											4
1	2	3	4	5	6	7		9	10	**11**			8	12		13										5
1	2	3	4	5	6	7			**10**	11			8			12	9									6
1	2	3	4	5	6	7		12	13	11			8			10	**9**									7
1	2	3	4	5	6	7		12	13	*11*			8			10	**9**	14								8
1	2	3	4	5	6	7			12	11			8			**10**	9									9
1	2	3	4	5	6	7		12	**10**	11			8				9	13								10
1	2	3	**4**	5	6	7			10	11			8				9	12								11
1	2	3	4	5	6	7		12	**10**	11			8				9	13								12
	2	3	**4**	5	6	7			10	11			8				9	12	13							13
1	2	3		5	6	7		12	13	11			8				**9**	4	10							14
1	2	3	12	5	6	7			13	11			**8**				9	4	10							15
1	2	3		5	6	7		12	13				8	11			**9**	4	10							16
1	2	3	12	5	6	7		13					8	**11**			9	4	10							17
1		3	12	5	6	**7**		9	*10*	11	2		8	13				4	14							18
1		3	12	5	6	7					2		**8**	13			9	4		10	11					19
1		3	12	5	*6*	7		13			**2**		8				9	4		10	11	14				20
		3		5	6	7		12		11	2		8				**9**	4		10						21
	2	3	12	5	6	7		13	10	*11*			**8**					4		9	14					22
	2	3	12	5	6	7			13				**8**				9	4		*10*	11	14				23
	2	3	8	5	6	7				11					12		**9**	4		10	13					24
	2	*3*	8	5		7				11			13		12		9	4		**10**	14	6				25
	2	3	12		6	**7**				11			8				9	4		10	13	5				26
	2				6	7		12		11			8				**9**	4		10	3	5				27
	2			5	6	7				11			8		12	13	**9**	4		10	3					28
	2			5	6	7				**11**			8		12		9	4		10	3					29
	2		8	5	6					11						12	9	4	**7**	10	3		13			30
	2			5	6	7				11			8		12	13	9	4		10	3					31
	2			5	6	7				11			*8*		12	13	**9**	4		10	3		14			32
	2			5	6	7				11			8			12	**9**			10	3		4			33
	2			5	6	7				11	12		8				9	4		10	3		13			34
	2			5	6	7				11			*8*		12	13	**9**	4		10	3		14			35
	2			5	6	**7**				11			8			12	9	4		10	3		13			36
	2			5	6	7				**11**					12	13	9	4		10	3		8			37
	2			5	6	7				11			8		12		**9**			10	3		4			38
	2			5	6	7				11			**8**				9	4		10	3		12			39
	2			5	6	7				11			13		12	14	9	4		*10*	3		**8**			40
	2			5		7					12		8		10	11	9	4			3	**6**				41
				5	6	7					*2*		8		12	13	**9**	4		10	3			14	11	42
				5	6	7							8		12	13	9	4		10	3			2	**11**	43
				5	6	7							8		12	**9**	13	*4*		10	3		14	2	11	44
				5	**6**	7							8			13	9	4		10	3	12		2	11	45
		12		5		7				*11*			8			13	9	4		10	**3**	6		2	14	46
6	37	26	15	44	43	45	4	6	12	35	5		38	3	1	5	38	31	5	27	23	5	4	4	4	
		1	8					11	7		3	2	3	4	14	15	1	5	2		4	3	7	1	1	
			2	5	1	8		2	3	5			4	1	1	2	11	7		20						

Oakes MC	Muscat KV	Naylor LM	Robinson CP	Lescott JP	Butler PJ	Newton SO'N	Dinning T	Roussel C	Proudlock AD	Kennedy MJ	Connelly SP	Ketsbaia T	Cameron C	Sinton A	Ndah GE	Miller K	Blake NA	Rae AS	Branch PM	Sturridge DC	Camara M	Pollet L	Andrews KJ	Halle G	Cooper KL	
				5	6	**7**			13				8			12	9	4		10	3			2	11	SF1
				5	6	7				13			8			12	9	4		10	3			**2**	11	SF2
				2	2	2							2				2	2		2	2			2	2	
									1	1						2										
																				1					1	

Oakes MC	Muscat KV	Naylor LM	Robinson CP	Lescott JP	Butler PJ	Newton SO'N	Dinning T	Roussel C	Proudlock AD	Kennedy MJ	Connelly SP	Ketsbaia T	Cameron C	Sinton A	Ndah GE	Miller K	Blake NA	Rae AS	Branch PM	Sturridge DC	Camara M	Pollet L	Andrews KJ	Halle G	Cooper KL	
	2				6	7		12		11			8			13	9	4		10	3	5				R3
	1				1	1				1			1				1	1		1	1	1				
								1								1										

Oakes MC	Muscat KV	Naylor LM	Robinson CP	Lescott JP	Butler PJ	Newton SO'N	Dinning T	Roussel C	Proudlock AD	Kennedy MJ	Connelly SP	Ketsbaia T	Cameron C	Sinton A	Ndah GE	Miller K	Blake NA	Rae AS	Branch PM	Sturridge DC	Camara M	Pollet L	Andrews KJ	Halle G	Cooper KL	
			4		6	7	8	13	10	11	**2**	9		12							3	5				R1
			1		1	1	1		1	1	1	1									1	1				
								1						1												
							1																			

2002-03

Division One

Manager: Dave Jones

	P	W	D	L	F	A	Pts
Portsmouth	46	29	11	6	97	45	98
Leicester City	46	26	14	6	73	40	92
Sheffield United	46	23	11	12	72	52	80
Reading	46	25	4	17	61	46	79
Wolverhampton Wanderers	46	20	16	10	81	44	76
Nottingham Forest	46	20	14	12	82	50	74
Ipswich Town	46	19	13	14	80	64	70
Norwich City	46	19	12	15	60	49	69
Millwall	46	19	9	18	59	69	66
Wimbledon	46	18	11	17	76	73	65
Gillingham	46	16	14	16	56	65	62
Preston North End	46	16	13	17	68	70	61
Watford	46	17	9	20	54	70	60
Crystal Palace	46	14	17	15	59	52	59
Rotherham United	46	15	14	17	62	62	59
Burnley	46	15	10	21	65	89	55
Walsall	46	15	9	22	57	69	54
Derby County	46	15	7	24	55	74	52
Bradford City	46	14	10	22	51	73	52
Coventry City	46	12	14	20	46	62	50
Stoke City	46	12	14	20	45	69	50
Sheffield Wednesday	46	10	16	20	56	73	46
Brighton & Hove Albion	46	11	12	23	49	67	45
Grimsby Town	46	9	12	25	48	85	39

Did you know that?

• Eighteen players scored competitive goals this season and Wolves reached the Premiership for the first time after a comprehensive 3–0 Play-off Final win over Sheffield United at the Millennium Stadium, Cardiff.

• Rotherham United defender Rob Scott 'equalised' for Wolves in the last minute of extra-time of the second-round League Cup tie at Millmoor. The Millers won the penalty shoot-out 4–2 much to Scott's relief. Wolves had led 3–1 with 11 minutes of normal time remaining.

• Two big-name signings made by Wolves this term were Paul Ince and Denis Irwin, both from Manchester United.

• Sir Jack Hayward handed over the chairmanship of the club to his son, Rick.

Match No.	Date		Venue	Opponents	Result		Scorers	Atten
1	Aug	11	A	Bradford City	D	0-0		13,
2		14	H	Walsall	W	3-1	Newton, Cameron 2	27,
3		17	H	Burnley	W	3-0	Irwin, Blake, Cooper	25,
4		24	A	Derby County	W	4-1	Rae 2, Miller, Cooper	29,
5		27	H	Sheffield Wednesday	D	2-2	Blake, Sturridge	27,
6		31	A	Wimbledon	L	2-3	Ingimarsson, Gier (og)	3,
7	Sep	14	A	Crystal Palace	L	2-4	Ingimarsson, Blake	16,
8		21	H	Reading	L	0-1		25,
9		24	H	Preston North End	W	4-0	Blake 2, Miller, Sturridge	23,
10		28	A	Leicester City	L	0-1		32,
11	Oct	5	H	Sheffield United	L	1-3	Ullathorne (og)	24,
12		19	A	Stoke City	W	2-0	Blake, Cameron	16,
13		26	H	Grimsby Town	W	4-1	Irwin, Miller, Ndah, Sturridge	23,
14		29	A	Gillingham	W	4-0	Blake 3, Cameron (pen)	10,
15	Nov	2	A	Watford	D	1-1	Cooper	16,
16		6	H	Portsmouth	D	1-1	Sturridge	27,
17		11	H	Brighton & Hove Albion	D	1-1	Miller	23,
18		16	A	Coventry City	W	2-0	Lescott, Rae	18,
19		23	H	Nottingham Forest	W	2-1	Miller, Sturridge	27,
20		30	A	Rotherham United	D	0-0		6,
21	Dec	7	H	Norwich City	W	1-0	Cole	25,
22		14	H	Coventry City	L	0-2		25,
23		21	A	Millwall	D	1-1	Kennedy	9,
24		26	A	Burnley	L	1-2	Butler	18,
25		28	H	Bradford City	L	1-2	Ndah	25,
26	Jan	1	H	Derby County	D	1-1	Ince	26,
27		11	A	Walsall	W	1-0	Ndah	11,
28		18	H	Wimbledon	D	1-1	Miller	23,
29	Feb	1	A	Sheffield Wednesday	W	4-0	Miller, Proudlock 2, Sturridge	21,
30		8	A	Brighton & Hove Albion	L	1-4	Miller	6,
31		19	A	Ipswich Town	W	4-2	Naylor, Miller 2, Ndah	27,
32		22	A	Preston North End	W	2-0	Miller, Ndah	16,
33		25	H	Watford	D	0-0		24,
34	Mar	1	H	Crystal Palace	W	4-0	Miller 3 (1 pen), Sturridge	26,
35		5	H	Ipswich Town	D	1-1	Ince	26,
36		12	A	Reading	W	1-0	Miller	19,
37		15	A	Portsmouth	L	0-1		19,
38		18	H	Stoke City	D	0-0		25,2
39		22	H	Gillingham	W	6-0	Blake, Miller 2, Cameron, Kennedy 2	25,
40	Apr	5	H	Rotherham United	D	0-0		25,9
41		8	A	Grimsby Town	W	1-0	Blake	4,9
42		11	A	Nottingham Forest	D	2-2	Blake, Cameron	27,2
43		19	H	Millwall	W	3-0	Newton 2, Cameron	27,0
44		21	A	Norwich City	W	3-0	Miller, Ndah, Sturridge	20,8
45		26	A	Sheffield United	D	3-3	Ndah, Sturridge 2 (1 pen)	22,2
46	May	4	H	Leicester City	D	1-1	Miller	28,

Appearanc

Sub appearanc

Two own-goals Goa

Irwin JD	Naylor LM	Ingimarsson I	Butler PJ	Lescott JP	Newton SO'N	Rae AS	Blake NA	Miller K	Cameron C	Ndah GE	Proudlock AD	Sturridge DC	Cooper KL	Ince PEC	Murray MW	Edworthy M	Clyde MG	Kennedy MJ	Andrews KJ	Melligan JJ	Cole CM	Pollet L	
2	3	4	6	5	7	8	9	**10**	11	12													1
2	3	4	6	5	7	8	9	**10**	11		13	12											2
2	3	4	6	5	7	8	9	**10**	*11*			12	13	14									3
2	3	11	6	5	7	4	9	12			13	**10**	14	*8*									4
2	3	4	6	5	**7**	8	9	12				10	11										5
2	3	4	6	5	**7**	8	9	12			13	10	11		1								6
2	3	11	6	5	**7**	*4*	9	13			12	10	14	8									7
2	3	11	6	5	7	4	12			**9**		10	13	8	1								8
2	3	12	6	5	7	4	9	13				10	11	**8**	1	14							9
2	3		6	5	7	4	9	12		13		**10**	11	8	1								10
3		4	6	5	**7**	8	9	10		*11*		12	14	13	1	2							11
3				5	7	4	9	**10**	11	13		12		8	1	2	6						12
3		12		5	7	**4**	9	*10*	11	13		14		8	1	2	6						13
3	12	13		5			9	*10*	4	**7**		14	11	8	1	2	6						14
3				5	12	13	9	*10*	4	**7**		14	11	8	1	2	6						15
3				5	12	4	9	10		*7*		13	**11**	8	1	2	6	14					16
3		4		5	12	8		10				9	**7**		1	2	6	11	13				17
3				5	7	4		**10**				9		8	1	2	6	11	12	13			18
3				5	**7**	8		10				9	12		1	2	6	11	4	13			19
3				5		4		**10**				9	7	8	1	2	6	11			12		20
3				5		4		**10**	13			12	7	8	1	2	6	*11*	14		9		21
3				5		4		**10**	8			12	13		1	2	6	11	7		9		22
3				5		4		12	13	14		10	**7**	8	1	2	6	11			*9*		23
3			12	5		4			13	14		10	*7*	8	1	2	6	11			9		24
	3			5				12	4	7		10	13	8	1	2	6	11			**9**		25
2	3		6	5	7			10	4	**9**				8	1			11			12		26
2	3		6	5	**7**			10	4	9	12			8	1			11					27
2	3		6	5	**7**			10	4	9	13		12	8	1			11					28
2	3		6	5	7	12		**10**	4		9	13		8	1			*11*	14				29
	3		6	5	7	12		10	4		9	13		8	1	**2**	14	11					30
2	3		6	5		*4*		**10**	7	9	12			8	1	13		11	14				31
2	3		6	5		**4**		10	7	9	12			8	1			11	13				32
2	3		6	5		**4**		10	7	9	12	13		*8*	1			11	14				33
2	3		6	5	*7*	12		10	**4**	9	13	14		8	1			11					34
2	3		6	5	7		**9**	10	4		12	13		8	1			11					35
2	3		6	5	7	4	**9**	10	*8*		12	13			1		14	11					36
3					12	4		10	**7**		13	9		8	1	2	6	11				5	37
2	3		6	5	7	**4**		10	12		13	9	14	8	1			11					38
2	3		6	5	7	12	9	*10*	**4**		13	14		8	1			11					39
2	3		6	5	7	12	9	*10*	4	14		13		**8**	1			11					40
2	3		6	5			9	**10**	4	7		12	13	8	1			11					41
2	3		6	5		4	9	**10**	7	12				8	1	13		11					42
2	3		6	5	*7*	12		10	4	9		13	14	**8**	1			11					43
2	3		6	5	7			10	4	**9**		12	13	8	1			11					44
	3		6	5		4			8	9		10	7		1	2		11					45
2	*3*		6		7	12	9	10	4			13		**8**	1	14		11				5	46
3	31	10	31	44	29	30	22	35	29	17	2	17	13	35	40	18	15	30	2		5	2	
	1	3	1		4	8	1	8	4	8	15	22	13	2		4	2	1	7	2	2		
2	1	2	1	1	3	3	12	19	7	7	2	10	3	2				3			1		

2002-03

Cont.

Match No.	Date		Venue	Opponents	Result		Scorers	Atte
Play-offs								
SF1	May	10	H	Reading	W	2-1	Murray (og), Naylor	2
SF2		14	A	Reading	W	1-0	Rae	24
F		26	N	Sheffield United	W	3-0	Blake, Miller, Kennedy	69

Final at the Millennium Stadium, Cardiff.

Appeara

Sub appeara

One own-goal G

Match No.	Date		Venue	Opponents	Result		Scorers	Atte
FA Cup								
R3	Jan	5	H	Newcastle United	W	3-2	Ndah, Ince, Kennedy	2
R4		25	H	Leicester City	W	4-1	Miller 2, Ndah 2	2
R5	Feb	16	H	Rochdale	W	3-1	Miller, Ndah, Proudlock	2
R6	Mar	9	A	Southampton	L	0-2		3

Appeara

Sub appeara

G

Match No.	Date		Venue	Opponents	Result		Scorers	Atte
League Cup								
R1	Sep	11	A	Swansea City	W	3-2	Rae, Blake, Pollet	
R2	Oct	1	A	Rotherham United	D	4-4	Newton (pen), Miller, Rae, Scott (og)	

R2 lost 4–2 on penalties aet

Appeara

Sub appeara

One own-goal G

	win JD	Naylor LM	Ingimarsson I	Butler PJ	Lescott JP	Newton SO'N	Rae AS	Blake NA	Miller K	Cameron C	Ndah GE	Proudlock AD	Sturridge DC	Cooper KL	Ince PEC	Murray MW	Edworthy M	Clyde MG	Kennedy MJ	Andrews KJ	Melligan JJ	Cole CM	Pollet L
SF1	2	3		**6**	5	13		9	*10*	4	7		14		8	1			11				12
SF2	2	3		6	5	**7**	14	9	*10*	4			13	12	8	1			11				
F	2	3		6	5	7		**9**	10	4		12	13		8	1			11				
	3	3		3	3	2		3	3	3	1				3	3			3				
						1	1					1	3	1									1
		1					1	1	1										1				

	win JD	Naylor LM	Ingimarsson I	Butler PJ	Lescott JP	Newton SO'N	Rae AS	Blake NA	Miller K	Cameron C	Ndah GE	Proudlock AD	Sturridge DC	Cooper KL	Ince PEC	Murray MW	Edworthy M	Clyde MG	Kennedy MJ	Andrews KJ	Melligan JJ	Cole CM	Pollet L
R3	2	3		**6**	5	7			10	4	9			13	8	1		12	11				
R4	2	3		6	5	7			10	4	**9**	12			8	1			11				
R5	2	3		6	5	**7**	12		10	4	9	13			8	1			11				
R6	2	3		6	5	7	12	*9*	10	8		14	13			1			11	**4**			
	4	4		4	4	4		1	4	4	3				3	4			4	1			
							2					3	1	1				1					
									3		4	1			1				1				

	win JD	Naylor LM	Ingimarsson I	Butler PJ	Lescott JP	Newton SO'N	Rae AS	Blake NA	Miller K	Cameron C	Ndah GE	Proudlock AD	Sturridge DC	Cooper KL	Ince PEC	Murray MW	Edworthy M	Clyde MG	Kennedy MJ	Andrews KJ	Melligan JJ	Cole CM	Pollet L
R1	2	3	11	6		**7**	4	9	13			12	10		8								5
R2	2	3	4	6	5	7	**8**	9	10		*11*		14		13	1	2						
		2	2	2	1	2	2	2	1		1		1		1	1	1						1
									1			1	1		1								
						1	2	1	1														1

2003-04

Premier League

Manager: Dave Jones

	P	W	D	L	F	A	Pts
Arsenal	38	26	12	0	73	26	90
Chelsea	38	24	7	7	67	30	79
Manchester United	38	23	6	9	64	35	75
Liverpool	38	16	12	10	55	37	60
Newcastle United	38	13	17	8	52	40	56
Aston Villa	38	15	11	12	48	44	56
Charlton Athletic	38	14	11	13	51	51	53
Bolton Wanderers	38	14	11	13	48	56	53
Fulham	38	14	10	14	52	46	52
Birmingham City	38	12	14	12	43	48	50
Middlesbrough	38	13	9	16	44	52	48
Southampton	38	12	11	15	44	45	47
Portsmouth	38	12	9	17	47	54	45
Tottenham Hotspur	38	13	6	19	47	57	45
Blackburn Rovers	38	12	8	18	51	59	44
Manchester City	38	9	14	15	55	54	41
Everton	38	9	12	17	45	57	39
Leicester City	38	6	15	17	48	65	33
Leeds United	38	8	9	21	40	79	33
Wolverhampton Wanderers	38	7	12	19	38	77	33

Did you know that?

• A crowd of 29,396 saw Wolves beat Manchester United 1–0 in the Premiership game on 17 January – the biggest turn-out at Molineux since the ground was redeveloped. At the same time, record receipts were registered – £399,408.

• Wolves had 10 non-British-born players on their books this season, including Henri Camara from Senegal, Ivo Ganea from Romania, the Icelander Joey Gudjonsson, the Norwegian Steffen Iversen, Hassan Kachloul from Morocco, the Ukrainian Oleg Luzny, Isaac Okoronkwo from Nigeria and the Portuguese international Rebelo Fernandes Jorge Manuel (better known as Silas).

• Wolves' highest Premiership placing was 15th – achieved after their 4–3 win over Leicester City in October.

Match No.	Date		Venue	Opponents	Result		Scorers
1	Aug	16	A	Blackburn Rovers	L	1-5	Iversen
2		23	H	Charlton Athletic	L	0-4	
3		27	A	Manchester United	L	0-1	
4		30	H	Portsmouth	D	0-0	
5	Sep	13	A	Southampton	L	0-2	
6		20	H	Chelsea	L	0-5	
7		27	A	Bolton Wanderers	D	1-1	Rae
8	Oct	4	H	Manchester City	W	1-0	Cameron
9		18	A	Fulham	D	0-0	
10		25	H	Leicester City	W	4-3	Cameron 2 (1 pen), Camara, Rae
11	Nov	1	A	Middlesbrough	L	0-2	
12		8	H	Birmingham City	D	1-1	Iversen
13		22	A	Everton	L	0-2	
14		29	H	Newcastle United	D	1-1	Blake
15	Dec	6	A	Tottenham Hotspur	L	2-5	Ince, Rae
16		14	A	Aston Villa	L	2-3	Rae, Kennedy
17		26	A	Arsenal	L	0-3	
18		28	H	Leeds United	W	3-1	Smith (og), Iversen 2
19	Jan	7	H	Blackburn Rovers	D	2-2	Butler, Rae
20		10	A	Charlton Athletic	L	0-2	
21		17	H	Manchester United	W	1-0	Miller
22		21	H	Liverpool	D	1-1	Miller
23		31	A	Portsmouth	D	0-0	
24	Feb	7	H	Arsenal	L	1-3	Ganea
25		10	A	Leeds United	L	1-4	Ganea
26		21	H	Fulham	W	2-1	Ince, Cort
27		28	A	Leicester City	D	0-0	
28	Mar	14	H	Aston Villa	L	0-4	
29		20	A	Liverpool	L	0-1	
30		27	A	Chelsea	L	2-5	Craddock, Camara
31	Apr	3	H	Southampton	L	1-4	Camara
32		10	A	Manchester City	D	3-3	Camara, Kennedy, Cort
33		12	H	Bolton Wanderers	L	1-2	Camara
34		17	H	Middlesbrough	W	2-0	Camara, Cort
35		25	A	Birmingham City	D	2-2	Cameron, Cort
36	May	1	H	Everton	W	2-1	Camara, Cort
37		9	A	Newcastle United	D	1-1	Ganea
38		15	H	Tottenham Hotspur	L	0-2	

Appea
Sub appear
One own-goal

FA Cup

R3	Jan	25	H	West Ham United	L	1-3	Ganea

Appea
Sub appear

League Cup

R2	Sep	23	H	Darlington	W	2-0	Rae, Gudjonsson
R3	Oct	28	H	Burnley	W	2-0	Craddock, Miller
R4	Dec	2	A	Arsenal	L	1-5	Rae

Appear
Sub appear

Irwin JD	Naylor LM	Cameron C	Craddock JD	Butler PJ	Newton SO'N	Ince PEC	Iversen S	Sturridge DC	Fernandes JM	Camara H	Luzhny O	Blake NA	Oakes MC	Rae AS	Cooper KL	Gudjonsson JK	Kennedy MJ	Kachloul H	Miller K	Clyde MG	Andrews KJ	Ganea IV	Jones PS	Cort CER	Okoronkwo I	Clarke L	Marshall A	
2	3	4	5	6	**7**	8	9	10	*11*	12	13	14																1
2	3	4	5	6	7	8	**9**	12	*11*			10	1	13	14													2
2	3	4	5	6	**7**	8			12	11		9	1	10														3
2	3	4	5	6	7	8				11		9	1	**10**		12												4
2	3	*4*	5	6	**7**	8	13		12			9	1	10		14	11											5
2	3	12	5	6	**7**	8	9		13	10			1			4	11											6
2	3	4	5	6	**7**	8	9						1	10			11	12	13									7
2	3	7	5	6	12	8				11		9	1	4				13	**10**									8
2	3	7	5	6						11		9	1	8		4	12		**10**									9
2	3	7	5	6	12					11		9	1	8		**4**		13	10									10
2	3		5	6		8	9		12	11			1	7		**4**	13		10									11
2	3		5	6	12	8	9			7			1	4			11		**10**	13								12
2	3		5	6	**7**	8	9			10		13	1	*4*		14	11		12									13
2	3		5	6						10		9	1	8		4	**11**		12		7							14
2	3	4	5	6		8		13		10		9	1	**7**			11		12									15
3	12	*4*	5	6		8		9	13	10	2		1	7			11		14									16
	3	4	5	6	12	8		13		10	2		1	7			11		**9**									17
	3	4	5	6	**7**	8	9			11	2		1					12	10									18
2	3	4	5	6	7		**9**			10		12	1	8		13	11											19
2	3	**4**	5		*7*	8				10	13	9	1	11			12			6		14						20
2	3		5	6	7	8	**9**						1	4			11		10			12						21
2	3	12	5	6	**7**	8	*9*		13				1	4			11		10			14						22
2	3	4	5	6		8	12							7			11		10			13	1	**9**				23
2	3	4	5	6			12							8			11		7			9	1	**10**				24
2	3	4	5	6			12		13					8			11		7			9	1	**10**				25
	3	12	5	6		8				7				4			11		10	2		13	1	**9**				26
2	3		5	6	12	8				**7**				4			11		*10*	13		14	1	9				27
2	3		5	6		8	13			7				4			11			12		9	1	10				28
	3		5	6	12	8				7				4			11		10	2		**9**	1	13				29
	3	12	5	6	13	8				7				**4**			11		*10*	2		9	1	14				30
2	3	12	5	6	13	8				7				4			11		10			*9*	1	14				31
12	3	4		6	7	8				10						14	11		13	**2**			1	9	5			32
2	3	4		6	7	8				10							11		12				1	9	5			33
12	3	4		6	7	8				10				13			11			**2**			1	9	5			34
	3	4		6	7	8				10	*2*			12			**11**		13			14	1	9	5			35
2	3	**4**		6	7	8				10				12			11					13	1	9	5			36
2	**3**	4		6	7	8				10				12		13	11					14	1	9	5			37
2	3	4	12	6	7	8				10				13			11					14	1	9	5			38
30	37	25	31	37	20	32	11	2	2	29	4	10	21	27		5	28		17	6	1	6	16	13	7			
2	1	5	1		8		5	3	7	1	2	3		6	1	6	3	4	8	3		10		3				
		4	1	1		2	4			7		1		5			2		2			3		5				

Irwin JD	Naylor LM	Cameron C	Craddock JD	Butler PJ	Newton SO'N	Ince PEC	Iversen S	Sturridge DC	Fernandes JM	Camara H	Luzhny O	Blake NA	Oakes MC	Rae AS	Cooper KL	Gudjonsson JK	Kennedy MJ	Kachloul H	Miller K	Clyde MG	Andrews KJ	Ganea IV	Jones PS	Cort CER	Okoronkwo I	Clarke L	Marshall A	
	3	4	12	6		8			7		**2**		1			13	11		*10*	5		9				14		R3
	1	1		1		1			1		1		1				1		1	1		1						
			1													1										1		
																						1						

Irwin JD	Naylor LM	Cameron C	Craddock JD	Butler PJ	Newton SO'N	Ince PEC	Iversen S	Sturridge DC	Fernandes JM	Camara H	Luzhny O	Blake NA	Oakes MC	Rae AS	Cooper KL	Gudjonsson JK	Kennedy MJ	Kachloul H	Miller K	Clyde MG	Andrews KJ	Ganea IV	Jones PS	Cort CER	Okoronkwo I	Clarke L	Marshall A	
	3	7	5		13		9		10		2		12	8		4	*11*								6	14		R2
	3		5	6		**8**	9		7	11	2		1	12		4			10							13		R3
	3		5	6	14	8		12		*11*		9		7		4	13		10		**2**						1	R4
	3	1	3	2		2	2		2	2	2	1	1	2		3	1		2		1				1		1	
					2			1					1	1			1									2		
			1											2		1			1									

2004-05

Championship

Manager: Dave Jones then Glenn Hodale (from December)

	P	W	D	L	F	A	Pts
Sunderland	46	29	7	10	76	41	94
Wigan Athletic	46	25	12	9	79	35	87
Ipswich Town	46	24	13	9	85	56	85
Derby County	46	22	10	14	71	60	76
Preston North End	46	21	12	13	67	58	75
West Ham United	46	21	10	15	66	56	73
Reading	46	19	13	14	51	44	70
Sheffield United	46	18	13	15	57	56	67
Wolverhampton Wanderers	46	15	21	10	72	59	66
Millwall	46	18	12	16	51	45	66
Queen's Park Rangers	46	17	11	18	54	58	62
Stoke City	46	17	10	19	36	38	61
Burnley	46	15	15	16	38	39	60
Leeds United	46	14	18	14	49	52	60
Leicester City	46	12	21	13	49	46	57
Cardiff City	46	13	15	18	48	51	54
Plymouth Argyle	46	14	11	21	52	64	53
Watford	46	12	16	18	52	59	52
Coventry City	46	13	13	20	61	73	52
Brighton & Hove Albion	46	13	12	21	40	65	51
Crewe Alexandra	46	12	14	20	66	86	50
Gillingham	46	12	14	20	45	66	50
Nottingham Forest	46	9	17	20	42	66	44
Rotherham United	46	5	14	27	35	69	29

Did you know that?

- Glenn Hoddle was appointed Wolves manager in December 2004 in place of Dave Jones. Ironically, both men had previously been in charge at Southampton.
- Wolves fielded four more overseas-born players this season – the Dane Mikkel Bischoff, Joachim Bjorkland from Sweden, Seyi Olofinjana from Nigeria and the South Korean international and World Cup star Ki-Hyeon Seol.
- Wolves' highest League position this term was ninth – claimed on the very last day after their 4–2 home win over Sheffield United.
- Joleon Lescott had the pleasure of scoring both home and away against Sheffield United, grabbing a dramatic late equaliser at Bramall Lane.

Match No.	Date		Venue	Opponents	Result		Scorers	Atten
1	Aug	8	A	Stoke City	L	1-2	Miller (pen)	17
2		11	H	Preston North End	D	2-2	Miller, Clarke	26
3		14	H	Leeds United	D	0-0		28
4		21	A	Burnley	D	1-1	Newton	13
5		28	H	Leicester City	D	1-1	Miller	27
6		30	A	Ipswich Town	L	1-2	Olofinjana	24
7	Sep	11	H	Wigan Athletic	D	3-3	Cameron, Miller 2	26
8		14	A	Brighton & Hove Albion	W	1-0	Miller	6
9		18	A	Plymouth Argyle	W	2-1	Sturridge, Cort (pen)	18
10		25	H	Cardiff City	L	2-3	Ince, Cort	27
11	Oct	2	A	West Ham United	L	0-1		29
12		15	A	Nottingham Forest	L	0-1		21
13		19	H	Derby County	W	2-0	Cooper 2 (1 pen)	26
14		23	H	Queen's Park Rangers	W	2-1	Cort 2	27,
15		30	A	Gillingham	L	0-1		9,
16	Nov	2	A	Sunderland	L	1-3	Miller	23,
17		6	H	Nottingham Forest	W	2-1	Cooper (pen), Bischoff	27
18		13	A	Rotherham United	W	2-1	Cooper, Cort	6
19		20	H	Coventry City	L	0-1		26
20		27	A	Sheffield United	D	3-3	Olofinjana, Lescott, Cort	18
21	Dec	4	H	Reading	W	4-1	Cameron, Olofinjana, Clarke 2	25
22		7	H	Millwall	L	1-2	Cooper (pen)	24,
23		11	A	Watford	D	1-1	Olofinjana	14,
24		18	H	Crewe Alexandra	D	1-1	Cort	25,
25		26	A	Cardiff City	D	1-1	Miller	16,
26		28	H	Brighton & Hove Albion	D	1-1	Miller	28,
27	Jan	1	H	Plymouth Argyle	D	1-1	Seol	27,
28		4	A	Wigan Athletic	L	0-2		10,
29		15	H	West Ham United	W	4-2	Miller 2, Ince, Cort	28,
30		22	A	Millwall	W	2-1	Olofinjana, Seol	13,
31	Feb	4	H	Sunderland	D	1-1	Seol	26,
32		19	H	Gillingham	D	2-2	Miller, Clarke	24,
33		22	A	Queen's Park Rangers	D	1-1	Cort	15,
34		26	H	Watford	D	0-0		25,
35	Mar	2	A	Derby County	D	3-3	Miller, Lescott, Cort	24,
36		5	A	Crewe Alexandra	W	4-1	Miller 2 (1 pen), Cort 2	8,
37		12	A	Preston North End	D	2-2	Craddock, Seol	16,
38		15	H	Burnley	W	2-0	Miller, Ince	24,
39		19	H	Stoke City	D	1-1	Cort	28,
40	Apr	2	A	Leeds United	D	1-1	Cort	29,
41		5	A	Leicester City	D	1-1	Lescott	22,
42		11	H	Ipswich Town	W	2-0	Cameron, Cort	25,
43		16	A	Coventry City	D	2-2	Naylor, Clarke	19,
44		23	H	Rotherham United	W	2-0	Miller 2	25,
45		30	A	Reading	W	2-1	Clarke, Ricketts	20,
46	May	8	H	Sheffield United	W	4-2	Miller, Cooper, Clarke, Lescott	27,
								Appearanc
								Sub appearanc
								Go

FA Cup

R3	Jan	8	H	Millwall	W	2-0	Cort, Seol	12,
R4		29	A	Arsenal	L	0-2		37,
								Appearanc
								Sub appearanc
								Go

League Cup

R1	Aug	23	A	Rochdale	W	4-2	Miller, Clarke, Ince, Andrews	3,
R2	Sep	21	A	Burnley	D	1-1	Seol	5,

R2 lost 4–2 on penalties aet

Appearanc

Sub appearanc

Go

Naylor LM	Olofinjana SG	Craddock JD	Bjorklund J	Newton SO'N	Cameron C	Sturridge DC	Miller K	Kennedy MJ	Cooper KL	Edwards RO	Clarke LM	Ince PEC	Andrews KJ	Lescott JP	Mulligan GT	Cort CER	Seol K-H	Lowe KS	Oakes MC	Bischoff M	Murray MW	Ricketts RA	
3	4	5	6	7	8	*9*	10	11	12	13	14												1
12	4	5	**6**	7	13		10	11	14	*3*	9	8											2
3	4	5		7	**11**		10		12	2	9	8	13										3
	4	5		7	11		**10**			3	9	8		6	12								4
3	4	5		7	**11**		10		12		9	8		6									5
3	4	5		7	11	12	10		13		9	8	14	6									6
3	**4**	5		7	12	13	10		14			8		6		9	11						7
3	4	5		7			10		12			8		6		9	**11**						8
3	4	5		7		*13*	10		12			8	14	6		9	**11**						9
3	4	5	12	7	13		10					8				9	11	2					10
3	*4*	5		7	12		10				13	8	14	6		9	**11**		1				11
				7	12		10	3	11			**8**	4	5		9	13	2	1	6			12
	8	5		12	4		10	3	7		13					9	**11**	2	1	6			13
	8			12	4		10	3	7					5		9	**11**	2	1	6			14
	8	14		7	4	12		3	11			13		5		9	10	**2**	1	*6*			15
	8			7	**4**	13	10	3	11			12		5		9		2	1	6			16
3	8			7	4	12	**10**		11					5		9		2	1	6			17
3	8	12		7	4		*10*		11		14			5		9	13	2	1	**6**			18
3	*8*	5		7	4		10	12	11				14	6		9	13	2	1				19
	8	5			7	**10**	12	3	11				4	6		9	13		1				20
12	**8**	5			7	10		3	11		13		4	6		9		2	1				21
	8	5			7	10	12	3	**11**		13		*4*	6		9	14		1				22
3	8	5				**10**	12	11	7				4	6		9	13	2	1				23
3	*8*	5		2	12		10	11	**7**		13		4	6		9	14		1				24
3	*8*	5		**2**	13		10	11	7				4	6		9	14		1				25
3		5		2	8		10	11	12		13		4	6		9	7		1				26
3		5		2	**8**		10	11			12		4	6		9	7		1				27
3	8	5			12		10	**11**			13	14	*4*	6		9	7		1				28
3	**4**	5			12		10	11				8		6		9	7				1		29
3	4	5					**10**	11			12	8	13	6		9	7		1				30
3	4	5		12	13		10	**11**				8		6		9	7		1				31
3	**8**	5			7		10		12	2	13		4	6		9	11		1				32
3	12	5			7		10		13	2	9	8	*4*	6		14	**11**		1				33
3		5			12		10	13	*11*	2	9	8	4	6		14	**7**		1				34
3	4	5					10	11		2		8		6		9	7		1				35
3	4	5					**10**	11	12		13	8	2	6		9	7		1				36
3	4	5					10	11	12	2	13	8		6		9	7		1				37
3	4	5					**10**	11		2		8		6		9	7		1			12	38
3	4	5					10	**11**		2	12	8		6		9	7		1			13	39
3	4	5			12		10	**11**		2		8		6		9	13		1			**7**	40
3	4	5			12		10	**11**		2	13	8		6		9	7		1				41
3	4	5			7		10			2	12	8		6		**9**	11		1				42
3	4	5			**7**		10	12			9	8		6			11		1	2		13	43
3	4	5			8		10	11	13	12	9			6			*7*		1	**2**		14	44
3	4	5			8		10			2	**9**			6			11		1	12		7	45
3	**4**	5			8		10		12	*2*	9			6		13	11		1	14		7	46
36	41	40	2	21	24	5	41	27	15	15	11	25	14	41		34	28	11	35	9	1	3	
2	1	2	1	3	13	6	3	3	15	2	17	3	6		1	3	9			2		4	
1	5	1		1	3	1	19		6		7	3		4		15	4			1		1	
3	**4**	5		13	12		10	11				8		6		9	7				1		R3
3	4	5	**2**	7	14		12	11			13	*8*		6		9	10		1				R4
2	2	2	1	1			1	2				2		2		2	2		1		1		
				1	2		1				1												
																1	1						
	12	5		7			10		11	3	9	**8**	4					2	1				R1
3	8	5	**6**	7	11						13		4			9	10	12	1				R2
1	1	2	1	2	1		1		1	1	1	1	2			1	1	1	2				
	1										1							1					
							1				1	1	1				1						

2005-06

Championship

Manager: Glenn Hoddle

	P	W	D	L	F	A	Pts
Reading	46	31	13	2	99	32	106
Sheffield United	46	26	12	8	76	46	90
Watford	46	22	15	9	77	53	81
Preston North End	46	20	20	6	59	30	80
Leeds United	46	21	15	10	57	38	78
Crystal Palace	46	21	12	13	67	48	75
Wolverhampton Wanderers	46	16	19	11	50	42	67
Coventry City	46	16	15	15	62	65	63
Norwich City	46	18	8	20	56	65	62
Luton Town	46	17	10	19	66	67	61
Cardiff City	46	16	12	18	58	59	60
Southampton	46	13	19	14	49	50	58
Stoke City	46	17	7	22	54	63	58
Plymouth Argyle	46	13	17	16	39	46	56
Ipswich Town	46	14	14	18	53	66	56
Leicester City	46	13	15	18	51	59	54
Burnley	46	14	12	20	46	54	54
Hull City	46	12	16	18	49	55	52
Sheffield Wednesday	46	13	13	20	39	52	52
Derby County	46	10	20	16	53	67	50
Queen's Park Rangers	46	12	14	20	50	65	50
Crewe Alexandra	46	9	15	22	57	86	42
Millwall	46	8	16	22	35	62	40
Brighton & Hove Albion	46	7	17	22	39	71	38

Did you know that?

- On 20 August 2005, Wolves' record of 21 unbeaten League games came to an end with a 2–0 reverse at Leeds.
- Former England international Darren Anderton scored Wolves' 7,000th goal in the Football League, on 28 December 2005 against Sheffield Wednesday.
- Almost a third of the players who appeared in Wolves' first team this season were non-British – and 16 players figured on the score sheet.
- Wolves scored four goals in 23 first-half minutes in their League game at Crewe in September.
- Paul Ince's dramatic late winning goal against Luton (at home) was his first of the season.

Match No.	Date		Venue	Opponents	Result		Scorers
1	Aug	6	A	Southampton	D	0-0	
2		9	H	Crystal Palace	W	2-1	Seol, Cort
3		13	H	Hull City	W	1-0	Delaney (og)
4		20	A	Leeds United	L	0-2	
5		27	A	Cardiff City	D	2-2	Lescott, Clarke
6		30	H	Queen's Park Rangers	W	3-1	Cort 3
7	Sep	10	A	Luton Town	D	1-1	Cort
8		13	H	Millwall	L	1-2	Cort
9		17	H	Leicester City	D	0-0	
10		24	A	Stoke City	W	3-1	Naylor, Cort, Miller
11		27	A	Crewe Alexandra	W	4-0	Cort 2, Miller 2
12		30	H	Burnley	L	0-1	
13	Oct	15	A	Sheffield United	L	0-1	
14		18	H	Derby County	D	1-1	Miller
15		22	H	Preston North End	D	1-1	Ganea
16		29	A	Watford	L	1-3	Seol
17	Nov	1	A	Brighton & Hove Albion	D	1-1	Cameron
18		5	H	Norwich City	W	2-0	Seol, Ganea
19		18	A	Derby County	W	3-0	Ndah, Ganea, Huddlestone
20		22	H	Sheffield United	D	0-0	
21		26	H	Southampton	D	0-0	
22	Dec	3	A	Ipswich Town	D	1-1	Cameron
23		10	A	Crystal Palace	D	1-1	Seol
24		17	H	Leeds United	W	1-0	Ganea
25		26	H	Reading	L	0-2	
26		28	A	Sheffield Wednesday	W	2-0	Miller, Anderton
27		31	H	Plymouth Argyle	D	1-1	Cameron
28	Jan	2	A	Coventry City	L	0-2	
29		13	H	Luton Town	W	2-1	Ince, Davies
30		21	A	Millwall	D	0-0	
31	Feb	4	A	Leicester City	L	0-1	
32		11	H	Crewe Alexandra	D	1-1	Kennedy
33		14	A	Burnley	W	1-0	Ince
34		18	H	Ipswich Town	W	1-0	Miller (pen)
35		25	A	Hull City	W	3-2	Cort, Miller, Aliadiere
36	Mar	4	A	Queen's Park Rangers	D	0-0	
37		7	H	Stoke City	D	0-0	
38		11	H	Cardiff City	W	2-0	Miller (pen), Rosa
39		18	A	Reading	D	1-1	Miller
40		25	H	Sheffield Wednesday	L	1-3	Cort
41	Apr	1	A	Plymouth Argyle	L	0-2	
42		8	H	Coventry City	D	2-2	Ince, Cameron
43		14	H	Watford	D	1-1	Aliadiere
44		17	A	Preston North End	L	0-2	
45		22	H	Brighton & Hove Albion	W	1-0	Miller (pen)
46		30	A	Norwich City	W	2-1	Kennedy, Rosa

One own-goal

FA Cup

R3	Jan	7	H	Plymouth Argyle	W	1-0	Clarke
R4		29	H	Manchester United	L	0-3	

League Cup

R1	Aug	23	H	Chester City	W	5-1	Miller, Cameron 2, Anderton, Ganea
R2	Sep	20	A	Watford	L	1-2	Miller

R2 aet

akes MC	Edwards RO	Naylor LM	Ricketts RA	Lescott JP	McNamara J	Seol K-H	Ince PEC	Cort CER	Miller K	Kennedy MJ	Olofinjana SG	Clarke LM	Craddock JD	Ndah GE	Cameron C	Davies MN	Anderton DR	Gyepes G	Ganea IV	Ross M	Huddlestone TA	Postma S	Gobern LT	Rosa D	Frankowski T	Aliadiere J	Jones DJ	Lowe KS	Murray MW	Ikeme C	
	2	3	4	5	6	**7**	8	9	10	11	12	13																			1
	12	3	4	5	6	7		9	*10*	11	8	13	**2**	14																	2
	2	3	4	5	6	7	8	9	**10**	11		12			13																3
	2	3	4	5	6	*7*		9	10		8	12		14	**11**	13															4
	2	12	13	5	6			9	*10*	3	8	14		**7**	4		11														5
	2	3	4	5	6			9	10	11	13	8		12			**7**														6
	2	3	4	5		*8*		9	**10**	11	13	12			14		7	6													7
		3	**4**	5	2	8		9		11	13	*10*		14	12		7	6													8
	2	3		5	6	12		9		11	8	*10*		**7**	4	13			14												9
	2	3	4	5		7		9	**10**	11				12	8			6													10
	2	3	4	5		7		9	10	11		13			**8**	12		6													11
	2	3	4	5		7		9	10	11		13			**8**	12		6													12
	2	3		5		7		9	**10**	11	8		6	12	*4*	14	13														13
	2	3		5		8		9	10	11		12				4	**7**	6	13												14
	2	3		5		*8*			10	11	12	14			13	4	**7**	6	9												15
	2	3		5		12			10	11	13	9	6				**7**	*4*		14	8										16
	2	3		5		12				11	**4**	10	6		13		7		9		8	1									17
	2	3		5		7				11		**10**	6		4				9		8	1	12								18
	2	3		5		7				11		**10**	6	12	4				9		8	1									19
	2	3		5		7				11		12	6	**10**	4		13	14	9		8	1									20
	2	3		5		12				11	13	14		10	4		**7**	6	*9*		8	1									21
	2	3		5		7				11		12		10	4		13	6	9		**8**	1									22
	2	3		5		8			10	11		12					7	6	**9**		4	1									23
	2	3	4	5		7			10						12		**11**	6	9		8	1									24
	2	3	**4**	5		8			10	11			14	13	12		7	*6*	9			1									25
	2	*3*		5		8	12		13	11			6	10	4		**7**		9		14	1									26
				5		13	12		10	11		*9*	2		4		**7**	6	14	3	8	1									27
	3			5		12			10	11		9	**2**		4		*7*	6	13		8	1		14							28
	3			5			8	9		11		**10**	6			7			12	2	4	1									29
	3	12		5		13	8	9	10	11			6			4	*7*			**2**		1		14							30
	2	3	4	5			8	9	**10**	11								6	12			1		13	7						31
	2	3		5		**7**	8	9	12	11			6						13	14		1		4	10						32
		3		5			8	9	10				6			11	12			2		1		**4**	7	13					33
	12	3	13	5				9	10				**6**			8	11			2		1		4	*7*	14					34
	6	3	12	5			8	9	*10*	13						4	11			2		1			14	**7**					35
	6	3	12	5			8	9	*10*	13						**4**	11			2		1			14	7					36
	6	3	13	5			12	*9*	10	11							**7**			2		1		4	14	8					37
	2	3	7	5			8		10							12		6				1		**4**	11	9					38
	2	3	7	5			8	12	**10**							4		6		13		1			11	9					39
	2	3	7	5			8	12	**10**	13						4		6		14		1			11	9					40
	12		13	5			8	9	*10*	11			6			4				2		1			14	7	**3**				41
		3	13	5		*7*	8	12		11			6		4	14				2		1			**10**	9					42
	6	3	12	5		13	**8**	14		11					7					2		1			*10*	9		4			43
	2		4	5		12		13	**10**	11					7	14				3		1			8	9		6			44
	2			5	12			13	10	11					7	4				3		*1*			8	9		**6**			45
	2	3		5	6	12		13	**10**	11					7					14				4	8	*9*			1		46
	39	38	17	46	9	22	15	24	33	37	6	10	17	6	20	12	20	19	11	13	12	29		6	12	12	1	3	1		
	3	2	8		1	10	3	7	2	3	7	14	1	8	7	8	4	1	7	5	1		1	3	4	2					
		1		1		4	3	11	10	2		1		1	4	1	1		4		1			2		2					
				5		7	8	13	10	11		9			4	2		6		3		1		12							R3
	2	3		5		**4**	8	*9*	10	11					12	13	7	6				1			14						R4
	1	1		2		2	2	1	2	2		1			1	1	1	2		1		2									
								1							1	1								1	1						
												1																			
	2			**5**	12	8			10	3		*9*		13	4	7	11	6	14											1	R1
	2	3	12	13		11			10		8		5	14	**4**	7		6	*9*			1									R2
	2	1		1		2			2	1	1	1	1		2	2	1	2	1			1								1	
			1	1	1									2					1												
									2						2		1		1												

2006-07

Championship

Manager: Mick McCarthy

	P	W	D	L	F	A	Pts
Sunderland	46	27	7	12	76	47	88
Birmingham City	46	26	8	12	67	42	86
Derby County	46	25	9	12	62	46	84
West Bromwich Albion	46	22	10	14	81	55	76
Wolverhampton Wanderers	46	22	10	14	59	56	76
Southampton	46	21	12	13	77	53	75
Preston North End	46	22	8	16	64	53	74
Stoke City	46	19	16	11	62	41	73
Sheffield Wednesday	46	20	11	15	70	66	71
Colchester United	46	20	9	17	70	56	69
Plymouth Argyle	46	17	16	13	63	62	67
Crystal Palace	46	18	11	17	59	51	65
Cardiff City	46	17	13	16	57	53	64
Ipswich Town	46	18	8	20	64	59	62
Burnley	46	15	12	19	52	49	57
Norwich City	46	16	9	21	56	71	57
Coventry City	46	16	8	22	47	62	56
Queens Park Rangers	46	14	11	21	54	68	53
Leicester City	46	13	14	19	49	64	53
Barnsley	46	15	5	26	53	85	50
Hull City	46	13	10	23	51	67	49
Southend United	46	10	12	24	47	80	42
Luton Town	46	10	10	26	53	81	40
Leeds United	46	13	7	26	46	72	36

Did you know that?

- Former Republic of Ireland defender Mick McCarthy was appointed manager (Wolves' 15th in 30 years) on 21 July 2006.
- Wolves' highest League placing during the season was third, after beating Leeds United 1–0 at Elland Road in September.
- Wolves lost to arch-rivals West Bromwich Albion in the Play-off semi-final and so missed out on a trip to the 'new' Wembley.
- Sir Jack Hayward sold the club to businessman and one-time Liverpool fanatic Steve Morgan for £10 (with a written clause in the deal).
- In June 2007 former player and chief executive Derek Dougan died aged 69.

Match No.	Date		Venue	Opponents	Result		Scorers	Attenda
1	Aug	5	A	Plymouth Argyle	D	1-1	Doumbe (og)	15,9
2		8	H	Ipswich Town	W	1-0	Bothroyd	19,1
3		11	H	Preston North End	L	1-3	Bothroyd	17,4
4		19	A	Burnley	W	1-0	Johnson	12,2
5		26	H	Luton Town	W	1-0	Johnson	19,3
6	Sep	10	A	Leeds United	W	1-0	Bothroyd	16,2
7		12	H	Derby County	L	0-1		21,5
8		16	A	Barnsley	L	0-1		11,3
9		23	H	Stoke City	W	2-0	Olofinjana, Clarke	19,4
10		30	A	Cardiff City	L	0-4		19,9
11	Oct	14	H	Colchester United	W	1-0	Bothroyd	19,3
12		17	H	Coventry City	W	1-0	Ward (og)	19,8
13		22	A	West Bromwich Albion	L	0-3		26,6
14		28	H	Sheffield Wednesday	D	2-2	Clarke 2	20,6
15	Nov	1	A	Southampton	L	0-2		18,9
16		4	H	Southend United	W	3-1	Craddock, Clarke 2	17,9
17		11	A	Hull City	L	0-2		16,9
18		18	A	Birmingham City	D	1-1	Craddock	22,2
19		24	H	Sunderland	D	1-1	Johnson	27,2
20		28	H	Crystal Palace	D	1-1	Gobern	17,8
21	Dec	2	A	Southend United	W	1-0	Craddock	9,4
22		9	H	Leicester City	L	1-2	Gobern	18,6
23		16	A	Queen's Park Rangers	W	1-0	Kightly	12,3
24		23	H	Norwich City	D	2-2	Henry, Craddock	22,9
25		26	A	Derby County	W	2-0	Olofinjana, Kightly	31,9
26		30	A	Colchester United	L	1-2	Collins	5,8
27	Jan	1	H	Barnsley	W	2-0	Henry, Olofinjana	20,0
28		13	A	Stoke City	D	1-1	Collins	15,8
29		20	H	Cardiff City	L	1-2	Olofinjana	16,
30		30	A	Norwich City	W	1-0	Kightly	23,3
31	Feb	3	H	Plymouth Argyle	D	2-2	Ward, Olofinjana	19,0
32		10	A	Preston North End	W	1-0	Olofinjana	15,7
33		17	H	Burnley	W	2-1	Kightly, Ward	19,5
34		20	A	Ipswich Town	W	1-0	Ward	20,6
35		24	H	Leeds United	W	1-0	Kightly	24,
36	Mar	3	A	Luton Town	W	3-2	Breen, Keogh, Henry	10,
37		11	H	West Bromwich Albion	W	1-0	Bothroyd	28,0
38		13	A	Coventry City	L	1-2	Kightly	22,
39		17	A	Sheffield Wednesday	D	2-2	McIndoe, Keogh	24,
40		31	H	Southampton	L	0-6		24,
41	Apr	7	A	Sunderland	L	1-2	Keogh	40,
42		9	H	Hull City	W	3-1	Bothroyd 2, Olofinjana	20,
43		14	A	Crystal Palace	D	2-2	Bothroyd 2	17,
44		22	H	Birmingham City	L	2-3	McIndoe 2	22,
45		28	H	Queen's Park Rangers	W	2-0	Keogh, Kightly	24,
46	May	6	A	Leicester City	W	4-1	Olofinjana, Kightly, McAuley (og), Keogh (pen)	30,
								Appearan
								Sub appearan
							Three own-goals	Go

FA Cup

R3	Jan	6	H	Oldham Athletic	D	2-2	Olofinjana, C Davies	14,
rep		16	A	Oldham Athletic	W	2-0	Potter, C Davies	9,
R4		28	H	West Bromwich Albion	L	0-3		28,
								Appearan
								Sub appearan
								Go

League Cup

R1	Aug	23	A	Chesterfield	D	0-0		4,
								Appearan
								Sub appearan

Lost 6–5 on penalties aet

urray MW	Clyde MG	Naylor LM	Clapham JR	Breen GP	Craddock JD	O'Connor KJA	Henry KLD	Cort CER	Bothroyd J	Ricketts RA	Edwards RO	Davies CM	Gobern LT	Olofinjana SG	Clarke LM	Jones DJ	Johnson JP	Potter DM	Ikeme C	Mulgrew CP	Little M	Wheater DJ	McIndoe M	Kightly M	McNamara J	Collins N	Davies MN	Fleming C	Ward S	Keogh A	Budtz J	Gleeson S	Frankowski T	Rosa D	
	2	3	4	**5**	6	7	8	9	10	*11*	12	13	14																								1
	2	3	4	5	6	**7**	8	9	*10*	11	12	14		13																							2
	2	3	4	5	6	7	8		10	11	12	*9*		13	14																						3
			3	5	6		8			7	2	12		4	9	11	**10**	13																				4
			3	5	6		8	9		12	2			4	13	11	10	**7**	14																	5
				5	6		8	9	13		2			4	12	11	**10**	7		*3*	14															6
				5	6		*8*	12	**10**	13	2			4	14	11	9	7			3															7
				5	6			12	10	11	*2*		**8**	4	13		9	7		14	3															8
				5	6		8			11	2	12	13	4	**10**		9	7		3																9
			12	5	6		8		13	*11*	2	14		4	**9**		10	7		3																10
			3	5	6		8		**10**	11	2	12	14	4	13		*9*	7																			11
			3	5	6		8		10	11	2	12		4	13		**9**	7																			12
			3	5	6		8		10	11	*2*	12		4	13		9	**7**			14														13
			3	5	*6*		8	12	**10**	11	2		13	4	9			7			14														14
			3	5			8	9		11	*2*		12	4	10		13	**7**			14	6													15
			3	5	6		8	9	12	*11*	2		7	4	**10**			13			14														16
			4	5	6		8	9		11	2	13	12		*10*		14	7		**3**																17
				5	6		8		10	12	13		11	4		**9**	14	*7*		3	2															18
			3	5	6		8		10		12	7	4	13	11	**9**				2															19
			3	5	6		8				12	7	4	10	11	**9**				2		13													20
			3	5	*6*		8		**10**		14	13		4	12		9				2		11	7												21
			3	5	6		8		10		12	7	4			**9**				2		11													22
				5	6				10		**9**		4	12			8			2		11	7	3											23
				5	6		8			12		9		*4*	10		13	14			2		11	**7**	**3**											24
				5			8				12		4	**9**			10			2		11	7	3	6										25
			12	5			8			7	13	14		*4*	*9*			10			2		11		**3**	6										26
				5			8				12	9		4			13	7			2		11	*10*	**3**	6	14									27
			12	5			8				13	9		4				7			2		11	10	**3**	6										28
			3				8					9		4			12	7			2		**11**	10		6		5	13								29
				5			8		12		13			4				7			2		11	10	3	6			14	**9**					30
			3				4		12		5			13		*11*		7			2		14	8		6			**10**	9					31
							2				5			4				8					**11**	7	3	6	12		10	9					32
					12		2		13		5			4				8					11	**7**	3	6	14		10	*9*					33
					13		2		12		5			4				8					11	**7**	3	6	14		*10*	9					34
					12		2		13		5			4				8					11	7	3	6			10	9					35
				5			8		12		2			4									11	7	3	6			**10**	9					36
				5	12				13		2			4				8					11	*7*	3	6	14		10	9					37
			12	5					13		2			4				8					*11*	**7**	3	6	14		10	9					38
			3	5	12				13		**2**			4				8					11	7		6			10	9	14				39
			3	5	12				13		2	14		4				8					11	7		6			*10*	9					40
			3	5					12		13		4				8			2		11	**7**		6			10	9	14				41
				5	6				10					4				8			2		*11*	7	**3**	12			13	9	1	14			42
				5	6				*10*					4				8			2		11	**7**	3	13	12		14	9	1				43
			12	**5**	6				10					4				8					11	7	3	2			13	9					44
				5	6				10					4				8			12		11	7	2	3			13	**9**		14			45
				5	6				*10*					4				8			12		11	7	**2**	3			14	9		13			46
	3	3	21	40	28	3	34	7	19	15	24	6	6	41	11	8	14	35		5	19	1	25	24	19	20		1	11	17	2				
			5		6			3	14	4	9	17	6	3	11		6	3	1	1	7		2			2	7		7		2	3		
				1	4		3		9					2	8	5		3					3	8		2			3	5				
				5			8			10	12	9		4			14	*7*			2		*11*		3	6	13							R3
			3	5			8			7	12	9		4			13	10			2		*11*			6	**14**							rep
				5			8			*10*		9		**4**			12	7			2		11		3	6	13		14						R4
			1	3			3			3		3		3				3			3		3		2	3								
											2						3										3		1					
													2		1				1																
			3		6		14			7	2	**9**		4	12		13	8	1		5												10	*11*	R1
			1		1					1	1	1		1				1	1		1												1	1	
							1									1		1																		

2007-08

Championship

Manager: Mick McCarthy

	P	W	D	L	F	A	Pts
West Bromwich Albion	46	23	12	11	88	55	81
Stoke City	46	21	16	9	69	55	79
Hull City	46	21	12	13	65	47	75
Bristol City	46	20	14	12	54	53	74
Crystal Palace	46	18	17	11	58	42	71
Watford	46	18	16	12	62	56	70
Wolverhampton Wanderers	46	18	16	12	53	48	70
Ipswich Town	46	18	15	13	65	56	69
Sheffield United	46	17	15	14	56	51	66
Plymouth Argyle	46	17	13	16	60	50	64
Charlton Athletic	46	17	13	16	63	58	64
Cardiff City	46	16	16	14	59	55	64
Burnley	46	16	14	16	60	67	62
Queens Park Rangers	46	14	16	16	60	66	58
Preston North End	46	15	11	20	50	56	56
Sheffield Wednesday	46	14	13	19	54	55	55
Norwich City	46	15	10	21	49	59	55
Barnsley	46	14	13	19	52	65	55
Blackpool	46	12	18	16	59	64	54
Southampton	46	13	15	18	56	72	54
Coventry City	46	14	11	21	52	64	53
Leicester City	46	12	16	18	42	45	52
Scunthorpe United	46	11	13	22	46	69	46
Colchester United	46	7	17	22	62	86	38

Did you know that?

- Wolves were embarrassingly dumped out of the League Cup by lowly Morecambe who two years earlier played Canvey Island in the Conference in front of 480 spectators!
- Wolves missed out on the Play-offs by one point or two goals. Their goal-difference was +5 against Watford's +6
- In May 2008, former Wolves goalkeeper Mark Kendall died from a heart attack at the age of 49.
- Wolves' average home League attendance this season was 23,496 – the second lowest at Molineux since 2000-01.
- Wolves' manager Mick McCarthy used 31 players in the first team this season and only goalkeeper Wayne Hennessey appeared in every League game.

Match No.	Date		Venue	Opponents	Result		Scorers	Atte
1	Aug	11	H	Watford	L	1-2	Olofinjana	23
2		19	A	Sheffield Wednesday	W	3-1	Eastwood, Kightly, Bothröyd	22
3		25	H	Blackpool	W	2-1	Eastwood 2	24
4	Sep	1	A	Stoke City	D	0-0		
5		15	A	Sheffield United	L	1-3	Elliott	26
6		18	H	Hull City	L	0-1		
7		22	H	Norwich City	W	2-0	Foley, Keogh	22
8		29	A	Plymouth Argyle	D	1-1	Elliott	13
9	Oct	2	A	Leicester City	D	0-0		21
10		6	H	Coventry City	W	1-0	N Collins	24
11		20	H	Charlton Athletic	W	2-0	Bothroyd, Henry	24
12		24	A	Cardiff City	W	3-2	Kightly 2, Craddock	15
13		27	A	Ipswich Town	L	0-3		23
14	Nov	3	H	Bristol City	D	1-1	Bothroyd	26
15		6	A	Southampton	D	0-0		19
16		10	H	Barnsley	W	1-0	N Collins	22
17		25	A	West Bromwich Albion	D	0-0		27
18		28	H	Colchester United	W	1-0	Elliott	20
19	Dec	1	H	Preston North End	W	1-0	Henry	22
20		4	A	Barnsley	L	0-1		9
21		8	H	Burnley	L	2-3	Gibson, Elliott (pen)	20
22		15	A	Queen's Park Rangers	D	0-0		13
23		22	H	Leicester City	D	1-1	Jarvis	23
24		26	A	Hull City	L	0-2		19
25		29	A	Norwich City	D	1-1	Keogh	24
26	Jan	1	H	Sheffield United	D	0-0		24
27		12	H	Crystal Palace	L	0-3		22
28		19	A	Scunthorpe United	W	2-0	D Edwards, Ebanks-Blake	7
29		29	H	Sheffield Wednesday	W	2-1	Keogh, Ebanks-Blake	22
30	Feb	2	A	Watford	L	0-3		18
31		9	H	Stoke City	L	2-4	Rob Edwards, Keogh	25
32		12	A	Blackpool	D	0-0		9
33		23	A	Crystal Palace	W	2-0	Gray, Kyle	15
34	Mar	1	A	Colchester United	W	1-0	Ebanks-Blake	5
35		4	H	Southampton	D	2-2	Ebanks-Blake 2	21
36		11	A	Preston North End	L	1-2	Keogh	12
37		15	A	Burnley	W	3-1	Olofinjana, Gray, Ebanks-Blake	12
38		18	H	Scunthorpe United	W	2-1	Gray, N Collins	21
39		22	H	Queen's Park Rangers	D	3-3	Keogh 2, Ebanks-Blake (pen)	24
40		29	A	Charlton Athletic	W	3-2	Ebanks-Blake 2, Henry	23
41	Apr	12	A	Bristol City	D	0-0		19
42		15	H	West Bromwich Albion	L	0-1		27
43		19	H	Ipswich Town	D	1-1	Ebanks-Blake	26
44		22	H	Cardiff City	W	3-0	Keogh, Ebanks-Blake, Kightly	20
45		26	A	Coventry City	D	1-1	Ebanks-Blake (pen)	27
46	May	4	H	Plymouth Argyle	W	1-0	Olofinjana	26

Appearar
Sub appearar
G

FA Cup

R3	Jan	5	H	Cambridge United	W	2-1	Kightly, N Collins	15
R4		26	A	Watford	W	4-1	Keogh 2, Elliott, Bothroyd	12
R5	Feb	16	A	Cardiff City	L	0-2		15

Appearar
Sub appearan
G

League Cup

R1	Aug	15	H	Bradford City	W	2-1	Eastwood, Craddock	9
R2		28	H	Morecambe	L	1-3	Keogh (pen)	11

R2 a.e.t.

Appearar
Sub appearar
G

Collins N	Ward D	Breen GP	Gray M	Kightly M	Olofinjana SG	Potter DM	Ward S	Keogh A	Elliott S	Edwards RO	Bothroyd J	Foley K	Eastwood F	Henry KLD	Craddock JD	Stack G	Gibson D	Jarvis M	Little M	Ebanks-Blake S	Edwards D	Jones DJ	Kyle K	Elokobi G	Mulgrew CP	Bennett E	Clapham JR	Gleeson S	Rosa D	
2	3	**4**	5	6	7	8	9	10	11	12	13																			1
2	3	**4**	5	6	7	8	9	10			14	2	*11*	13																2
2	3	4	**5**	6	7	8	*9*	10			14	2	11	13																3
3	4		6	**7**		9	10	12			2	**11**	8																	4
5	3	4		6	7		9	10	**11**		12	2	13	8																5
8	4	12	6	**7**		*9*	10	14		13	2	11	8																	6
		3	5	6	7		9	10	11			2		8	4															7
		3	5	6	7	12	**9**	10	11		13	2		8	4															8
		3	5	6	7		9	10	**11**			2	12	8	4															9
2		3	**5**	6	7		*9*	10	11			2	14	8	4	13														10
	3			6	7			10			**11**	2		8	4		9	12												11
	3			6	7	14	12	10			*11*	2	13	8	4		**9**													12
	3			*6*	7		9	14			11	2	10	8	**4**			13	12											13
	3			6	7	13	*9*	10			**11**	2	14	8	4			12												14
	3			**6**	7	13	9	*10*			14	2	11	8	4			12												15
	3			6	7	13	9	12			**11**	2	10	8	4															16
	3			**6**	7		10		13		11	2	12	8	4		9													17
	3		13			6	9	12	**11**			2	10	8	4		**7**													18
	3		5		7	14	9	13	11			2	*10*	8			**6**	12												19
	3		5		7	11	*9*	10	12			2	14	8			13	**6**												20
	3		5		7		9	14	10		*11*	2	12	8			**6**	13												21
	3		5		7		9	12	10		**11**	2		8			6													22
	3		*5*		7		14	13	**10**		11	2	12	8			6	9												23
	3				*7*		13	10	12	5	11	2	9	8			14	**6**												24
	3		5		7		9	**10**	12	13	11	2		8			6													25
	3		5		7		9	**10**	12		11	2	13	8			6													26
	3		5			7	9	14			10	2	13	8			**6**	12		*11*										27
	3		**5**				13	10	9	12		2		8				6		11	7									28
	3		5					*10*	9	12	14	2		8				6		11	7	13								29
	3		5					10	**9**	4	13	2		8				6		11	7		12							30
	3		5					**10**	13	4		2	12	8				6		11	7		9							31
	3	4			12			**10**				2	13	8				6		11	7		9	5						32
		3	9			6			*10*			14		8	4	13				**11**	7		12	5						33
		3	9			10			6			12		8	**4**		13			*11*	7		14	5						34
		3				13		12	*6*			2	14	8				9		11	7		**10**	5						35
		3	*9*			10		12	6					8	4		13	14		11	**7**			5						36
	3		**9**		*7*	6		10				2	14	8			12			11			13	5						37
	3		9		7	**6**		10				2	13	8				12		*11*			14	5						38
			9		7			10		4		*2*	13	8	12			6		11			14	5						39
			9		7			10				2	13	8	4		12	6		*11*			14	5						40
			9		7			10				2	12		4		8	6		11				5						41
			9		7			10				2	12		4		8	6		11			13	5						42
		12	9	13	7			10				2			4			6		*11*	**8**		14	5						43
		3		**6**	7		12	10	13			*2*			4		8	9		11				5						44
		3	12	**6**	7		14	10	13			2			4		8	*9*		11				5						45
		3	13	6	7			**10**	14			*2*	12	8	4			9		11				5						46
	30	18	29	20	35	11	23	33	18	4	13	42	10	38	22		15	17		20	10		3	15						
		1	4	1	1	7	6	10	11	4	9	2	21	2	1	2	6	9	1			1	9							
			3	4	3			8	4	1	3	1	3	3	1		1	1		12	1		1							
	3		5	13		7	9	**10**		14	11	2	12				8	*6*												R3
	3		12	13		7		10	9	6	*11*	2		8			14	**5**												R4
		2	5		**7**	8		11	13		10	*4*	12	6	3		14						9							R5
	2	1	2		1	3	1	3	1	1	3	3		2	1		1	2					1							
			1	2					1	1			2				2														
				1				2	1		1																				
				6		7	13	10		4		2	11	**8**	3	1									**5**	9	12			R1
			5	13		12		10		3		2	11	8		1									*9*	6		**7**	14	R2
			1	1		1		2		2		2	2	2	1	2									2	2		1		
				1		1	1																				1		1	
								1					1		1																

Honours

Club Records

- (Old) Division One champions: 1953–54, 1957–58, 1958–59
- FA Cup winners: 1892–93, 1907–08, 1948–49, 1959–60
- FA Cup runners-up: 1888–89, 1895–96, 1920–21, 1938–39
- (Old) Division Two champions: 1931–32, 1976–77
- Division One Play-off winners: 2002–03
- (Old) Division Three champions: 1988–89
- (Old) Division Three North champions: 1923–24
- (Old) Division Four champions: 1987–88
- League Cup winners: 1973–74, 1979–80
- Sherpa Van Trophy winners: 1987–88
- Texaco Cup winners: 1970–71
- UEFA Cup runners-up: 1971–72
- FA Charity Shield winners: 1949–50 (shared), 1954–55 (shared), 1959–60, 1960–61 (shared)

NB: Wolves are the only club to have won titles in five different divisions of the Football League.

No Mean Rivals

West Bromwich Albion are by far Wolves' fiercest and, indeed, oldest rivals. The clubs first met at a competitive level as long ago as January 1886 when Albion won a fourth-round FA Cup tie 3–1 at Stoney Lane. The first League encounters took place in the inaugural season of 1888–89 when Wolves completed the double over the Baggies, winning 2–1 at home and 3–1 away.

At the end of the 2007–08 season this was Wolves' playing record against Albion:

Competition	P	W	D	L	F	A
Football League	142	51	39	52	222	218
Play–offs	2	0	0	2	2	4
FA Cup	11	1	2	8	7	19
Charity Shield	1	0	1	0	4	4
Totals	**156**	**52**	**42**	**62**	**235**	**245**

There has also been relatively strong rivalry between Wolves and Aston Villa. Both were founder members of the Football League and played against each other almost every season leading up to 1983–84. But since then the two clubs have hardly been in the same division. Birmingham City have also got old ties with Wolves as the clubs have played in the same division for much of their respective histories, but 2006–07 saw the rivalry exercised for only the second time in five seasons. In contrast, Walsall and Wolves have rarely met in League action due to the Saddlers spending most of their life in the lower Divisions. Staffordshire neighbours Stoke City, also one of the 12 founder members of the Football League in 1888, are not regarded as fierce rivals like

Albion (or even Villa), but nevertheless there is still a very strong rivalry between the two clubs which dates back to 1882–83 when the teams first met in a friendly.

Players' Records

Appearances

- Most senior appearances: Derek Parkin – 607+2 (1968–82).
- Most League appearances: Derek Parkin – 500+1 (1968–82).
- Most consecutive appearances: Phil Parkes – 171 (127 League) between September 1970 and September 1973.

Most full/senior international caps won as a Wolves player

- England – Billy Wright, 105 (90 as captain, 1939–59).
- Scotland – Kenny Miller, 25 (2002–06).
- Wales – Paul Jones, 45 (1997–2006).
- Northern Ireland – Derek Dougan, 26 (1966–75).
- Republic of Ireland – Robbie Keane, 9 (1998–99).

Goalscoring

- Most goals scored for club (all senior competitions): Steve Bull – 306 (1986–99).
- Most League goals scored: Steve Bull – 250 (1986–99).
- Most goals scored in a season: Steve Bull – 52 (1987–88).
- Most League goals scored in a First Division season: Dennis Westcott – 38 (1946–47).
- Most goals scored in the FA Cup: John Richards – 24 (1969–83).
- Most goals scored in the League Cup: John Richards – 18 (1969–83) and Steve Bull – 18 (1986–99).
- Most hat-tricks scored (all competitions): Steve Bull – 18 (1986–99).
- Most goals in European competitions: Derek Dougan – 12 (1967–75).
- Most goals scored in a League game: 5 – by Joe Butcher versus Accrington Stanley, 1892 (Division One), Tom Phillipson versus Bradford City, 1926 (Division Two), Billy Hartill versus Notts County, 1929 (Division Two) and Hartill (again) versus Aston Villa, 1934 (Division One).
- Fastest recorded goal: 12 seconds, by John Richards versus Burnley – 1976–77 (Division Two).

Club Records

- Most League goals scored in a season: 115 (Division Two, 1931–32).
- Most points gained in a season: 2 for a win: 64 (Division One, 1957–58); 3 for a win: 92 (Division Three, 1988–89).
- Best home League win: 10–1 versus Leicester City, Division One, 15 April 1937.
- Best away League win: 9–1 versus Cardiff City, Division One, 3 September 1955.
- Heaviest home League defeat: 0–8 versus West Bromwich Albion, Division One, 27 December 1893.
- Heaviest away League defeat: 1–10 versus Newton Heath, Division One, 15 October 1892.

- Biggest home FA Cup win: 14–0 versus Crosswell's Brewery, second round, 13 November 1886.
- Biggest away FA Cup win: 4–0 versus Swansea Town, third round, 8 January 1938; 4–0 versus Darlington, third round, 14 January 1998.
- Most goals in an away FA Cup tie: 5–2 versus Grimsby Town, third round, 8 January 1955.
- Most FA Cup goals on neutral territory: 5–0 versus Grimsby Town, semi-final 25 March 1939, at Old Trafford.
- Heaviest home FA Cup defeat: 0–4 versus Sheffield United, third round, 23 March 1901.
- Most goals conceded at home in the FA Cup: 3–6 versus Derby County, third round, 14 January 1933.
- Heaviest away FA Cup defeat: 0–6 versus Rotherham United, first round, 16 November 1985.
- Biggest home League Cup win: 6–1 versus Shrewsbury Town, second round, First leg, 24 September 1991.
- Biggest away League Cup win: 5–1 versus Fulham, second round, second leg, 3 October 1995.
- Heaviest home League Cup defeat: 1–3 versus Fulham, second round, 11 September 1974; 1–3 versus Luton Town, second round, 30 August 1977.
- Heaviest away League Cup defeat: 0–5 versus Fulham, third round, 5 October 1966; 0–5 versus Sunderland, second round, second leg, 27 October 1982.
- Highest transfer fee paid: £3.5 million to Bristol City for Ade Akinbiyi, September 1999.
- Highest transfer fee received: £6 million from Coventry City for Robbie Keane, August 1999.
- Record attendance at Molineux: 61,315 versus Liverpool, FA Cup fifth round, 11 February 1939.
- Lowest attendance at Molineux: 900 versus Notts County, League, 17 October 1891 and Blackburn Rovers, League, 28 November 1891.
- Youngest League player: Jimmy Mullen, 16 years, 43 days versus Leeds United, 18 February 1939.
- Oldest League player: Archie Goodall, 41 years, 116 days versus Everton, 2 December 1906.
- Wolves had 26 changes of manager between 1877 and 2006.
- Longest-serving manager: Jack Addenbrooke, 37 years, 1885–1922.

Wolves in the FA Cup (pre-League days: 1883–88)

1883–84

27 October round one v Long Eaton Rangers (home) won 4–1
Brodie (2), J. Griffiths (2)
I. Griffiths, Cliff, C. Mason, Davidson, Baynton, Blackham, Hill, Lowder, Brodie, Hadley, J. Griffiths.
Att: 2,000

1 December round two v Wednesbury Old Athletic (away) lost 2–4
Brodie (2)
I. Griffiths, Cliff, C. Mason, Davidson, Baynton, Blackham, Waldron, Lowder, Brodie, Hadley, J. Griffiths.
Att: 1,000

1884–85

8 November round one v Derby St Luke's (home) drew 0–0
I. Griffiths, Cliff, C. Mason, Davidson, J. Aston, Pearson, Deans, Baynton, Stanford, Hadley, Lowder.
Att: 3,000

22 November round-one replay v Derby St Luke's (away) lost 2–4
Brodie, Brazier
I. Griffiths, Cliff, C. Mason, Davidson, Baynton, Pearson, Deans, H. Aston, Brodie, Brazier, Stanford.
Att: 1,000

1885–86

31 October round one v Derby St Luke's (home) won 7–0
H. Aston (2), Brodie (2), J. Aston, Horton, H. Wood
I. Griffiths, C. Mason, Hawkins, Pearson, J. Aston, Evans, H. Aston, Horton, Brodie, H. Wood, G. Wood.
Att: 2,000

21 November round two v Stafford Road (home) won 4–2
J. Aston (2), H. Aston, H. Wood
I. Griffiths, C. Mason, Hawkins, Pearson, J. Aston, Evans, H. Aston, Horton, Brodie, H. Wood, G. Wood.
Att: 3,000

12 December round three v Walsall Town (home) won 2–1
Lowder, Brodie
I. Griffiths, C. Mason, Hawkins, Pearson, J. Aston, Evans, H. Aston, Lowder, Brodie, H. Wood, G. Wood.
Att: 2,500

2 January round four v West Bromwich Albion (away) lost 1–3
H. Aston
I. Griffiths, C. Mason, Lowder, Davidson, J. Aston, Pearson, H. Aston, Brazier, Brodie, H. Wood, G. Wood.
Att: 5,196

1886–87

30 October round one v Matlock (home) won 6–0
Brodie (2), B Griffiths (2), Allen, Hunter
I. Griffiths, Baugh, C. Mason, Lowder, Allen, Pearson, Hunter, Knight, Brodie, H. Wood, B. Griffiths.
Att: 2,500

13 November round two v Crosswells Brewery (home) won 14–0
Hunter (4), Brodie (3), Knight (3), B. Griffiths (2), Allen, Law (og)
I. Griffiths, Baugh, C. Mason, Lowder, Allen, Pearson, Hunter, Knight, Brodie, H. Wood, B. Griffiths.
Att: 2,000

11 December round three v Aston Villa (away) drew 2–2
B. Griffiths, Brodie
I. Griffiths, Baugh, C. Mason, Lowder, Allen, Pearson, Hunter, Knight, Brodie, H. Wood, B. Griffiths.
Att: 5,000

15 January round-three replay v Aston Villa (home) drew 1–1 aet
Brodie
I. Griffiths, Baugh, C. Mason, Lowder, Allen, Pearson, Hunter, Knight, Brodie, H. Wood, B. Griffiths.
Att: 7,000

22 January round-three second replay v Aston Villa (home) drew 3–3 aet
B. Griffiths (2), Knight
I. Griffiths, Baugh, C. Mason, Lowder, Allen, Pearson, Hunter, Knight, Brodie, H. Wood, B. Griffiths.
Att: 6,000

29 January round-three third replay v Aston Villa (away) lost 0–2
I. Griffiths, Baugh, C. Mason, Lowder, Allen, Pearson, Hunter, Knight, Brodie, H. Wood, G. Wood.
Att: 11,500

1887–88

15 October round one v Walsall Town (away) won 2–1
Smallwood (og), Hunter
Llowarch, Baugh, C. Mason, Fletcher, Allen, Lowder, Hunter, Shaw, Danks, H. Wood, B. Griffiths.
Att: 2,000

5 November round two v Aston Shakespeare (home) won 3–0
Hunter, Shaw, B. Griffiths
Llowarch, Baugh, C. Mason, Fletcher, Allen, Lowder, Hunter, Shaw, Danks, H. Wood, B. Griffiths.
Att: 2,500

26 November round three v West Bromwich Albion (away) lost 0–2
Llowarch, Baugh, C. Mason, Fletcher, Allen, Lowder, Hunter, Shaw, Danks, H. Wood, B. Griffiths.
Att: 7,429

Wolves in Wartime

Playing record in World War One Midland Victory League

Season	P	W	D	L	F	A
1918–19	6	2	3	1	9	9

Playing record in World War Two Regional League, Football League South and Cup competitions

Season	P	W	D	L	F	A
1939–40	35	20	6	9	85	56
1941–42	37	19	4	14	81	66
1942–43	35	10	6	19	66	86
1943–44	38	8	9	21	58	98
1944–45	42	18	12	12	77	58
1945–46	42	20	11	11	55	48

* FA Cup results from 1945–46 not included.
* Wolves did not play football in season 1940–41.

Fact File

- Wolves won the Midland Regional League title in 1939–40 with a record 19 wins and three draws from their 28 fixtures. Dennis Westcott top scored with 27 goals, including four hat-tricks.
- Wolves won the Football League Wartime Cup in 1941–42. They beat Sunderland 6–3 on aggregate in the two-leg Final (2–2 draw at Roker Park, 4–1 victory at Molineux). Wolves defeated Manchester United 6–5 on aggregate in the second round and West Bromwich Albion 7–0 on aggregate in the semi-final.
- Wolves' heaviest defeats in Wartime football were 9–3 at Stoke in January 1944, 8–1 at Crewe Alexandra in April 1943 and 8–2 against West Bromwich Albion (away) in November 1941.
- Wolves' biggest win during Wartime competition was 11–1 versus Everton (home) in March 1942 when guest players Jack Rowley (5) and Frank Broome (3) led the goal chase.
- Jack Rowley (guesting from Manchester United) scored all Wolves' goals in their 8–1 win over Derby County in November 1942.
- The average age of Wolves' first team against Leicester City in September 1941 was just 17 years, one month. Derek Ashton, at 18½ years old, was the oldest.
- Scotsman Cameron Buchanan made his senior debut for Wolves against West Bromwich Albion at the age of 14 years, 57 days in September 1942 – the youngest-ever player in a competitive match at that time.
- The first official transfer to take place during World War Two was that of Bob King, who switched from Northampton Town to Wolves for £2,000 in November 1939.
- Wolves recruited a total of 42 guest players during World War Two.

Wartime Appearances and Goalscorers

The top-10 appearance-makers and champion goalscorers for Wolves during World War Two are as follows:

Appearances

147	Derek Ashton
125	Angus McLean
122	Billy Crook
111	Billy Wright
110	Jack Alderton
100	Jimmy Dunn
93	Cyril Sidlow
84	Jimmy Mullen
71	Dennis Westcott
62	Tom Galley

Goalscorers

89	Dennis Westcott
40	Dicky Dorsett
33	Billy Wright
28	Jimmy Mullen
18	Jack Acquaroff
17	Jack Rowley
16	Ray Chatham
16	Jimmy Dunn
14	Emilio Aldecoa
13	Tom Galley

Football League Play-offs

1994–95

14 May semi-final first leg v Bolton Wanderers (home) won 2–1
Bull, Venus
Stowell, Thompson, Venus, Rankine, Richards, Shirtliff, Goodman, D. Kelly, Bull, Cowans, Dennison.
Att: 26,153

17 May semi-final second leg v Bolton Wanderers (away) lost 0–2 aet
Stowell, Thompson, Venus, Rankine, Richards, Shirtliff, Goodman, D. Kelly, Bull, Cowans, Dennison (Wright).
Att: 20,041

1996–97

10 May semi-final first leg v Crystal Palace (away) lost 1–3
Smith
Stowell, Smith, Thompson, Atkins, Williams, Curle, Osborn, Ferguson, Bull (Foley), Roberts, Thomas.
Att: 22,312

14 May semi-final second leg v Crystal Palace (home) won 2–1
Atkins, Williams
Stowell, Smith, Thomas, Atkins, Williams, Curle, Goodman, Ferguson, Bull, Roberts, Osborn (Foley).
Att: 26,403

2001–02

28 April semi-final first leg v Norwich City (away) lost 1–3
Sturridge
Oakes, Halle, Camara, Lescott, Butler, Cameron, Newton (Miller), Rae, Blake (Proudlock), Sturridge, Cooper.
Att: 20,127

1 May semi-final second leg v Norwich City (home) won 1–0
Cooper
Oakes, Halle (Miller), Camara, Lescott, Butler, Cameron, Newton (Kennedy), Rae, Blake, Sturridge, Cooper.
Att: 27,418

2002–03

10 May semi-final first leg v Reading (home) won 2–1
Murty (og), Naylor
Murray, Irwin, Naylor, Ince, Butler (Pollet), Lescott, Ndah (Newton), Cameron, Blake, Miller (Sturridge), Kennedy.
Att: 27,678

14 May semi-final second leg v Reading (away) won 1–0
Rae
Murray, Irwin, Naylor, Ince, Butler, Lescott, Newton (Cooper), Cameron, Blake (Sturridge), Miller (Rae), Kennedy.
Att: 24,060

26 May Final v Sheffield United (Millennium Stadium) won 3–0
Kennedy, Blake, Miller
Murray, Irwin, Naylor, Ince, Butler, Lescott, Newton, Cameron, Blake (Proudlock), Miller (Sturridge), Kennedy.
Att: 69,473

2006–07

13 May semi-final first leg v West Bromwich Albion (home) lost 2–3
Craddock, Olofinjana
Hennessey, Collins, McNamara (Little), Olofinjana, Breen, Craddock, Kightly, Potter, Keogh, Bothroyd (Ward), McIndoe.
Att: 27,750

16 May semi-final second leg v West Bromwich Albion (away) lost 0–1
Hennessey, Collins, McNamara (Mulgrew), Olofinjana, Breen, Craddock, Kightly (Ward), Potter, Keogh, Bothroyd, McIndoe (Gleeson).
Att: 27,415

European Competitions

European Cup

1958–59

12 November round one first leg v FC Schalke 04 (home) drew 2–2
Broadbent (2)
Sidebottom, Stuart, Harris, Slater, Wright, Flowers, Deeley, Broadbent, Jackson, Mason, Mullen.
Att: 45,767

18 November round one second leg v FC Schalke 04 (away) lost 1–2
Jackson
Finlayson, Stuart, Harris, Clamp, Wright, Flowers, Deeley, Broadbent, Jackson, Mason, Mullen.
Att: 25,000

1959–60

30 September preliminary round one first leg v Vorwaerts (away) lost 1–2
Broadbent
Finlayson, Stuart, Harris, Flowers, Showell, Clamp, Lill, Mason, Murray, Broadbent, Deeley.
Att: 65,000

7 October preliminary round one first leg v Vorwaerts (home) won 2–0
Mason, Broadbent
Finlayson, Stuart, Harris, Slater, Showell, Flowers, Lill, Mason, Murray, Broadbent, Deeley.
Att: 55,747

11 November round one first leg v Red Star Belgrade (away) drew 1–1
Deeley
Finlayson, Stuart, Harris, Clamp, Showell, Flowers, Deeley, Mason, Murray, Broadbent, Horne.
Att: 62,000

24 November round one second leg v Red Star Belgrade (home) won 3–0
Mason (2), Murray
Finlayson, Stuart, Harris, Clamp, Showell, Flowers, Deeley, Mason, Murray, Broadbent, Horne.
Att: 55,519

10 February round two first leg v Barcelona (away) lost 0–4
Finlayson, Stuart, Harris, Clamp, Showell, Flowers, Deeley, Mason, Murray, Broadbent, Horne.
Att: 80,000

2 March round two second leg v Barcelona (home) lost 2–5
Murray, Mason
Sidebottom, Showell, Harris, Clamp, Slater, Flowers, Deeley, Mason, Murray, Broadbent, Horne.
Att: 55,535

European Cup-Winners' Cup

1960–61

12 October quarter-final first leg v FK Austria (away) lost 0–2
Sidebottom, Kelly, Showell, Kirkham, Stuart, Flowers, Mannion, Murray, Farmer, Broadbent, Deeley.
Att: 25,000

30 November quarter-final second leg v FK Austria (home) won 5–0
Kirkham (2), Mason, Broadbent (2)
Sidebottom, Stuart, Harris, Clamp, Slater, Kirkham, Deeley, Mason, Farmer, Broadbent, Durandt.
Att: 31,699

29 March semi-final first leg v Glasgow Rangers (away) lost 0–2
Finlayson, Stuart, Showell, Clamp, Slater, Flowers, Deeley, Murray, Farmer, Mason, Durandt.
Att: 79,229

19 April semi-final second leg v Glasgow Rangers (home) drew 1–1
Broadbent
Finlayson, Stuart, Showell, Clamp, Slater, Flowers, Deeley, Mason, Murray, Broadbent, Durandt.
Att: 45,163

UEFA Cup
1971–72

15 September round one first leg v Academica Coimbra (home) won 3–0
McAlle, Dougan, Richards
Parkes, Shaw, Parkin, Bailey, Munro, McAlle, Sunderland, O'Grady, Richards, Dougan, Wagstaffe.
Att: 23,349

29 September round one second leg v Academica Coimbra (away) won 4–1
McAlle, Dougan (3)
Parkes, Shaw, Parkin, Bailey, Munro, McAlle, Hegan, O'Grady, McCalliog, Dougan, Wagstaffe.
Att: 11,466

20 October round two first leg v FC Den Haag (away) won 3–1
McCalliog, Dougan, Hibbitt
Parkes, Shaw, Parkin, Bailey, Taylor (Wilson), McAlle, McCalliog (Hibbitt), O'Grady, Richards, Dougan, Wagstaffe.
Att: 16,466

3 November round two second leg v FC Den Haag (home) won 4–0
Weiner (og), Mansveld (og), Van Den Burgh (og), Dougan
Parkes, Taylor, Parkin, Bailey, Munro, McAlle, McCalliog, Hibbitt, Dougan, Curran, Wagstaffe.
Att: 20,299

24 November round three first leg v Carl Zeiss Jena (away) won 1–0
Richards
Parkes, Shaw, Parkin, Bailey, Munro, McAlle, McCalliog, Hibbitt, Richards, Dougan, Wagstaffe (Daley).
Att: 9,764

8 December round three second leg v Carl Zeiss Jena (home) won 3–0
Dougan (2), Hibbitt
Parkes, Shaw, Parkin, Bailey, Munro, McAlle, McCalliog, Hibbitt (Sunderland), Richards, Dougan, Wagstaffe.
Att: 24,135

7 March round four first leg v Juventus (away) drew 1–1
McCalliog
Parkes, Shaw, Taylor (Sunderland), Hegan, Munro, McAlle, McCalliog, Hibbitt, Richards, Dougan, Wagstaffe.
Att: 35,000

22 March round four second leg v Juventus (home) won 2–1
Hegan, Dougan
Parkes, Shaw, Parkin (Taylor), Hegan, Munro, McAlle, McCalliog, Hibbitt, Richards, Dougan, Wagstaffe.
Att: 40,421

5 April semi-final first leg v Ferencvaros (away) drew 2–2
Munro, Richards
Parkes, Shaw, Taylor, Hegan, Munro, McAlle, McCalliog, Hibbitt, Richards, Dougan, Wagstaffe.
Att: 44,763

19 April semi-final second leg v Ferencvaros (home) won 2–1
Munro, Daley
Parkes, Sunderland, Taylor, Hegan, Munro, McAlle, McCalliog, Hibbitt, Richards, Dougan, Daley.
Att: 28,262

3 May Final first leg v Tottenham Hotspur (home) lost 1–2
McCalliog
Parkes, Shaw, Taylor, Hegan, Munro, McAlle, McCalliog, Hibbitt, Richards, Dougan, Wagstaffe.
Att: 38,362

17 May Final second leg v Tottenham Hotspur (away) drew 1–1
Wagstaffe
Parkes, Shaw, Taylor, Hegan, Munro, McAlle, McCalliog, Hibbitt (Bailey), Richards, Dougan (Curran), Wagstaffe.
Att: 52,891

1973–74

26 September round one first leg v Belenenses (away) won 2–0
Richards, Dougan
Pierce, Taylor, Parkin, Bailey (Hegan), Munro, McAlle, McCalliog, Hibbitt, Richards, Dougan, Wagstaffe.
Att: 8,925

3 October round one second leg v Belenenses (home) won 2–1
McCalliog, Eastoe
Pierce, Taylor, Parkin, Sunderland, Munro, McAlle, McCalliog, Hibbitt, Eastoe, Dougan, Wagstaffe.
Att: 16,010

24 October round two first leg v Locomotiv Leipzig (away) lost 0–3
Parkes, Palmer, Parkin, Hegan, Munro, McAlle, McCalliog, Hibbitt, Sunderland (Eastoe), Dougan, Daley.
Att: 16,860

7 November round one second leg v Locomotiv Leipzig (home) won 4–1
Hibbitt, Kindon, Dougan, Munro
Parkes, Palmer, Parkin, Powell, Munro, McAlle, Hibbitt, Sunderland (Daley), Kindon, Dougan, Wagstaffe.
Att: 14,530
* Wolves lost on the away-goals rule

1974–75

18 September round one first leg v FC Porto (away) lost 1–4
Bailey
Parkes, Palmer, Parkin, Bailey, Munro, McAlle, Hibbitt, Powell (Daley), Sunderland, Dougan (Kindon), Farley.
Att: 39,529

2 October round one second leg v FC Porto (home) won 3–1
Bailey, Dougan, Daley
Parkes, Palmer, Parkin, Bailey, Munro, McAlle, Hibbitt, Daley, Richards, Dougan, Sunderland.
Att: 15,924

1980–81

17 September round one first leg v PSV Eindhoven (away) lost 1–3
Gray
Bradshaw, Palmer, Parkin (Brazier), Thomas, Hughes, Berry, Villazan, Carr, Gray, Richards (Clarke), Eves.
Att: 28,890

1 October round one second leg v PSV Eindhoven (home) won 1–0
Eves
Bradshaw, Palmer, Parkin, Daniel, Hughes, Villazan, Hibbitt (Atkinson), Carr (Brazier), Gray, Richards, Eves.
Att: 19,558

Wolves' Record in other Senior Competitions

FA Charity Shield

1949–50

19 October v Portsmouth (Highbury) drew 1–1
Hancocks
Parsons, Kelly, Springthorpe, Russell, Shorthouse, W. Crook, Hancocks, Smyth, Pye, Dunn, Mullen.
Att: 35,140

1954–55

29 September v West Bromwich Albion (home) drew 4–4
Hancocks, Swinbourne 2, Deeley
Williams, Guttridge, Shorthouse, Flowers, Russell, Clamp, Hancocks, Broadbent, Swinbourne, Deeley, Wilshaw.
Att: 45,035

1958–59

6 October v Bolton Wanderers (away) lost 1–4
Durandt
Finlayson, Stuart, Harris, Flowers, Wright, Clamp, Mannion, Durandt, Murray, Mason, Horne.
Att: 36,029

1959–60

15 August v Nottingham Forest (home) won 3–1
Lill, Murray, Broadbent
Finlayson, Stuart, Jones, Clamp, Showell, Flowers, Lill, Mason, Murray, Broadbent, Deeley.
Att: 32,329

1960–61

13 August v Burnley (away) drew 2–2
Murray, Deeley
Sidebottom, Showell, Harris, Kirkham, Stuart, Clamp, Mannion, Stobart, Murray, Broadbent, Deeley.
Att: 19,873

Anglo-Italian Cup

1969–70

Group

1 May v Fiorentina (home) won 2–1
Dougan, Wagstaffe
Parkes, Shaw, Parkin, Bailey (Walker), Holsgrove, Munro, Lutton, McCalliog, Dougan, Curran, Wagstaffe.
Att: 14,262

9 May v Lazio (home) won 1–0
Bailey
Parkes, Shaw, Parkin, Bailey, Holsgrove, Munro, McCalliog, Walker (Richards), Dougan, Curran, Wagstaffe.
Att: 11,953

16 May v Fiorentina (away) won 3–1
Richards, Dougan, Curran
Parkes, Taylor (Shaw), Parkin, Bailey, Holsgrove, Munro, McCalliog, Richards, Dougan, Curran, Wagstaffe.
Att: 13,120

21 May v Lazio (away) lost 0–2
Parkes, Taylor, Parkin, Bailey, Holsgrove, Munro, Richards, Walker, Dougan, Curran (Lutton), Wagstaffe.
Att: 43,073
* Wolves failed to qualify for the next stage

1992–93

15 September preliminary round v Tranmere Rovers (away) lost 1–2
Birch
Stowell, Ashley, Edwards, Downing (Dennison), Westley, Mountfield, Birch, Cook, Bull, Roberts, Rankine.
Att: 3,361

30 September preliminary round v Peterborough United (home) won 2–0
Taylor, Bull
Jones, Ashley, Thompson, Downing (Burke), Madden, Mountfield, Birch, Cook, Bull, Taylor (Roberts), Dennison.
Att: 3,091
* Wolves failed to qualify for the next stage

1993–94

31 August preliminary round v Stoke City (home) drew 3–3
D. Kelly, Bull, Keen
Stowell, Rankine, Thompson, Burke, Blades, Venus, Birch (Cook), Thomas, Regis (Bull), D. Kelly, Keen.
Att: 9,092

14 September preliminary round v Birmingham City (away) drew 2–2
Burke, Mills
Stowell, Ashley, Venus, Burke, Blades, Shirtliff, Birch, Thomas, Mills, Rankine, Keen.
Att: 2,710
* Wolves failed to qualify for the next stage

1994–95

Group A

24 August v Lecce (away) won 1–0
D. Kelly
Jones, Smith, Thompson, Ferguson, Blades, Shirtliff, Venus (Emblen), Thomas, Rankine (Birch), D. Kelly, Froggatt.
Att: 1,795

6 September v Ascoli (home) lost 0–1
Jones, Smith, Thompson, Ferguson, Blades, Shirtliff, Emblen, Birch, Stewart, Keen, Venus.
Att: 9,599

5 October v Venezia (away) lost 1–2
Venus
Jones, Rankine, Thompson, Venus, Blades, Bennett, Birch, Ferguson, Bull, Mills, Keen.
Att: 750

15 November v Atalanta (home) drew 1–1
Mills
Stowell, Emblen, Thompson, Ferguson (Rankine), Blades, Venus, Birch, Thomas, Mills, Stewart, Froggatt.
Att: 7,285
* Wolves failed to qualify for the next stage

Texaco Cup

1970–71

16 September round one first leg v Dundee (away) won 2–1
McCalliog, Dougan
Parkes, Shaw, Parkin, Bailey, Munro, McAlle, McCalliog, Hibbitt, Dougan, Gould, Walker.
Att: 9,892

29 September round one second leg v Dundee (home) drew 0–0
Parkes, Shaw, Parkin, Bailey, Munro, McAlle, McCalliog, Hibbitt, Gould (Richards), Dougan, Wagstaffe.
Att: 13,042

21 October round two first leg v Morton (away) won 3–0
Gould (2), Dougan
Parkes, Shaw, Parkin, Bailey, Munro, McAlle, McCalliog, Hibbitt, Gould, Dougan, Wagstaffe.
Att: 10,145

3 November round one second leg v Morton (home) lost 1–2
Curran
Parkes, Shaw, Parkin, Bailey, Munro, McAlle, McCalliog, Hibbitt, Gould, Dougan (Curran), Wagstaffe.
Att: 13,821

1 December semi-final first leg v Derry City (away) won 1–0
Gould
Parkes, Taylor, Shaw, Wilson, Munro, McAlle, McCalliog, Richards, Gould, Curran, Walker.
Att: 10,096

23 March semi-final second leg v Derry City (home) won 4–0
Parkin, Gould, Curran, O'Grady
Parkes, Shaw, Parkin, Bailey, Munro, McAlle, McCalliog, O'Grady, Gould, Curran, Wagstaffe.
Att: 15,784

14 April Final first leg v Hearts (away) won 3–1
Curran (2), Bailey
Parkes, Taylor, Parkin, Bailey, Munro, McAlle, McCalliog, O'Grady, Gould, Curran (Dougan), Wagstaffe.
Att: 26,057

3 May Final second leg v Hearts (home) lost 0–1
Parkes, Shaw, Parkin, Bailey, Munro, McAlle, McCalliog, Hibbitt, Gould, Dougan, Wagstaffe (O'Grady).
Att: 28,462

1972–73

12 September round one first leg v Kilmarnock (home) won 5–1
McCalliog, Dougan (2), Richards (2)
Parkes, Shaw, Taylor, Bailey, Owen, McAlle, McCalliog, Hibbitt, Richards, Dougan, Kindon.
Att: 8,734

26 September round one second leg v Kilmarnock (away) drew 0–0
Parkes, Shaw, Taylor, Bailey, Owen, McAlle, Hegan, Hibbitt, Richards, Dougan, Kindon.
Att: 4,435

24 October round two first leg v Ipswich Town (away) lost 1–2
Richards
Parkes, Shaw, McAlle, Bailey, Munro, Owen, McCalliog, Sunderland, Eastoe, Richards, Kindon.
Att: 14,425

7 November round two second leg v Ipswich Town (home) lost 0–1
Parkes, Shaw, McAlle, Bailey, Munro, Jefferson, McCalliog, Hibbitt (Dougan), Richards, Kindon, Wagstaffe.
Att: 12,029

Watney Cup

1972–73

29 July round one v Bristol Rovers (away) lost 0–2
Parkes, Taylor, Parkin, Bailey, Munro, McAlle, Hegan, Daley, Richards, Kindon, Wagstaffe.
Att: 12,489

Freight Rover Trophy

1985–86

Group

14 January v Exeter City (away) drew 1–1
D. Edwards
Flowers, Cartwright, Palmer, Streete, Clarke, Whitehead, Ryan, Raynes, Rosario (Herbert), D. Edwards, Crainie.
Att: 1,278

22 January v Torquay United (home) drew 1–1
Cartwright
Flowers, Palmer, Clarke, Streete, Zelem, Cartwright, Eli (Holmes), Whitehead, Rosario, D. Edwards, Purdie.
Att: 1,618

1986–87

2 December preliminary round v Cardiff City (a) won 1–0
Bull
Barrett, Stoutt, Barnes, Clarke, Powell, Zelem, Purdie, Thompson, Bull, Mutch, Dougherty.
Att: 1,201

16 December preliminary round v Bournemouth (home) won 4–3
Bull (2), Dougherty (2)
Barrett, Oldroyd, Barnes, Powell, Stoutt, Clarke, Purdie, Thompson, Bull, Mutch, Dougherty.
Att: 1,923

26 January round one v Hereford United (home) lost 0–1
Barrett, Stoutt, Clarke, Streete, Brindley, Robertson, Thompson, N. Edwards, Bull, Mutch, Forman (Holmes).
Att: 2,892

Sherpa Van Trophy

1987–88

27 October preliminary round v Swansea City (away) drew 1–1
Bull
Kendall, Stoutt, Thompson, Streete, Robertson, Holmes, Dennison, Vaughan, Bull, Mutch, Downing (Gallagher).
Att: 2,886

24 November preliminary round v Bristol City (home) won 3–1
Bull (2), Vaughan
Kendall, Stoutt, Thompson, Streete, Clarke, Robinson, Dennison, Vaughan, Bull (Holmes), Mutch, Gallagher.
Att: 5,174

19 January round one v Brentford (home) won 4–0
Bull (3), Dennison
Kendall, Bellamy, Thompson, Streete, Robertson, Robinson, Dennison, Vaughan, Bull, Mutch, Downing (Holmes).
Att: 6,298

9 February Area South quarter-final v Peterborough United (home) won 4–0
Bull (2), Mutch, Dennison
Kendall, Bellamy, Thompson, Brindley, Robertson, Robinson, Dennison, Vaughan, Bull (Gallagher), Mutch, Downing (Holmes).
Att: 6,155

8 March Area South semi-final v Torquay United (home) won 1–0
Bull
Kendall, Stoutt, McDonald, Streete, Bellamy, Robinson, Dennison, Vaughan, Bull, Mutch, Holmes.
Att: 11,039

12 April Area Final first leg v Notts County (away) drew 1–1
Bull
Kendall, Bellamy, Thompson, Streete, Robertson, Robinson, Dennison, Downing, Bull, Mutch, Holmes.
Att: 10,041

19 April Area Final second leg v Notts County (home) won 3–0
Bull (2), Downing
Kendall, Bellamy, Thompson, Streete, Robertson, Robinson, Dennison, Downing, Bull, Mutch, Holmes.
Att: 8,413

29 May Final v Burnley (Wembley) won 2–0
Mutch, Dennison
Kendall, Bellamy, Thompson, Streete, Robertson (Gallagher), Robinson, Dennison, Downing (Vaughan), Bull, Mutch, Holmes.
Att: 80,841

1988–89

30 November preliminary round v Hereford United (away) drew 2–2
Thompson, Bull
Kendall, Bellamy, Venus, Streete, Robertson, Vaughan, Thompson, Downing, Bull, Mutch, Dennison.
Att: 4,215

13 December preliminary round v Port Vale (home) won 5–1
Bull (4), Mutch
Kendall, Bellamy, Venus, Streete, Robertson, Robinson (Vaughan), Thompson (Downing), Gooding, Bull, Mutch, Dennison.
Att: 9,734

24 January round one v Bristol City (home) won 3–0
Bull (3)
Kendall, Bellamy, Venus, Streete, Robertson (Robinson), Vaughan, Thompson, Gooding (Downing), Bull, Mutch, Dennison.
Att: 14,216

21 February round two v Northampton Town (home) won 3–1 aet
Vaughan, Gooding, Dennison
Kendall, Bellamy, Venus, Streete, Downing, Vaughan, Thompson, Gooding (Robinson), Bull, Mutch, Dennison (Kelly).
Att: 16,815

22 March semi-final v Hereford United (away) won 2–0
Bull, Mutch
Hansbury, Bellamy, Venus, Streete, Steele, Vaughan, Thompson, Gooding, Bull, Mutch, Dennison.
Att: not known

12 April Area Final first leg v Torquay United (away) won 2–1
Bull (2)
Hansbury, Thompson, Venus, Streete, Robertson, Vaughan, Chard, Downing (Gooding), Bull, Mutch, Dennison.
Att: 4,612

18 April Area Final second leg v Torquay United (home) lost 0–2
Hansbury, Thompson, Venus (Chard), Bellamy, Robertson, Vaughan, Steele (Downing), Gooding, Bull, Mutch, Dennison.
Att: 22,532

Zenith Data Systems Cup

1989–90

7 November round one v Sheffield United (away) lost 0–1
Kendall, Bennett (Paskin), Venus, Bellamy, Westley, Downing (Vaughan), Thompson, Cook, Bull, Mutch, Dennison.
Att: 4,926

1990–91

27 November round one v Leicester City (away) won 1–0
Bull
Stowell, Roberts, Steele, Bellamy, Stancliffe (Hindmarch), Downing, Thompson, Cook, Bull, Taylor, Dennison.
Att: 4,705

18 December round two v Leeds United (home) lost 1–2
Cook
Stowell, Roberts, Thompson, Bellamy, Stancliffe (Bennett), Downing, Steele, Cook, Bull, Taylor, Dennison.
Att: 11,080

1991–92

1 October round one v Grimsby Town (away) lost 0–1
Stowell, Ashley, Venus, Bennett, Madden, Downing, Birch, Cook, Bull, Dennison (Burke), Bellamy.
Att: 1,593

FA Cup third-place play-off 1973–74*

18 August v Arsenal (away) won 3–1
Dougan 2, McCalliog
Parkes, Palmer, Parkin, Hegan, Jefferson, Taylor, McCalliog, Sunderland, Richards, Dougan (Hibbitt), Wagstaffe.
Att: 21,038

*Played at the start of the 1973–74 season for the 1972–73 season.

Wolves Abroad (post-World War Two)

(Match venue is given if known to be different from the location of the 'host' team)

1946 Swedish Tour

19 June v Gothenburg Alliance lost 0–3
Williams, Morris, McLean, Galley, Cullis, Wright, King, Pye, Westcott, Dorsett, Hancocks.
Att: 13,041

23 June v Sundsvall XI won 7–1
Westcott (2), Hancocks (2), Galley (pen), Pye, Ramscar
Williams, Morris, McLean, W. Crook, Galley, Miller, Hancocks, Pye, Westcott, Ramscar, King.
Att: 3,837

25 June v Gavle XI drew 2–2
Westcott (2)
Williams, Morris, McLean, W. Crook, Galley, Miller, Hancocks, Pye, Westcott, Ramscar (McIntosh), Chatham.
Att: 5,620

30 June v Djurgarden lost 1–3 in Stockholm
Pye
Williams, Morris, Ratcliffe, Galley, McLean, W. Crook, Hancocks, Pye, Westcott (Kirkham), Ramscar, Chatham.
Att: 10,837

3 July v Malmo won 3–2
Westcott (2), Chatham
Williams, Morris, Ratcliffe, W. Crook, Galley, McLean, Hancocks, Pye, Westcott (King), Ramscar, Chatham.
Att: 6,800

1948

13 April v Dundela lost 0–2 in Belfast
Elliott, Paxton, W. Crook, Baxter, Simpson, Russell, Mynard, Forbes, Reid, Smyth, Clews.
Att: 10,000

1948 Dutch and French Tour

12 May v Dutch FA XI won 3–2 in Rotterdam
Pye (2), Sluijs (og)
Williams, Kelly, Pritchard, W. Crook, Shorthouse, Chatham, Smith, Dunn, Pye, Smyth, Mullen.
Att: 60,000

14 May v Dutch National XI won 1–0 in Amsterdam
Pye
Williams, Kelly, McLean, W. Crook, Shorthouse, Chatham, Smith, Dunn, Pye, Stevenson, Mullen.
Att: 50,000

19 May v Stade Francaise lost 1–3 in Paris
Mullen
Williams, Kelly, Pritchard, W. Crook, McLean, Chatham, Smith, Dunn, Pye, Stevenson, Mullen.
Att: 4,000

1949 Irish Tour

13 May v Dublin Bohemians drew 1–1
Smith
Parsons, McLean, Pritchard, Russell, Shorthouse, W. Crook, Smith, Walker, Smyth, Dunn, Clews.
Att: not known

19 May v Munster Select won 3–2 in Cork
Clews, Pye, Smith
Parsons, Kelly, McLean, Russell, Shorthouse, W. Crook, Smith, Smyth, Pye, Dunn, Clews.
Att: 9,800

1949

1 November v Entente Anversoise lost 1–2 in Antwerp

Wright

Sims, Kelly, McLean, Russell, Shorthouse, Wright, Smith, Forbes, Pye, Smyth, Mullen.

Att: 40,256

1950

1 November v Antwerp drew 2–2

Walker, Mullen

Williams, McLean, Pritchard, Baxter, Russell, Wright, Smith, Walker, Swinbourne, Dunn, Mullen.

Att: 35,500

1951 South African Tour

19 May v Southern Transvaal won 4–1 in Johannesburg

Swinbourne (2), Pye, Smyth

Parsons, McLean, Short, Baxter, Russell, Wright, Smith, Dunn, Swinbourne, Pye, Mullen.

Att: 35,000

24 May v Orange Free State and Basutoland won 4–0 in Bloemfontein

Swinbourne (2), Smyth, Walker

Parsons, Shorthouse, Short, Russell, Baxter, Deeley, Broadbent, Walker, Swinbourne, Smyth, Smith.

Att: 5,300

26 May v Natal won 3–1 in Durban

Swinbourne (3)

Parsons, McLean, Short, Baxter, Russell, Wright, Broadbent, Dunn, Swinbourne, Pye, Mullen.

Att: 25,000

31 May v Northern Transvaal won 7–0 in Pretoria

Pye (3), Swinbourne (2), Smith, Broadbent

Parsons, McLean, Pritchard, Russell, Baxter, Wright, Smith, Broadbent, Swinbourne, Pye, Mullen.

Att: not known

2 June v Western Province won 4–0 in Cape Town

Pye (2), Walker, Smith

Parsons, Short, Pritchard, Deeley, McLean, Wright, Smith, Walker, Smyth, Pye, Mullen.

Att: 8,250

6 June v South West Districts won 11–0 in Mossel Bay

Walker (3), Broadbent (3), Dunn (2), Mullen, Smyth, Cullis

Parsons, Short, Pritchard, Cullis, Shorthouse, Deeley, Dunn, Broadbent, Smyth, Walker, Mullen.

Att: 1,500

9 June v Eastern Province won 5–1 in Port Elizabeth

Mullen, Pye, Swinbourne, Dunn, Smith

Parsons, Shorthouse, McLean, Wright, Russell, Deeley, Mullen, Pye, Swinbourne, Dunn, Smith.

Att: 8,000

13 June v Border Frontier State won 2–0 in East London

Baxter, Walker

Parsons, Short, Pritchard, Cullis, Shorthouse, Baxter, Broadbent, Dunn, Smyth, Walker, Smith.

Att: 6,000

16 June v Eastern Transvaal won 13–0 in Benoni

Swinbourne (6), Pye (4), Smith (2), Wright

Parsons, Short, Shorthouse, Russell, Baxter, Wright, Smith, Smyth, Swinbourne, Pye, Dunn.

Att: not known

20 June v Natal won 2–1 in Pietermaritzburg

Smyth (2)

Parsons, Short, Shorthouse, Russell, Baxter, Deeley, Smith, Broadbent, Swinbourne, Smyth, Dunn.

Att: not known

23 June v South Africa XI won 4–1 in Durban
Smith (2), Swinbourne, Pye
Parsons, Short, Pritchard, Baxter, Shorthouse, Wright, Smith, Dunn, Swinbourne, Pye, Broadbent.
Att: 29,000

30 June v South Africa XI won 1–0 in Johannesburg
Dunn
Parsons, Short, Pritchard, Baxter, Shorthouse, Wright, Smith, Dunn, Swinbourne, Pye, Broadbent.
Att: not known

1952

8 October v Dutch XI drew 2–2 in Rotterdam
Smith, Broadbent
Williams, Short, Pritchard, Chatham, Shorthouse, Wright, Smith, Broadbent, Swinbourne, Dunn, Mullen.
Att: 52,000

1954 Scandinavian Tour*

29 April v Aarhus XI won 5–0
Swinbourne (3), Smith (2)
Dwyer, Stuart, Pritchard, Shorthouse, Flowers, Clamp, McDonald, Broadbent, Swinbourne, Smith, Deeley.
Att: not known

4 May v Helsingborg won 5–0
Broadbent, Smith (2), McDonald, Swinbourne
Dwyer, Pritchard, Stuart, Clamp, Shorthouse, Flowers, Broadbent, Deeley, Smith, Swinbourne, McDonald.
Att: 10,192

6 May v Copenhagen XI drew 2–2
Broadbent, McDonald
Dwyer, Stuart, Pritchard, Shorthouse, Flowers, Clamp, McDonald, Broadbent, Swinbourne, Smith, Deeley.
Att: not known
** The game against Helsingborg was played in Sweden and the other two were in Denmark.*

1955 Soviet Union Tour

7 August v Moscow Spartak lost 0–3
Williams, Stuart, Shorthouse, Slater, Wright, Flowers, Smith, Broadbent, Swinbourne, Wilshaw, Mullen.
Att: 70,000

12 August v Moscow Dynamo lost 2–3
Wilshaw (2)
Williams, Stuart, Shorthouse, Slater, Wright, Flowers, McDonald (Smith), Broadbent, Swinbourne, Wilshaw, Smith (Mullen).
Att: 40,000

1957

19 March v Valencia lost 1–3
Broadbent
Finlayson, Stuart, Harris, Clamp, Wright, Flowers, Hooper, Broadbent, Murray (Bonson), Booth, Deeley.
Att: not known

1957 South African and Rhodesian Tour

4 May v Southern Transvaal won 5–2 in Johannesburg
Murray (5)
Finlayson, Stuart, Harris, Clamp, Showell, Flowers, Hooper, Broadbent, Murray, Booth, Mullen.
Att: 6,000

8 May v Combined Northern and Eastern Transvaal won 1–0 in Pretoria
Murray
Dwyer, Stuart, Jones, Clamp, Showell, Flowers, Hooper, Mason, Murray, Broadbent, Mullen.
Att: not known

11 May v Natal won 5–1 in Durban
Broadbent (3), Deeley (2)
Finlayson, Jones, Harris, Clamp, Showell, Flowers, Deeley, Booth, Murray, Broadbent, Mullen.
Att: not known

15 May v Western Province won 6–0 in Cape Town
Mullen (2), Booth (2), Broadbent, Hooper
Dwyer, Stuart, Harris, Jones, Showell, Flowers, Hooper, Booth, Murray, Broadbent, Mullen.
Att: not known

18 May v South African XI won 4–1 in Johannesburg
Broadbent (3), Deeley
Finlayson, Stuart, Harris, Clamp, Showell, Flowers, Deeley, Booth (Hooper), Murray, Broadbent, Mullen.
Att: not known

21 May v President's XI won 7–3 in Johannesburg
Deeley (2), Murray (2), Mason (2), Showell
Dwyer, Harris, Tether, Jones, Stuart, Flowers, Deeley, Mason, Showell (Clamp), Murray, Broadbent.
Att: 7,000

24 May v Southern Rhodesia won 10–1 in Bulawayo
Deeley (3), Mullen (2), Broadbent (2), Murray, Turnbull (og), Mason
Finlayson, Stuart, Harris, Flowers, Wright, Clamp, Deeley, Booth (Mason), Murray, Broadbent, Mullen.
Att: 10,000

26 May v Northern Rhodesia won 11–1 in Kitwe
Mullen (4), Deeley (3), Murray (2), Booth (2)
Finlayson, Stuart, Harris, Clamp, Wright, Flowers, Deeley, Booth, Murray, Broadbent, Mullen.
Att: 14,000

1957

20 November v Anderlecht lost 0–2
Dwyer, Stuart, Harris, Clamp, Wright, Flowers, Deeley, Broadbent, Murray, Thomson, Hooper.
Att: 38,000

11 December v Real Madrid drew 2–2
Mason, Mullen
Finlayson, Stuart, Harris, Clamp (Showell), Wright, Flowers, Deeley, Broadbent, Murray, Mason, Mullen.
Att: 60,000

1958 European Tour

4 May v Grasshoppers won 3–1 in Zurich
Broadbent, Flowers, Booth
Finlayson, Stuart, Harris, Clamp, Showell, Flowers, Deeley, Broadbent, Murray, Booth, Mullen (Henderson).
Att: 25,000

7 May v Servette won 4–1 in Geneva
Lill, Mason (2), Booth
Finlayson, Stuart, Harris, Howells, Showell, Flowers, Lill, Booth, Murray, Mason, Mullen.
Att: 16,500

11 May v Stuttgart won 4–3
Booth, Henderson, Mason, Mullen
Finlayson, Stuart, Harris, Howells, Showell, Flowers, Deeley, Booth, Henderson, Mason, Mullen.
Att: 40,000

14 May v Beerschot lost 1–2 in Brussels
Booth
Finlayson, Stuart, Harris, Howells, Showell, Flowers, Deeley, Booth, Murray, Mason, Henderson.
Att: 4,000

15 May v Juventus lost 1–5 in Brussels
Booth
Finlayson, Jones, Harris, Howells, Flowers, Thomson, Deeley, Booth, Murray, Henderson, Mullen.
Att: 5,000

1959 West German and Swiss Tour

1 May v Stuttgart lost 1–3
Deeley
Finlayson, Stuart, Harris, Jones, Showell, Thomson, Lill, Mason, Murray, Booth, Deeley.
Att: 22,000

6 May v Grasshoppers won 6–2 in Zurich
Mason (2), Lill, Jones, Booth, Murray
Finlayson, Stuart, Harris, Clamp, Showell, Jones, Mannion, Mason, Murray, Booth, Lill.
Att: 10,000

13 May v First Nuremberg won 3–1
Lill, Mason, Booth
Finlayson, Stuart, Harris, Clamp, Showell, Jones, Mannion, Booth, Murray, Mason, Lill.
Att: not known

1961

8 May v Ards won 4–1 in Northern Ireland
Deeley, Broadbent, Kirkham, Stobart
Finlayson, Stuart, Showell, Kirkham, Woodfield, Clamp, Stobart, Murray, Farmer, Broadbent, Deeley.
Att: 7,000

1963

9 February v Coventry won 3–0 in Cork
Flowers, Stobart, Crowe
Finlayson, Showell, Thomson, Kirkham, Woodfield, Flowers, Broadbent, Crowe, Farmer, Stobart, Wharton.
Att: not known

20 February v Coventry won 6–3 at Celtic Park, Belfast
Wharton (2), Hinton (2), Farmer, Crowe
Davies, Showell, Thomson, Kirkham, Woodfield, Flowers, Wharton, Crowe, Farmer, Stobart, Hinton.
Att: 5,500

1963 US and Canadian Tour

23 May v Montreal Cantalia won 5–1
Crowe (2), Farmer, Wharton, G. Harris
Wolves 15 (all used): Davies, G. Harris, J. Harris, Showell, Knighton, Kirkham, Goodwin, Woodfield, Broadbent, Stobart, Crowe, Murray, Wharton, Farmer, Knowles.
Att: 2,500

26 May v Schalke 04 won 4–2 in New York
Murray (2), Wharton, Broadbent
Davies, Showell, G. Harris, Goodwin, Woodfield, Kirkham, Crowe, Murray, Farmer, Broadbent, Wharton.
Att: 8,200

30 May v Ukranian Nationals won 3–2 in Philadelphia
Krawec (og), Farmer (2)
Finlayson (Davies), Showell, G. Harris, Goodwin, Woodfield, Kirkham, Crowe, Murray, Farmer, Knowles, Wharton.
Att: 5,000

2 June v American Soccer League XI won 5–0 in Randalls Island, New York
Farmer (2), G. Harris, Crowe, Stobart
Finlayson, Showell, G. Harris, Goodwin, Woodfield, Kirkham, Crowe, Stobart, Farmer, Broadbent, Wharton.
Att: 4,526

5 June v Catholic Youth Council won 6–0 in St Louis
Crowe (2), Farmer (2), Broadbent, Wharton
Davies, Showell, G. Harris, Goodwin, Woodfield, Kirkham, Crowe, Murray, Farmer, Broadbent, Wharton.
Att: 3,500

9 June v Mexican City Select won 3–0 in San Francisco
Farmer, Crowe, Wharton
Davies, Showell, G. Harris, Goodwin, Woodfield, Kirkham, Crowe, Murray, Farmer, Broadbent, Wharton.
Att: 7,000

15 June v Bangu drew 2–2 in Vancouver
Crowe, Murray
Davies, Showell, G. Harris, Goodwin, Woodfield, Kirkham, Crowe, Murray, Farmer, Broadbent, Wharton.
Att: 19,339

17 June v West Victoria AS won 2–1 in Victoria, British Columbia
Stobart, Murray
Finlayson, Showell, J. Harris, Goodwin, Woodfield, Knighton, Wharton, Kirkham, Stobart, Broadbent, G. Harris.
Att: 3,000

19 June v Vancouver All Stars won 4–1 in Vancouver
Farmer (2), Murray, Stobart
Davies, Showell, G. Harris, Goodwin, Woodfield, Kirkham, Crowe, Murray, Farmer (Stobart), Broadbent, Wharton.
Att: 12,000

22 June v Bangu won 4–1 in Toronto
Stobart (2), Farmer, G Harris
Davies, Showell, G. Harris, Goodwin, Woodfield, Kirkham, Crowe, Murray, Farmer, Stobart, Wharton.
Att: 10,226

1963

9 October v Honved lost 1–2
Crawford
Davies, Thomson, G. Harris (Showell), Goodwin, Woodfield, Flowers, Wharton, Crowe, Crawford, Murray, Hinton.
Att: 31,000

1964 Caribbean Tour

21 May v Chelsea won 3–1 in Bridgetown, Barbados
Le Flem, Crawford (2)
Line up and att: not known

24 May v Trinidad won 4–0 in Pointe a Pierre, Trinidad
Crawford (3), Stobart
Davies, Showell, Harris, Woodruff, Woodfield, Kirkham, Wharton, Crowe, Crawford, Melia, Stobart.
Att: 12,000

25 May v Chelsea lost 2–3 in Port of Spain, Trinidad
Le Flem, Knowles
Davies, Showell, Harris, Broadbent, Woodfield, Woodruff, Crowe, Knowles, Crawford, Melia, Le Flem.
Att: 25,000

27 May v Chelsea won 4–2 in Kingston, Jamaica
Crawford (2), Le Flem, Upton (og)
Line up not known
Att: 13,000

29 May v Jamaica won 8–4 in Kingston, Jamaica
Scorers, line up and att: not known

1965

8 August v Kaiserslautern won 3–2
Knowles, Miller, McIlmoyle
McLaren, Knighton, Thomson, Flowers, Woodfield, Miller, Wharton, Woodruff, McIlmoyle, Knowles, Wagstaffe.
Att: 6,000

1966 Swiss Tour

9 August v FC Zurich lost 1–3
Knighton
McLaren (Davies), J. Wilson (Knighton), Thomson, Bailey, Flowers, Holsgrove, Wharton, Hunt, McIlmoyle, Knowles, Wagstaffe.
Att: not known

12 August v Servette drew 1–1 in Lausanne
Hunt
Davies (McLaren), J. Wilson (Knighton), Thomson, Bailey, Hawkins, Flowers, Wharton, Hunt, McIlmoyle (L. Wilson), Knowles, Wagstaffe.
Att: not known

1967 United Soccer Association League

In this tournament, Wolves played as Los Angeles Wolves and played their home games in LA. They won the Western Division and faced Eastern Division winners Aberdeen in the Final at the Los Angeles Coloseum.

27 May v Bangu drew1–1 in Houston
Woodfield
Parkes, Taylor, Thomson, Holsgrove, Woodfield, Burnside, Wharton, Hunt, Dougan, Knowles, Wagstaffe.
Att: 34,965

4 June v Cerro won 2–1 in Los Angeles
Hunt, Burnside
Parkes, Taylor, Thomson, Holsgrove, Hawkins, Burnside, Wharton, Hunt, Dougan, Knowles, Wagstaffe.
Att: 7,000

7 June v Stoke drew 0–0 in Cleveland
Davies, L. Wilson, Thomson, Holsgrove, Hawkins, Burnside, Wharton, Hunt (Evans), Dougan, Knowles (Buckley), Wagstaffe.
Att: 4,128

11 June v Hibernian won 2–1 in Toronto
Thomson, Dougan
Parkes, L. Wilson, Thomson, Holsgrove, Hawkins, Burnside (Davies), Wharton, Evans (Allen), Dougan, Knowles, Wagstaffe.
Att: 5,000

14 June v Sunderland won 5–1 in Los Angeles
Buckley (2), Hunt, Dougan, Knowles
Davies, L. Wilson, Thomson, Holsgrove, Hawkins, Burnside, Wagstaffe, Hunt, Dougan, Knowles, Buckley.
Att: 6,000

18 June v Glentoran won 4–1 in Los Angeles
Thomson, Dougan, Hunt, Knowles
Davies, L. Wilson (Taylor), Thomson, Holsgrove, Hawkins, Burnside, Wagstaffe (Wharton), Hunt, Dougan, Knowles, Buckley.
Att: 5,381

20 June v Aberdeen drew 1–1 in Washington DC
Burnside
Davies, L. Wilson, Thomson, Holsgrove, Hawkins, Burnside, Wharton (Buckley), Hunt (Evans), Dougan, Knowles, Wagstaffe (Taylor).
Att: 7,847

25 June v Shamrock Rovers drew 1–1 in Los Angeles
Wharton (pen)
Parkes, Taylor, Thomson, Holsgrove, Woodfield, Burnside, Wharton, Hunt, Dougan, Knowles, Wagstaffe.
Att: 8,000

28 June v ADO The Hague lost 0–1 in San Francisco
Davies, Taylor, Thomson, Holsgrove, Woodfield, Burnside, Wharton, Hunt, Dougan, Knowles, Wagstaffe (Buckley). L. Wilson replaced Buckley.
Att: 7,123

30 June v ADO The Hague won 2–0 in Los Angeles
Wharton, Davies
Parkes, Taylor, Thomson, Bailey (Davies), Holsgrove, Woodfield, Wharton, L. Wilson, Evans, Knowles, Burnside.
Att: 12,000

5 July v Cagliari drew 2–2 in Los Angeles
Hunt, Wharton (pen)
Davies, Taylor, Thomson, Bailey, Woodfield, Holsgrove, Wharton, Hunt, Dougan, Knowles (Wagstaffe), Burnside.
Att: 11,000

9 July v Dundee United drew 2–2 in Dallas
Knowles, Thomson
Parkes, Taylor, Thomson, Bailey, Holsgrove, L. Wilson, Wharton, Hunt, Dougan, Knowles, Burnside.
Att: 7,946

10 July v Aberdeen lost 0–3 in Washington DC
Davies, Taylor, Thomson, Bailey, Woodfield, Holsgrove, Wharton, Hunt, Dougan, Knowles, Burnside.
Att: 7,641
(This was a re-staging of the 20 June meeting of the clubs in which Wolves were found to have infringed the rules by fielding three substitutes).

14 July v Aberdeen won 6–5 in Los Angeles (in sudden death after extra-time)
Knowles, Burnside (3), Dougan, Thomson
Parkes, Taylor, Thomson, Holsgrove, Woodfield, Burnside, Wharton, Hunt, Dougan, Knowles, Wagstaffe.
Att: 17,824

1969 US Tournament

2 May v West Ham lost 2–3 in Baltimore
Knowles, Bailey
Parkes, L. Wilson, Parkin, Bailey, Woodfield, McAlle, Walker, Knowles, D. Clarke (Farrington), Curran, Wagstaffe.
Att: 5,128

4 May v Dundee United won 4–2 in Kansas City
Knowles (2), Wilson, Bailey
Parkes, Parkin, Taylor, Bailey, Holsgrove, Munro, Farrington, L. Wilson (Walker), Knowles, Curran (D. Clarke), Wagstaffe.
Att: 3,221

8 May v West Ham won 4–2 in Kansas City
McAlle (2), Bailey, Curran
Parkes, L. Wilson, Parkin, Bailey, Holsgrove, McAlle, Walker, Munro, Knowles, Curran, Wagstaffe.
Att: 1,417

11 May v Kilmarnock won 3–2 in Kansas City
Curran (2), Farrington
Parkes, L. Wilson, Parkin, Bailey, Woodfield, McAlle (Holsgrove), Farrington, Knowles (Walker), Munro, Curran, Wagstaffe.
Att: 5,834

14 May v Aston Villa won 2–1 in Atlanta
Knowles (pen), Dougan
Parkes, L. Wilson, Parkin, Bailey, Holsgrove, McAlle, Knowles, Munro, Dougan, Curran (Woodfield), Wagstaffe (Walker).
Att: 1,869

16 May v Kilmarnock won 3–0 in St Louis
Dougan, Wagstaffe, Curran
Parkes, Taylor (L. Wilson), Parkin, Bailey, Woodfield, McAlle, Knowles, Munro, Dougan, Curran, Wagstaffe (Walker).
Att: 3,224

24 May v Aston Villa won 5–0 in Kansas City
Dougan, Curran (2), Knowles, Woodfield
Parkes, L. Wilson, Parkin, Bailey, Holsgrove, McAlle, Knowles, Munro (Woodfield), Dougan, Curran, Wagstaffe (Walker).
Att: 1,219

25 May v Kansas City Spurs drew 1–1 in Kansas City
Dougan
Line up and att: not known
(friendly, not part of the tournament)

31 May v Dundee United lost 2–3 in Dallas
Dougan (2)
Line up not known
Att: 2,659

1970 Yugoslav Tour

15 April v Zeljeznicar Sarajevo won 1–0
McCalliog
Line up not known
Att: 7,000

17 April v Sloboda lost 1–3 in Tuzla
D. Clarke
Oldfield, Taylor, Parkin, Bailey, Holsgrove, Munro, Hibbitt, McCalliog, Richards (D. Clarke), Curran, Walker. Richards returned to replace Hibbitt, who also returned later in the game.
Att: not known

22 April v Skopje lost 2–5
Curran (pen), McCalliog
Oldfield, Wilson, Parkin, Bailey (McAlle), Holsgrove, Munro, Hibbitt (Woodfield), McCalliog, D. Clarke (Chung), Curran, Richards.
Att: not known

1970 West German and Dutch Tour

29 July v Stuttgart 2–0
Parkes, Wilson, Parkin, Bailey, Holsgrove, Munro (Woodfield), Hegan (Richards), McCalliog, Dougan (Gould), Curran, Walker (Lutton).
Att: not known

1 August v Hanover lost 1–4
Curran
Oldfield, Wilson, Parkin, Bailey, Holsgrove, Munro, Hegan, McCalliog, Dougan, Curran (Gould), Walker (Lutton).
Att: not known

4 August v Groningen lost 0–1
Munro, Bailey, Parkin, Woodfield, Holsgrove, Hegan (Richards), McCalliog (L. Wilson), Curran (Dougan), Gould, Walker, Lutton.
Att: 6,000

1971

24 February v Marsa won 5–1 in Valetta, Malta
Gould (2), Hibbitt (2), Holsgrove
Parkes, Shaw, Taylor, Bailey, Holsgrove, McAlle, Hibbitt, O'Grady, Richards, Gould, Wagstaffe. Sub: Curran.
Att: 5,000

5 May v Israel National XI won 3–1 in Tel Aviv
Parkin, Walker, Gould
Parkes, Shaw, Parkin, McCalliog, Munro, McAlle, O'Grady (Hibbitt), Walker, Gould, Dougan (Curran), Wagstaffe.
Att: 22,000

1971 Swedish Tour

19 July v Örgryte won 2–1
Gould, McCalliog (pen)
Parkes, Shaw, Parkin, Bailey, Munro, McAlle, McCalliog, Hibbitt, Dougan, Gould (Daley), Wagstaffe.
Att: 3,000

22 July v GAIS drew 3–3 (Wolves won 3-2 on penalties)
Richards (2), Parkin
Parkes, Shaw, Parkin, Bailey, Munro, McAlle, Hibbitt, McCalliog, Dougan, Richards, Daley.
Att: 8,545

23 July v Karlstad won 2–1
Parkin, Richards
Line up not known
Att: 3,403

1972

31 January v Jersey Select XI won 9–0
McCalliog (4), Dougan (2), Sunderland, Hibbitt, Richards
Parkes, Shaw, Parkin, Sunderland, Munro, McAlle, McCalliog, Hibbitt, Richards, Dougan, Wagstaffe.
Att: not known

9 February v PAOK Salonika drew1–1 in Greece
Dougan
Parkes, Taylor, Parkin, Sunderland, Munro, McAlle, McCalliog, Hibbitt, Richards, Dougan, Wagstaffe. Subs: Daley, Curran.
Att: 15,000

1972 US Tour

21 May v Aberdeen lost 1–3 in San Francisco
McCalliog
Parkes, Shaw, Taylor (Parkin), Bailey, Munro, McAlle, Hibbitt (Sunderland), McCalliog (Daley), Curran (Eastoe), Richards, Wagstaffe.
Att: 1,500

24 May v Aberdeen lost 0–3 in Seattle
Parkes, Shaw (Taylor), Parkin, Bailey, Munro, McAlle, Sunderland (Daley), Hibbitt (Eastoe), Richards, Curran, Wagstaffe.
Att: 6,000

26 May v Aberdeen won 3–0 in Vancouver
Hibbitt, Richards, Curran
Parkes, Taylor, Parkin (Shaw), Bailey (Sunderland), Munro, McAlle, Hibbitt (Daley), McCalliog, Richards, Curran (Eastoe), Wagstaffe.
Att: 9,195

28 May v Aberdeen won 4–0 in Los Angeles
Richards (3), Munro
Parkes, Taylor, Parkin (Shaw), Sunderland (Bailey), Munro, McAlle, McCalliog, Daley, Richards, Curran (Eastoe), Wagstaffe.
Att: 4,500

1972 New Zealand and Australian Tour

3 June v Auckland won 3–2
Dougan (2), Curran
Line up not known
Att: 14,000

5 June v Wellington won 6–0
Dougan (2), McCalliog (2), Eastoe (2)
Line up and att: not known

7 June v South Island won 2–0 in Christchurch
Eastoe, Munro
Line up and att: not known

11 June v Australian National XI lost 0–1 in Melbourne
Parkes, Shaw, Parkin, Hegan, Munro, (Taylor), McAlle, McCalliog, Sunderland, Curran, Dougan, Daley (Wagstaffe).
Att: 10,269

12 June v Australian National XI drew 2–2 in Sydney
Munro, Curran
Parkes, Taylor, Parkin, Hegan, Munro, McAlle, McCalliog, Sunderland (Hibbitt), Curran, Dougan (Eastoe), Wagstaffe.
Att: 16,134

14 June v Queensland XI won 6–2 in Brisbane
Eastoe (3), Dougan, McCalliog, Hibbitt
Line up and att: not known

17 June v South Australia won 3–2 in Adelaide
Hegan, Hibbitt, Sunderland
Line up and att: not known

19 June v Western Australia won 3–0 in Perth
McCalliog, Wagstaffe, Eastoe
Line up not known
Att: 15,346

1972 Swedish Tour

25 July v GAIS (Rous Cup semi-final) drew 1–1 (Wolves won 4–3 on pens) in Gothenburg
Soderblom (og)
Line up not known
Att: 3,847

27 July v Everton (Rous Cup Final) won 2–1 in Gothenburg
Richards, Hibbitt
Line up not known
Att: 3,133

1973 Swedish Tour

30 July v Örgryte (Rous Cup semi-final) won 3–1 in Gothenburg
McCalliog (2, 1 pen), Richards
Line up not known
Att: 3,824

1 August v Leicester (Rous Cup Final) won 1–0 in Gothenburg
Sunderland
Line up and att not known

3 August v Trollhättans IF won 4–1
Dougan, Richards, McCalliog, Sunderland
Pierce, Taylor, Parkin, Hibbitt, Munro, McAlle, McCalliog, Sunderland, Richards, Dougan, Kindon.
Att: 2,161

6 August v Stockholm XI won 1–0
Richards
Parkes, Taylor, Parkin, Hegan, Munro, McAlle, McCalliog, Hibbitt, Richards, Dougan, Kindon.
Att: 3,840

1973

20 August v Bruges lost 0–1
Parkes, Palmer, Parkin, Hegan, Jefferson, Taylor, McCalliog (Sunderland), Hibbitt, Richards, Dougan (Powell), Wagstaffe.
Att: 5,000

1975 Norwegian Tour

14 May v Mjondalen Idrettsforening won 1–0
Kindon
Parkes, Taylor (Williams), Parkin, Bailey, Jefferson, McAlle, Hibbitt (Daley), Carr, Richards, Kindon, Wagstaffe (Farley).
Att: 2,000

17 May v Odds Ballklubb won 8–2 in Skien
Richards (3), Kindon (2), Hibbitt, Carr (pen), Parkin (pen)
Parkes, Williams (Taylor), Parkin, Bailey, Jefferson, McAlle, Hibbitt (Daley), Carr, Richards, Kindon, Wagstaffe (Farley).
Att: 6,000

21 May v Alesund won 3–1
Kindon (2), Farley
Line up and att not known

1975 Swedish Tour

21 July v Norrkoping won 3–0
Hibbitt (pen), Richards, Kindon
Line up not known
Att: 4,350

23 July v Kalmar won 1–0
Richards
Parkes, Parkin, McNab, Bailey, Munro (Jefferson), McAlle, Hibbitt, Carr, Richards, Sunderland, Wagstaffe.
Att: 4,483

24 July v Malmo won 2–1
Kindon, Sunderland
Garnham, Palmer, McNab (Parkin), Daley, Munro (McAlle), Jefferson, Hibbitt, Carr (Wagstaffe), Sunderland, Kindon, Farley.
Att: not known

26 July v IS Halmia won 2–1
Kindon (2)
Parkes (Garnham), Palmer, McNab (Daley), Bailey, Munro, McAlle, Sunderland, Carr, Richards, Kindon, Wagstaffe.
Att: not known

29 July v Helsingborg won 4–0
Richards (3), Carr
Parkes (Garnham), Parkin, McNab (Palmer), Bailey, Munro, McAlle (Jefferson), Sunderland (Farley), Carr, Richards, Kindon, Daley.
Att: 3,041

1976 Swedish Tour

24 July v Leksand won 9–1
Gould (4), Kindon (2), Daley, Richards, Sunderland
Pierce, Palmer, Parkin, Daley, Bailey, Brazier, Hibbitt, Carr, Richards (Gould), Kindon, Farley (Sunderland).
Att: not known

26 July v Hudiksvall won 1–0
Kindon
Pierce, Palmer, Parkin, Daley, Bailey, Berry, Patching (Carr), O'Hara (Hibbitt), Bell (Kindon), Gould (Richards), Sunderland.
Att: not known

27 July v Domsjo XI won 3–0
Kindon, Richards, Gould
Garnham, Palmer, Parkin, Daley (Patching), Bailey (Berry), Brazier, Hibbitt (O'Hara), Carr, Richards (Gould), Kindon (Bell), Sunderland.
Att: not known

29 July v OPE won 4–0
Hibbitt (2), Palmer, Gould
Pierce, Palmer, Parkin, Daley, Brazier, Berry, Hibbitt (Patching), Carr (Bell), Gould, Kindon (Richards), Sunderland (O'Hara).
Att: 600

1977 Norwegian Tour

17 May v Odd won 4–2 in Skien
Richards (2), Todd, Brazier
Parkes, Palmer, Parkin, Daley (Wright), Brazier, Berry, Hibbitt, Richards (Gould), Kindon (Bell), Todd, Carr.
Att: not known

18 May v Vinstra won 5–0
Gould (2), Richards, Hibbitt, Bell
Parkes, Palmer, Parkin (Daly), Brazier, Berry, Daley, Hibbitt, Richards (Gould), Kindon (Bell), Todd (Wright), Carr.
Att: 3,60

19 May v Grue won 6–0
Hibbitt (2), Sunderland (2), Bell, Gould
Parkes, Palmer, Daly, Daley, Brazier, Parkin, Hibbitt (Bell), Richards (Gould), Sunderland, Todd, Carr (Wright).
Att: 3,800

1977 Swedish Tour

22 July v Norrkoping lost 0–2
Parkes, Palmer, Parkin, Daley, Munro, Brazier (Daly), Hibbitt, Gould (Sunderland), Kindon, Patching (Todd), Carr.
Att: 3,000

25 July v Orebro lost 0–2
Taylor, Palmer, Daly (Munro), Daley, Parkin, McAlle, Todd (Patching), Carr, Richards, Kindon (Gould), Sunderland.
Att: 3,993

27 July v Stockholm Alliance drew 0–0
Line up not known
Att: 4,864

28 July v Gavle XI won 3–1
Richards (2), Daley
Taylor, Palmer, Daly, Daley (Carr), Brazier, McAlle (Kindon), Patching, Todd, Richards, Gould, Sunderland.
Att: 3,138

1 August v Sirius won 4–1 in Uppsala
Richards (2), Kindon, Gould
Parkes, Palmer, Daly, Daley, Parkin, McAlle, Hibbitt (Patching), Carr, Richards (Gould), Kindon, Sunderland (Todd).
Att: 3,332

2 August v Vasteras won 7–1
Richards, Kindon, Daley, Hibbitt, Sunderland, Carr, Gould
Parkes, Palmer (Daly), Parkin, Daley, Munro, McAlle (Brazier), Hibbitt, Richards (Kindon), Sunderland (Gould), Patching (Todd), Carr.
Att: 3,174

1978 Norwegian Tour

14 May v Ski-Kolbotn won 4–0 in Oslo
Rafferty, Moss, Black, Daley
Bradshaw, Palmer, Parkin, Daley, Hazell (Berry), McAlle, Car, Rafferty, Richards (Bell), Patching (Moss), Eves (Black).
Att: not known

15 May v Gvand won 4–1
Black (2), Bell, Eves
Bradshaw, Palmer, Parkin, Daley, Berry, McAlle (Hazell), Moss (Patching), Carr, Richards (Bell), Rafferty (Black), Eves.
Att: not known.

18 May v Molde lost 0–1
Line up and att: not known

1978 Swedish and Danish Tour (Sweden unless stated)

18 July v Kristianstad won 3–1
Daniel (pen), Todd, Eves
Bradshaw, Daniel, Palmer, Parkin (Arkwright), Hazell, McAlle, Todd, Carr (Clarke), Rafferty, Eves, Black.
Att: not known

20 July v Karlskrona won 2–0
Parkin, Todd
Bradshaw, Daniel, Palmer, Parkin, Brazier, Berry, Todd (Arkwright), Carr, Rafferty (Eves), Bell, Black.
Att: not known

22 July v Trelleborg won 3–1
Todd, Eves, Rafferty
Bradshaw, Palmer, Parkin, Daniel, Hazell, McAlle, Todd, Carr, Rafferty, Eves, Black (Hibbitt).
Att: 3,012

23 July v Folkets Lag won 3–1
Scorers, line up and att not known

25 July v Mjallby drew 1–1
Berry
Bradshaw, Daniel, Palmer, Parkin (McAlle), Brazier, Berry, Hibbitt (Todd), Carr, Clarke, Bell (Rafferty), Arkwright (Black).
Att: not known

27 July v Hvidovre won 5–1 in Copenhagen
Eves (3), Carr, Rafferty
Bradshaw, Daniel, Palmer, Parkin, Hazell, McAlle, Hibbitt, Carr, Rafferty, Eves, Todd.
Att: not known

1980 Greece

15 April v AEK Athens drew 2–2
Gray (2)
Line up and att: not known

1980 Bilbao Tournament

7 August v Borussia Monchengladbach lost 3–4
Gray, Hughes, Eves
Bradshaw, Palmer, Parkin, Daniel, Hughes, Berry, Brazier, Carr (Villazan), Gray (Richards), Clarke, Eves (Thomas).
Att: not known

8 August v Athletico Bilbao lost 0–1
Bradshaw, Palmer (Carr), Parkin (Berry), Daniel, Hughes, McAlle, Brazier, Villazan, Richards, Clarke, Thomas (Eves).
Att: not known

1981 US

16 May v Jacksonville Teamen lost 1–4
Richards
Line up not known
Att: 2,000

Northern Ireland

4 August v Linfield drew 1–1
Richards
Bradshaw, Palmer, Hollifield (Humphrey), Daniel (Atkinson), Villazan, Berry, Teasdale (Moss), Carr, Gray, Richards, Matthews.
Att: 6,000

1982 Northern Ireland

18 August v Dundalk won 1–0
Coy
Burridge, Humphrey, Coy, Gallagher, Atkinson, Cartwright, Palmer, Wintersgill, Clarke, Eves, Livingstone (Butler).
Att: 1,756

19 October v Glentoran won 3-2
Eves (2), Clarke
Burridge, Humphrey, Palmer, Hibbitt, Pender, Coy, Daniel, Eves (Miller), Gray, Clarke (Rudge), Butler.
Att: 2,204

1983 Swedish Tour

31 July v Vargarna won 3-2
Livingstone (2), Eves
Bradshaw (Burridge), Humphrey, Palmer, Cartwright (Rudge), Pender, Dodd, Kellock (Hibbitt), Daniel (Matthews), Livingstone, Eves, Towner (Butler).
Att: 1,440

4 August v Nykoping Alliance won 6–0
Gray (2), Livingstone, Kellock, Dodd, Hibbitt
Bradshaw, Humphrey, Daniel, Rudge (Butler), Palmer, Dodd, Hibbitt, Kellock, Gray (Towner), Livingstone, Matthews.
Att: 2,063

6 August v Krylbo won 5–1
Matthews (2), Kellock, Livingstone, Gray
Bradshaw, Humphrey, Daniel, Cartwright, Dodd, Palmer, Towner (Livingstone), Rudge, Kellock (Gray), Matthews, Butler.
Att: 1,448

7 August v Ludvika won 2–0
Gray (2)
Burridge, Daniel, Palmer, Rudge, Dodd, Hibbitt (Matthews), Towner, Cartwright, Gray, Livingstone (Kellock), Butler.
Att: 2,310

10 August v Vasteras XI lost 1–3
Gray
Burridge, Humphrey, Daniel, Palmer, Dodd, Towner (Pender), Cartwright, Gray, Livingstone, Rudge, Butler (Kellock).
Att: 3,377

1983 Irish Tour

14 August v Drogheda United won 4–0
Hibbitt, Smith, Gray, Palmer (pen)
Line up and att: not known

17 August v Bohemians lost 0–1 in Dublin
Bradshaw, Humphrey, Daniel, Smith, Pender, Palmer, Hibbitt (Dodd), Clarke, Eves, Rudge, Towner.
Att: 900

19 August v Athlone drew 1–1
Clarke
Burridge, Humphrey, Pender (Butler), Dodd, Palmer, Smith, Daniel, Rudge, Clarke (Livingstone), Gray (Cartwright), Eves.
Att: 950

1984 Kuwaiti Tour

21 February v Kuwait National XI drew 0–0
Burridge, Buckland, Daniel, Hibbitt, Pender, Dodd, Towner, Clarke, Troughton, Eves (Humphrey), Crainie (Rudge).
Att: 2,000

23 February v Kuwait National XI drew 0–0
Flowers, Buckland, Palmer, Rudge, Rodger, Dodd, Towner, Wintersgill, Troughton, Eves, Crainie.
Subs (all used): Daniel, Hibbitt, Clarke.
Att: 1,500

3 October v Norrkoping won 1–0
Buckland
Line up not known
Att: 890

1985 Maltese Tour

18 May v Xewkija Tigers won 2–1 in Gozo
Ainscow, Crainie
Barrett, Humphrey, Buckland, Zelem, Pender, Cartwright (Herbert), Ryan, Campbell Chapman, Ainscow, Crainie, Stoutt (Dougherty).
Att: 1,200

24 May v Gozo and Maltese Select won 3–0 in Gozo
Buckland, Ainscow, Campbell Chapman
Barrett, Wright, Stoutt, Zelem, Pender, Herbert, Dougherty (Cavan Chapman), Campbell Chapman, Ainscow, Crainie (Ryan), Buckland (Cartwright).
Att: 1,000

28 May v Shrewsbury lost 2–5 in Marsa
Campbell Chapman, Buckland
Barrett, Cartwright, Buckland, Zelem, Pender, Herbert, Dougherty, Campbell Chapman, Ainscow, Crainie, Stoutt.
Att: 400

1990 Northern Ireland

10 August v Glenavon won 4–2
Bull (2), Dennison, Mutch
Stowell, Bennett, Thompson, Bellamy, Hindmarch, Venus (Stobart), Paskin (Steele), Cook (Downing), Bull, Mutch, Dennison.
Att: 500

1991 Swedish Tour

26 July v Bracke won 8–0
Taylor (3), Burke (2), Bennett, Bull, Dennison
Line up not known
Att: 350

29 July v Spoland won 5–0
Bull (2), Bellamy, Downing, Dennison
Jones, Ashley, Venus, Westley, Bellamy, Downing, Thompson, Cook, Bull, McLoughlin (Mutch), Dennison (Burke).
Att: 1,200

31 July v Timra XI won 4–1
Thompson (pen), Taylor, Bull, Burke
Line up not known
Att: 630

2 August v Vemdalen XI won 10–0
McLoughlin (4), Steele (2), Venus, Bellamy, Dennison, Bull
Line up not known
Att: 750

3 August v Husum won 6–0
Mutch (2), Hindmarch, Downing, Bull, Burke
Line up not known
Att: 987

1992 Gibraltar

27 January v Gibraltar XI won 5–2
Burke (2), Bull, Bennett Birch
Jones, Thompson, Venus, Bennett, Madden (Smith), Mountfield (B. Roberts), Steele, Birch, Bull, Burke, Dennison.
Att: 1,000

1993 Swedish Tour

21 July v Vaxjo Norra won 5–2
Bull (2), Mills (2), Birch
Line up not known
Att: 333

22 July v Nymbro won 3–1
Burke, Bull, D. Kelly
Stowell, Ashley, Edwards, Burke, Mountfield, Blades (Venus), Keen, Cook, Bull, D. Kelly, Thomas.
Att: 1,004

25 July v Ljungby won 3–0 (match abandoned after 82 minutes)
Mills (2), Birch
Jones, Simkin, Edwards, Rankine, Mountfield (Ashley), Blades (Venus), Birch, Thomas (Cook), Mills (Bull), D. Kelly (Roberts), Keen (Burke).
Att: 400

26 July v Saxemara won 3–1
Bull, D. Kelly, Thomas
Stowell, Simkin (Ashley), Venus, Burke, Mountfield, Blades, Keen (Birch), Cook, Bull, D. Kelly, Thomas. Sub: Mills.
Att: 1,557

28 July v Valdermarsvik won 8–1
Roberts (3), Edwards (2), Mountfield, Cook (pen), Mills
Line up not known
Att: 518

1994 Danish and Swedish Tour

19 July v Hvidovre won 2–1 in Copenhagen
Bull (2)
Jones (Stowell), Thompson, Venus, Rankine (Smith), Blades (Emblen), Shirtliff, Keen (Simkin), Cook (Ferguson), Bull (Daley), Mills, Froggatt: (Dennison).
Att: not known

20 July v Solve won 6–1
Dennison (2), Daley (2), Mills, Froggatt
Stowell (Jones), Rankine (Venus), Smith, Keen (Marsden), Blades, Emblen, Dennison, Thomas (Cook), Daley, Mills, Froggatt: (Ferguson).
Att: 400

23 July v Smedby BoIK won 9–0
Bull (5), Mills (3), Thompson
Jones, Rankine (Simkin), Thompson, Ferguson, Shirtliff, Emblen, Keen, Thomas, Bull, Mills, Cook.
Att: 500

25 July v Kristianstad won 2–0
Daley, Bull
Stowell, Simkin (Smith), Thompson, Ferguson (Keen), Blades, Venus, Daley, Cook, Bull, Mills (Rankine), Dennison.
Att: 1,103

27 July v Asarum won 3–1
Mills (3)
Stowell, Smith, Thompson, Ferguson (Dennison), Blades, Shirtliff, Keen, Thomas, Bull, Mills, Froggatt.
Att: 1,200

1996 Austrian and German Tour*

19 July v Abtenau won 4–0
Osborn, Bull (2), Froggatt
Stowell, Smith, Froggatt, (Thompson), Venus, Emblen, Popovic, Atkins (Wright), Robinson (Rankine), Bull, Roberts, Osborn.
Att: not known

21 July v Spittal won 2–1
Roberts, Foley
Stowell, Thompson, Froggatt, (Pearce), Venus, Emblen (Smith), Popovic, Atkins (Rankine), Osborn, Ferguson (Wright), Bull, Roberts (Foley).
Att: not known

24 July v Kotzting won 3–1
Roberts, Bull, Ferguson
Stowell, Smith, Froggatt, (Pearce), Venus, Atkins, Popovic, Wright, Ferguson (Thompson), Bull (Foley), Roberts, Osborn (Rankine).
Att: not known

26 July v Weismain won 4–0
Froggatt, Thompson, Bull (2)
Stowell, Smith, Froggatt, Venus, Atkins, Popovic, Wright, Thompson, Bull, Roberts, Osborn. Subs: Ferguson, Rankine.
Att: not known
* *The first two games above were played in Austria, the second two in Germany.*

1998 Austrian and German Tour

15 July v Wustenrot Salzburg lost 0–2
Stowell, Muscat, Froggatt (Naylor), Sedgley (Curle), Emblen, Williams, Simpson (Ferguson), Atkins, Bull (Paatelainen), Freedman (Claridge), Osborn. Subs: Richards, Robinson.
Att: not known

18 July v Lask Linz lost 0–2 in Grieskirchen, Austria
Stowell, Muscat, Naylor, Richards, Williams (Paatelainen), Curle, Ferguson, Emblen (Robinson), Bull, Claridge, Osborn (Froggatt). Subs: Simpson, Atkins.
Att: 2,000

22 July v Carl Zeiss Jena won 1–0 in Schleiz, Germany
Bull
Stowell, Muscat, Naylor, Atkins, Richards, Curle, Corica (Robinson), Simpson (Osborn), Bull, Claridge, Froggatt. Subs: Emblen, Williams.
Att: not known

24 July v Union Berlin won 2–1
Robinson, Simpson
Stowell, Muscat, Naylor (Simpson), Richards, Emblen, Williams, Froggatt, Robinson (Ferguson), Bull, Claridge (Corica), Osborn (Atkins).
Att: 2,200

1999 Swedish Tour

13 July v Olofstrom won 3–2
Ekelund, Emblen, Sinton (pen)
Stowell, Muscat (Bazeley), Emblen, Curle (Green), Van kiel (Naylor), Taylor (Niestroj), Robinson (Osborn), Corica (Robinson), Simpson (Sinton), Keane (Jones), Ekelund (Flo).
Att: 700

14 July v Hassleholm won 3–2
Robinson, Jones, Keane
Murray, Muscat (Green), Curle (Naylor), Emblen, Van Kiel, Bazeley (Niestroj), Robinson (Corica), Osborn (Taylor), Sinton (Simpson), Flo (Jones), Ekelund (Keane).
Att: 558

16 July v Bromolla won 3–0
Van Kiel, Ekelund (2)
Stowell, Muscat (Taylor), Curle, Emblen (Green), Van Kiel (Naylor), Niestroj (Bazeley), Osborn (Corica), Taylor (Robinson), Simpson, Keane (Jones), Ekelund.
Att: 550

17 July v Solve XI won 4–3
Taylor, Flo, Keane, Muscat (pen)
Murray, Bazeley (Niestroj), Green, Curle (Van Kiel), Naylor, Taylor (Simpson), Robinson (Osborn), Corica, Sinton (Muscat), Jones (Keane), Ekelund (Flo).
Att: 500

2000 Irish Tour

17 July v Waterford won 2–0
Robinson, Titi
Oakes, Green, Ulfstein, Titi, Camara, Taylor (Andrews), Osborn (Robinson), Leitch, Simpson (Lescott), Emblen, Branch (Sinton).
Att: 2,500

19 July v Cork drew 0–0
Oakes, Muscat (Green), Pollet (Osborn), Titi (Lescott), Naylor (Camara), Bazeley (Ulfstein), Robinson, Osborn (Andrews), Leitch (Emblen), Sinton (Simpson), Branch (Taylor).
Att: 4,250

21 July v Kilkenny won 2–0
Robinson, Branch
Oakes (Murray), Muscat (Titi), Pollet (Sedgley), Lescott (Ulfstein), Camara (Naylor), Bazeley (Green), Emblen (Andrews), Robinson, Leitch (Osborn), Sinton (Simpson), Branch.
Att: 2,200

2001 Portuguese Tour

16 July v Espinho drew 2–2 in Caldas
Roussel, Robinson
Bywater (Oakes), Bazeley (Connelly), Clyde (Butler), Pollet (Lescott), Sinton (Naylor), Branch (Ketsbaia), Markovic (Dinning), Andrews (Robinson), Melligan (Kennedy), Ketsbaia (Proudlock), Roussel.
Att: 1,500

18 July v Leiria lost 0–2
Oakes, Connelly, Butler, Lescott (Clyde), Naylor, Bazeley (Branch), Robinson (Melligan), Andrews (Markovic), Kennedy, Proudlock (Roussel), Larkin.
Att: 2,000

21 July v Alverca lost 1–2
Proudlock
Bywater (Oakes), Connelly, Butler, Pollet (Lescott), Naylor, Branch (Melligan), Dinning (Andrews), Markovic (Robinson), Kennedy, Ketsbaia (Larkin), Proudlock. Subs: Clyde, Roussel.
Att: 2,500

2001 Belgium

31 July v Royal Antwerp drew 2–2
Suarez, Roussel
Bywater, Connelly (Bazeley), Butler, Pollet, Camara, Branch (Ketsbaia), Andrews, Dinning, Kennedy (Sinton), Roussel (Robinson), Suarez (Proudlock). Sub: Oakes.
Att: 3,500

2002 Portuguese Tour

18 July v Sporting Lisbon lost 1–5
Newton
Oakes, Edworthy (Connelly), Naylor (Camara), Clingan (Newton), Pollet, Butler (Ingimarsson), Cooper, Rae, Blake (Ndah), Cameron (Proudlock), Sturridge (Miller). Subs: Howarth, Lescott.
Att: 1,800

21 July v Maritimo lost 0–1 in Rio Maior, Lisbon
Oakes (Howarth), Edworthy (Connelly), Naylor (Camara), Ingimarsson, Lescott, Pollet (Butler), Newton (Ndah), Rae, Sturridge (Proudlock), Miller (Clingan), Cooper.
Att: 1,500

2004 Norwegian Tour

17 July v Tromso won 3–2 in Nordreisa
Craddock, Ganea (2)
Jones, Clyde, Craddock, Booth, Kennedy, Newton, Ince (Clingan), Andrews, Cooper (Naylor), Miller (Mulligan), Ganea (Gobern, 82). Subs: Ikeme, Flynn, O'Connor, Lowe, Townsend.
Att: 1,800

19 July v Bodo Glimt lost 0–2
Jones (Ikeme), Clyde (Lowe), Booth (Mawene), Lescott (Craddock), Naylor; Cooper (Kennedy), Andrews (Ince), Clingan (O'Connor), Gobern (Newton); Mulligan (Ganea), Ndah (Miller).
Att: 1,177

21 July v Lyn lost 1–2 in Oslo
Ince
Jones, Lowe (Gobern), Mawene, Craddock, Kennedy, Newton, Andrews, Ince, Cooper, Ganea (Mulligan), Miller.
Att: 828

2005 Netherlands

27 July v Den Haag lost 0–3
Hennessey (Ikeme), McNamara (Rafferty), Edwards, Lowe, Kennedy, Cameron, Ince, Ricketts, Ndah (Gobern), Cort (Ganea), Seol (Clarke).
Att: 2,700

2007 Irish Tour

18 July v Bray Wanderers won 4–0
Eastwood (2), Bothroyd (2)
Murray, Edwards (Little), Mulgrew (L. Collins), D. Ward (N. Collins), Breen (Craddock), Potter (Gleeson), Jarvis (Kightly), Henry, Keogh (Bothroyd), Eastwood, S. Ward (Jones).
Att: 3,459

22 July v Bohemians drew 1–1 in Dublin
S. Ward
Murray (Hennessey), Little (Edwards), L. Collins (Mulgrew), Olofinjana (Potter), N. Collins (D. Ward), Craddock (Breen), Kightly, Gleeson (Henry), Elliott (Keogh), Bothroyd (Eastwood), Jones (S. Ward).
Att: 2,200

International Wolves

Details of international/major representative honours gained by players while they were associated with Wolves. (Loan players are included.)

Full International Appearances

Australia

Steve Corica (1), Kevin Muscat (10).
Goals: Muscat 4 (including hat-trick of penalties).

England

Harry Allen (5), Tom Baddeley (5), Dicky Baugh (1), Billy Beats (2), Peter Broadbent (7), Jack Brodie (3), Steve Bull (5+8 sub), Eddie Clamp (4), Chris Crowe (1), Stan Cullis (12), Norman Deeley (2), Arthur Fletcher (2), Ron Flowers (48+1 sub), Tom Galley (2), Johnny Hancocks (3), Alan Hinton (1), Emlyn Hughes (1+2 sub), Revd Kenneth Hunt (2), George Kinsey (2), Arthur Lowder (1), Charlie Mason (3), Bill Morris (3), Jimmy Mullen (11+1 sub), Jesse Pye (1), John Richards (1), Billy Crispin Rose (4), Bill Slater (12), Tom Smalley (1), Bobby Thomson (8), Dick Topham (1), Bert Williams (24), Dennis Wilshaw (12), Harry Wood (3), Billy Wright (105).
Goals: Flowers 10, Wilshaw 10, Mullen 6, Bull 4, Wright 3, Broadbent 2, Hancocks 2, Brodie 1, Galley 1, Wood 1.

Finland

Mixu Paatelainen (3+1 sub).

Georgia

Temuri Ketsbaia (8), 1 goal.

Grenada

Jason Roberts (3), 5 goals.

Hungary

Gabor Gyepes (2), Devres Rosa (1).

Iceland

Joey Gudjonsson (2), Ivar Igimarsson (4).

Ireland

Billy Halligan (1).

New Zealand

Rikki Herbert (11).

Nigeria

Ade Akinbiyi (2), Isaac Okoronkwo (4), Seyi Olofinjana (2).

Northern Ireland

Jackie Brown (3), Mark Clyde (3), Robbie Dennison (12+6 sub), Derek Dougan (26), Danny Hegan (6), Bertie Lutton (2), David Martin (2), Peter McParland (1), Sammy Smyth (8).
Goals: Smyth 5, Dougan 4, Brown 1.

Norway
Haavard Flo (1), Steffen Iversen (5).
Goals: Iversen 2.

Poland
Tomasz Frankowski (2).

Republic of Ireland
David Connolly (1+4 sub), Maurice Daly (2), Stephen Gleeson (0+2 sub), David Jordan (2), Robbie Keane (10+2 sub), Andrew Keogh (4+3 sub), Mark Kennedy (2+1 sub), Mick Kearns (2), David Kelly (3+1 sub), Jimmy Kelly (5), Darren Potter (3+2 sub).
Goals: Keane 2, Connolly 1, D. Kelly 1, Keogh 1.

Romania
Vio Ganea (3).

Saudi Arabia
Sami Al Jaber (4).

Scotland
Colin Cameron (11+6 sub), Hugh Curran (4+1 sub), Andy Gray (8+5 sub), Jim McCalliog (1), Jackie McNamara (3), Kenny Miller (18+7 sub), Frank Munro (6+3 sub).
Goals: Miller 7, Gray 4, Cameron 1, Curran 1.

Senegal
Henri Camara (3).

South Africa
Mark Williams (3+1), 3 goals.

South Korea
Ki-Hyeon Seol (14), 2 goals.

Ukraine
Oleg Luzhny (2).

Wales
George Berry (3+1 sub), Nathan Blake (2+6 sub), John Bowdler (2), Craig Davies (0+1 sub), Joe Davies (2), Freddy Eastwood (9), David Edwards (2+1 sub), Rob Edwards (4+5 sub), Ryan Green (2), Wayne Hennessey (9+1 sub), Bryn Jones (10), Paul Jones (8), Albert Lumberg (1), John Matthias (1), Teddy Peers (8), Charlie Phillips (10), David Richards (11), Dick Richards (5), Carl Robinson (3+5 sub), Sam Vokes (0+2), Adrian Williams (4+1 sub), Eric Young (1).
Goals: Eastwood 4, Phillips 4, Jones 3, Bowdler 2, Blake 1, Dick Richards 1, Williams 1.

Rest of the United Kingdom
Billy Wright (1).

United Kingdom
Derek Dougan (1).

Unofficial Internationals

England

Billy Beats (1), Alan Hinton (1), Billy Wooldridge (1).

England XI

Joe Blackett (1), Hill Griffiths (1), Jack Miller (1).

England (v Young England)

Peter Broadbent (2), Eddie Clamp (1), Ron Flowers (7), Johnny Kirkham (1), Nigel Sims (1), Bill Slater (1), Bobby Thomson (1), Billy Wright (3).

England World Cup XI

Jimmy Mullen (1), Bert Williams (1), Billy Wright (1).

Scotland XI

Hugh Curran (1).

Under-23 Internationals

England

Colin Booth (0+1 sub), Peter Broadbent (1), Ted Farmer (2), Ron Flowers (2), Gerry Harris (4), Kenny Hibbitt (0+1 sub), Alan Hinton (3), Ernie Hunt (2), Johnny Kirkham (2), Peter Knowles (4), Gerry Mannion (2), Jimmy Murray (2), Geoff Palmer (2), Derek Parkin (5), Barry Powell (3+1 sub), John Richards (5+1 sub), Alan Sunderland (0+1 sub), Bobby Thomson (15).
Goals: Farmer 4, Hinton 3, Murray 2, Knowles 1, Mannion 1, Richards 1.

Republic of Ireland

Stephen Ward (3+1 sub).
Goal: Ward 1.

Scotland

Frank Munro (3+1 sub).

Under-21 Internationals

England

Paul Bradshaw (2), Steve Bull (5), Bob Hazell (1), Michael Kightly (1+2 sub), Joleon Lescott (0+2 sub), Matt Murray (4+1 sub), Andy Mutch (1), Lee Naylor (3), Dean Richards (4), John Richards (2), Alan Sunderland (1).
Goals: Bull 3, Hazell 1.

Northern Ireland

Sammy Clingan (5+1 sub), Mark Clyde (5), Tom Stewart (3+2 sub).
Goals: Stewart 1.

Republic of Ireland

Hugh Atkinson (1), Glenn Crowe (1+1 sub), Maurice Daly (1), Dominic Foley (8+1 sub), Darren Gibson (1), Stephen Gleeson (4), Robbie Keane (5), Andy Keogh (2), John Melligan (0+1 sub), Kevin O'Connor (2), John Pender (1), Mark Salmon (1+1 sub), Stephen Ward (1).
Goals: Gleeson 2, Foley 1, Keane 1, Keogh 1.

Scotland
Charlie Mulgrew (7+1 sub).
Goals: Mulgrew 2.

Wales
Craig Davies (1), David Edwards (1), Ryan Green (16), Wayne Hennessey (5), Carl Robinson (8+1 sub).

B Internationals

England
Peter Broadbent (1), Steve Bull (4+1 sub), Steve Daley (5+1 sub), Mel Eves (1+2 sub), Bob Hazell (1), Harry Hooper (1), Jimmy Mullen (3), Andy Mutch (2+1 sub), Jesse Pye (3), John Richards (3), Roy Swinbourne (1), Bert Williams (1), Dennis Wilshaw (2), Billy Wright (2).
Goals: Bull 2, Daley 2, Wilshaw 2, Eves 1, Hooper 1, Mullen 1, Swinbourne 1.

Northern Ireland
Robbie Dennison (1).

Republic of Ireland
Noel Dwyer (1), Robbie Keane (1), David Kelly (1), Darren Potter (0+1 sub), Stephen Ward (0+1 sub).

Scotland
Neill Collins (0+1 sub), Dougie Freedman (0+1 sub), Kenny Miller (1).

Wales
Carl Robinson (2).

Wartime and Victory Internationals

England
Sammy Brooks (1), Stan Cullis (20), Jimmy Mullen (3), Frank Taylor (1), Dennis Westcott (4), Bert Williams (4), Billy Wright (4).
Goals: Westcott 5.

Scotland
John Harris (1).

Wales
Teddy Peers (2), Cyril Sidlow (11).

All British XI
Stan Cullis (1).

Inter-League Matches

Football League
George Ashall (1), Tom Baddeley (3), Mike Bailey (3), Billy Beats (5), Peter Broadbent (2), Sammy Brooks (1), Steve Bull (3), Eddie Clamp (1), Stan Cullis (3), Ron Flowers (13), Tom Galley (1), Joe Gardiner (1), Hill Griffiths (1), Johnny Hancocks (2), Harry Hooper (1), Revd Kenneth Hunt (1), Joey Jones (1), Billy Malpass (1), Jack Miller (1), Jimmy Mullen (1), Jimmy Murray (1), Derek Parkin (1), Jesse Pye (1), John

Richards (1), Cecil Shaw (1), Jamie Smith (1), Bobby Thomson (4), Dave Wagstaffe (1), Dennis Westcott (1), Bert Williams (5), Harry Wood (4), Billy Wooldridge (1), Billy Wright (21), David Wykes (1).
Goals: Beats 4, Wooldridge 3, Bailey 1, Broadbent 1, Murray 1, Pye 1, Westcott 1, Wood 1, Wright 1, Wykes 1.

Football League Select XI

Billy Harrison (2).

Football League XI

Stan Cullis (2), Dicky Dorsett (1), Tom Galley (1), Joe Gardiner (1), Billy Hartill (1), Alex Scott (1), Dennis Westcott (2).

Youth Internationals (at Under-16, 17, 18 and 20 Levels)

England

C. Beavon, J. Bray, W. Clarke, V. Cockcroft, L. Cocker, A. Corbett, C. Dangerfield, A. Dickson, P. Eastoe, A. Evans, T. Flowers, I. Hall, R. Hazell, A. Hinton, T. Jewkes, M. Jones, J. Kirkham, P. Knowles, J. Lescott, M. Little, G. Mannion, H. Middleton, C. Moss, M. Murray, L. Naylor, M. Patching, A. Proudlock, B. Perry, J. Skull, C. Tether.

Northern Ireland

D. Beattie, D. Clements, S. Devine, C. Gilmore, C. Hagan, G. Haveron, G. Simms, M. McCain, S. Troughton, J. Willis.

Republic of Ireland

K. Andrews, K. Coleman, G. Crowe, S. Crowe, M. Daly, S. Gleeson, S. Hackett, F. Hayes, R. Keane, A. Kernan, C. Larkin, J. Melligan, K. O'Connor, J. Pender, G. Quinn.

Scotland

P. Buckley, D. Devlin, W. Livingstone.

Wales

J. Easter, R. Green, W. Hennessey, D. Keith, C. Robinson.

Junior International

England

E. Cutler, W. Rotton.

Amateur Internationals

England

Percy Corbett (7), Billy Holmes (3), Revd Kenneth Hunt (20), Dick Topham (2), Bill Slater (6).

United Kingdom (Olympic Games)

Revd Kenneth Hunt (3).

Wolves Players' Career Records

The following is a list of players who have played for Wolves at competitive level between 1883 and 2008. 'Other matches' are the European Cup, European Cup-winners' Cup, UEFA Cup, Anglo-Italian Cup, Texaco Cup, Watney Cup, Freight Rover Trophy, Zenith Data Systems Cup, Sherpa Van Trophy, Football League Play-offs and FA Charity Shield.

Player	Birthplace	Date of Birth	Died	With club	From	To	League A	League G	FAC A	FAC G	FLC A	FLC G	Others A	Others G	Total A	Total G
Ainscow, Alan	Bolton	15/07/1953		1984–85	Eastern FC	Blackburn Rovers	56 +2	5	3	1	3 +1	0	0	0	62 +3	6
Akinbiyi, Ade	Hackney	10/10/1974		1999–2000	Bristol City	Leicester City	36 +1	16	3	0	0	0	0	0	39 +1	16
Alderton, James	Wingate	06/12/1924		1941–47	Juniors	Coventry City	11	4	0	0	0	0	0	0	11	4
Aliadiere, Jeremie	Rambouillet (France)	30/03/1983		2006	Arsenal (L)	Arsenal	12 +2	2	0	0	0	0	0	0	12 +2	2
Al-Jaber, Sami A.	Riyadh (SA)	11/12/1972		2000–01	Al Hilal (L)	Al Hilal	0 +4	0	0	0	1	0	0	0	1 +4	0
Allen, Harry	Walsall	19/01/1866	1895	1886–94	Walsall Town Swifts	Retired	123	8	30	5	0	0	0	0	153	13
Anderson, Edward	Newcastle	17/07/1911	1979	1930–31	Worksop Town	Torquay United	2	0	0	0	0	0	0	0	2	0
Anderson, Nicholas	Wolverhampton	1865	1921	1888–89	Local	Local	2	0	0	0	0	0	0	0	2	0
Anderton, Darren	Southampton	03/03/1972		2005–06	Birmingham City	Bournemouth	20 +4	1	1	0	1	1	0	0	22 +4	2
Andrews, Keith	Dublin	13/09/1980		1997–2005	School	Hull City	41 +24	0	4	0	3	1	0	0	48 +24	1
Annis, Walter	Wolverhampton	13/05/1874	1950	1898–1905	Stafford Road	Cradley Heath	138	1	9	0	0	0	0	0	147	1
Arkwright, Ian	Shafton, Yorks	18/09/1959		1977–79	Juniors	Wrexham	3 +1	0	0	0	0	0	0	0	3 +1	0
Arrowsmith, Arthur	Wolverhampton	23/05/1880	1954	1908–09	Stoke	Willenhall Swifts	1	0	0	0	0	0	0	0	1	0
Ashall, George	Kilamarsh	29/09/1911	1998	1935–38	Frickley Colliery	Coventry City	84	14	10	5	0	0	0	0	94	19
Ashley, Kevin	Birmingham	31/12/1968		1990–94	Birmingham City	Peterborough	87 +1	1	1 +1	0	5	0	4	0	97 +2	1
Ashton, Derek	Worksop	04/07/1922		1941–46	Worksop Schools	Aston Villa	0	0	4	0	0	0	0	0	4	0
Astill, Leonard	Wolverhampton	30/12/1916	1988	1931–35	Juniors	Blackburn Rovers	2	0	0	0	0	0	0	0	2	0
Aston, Harry	Bloxwich	20/10/1855	1914	1885–86	West Bromwich Albion	Burslem Port Vale	0	0	5	4	0	0	0	0	5	4
Aston, Jack	Wednesbury	23/03/1863	1935	1884–86	Local	Willenhall	0	0	5	3	0	0	0	0	5	3
Atkins, Mark	Doncaster	14/08/1968		1995–99	Blackburn Rovers	York City	115 +11	8	11 +1	0	12 +1	2	2	1	140 +13	11

Player	Birthplace	Date of Birth	Died	With club	From	To	League		FAC		FLC		Others		Total	
							A	G	A	G	A	G	A	G	A	G
Atkinson, Hugh	Dublin	08/11/1960		1978–82	Dundrum Boys	Exeter City	38 +8	3	4	0	1	0	0 +1	0	43 +9	3
Baddeley, Thomas	Stoke	02/11/1874	1946	1896–1907	Burslem Port Vale	Bradford	296	0	19	0	0	0	0	0	315	0
Bailey, Herbert	Wolverhampton	01/09/1870	1942	1891–92	Local	Willenhall Pickwick	1	0	0	0	0	0	0	0	1	0
Bailey, Michael	Wisbech	27/02/1942		1966–77	Charlton Athletic	Minnesota Kicks	360 +1	19	18 +2	2	29	0	25 +1	4	432 +4	25
Baillee, Joseph	Dumfries	26/02/1929	1966	1954–56	Celtic	Bristol City	1	0	0	0	0	0	0	0	1	0
Baker, Charles	Stafford	10/02/1870	1940	1891–93	Stoke	Stoke	37	6	4	4	0	0	0	0	41	10
Baker, Jack	Trethomas	27/03/1904	1975	1926–29	Lovells Athletic	Coventry City	16	0	1	0	0	0	0	0	17	0
Bansford, George	Wednesfield	23/05/1894	1965	1919–20	Bushbury	Lanesfield	1	0	0	0	0	0	0	0	1	0
Barker, George	Blakenhall	23/02/1875	1953	1900–01	Bristol City	Retired	13	0	3	0	0	0	0	0	16	0
Barlow, Herbert	Kilnhurst	22/07/1916	2004	1938–39	Barnsley	Portsmouth	3	1	0	0	0	0	0	0	3	1
Barnes, David	Paddington	16/11/1961		1984–87	Ipswich Town	Aldershot	86 +2	4	6	0	7	0	6	0	105 +2	4
Barraclough, William	Hull	03/01/1909	1969	1928–34	Hull City	Chelsea	172	18	11	1	0	0	0	0	183	19
Barrett, Scott	Ilkeston	02/04/1963		1984–87	Notts County	Stoke City	30	0	1	0	1	0	3	0	35	0
Barron, James	Tanobie, Durham	19/10/1943		1961–65	Newcastle West End	Chelsea	8	0	0	0	0	0	0	0	8	0
Bartley, Jack	New Washington	11/02/1902	1977	1928–30	Spennymoor United	Walsall	2	0	0	0	0	0	0	0	2	0
Bartram, Vincent	Birmingham	07/08/1968		1985–91	Oldswinford	Bournemouth	5	0	3	0	2	0	0	0	10	0
Bate, William	West Bromwich	05/05/1895	1963	1919–20	Darlaston	West Smethwick	11	0	0	0	0	0	0	0	11	0
Baugh, Richard snr	Wolverhampton	14/02/1864	1929	1886–96	Stafford Road	Walsall	185	1	42	0	0	0	0	0	227	1
Baugh, Richard jnr	Wolverhampton	06/03/1902	1972	1918–24	Stafford Road	West Bromwich Albion	108	4	12	0	0	0	0	0	120	4
Baxter, Thomas	Mansfield	01/02/1903	1987	1927–29	Mansfield Town	Port Vale	50	14	3	1	0	0	0	0	53	15
Baxter, William	Methill, Fife	21/09/1924	2002	1945–53	Juniors	Aston Villa	43	1	4	0	0	0	0	0	47	1
Bayly, Martin	Dublin	14/09/1966		1982–85	Little Bray	Coventry City	9 +1	0	0	0	1	0	0	0	10 +1	0
Baynham, Albert	Wolverhampton	18/03/1880	1944	1903–06	Halesowen	St Peter's FC	71	2	6	2	0	0	0	0	77	4
Baynton, Jack	Rushock Wood	06/03/1859	1932	1877–89	St Luke's	Retired	18	0	10	0	0	0	0	0	28	0
Bazeley, Darren	Northampton	05/10/1972		1999–2001	Watford	Non-League	69 +1	4	3	0	7	0	0	0	79 +1	4
Beasant, David	Willesden	20/03/1959		1993	Chelsea (L)	Chelsea	4	0	1	0	0	0	0	0	5	0
Beats, William	Wolstanton	13/11/1871	1939	1894–1903	Burslem Port Vale	Bristol Rovers	199	67	19	6	0	0	0	0	218	73
Beattie, John	Newhills (Scotland)	28/05/1912	1992	1933–34	Aberdeen	Blackburn Rovers	44	13	2	0	0	0	0	0	46	13
Bell, John	Dundee	10/06/1877	1940	1894–95	Bacup	Grimsby Town	6	2	0	0	0	0	0	0	6	2
Bell, Norman	Sunderland	16/11/1955		1971–81	Juniors	Blackburn Rovers	58 +22	17	14 +4	7	0 +2	0	0	0	72 +28	24
Bellamy, Gary	Worksop	04/07/1962		1987–92	Chesterfield	Leyton Orient	133 +3	9	3	0	9	0	16	0	161 +3	9

Player	Birthplace	Date of Birth	Died	With club	From	To	League A	League G	FAC A	FAC G	FLC A	FLC G	Others A	Others G	Total A	Total G
Bellis, George	Khadki, India	08/06/1904	1969	1929–32	Wrexham	Burnley	42	0	1	0	0	0	0	0	43	0
Bennett, Elliott	Telford	18/12/1988		2005–	School	Still with club	0	0	0	0	2	0	0	0	2	0
Bennett, Michael	Bolton	24/12/1962		1983–84	Bolton Wanderers	Cambridge United	6	0	0	0	2	0	0	0	8	0
Bennett, Thomas	Falkirk	12/12/1969		1988–95	Aston Villa	Stockport County	103 +12	29	5 +2	0	7	0	3 +1	0	118 +15	2
Benton, Jack	Wolverhampton	08/01/1865	1930	1888–89	Willenhall	Blakenhall	1	0	0	0	0	0	0	0	1	0
Berry, George	Rostrop, Germany	19/11/1957		1975–72	Juniors	Stoke City	124	4	21	2	14	0	1	0	160	6
Best, Robert	Mickley	12/09/1891	1965	1922–23	Sunderland	Durham City	22	0	1	0	0	0	0	0	23	0
Betteley, Richard	Bradley	14/07/1880	1942	1901–06	Bilston United	West Bromwich Albion	115	1	8	0	0	0	0	0	123	1
Bevin, Frederick	Walsall	03/04/1880	1947	1903–06	Darlaston	Stourbridge	35	8	3	1	0	0	0	0	38	9
Bicknell, Roy	Doncaster	19/02/1926	2005	1942–47	Juniors	Charlton Athletic	0	0	1	0	0	0	0	0	1	0
Biggins, Stephen	Lichfield	20/06/1954		1985	Derby County (L)	Derby County	4	0	0	0	0	0	0	0	4	0
Birch, Alan	West Bromwich	12/08/1956		1981–82	Chesterfield	Barnsley	13 +2	0	1	0	2	0	0	0	16 +2	0
Birch, Brian	Salford	18/11/1931		1952	Manchester United	Lincoln City	3	1	0	0	0	0	0	0	3	1
Birch, Paul	West Bromwich	20/11/1962		1991–96	Aston Villa	Doncaster Rovers	128 +14	15	2 +1	0	11 +1	3	8 +1	1	149 +17	19
Bird, Horace	Smethwick	07/02/1895	1964	1919–20	Walsall	Bloxwich Strollers	3	0	0	0	0	0	0	0	3	0
Bischoff, Mikkel	Copenhagen	03/02/1982		2004–05	Manchester City (L)	Manchester City	9 +2	1	0	0	0	0	0	0	9 +2	1
Bishop, Alfred	Stourbridge	08/04/1866	1938	1905–20	Halesowen	Wrexham	357	6	25	0	0	0	0	0	382	6
Bissett, George	Cowdenbeath	25/01/1887	1946	1921–24	Manchester United	Pontypridd	41	10	3	0	0	0	0	0	44	10
Björklund, Joachim	Vaxjo (Sweden)	15/03/1971		2004–05	Sunderland	Retired	2 +1	0	1	0	1	0	0	0	4 +1	0
Black, David	Irvine	22/03/1868	1940	1893–97	Middlesbrough	Burnley	74	15	10	2	0	0	0	0	84	17
Black, John	Helensburgh	10/11/1957		1975–80	Juniors	Bradford City	5 +1	0	0	0	0	0	0	0	5 +1	0
Blackett, Joseph	Newcastle	09/06/1875	1950	1896–1900	Loughborough Town	Derby County	96	11	7	1	0	0	0	0	103	12
Blackham, Arthur	Blakenhall	02/07/1859	1938	1883–84	Stafford Royal	Retired	0	0	2	0	0	0	0	0	2	0
Blackwell, Steven	Wolverhampton	08/06/1967		1982–85	Juniors	Wednesfield	0 +1	0	0	0	0	0	0	0	0 +1	0
Blades, Paul	Peterborough	05/01/1965		1992–95	Norwich City	Rotherham United	103 +4	2	9	1	4 +1	0	6	0	122 +5	3
Blair, Andrew	Kirkcaldy	18/12/1959		1983	Aston Villa (L)	Aston Villa	10	0	0	0	0	0	0	0	10	0
Blake, Mark	Nottingham	16/12/1970		1991	Aston Villa (L)	Aston Villa	2	0	0	0	0	0	0	0	2	0
Blake, Nathan	Cardiff	27/01/1972		2001–04	Blackburn Rovers	Leicester City	70 +5	24	2	0	3	1	5	1	80 +5	26
Blunt, William	Bilston	05/08/1886	1962	1908–12	Stafford Rangers	Bristol Rovers	58	38	3	4	0	0	0	0	61	42
Bonson, Joseph	Barnsley	19/06/1936	1991	1953–57	Juniors	Cardiff City	10	3	2	2	0	0	0	0	12	5
Boon, Reginald	Wolverhampton	06/02/1880	1947	1905–06	Stafford Rangers	Tettenhall	3	1	0	0	0	0	0	0	3	1

Player	Birthplace	Date of Birth	Died	With club	From	To	League		FAC		FLC		Others		Total	
							A	G	A	G	A	G	A	G	A	G
Booth, Charles	Gainsborough	15/08/1869	1898	1889–91	Gainsborough Trinity	Woolwich Arsenal	61	9	12	1	0	0	0	0	73	10
Booth, Colin	Middleton	30/12/1934		1950–59	Juniors	Nottingham Forest	78	26	4	1	0	0	0	0	82	27
Boswell, Alan	Wednesbury	08/08/1943		1968–69	Shrewsbury Town	Bolton Wanderers	10	0	0	0	0	0	0	0	10	0
Boswell, William	Cradley Heath	05/08/1902	1977	1925–27	Walsall	Gillingham	9	5	0	0	0	0	0	0	9	5
Bothroyd, Jay	Islington	07/05/1982		2006–	Charlton Athletic	Still with club	32 +23	12	3	1	0	0	2	0	37 +23	13
Botto, Lewis	Jarrow	12/07/1898	1953	1927–29	Shildon	Norwich City	16	0	0	0	0	0	0	0	16	0
Bottrill, Walter	Elston	08/01/1903	1975	1930–33	York City	Huddersfield Town	101	42	8	2	0	0	0	0	109	44
Bould, George	Tettenhall	17/09/1885	1949	1907–08	Penkridge	Darlaston	6	1	0	0	0	0	0	0	6	1
Bowdler, John	Shrewsbury	24/04/1869	1927	1890–92	Shrewsbury Town	Blackburn Rovers	24	3	1	0	0	0	0	0	25	3
Bowen, George	Walsall	13/07/1875	1945	1899–1901	Bridgtown Amateurs	Liverpool	51	14	5	2	0	0	0	0	56	16
Bowen, Thomas	West Bromwich	16/01/1900	1976	1924–28	Walsall	Coventry City	86	24	8	0	0	0	0	0	94	24
Boxley, Frank	Cradley Heath	17/08/1887	1950	1909–12	Cradley St Luke's	Shrewsbury Town	67	0	7	0	0	0	0	0	74	0
Bradbury, Shaun	Birmingham	11/02/1974		1992–94	Juniors	Hereford United	2	2	0	0	1	0	0	0	3	2
Bradford, John	Pilsley	09/04/1895	1969	1924–27	Grimsby Town	Bournemouth	77	0	3	0	0	0	0	0	80	0
Bradley, Claude	Walsall	19/05/1868	1922	1891–92	Birchills FC	Dudley Town	6	0	0	0	0	0	0	0	6	0
Bradley, Patrick	Coatbridge	03/09/1901	1970	1924–27	Coatbridge	Gillingham	5	0	0	0	0	0	0	0	5	0
Bradshaw, Paul	Altrincham	28/04/1956		1977–84	Blackburn Rovers	Vancouver White Caps	200	0	23	0	18	0	2	0	243	0
Branch, Michael	Liverpool	18/10/1978		1999–03	Everton	Bradford City	61 +11	10	4	0	2 +1	0	0	0	67 +12	10
Brazier, Colin	Solihull	06/06/1967		1973–81	Northfield Town	Jacksonville Town	69 +9	2	4 +2	0	2 +3	0	0 +2	0	75 +16	2
Brazier, Gilbert	Beckbury	15/08/1860	1923	1884–86	Shifnal	Lyttleton Rangers	0	0	2	1	0	0	0	0	2	1
Breakwell, Arthur	Dudley	22/03/1882	1954	1904–07	Sedgley	Brierley Hill	24	3	0	0	0	0	0	0	24	3
Breen, Gary	Hendon	12/12/1973		2006–	Sunderland	Still with club	58 +1	1	4	0	0	0	2	0	64 +1	1
Brewster, George	Culsalmund	07/10/1893	1963	1922–23	Everton	Lovells Athletic	11	0	2	0	0	0	0	0	13	0
Brice, Gordon	Bedford	04/05/1924		1947–48	Luton Town	Reading	12	0	0	0	0	0	0	0	12	0
Brindley, Christopher	Stafford	05/07/1969		1986–88	Hednesford Town	Telford United	7	0	0	0	0	0	2	0	9	0
Broadbent, Peter	Dover	15/05/1933		1951–65	Brentford	Shrewsbury Town	452	127	31	10	0	0	14	8	497	145
Brocksopp, Arthur	Wolverhampton	26/01/1870	1933	1894–95	Ironbridge	Willenhall	3	0	0	0	0	0	0	0	3	0
Brodie, Charles	Duntocher	22/02/1937	2000	1961	Aldershot	Northampton Town	1	0	0	0	0	0	0	0	1	0
Brodie, John	Wightwick	30/08/1862	1925	1877–91	St Luke's	Retired	42	22	23	22	0	0	0	0	65	44
Brookes, Albert	Birmingham	12/12/1888	1948	1910–15	Small Heath Town	Newport County	13	0	1	0	0	0	0	0	14	0
Brooks, Arthur	Sheffield	16/11/1890	1949	1913–15	Rotherham County	Newport County	15	0	3	0	0	0	0	0	18	0

Player	Birthplace	Date of Birth	Died	With club	From	To	League A	League G	FAC A	FAC G	FLC A	FLC G	Others A	Others G	Total A	Total G
Brooks, Samuel	Brierley Hill	28/03/1890	1960	1910–22	Cradley Heath	Tottenham Hotspur	224	50	22	3	0	0	0	0	246	53
Brown, Henry	Workington	23/05/1918	1963	1938–46	Workington	Hull City	2	0	0	0	0	0	0	0	2	0
Brown, John	Belfast	08/11/1914	1990	1934–36	Belfast Celtic	Coventry City	27	6	4	1	0	0	0	0	31	7
Brown, William	Burnbank	17/11/1902	1985	1928–29	Coventry City	Norwich City	33	0	1	0	0	0	0	0	34	0
Bryan, John	Wolverhampton	01/10/1867	1931	1898–1901	St Stephen's FC	Blakenhall	9	2	1	0	0	0	0	0	10	2
Bryant, William	Shildon	26/11/1913	1975	1931–33	Cockfield FC	Wrexham	5	0	0	0	0	0	0	0	5	0
Bryce, Frederick	Flint	16/09/1908	1970	1927–28	Denbigh	Nuneaton Borough	2	0	0	0	0	0	0	0	2	0
Buckland, Mark	Cheltenham	18/08/1961		1984–85	AP Leamington	Kidderminster Harriers	44 +6	5	2	0	4	0	0	0	50 +6	5
Buckley, Patrick	Leith	12/08/1946		1964–68	Third Lanark	Sheffield United	28 +1	8	0	0	0	0	0	0	28 +1	8
Budtz, Jan	Denmark	20/04/1979		2007	Doncaster Rovers (L)	Doncaster Rovers	2 +2	0	0	0	0	0	0	0	2 +2	0
Bull, Stephen	Tipton	28/03/1965		1986–99	West Bromwich Albion	Hereford United	461 +13	250	18 +2	7	32 +1	18	33 +1	31	544 +17	306
Bunch, Walter	Weston-super-Mare	15/08/1872	1937	1895–99	Blakenhall	Walsall	7	0	0	0	0	0	0	0	7	0
Burke, Mark	Solihull	12/02/1969		1991–94	Middlesbrough	Port Vale	53 +15	11	2	0	3	2	2 +2	1	60 +17	14
Burleigh, James	Wolverhampton	24/02/1869	1917	1890–92	Stafford Royal	Willenhall	2	0	0	0	0	0	0	0	2	0
Burns, William	Newtonards	15/11/1904	1969	1925–26	Glentoran	US	1	0	0	0	0	0	0	0	1	0
(2 spells)				1928–29	Shelbourne Ards	Workington	3	0	0	0	0	0	0	0	3	0
Burnside, David	Bristol	10/12/1939		1966–68	Crystal Palace	Plymouth Argyle	38 +2	5	1	0	2	0	0	0	41 +2	5
Burridge, John	Workington	03/12/1951		1982–84	Queen's Park Rangers	Sheffield United	74	0	5	0	2	0	0	0	81	0
Burrill, Frank	London	16/06/1894	1955	1920–23	Southend United	Charlton Athletic	61	16	8	1	0	0	0	0	69	17
Burton, Stanley	Wombwell	03/03/1912	1977	1938–39	Doncaster Rovers	West Ham United	28	3	4	1	0	0	0	0	32	4
Butcher, Joseph	Willenhall	13/02/1975	1945	1892–95	Wolverhampton East End	West Bromwich Albion	65	26	11	4	0	0	0	0	76	30
Butler, Paul	Stockton	09/06/1964		1982–85	Juniors	Hereford United	18 +11	2	0	0	3 +3	0	0	0	21 +14	2
Butler, Paul	Manchester	02/11/1972		2000–04	Sunderland	Leeds United	123 +1	3	7	0	5	0	5	0	140 +1	3
Buttery, Arthur	Hednesford	20/12/1908	1976	1929–32	Hednesford Town	Bury	10	6	0	0	0	0	0	0	10	6
Caddick, William	Wolverhampton	14/03/1903	1990	1920–27	Wellington Town	Wellington Town	147	4	7	0	0	0	0	0	154	4
Callanan, William	Featherstone	11/06/1885	1960	1907–08	Willenhall Pickwick	Bilston Town	3	0	0	0	0	0	0	0	3	0
Camara, Henri	Senegal	10/05/1977		2003–05	Sedan	Wigan Athletic	29 +1	7	0	0	2	0	0	0	31 +1	7
Camara, Mohamed	Conakry, Guinea	25/06/1975		2000–03	Le Havre	Burnley	27 +18	0	1 +1	0	2 +1	0	2	0	32 +20	0
Cameron, Colin	Kirkcaldy	23/10/1972		2001–06	Heart of Midlothian	Coventry City	136 +32	22	8 +3	0	4	2	5	0	153 +35	24
Canavon, Alfred	Coventry	15/12/1904	1971	1925–28	Stafford Rangers	Shrewsbury Town	13	0	2	0	0	0	0	0	15	0
Cannon, Alfred	Cannock	25/05/1865	1930	1888–89	Easington	Springfield FC	7	0	0	0	0	0	0	0	7	0

Player	Birthplace	Date of Birth	Died	With club	From	To	League A	League G	FAC A	FAC G	FLC A	FLC G	Others A	Others G	Total A	Total G
Carr, William	Cambridge	06/01/1950		1975–82	Coventry City	Millwall	231 +6	21	28 +1	4	21	1	2	0	282 +7	26
Carter, Ernest	Harrington	22/04/1895	1958	1921–23	Ashington	Durham Town	17	0	0	0	0	0	0	0	17	0
Cartwright, Archibald	Wolverhampton	02/02/1865	1923	1907–08	Willenhall Pickwick	Bilston Town	2	0	0	0	0	0	0	0	2	0
Cartwright, Ian	Birmingham	13/11/1964		1980–86	Brierley Hill	Northfield	59 +2	3	1	0	4	0	2	1	66 +2	4
Caswell, Brian	Wednesbury	14/02/1956		1987	Leeds United (L)	Leeds United	1	0	0	0	0	0	0	0	1	0
Chadburn, John	Mansfield	12/02/1873	1923	1897–1900	Notts County	West Bromwich Albion	11	1	1	0	0	0	0	0	12	1
Chadwick, Wilfred	Bury	07/10/1900	1975	1926–29	Leeds United	Stoke City	97	44	4	0	0	0	0	0	101	44
Chapman, Campbell	Sutton-in-Ashfield	28/06/1963		1984–86	Bilston Town	Crewe Alexandra	46 +6	4	3	0	2	0	0	0	51 +6	4
Chapman, Cavan	Emsworth	11/09/1967		1983–86	Juniors	West Bromwich Albion (tr)	1	0	0	0	0	0	0	0	1	0
Chard, Philip	Corby	16/10/1960		1988–89	Northampton Town	Northampton Town	26 +8	5	0	0	3 +1	0	1 +1	0	30 +10	5
Charnley, Samuel	Craigneuk	18/11/1902	1977	1925–28	Burnbank Athletic	York City	52	1	3	0	0	0	0	0	55	1
Chatham, Raymond	Wolverhampton	20/07/1924	1999	1940–54	Oxley FC	Notts County	76	0	10	2	0	0	0	0	86	2
Clamp, Edwin	Coalville	14/09/1934	1995	1949–61	School	Arsenal	214	23	14	2	0	0	13	0	241	25
Clapham, James	Lincoln	07/12/1975		2006–07	Birmingham City	Still with club	21 +5	0	1	0	1 +1	0	0	0	23 +6	0
Claridge, Stephen	Portsmouth	04/10/1966		1998	Leicester City	Portsmouth	4 +1	0	1	0	0	0	0	0	5 +1	0
Clarke, Derek	Willenhall	19/02/1950		1968–70	Walsall	Oxford United	2 +3	0	0	0	0	0	0	0	2 +3	0
Clarke, Leon M.	Birmingham	10/02/1985		2002–07	School	Sheffield Wednesday	32 +42	13	1 +2	1	2 +4	1	0	0	35 +48	15
Clarke, Nicholas	Willenhall	20/08/1967		1983–91	School	Mansfield Town	73 +8	1	2 +1	0	5	0	8	0	88 +9	1
Clarke, Wayne	Willenhall	28/02/1961		1976–84	School	Birmingham City	129 +19	30	9 +2	1	8 +2	2	0 +1	0	146 +24	33
(2 spells)				1991	Manchester City (L)	Manchester City	1	0	0	0	0	0	0	0	1	0
Clayton, Gordon	Sunderland	09/07/1910	1976	1932–37	Shotton Colliery	Aston Villa	47	34	8	5	0	0	0	0	55	39
Clews, Malcolm	Tipton	12/03/1931		1946–54	Juniors	Lincoln City	1	0	0	0	0	0	0	0	1	0
Cliff, Thomas	Wolverhampton	22/12/1860	1934	1883–85	St Luke's	Excelsior FC	0	0	4	0	0	0	0	0	4	0
Clyde, Mark G.	Limavady	27/12/1982		1999–2007	School	Retired	41 +6	0	4 +1	0	2	0	0	0	47 +6	0
Coady, Michael	Dipton, Durham	01/10/1958		1985–88	Sydney Olympic	Lincoln City	14 +1	1	0	0	0	0	0	0	14 +1	1
Cock, Donald	Hayle	08/07/1896	1974	1927	Clapton Orient	Newport County	3	1	0	0	0	0	0	0	3	1
Cocker, Leslie	Wolverhampton	18/09/1939		1956–60	Juniors	Wellington Town	1	0	0	0	0	0	0	0	1	0
Cole, Carlton	Croydon	12/12/1983		2002–03	Chelsea (L)	Chelsea	5 +2	1	0	0	0	0	0	0	5 +2	1
Coleman, Simon	Worksop	19/10/1966		1997	Bolton Wanderers (L)	Bolton Wanderers	3 +1	0	0	0	0	0	0	0	3 +1	0
Coley, William	Wolverhampton	17/09/1916	1974	1931–37	Belle Vue Rovers	Bournemouth	2	0	0	0	0	0	0	0	2	0
Colley, Robert	Wednesfield	18/12/1875	1941	1899–1901	Juniors	Newtown	8	2	0	0	0	0	0	0	8	2

Player	Birthplace	Date of Birth	Died	With club	From	To	League		FAC		FLC		Others		Total	
							A	G	A	G	A	G	A	G	A	G
Collins, Edward	Wolverhampton	16/06/1884	1955	1907–15	Brownhills Albion	Sunbeam Motors	284	0	23	0	0	0	0	0	307	0
Collins, Neill	Irvine	02/09/1983		2006–	Sunderland	Still with club	54 +7	5	5	1	1	0	2	0	62 +7	6
Connelly, Sean P.	Sheffield	26/06/1970		2001–02	Stockport County	Tranmere Rovers	11 +3	0	0	0	1	0	0	0	12 +3	0
Connolly, David	Willesden	06/06/1977		1998	Feyenoord (L)	Feyenoord	18 +14	6	0 +1	0	2	0	0	0	20 +15	6
Conway, Arthur	Stirchley	01/04/1885	1954	1908–09	Aston Villa	Halesowen	30	0	0	0	0	0	0	0	30	0
Cook, Paul	Liverpool	22/02/1967		1989–94	Norwich City	Coventry City	191 +2	19	5 +2	0	7	1	6 +1	1	209 +5	21
Cooper, Jeremiah	Heath Town	01/08/1865	1932	1888–91	Amblecote Nomads	Stourbridge	24	6	2	0	0	0	0	0	26	6
Cooper, Kevin	Derby	08/02/1975		2002–05	Wimbledon	Cardiff City	32 +30	9	0 +1	0	1	0	2 +1	1	35 +32	10
Corbett, Percy	Penn	23/02/1885	1948	1905–10	Wulfurians	Retired	6	3	2	0	0	0	0	0	8	3
Corfield, Sidney	Tipton	24/06/1883	1941	1905–09	West Bromwich Albion	Wrexham	44	3	3	0	0	0	0	0	47	3
Corica, Stephen	Innisfail (Australia)	24/03/1973		1995–2000	Leicester City	Hiroshima A (Japan)	80 +20	5	4 +2	0	5 +1	0	0	0	89 +23	5
Cort, Carl	Southwark	01/11/1977		2004–07	Newcastle United	Leicester City	78 +16	31	3 +1	1	1	0	0	0	82 +17	32
Counden, Cuthbert	Sunderland	03/04/1905	1978	1928–29	Southampton	Southend United	43	1	0	0	0	0	0	0	43	1
Cowans, Gordon	Cornworth	27/10/1958		1994–95	Derby County	Sheffield United	31 +6	0	5	1	2	0	2	0	40 +6	1
Coy, Robert	Birmingham	30/11/1961		1977–84	Juniors	Chester City	40 +3	0	0	0	4	0	0	0	44 +3	0
Crabtree, John	Bournbrook	12/09/1887	1954	1912–15	Bournville	Kings Heath	10	0	1	0	0	0	0	0	11	0
Craddock, Jody	Redditch	25/07/1975		2003–	Sunderland	Still with club	138 +11	7	5 +1	0	8	2	2	1	153 +12	10
Crainie, Daniel	Kilsyth	24/05/1962		1983–85	Celtic	Dundee	63 +1	4	4	0	3 +1	0	1	0	71 +2	4
Crawford, Raymond	Portsmouth	13/07/1936		1963–65	Ipswich Town	West Bromwich Albion	57	39	4	2	0	0	0	0	61	41
Crew, William	Little Lever	26/11/1901	1961	1923–24	Bolton Wanderers	Tranmere Rovers	7	0	1	0	0	0	0	0	8	0
Crook, Alfred	Brewood	13/08/1923		1942–49	Boulton & Paul's	Retired	1	0	1	0	0	0	0	0	2	0
Crook, Mark	Morby	29/06/1903	1977	1929–34	Swindon Town	Luton Town	78	14	3	2	0	0	0	0	81	16
Crook, William	Cannock	07/06/1926		1940–54	Boulton & Paul's	Walsall	196	2	24	1	0	0	1	0	221	3
Cross, Charles	Coventry	15/05/1900	1979	1928–29	Crystal Palace	Merthyr Town	3	0	0	0	0	0	0	0	3	0
Crowe, Christopher	Newcastle	11/10/1939	2003	1962–64	Blackburn Rovers	Nottingham Forest	83	24	2	0	0	0	0	0	85	24
Crowe, Glen	Dublin	25/12/1977		1994–99	School	Plymouth Argyle	6 +4	1	0	0	0	0	0	0	6 +4	1
Crump, William	Smethwick	10/02/1874	1943	1894–95	Wednesfield	Bloxwich Strollers	1	0	0	0	0	0	0	0	1	0
Cullis, Stanley	Ellesmere Port	25/10/1916	2001	1934–48	Ellesmere Port Wednesday	Retired	152	0	19	0	0	0	0	0	171	0
Curle, Keith	Bristol	14/11/1963		1996–2000	Manchester City	Sheffield United	148 +2	9	11	1	7	1	2	0	168 +2	11
Curnow, John	Lingdale	31/01/1910	1990	1934–36	Lingdale	Blackpool	6	0	2	0	0	0	0	0	8	0
Curran, Hugh	Glasgow	25/09/1943		1969–72	Norwich City	Oxford United	77 +5	40	2	0	4	2	8 +2	5	91 +7	47

Player	Birthplace	Date of Birth	Died	With club	From	To	League A	League G	FAC A	FAC G	FLC A	FLC G	Others A	Others G	Total A	Total G
Curtis, Frank	Llanelli	12/11/1890	1957	1914–19	Llanelli	Reading	40	25	2	0	0	0	0	0	42	25
Cutler, Eric	Wolverhampton	01/01/1898	1965	1919–21	Fallings Rangers	Bilston Town	18	4	0	0	0	0	0	0	18	4
Daley, Anthony	Birmingham	18/10/1967		1994–98	Aston Villa	Watford	16 +5	3	0 +2	0	4	1	0	0	20 +7	4
Daley, Stephen	Barnsley	15/04/1953		1969–79	School	Manchester City	191 +21	38	18 +1	3	5 +1	0	4 +3	2	218 +26	43
Daly, Maurice	Dublin	28/11/1955		1973–78	Home Farm	Sweden	28 +4	0	2 +1	1	1	0	0	0	31 +5	1
Daniel, Peter	Hull	12/12/1955		1978–84	Hull City	Sunderland	157	13	19	1	17	2	1	0	194	16
Danks, Robert	Bilston	12/03/1865	1936	1887–88	Saltley College	Burslem Port Vale	0	0	3	0	0	0	0	0	3	0
Davidson, Alfred	Wolverhampton	23/01/1861	1933	1883–86	St Luke's	Wednesfield SL	0	0	5	0	0	0	0	0	5	0
Davies, Craig	Burton upon Trent	09/01/1986		2006–07	Verona (L)	Verona	6 +17	0	3	2	1	0	0	0	10 +17	2
Davies, Frederick	Liverpool	22/08/1939		1957–68	Borough United	Cardiff City	156	0	15	0	2	0	0	0	173	0
Davies, Harold	Wednesbury	12/04/1873	1963	1898–1901	Bamford Athletic	Shrewsbury Town	66	0	6	0	0	0	0	0	72	0
Davies, Josiah	Cefn Mawr	12/07/1865	1943	1890–92	West Bromwich Albion	Kidderminster Olympic	34	0	5	0	0	0	0	0	39	0
Davies, Kenneth	Doncaster	20/09/1923		1943–46	Doncaster Town	Walsall	0	0	2	2	0	0	0	0	2	2
Davies, Mark	Willenhall	18/02/1988		2003–	School	Still with club	12 +15	1	1 +4	0	2	0	0	0	15 +19	1
Davies, Richard	Quarrington Hill	12/01/1876	1940	1898–1901	Bristol St George	Reading	11	2	0	0	0	0	0	0	11	2
Davies, Royston	Penydarren	19/10/1903	1944	1929–30	Ebbw Vale	Reading	9	0	0	0	0	0	0	0	9	0
Davison, Thomas	West Stanley	03/10/1901	1971	1923–25	Durham City	Derby County	9	1	1	0	0	0	0	0	10	1
De Wolf, Johannes	Schneidam	10/10/1962		1994–96	Feyenoord	Feyenoord	27 +1	5	4	0	1	0	0	0	32 +1	5
Deacon, James	Glasgow	23/01/1906	1976	1929–34	Darlington	Southend United	149	52	9	4	0	0	0	0	158	56
Deacon, Richard	Glasgow	26/06/1911	1986	1930–31	Cockfield	West Ham United	3	1	0	0	0	0	0	0	3	1
Deakin, Enoch	Wolverhampton	02/05/1888	1945	1910–11	Billbrook	Willenhall Pickwick	5	1	0	0	0	0	0	0	5	1
Dean, John	Wolverhampton	22/09/1880	1958	1901–03	Willenhall White Star	Darlaston	4	0	0	0	0	0	0	0	4	0
Deans, Harold	Wolverhampton	30/12/1864	1923	1884–85	Local	Wednesbury Town	0	0	2	0	0	0	0	0	2	0
Deeley, Norman	Wednesbury	30/11/1933	2007	1948–62	School	Leyton Orient	206	66	16	6	0	0	15	3	237	75
Dennison, Robert	Banbridge	30/04/1965		1986–97	West Bromwich Albion	Hednesford Town	264 +29	40	16 +2	2	12 +4	3	24 +2	4	316 +37	49
Devey, William	Birmingham	12/04/1865	1935	1891–92	Small Heath	Aston Villa	41	17	1	1	0	0	0	0	42	18
Diaz, Isidro	Valencia (Spain)	15/05/1972		1997	Wigan Athletic (L)	Wigan Athletic	1	0	0	0	0	0	0	0	1	0
Dinning, Anthony	Wallsend	12/04/1975		2000–01	Stockport County	Wigan Athletic	35	6	1	0	1	1	0	0	37	7
Dodd, Alan	Stoke-on-Trent	20/09/1953		1982–85	Stoke City	Stoke City	88	5	5	0	6	1	0	0	99	6
Dorsett, Richard	Brownhills	03/12/1919	1998	1935–47	Juniors	Aston Villa	46	32	6	3	0	0	0	0	52	35
Dougan, Derek	Belfast	20/01/1938	2007	1967–75	Leicester City	Retired	244 +14	95	12	4	22	7	29 +2	17	307 +16	123

Player	Birthplace	Date of Birth	Died	With club	From	To	League A	League G	FAC A	FAC G	FLC A	FLC G	Others A	Others G	Total A	Total G
Dougherty, Paul	Leamington Spa	12/05/1964		1982–87	Juniors	San Diego	24 +17	3	2	0	1 +1	0	2	2	29 +18	5
Dowe, Jens	Rostock (Germany)	01/06/1968		1996–97	HSV Hamburg	Sturm Graz	5 +3	0	0	0	0	0	0	0	5 +3	0
Dowen, John	Wolverhampton	12/11/1914	1994	1931–35	Courtalds FC	West Ham United	8	0	0	0	0	0	0	0	8	0
(2 spells)				1936–38	West Ham United	Hull City	4	0	0	0	0	0	0	0	4	0
Downing, Keith	Oldbury	23/07/1965		1987–93	Notts County	Birmingham City	169 +22	8	7	2	9 +3	0	15 +3	1	200 +28	11
Dudley, Robert	Audley	13/03/1864	1910	1889	Audley Welfare	Warwick County	1	0	0	0	0	0	0	0	1	0
Dunn, Edwin	Coventry	11/06/1891	1964	1914–19	Cannock Town	Rugby Town	14	3	2	0	0	0	0	0	16	3
Dunn, James	Edinburgh	25/11/1923		1941–52	St Theresa's	Derby County	123	33	20	7	0	0	0	0	143	40
Dunn, Richard	Birmingham	18/11/1890	1959	1912–13	Cannock	Hednesford Thistle	1	0	0	0	0	0	0	0	1	0
Dunn, Thomas	Falkirk	15/05/1872	1938	1891–95	East Stirlingshire	Burnley	88	0	14	0	0	0	0	0	102	0
Durandt, Clifford	Johannesburg	16/04/1940	2002	1957–63	Marist Brothers	Charlton Athletic	43	9	2	0	0	0	4	1	49	10
Dwyer, Noel	Dublin	30/10/1934	1992	1953–57	Ormeau FC	West Ham United	5	0	0	0	0	0	0	0	5	0
Eastoe, Peter	Dorden, Tamworth	02/08/1953		1970–74	Warton Hatters	Swindon Town	4 +2	0	0	0	0	0	1 +1	1	6 +3	1
(2 spells)				1985	West Bromwich Albion (L)	West Bromwich Albion	8	0	0	0	0	0	0	0	8	0
Eastwood, Frederick	Epsom	29/10/1983		2007–08	Southend United	Coventry City	10 +21	3	0 +2	0	2	1	0	0	12 +23	4
Ebanks-Blake, Sylvan	Cambridge	29/03/1986		2008–	Plymouth Argyle	Still with club	20	12	0	0	0	0	0	0	20	12
Eccles, George	Newcastle-under-Lyme	01/09/1874	1945	1896–98	Burslem Port Vale	Everton	36	1	1	0	0	0	0	0	37	1
Edge, Robert	Wolverhampton	04/07/1871	1950	1893–97	St Phillip's Church	Loughborough	24	8	1	0	0	0	0	0	25	8
Edmonds, George	Holborn	04/04/1893	1989	1920–23	Watford	Fulham	115	38	11	4	0	0	0	0	126	42
Edwards, David	Pontesbury	03/02/1986		2008–	Luton Town	Still with club	10	1	0	0	0	0	0	0	10	1
Edwards, Dean	Wolverhampton	25/02/1962		1985–87	Telford United	Exeter City	28 +3	9	0 +1	0	0	0	2	1	30 +4	10
Edwards, Evan	Merthyr	14/12/1898	1958	1923–25	Merthyr Town	Mid-Rhondda	63	12	7	1	0	0	0	0	70	13
Edwards, Neil	Rowley Regis	14/03/1966		1985–88	Oldswinford	Kettering Town	26 +3	7	3	0	2 +1	0	1	0	32 +4	7
Edwards, Paul	Birkenhead	25/12/1963		1992–94	Coventry City	West Bromwich Albion	43 +3	0	2	0	2	0	1	0	48 +3	0
Edwards, Robert	Telford	25/12/1982		2004–	Aston Villa	Still with club	82 +18	1	2 +3	0	6	0	0	0	90 +21	1
Edworthy, Marc	Barnstaple	24/12/1972		2002–03	Coventry City	Norwich City	18 +4	0	0	0	1	0	0	0	19 +4	0
Eli, Roger	Bradford	11/09/1965		1986–87	Leeds United	Cambridge United	16 +2	0	0	0	1 +1	0	1	0	18 +3	0
Elliott, Edward	Carlisle	24/05/1919	1984	1946–48	Carlisle United	Chester	7	0	0	0	0	0	0	0	7	0
Elliott, Stephen	Dublin	06/01/1984		2007–	Sunderland	Still with club	18 +11	4	1 +1	1	0	0	0	0	19 +12	5
Ellis, John	Tyldesley	25/01/1908	1994	1930–34	West Bromwich Albion (A)	Bristol Rovers	26	0	0	0	0	0	0	0	26	0
Elokobi, George Nganguo	Cameroon	31/01/1986		2008–	Colchester United	Still with club	15	0	0	0	0	0	0	0	15	0

Player	Birthplace	Date of Birth	Died	With club	From	To	League A	League G	FAC A	FAC G	FLC A	FLC G	Others A	Others G	Total A	Total G
Emblen, Neil	Bromley	19/06/1971		1993–97	Millwall	Crystal Palace	80 +8	9	7 +2	0	2 +2	1	2 +1	0	91 +13	10
(2 spells)				1998–2001	Crystal Palace	Norwich City	102 +12	7	6 +1	0	8 +1	1	0	0	116 +14	8
Evans, Alun	Stourport	30/09/1949		1965–68	Aston Villa	Liverpool	20 +2	4	0	0	0	0	0	0	20 +2	4
Evans, Anthony	Liverpool	11/01/1954		1984–85	Crystal Palace	Swindon Town	20 +3	5	1	0	3	1	0	0	24 +3	6
Evans, Jasper	Wednesbury	22/09/1861	1923	1885–87	Wednesbury Town	West B Standard	0	0	3	0	0	0	0	0	3	0
Eves, Melvyn	Wednesbury	10/09/1956		1973–84	Juniors	Sheffield United	169 +11	44	19	5	12 +1	3	2	1	202 +12	53
Farley, John	Middlesbrough	21/09/1951		1974–78	Watford	Hull City	35 +5	0	1	0	1	0	1	0	38 +5	0
Farmer, Edward	Rowley Regis	21/01/1940		1956–64	Wednesbury Youth Club	Retired	57	44	2	0	0	0	3	0	62	44
Farrington, John	Lynemouth	19/06/1947		1965–69	Juniors	Leicester City	31 +3	2	0	0	4	3	0	0	35 +3	5
Farrow, George	Whitburn	04/10/1913	1980	1932–33	Stockport County	Bournemouth	11	0	1	0	0	0	0	0	12	0
Fazackerley, Stanley	Preston	03/10/1891	1946	1922–25	Everton	Derby County	70	29	7	3	0	0	0	0	77	32
Featherby, Leonard	King's Lynn	28/07/1905	1972	1929–30	Merthyr Town	Reading	21	6	0	0	0	0	0	0	21	6
Fellows, Arthur	Wednesfield	12/05/1880	1947	1901–03	Willenhall Pickwick	Darlaston	54	8	1	0	0	0	0	0	55	8
Ferguson, Darren	Glasgow	09/02/1972		1994–99	Manchester United	Wrexham	94 +23	4	9 +2	3	13 +2	2	6	0	122 +27	9
Ferguson, John	Rowland's Gill	12/12/1904	1981	1928–29	Spen Black & White	Watford	20	4	0	0	0	0	0	0	20	4
Ferres, Walter	Bloxwich	13/10/1886	1961	1907–08	Willenhall Swifts	Wednesfield	2	0	0	0	0	0	0	0	2	0
Finlayson, Malcolm	Dumbarton	14/06/1930		1956–64	Millwall	Retired	179	0	14	0	0	0	10	0	203	0
Fleming, Craig	Halifax	06/10/1971		2007	Norwich City (L)	Norwich City	1	0	0	0	0	0	0	0	1	0
Fleming, George	Bannockburn	20/05/1869	1934	1894–1901	East Stirlingshire	Liverpool	171	7	16	0	0	0	0	0	187	7
Fletcher, Albert	Wolverhampton	04/06/1867	1938	1886–91	Willenhall Pickwick	Retired	59	1	17	1	0	0	0	0	76	2
Flo, Håvard	Strin (Norway)	04/04/1970		1999–2001	Werder Bremen	Sogndal	27 +11	9	1 +2	1	2	0	0	0	30 +13	10
Flowers, Ronald	Edlington	28/07/1934		1950–67	Wath Wanderers	Northampton Town	467	33	31	4	0	0	14	0	512	37
Flowers, Timothy	Kenilworth	03/02/1967		1983–86	Juniors	Southampton	63	0	2	0	5	0	2	0	72	0
Foley, Dominic	Cork	07/07/1976		1995–99	St James Gate FC	Watford	4 +16	3	0 +1	0	0 +3	0	0 +2	0	4 +22	3
Foley, Kevin	Luton	01/11/1984		2007–	Luton Town	Still with club	42 +2	1	3	0	2	0	0	0	47 +2	1
Forbes, William	Glasgow	25/05/1922		1946–49	Dunfermline Athletic	Preston North End	71	23	4	0	0	0	0	0	75	23
Ford, Clive	Oldbury	10/04/1945		1960–64	West Bromwich Boys	Walsall	2	0	0	0	0	0	0	0	2	0
Forman, Matthew	Evesham	08/09/1967		1986–88	Aston Villa	Burton Albion	24 +1	4	3	1	0	0	1	0	28 +1	5
Forshaw, Richard	Preston	20/08/1895	1959	1929–30	Everton	Hednesford Town	6	4	0	0	0	0	0	0	6	4
Fownes, Walter	Coseley	18/03/1885	1951	1906–11	Wood Green Rovers	Willenhall	12	0	0	0	0	0	0	0	12	0
Fox, Victor	Middlesbrough	08/01/1898	1949	1924–30	Middlesbrough	Newport County	44	0	5	0	0	0	0	0	49	0

Player	Birthplace	Date of Birth	Died	With club	From	To	League A	League G	FAC A	FAC G	FLC A	FLC G	Others A	Others G	Total A	Total G
Francis, Ernest	Wolverhampton	12/02/1890	1960	1912–14	St Peter's FC	Halesowen	10	3	0	0	0	0	0	0	10	3
Frankowski, Tomasz	Bialystok (Poland)	16/08/1974		2006–	Elche (Spain)	Still with club	12 +4	0	0 +1	0	1	0	0	0	13 +5	0
Freedman, Douglas	Glasgow	21/01/1974		1997–98	Crystal Palace	Nottingham Forest	25 +4	10	5 +1	2	0	0	0	0	30 +5	12
Froggatt, Stephen	Lincoln	09/03/1973		1994–98	Aston Villa	Coventry City	99 +7	7	3	0	10 +1	2	2	0	114 +8	9
Gallagher, John (Jackie)	Wisbech	06/04/1958		1987–89	Wisbech Town	Kettering Town	10 +17	4	2 +1	1	0 +2	0	1 +3	0	13 +23	5
Gallagher, Joseph	Liverpool	11/01/1955		1981–82	Birmingham City	West Ham United	31	0	1	0	2	1	0	0	34	1
Galley, John	Clowne	07/05/1944		1959–64	Juniors	Rotherham United	5	2	1	0	0	0	0	0	6	2
Galley, Thomas	Cannock	04/08/1915	2000	1934–47	Cannock Town	Grimsby Town	183	41	21	8	0	0	0	0	204	49
Galvin, David	Denaby	05/10/1946		1965–66	Juniors	Gillingham	5	0	0	0	0	0	0	0	5	0
Ganea, Ioan Viorel	Fagaras (Romania)	10/08/1973		2004–07	Bursapor	Dinamo Bucharest	17 +17	7	2 +1	1	1 +1	1	0	0	20 +19	9
Gardiner, John	Hamilton	11/07/1904	1976	1928–29	Coventry City	Norwich City	3	0	0	0	0	0	0	0	3	0
Gardiner, Joseph	Bearpark	23/08/1916	1997	1932–44	Juniors	Retired	121	2	18	0	0	0	0	0	139	0
Gardner, Donald	Jamaica	30/08/1955		1972–75	Juniors	Unknown	1 +2	0	0	0	0	0	0	0	1 +2	0
Garratly, George	Walsall	10/10/1888	1952	1909–20	Walsall	Hednesford Town	217	6	15	0	0	0	0	0	232	6
George, Noel	Lichfield	26/12/1897	1929	1919–28	Hednesford Town	Retired	222	0	20	0	0	0	0	0	242	0
Getgood, George	Coylton	15/11/1892	1970	1923–25	Southampton	Kidderminster Harriers	55	1	4	0	0	0	0	0	59	1
Gibbons, Leonard	Wirral	27/11/1930		1946–53	Amateur football	Dudley Town	25	0	4	0	0	0	0	0	29	0
Gibson, Darron	Derry	25/10/1987		2007–08	Manchester United (L)	Manchester United	15 +6	1	1 +2	0	0	0	0	0	16 +8	1
Gilkes, Michael	Hackney	20/07/1965		1997–99	Reading	Millwall	33 +5	1	2	0	1	0	0	0	35 +6	1
Gill, James	Bury	12/12/1901	1970	1921–22	Exeter City	Stourbridge	7	0	0	0	0	0	0	0	7	0
Gleeson, Stephen	Dublin	03/08/1988		2004–	School	Still with club	0 +3	0	0	0	1	0	0 +1	0	1 +4	0
Gobern, Lewis	Birmingham	28/01/1985		2002–	School	Still with club	6 +7	2	0	0	0	0	0	0	6 +7	2
Goddard, George	Gomshall	20/12/1903	1987	1933–34	Brentford	Sunderland	17	12	1	0	0	0	0	0	18	12
Goddard, Raymond	Ecclesfield	17/10/1920	1974	1938–46	Red Rovers	Chelsea	4	0	0	0	0	0	0	0	4	0
Gold, William	Birkenshaw	11/03/1914	1978	1936–37	Bournemouth	Chelsea	10	0	6	0	0	0	0	0	16	0
Gomez, Fernando	Burgos (Spain)	11/09/1965		1998–99	Valencia	CE Castello	17 +2	2	1	0	2	0	0	0	20 +2	2
Goodall, Archibald	Belfast	18/06/1864	1929	1905–06	Glossop	Retired	7	0	0	0	0	0	0	0	7	0
Gooding, Michael	Newcastle	12/04/1959		1988–89	Peterborough United	Reading	43 +1	4	0	0	4	0	5 +1	1	52 +2	5
Goodman, Donald	Leeds	09/05/1966		1994–98	Sunderland	Hiroshima Antlers	115 +10	33	16 +1	2	8 +1	4	3	0	142 +12	39
Goodwin, Frederick	Stockport	04/01/1944		1959–66	School	Stockport County	44 +1	0	2	0	0	0	0	0	46 +1	0
Gorman, James	Stourbridge	c.1883		1906–07	Halesowen	Stoke	9	4	0	0	0	0	0	0	9	4

Player	Birthplace	Date of Birth	Died	With club	From	To	League		FAC		FLC		Others		Total	
							A	G	A	G	A	G	A	G	A	G
Gould, Robert	Coventry	12/06/1946		1970–71	Arsenal	West Bromwich Albion	39 +1	18	2 +1	2	1	0	8	5	50 +2	25
(2 spells)				1975–77	West Ham United	Bristol Rovers	24 +10	13	6	1	1	0	0	0	31 +10	14
Gray, Andrew	Glasgow	03/11/1955		1979–85	Aston Villa	Everton	130 +3	38	13	3	14	3	2	1	159 +3	45
Gray, Michael	Sunderland	03/08/1974		2007–	Blackburn Rovers	Still with club	29 +4	3	2 +1	0	1	0	0	0	32 +5	3
Greatwich, Frank	Wolverhampton	07/07/1874	1933	1897–98	Blackthorn Rovers	Walsall	2	0	0	0	0	0	0	0	2	0
Green, Alfred	Wolverhampton	22/09/1873	1942	1894–96	Hartshill Unity	Hereford Thistle	2	0	0	0	0	0	0	0	2	0
Green, Francis	Ashington	11/05/1902	1982	1927–29	Frickley Colliery	Crewe Alexandra	37	17	1	0	0	0	0	0	38	17
Green, John	St Helens	13/09/1884	1952	1919–20	Prescot Cables	Formby	6	1	0	0	0	0	0	0	6	1
Green, Ryan	Cardiff	20/02/1980		1996–2001	School	Millwall	6 +2	0	0 +2	0	2	0	0	0	8 +4	0
Greene, Christopher	Dublin	01/12/1911	1975	1933–36	Southport	Swansea Town	7	2	0	0	0	0	0	0	7	2
Gregory, John	Wolverhampton	20/12/1887	1950	1908–10	Victoria Swifts	Dudley Town	1	0	0	0	0	0	0	0	1	0
Gregory, Valentine	Hendon	14/02/1888	1940	1920–25	Arsenal	Retired	96	2	10	0	0	0	0	0	106	2
Griffin, Alfred	Walsall	03/06/1871	1945	1892–96	Walsall Town Swifts	Walsall	69	12	7	2	0	0	0	0	76	14
Griffiths, Bernard	Pendeford	23/06/1868	1934	1886–88	Wolverhampton Rangers	Lanesfield	0	0	8	8	0	0	0	0	8	8
Griffiths, Hillary	Wednesfield	04/08/1871	1940	1889–1901	Wednesfield Rovers	Burton Swifts	181	1	20	0	0	0	0	0	201	1
Griffiths, Isaac	Willenhall	15/03/1862	1932	1883–91	Wolverhampton Rangers	Retired	1	0	14	0	0	0	0	0	15	0
Griffiths, Jabez	Wednesfield	12/08/1872	1946	1883–84	Wednesfield Rovers	Stafford	13	2	0	0	0	0	0	0	13	2
Griffiths, John	Wednesfield	27/10/1890	1956	1913–19	Willenhall	Retired	13	2	0	0	0	0	0	0	13	2
Griffiths, John	Fenton	15/09/1909	1975	1929–32	Shirebrook	Bolton Wanderers	5	0	1	0	0	0	0	0	6	0
Griffiths, Joseph	New Tredegar	12/02/1910	1980	1930–31	Tredegar Bay	Stockport County	1	0	0	0	0	0	0	0	1	0
Grosvenor, Sydney	Wolverhampton	18/01/1882	1955	1903–06	Willenhall Swifts	Walsall	2	0	0	0	0	0	0	0	2	0
Groves, Albert	Newport	15/01/1886	1960	1909–20	Aberdare Athletic	Walsall	200	18	17	2	0	0	0	0	217	20
Gudjohnsson, Johannes	Akranes (Iceland)	25/05/1980		2003–04	Real Betis (L)	Real Betis	5 +6	0	1 +1	0	3	1	0	0	9 +7	1
Guelliam, Richmond	Wolverhampton	13/11/1880	1941	1901–02	Birch Coppice	Wren's Nest	2	1	0	0	0	0	0	0	2	1
Gummery, Walter	Worcester	01/05/1900	1974	1923–26	Worcester City	Accrington Stanley	10	1	0	0	0	0	0	0	10	1
Guttridge, William	Darlaston	04/03/1931		1947–54	Metroshafts Works	Walsall	6	0	0	0	0	0	1	0	7	0
Gyepes, Gabor	Budapest	26/06/1981		2005–07	Ferencvaros	Released	19 +1	0	2	0	2	0	0	0	23 +1	0
Hadley, Edmund	Tettenhall	20/09/1865	1929	1883–85	Wednesfield Rovers	Bilston Saints	0	0	3	0	0	0	0	0	3	0
Hales, Frank	Oldbury	13/11/1898	1960	1920–22	Hardy Spicer FC	Darlaston	2	1	0	0	0	0	0	0	2	1
Halle, Gunnar	Larvik (Nor)	11/08/1965		2002	Bradford City (L)	Bradford City	4 +1	0	0	0	0	0	2	0	6 +1	0
Halligan, William	Athlone	13/04/1886	1950	1911–13	Derby County	Hull City	67	34	6	7	0	0	0	0	73	41

Player	Birthplace	Date of Birth	Died	With club	From	To	League		FAC		FLC		Others		Total	
							A	G	A	G	A	G	A	G	A	G
Hamilton, John	Ayr	22/12/1872	1931	1894	Ayr United	Derby County	4	0	0	0	0	0	0	0	4	0
Hampton, John	Wolverhampton	11/10/1899	1961	1920–27	Oakengates	Derby County	49	0	2	0	0	0	0	0	51	0
Hancocks, John	Oakengates	30/04/1919	1994	1946–57	Walsall	Wellington Town	343	157	33	8	0	0	2	2	378	167
Handysides, Ian	Jarrow	14/12/1962	1990	1986	Birmingham City (L)	Birmingham City	11	2	0	0	0	0	0	0	11	2
Hankin, Raymond	Wallsend	21/02/1956		1985–86	Peterborough United	Whitby Town	9 +1	1	0	0	0	0	0	0	9 +1	1
Hann, William	Wolverhampton	01/01/1905	1998	1925–27	Wesley Methodists	Darlaston	14	2	0	0	0	0	0	0	14	2
Hansbury, Roger	Barnsley	26/01/1955		1989	Birmingham City (L)	Birmingham City	3	0	0	0	0	0	0	0	3	0
Hardware, James	Finchfield	04/09/1896	1959	1907–10	Hurst Lane Social	Bilston United	9	0	0	0	0	0	0	0	9	0
Hargreaves, Harold	Higham	03/02/1899	1975	1921–23	Nelson	Pontypridd	53	8	2	0	0	0	0	0	55	8
Harper, George	Birmingham	12/05/1877	1949	1897–1901	Hereford Thistle	Grimsby Town	61	19	5	2	0	0	0	0	66	21
Harrington, John	Hednesford	22/10/1901	1976	1923–28	Hednesford Town	Northampton	107	10	10	0	0	0	0	0	117	10
Harris, George	Redditch	01/07/1875	1910	1896–1900	Aston Villa	Grimsby Town	7	0	0	0	0	0	0	0	7	0
Harris, Gerald	Claverley	08/10/1935		1953–66	Bobbington FC	Walsall	235	2	24	0	0	0	11	0	270	2
Harris, John D.	Upper Gornal	03/04/1939		1955–65	Juniors	Walsall	3	0	0	0	0	0	0	0	3	0
Harris, John W.	Redcar	19/03/1896	1933	1924–26	Bilston Central	Watford	6	2	0	0	0	0	0	0	6	2
Harris, Walter	Wolverhampton	28/01/1888	1938	1908–09	Redditch	Dudley Town	5	1	0	0	0	0	0	0	5	1
Harrison, William	Wybunbury	29/08/1884	1948	1907–20	Crewe Alexandra	Manchester United	317	43	28	6	0	0	0	0	345	49
Hartill, William	Wolverhampton	18/07/1905	1980	1928–35	Army football	Everton	221	162	13	8	0	0	0	0	234	170
Hartland, Frederick	West Bromwich	12/06/1902	1970	1920–22	West Bromwich Albion	Smethwick Highfield	1	0	0	0	0	0	0	0	1	0
Harwood, Irvine	Bradford	05/12/1905	1973	1933–34	Bradford City	Bristol Rovers	6	0	0	0	0	0	0	0	6	0
Hassall, Josuah	Wednesfield	12/01/1874	1938	1892–95	Heath Moor	Retired	48	0	4	0	0	0	0	0	52	0
Hatfield, Ernest	Bradford	16/01/1905	1984	1930–31	Sheffield Wednesday	Southend United	3	0	1	0	0	0	0	0	4	0
Hatton, Robert	Hull	10/04/1947		1963–67	Wath Wanderers	Bolton Wanderers	10	7	2	1	1	0	0	0	13	8
Hawkins, Arthur	Wolverhampton	12/08/1882	1944	1905–07	Bloxwich Strollers	Kidderminster Harriers	20	9	0	0	0	0	0	0	20	9
Hawkins, George	West Bromwich	05/07/1862	1918	1885–86	Wednesbury OA	Walsall Vics	0	0	3	0	0	0	0	0	3	0
Hawkins, Graham	Darlaston	05/03/1946		1961–67	Juniors	Preston North End	28 +6	0	0	0	1	0	0	0	29 +6	0
Hayes, Walter	Oldbury	12/04/1894	1954	1912–14	Hednesford Town	Preston North End	2	0	0	0	0	0	0	0	2	0
Haynes, Harold	Walsall	21/04/1873	1902	1893–95	Walsall Town Swifts	Small Heath	24	2	0	0	0	0	0	0	24	2
Haywood, Adam	Horninglaw	23/03/1875	1932	1901–05	Burton Swifts	West Bromwich Albion	107	28	6	0	0	0	0	0	113	28
Hazell, Robert	Kingston (Jamaica)	14/06/1959		1975–79	Juniors	Queen's Park Rangers	32 +1	1	3	0	0	0	0	0	35 +1	1
(2 spells)				1985	Leicester City (L)	Leicester City	1	0	0	0	0	0	0	0	1	0

Player	Birthplace	Date of Birth	Died	With club	From	To	League		FAC		FLC		Others		Total	
							A	G	A	G	A	G	A	G	A	G
Heath, Joseph	Bristol	02/04/1869	1930	1891–93	Wednesbury Old Athletic	Arsenal	8	4	4	1	0	0	0	0	12	5
Hedley, George	Southbank	20/07/1876	1942	1906–13	Southampton	Retired	193	65	21	9	0	0	0	0	214	74
Heelbeck, Leslie	Scarborough	13/05/1911	1998	1932–34	Carlisle United	Rotherham United	8	0	0	0	0	0	0	0	8	0
Hegan, Daniel	Coatbridge	14/06/1943		1970–73	West Bromwich Albion	Sunderland	49 +4	6	3	0	3	1	10 +1	1	65 +5	8
Hellin, Matthew	Merthyr Tydfil	12/09/1966		1986–87	Aston Villa	Merthyr Town	1	0	0	0	0	0	0	0	1	0
Hemingway, Cyril	Rotherham	12/11/1904	1974	1930–31	Exeter City	Torquay United	4	0	0	0	0	0	0	0	4	0
Henderson, Charles	Durham	12/04/1870	1943	1895–96	Bolton Wanderers	Sheffield United	30	9	6	2	0	0	0	0	36	11
Henderson, John	Montrose	17/01/1932	2005	1958	Portsmouth	Arsenal	9	3	0	0	0	0	0	0	9	3
Hennessey, Wayne	Angelsey	24/01/1987		2003–	School	Still with club	46	0	3	0	0	0	2	0	51	0
Henry, Karl	Wolverhampton	26/11/1982		2006–	Stoke City	Still with club	72 +2	6	5	0	2 +1	0	0	0	79 +3	6
Henshall, Albert	Wellington	13/09/1882	1954	1905–07	Whitchurch	Wellington Town	2	0	0	0	0	0	0	0	2	0
Henson, George	Stony Stratford	25/12/1911	1990	1934–36	Northampton Town	Swansea Town	6	1	0	0	0	0	0	0	6	1
Herbert, Rikki	Wellington (NZ)	10/04/1961		1984–86	Sydney Olympic	Wellington (NZ)	44 +1	0	3	0	0	0	0 +1	0	47 +2	0
Hetherington, John	Rotherham	07/08/1906	1977	1928–35	Dalton United	Preston North End	94	24	1	0	0	0	0	0	95	24
Heywood, David	Wolverhampton	25/07/1967		1983–86	Juniors	Burton Albion	7	0	1	0	0	0	0	0	8	0
Hibbitt, Kenneth	Bradford	03/01/1951		1968–84	Bradford Park Avenue	Coventry City	447 +19	89	46 +1	10	35 +1	12	24 +1	3	552 +22	114
Higgs, Harold	Stourbridge	15/11/1900	1969	1919–20	Halesowen	Darlaston	3	0	0	0	0	0	0	0	3	0
Higham, Frank	Daventry	04/09/1905	1968	1925–28	Walsall	Coventry City	37	2	5	0	0	0	0	0	42	2
Hill, Albert	Rotherham	17/07/1907	1977	1928–30	Yorkshire Amateurs	Wrexham	2	0	0	0	0	0	0	0	2	0
Hill, James	Aldridge	10/03/1888	1952	1909–11	Blakenhall	Darlaston	3	0	0	0	0	0	0	0	3	0
Hill, James W.	Wolverhampton	23/04/1862	1930	1877–84	Spittall Strollers	Retired	0	0	1	0	0	0	0	0	1	0
Hindmarch, Robert	Morpeth	27/04/1961	2002	1990–93	Derby County	Telford United	40	2	1	0	2	0	0 +1	0	43 +1	2
Hinton, Alan	Wednesbury	06/10/1942		1959–64	Juniors	Nottingham Forest	75	29	3	0	0	0	0	0	78	29
Hodnett, Joseph	Wolverhampton	18/07/1896	1943	1919–23	Willenhall	Pontypridd	75	5	10	0	0	0	0	0	85	5
Hollifield, Michael	Middlesbrough	02/05/1961		1977–83	Juniors	Hull City	21	0	4	0	0	0	0	0	25	0
Hollingworth, Reginald	Rainworth	17/10/1909	1969	1928–36	Sutton Junction	Retired	167	7	13	1	0	0	0	0	180	8
Holmes, Michael	Blackpool	09/09/1965		1985–88	Burnley	Huddersfield Town	74 +9	13	3 +1	0	3	0	9 +5	0	89 +15	13
Holsgrove, John	Southwark	27/09/1945		1965–71	Crystal Palace	Sheffield Wednesday	178 +2	7	10	0	8	0	4	0	200 +2	7
Holt, Sidney	Cornworthy	12/09/1885	1949	1907–08	Buckfastleigh	Torquay United	8	0	0	0	0	0	0	0	8	0
Holyhead, Joseph	Wolverhampton	15/08/1880	1951	1902–03	Wednesbury Town	Port Vale	6	0	0	0	0	0	0	0	6	0
Homer, Sidney	Bloxwich	14/01/1903	1983	1925–27	Bloxwich Strollers	Bristol Rovers	29	2	0	0	0	0	0	0	29	2

Player	Birthplace	Date of Birth	Died	With club	From	To	League A	League G	FAC A	FAC G	FLC A	FLC G	Others A	Others G	Total A	Total G
Hooper, Harold	Pittington	14/06/1933		1956–57	West Ham United	Birmingham City	39	19	2	0	0	0	0	0	41	19
Hopkins, John	Liverpool	11/11/1882	1953	1904–07	Liverpool United	New Brompton	43	14	4	0	0	0	0	0	47	14
Horne, Desmond	Johannesburg	12/12/1939		1958–61	J'burg Railway Club	Blackpool	40	16	7	2	4	0	1	0	52	18
Horton, Thomas	Birmingham	10/01/1863	1930	1885–86	Crosswells Brewery	WB Standard	0	0	2	1	0	0	0	0	2	1
Hoskins, Albert	Southampton	16/09/1885	1968	1908–10	Shrewsbury Town	Dudley Town	14	2	0	0	0	0	0	0	14	2
Howell, Henry	Smethwick	29/11/1890	1932	1913–21	Stoke	Southampton	38	6	3	2	0	0	0	0	41	8
Howells, Ronald	Rhondda	03/08/1935		1953–58	Nuneaton Borough	Portsmouth	9	0	0	0	0	0	0	0	9	0
Howells, William	Shrewsbury	13/12/1879	1949	1900–01	Wellington Town	Willenhall Pickwick	1	0	0	0	0	0	0	0	1	0
Huddlestone, Thomas	Nottingham	28/12/1986		2005–06	Tottenham Hotspur (L)	Tottenham Hotspur	12 +1	1	0	0	0	0	0	0	12 +1	1
Hughes, Emlyn	Barrow	28/08/1947	2004	1979–81	Liverpool	Rotherham United	56 +2	2	5	0	12	0	2	0	75 +2	2
Hughes, Harold	Nantwich	14/09/1881	1948	1905–06	Crewe Alexandra	Leamington Town	9	0	0	0	0	0	0	0	9	0
Hughes, William	Stourbridge	11/04/1890	1961	1913–14	Bolton Wanderers	Retired	21	10	3	0	0	0	0	0	24	10
Humphrey, John	Paddington	31/01/1961		1977–85	Bourne Hall FC	Charlton Athletic	149	3	7	0	8	0	0	0	164	3
Hunt, Revd Kenneth	Oxford	24/02/1884	1949	1906–20	Leyton FC	Crystal Palace	50	1	11	1	0	0	0	0	61	2
(As an amateur, he had six separate spells with Wolves over a period of 14 years)																
Hunt, Roger (Ernie)	Swindon	17/03/1943		1965–68	Swindon Town	Everton	74	32	7	3	1	0	0	0	82	35
Hunter, Thomas	Walsall	12/09/1863	1918	1886–89	Walsall	Stourbridge	20	4	15	9	0	0	0	0	35	13
Ikeme, Carl	Sutton Coldfield	08/06/1986		2003–	School	Still with club	0 +1	0	0	0	2	0	1	0	3 +1	0
Ince, Paul	Ilford	21/10/1967		2002–06	Middlesbrough	Swindon Town	107 +8	10	8	1	4 +1	1	3	0	122 +9	12
Ingimarsson, Ivar	Reykjavik (Iceland)	20/08/1977		2002–03	Brentford	Reading	10 +3	2	0	0	2	0	0	0	12 +3	2
Irwin, Denis	Cork	31/10/1965		2002–04	Manchester United	Retired	73 +2	2	5	0	1 +1	0	3	0	82 +3	2
Iversen, Steffen	Oslo (Norway)	10/11/1976		2003–04	Tottenham Hotspur	Valerengen (Norway)	11 +5	4	1 +1	0	2	0	0	0	14 +6	4
Iverson, Robert	Folkestone	17/10/1910	1953	1934–37	Lincoln City	Aston Villa	35	7	2	0	0	0	0	0	37	7
Ivill, Edward	Little Hutton	07/12/1898	1979	1932–33	Oldham Athletic	Charlton Athletic	4	0	0	0	0	0	0	0	4	0
Jackson, Alan	Swadlincote	22/08/1938		1953–59	Juniors	Bury	4	1	0	0	0	0	2	1	6	2
Jackson, Joseph	Wolverhampton	22/04/1966		1981–84	Juniors	Bilston United	1	0	0	0	0	0	0	0	1	0
James, Ernest	Wolverhampton	14/10/1885	1956	1904–06	Stafford Road	Langley Green	17	0	0	0	0	0	0	0	17	0
Jarvis, Matthew	Middlesbrough	22/05/1986		2007–	Gillingham	Still with club	17 +9	1	2	0	0	0	0	0	19 +9	1
Jeavons, William	Wolverhampton	15/03/1886		1907–09	Hurst Hill	Dudley Town	8	0	0	0	0	0	0	0	8	0
Jefferson, Derek	Morpeth	05/09/1948		1972–76	Ipswich Town	Hereford United	41 +1	0	4	0	5	0	1	0	51 +1	0
Johnson, Jemal	Paterson (US)	03/05/1984		2006–07	Blackburn Rovers	MK Dons	14 +6	3	0 +3	0	0 +1	0	0	0	14 +10	3

Player	Birthplace	Date of Birth	Died	With club	From	To	League		FAC		FLC		Others		Total	
							A	G	A	G	A	G	A	G	A	G
Johnson, Martin	Windy Nook	09/10/1904	1978	1928–30	Durham City	North Shields	8	2	0	0	0	0	0	0	8	2
Johnson, Thomas	Wolverhampton	01/11/1867	1936	1888–90	Bourne Rovers	Shallington	1	0	0	0	0	0	0	0	1	0
Johnston, James	Edinburgh	11/09/1869	1929	1891–93	St Bernard's	East Stirlingshire	16	5	3	1	0	0	0	0	19	6
Jones, Brynmor	Penyard	14/02/1912	1985	1933–38	Glenavon	Arsenal	163	52	14	5	0	0	0	0	177	57
Jones, Daniel	Wordsley	14/07/1986		2003–	School	Still with club	9 +1	0	0	0	0	0	0	0	9 +1	0
Jones, Eric	Birmingham	05/02/1915	1985	1936–37	Kidderminster Harriers	Portsmouth	3	0	0	0	0	0	0	0	3	0
Jones, Gwynfor	Llandwrog	20/03/1935		1955–62	Caernarvon Town	Bristol Rovers	21	0	0	0	0	0	0	0	21	0
Jones, Harold	Codsall	16/06/1889	1950	1909–12	Codsall Villa	Darlaston	4	0	0	0	0	0	0	0	4	0
Jones, Jackery	Wellington	16/03/1877	1945	1900–19	Lichfield	Retired	314	16	22	0	0	0	0	0	336	16
Jones, James	Cheslyn Hay	16/09/1892	1955	1911–20	Walsall Wood	Shirebrook	36	1	0	0	0	0	0	0	36	1
Jones, John.	Wolverhampton	23/09/1889	1966	1918–21	Bristol City	Bilston Town	36	0	0	0	0	0	0	0	36	0
Jones, Joseph	Wellington	17/08/1880	1941	1898–1903	Lanesfield	Retired	15	1	0	0	0	0	0	0	15	1
Jones, Mark	Willenhall	07/09/1979		1994–99	School	Cheltenham Town	0 +3	0	0	0	0 +2	0	0	0	0 +5	0
Jones, Paul	Walsall	09/09/1965		1989–90	Walsall	Kettering Town	7 +7	0	0 +1	0	0	0	0	0	7 +8	0
Jones, Paul S.	Chirk	18/04/1967		1991–96	Kidderminster Harriers	Stockport County	33	0	5	0	2	0	4	0	44	0
(2 spells)				2004–06	Southampton	Queen's Park Rovers	26	0	0	0	0	0	0	0	26	0
Jordan, David	Belfast	12/12/1912	1989	1936–37	Hull City	Crystal Palace	3	0	0	0	0	0	0	0	3	0
Jordan, Revd William	Langley	09/12/1885	1949	1912–13	Everton	Retired	3	2	0	0	0	0	0	0	3	2
Juggins, Eleander	Bilston	14/04/1879	1946	1904–07	Darlaston	Coventry City	22	0	0	0	0	0	0	0	22	0
Kachloul, Hassan	Agadir (Morocco)	19/02/1973		2003	Aston Villa (L)	Aston Villa	0 +4	0	0	0	0	0	0	0	0 +4	0
Kay, Albert	Sheffield	22/11/1895	1975	1921–32	Willenhall	Retired	278	2	17	0	0	0	0	0	295	2
Keane, Robert	Dublin	08/07/1980		1995–99	Juniors	Coventry City	66 +7	24	3 +2	2	7 +2	3	0	0	76 +11	29
Kearns, Michael	Banbury	26/11/1950		1979–82	Walsall	Walsall	9	0	1	0	0	0	0	0	10	0
Keen, Kevin	Amersham	25/02/1967		1993–94	West Ham United	Stoke City	37 +5	7	5	1	2 +1	0	4	1	48 +6	9
Keeley, Arthur	Cheshire	11/07/1915	1942	1935–37	Ellesmere Port	Bournemouth	2	0	0	0	0	0	0	0	2	0
Keetley, Joseph	Derby	28/06/1897	1958	1925	Liverpool	Wrexham	10	5	0	0	0	0	0	0	10	5
Kellock, William	Glasgow	07/02/1954		1983	Luton Town	Southend United	12	3	0	0	0	0	0	0	12	3
Kelly, David	Birmingham	25/11/1965		1993–95	Newcastle United	Sunderland	76 +7	26	11	6	5	2	4	2	96 +7	36
Kelly, James	Liverpool	14/02/1973		1992–97	Walsall	Hednesford Town	4 +3	0	0	0	1	0	0	0	5 +3	0
Kelly, James	Aldergrove (NI)	06/02/1954		1971–76	Cliftonville	Walsall	20 +2	0	1	0	0	0	0	0	21 +2	0
Kelly, Lawrence	Wolverhampton	28/04/1935		1940–50	Juniors	Huddersfield Town	60	0	9	0	0	0	1	0	70	0

Player	Birthplace	Date of Birth	Died	With club	From	To	League A	League G	FAC A	FAC G	FLC A	FLC G	Others A	Others G	Total A	Total G
Kelly, Philip	Dublin	10/07/1939		1957–62	Sheldon Town	Norwich City	16	0	1	0	0	0	1	0	18	0
Kelly, Robert	Birmingham	21/12/1964		1987–90	Leicester City	Burton Albion	13 +3	2	0	0	0	0	3 +1	1	16 +4	3
Kemp, Frederick	Salerno, Italy	27/02/1948		1961–65	Juniors	Southampton	3	0	1	0	0	0	0	0	4	0
Kendall, Mark	Blackwood (Wales)	20/09/1958	2008	1986–90	Newport County	Swansea City	147	0	5	0	8	0	17	0	177	0
Kennedy, Mark	Dublin	15/05/1976		2001–06	Manchester City	Crystal Palace	157 +10	12	12	1	3 +1	0	3 +1	1	175 +12	14
Kenning, Michael	Birmingham	18/08/1940		1968–69	Norwich City	Charlton Athletic	35 +6	5	3	0	2	1	0	0	40 +6	6
Kent, Michael	Dinnington	01/12/1951		1968–73	Wath Wanderers	Sheffield Wednesday	0 +2	0	0	0	0	0	0	0	0 +2	0
Keogh, Andrew	Dublin	16/05/1986		2007–	Scunthorpe United	Still with club	50 +10	13	3	2	2	1	2	0	57 +10	16
Kernan, Anthony	Letterkenny (Ireland)	31/08/1963		1980–82	Juniors	St Cuthbert's (Ireland)	1	0	0	0	0	0	0	0	1	0
Ketsbaia, Temuri	Georgia	18/03/1968		2000–01	Newcastle United	Dundee	14 +10	3	0	0	4 +1	1	0	0	18 +11	4
Kerr, Robert	Larkhall (Scotland)	12/12/1904	1973	1925–27	Hearts	Clapton Orient	18	7	0	0	0	0	0	0	18	7
Kightly, Michael	Basildon	24/01/1986		2006	Grays Athletic	Still with club	44 +1	12	0 +2	1	1 +1	0	2	0	7 +4	13
Kindon, Stephen	Warrington	17/12/1950		1972–77	Burnley	Burnley	111 +27	28	5 +5	1	9 +3	1	6 +1	1	131 +36	31
King, Andrew	Luton	14/08/1956		1985	SC Cambuur (Netherlands)	Luton Town	28	10	0	0	2	0	0	0	30	10
King, Robert	Northampton	19/09/1919	1988	1939–47	Northampton Town	Northampton Town	6	3	7	1	0	0	0	0	13	4
Kirkham, John	Wednesbury	13/05/1941		1956–65	School	Peterborough United	100	12	9	1	0	0	3	2	112	15
Kirkham, Reginald	Ellesmere Port	16/06/1918	1982	1937–38	Ellesmere Port Town	Bournemouth	13	5	2	0	0	0	0	0	15	5
Kinsey, George	Burton upon Trent	20/06/1866	1911	1891–94	Mitchell's St George	Aston Villa	72	3	11	0	0	0	0	0	83	3
Knight, Thomas	Wolverhampton	14/08/1864	1922	1886–90	Willenhall Pickwick	Retired	21	8	12	9	0	0	0	0	33	17
Knighton, Kenneth	Darton	20/02/1944		1960–66	Juniors	Oldham Athletic	13 +3	0	0	0	0	0	0	0	13 +3	0
Knowles, Peter	Fitzwilliam	30/09/1945		1963–69	Wath Wanderers	Retired	171 +3	61	11	3	6	0	0	0	188 +3	64
Kubicki, Dariusz	Kozuchow, Poland	06/06/1963		1997–98	Sunderland	Carlisle	12	0	0	0	0	0	0	0	12	0
Kyle, Kevin	Stranraer	07/06/1981		2008 (L)	Coventry City	Still with club	3 +9	1	1	0	0	0	0	0	4 +9	1
Laking, George	Harthill	17/03/1913	1997	1934–36	Dinnington	Middlesbrough	27	0	2	0	0	0	0	0	29	0
Lange, Anthony	West Ham	10/12/1964		1989–92	Aldershot	West Bromwich Albion	8	0	0	0	2	0	0	0	10	0
Langford, Thomas	Wolverhampton	04/10/1892	1960	1914–20	Bargoed Town	Stalybridge Celtic	7	3	0	0	0	0	0	0	7	3
Langley, Thomas	Lambeth	08/02/1958		1984–86	Coventry City	South China	22 +1	4	2	0	2 +1	0	0	0	26 +2	4
Langley, William	Wolverhampton	11/09/1918	1980	1936–38	Tunbridge Wells Rovers	Bournemouth	7	3	0	0	0	0	0	0	7	3
Larkin, Colin	Dundalk	27/04/1982		1997–2002	Juniors	Mansfield Town	1 +2	0	0	0	0 +1	1	0	0	1 +3	1
Law, Brian	Merthyr Tydfil	01/01/1970		1994–97	Queen's Park Rangers	Millwall	26 +5	1	7	0	1 +1	0	0	0	34 +6	1
Lawrence, Joseph	Willenhall	29/01/1871	1931	1891–93	Wolverhampton Rangers	Darlaston	2	0	0	0	0	0	0	0	2	0

Player	Birthplace	Date of Birth	Died	With club	From	To	League		FAC		FLC		Others		Total	
							A	G	A	G	A	G	A	G	A	G
Lax, George	Pontefract	13/03/1905	1968	1929–31	Frickley Colliery	Barnsley	61	1	5	0	0	0	0	0	66	1
Layton, William	Newton	11/08/1881	1961	1904–06	Shrewsbury Town	Coventry City	29	4	5	0	0	0	0	0	34	4
Lazarus, Mark	Stepney	05/12/1938		1961–62	Queen's Park Rangers	Brentford	9	3	0	0	0	0	0	0	9	3
Lea, Thomas	Oswestry	15/05/1893	1964	1913–21	Oswestry Town	Bristol Rovers	47	3	11	1	0	0	0	0	58	4
Leadbeater, Richard	Gornal, Dudley	21/10/1977		1994–98	Juniors	Hereford United	0 +1	0	0	0	0	0	0	0	0 +1	0
Lees, Harry	Nottingham	11/05/1895	1965	1923–27	Ebbw Vale	Darlington	120	40	9	3	0	0	0	0	129	43
Le Flem, Richard	Bradford on Avon	12/07/1942		1964–65	Nottingham Forest	Middlesbrough	19	5	0	0	0	0	0	0	19	5
Legge, Albert	Hednesford	19/01/1901	1998	1922–28	Lewisham Athletic	Gillingham	53	5	3	0	0	0	0	0	58	5
Lescott, Joleon	Birmingham	16/08/1982		1997–2006	School	Everton	206 +6	13	10	0	7 +1	0	5	0	228 +7	13
Lester, Frank	Wednesbury	23/04/1870	1940	1894–95	Fallings Heath	Walsall	1	0	0	0	0	0	0	0	1	0
Lewis, Norman	Wolverhampton	13/06/1908	1972	1928–29	Sunbeam FC	Stoke City	29	0	1	0	0	0	0	0	30	0
Lill, Michael	Barking	03/08/1936	2004	1954–60	Storey Athletic	Everton	30	15	1	1	0	0	3	0	34	16
Little, Mark	Worcester	20/08/1988		2003–	School	Still with club	19 +8	0	3	0	1	0	0 +1	0	23 +9	0
Livingstone, William	Coventry	13/08/1964		1980–84	Juniors	Derby County	21 +3	4	0	0	1	0	0	0	22 +3	4
Llowarch, Albert	Nechells	20/09/1865	1933	1887–88	Nechells Park	Willenhall	0	0	3	0	0	0	0	0	3	0
Lloyd, Arthur	Smethwick	15/07/1881	1945	1905–08	Halesowen Town	Hednesford Town	79	3	1	0	0	0	0	0	80	3
Lloyd, Herbert	Cannock Chase	13/03/1888	1960	1913–14	Crystal Palace	Hednesford Town	8	1	0	0	0	0	0	0	8	1
Lockett, William	Tipton	23/04/1893	1974	1913–14	Dudley College	Northampton Town	6	2	0	0	0	0	0	0	6	2
Lockhart, Keith	Wallsend	19/07/1964		1986	Cambridge United	Hartlepool United	24 +1	4	3	0	2	1	0	0	29 +1	5
Lomax, Geoffrey	Droylsden	06/07/1964		1985	Manchester City (L)	Manchester City	5	0	0	0	0	0	0	0	5	0
Lowder, Arthur	Wolverhampton	11/02/1863	1926	1882–91	St Luke's	Retired	46	1	25	2	0	0	0	0	71	3
Lowe, Keith	Wolverhampton	13/09/1985		2002–07	School	Port Vale (L)	14	0	0	0	1 +1	0	0	0	15 +1	0
Lowton, Wilfred	Exeter	03/10/1899	1963	1929–35	Exeter City	Exeter City	198	25	11	2	0	0	0	0	209	27
Lumberg, Albert	Connah's Quay	20/05/1901	1986	1930–33	Wrexham	Brighton & Hove Albion	20	0	2	0	0	0	0	0	22	0
Lunn, Thomas	Bishop Auckland	09/07/1883	1960	1904–11	Brownhills Athletic	Tottenham Hotspur	129	0	13	0	0	0	0	0	142	0
Lutterloch, Bert	Poplar, London	12/08/1910	1996	1934–35	Lille (France)	Aldershot	2	0	0	0	0	0	0	0	2	0
Lutton, Robert	Banbridge (NI)	13/07/1950		1965–71	School	Brighton & Hove Albion	16 +5	1	0	0	2	0	1 +1	0	19 +6	1
Luzhny, Oleg	Ukraine	05/08/1968		2003–04	Arsenal	Retired	4 +2	0	2	0	2	0	0	0	8 +2	0
Lyden, Joseph	Bury	22/04/1870	1934	1896–97	Bolton Wanderers	Darlaston	8	3	0	0	0	0	0	0	8	3
McAlle, John	Liverpool	31/01/1950		1965–81	Juniors	Sheffield United	394 +12	0	43 +1	0	27	1	31	2	495 +13	3
McAloon, Gerald	Glasgow	13/09/1916	1987	1939–46	Brentford	Brentford	2	1	0	0	0	0	0	0	2	1

Player	Birthplace	Date of Birth	Died	With club	From	To	League A	League G	FAC A	FAC G	FLC A	FLC G	Others A	Others G	Total A	Total G
McCall, William	Wallacetown	05/05/1898	1967	1922–23	Blackburn Rovers	Southampton	15	1	1	0	0	0	0	0	16	1
McCalliog, James	Glasgow	23/09/1946		1969–74	Sheffield Wednesday	Manchester United	158 +5	34	9	4	9 +1	4	28	6	204 +6	48
McDonald, John	Maltby	27/08/1921	1995	1936–39	Juniors	Bournemouth	2	0	0	0	0	0	0	0	2	0
McDonald, Robert	Aberdeen	13/04/1955		1987–88	Leeds United (L)	Leeds United	6	0	0	0	0	0	1	0	7	0
McDonald, Thomas	Cowdenbeath	24/05/1930		1954–56	Hibernian	Leicester City	5	1	1	1	0	0	0	0	6	2
McDougall, Alexander	Flemington	12/09/1900	1971	1925–28	Wishaw Juniors	Derby County	20	1	2	0	0	0	0	0	22	1
McGarvey, Scott	Glasgow	22/04/1963		1984	Manchester United (L)	Manchester United	13	2	0	0	0	0	0	0	13	2
McIlmoyle, Hugh	Port Glasgow	29/01/1940		1964–67	Carlisle United	Carlisle United	90	35	12 +1	10	2	0	0	0	104 +1	45
McIndoe, Michael	Edinburgh	02/12/1979		2006–07	Barnsley	Bristol City	25 +2	3	3	0	0	0	2	0	30 +2	3
McIntosh, Alexander	Dunfermline	14/04/1916	1980	1937–47	Folkestone Town	Birmingham City	44	7	6	2	0	0	0	0	50	9
McLean, Angus	Hawarden	20/09/1925	1979	1942–51	Hilton Main	Aberystwyth Town	144	2	14	0	0	0	0	0	158	2
McLoughlin, Paul	Bristol	23/12/1963		1989–91	Hereford United	Mansfield Town	12 +16	4	0	0	0 +1	0	0	0	12 +17	4
McMahon, Douglas	Winnepeg (Canada)	01/02/1915	1975	1938–39	Caledonian Jnrs	Union Western	1	0	0	0	0	0	0	0	1	0
McMain, Joseph	Preston	11/09/1875	1953	1896–99	Kettering Town	Notts County	46	19	5	0	0	0	0	0	51	19
McMillan, Stuart	Leicester	17/09/1896	1963	1922–24	Gillingham	Bradford City	36	5	3	0	0	0	0	0	39	5
McNab, Robert	Huddersfield	20/07/1943		1975–76	Arsenal	San Antonio (US)	13	0	0	0	3	0	0	0	16	0
McNamara, Jackie	Glasgow	24/10/1973		2005–07	Celtic	Aberdeen	28 +1	0	2	0	0 +1	0	2	0	32 +2	0
McParland, Peter	Newry (NI)	25/04/1934		1962–63	Aston Villa	Plymouth Argyle	21	10	0	0	0	0	0	0	21	10
McVeigh, James	Sheffield	02/07/1949		1966–70	School	Gillingham	2	0	0	0	0	0	0	0	2	0
MacLaren, David	Auchterarder	12/06/1934		1965–66	Plymouth Argyle	Southampton	44	0	3	0	0	0	0	0	47	0
Madden, Lawrence	Hackney	28/09/1955		1991–93	Sheffield Wednesday	Darlington	62 +5	1	3	0	4	0	2	0	71 +5	1
Maguire, James	Meadowfield	23/07/1917	1990	1936–47	Willington	Swindon Town	79	7	6	2	0	0	0	0	85	9
Malpass, William	Wednesbury	05/03/1867	1939	1891–99	Wednesbury Old Athletic	Retired	133	6	22	3	0	0	0	0	155	9
Mannion, Gerard	Warrington	21/12/1939	1994	1957–61	School	Norwich City	17	7	1	0	0	0	3	0	21	7
Mardenborough, Stephen	Birmingham	11/09/1964		1983–84	Birmingham City	Swansea City	9	1	0 +1	0	0 +1	0	0	0	9 +2	1
Marr, Andrew	Gateshead	14/04/1892	1960	1913–15	Coventry City	Townstall	3	0	0	0	0	0	0	0	3	0
Marsden, Christopher	Sheffield	03/01/1969		1994	Huddersfield Town	Notts County	8	0	3	0	0	0	0	0	11	0
Marsden, Frederick	Blackburn	06/09/1911	1989	1935–36	Accrington Stanley	Bournemouth	1	0	0	0	0	0	0	0	1	0
Marshall, Andrew	Bury St Edmunds	14/04/1975		2003	Ipswich Town (L)	Ipswich Town	1	0	0	0	0	0	0	0	1	0
Marshall, George	Walker-on-Tyne	03/03/1896	1966	1919–24	Southend United	Walsall	102	1	9	0	0	0	0	0	111	1
Marshall, John	Ely	12/12/1917	1980	1938–39	Norwich City	Basingstoke	1	0	0	0	0	0	0	0	1	0

Player	Birthplace	Date of Birth	Died	With club	From	To	League A	League G	FAC A	FAC G	FLC A	FLC G	Others A	Others G	Total A	Total G
Marshall, William	Hucknall	16/02/1905	1959	1928–30	Southport	Port Vale	52	13	2	0	0	0	0	0	54	13
Marson, Frederick	Darlaston	18/01/1900	1976	1923–25	Darlaston	Sheffield Wednesday	8	4	0	0	0	0	0	0	8	4
Martin, David	Belfast	01/02/1914	1991	1934–36	Belfast Celtic	Nottingham Forest	25	17	2	1	0	0	0	0	27	18
Martin, James	Basford	02/12/1898	1969	1923–24	Aberdare Athletic	Reading	11	6	0	0	0	0	0	0	11	6
Martin, Tudor	Caerau	20/04/1904	1979	1930–32	Newport County	Swansea Town	15	9	0	0	0	0	0	0	15	9
Mason, Charles	Wolverhampton	13/04/1863	1941	1877–92	St Luke's	Retired	75	1	33	1	0	0	0	0	108	2
Mason, James	Wolverhampton	22/01/1885	1934	1907–09	Wednesfield Rangers	Bristol Rovers	8	1	0	0	0	0	0	0	8	1
Mason, Jeremiah	Wolverhampton	11/09/1865	1942	1899–91	St Luke's	Willenhall Swifts	7	0	0	0	0	0	0	0	7	0
Mason, Robert	Tipton	22/03/1936		1951–62	School	Chelmsford City	146	44	14	5	0	0	13	5	173	54
Masters, Neil	Ballymena	25/05/1972		1993–97	Bournemouth	Gillingham	10 +2	0	0	0	0	0	0	0	10 +2	0
Matthews, Michael	Hull	25/09/1960		1976–84	School	Scunthorpe United	72 +4	7	2	0	5	0	0	0	79 +4	7
Matthias, John	Broughton	12/04/1878	1938	1897–1901	Shrewsbury Town	Wrexham	43	0	2	0	0	0	0	0	45	
May, George	Aston, Birmingham	11/02/1891	1959	1908–10	Verity Athletic	Nuneaton Town	16	0	0	0	0	0	0	0	16	0
Mayson, Thomas	Whitehaven	08/12/1886	1972	1921–22	Pontypridd	Aberdare Athletic	2	0	0	0	0	0	0	0	2	0
Meek, Hugh	Belfast	13/10/1903	1980	1925–26	Glentoran	Shelbourne	6	1	2	0	0	0	0	0	8	1
Melia, James	Liverpool	01/11/1937		1964–65	Liverpool	Southampton	24	4	0	0	0	0	0	0	24	0
Melligan, John	Dublin	11/02/1982		1998–2004	School	Cheltenham Town	0 +2		0	0	0	0	0	0	0 +2	0
Melrose, James	Glasgow	07/10/1958		1984	Celtic (L)	Celtic	6 +1	2	0	0	2	2	0	0	8 +1	4
Metcalf, Thomas	Burton upon Trent	04/04/1878	1942	1906–09	Salisbury City	Bristol Rovers	9	0	0	0	0	0	0	0	9	0
Micklewright, William	Reading	23/03/1890	1959	1910–11	Wellington Town	Abingdon	5	0	0	0	0	0	0	0	5	0
Middleton, Henry	Birmingham	18/03/1937		1954–59	School	Scunthorpe United	1	0	0	0	0	0	0	0	1	0
Miller, David	Middlesbrough	21/01/1921	1989	1945–47	Middlesbrough	Derby County	2	0	0	0	0	0	0	0	2	0
Miller, George	Larkhall	20/05/1939		1964–66	Dunfermline Athletic	Dunfermline Athletic	37	3	8	0	0	0	0	0	45	3
Miller, John	Hednesford	11/03/1875	1949	1895–1905	Hednesford Town	Stoke	251	47	18	2	0	0	0	0	269	49
Miller, Kenneth	Edinburgh	23/12/1979		2001–06	Rangers	Celtic	134 +38	53	10 +2	5	6 +1	5	3 +2	0	153 +43	63
Mills, Lee	Mexborough	10/07/1970		1992–95	Stocksbridge FC	Derby County	12 +13	2	3 +1	1	1	0	3	1	19 +14	4
Mitton, John	Todmorden	07/11/1895	1983	1924–27	Sunderland	Southampton	100	6	7	0	0	0	0	0	107	6
Morris, William	Handsworth	26/03/1913	1995	1933–47	West Bromwich Albion (A)	Dudley Town	175	2	22	1	0	0	0	0	197	3
Morrissey, John	Liverpool	08/03/1965		1985	Everton	Tranmere Rovers	5 +5	1	0	0	1	0	0	0	6 +5	1
Moss, Craig	Birmingham	11/03/1961		1977–82	School	Worcester City	4	0	0	0	0	0	0	0	4	0
Mountfield, Derek	Liverpool	02/11/1962		1991–94	Aston Villa	Carlisle United	79 +4	4	2	0	4	1	2	0	87 +4	5

Player	Birthplace	Date of Birth	Died	With club	From	To	League A	League G	FAC A	FAC G	FLC A	FLC G	Others A	Others G	Total A	Total G
Mulgrew, Charles	Glasgow	06/03/1986		2006–	Celtic	Still with club	5 +1	0	0	0	2	0	0 +1	0	7 +2	0
Mulholland, Thomas	Wolverhampton	31/07/1880	1950	1912–13	Brierley Hill Colliery	Brewood	6	1	0	0	0	0	0	0	6	1
Mullen, James	Newcastle	06/01/1923	1987	1937–59	School	Retired	445	98	38	14	0	0	3	0	486	112
Mulligan, Gary	Dublin	23/04/1985		2000–05	School	Sheffield United	0 +1	0	0	0	0	0	0	0	0 +1	0
Munro, Francis	Broughty Ferry	25/10/1947		1967–77	Aberdeen	Celtic	290 +6	14	20	0	23	2	32	3	365 +6	19
Murray, James	Eythorne (Kent)	11/10/1935		1953–63	School	Manchester City	273	155	14	7	0	0	12	4	299	166
Muscat, Kevin	Crawley	07/08/1973		1997–2002	Crystal Palace	Glasgow Rangers	178 +2	14	11	0	10	1	0	0	199 +2	15
Murray, Matthew	Solihull	02/05/1981		1996–	School	Still with club	87	0	8	0	2	0	3	0	100	0
Mutch, Andrew	Liverpool	28/12/1963		1986–93	Southport	Swindon Town	277 +12	96	11 +1	2	14	4	23	4	325 +13	106
Myers, James	Barnsley	05/03/1920	1989	1938–39	Barnsley	Cardiff City	3	0	0	0	0	0	0	0	3	0
Mynard, Leslie	Kidderminster	19/12/1925	2002	1945–49	Bewdley	Derby County	3	0	0	0	0	0	0	0	3	0
Naylor, Lee	Walsall	19/03/1980		1995–2007	School	Celtic	270 +23	7	18	1	19	0	3	1	310 +23	9
Ndah, George	Dulwich	23/12/1974		1999–2003	Swindon Town	Retired	44 +29	14	3 +1	4	1 +1	0	1	0	49 +31	18
Needham, Archibald	Sheffield	02/08/1881	1950	1910–11	Glossop North End	Brighton & Hove Albion	32	6	3	1	0	0	0	0	35	7
Needham, John	Newstead	04/03/1887	1961	1910–20	Birmingham	Hull City	187	57	15	4	0	0	0	0	202	61
Neil, Patrick	Portsmouth	24/10/1937		1956–57	Portsmouth	Pegasus (A)	4	1	0	0	0	0	0	0	4	1
Nelson, John	Chorley	15/03/1806	1984	1932–35	Preston North End	Luton Town	74	4	1	0	0	0	0	0	75	4
Newell, Percy	Wolverhampton	31/01/1901	1979	1920–23	Stourbridge	Stourbridge	10	0	0	0	0	0	0	0	10	0
Newton, Shaun	Camberwell	20/08/1975		2001–05	Charlton Athletic	West Ham United	115 +15	12	8 +1	0	5 +2	1	7 +1	2	135 +19	15
Nicholls, Alfred	Birmingham	15/02/1875	1946	1896–97	Wednesbury Old Athletic	Walsall Alma	3	2	0	0	0	0	0	0	3	2
Nielsen, Allan	Esbjerg (Denmark)	13/03/1971		2000	Tottenham Hotspur (L)	Tottenham Hotspur	7	2	0	0	0	0	0	0	7	2
Niestroj, Robert	Oppeln (Germany)	02/12/1974		1998–2000	Fortuna Dusseldorf	Nurnberg	2 +4	0	1	0	0	0	0	0	3 +4	0
Nightingale, John	Oldbury	12/06/1899	1967	1919–20	Kidderminster Harriers	Shrewsbury Town	3	0	0	0	0	0	0	0	3	0
Nixon, Eric	Manchester	04/10/1962		1986	Manchester City (L)	Manchester City	16	0	0	0	0	0	0	0	16	0
North, Stacey	Luton	25/11/1974		1985	Luton Town (L)	Luton Town	3	0	0	0	0	0	0	0	3	0
Nurse, Daniel	Tipton	23/06/1873	1959	1894–1901	Coseley	West Bromwich Albion	39	1	0	0	0	0	0	0	39	1
Oakes, Michael	Northwich	30/10/1973		1999–07	Aston Villa	Cardiff City	198 +1	0	9	0	9 +1	0	2	0	218 +2	0
O'Connor, John	Wolverhampton	11/01/1901	1977	1924–26	Quarry Bank	Gillingham	11	2	0	0	0	0	0	0	11	2
O'Connor, Kevin	Dublin	19/10/1985		2001–	School	Still with club	3	0	0	0	0	0	0	0	3	0
O'Grady, Michael	Leeds	11/10/1942		1969–72	Leeds United	Rotherham United	28 +5	5	1	1	3	0	1 +1	1	35 +6	6
O'Hara, Gerald	Wolverhampton	03/12/1956		1972–78	School	Hereford United	7 +2	0	2	0	0	0	0	0	9 +2	0

Player	Birthplace	Date of Birth	Died	With club	From	To	League A	League G	FAC A	FAC G	FLC A	FLC G	Others A	Others G	Total A	Total G
Okoronkwo, Isaac	Nbene (Nigeria)	01/05/1978		2003–05	Shaktar Donetsk	Alania Vladikavkaz	7	0	0	0	1	0	0	0	8	0
Oldershaw, William	Walsall	03/11/1867	1934	1889–90	Walsall Alma	Wednesbury Town	1	0	0	0	0	0	0	0	1	0
Oldfield, John	Lindrick	19/08/1943		1969–71	Huddersfield Town	Bradford City	19	0	0	0	0	0	0	0	19	0
Oldroyd, Darren	Ormskirk	01/11/1966		1986–87	Everton	Southport	10	0	0	0	2	0	1	0	13	0
Olofinjana, Seyi	Lagos (Nigeria)	30/06/1980		2004–08	SK Brann Bergen	Stoke City	123 +12	16	6	1	3 +1	0	2	1	134 +13	18
Ordish, Cyril	Chesterfield	23/05/1915	1992	1936–38	Chesterfield	Reading	2	0	0	0	0	0	0	0	2	0
Osborn, Simon	Croydon	19/01/1972		1995–2001	Queen's Park Rangers	Tranmere Rovers	151 +11	1	11 +1	0	7	3	2	0	171 +12	4
Owen, Brian	Uxbridge	02/11/1944		1972–73	Colchester United	Retired	4	0	0	0	0	0	3	0	7	0
Owen, Trevor	Llangollen	05/05/1873	1930	1899–1900	Crewe Alexandra	Crewe Alexandra	11	3	1	0	0	0	0	0	12	3
Owen, William	Brierley Hill	12/03/1969	1930	1893–98	Loughborough	Everton	106	7	11	1	0	0	0	0	117	8
Paatelainen, Mika M	Helsinki	03/02/1967		1997–99	Bolton Wanderers	Hibernian	10 +13	0	4 +1	4	4 +1	1	0	0	18 +15	5
Palmer, Geoffrey	Cannock	11/07/1954		1970–74	School	Burnley	389 +5	13	38	0	33	2	6	0	466 +5	15
(2 spells)				1985–87	Burnley	Cannock Police Force	21 +1	0	0	0	0	0	2	0	23 +1	0
Parfitt, George	Longton	22/06/1890	1954	1913–20	Newcastle St George	Cocknage	4	0	0	0	0	0	0	0	4	0
Parker, William	Liverpool	27/05/1915	1980	1938–43	Hull City	Killed during WW2	3	0	0	0	0	0	0	0	3	0
Parkes, Philip	West Bromwich	14/07/1947		1962–78	School	Retired	303	0	23	0	23	0	33	0	382	0
Parkin, Derek	Newcastle upon Tyne	02/01/1948		1968–82	Huddersfield	Stoke City	500 +1	6	45 +1	1	35	2	27	1	607 +2	10
Parsonage, Harold	Birmingham	13/10/1889	1979	1911–13	Walsall	Dudley Town	20	6	0	0	0	0	0	0	20	6
Parsons, Dennis	Birmingham	29/05/1925	1980	1944–51	BSA	Hereford United	23	0	3	0	0	0	1	0	27	0
Paskin, John	Cape Town (SA)	01/02/1962		1989–92	West Bromwich Albion	Wrexham	21 +13	2	2	0	2 +1	0	0 +1	0	25 +15	2
Patching, Martin	Rotherham	01/11/1958		1974–80	School	Watford	78 +12	10	5 +3	1	3	0	0	0	86 +15	11
Payne, Charles	Wednesfield	20/02/1888	1959	1907–10	Victoria Swifts	Blakenhall	12	1	0	0	0	0	0	0	12	1
Peacock, Darren	Bristol	03/02/1978		2000	Blackburn Rovers (L)	Blackburn Rovers	2 +2	0	0	0	1	0	0	0	3 +2	0
Pearce, Dennis	Wolverhampton	10/09/1974		1995–97	Aston Villa	Notts County	7 +2	0	1	0	1	0	0	0	9 +2	0
Pearson, Alfred	Wolverhampton	25/07/1861	1930	1884–87	St Luke's	Stafford Road	0	0	12	0	0	0	0	0	12	0
Pedley, John	West Bromwich	15/02/1881	1956	1905–10	Wednesbury Old Athletic	Wrexham	156	26	12	2	0	0	0	0	168	28
Peers, Edward	Connah's Quay	31/12/1886	1935	1911–21	Connah's Quay	Port Vale	186	0	12	0	0	0	0	0	198	0
Pemble, Arthur	Bridgnorth	06/06/1885	1951	1909–10	Beacon Rangers	Willenhall Pickwick	2	0	0	0	0	0	0	0	2	0
Pender, John	Luton	19/11/1963		1981–85	Lichfield Social	Charlton Athletic	115 +2	3	7	1	5	0	0	0	127 +2	4
Perrett, William	Willenhall	22/09/1888	1945	1909–12	Bilston United	Dudley Town	4	0	0	0	0	0	0	0	4	0
erry, Walter	West Bromwich	11/10/1868	1928	1889–90	West Bromwich Albion	Warwick County	8	3	0	0	0	0	0	0	8	3

Player	Birthplace	Date of Birth	Died	With club	From	To	League		FAC		FLC		Others		Total	
							A	G	A	G	A	G	A	G	A	G
Pheasant, Edward	Darlaston	15/02/1877	1910	1894–1904	Wednesbury Old Athletic	West Bromwich Albion	159	19	9	0	0	0	0	0	168	19
Phillips, Cuthbert	Victoria (Wales)	23/06/1910	1969	1929–36	Ebbw Vale	Aston Villa	191	59	11	6	0	0	0	0	202	65
Phillipson, Thomas	Ryton	31/10/1898	1965	1923–28	Swindon Town	Sheffield United	144	104	15	7	0	0	0	0	159	111
Picken, Albert	Wellington	22/01/1900	1966	1921–25	Audley FC	Bolton Wanderers	12	0	0	0	0	0	0	0	12	0
Pickerell, John	Bilston	30/01/1875	1940	1890	Dudley Road	Swifts (Trial)	1	0	0	0	0	0	0	0	1	0
Pierce, Gary	Bury	02/03/1951		1973–79	Huddersfield Town	Barnsley	98	0	5	0	6	0	2	0	111	0
Pilsbury, Charles	Bilston	27/04/1881	1949	1903–04	Dudley Central	Burton Swifts	1	1	0	0	0	0	0	0	1	1
Pincott, Frederick	Bristol	19/03/1913	1987	1931–34	Bristol Royal Vics	Bournemouth	2	0	0	0	0	0	0	0	2	0
Platt, D. Frederick	Wolverhampton	31/01/1869	1912	1897–1900	Lanesfield Boys	Oxley FC	6	0	0	0	0	0	0	0	6	0
Pollet, Ludovic	Vieux-Conde (France)	18/06/1970		1999–2003	Le Havre (T)	Le Havre	74 +4	7	5	0	2	1	0 +1	0	81 +5	8
Pope, Frank J.	Brierley Hill	12/11/1884	1953	1900–03	Cradley Heath	Stourbridge	5	0	0	0	0	0	0	0	5	0
(2 spells)				1905–06	Stourbridge	Notts County	8	1	0	0	0	0	0	0	8	1
Poppitt, James	Wellington	13/03/1875	1930	1900–02	Wellington Town	Swindon Town	21	3	0	0	0	0	0	0	21	3
Postma, Stefan	Utrecht (Netherlands)	10/06/1976		2005–06	Aston Villa	ADO The Hague	29	0	2	0	1	0	0	0	32	0
Potter, Darren	Liverpool	21/12/1984		2006–	Liverpool	Still with club	46 +10	0	6	1	1 +2	0	2	0	55 +12	1
Potts, Arthur	Cannock	26/05/1888	1981	1920–22	Manchester United	Walsall	35	9	7	1	0	0	0	0	44	10
Powell, Barry	Kenilworth	29/01/1954		1970–75	School	Coventry City	58 +6	7	4	0	6 +2	1	2	0	70 +8	8
(2 spells)				1986–88	South China	Retired	10 +4	0	0 +1	0	0	0	2	0	12 +5	0
Preece, John	Wolverhampton	30/04/1914	1981	1934–35	Sunbeam Motors	Bristol Rovers	2	0	0	0	0	0	0	0	2	0
Preston, Henry	Ironbridge	04/04/1880	1949	1901–05	Trowbridge	Kidderminster Harriers	26	1	0	0	0	0	0	0	26	1
Price, Arthur	Birmingham	25/05/1883	1941	1907	Moor Green	Acocks Green	1	0	0	0	0	0	0	0	1	0
Price, Frederick	Brierley Hill	20/11/1888	1955	1912–20	Dudley Town	Port Vale	116	0	8	0	0	0	0	0	124	0
Price, Frederick T.	Ibstock	24/10/1901	1985	1925–27	Southampton	Chesterfield	39	8	2	0	0	0	0	0	41	8
Price, John	Blackburn	27/07/1900	1958	1920–22	Barnoldswick Town	Heanor Town	13	1	0	0	0	0	0	0	13	1
Pritchard, Roy	Dawley	09/05/1925	1993	1941–56	School	Aston Villa	202	0	21	0	0	0	0	0	223	0
Pritchard, Thomas	Wellington	18/06/1904	1980	1927–29	Newport County	Charlton Athletic	56	3	2	0	0	0	0	0	58	3
Proudlock, Adam	Telford	09/05/1981		1997–2003	School	Sheffield Wednesday	42 +29	13	2 +3	2	4 +2	2	0 +2	0	48 +36	17
Purdie, Jonathan	Corby	22/02/1967		1985–88	Arsenal	Oxford United	82 +7	12	2	0	5	1	5 +2	0	94 +9	13
Pye, Jesse	Rotherham	22/12/1919	1984	1946–52	Notts County	Luton Town	188	90	20	5	0	0	1	0	209	95
Radford, Walter	Wolverhampton	11/07/1886	1940	1905–10	Juniors	Southport Central	85	41	9	7	0	0	0	0	94	48
Rae, Alexander	Glasgow	30/09/1969		2001–04	Sunderland	Glasgow Rangers	61 +13	10	1 +2	0	2	2	2 +1	1	66 +16	13

Player	Birthplace	Date of Birth	Died	With club	From	To	League A	League G	FAC A	FAC G	FLC A	FLC G	Others A	Others G	Total A	Total G
Rafferty, William	Port Glasgow	30/12/1950		1978–79	Carlisle United	Newcastle United	41 +3	6	3	2	3	0	0	0	47 +3	8
Ramscar, Frederick	Salford	24/01/1919	1989	1945–47	Stockport County	Queen's Park Rangers	16	1	1	0	0	0	0	0	17	1
Rankine, S. Mark	Doncaster	30/09/1969		1992–96	Doncaster Rovers	Preston North End	112 +20	1	14 +2	0	9 +1	0	7 +2	0	142 +25	1
Ratcliffe, Patrick	Dublin	31/12/1919	2000	1946–47	Notts County	Plymouth Argyle	2	0	0	0	0	0	0	0	2	0
Raybould, Thomas	Wilden	13/07/1884	1944	1905–07	Kidderminster Harriers	Grimsby Town	15	1	0	0	0	0	0	0	15	1
Raynes, William	Sheffield	30/10/1964		1985–86	Rotherham United	Dallas (US)	6 +1	1	0	0	0	0	1	0	7 +1	1
Redfearn, Leslie	Burton upon Trent	06/12/1911	1989	1931–33	Stafford Rangers	Southend United	6	1	0	0	0	0	0	0	6	1
Reed, Johnson	Brusselton	11/05/1908	1987	1931	Spennymoor United	Walsall	1	0	0	0	0	0	0	0	1	0
Regis, Cyrille	Maripiasoula (FG)	09/02/1958		1993–94	Aston Villa	Wycombe Wanderers	8 +11	2	1 +2	0	0	0	1	0	10 +13	2
Reynolds, Charles J.	Wolverhampton	30/04/1873	1939	1893–95	Church Taverners	Berwick Rangers	14	5	0	0	0	0	0	0	14	5
Rhodes, Leonard	Darlaston	22/02/1900	1970	1920–22	Willenhall	Shrewsbury Town	19	1	0	0	0	0	0	0	19	1
Rhodes, Richard	Wolverhampton	22/06/1908	1993	1926–35	Redditch United	Sheffield United	149	7	10	0	0	0	0	0	159	7
Richards, David (Dai)	Abercanaid	31/10/1906	1969	1927–35	Merthyr Town	Brentford	219	5	10	0	0	0	0	0	229	5
Richards, Dean	Bradford	09/06/1974		1992–99	Bradford City	Southampton	78 +3	4	9 +1	0	7	0	2	0	96 +4	4
Richards, John	Warrington	09/11/1950		1967–83	School	Maritimo Funchal	365 +20	144	42 +2	24	32 +1	18	22 +2	8	461 +25	194
Richards, Richard	Glyncorrwg	14/02/1890	1934	1913–22	Oswestry Town	West Ham United	88	22	6	4	0	0	0	0	94	26
Richards, William	Abercanaid	14/08/1905	1956	1927–29	Merthyr Town	Coventry City	30	2	1	0	0	0	0	0	31	2
Richardson, Jonathan	Durham	22/11/1905	1976	1928–30	Spennymoor B & W	Southend United	3	0	0	0	0	0	0	0	3	0
Ricketts, Rohan	Clapham	22/12/1982		2005–07	Tottenham Hotspur	Barnsley	35 +16	1	3	0	1 +1	0	0	0	39 +17	1
Riley, Alfred	Stafford	07/12/1889	1958	1913–23	Stafford Rangers	Retired	112	1	12	0	0	0	0	0	124	1
Roberts, Brian	Manchester	06/11/1955		1990–91	Birmingham City	Retired	17 +4	0	1	0	0	0	2	0	20 +4	0
Roberts, Darren	Birmingham	12/10/1969		1992–94	Burton Albion	Doncaster Rovers	12 +9	5	0	0	0 +1	0	1 +1	0	13 +11	5
Roberts, Iwan	Bangor (Wales)	26/06/1968		1996–97	Leicester City	Norwich City	24 +9	12	0 +1	0	2	0	2	0	28 +10	12
Roberts, John	Wednesbury	1873	1951	1894–95	Tipton Excelsior	Ewells FC	1	0	0	0	0	0	0	0	1	0
Roberts, John	Walsall	1885	1959	1906–07	Darlaston	Bristol Rovers	24	14	1	0	0	0	0	0	25	14
Robertson, Alistair	Philipstoun (Scotland)	09/09/1952		1986–90	West Bromwich Albion	Worcester City	107	0	7	0	8	0	14	0	136	0
Robinson, Carl	Llandrindod Wells	13/10/1976		1993–2002	School	Portsmouth	125 +39	19	14	3	12 +1	1	0	0	151 +40	23
Robinson, Philip	Stafford	06/01/1967		1987–89	Aston Villa	Notts County	63 +8	8	3	1	6	0	8 +2	0	80 +10	9
Robson, David	Ayr	21/06/1869	1923	1893–95	Ardwick	Ardwick	5	0	0	0	0	0	0	0	5	0
Rodger, Graham	Glasgow	01/04/1967		1983–85	School	Coventry City	1	0	0	0	0	0	0	0	1	0
Romano, Serge	Metz (France)	25/05/1964		1996–98	Martigues (France)	Lyon	1 +3	0	0	0	1	0	0	0	2 +3	0

Player	Birthplace	Date of Birth	Died	With club	From	To	League A	League G	FAC A	FAC G	FLC A	FLC G	Others A	Others G	Total A	Total G
Rooney, Joseph	Newcastle	1920	1943	1938–43	Romsley	Killed during WW2	2	0	0	0	0	0	0	0	2	0
Roper, Francis	Walsall	1899	1956	1919–20	Pleck Wolverhampton	Rangers	1	0	0	0	0	0	0	0	1	0
Rosa, Denes	Budapest	07/04/1977		2006–	Ferencvaros	Still with club	6 +3	2	0 +1	0	1 +1	0	0	0	7 +5	1
Rosario, Robert	Hammersmith	04/03/1966		1986	Norwich City (L)	Norwich City	2	1	0	0	0	0	2	0	4	1
Rose, William	St Pancras	03/04/1861	1937	1889–96	Stoke	Retired	134	0	21	0	0	0	0	0	155	0
Ross, Maurice	Dundee	03/02/1981		2005–06	Sheffield Wednesday	Millwall	13 +5	0	1	0	0	0	0	0	14 +5	0
Ross, Stuart	Woking	11/09/1945		1965–71	School	Old Wulfrunians	1 +2	0	0	0	0	0	0	0	1 +2	0
Rostance, John	Penkridge	05/1888	1961	1913–20	Siemens FC	Hednesford Town	9	0	0	0	0	0	0	0	9	0
Rotton, William	Wednesbury	20/10/1909	1969	1927–28	Local	Shrewsbury Town	4	1	0	0	0	0	0	0	4	1
Rouse, Valentine	Hoddesden	14/02/1898	1961	1921–22	Pontypridd	Stoke	5	0	0	0	0	0	0	0	5	0
Roussel, Cedric	Mons (Belgium)	06/01/1978		2001–02	Coventry City	RAEC Mons (Bel)	9 +17	2	0 +1	0	0 +1	0	0	0	9 +19	2
Rowbotham, Harold	Heath Town	04/1881	1950	1900–03	Hunslet	Fulham	6	1	0	0	0	0	0	0	6	1
Rowley, Kenneth	Pelsall	29/08/1926	1995	1946–51	Elkington's FC	Birmingham City	1	0	2	0	0	0	0	0	3	0
Rudge, Dale	Wolverhampton	09/09/1963		1979–84	Staffs Boys	Preston North End	23 +4	0	1	0	1	0	0	0	25 +4	0
Russell, Edward	Cranwell	15/07/1928		1945–51	St Chad's	Middlesbrough	30	0	4	0	0	0	1	0	35	0
Russell, Peter	Sedgley	16/01/1935		1950–56	School	Notts County	3	0	1	0	0	0	0	0	4	0
Rutter, Hubert	Walsall	1869	1935	1891	Bradley Swifts	Ashwood Villa	2	0	0	0	0	0	0	0	2	0
Ryan, Derek	Dublin	02/01/1967		1982–87	School	Ireland (hurling)	23 +10	5	1	0	4 +1	0	1	0	28 +11	5
Sambrook, John	Wednesfield	10/03/1899	1973	1919–21	Willenhall Town	Liverpool	21	7	0	0	0	0	0	0	21	7
Samways, Vincent	Bethnal Green	27/10/1968		1995	Everton (L)	Everton	3	0	0	0	0	0	0	0	3	0
San Juan Garcia Jesus	Zaragoza (Spain)	22/08/1971		1997–98	Real Zaragoza	Real Zaragoza	4	0	0	0	2 +1	1	0	0	6 +1	1
Scott, Alexander	Liverpool	29/10/1913	1962	1935–47	Burnley	Crewe Alexandra	119	0	10	0	0	0	0	0	129	0
Scott, Henry	Newburn	04/08/1897	1969	1925–26	Sunderland	Hull City	35	6	2	0	0	0	0	0	37	6
Seal, James	Pontefract	09/12/1950		1966–71	School	Barnsley	1	0	0	0	0	0	0	0	1	0
Sedgley, Stephen	Enfield	26/05/1968		1997–2000	Ipswich Town	Kingstonian	91 +10	8	8 +1	1	7	0	0	0	106 +11	9
Segers, Johannes	Eindhoven (Ne'rlands)	30/11/1961		1997–98	Wimbledon	Woking	11	0	2	0	0	0	0	0	13	0
Seol, Ki-Hyeon	South Korea	08/01/1979		2004–05	RSC Anderelecht	Reading	28 +9	4	2	1	1	1	0	0	31 +9	6
Shaw, Bernard	Sheffield	14/03/1945		1969–76	Sheffield United	Sheffield Wednesday	113 +3	2	7	0	9	0	23 +1	0	152 +4	2
Shaw, Bertram	Lower Gornal	1863	1948	1887–88	Gornal Wood	Willenhall	0	0	3	1	0	0	0	0	3	1
Shaw, Cecil	Mansfield	22/06/1911	1977	1930–37	Rufford Colliery	West Bromwich Albion	177	8	6	0	0	0	0	0	183	8
Shaw, Harold	Hednesford	05/02/1906	1960	1923–30	Hednesford Town	Sunderland	235	0	14	0	0	0	0	0	249	0

Player	Birthplace	Date of Birth	Died	With club	From	To	League A	League G	FAC A	FAC G	FLC A	FLC G	Others A	Others G	Total A	Total G
Sheargold, Arthur	Tipton	04/1888	1954	1910–12	Connah's Quay	Dudley Town	4	0	0	0	0	0	0	0	4	0
Shelton, John	Wolverhampton	1884	1918	1907–11	Compton Rovers	Port Vale	83	16	11	1	0	0	0	0	94	17
Shinton, Bertram	Wednesbury	11/1885	1961	1909–10	Ettingshall Church	Halesowen	1	1	0	0	0	0	0	0	1	1
Shirtliff, Peter	Chapeltown	06/04/1961		1993–95	Sheffield Wednesday	Barnsley	67 +2	0	7	0	4	0	5	0	83 +2	0
Short, John	Barnsley	18/02/1928	1976	1948–54	Wath Wanderers	Stoke City	98	0	9	2	0	0	0	0	107	2
Shorthouse, William	Bilston	27/05/1922		1941–57	Wath Wanderers	Retired	344	1	30	0	0	0	2	0	376	1
Showell, George	Bilston	09/02/1934		1949–65	SE Staffs	Bristol City	200	3	7	0	9	0	2	0	218	3
Sidebottom, Geoffrey	Mapplewell	29/12/1936		1954–61	Wath Wanderers	Aston Villa	28	0	2	0	0	0	5	0	35	0
Sidlow, Cyril	Colwyn Bay	26/11/1915	2005	1937–46	Llandudno Town	Liverpool	4	0	0	0	0	0	0	0	4	0
Silas Rebelo Fernandes	Lisbon	01/09/1976		2003–04	Uniao Leiria (Port)	CS Maritimo	2 +7	0	1 +2	0	2	0	0	0	5 +9	0
Simkin, Darren	Walsall	24/03/1970		1992–94	Blakenhall Town	Shrewsbury Town	14 +1	0	0	0	1	0	0	0	15 +1	0
Simpson, Alexander	Glasgow	24/11/1924	2008	1947–49	Benburb FC	Notts County	2	0	0	0	0	0	0	0	2	0
Simpson, Paul	Carlisle	26/07/1966		1997–2001	Derby County	Blackpool	32 +20	6	2 +5	0	2 +1	0	0	0	36 +26	6
Sims, Nigel	Caton-in-the-Elms	09/08/1931		1948–56	Stapenhill	Aston Villa	38	0	1	0	0	0	0	0	39	0
Sinclair, Nicholas	Manchester	03/01/1960		1984	Oldham Athletic (L)	Oldham Athletic	1	0	0	0	0	0	0	0	1	0
Sinton, Andrew	Cramlington	19/03/1966		1999–2002	Tottenham Hotspur	Burton Albion	62 +10	3	5	0	3 +2	0	0	0	70 +12	3
Slater, Robert	Ormskirk	22/11/1964		1997–99	Southampton	Retired	4 +2	0	0 +1	0	0	0	0	0	4 +3	0
Slater, William	Clitheroe	29/04/1927		1952–63	Brentford	Brentford	310	24	23	1	0	0	6	0	339	25
Small, Michael	Birmingham	02/03/1962		1993	West Ham United (L)	West Ham United	2 +1	1	0	0	1	0	0	0	3 +1	1
Smalley, Thomas	Kingsley (Yorks)	13/01/1912	1984	1931–38	South Kirby	Norwich City	179	11	17	1	0	0	0	0	196	12
Smart, Bertram	Hednesford	15/04/1890	1950	1912–14	Hednesford SM	Bloxwich Strollers	3	0	0	0	0	0	0	0	3	0
Smart, Frederick	Birmingham	1899	1969	1919–21	Redditch	Aston Villa	7	2	0	0	0	0	0	0	7	2
Smith, Alun	Aberaman	12/1906	1971	1930–31	Merthyr Town	Caerphilly	4	0	0	0	0	0	0	0	4	0
Smith, Arthur	Merthyr	27/10/1911	1975	1929–34	Aberdare Athletic	Bristol Rovers	26	0	1	0	0	0	0	0	27	0
Smith, Edwin	Wednesbury	24/12/1880	1955	1903–06	Bilston United	Darlaston	12	0	3	0	0	0	0	0	15	0
Smith, Gordon	Glasgow	03/07/1954		1982–84	Tottenham Hotspur	Cape Town	35 +3	3	2	0	2	0	0	0	39 +3	3
Smith, James	Birmingham	17/09/1974		1991–97	School	Crystal Palace	81 +6	0	2	0	10 +1	0	4	1	97 +7	1
Smith, John	Penn	04/1875	1929	1897–98	Springfield RS	Dudley Town	1	0	0	0	0	0	0	0	1	0
Smith, John	Wednesfield	10/1882	1954	1902–06	Stafford Road	Birmingham	104	38	10	5	0	0	0	0	114	43
Smith, Leslie	Halesowen	24/12/1927	2008	1945–56	Juniors	Aston Villa	88	22	6	2	0	0	0	0	94	24
Smith, Reginald	Westbury	08/02/1916	1979	1937–38	Bristol City	Tranmere Rovers	2	0	0	0	0	0	0	0	2	0

Player	Birthplace	Date of Birth	Died	With club	From	To	League A	League G	FAC A	FAC G	FLC A	FLC G	Others A	Others G	Total A	Total G
Smith, Richard	Reading	22/10/1967		1983–86	School	Moor Green	0 +1	0	0	0	0	0	0	0	0 +1	0
Smith, William	Bilston	11/1872	1936	1896–99	Willenhall	Portsmouth	58	19	4	0	0	0	0	0	62	19
Smith, William C.	Aberaman	09/1912	1980	1932–33	Denaby United	Southend United	5	0	0	0	0	0	0	0	5	0
Smyth, Samuel	Belfast	25/02/1925		1947–51	Dundela	Liverpool	102	34	13	9	0	0	1	0	116	4
Spiers, Cyril	Witton, B'ham	04/04/1902	1967	1933–35	Tottenham Hotspur	Retired	8	0	0	0	0	0	0	0	8	0
Springthorpe, Terence	Draycott (Salop)	04/12/1923		1939–50	School	Coventry City	35	0	2	0	0	0	1	0	38	0
Stack, Graham	Hempstead	26/09/1981		2007–08	Reading (L)	Reading	0 +2	0	0	0	2	0	0	0	2 +2	0
Stancliffe, Paul	Sheffield	05/05/1958		1990	Sheffield United (L)	Sheffield United	17	0	1	0	0	0	2	0	20	0
Stanford, Sidney	Wolverhampton	1860	1935	1884–86	Mossley White Star	Lanesfield	0	0	2	0	0	0	0	0	2	0
Stanley, John	Crewe	23/02/1883	1948	1905–09	Crewe Alexandra	Bolton Wanderers	20	0	2	0	0	0	0	0	22	0
Steele, Timothy	Coventry	01/12/1967		1989–93	Shrewsbury Town	Bradford City	53 +22	6	1	0	5	3	4	0	63 +22	9
Steen, Alan	Crewe	26/06/1922		1937–46	Juniors	Luton Town	1	1	0	0	0	0	0	0	1	1
Stevenson, Ernest	Rotherham	28/12/1923	1989	1943–48	Wath Wanderers	Cardiff City	8	0	1	0	0	0	0	0	9	0
Stewart,Paul	Manchester	07/10/1964		1994–95	Liverpool	Burnley (L)	5 +3	2	0	0	0	0	0	0	5 +3	2
Stobart, Barry	Doncaster	06/06/1938		1953–64	School	Manchester City	49	20	4	2	0	0	1	0	54	22
Stockin, Ronald	Birmingham	27/06/1931		1952–54	Walsall	Cardiff City	21	7	0	0	0	0	0	0	21	7
Stokes, David	Ketley	03/1880	1956	1920–21	Brierley Hill	Retired	7	0	0	0	0	0	0	0	7	0
Stoutt, Stephen	Halifax	05/04/1964		1985–88	Huddersfield Town	Grimsby Town	91 +3	5	7	0	6	0	10	0	114 +3	5
Stowell, Michael	Portsmouth	19/04/1965		1989	Everton (L)	Everton	7	0	0	0	0	0	0	0	7	0
(2 spells)				1990–2001	Everton	Bristol City	377 +1	0	22	0	30	0	11	0	440 +1	0
Streete, Floyd	Jamaica	05/05/1959		1985–90	Derby County	Reading	157 +2	7	6	0	9	0	20	0	192 +2	7
Streets, John	Nottingham	22/11/1883	1949	1913–14	Long Eaton Rangers	Notts County	2	0	0	0	0	0	0	0	2	0
Stringer, James	Netherton	12/05/1878	1933	1900–05	Netherton Rovers	West Bromwich Albion	15	0	1	0	0	0	0	0	16	0
Stuart, Edward	Middlebury (SA)	12/05/1931		1951–62	Rangers (SA)	Stoke City	287	1	21	0	11	0	3	0	322	1
Sturridge, Dean	Birmingham	27/07/1973		2001–05	Leicester City	Queen's Park Rangers	51 +31	31	1 +1	0	1 +2	0	2 +3	1	55 +37	32
Sunderland, Alan	Mexborough	01/07/1953		1969–77	School	Arsenal	139 +19	30	16	0	13 +1	4	8 +2	0	176 +22	34
Swallow, John	Wednesbury	07/1873	1944	1895–96	White Star FC	Darlaston	2	0	0	0	0	0	0	0	2	0
Swift, George	Oakengates	03/02/1870	1942	1891–94	Crewe Alexandra	Loughborough	59	1	7	0	0	0	0	0	66	1
Swift, Walter	Coseley	03/1874	1938	1894–1902	Coseley	Bilston United	1	1	0	0	0	0	0	0	1	0
Swinbourne, Royston	Denaby Main	25/08/1929		1944–57	Wath Wanderers	Retired	211	107	18	5	0	0	1	2	230	114
Tagg, Ernest	Crewe	15/09/1917		1938–39	Crewe Alexandra	Bournemouth	1	0	0	0	0	0	0	0	1	0

Player	Birthplace	Date of Birth	Died	With club	From	To	League A	League G	FAC A	FAC G	FLC A	FLC G	Others A	Others G	Total A	Total G
Tatem, Frank	West Bromwich	1888	1941	1907–09	Willenhall Pickwick	Brierley Hill	2	0	0	0	0	0	0	0	2	0
Taylor, Colin	Liverpool	25/12/1971		1987–93	Juniors	Telford United	7 +12	2	0	0	0 +2	0	3	1	10 +14	3
Taylor, Douglas	Wolverhampton	20/04/1931		1949–55	West Bromwich Albion (A)	Walsall	3	0	0	0	0	0	0	0	3	0
Taylor, Frank	Hemsworth	30/04/1916	1970	1936–44	School	Retired	48	0	6	0	0	0	0	0	54	0
Taylor, Gerald	Hull	15/08/1947		1962–76	School	Police force	151 +3	1	12 +1	0	8	0	16 +2	0	187 +6	1
Taylor, John	Barnsley	15/02/1914	1978	1931–38	Wordsboro' Bridge	Norwich City	79	0	10	0	0	0	0	0	89	0
Taylor, John E.	Chilton	11/09/1924		1949–52	Luton Town	Notts County	10	1	0	0	0	0	0	0	10	1
Taylor, Robert A.	Norwich	30/04/1971		2000–01	Manchester City	Grimsby Town	5 +4	0	0	0	3	3	0	0	8 +4	3
Taylor, Scott D.	Portsmouth	28/11/1970		1999–2001	Leicester City	Cambridge United	21 +11	3	0	0	2	0	0	0	23 +11	3
Teasdale, John	Glasgow	15/10/1962		1980–82	Nairn County	Walsall	6 +2	0	0	0	0	0	0	0	6 +2	0
Tennant, William	Wolverhampton	12/07/1865	1927	1896–97	Hartshill Unity	Walsall	39	0	6	0	0	0	0	0	45	0
Tether, Colin	Stourbridge	11/08/1939		1954–60	School	Oxford United	1	0	0	0	0	0	0	0	1	0
Thetis, Jean-Manuel	Dijon (France)	05/11/1971		2000	Ipswich Town (L)	Ipswich Town	3	0	0	0	0	0	0	0	3	0
Thomas, Albert	Birmingham	1900	1969	1920–22	Hall Green	Stourbridge	11	0	0	0	0	0	0	0	11	0
Thomas, David	Kirkby-in-Ashfield	05/10/1950		1979–80	Everton	Vancouver White Caps	10	0	1	0	4	0	1	0	16	0
Thomas, Geoffrey	Manchester	05/08/1964		1993–97	Crystal Palace	Nottingham Forest	36 +10	8	1	0	1	0	6	0	44 +10	8
Thompson, Andrew	Cannock	09/11/1967		1986–97	West Bromwich Albion	Tranmere Rovers	356 +20	43	20	1	22	0	33	1	431 +20	45
Thompson, David	Catterick Camp	12/03/1945		1960–66	Juniors	Southampton	8	1	2	0	0	0	0	0	10	1
Thompson, Harold	Mansfield	29/04/1915	1990	1933–38	Mansfield Town	Sunderland	69	16	4	1	0	0	0	0	73	17
Thomson, Robert A.	Smethwick	05/12/1943		1959–69	Juniors	Birmingham City	277 +1	2	20	1	2	0	0	0	299 +1	2
Thomson, Robert G.	Dundee	21/03/1937		1954–59	Airdrieonians	Aston Villa	1	1	0	0	0	0	0	0	1	1
Thomson, Samuel	Lugar	14/02/1862	1943	1890–91	Preston North End	Everton	21	9	3	0	0	0	0	0	24	9
Thorpe, Albert	Pilsley	14/07/1910	1971	1928–29	Shirebrook	Mansfield Town	1	0	0	0	0	0	0	0	1	0
Timmins, Benjamin	Great Barr	08/1898	1965	1924–26	Walsall	Kidderminster Harriers	11	0	0	0	0	0	0	0	11	0
Todd, Kenneth	Butterknowle	24/08/1957		1973–78	Juniors	Port Vale	4 +1	1	0	0	0	0	0	0	4 +1	1
Todd, Mark	Belfast	04/12/1967		1991	Sheffield United (L)	Sheffield United	6 +1	0	0	0	0	0	0	0	6 +1	0
Tomkyes, Thomas	Heath Town	1867	1958	1887–89	Stafford Road	Stafford Road	1	0	0	0	0	0	0	0	1	0
Tonks, John	Wednesfield	27/07/1872	1948	1894–1900	Walsall Unity	Walsall	106	20	13	3	0	0	0	0	119	23
Tootill, Alfred	Ramsbottom	12/11/1908	1975	1929–33	Accrington Stanley	Fulham	138	0	5	0	0	0	0	0	143	0
Topham, Robert	Ellesmere Port	03/11/1867	1951	1891–96	Corinthians	Corinthians	23	14	9	5	0	0	0	0	32	19
Towner, Anthony	Brighton	02/05/1965		1983–84	Rotherham United	Charlton Athletic	25 +6	2	3	0	1	0	0	0	29 +6	2

Player	Birthplace	Date of Birth	Died	With club	From	To	League A	League G	FAC A	FAC G	FLC A	FLC G	Others A	Others G	Total A	Total G
Troughton, Samuel	Lisburn (NI)	27/03/1964		1983–84	Glentoran	Glentoran	17	2	3	0	0	0	0	0	20	2
Tudor, Shaun	Wolverhampton	10/02/1982		1997–2001	School	Cambridge United	0 +1	0	0	0	0	0	0	0	0 +1	0
Tuft, William	Wolverhampton	1874	1954	1897–1900	Coseley United	Walsall	8	0	0	0	0	0	0	0	8	0
Turner, John	Swallownest	1906	1975	1928–29	Stockport County	Watford	7	0	0	0	0	0	0	0	7	0
Turner, Mark	Bebbington	04/10/1972		1991–94	Paget Rangers	Northampton Town	1	0	0	0	0	0	0	0	1	0
Tyler, Sidney	Wolverhampton	07/12/1904	1971	1924–27	Manchester United	Gillingham	18	0	0	0	0	0	0	0	18	0
Utterson, James	Gateshead	26/11/1914	1935	1934–36	Glenavon	Died	12	0	2	0	0	0	0	0	14	0
Van der Laan, Robin	Scheidan (Ne'lands)	05/09/1968		1996	Derby County (L)	Derby County	7	0	0	0	0	0	0	0	7	0
Vaughan, Nigel	Caerleon	20/05/1959		1987–90	Cardiff City	Hereford United	86 +7	10	3	1	8	0	11 +3	2	108 +10	13
Venus, Mark	Hartlepool	06/04/1967		1987–97	Leicester City	Ipswich Town	271 +16	7	15 +1	0	17 +1	1	17	2	320 +18	10
Veysey, Arthur	Willenhall	1884	1944	1904–05	Featherstone Boys	Oxley	2	2	0	0	0	0	0	0	2	2
Villazan, Rafael	Uruguay	19/09/1957		1980–82	Huelva SC	Nacional	20 +3	0	0	0	2	0	2	0	24 +3	0
Wagstaffe, David	Manchester	05/04/1943		1964–76	Manchester City	Blackburn Rovers	324	26	31	2	23	1	26	2	404	31
Wake, Bertram	Wolverhampton	1888	1955	1907–09	Blackpool	Bloxwich	4	1	0	0	0	0	0	0	4	1
Waldron, Joseph	Wolverhampton	1861	1935	1883–84	Springfield RS	White Horse	0	0	1	0	0	0	0	0	1	0
Walker, Alfred	London	1887	1961	1909–11	Brentford	Port Vale	32	2	3	0	0	0	0	0	35	2
Walker, David	Oakdene	02/07/1884	1935	1904–05	Birchfield Villa	Bristol Rovers	2	0	0	0	0	0	0	0	2	0
Walker, George	Wednesfield	1877	1945	1900–05	Willenhall Pickwick	Crystal Palace	121	2	11	0	0	0	0	0	132	2
Walker, John	Gornal	1882	1960	1902–04	Coseley Town	Dudley Town	2	0	0	0	0	0	0	0	2	0
Walker, John	Glasgow	07/12/1928		1947–52	Campsie BW	Southampton	37	21	7	5	0	0	0	0	44	26
Walker, Paul	Bradford	03/04/1949		1966–71	Bradford Park Avenue	Watford	17 +9	0	0	0	0 +1	0	4 +1	0	21 +11	0
Walker, Wilfred	Waddington	1907	1980	1929–31	Grantham	New Brighton	1	0	0	0	0	0	0	0	1	0
Wallace, Ian	Wellington	12/09/1948		1964–67	School	Wrockwardine Wood	0 +1	0	0	0	0	0	0	0	0 +1	0
Walters, Mark	Birmingham	02/06/1964		1994	Liverpool (L)	Liverpool	11	3	0	0	0	0	0	0	11	3
Ward, Darren	Harrow	13/09/1978		2007–	Crystal Palace	Still with club	30	0	2	0	0	0	0	0	32	0
Ward, Samuel	Wolverhampton	1880	1938	1906–10	Springfield FC	Dudley Town	45	1	2	0	0	0	0	0	47	1
Ward, Stephen	Dublin	20/08/1985		2007–	Bohemians	Still with club	34 +13	3	1 +1	0	0 +1	0	0	0	35 +15	3
Waring, Thomas	Birkenhead	12/10/1906	1980	1936	Aston Villa	Tranmere Rovers	10	3	0	0	0	0	0	0	10	3
Wassell, Kim	Wolverhampton	09/06/1957		1985	Swansea City	ROPS (Finland)	2	0	0	0	0	0	0	0	2	0
Watkiss, Stuart	Wolverhampton	08/05/1966		1982–86	School	Crewe Alexandra	2	0	0	0	0	0	0	0	2	0
Watson, Edward	Felling-on-Tyne	28/04/1895	1971	1921–29	Pontypridd	Coventry City	193	4	13	0	0	0	0	0	206	4

Player	Birthplace	Date of Birth	Died	With club	From	To	League A	League G	FAC A	FAC G	FLC A	FLC G	Others A	Others G	Total A	Total G
Weare, Arthur	Newport (Wales)	21/09/1912	1979	1933–37	Lovells Athletic	West Ham United	42	0	0	0	0	0	0	0	42	0
Weaver, Reginald	Clutton	14/09/1905	1970	1927–29	Newport County	Chelsea	50	29	1	0	0	0	0	0	51	29
Weaver, Walter	Birkenhead	09/11/1898	1965	1926–27	Burnley	Accrington Stanley	43	11	4	2	0	0	0	0	45	13
Westcott, Dennis	Wallasey	02/07/1917	1960	1937–48	New Brighton	Blackburn Rovers	128	105	16	19	0	0	0	0	144	124
Westley, Shane	Canterbury	16/06/1965		1989–92	Southend United	Brentford	48 +2	1	0	0	5	1	2	0	55 +2	2
Westwood, Christopher	Dudley	13/02/1977		1993–98	School	Telford United	3 +1	1	0	0	1 +1	0	0	0	4 +2	1
Wharton, Guy	Broomfield	05/12/1915	1990	1936–38	Chester	Portsmouth	29	2	6	0	0	0	0	0	35	2
Wharton, Terence	Bolton	01/07/1942		1957–67	School	Bolton Wanderers	223 +1	69	16	9	2	1	0	0	241 +1	79
Whatmore, Ernest	Kidderminster	25/04/1900	1991	1922–23	Stourbridge	Shrewsbury Town	2	0	0	0	0	0	0	0	2	0
Wheater, David	Redcar	14/02/1987		2006	Middlesbrough (L)	Middlesbrough	1	0	0	0	0	0	0	0	1	0
(2 spells)				2007	Middlesbrough (L)	Middlesbrough										
White, Edward	Wolverhampton	1900	1970	1922–23	Wellington Town	Wellington Town	11	3	0	0	0	0	0	0	11	3
White, Joseph	Wolverhampton	1903	1974	1922–23	Wellington Town	Retired	1	0	0	0	0	0	0	0	1	0
White, Robert	Walbottle	11/08/1902	1977	1929–30	Yeovil & Petters	Watford	3	2	0	0	0	0	0	0	3	2
White, Walter	Halesowen	1864	1925	1888–90	Coombs Wood	Cradley St Luke's	4	2	0	0	0	0	0	0	4	2
Whitehead, Clive	Northfield	24/11/1955		1986	West Bromwich Albion (L)	West Bromwich Albion	2	0	0	0	0	0	2	0	4	0
Whitehouse, John	West Bromwich	15/08/1878	1950	1900–06	Wednesbury Town	Halesowen	147	0	8	1	0	0	0	0	155	1
Whitfield, Kenneth	Spennymoor	24/03/1930	1995	1947–53	Shildon Colliery	Manchester City	9	3	1	1	0	0	0	0	10	4
Whittaker, Percy	Rotherham	19/11/1905	1976	1930–33	Wath Wanderers	Reading	6	0	5	0	0	0	0	0	11	0
Whittam, Ernest	Wealdstone	07/01/1911	1977	1935–36	Mansfield Town	Bournemouth	1	0	0	0	0	0	0	0	1	0
Whittingham, Guy	Evesham	10/11/1964		1994	Aston Villa (L)	Aston Villa	13	8	1	0	0	0	0	0	14	8
Wignall, Frank	Chorley	21/08/1939		1968–69	Nottingham Forest	Derby County	32	15	1 +1	1	2	0	0	0	35 +1	16
Wildman, Frank	South Kirby	11/08/1910	1980	1932–35	South Kirby Colliery	Reading	54	0	2	0	0	0	0	0	56	0
Wildsmith, Thomas	Sheffield	08/01/1913	1979	1932–33	Hadfield Sports	Bristol Rovers	1	0	0	0	0	0	0	0	1	0
Wilkes, G. Harold	West Bromwich	1882	1942	1905–06	West Bromwich Albion (am)	Dudley Town	1	0	0	0	0	0	0	0	1	0
William, Walter J.	Wolverhampton	18/07/1906	1982	1927–28	Wednesfield Rovers	Gillingham	3	0	0	0	0	0	0	0	3	0
Williams, Adrian	Reading	16/08/1971		1996–99	Reading	Reading	26 +1	0	2 +2	0	3	0	2	1	33 +3	1
Williams, Bertram	Bilston	31/01/1920		1945–57	Walsall	Retired	381	0	38	0	0	0	1	0	420	0
Williams, Evan	Dumbarton	15/07/1943		1966–69	Dumbarton	Aston Villa	13	0	0	0	2	0	0	0	15	0
Williams, George	Wolverhampton	1882	1939	1904–06	Blakenhall	Tettenhall Rangers	46	0	5	0	0	0	0	0	51	0
Williams, Leonard	Rotherham	1902	1970	1927–30	Stockport County	Swansea Town	49	0	1	0	0	0	0	0	50	0

Player	Birthplace	Date of Birth	Died	With club	From	To	League A	League G	FAC A	FAC G	FLC A	FLC G	Others A	Others G	Total A	Total G
Williams, Mark	Johannesburg	11/08/1966		1995–96	RWD Molenbeek	Released	5 +7	1	1	0	2 +1	1	0	0	8 +8	1
Williams, Nigel	Canterbury	29/07/1954		1970–76	School	Gillingham	3	0	0	0	0	0	0	0	3	0
Williams, Walter	Stafford	22/08/1883	1949	1905–08	Ettingshall	Darlaston	34	4	0	0	0	0	0	0	34	4
Wilshaw, Dennis	Stoke-on-Trent	11/03/1926	2004	1943–57	Packmoor Boys Club	Stoke City	211	106	7	7	0	0	1	0	219	113
Wilson, Frank	Birmingham	1871	1949	1892–93	Elwells	Castle Blues	2	0	0	0	0	0	0	0	2	0
Wilson, Joseph	Workington	06/07/1937		1965–67	Nottingham Forest	Newport County	59	0	3	0	2	0	0	0	64	0
Wilson, Leslie	Manchester	10/07/1947		1963–71	School	Bristol City	89 +11	7	4 +1	0	8	1	1	0	102 +12	8
Wintersgill, David	Northallerton	19/09/1965		1981–84	School	Wimbledon (trial)	3 +1	0	0	0	0	0	0	0	3 +1	0
Withe, Peter	Liverpool	30/08/1951		1973–75	Barrow	Birmingham City	12 +5	3	0	0	0	0	0	0	12 +5	3
Wood, George	Wolverhampton	25/04/1862	1950	1885–87	Wolves Druids	Wednesbury Town	0	0	5	0	0	0	0	0	5	0
Wood, Harold	Walsall	02/08/1868	1951	1885–91	Kidderminster Harriers	Walsall	60	35	27	11	0	0	0	0	87	46
(2 spells)				1891–98	Walsall	Southampton	181	75	21	5	0	0	0	0	202	80
Woodfield, David	Leamington Spa	11/10/1943		1959–71	School	Watford	247 +3	13	19	1	7	1	0	0	273 +3	5
Woodhall, George	West Bromwich	05/09/1863	1924	1892–94	West Bromwich Albion	Berwick Rangers (NL)	18	1	0	0	0	0	0	0	18	1
Woodruff, Robert	Highworth	09/11/1940		1964–66	Swindon Town	Crystal Palace	63	18	9	3	0	0	0	0	72	21
Woodward, Maurice	Enderby	23/02/1892	1968	1919–22	Southend United	Bristol Rovers	33	1	4	0	0	0	0	0	37	1
Wooldridge, William	Netherton	19/08/1878	1945	1899–1911	Cradley St Luke's	Retired	328	81	28	9	0	0	0	0	356	90
Worrall, Arthur	Wolverhampton	08/09/1870	1935	1889–91	Fallings Heath Rovers	Burton Swifts	29	10	8	3	0	0	0	0	37	13
Worton, Thomas	Wolverhampton	04/02/1878	1940	1895–1901	School	West Bromwich Albion	57	12	2	0	0	0	0	0	59	12
Wrigglesworth, William	South Elmshall	12/11/1912	1980	1934–37	Chesterfield	Manchester United	56	21	2	1	0	0	0	0	58	22
Wright, Darren	West Bromwich	14/03/1968		1983–86	School	Wrexham	1	0	0	0	0	0	0	0	1	0
Wright, Harold	West Bromwich	12/10/1888	1950	1919–20	West Bromwich Albion	Newport County	18	4	3	0	0	0	0	0	21	4
Wright, Horace	Pontefract	06/09/1918	1987	1937–46	Woodbourne Athletic	Exeter City	8	1	0	0	0	0	0	0	8	1
Wright, Jermaine	Greenwich	21/10/1975		1994–98	Millwall	Crewe Alexandra	4 +16	0	0	0	1 +3	1	0 +1	0	5 +20	1
Wright, Stephen	Belshill	27/08/1971		1998	Glasgow Rangers (L)	Glasgow Rangers	3	0	0	0	0	0	0	0	3	0
Wright, William	Ironbridge	06/02/1924	1994	1939–59	Cradley Heath	Retired	490	13	48	3	0	0	3	0	541	16
Wykes, David	Walsall	15/09/1867	1895	1888–95	Wednesbury Town	Died	151	57	28	12	0	0	0	0	179	69
Young, Eric	Singapore	25/03/1960		1995–97	Crystal Palace	Egham Town	31	2	4	0	5	0	0	0	40	2
Young, Robert	Lanarkshire	07/09/1886	1955	1911–14	Everton	Retired	67	10	6	1	0	0	0	0	73	11
Yule, Thomas	Douglaswater	04/02/1888	1959	1911–13	Lincoln City	Port Vale	33	7	0	0	0	0	0	0	33	7
Zelem, Peter	Manchester	13/02/1962		1985–87	Chester City	Preston North End	45	1	3	0	4	0	2	0	54	1

A total of 929 footballers have played in competitive matches for Wolves over a period of 125 years.

Roll of Honour

Peter Emery
Stuart Parry
Eric & Ann Matthews
John Ward
John-Si-Max Davies
John Parkes
John Withers
Rosemary Crump
Peter Bagnall
Patrick Donnellan
Philip Bullock
Jamie Sakalys
Robert H. Green
Andrew Porter
Michael Ashmore
Alwyn Hill
Pete Walton
Graham S. Warner
Darren Maydew
Poppy Wigstead
Robbie Mullin
Paul Willis
Leslie E. Dainty
Graham Robert Hunt
Michael Wright
Timothy James Page
Les Archer
John A. Clifford
Alan Hazelwood
Andrew Dent
Michael Ashmore
Andrew Porter
Gary J. Smith
Paul R.A. Smith
Zachary L. Sheppard
Kenneth Taylor
Ken Cooper
Barry 'Wolfie Bal' Hudson
James Ratcliff
John Eva
Neill & Ann Morris-Hobley
Rick Croft
Paul Harrison
Kevin Wallsgrove
Paul James Foster
Ian Lickis
Ken Bedford
Adrian Whitehurst
Ian Shepherd
Stephen Wildman R.I.P. 06
Nick Hone
Keith Alexander Owen
Roy S. Davies
David Middlemass
Martin Wood
Natalie Wood
Ian Degg
Egerton Dominoes Champion
Hesson Dominoes Runner-Up
Craig A. Roberts
Robert Philip Samuel
David Martin
Colin & Liam, Oswestry Wolves
Gary Anthony Bullock
David John Thomas
Mat Derrick
Andrew Groom
Pop Masaun
Andy Pugh
Thomas Adrian Sage

Stan Pugh
Barry & Lynette Goss
Richard Alan Sharp
David Lloyd-Williams
Bob (pafkab) Morgan
Danilo 'Dan' Ronzani
David Carswell
Ian B. Ward
John Stanley Gibbons
Peter Mayhew
Jim Sibley
Christopher Davison
David Farmer
Leslie Lord
Thanks Dad, Patrick Quirke
The Carvey Family
Kevin Jones
Ryan Leah
Anthony Holman
Albert Camilleri
Christer Hibbitt Herentz
Peter Rendell
Billy Rendell
N.R. Pennington
David Lane
Gary Lester
Kevin Defty
Philip A.J. O'Connor
Richard Ralph
Adam Haggar
Roy Singleton
Mark Singleton
Kevin Singleton
Ray Finch (in memory of Frank A. Court)
Robert Charles
Stuart Cork
Harvey James Martin
Douglas Hamerton
Robert Charles
John Clarke
Timothy Robert Hazlewood
David William Day
Stephen Paul Walker
George Voulgaris
Robert Blackhall
Keith Littlehales
Dave R.J. Watson
Alwyn Hill
Paul Justin Edwards
Andrew Blews
Paul Blews
Arthur Blews
Irene Blews
Stephen Grainger
Lisa Flintham
Lynn Grainger
Alan Grainger
Gavin Hill
London Wolves
Steve Caron
James Caron
Matthew Caron
Daniel Caron
Glenn Aston
Bryan Bridges
Maurice John Briscoe
R.J. Castle
David Cleveland
The Cowley Family
Bob Crockett
John A. Cross
Brian N. Daniels
The Davies Family
The Dungar Family
Paul Wayne Dunne
Steve Edwards
Steve English
F.D. Gilson (SLH)

Ken Gregory
David Harper
Graham Harridence
Reg, Amy and Greg Harris
Neil Harrison
Gail Henshall
David Instone
Glen Jones
Graham Jones
Kenneth Jones
Stan Journeaux (Jersey)
David Keeling
Brian Key
Alec Kokinis
Derek Lawton
Tony Lewis
Peter C Lowe
Ian Mason
Eric 'Barrs' Millington
Simon Patten
Douglas John Pearl
Jack T. Raby
Arthur Edward Salusbury
Michael Sampson
Peter John Schofield
Dave Snow
Glyn Tunney
Adrian Turner
Tony Turpin
Simon Ashley Walters
David Watkiss
Leslie Westwood (Grand pop)
Tony White
Dave Wilkins
Peter and Joan Williams
Les Wilson
Ron Peacock